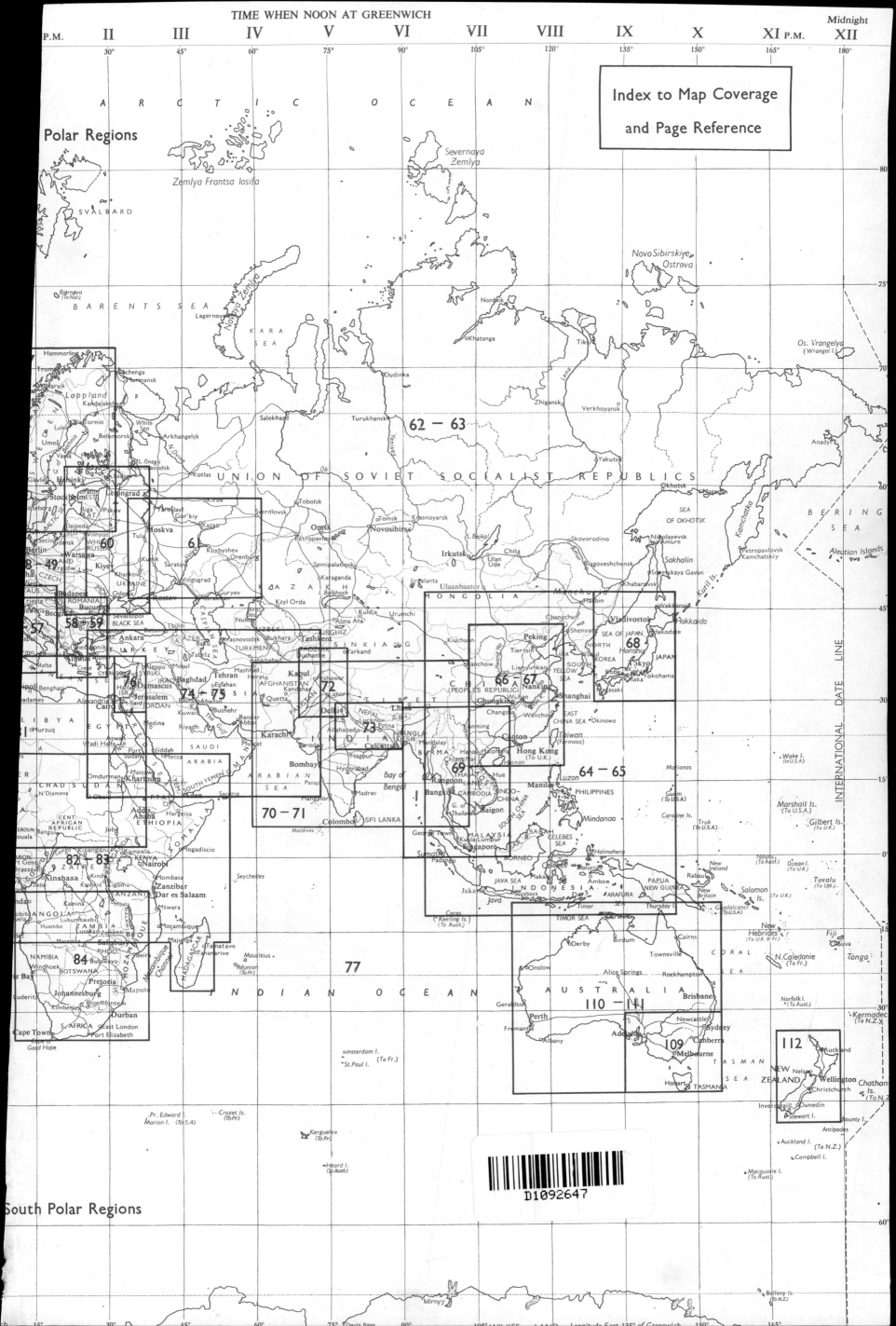

THE
WORLD ATLAS

JOHN C. BARTHOLOMEW, M.A., F.R.S.E.
DIRECTOR, THE GEOGRAPHICAL INSTITUTE, EDINBURGH

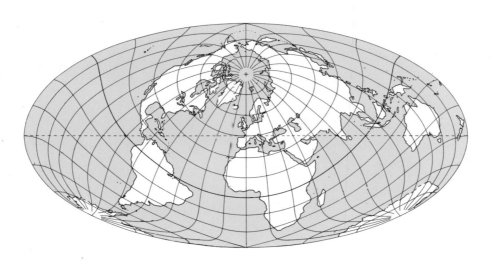

ELEVENTH EDITION

JOHN BARTHOLOMEW & SON LTD
EDINBURGH
1977

As Edinburgh World Atlas
First Edition – 1954
Eighth Edition – 1973

As The World Atlas
Ninth Edition – 1974
Tenth Edition – 1975
Eleventh Edition - 1977

© 1977 JOHN BARTHOLOMEW & SON LTD
PRINTED IN GREAT BRITAIN
AT THE GEOGRAPHICAL INSTITUTE, EDINBURGH
ISBN 0 85152 780 9
6666

FOREWORD

THIS Atlas, planned originally for academic purposes, has become so popular among general readers throughout the world, on account of its fresh scientific approach to many world problems, that it is now issued as a library and general reference atlas under the present modified title.

A humanistic viewpoint is given to all continental areas by showing density of population along with its vegetational, climatic and physical backgrounds. Special introductory maps show racial distinctions along with mineral and agricultural resources of the world.

Students of cartography will find matter of interest in the new projections employed. These to the number of four are designed to show more realistic relations of the inhabited land masses, as in the *Nordic* Projection on pages 22-23, which reveals the proximity of the Soviet Union to the United States; another, the *Regional* on pages 14-15, claims to show conformal properties (truth to shape) in the best manner possible; while another, the *Atlantis* on page 11, is ideal for displaying world air communications centred on the Atlantic Ocean.

Place-names are spelt on the most rational system possible, *viz.*, to conform with the local usage of the country in question; traditional or English forms are given in brackets where these are of sufficient importance.

A new form of co-ordinate system for the ready location of positions has been introduced and is explained on page 1; being related to time, it is known as the "Hour System".

THE GEOGRAPHICAL INSTITUTE,
EDINBURGH, July 1954.

JOHN BARTHOLOMEW.

PREFACE TO SEVENTH EDITION

Recent strides in the advancement of our knowledge of the earth and its resources are reflected in a series of new world maps illustrating structure, seismology, relief, continental drift, minerals, energy, food and soils. The British Isles likewise have a comparable series of new maps.

In conformity with the metrication of units of measurement, all temperature maps have been redrawn in degrees Celsius (°C) and spot heights have been altered from feet to metres.

JOHN C. BARTHOLOMEW

EDINBURGH, September 1970.

CONTENTS

The contraction " M " is used to denote scale of map in millionths.

PAGE

1 GEOGRAPHICAL CO-ORDINATES
2–3 GEOGRAPHICAL TERMS
4 CLIMATIC TABLES
5 STATES AND POPULATION
6 WORLD EXPLORATION (Old World)
7 WORLD EXPLORATION (New World)
8–9 MAP PROJECTIONS
10 MAP PROJECTIONS (modern)
11 WORLD AIRWAYS
12 ASTRONOMICAL CHARTS

THE WORLD
13 (a) STRUCTURE   1 : 130 M.
   (b) SEISMOLOGY   1 : 130 M.
14–15 PHYSIOGRAPHY   1 : 90 M.
   Drainage Regions, Continental Drift
16–17 TEMPERATURE AND AIR MOVEMENTS
   Air Pressure and Winds, January, July
   Temperature, January, July
   Air Masses and Fronts
   Storm Tracks
   Temperature Extremes
   Amount of Cloud
18–19 RAINFALL AND OCEANOGRAPHY
   Climatic Regions
   Length of Growing Seasons
20–21 ECONOMIC RESOURCES
   Minerals   Food
   Energy   Soils
22–23 ETHNOLOGY   1:140 M.
   Cephalic Index, Religions
24–25 STATES OF THE WORLD
   Changes of Sovereignty
   Time Zones
26 NORTH POLAR REGIONS   1 : 30 M.
   Temperature, January, July
27 SOUTH POLAR REGIONS   1 : 30 M.
   Temperature, January, July

EURASIA
28 VEGETATION   1 : 45 M.
   Rainfall, January, July
29 POPULATION   1 : 45 M.
   Temperature, January, July
30–31 EURASIA   1 : 30 M.
   Races

EUROPE
32–33 EUROPE   1 : 15 M.
34 NORTH–WEST EUROPE   1 : 10 M.
35 BRITISH ISLES   1 : 6 M.
   Geology
   Structure and
   Land Use
36 Climate
   Population
   Energy
   Industry   1 : 8 M.
37 NORTH ENGLAND   1 : 1¼ M.
   Isle of Man
38–39 SOUTH ENGLAND AND WALES   1 : 1¼ M.
   Channel Islands
40–41 SCOTLAND   1 : 1¼ M.
   Shetland, Fair Isle, St Kilda
42–43 IRELAND   1 : 1¼ M.
   Population
44 THE LOW COUNTRIES   1 : 1¼ M.
45 SWITZERLAND   1 : 1¼ M.
46–47 SCANDINAVIA AND THE BALTIC   1 : 4½ M.
   Iceland, The Faeroes
48–49 GERMANY, POLAND & CZECHOSLOVAKIA   1·3 M.
50–51 CENTRAL EUROPE & MEDITERRANEAN   1 : 10 M.
52–53 IBERIAN PENINSULA   1 : 3 M.
54–55 FRANCE AND NORTH ALGERIA   1 : 3 M.
   Corsica

PAGE

EUROPE—continued
56–57 ITALY AND THE ADRIATIC   1 : 3 M.
58–59 THE BALKANS AND LOWER DANUBE   1 : 3 M.
60 EUROPEAN RUSSIA   1 : 6 M.
61 VOLGA BASIN   1 : 6 M.

ASIA
62–63 SOVIET UNION   1 : 17½ M.
64–65 THE FAR EAST   1 : 15 M.
66–67 EAST CHINA   1 : 6 M.
68 JAPAN   1 : 6 M.
69 INDO-CHINA   1 : 10 M.
   Singapore
70–71 INDIA, PAKISTAN AND SRI LANKA   1 : 10 M.
   Races, Population, Religions
72 PUNJAB AND KASHMIR   1 : 4 M·
73 PLAIN OF THE GANGES   1 : 4 M.
74–75 THE MIDDLE EAST   1 : 10 M.
76 THE LEVANT COAST   1 : 2½ M.
77 INDIAN OCEAN   1 : 40 M.
   Islands

AFRICA
78 VEGETATION   1 : 35 M.
   Rainfall, January, July
79 POPULATION   1 : 35 M.
   Temperature, January, July
80–81 NORTH-WEST AFRICA   1 : 12½ M.
   Azores (Açores), Cape Verde Is.
82–83 CENTRAL AND EAST AFRICA   1 : 12½ M.
   Ascension, St Helena, Madagascar
84 SOUTH AFRICA   1 : 12½ M.
   The Cape, Witwatersrand

NORTH AMERICA
85 ATLANTIC OCEAN   1 : 48 M.
86 VEGETATION   1 : 34 M.
   Rainfall, January, July
87 POPULATION   1 : 34 M.
   Temperature, January, July
88–89 CANADA   1 : 12½ M.
90 GULF OF ST LAWRENCE   1 : 5 M.
91 GREAT LAKES   1 : 5 M.
92 PACIFIC COAST   1 : 5 M.
93 NORTH CENTRAL STATES   1 : 5 M.
94–95 MIDDLE WEST STATES   1 : 5 M.
96 MIDDLE ATLANTIC STATES   1 : 2½ M.
97 SOUTHERN STATES   1 : 5 M.
98–99 UNITED STATES OF AMERICA   1 : 12½ M.
   Hawaiian Is., San Francisco,
   Alaska, New York
100 MEXICO   1 : 10 M.
101 THE CARIBBEAN   1 : 10 M.
   The Panama Canal

SOUTH AMERICA
102 VEGETATION   1 : 32 M.
   Rainfall, January, July
103 ARGENTINA AND CHILE   1 : 12½ M.
   South America Population
104–105 BRAZIL & NORTH ANDEAN STATES   1 : 12½ M.
   South America Temperature, Jan., July

AUSTRALASIA
106–107 PACIFIC OCEAN   1 : 45 M.
   Islands
108 VEGETATION   1 : 28 M.
   Temperature, January, July
   Rainfall, January, July
109 SOUTH-EAST AUSTRALIA   1 : 5 M.
   Tasmania
110–111 AUSTRALIA   1 : 12½ M.
   Population
112 NEW ZEALAND   1 : 5 M.
   Population

INDEX OF GEOGRAPHICAL NAMES

GEOGRAPHICAL CO-ORDINATES

THE most ancient function of geography has probably been to describe the location of places on the earth's surface. Thus it came about that early Greek philosophers, absorbed in conjectures as to the size and shape of the world they lived in, hit on the method of measuring its estimated circumference by 360 degrees to the circle. Any locality could then be determined by reference to a prime meridian and the number of degrees from the Equator. This method was adopted by Claudius Ptolemy of Alexandria in his tables and maps; and with modifications is much the same as the system of latitude and longitude in use to-day. That it should have survived so long is testimony of its efficiency, especially for navigational purposes. For more ordinary use, however, it is surprising that a simpler and more easily quoted system has not been adopted. True, there have been attempts in that direction. The circle has been divided into 100, which would help if all maps were so printed. More noteworthy are the systems of Military and National Grids, which served an essential purpose during both World Wars. For civilian and international use, however, these grids stand at great disadvantage. Being imposed in right-angled pattern on a particular projection of limited area, they are not suitable for extending to other areas. For instance, a grid planned for Great Britain on Transverse Mercator's Projection would not at the same time be suitable for Germany. Moreover, unless the grid were printed on all maps in common use it would be of little service to the man-in-the-street.

To avoid these disadvantages, therefore, the system used in this atlas has been devised. It has the merit of being international. It is related to the World Grid, based on Greenwich, and can thus be used on any map, if necessary without being specially so printed. It avoids the confusing factor of reading east and west of a prime meridian. Its formula is compact and simple to understand. Finally, it is capable of infinite precision by the use of decimal subdivision.

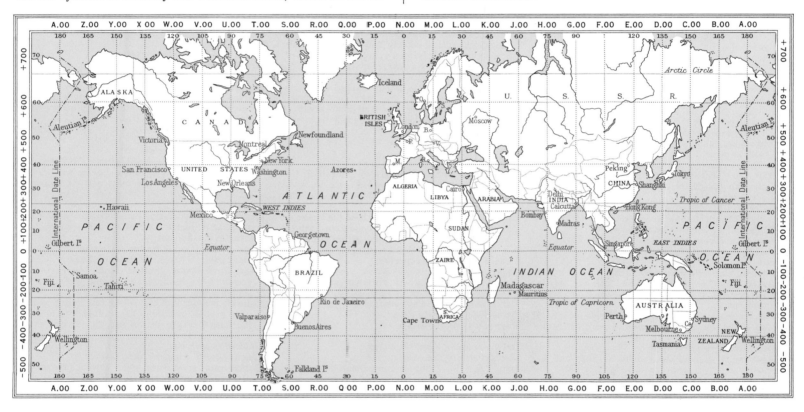

RULES FOR USE OF "HOUR" CO-ORDINATES

1. The World is divided into twenty-four *hour* zones, each of 15° longitude and denoted by a letter of the alphabet, omitting I and O which may be confused with numerals. Starting point of the A zone is the meridian 180° E. of Greenwich, associated with the International Date Line. All readings are made East to West, *i.e.*, with transit of the Sun, Greenwich being N.

2. Every *hour* zone of 15° is subdivided longitudinally, *i.e.*, by *Westings* into 90 units, reading likewise East to West. For greater precision these may be divided into further decimal parts. The units are marked in the top and bottom margins of each map.

It will be found that 60 units *Westing* = 10° of longitude

06	,,	= 1°	,,
01	,,	= 10′	,,
001	,,	= 1′	,,
0001	,,	= 6″	,,

3. In the co-ordinate of latitude the quadrant from Equator to Pole is divided into 90 parts, each of which is then subdivided into 10 units.

Thus 100 units *Northing* = 10° of latitude

010	,,	= 1°	,,
001	,,	= 6′	,,
0001	,,	= 36″	,,

The coupling sign + or − marks this co-ordinate, meaning North or South respectively from the Equator. These *Northing* or *Southing* units are marked on the East and West sides of the Atlas maps. Further decimal subdivisions may also be used.

4. The complete co-ordinate is given by the *hour* figure or *Westing*, followed by the latitude figure or *Northing*,

thus M 89 + 522 = Cambridge, England
and T 12 + 389 = Washington, D.C.

As the *hour* letter and the + or − are both treated as if they were decimal points, it is important to include the initial 0's so that all readings less than 10 should be written 05, 001, or as the case may be.

5. Readings apply to the space between the last digit given and the next digit; but, where greater precision on a larger scale is required, as in the case of the annexed One-Inch section of the English Lake District readings may be made to several places of decimals. Here the Church at Grasmere becomes N 1813 + 54456.

6. The above system, as used in this Atlas, is intended to assist travellers, writers, or scientific and commercial interests in their work. Free permission is accordingly given by the author for its use anywhere without restriction. It may be described as Bartholomew's Hour System of Geographical Co-ordinates.

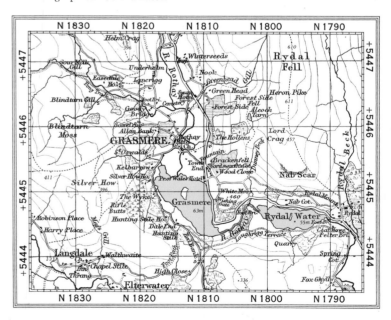

GEOGRAPHICAL TERMS

Abad *(Persian)*, town.
Aborigines, the earliest inhabitants of a country.
Ada *(Turkish)*, island.
Aiguille *(French)*, needle; applied to certain pinnacle-shaped mountain peaks.
Ain, Bir *(Arabic)*, a well or spring.
Ainu, a race inhabiting N. Hokkaido and S. Sakhalin.
Air Mass, an extensive body of air, moving or stationary, having throughout similar characteristics of temperature and humidity.
Akaba *(Arabic)*, pass.
Alf, älv, elf, elv *(Swedish* and *Norse)*, river.
Alluvium, fine sand or silt deposited, largely during flood periods, by streams and rivers.
Anticline, an arch of strata on both sides of which the rocks dip downwards.
Anticyclone, a high pressure system occuring in the zone of the "Westerlies", usually accompanied by fine weather. Wind tends to move outwards in clockwise direction in the Northern Hemisphere, anticlockwise in the Southern.
Antipodes, that part of the earth diametrically opposite to our feet, on the same meridian, but with latitude and seasons reversed, *e.g.* New Zealand is the antipodes of Great Britain.
Arctic Circle, constituted by the parallel 66°32′ N., separating North Temperate and North Frigid Zones. North of this at mid-summer the sun does not set during the 24 hours, while at mid-winter it does not rise. In the Southern Hemisphere the same conditions apply S. of the **Antarctic Circle,** 66°32′ S.
Artesian Well, a water supply obtained by tapping porous rock strata from which the water rises by natural pressure. Derived from Artois in France.
Atolls, circular coral reefs enclosing a central lagoon connected with the outside sea by an opening. Found mostly in the Pacific Ocean.
Avalanches, masses of loosened snow and ice mixed with earth and stone, precipitated with destructive force down mountain sides.
Axis, the imaginary line running from pole to pole through the centre of and on which the earth revolves.
Aztecs, the highly civilised dominant race in Mexico at the time of the Spanish invasion in 1519.
Bahia *(Portuguese* and *Spanish)*, bay.
Bahr *(Arabic)*, sea, lake, river.
Bal, Bally, Baile *(Celtic)*, town, village.
Ban *(Siamese)*, village.
Bandar, Nagar, Pura *(Indian)*, town.
Bantu, *i.e.*, "people"; correlated races of Africa between lat. 5° N. and 25° S. They include Xhosas and Zulus.
Bar, gravel, sand or mud deposited across the mouth of a river by currents or wave action; often impedes navigation.
Bas *(French)*, low, low-lying.
Basin, area of land drained by a river, and its tributaries.
Basin of Inland Drainage, an area of land which has no surface drainage outlet to the sea.
Basques, an ancient race with a distinct language inhabiting N.E. Spain and S.W. France, on the shores of the Bay of Biscay.
Basutos, a branch of the Bantu race occupying Lesotho.
Batang *(Malay)*, river.
Beaches, Raised, small platforms of land, formerly sea shore, now left dry through a rise of the land level.
Beaufort Scale, a scale of 13 symbols used in weather maps to portray the force of the wind from calm to more than 120 kilometres per hour.
Bedouins, nomadic tribes of Arabia and North Africa.
Beled *(Arabic)*, country, village.
Ben, Beinn *(Celtic)*, mountain.
Bender *(Persian)*, harbour, landing-place.
Black Earth, fertile soil in S. Russia and parts of Romania and Hungary on which heavy grain crops are grown.
Boers, descendants of the early Dutch colonists in South Africa.
Bora, a cold, dry, northerly wind, blowing in winter and spring along the Dalmatian coast of the Adriatic Sea.
Bore or **Eagre,** a tidal wave arising in the estuaries of certain rivers.
Boulder Clay, a glacial deposit, consisting of boulders of various sizes embedded in finer material, laid down under a glacier or ice cap and often found to great depths in glaciated valleys.
Brdo *(Czech.)*, a hill.
Brunn *(German)*, a spring, well.
Bugt, Bukt *(Danish* and *Swedish)*, a bay.
Buran, snow blizzards of winter occuring in Russia and Siberia.
Burun *(Turkish)*, a headland, promontory.
Bush, The, interior uncultivated scrubland.
Bushmen, or in Afrikaans **Boesmanne** an aboriginal Negrito nomadic race of south central Africa, now mostly in the Kalahari desert.
Butte *(French* and *Amer.)*, an isolated hill or peak.
Cabo *(Portoguese* and *Spanish)*, a cape.
Campo *(Italian* and *Spanish)*, a plain.
Campos, grasslands of S.E. Brazil.
Canon or Canyon *(Spanish)*, a deep gorge or ravine with lofty sides. Formed by rapid erosion of the softer strata in a dry region, *e.g.*, Colorado Canon.
Catingas, open forest lands on the plateaux of Eastern Brazil, north of 15° S. Drier and warmer than the adjoining **Cerrados**; they contain cactus, mimosa and other types of dry vegetation.
Cephalic Index, the shape of the head expressed by a number which is obtained by giving the breadth of the head as a percentage of its length.
Cerrados, semi-dry plateaux of S.E. Brazil covered with grass and trees of stunted growth.
Chart, map of the sea for use of navigators.
Chinook, a warm, dry west wind blowing down the east slopes of the Rocky Mountains.
Chotts, *see* Shotts.
Chow *(Chinese)*, town of the second rank.
Chrebet *(Russian)*, a chain; mountain range.
Cidade *(Portuguese)*, town.
Cima, Pizzo *(Italian)*, mountain peak.
Cirrus Clouds, very lofty (eight to ten kilometres high) fibrous looking clouds, associated with fine weather.
Città *(Italian)*, town, city.
Ciudad *(Spanish)*, city, town.
Climate, the generalisation of day to day weather conditions.
Col *(French)*, **Colle** *(Italian)*, a pass or neck.
Cold Front, the sloping boundary between an advancing mass of cold air and warmer air under which the cold air forms a wedge.
Continental Shelf, a sea-covered platform extending from the coast-line of all continents. It varies in width and the edge is usually marked by the isobath for 200 metres.
Contour, a line on a map joining all points which are situated at the same height above sea-level.
Cordillera *(Spanish)*, mountain range.
Crater, the cup-shaped cavity forming the mouth of a volcano.
Creek *(Amer.)*, a stream or small river.
Crevasse, rent or fissure in a glacier or ice sheet.
Cumulus Clouds, massive rounded clouds (approx. 1500 metres high), associated with hot weather and rising air-currents.
Cycle of Erosion, the development of the landscape by the various processes of denudation from the youthful stage, after a period of instability and mountain building, through maturity till the surface is reduced to a peneplane.
Cyclone, a low pressure system, or **depression,** generally associated with stormy or wet weather. Winds tend to blow inwards in anti-clockwise direction in N. Hemisphere; clockwise in South.
Daban *(Mongolian)*, a pass.
Dagh *(Turkish)*, mountain.
Dake, Take *(Japanese)*, mountain.
Dal *(Norwegian, Swedish)*, valley.
Darya *(Persian)*, sea, stream, river.
Date Line, this follows approximately the 180° meridian from Greenwich, and marks the point where according to international convention the day begins. A ship crossing this line eastwards goes back a day, while westward it goes forward a day.
Declineation, the deviation of the compass needle from True North.
Delta, a triangular or finger-shaped tract of mud and detritus deposited by a river at its mouth when it no longer has sufficient speed to keep them in suspension.
Denudation, the slow process of laying bare and levelling down the physical features of the earth's surface by natural forces.
Depression, a localised and mobile low pressure system occuring in the zone of the "Westerlies" associated with rain and stormy weather.
Derbend *(Persian, Turkish)*, pass.
Desert, a barren area of land, practically devoid of rainfall or vegetation.
Dip, the angle between the downward slope of a stratum of rock and the horizontal.
Dogger Bank, important fishing ground in North Sea, depth varies from 11 to 36 metres.
Doldrums, nautical term for a region of calms and baffling winds near the equator between the N.E. and S.E. Trade Winds.
Dolina *(Slav.)*, a large hollow or basin caused by the dissolving of limestone. Cultivated if not occupied by a pond.
Donga *(Afrikaans)*, ravine, gulley.
Dorp *(Dutch)*, **Dorf** *(German)*, village.
Dunes, mounds formed by wind-blown sand; capable of considerable advances over level ground unless arrested by the planting of suitable vegetation.
Earthquake, disturbance of the earth's surface generally occuring along faults or lines of weakness in the earth's crust. Sometimes cause great destruction, especially on alluvial ground.
Eiland *(Dutch)*' island.
Ennis *(Irish)*, island.
Equator, imaginary line circumscribing the globe midway between the poles and at its greatest circumference (40 074.72 km). It constitutes the zero from which latitudes N. and S. are calculated.
Equinox, one of the two periods of the year when day and night are of equal duration owing to the sun's crossing the Equator. 20th March and 22nd September.
Erosion, the wearing away of surface features of the earth by the action of wind, water or ice.
Escarpment, the steep face of a hill or range which on the other side slopes gently downwards *e.g.,* Cotswold and Chiltern escarpments.
Eskimos or **Esquimaux,** an aboriginal race inhabiting the Arctic coasts of America, especially of Greenland and Alaska. They live chiefly by fishing.
Estuary, the lower reaches of a river affected by the tides.
Falu *(Hungarian)*, village.
Fault, a break or crack in the earth's surface.
Fell *(Norwegian,* **Fjeld**; *Swedish,* **Fjäll**), mountain.
Fen *(Anglo-Saxon)*, swampy or boggy land.
Fiume *(Italian)*, river.
Fjord, old glacial valley filled by the sea. Sides often steepened by faulting.
Flood Plain, the generally flat area in the bottom of a valley which is covered by water when the river draining it is in flood.
Föhn, a dry warm wind in the valleys of the Alps, blowing in winter from the south.
Fork, the junction of two streams or rivers of approximately the same size.
Fu *(Chinese)*, town of importance.
Ganga *(Indian)*, river.
Gap, *see* **Pass.**
Gawa, Kawa *(Japanese)*, river.
Gebel, Jebel *(Arabic)*, rock, mountain.
Geysers, intermittent spouting hot springs associated with volcanic activity as in Iceland.
Glaciers, rivers of ice originating in snowfields, and moving slowly down valleys until they melt, or on reaching the sea break off as icebergs.
Gol, Song *(Mongolian)*, river.
Gora *(Slav.)*, mountain.
Gorod, Grad *(Slav.)*, town.
Gran Chaco, "the great hunting place", is an extensive area between Argentina, Bolivia and Paraguay consisting for the most part of swampy plains with varied vegetation; rich in animal and bird life.
Grand Banks, submarine banks situated south-east of Newfoundland. One of the best cod fishing grounds in the world.
Great Circle, a circle on the earth's surface whose plane passes through the centre of the earth.
Great Circle Route, shortest distance between two points on the earth, hence used for preference by shipping and air services.
Growing Season, that part of the year during which plant growth is possible. The main factors limiting the length of the period are the occurence of killing frosts and drought.
Guba *(Russian)*, bay.
Gulch *(Amer.)*, a narrow, deep ravine.
Gulf Stream, great warm water current originating in the Gulf of Mexico and flowing across the Atlantic to North-West Europe.
Gunung *(Malay)*, mountain.
Hachures, closely drawn lines sometimes used on maps to denote ground relief. They should follow the direction of slope and vary in intensity with the gradient.
Haf *(Swedish)*, sea.
Hai, Hu *(Chinese)*, sea or lake.
Hamn *(Swedish)*, harbour.
Harmattan, a hot dry wind laden with clouds of reddish dust from the desert blowing over the Guinea Lands in December, January and February. It is an extension of the N.E. Trade wind.
Havn *(Danish)*' harbour.
Havre *(French)*, harbour, port.
Hegy *(Hungarian)*, mountain.
Height of Land *(Amer.)*, a watershed or divide.
Hinterland, region inland from a coast. Often deciding factor in location or growth of a port.
Ho *(Chinese)*, river.
Hoek *(Dutch)*, cape.
Höhe *(German)*, height, hill.
Horse Latitudes, regions of calms and variable winds between 25° and 40° N. and S. on the polar margins of the Trade Winds.
Horst, a block of rock left upstanding by the down faulting of rocks on either side. Exact opposite of rift valley.
Hottentots, an indigenous race in western South Africa.
Hsi *(Chinese)*, west.
Hsien *(Chinese)*, town of the third class.
Humidity, the amount of water vapour in the air. Relative Humidity is percentage of moisture contained as compared with that contained in air completely saturated at the given temperature.
Hurricane or **Typhoon,** a violent and destructive tropical cyclone which occasionally blows in the Gulf of Mexico and the China Seas (where it is known as Typhoon) in August, September or October.
Icebergs, detached masses of ice floating in the Polar Seas, carried along by ocean currents. Originate from glaciers, terminating in the sea. Danger to navigation in Atlantic.
Inch, Innis *(Celtic)*, island.

GEOGRAPHICAL TERMS—*continued*

Irmak *(Turkish)*, river.
Isla *(Spanish)*, **Isola** *(Italian)*, island.
Isobars, lines connecting points having the same barometric pressure at a given time.
Isobaths, lines connecting points of the ocean of equal depths.
Isohyets, lines connecting points with equal rainfall over given period.
Isotherms, lines connecting points of equal temperature at a given time.
Jaur, Javr, Järvi *(Finnish)*, lake.
Jesero *(Serbian)*, lake.
Joch *(German)*, mountain ridge; pass.
Joki *(Finnish)*, river.
Jug *(Serbian)*, **Yug** *(Russian)*, south.
Kahli *(Arabic)*, desert.
Kampong *(Malay)*, village.
Karroos, terraced plains between the mountains in South Africa. Desert in dry season, but develop vegetation in wet season and are used as sheep pasture.
Karst, the porous limestone region of the Dinaric Alps north-east of Adriatic Sea. Also applied to similar types of country in other lands where the river system disappears underground.
Kato *(Greek)*, under.
Khamsin *(Arabic)*, "Fifty"), name given to Sirocco in Lower Egypt where it blows for fifty days between April and June.
Kiang *(Chinese)*, river.
Koppie *(S. African)*, a small hill.
Kraal, a native dwelling in South Africa.
Kuh *(Persian)*, mountain.
Kul *(Turkish)*, lake.
Kum or **Qum** *(Turkish)*, sand.
La *(Tibetan)*, pass.
Lac *(French)*, **Lacul** *(Romanian)*, lake.
Lago *(Italian, Portuguese, Spanish)*, lake.
Lande *(French)*, heath or waste land.
Latitude, the angular distance of a place N. or S. of the equator measured on its meridian. Each degree represents sixty geographical or nautical miles equal to 69.172 statute miles (111.319 km).
Levante *(Italian)*, east.
Levees, embankments, natural or artificial, erected along the banks of rivers and built, as on the Mississippi, to prevent flooding.
Llanos, grasslands of the N.W. Orinoco Basin.
Loch, Lough *(Celtic)*, lake.
Loess, a post glacial wind-blown soil of great fertility; found in N. European Plain and in the Hwang Ho Valley of China.
Long Forties, a portion of the North Sea, so known to fishermen because the depth of water approximates 40 fathoms (73 metres).
Longitude, the angular distance of any place on the globe eastward or westward from a standard meridian, as in Great Britain that of Greenwich. Each degree of longitude represents 4 minutes of time, so that 15° of longitude represent an hour.
Magyars, native name of Hungarians.
Mallee, type of Australian scrub growing in the Murray-Darling and other areas. It is characterised by low-growing eucalyptus and other gum trees.
Maoris, the aboriginal inhabitants of New Zealand.
Marais *(French)*, marsh.
Mean Annual Rainfall, the average amount of rain which falls in a year. The average is deduced from observations taken over a considerable period.
Meander, the winding about of a river in its flood plain when it has reached its base line of erosion but still has energy for further corrosion.
Medine *(Arabic)*, town.
Mer *(French)*, **Meer** *(German)*, sea.
Meridian, an imaginary line represented by a portion of a circle passing through the earth's two poles and on which all places have noon at the same time.
Miasto *(Polish)*, village.
Mile (geographical) = 1 minute of latitude, or 6080 feet (1.15 statute miles)(1.9 kilometres).
Millibar, a standard unit of barometric pressure. Average pressure is approximately 1013 millibars or 76 cms of mercury.
Mistral, a violent, dry, cold wind blowing in winter down the Rhône Valley which acts as a funnel when a depression lies over the Mediterranean.
Monsoon, seasonal winds blowing over the S.E. half of Asia. General direction October to March from N.E., April to September from S.W.
Mont *(French)*, **Monte** *(Italian)*, mount.
Monte, a type of deciduous hardwood forest situ-

ated in the higher portions of the **Gran Chaco**, moister than **Cerrados**.
Montagna *(Italian)*, mountain range.
Moraine, the waste material deposited by a glacier.
Morye *(Russian)*, sea.
Muang *(Siamese)*, town.
Myo *(Burmese)*, town.
Nagar *(Indian)*, town.
Nahr *(Arabic)*, river
Nam *(Siamese)*, river.
Nan *(Chinese)*, south.
Näs *(Scandinavian)*, cape.
Natural Scale, *see* Representative Fraction.
Neap-Tides, period of lowest tide-range, when sun and moon are at right angles, as seen from the earth.
Negeri *(Malay)*, town.
Nejd *(Arabic)*, high plain.
Nimbus, dark water-laden rain cloud.
Nor *(Mongol.)*, lake.
Nos *(Russian)*, cape.
Oasis, fertile spot in a desert owing its existence to a spring or well.
Occluded Front, a line along which warm air of the atmosphere has been raised from the earth's surface by the junction of cold and warm fronts.
Ola *(Mongolian)*, mountain range.
Oxbow Lake, remains of a pronounced meander which has been short circuited by the river cutting through its neck. They occur on a river like the Mississippi.
Ozero *(Russian)*, lake.
Pack Ice, sea ice which has drifted from its original position. It takes the form of floes of various sizes and can be either loosely or tightly packed together.
Pampa *(Argentina)*, dreary expanse of treeless grass plain, and salt steppe, lat. 30° to 40° S., between the Andes and the Atlantic Ocean.
Pampero, a cold south-westerly wind that sweeps over the pampas in Central South America.
Pass, a depression or **Gap** in a mountain range which serves as way for communication between the lands on either side.
Peneplane, the almost level surface which, if the normal course of denudation is undisturbed, results from the erosion of a landscape by running water. The gradient of a river draining a peneplane is just great enough for the flow of water to be maintained.
Pizzo *(Italian)*, peak.
Plain, an area of flat or undulating ground usually at low level.
Planina *(Bulg., Serb.)*, mountain range.
Plateau, an area of relatively flat ground at considerable altitude, sometimes called a Tableland.
Polder, land recovered from the sea in Holland, and protected by dykes from being again flooded.
Ponente *(Italian)*, evening, west.
Pont, Ponte *(French, Span., Italian)*, bridge.
Potomos *(Greek)*, river.
Prairie, a series of grassy plains stretching eastwards from the Rocky Mountains in Canada and U.S.A.
Primeval Forest, a forest which has not been interfered with by man and is allowed to remain in its natural state.
Pristan *(Russian)*, port, harbour.
Projection, is the process of transferring the outline of the features on the earth's spherical surface on to a flat surface, thus constituting a map.
Pueblo *(Spanish)*, village.
Pulau *(Malay)*, island.
Puna, a high plateau between the E. and W. Andes in Bolivia and Peru.
Pur, Pura *(Indian)*, town.
Ras *(Arabic)*, cape.
Reef, a ridge of rock or coral generally covered by sea, but exposed at low tide.
Representative Fraction, a fraction representing a distance of unit lengths on a map over its corresponding length on the earth's surface.
Ria, river valley drowned by the sea owing to a fall in the land level.
Rieka *(Slav.)*, river.
Rift Valley, valley with steep walls caused by the sinking of land between two parallel geological faults.
Rio *(Portuguese, Spanish)*, river.
River Capture, process by which one river having more rapid powers of erosion than another cuts into the head waters of the latter and steals certain of its tributaries.
Riviera, narrow strip of sea coast between Toulon

and Spezia, noted for mild climate in winter.
Roaring Forties, nautical name of steady north-westerly winds between lat. 40° and 60° S. Equivalent to Westerlies of N. Hemisphere.
Ross *(Celtic)*, promontory.
Saki *(Japanese)*, cape.
Sargasso Sea, an area of calms and floating seaweed in the N. Atlantic, east of the Bahamas and the Antilles Current.
Savannas, grasslands of the sub-tropics.
Sea Level, the mean level of the sea between high and low tide.
Selo *(Russian)*, village.
Selva *(Portuguese)*, forest. The name of Selvas is given to the vast rain forests of the Amazon basin.
Shan *(Chinese)*, mountain range.
Shotts *(Arabic)*, salt marshy lakes of N. Algeria and Tunisia.
Sierra *(Spanish)*, **Serra** *(Portuguese)*, mountain range.
Silt, material, finer than sand, which is often carried in suspension by rivers and deposited by them, on flood plains and deltas, when the river has lost the force required to hold the load.
Sirocco, a hot southerly wind blowing off Africa in Southern Mediterranean Countries.
Sjö *(Swedish)*, lake.
Slieve *(Irish)*, mountain.
Snow Line, the lower limit in altitude of the region which is never free from snow.
Spring Tides, period of highest tides at new or at full moon time, *i.e.* when sun and moon are pulling in line with the earth.
Stad, Stadt *(Dutch, Swedish, German)*, town.
Steppe, large expanses of grassland as in European Russia and S.W. Siberia.
Strath *(Celtic)*, broad valley of a river.
Stratus, cloud in the form of a level or horizontal sheet.
Sudd, large floating islands of vegetable matter which impede navigation on the Upper White Nile.
Syd *(Danish-Norwegian)*, south.
Sziget *(Hungarian)*, island.
Taiga, coniferous forest belt south of the Tundra, chiefly used for hunting.
Tanjong *(Malay)*, cape.
Tind *(Norwegian)*, peak.
Trade Winds, regular steady winds in the tropics, between latitudes 30° N. and 30° S. blowing to the equator, from N.E. in N. Hemisphere and S.E. in Southern.
Tributary, a river or stream which flows into and thus becomes part of a larger river.
Tropics, the parallels 23½° N., **Tropic of Cancer**, and 23½° S., **Tropic of Capricorn**, are "turning points" in the apparent seasonal movements of the sun. On June 22nd at noon it is vertically over all points on the Northern Tropic, on December 22nd at noon it is vertically over all points on the Southern Tropic.
Tundra, treeless plains along Arctic and Antarctic coasts; hard frozen in winter, and only partly thawed in summer; scanty vegetation of lichens and mosses.
Tung *(Chinese)*, east.
Ula *(Mongol.)*, mountain.
Vatn *(Norwegian)*, lake.
Veld, grassy plain in South Africa.
Volcano, a vent in the earth's crust through which molten rock, ashes and steam are ejected from the hot interior.
Wadi, Oued *(Arabic)*, a water-course.
Wallace's Line, an imaginary line dividing the characteristic flora and fauna of Asia from that of Australasia. It passes between the islands of Bali and Lombok, thence through the Strait of Macassar between Borneo and Celebes and south of the Philippine Islands. Named after Alfred Russel Wallace the noted scientist.
Warm Front, the sloping boundary in the atmosphere between an advancing mass of warm air and colder air over which the warm air rises.
Watershed, the land-form separating head streams of two river systems. Also known as **waterparting** or **divide**.
Westerlies, predominantly westerly winds in the northern and southern hemispheres N. of 30° N. and S. of 30° S.
Zee *(Dutch)*, sea.

CLIMATIC TABLES

A selection of characteristic stations in different parts of the world, giving Mean Temperature in degrees Celsius (°C),
and Mean Rainfall in millimetres for each month of the year.

Climatic Type	Station	Lat.	Alt in m.		Jan.	Feb.	Mar.	April	May	June	July	Aug.	Sept.	Oct.	Nov.	Dec.	Year
SUB-POLAR	Nome, Alaska	64.30N	7	°C	−17.1	−14.6	−13.2	−8.2	1.3	7.1	10.1	9.7	5.1	−1.7	−9.8	−14.3	−3.8
				mm	25	28	23	15	23	30	74	76	58	38	25	28	445
	North Cape, Norway	71.6 N	6	°C	−3.6	−4.2	−3.4	−0.3	2.8	6.8	9.9	10.0	6.6	2.1	−1.1	−2.9	1.9
				mm	58	61	58	46	48	46	66	58	84	76	74	66	747
WEST MARITIME	Stanley Harbour, Falkland Is.	51.41s	2	°C	9.7	9.8	8.6	6.7	4.7	3.1	2.6	3.0	4.1	5.3	6.8	8.3	6.1
				mm	71	58	56	61	76	61	56	53	33	38	53	71	686
	Ben Nevis, Scotland	56.48N	1344	°C	−4.4	−4.6	−4.5	−2.3	0.7	4.2	4.7	4.4	3.3	−0.8	−2.0	−3.9	−0.5
				mm	480	340	391	221	196	193	279	348	394	386	399	478	4105
	Christchurch, N.Z.	43.31s	6	°C	16.3	15.9	14.5	11.9	8.8	6.4	5.9	6.8	9.4	11.7	13.6	15.7	11.4
				mm	56	46	53	51	66	71	46	41	41	46	51		640
	Edinburgh, Scotland	55.55N	80	°C	3.9	4.2	5.2	7.4	10.1	13.2	14.8	14.6	12.6	9.2	6.3	4.4	8.8
				mm	43	41	48	36	51	48	69	79	51	66	53	53	635
	Paris, France	48.50N	50	°C	2.5	3.9	6.2	10.3	13.4	16.9	18.6	18.0	15.0	10.3	6.0	2.9	10.3
				mm	36	28	36	38	48	53	51	48	48	53	48	41	528
	Valdivia, Chile	39.46s	43	°C	15.3	14.9	13.7	11.9	10.8	9.2	7.8	7.9	9.6	10.6	11.8	13.7	11.4
				mm	74	81	163	236	389	445	391	343	185	127	112	122	2667
	Valentia, Ireland	51.56N	9	°C	6.9	6.8	7.2	8.9	11.1	13.7	14.9	14.9	13.7	10.8	8.6	7.5	10.4
				mm	140	132	114	94	79	81	97	122	104	142	140	165	1415
	Victoria, B.C.	48.24N	26	°C	3.8	4.6	6.3	8.8	11.6	13.9	15.7	15.4	13.3	10.2	6.9	5.1	9.6
				mm	117	81	64	41	30	23	10	15	46	64	147	147	787
SEMI-CONTINENTAL	Chicago, Illinois	41.53N	251	°C	−3.6	−2.8	2.6	8.6	14.7	20.0	23.3	22.7	19.1	12.7	5.3	−0.9	10.1
				mm	53	53	66	74	91	84	86	76	79	66	61	53	841
	Nashville, Tennessee	36.10N	175	°C	3.8	4.9	9.7	14.9	20.2	24.4	26.1	25.3	22.2	15.8	9.4	5.1	15.2
				mm	119	127	130	112	97	107	104	89	89	61	89	99	1204
COLD CONTINENTAL	Warsaw, Poland	52.13N	119	°C	−3.1	−1.9	1.8	7.9	14.1	17.2	18.8	17.5	13.5	7.9	2.2	−1.2	7.9
				mm	33	25	33	41	51	61	86	66	46	41	36	36	478
	Moscow, U.S.S.R.	55.50N	146	°C	−10.8	−9.0	−4.3	3.4	11.8	15.6	18.0	15.8	9.7	3.7	−2.8	−7.9	3.6
				mm	33	30	36	36	46	66	81	79	53	53	46	41	599
	Verkhoyansk, U.S.S.R.	67.33N	101	°C	−50.5	−44.0	−31.0	−13.3	1.6	13.1	15.6	10.0	1.9	−15.0	−36.5	−46.4	−16.2
				mm	5	3	0	3	5	13	30	23	5	5	5	5	99
	Winnipeg, Manitoba	49.53N	232	°C	−15.6	−17.7	−9.4	3.2	11.1	16.8	19.1	17.7	12.1	4.8	−5.9	−14.5	1.4
				mm	23	18	30	36	51	79	79	56	56	36	28	23	513
EAST MARITIME	Miyako, Japan	39.38N	30	°C	−0.6	−0.3	2.6	8.2	12.3	16.0	19.9	22.1	18.5	12.6	7.2	2.2	10.0
				mm	69	66	89	99	119	127	135	178	216	170	81	64	1412
	St John's, Newfoundland	47.34N	38	°C	−4.7	−5.3	−2.4	1.6	6.1	10.6	15.2	15.4	12.1	7.4	2.8	−1.7	4.8
				mm	137	127	117	109	91	91	97	94	97	137	152	137	1382
PRAIRIE STEPPE	Bahia Blanca, Argentina	38.43s	15	°C	23.2	22.2	19.4	15.3	11.5	8.4	8.1	9.4	12.2	14.9	18.6	21.7	15.4
				mm	51	56	66	56	30	23	25	25	41	58	51	53	533
	Calgary, Alberta	51.2 N	1033	°C	−10.9	−9.2	−3.7	4.6	9.5	13.5	16.2	15.2	10.4	5.4	−2.4	−7.0	3.4
				mm	13	15	18	20	58	74	66	64	33	18	18	13	401
	Semipalatinsk, U.S.S.R.	50.26N	180	°C	−17.5	−16.8	−9.8	3.5	14.0	20.0	22.2	19.6	12.7	3.4	−6.6	−14.4	2.5
				mm	13	5	10	10	20	23	28	10	15	15	15	20	185
MANCHURIAN	Peking, China	39.55N	40	°C	−4.7	−1.5	5.0	13.7	19.9	24.5	26.0	24.7	19.8	12.5	3.6	−2.6	11.7
				mm	3	5	5	15	36	76	239	160	66	15	8	3	632
HUMID TEMPERATE	Brisbane, Australia	27.28s	42	°C	25.1	24.7	23.5	21.3	18.1	15.7	14.7	15.8	18.5	21.0	23.1	24.7	20.5
				mm	160	157	142	91	71	66	58	53	53	66	94	122	1135
	Charleston, S. Carolina	32.47N	15	°C	9.9	10.7	14.2	17.7	22.3	25.6	27.0	26.7	24.6	19.4	14.3	10.6	18.6
				mm	79	84	86	74	86	122	180	168	127	91	61	74	1229
	Wuhan, China	30.35N	36	°C	3.8	4.5	9.6	16.2	21.7	25.7	28.6	28.5	24.4	18.2	12.1	6.3	16.6
				mm	53	28	71	122	127	178	218	117	56	99	28	15	1113
MEDITERRANEAN	Adelaide, Australia	34.55s	43	°C	23.4	23.3	21.1	17.8	14.3	11.9	10.8	12.1	13.9	16.6	19.4	21.7	17.2
				mm	20	15	28	46	71	76	66	61	46	46	25	20	521
	Athens, Greece	37.58N	107	°C	9.1	9.7	11.3	14.8	19.1	23.5	26.7	26.4	22.9	18.9	14.1	11.2	17.4
				mm	53	43	30	23	20	18	8	8	13	18	41	66	394
	Gibraltar	36.6 N	15	°C	12.8	13.3	14.1	15.9	18.2	20.8	23.0	23.8	22.2	18.7	15.8	13.4	17.6
				mm	130	107	122	69	43	13	0	3	36	84	163	140	897
	Marseilles, France	43.18N	75	°C	6.9	7.9	10.0	12.8	16.3	19.7	22.2	21.3	19.4	14.8	10.6	7.6	14.1
				mm	41	38	48	56	43	28	18	20	61	97	71	53	574
	Sacramento, California	38.35N	22	°C	8.1	10.2	12.6	14.7	18.0	21.6	22.9	22.3	20.6	16.0	11.6	8.4	15.6
				mm	97	71	71	38	18	3	0	0	8	20	48	97	472
SEMI-ARID	Alice Springs, Australia	23.38s	587	°C	28.5	27.8	24.8	20.1	15.4	12.4	11.4	14.7	18.6	22.9	26.1	27.9	20.9
				mm	46	43	30	20	18	15	10	10	18	25	41		284
	Denver, Colorado	39.45N	1613	°C	−1.2	−0.2	3.8	8.6	13.7	19.6	22.3	21.6	16.9	10.3	4.0	−0.2	9.9
				mm	10	13	25	53	61	36	46	36	25	25	15	18	363
	Kabul, Afghanistan	34.35N	1905	°C	−0.7	2.1	8.2	14.9	20.0	22.9	24.8	24.2	20.4	14.6	10.4	4.7	13.9
				mm	25	20	119	56	15	5	5	5	0	3	25	5	284
	Karachi, Pakistan	24.51N	4	°C	18.5	20.2	23.9	27.0	29.3	30.4	29.1	28.0	27.8	26.7	23.3	19.7	25.3
				mm	15	10	8	3	3	18	71	43	15	0	3	3	188
	Madrid, Spain	40.24N	655	°C	4.6	6.5	8.7	12.2	16.1	20.8	25.1	24.8	19.6	13.4	8.4	5.0	13.7
				mm	33	33	41	41	43	33	10	13	36	46	51	41	422
	Tombouctou, Mali	16.37N	250	°C	21.7	23.1	28.4	33.1	34.7	34.3	31.8	30.3	31.8	31.6	27.1	21.7	29.1
				mm	0	0	3	0	8	23	89	71	28	10	0	0	229
DESERT	Esfahān, Iran	32.40N	1773	°C	1.2	5.3	9.4	15.6	20.7	25.2	27.8	25.6	22.4	16.1	9.1	4.4	15.2
				mm	18	13	23	15	5	0	0 .	0	0	3	15	23	114
	Swakopmund, S.W. Africa	22.40s	6	°C	17.0	17.3	17.4	15.5	15.9	14.7	13.6	12.7	13.4	14.5	14.8	16.4	15.2
				mm	0	3	5	0	0	0	0	0	0	0	3	0	18
	Yuma, Arizona	32.45N	43	°C	12.6	15.1	18.1	21.2	24.9	29.3	32.7	32.3	28.8	22.4	16.1	13.2	22.3
				mm	13	10	8	3	0	0	5	15	8	5	8	10	84
DRY TROPICAL	Bombay, India	18.55N	11	°C	24.2	24.3	26.4	28.4	29.9	28.9	27.4	27.1	27.2	28.0	27.0	25.2	27.0
				mm	3	0	3	0	18	523	693	406	300	61	10	0	2017
	Cuyaba, Brazil	15.36s	165	°C	27.2	27.1	27.1	26.8	25.3	24.1	24.4	25.7	27.8	27.6	27.8	28.4	26.4
				mm	251	211	211	102	53	5	5	30	51	114	152	206	1389
	Darwin, N. Australia	12.28s	30	°C	28.8	28.6	28.9	28.9	27.7	26.1	25.2	26.3	28.1	29.6	29.9	29.5	28.1
				mm	404	330	257	104	18	3	3	3	13	56	122	262	1570
	Manila, Philippines	14.35N	14	°C	24.8	25.3	26.6	28.1	28.6	27.8	27.1	27.1	26.8	26.6	25.8	25.1	26.5
				mm	20	10	20	33	114	234	406	363	170	132	76		2032
	Veracruz, Mexico	19.10N	15	°C	21.9	22.9	23.8	26.1	27.2	27.5	27.6	27.7	26.9	24.7	23.8	21.6	25.2
				mm	10	15	15	3	109	318	376	226	295	229	81	51	1727
WET TROPICAL	Georgetown, Guyana	6.50N	23	°C	25.8	25.8	26.1	26.4	26.3	26.0	26.1	26.5	27.2	27.3	26.9	26.1	26.4
				mm	201	117	183	152	282	297	251	165	79	79	170	282	2253
	Lagos, Nigeria	6.27N	8	°C	27.2	27.9	28.5	28.1	27.7	26.3	25.4	25.4	25.8	26.4	27.4	27.5	26.9
				mm	28	53	94	147	267	472	272	71	135	196	66	20	1819
	Singapore	1.24N	3	°C	25.7	26.1	26.8	27.1	27.5	27.3	27.2	27.0	26.9	26.7	26.3	25.9	26.7
				mm	216	155	165	175	183	170	173	216	180	208	254	264	2360
MOUNTAIN	Bogota, Colombia	4.36N	2661	°C	14.2	14.4	14.8	14.8	14.7	14.5	14.0	13.9	13.9	14.4	14.6	14.5	14.4
				mm	58	61	104	145	114	61	51	56	61	163	117	66	1057
	Darjeeling, India	27.3 N	2248	°C	4.5	5.3	9.8	13.4	14.6	15.5	16.4	16.1	15.2	12.9	8.8	5.4	11.5
				mm	20	28	51	104	198	615	805	660	465	135	5	5	3094
	Johannesburg, S. Africa	26.11s	1806	°C	19.2	18.6	17.4	15.4	12.4	10.4	10.3	12.4	15.2	17.0	17.5	18.4	15.3
				mm	157	132	112	43	20	3	13	13	25	66	127	137	843
	Mexico City, Mexico	19.26N	2278	°C	12.2	13.8	15.8	17.9	18.3	17.7	16.9	16.7	16.2	14.8	13.6	11.9	15.5
				mm	5	5	15	15	48	99	104	119	104	46	13	5	587

STATES AND POPULATIONS

	area (sq. km)	POPULATION
AFGHANISTAN	657 500	17 600 000
ALBANIA	28 748	2 170 000
ALGERIA	2 381 730	14 600 000
ANDORRA	453	20 000
ANGOLA	1 246 700	5 673 000
ARGENTINA	2 778 412	24 000 000
AUSTRALIA	7 686 900	12 959 000
Australian Capital Terr.	2 432	158 000
New South Wales	801 432	4 663 000
Northern Territory	1 347 515	93 000
Queensland	1 727 520	1 869 000
South Australia	984 381	1 186 000
Tasmania	68 332	392 200
Victoria	227 620	3 546 000
Western Australia	2 527 623	1 053 000
AUSTRIA	83 849	7 456 000
BAHAMAS, THE	11 400	171 000
BAHRAIN	598	216 000
BANGLADESH	142 776	75 000 000
BARBADOS	430	238 141
BELGIUM	30 513	9 676 000
BELIZE	22 963	126 000
BENIN	112 600	2 800 000
BERMUDA	53	55 000
BHUTAN	46 600	1 000 000
BOLIVIA	1 098 580	5 100 000
BOTSWANA	600 000	700 000
BRAZIL	8 511 965	98 000 000
BRUNEI	5 765	142 000
BULGARIA	110 912	8 490 000
BURMA	678 034	28 870 000
BURUNDI	27 834	3 800 000
CAMBODIA	181 305	7 200 000
CAMEROUN	475 500	6 200 000
CANADA	9 976 169	21 568 000
Alberta	661 188	1 627 900
British Columbia	948 600	2 184 600
Manitoba	650 090	988 200
New Brunswick	73 437	634 600
Newfoundland	404 519	522 100
Northwest Territories	3 379 689	34 800
Nova Scotia	55 490	789 000
Ontario	1 068 587	7 703 000
Prince Edward Island	5 657	111 600
Quebec	1 549 677	6 027 800
Saskatchewan	651 903	926 200
Yukon	536 327	18 400
CAPE VERDE ISLANDS	4 033	272 000
CENT. AFRICAN REP.	623 018	1 520 000
CHAD	1 284 000	3 710 000
CHILE	756 945	10 000 000
CHINA	9 560 975	750 000 000
Inner Mongolia	450 000	9 000 000
Sinkiang	1 646 790	8 000 000
Tibet	1 221 600	1 250 000
COLOMBIA	1 138 914	22 500 000
CONGO	342 000	1 000 000
COSTA RICA	50 900	1 800 000
CUBA	114 524	8 553 395
CYPRUS	9 255	600 000
CZECHOSLOVAKIA	127 870	14 362 000
DENMARK	43 069	4 976 000
DOMINICAN REP.	48 442	4 200 000
ECUADOR	281 341	6 500 000
EGYPT	1 000 253	34 700 000
EL SALVADOR	21 393	3 700 000
EQUATORIAL GUINEA	28 051	290 000
ETHIOPIA	1 221 900	26 400 000
FAEROES	1 373	38 000
FALKLAND ISLANDS	11 961	2 105
FIJI	18 272	533 000
FINLAND	337 032	4 706 000
FRANCE	549 430	51 600 000
FRENCH GUIANA	91 000	51 000
FRENCH TERR. OF AFARS & ISSAS	23 000	81 000
GABON	267 000	500 000
GAMBIA, THE	11 295	364 000
EAST GERMANY	108 173	17 042 000
WEST GERMANY	248 533	61 682 000
GHANA	238 539	9 600 000
GIBRALTAR	6	26 833
GILBERT IS.&TUVALU	886	56 000
GREECE	131 944	9 000 000
GREENLAND	2 175 600	47 000
GUATEMALA	108 889	5 500 000
GUINEA	245 857	3 920 000
GUINEA-BISSAU	36 125	560 000
GUYANA	214 970	700 000
HAITI	27 750	5 000 000
HONDURAS	112 088	2 700 000

	area (sq. km)	POPULATION
HONG KONG	1 032	4 078 000
HUNGARY	93 030	10 415 000
ICELAND	103 000	200 000
INDIA	3 268 000	564 008 000
INDONESIA	1 904 334	129 000 000
IRAN	1 648 180	30 550 000
IRAQ	438 446	9 800 000
IRELAND, Rep. of	68 893	3 000 000
ISRAEL	20 700	3 080 000
ITALY	301 224	55 000 000
IVORY COAST	322 463	4 500 000
JAMAICA	11 525	2 040 000
JAPAN	372 077	106 958 000
JORDAN	97 740	2 467 000
KENYA	582 600	11 800 000
KOREA, NORTH	127 158	14 500 000
KOREA, SOUTH	98 431	33 400 000
KUWAIT	16 000	800 000
LAOS	236 800	2 962 000
LEBANON	10 400	2 855 000
LESOTHO	30 340	1 200 000
LIBERIA	111 000	1 300 000
LIBYA	1 759 540	2 100 000
LIECHTENSTEIN	160	21 350
LUXEMBOURG	2 586	345 000
MADAGASCAR	594 180	7 655 000
MALAWI	126 338	4 530 000
MALAYSIA	333 507	10 800 000
MALI	1 240 000	5 300 000
MALTA	316	326 000
MAURITANIA	1 030 700	1 400 000
MAURITIUS	1 865	836 000
MEXICO	1 967 183	52 500 000
MONACO	15	23 000
MONGOLIA	1 565 000	1 290 000
MOROCCO	458 730	15 700 000
MOZAMBIQUE	784 961	8 234 000
NEPAL	141 400	11 500 000
NETHERLANDS	40 893	13 270 000
NETHERLANDS ANTILLES	1 019	225 000
NEW HEBRIDES	14 760	84 000
NEW ZEALAND	268 680	2 900 000
NICARAGUA	148 000	2 210 000
NIGER	1 267 000	4 200 000
NIGERIA	923 773	58 000 000
NORWAY	324 219	3 918 000
OMAN	212 000	660 000
PAKISTAN	803 994	58 000 000
PANAMA	75 650	1 500 000
PANAMA CANAL ZONE	1 676	50 000
PAPUA-NEW GUINEA	461 700	2 467 000
PARAGUAY	406 752	2 500 000
PERU	1 285 215	14 400 000
PHILIPPINES	299 400	40 600 000
POLAND	312 700	32 900 000
PORTUGAL	92 082	9 700 000
PUERTO RICO	8 891	2 770 000
QATAR	22 000	80 000
RHODESIA	390 622	5 780 000
ROMANIA	237 500	20 600 000
RWANDA	26 330	3 800 000
SAN MARINO	61	19 000
SAUDI ARABIA	2 263 600	7 200 000
SENEGAL	197 161	3 925 000
SIERRA LEONE	73 326	2 550 000
SIKKIM	7 298	205 000
SOLOMON IS.	29 785	163 000
SOMALI REPUBLIC	637 660	2 790 000
SOUTH AFRICA, Rep. of	1 221 042	22 700 000
Cape of Good Hope	721 004	5 363 000
Natal	86 967	2 980 000
Orange Free State	129 153	1 387 000
Transvaal	283 918	6 273 000
SOUTH-WEST AFRICA (Namibia)	824 295	630 000
SPAIN	504 748	34 600 000
SRI LANKA	65 610	13 033 000
SUDAN	2 505 813	16 700 000
SURINAM	17 400	385 000
SWAZILAND	173 400	408 000
SWEDEN	449 793	8 127 000
SWITZERLAND	41 288	6 270 000
SYRIA	185 680	6 600 000
TAIWAN	35 961	14 990 000
TANZANIA	939 700	14 000 000
THAILAND	514 000	38 000 000
TOGO	56 000	2 004 711
TRINIDAD & TOBAGO	5 128	1 070 000
TUNISIA	164 150	5 300 000
TURKEY	780 576	37 010 000

	area (sq. km)	POPULATION
UGANDA	236 037	9 764 000
UNION OF SOVIET SOCIALIST REPS.	22 400 000	246 300 000
Armenian S.S.R.	29 759	2 600 000
Azerbaijan S.S.R.	86 853	5 300 000
Byelorussian S.S.R.	207 588	9 100 000
Estonian S.S.R.	45 092	1 357 000
Georgian S.S.R.	69 670	4 800 000
Kazakh S.S.R.	2 717 000	13 500 000
Kirghiz S.S.R.	198 652	3 100 000
Latvian S.S.R.	64 000	2 365 000
Lithuanian S.S.R.	65 190	3 129 000
Moldavian S.S.R.	33 800	3 700 000
Russian S.F.S.R.	17 077 962	130 090 000
Tadzhik S.S.R.	143 072	3 100 000
Turkmen S.S.R.	487 956	2 300 000
Ukrainian S.S.R.	604 000	47 900 000
Uzbek S.S.R.	447 000	12 500 000
UNITED ARAB EMIRATES	83 660	180 000
UNITED KINGDOM OF GT. BRITAIN & N. IRELAND	230 608	55 356 000
England and Wales	130 362	48 604 000
Scotland	78749	5 224 000
Northern Ireland	14147	1 528 000
Channel Islands	195	125 240
Isle of Man	588	49 743
UNITED STATES OF AMERICA	9 363 353	209 000 000
Alabama	133 167	3 444 165
Alaska	1 518 800	302 173
Arizona	295 022	1 772 482
Arkansas	137 539	1 923 295
California	411 012	19 953 134
Colorado	269 998	2 207 259
Connecticut	12 973	3 032 217
Delaware	5 328	548 104
District of Columbia	174	756 510
Florida	151 670	6 789 443
Georgia	152 488	4 589 575
Hawaii	16 705	769 913
Idaho	216 412	713 008
Illinois	146 075	11 113 976
Indiana	93 993	5 193 669
Iowa	145 791	2 825 041
Kansas	213 063	2 249 071
Kentucky	104 623	3 219 311
Louisiana	125 674	3 643 180
Maine	86 027	993 663
Maryland	27 394	3 922 399
Massachusetts	21 386	5 689 170
Michigan	150 779	8 875 083
Minnesota	217 735	3 805 069
Mississippi	123 584	2 216 912
Missouri	180 486	4 677 399
Montana	381 084	694 409
Nebraska	200 017	1 483 791
Nevada	286 296	488 738
New Hampshire	24 097	737 681
New Jersey	20 295	7 168 164
New Mexico	315 113	1 016 000
New York	128 401	18 241 266
North Carolina	136 197	5 082 059
North Dakota	183 022	617 716
Ohio	106 765	10 652 017
Oklahoma	181 090	2 559 253
Oregon	251 180	2 091 385
Pennsylvania	117 412	11 793 909
Rhode Island	3 144	949 723
South Carolina	80 432	2 590 516
South Dakota	199 551	666 257
Tennessee	109 412	3 924 164
Texas	692 403	11 196 730
Utah	219 932	1 059 273
Vermont	24 887	444 732
Virginia	105 816	4 648 494
Washington	176 617	3 409 169
West Virginia	62 629	1 744 237
Wisconsin	145 438	4 417 933
Wyoming	253 597	332 416
UPPER VOLTA	274 122	5 600 000
URUGUAY	186 926	3 000 000
VATICAN CITY	0.44	1 000
VENEZUELA	912 050	11 000 000
VIETNAM	329 650	41 000 000
YEMEN	195 000	5 750 000
YEMEN, SOUTH	160 300	1 280 000
YUGOSLAVIA	255 804	20 800 000
ZAIRE	2 345 409	22 800 000
ZAMBIA	752 262	4 500 000

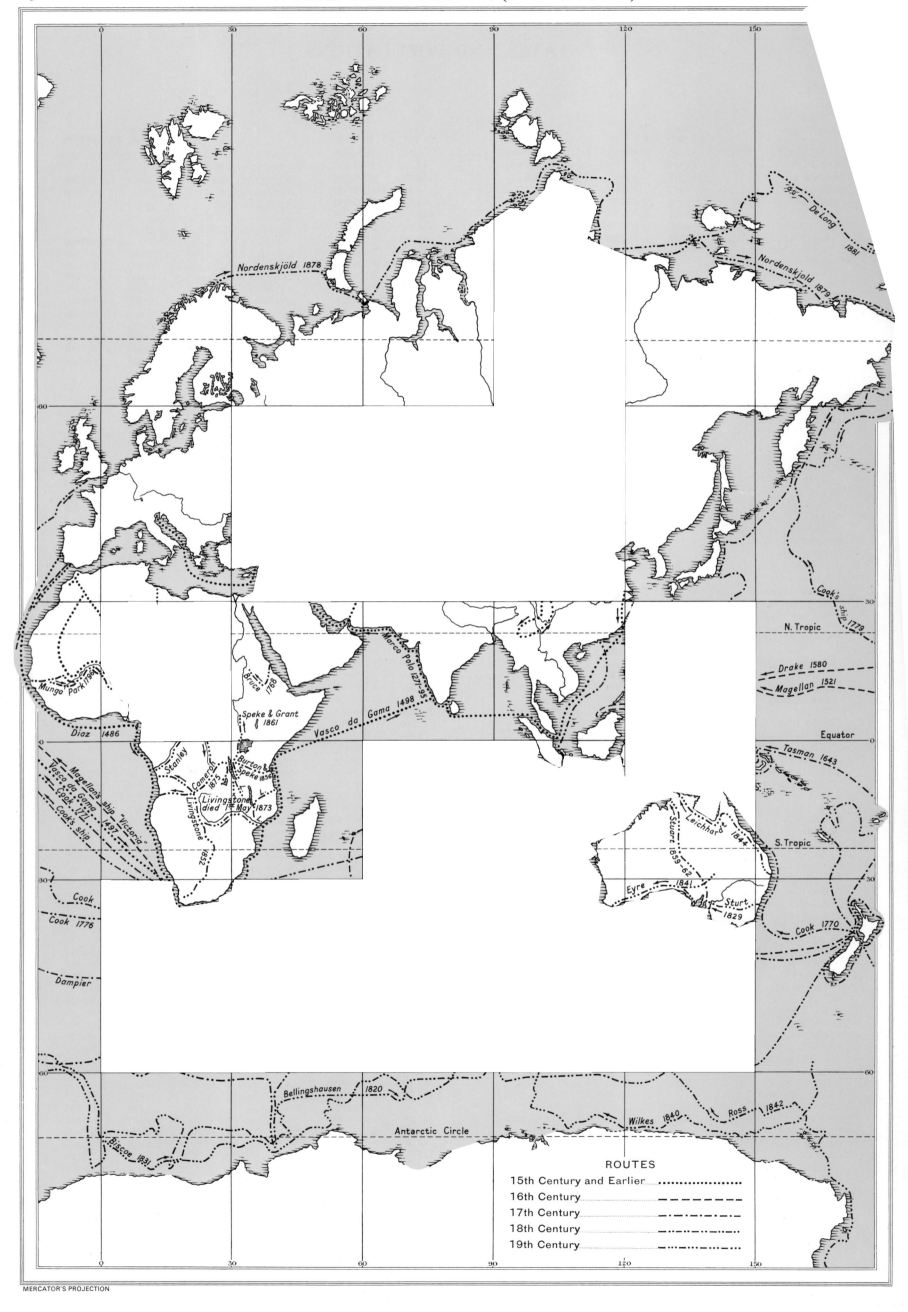

Nordenskjöld 1878

De Long 1881

Nordenskjöld 1879

Cook's ship 1779

N. Tropic

Drake 1580

Magellan 1521

Marco Polo 1277-95

Bruce 1768

Speke & Grant 1861

Vasco da Gama 1498

Mungo Park 1796

Diaz 1486

Equator

Tasman 1643

Stanley 1875

Cameron 1875

Burton & Speke 1856

Livingstone died 1st May 1873

Livingstone 1852

Magellan's ship "Victoria"

Vasco de Gama 1497

Cook 1772

Cook's ship

Leichhar 1844

Stuart 1859-62

S. Tropic

Eyre 1841

Sturt 1829

Cook 1770

Cook

Cook 1776

Dampier

Bellingshausen 1820

Wilkes 1840

Ross 1842

Antarctic Circle

Biscoe 1831

ROUTES

15th Century and Earlier	·················
16th Century	‑ ‑ ‑ ‑ ‑
17th Century	‑·‑·‑·‑
18th Century	‑··‑··‑··
19th Century	‑···‑···‑···

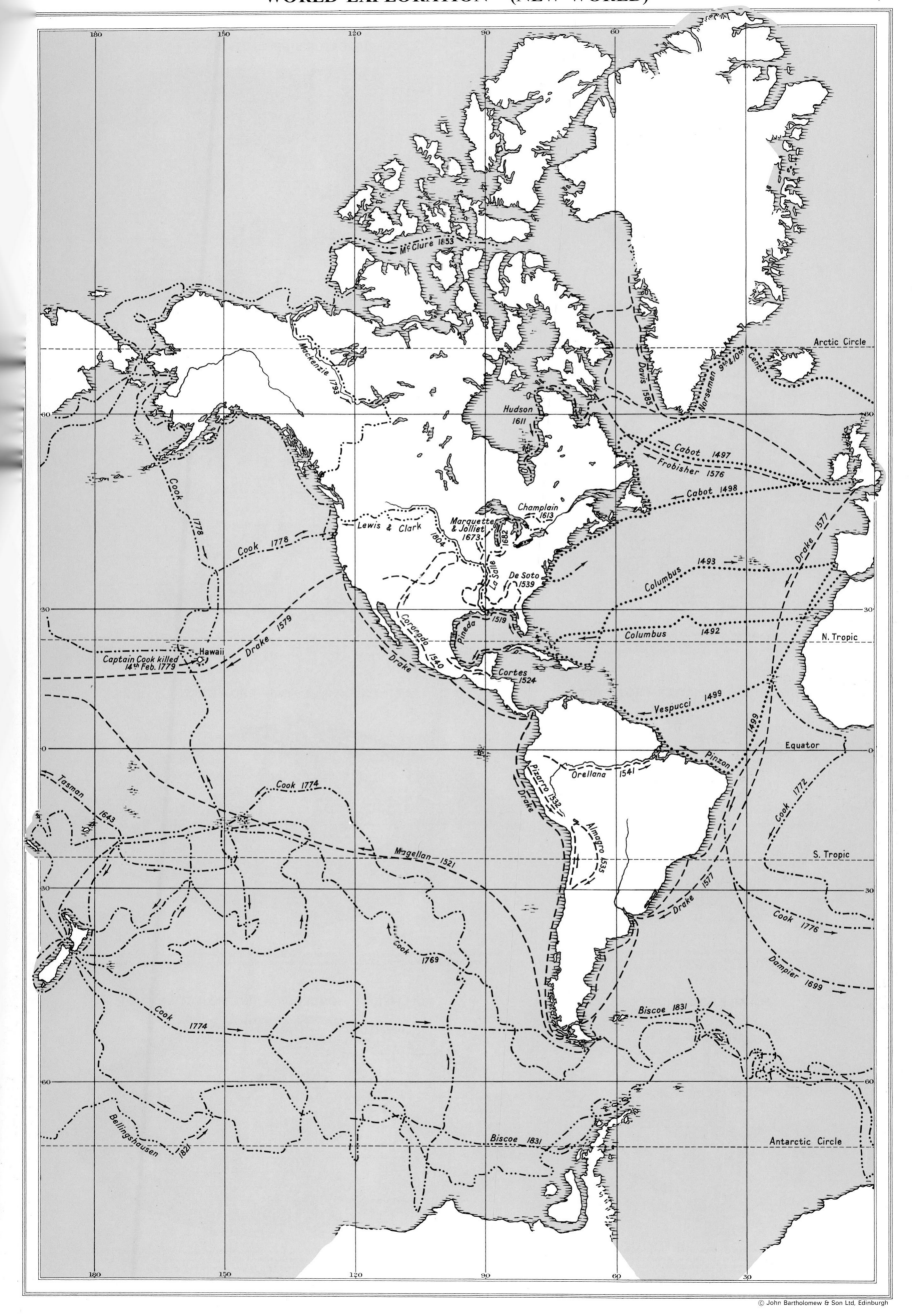

STEREOGRAPHIC PROJECTION

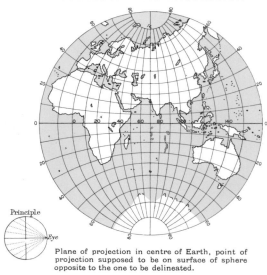

Plane of projection in centre of Earth, point of projection supposed to be on surface of sphere opposite to the one to be delineated.

ORTHOGRAPHIC PROJECTION

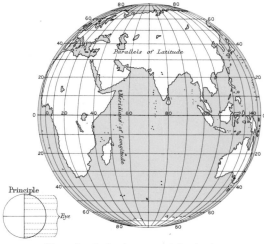

Plane of projection in centre of Earth, the eye or point of projection supposed to be at infinite distance so that lines of projection are all parallel.

EQUIDISTANT OR GLOBULAR PROJECTION

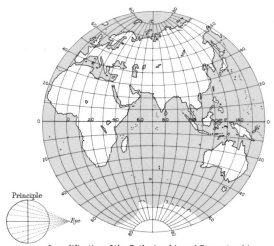

A modification of the Orthographic and Stereographic in which the point of projection is supposed to be removed to a point outside of the opposite surface of the sphere.

POLAR PROJECTIONS

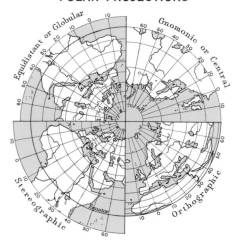

The Gnomonic Projection cannot be made to include the whole hemisphere. The Stereographic and Globular Projections can be extended to include more than the hemisphere.

MERCATOR'S PROJECTION

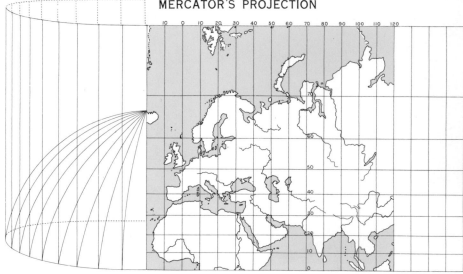

The plane of projection is the surface of an imaginary cylinder surrounding the globe and touching its surface at the Equator. At the Equator its scale agrees with the globe, but as each parallel of latitude becomes a great circle equal to the Equator, the scale increases as we go North and South. The latitude is, however, increased in same proportion as the longitude. Mercator's projection is the only one which gives the true direction of one point in relation to another, and is therefore most used for the purposes of navigation.

GALL'S STEREOGRAPHIC PROJECTION

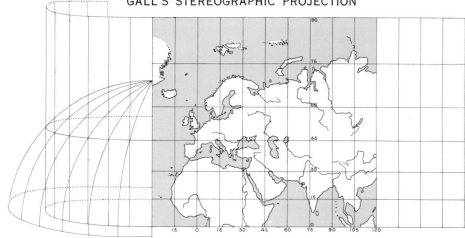

This is another Cylindrical Projection, but the cylinder, instead of touching the sphere only at the Equator as in Mercator's, is supposed to be sunk into its surface so that it cuts its surface half way between the Equator and the poles, and thus coincides with the two parallels of 45° N. and S. Lat. The parallels are projected stereographically.

SANSON'S (SINUSOIDAL) PROJECTION

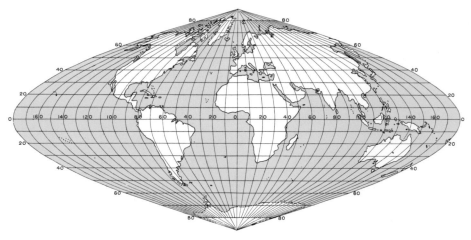

The parallels are drawn at their true distances from the Equator and along each of these. correct distances are measured through which the meridians are drawn. The projection is obviously equal-area.

MOLLWEIDE'S HOMOLOGRAPHIC PROJECTION

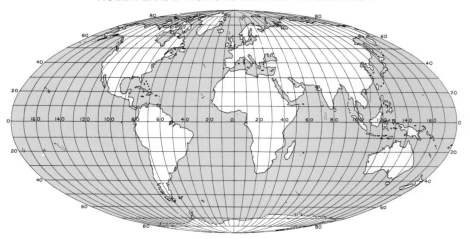

This is an equal area projection. The complete circle on the map is made to equal the world hemisphere. Parallels are so drawn that the zone enclosed by them bears the same relation to the area of the circle as the similar zone on the Earth bears to the hemisphere. The meridians are ellipses cutting the parallels at equal distances.

CONIC PROJECTION WITH ONE STANDARD PARALLEL

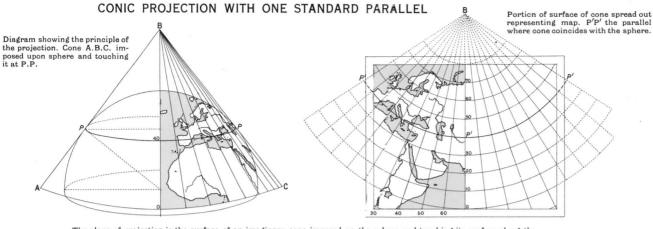

Diagram showing the principle of the projection. Cone A.B.C. imposed upon sphere and touching it at P.P.

Portion of surface of cone spread out representing map. P'P' the parallel where cone coincides with the sphere.

The plane of projection is the surface of an imaginary cone imposed on the sphere and touching its surface along the parallel of 40° P.P. Distances measured along that parallel on the map are absolutely correct as they exactly coincide with the globe. But the scale is distorted to the North and South of tangential parallel according to distance away from it.

CONIC PROJECTION WITH TWO STANDARD PARALLELS

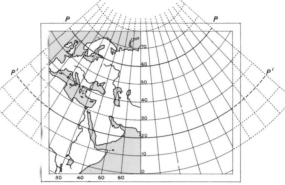

Diagram showing the principle of the projection. Cone A.B.C. imposed upon sphere and touching it at P.P. P'P'.

Portion of surface of cone spread out representing map. P.P. P'P' the parallels where the cone coincides with the sphere.

In this case the cone is supposed to cut the sphere along two parallels PP. and P'P', which, however, are plotted their true distance apart (i.e. the distance along the arc PP', not the chord). The map has therefore the advantage of coinciding with the globe along two parallels instead of one as in the Simple Conic.

LENGTH OF DEGREES OF LONGITUDE AT VARIOUS DEGREES OF LATITUDE

Pole 90°	0		
85°	6·05	Miles	9.74km
80°	12·05	,,	19.4km
75°	17·96	,,	28.9km
70°	23·73	,,	38.26km
65°	29·31	,,	47.17km
60°	34·67	,,	55.8km
55°	39·77	,,	64.0km
50°	44·55	,,	71.7km
45°	48·99	,,	78.84km
40°	53·06	,,	85.39km
35°	56·72	,,	91.28km
30°	59·96	,,	96.49km
25°	62·73	,,	101.0km
20°	65·03	,,	104.65km
15°	66·83	,,	107.6km
10°	68·13	,,	109.64km
5°	68·91	,,	110.9km
0° Equator	69·17	,,	111.32km

BONNE'S PROJECTION

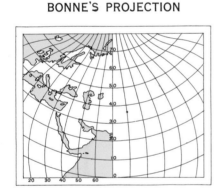

This is a development of the Conic Projection and differs from the pure Conic in that instead of distances being correctly measured along one parallel, true distances are measured along each parallel.

VAN DER GRINTEN'S PROJECTION

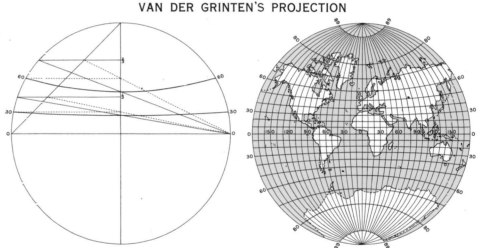

This projection strikes a mean between Mercator's and Mollweide's. It has neither the great exaggeration of land areas towards the Pole, of the former, nor the excessive angular distortion of the latter.

COVERING OF A 2½ INCH WORLD GLOBE IN GORES

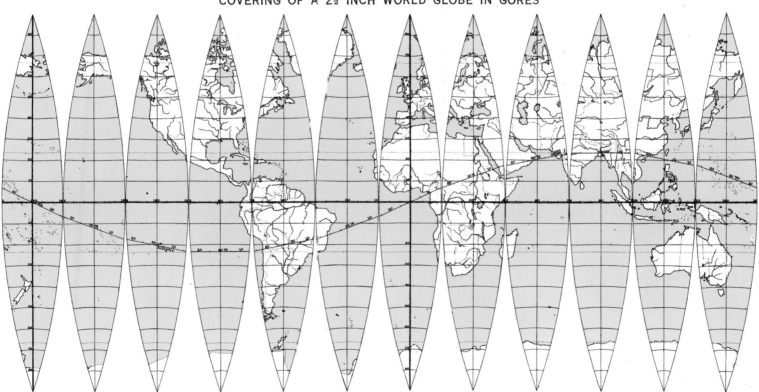

Note—These Gores are designed to be cut out and mounted on a Globe 2½ inches in diameter, which they will exactly cover.

LAMBERT'S AZIMUTHAL PROJECTION

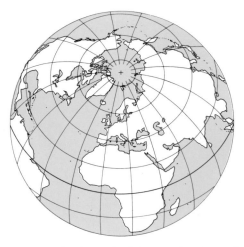

This projection is calculated from a selected central point as in a Polar, the crossing of degree lines being calculated to retain equal-area properties. It gives excellent treatment of large continental masses, but necessarily leads to some distension in circumferential areas.

BARTHOLOMEW'S ATLANTIS PROJECTION

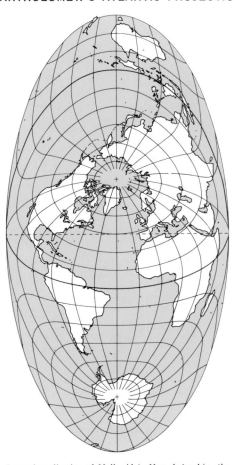

A novel application of Mollweide's Homolographic, the main axis being taken as a transverse great circle running through the poles. The minor axis lies on an oblique great circle touching 45°N. It is equal-area and shows the land masses in unbroken formation with regard to the N. Atlantic Ocean.

TETRAHEDRAL PROJECTION

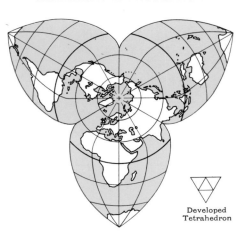

Developed
Tetrahedron

One of the simplest yet most natural developments of the Globe. Prof. J. W. Gregory was first to point out the Earth's affinity to a tetrahedron, whose edges represented the main lines of mountain folding.

AITOFF'S PROJECTION

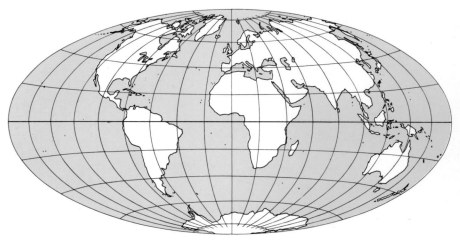

This is developed from Lambert's equal-area treatment of the hemisphere. Co-ordinates on the "X" axis are doubled while those on the "Y" remain as they were. The result is an ellipse containing an equal-area grid which may be subdivided for the whole world.

BARTHOLOMEW'S NORDIC PROJECTION

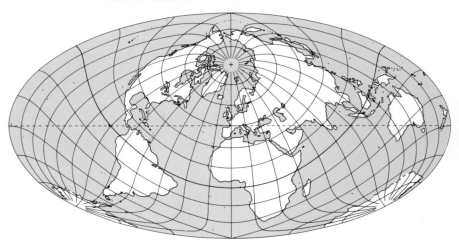

Like Aitoff's, this is a development of Lambert's Azimuthal. The main axis, however, instead of following the Equator becomes an oblique great circle, in this case touching 45° N. and 45° S. It is equal-area and gives a good basis for distributional maps, particularly in the north temperate and circum-polar areas.

BARTHOLOMEW'S RE-CENTRED SINUSOIDAL PROJECTION

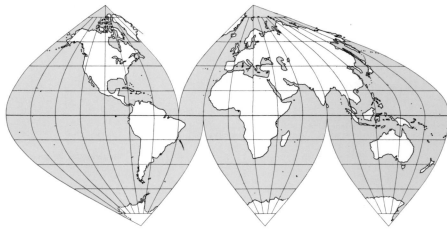

The equal-area properties and simple construction of the Sinusoidal are here applied to each continental mass separately so as to preserve optimum conformity. It was developed from Prof. Paul Goode's idea of the "Interrupted Homolographic" over which it claims certain advantages for purposes of land distribution.

BARTHOLOMEW'S REGIONAL PROJECTION

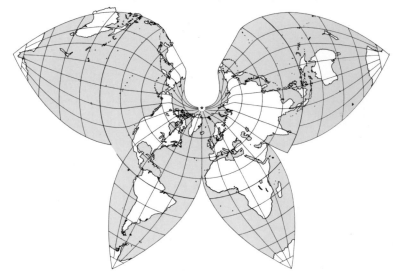

This arrangement claims to combine the best conformal properties with those as near equal-area as possible. It recognises that the chief field of man's development is in the North Temperate Zone and from a cone cutting the globe along two selected parallels it is continued on interrupted lines to complete the Earth.

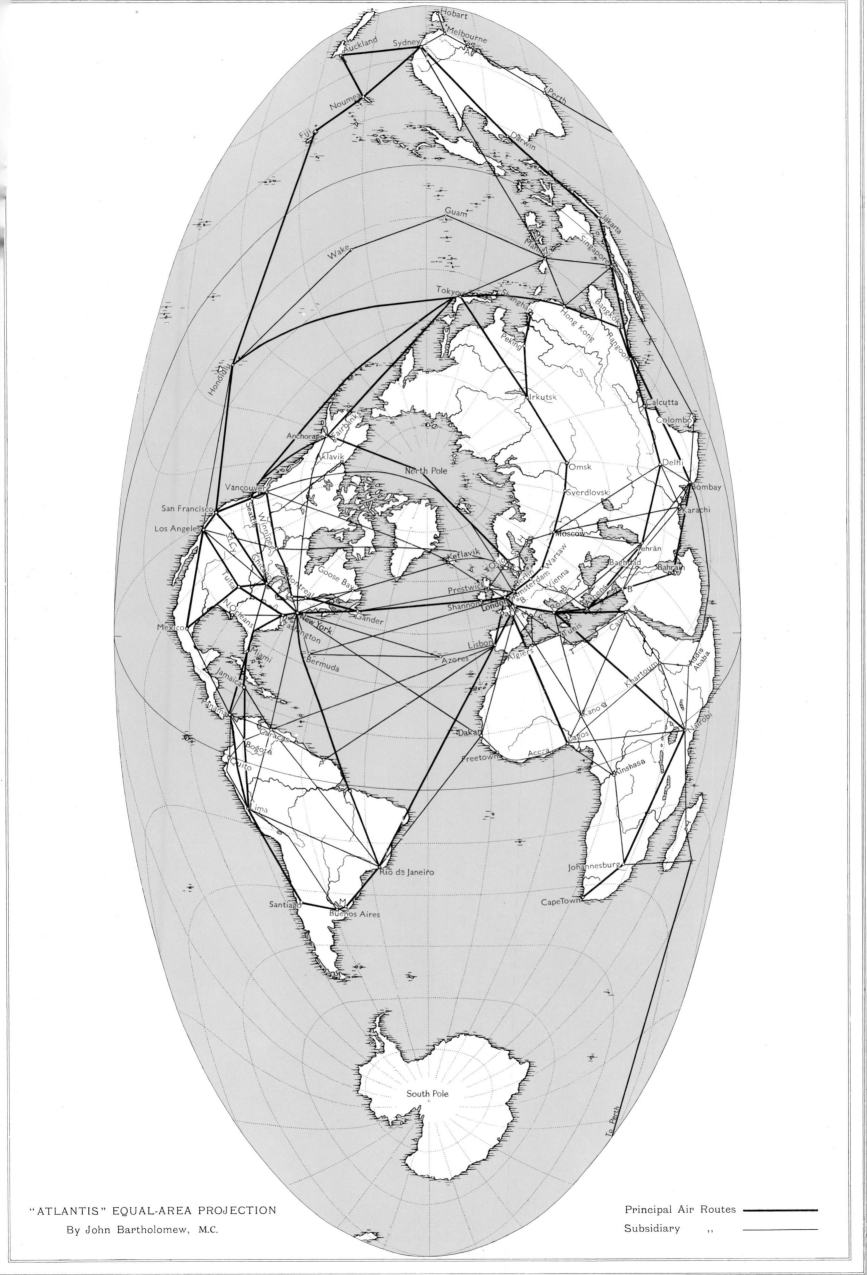

"ATLANTIS" EQUAL-AREA PROJECTION

By John Bartholomew, M.C.

Principal Air Routes ─────

Subsidiary   ,,   ───────

1:120M

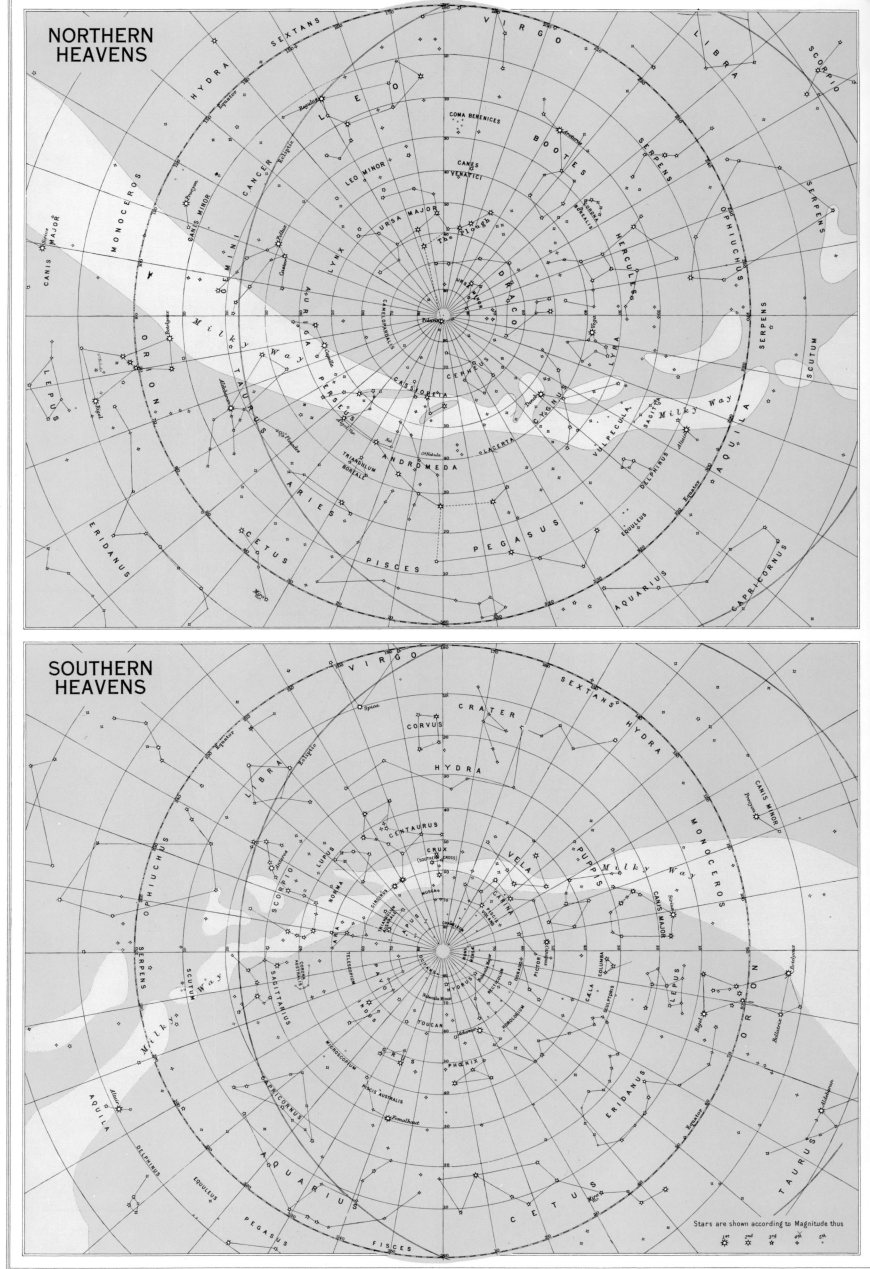

NORTHERN HEAVENS

SOUTHERN HEAVENS

Stars are shown according to Magnitude thus

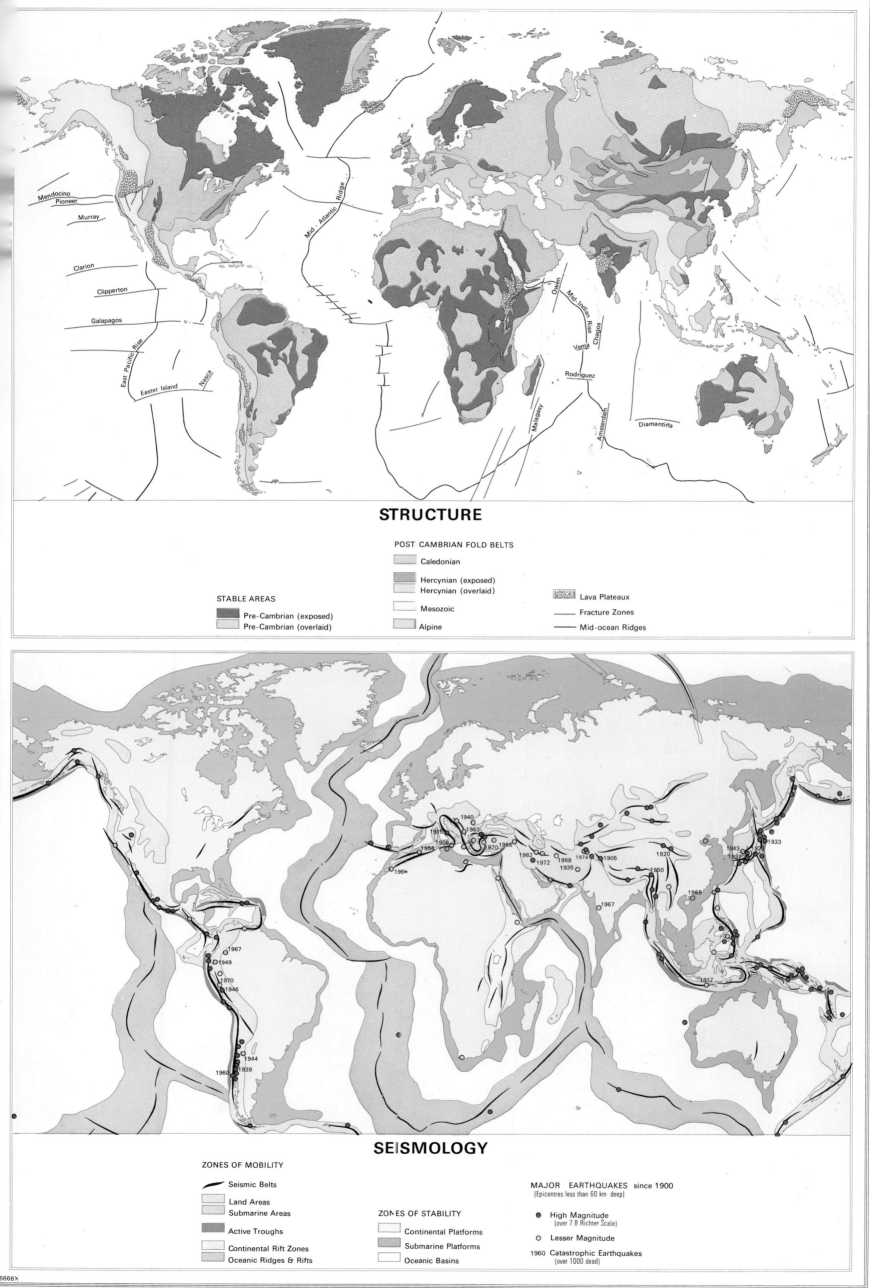

STRUCTURE

POST CAMBRIAN FOLD BELTS

Caledonian

Hercynian (exposed)

Hercynian (overlaid)

STABLE AREAS

Mesozoic

Pre-Cambrian (exposed)

Pre-Cambrian (overlaid)

Alpine

Lava Plateaux

Fracture Zones

Mid-ocean Ridges

SEISMOLOGY

ZONES OF MOBILITY

Seismic Belts

Land Areas

Submarine Areas

Active Troughs

ZONES OF STABILITY

Continental Rift Zones

Continental Platforms

Oceanic Ridges & Rifts

Submarine Platforms

Oceanic Basins

MAJOR EARTHQUAKES since 1900
(Epicentres less than 60 km deep)

● High Magnitude
(over 7.8 Richter Scale)

○ Lesser Magnitude

1960 Catastrophic Earthquakes
(over 1000 dead)

6666x

1:140M

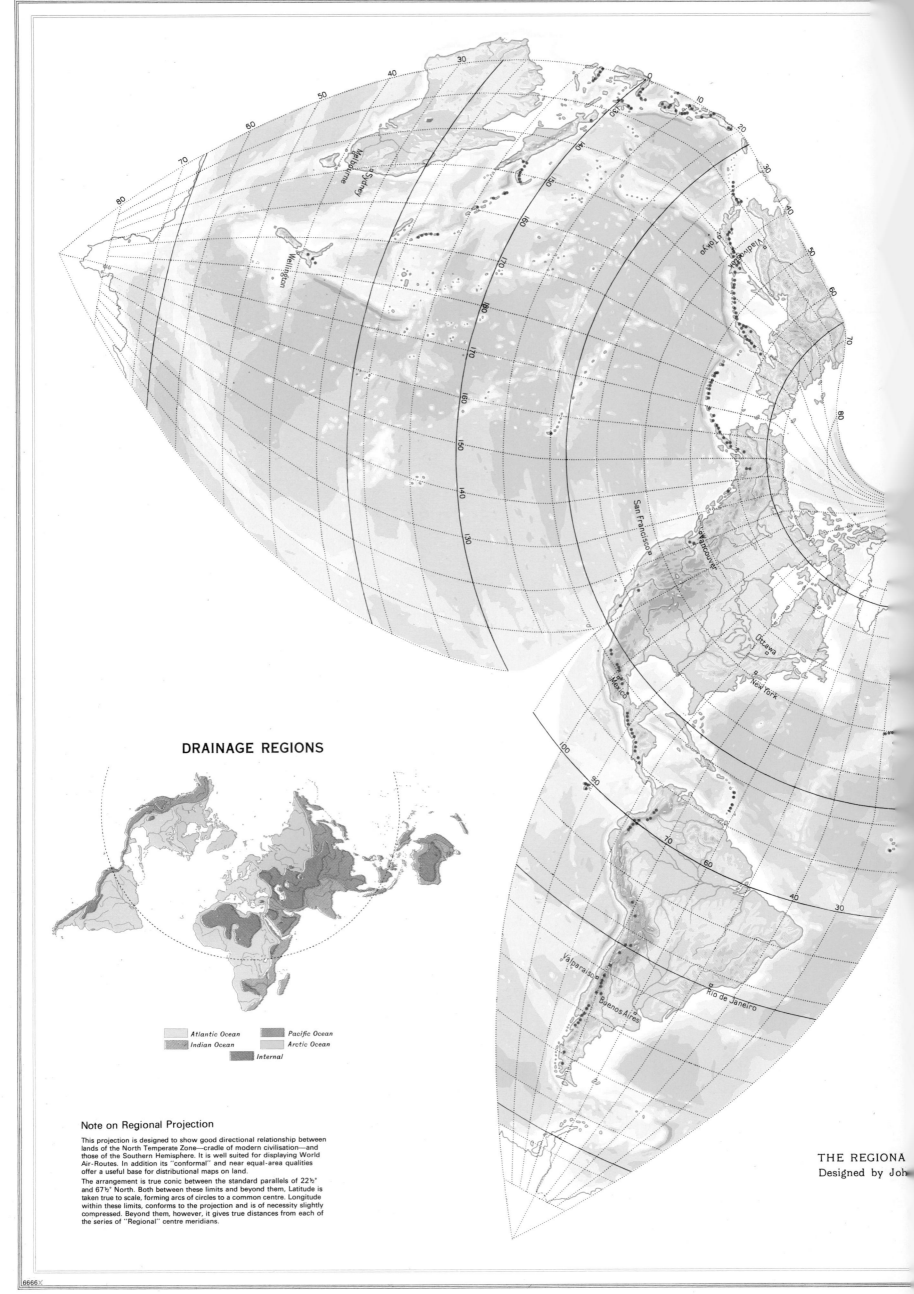

DRAINAGE REGIONS

Atlantic Ocean   Pacific Ocean
Indian Ocean   Arctic Ocean
Internal

Note on Regional Projection

This projection is designed to show good directional relationship between lands of the North Temperate Zone—cradle of modern civilisation—and those of the Southern Hemisphere. It is well suited for displaying World Air-Routes. In addition its "conformal" and near equal-area qualities offer a useful base for distributional maps on land.

The arrangement is true conic between the standard parallels of 22½° and 67½° North. Both between these limits and beyond them, Latitude is taken true to scale, forming arcs of circles to a common centre. Longitude within these limits, conforms to the projection and is of necessity slightly compressed. Beyond them, however, it gives true distances from each of the series of "Regional" centre meridians.

THE REGIONA
Designed by Joh

Metres 7000 5000 4000 3000 1000   0
Feet 22960 16400 13120 9840 3280   0

1:9(

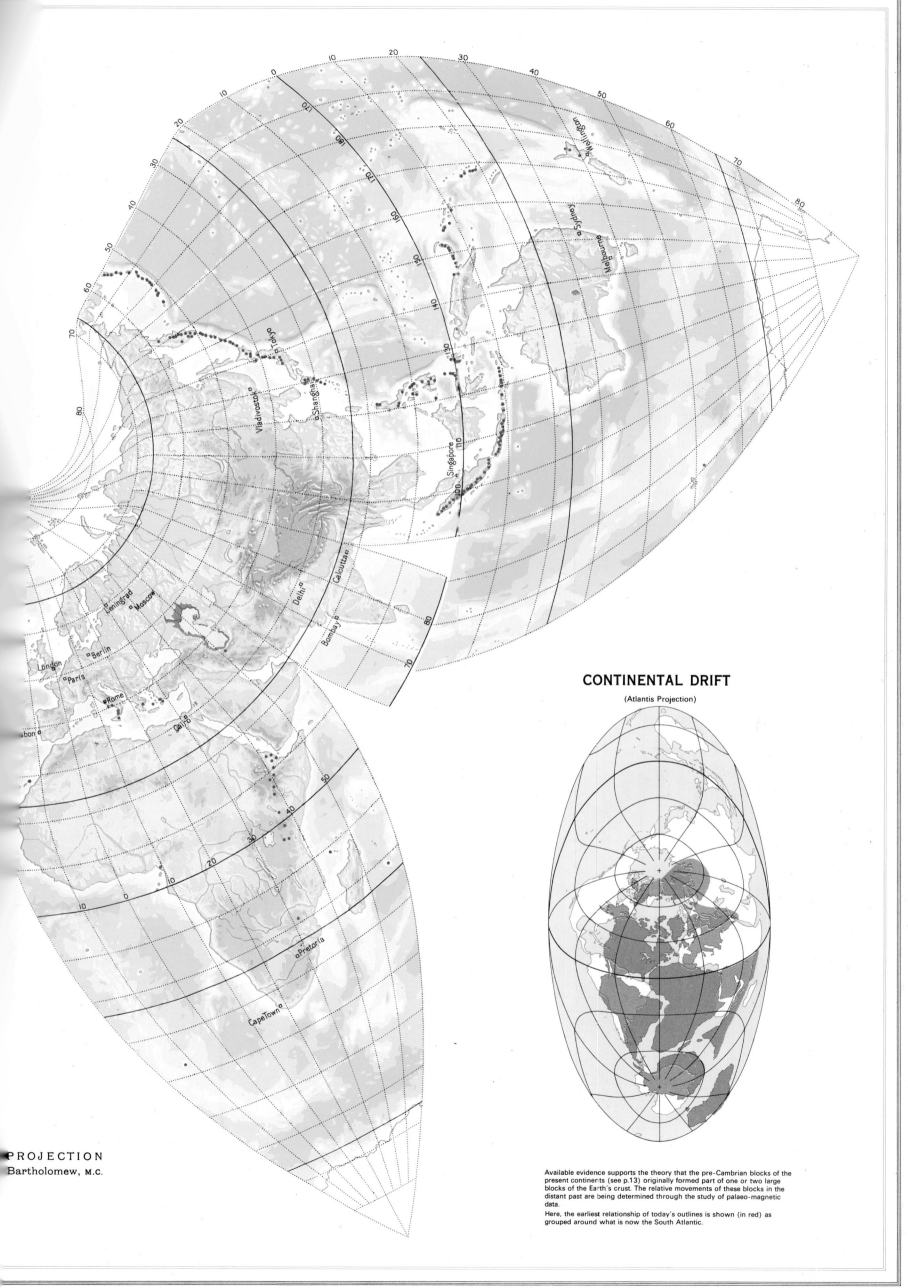

London
Paris
Rome
Berlin
Cairo
Lisbon
Leningrad
Moscow
Vladivostok
Tokyo
Shanghai
Singapore
Delhi
Calcutta
Bombay
Pretoria
CapeTown
Wellington
Kaupf/Sa
Melbourne

PROJECTION
Bartholomew, M.C.

CONTINENTAL DRIFT

(Atlantis Projection)

Available evidence supports the theory that the pre-Cambrian blocks of the present continents (see p.13) originally formed part of one or two large blocks of the Earth's crust. The relative movements of these blocks in the distant past are being determined through the study of palaeo-magnetic data.

Here, the earliest relationship of today's outlines is shown (in red) as grouped around what is now the South Atlantic.

| 0 | 200 | 500 | 1000 | 2000 | 4000 Metres |

| 0 | 660 | 1640 | 3280 | 6560 | 13120 Feet |

• Active Volcanoes

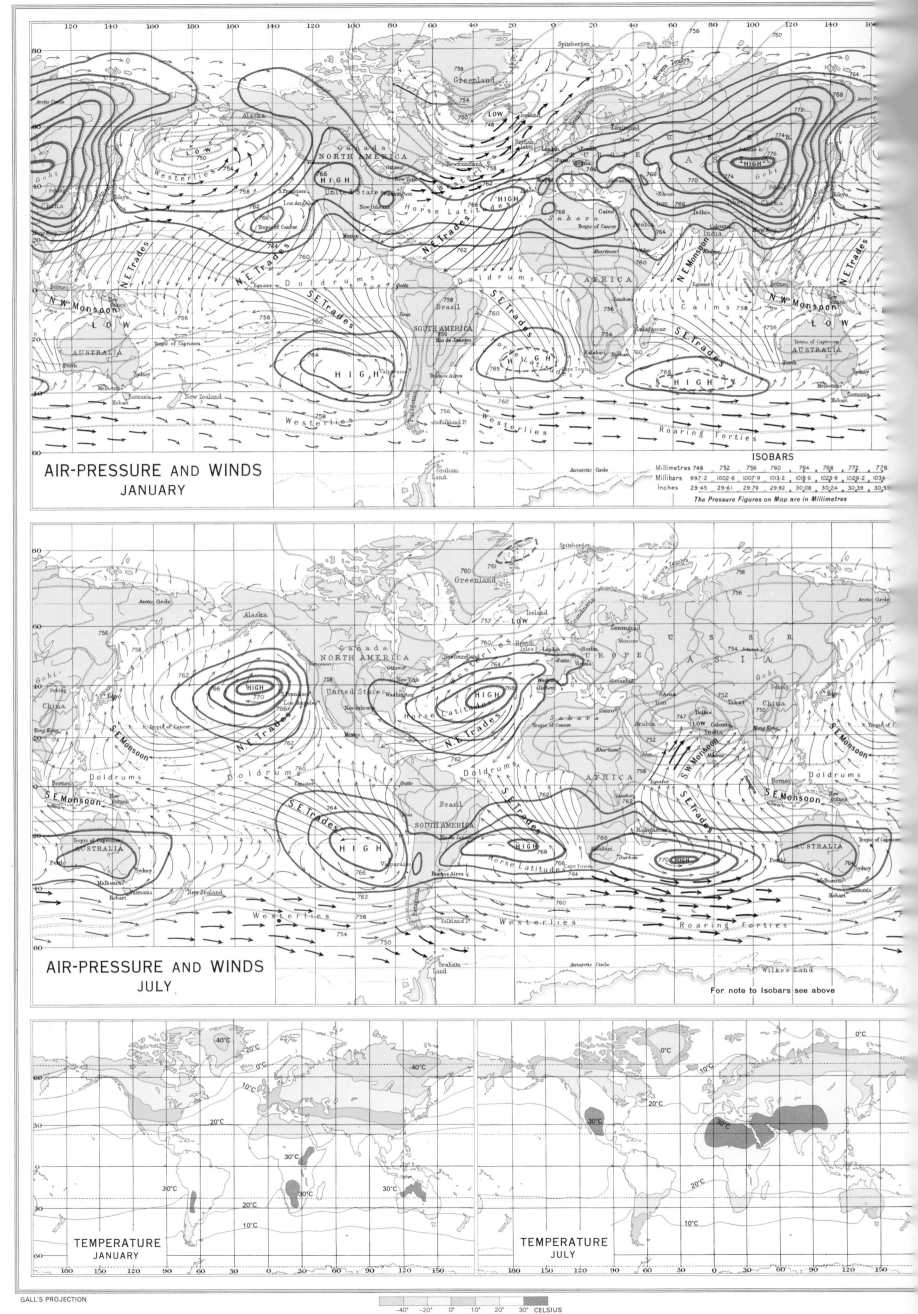

AIR-PRESSURE AND WINDS
JANUARY

ISOBARS

Millimetres	748	752	756	760	764	768	772	776
Millibars	997·2	1002·6	1007·9	1013·2	1018·6	1023·9	1029·2	1034·
Inches	29·45	29·61	29·76	29·92	30·08	30·24	30·39	30·55

The Pressure Figures on Map are in Millimetres

AIR-PRESSURE AND WINDS
JULY

For note to Isobars see above

TEMPERATURE
JANUARY

TEMPERATURE
JULY

−40° −20° 0° 10° 20° 30° CELSIUS

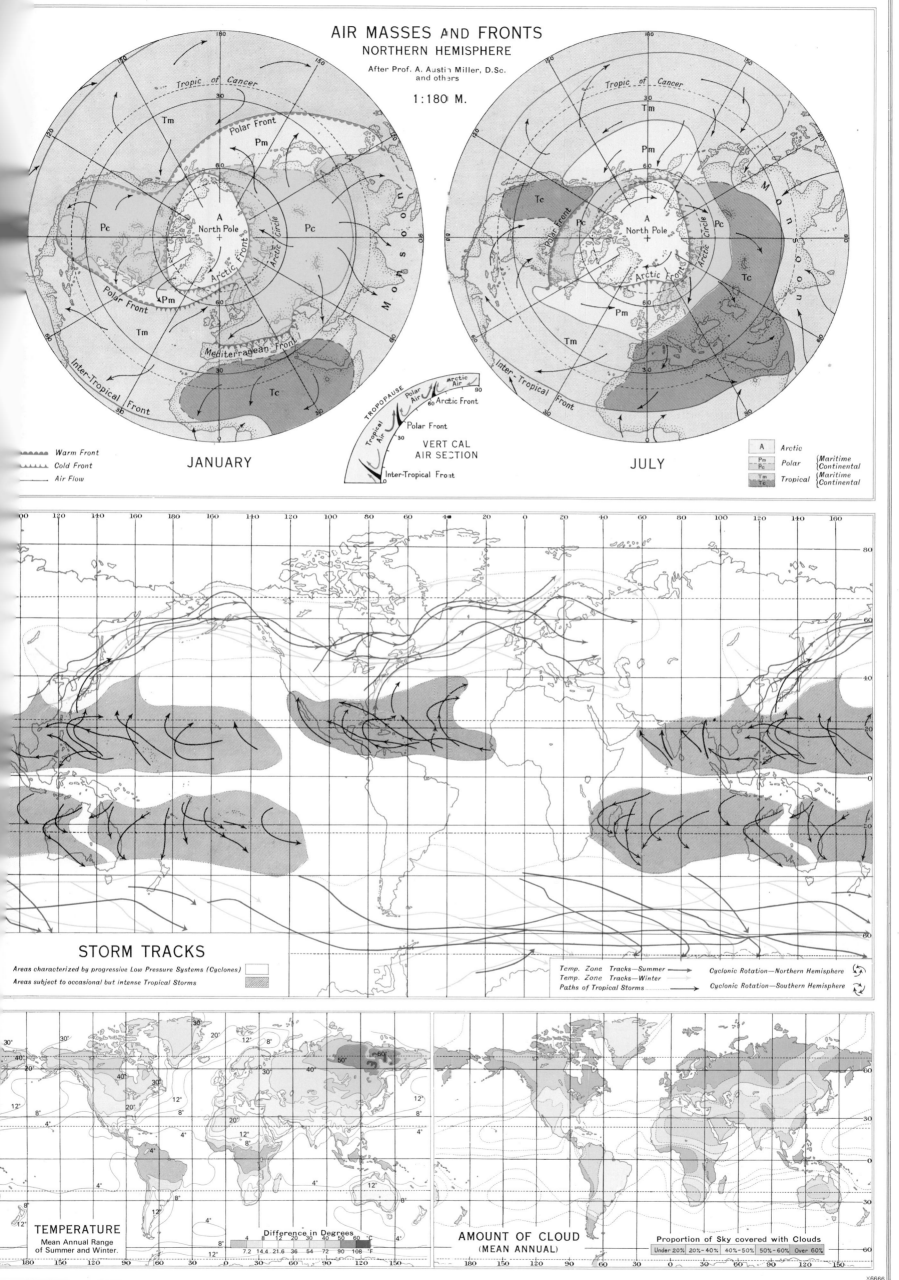

AIR MASSES AND FRONTS
NORTHERN HEMISPHERE
After Prof. A. Austin Miller, D.Sc.
and others
1:180 M.

JANUARY

JULY

VERTICAL
AIR SECTION

Warm Front
Cold Front
Air Flow

A — Arctic
Pm / Pc — Polar (Maritime / Continental)
Tm / Tc — Tropical (Maritime / Continental)

STORM TRACKS

Areas characterized by progressive Low Pressure Systems (Cyclones)
Areas subject to occasional but intense Tropical Storms

Temp. Zone Tracks—Summer
Temp. Zone Tracks—Winter
Paths of Tropical Storms

Cyclonic Rotation—Northern Hemisphere
Cyclonic Rotation—Southern Hemisphere

TEMPERATURE
Mean Annual Range
of Summer and Winter.

Difference in Degrees
°C
°F

AMOUNT OF CLOUD
(MEAN ANNUAL)

Proportion of Sky covered with Clouds
Under 20% 20%–40% 40%–50% 50%–60% Over 60%

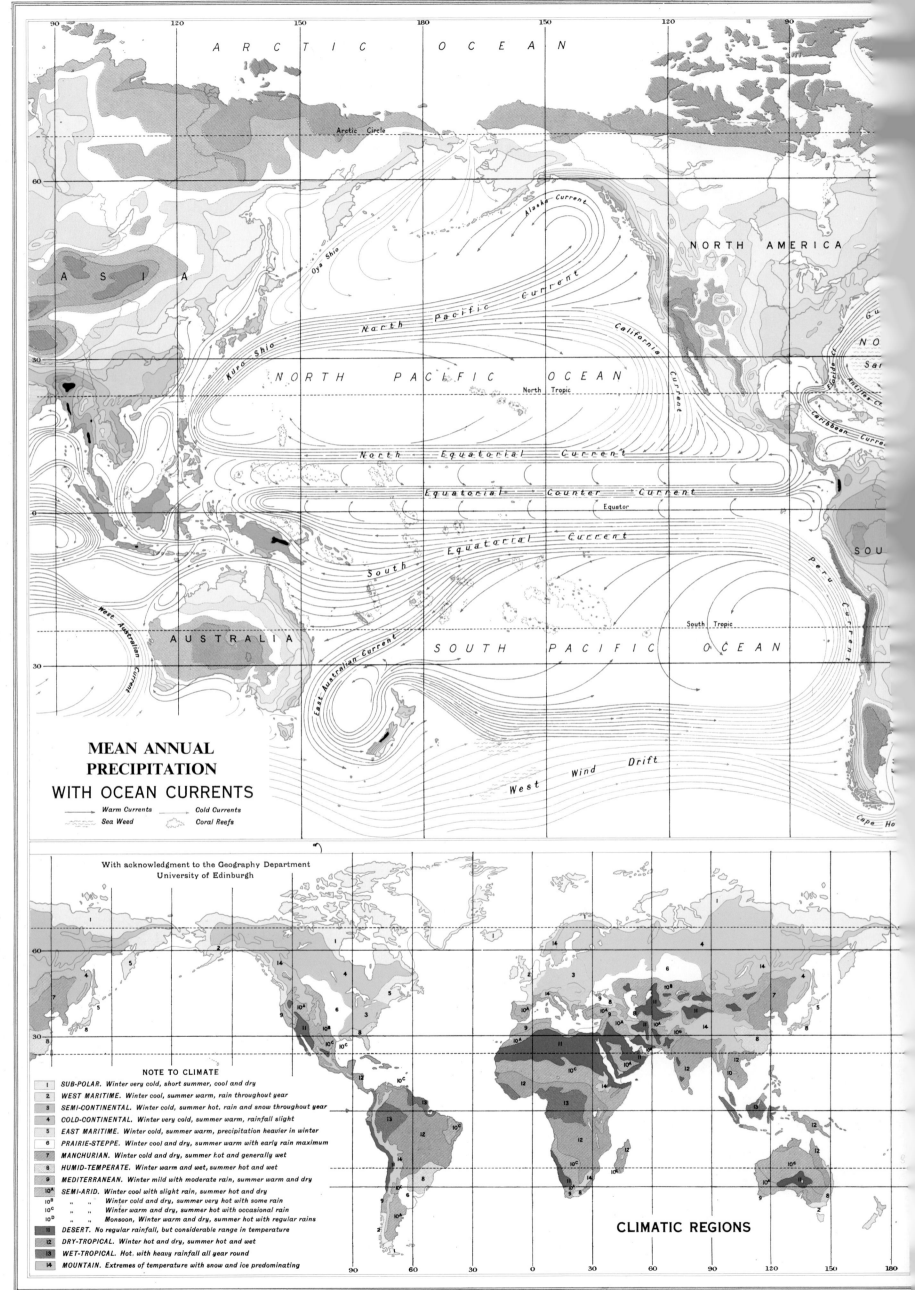

MEAN ANNUAL
PRECIPITATION
WITH OCEAN CURRENTS

→ Warm Currents   → Cold Currents
Sea Weed   Coral Reefs

With acknowledgment to the Geography Department
University of Edinburgh

NOTE TO CLIMATE

1	SUB-POLAR.	Winter very cold, short summer, cool and dry
2	WEST MARITIME.	Winter cool, summer warm, rain throughout year
3	SEMI-CONTINENTAL.	Winter cold, summer hot, rain and snow throughout year
4	COLD-CONTINENTAL.	Winter very cold, summer warm, rainfall slight
5	EAST MARITIME.	Winter cold, summer warm, precipitation heavier in winter
6	PRAIRIE-STEPPE.	Winter cool and dry, summer warm with early rain maximum
7	MANCHURIAN.	Winter cold and dry, summer hot and generally wet
8	HUMID-TEMPERATE.	Winter warm and wet, summer hot and wet
9	MEDITERRANEAN.	Winter mild with moderate rain, summer warm and dry
10A	SEMI-ARID.	Winter cool with slight rain, summer hot and dry
10B	" "	Winter cold and dry, summer very hot with some rain
10C	" "	Winter warm and dry, summer hot with occasional rain
10D	" "	Monsoon. Winter warm and dry, summer hot with regular rains
11	DESERT.	No regular rainfall, but considerable range in temperature
12	DRY-TROPICAL.	Winter hot and dry, summer hot and wet
13	WET-TROPICAL.	Hot, with heavy rainfall all year round
14	MOUNTAIN.	Extremes of temperature with snow and ice predominating

CLIMATIC REGIONS

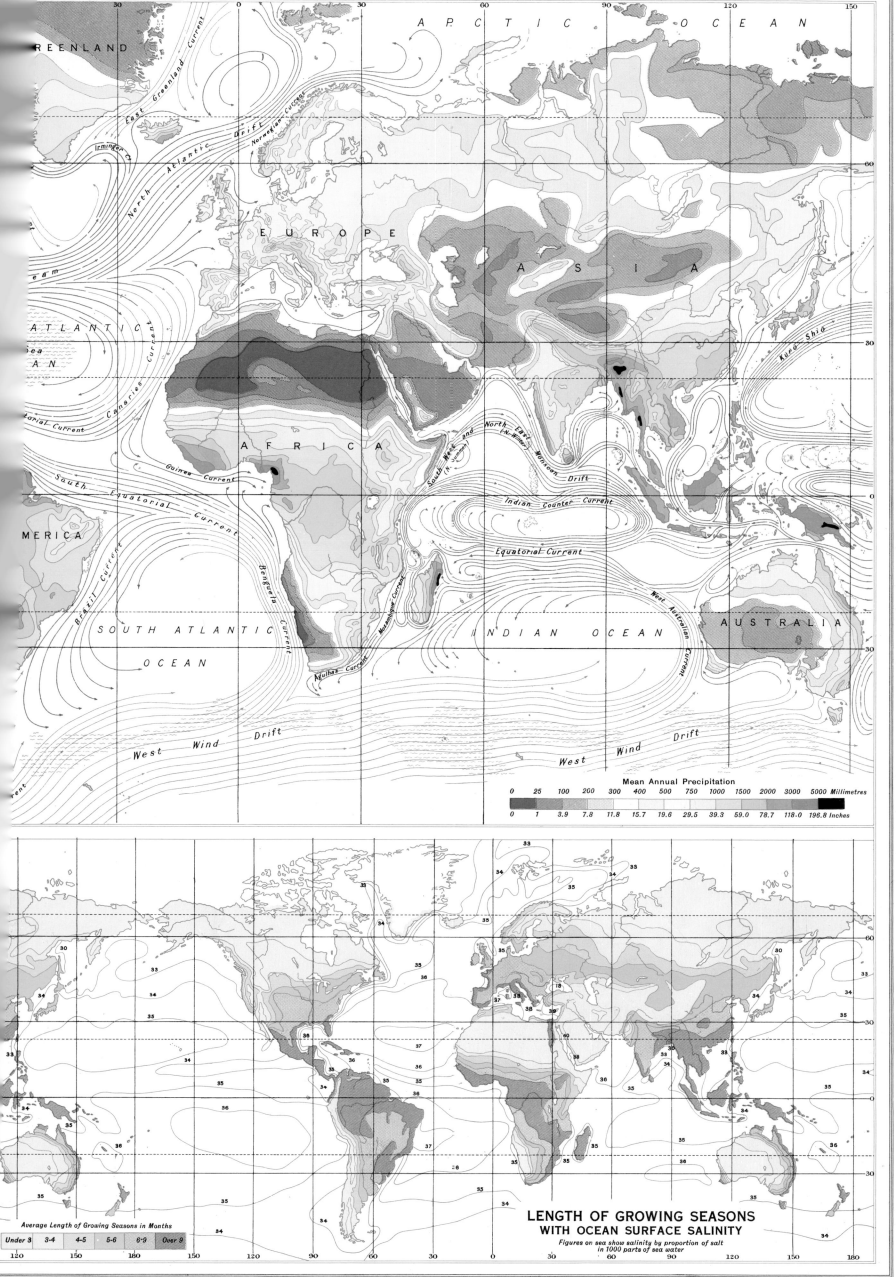

A R C T I C   O C E A N

GREENLAND

East Greenland Current

Irminger C.

North Atlantic Drift

Norwegian Current

EUROPE

ASIA

ATLANTIC

Sea

Canaries Current

AFRICA

Equatorial Current

Guinea Current

South Equatorial Current

MERICA

Brazil Current

Benguela Current

Mozambique Current

Aguilhas Current

South West and North (N. Summer)

East (N. Winter) Monsoon Drift

Indian Counter Current

Equatorial Current

West Australian Current

Kuro Shio

INDIAN   OCEAN

AUSTRALIA

SOUTH   ATLANTIC

OCEAN

West   Wind   Drift

West   Wind   Drift

Mean Annual Precipitation

| 0 | 25 | 100 | 200 | 300 | 400 | 500 | 750 | 1000 | 1500 | 2000 | 3000 | 5000 Millimetres |

| 0 | 1 | 3.9 | 7.8 | 11.8 | 15.7 | 19.6 | 29.5 | 39.3 | 59.0 | 78.7 | 118.0 | 196.8 Inches |

LENGTH OF GROWING SEASONS
WITH OCEAN SURFACE SALINITY
*Figures on sea show salinity by proportion of salt
in 1000 parts of sea water*

Average Length of Growing Seasons in Months

| Under 3 | 3-4 | 4-5 | 5-6 | 6-9 | Over 9 |

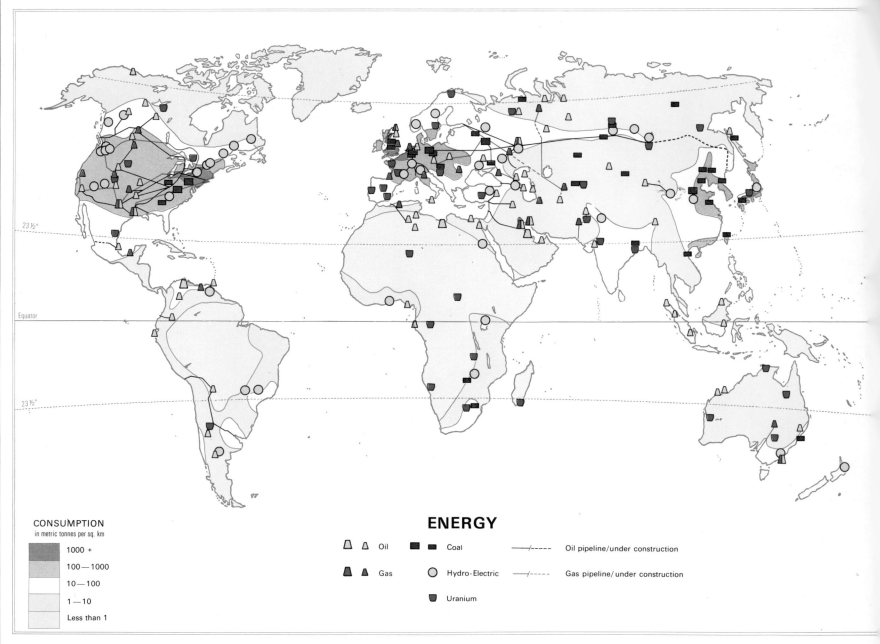

ENERGY

CONSUMPTION
in metric tonnes per sq. km

	1000 +
	100 — 1000
	10 — 100
	1 — 10
	Less than 1

Oil   Coal   Oil pipeline/under construction

Gas   Hydro-Electric   Gas pipeline/under construction

Uranium

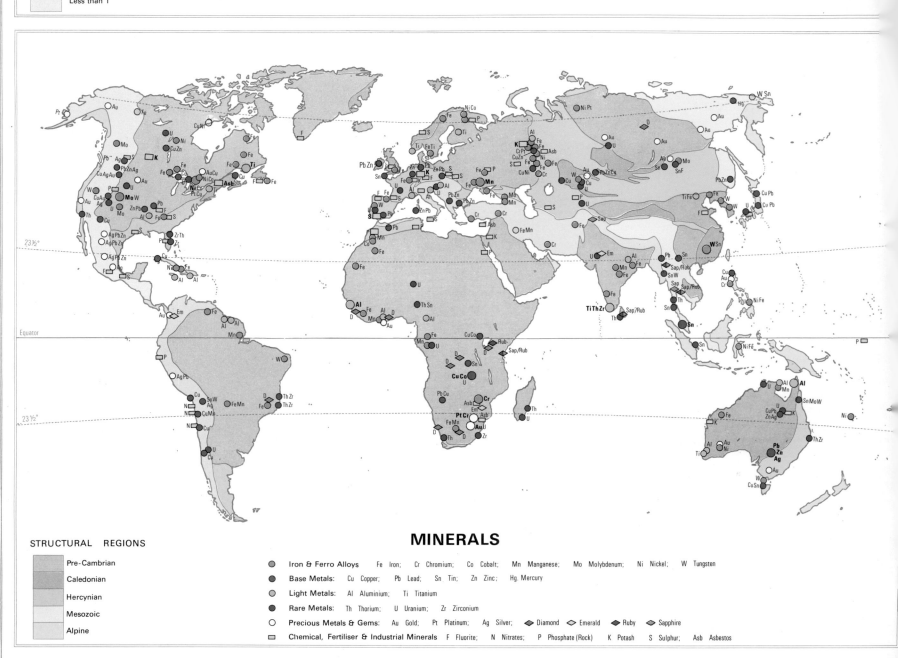

MINERALS

STRUCTURAL REGIONS

	Pre-Cambrian
	Caledonian
	Hercynian
	Mesozoic
	Alpine

Iron & Ferro Alloys   Fe Iron;   Cr Chromium;   Co Cobalt;   Mn Manganese;   Mo Molybdenum;   Ni Nickel;   W Tungsten

Base Metals: Cu Copper;   Pb Lead;   Sn Tin;   Zn Zinc;   Hg. Mercury

Light Metals: Al Aluminium;   Ti Titanium

Rare Metals: Th Thorium;   U Uranium;   Zr Zirconium

Precious Metals & Gems: Au Gold;   Pt Platinum;   Ag Silver;   Diamond   Emerald   Ruby   Sapphire

Chemical, Fertiliser & Industrial Minerals   F Fluorite;   N Nitrates;   P Phosphate (Rock)   K Potash   S Sulphur;   Asb Asbestos

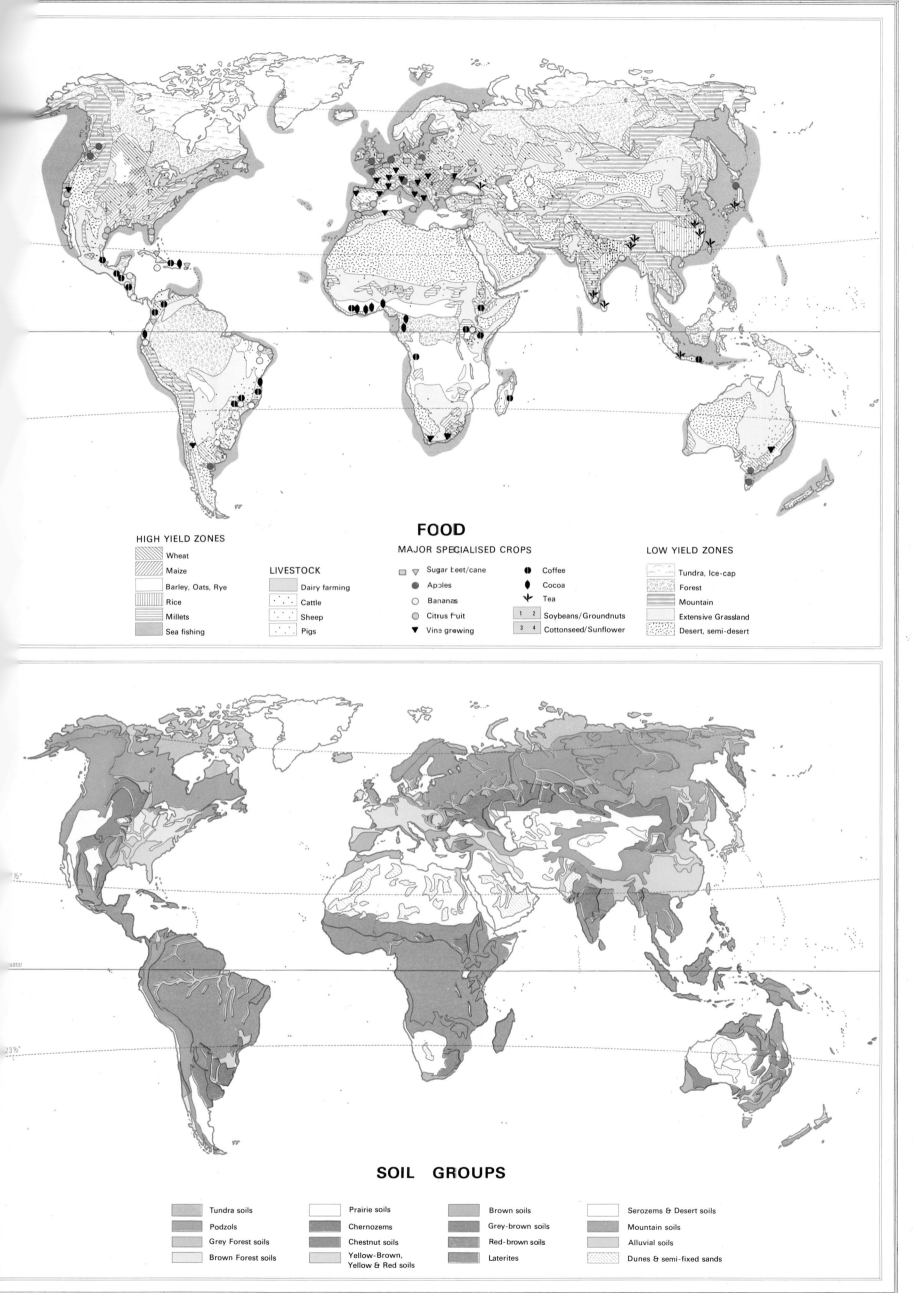

FOOD

HIGH YIELD ZONES
- Wheat
- Maize
- Barley, Oats, Rye
- Rice
- Millets
- Sea fishing

LIVESTOCK
- Dairy farming
- Cattle
- Sheep
- Pigs

MAJOR SPECIALISED CROPS
- Sugar beet/cane
- Apples
- Bananas
- Citrus Fruit
- Vine growing
- Coffee
- Cocoa
- Tea
- 1 2 Soybeans/Groundnuts
- 3 4 Cottonseed/Sunflower

LOW YIELD ZONES
- Tundra, Ice-cap
- Forest
- Mountain
- Extensive Grassland
- Desert, semi-desert

SOIL GROUPS

- Tundra soils
- Podzols
- Grey Forest soils
- Brown Forest soils
- Prairie soils
- Chernozems
- Chestnut soils
- Yellow-Brown, Yellow & Red soils
- Brown soils
- Grey-brown soils
- Red-brown soils
- Laterites
- Serozems & Desert soils
- Mountain soils
- Alluvial soils
- Dunes & semi-fixed sands

© John Bartholomew & Son Ltd, Edinburgh

1:135M

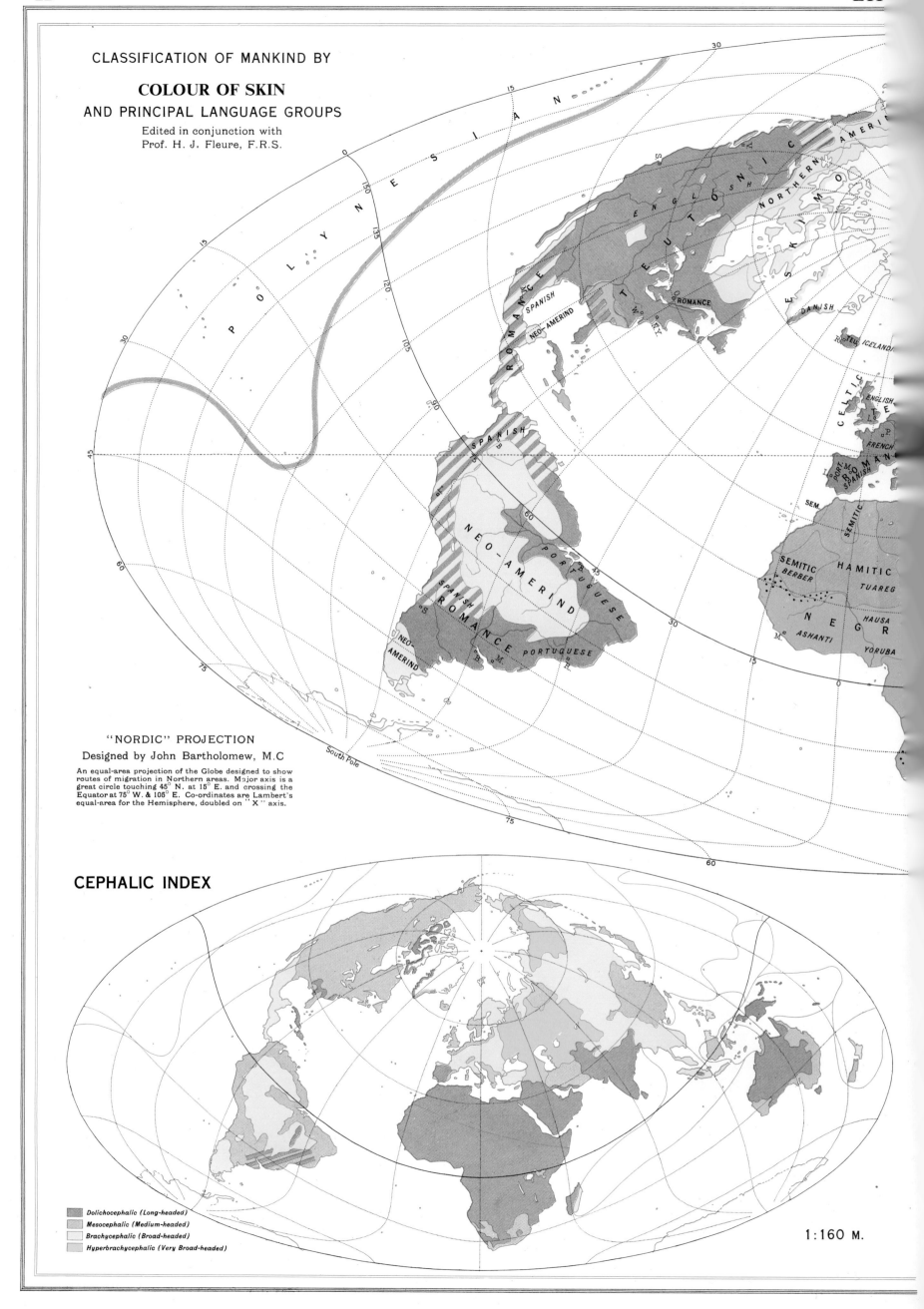

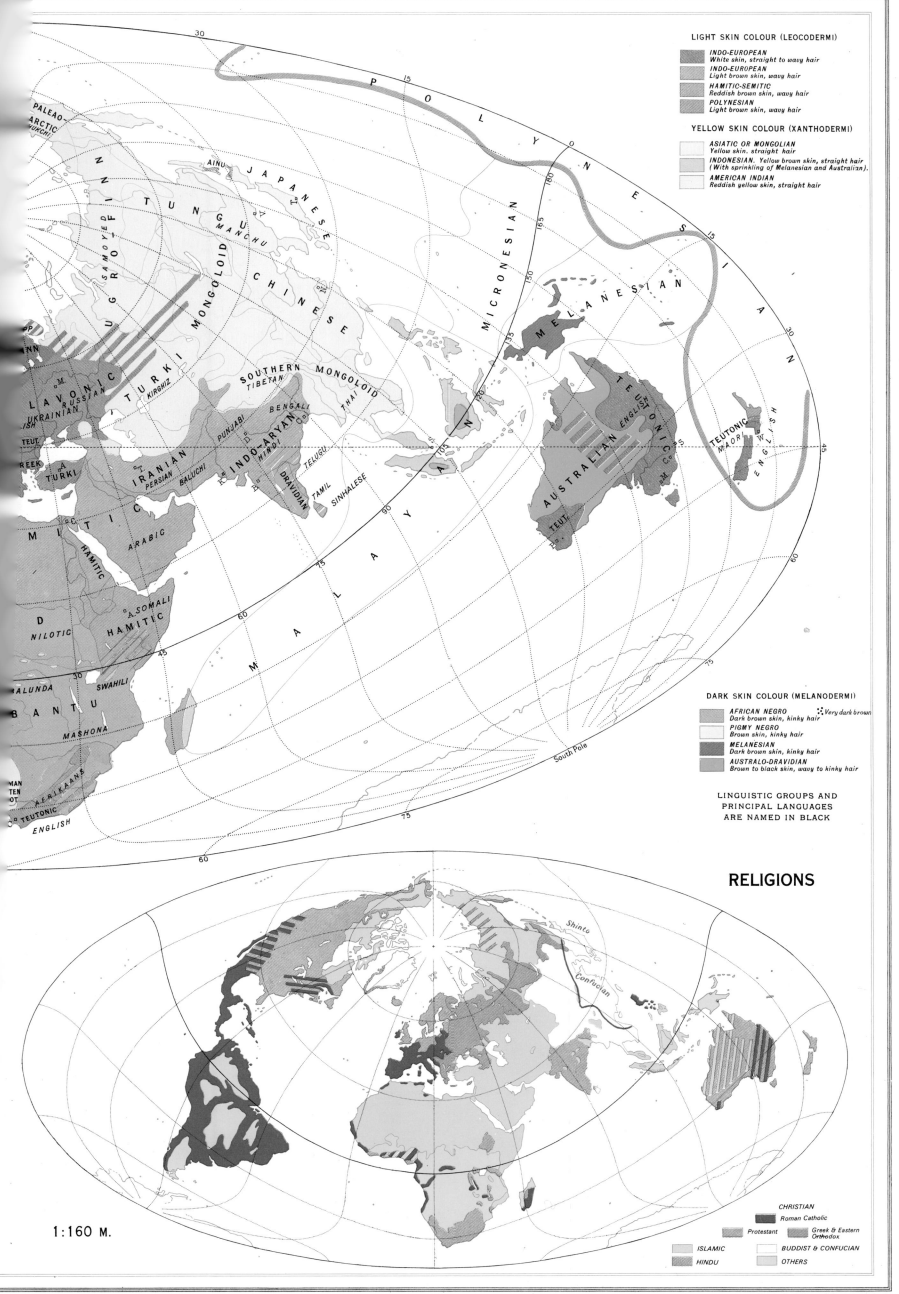

LIGHT SKIN COLOUR (LEOCODERMI)

INDO-EUROPEAN
White skin, straight to wavy hair
INDO-EUROPEAN
Light brown skin, wavy hair
HAMITIC-SEMITIC
Reddish brown skin, wavy hair
POLYNESIAN
Light brown skin, wavy hair

YELLOW SKIN COLOUR (XANTHODERMI)

ASIATIC OR MONGOLIAN
Yellow skin, straight hair
INDONESIAN. *Yellow brown skin, straight hair*
(With sprinkling of Melanesian and Australian).
AMERICAN INDIAN
Reddish yellow skin, straight hair

DARK SKIN COLOUR (MELANODERMI)

AFRICAN NEGRO   ∴ *Very dark brown*
Dark brown skin, kinky hair
PIGMY NEGRO
Brown skin, kinky hair
MELANESIAN
Dark brown skin, kinky hair
AUSTRALO-DRAVIDIAN
Brown to black skin, wavy to kinky hair

LINGUISTIC GROUPS AND
PRINCIPAL LANGUAGES
ARE NAMED IN BLACK

RELIGIONS

1:160 M.

CHRISTIAN
Roman Catholic
Protestant   Greek & Eastern
                       Orthodox
ISLAMIC   BUDDIST & CONFUCIAN
HINDU   OTHERS

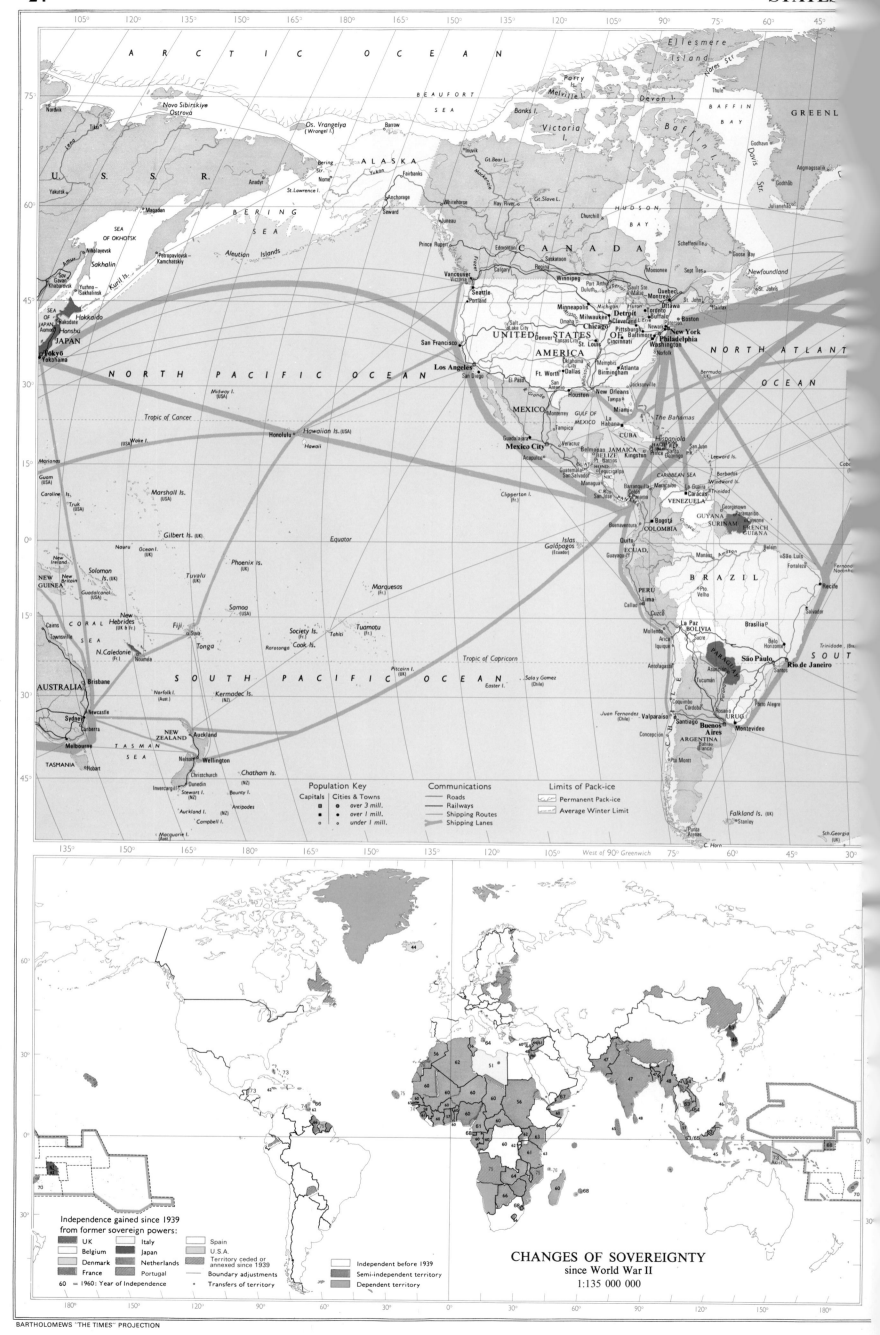

ARCTIC OCEAN

BEAUFORT SEA

Ellesmere Island

GREENL

BAFFIN BAY

U.S.S.R.

ALASKA

BERING SEA

CANADA

SEA OF OKHOTSK

HUDSON BAY

JAPAN
Tōkyō
Yokohama

NORTH PACIFIC OCEAN

UNITED STATES OF AMERICA

New York
Philadelphia
Washington

NORTH ATLANT

OCEAN

Los Angeles
San Diego

MEXICO

GULF OF MEXICO

CUBA

The Bahamas

Tropic of Cancer

Honolulu   Hawaiian Is. (USA)

Hawaii

Mexico City

Marianas

Guam (USA)

Caroline Is.

Marshall Is. (USA)

Truk (USA)

Gilbert Is. (UK)

Equator

CARIBBEAN SEA

VENEZUELA

GUYANA
SURINAM
FRENCH GUIANA

COLOMBIA

ECUAD.

Islas Galápagos (Ecuador)

NEW GUINEA

Solomon Is. (USA)

Nauru

Ocean I. (UK)

Tuvalu (UK)

Phoenix Is. (UK)

Marquesas (Fr.)

PERU

Lima
Callao

BRAZIL

Recife

Samoa (USA)

Fiji

Society Is. (Fr.)   Tahiti

Tuamotu (Fr.)

Brasília

BOLIVIA
La Paz
Sucre

AUSTRALIA

CORAL SEA

New Hebrides (UK & Fr.)

N. Caledonie

Tonga

Cook Is. (UK)

Rarotonga

Tropic of Capricorn

Pitcairn I. (UK)

Easter I. (Chile)

Sala y Gomez (Chile)

São Paulo
Rio de Janeiro

SOUT

SOUTH PACIFIC OCEAN

Brisbane

Norfolk I. (Aust.)

Kermadec Is. (NZ)

Sydney
Canberra

Newcastle

TASMAN SEA

Melbourne

TASMANIA   Hobart

NEW ZEALAND

Auckland

Nelson   Wellington

Christchurch

Chatham Is.

Dunedin

Invercargill   Stewart I. (NZ)

Bounty I. (NZ)

Antipodes

Valparaíso
Santiago

URUG
Buenos Aires
Montevideo

ARGENTINA

Falkland Is. (UK)

Stanley

C. Horn

Population Key		Communications	Limits of Pack-ice
Capitals	Cities & Towns	—— Roads	Permanent Pack-ice
■ over 3 mill.	● over 3 mill.	—— Railways	Average Winter Limit
■ over 1 mill.	● over 1 mill.	Shipping Routes	
▪	∘ under 1 mill.	Shipping Lanes	

CHANGES OF SOVEREIGNTY
since World War II
1:135 000 000

Independence gained since 1939
from former sovereign powers:

▨ UK		▨ Italy	▨ Spain
▨ Belgium		▨ Japan	▨ U.S.A.
▨ Denmark		▨ Netherlands	Territory ceded or annexed since 1939
▨ France		▨ Portugal	Boundary adjustments

60 = 1960: Year of Independence   · · · Transfers of territory

☐ Independent before 1939
▨ Semi-independent territory
▨ Dependent territory

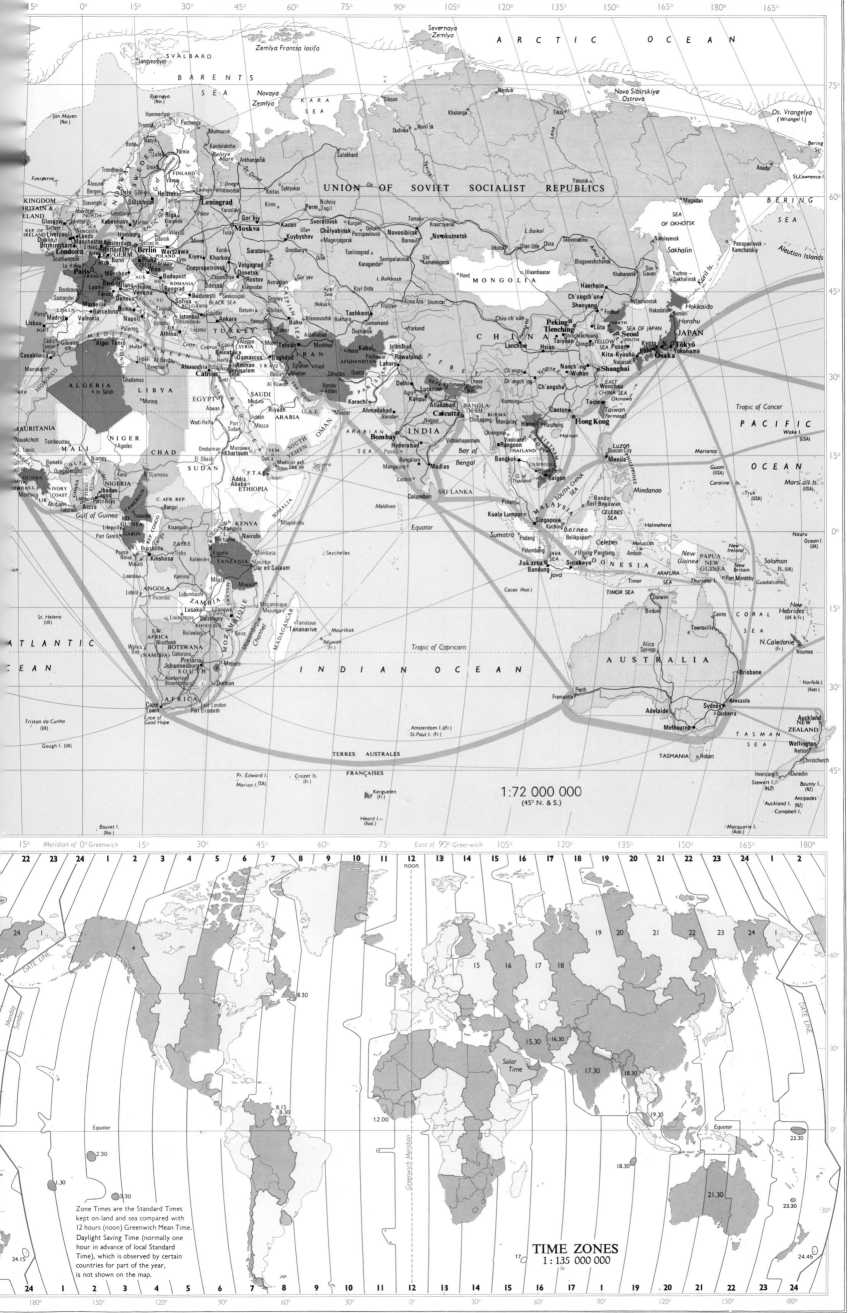

ARCTIC OCEAN

BARENTS SEA

UNION OF SOVIET SOCIALIST REPUBLICS

MONGOLIA

CHINA

JAPAN

PACIFIC OCEAN

ALGERIA LIBYA EGYPT SAUDI ARABIA

Tropic of Cancer

INDIA

Bay of Bengal

Equator

INDIAN OCEAN

Tropic of Capricorn

AUSTRALIA

NEW ZEALAND

1:72 000 000
(45° N. & S.)

Meridian of 0° Greenwich   East of 90° Greenwich

TIME ZONES
1:135 000 000

Zone Times are the Standard Times
kept on land and sea compared with
12 hours (noon) Greenwich Mean Time.
Daylight Saving Time (normally one
hour in advance of local Standard
Time), which is observed by certain
countries for part of the year,
is not shown on the map.

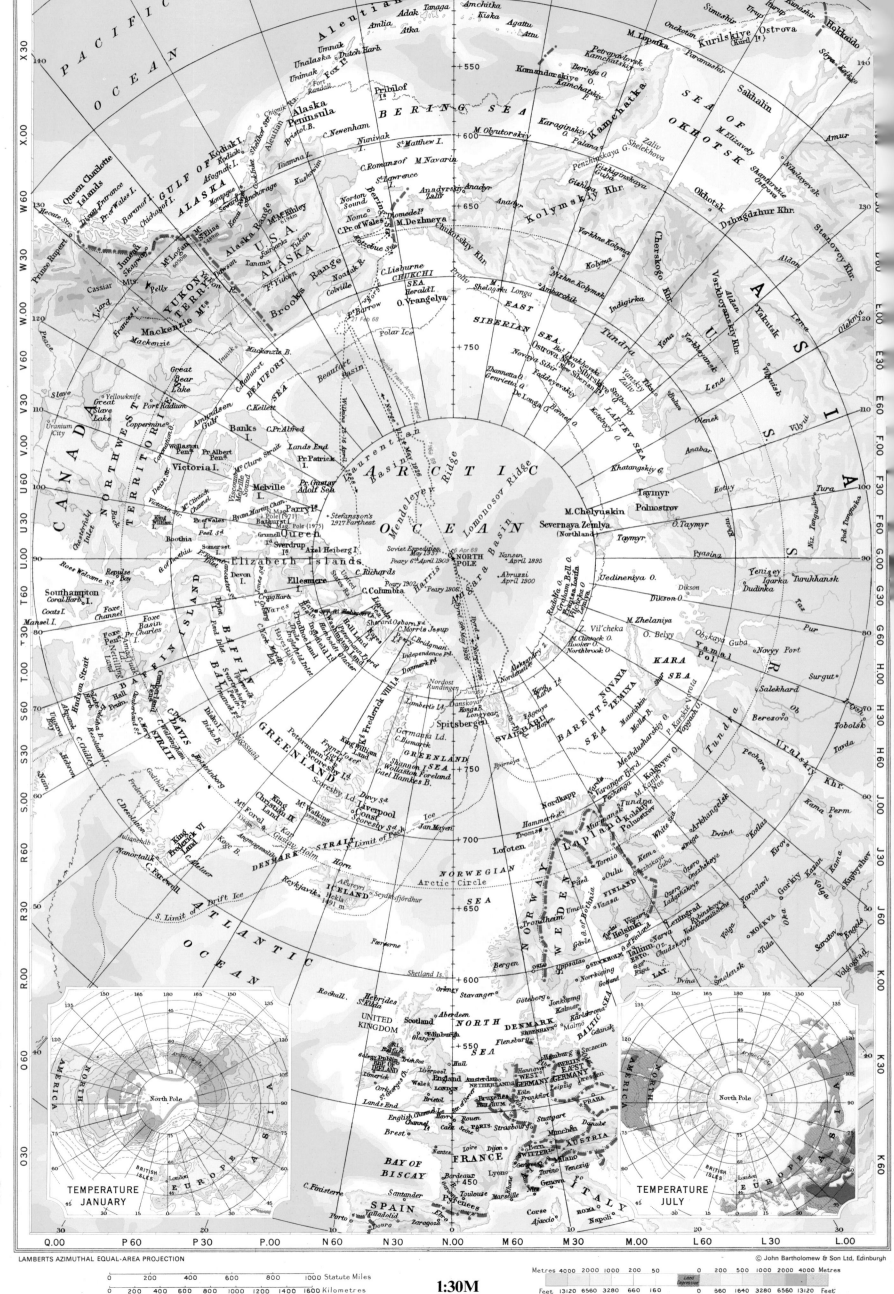

TEMPERATURE
JANUARY

TEMPERATURE
JULY

LAMBERTS AZIMUTHAL EQUAL·AREA PROJECTION

© John Bartholomew & Son Ltd, Edinburgh

1:30M

0 200 400 600 800 1000 Statute Miles

0 200 400 600 800 1000 1200 1400 1600 Kilometres

Metres 4000 2000 1000 200 50   0   200 500 1000 2000 4000 Metres

Feet 13120 6560 3280 660 160   0   660 1640 3280 6560 13120 Feet

ATLANTIC OCEAN

Northern Limit of Pack Ice

Falkland Islands
South Georgia
Shag Rocks
Grytviken
Traversay Is.
Saunders I.
Montagu I.
Bristol I.
Thule I.
South Sandwich Islands

S C O T I A   S E A

Dependencies (To UK.)

South Orkneys
Laurie I.
Coronation I.

BRITISH ANTARCTIC

WEDDELL SEA

TERRITORY (To Gt Br.)

Bouvet I. (To Nor.)

Pr. Edward Is. (To S Af.)

Antarctic Circle

Mørdheim
K. Norvegia
Princess Martha Land
Cr. Princess Martha Land
Princess Astrid Land
Queen Maud Land
Princess Ragnhild Ld.
Pr. Harald Ld.
Cr. Prince Olav Land
C. Ann

Coats Land

Halley Bay
Vahsel Bay
Luitpold Coast
Gould Coast
Shackleton
Slessor Gl.
Recovery Gl.

Enderby Land

Kemp Land

Mawson

Mac Robertson Land
Lars Christensen Coast

Clarence I.
Elephant I.
King George I.
Joinville I.
Dundee I.
Trinity Peninsula
James Ross I.
Livingston I.
Deception I.
Smith I.
Oscar II Coast

South Shetlands

Staten I.
Diego
Cape Horn
te I
nderry I

Drake Str.
Bransfield Str.

ANTARCTIC PENINSULA

de Gerlache Str.
Biscoe
Toubet Cst.
Biscoe 1832
Stonington I.
Eternity Ra.
Georges VI St.
Marguerite
Adelaide I.
Palmer Ld.

Alexander Island
Charcot I.
Wilkins Str.
English Coast

Filchner Ice Shelf
Berkner Island
Ronne Ice Shelf
Ronne Entrance
Bryan Coast

Bellingshausen Sea

Eights Coast
Sentinel Ra.
Ellsworth Mts.
Peter I Øy

Ellsworth Highland

Thurston I.
C. Flying Fish
Peacock Sd.
Pine I.B.
Bear I.
Cook 1774
Amundsen Sea
C. Leahy
C. Dart
Getz Ice Shelf
Wrigley Gulf
Ford Ranges
Guest Pen.
Bay of Whales

Hollick Kenyon Plateau

Byrd Land

Rockefeller Plateau
Marie Byrd Land

King Edward VII Land

Roosevelt I.

ROSS SEA

A N T A R C T I C A

Amundsen, Dec. 1911
Scott, Jan. 1912
Hillary, 4th Jan. 1958
Fuchs, 19th Jan. 1958

SOUTH POLE

South Polar Plateau 3200 m.

Queen Maud Mts.
Mt Fridtjof Nansen 4068 m.
Commonwealth Range
Queen Alexandra Range
Mt Markham 4350 m.
Beardmore Gl.

Ross Ice Shelf

AUSTRALIAN TERRITORY

Kaiser Wilhelm II Land
Posadowsky Bay
Drygalski I.
Queen Mary Land
Davis Sea

King Leopold and Queen Astrid Cst.

Princess Elizabeth Land

Mackenzie Bay
Ingrid Christensen Cst.
Prydz Bay
Lambert Gl.

Colbeck Arch.

Knox Coast
Mill I.
Bowman I.

Wilkes Land

Sabrina Coast

Banzare Coast

INDIAN OCEAN

Ross I.
C. Crozier
Mt Murdo Sd.
Mt Erebus (Vol.) 3794 m.
Franklin I.
Lady Newnes B.
Coulman I.
Ross I.
Possession I.
C. Adare

Mt Melbourne 2734 m.
Mt Brewster
Mt Sabine 3850 m.

VICTORIA LAND

AUST. TERR.

Terre Adélie
South Magnetic Pole (1975)

Oates Ld.
King George V Land
C. North

ROSS DEPENDENCY (To New Zealand)

Scott I.

Antarctic Circle

Belleny Is.
Young I.

PACIFIC OCEAN

Northern Limit of Pack Ice

Macquarie I. (To Tasmania)
Bishop & Clerk
Judge & Clerk

Campbell I.
Auckland Is.

Northern Limit of Drift Ice

Antipodes I.
Bounty I.
The Snares
Foveaux Str.
Invercargill
Stewart I.
Dunedin
Timaru
Mt Cook 3764 m.
Hokitika

SOUTH ISLAND

Chatham Is. (To N.Z.)

C. Palliser
Nelson
NEW ZEALAND
Wellington
Cook Strait
Napier
Mt Egmont
New Plymouth

NORTH ISLAND

Waikato R.
B. of Plenty
Auckland
C. Maria Van Dieman

Note.
Under the Antarctic Treaty of 1959 all territorial claims are held in abeyance in the interest of international co-operation for scientific purposes.

TEMPERATURE JANUARY
South Pole
Antarctic Circle

TEMPERATURE JULY
South Pole
Antarctic Circle

C° F°
20 68
10 50
0   32
-10 14
-20 -4
-30 -22
-40 -40
-60 -76

LAMBERT'S AZIMUTHAL EQUAL-AREA PROJECTION

© John Bartholomew & Son Ltd, Edinburgh

0 200 400 600 800 1000 Statute Miles
0 200 400 600 800 1000 1200 1400 1600 Kilometres

1:30M

Metres 4000 2000 1000 200 50 0 200 500 1000 2000 4000 Metres
Feet 13120 6560 3280 660 160 0 660 1640 3280 6560 13120 Feet

Antarctic Bases (1970-71) are shown by a red dot.

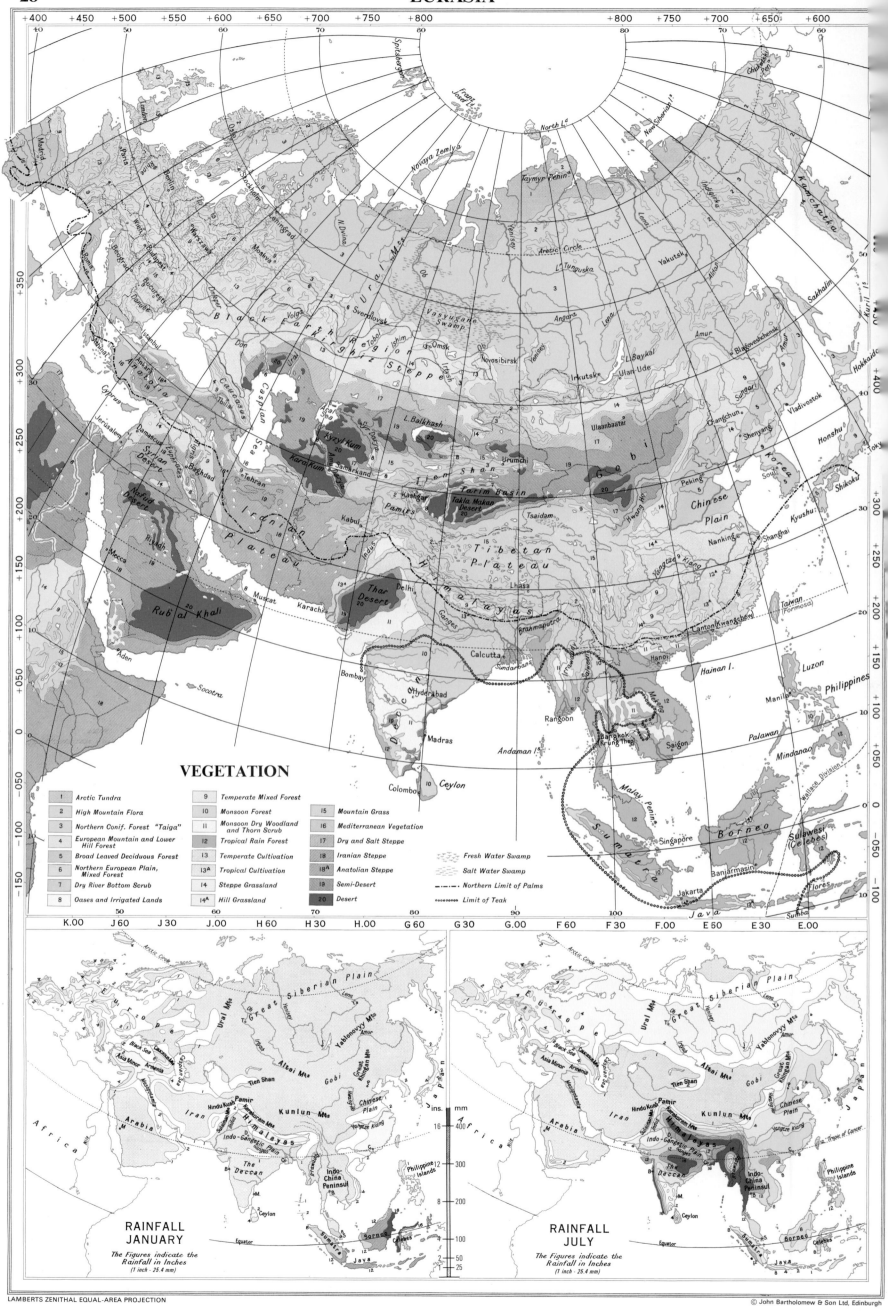

VEGETATION

1	Arctic Tundra	
2	High Mountain Flora	
3	Northern Conif. Forest "Taiga"	
4	European Mountain and Lower Hill Forest	
5	Broad Leaved Deciduous Forest	
6	Northern European Plain, Mixed Forest	
7	Dry River Bottom Scrub	
8	Oases and Irrigated Lands	
9	Temperate Mixed Forest	
10	Monsoon Forest	
11	Monsoon Dry Woodland and Thorn Scrub	
12	Tropical Rain Forest	
13	Temperate Cultivation	
13A	Tropical Cultivation	
14	Steppe Grassland	
14A	Hill Grassland	
15	Mountain Grass	
16	Mediterranean Vegetation	
17	Dry and Salt Steppe	
18	Iranian Steppe	
18A	Anatolian Steppe	
19	Semi-Desert	
20	Desert	

- Fresh Water Swamp
- Salt Water Swamp
- Northern Limit of Palms
- Limit of Teak

RAINFALL JANUARY

The Figures indicate the Rainfall in Inches
(1 inch - 25.4 mm)

RAINFALL JULY

The Figures indicate the Rainfall in Inches
(1 inch - 25.4 mm)

LAMBERTS ZENITHAL EQUAL-AREA PROJECTION

© John Bartholomew & Son Ltd, Edinburgh

0   200   400   600   800   1000 Statute Miles

1:45M

0 200 400 600 800 1000 1200 1400 1600 Kilometres

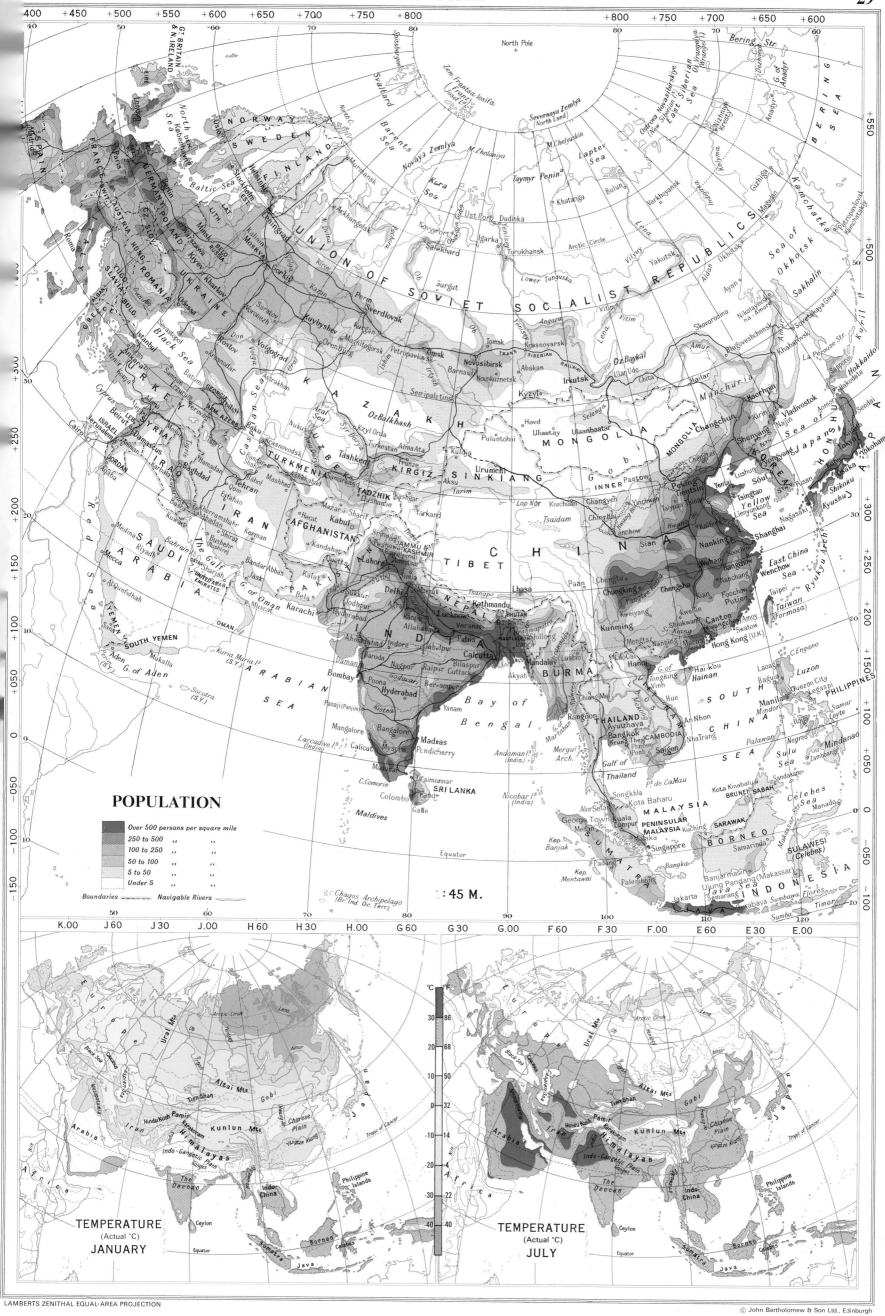

BRITISH ISLES

MOROCCO PORTUGAL SPAIN ALGERIA TUNISIA LIBYA FEZZAN CYRENAICA EGYPT

MEDITERRANEAN SEA

FRANCE ITALY YUGOSLAVIA ROMANIA BULGARIA GREECE TURKEY

NORWAY SWEDEN FINLAND POLAND BELORUSSIA LITHUANIA

NORTH SEA BALTIC SEA BLACK SEA Sea of Azov

E U R O P E

MOSKVA

U N I O N   O F   S O V I E T   S O C

SVALBARD (TO NORWAY) BARENTS SEA Novaya Zemlya Kara Sea ARCTIC

Khrebet Sibir

Aral Sea KIRGIZ Balkhash KAZAKH

CASPIAN SEA GEORGIA AZERBAIJAN

A F R I C A SUDAN CHAD ETHIOPIA

RED SEA HEJAZ ARABIA NAJD HASA Rub' al Khali RUB

SOUTH YEMEN Gulf of Aden

SYRIA IRAQ BAGHDAD IRAN (PERSIA) Plateau of Iran Lut Desert Great Salt Desert TEHRAN KABUL AFGHANISTAN BALUCHISTAN MAKRAN

TURKMEN UZBEK TADZHIK Pamir SINKIANG Tarim Basin Takla Makan TIBET KUNLUN

UNITED ARAB EMIRATES OMAN QATAR BAHRAIN Gulf of Oman Muscat

Karachi DELHI I N D I A NEPAL Thar Desert

ARABIAN SEA Bombay Poona Hyderabad Madras BAY OF BENGAL

Laccadive Islands (To India) SRI LANKA Colombo Maldives

I N D I A N   O C E

RACES

Chinese
Other Eastern
Nomadic Mongols
Dravidian & Oceanic
Semetic
Celto-Teutonic
Romanic
Slavonic
Indo-Iranian
Greco-Albanian
Aryan

Irish Scots Lapps Finns Samoyedes Yukagirs Chukchi Yakuts Tunguses Gilyaks Manchu Tatars Kirghiz Usbegs Kalmuks Mongols Japanese Afghans Tibetans Burmese Arabs Hindus Baluchi Siamese Dyaks

LAMBERTS AZIMUTHAL EQUAL-AREA PROJECTION

6666

0 100 200 400 600 800 1000 Statute Miles
0 200 400 600 800 1000 1200 1400 1600 Kilometres

Metres 2000 200 50 0 200 500 1000 2000 4000 6000 Metres
Feet 6560 660 160 0 660 1640 3280 6560 13120 19690 Feet
Land Depression

Longitude East 70 of Greenwich

1:30

OCEAN

IST REPUBLICS

MONGOLIA

INNER MONGOLIA

The Gobi

MANCHURIA

CHINA

HIN A

BURMA

THAILAND

CAMBODIA

INDO CHINA

MALAYSIA

PENINSULAR MALAYSIA

SUMATRA

BORNEO (KALIMANTAN)

SARAWAK

SABAH

JAVA

PHILIPPINES

Luzon

Mindanao

Palawan

NEW GUINEA

IRIAN JAYA

PAPUA NEW GUINEA

JAPAN

Hokkaido

Honshu

Shikoku

Kyushu

SAKHALIN

TAIWAN (FORMOSA) (China Nat. Rep.)

NORTH SEA OF JAPAN

SOUTH

YELLOW SEA

EAST CHINA SEA

SOUTH CHINA SEA

SEA OF OKHOTSK

BERING SEA

NORTH PACIFIC OCEAN

SULU SEA

CELEBES SEA

JAVA SEA

BANDA SEA

ARAFURA SEA

CORAL SEA

INDIAN OCEAN

Gulf of Tongking

Gulf of Thailand

Gulf of Martaban

Kuriliskiye Ostrova

Aleutian Islands

Kamchatka

Cherskogo Khr.

Verkhoyanskiy Khr.

Lena

Nan Shan

Chin Ling Shan

Tropic of Cancer

Equator

Mariannas or Ladrones Is.

Caroline Islands

Peking (Pei-ching) (Tientsin)

Nanking

Shanghai

Canton (Kwangchow)

Hong Kong (U.K.)

Macao (Port.)

Hanoi

Vientiane

Bangkok (Krung Thep)

Phnom Penh

Saigon

Rangoon

Kuala Lumpur

Singapore

Jakarta

Manila

Quezon City

Seoul

Tokyo

Yokohama

Osaka

Nagoya

Ulaanbaatar

Yakutsk

Irkutsk

Ulan Ude

Khabarovsk

Vladivostok

Kunming

Chungking

Chengtu

Hankow

Wuhan

Tsingtao

Nagasaki

Kagoshima

International Boundaries

State Boundaries

© John Bartholomew & Son Ltd, Edinburgh

M

0   100 200 300 400 500 600 700 800 Kilometres

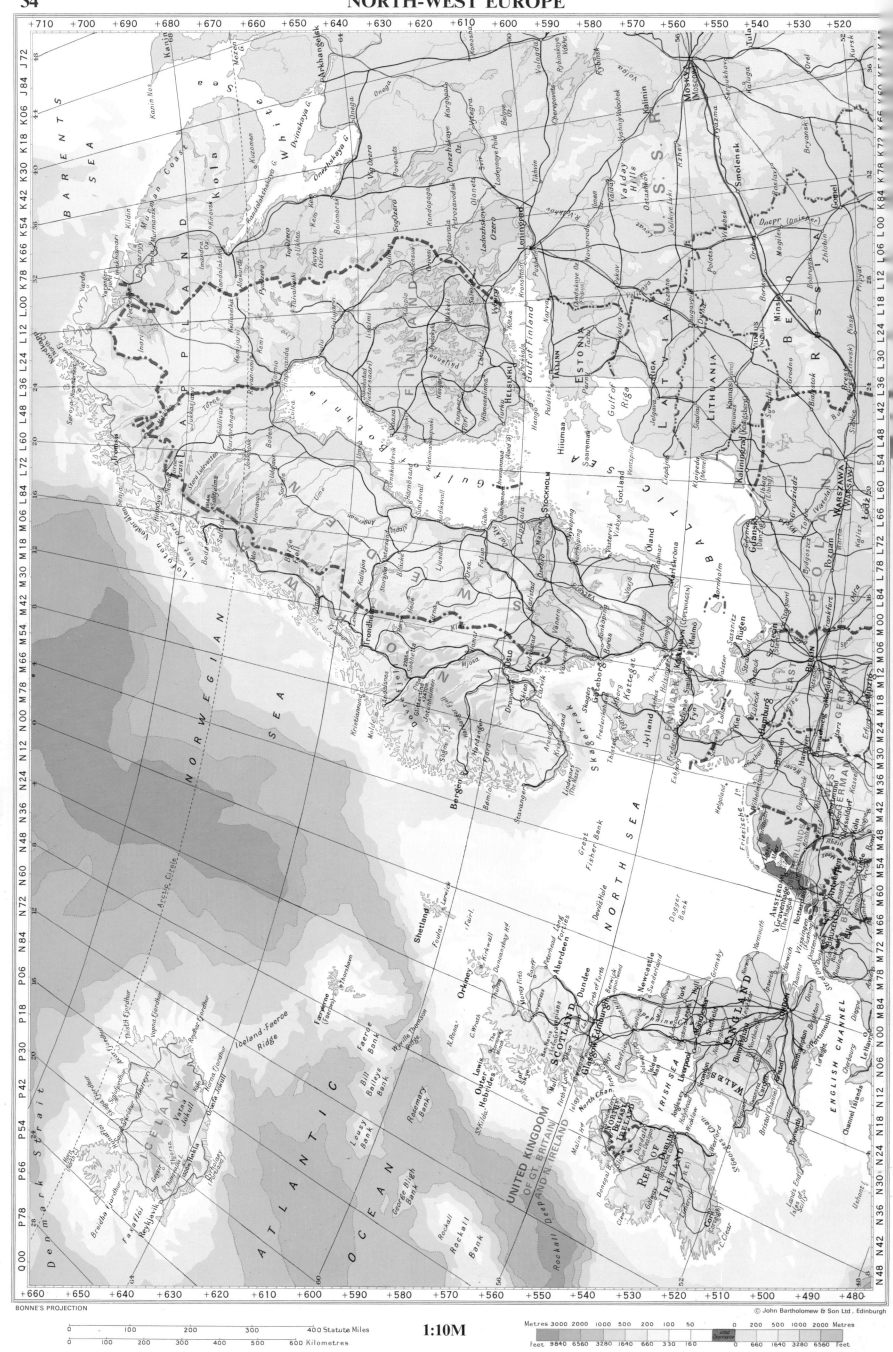

BONNE'S PROJECTION

1:10M

© John Bartholomew & Son Ltd., Edinburgh

| 0 | 100 | 200 | 300 | 400 Statute Miles |
| 0 | 100 | 200 | 300 | 400 | 500 | 600 Kilometres |

| Metres | 3000 | 2000 | 1000 | 500 | 200 | 100 | 50 | | | 0 | 200 | 500 | 1000 | 2000 Metres |
| Feet | 9840 | 6560 | 3280 | 1640 | 660 | 330 | 160 | | | 0 | 660 | 1640 | 3280 | 6560 Feet |

LAND USE

1:6M

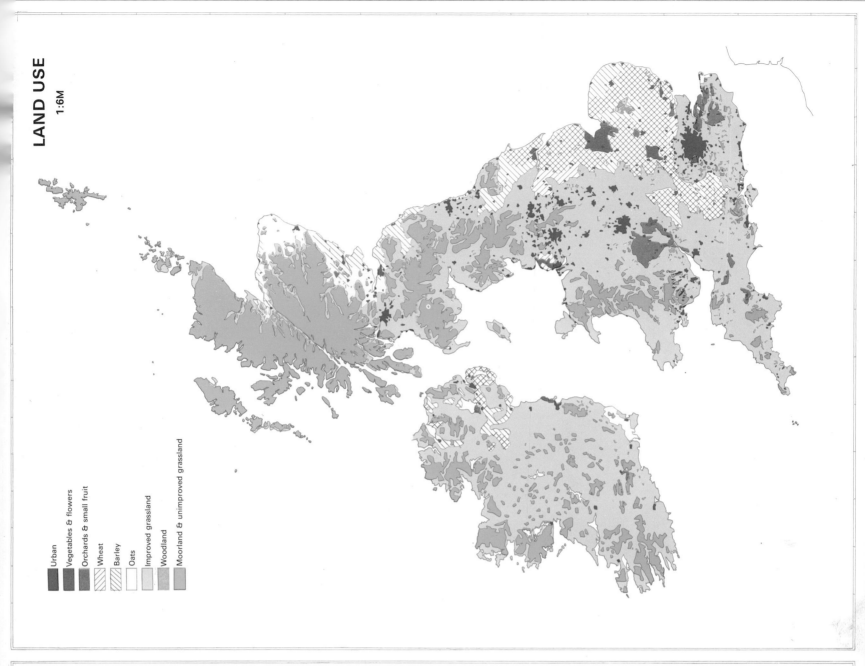

- Urban
- Vegetables & flowers
- Orchards & small fruit
- Wheat
- Barley
- Oats
- Improved grassland
- Woodland
- Moorland & unimproved grassland

STRUCTURE

1:6M

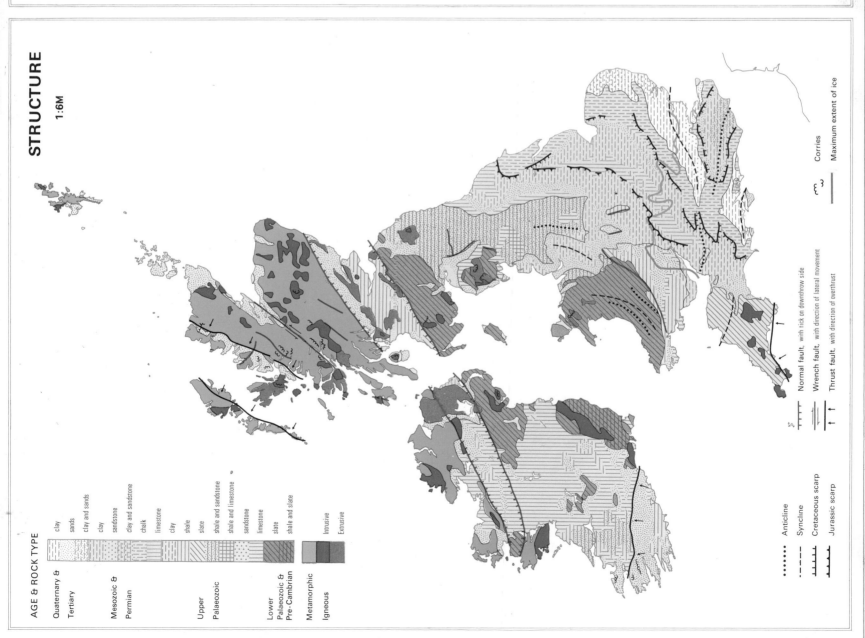

AGE & ROCK TYPE

Quaternary &	clay
Tertiary	sands
	clay and sands
Mesozoic &	clay
	sandstone
Permian	clay and sandstone
	chalk
	limestone
	clay
	shale
Upper	slate
Palaeozoic	shale and sandstone
	shale and limestone
Lower	sandstone
Palaeozoic &	limestone
Pre-Cambrian	slate
	shale and slate
Metamorphic	
Igneous	Intrusive
	Extrusive

- Anticline
- Syncline
- Cretaceous scarp
- Jurassic scarp

- Normal fault, with tick on downthrow side
- Wrench fault, with direction of lateral movement
- Thrust fault, with direction of overthrust

- Corries
- Maximum extent of ice

© John Bartholomew & Son Ltd., Edinburgh

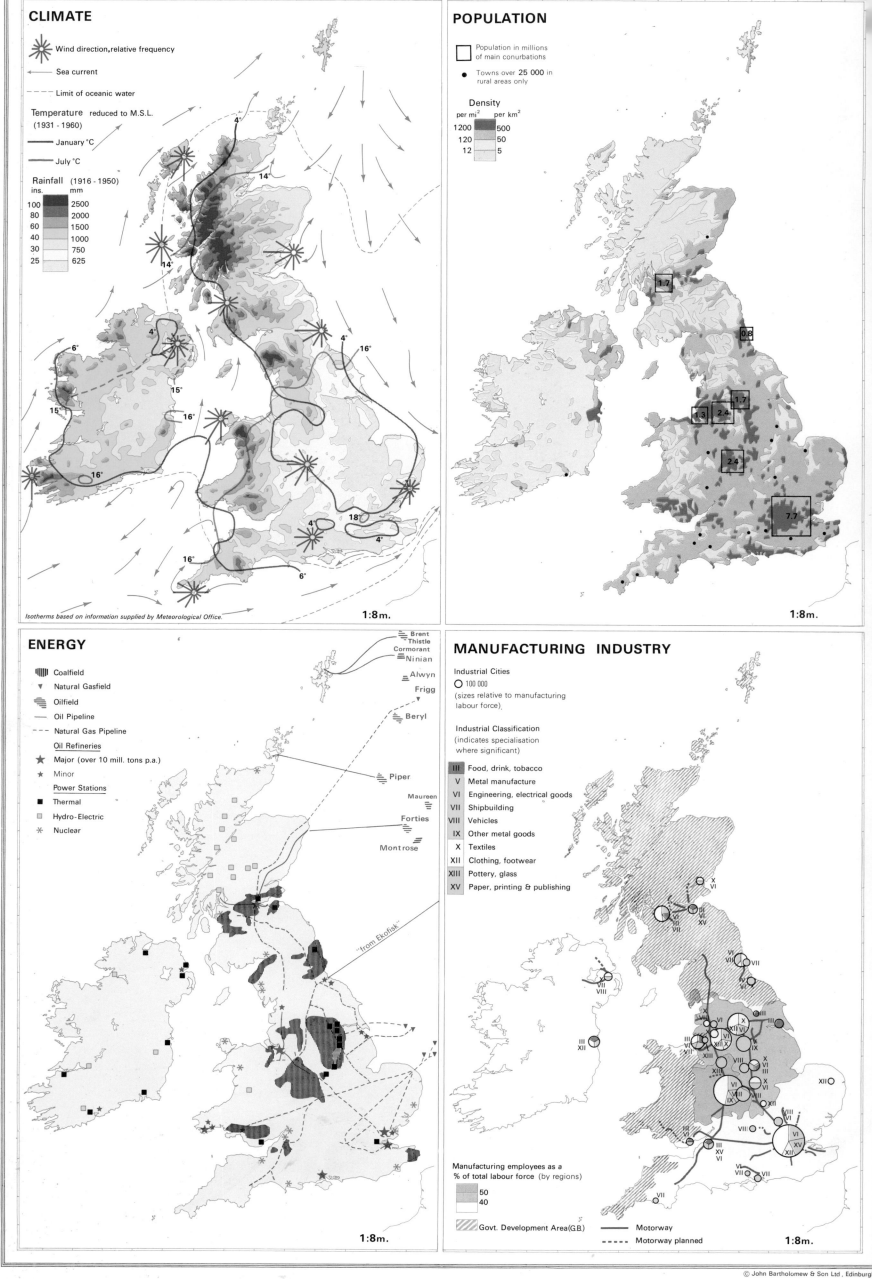

CLIMATE

- ✳ Wind direction, relative frequency
- ← Sea current
- --- Limit of oceanic water

Temperature reduced to M.S.L.
(1931 - 1960)
— January °C
— July °C

Rainfall (1916 - 1950)

ins.	mm
100	2500
80	2000
60	1500
40	1000
30	750
25	625

Isotherms based on information supplied by Meteorological Office.

1:8 m.

POPULATION

- ☐ Population in millions of main conurbations
- • Towns over 25 000 in rural areas only

Density

per mi²	per km²
1200	500
120	50
12	5

1:8 m.

ENERGY

- ⊪ Coalfield
- ▼ Natural Gasfield
- ▱ Oilfield
- — Oil Pipeline
- --- Natural Gas Pipeline

Oil Refineries
- ★ Major (over 10 mill. tons p.a.)
- ★ Minor

Power Stations
- ■ Thermal
- ☐ Hydro-Electric
- ✳ Nuclear

Brent
Thistle
Cormorant
Ninian
Alwyn
Frigg
Beryl
Piper
Maureen
Forties
Montrose

"from Ekofisk"

1:8 m.

MANUFACTURING INDUSTRY

Industrial Cities
- ○ 100 000
(sizes relative to manufacturing labour force)

Industrial Classification
(indicates specialisation where significant)

III	Food, drink, tobacco
V	Metal manufacture
VI	Engineering, electrical goods
VII	Shipbuilding
VIII	Vehicles
IX	Other metal goods
X	Textiles
XII	Clothing, footwear
XIII	Pottery, glass
XV	Paper, printing & publishing

Manufacturing employees as a
% of total labour force (by regions)

	50
	40

▨ Govt. Development Area (G.B.)

— Motorway
--- Motorway planned

1:8 m.

1:8 M

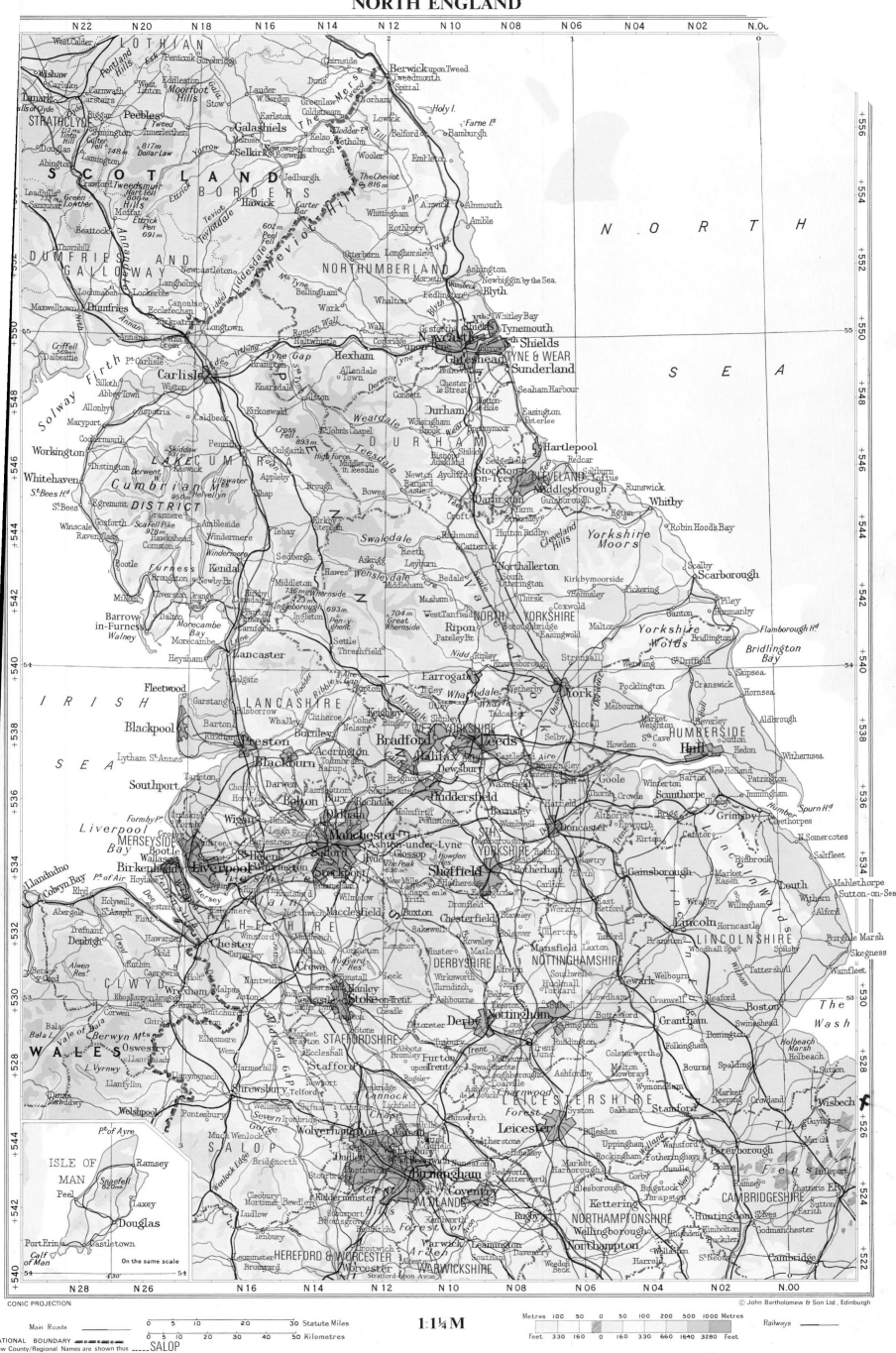

CONIC PROJECTION

Main Roads

NATIONAL BOUNDARY

New County/Regional Names are shown thus ------ SALOP

1:1¼M

Metres 100 50 0 50 100 200 500 1000 Metres

Feet 330 160 0 160 330 660 1640 3280 Feet

Railways

© John Bartholomew & Son Ltd., Edinburgh

N 36   N 34   N 32   N 30   N 28   N 26   N 24   N 22   N 20   N 18

M 88
558+

Lambay I.
Howth Hd
(e Atha Cliath)

Bray
Kilcoole

WICKLOW
Lugnaquilla
Wicklow
Wicklow Hd
Rathdrum
Aughrim
Arklow
Shillelagh
Corey
Ferns
Cahore Pt

R.Slaney
Enniscorthy

Wexford Harb.
Wexford
Rosslare Harb.
Greenore Pt
Carnsore Pt

ST GEORGE'S CHANNEL

Lambay I.
Amlwch
Cemaes
Holyhead
Holyhead Mt
219 m
Holy I.
Anglesey
Llanfair-fechan
Llanerchymedd
Gt Ormes
Hd
Llandudno
Colwyn Bay
Rhyl
Pt of Air
Abergele
Llangefni Beaumaris
Menai Brd
Bangor
Gaerwen
Dinorwic
Bethesda
Llanrwst
Menai Str.
Caernarfon
Llanberis
Llanllyfni
Snowdon
1085 m
Beddgelert
Porthmadog
Nevin Peninsula
Criccieth
Lleyn Peninsula
Pwllheli
Tremadog
Bay
Porth
Neigwl
Penkilan Hd
Bardsey
Barmou

Cardigan
Bay

Tywy
Aber

Aberystwyth

Llanrhystyd

Aberaeron
New Quay
Ystrad
Sarnau
Lampeter
St Dogmaels
Cardigan
Newcastle
Emlyn
Llandyssul
Pencader
Fishguard B.
Strumble Hd
Newport
Fishguard
Mathry
Crymmych Arms
DYFED
St Davids Hd
St Davids
Ramsey I.
St Brides
Bay
Haverfordwest
Skomer I.
Milford
Haven
Milford Haven
Pembroke
Dock
Narberth
Saundersfoot
Tenby
Pembroke
Langharne
St Govans Hd
Carmarthen Bay

Aberystwyth

WALES
Devils
Bridge
Ystwyth
Llanidloes
Rhayader
Res.
POWYS
Res.
Newbridge
on Wye
Llandrindod
New Radnor
Builth
Wells
Garth
Llanwrtyd Wells
Pumsaint
Mynydd Eppynt
Talgarth
Llandovery
Brecon
Black Mts
Brecon
Beacons
Llandeilo
Black Mt
Brynamman
Usk
Ammanford
Santardawe
Kidwelly
Llanelli
Llanelli
Burry Inlet
Llanelli
Port
Burry Inlet
Neath
Bridgend
Gower
Port
Eynon
Swansea Bay
Mumbles
Worms Hd
Nash Pt

WALES

SALOP
Much Wenlock
Church
Stretton
Craven
Arms
Clun Forest
Clun
Wenlock Edge
Bridgnorth
Cleobury
Mortimer
Bewd
Bishops
Castle
Knighton
Presteigne
Ludlow
Leominster
Pembridge
Kington
Weobley
Leintwardine
Tenbury
Temg
HEREFORD
Bromyard
Marden
Gre
Maly
Ma
Hay on Wye
Hereford
Ledbury
Ross on Wye
Peterstow
Cinderford
Newnham
Forest
of Dean
Blakeney
Lydney
Berkeley
Tintern
Chepstow
Thornbury
AVON
Severn
Bristol
Portishead
Clevedon

Black Mts
Abergavenny
Monmouth
Pontrilas
GWENT
Usk
Crickhowell
Ebbw
Vale
Blaenavon
Dowlais
Merthyr
Tydfil
Aberdare
Mountain Ash
Pontypool
Bargoed
Rhondda
New
Bridge
Caerphilly
Pontypridd
Llantrisant
Newport
Cardiff
Penarth
STH GLAM.
Cowbridge
Barry
Aberthaw
Porthcawl

Caerleon

Keynsham
Bath
Bathfield
Weston
super-Mare
Blagdon
Res.
Chew Valley
Mendip Hills
Wells
Glastonbury
Shepton
Mallet
Frome
Bru

BRISTOL CHANNEL

Lynton
Foreland
Porlock
Minehead
Watchet
Bridgwater
Bay
Burnham
Lundy
Ilfracombe
Morte Pt
Combe
Martin
Parracombe
Dunkery
Beacon
Dulverton
Exton
Exmoor
Brendon
Hills
Quantock
Hills
Cheddar
Wiveliscombe
Williton
SOMERSET
Bridgwater
Street
Sedgemoor
Somerton
Langport
Wincanton
Milborne
Glastonbury
Shepton
Mallet
Castle
Cary

Bideford
Bay
Westward Ho!
Barnstaple
Bampton
Wellington
Taunton
Ilchester
Martock
Yeovil
Sherborne
Blackmoor
Yetminster
DOR

Hartland Pt
Hartland
Clovelly
Appledore
Bideford
Great
Torrington
Witheridge
St Molton
Wivelscombe
Durston
Wellington
Uffculme
Blackdown
Hills
Ilminster
Chard
Crewkerne
Sherborne
Beaminster
Cerne Abt
Maiden
Newton
Dorc

Bradworthy
Bude
Stratton
Merton
Chumleigh
Tiverton
Lapford
Crediton
Bow
Bradninch
Honiton
Axminster
Colyton
Lyme
Regis
Bridport
Abbotsbury
Chesil
Bank
Portland Isle
Portl

Stratton
Holsworthy
Hatherleigh
Okehampton
Sourton
Yes Tor
Lifton
Lydford
Hampstead
Princetown
Dartmoor
Moretonhampstead
Bovey Tracey
Dart
Ashburton
Crediton
Thorverton
Exeter
St Mary
Exminster
Topsham
Exmouth
Budleigh Salterton
Sidmouth
Seaton
Lyme Bay
Whitstone
Boscastle
Tintagel Hd
Camelford
St Teath
Port Isaac
Padstow
St Columb
Newquay
Wadebridge
Bodmin
Moors
Bodmin
Gunnislake
Callington
Liskeard
Tavistock
Yelverton
Newton
Abbot
Teignmouth
Dawlish
Torquay
Paignton
Torbay
Brixham
Kingswear
Dartmouth
Start Bay
Salcombe
Start Pt
Prawle Pt
CORNWALL

Perranporth
St Agnes
St Day
Redruth
Truro
Newlyn
St Austell
Grampound
Tregoney
Mevagissey
St Blazey
W.Looe
Lostwithiel
Fowey
E.Looe
Polperro
St Germans
Saltash
Devonport
Plymouth
Oreston
Plymouth Snd
Bigbury
Bay
Kingsbridge
Camborne
Penryn
Falmouth
Falmouth B.
Dodman Pt
Eddystone Lt Hoe
E N

St Ives B.
St Ives
Hayle
Marazion
Penzance
Mounts
Bay
Helston
Lizard
Lizard Pt
C.Cornwall
St Just
Longships Lt Ho
Land's End
Sennen
Wolf
Rock Lt Ho

Tresco
St Martins
Hugh Town
St Marys
Bishop
Rock
Lt Ho
St Agnes
Isles
of Scilly

N 38   N 36   N 34   N 32   N 30   N 28   N 26   N 24   N 22   N 20   N 18   N 16   N 14

CONIC PROJECTION

Main Roads ———
Railways ———

0 5 10   20   30   40   50 Statute Miles
0 5 10 20 30 40 50 60 70 80 Kilometres

1:1¼

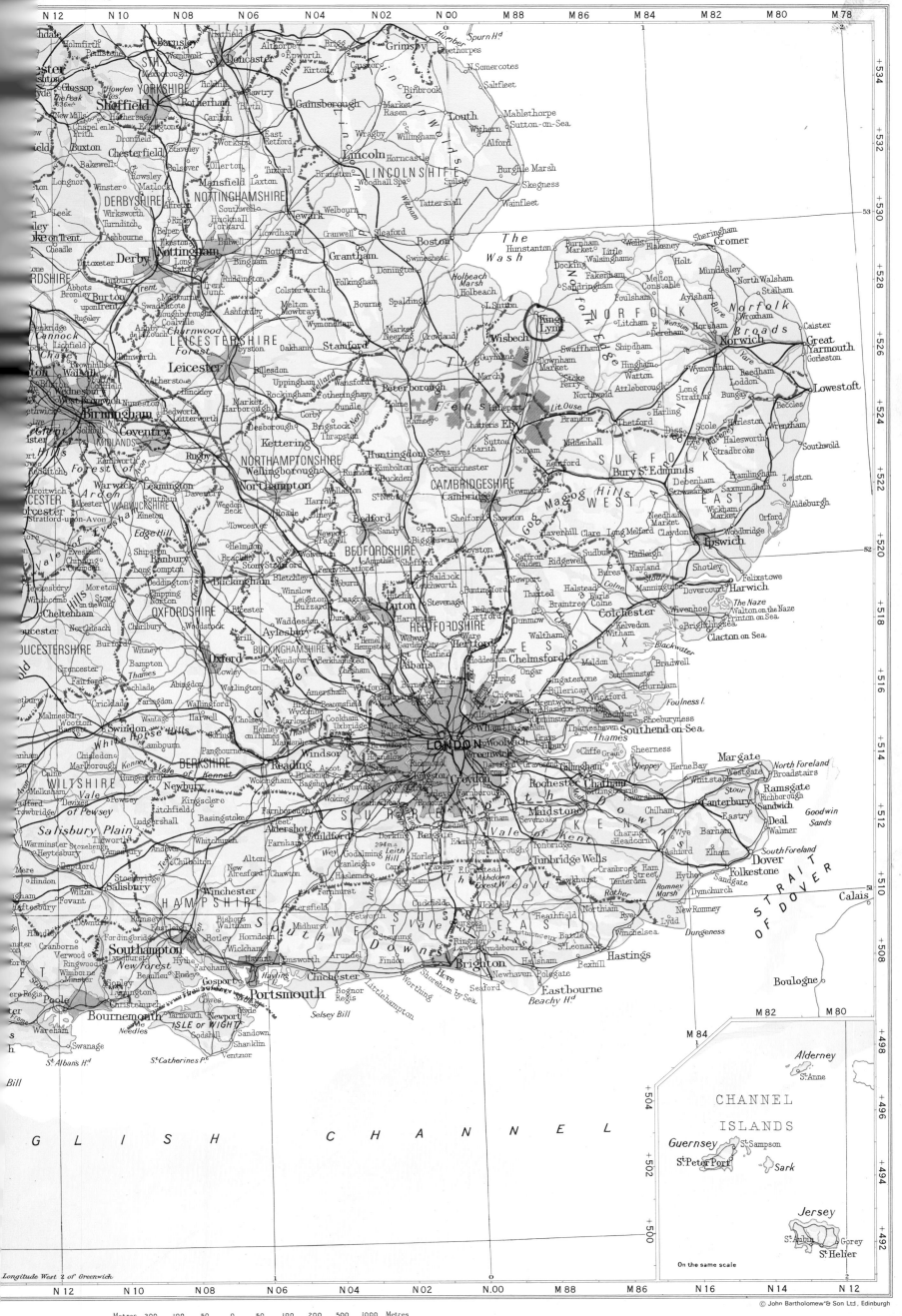

Holmfirth
Hallstone
Wombwell Barnsley
Whitfield Altthorpe Brigg Grimsby Humber Spurn Hd
Glossop Mexborough Doncaster Trent Epworth Cleethorpes
The Peak Howden YORKSHIRE Tickhill Kirton N.Somercotes
636 m Res Saltfleet
New Mills Sheffield Rotherham Sawtry Gainsborough Market Louth Mablethorpe
Chapel en le Carlton Rasen Witham Sutton-on-Sea
Buxton Chesterfield Staveley East Worksop Wragby Willingham Alford
Bakewell Bolsover Retford Lincoln Horncastle Burghle Marsh
Longnor Rowsley Ollerton Tuxford Branston LINCOLNSHIRE Spilsby Skegness
Leek Winster Matlock Mansfield Taxton Woodhall Spa Tattershall Wainfleet
Ashbourne Southwell Sleaford Boston
DERBYSHIRE Wirksworth Hucknall Newark Welbourn The Wash
Turnditch Ripley Torkard Lowdham Cranwell
Belper Bulwell Bingham Donington Hunstanton Burnham Wells Sheringham Cromer
Uttoxeter Derby Nottingham Bottesford Grantham Spalding Market Docking Fakenham Little Blakeney Holt Mundesley
Abbots Long Eaton Swineshead Holbeach Walsingham Melton North Walsham
Bromley Burton Swadlincote Melton Colsterworth Holbeach Marsh Sandringham Constable Aylsham Stalham
upon Trent Coalville Mowbray Bourne L.Sutton Foulsham Dereham Norfolk Wroxham
Rugeley Loughborough Wymondham Crowland Kings Swaffham Shipdham Horsham Broads Caister
Cannock Ashby Charnwood Oakham Stamford Market Lynn Downham Norwich Great
Chase Lichfield Forest Deeping Wisbech Market Hingham Watton Yarmouth
Walsall LEICESTERSHIRE Uppingham Peterborough March Stoke Wymondham Reedham Gorleston
West Bromwich Leicester Billesdon Rockingham Fotheringhay Guyhirn Ferry Long Loddon Lowestoft
Birmingham Hinckley Market Oundle Holme The Northwold Stratton Beccles
Coventry Nuneaton Harborough Corby Thrapston Ramsey Fens Lit. Ouse Attleborough Bungay Wrentham
MIDLANDS Bedworth Desborough Brigstock Chatteris Ely Brandon Diss Scole Harleston Halesworth Southwold
Solihull Lutterworth Kettering Nene Sutton Mildenhall Thetford Harling SUFFOLK Stradbroke
Kenilworth Rugby NORTHAMPTONSHIRE Huntingdon St.Ives Earith Soham Bury St. Edmunds WEST EAST Leiston
Forest of Warwick Leamington Wellingborough Godmanchester Newmarket Debenham Framlingham
Arden Daventry Northampton Weedon Rushden Kimbolton CAMBRIDGESHIRE Stowmarket Saxmundham
Alcester WARWICKSHIRE Beck Wollaston Buckden Cambridge Gog Magog Hills Needham Aldeburgh
Stratford-upon-Avon Kineton Roade Harrold St.Neots Shelford Sawston Market Orford
Towcester Bedford Potton Haverhill Clare Long Melford Woodbridge
Evesham Edge Hill Olney Biggleswade Saffron Sudbury Ipswich
Shipston Banbury Bletchley BEDFORDSHIRE Shefford Royston Walden Ridgewell Nayland Shotley
EVESHAM Long Compton Brackley Stony Stratford Ampthill Byres Colne Felixstowe
HILLS Moreton Chipping Buckingham Woburn Hitchin Buntingford Newport Halstead Manningtree Harwich
Cheltenham in the Marsh Norton Bicester Winslow Leighton Luton Stevenage Thaxted Braintree Colne Wivenhoe Dovercourt
Deddington Buzzard Leagrave Bishops Dunmow The Naze
Moreton Waddesdon Dunstable Harpenden Stortford Colchester Walton on the Naze
Northleach Charlbury Woodstock Aylesbury Hemel Welwyn HERTFORDSHIRE Harlow Kelvedon Frinton-on-Sea
GLOUCESTERSHIRE Witney Brill Hempstead Garden City Ware Hoddesdon ESSEX Brightlingsea
Burford OXFORDSHIRE Thame Berkhamsted Hatfield Hertford Ongar Maldon Clacton on Sea
Cirencester Bampton Oxford BUCKINGHAMSHIRE Wendover Chesham St. Epping Ingatestone Southminster
Fairford Cowley Chilter Albans Chigwell Billericay Burnham
Cricklade Abingdon Thames Amersham Watford Brentwood Basildon Rayleigh Bradwell Blackwater
Lechlade Faringdon Wallingford Beaconsfield Barnet Wickford
Wantage Marlow Cookham Uxbridge Enfield Ilford Romford Shoeburyness
Swindon Harwell Chalsey Henley Maidenhead Brentford Woolwich Grays Thames Southend-on-Sea
White Horse Hills Pangbourne on Thames Windsor Hounslow Dartford Tilbury Foulness I.
Chiseldon Kennet Reading Ascot Staines LONDON Greenwich Gravesend Gillingham Thameshaven
Marlborough Newbury Wokingham Bracknell Weybridge Richmond Croydon Woolwich Rochester Chatham Sheppey Herne Bay Margate
WILTSHIRE Vale of Bagshot Kingston Dartford Gillingham Grain Whitstable Westgate North Foreland
Calne Kennet Hungerford SURREY Farnborough Epsom the Sittingbourne Sheerness Broadstairs
Melksham Vale Pewsey Kingsclere Aldershot Dorking Reigate Redhill Maidstone Faversham Ramsgate
Trowbridge of Pewsey Basingstoke Guildford Westerham Sevenoaks Chilham Canterbury Richborough
Devizes Ludgershall Whitchurch Godalming Leith KENT Charing Wye Sandwich
Salisbury Plain Andover Farnham Hill 294 m Edenbridge Vale of Kent Barham Deal
Warminster Tidworth Alton Cranleigh Horley Tonbridge Ashford Headcorn The Downs Walmer
Heytesbury Amesbury New Chawton Capel Crawley Tunbridge Wells Goodwin
Mere Deptford Stonehenge Alresford Haslemere E. Grinstead Cranbrook Ham South Foreland Sands
Hindon Wilton Winchester Petersfield Fernhurst Cuckfield Ashdown Street Tenterden Dover
Shaftesbury Fovant Salisbury SUSSEX Forest The Hawkhurst Hythe STRAIT
Downton HAMPSHIRE Midhurst Weald Northiam Dymchurch Folkestone OF DOVER
Handley Romsey Bishops South WEST Uckfield Rother Rye Sandgate
Cranborne Eastleigh Waltham Downs Burgess Heathfield Battle New Romney Calais
Verwood Botley Wickham Midhurst Hill Ringmer Romney Marsh Lydd
Fordingbridge Southampton Horndean SUSSEX Lewes Hailsham Winchelsea Dungeness
Ringwood Hythe Emsworth Arundel Findon St.Leonards Polegate Hastings
Wimborne New Forest Fareham Chichester Worthing Brighton Hove Newhaven Bexhill
Minster Lyndhurst Gosport Hayling Littlehampton Shoreham by Sea Seaford Eastbourne
Poole Bournemouth Yarmouth Newport Portsmouth Bognor Selsey Bill Beachy Hd
Wareham Christchurch Needles ISLE of WIGHT Regis
Swanage Cowes Sandown
St.Albans Hd St Catherines Pt Sodshill Shanklin Ventnor

ENGLISH CHANNEL

CHANNEL ISLANDS
Alderney St.Anne
Guernsey St.Sampson
St.Peter Port Sark
Jersey
St.Aubin Gorey St. Helier
On the same scale

Longitude West 2 of Greenwich

© John Bartholomew & Son Ltd., Edinburgh

M

Metres 200 100 50 0 50 100 200 500 1000 Metres
Feet 660 330 160 0 160 330 660 1640 3280 Feet

NATIONAL BOUNDARY
COUNTY/REGION BOUNDARY .... SALOP

CONIC PROJECTION

Main Roads ——
Railways ——

0 5 10 20 30 40 50 Statute Miles
0 5 10 20 30 40 50 60 70 80 Kilometres

1:1¼

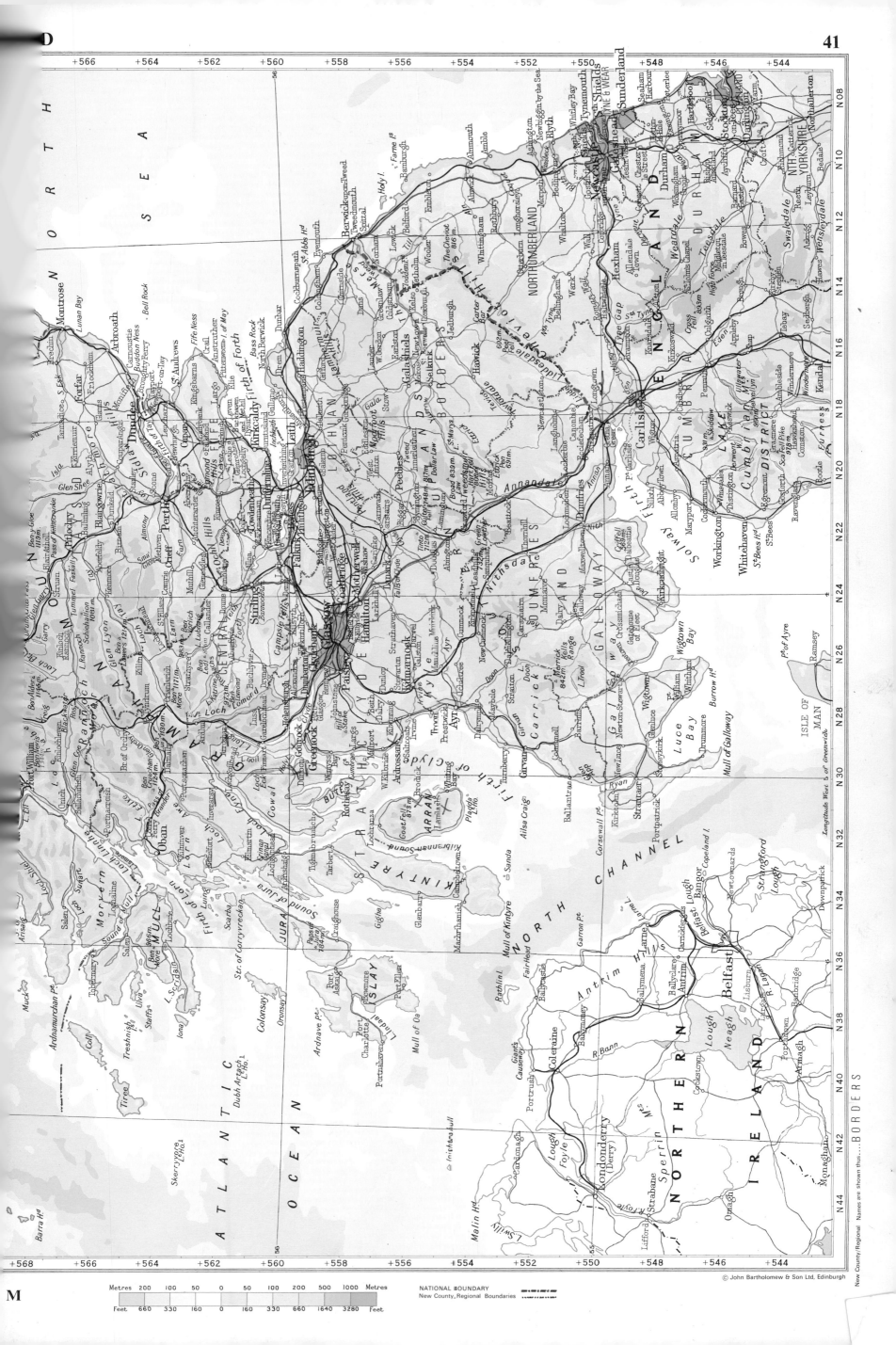

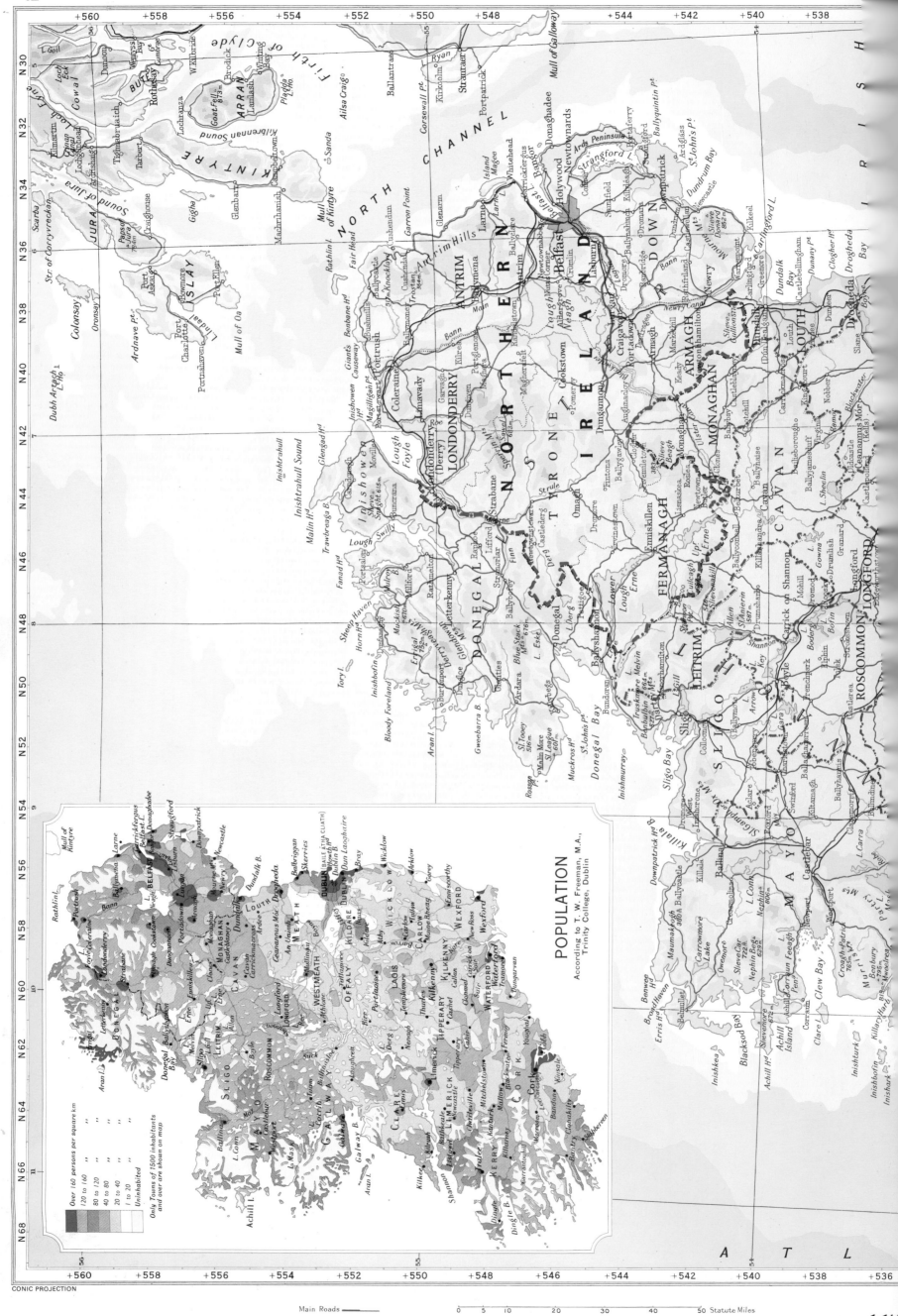

+560 +558 +556 +554 +552 +550 +548 +544 +542 +540 +538

N 30
N 32
N 34
N 36
N 38
N 40
N 42
N 44
N 46
N 48
N 50
N 52
N 54
N 56
N 58
N 60
N 62
N 64
N 66
N 68

NORTH CHANNEL

NORTHERN IRELAND

ANTRIM
Belfast
LONDONDERRY (DERRY)
TYRONE
DOWN
ARMAGH
MONAGHAN
FERMANAGH
CAVAN
LEITRIM
SLIGO
LONGFORD
ROSCOMMON
MAYO
DONEGAL

IRISH

ATL

POPULATION

According to T. W. Freeman, M.A.,
Trinity College, Dublin

Over 160 persons per square km
120 to 160 " "
80 to 120 " "
40 to 80 " "
20 to 40 " "
1 to 20 " "
Uninhabited

Only Towns of 1500 inhabitants
and over are shown on map

BELFAST
DUBLIN (BAILE ÁTHA CLIATH)
ANTRIM
DOWN
ARMAGH
MONAGHAN
CAVAN
FERMANAGH
TYRONE
LONDONDERRY
DONEGAL
LEITRIM
SLIGO
MAYO
ROSCOMMON
LONGFORD
WESTMEATH
MEATH
LOUTH
DUBLIN
KILDARE
WICKLOW
OFFALY
LAOIS
CARLOW
WEXFORD
KILKENNY
TIPPERARY
WATERFORD
LIMERICK
CORK
KERRY
CLARE
GALWAY

+560 +558 +556 +554 +552 +550 +548 +546 +544 +542 +540 +538 +536

CONIC PROJECTION

Main Roads ———
Railways ·······

0 5 10   20   30   40   50 Statute Miles
0 5 10 20 30 40 50 60 70 80 Kilometres

1:1¼

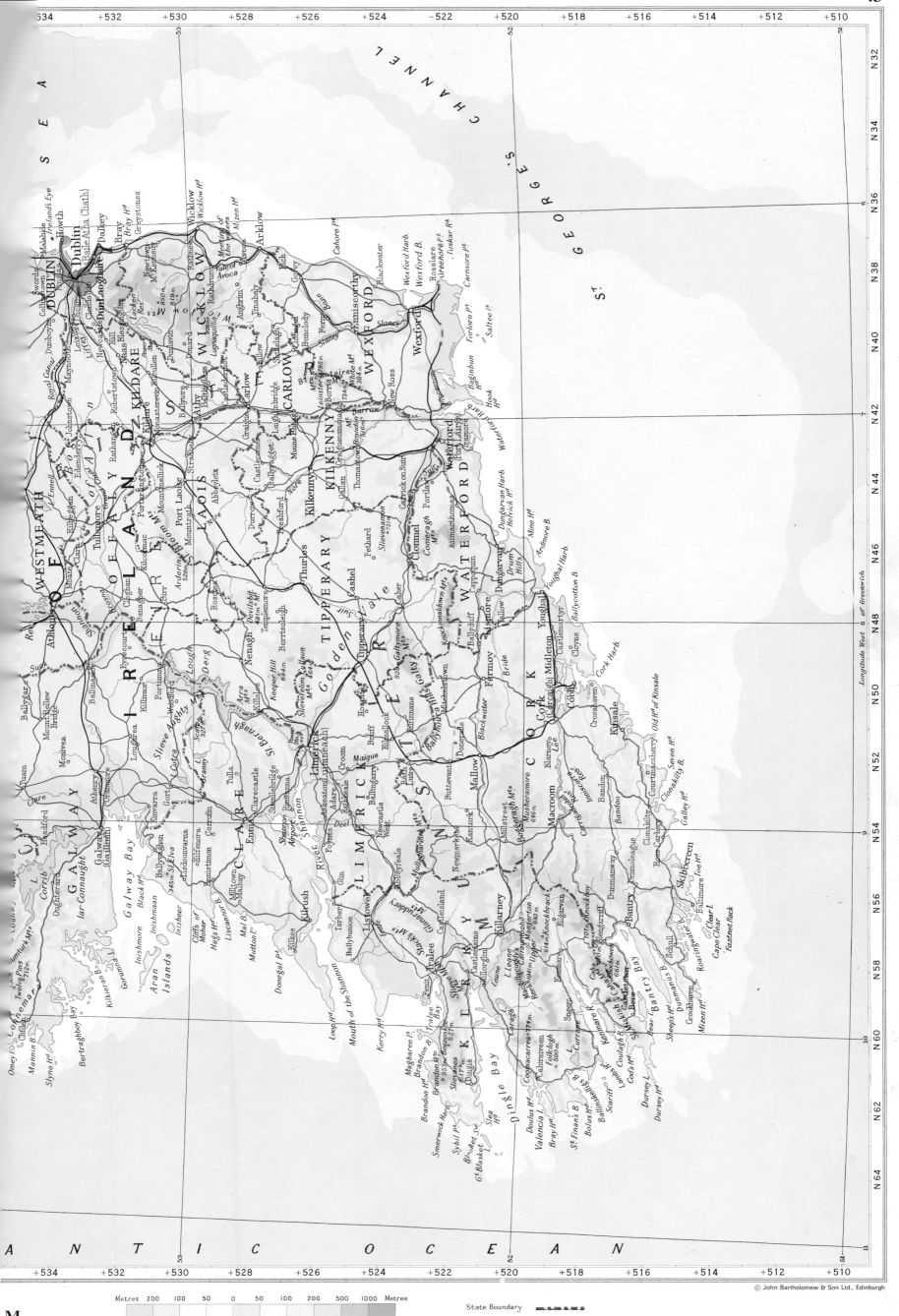

43

N 32
N 34
N 36
N 38
N 40
N 42
N 44
N 46
N 48
N 50
N 52
N 54
N 56
N 58
N 60
N 62
N 64

+534 +532 +530 +528 +526 +524 −522 +520 +518 +516 +514 +512 +510

GEORGE'S CHANNEL

St.

IRISH SEA

DUBLIN

WICKLOW

KILDARE

CARLOW

WEXFORD

KILKENNY

WATERFORD

WESTMEATH

OFFALY

LAOIS

TIPPERARY

CORK

CLARE

LIMERICK

KERRY

GALWAY

ATLANTIC OCEAN

Longitude West 8 of Greenwich.

M

Metres 200 100 50 0 50 100 200 500 1000 Metres
Feet 660 330 160 0 160 330 660 1640 3280 Feet

State Boundary
County Boundaries

© John Bartholomew & Son Ltd., Edinburgh

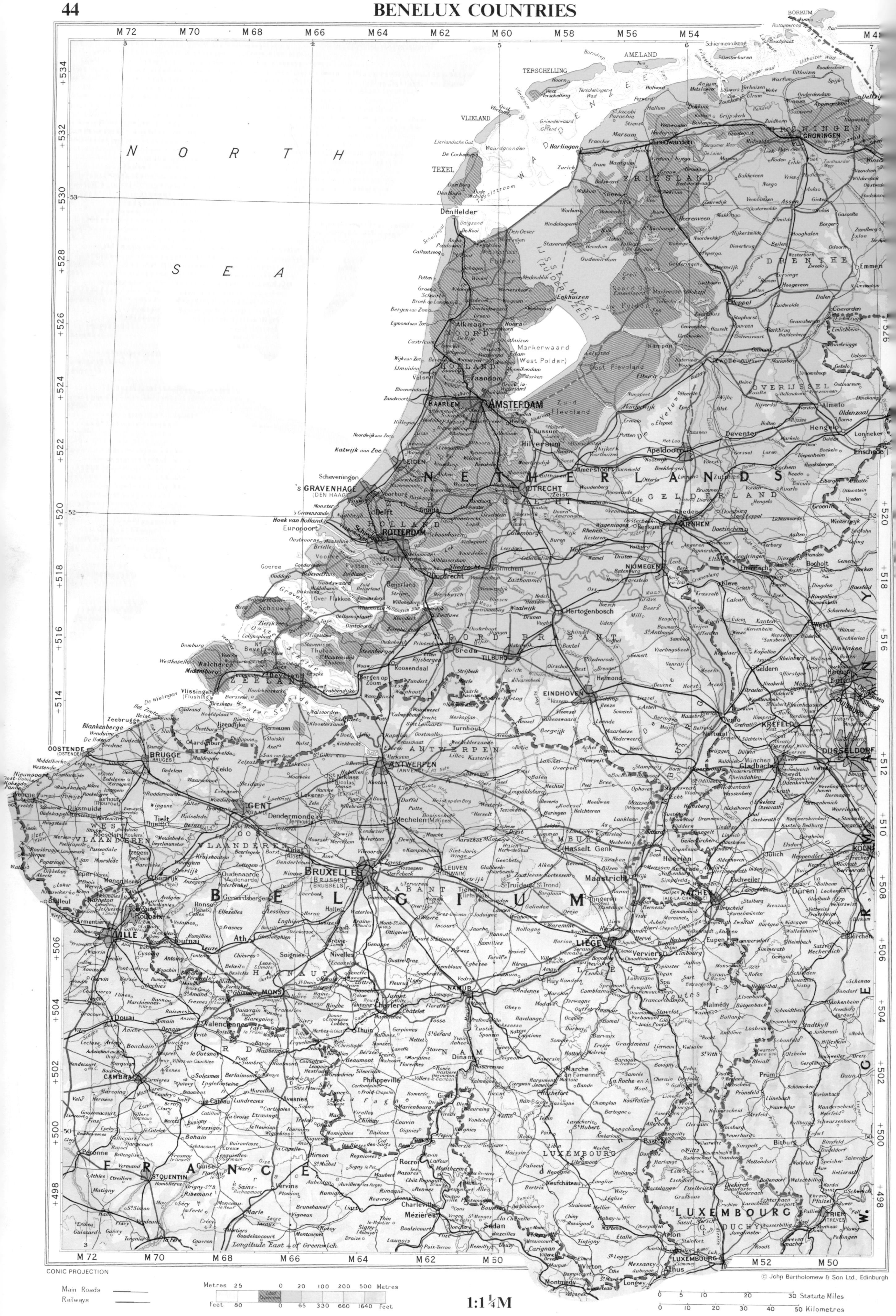

NORTH

SEA

NETHERLANDS

BELGIUM

FRANCE

LUXEMBOURG

GERMANY

CONIC PROJECTION

Main Roads

Railways

| Metres | 25 | | 0 | 20 | 100 | 200 | 500 Metres |
| Feet | 80 | | 0 | 65 | 330 | 660 | 1640 Feet |

1:1¼M

0 5 10 20 30 Statute Miles

0 10 20 30 40 50 Kilometres

© John Bartholomew & Son Ltd., Edinburgh

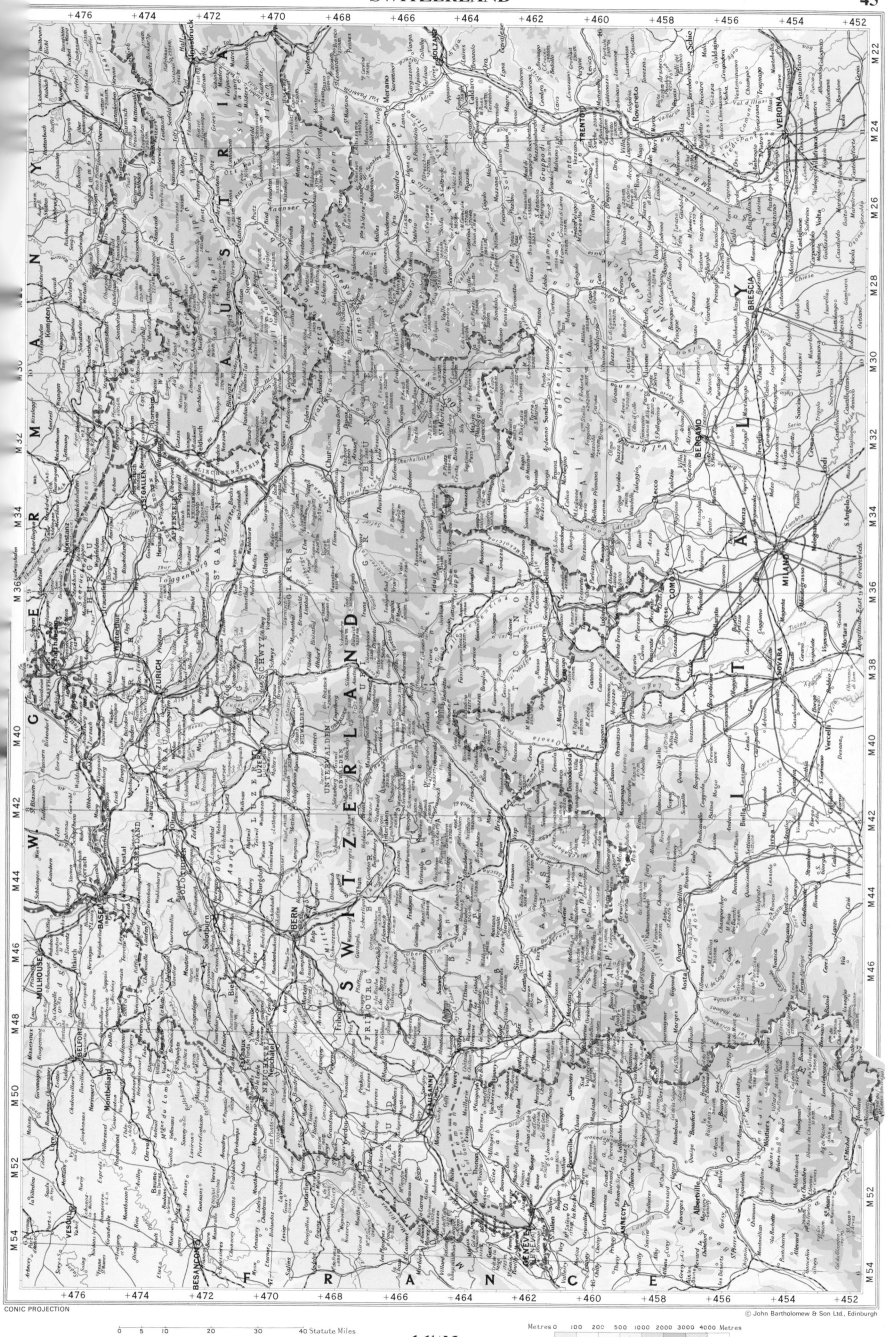

0   5   10   20   30   40 Statute Miles

0 10 20   30   40   50   60 Kilometres

1:1¼M

Metres 0   100 200 500 1000 2000 3000 4000 Metres

Feet 0   330 660 1640 3280 6560 9840 13120 Feet

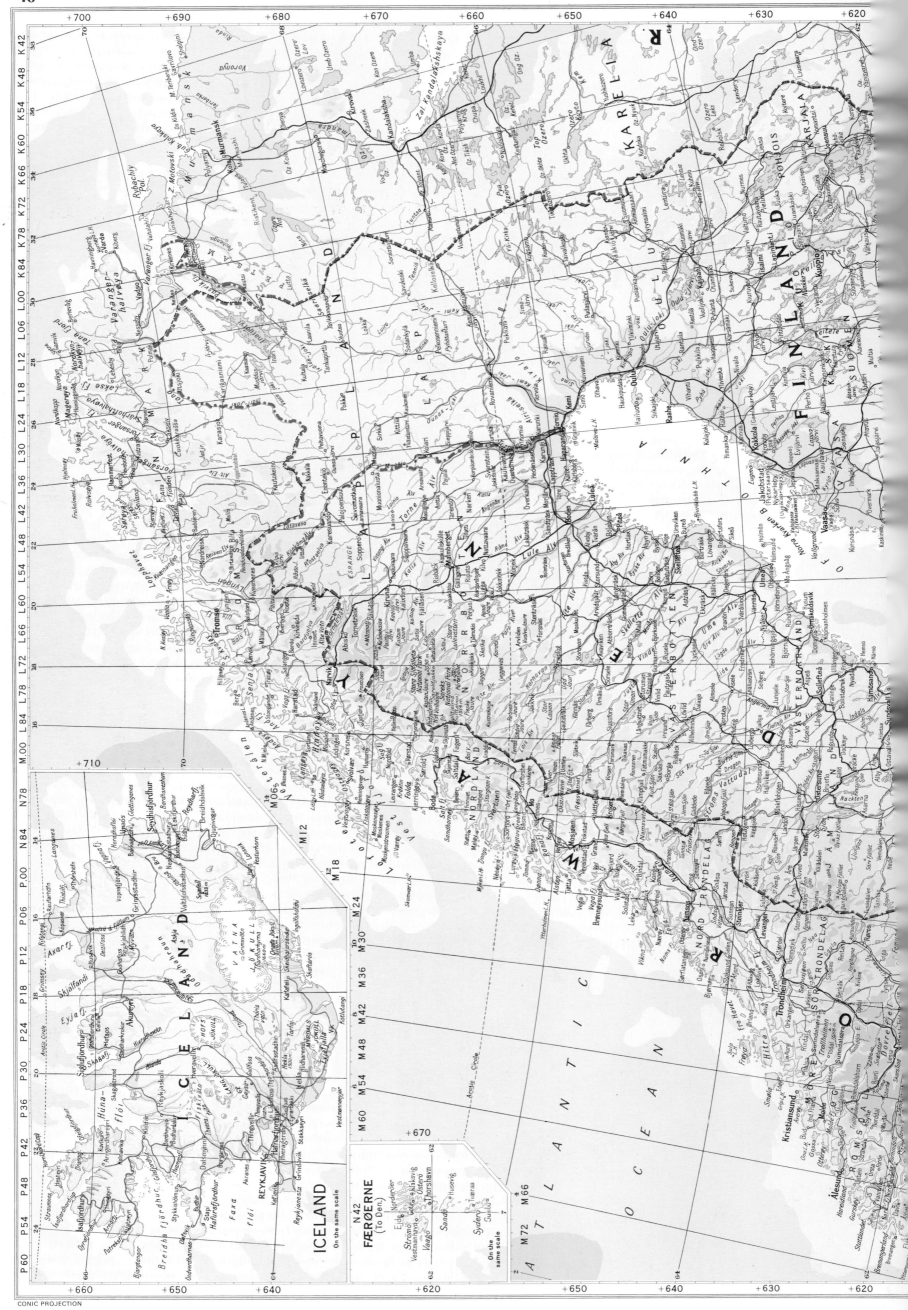

ICELAND
On the same scale

FERØERNE
(To Den.)
On the same scale

CONIC PROJECTION

Main Roads ———
Railways ———

0	20	40	60	80	100	120	140	160	180 Statute Miles

0	20	40	80	120	160	200	240	280 Kilometres

1:4½

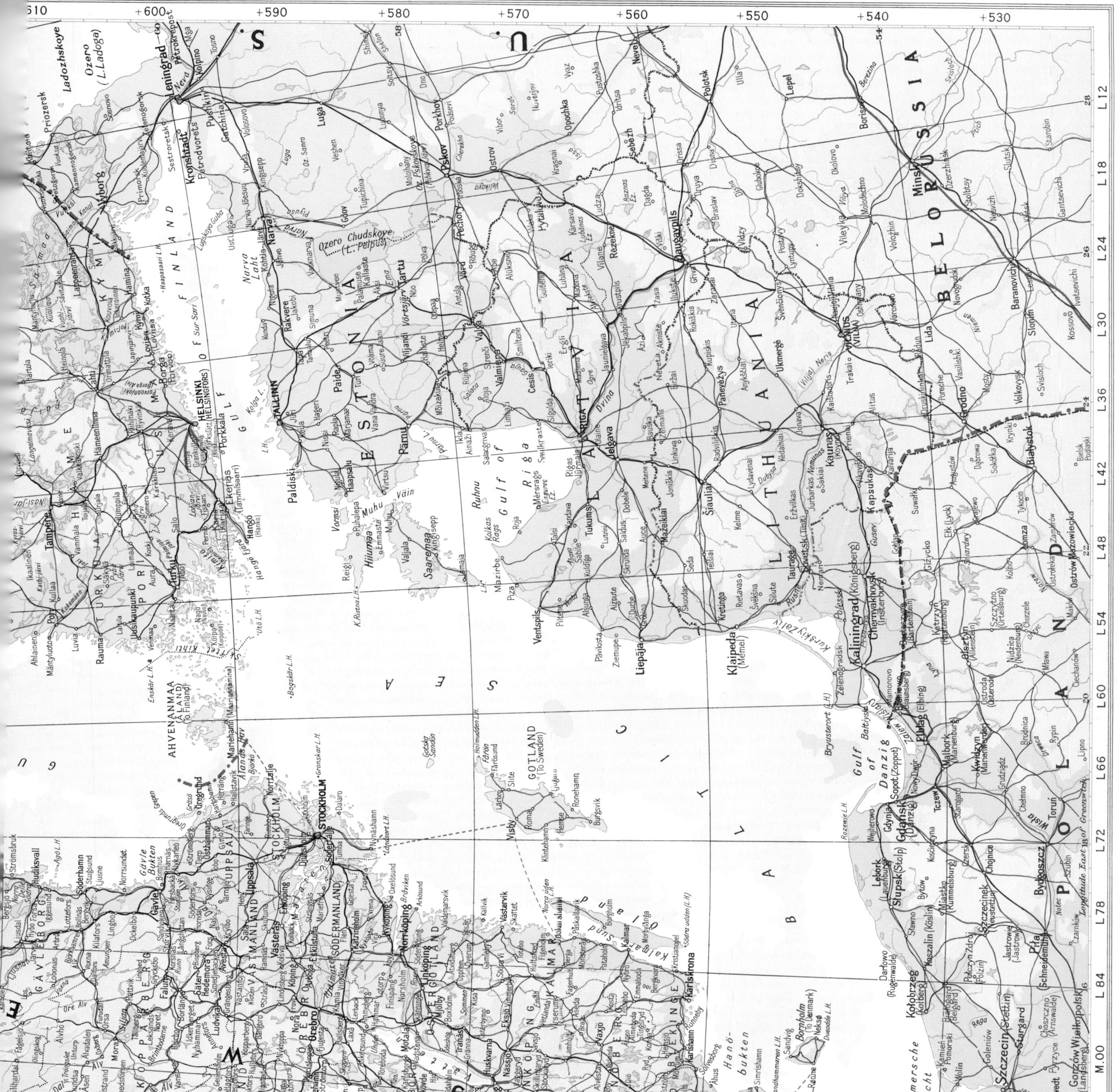

Metres 2000 200 50 0 100 200 500 1000 2000 Metres

Feet 6560 660 160 0 330 660 1640 3280 6560 Feet

International Boundaries

State Boundaries

© John Bartholomew & Son Ltd., Edinburgh

M

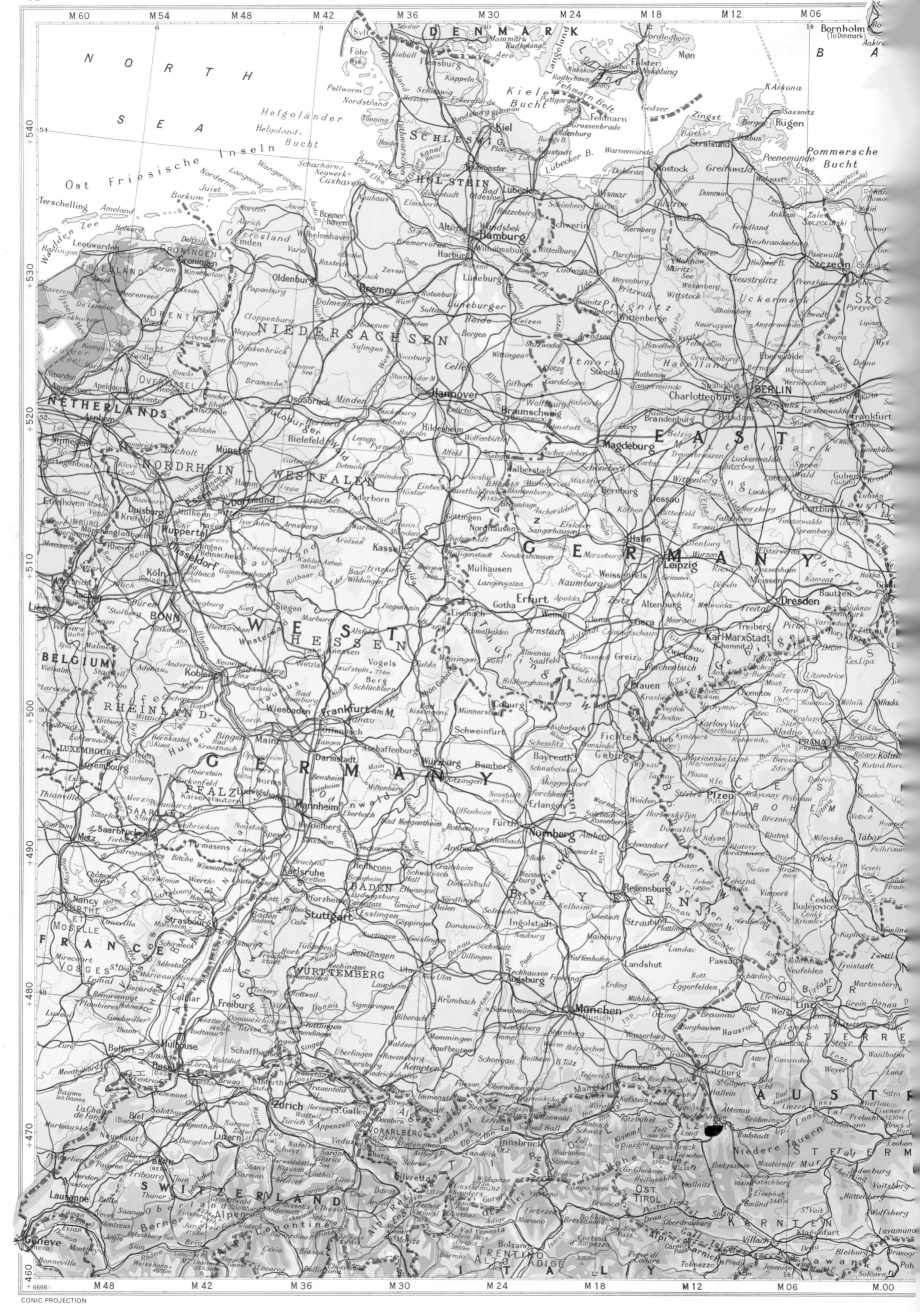

Main Roads ——————
Railways ——————

0 10 20 30 40 50 60 70 80 90 100 110 120 Statute Miles
0 10 20   40   60   80   100   120   140   160 Kilometres

1:3

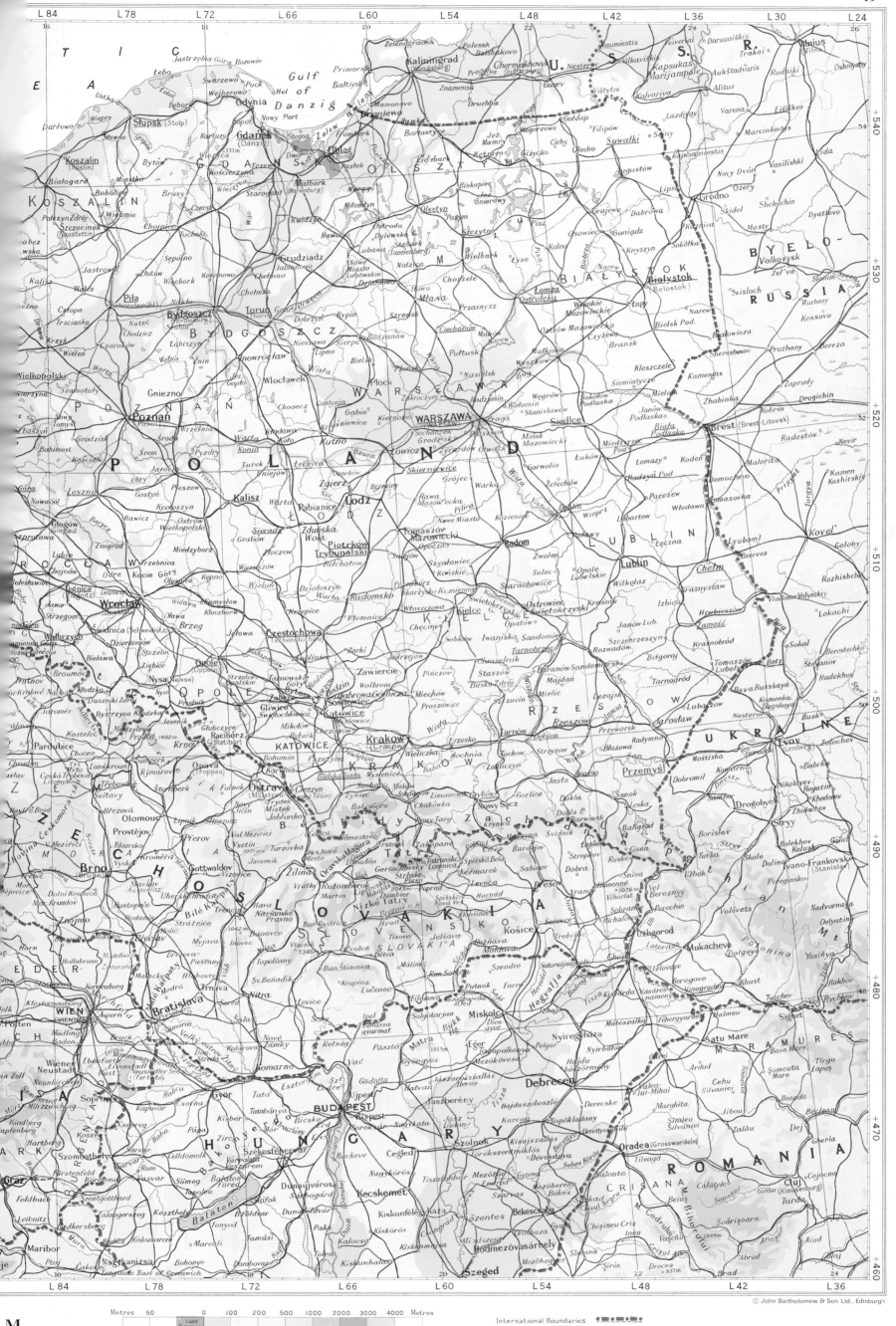

M

| Metres | 50 | 0 | 100 | 200 | 500 | 1000 | 2000 | 3000 | 4000 | Metres |

Land Depression

| Feet | 100 | 0 | 330 | 660 | 1640 | 3280 | 6560 | 9840 | 13120 | Feet |

International Boundaries

State Boundaries

© John Bartholomew & Son Ltd., Edinburgh

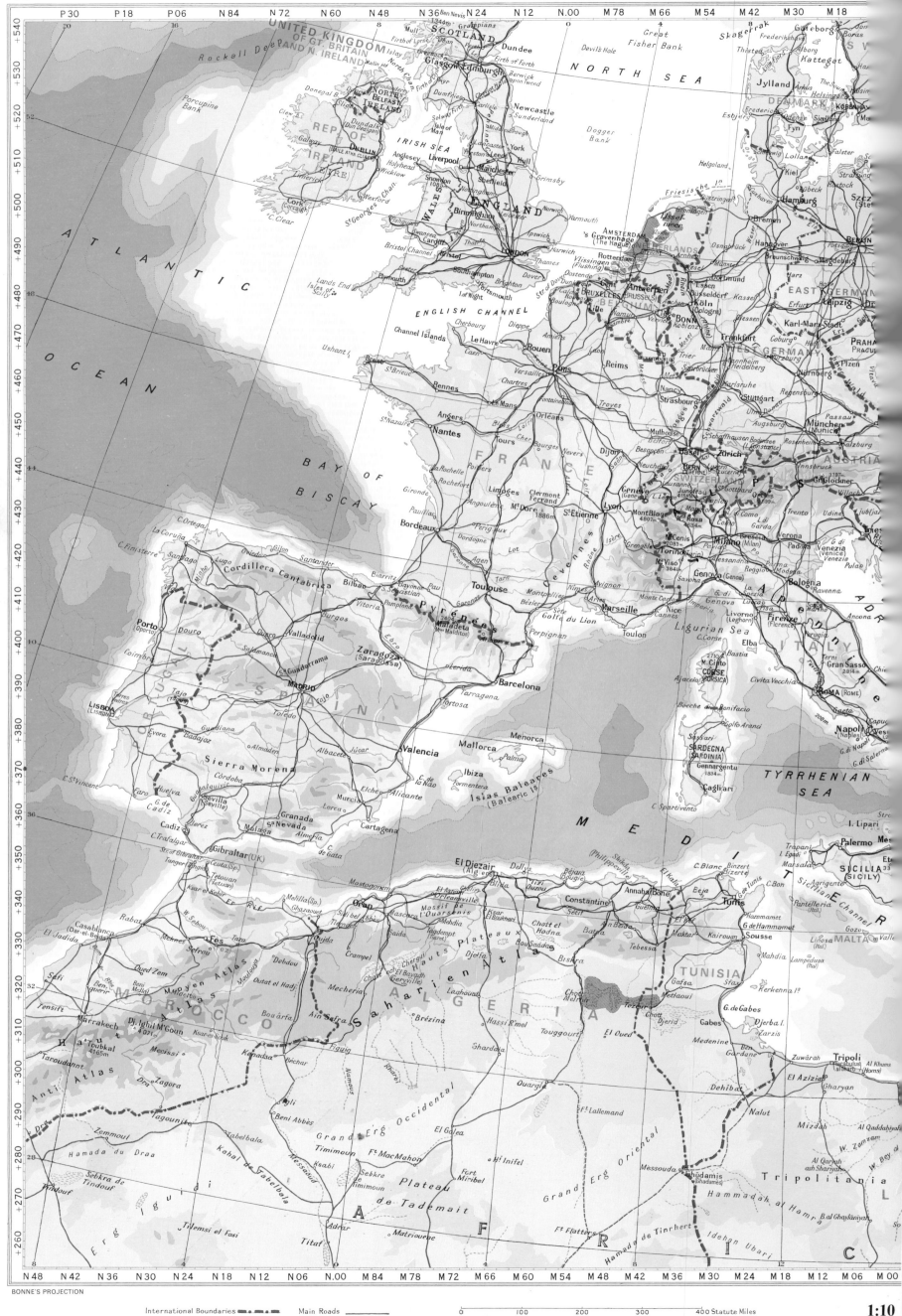

International Boundaries ▬▪▬▪ Main Roads ─────
State Boundaries ─·─·─ Railways ─────

0   100   200   300   400 Statute Miles
0   100   200   300   400   500   600 Kilometres

© John Bartholomew & Son Ltd., Edinburgh

Metres	5000	4000	3000	2000	1000	500	200	100	50	0	200	500	1000	2000	3000	4000	Metres
Feet	16400	13120	9840	6560	3280	1640	660	330	160	0	660	1640	3280	6560	9840	13120	Feet

Main Roads ————
Railways ————

0 10 20 30 40 50 60 70 80 90 100 110 120 Statute Miles

0 10 20 40 60 80 100 120 140 160 180 Kilometres

1:3

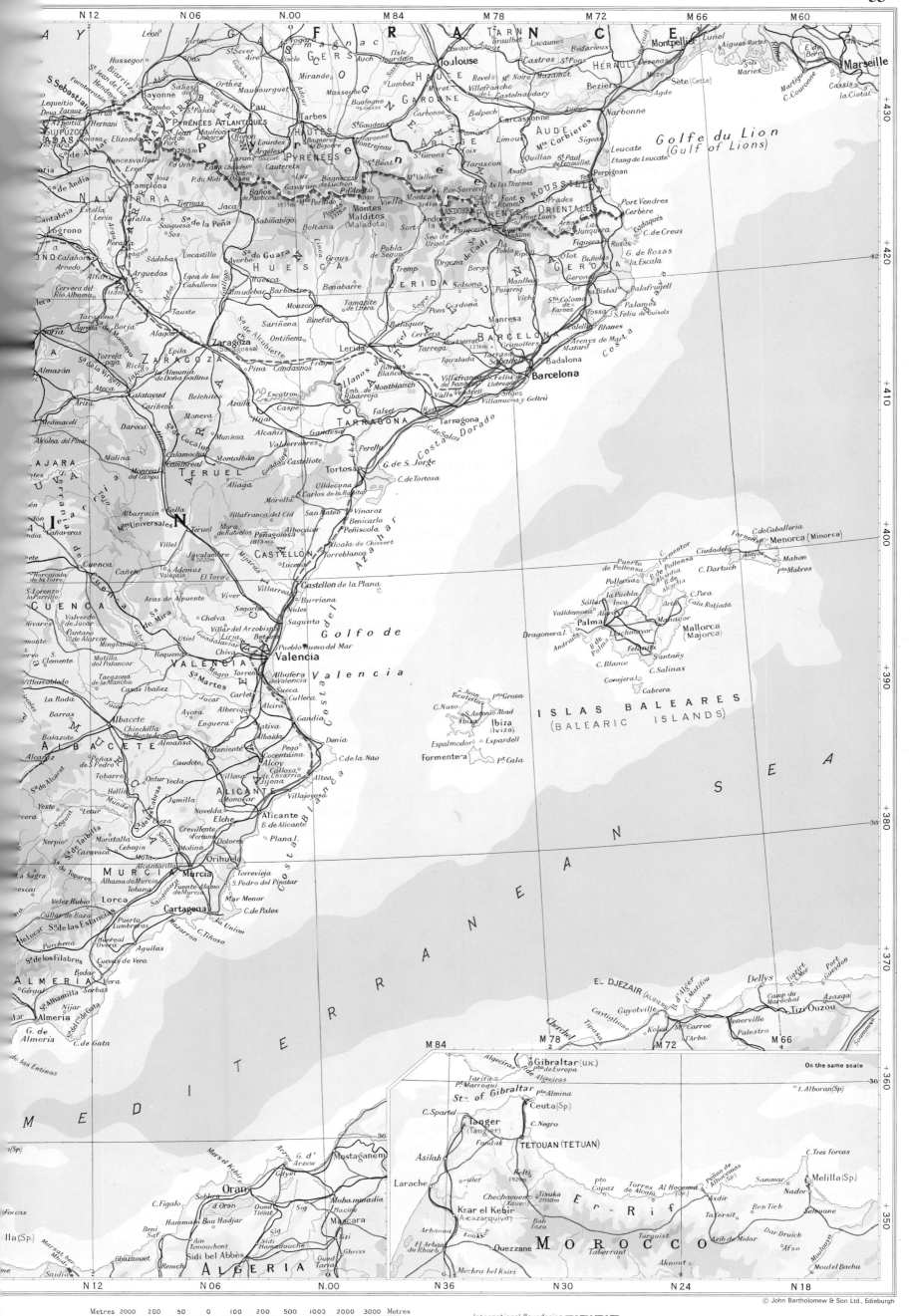

AY
León   Tartas
Hossegor   St-Sever   Isle Jourdain   T²   Lacaune   Bédarieux   Montpellier Tunel   Aigues-Mortes   E. de Berre   Marseille
S. Sebastián   St-Jean-de-Luz   Dax   Aire   Lisle   Auch   M^{ts} Noire   Mazamet   Hérault   C. Couronne   la Ciotat
Biarritz   Orthez   Maubourguet   Mirande   Lombez   Toulouse   Revel   Castres   St-Pons   Béziers   Sète (Cette)   Cassis
Lequeitio   St-Palais   Bayonne   Pau   Tarbes   Boulogne-s-Gesse   Muret   Villefranche-de-Laur.   Castelnaudary   Narbonne   C. Croisette   Martigues
Deva Zarauz   Fuenterrabia   Pamplona   Lourdes   Bagnères-de-Bigorre   Carbonne   St-Gaudens   Belpech   Carcassonne

GUIPÚZCOA
Hernani   Elizondo   St-Jean-Pied-de-Port   Bagnères-de-Luchon   St-Girons   Foix   Limoux   M^{ts} Corbières   Leucate   Golfe du Lion (Gulf of Lions)
NAVARRA   PYRÉNÉES ATLANTIQUES   HAUTES PYRÉNÉES   ARIÈGE   Axat   St-Paul-de-Fenouillet   Etang de Leucate
Pamplona   Tiermas   Jaca   Baños de Panticosa   Viella   Montcalm 3141m   Perpignan   Port Vendres   Cerbère
Estella   Lerín   Tafalla   Sangüesa   Sos   Sabiñánigo   Boltaña   Andorra   Seo de Urgel   Puigcerdá   PYRÉNÉES ORIENTALES   C. de Creus

(map content — place names throughout the Iberian Peninsula, southern France, Balearic Islands, and North Africa)

HUESCA   Ayerbe   Graus   Pobla de Segur   Organá   Berga   Manresa   GERONA   Figueras   Rosas   G. de Rosas   la Escala
ZARAGOZA   Zaragoza   Lérida   LÉRIDA   Cervera   Manresa   Vich   BARCELONA   Gerona   Palafrugell   Palamós

Barcelona
TARRAGONA   Tarragona   Costa Dorada   Costa Brava

TERUEL   Teruel   CASTELLÓN   Castellón de la Plana

CUENCA   VALENCIA   Valencia   Golfo de Valencia

ALBACETE   ALICANTE   Alicante

MURCIA   Murcia   Cartagena

ALMERÍA   Almería   G. de Almería

ISLAS BALEARES (BALEARIC ISLANDS)
Menorca (Minorca)   Mahón
Palma   Mallorca (Majorca)
Ibiza (Iviza)   Formentera
Cabrera

MEDITERRANEAN SEA

On the same scale
Algeciras   Gibraltar (U.K.)   I. Alborán (Sp)
Tarifa   St. of Gibraltar   Ceuta (Sp)
C. Spartel   Tanger (Tanger)
Asilah   TETUAN (TETUAN)   Melilla (Sp)   Nador
EL DJEZAIR   Oran   ALGERIA   MOROCCO   Er-Rif

© John Bartholomew & Son Ltd., Edinburgh

Metres	2000	200	50	0	100	200	500	1000	2000	3000 Metres
Feet	6560	660	160	0	330	660	1640	3280	6560	9840 Feet

International Boundaries
State Boundaries

M

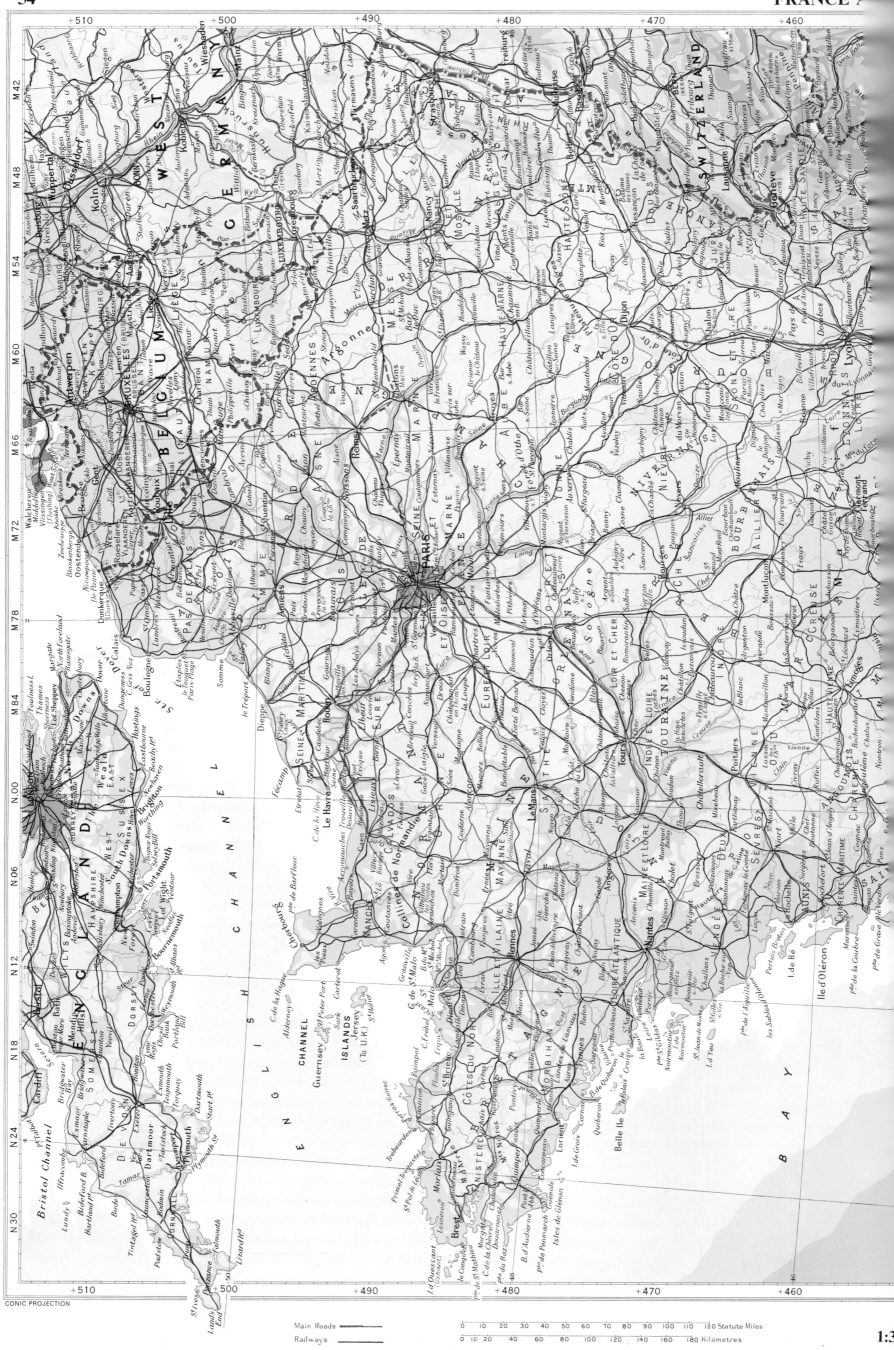

CONIC PROJECTION

Main Roads ━━━━
Railways ━━━━

0 10 20 30 40 50 60 70 80 90 100 110 120 Statute Miles
0 10 20 40 60 80 100 120 140 160 180 Kilometres

1:3

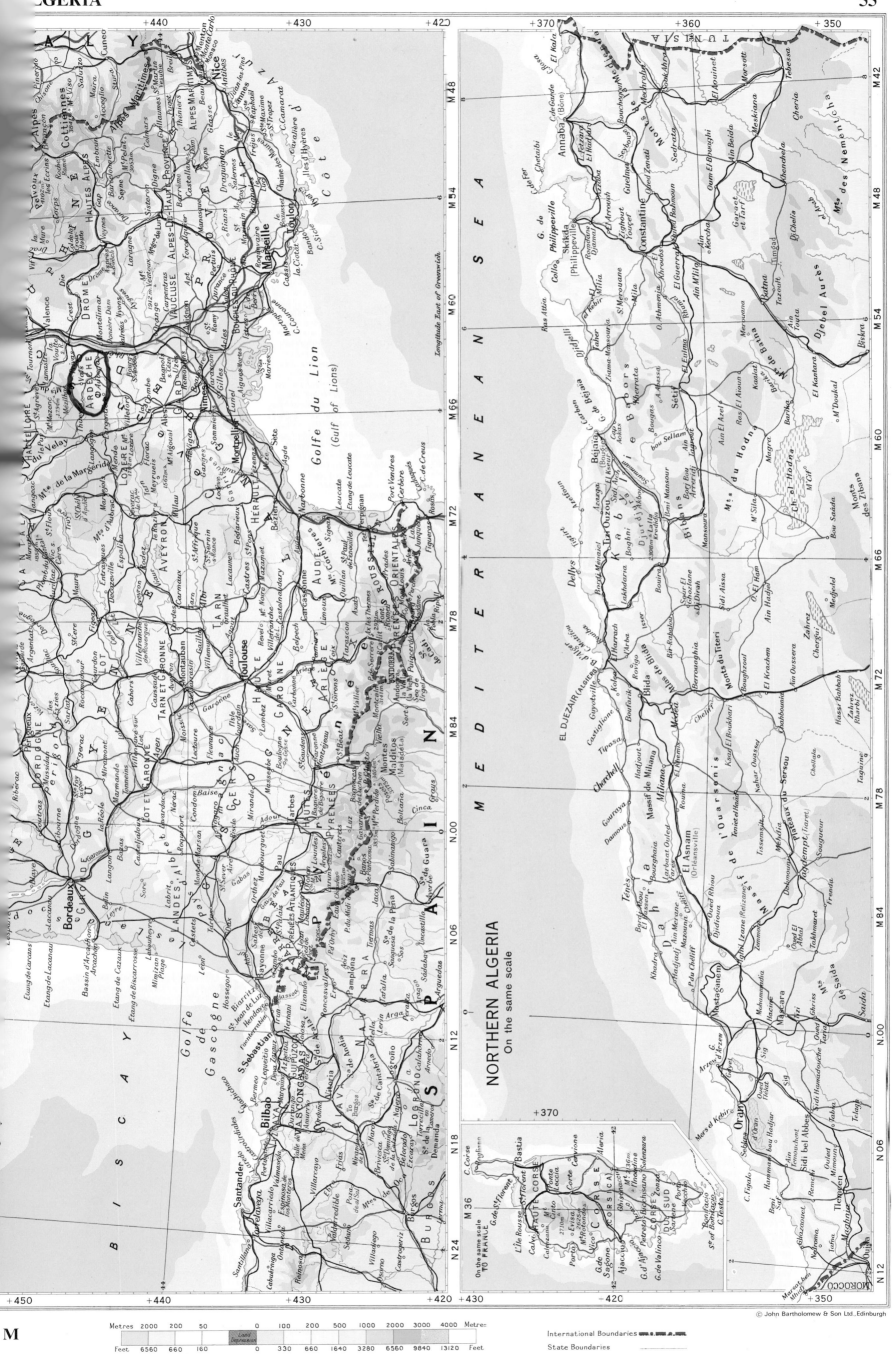

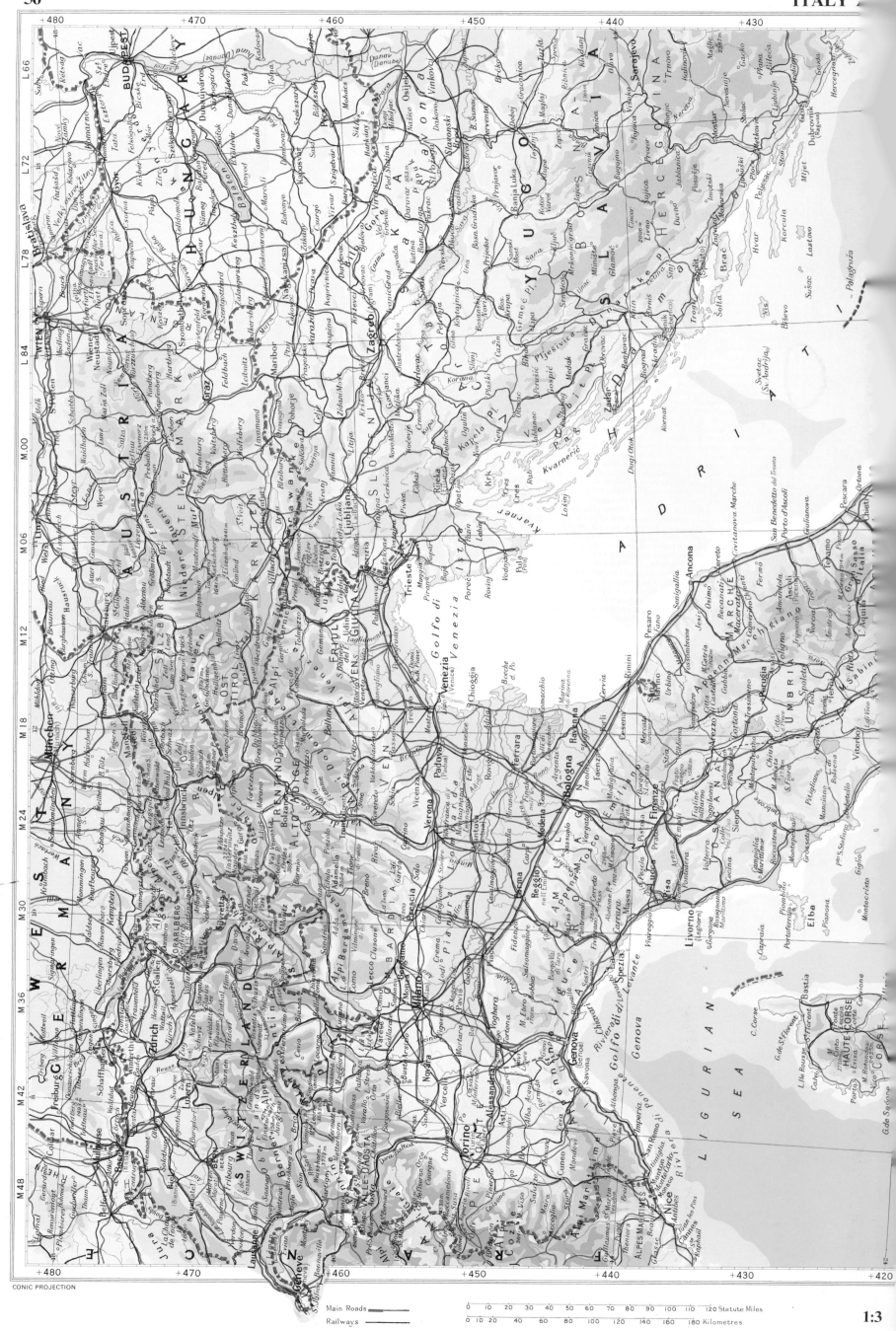

Main Roads ———
Railways ———

0 10 20 30 40 50 60 70 80 90 100 110 120 Statute Miles

0 10 20 40   60   80   100   120   140   160 180 Kilometres

1:3

Metres 2000 200 50 0 100 200 500 1000 2000 3000 4000 Metres

Feet 6560 660 160 0 330 660 1640 3280 6560 9840 13120 Feet

International Boundaries

State Boundaries

© John Bartholomew & Son Ltd., Edinburgh

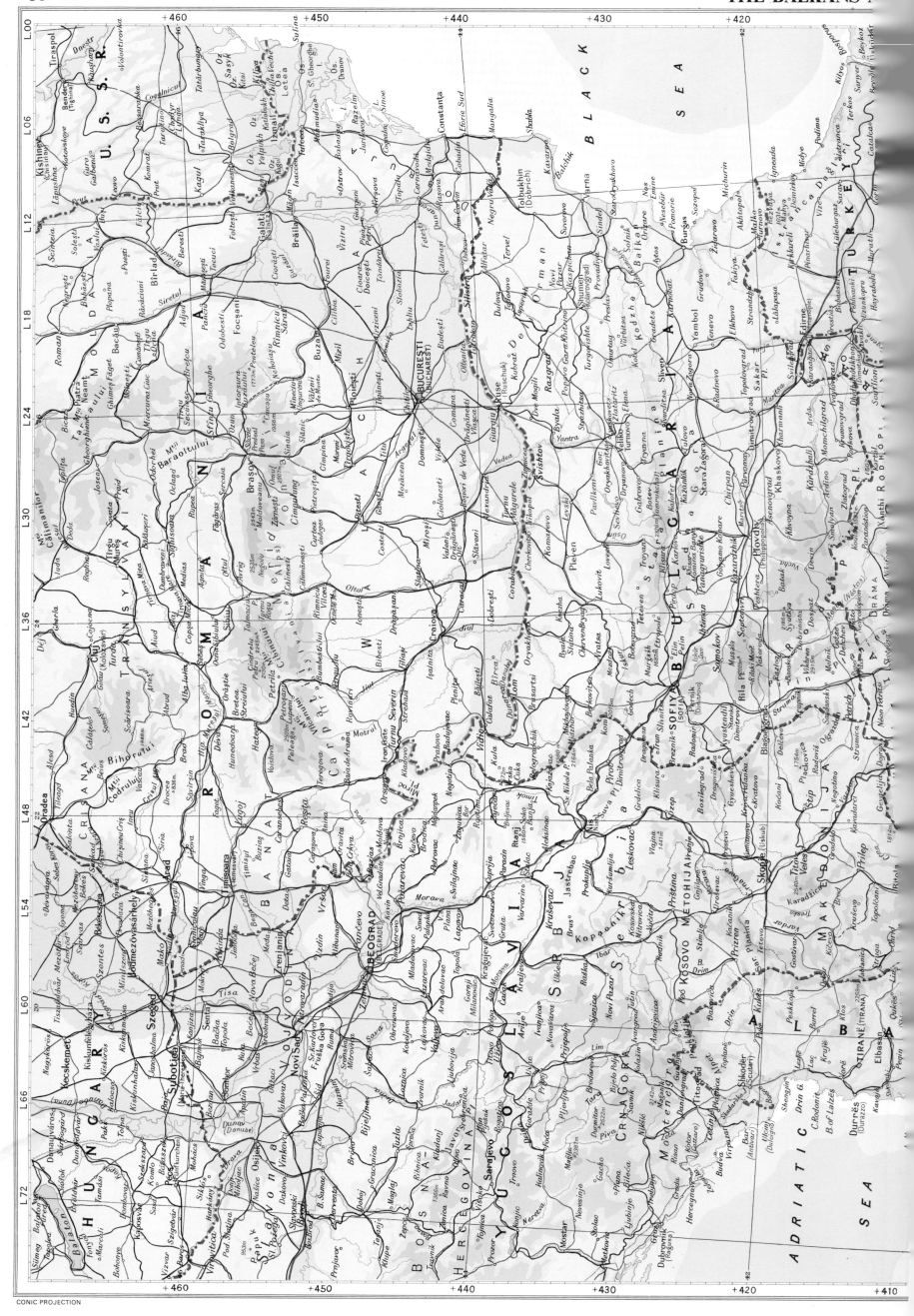

Main Roads _____
Railways _____

0 10 20 30 40 50 60 70 80 90 100 110 120 Statute Miles
0 10 20 40 60 80 100 120 140 160 180 Kilometres

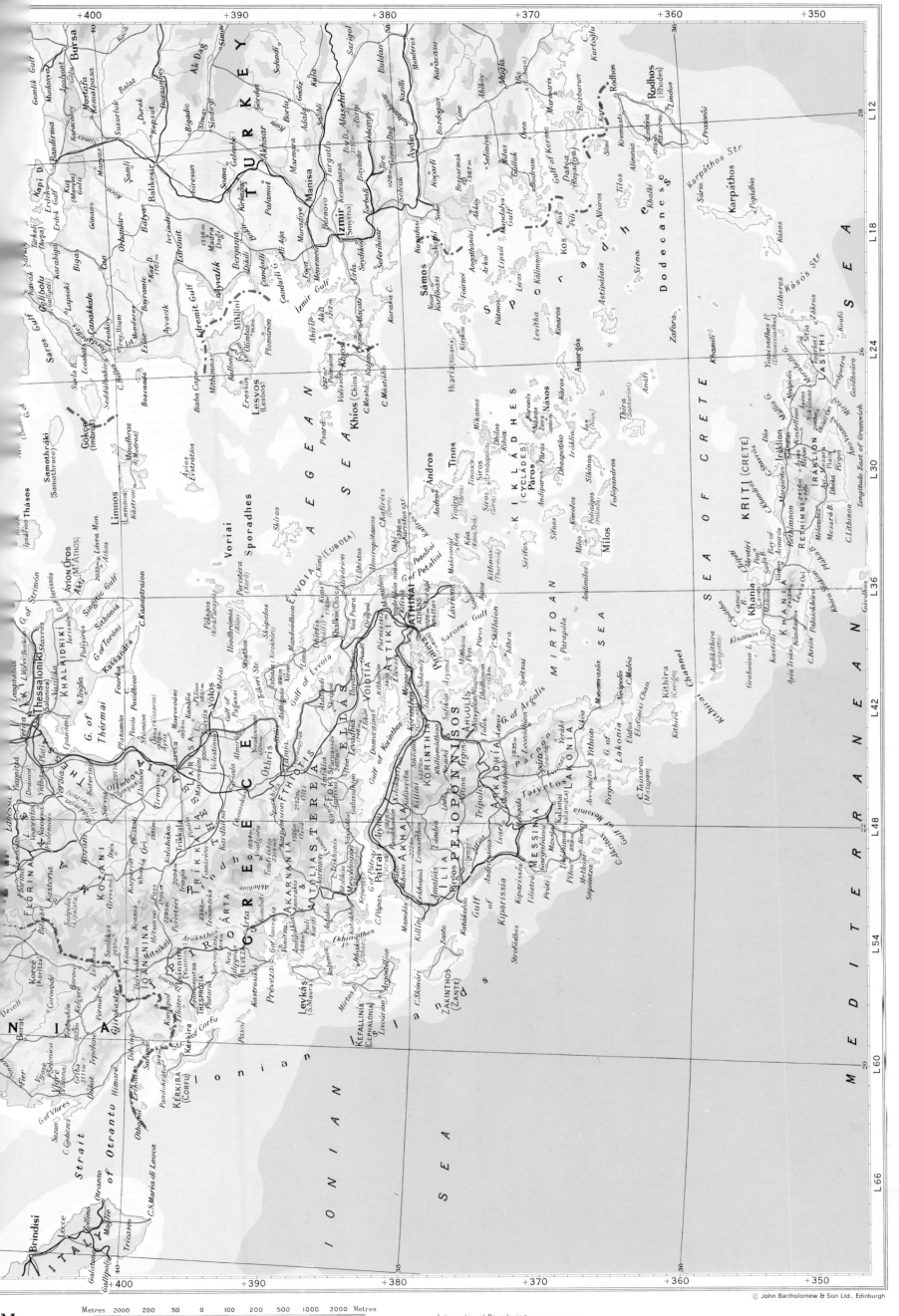

M

Metres	2000	200	50	0	100	200	500	1000	2000	Metres
Feet	6560	660	160	0	330	660	1640	3280	6560	Feet

International Boundaries

State Boundaries

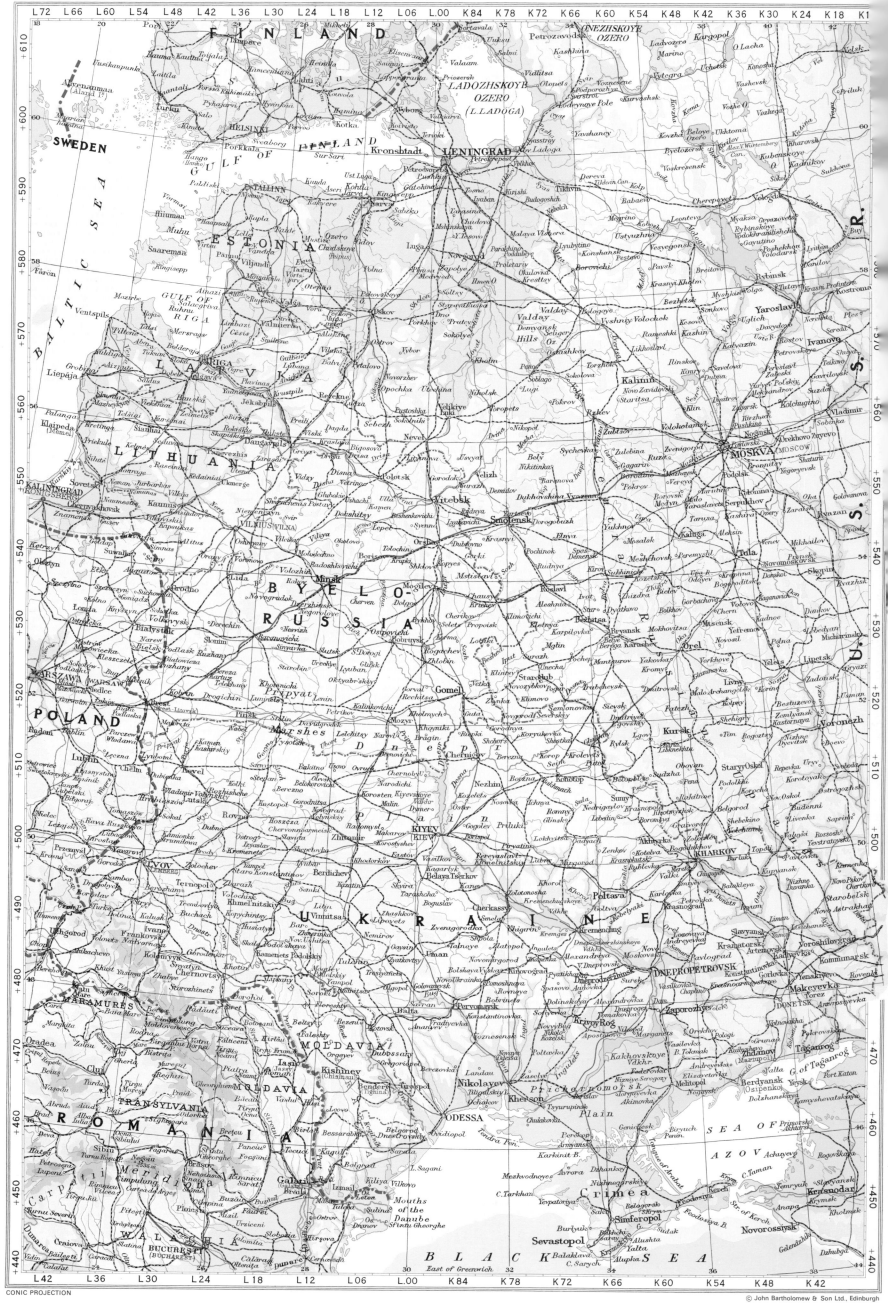

© John Bartholomew & Son Ltd., Edinburgh

1:6M

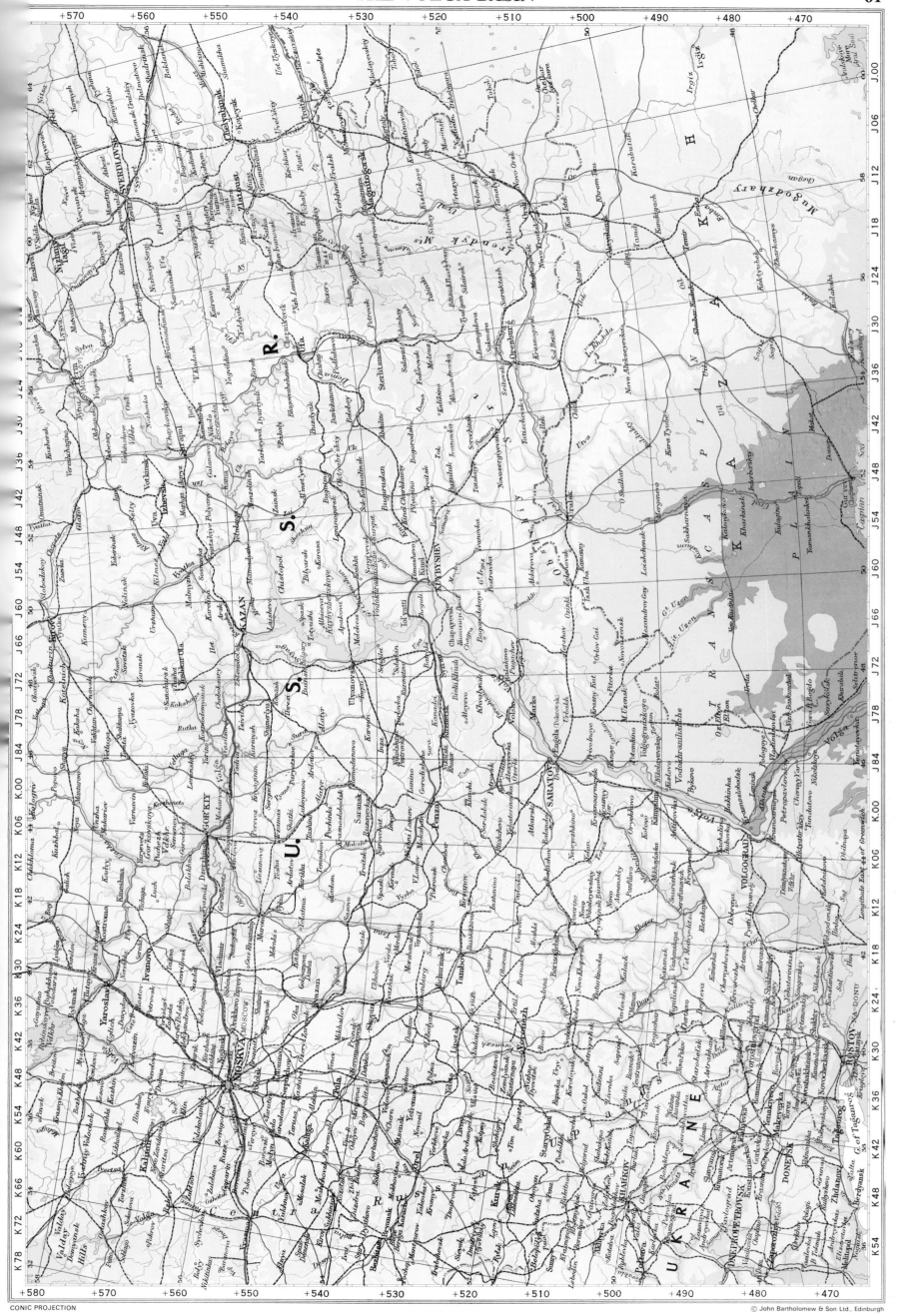

CONIC PROJECTION

0 20 40 60 80 100 120 140 160 Statute Miles

0 20 40 80 120 160 200 240 Kilometres

1:6M

Metres 0 100 200 530 1000 Metres

Land Depression

Feet 0 330 660 1640 3280 Feet

© John Bartholomew & Son Ltd., Edinburgh

SCOTLAND

DENMARK

NORTH SEA

Skagerrak

NORWAY

SWEDEN

NORWEGIAN SEA

Jan Mayen (Norway)

Spitsbergen

SVALBARD (to Norway)

BARENTS SEA

ZEMLYA FRANTSA IOSIFA (FRANZ JOSEF LAND)

ARCTIC

NOVAYA ZEMLYA

KARA SEA

Gulf of Bothnia

BALTIC SEA

FINLAND

KAREL'SKAYA A.S.S.R.

Beloye More

Arkhangel'sk

Murmansk

KOL'SKIY POLUOSTROV

POLAND

LATVIYSKAYA S.S.R.

LITOVSKAYA S.S.R.

Leningrad

Kaliningrad

RUSSIAN SOVIET FEDERAL SOCIALIST

Z a p a d n o - S i b i r s k a y a

Moskva

Kalinin

Yaroslavl'

UKRAINSKAYA S.S.R.

Moldavskaya S.S.R.

BLACK SEA

Khar'kov

Kiyev

Voronezh

Gor'kiy

MORDOVSKAYA A.S.S.R.

TATARSKAYA A.S.S.R.

Perm

Sverdlovsk

Ob'

Tyumen'

Omsk

Tomsk

Novosibirsk

Kemerovo

Novokuznetsk

Ob'

Azovskoye More

Rostov-na-Donu

Volgograd

Saratov

KALMYTSKAYA A.S.S.R.

Astrakhan'

BASHKIRSKAYA A.S.S.R.

Ufa

Magnitogorsk

Chelyabinsk

Troitsk

Kustanay

Petropavlovsk

Kurgan

Barnaul

Biysk

Gorno-Altaysk

ALTAY

CASPIAN SEA

TURKEY

IRAQ

Baghdad

IRAN (PERSIA)

GRUZINSKAYA S.S.R.

Tbilisi

Baku

AZERBAYDZHANSKAYA S.S.R.

Yerevan

ARMYANSKAYA S.S.R.

Mashhad

TURKMENSKAYA S.S.R.

Ashkhabad

Kara Kum

Kyzyl Kum

UZBEKSKAYA S.S.R.

Aral'skoye More (Aral Sea)

KARA-KALPAKSKAYA A.S.S.R.

KAZAKHSKAYA S.S.R.

Karaganda

Semipalatinsk

Ust'-Kamenogorsk

Balkhash

Oz. Balkhash

Tashkent

Samarkand

Dushanbe

TADZHIKSKAYA S.S.R.

KIRGIZSKAYA S.S.R.

Frunze

Alma-Ata

DZUNGARIA

TIAN SHAN

SINKIANG

Pamir

AFGHANISTAN

Kabul

Hindu Kush

Takla Makan

THE GULF

CONIC PROJECTION

Main Roads

Railways

0 100 200 300 400 500 600 Statute Miles

0 100 200 300 400 500 600 700 800 900 1000 Kilometres

1:17½

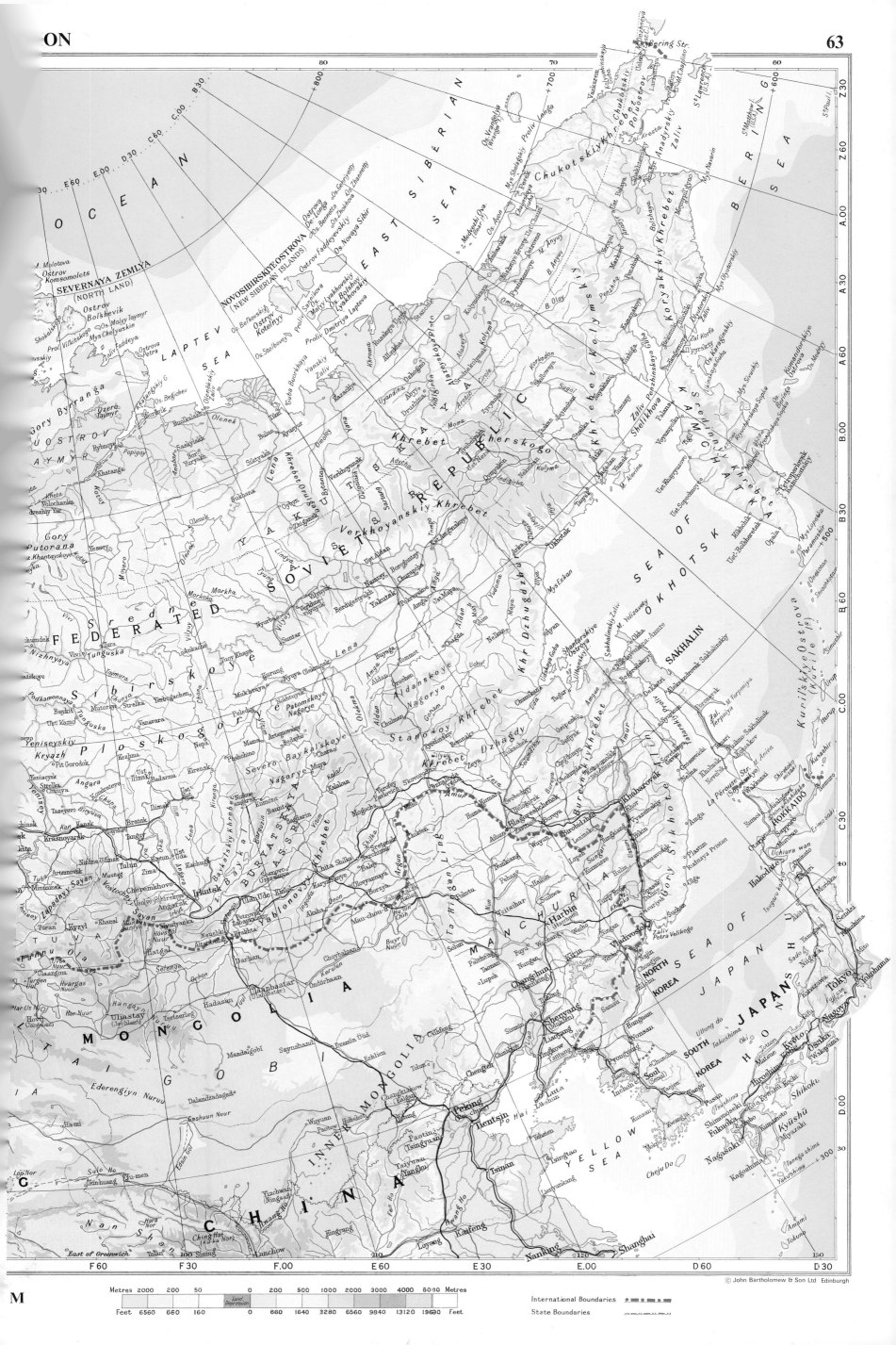

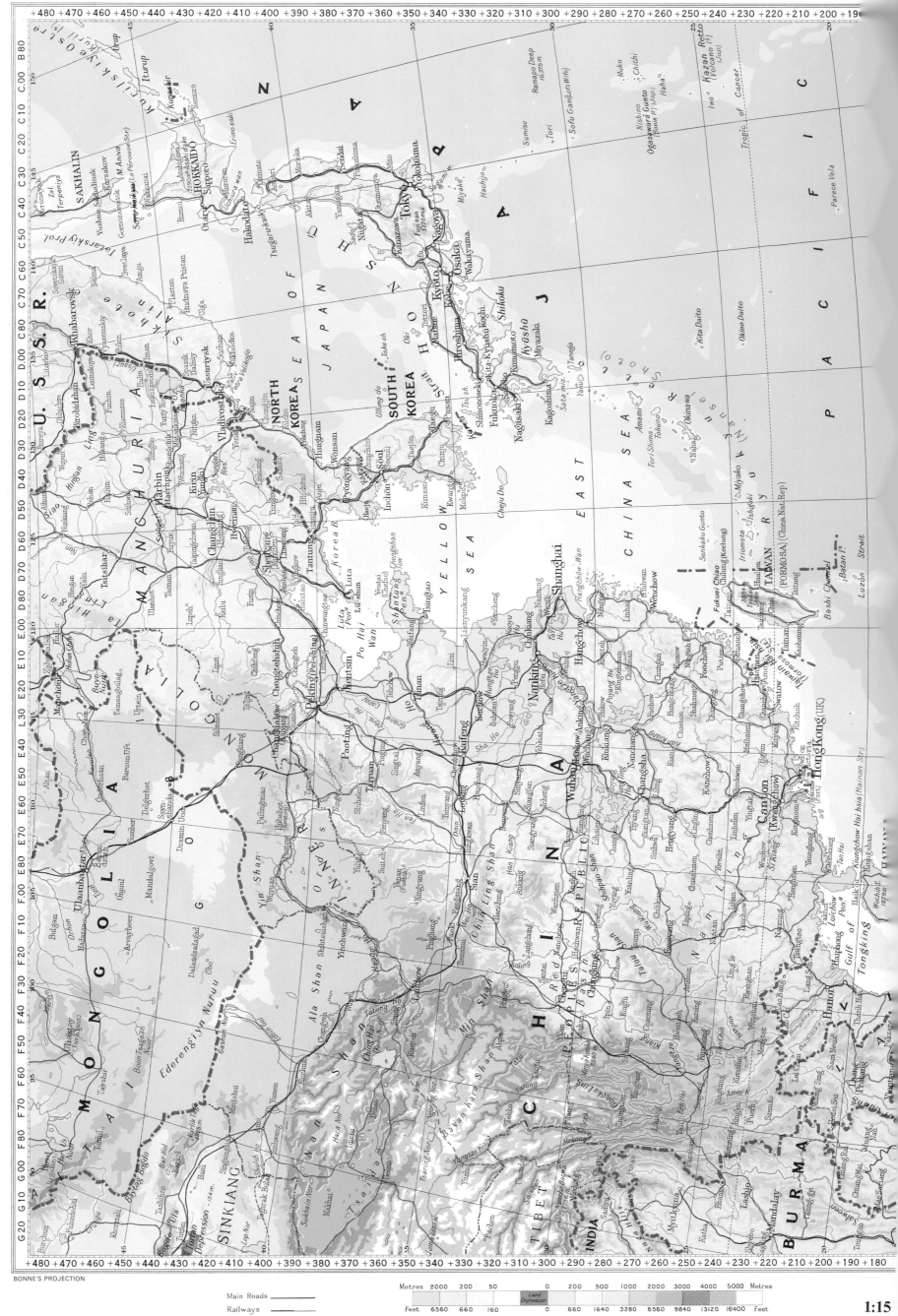

Main Roads _____
Railways _____

Metres	2000	200	50	0	200	500	1000	2000	3000	4000	5000	Metres
Feet	6560	660	160	0	660	1640	3280	6560	9840	13120	16400	Feet

Land Depression

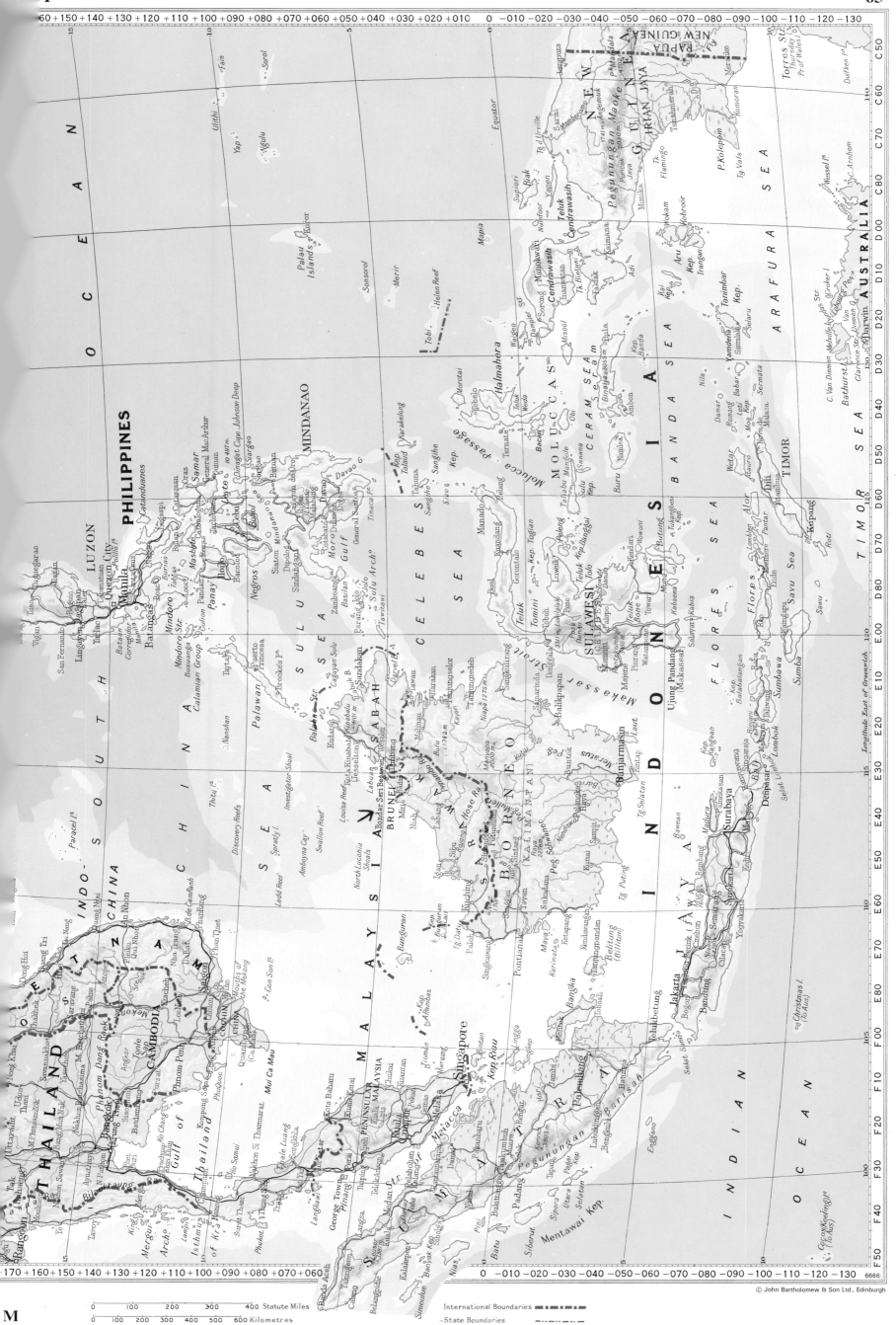

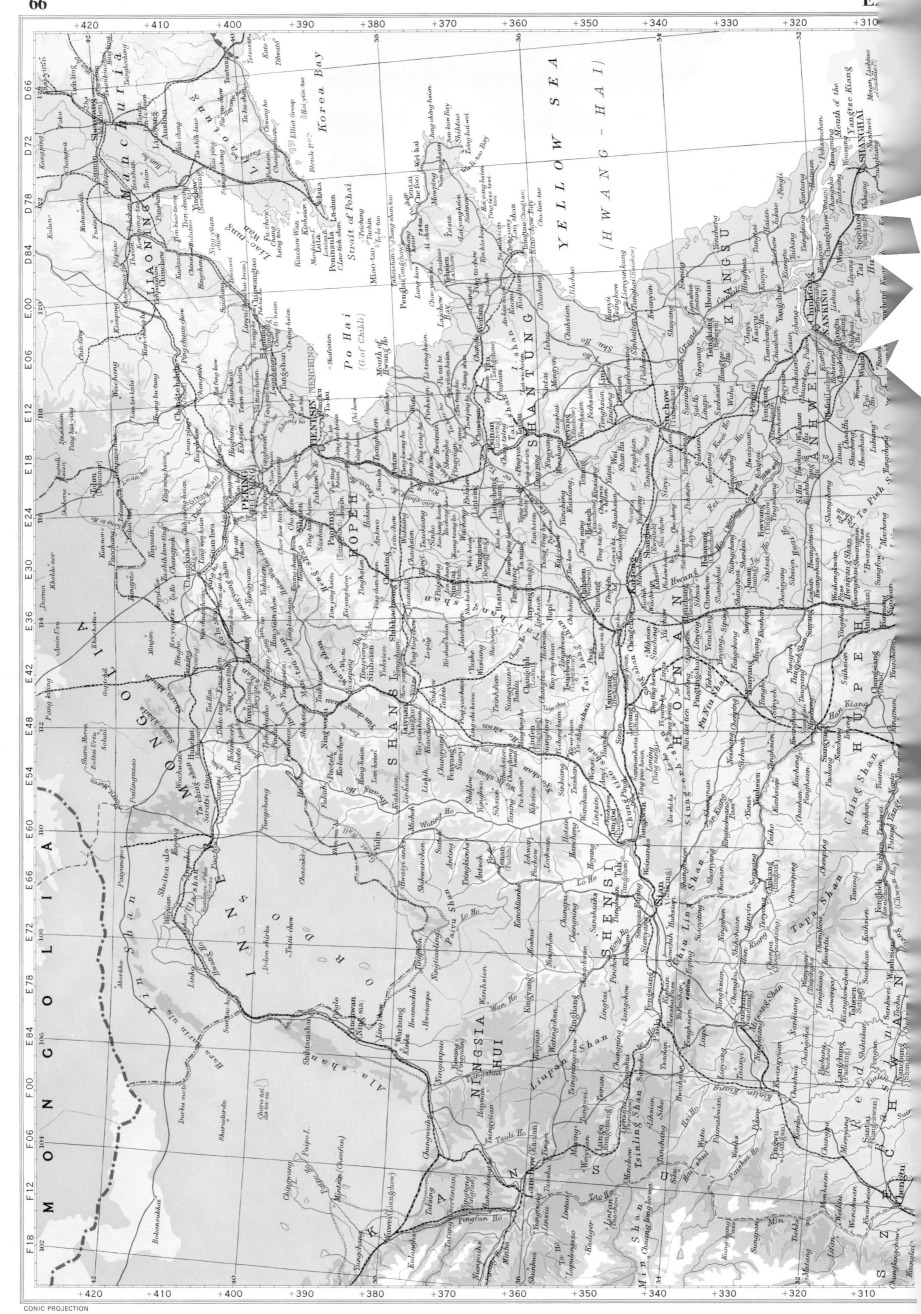

CONIC PROJECTION

Main Roads ————————
Railways ————————

0 20 40 60 80 100 120 140 160 180 200 220 240 Statute Miles
0 20 40   80   120   160   200   240   280   320   360 Kilometres

1:6

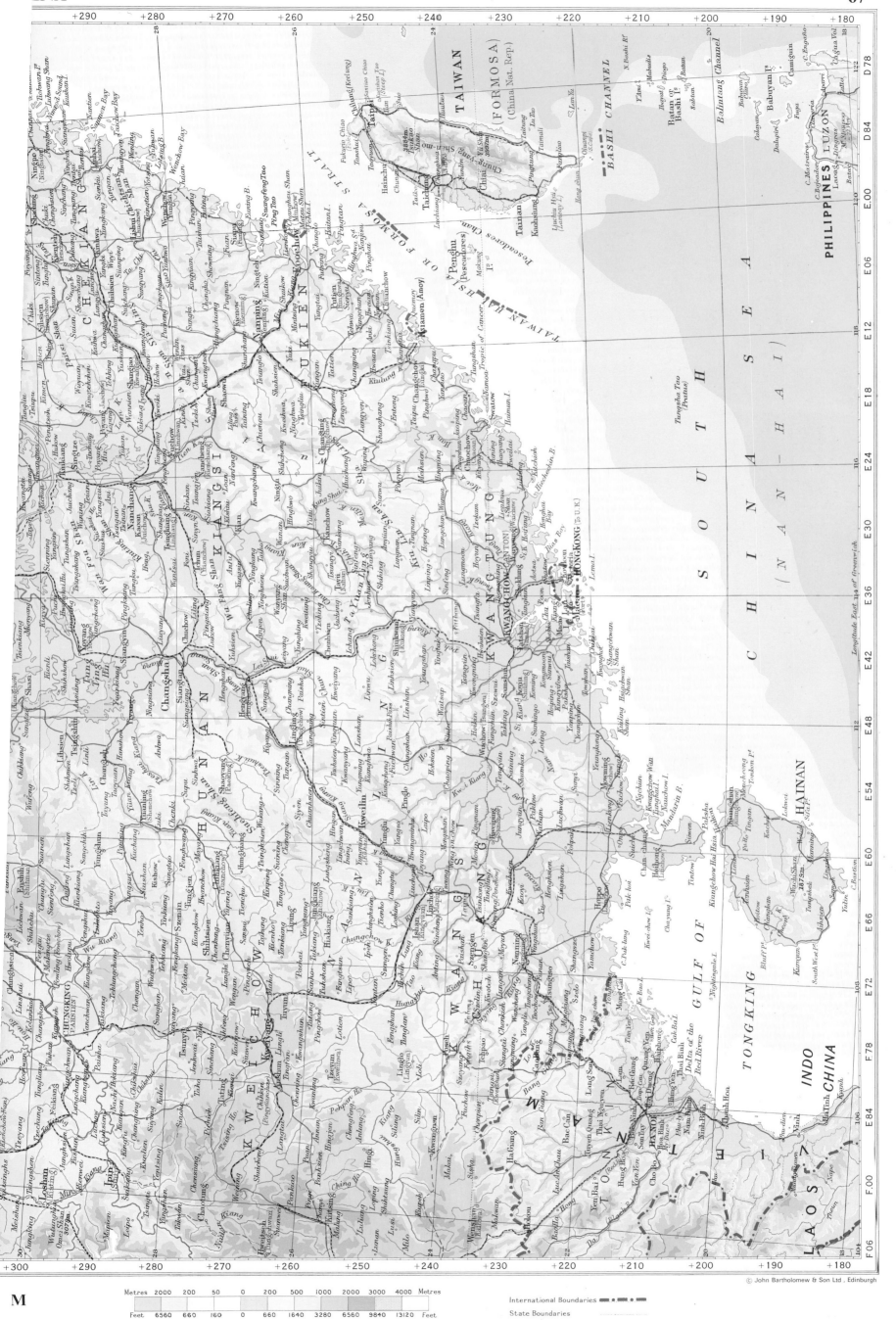

Metres 2000 200 50 0 200 500 1000 2000 3000 4000 Metres
Feet 6560 660 160 0 660 1640 3280 6560 9840 13120 Feet

International Boundaries ▬▪▬▪▬
State Boundaries

© John Bartholomew & Son Ltd . Edinburgh

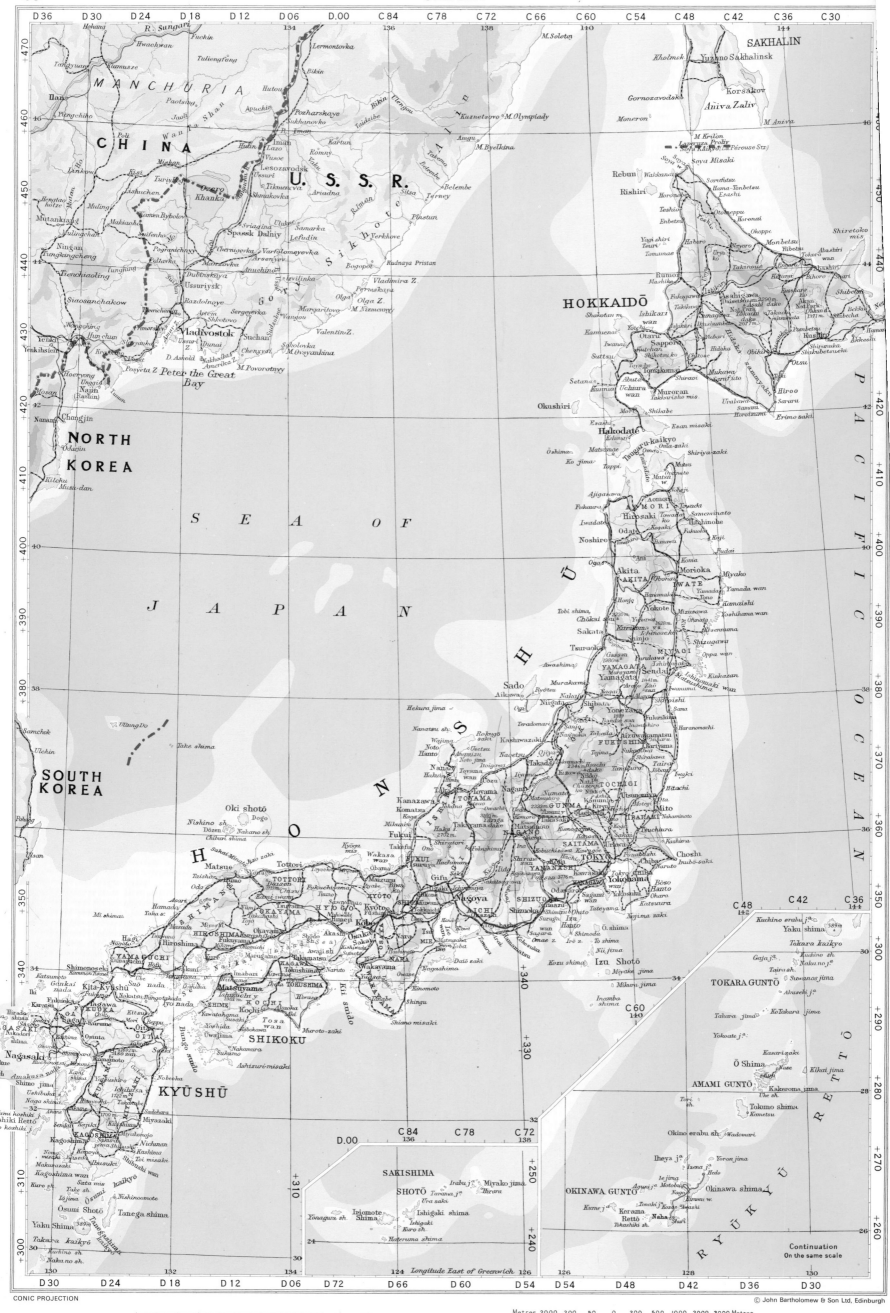

© John Bartholomew & Son Ltd, Edinburgh

0 20 40 60 80 100 120 140 160 180 Statute Miles

0 20 40 80 120 160 200 240 280 Kilometres

1:6M

Metres 2000 200 50 0 200 500 1000 2000 3000 Metres

Feet 6560 660 160 0 660 1640 3280 6560 9840 Feet

CONIC PROJECTION

1:10M

© John Bartholomew & Son Ltd., Edinburgh

RELIGIONS

Hindu
Sikh
Muhammadan
Buddhist
Christian
Animist

CONIC PROJECTION

Main Roads ⎯⎯⎯
Railways ⎯⎯⎯⎯⎯

0   100   200   300   400 Statute Miles
0 100 200 300 400 500 600 Kilometres

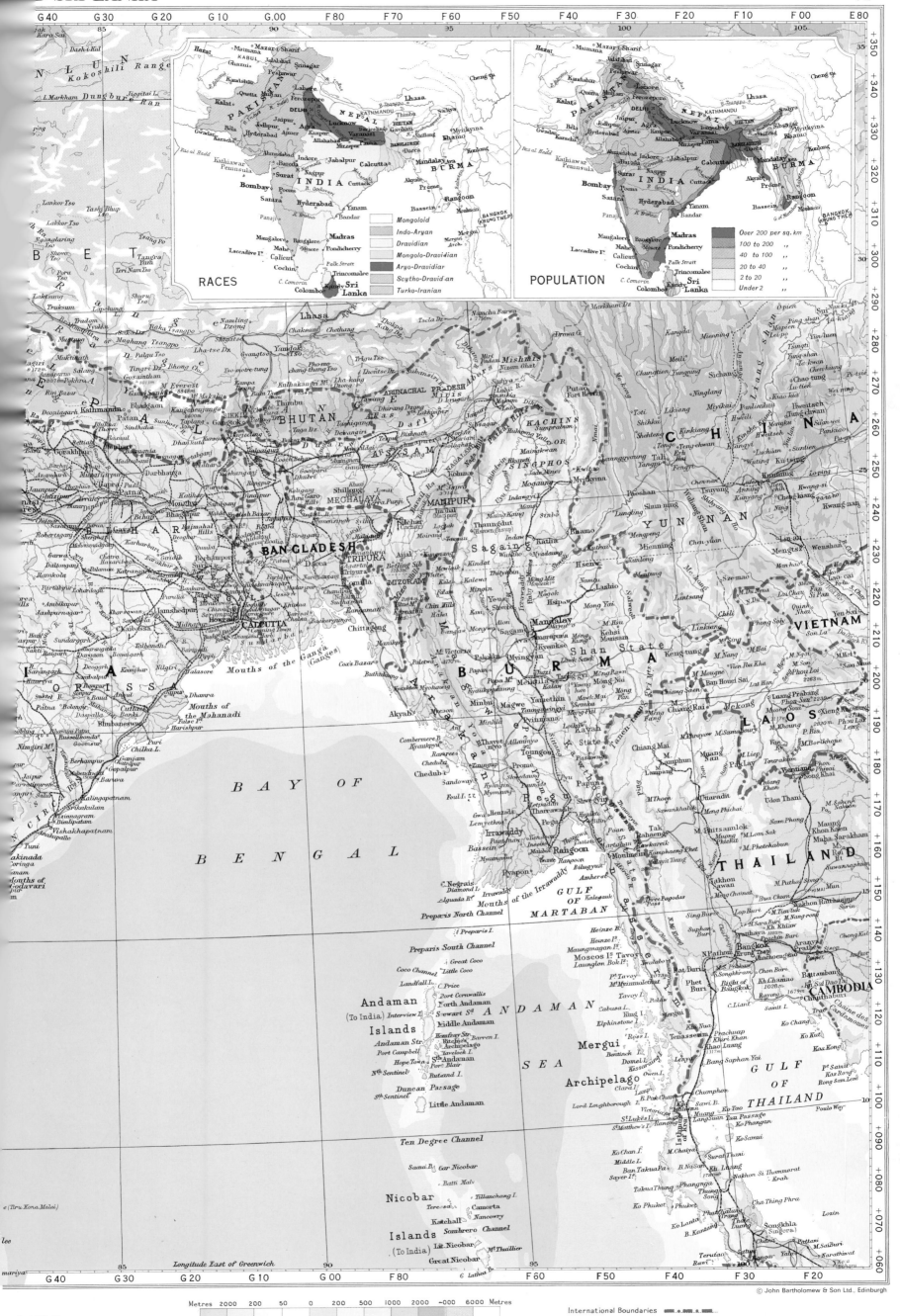

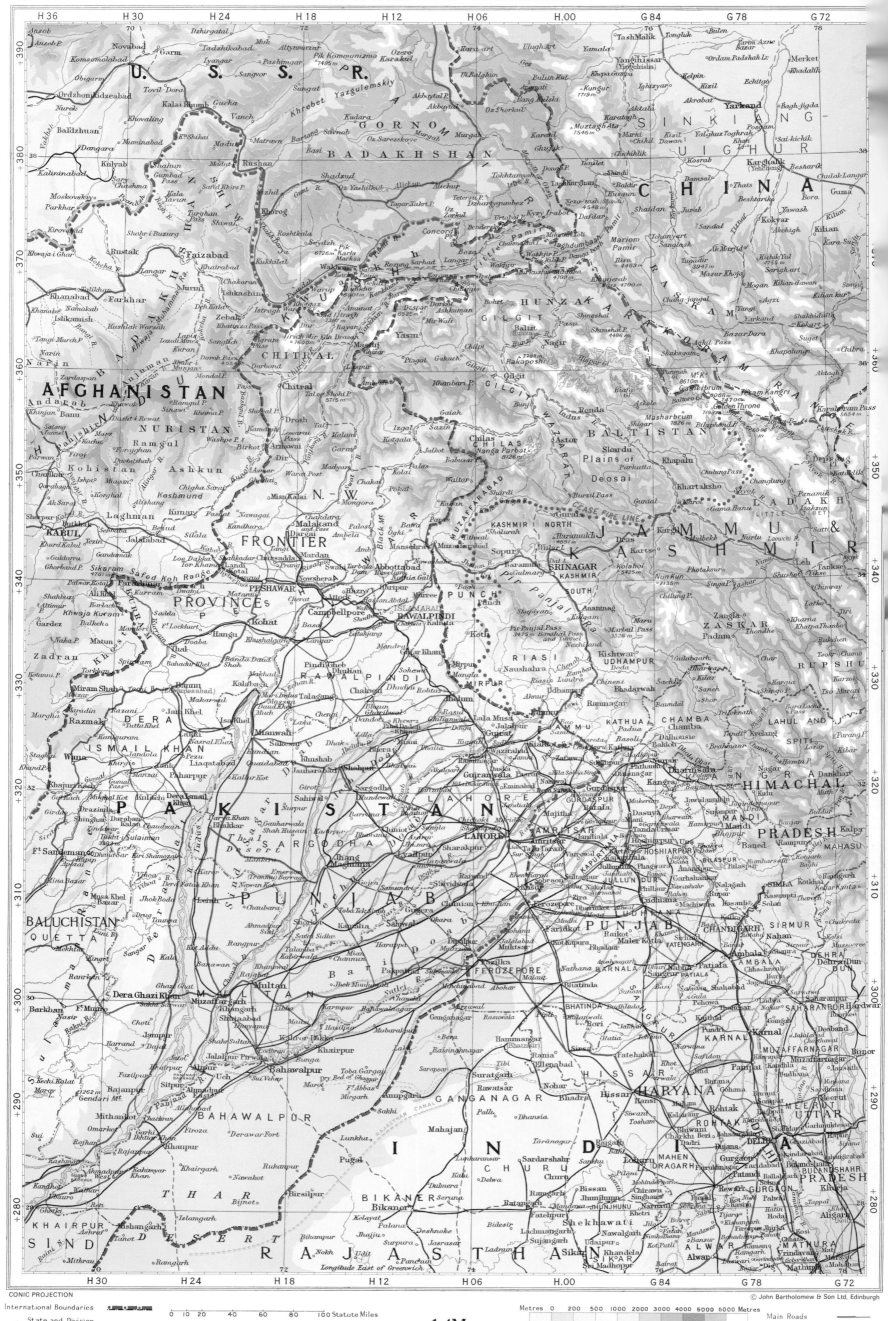

© John Bartholomew & Son Ltd, Edinburgh

CONIC PROJECTION

International Boundaries

State and Division
Boundaries

0 10 20   40   60   80   100 Statute Miles

0 10 20 40   60   80   100 120 140 160 Kilometres

1:4M

Metres 0   200   500 1000 2000 3000 4000 5000 6000 Metres

Feet   0   660 1640 3280 6560 9840 13120 16400 19690 Feet

Main Roads

Irrigation Canals

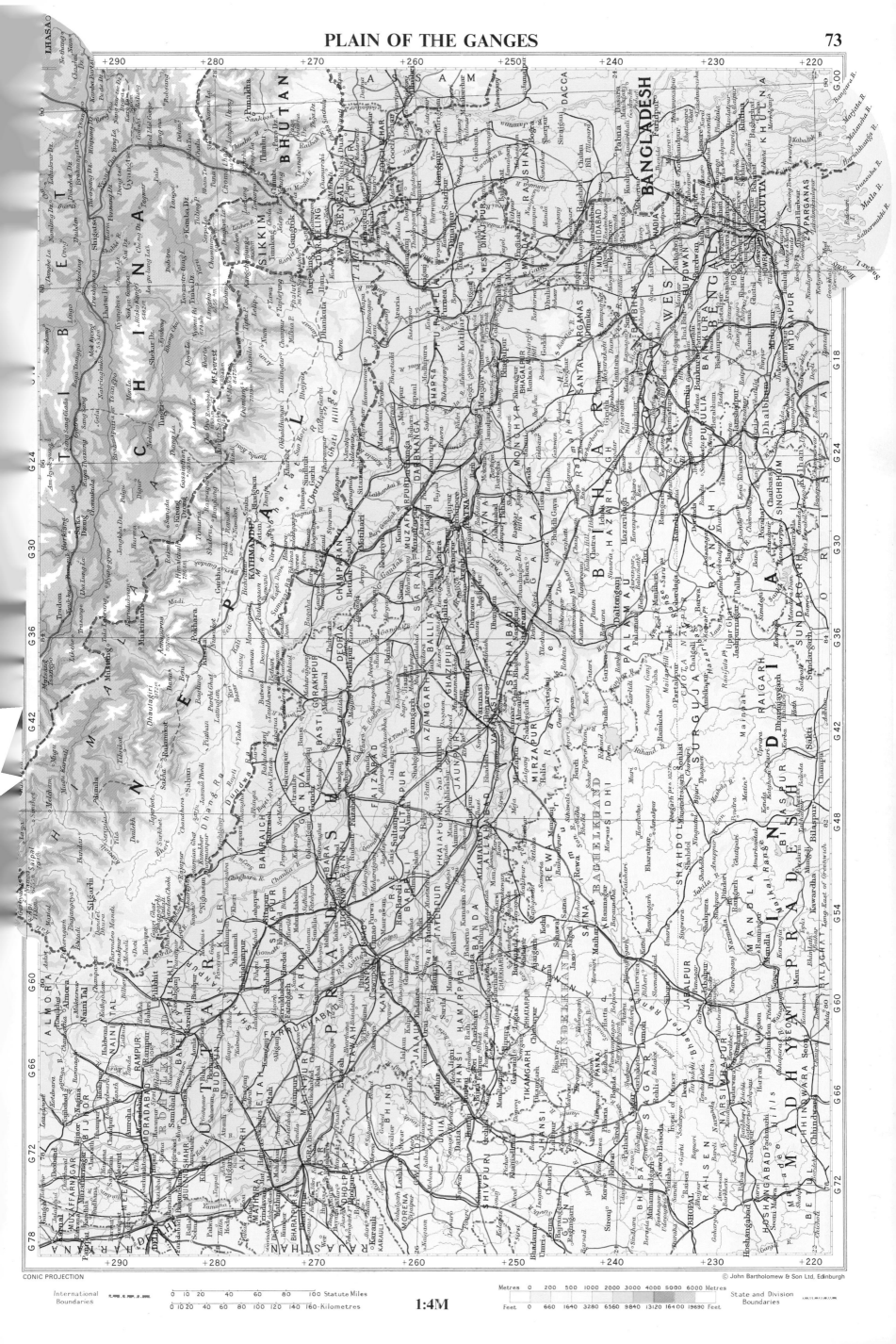

CONIC PROJECTION

International Boundaries

0 10 20 40 60 80 100 Statute Miles
0 10 20 40 60 80 100 120 140 160 Kilometres

1:4M

Metres 0 200 500 1000 2000 3000 4000 5000 6000 Metres

Feet 0 660 1640 3280 6560 9840 13120 16400 19690 Feet

State and Division Boundaries

© John Bartholomew & Son Ltd. Edinburgh

MEDITERRANEAN SEA

BLACK SEA

AEGEAN SEA

RED SEA

TURKEY

ANATOLIA

GEORGIA

ARMENIA

AZERBAIJAN

U.

CYPRUS

SYRIA

LEBANON

ISRAEL

JORDAN

IRAQ

KUWAIT

SAUDI ARABIA

EGYPT

LOWER EGYPT

UPPER EGYPT

Delta of the Nile

Libyan Plateau

Qattara Depression

Eastern Desert

Sinai

Nubian Desert

Batyuda Desert

Kordofan

SUDAN

ETHIOPIA

YEMEN

SOUTH

Nafud

Rub' al Khali

JABAL SHAMMAR

HIJAZ

Lake Nasser

Istanbul
Edirne
Ankara
Izmir
Konya
Adana
Erzurum
Tabriz
Tbilisi (Tiflis)
Yerevan
Mosul
Kirkuk
Baghdad
Basra
Aleppo (Haleb)
Hama
Homs
Tripoli
Beirût
Damascus
Haifa
Tel Aviv
Jerusalem
Amman
Alexandria
CAIRO
Port Said
Suez
Asyut
Luxor
Aswân
Wadi Halfa
Dongola
Khartoum
Omdurman
Kassala
Massawa
Medina (Al Madinah)
Mecca (Makkah)
Jidda (Jeddah)
Riyadh (Ar Riyad)
Kuwait
Sana'

Nicosia
Latakia

Baghdad

Red Sea

Main Roads
Railways

| 0 | 100 | 200 | 300 | 400 Statute Miles |
| 0 | 100 | 200 | 300 | 400 | 500 | 600 Kilometres |

1:10

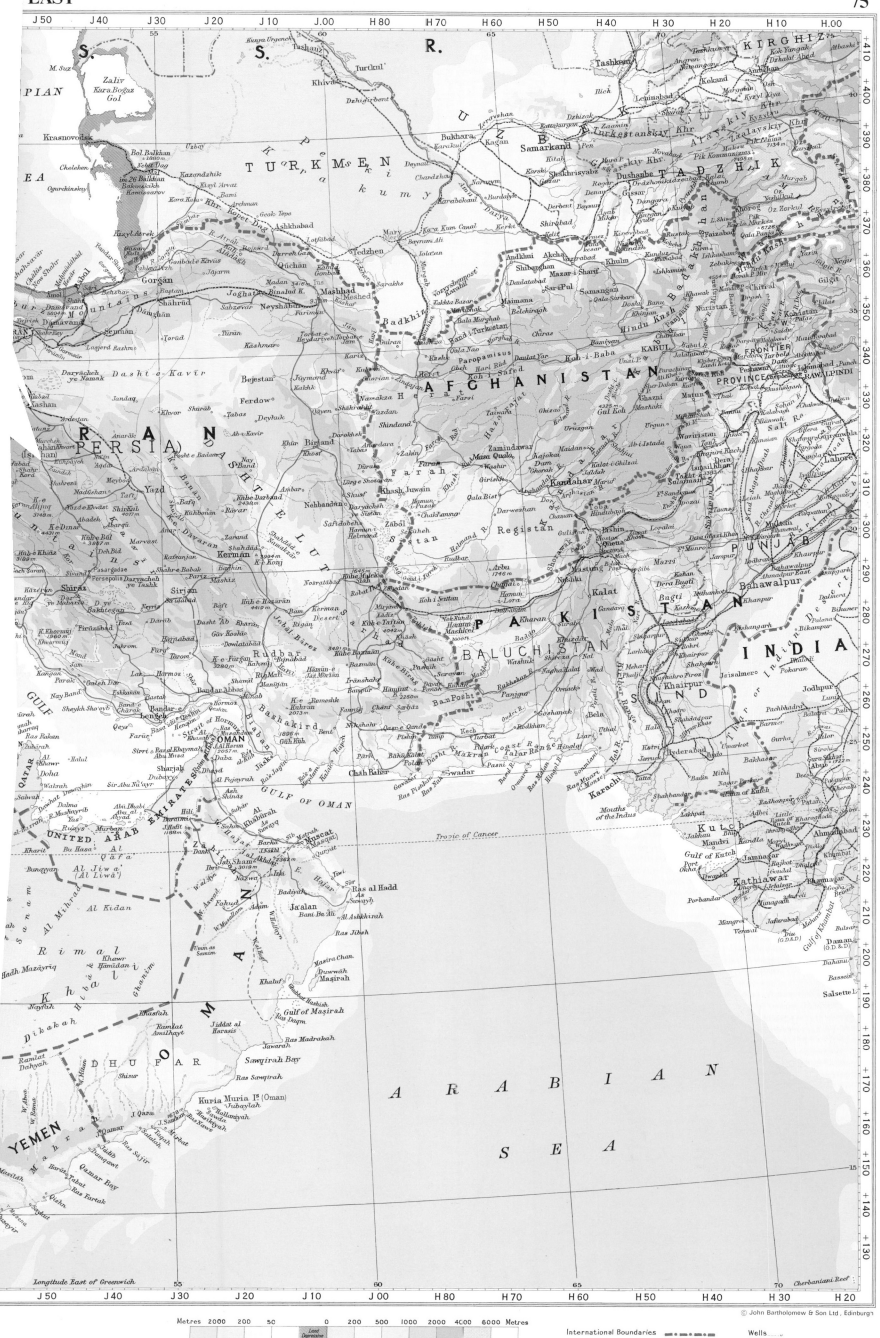

© John Bartholomew & Son Ltd., Edinburgh

Metres	2000	200	50		0	200	500	1000	2000	4000	6000	Metres		International Boundaries		Wells
				Land	Depression										
Feet	6560	660	160		0	660	1640	3280	6560	13120	19690	Feet		State Boundaries		

© John Bartholomew & Son Ltd., Edinburgh

0   10   20   30   40   50   60   70   80 Statute Miles
0   10 20 30 40 50 60 70 80 90 100 110 120 Kilometres

1:2½ M

Metres 2000 200 50   0   100 200 500 1000 2000 3000 Metres
Feet 6560 660 160   0   330 660 1640 3280 6560 9840 Feet

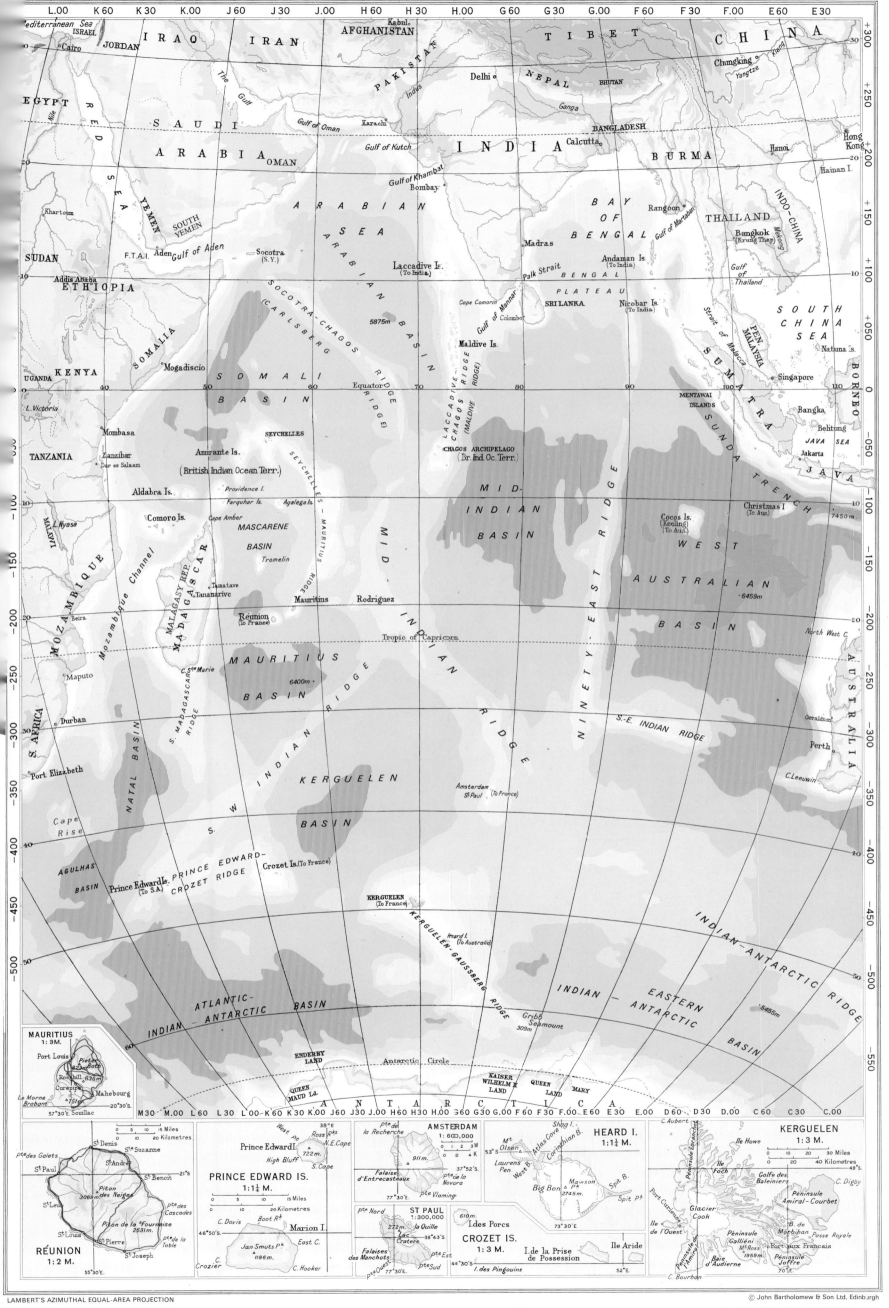

L.00 K 60 K 30 K.00 J 60 J 30 J.00 H 60 H 30 H.00 G 60 G 30 G.00 F 60 F 30 F.00 E 60 E 30

editerranean Sea
ISRAEL
Cairo
JORDAN
IRAQ
IRAN
AFGHANISTAN
Kabul
TIBET
CHINA
Chungking
Yangtze
+300
EGYPT
RED SEA
SAUDI
ARABIA
OMAN
PAKISTAN
Indus
Delhi
NEPAL
BHUTAN
Ganga
BANGLADESH
INDIA
BURMA
Hanoi
Hainan I.
Hong Kong
+250
+200
Khartoum
YEMEN
SOUTH YEMEN
F.T.A.I. Aden Gulf of Aden
Socotra (S.Y.)
Gulf of Oman
Karachi
Gulf of Kutch
Bombay
Gulf of Khambat
ARABIAN
SEA
BAY
OF
BENGAL
Rangoon
Gulf of Martaban
THAILAND
Bangkok (Krung Thep)
Mekong
INDO-CHINA
+150
SUDAN
Addis Ababa
ETHIOPIA
SOMALIA
Mogadiscio
SOCOTRA-CHAGOS RIDGE
(CARLSBERG RIDGE)
ARABIAN BASIN
5875m
Madras
Laccadive Is. (To India)
Cape Comorin
Gulf of Mannar
Gulf of Colombo
SRI LANKA
Palk Strait
BENGAL
PLATEAU
Andaman Is. (To India)
Nicobar Is. (To India)
Gulf of Thailand
PEN. MALAYSIA
Strait of Malacca
SOUTH CHINA SEA
Natuna Is.
+100
+050
UGANDA
KENYA
L. Victoria
Equator
SOMALI
BASIN
LACCADIVE-CHAGOS RIDGE (MALDIVE RIDGE)
Maldive Is.
MID-INDIAN BASIN
Singapore
SUMATRA
SUNDA TRENCH
Bangka
Belitung
BORNEO
0
-050
TANZANIA
Mombasa
Zanzibar
Dar es Salaam
SEYCHELLES
Amirante Is.
(British Indian Ocean Terr.)
SEYCHELLES - MAURITIUS RIDGE
CHAGOS ARCHIPELAGO (Br. Ind. Oc. Terr.)
JAVA SEA
Jakarta
JAVA
MALAWI
L. Nyasa
Aldabra Is.
Providence I.
Farquhar Is. Agalega Is.
Comoro Is. Cape Amber
MASCARENE BASIN
Tromelin
MAURITIUS RIDGE
MID-INDIAN BASIN
WEST AUSTRALIAN BASIN
Cocos Is. (Keeling) (To Aus.)
6459m
Christmas I. (To Aus.)
7450m
-100
-150
MOZAMBIQUE
Beira
Mozambique Channel
MALAGASY REP. MADAGASCAR
Tamatave
Tananarive
Réunion (To France)
Mauritius
Rodriguez
Tropic of Capricorn
MID-INDIAN RIDGE
NINETY-EAST RIDGE
North West C.
-200
S. AFRICA
Maputo
Durban
S. MADAGASCAR RIDGE
NATAL BASIN
C. Ste Marie
MAURITIUS BASIN
6400m
S.W. INDIAN RIDGE
S.E. INDIAN RIDGE
Geraldton
AUSTRALIA
-250
-300
Port Elizabeth
Cape Rise
KERGUELEN BASIN
Amsterdam St Paul (To France)
Perth
C. Leeuwin
-350
AGULHAS BASIN
Prince Edward Is. (To S.A.)
PRINCE EDWARD-CROZET RIDGE
Crozet Is. (To France)
-400
KERGUELEN (To France)
KERGUELEN-GAUSSBERG RIDGE
Heard I. (To Australia)
INDIAN-ANTARCTIC RIDGE
-450
ATLANTIC-INDIAN-ANTARCTIC BASIN
INDIAN-EASTERN-ANTARCTIC BASIN
Gribb Seamount 309m
5455m
-500
ENDERBY LAND
Antarctic Circle
KAISER WILHELM II LAND
QUEEN MARY LAND
-550
QUEEN MAUD Ld.
ANTARCTICA
M30 M.00 L60 L30 L.00 K 60 K 30 K.00 J60 J30 J.00 H60 H30 H.00 G60 G30 G.00 F60 F30 F.00 E60 E30 E.00 D60 D30 D.00 C60 C30 C.00

MAURITIUS 1:3M.
Port Louis
Pieters Bott 823m
Rose Hill 635m
Curepipe
Le Morne Brabant 556m
Souillac
Mahebourg
20°30'S.
57°30'E.

RÉUNION 1:2 M.
St Denis
pte des Galets
St Paul
St Leu
Piton des Neiges 3069m
Piton de la Fournaise 2631m
St Louis
St Pierre
St Joseph
St Suzanne
St André
St Benoit
pte des Cascades
38°E.
21°S.
55°30'E.

PRINCE EDWARD IS. 1:1¼ M.
Prince Edward I. 722m High Bluff
N.E. Cape
Ross Rks.
West pt.
S. Cape
C. Davis
Boot Rk.
Marion I.
Jan Smuts Pk. 1186m
East C.
C. Crozier
C. Hooker
46°50'S.
37°30'E.

AMSTERDAM 1:300,000
pte de la Recherche
911m.
Falaise d'Entrecasteaux
pte Vlaming
37°52'S.
77°30'E.

ST PAUL 1:300,000
pte Nord
la Quille
Lac Cratère
610m.
212m.
pte Est
pte Sud
38°43'S.
77°30'E.

CROZET IS. 1:3 M.
Shag I.
Atlas Cove
Corinthian B.
I. des Porcs
Falaises des Manchots
I. de la Prise de Possession
I. des Pingouins
I. Aride
44°30'S.
52°E.

HEARD I. 1:1¼ M.
C. Aubert
Mt Olsen
Laurens Pen.
West pt.
Big Ben
Mawson Pk. 2745m.
Spit B.
Spit pt.
53°S.
73°30'E.

KERGUELEN 1:3 M.
Ile Howe
Péninsule Loranchet
Golfe des Baleiniers
Péninsule Amiral-Courbet
Glacier Cook
C. Digoy
Ile de l'Ouest
Port Curieuse
Péninsule Gallieni
Mt Ross 1959m.
Péninsule Jeanne d'Arc
B. de Morbihan
Passe Royale
Port aux Français
Péninsule Joffre
Baie d'Audierne
C. Bourbon
49°S.
70°E.

LAMBERT'S AZIMUTHAL EQUAL-AREA PROJECTION

0 200 400 600 800 1000 1200 1400 1600 Statute Miles
0 400 800 1200 1600 2000 2400 Kilometres
1:40M

Metres 6000 5000 4000 3000 2000 1000 200 0 200 1000 2000 4000 6000 Metres
Land Depression
Feet 19690 16400 13120 9840 6560 3280 660 0 660 3280 6560 13120 19690 Feet

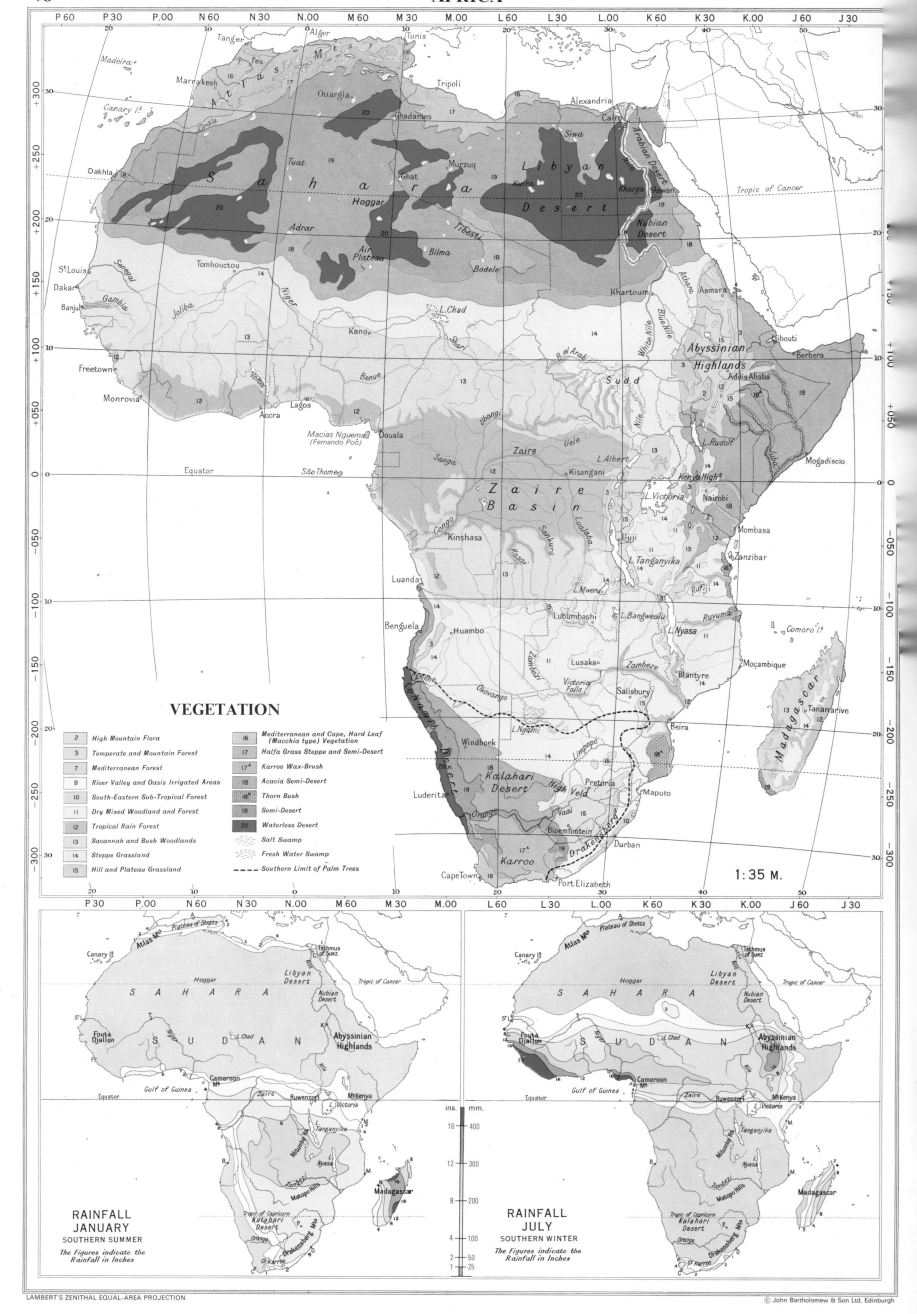

VEGETATION

2 High Mountain Flora	16 Mediterranean and Cape, Hard Leaf (Macchia type) Vegetation
3 Temperate and Mountain Forest	17 Halfa Grass Steppe and Semi-Desert
7 Mediterranean Forest	17^A Karroo Wax-Brush
8 River Valley and Oasis Irrigated Areas	18 Acacia Semi-Desert
10 South-Eastern Sub-Tropical Forest	18^A Thorn Bush
11 Dry Mixed Woodland and Forest	19 Semi-Desert
12 Tropical Rain Forest	20 Waterless Desert
13 Savannah and Bush Woodlands	Salt Swamp
14 Steppe Grassland	Fresh Water Swamp
15 Hill and Plateau Grassland	- - - Southern Limit of Palm Trees

1 : 35 M.

RAINFALL
JANUARY
SOUTHERN SUMMER
The Figures indicate the
Rainfall in Inches

RAINFALL
JULY
SOUTHERN WINTER
The Figures indicate the
Rainfall in Inches

ins. mm.

LAMBERT'S ZENITHAL EQUAL-AREA PROJECTION

© John Bartholomew & Son Ltd, Edinburgh

0 200 400 600 800 1000 Statute Miles

1:35M

0 200 400 600 800 1000 1200 1400 1600 Kilometres

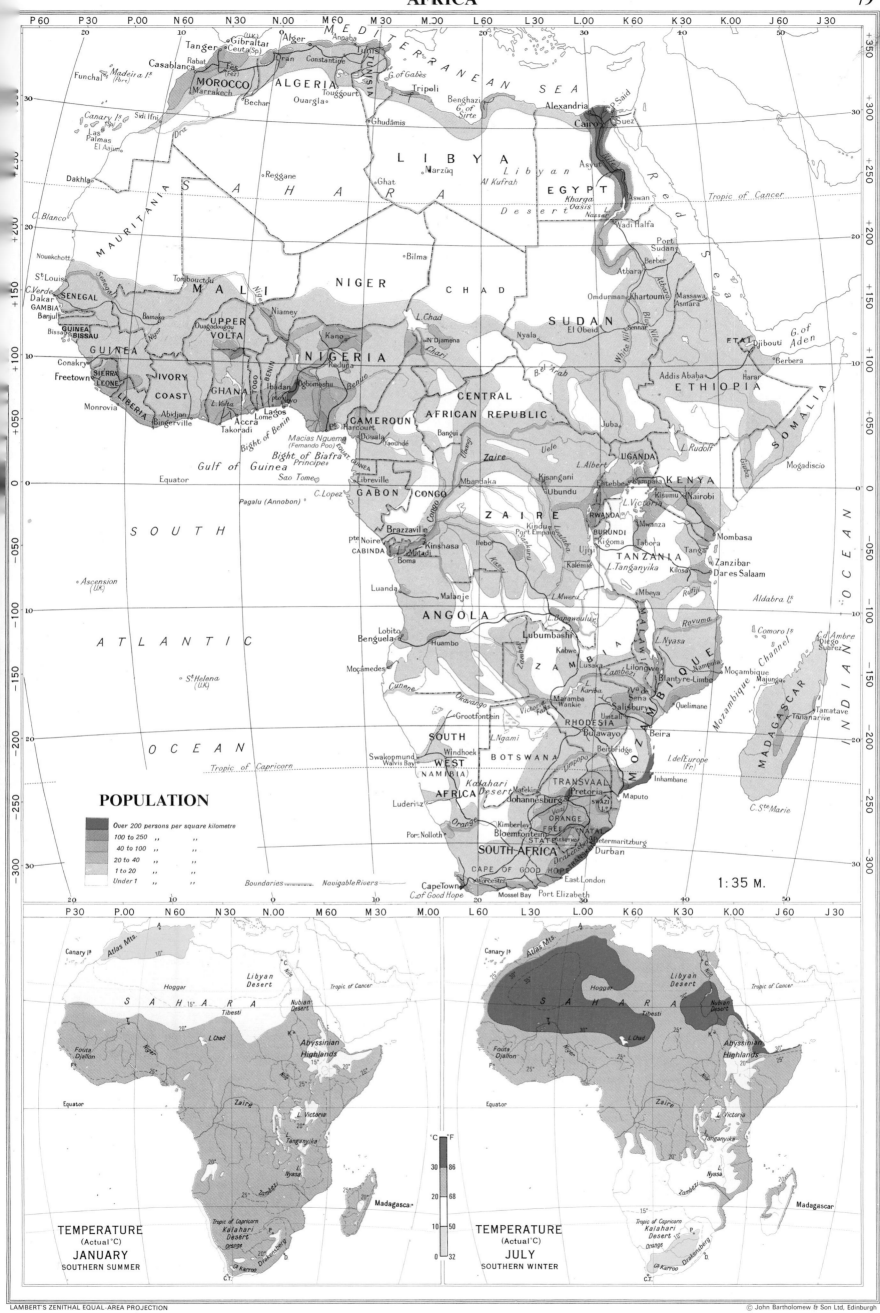

| | | | | | | | | | | | | | | | |
P 60 | P 30 | P.00 | N 60 | N 30 | N.00 | M 60 | M 30 | M.00 | L 60 | L 30 | L.00 | K 60 | K 30 | K.00 | J 60 | J 30

MEDITERRANEAN SEA

Tanger Gibraltar (U.K) Alger Annaba Tunis
Ceuta(Sp) Oran Constantine
Casablanca Rabat Fes(Fez) TUNISIA G.of Gabes Tripoli
Funchal Madeira Is (Port) MOROCCO ALGERIA Touggourt Benghazi G.of Sirte
Canary Is Sidi Ifni Marrakech Bechar Ouargla Ghudâmis
Las Palmas El Aaiun Dra Reggane Marzûq Ghat Libyan Desert Al Kufrah EGYPT Kharga Oasis Nasser
Dakhla MAURITANIA S A H A R A LIBYA Bilma

Nouakchott
St Louis SENEGAL Tombouctou MALI NIGER CHAD SUDAN Port Sudan
C.Verde Dakar Bamako Niger Niamey L.Chad Nyala El Obeid Omdurman Khartoum Atbara Berber Massawa Asmara
GAMBIA Banjul UPPER VOLTA Ouagadougou Kano N'Djamena Chari B.el Arab ETH. Djibouti Berbera
GUINEA-BISSAU GUINEA Conakry Kaduna NIGERIA CENTRAL AFRICAN REPUBLIC Addis Ababa Harar
Freetown SIERRA LEONE IVORY COAST GHANA TOGO BENIN Ibadan Ogbomosho Juba ETHIOPIA
Monrovia LIBERIA Abidjan Accra Lome Lagos Benue CAMEROUN Douala Yaoundé Bangui Uele SOMALIA
Bingerville Takoradi Bight of Benin Macias Nguema Harcourt Zaire L.Albert UGANDA L.Rudolf Mogadiscio
Equator Bight of Biafra Principe Libreville GABON CONGO Kisangani Kampala KENYA
Sao Tome C.Lopez Mbandaka Ubundu L.Victoria Kisumu Nairobi
Pagalu (Annobon) Brazzaville ZAIRE RWANDA Mombasa
Pte Noire Kinshasa Kindu BURUNDI Mwanza
CABINDA Matadi Ilebo Kigoma Tabora TANZANIA Zanzibar
Boma Kalemie L.Tanganyika Dar es Salaam
Luanda Malanje L.Mweru Mbeya Rufiji Aldabra Is
ANGOLA L.Bangweulu Rovuma Comoro Is
Lobito Lubumbashi Kabwe MALAWI L.Nyasa Nampula Diego Suarez
Benguela Huambo ZAMBIA Lilongwe MOZAMBIQUE Majunga
Moçâmedes Lusaka Zambezi Blantyre-Limbe Moçambique MADAGASCAR Tamatave
Cunene Okavango Kariba Sena Quelimane Tananarive
Grootfontein L.Ngami Victoria Falls Wankie Salisbury Beira
SOUTH WEST AFRICA Windhoek RHODESIA Bulawayo Umtali I.del'Europe
Swakopmund Walvis Bay BOTSWANA Beitbridge Inhambane C.Ste Marie
NAMIBIA Kalahari Desert Limpopo Maputo
POPULATION TRANSVAAL Pretoria SWAZI
Luderitz Mafeking Johannesburg
ORANGE Vaal
Por.Nolloth Kimberley FREE NATAL
Bloemfontein STATE LESOTHO Pietermaritzburg
SOUTH AFRICA Durban
CAPE OF GOOD HOPE East London
Boundaries Navigable Rivers CapeTown Worcester Port Elizabeth
C.of Good Hope Mossel Bay 1:35 M.

POPULATION

- Over 200 persons per square kilometre
- 100 to 250 ,, ,, ,,
- 40 to 100 ,, ,, ,,
- 20 to 40 ,, ,, ,,
- 1 to 20 ,, ,, ,,
- Under 1 ,, ,, ,,

Tropic of Cancer

Red Sea
G.of Aden
INDIAN OCEAN
Mozambique Channel

SOUTH ATLANTIC OCEAN
Ascension (U.K)
St Helena (U.K)
Tropic of Capricorn

TEMPERATURE
(Actual °C)
JANUARY
SOUTHERN SUMMER

Canary Is Atlas Mts
Hoggar Libyan Desert Tropic of Cancer
S A H A R A Tibesti Nubian Desert
Fouta Djallon Niger L.Chad Abyssinian Highlands
Equator Zaire
L.Victoria
Tanganyika
Nyasa
Zambezi
Madagascar
Tropic of Capricorn Kalahari Desert
Orange Gt.Karroo
C.T.

°C °F
30 — 86
20 — 68
10 — 50
0 — 32

TEMPERATURE
(Actual °C)
JULY
SOUTHERN WINTER

Canary Is Atlas Mts
Hoggar Libyan Desert Tropic of Cancer
S A H A R A Tibesti Nubian Desert
Fouta Djallon Niger L.Chad Abyssinian Highlands
Equator Zaire
L.Victoria
Tanganyika
Nyasa
Zambezi
Madagascar
Tropic of Capricorn Kalahari Desert
Orange Gt.Karroo
C.T.

LAMBERT'S ZENITHAL EQUAL-AREA PROJECTION

© John Bartholomew & Son Ltd, Edinburgh

0 200 400 600 800 1000 Statute Miles
1:35M
0 200 400 600 800 1000 1200 1400 1600 Kilometres

AÇORES (AZORES)
(Portugal)

On the same scale

MADEIRA
(Portugal)

ISLAS CANARIAS
(CANARY ISLANDS)
(Spain)

CAPE VERDE ISLANDS

On the same scale

6666X

LAMBERT'S AZIMUTHAL EQUAL-AREA PROJECTION

Main Roads
Railways

| 0 | 50 | 100 | 200 | 300 | 400 | 500 Statute Miles |
| 0 | 50 100 | 200 | 300 | 400 | 500 | 600 | 700 | 800 Kilometres |

1:12½

MOROCCO
ALGERIA
SAHARA
MAURITANIA
MALI
SENEGAL
GAMBIA
GUINEA-BISSAU
GUINEA
SIERRA LEONE
LIBERIA
IVORY COAST
GHANA
UPPER VOLTA
TOGO
BENIN
NIGER

ATLANTIC OCEAN
BIGHT OF BENIN
GULF OF GUINEA

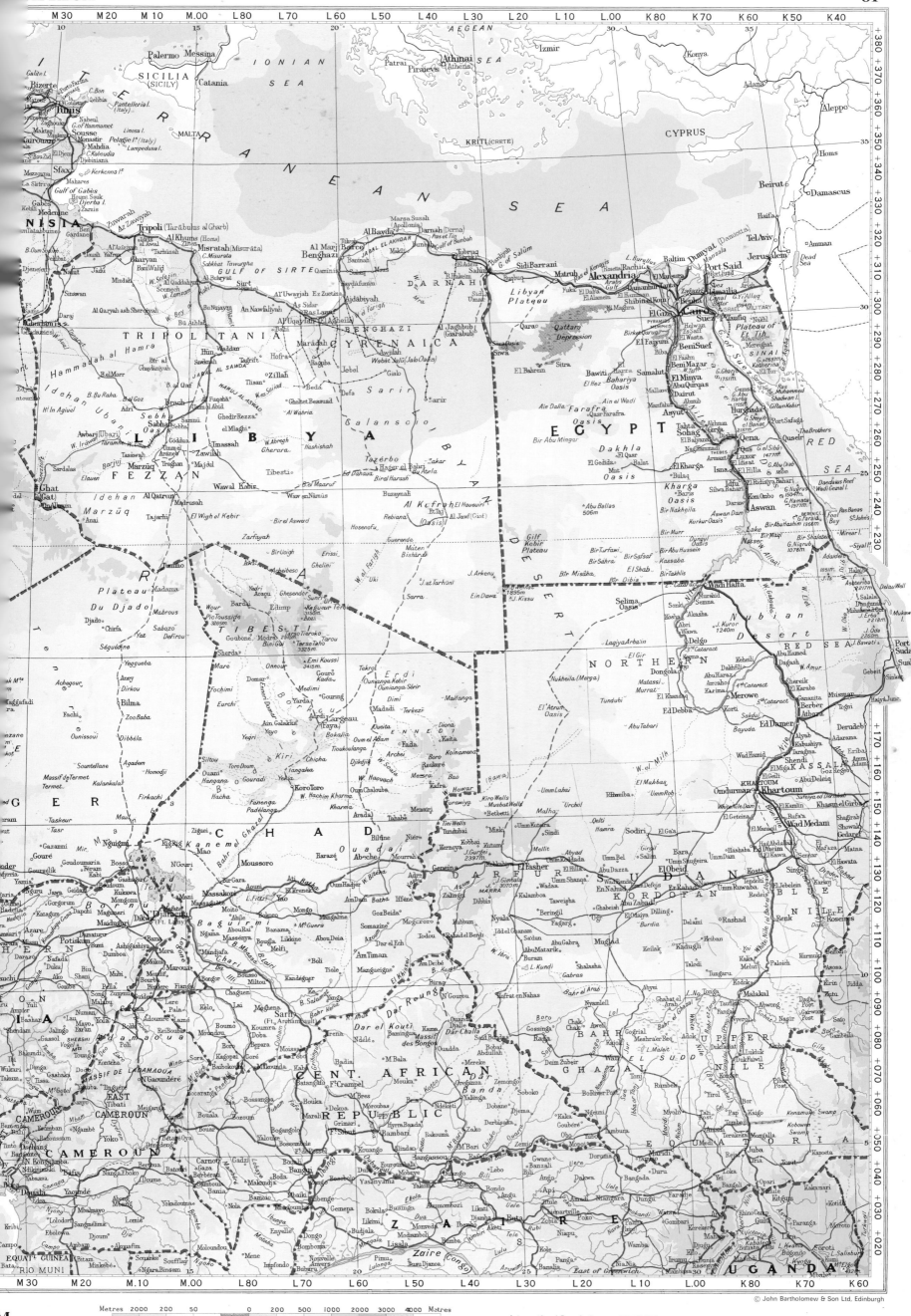

M 30 M 20 M 10 M.00 L 80 L 70 L 60 L 50 L 40 L 30 L 20 L 10 L.00 K 80 K 70 K 60 K 50 K 40

MEDITERRANEAN SEA

IONIAN SEA

AEGEAN SEA

SICILIA (SICILY)

KRITI (CRETE)

CYPRUS

TRIPOLITANIA

CYRENAICA

LIBYA

FEZZAN

EGYPT

RED SEA

Libyan Plateau

Qattara Depression

SINAI

Sarir Calanscio

LIBYAN DESERT

TIBESTI

NORTHERN

Nubian Desert

RED SEA

Plateau Du Djado

Du Djado

ENNEDI

CHAD

OUADAI

DARFUR

SUDAN

KORDOFAN

BLUE NILE

Lake Chad

KANEM

BAGIRMI

KASSALA

KHARTOUM

Omdurman

CENT. AFRICAN REPUBLIC

BAHR EL GHAZAL

UPPER NILE

CAMEROUN

ZAIRE (Congo)

EQUATORIA

UGANDA

RIO MUNI

EQUAT. GUINEA

M 30 M 20 M.10 M.00 L 80 L 70 L 60 L 50 L 40 L 30 L 20 L 10 L.00 K 80 K 70 K 60

M

Metres 2000 200 50 Land Depression 0 200 500 1000 2000 3000 4000 Metres

Feet 6560 660 160 0 660 1640 3280 6560 9840 13120 Feet

© John Bartholomew & Son Ltd. Edinburgh

International Boundaries

State Boundaries

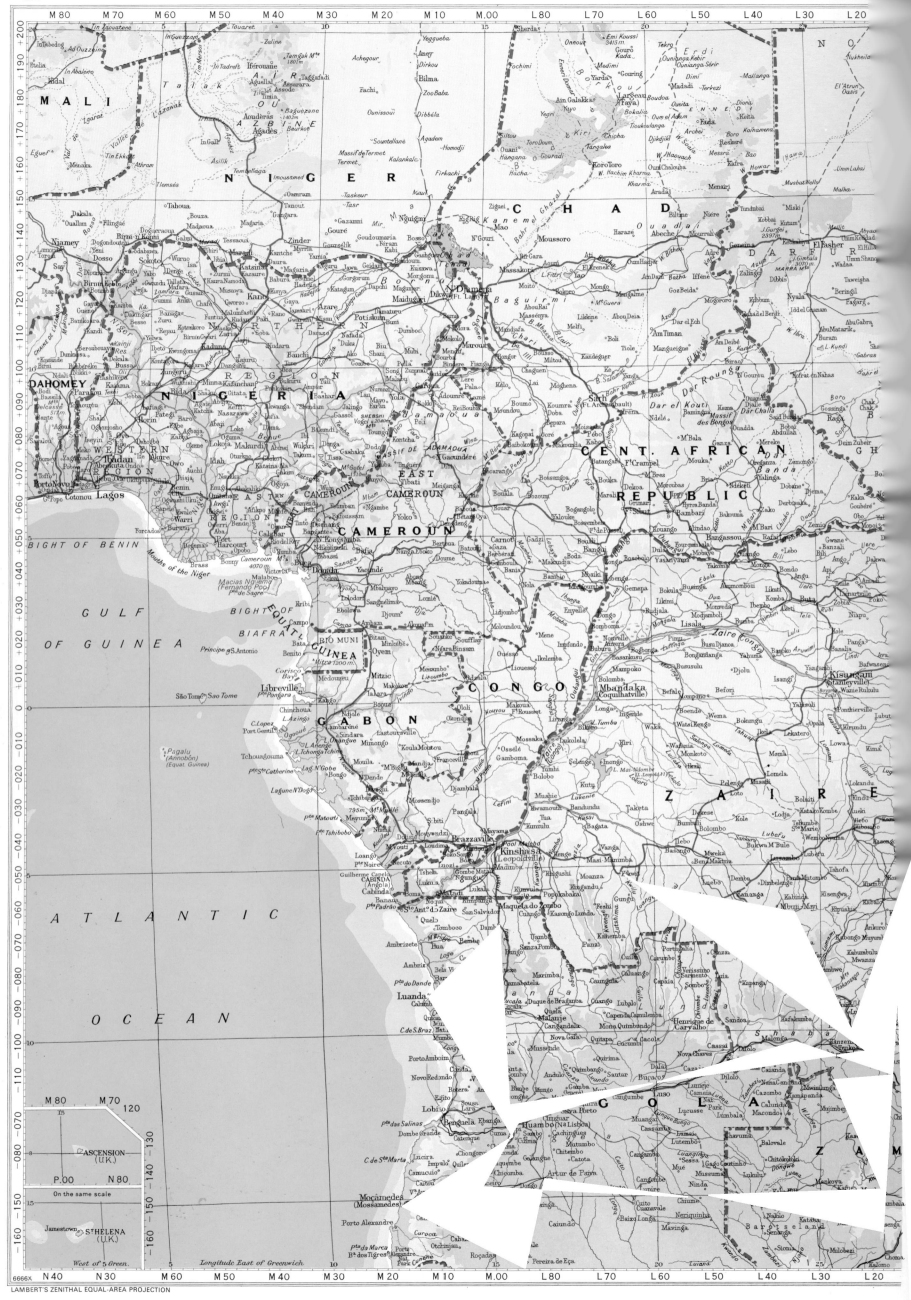

LAMBERT'S ZENITHAL EQUAL-AREA PROJECTION

Main Roads ————
Railways ————

0   50   100   200   300   400   500 Statute Miles
0 50 100   200   300   400   500   600   700   800 Kilometres

1:12½

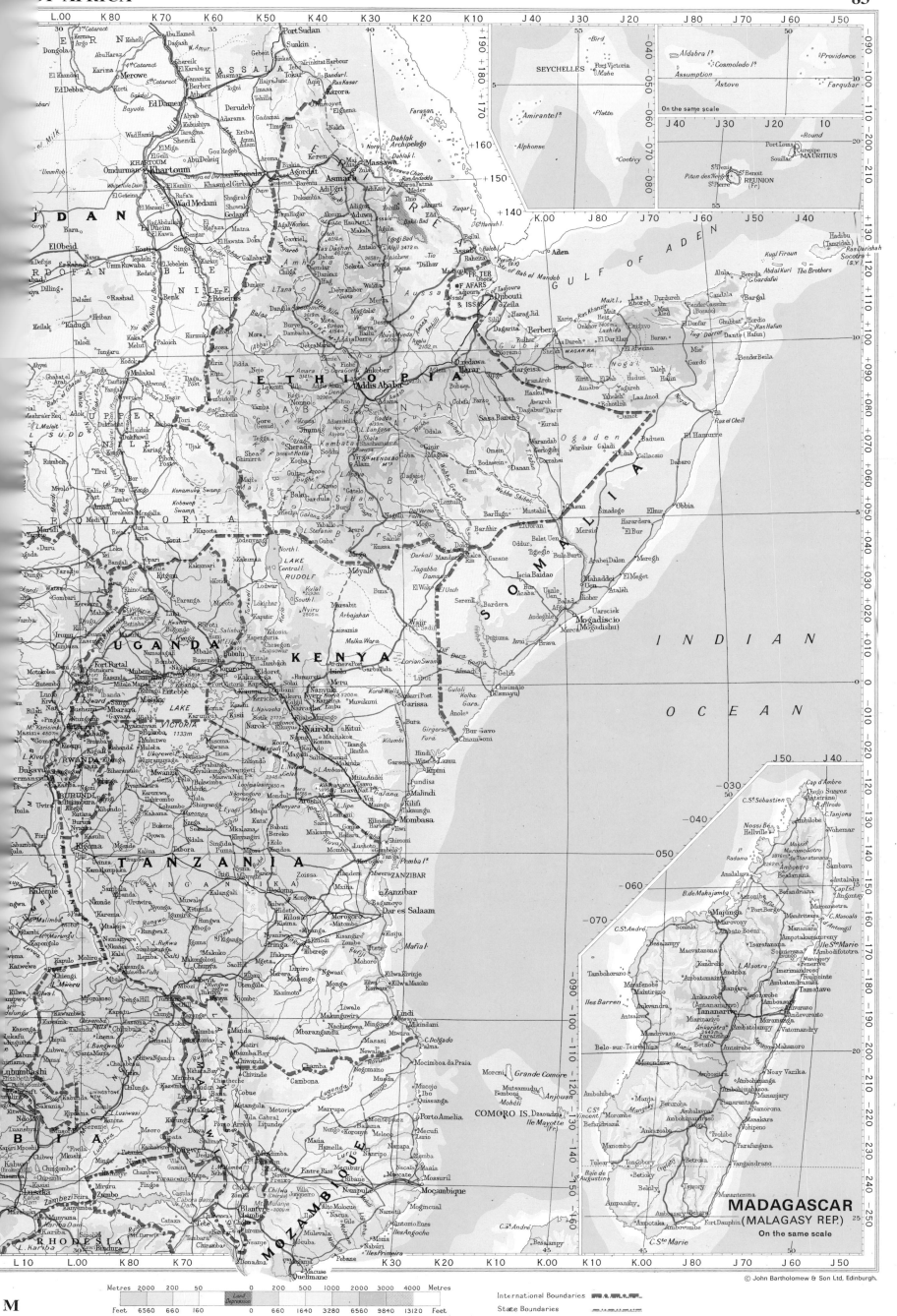

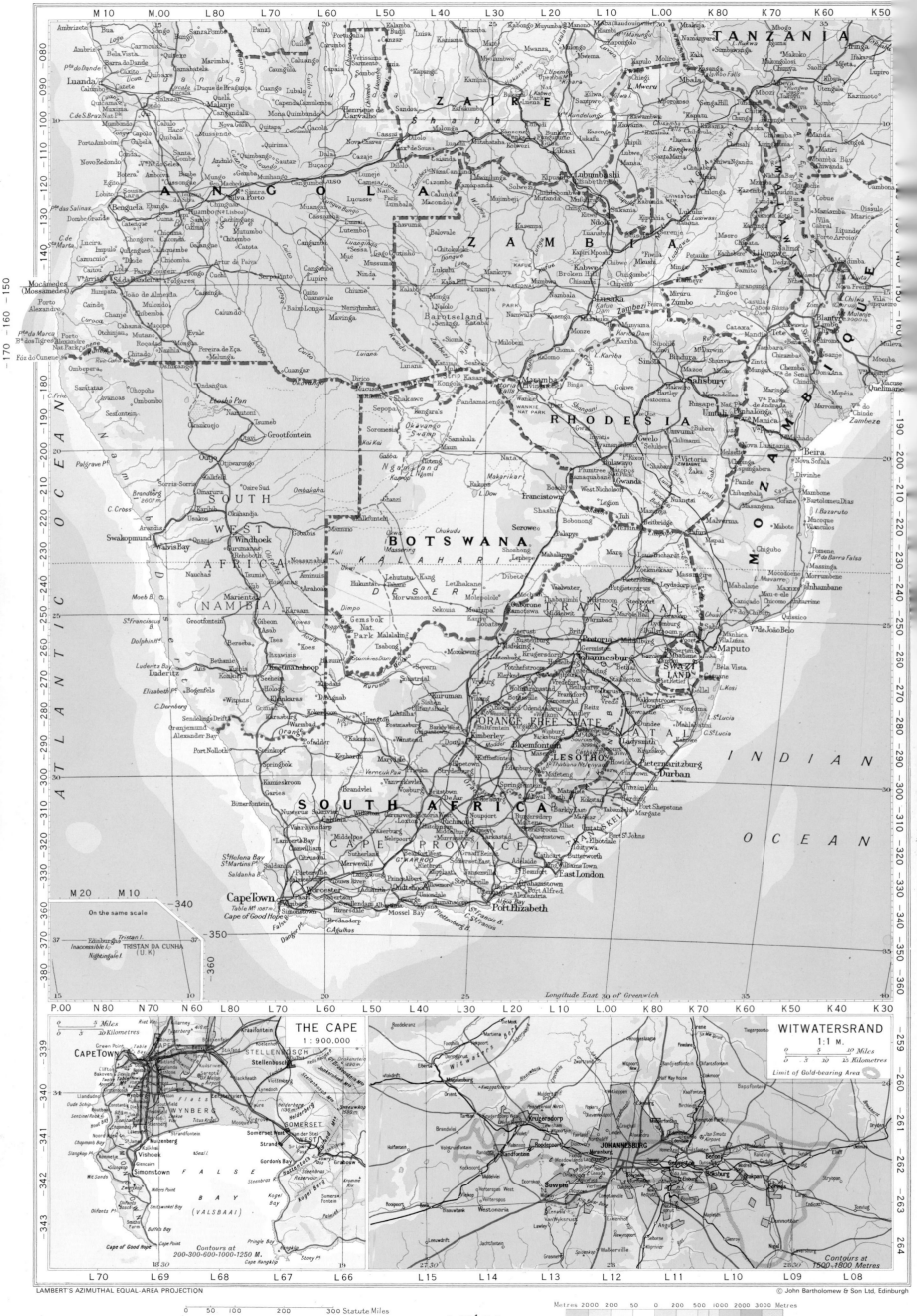

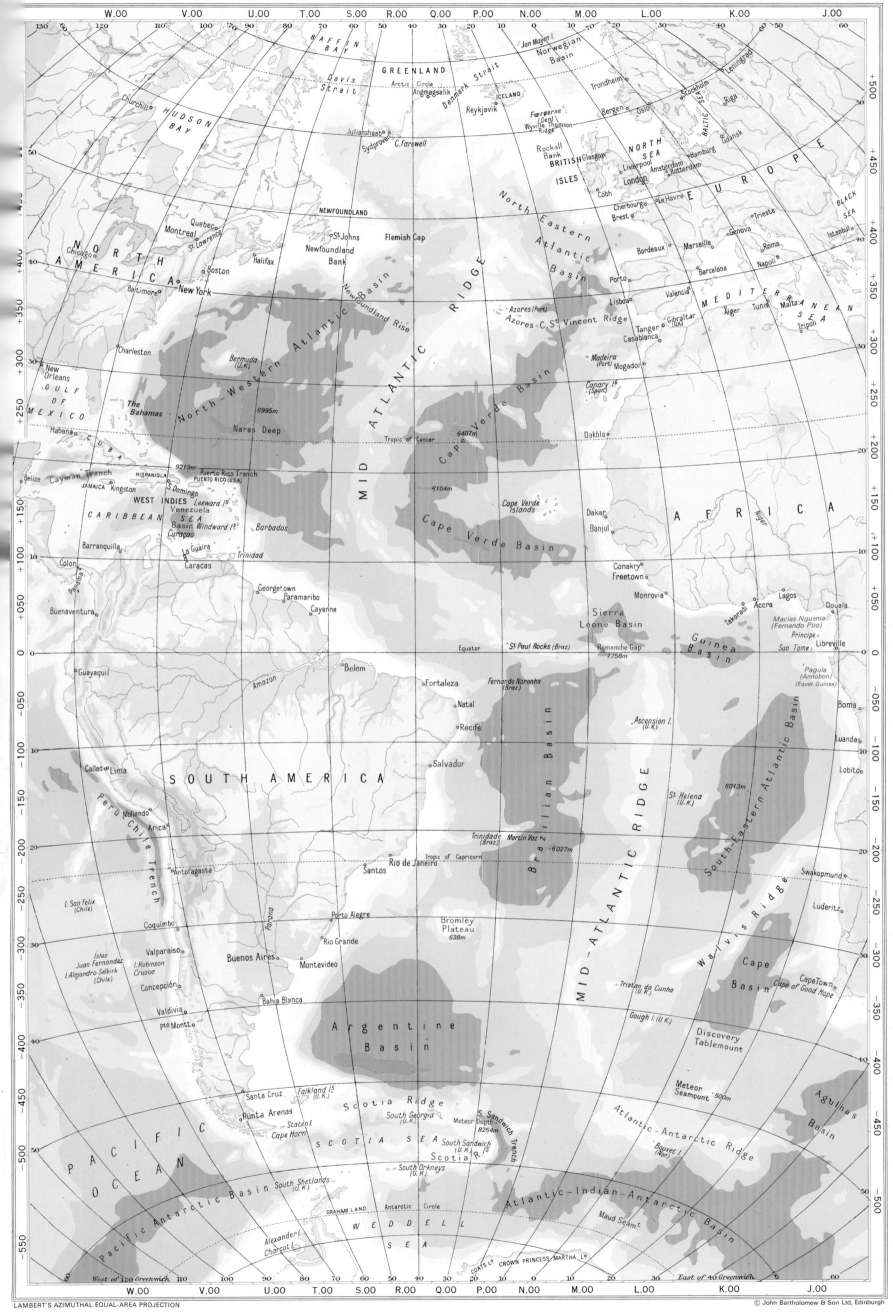

W.00 V.00 U.00 T.00 S.00 R.00 Q.00 P.00 N.00 M.00 L.00 K.00 J.00

130 120 110 100 90 80 70 60 50 40 30 20 10 0 10 20 30 40 50 60

+500
+450
+400
+350
+300
+250
+200
+150
+100
+050
0
-050
-100
-150
-200
-250
-300
-350
-400
-450
-500
-550

BAFFIN BAY
GREENLAND
Arctic Circle
Davis Strait
Angmagssalik
Denmark Strait
Jan Mayen I.
Norwegian Basin
Julianshaab
Sydprøven
C. Farewell
Reykjavik
ICELAND
Færøerne (Den)
Wyville Thomson Ridge
Trondheim
Bergen
Oslo
Stockholm
Leningrad
Riga
BALTIC SEA
Gdansk
Hamburg
Amsterdam
Rotterdam
London
Liverpool
Glasgow
BRITISH ISLES
Rockall Bank
NORTH SEA
NORTH EASTERN ATLANTIC BASIN
Cóbh
Cherbourg
Le Havre
Brest
EUROPE
BLACK SEA
Istanbul
Trieste
Roma
Napoli
Genova
Marseille
Barcelona
Bordeaux
Porto
Lisboa
Valencia
MEDITERRANEAN SEA
Alger
Tunis
Malta
Tripoli

HUDSON BAY
Churchill
Quebec
Montreal
St. Lawrence
St. Johns
NEWFOUNDLAND
Flemish Cap
Newfoundland Bank
Halifax
Boston
NORTH AMERICA
Chicago
Baltimore
New York
Charleston
New Orleans
GULF OF MEXICO
The Bahamas
Habana
CUBA
Belize
Cayman Trench
JAMAICA
Kingston
HISPANIOLA
S. Domingo
9219m
Puerto Rico Trench
PUERTO RICO (U.S.A.)
WEST INDIES
Leeward Is.
Venezuela
CARIBBEAN SEA
Barranquilla
Colon
Panama
Buenaventura
Guayaquil
Callao
Lima
Moliendo
Arica
Antofagasta
I. San Felix (Chile)
Coquimbo
Valparaiso
I. Robinson Crusoe
Islas Juan Fernandez
I. Alejandro Selkirk (Chile)
Concepción
Valdivia
pto Montt
PACIFIC OCEAN
Santa Cruz
Punta Arenas
Staten I.
Cape Horn
South Shetlands (U.K.)
Pacific-Antarctic Basin
GRAHAM LAND
Alexander I.
Charcot I.
Basin Windward Is.
Curaçao
La Guaira
Caracas
Trinidad
Georgetown
Paramaribo
Cayenne
Amazon
Belem
SOUTH AMERICA
Fortaleza
Natal
Recife
Salvador
Parana
Porto Alegre
Rio Grande
Buenos Aires
Montevideo
Bahia Blanca
Argentine Basin

Bermuda (U.K.)
6995m
Nares Deep
North-Western Atlantic Basin
Newfoundland Rise
MID ATLANTIC RIDGE
Azores (Port.)
Azores-C. St Vincent Ridge
Tropic of Cancer
6407m
Madeira (Port.)
Mogador
Canary Is. (Span.)
Dakhla
Cape Verde Basin
5104m
Cape Verde Islands
Dakar
Banjul
AFRICA
Niger
Conakry
Freetown
Monrovia
Takoradi
Accra
Lagos
Douala
Macias Nguama (Fernando Poo)
Principe
São Tomé
Libreville
Sierra Leone Basin
Equator
St. Paul Rocks (Braz)
Romanche Gap
7758m
Guinea Basin
Pagula (Annobon) (Equat Guinea)
Boma
Fernando Noronha (Braz)
Ascension I. (U.K.)
Luanda
Lobito
Brazilian Basin
St Helena (U.K.)
6013m
South-Eastern Atlantic Basin
Trinidade (Braz)
Martin Vaz (Braz)
6027m
Tropic of Capricorn
Rio de Janeiro
Santos
Bromley Plateau 638m
MID-ATLANTIC RIDGE
Tristan da Cunha (U.K.)
Walvis Ridge
Swakopmund
Lüderitz
Cape Basin
Cape Town
Cape of Good Hope
Gough I. (U.K.)
Discovery Tablemount
Meteor Seamount 500m
Agulhas Basin
Falkland Is. (U.K.)
Scotia Ridge
South Georgia (U.K.)
Meteor Depth 8264m
S. Sandwich Is. (U.K.)
Atlantic-Antarctic Ridge
Bouvet I. (Nor)
SCOTIA SEA
South Sandwich (U.K.)
Scotia R.
South Orkneys (U.K.)
Atlantic-Indian-Antarctic Basin
Maud Seamt.
WEDDELL SEA
COATS LD.
CROWN PRINCESS MARTHA Ld.
Antarctic Circle

West of 120 Greenwich 110 100 90 80 70 60 50 40 30 20 10 0 10 20 30 40 50 60 East of 40 Greenwich

W.00 V.00 U.00 T.00 S.00 R.00 Q.00 P.00 N.00 M.00 L.00 K.00 J.00

LAMBERT'S AZIMUTHAL EQUAL-AREA PROJECTION

© John Bartholomew & Son Ltd, Edinburgh

0 200 400 600 800 1000 Statute Miles
0 400 800 1200 1600 Kilometres

1:48M

Metres 6000 5000 4000 2000 200 0 200 1000 2000 4000 Metres
Feet 19690 16400 13120 6560 660 0 660 3280 6560 13120 Feet

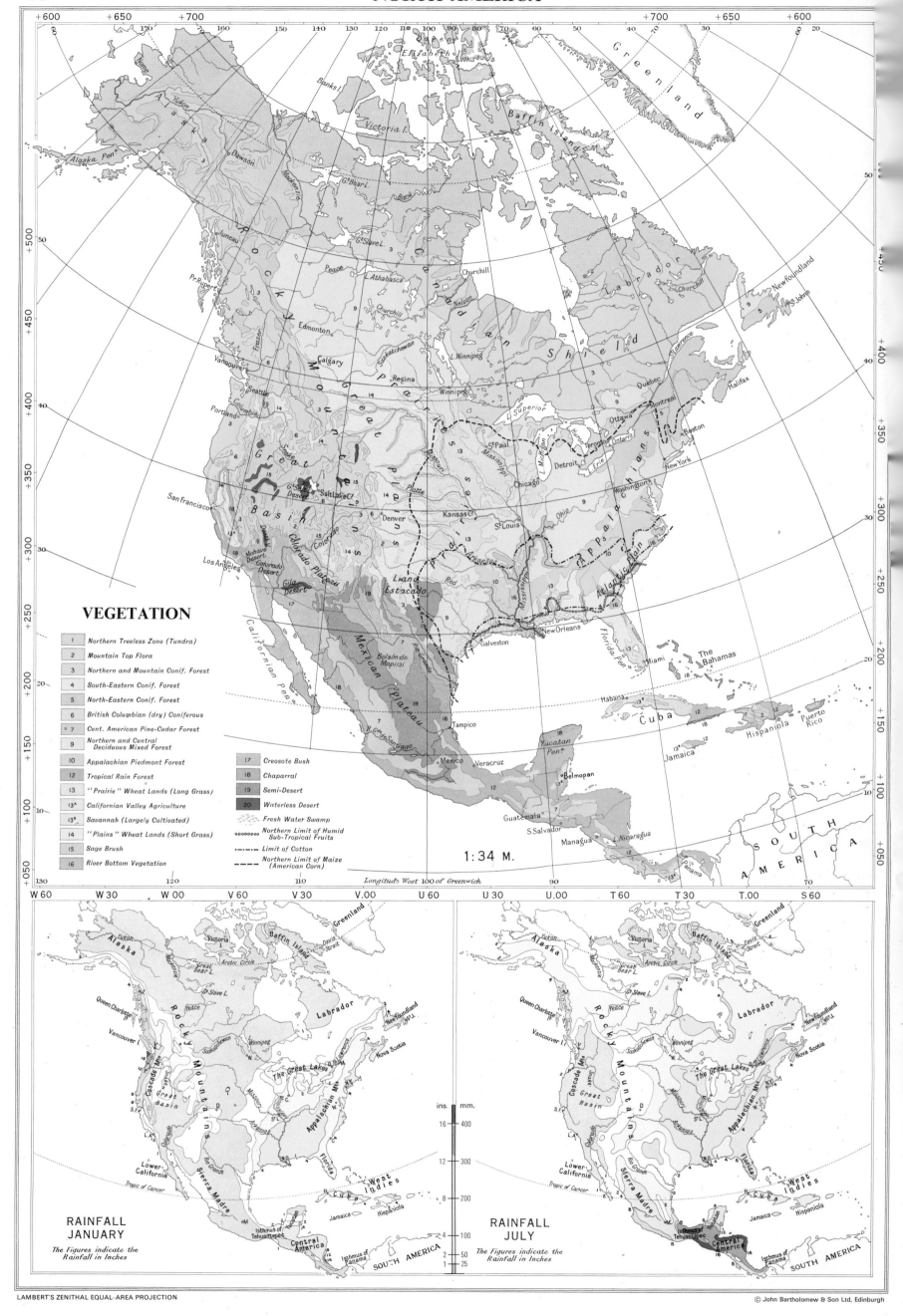

VEGETATION

1	Northern Treeless Zone (Tundra)
2	Mountain Top Flora
3	Northern and Mountain Conif. Forest
4	South-Eastern Conif. Forest
5	North-Eastern Conif. Forest
6	British Columbian (dry) Coniferous
7	Cent. American Pine-Cedar Forest
9	Northern and Central Deciduous Mixed Forest
10	Appalachian Piedmont Forest
12	Tropical Rain Forest
13	"Prairie" Wheat Lands (Long Grass)
13ᴬ	Californian Valley Agriculture
13ᴮ	Savannah (Largely Cultivated)
14	"Plains" Wheat Lands (Short Grass)
15	Sage Brush
16	River Bottom Vegetation

17	Creosote Bush
18	Chaparral
19	Semi-Desert
20	Waterless Desert
	Fresh Water Swamp
	Northern Limit of Humid Sub-Tropical Fruits
	Limit of Cotton
	Northern Limit of Maize (American Corn)

1:34 M.

RAINFALL
JANUARY

The Figures indicate the Rainfall in Inches

ins.   mm.

RAINFALL
JULY

The Figures indicate the Rainfall in Inches

LAMBERT'S ZENITHAL EQUAL-AREA PROJECTION

© John Bartholomew & Son Ltd, Edinburgh

0   200   400   600   800 Statute Miles

1:34M

0   200   400   600   800   1000   1200 Kilometres

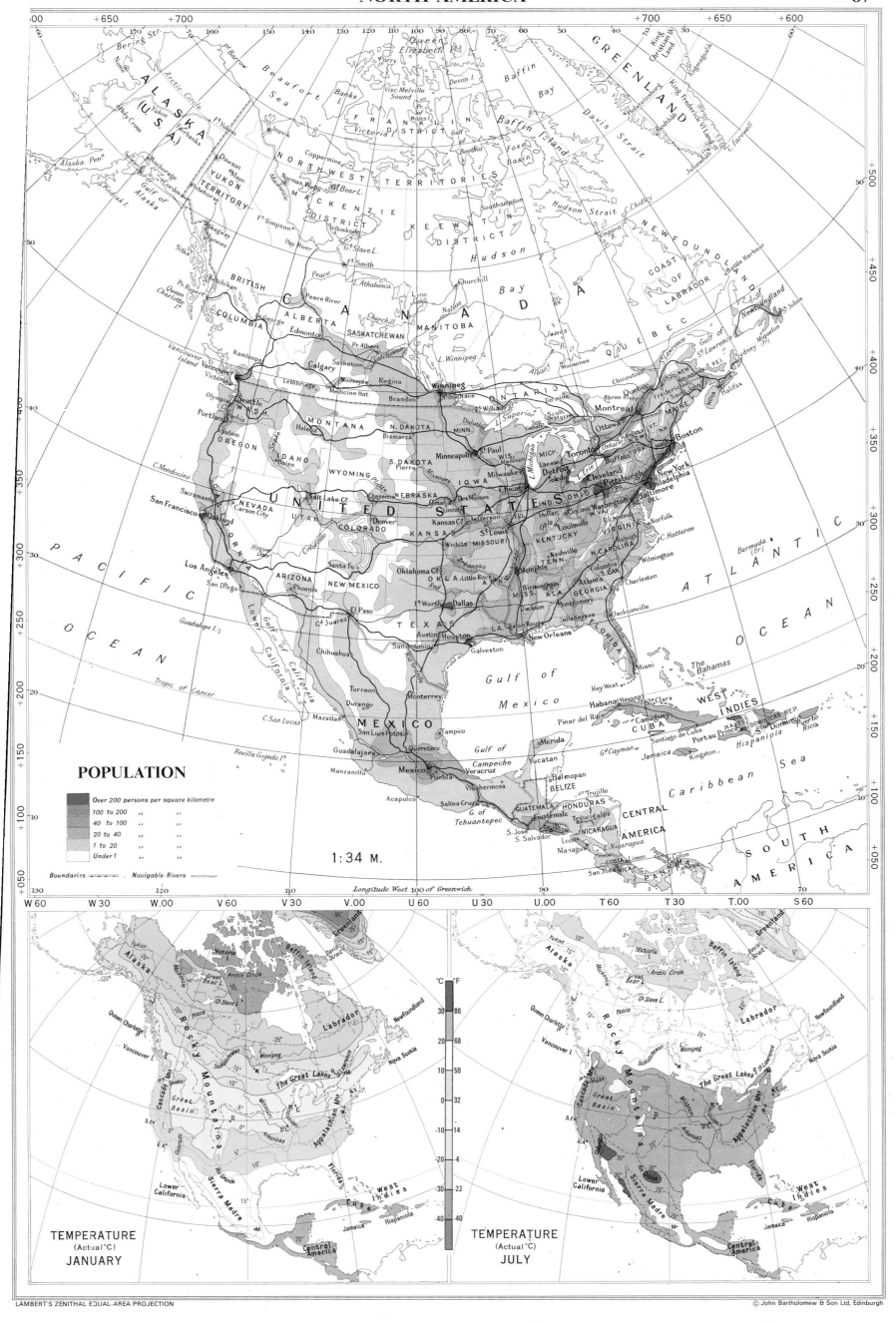

POPULATION

Over 200 persons per square kilometre
100 to 200 ,, ,, ,,
40 to 100 ,, ,, ,,
20 to 40 ,, ,, ,,
1 to 20 ,, ,, ,,
Under 1 ,, ,, ,,

Boundaries .... Navigable Rivers ———

1:34 M.

TEMPERATURE
(Actual °C)
JANUARY

TEMPERATURE
(Actual °C)
JULY

LAMBERT'S ZENITHAL EQUAL-AREA PROJECTION

© John Bartholomew & Son Ltd, Edinburgh

0   200   400   600   800 Statute Miles

1:34M

0   200 400 600 800 1000 1200 Kilometres

Y 30 Y.00 X 60 X 30 X.00 W 60 W 30 W.00 V 60 V 30 V.00 U 60

155 150 145 140 135 110 120 115 Borden I. 105 Ellef Ringnes I. 100

BEAUFORT SEA

Brooks Range

UNITED STATES

ALASKA

QUEEN ELIZABETH ISLANDS

PARRY ISLAND

Melville Island

Banks Island

Victoria Island

NORTHWEST

FRANKLIN DISTRICT

Prince of Wales Island

Amundsen Gulf

King William I.

YUKON TERRITORY

MACKENZIE DISTRICT

Great Bear Lake

Great Slave Lake

PACIFIC OCEAN

Alexander Archipelago

Prince of Wales I.

Queen Charlotte Islands

Vancouver Island

BRITISH COLUMBIA

SASKATCHEWAN

Prince Albert

MANITOBA

Lake Winnipeg

Wood Buffalo Park

L. Athabasca

Reindeer Lake

Portland

Columbia R.

Plateau

IDAHO

Boise

WYOMING

Bad Lands

DAKOTA

W 40 W 30 W 20 W 10 W.00 V 80 V 70 V 60 V 50 V 40 V 30 V 20 V 10 V.00 U 80 U 70 U 60 U 50 U 40 U 30

CONIC PROJECTION

Main Roads _____
Railways _____

0 50 100 200 300 400 500 Statute Miles
0 50 100 200 300 400 500 600 700 800 Kilometres

1:12½

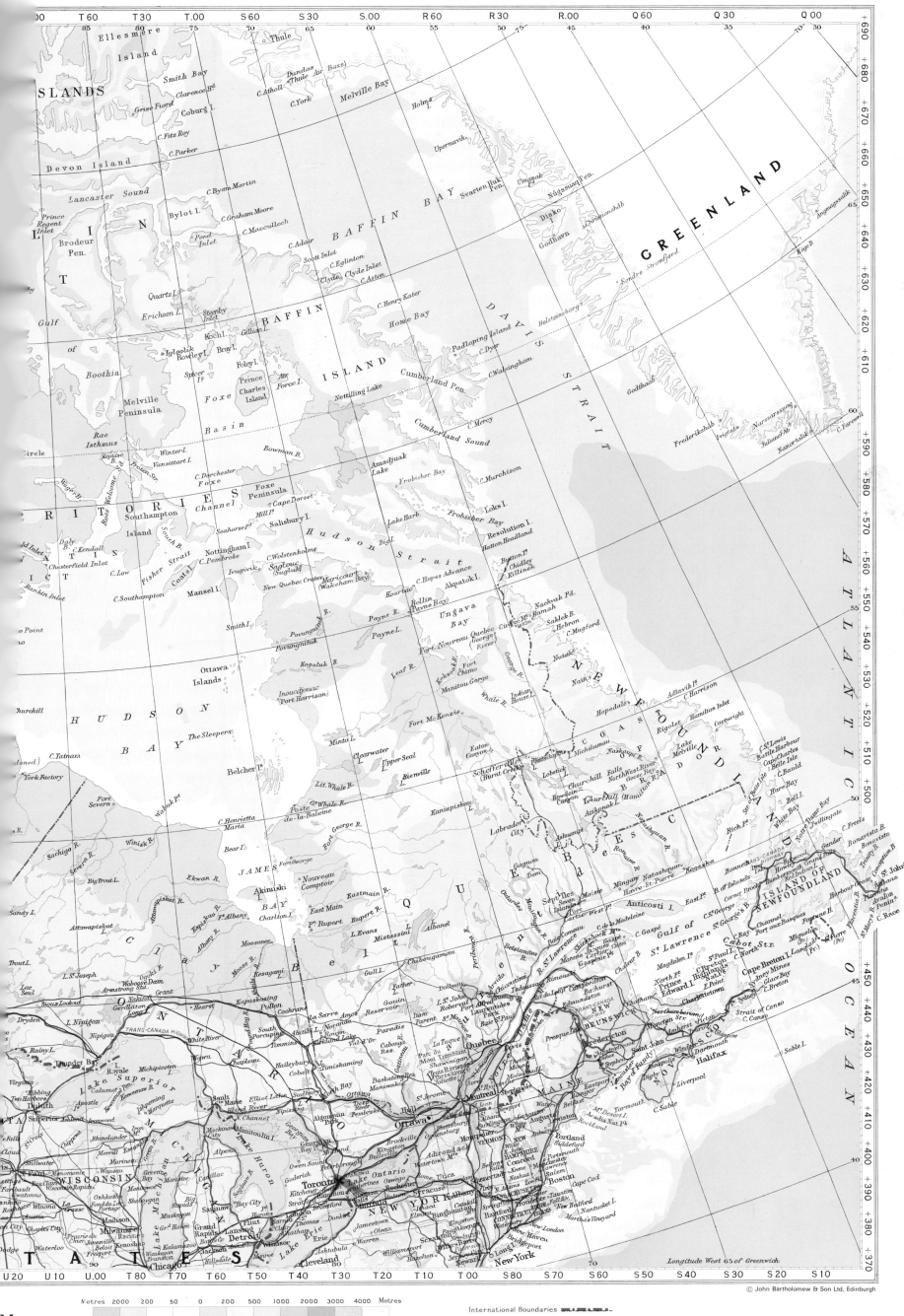

GREENLAND

ATLANTIC OCEAN

BAFFIN BAY

DAVIS STRAIT

BAFFIN ISLAND

Ellesmere Island

Devon Island

HUDSON BAY

JAMES BAY

NEWFOUNDLAND

QUÉBEC

ONTARIO

NEW BRUNSWICK

NOVA SCOTIA

ISLAND OF NEWFOUNDLAND

MAINE

VERMONT

NEW HAMPSHIRE

MASSACHUSETTS

CONNECTICUT

NEW YORK

WISCONSIN

MICHIGAN

UNITED STATES

Toronto

Detroit

Chicago

Cleveland

Montreal

Ottawa

Quebec

Halifax

Boston

New York

Longitude West of 65 of Greenwich

© John Bartholomew & Son Ltd, Edinburgh

Metres 2000 200 50 0 200 500 1000 2000 3000 4000 Metres
Feet 6560 660 160 0 660 1640 3280 6560 9840 13120 Feet

International Boundaries
Province Boundaries

M

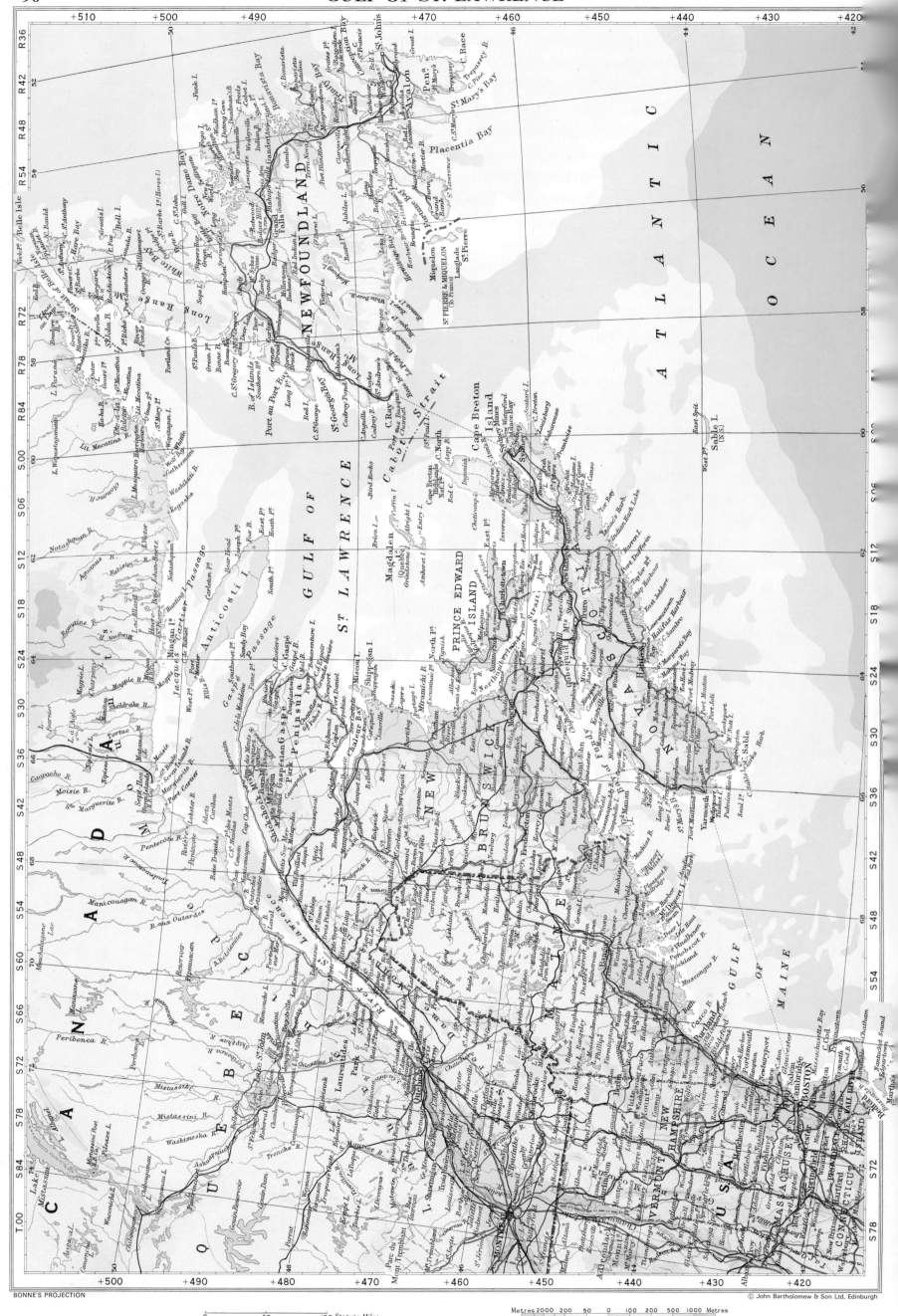

© John Bartholomew & Son Ltd, Edinburgh

BONNE'S PROJECTION

1:5M

0   50   100 Statute Miles
0   50   100   150 Kilometres

Metres 2000 200 50 0 100 200 500 1000 Metres
Feet 6560 660 160 0 330 660 1640 3280 Feet

CANADA

QUEBEC

ONTARIO

MINNESOTA

WISCONSIN

MICHIGAN

ILLINOIS

INDIANA

OHIO

PENNSYLVANIA

WEST VIRGINIA

MARYLAND

DELAWARE

NEW JERSEY

NEW YORK

MAINE

VERMONT

NEW HAMPSHIRE

MASSACHUSETTS

CONNECTICUT

RHODE ISLAND

LAKE SUPERIOR

LAKE HURON

LAKE MICHIGAN

LAKE ERIE

LAKE ONTARIO

Georgian Bay

North Channel

Green Bay

Saginaw Bay

Thunder Bay

White Fish Bay

Whitefish Bay

ATLANTIC OCEAN

Long Island

Isle Royale National Park

Apostle Is.

Manitoulin I.

Algonquin Park

Parc du Mont Tremblant

Verendrye Park

Montreal

Ottawa

Toronto

Hamilton

Buffalo

Rochester

Syracuse

Albany

Boston

New York

Philadelphia

Baltimore

Washington

Pittsburgh

Cleveland

Detroit

Toledo

Chicago

Milwaukee

Cincinnati

Indianapolis

Columbus

Springfield

St Louis

Duluth

Sault Ste Marie

Kingston

Bartholomew

BONNE'S PROJECTION

© John Bartholomew & Son Ltd, Edinburgh

1:5M

| Statute Miles | 0 | 50 | 100 |

| Kilometres | 0 | 50 | 100 | 150 |

| Metres 200 | 50 | 0 | 100 | 200 | 500 | 1000 Metres |

| Feet 660 | 160 | 0 | 330 | 660 | 1640 | 3280 Feet |

WASHINGTON   OREGON   IDAHO   MONTANA   NEVADA   UTAH   CALIFORNIA   ARIZONA

PACIFIC OCEAN

SEATTLE   Tacoma   Olympia   PORTLAND   Salem   Eugene   Spokane   Boise   SAN FRANCISCO   Oakland   Sacramento   Stockton   Fresno   Bakersfield   LOS ANGELES   Long Beach   San Diego   Las Vegas   SALT LAKE CITY   Reno   Carson City

BONNE'S PROJECTION

Metres 2000 200 50   0   100 200 500 1000 2000 3000 4000 Metres
Feet 6560 660 160   0   330 660 1640 3280 6560 9840 13120 Feet
Land Depression

Longitude West of Greenwich

1:5M

© John Bartholomew & Son Ltd, Edinburgh

BONNE'S PROJECTION

© John Bartholomew & Son Ltd. Edinburgh

X6666

1:5M

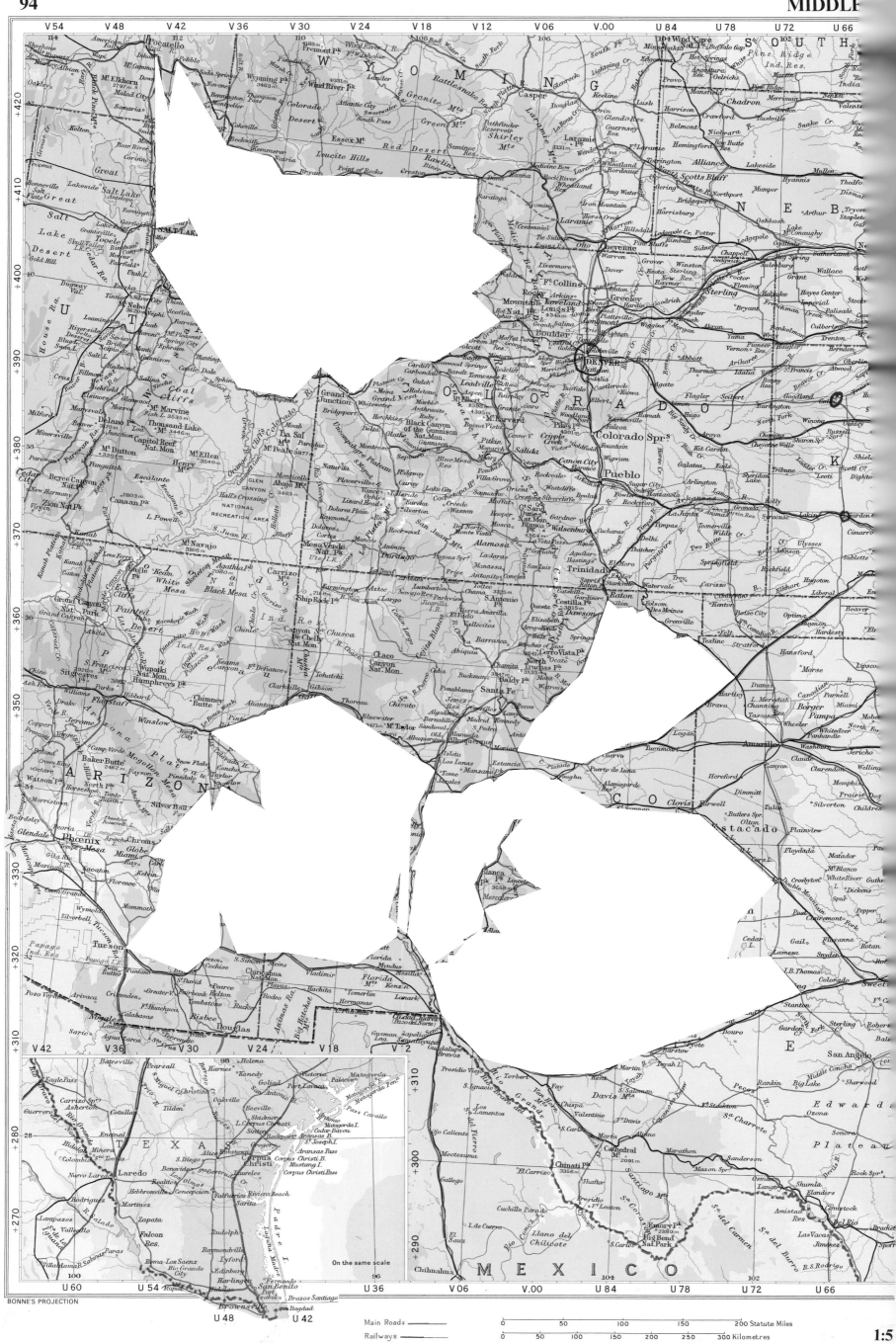

Main Roads ———
Railways ———

| | 0 | 50 | 100 | 150 | 200 Statute Miles |
| 0 | 50 | 100 | 150 | 200 | 250 | 300 Kilometres |

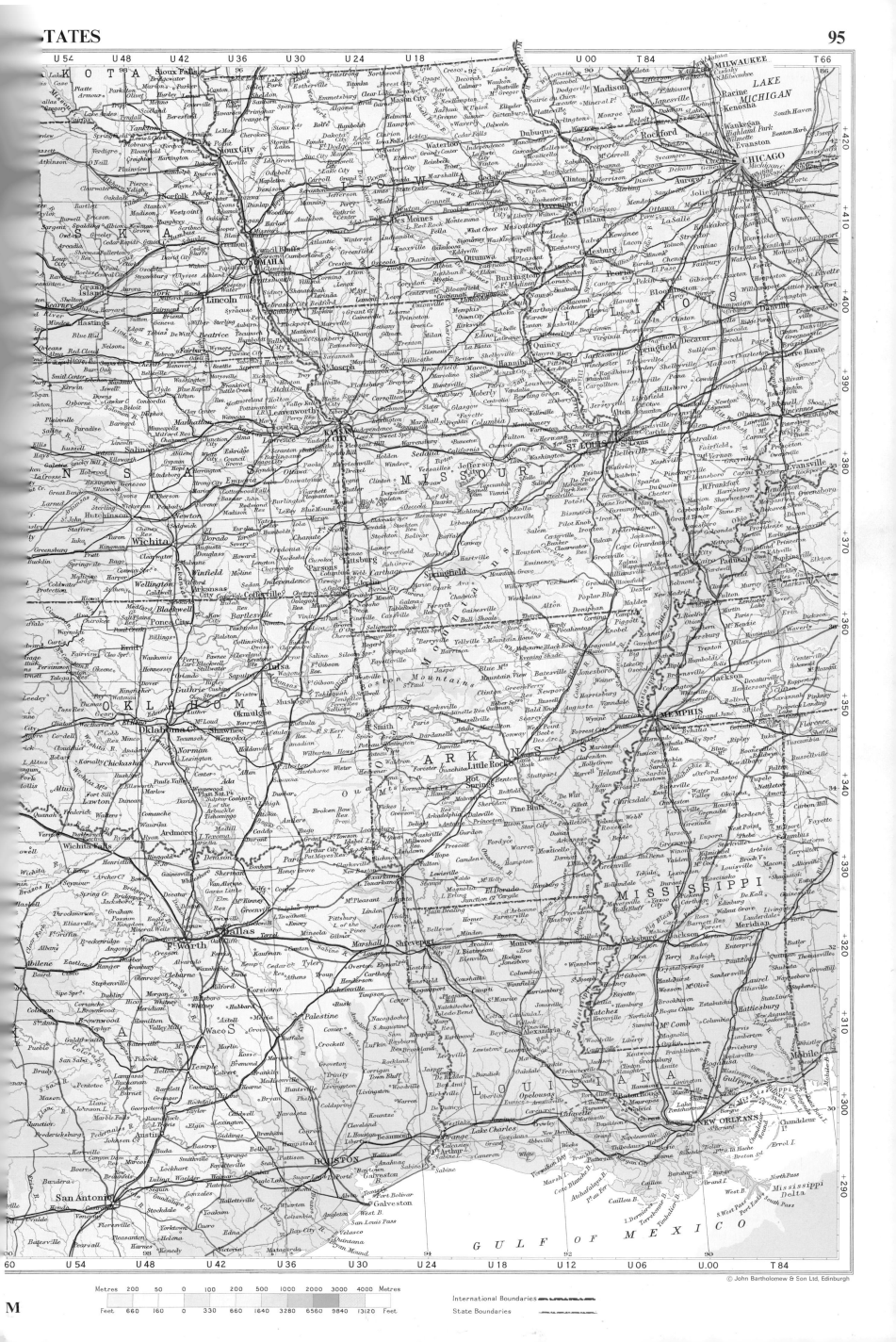

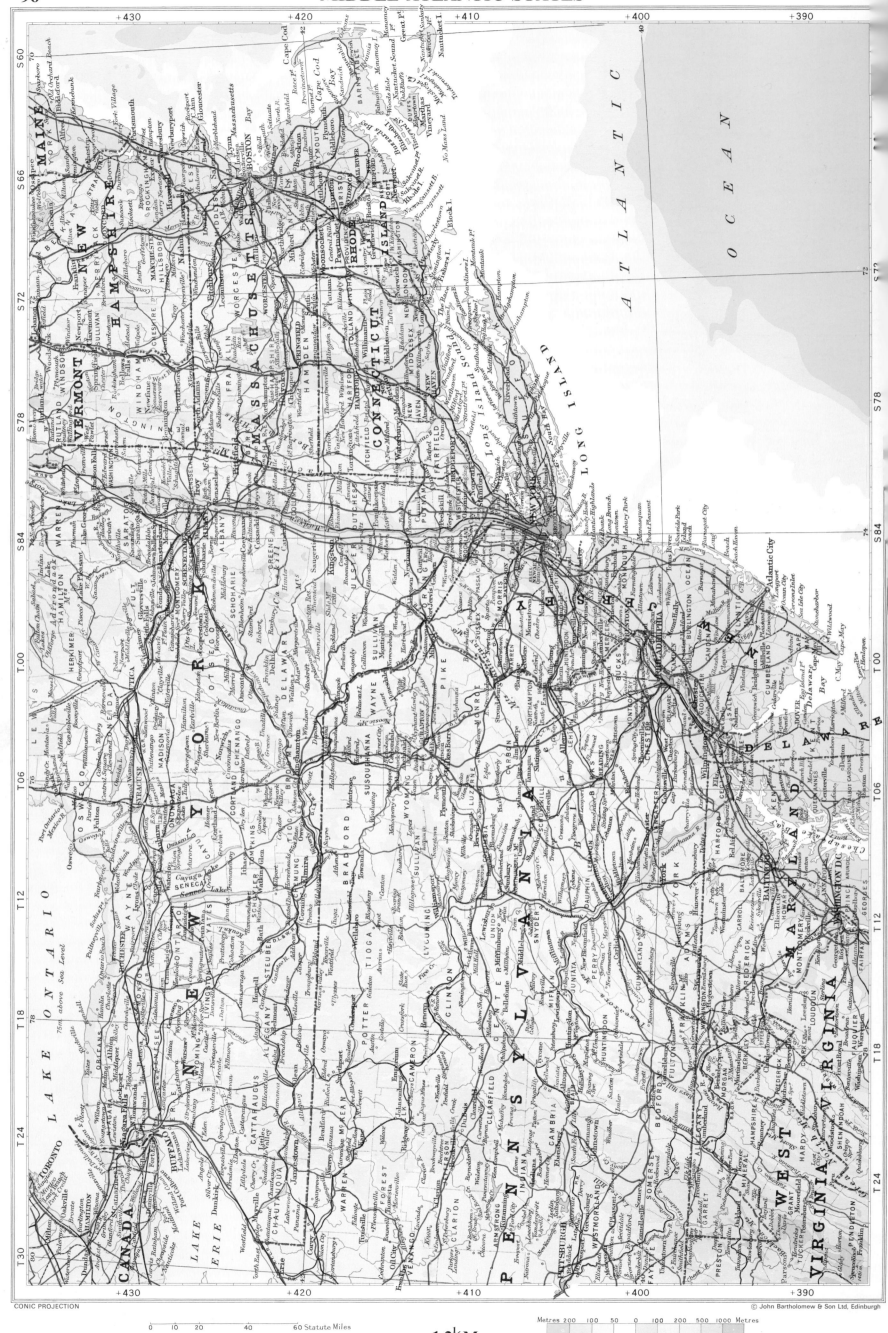

CONIC PROJECTION

	0	10	20	40	60 Statute Miles
	0	10	20	40	60	80	100 Kilometres

1:2½M

Metres	200	100	50	0	100	200	500	1000	Metres
Feet	660	330	160	0	330	660	1640	3280	Feet

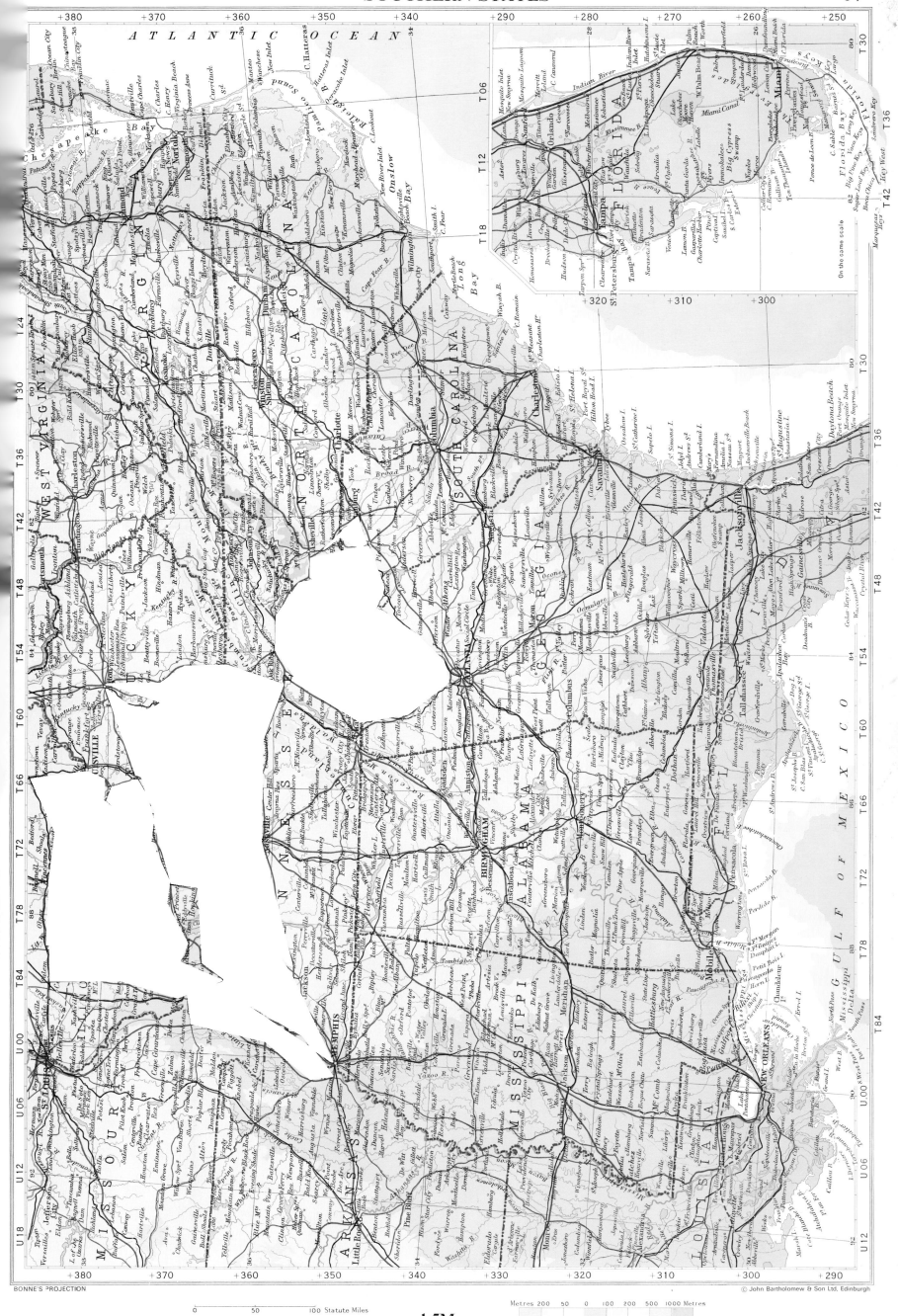

BONNE'S PROJECTION

1:5M

Statute Miles
0   50   100

Kilometres
0   50   100   150

Metres 200 50 0 100 200 500 1000 Metres
Feet 660 160 0 330 660 1640 3280 Feet

6

ATLANTIC OCEAN

GULF OF MEXICO

THE BAHAMAS

Tropic of Cancer

NEW YORK

0 2 4 km
0 1 2 Miles

HUDSON RIVER

EAST RIVER

LONG ISLAND

UPPER BAY

LOWER BAY

JAMAICA BAY

U.S.S.R.

Arctic Circle

Chukchi Sea

ALASKA

Brooks Range

Bering Sea

Alaska Range

Aleutian Is.

CANADA

Rocky Mts.

Gulf of Alaska

ALASKA
1:25 M

0 50 100 200 300 Miles
0 200 400 Kilometres

© John Bartholomew & Son Ltd, Edinburgh

Metres 2000 200 50 Land 0 200 500 1000 2000 3000 4000 Metres
                        Depression
Feet 6560 660 160 0 560 1640 3280 6560 9840 13120 Feet

International Boundaries
State Boundaries

GULF OF MEXICO

PACIFIC OCEAN

UNITED STATES

MEXICO

TEXAS

LOUISIANA

MISSISSIPPI

SONORA

CHIHUAHUA

COAHUILA

DURANGO

SINALOA

NUEVO LEON

TAMAULIPAS

ZACATECAS

S. LUIS POTOSI

NAYARIT

JALISCO

MICHOACAN

GUERRERO

HIDALGO

VERA CRUZ

OAXACA

CHIAPAS

TABASCO

CAMPECHE

YUCATAN

QUINTANA ROO

GUATEMALA

HONDURAS

BELIZE

SALVADOR

BAJA CALIFORNIA

BAJA CALIFORNIA (SUR)

Gulf of California

Gulf of Campeche

Gulf of Tehuantepec

Tropic of Cancer

Sierra Madre Occidental

Sierra Madre Oriental

Yucatan Channel

West of 100 Greenwich

Revilla Gigedo Is. (To California)

Bonne's Projection

© John Bartholomew & Son Ltd, Edinr.

1:10M

0   100   200   300 Statute Miles
0   100   200   300   400   500 Kilometres

Metres 2000 200 50 0 200 500 1000 2000 3000 4000 Metres
Feet 6560 660 160 0 660 1640 3280 6560 9840 13120 Feet

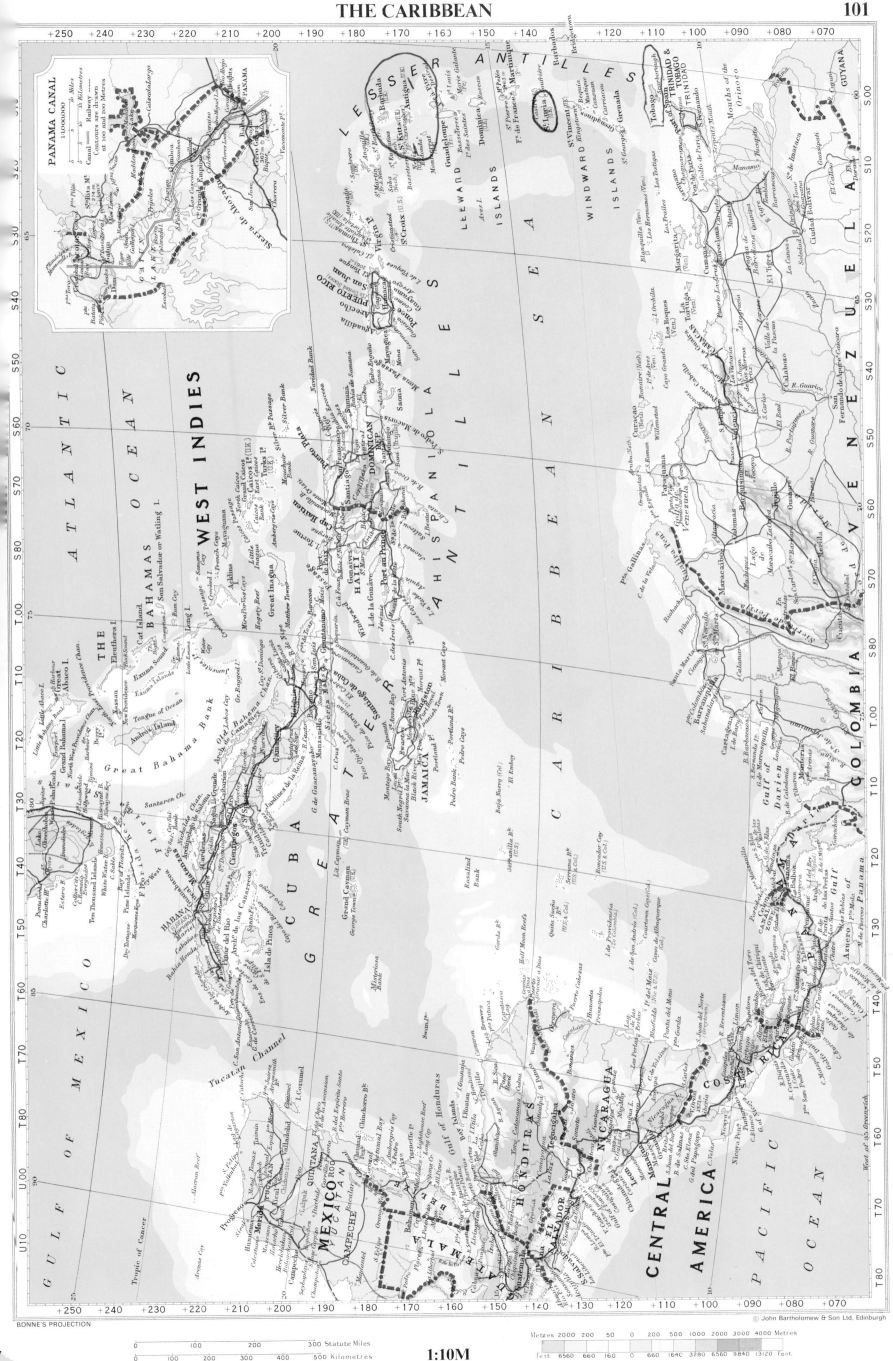

BONNE'S PROJECTION

© John Bartholomew & Son Ltd, Edinburgh

1:10M

VEGETATION

1	Antarctic Tundra
2ᴬ	Andean Mountain Zone, Paramos (wet)
2ᴮ	,, ,, ,, Punas (dry)
2ᶜ	,, ,, ,, Tola (arid)
3	Hill Tropical Forest
5	Catingas
6	Chaco
7	Inter-Andean Basin Cultivation
9	Park Land
10	Temperate Forest
11	Mixed Tropical Forest
12	Tropical Rain Forest

13	Pampas (Rich Grass)
14	Llanos (Plateau Grass)
15	Campos Cerrados and Savannah
16	Mediterranean Type Vegetation
17	"Monte," Xerophil Bush
17ˢ	Salt Swamp
18	Patagonian Steppe
19	Semi-Desert
20	Waterless Desert
	Fresh Water Swamp
- - - -	Southern Limit of Hevea (Wild Rubber)
-·-·-·	Southern Limit of Quebracho
ooooooo	Extent of Yerba Maté

1 : 32 M.

RAINFALL
JANUARY
SOUTHERN SUMMER
The Figures indicate the
Rainfall in Inches

ins.	mm.
16	400
12	300
8	200
4	100
2	50
1	25

RAINFALL
JULY
SOUTHERN WINTER
The Figures indicate the
Rainfall in Inches

LAMBERT'S ZENITHAL EQUAL-AREA PROJECTION

© John Bartholomew & Son Ltd, Edinburgh

0   200   400   600   800 Statute Miles   1:32M   0   200   400   600   800   1000   1200 Kilometres

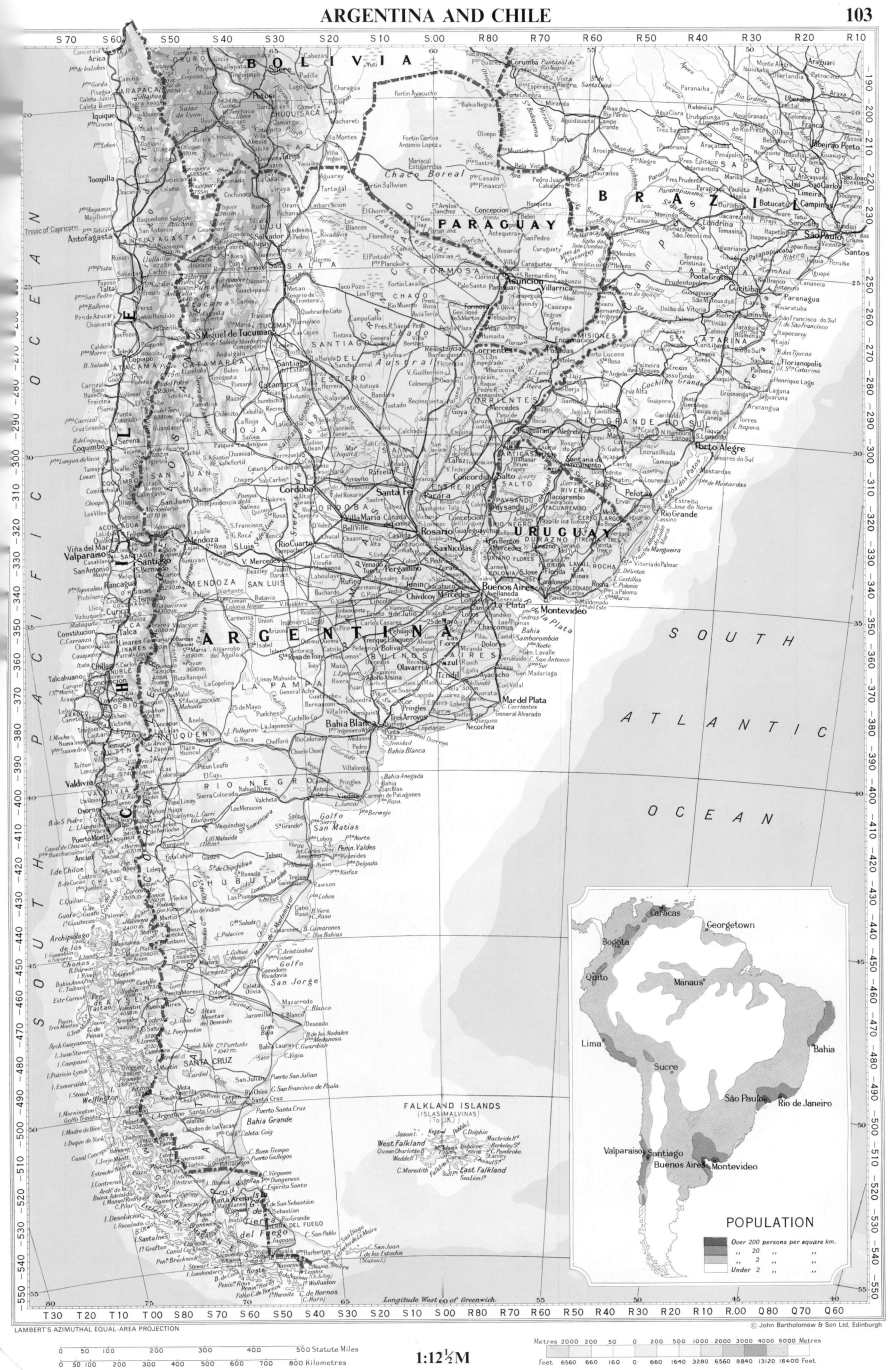

POPULATION

	Over 200 persons per square km.
	,, 20 ,, ,,
	,, 2 ,, ,,
	Under 2 ,,

LAMBERT'S AZIMUTHAL EQUAL-AREA PROJECTION

© John Bartholomew & Son Ltd, Edinburgh

0 50 100   200   300   400   500 Statute Miles

0 50 100 200 300 400 500 600 700 800 Kilometres

1:12½M

Metres 2000 200 50 0 200 500 1000 2000 3000 4000 5000 Metres

Feet 6560 660 160 0 660 1640 3280 6560 9840 13120 16400 Feet

GALAPAGOS ISLANDS
(ARCHIPIÉLAGO DE COLÓN)
(To Ecuador)

On the same scale

LAMBERT'S ZENITHAL EQUAL-AREA PROJECTION

Main Roads
Railways

0   50 100   200   300   400   500 Statute Miles
0 50 100 200 300 400 500 600 700 800 Kilometres

1:12½

TEMPERATURE
(Actual °C)
JANUARY
SOUTHERN SUMMER

TEMPERATURE
(Actual °C)
JULY
SOUTHERN WINTER

© John Bartholomew & Son Ltd, Edinburgh

International Boundaries
State Boundaries

Metres 2000 200 50   0   200 500 1000 2000 3000 4000 5000 Metres

Feet 6560 660 160   0   660 1640 3280 6560 9840 13120 16400 Feet

M

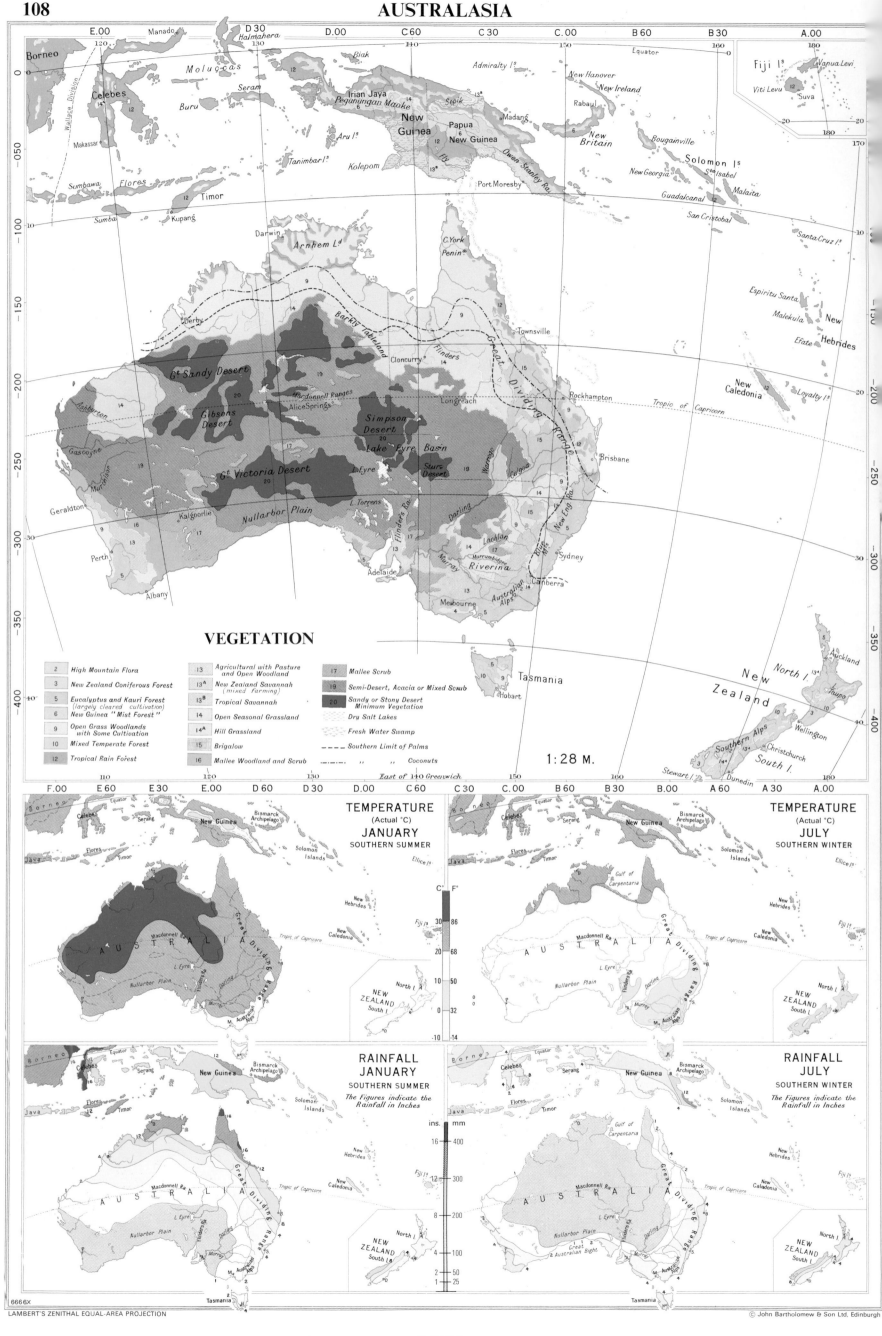

VEGETATION

2	High Mountain Flora	
3	New Zealand Coniferous Forest	
5	Eucalyptus and Kauri Forest (largely cleared cultivation)	
6	New Guinea "Mist Forest"	
9	Open Grass Woodlands with Some Cultivation	
10	Mixed Temperate Forest	
12	Tropical Rain Forest	
13	Agricultural with Pasture and Open Woodland	
13A	New Zealand Savannah (mixed farming)	
13B	Tropical Savannah	
14	Open Seasonal Grassland	
14A	Hill Grassland	
15	Brigalow	
16	Mallee Woodland and Scrub	
17	Mallee Scrub	
19	Semi-Desert, Acacia or Mixed Scrub	
20	Sandy or Stony Desert Minimum Vegetation	

Dry Salt Lakes
Fresh Water Swamp
– – – Southern Limit of Palms
" " " Coconuts

1 : 28 M.

TEMPERATURE
(Actual °C)
JANUARY
SOUTHERN SUMMER

TEMPERATURE
(Actual °C)
JULY
SOUTHERN WINTER

C° F°
30 86
20 68
10 50
0   32
-10 -14

RAINFALL
JANUARY
SOUTHERN SUMMER
The Figures indicate the Rainfall in Inches

RAINFALL
JULY
SOUTHERN WINTER
The Figures indicate the Rainfall in Inches

ins. mm
16   400
12   300
8   200
4   100
2   50
1   25

LAMBERT'S ZENITHAL EQUAL-AREA PROJECTION

© John Bartholomew & Son Ltd, Edinburgh

6666X

0   200   400   600   800 Statute Miles

1:28M

0   200   400   600   800   1000   1200 Kilometres

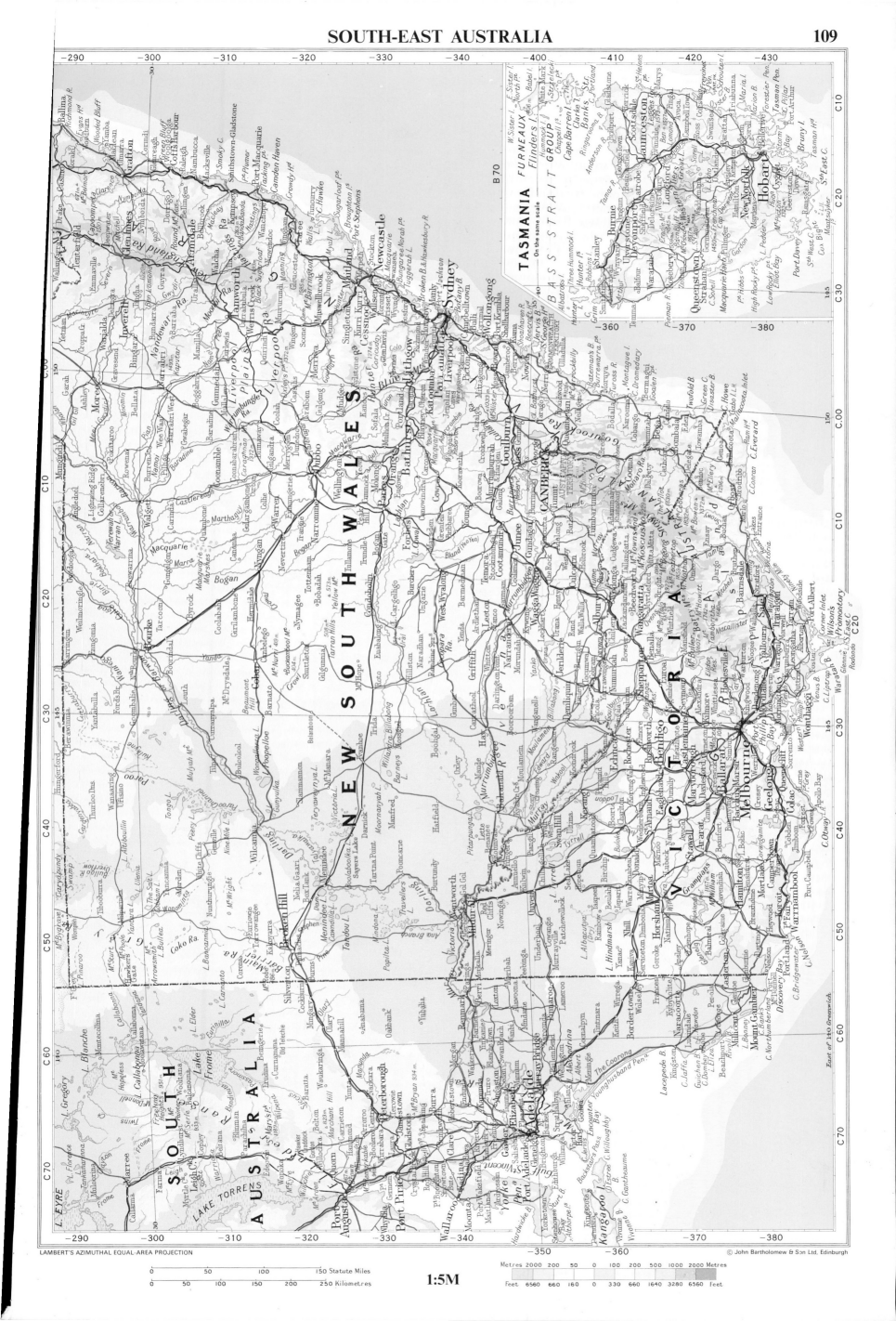

TASMANIA
FURNEAUX
On the same scale

LAMBERT'S AZIMUTHAL EQUAL-AREA PROJECTION

© John Bartholomew & Son Ltd, Edinburgh

0	50	100	150 Statute Miles
0	50	100	150	200	250 Kilometres

1:5M

Metres 2000 200 50 0 100 200 500 1000 2000 Metres
Feet 6560 660 160 0 330 660 1640 3280 6560 Feet

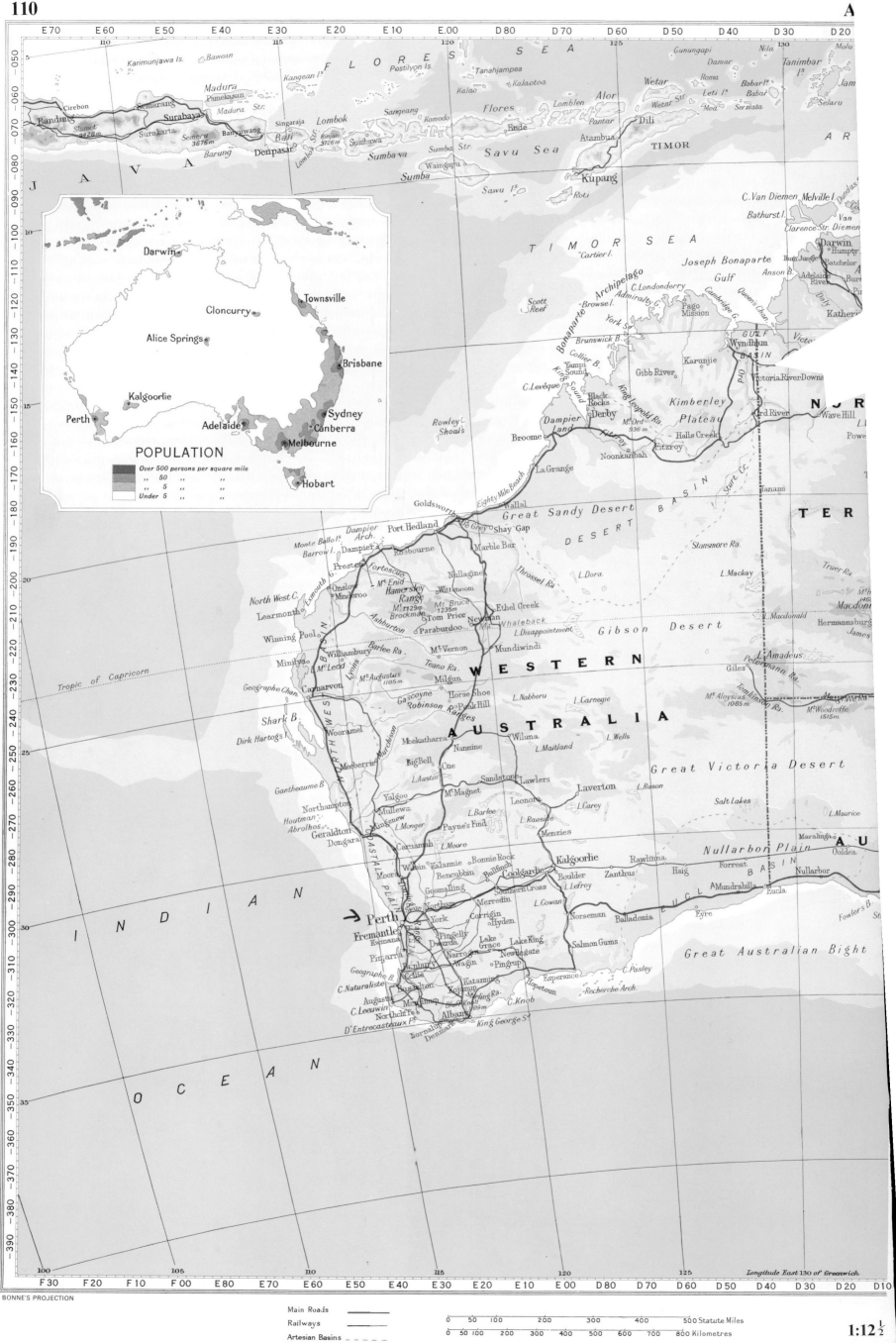

D 00   C 80   C 70   C 60   C 50   C 40   C 30   C 20   C 10   C 00   B 80   B 70   B 60   B 50   B 40

135   140   145   150   155

050 060 070 -110 -130 -140 -150 -160 -170 -180 -190 -200 -210 -220 -230 -240 -250 -260 -270 -280 -290 -300 -310 -320 -330 -340 -350 -360 -370 -380 -390

IRIAN JAYA

NEW GUINEA

PAPUA NEW GUINEA

De Jong pt.   Mapi   Digul   Kikori   Huon Pen.ª   Finschhafen   **NEW BRITAIN**

Kolepom   Komoran   Merauke   Gaima   Wabuda   Daru   Kiwai I.   Kerema   Morobe   Lae   Salamana   Wan—a.

SOLOMON ISLANDS

Buka   Bougainville I.   Kieta   Choiseul I.

SOLOMON SEA

Strachan I.   Boigu   Saibai   Great N.E. Channel   Mt. Albert Edward 3993m.   Buna   Kiriwina   Trobriand or Kiriwina Is.   Vella Lavella   Kolombangara   New Georgia

Jervis I.   Banks I.   Mt. Victoria 4073m.   Kokoda   Tufi   Goodenough I.   Fergusson I.   Woodlark I.   Rendova I.   Santa Isabel I.

Torres Strait   Thursday I.   Pr. of Wales I.   York   Somerset   Abau   Normanby I.   D'Entrecasteaux   Russel Is.

Port Moresby   Owen Stanley Ra.   Milne B.   Samarai   Louisiade   Arch.   Tagula I.   Rossel I.   Guadalcanal I.   Tulagi

Wessel¹   C. Arnhem   Duifken Pt.   **Cape York**   Weipa   C. Grenville   Rennell I.

CORAL SEA   **PACIFIC OCEAN**

Gulf of Carpentaria   Groote Eylandt   Archer   **York Peninsula**   Coen   C. Direction   Princess Charlotte B.   C. Melville   Willis Group

Roper   Limmen Bight   Musgrave   Cook's Passage   C. Flattery   Coringa Is.

Borroloola   Sir Edward Pellew Group   Mitchell River   Laura   **Cooktown**

ERN TERRITORY   Anthony Lagoon   Burketown   Mornington I.   Wellesley Is.   Walsh   Port Douglas   Mareeba   Cairns   Palm Is.   Flinder's Passage   Chesterfield Is. (Fr.)

Brunette Downs   Normanton   Atherton   Mt. Bartle Frere   Atherton Plateau   Innisfail   Tully   Cardwell   Halifax Bay   Magnetic I.

Frewena   Croydon   Georgetown   Forsayth   Ingham

McDouall Ra.   Soudan   Camooweal   Wurung   Gilberton   **Townsville**   Ayr   Bowen

Davenport Ra.   Lake Nash   Mt. Isa   Cloncurry   Julia Creek   Richmond   Hughenden   Charters Towers   Collinsville   Whitsunday I.   Hayman I.   Proserpine   Repulse B.

Mary Kathleen   Dobbyn   Prairie   Mt. Dalrymple 1277m.   Mackay   Sarina

Urandangi   Dajarra   Selwyn Ra.   Selwyn   Kynuna   Winton   L. Buchanan   Clermont   St. Lawrence   Northumberland Is.

Jervois Ra.   Boulia   Collingwood   Aramac   L. Galilee   Marlborough   C. Manifold

Arltunga   **QUEENSLAND**   Longreach   Barcaldine   Jericho   Emerald   Capricorn Channel   Heron I.

lice Springs   Bedourie   Isisford   Barcoo   Blackall   Springsure   **Rockhampton**   Yeppoon

Bundooma   L. Philippi   Monkira   Diamantina Ra.   Windorah   Jundah   Yaraka   Tambo   Gladstone

Simpson Desert   Birdsville   **AUSTRALIAN**   Adavale   Welford   Bundaberg   Tropic of Capricorn

Finke   Albunga   Yamma Yamma   Augathella   Injune   Theodore   Childers   Fraser or Sandy I.

Peera Peera   Poolanna   Clifton Hills   McGregor Ra.   **Charleville**   Morven   Mitchell   Roma   Miles   Taroom   Gayndah   Murgon   Maryborough   Hervey G.ᵗ Sandy C.

Oodnadatta   Lake Eyre Basin   Quilpie   Wyandra   Kingaroy   Gympie

SOUTH AUSTRALIA   Mt. Dutton   Warburton   L. Eyre   Sturt Range   **GREAT DIVIDING RANGE**   Darling Downs   Dalby   Cooroy   Moreton B.

William Creek   Etadunna   Cooper Cr.   Thargomindah   Cunnamulla   Goondiwindi   Toowoomba   **Brisbane**

Strangways Spr.   L. Gregory   Bollon   St. George   Warwick   Ipswich   Southport

Bopeechee   L. Blanche   Marree   Nockatunga   Dirranbandi   Stanthorpe   Tenterfield   Murwillumbah   C. Byron

Leigh Cr.   L. Callabonna   Milparinka   Wanaaring   Mungindi   Moree   Glen Innes   Casino   Lismore

Marcoola   Kingoonya   L. Frome   Bourke   Brewarrina   Barwon   Inverell   Grafton

Everard   L. Torrens   Darling   Louth   Walgett   Narrabri   Ben Lomond 1520m.   Coff's Harbour

L. Gairdner   Woomera   Wilcannia   Cobar   Coonamble   Gunnedah   Armidale   Round Mt. 1585m.

Ceduna   Gawler Range   Hawker   Cockburn   **Broken Hill**   Nyngan   Dubbo   Tamworth   Black Sugarloaf 1442m.   Kempsey   Port Macquarie

Buckleboo   Iron Knob   Menindee   Ivanhoe   Nymagee   Oxley Mt. Barrington 1372m.   C. Hawke

Kyancutta   Wyalla   Port Augusta   Peterborough   **NEW SOUTH WALES**   Parkes   Orange   Muswellbrook   Taree

Cowell   Port Pirie   Poonearie   Hillston   Condobolin   Forbes   Bathurst   Maitland   Cessnock

Eyre Pen.   Whyalla   Crystal Brook   Morgan   Hay   Young   Lithgow   **Newcastle & Port Hunter**

Cummins   Renmark   Wentworth   MURRAY RIVER   Balranald   Griffith   Cowra   Katoomba   Parramatta   Port Jackson

Port Lincoln   C. Catastrophe   Yorke Pen.   **Adelaide**   Mildura   Swan Hill   Deniliquin   Leeton   Narrandera   Junee   Wagga Wagga   Goulburn   Liverpool   Picton   **Sydney**

Investigator Str.   Victor Harbour   Murray Bridge   L. Alexandrina   Swan Hill   Aerang   Riverina   Culcairn   Nowra   **Wollongong**   Port Kembla

Kangaroo I.   Encounter Bay   Kingston   Bordertown   Nhill   Charlton   Shepparton   Wangaratta   Albury   Tumut   **CANBERRA (AUS. CAPITAL TERR.)**   Jervis B.

Beachport   Naracoorte   Horsham   **VICTORIA**   **Bendigo**   Seymour   Benalla   Mt. Bogong   Mt. Kosciusko 2229m.   Cooma   Bega

Millicent   Hamilton   Maryborough   Castlemaine   Australian Alps   Orbost   Bonitala   C. Howe

Mt. Gambier   **Ballarat**   Geelong   **Melbourne**   Warragul   Sale   Bairnsdale

Portland   Colac   Port Phillip   Traralgon   Woodside   Ninety Mile Beach

Warrnambool   C. Otway   Wonthaggi   Port Albert   Wilson's Prom.

Bass Strait   King I.   Flinders I.   Furneaux Group   Banks Str.   **TASMAN SEA**

Lord Howe I.

C. Grim   Hunter I.   C. Barren   C. Portland

Smithton   Burnie   Scottsdale   St. Marys

Queenstown   Devonport   Cradle Mt. 1545m.   Ben Lomond 1573m.   Launceston   Swansea

Strahan   **TASMANIA**   New Norfolk   Oyster B.

Macquarie Harbour   **Hobart**   Bruny I.

Franklin   South West C.   South East C.   Catamaran

D 00   C 80   C 70   C 60   C 50   C 40   C 30   C 20   C 10   C 00   B 80   B 70   B 60   B 50   B 40   B 30   B 20   B 10   B 00   A 80

135   140   145   150   155   160   165

© John Bartholomew & Son Ltd. Edinburgh

Metres 2000   200   50   Land Depression   0   200   500   1000   2000   3000 Metres

Feet 6560   660   160   0   660   1640   3280   6560   9840 Feet

International Boundaries

State Boundaries

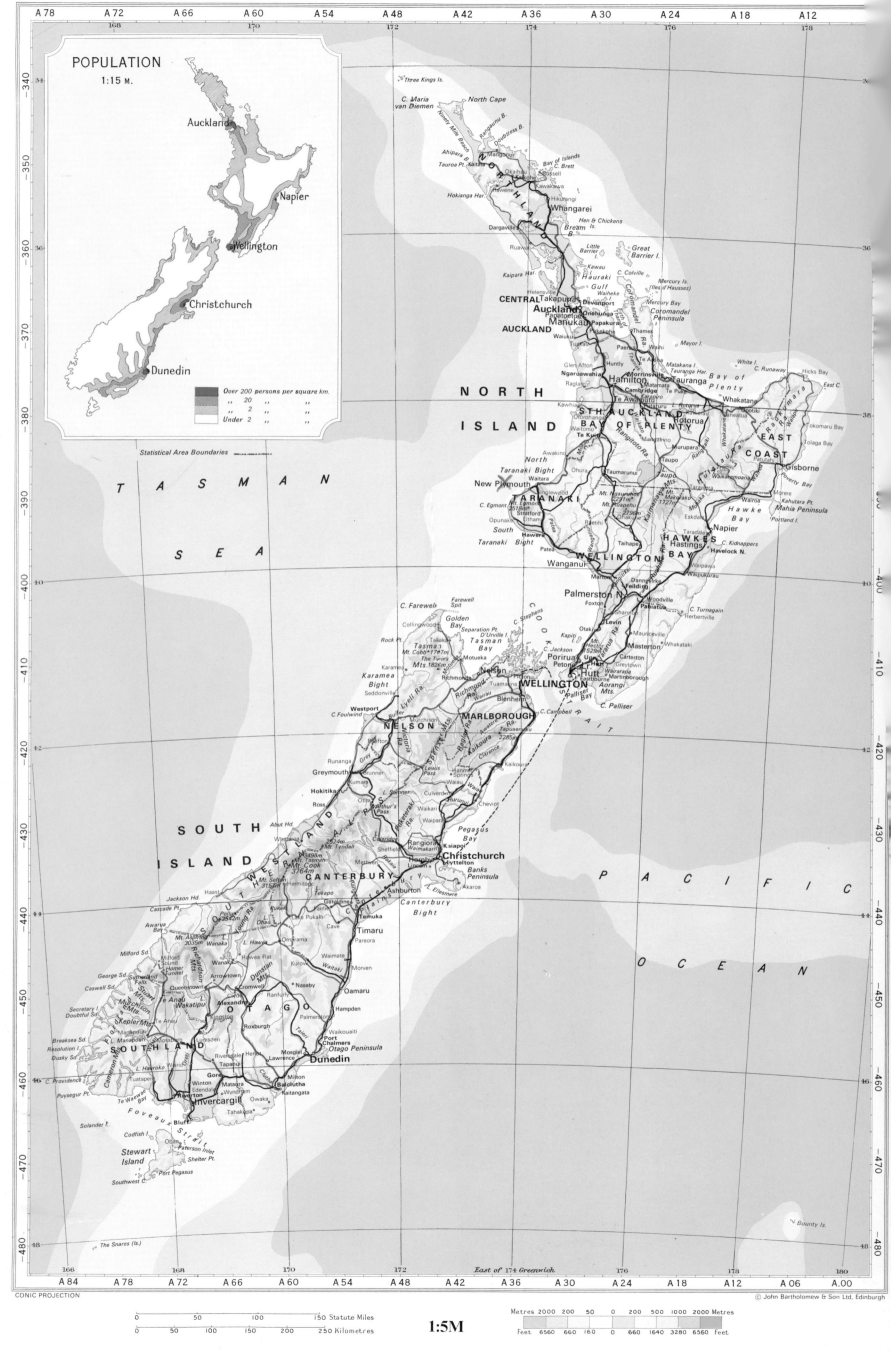

POPULATION
1:15 M.

Auckland

Napier

Wellington

Christchurch

Dunedin

Over 200 persons per square km.
„ 20 „ „
„ 2 „ „
Under 2 „ „

Statistical Area Boundaries

CONIC PROJECTION

0   50   100   150 Statute Miles
0   50   100   150   200   250 Kilometres

1:5M

Metres 2000 200 50 0 200 500 1000 2000 Metres
Feet 6560 660 160 0 660 1640 3280 6560 Feet

© John Bartholomew & Son Ltd, Edinburgh

GENERAL INDEX

For explanatory notes on the use of Index see page 1 of Atlas.

LIST OF ABBREVIATIONS

Aachen, *W. Germany* M53+507 **48**
Aagerbate, *Syria* K45+350 **76**
Aalen, *W. Germany* M30+488 **48**
Aalsmeer, *Netherlands* M62+523 **44**
Aalst (Alost), *Belgium* M66+509 **44**
Aalten, *Netherlands* M51+519 **44**
Aarau, *Switzerland* M42+474 **45**
Aarberg, *Switzerland* M46+470 **45**
Aarburg, *Switzerland* M43+473 **45**
Aardenburg, *Netherlands* M69+513 **44**
Aare, R., *Switzerland* M44+472 **45**
Aargau, canton, *Switzerland* M41+474 **45**
Aba, *Zaire* K88+036 **83**
Abacaxis, *Brazil* R82-040 **104**
Abaco I., Gt., *Bahamas, The* T13 + 263 **101**
Abaco I., Lit., *Bahamas, The* T17 + 268 **101**
Abadan, *Iran* J70+303 **74**
Abadeh, *Iran* J44+312 **75**
Abaete, *Brazil* R23-016 **105**
Abajo Mts., *Utah* V27+378 **94**
Abajo Pk., *Utah* V27+376 **98**
Abakan, *U.S.S.R.* F83+537 **63**
Abancay, *Peru* S78-137 **104**
Abarqu, *Iran* J40+311 **75**
Abashiri, *Japan* C34+440 **68**
Abashiri Bay, *Japan* C32+442 **68**
Abau, *Papua New Guinea* C09-102 **111**
Abaya L., *Ethiopia* K42+062 **83**
Abbasabad, *Iran* J52+366 **75**
Abbeville, *France* M79+501 **54**
Abbeville, *Georgia* T50+320 **97**
Abbeville, *Louisiana* U12+300 **95**
Abbeyfeale, *Ireland, Rep.* N56+524 **43**
Abbeyleix, *Ireland, Rep.* N44+529 **43**
Abbot Ice Shelf, *Antarctica* T80-730 **27**
Abbottabad, *Pakistan* H11+342 **72**
Abdul Aziz, Jebel, *Syria* K30+365 **74**
Abdulino, *U.S.S.R.* J35+537 **61**
Abeche, *Chad* L56+138 **81**
Abeele, *Belgium* M74+508 **44**
Abelessa, *Algeria* M62+226 **80**
Abengourou, *Ivory Coast* N22+068 **80**
Abeokuta, *Nigeria* M70+072 **80**
Aberaeron, *Wales* N26+522 **38**
Aberdare, *Wales* N21+517 **38**
Aberdeen, *Mississippi* T81+338 **97**
Aberdeen, *Montana* V14+450 **93**
Aberdeen, *S. Dakota* U51+455 **93**
Aberdeen, *Washington* W23+470 **92**
Aberdeen, *Scotland* N12+571 **40**
Aberdeen L., *N.-W. Terr.* U55+645 **88**
Aberfeldy, *Scotland* N23+566 **41**
Aberfoyle, *Scotland* N26+562 **41**
Abergavenny, *Wales* N18+518 **38**
Aberystwyth, *Wales* N24+524 **38**
Abha, *Saudi Arabia* K12+181 **74**
Abidjan, *Benin* N24 + 054 **80**
Abi-i-Istada L., *Afghanistan* H42+325 **75**
Abilene, *Kansas* U44+389 **95**
Abilene, *Texas* U58+324 **95**
Abingdon, *Virginia* T42+367 **97**
Abington, *Massachusetts* S65+421 **96**
Abisko, *Sweden* L66+683 **46**
Abitibi L., *Ontario* T28+488 **89**
Abitibi R., *Ontario* T40+500 **89**
Abomey, *Benin* M78 + 072 **80**
Aboyne, *Scotland* N17+571 **40**
Abqaiq, *Saudi Arabia* J61+262 **74**
Abrantes, *Portugal* N49+395 **52**
Abrets, les, *France* M57+456 **54**
Abrud, *Romania* L42+469 **58**
Abruzzi, dep., *Italy* M07+420 **56**
Abtenau, *Austria* M10+475 **48**
Abu, *India* H14+246 **70**

Abu Deleiq, *Sudan* K68+158 **81**
Abu Dhabi, *U.A.E.* J33+245 **75**
Abu ed Duhur, *Syria* K48+357 **76**
Abu el Jirdhan, *Jordan* K55+303 **76**
Abu Jifan, *Saudi Arabia* J73+246 **74**
Abu Kemal, *Syria* K24+345 **74**
Abul Abyadh I., *U.A.E.* J38+243 **75**
Abu Mombasi, *Zaire* L46+034 **82**
Abuna, *Brazil* S32-098 **104**
Abu Qurqas, *Egypt* K68+278 **81**
Abuya Myeda, mt., *Ethiopia* K30+106 **83**
Abu Zabad, *Sudan* L04+122 **81**
Abyei, *Sudan* L08+096 **81**
Abyy, *U.S.S.R.* C30+685 **63**
Abyn, *Sweden* L52+650 **46**
Acajutla, *Salvador* T88+136 **101**
Acambaro, *Mexico* U64+200 **100**
Acaponeta, *Mexico* V02+225 **100**
Acapulco, *Mexico* U59+168 **100**
Acara & R., *Brazil* R20-022 **105**
Acarigua, *Venezuela* S55+095 **104**
Acatlan, *Mexico* U49+182 **100**
Accomac, *Virginia* T04+377 **97**
Accra, *Ghana* N02+056 **80**
Accrington, *England* N14+538 **37**
Achaguas, *Venezuela* S49+075 **104**
Achao, *Chile* S81-424 **103**
Achill & I., *Ireland, Rep.* N60+539 **42**
Achinsk, *U.S.S.R.* F86+564 **63**
Achray, *Ontario* T17+459 **91**
Acklins, I., *Bahamas, The* S84 + 225 **101**
Aconcagua, mt., *Argentina* S60-325 **103**
Acores, Is., *Atlantic Ocean* P70+390 **80**
Acoyapa, *Nicaragua* T61+120 **101**
Acre & B., *Israel* K60+329 **76**
Actaeon Group, *Tuamotu*
Archipelago X05-228 **107**
Acton Vale, *Quebec* S75+457 **91**
Ada, *Minnesota* U39+473 **93**
Ada, *Oklahoma* U40+348 **95**
Adair, C., *N.-W. Territories* S68+713 **89**
Adairville, *Kentucky* T71+367 **97**
Adak, I., *Aleutian Is.* Z70+514 **99**
Adalia. *See* Antalya
Adam, *Oman* J15+223 **75**
Adama, *Ethiopia* K34+084 **83**
Adamello, mt., *Italy* M27+462 **56**
Adammaby, *New S. Wales* C08-360 **109**
Adams, *New York* T06+438 **91**
Adam's Bridge, *India-*
Sri Lanka G63+091 **70**
Adams, Mt., *Washington* W09+452 **92**
Adams, Pk., *Sri Lanka* G58+069 **70**
Adana, *Turkey* K58+370 **74**
Ada-Pazari, *Turkey* K88+408 **74**
Adare, *Ireland, Rep.* N53+525 **43**
Adare, C., *Antarctica* A55-710 **27**
Addis Ababa, *Ethiopia* K38+090 **83**
Addis Derra, *Ethiopia* K38+102 **83**
Addison, *New York* T13+421 **96**
Adelaer, C., *Greenland* Q65+610 **26**
Adelaide, *Cape Province* L22-328 **84**
Adelaide, *S. Australia* C69-350 **109**
Adelaide, I., *Antarctica* S50-670 **27**
Adelaide Pen., *N.-W. Terr.* U45-674 **88**
Adelboden, *Switzerland* M45+465 **45**
Adelie Ld., *Antarctica* C60-680 **27**
Adelong, *New South Wales* C12-354 **109**
Ademuz, *Spain* N08+401 **53**
Aden, *Yemen, South* K00 + 127 **74**
Aden, G. of, *Africa-Arabia* J60-130 **30**
Adh Dhahiriya, *Jordan* K60+314 **76**
Adhoi, *India* H27+234 **70**
Adhra, *Syria* K51+336 **76**

Adi, I., *New Guinea* D08-042 **65**
Adi Kaie, *Ethiopia* K34+146 **83**
Adilabad, *India* G67+197 **70**
Adirondack Mts., *New York* S84+444 **91**
Adi Ugri, *Ethiopia* K38+148 **83**
Admiralty G., *W. Australia* D54-142 **110**
Admiralty Is., *Pacific Ocean* C15-023 **106**
Adolfo Alsina, *Argentina* S16-371 **103**
Adoni, *India* G76+156 **70**
Adoumre, *Cameroun* M08+092 **81**
Adour R., *France* N08+434 **55**
Adra, *Spain* N19+367 **52**
Adraj, *Saudi Arabia* J55+201 **75**
Adrano, *Sicily* M01+376 **57**
Adrar, *Algeria* N02+276 **80**
Adria, *Italy* M18+451 **56**
Adrian, *Michigan* T55+419 **91**
Adriatic Sea, *Italy* L84+425 **56**
Aduwa, *Ethiopia* K36+140 **83**
Aegean Sea, *Greece* L30+385 **59**
Aegina, I., *Greece* L39+377 **59**
Aeltre, *Belgium* M69+511 **44**
Ærøskøbing, *Denmark* M27+549 **47**
Aerschot, *Belgium* M61+510 **44**
Aesch, *Switzerland* M44+475 **45**
Afferden, *Netherlands* M54+516 **44**
Affua, *Brazil* R31-004 **105**
Afghanistan, *Asia* H60+340 **75**
Afif, *Saudi Arabia* K12+239 **74**
Afogados de Ingazeira,
Brazil Q46-078 **105**
Afognak I., *Alaska* Y20+582 **99**
Afrin, *Syria* K49+365 **76**
Afula, *Israel* K58+326 **76**
Afyon, *Turkey* K87+387 **74**
Agab Workei, *Ethiopia* K48+136 **83**
Agades, *Niger* M42+168 **80**
Agadir, *Morocco* N58+304 **80**
Agartala, *India* F82+239 **71**
Agathla Pk., *Arizona* V32+368 **94**
Agattu, I., *Aleutian Is.* A40+518 **99**
Agawa, *Ontario* T57+476 **91**
Agde, *France* M69+433 **55**
Agen, *France* M86+442 **55**
Aghda, *Iran* J38+325 **75**
Agiabampo, *Mexico* V25+264 **100**
Agira, *Sicily* M03+376 **57**
Agno, *Switzerland* M37+460 **45**
Agordat, *Ethiopia* K42+154 **83**
Agra, *India* G72+272 **73**
Agram. *See* Zagreb
Agrigento, *Sicily* M08+373 **57**
Agrihan, I., *Mariana Is.* C25+180 **106**
Agrinion, *Greece* L52+387 **59**
Agropoli, *Italy* M00+404 **57**
Agua Clara, *Brazil* R47-204 **105**
Aguadas, *Colombia* T03+056 **104**
Aguadilla, *Puerto Rico* S42+185 **101**
Aguadulce, *Panama* T33+082 **101**
Agua Limpa, *Brazil* R26-042 **105**
Agua Prieta, *Mexico* V27+312 **100**
Aguaray, *Argentina* S22-222 **103**
Aguascalientes, *Mexico* U74+218 **100**
Agudo, *Spain* N29+390 **52**
Agudos, *Brazil* R24-224 **105**
Aguilar, *Spain* N28+375 **52**
Aguilar de Campós, *Spain* N26+428 **52**
Aguilas, *Spain* N10+374 **53**
Aguirre, B., *Argentina* S35-550 **103**
Agulhas, *Cape Province* L60-348 **84**
Agusta, *W. Australia* E29-340 **110**
Ahar, *Iran* J77+385 **74**
Ahmadnagar, *India* H01+191 **70**
Ahmadpur East, *Pakistan* H23+291 **72**

Ahmadabad, *India* H14 + 230 **70**
Ahraura, *India* G42+250 **73**
Ahtopol, *Bulgaria* L13+421 **58**
Ahuachapan, *Salvador* T89+140 **101**
Ahualulco, *Mexico* U85+207 **100**
Ahus, *Sweden* M04+559 **47**
Ahvaz, *Iran* J67+313 **74**
Ahvenanmaa, *Finland* L60+603 **47**
Ahwar, *Yemen, South* J80+ 135 **74**
Aigle, *Switzerland* M48+463 **45**
Aihunkiu, *China* D45+489 **64**
Aijal, *India* F73+239 **71**
Aikawa, *Japan* C71+380 **68**
Ailsa Craig, I., *Scotland* N31+552 **41**
Aim, *U.S.S.R.* D06+588 **63**
Ain, dep., *France* M56+461 **54**
Ain Gallaka, *Chad* L70+180 **81**
Ain Safra, *Mauritania* N72+194 **80**
Ainsworth, *Nebraska* U60+426 **95**
Aintree, *England* N18+535 **37**
Aira, *Ethiopia* K58+090 **83**
Airdrie, *Scotland* N24+558 **41**
Aire, *France* N02+437 **55**
Aire R., *England* N07+537 **37**
Airolo, *Switzerland* M38+465 **45**
Aishihik L., *Yukon* X12+612 **88**
Aisne, dep., *France* M68+495 **54**
Aitkin, *Minnesota* U22+465 **93**
Aiun, El, *Western Sahara* N80 + 270 **80**
Aix, *France* M57+435 **55**
Aix, Mt., *Washington* W07+469 **92**
Aix-la-Chapelle. *See* Aachen
Aiyina, I., *Greece* L39+377 **59**
Aiyion, *Greece* L48+383 **59**
Aizpute, *Latvia* L50+567 **47**
Aizuwakamatsu, *Japan* C60+375 **68**
Ajaccio & G. d', *Corsica* M38+419 **57**
Ajaigarh, *India* G58+249 **73**
Ajanta, *India* G85+205 **70**
Ajanta Ra. *See* Sahiadriparvat
Ajibba, *Saudi Arabia* K04+273 **74**
Ajigasawa, *Japan* C58+408 **68**
Ajlun, *Jordan* K56+323 **76**
Ajmer, *India* H02+263 **70**
Ajodhya, (Ayodhya), *India* G46+267 **73**
Ajoewa, *Surinam* R72+026 **105**
Akalkot, *India* G83+176 **70**
Akan Nat. Park, *Japan* C36+435 **68**
Akanthou, *Cyprus* K67+354 **76**
Akaoka, *Japan* D08+335 **68**
Akarnania and Aitolia,
Greece L51+388 **59**
Akaroa, *New Zealand* A42-437 **112**
Akashi, *Japan* D00+347 **68**
Akbarpur, *India* G60+263 **73**
Akcha, *Afghanistan* H53+369 **75**
Akhdhar, Jebel, *Oman* J14+232 **75**
Akhisar, *Turkey* L13+389 **74**
Akhterine, *Syria* K46+365 **76**
Akhtyrka, *Ukraine* K61+504 **60**
Akimiski I., *N.-W. Terr.* T38+532 **89**
Akita, *Japan* C59+397 **68**
Akkrum, *Netherlands* M55+530 **44**
Aklavik, *N.-W. Territories* W86+689 **88**
Ako, *Nigeria* M06+104 **82**
Akola, *India* G77+207 **70**
Akpatok I., *North-West*
Territories S49+603 **89**
Akra, Jebel el, *Turkey* K54+359 **74**
Akron, *Colorado* U80+402 **94**
Akron, *Ohio* T39+411 **91**
Akrotiri Pen., *Crete* L35+356 **59**
Aksaray, *Turkey* K66+383 **74**
Aksehir, *Turkey* K82+383 **74**

Aksha, *U.S.S.R.* E40+503 63
Aksı, *Estonia* L20+585 47
Akti, *Greece* L35+403 59
Aktyubinsk, *Kazakh.* J17+504 62
Akure, *Nigeria* M58+072 80
Akureyri, *Iceland* P19+657 46
Akyab, *Burma* F73+202 71
Alabama, state, *U.S.A.* T70+326 99
Alabama R., *Alabama* T74+313 99
Alaejos, *Spain* N31+413 52
Alagoa de Baixo, *Brazil* Q44-082 105
Alagoas, *Brazil* Q35-096 105
Alagoinhas, *Brazil* Q50-122 105
Alagon, *Spain* N07+417 53
Alaja, *Syria* K55+358 76
Alajuela, *Costa Rica* T55+100 101
Alakurtii, *U.S.S.R.* K85+672 62
Alakpa, *Nigeria* M64+086 82
Al' Ala, *Saudi Arabia* K41+267 74
Alameda, *California* W14+377 92
Alameda, *Saskatchewan* U74+496 88
Alamogordo, *New Mexico* V06+330 94
Alamogorda Res., *New Mex.* U87+346 94
Alamos, *Mexico* V24+271 100
Alamosa, *Colorado* V06+374 94
Åland, *See Ahvenanmeri*
Ålands Hav. *Sweden-Finland* L64+600 47
Alapaevsk, *U.S.S.R.* H80+578 61
Alasehir, *Turkey* L09+384 74
Ala Shan, *China* F10+394 64
Al Ashkharah, *Oman* J03+219 75
Alaska, state, *U.S.A.* Y00+630 99
Alaska, G. of, *Alaska* X60+586 99
Alaska Pen., *Alaska* Y60+560 99
Alaska Ra., *Alaska* Y25+610 99
Alaska Highway, *Alaska-Can.* X38+632 88
Alatyr, *U.S.S.R.* J80+548 61
Alavus, *Finland* L38+626 46
Alawoona, *S. Australia* C57-348 109
Al 'Ayn, *Oman* J31+196 75
Alaysky Khrebet., *Kirgiz* H20+400 62
Alazeiskoye Plat., *U.S.S.R.* C10+680 63
Albacete, *Spain* N11+390 53
Alba de Tormes, *Spain* N33+408 52
Albaida, *Spain* N03+389 53
Alba Iulia, *Romania* L39+461 58
Albanel L., *Quebec* S78+511 90
Albania, *S. Europe* L60+410 51
Albany, *Alabama* T70+342 99
Albany, *Georgia* T55+315 97
Albany, *Kentucky* T61+367 97
Albany, *Missouri* U26+403 95
Albany, *New York* S83+426 91
Albany, *Oregon* W19+446 92
Albany, *W. Australia* E13-350 110
Albany R., *Ontario* T52+514 89
Albarracin, *Spain* N09+405 53
Al Bayda', *Libya* L49+326 81
Albemarle Sd., *N. Carolina* T08+360 97
Albergaria a-Velha, *Portugal* N50+407 52
Alberique, *Spain* N03+391 53
Albert, *New Brunswick* S28+457 90
Albert L., *Zaire* K86+014 83
Albert, Mt., *Quebec* S37+489 90
Alberta, prov., *Canada* - 88
Alberta Mt., *Alberta* V75+526 88
Albert Edward, Mt.,
  Papua New Guinea C18-084 111
Albert Lea, *Minnesota* U20+437 93
Alberton, *Prince Edward I.* S24+468 90
Alberton, *Victoria* C20-386 109
Albertville, *France* M52+457 54
Albi, *France* M77+439 55
Albia, *Iowa* U17+410 95
Albina, *Surinam* R56+054 105
Albion, *Michigan* T59+423 91
Albion, *New York* T19+432 91
Albocácer, *Spain* N00+403 53
Alborg, *Denmark* M30+570 47
Albufeira, *Portugal* N49+371 52
Albufera de Mexcaltitlan, *Mex.* V04+220 100
Albuñol, *Spain* N19+368 52
Albuquerque, *New Mexico* V10+350 94
Alburquerque, *Spain* N42+392 52
Albury, *New South Wales* C19-360 109
Alcacer do Sal, *Portugal,* N51+384 52
Alcala de Chisvert, *Spain* M99+403 53
Alcala de Henares, *Spain* N20+405 52
Alcamo, *Sicily* M12+380 57
Alcañices, *Spain* N38+417 52
Alcañiz, *Spain* N01+410 53
Alcantara, *Brazil* Q87-024 105
Alcantara, *Spain* N41+397 52
Alcantarilla, *Spain* N07+380 53
Alcaraz, *Spain* N15+387 53
Alcázar de San Juan, *Spain* N19+394 52
Alcazarquivir, (Ksar-el-Kebir,)
  Morocco N36+350 80
Alcira, *Spain* N03+391 53
Alcobaça, *Portugal* N54+395 52
Alcolea del Pinar, *Spain* N15+410 53
Alcoutim, *Portugal* N45+375 52
Alcoy, *Spain* N03+387 53
Aldabra Is., *Indian Ocean* J76-093 77
Aldama, *Chihuahua, Mexico* V06+288 100
Aldama, *Tamaulipas, Mexico* U49+229 100
Aldan & R., *U.S.S.R.* D58+588 63
Aldeburgh, *England* M80+522 39
Aldeia Cumare, *Brazil* R34-109 105
Alderney I., *Channel Is.* N13+497 54
Aldershot, *England* N05+512 39
Al Dola, *Yemen, South* J85 + 146 74
Aledo, *Illinois* U04+412 95
Alegrete, *Brazil* R65-298 103
Aleih, *Lebanon* K56+338 76
Alejandro Selkirk, I., *Chile* T35-338 107
Aleksandrov, *U.S.S.R.* K38+564 60
Aleksandrovsk Sakhalinskiy,
  U.S.S.R. C46+510 63
Aleksandry Zemlya, *Arctic Oc.* K00+808 62
Alekseyeka, *Kazakh.* H25+520 62
Alemquer, *Brazil* R59-019 105
Alencon, *France* M89+484 54
Alenquer, *Portugal* N54+390 52
Aleppo, *Syria* K47+362 76
Ales, *France* M65+441 55
Aleshki, *U.S.S.R.* K19+516 61
Alessandria, *Italy* M38+449 56
Ålesund, *Norway* M53+625 46
Aletschhorn, mt., *Switzerland* M42+465 45

Aleutian Is., *Bering Sea* A00+512 99
Aleutian Ra., *Alaska* Y40+580 26
Alexander Arch., *Alaska* X05+575 99
Alexander I., *Antarctica* S60-700 27
Alexandra, *New Zealand* A63-452 112
Alexandra, *Victoria* C26-372 109
Alexandretta. *See Iskenderun*
Alexandria, *Egypt* L00+310 81
Alexandria, *Louisiana* U14+312 95
Alexandria, *Minnesota* U32+459 93
Alexandria, *Ontario* S88+453 91
Alexandria, *Virginia* T13+388 96
Alexandrina, L., *S. Aust.* C65-355 109
Alexandroúpolis, *Greece* L25+408 59
Alexveeka, *U.S.S.R.* J82+522 61
Aleysk, *U.S.S.R.* G44+525 62
Al Falluja, *Iraq* K07+334 74
Alfaro, *Spain* N11+422 53
Alfred, *Maine* S64+435 96
Alfredo Chaves, *Brazil* R40-290 103
Alga, *Kazakh* J16+498 62
Älgård, *Norway* M55+588 47
Algauer Alpen, *Austria, etc.* M29+474 48
Algeciras, *Spain* N33+361 52
Algeria, *N.-W. Africa* M70+280 80
Al Ghail, *Yemen* K00+161 74
Alghero, *Sardinia* M40+405 57
Algiers (El Djezair), *Algeria* M72+366 55
Algoa B., *Cape Province* L24-338 84
Algoma, *Ontario* T47+462 91
Algoma, *Wisconsin* T75+446 91
Algona, *Iowa* U26+430 95
Algonquin Park, *Ontario* T22+456 91
Alguada Reef, *Burma* F65+158 71
Alhama de Granada, *Spain* N24+370 52
Al Harsha, *Saudi Arabia* J52+196 75
Al Hauta, *Yemen, South* J70 + 159 74
Al Hillah, *Iraq* K03+325 74
Alia, *Sicily* M08+378 57
Aliabad, *Iran* J50+366 75
Aliaga, *Spain* N04+407 53
Alibag, *India* H13+187 70
Alicante, *Spain* N03+384 53
Alice, *Texas* U48+278 94
Alice Springs, *N. Terr., Aust.* D06-237 111
Aliceville, *Alabama* T80+331 95
Alicudi, I., *Italy* M04+386 57
Aliganj, *India* G65+275 73
Aligarh, *India* G73+278 72
Ali Khel, *Afghanistan* H32+340 75
Alimnia, I., *Greece* L13+363 59
Aling Kangri, *Tibet* G55+328 70
Alingsäs, *Sweden* M15+579 47
Alipur Duar, *India* G02+265 73
Alipur, *Pakistan* H24+294 72
Alipura, *India* G64+252 73
Alirajpur, *India* H03+222 70
Alivérion, *Greece* L36+385 59
Al Jesab, *Saudi Arabia* J86+150 74
Aljustrel, *Portugal* N49+379 52
Alken, *Belgium* M58+509 44
Al Khubba, *Saudi Arabia* J45+222 75
Alkmar, *Netherlands* M61+526 44
Allahabad, *India* G49+254 73
Allanmyo, *Burma* F58+194 71
Allard, *Montana* U34+283 68
Allariz, *Spain* N47+422 52
Allata, *Ethiopia* K38+066 83
Allaykha, *U.S.S.R.* C15+708 63
Alle, *Belgium* M60+498 44
Allegan, *Michigan* T65+426 91
Alleghany Mts., *U.S.A.* T41+370 99
Allegheny R., *Penn., etc.* T23+420 96
Allen, Bog of, *Ireland, Rep.* N43+534 43
Allen L., *Ireland, Rep.* N48+541 42
Allenby Bridge, *Jordan* K57+319 76
Allende, *Mexico* V03+268 100
Allentown, *Pennsylvania* T03+406 96
Alleppey, *India* G82+096 70
Alliance, *Nebraska* U77+422 94
Alliance, *Ohio* T37+409 91
Allier, dep. *France* M73+464 54
Allier, R., *France* M69+453 54
Alliston, *Ontario* T29+442 91
Alloa, *Scotland* N23+561 41
All Pines, *Belize* T80+168 101
Allumette I., *Quebec* T12+458 91
Alma, *Michigan* T58+434 91
Alma, *New Brunswick* S29+456 90
Alma Ata, *Kazakh.* G78+431 62
Almaden, *Spain* N29+388 52
Almagro, *Spain* N22+389 52
Almansa, *Spain* N07+389 53
Al Mat, *Iraq.* K28+330 74
Almazán, *Spain* N15+415 53
Almeirim, *Brazil* R45-015 105
Almeirim, *Portugal* N52+392 52
Almelo, *Netherlands* M50+524 44
Almeria & Gulf, *Spain* N09+369 53
Al'met'yevsk, *U.S.S.R.* J60+547 61
Almirante, *Panama* T44+094 101
Almiropótamos, *Greece* L35+383 59
Almiros, *Greece* L43+392 59
Almodôvar, *Portugal* N48+375 52
Almodôvar, *Spain* N25+388 52
Almond R., *Scotland* N21+564 41
Almont, *N. Dakota* U69+467 93
Almonte, *Ontario* T07+452 91
Almora, *India* G62+296 73
Almorox, *Spain* N26+402 52
Almudebar, *Spain* N04+421 53
Almunia de Doña Godina, la,
  Spain N08+415 53
Al Musayyib, *Iraq* K04+329 74
Al Muwaila, *Saudi Arabia* K57+277 74
Alness, *Scotland* N26+577 40
Alnwick, *England* N10+554 37
Alocèn, *Spain* N17+405 53
Aloja, *Latvia* L31+578 47
Alon, *Burma* F59+221 71
Alor. *See Iliodhrómia, I.*
Alor, I., *Indonesia* D60-084 65
Alora, *Spain* N28+368 52
Alor Setar, *Malaya* F28+062 69
Alost, *Belgium* M66+509 44
Aloysius, Mt., *W. Australia* D43-260 110
Alpena, *Michigan* T51+451 91
Alpes-Maritimes, dep., *Fr.* M48+438 55
Alphen, *Netherlands* M62+521 44
Alpine, *Texas* U83+304 98
Alps, mts., *Cent. Europe* M42+460 50

Al Qatrun, *Libya* M02+250 81
Al Qayyula, *Iraq* K11+359 74
Al Qunfidhah, *Saudi Arabia* K23+192 74
Al Qurnah, *Iraq* J75+310 74
Als, I., *Denmark* M30+549 47
Al Selail, *Saudi Arabia* K00+194 74
Alsten, *Norway* M15+660 46
Alston, *England* N15+548 37
Alsunga, *Latvia* L51+570 47
Alta Gracia, *Argentina* S26-316 103
Altagracia, *Venezuela* S69+107 105
Altagracia de Orituco, *Venez.* S38+099 104
Altai, Mts., *Central Asia* G20+505 62
Altamachi, *Bolivia* S38-167 104
Altamaha R., *Georgia* T43+318 99
Altamira, *Brazil* R44-032 105
Altamura, *Italy* L80+408 57
Altan Bulag, *Mongolia* E81+503 63
Altar, *Mexico* V40+307 100
Altata, *Mexico* V18+246 100
Altdorf, *Switzerland* M38+469 45
Altea, *Spain* N00+386 53
Altenburg, *E. Germany* M16+510 48
Altin Kopru, *Iraq* K05+358 74
Altmark, *E. Germany* M21+527 48
Alto Molocue, *Mozambique* K44-156 83
Alton, *Illinois* U01+390 95
Alton, *Missouri* U09+367 97
Altona, *Germany* M30+535 48
Altona, *New York* S82+449 91
Altoona, *Pennsylvania* T21+405 96
Alturas, *California* W03+415 92
Altus, *Oklahoma* U56+346 95
Altyn Tagh, *China* G30+380 30
Al Ugla, *Saudi Arabia* K43+258 74
Al 'Uj, *Saudi Arabia* J66+228 74
Alüksne, *Latvia* L18+574 47
Alula, *Somalia* J56+118 83
Alumine, *Argentina* S66-392 103
Alupka, *U.S.S.R.* K65+444 60
Alushta, *U.S.S.R.* K63+446 60
Alva, *Oklahoma* U52+368 95
Alvarado, *Mexico* U35+188 100
Alvear, *Argentina* S22-352 103
Älvesta, *Sweden* M03+569 47
Alvho, *Sweden* M01+615 47
Alvin, *Texas* U32+294 95
Alvito, *Portugal* N48+383 52
Alvord, L., *Oregon* V82+424 92
Alwar, *India* G81+275 72
Alward, *New Brunswick* S33+462 90
Alyab, *Sudan* K68+172 81
Alyth, *Scotland* N19+566 41
Alytus, *Lithuania* L36+544 47
Amadeus L., *N. Terr., Aust.* D25-246 110
Amadi, *Sudan* K88+056 81
Amadiyah, *Iraq* K10+371 74
Amadjuak, *N.-W. Territories* S75+641 89
Amadjuak L., *N.-W. Terr.* S65+648 89
Amakusa Nada, *Japan* D32+325 68
Amål, *Sweden* M14+591 47
Amalfi, *Italy* M03+407 57
Amalias, *Greece* L52+378 59
Amami Gunto, *Japan* D34+283 68
Amanalco, *Mexico* U60+192 100
Amantea, *Italy* L84+392 57
Amapa, *Brazil* R34+020 105
Amapala, *Honduras* T76+133 101
Amarah, *Iraq* J77+320 74
Amarante, *Brazil* Q77-063 105
Amarapura, *Burma* F53+218 71
Amaravti, *India* G73+210 70
Amargosa, *Brazil* Q59-130 105
Amarillo, *Texas* U68+352 94
Amarracão, *Brazil* Q70-030 105
Amasra, *Turkey* K74+418 74
Amasya, *Turkey* K55+406 74
Amatique, G. de, *Guatemala* T82+160 100
Amatitlan, *Guatemala* U04+145 100
Amazon, Mths. of the, *Brazil* R30+006 105
Amazonas, R., *Brazil* R53-020 105
Amb, *Pakistan* H12+343 72
Ambala, *India* G79+304 72
Ambam, *Cameroun* M22+024 82
Ambar, *Iran* J06+318 75
Ambarchik, *U.S.S.R.* B15+697 63
Ambato, *Ecuador* T22-013 104
Ambato Boéni, *Madagascar* J80-164 83
Amberg, *Germany* M18+494 48
Ambergris Cay, *Bahamas, The* S70 + 212 101
Ambergris Cay, *Belize* T78+180 101
Ambérieu, *France* M58+460 54
Ambert, *France* M68+455 54
Ambikapur, *India* G41+231 73
Ambilobe, *Madagascar* J66-132 83
Ambleside, *England* N18+544 37
Amblève, *Belgium* M55+504 44
Ambohimahasoa, *Madagascar* J78-212 83
Ambon, I., *Indonesia* D41-037 65
Ambositra, *Madagascar* J76-206 83
Ambrim, I., *New Hebrides* A67+169 106
Ambriz, *Angola* M10-080 82
Ambrizete, *Angola* M12-074 82
Amchitka, I., *Aleutian Is.* A05+508 99
Amd, *Yemen, South* J72 + 154 74
Amderma, *U.S.S.R.* H82+698 62
Ameca, *Mexico* U85+205 100
Ameland I., *Netherlands* M55+534 44
Amelia, *Italy* M16+426 56
Amelia, *Virginia* T18+374 97
American Falls, *Utah* V47+428 94
American Fork, *Utah* V41+404 94
Americus, *Georgia* T56+320 99
Amerongen, *Netherlands* M57+520 44
Amersfoort, *Netherlands* M58+522 44
Amersham, *England* N04+517 39
Ames, *Iowa* U22+420 95
Amesbury, *Massachusetts* S65+429 96
Amethi, *India* G49+262 73
Amfíklia. *Greece* L44+387 59
Amfilokhia, *Greece* L53+389 59
Amga & R., *U.S.S.R.* D18+610 63
Amgu, *U.S.S.R.* C74+457 63
Amherst, *Burma* F45+160 71
Amherst, *Massachusetts* S75+429 96
Amherst, *Nova Scotia* S25+458 90
Amherst I., *Ontario* T10+441 91
Amherstburg, *Ontario* T49+422 91
Amiens, *France* M76+499 54

Amik Lake, *Ontario* T28+456 91
Amindivi I., *Indian Oc.* H14+110 70
Amingaon, *India* F79+263 71
Aminuis, *S.-W. Africa* L64-236 84
Amirante Is., *Indian Ocean* J40-060 77
Amla, *Saudi Arabia* K11+206 74
Amlah, *Saudi Arabia* J89+173 74
Amlwch, *Wales* N26+534 38
Amm Adam, *Sudan* K54+164 81
Amman, *Jordan* K54+319 76
Ammanford, *Wales* N24+518 38
Amol, *Iran* J46+364 75
Amorgós, I., *Greece* L24+372 59
Amos, *Quebec* T18+488 89
Amoy. *See Hsiamen.*
Amparo, *Brazil* R10-225 105
Amqui, *Quebec* S44+485 90
Amraho, *Sudan* K78+186 81
Amran, *Yemen* K06+157 74
Amreli, *India* H23+214 70
Amriswil, *Switzerland* M34+475 45
Amritsar, *India* H01+316 72
Amroha, *India* G70+286 73
Amstelveen, *Netherlands* M61+523 44
Amsterdam, *Netherlands* M60+524 44
Amsterdam, *New York* S85+429 96
Amsterdam, I., *Indian Ocean* G75-380 77
Am Timan, *Chad* L60+110 81
Amu Darya, *Turkmen* H75+400 62
Amund Rngnes I.,
  North-West Territories U45+782 88
Amundsen G., *N.-W. Terr.* W10+706 88
Amundsen Sea, *Antarctica* V20-720 27
Amur, R., *U.S.S.R. - China* D60+528 63
Amyun, *Lebanon* K55+343 76
An, *Burma* F66+198 71
Anabama, *S. Australia* C59-328 109
Anabta, *Jordan* K59+323 76
Anaconda, *Montana* V48+461 92
Anadarko, *Oklahoma* U48+350 95
Anadyr & R., *U.S.S.R.* A15+645 63
Anadyrskiy Zaliv, *U.S.S.R.* Z80+640 63
Anáfi. I., *Greece* L25+364 59
Anah, *Iraq* K18+345 74
Anai, *Libya* M20+240 81
Anaimalai Hills, *India* G80+106 70
Anaiza, *Saudi Arabia* K05+262 74
Anakapalle, *India* G42+177 71
Analalava, *Madagascar* J74-148 83
Anama. *Brazil* S08-035 104
Anambas Kep., *Indonesia* E84+030 65
Anamizu, *Japan* C78+372 68
Anamosa, *Iowa* U08+422 95
Anandpur, *India* G81+312 72
Anantapur, *India* G74+146 70
Anar, *Iran* J28+309 75
Anarak, *Iran* J38+333 75
Anardarra, *Afghanistan* H80+328 75
Añatolia, *Turkey* K80+390 74
Anatuya, *Argentina* S17-284 103
Anchorage, *Alaska* Y00+612 99
Anchuras, *Spain* N29+395 52
Ancohuma, mt., *Bolivia* S51-160 104
Ancon, *Peru* T14-118 104
Ancona, *Italy* M09+435 56
Ancud, *Chile* S82-418 103
And Fd., *Norway* L83+692 46
Andacolla, *Argentina* S64-371 103
Andalgala, *Argentina* S38-275 103
Andalsnes, *Norway* M44+626 46
Andaman Is. and Sea,
  Bay of Bengal F65+124 71
Andeer, *Switzerland* M33+466 45
Andelfingen, *Switzerland* M38+476 45
Andenne, *Belgium* M59+505 44
Andermatt, *Switzerland* M38+466 45
Anderson, *Indiana* T64+401 91
Anderson, *S. Carolina* T46+345 97
Anderson R., *N.-W. Terr.* W40+684 88
Andes, Cord. de los,
  South America S70-429 103
Andevoranto, *Madagascar* J66-189 83
Andhra Pradesh, *India* G70+167 70
Andikithira, I., *Greece* L40+358 59
Andimilos, I., *Greece* L35+368 59
Andiparos, I., *Greece* L30+370 59
Andizhan, *Uzbek* H15+409 62
Andkhui, *Afghanistan* H59+369 75
Andoas Nuevo, *Ecuador* T11-023 104
Andorra & rep., *Pyrenees* M81+425 53
Andover, *England* N09+512 39
Andover, *Massachusetts* S67+427 96
Andover, *S. Dakota* U47+454 93
Andøya, *Norway* L86+691 46
Andrade, *Mozambique* K60-186 84
Andreanof Is., *Aleutian Is.* Z73+513 99
Andreas, C., *Cyprus* K62+357 76
Andreyevka, *Ukraine* K57+488 60
Andria, *Italy* L83+412 57
Andriba, *Madagascar* J78-176 83
Andritsaina, *Greece* L45+374 59
Andros I., *Bahamas, The* T18 + 244 101
Andros, I., *Greece* L31+378 59
Androscoggin R., *Maine* S66+444 90
Anegada, B., *Argentina* S10-402 103
Anegada, I., *Virgin Is.* S26+188 101
Aneiza, Jebel, *Iraq* K34+322 74
Anelo, *Argentina* S53-383 103
Aneta, *N. Dakota* U48+477 93
Aney, *Niger* M14+192 81
Angalê, *Cent. Afr. Rep.* L54+098 81
Angangueo, *Mexico* U62+195 100
Angaston, *S. Australia* C66-345 109
Angel Fall, *Venezuela* S15+056 104
Angel de la Guarda, I., *Mex.* V50+292 100
Angelholm, *Sweden* M13+562 47
Angemuk, mt., *New Guinea* C70+036 65
Angers, *France* N04+475 54
Angikuni L., *N.-W. Terr.* U60+628 88
Angkor, *Khmer* F06+134 69
Angledool, *New S. Wales* C12-291 109
Anglesey, I., *Wales* N27+533 38
Angliers, *Quebec* T25+475 91
Angmagssalik, *Greenland* Q55+660 26
Angol, *Chile* S76-299 103
Angola, *New York* T24+426 96
Angola, *W. Africa* L76-100 83
Angora. *See Ankara*
Angoulême, *France* M89+456 54
Angoumois, prov., *France* M89+459 54
Angra, *Brazil* Q86-229 105

Index

Anguilla, I., *Leeward Is.* S18+183 **101**
Angul, *India* G30+208 **71**

Anhalt, *Germany* M18+517 **48**
Anholt, I., *Denmark* M20+567 **47**
Anhwei, prov., *China* E18+320 **66**
Animas Ra., *New Mexico* V22+316 **94**
Anina, *Romania* L49+451 **58**
Anita, *Montana* V18+459 **93**
Anjengo, *India* G80+087 **70**
Anjou, prov., *France* N03+473 **54**
Anjouan I., *Comora Is.* K04-122 **83**
Anjozorobe, *Madagascar* J74-184 **83**
Ankacho, *U.S.S.R.* E72+632 **63**
Ankang, *China* E65+327 **66**
Ankara, *Turkey* K73+399 **74**
Anking (Hwaining), *China* E17+305 **67**
Ankober, *Ethiopia* K30+094 **83**
Ankwo, *China* E28+384 **66**
Anlier, *Belgium* M56+498 **44**
Anlu, *China* E37+313 **66**
Anlu. *See* Chungsiang
Ann C., *Antarctica* J55-660 **27**
Ann, C., *Massachusetts* S63+427 **96**
Anna, *Illinois* T85+374 **97**
Anna, *U.S.S.R.* K27+514 **61**
Annai, *Guyana* R85+039 **104**
An Najaf, *Iraq* K04+320 **74**
Annam, *Vietnam* E80+174 **69**
Annan & R., *Scotland* N20+550 **41**
Annapolis, *Brazil* R24-164 **105**
Annapolis, *Maryland* T09+390 **96**
Annapolis, *Nova Scotia* S33+447 **90**
Annapurna, Mt., *Nepal* G38+285 **71**
Ann Arbor, *Michigan* T52+423 **91**
Annecy & L. d', *France* M53+459 **54**
Anniston, *Alabama* T65+336 **97**
Annobon I., *See* Pagalu
Annonay, *France* M62+452 **55**
Annuello, *Victoria* C43-348 **109**
An Numas, *Saudi Arabia* K16+193 **74**
Anoka, *Minnesota* U22+452 **93**
Anole, *Somalia* K18-008 **83**
Ano Viannos, *Crete* L27+350 **59**
Anpehi, *China* E65+410 **66**
Ansariya, Jebel el, *Syria* K53+356 **76**
Ansbach, *W. Germany* M27+493 **48**
Anshan, *China* D75+412 **64**
Anshun, *China* E84+263 **67**
Ansi, *China* F54+407 **64**
Ansin, *China* E25+389 **66**
Anson B., *N. Terr., Aust.* D29-134 **110**
Ansongo, *Mali* M88+156 **80**
Ansonia, *Connecticut* S78+413 **96**
Anstruther, *Scotland* N16+562 **41**
Anta, *Peru* S74-134 **104**
Antakya (Antioch), *Turkey* K53+362 **76**
Antalo, *Ethiopia* K32+132 **83**
Antalya, *Turkey* K86+369 **74**
Antalya, G. of, *Turkey* K84+367 **74**
Antarctic Peninsula, *Antarctica* S25-660 **27**
Antelope I., *Utah* V43+410 **94**
Antequera, *Paraguay* R73-240 **103**
Antequera, *Spain* N27+370 **52**
Anthony, *Kansas* U48+371 **95**
Anthony Lagoon, *N.T., Aust.* C87-178 **111**
Antibes, *France* M47+436 **55**
Anticosti I., *Quebec* S18+495 **90**
Antigo, *Wisconsin* T85+451 **91**
Antigonish, *Nova Scotia* S12+456 **90**
Antigua, I., *Leeward Is.* S10+170 **101**
Antilhue, *Chile* S78-398 **103**
Antilla, *Cuba* T05+209 **101**
Antilles, Greater, *West Indies* - **101**
Antilles, Lesser, *West Indies* - **101**
Antioquia, *Colombia* T05+064 **104**
Antipodes Is., *Pacific Ocean* A04-500 **106**
Antivari. *See* Bar
Antlers, *Oklahoma* U34+343 **95**
Antofagasta, *Chile* S62-235 **103**
Antofagasta de la S., *Arg.* S44-261 **103**
Antofalla, mt., *Argentina* S48-256 **103**
Antoing, *Belgium* M69+506 **44**
Antongil, B. d', *Madagascar* J60-158 **83**
Antonito, *Colorado* V06+370 **94**
Antrain, *France* N09+485 **54**
Antrim & co., *N. Ireland* N37+547 **42**
Antrim Hills, *N. Ireland* N36+550 **42**
Antsirabe, *Madagascar* J78-198 **83**
Antsirana, *Madagascar* J64-124 **83**
Antsla, *Estonia* L20+578 **47**
Antung, *China* *See* Tantung
Antwerp. *See* Antwerpen
Antwerpen, & prov., *Belg.* M63+512 **44**
Anupgarh, *India* H11+292 **72**
Anupshahr, *India* G71+283 **73**
Anuradhapura, *Sri Lanka* G58+084 **70**
Anvers. *See* Antwerpen
Anyang, *China* E33+361 **66**
Anyi, *China* E54+351 **66**
Anykščiai, *Lithuania* L29+556 **47**
Anzhero Sudzhensh, *U.S.S.R.* G21+560 **62**
Aomori, *Japan* C56+408 **68**
Aonla, *India* G65+283 **73**
Aosta, *Italy* M46+457 **56**
Aoudèras, *Niger* M40+176 **80**
Aouni, *Chad* G80+130 **81**
Apakova, *U.S.S.R.* J61+545 **61**
Apalachee B., *Florida* T54+300 **97**
Apalachicola & B., *Florida* T60+297 **97**
Aparri, *Philippines* D80+183 **65**
Apataki I., *Tuamotu Arch.* X70-150 **107**
Apatin, *Yugoslavia* L66+457 **58**
Ape, *Latvia* L19+575 **47**
Apeldoorn, *Netherlands* M54+522 **44**
Apennines, mts., *Italy* M18+440 **50**
Api, mt., *Nepal* G54+300 **73**
Apiai, *Brazil* R23-244 **103**
Apodi, *Brazil* Q47-055 **105**
Apollo Bay, *Victoria* C38-388 **109**
Apolo, *Bolivia* S51-146 **104**
Apostle Is., *Wisconsin* U02+470 **91**
Apostoles, *Argentina* R65-278 **103**
Apoteri, *Guyana* R82+040 **104**
Apozai, *Pakistan* H34+312 **70**
Appalachian Mts., *U.S.A.* T54+346 **99**
Appenzell & canton, *Switz.* M34+473 **45**
Appleby, *England* N15+546 **37**
Applecross, *Scotland* N35+574 **40**
Appleton, *Wisconsin* T81+443 **91**

Appleton City, *Missouri* U24+382 **95**
Approuague, *Fr. Guiana* R41+042 **105**
Apsley, *Tasmania* C17-424 **109**
Apsley, *Victoria* C53-370 **109**
Apt, *France* M58+439 **55**
Apuhi, *Brazil* R88-052 **104**
Aqaba, *Jordan* K60+295 **76**
Aqiq, *Sudan* K40+180 **83**
Aqraba, *Jordan* K58+321 **76**
Aqua, *Mexico* V06+296 **100**
Aquidauana, *Brazil* R65-205 **105**
Aquila, L', *Italy* M10+424 **56**
Aquin, *Haiti* S80+182 **101**
Arabia, pen., *S.W. Asia* - **74**
Arabian Sea, *S. Asia* H60+150 **30**
Aracaju, *Brazil* Q43-109 **105**
Aracati, *Brazil* Q47-046 **105**
Arad, *Romania* L52+462 **58**
Arada, *Chad* L56+150 **81**
Arafura Sea, *Indonesia* D00-094 **65**
Aragua de Barcelona, *Venez.* S29+094 **104**
Araguaia, R., *Brazil* R24-070 **105**
Araguari, *Brazil* R19-187 **105**
Arak, *Iran* J62+341 **74**
Arakaka, *Guyana* S00+078 **104**
Arakan, *Burma* F60+200 **71**
Arakan Yoma, *Burma* F66+205 **71**
Araks, R., *Iran* J78+390 **62**
Aralsk, *Kazakh* H80+468 **62**
Aralskoye More (Aral Sea),
  Kazakh-Uzbek J00+450 **62**
Aramac, *Queensland* C28-225 **111**
Arambagh, *India* G13+229 **73**
Aran I., *Ireland, Rep.* N51+550 **42**
Aran Is., *Ireland, Rep.* N58+531 **43**
Aranda de Duero, *Spain* N22+417 **52**
Arani, *Bolivia* S34-175 **104**
Aranjuez, *Spain* N22+400 **52**
Aran Mawddwy, *Wales* N22+528 **38**
Aransas B., *Texas* U42+280 **94**
Araouane, *Mali* N22+186 **80**
Arapiraca, *Brazil* Q41-048 **105**
Arapey, *Uruguay* R75-309 **103**
Arapkir, *Turkey* K40+390 **74**
Arapuni, *New Zealand* A28-380 **112**
Ararangua, *Brazil* R27-289 **103**
Ararat, *Victoria* C42-373 **109**
Ararat, mt., *Turkey* K04+398 **74**
Araria, *India* G15+262 **73**
Arassuahy, *Brazil* Q72-169 **105**
Araty, *Brazil* S64-079 **104**
Arauca, *Colombia* S64+070 **104**
Arauco, *Chile* S80-372 **103**
Aravalli Ra., *India* H10+254 **70**
Araxa, *Brazil* R12-196 **105**
Arbatax, *Sardinia* M31+399 **57**
Arbil, *Iraq* K06+363 **74**
Arboga, *Sweden* L85+594 **47**
Arbois, *France* M56+469 **54**
Arbon, *Switzerland* M33+475 **45**
Arbroath, *Scotland* N16+565 **41**
Arcade, *New York* T21+425 **91**
Arcadia, *Michigan* T67+445 **91**
Arcadia, *Wisconsin* U07+442 **93**
Arcen, *Netherlands* M53+515 **44**
Archbald, *Pennsylvania* T04+415 **96**
Archidona, *Spain* N26+37 **52**
Arcot, *India* G64+129 **70**
Arctic Ocean - **26**
Arctic Red River, *N.-W. Terr.* W80+672 **88**
Ardabil, *Iran* J71+383 **74**
Ardahan, *Turkey* K14+412 **74**
Ardakan, *Iran* J35+324 **75**
Årdal, *Norway* M43+612 **47**
Ardal, *Iran* J55+321 **75**
Ardara, *Ireland, Rep.* N51+548 **42**
Ardatov, *U.S.S.R.* K11-552 **61**
Ardèche, dep., *France* M64+446 **55**
Ardee, *Ireland, Rep.* N39+539 **42**
Arden, Forest of, *England* N11+523 **37**
Ardennes, dep., *France* M61+496 **54**
Ardennes Mts., *Belg., etc.* M57+499 **44**
Arderin, *Ireland, Rep.* N46+530 **43**
Ardez, *Switzerland* M29+468 **45**
Ardgay, *Scotland* N26+579 **40**
Ardglass, *N. Ireland* N34+543 **42**
Ardino, *Bulgaria* L29+416 **58**
Ardistan, *Iran* J46+335 **75**
Ardlethan, *New S. Wales* C19-344 **109**
Ardmore, *Oklahoma* U41+342 **95**
Ardmore B., *Ireland, Rep.* N46+519 **43**
Ardrishaig, *Scotland* N33+560 **41**
Ardrossan, *Scotland* N29+556 **41**
Ardrossan, *S. Australia* C73-344 **109**
Ardud, *Romania* L43+476 **49**
Arecibo, *Puerto Rico* S40+185 **101**
Areia, *Brazil* Q58-133 **105**
Areia Branco, *Brazil* Q43-050 **105**
Areião, *Brazil* R26-044 **105**
Arenales, *Argentina* S09-343 **103**
Arenales, mt., *Chile* S80-471 **103**
Arenas de San Pedro, *Spain* N31+402 **52**
Arendal, *Norway* M37+584 **47**
Arenys de Mar, *Spain* M75+416 **53**
Arequipa, *Peru* S70-163 **104**
Arévalo, *Spain* N28+410 **52**
Arezzo, *Italy* M 9+434 **56**
Argentan, *France* N00+487 **54**
Argentat, *France* M78+451 **55**
Argentina, rep., *S. America* - **103**
Argentino, L., *Argentina* S75-503 **103**
Argent-sur-Saulcre, *France* M75+475 **54**
Argo, *Sudan* K88+192 **81**
Argolis, G of, *Greece* L42+372 **59**
Argonne, *France* M60+493 **54**
Argos, *Greece* L44+376 **59**
Arguedas, *Spain* N10+424 **53**
Argun, R., *U.S.S.R.-China* E04+510 **63**
Argungu, *Nigeria* M62+128 **80**
Argyll, co., *See* Strathclyde
Århus, *Denmark* M29+561 **47**
Ariake Wan, *Japan* D23+313 **68**
Ariano Irpino, *Italy* M00+412 **57**
Arica, *Chile* S62-186 **103**
Arica, *Colombia* S70-021 **104**
Ariège, dep., *France* M80+430 **55**
Arikemes, *Brazil* S19-099 **104**
Arilje, *Yugoslavia* L59+437 **58**
Arima, *Brazil* S22-057 **104**
Arinda, *Guyana* R82+047 **104**
Aripuana, *Brazil* S02-052 **104**

Arivechi, *Mexico* V24+290 **100**
Ariza, *Spain* N13+413 **53**
Arizona, *Argentina* S32-356 **103**
Arizona, state, *U.S.A.* V50+347 **98**
Arizona Plat., *Arizona* V36+446 **94**
Arizpe, *Mexico* V30+304 **100**
Arka, *Yemen, South* J76+136 **74**
Arka, *U.S.S.R.* C48+601 **63**
Arkabutla Res., *Mississippi* U01+348 **95**
Arkadelphia, *Arkansas* U18+342 **95**
Arkadhia, *Greece* L46+374 **59**
Arkaig L., *Scotland* N31+570 **40**
Arkansas, state, *U.S.A.* U20+350 **99**
Arkansas R., *Arkansas, etc.* U20+354 **99**
Arkansas City, *Arkansas* U07+336 **97**
Arkansas City, *Kansas* U42+370 **95**
Arkhangelsk, *U.S.S.R.* K25+647 **62**
Arklow, *Ireland, Rep.* N37+528 **43**
Arkoi, I., *Greece* L19+374 **59**
Arles, *France* M62+437 **55**
Arlon, *Belgium* M55+497 **44**
Arltunga, *N. Terr., Aust.* D02-232 **111**
Armagh & co., *N. Ireland* N40+543 **42**
Armenia, *Colombia* T04+048 **104**
Armenia, *U.S.S.R.* K05+405 **74**
Armentieres, *France* M73+507 **54**
Armidale, *New S. Wales* B81-305 **109**
Armiros, B of, *Crete* L34+354 **59**
Armistico, *Paraguay* R57-249 **103**
Armori, *India* G60+205 **70**
Armstrong, *Ontario* T83+502 **89**
Armyanskaya, rep., *U.S.S.R.* K00+400 **62**
Arnaudville, *Louisiana* U11+304 **97**
Arnauti, C., *Cyprus* K76+351 **76**
Arnawai, *Pakistan* H20+353 **72**
Arnhem, *Netherlands* M55+520 **44**
Arnhem, C., *N. Terr., Aust.* C78-122 **111**
Arnhem Ld., *N. Terr., Aust.* D10-130 **110**
Arnissa, *Greece* L49+408 **59**
Arnöy, *Norway* L56+701 **46**
Arnprior, *Ontario* T08+454 **91**
Arnsberg, *W. Germany* M42+514 **48**
Arnstadt, *E. Germany* M24+508 **48**
Arolla, *Switzerland* M45+460 **45**
Aroostook, *New Brunswick* S46+468 **90**
Arorae, I., *Gilbert Is.* A20-030 **106**
Arosa, *Switzerland* M32+468 **45**
Arouelli, *Chad* L44+186 **81**
Aroya, *Colorado* U79+338 **94**
Arrah, *India* G32+255 **73**
Arran I., *Scotland* N31+556 **41**
Arras, *France* M73+503 **54**
Arrayas, *Brazil* R11-131 **105**
Arroba, *Spain* N27+391 **52**
Arromanches, *France* N05+493 **54**
Arronches, *Portugal* N44+391 **52**
Arrow L., *Ireland, Rep.* N50+541 **42**
Arrowsmith, Mt., *N.S.W.* C51-301 **109**
Arrowtown, *New Zealand* A67-449 **112**
Arroyo, *Puerto Rico* S35+180 **101**
Års, *Denmark* M33+568 **47**
Arsk, *U.S.S.R.* J60+561 **61**
Arta, *Greece* L54+392 **59**
Artawiya, *Saudi Arabia* J88+266 **74**
Artemovsk, *U.S.S.R.* F68+545 **63**
Artemovsk, *Ukraine* K42+486 **60**
Artemovski, *U.S.S.R.* E32+582 **63**
Artemovski, *U.S.S.R.* H79+573 **61**
Artenay, *France* M79+481 **54**
Artesia, *New Mexico* U86+328 **94**
Artibonite, R., *Haiti* S74+190 **101**
Artigas, *Uruguay* R69-304 **103**
Artillery L., *N.-W. Terr.* V17+636 **88**
Artois, prov., *France* M76+503 **54**
Artvin, *Turkey* K20+412 **74**
Aru, *Zaire* K84+028 **83**
Aruanã, *Brazil* R36-148 **105**
Aru Kep., *Indonesia* D04-063 **65**
Arumá, *Brazil* S13-046 **104**
Arundel, *England* N04+508 **39**
Arundel, *Quebec* S88+460 **91**
Aruppukkottai, *India* G72+095 **70**
Arusha, *Tanzania* K50-034 **83**
Aru Tso, *Tibet* G46+339 **71**
Arvada, *Wyoming* V07+446 **93**
Arvida, *Quebec* S67+484 **90**
Arvika, *Sweden* M14+597 **47**
Arvilla, *N. Dakota* U45+479 **93**
Arzamas, *U.S.S.R.* K07+554 **61**
Arzeu, *Algeria* N02+358 **80**
Arzua, *Spain* N49+429 **52**
As, *Belgium* M57+510 **44**
Aš, *Czechoslovakia* M17+502 **48**
Asahigawa, *Japan* C46+437 **68**
Asansol, *India* G18+237 **73**
Åsarna, *Sweden* M04+627 **46**
Asbestos, *Quebec* S70+458 **91**
Asbury Park, *New Jersey* S84+402 **96**
Ascension, *Bolivia* S19-156 **104**
Ascension, B. de la, *Mexico* T74+196 **100**
Ascension I., *Atlantic Ocean* N87-080 **85**
Aschaffenburg, *W. Germany* M35+499 **48**
Ascoli, *Italy* M09+428 **56**
Ascona, *Switzerland* M37+462 **45**
Ascot, *England* N04+514 **39**
Ascotan, *Chile* S50-215 **103**
Aseda, *Sweden* L88+572 **47**
Åsele, *Sweden* L76+641 **46**
Åsen, *Sweden* M07+613 **47**
Asenovgrad, *Bulgaria* L31+420 **58**
Ashburton, *England* N23+505 **38**
Ashburton, *New Zealand* A49-439 **112**
Ashburton, R., *W. Aust.* E20-230 **110**
Ashdod, *Israel* K62+318 **76**
Asheboro, *N. Carolina* T29+357 **97**
Asheville, *N. Carolina* T45+356 **97**
Ash Fork, *Arizona* V45+352 **94**
Ashkhabad, *Turkmen* J10+380 **62**
Ashland, *Kansas* U58+372 **95**
Ashland, *Kentucky* T46+385 **97**
Ashland, *Maine* S51+466 **90**
Ashland, *Montana* V08+456 **93**
Ashland, *Ohio* T44+409 **91**
Ashland, *Oregon* W16+422 **92**
Ashland, *Pennsylvania* T08+408 **96**
Ashland, *Virginia* T15+376 **97**
Ashland, *Wisconsin* U09+466 **93**
Ashland City, *Tennessee* T72+363 **97**
Ashley, *New S. Wales* C01-292 **109**

Ashley, *N. Dakota* U56+461 **93**
Ashraf, *Iran* J39+367 **75**
Ash Shihr, *Yemen, South* J62 + 148 **74**
Ashtabula, *Ohio* T35+418 **91**
Ashton-under-Lyne, *England* N12+535 **37**
Ashton, *Idaho* V40+441 **93**
Ashuanipi L., *Labrador* S37+528 **89**
Ashuradeh, *Iran* J37+369 **75**
Ashville, *Alabama* T67+338 **97**
Asinara, I. & G. di, *Sardinia* M39+409 **57**
Asino, *U.S.S.R.* G24+570 **62**
Asir, *Saudi Arabia* K20+203 **74**
Askeaton, *Ireland, Rep.* N54+526 **43**
Askersund, *Sweden* M01+589 **47**
Askvoll, *Norway* M59+614 **47**
Aslandus, *Iran* J76+394 **74**
Asmara, *Ethiopia* K36+152 **83**
Aspern, *Austria* L81+483 **49**
Aspiring, Mt., *New Zealand* A68-444 **112**
Aspres-sur-Buech, *France* M56+445 **55**
Assab, *Ethiopia* K14+130 **83**
As Sabya, *Yemen* K14+172 **74**
Assam, *India* F70+255 **71**
As Sauda, *Yemen* K07+160 **74**
Assaye, *India* G84+203 **70**
Asse, *Belgium* M65+509 **44**
Assen, *Netherlands* M52+530 **44**
Asshur, *Iraq* K14+356 **74**
Assiniboia, *Saskatchewan* V05+496 **88**
Assiniboine, Mt., *Alberta* V63+507 **88**
Assiniboine R., *Manitoba* U50+498 **88**
Assinica L., *Quebec* T01+504 **90**
Assu & R., *Brazil* Q71-056 **105**
Assumar, *Portugal* N44+391 **52**
Assynt L., *Scotland* N30+582 **40**
Asten, *Netherlands* M56+514 **44**
Asti, *Italy* M41+449 **56**
Astipálaia, I., *Greece* L22+366 **59**
Aston, C., *N.-W. Territories* S44+700 **89**
Astor, *Kashmir* H01+353 **72**
Astorga, *Spain* N36+425 **52**
Astoria, *Oregon* W23+462 **92**
Astrakhan, *U.S.S.R.* J73+463 **62**
Åsträsk, *Sweden* L60+646 **46**
Astros, *Greece* L44+374 **59**
Astudillo, *Spain* N26+422 **52**
Aswân, *Egypt* K72+238 **81**
Asyût, *Egypt* K82+270 **81**
Atacama, Des., *Chile* S56-200 **103**
Atakpame, *Togo* M84+076 **80**
Atalaia, *Brazil* Q36-094 **105**
Atalándi, *Greece* L42+387 **59**
Atambua, *Timor I., Indon.* D62-090 **65**
Atar, *Mauritania* N78+206 **80**
Atara, *Yemen* J89+145 **74**
Ataran, R., *Burma* F42+160 **71**
Atbara, *Sudan* K66+178 **81**
Atbasar, *Kasakh.* H39+518 **62**
Atchafalaya B., *Louisiana* U08+294 **95**
Atchison, *Kansas* U31+396 **95**
Ateca, *Spain* N11+413 **53**
Ath, *Belgium* M67+506 **44**
Athabasca, *Alberta* V49+549 **88**
Athabasca, L., *Alta.-Sask.* V30+592 **88**
Athabasca R., *Alberta* V65+544 **88**
Athboy, *Ireland, Rep.* N41+536 **42**
Athenry, *Ireland, Rep.* N52+533 **43**
Athens. *See* Athinai
Athens, *Georgia* T51+339 **97**
Athens, *Tennessee* T57+354 **97**
Atherton Plat., *Queensland* C30-176 **111**
Athinai, *Greece* L38+380 **59**
Athleague, *Ireland, Rep.* N49+535 **43**
Athlone, *Ireland, Rep.* N48+534 **43**
Athna, *Cyprus* K67+350 **76**
Athol, *Massachusetts* S73+426 **96**
Athol, *New Zealand* A68-455 **112**
Atholl, Forest of, *Scotland* N24+568 **41**
Athy, *Ireland, Rep.* N42+530 **43**
Atico, *Peru* S82-162 **104**
Atienza, *Spain* N18+412 **52**
Atikonak L., *Labrador* S27+528 **89**
Atka, *U.S.S.R.* B80+607 **63**
Atka, I., *Aleutian Is.* Z55+519 **99**
Atkarsk, *U.S.S.R.* K00+518 **61**
Atlanta, *Georgia* T56+337 **97**
Atlanta, *Michigan* T55+450 **91**
Atlantic, *Iowa* U30+414 **95**
Atlantic City, *New Jersey* S86+394 **96**
Atlin, *British Columbia* W81+597 **88**
Atlit, *Israel* K60+327 **76**
Atoka, *Oklahoma* U36+344 **95**
Atrauli, *India* G70+280 **73**
Attalla, *Alabama* T63+336 **97**
Attawapiskat, L. & R., *Ont.* T78+520 **89**
Attica, *Indiana* T73+403 **95**
Attica, *New York* T20+428 **96**
Attiki, *Greece* L41+382 **59**
Attleboro, *Massachusetts* S68+419 **96**
Attleborough, *England* M84+525 **39**
Attock, *Pakistan* H16+339 **72**
Attu, I., *Aleutian Is.* A40+524 **99**
Atukesi, *Japan* C31+430 **68**
Atupi, *Brazil* R55+014 **105**
Aube, dep., *France* M64+482 **54**
Aubel, *Belgium* M55+507 **44**
Aubenas, *France* M63+446 **55**
Aubonne, *Switzerland* M52+465 **45**
Auburn, *Alabama* T63+326 **97**
Auburn, *Indiana* T60+414 **91**
Auburn, *Maine* S61+441 **90**
Auburn, *Nebraska* U35+404 **95**
Auburn, *New York* T10+429 **96**
Aubusson, *France* M77+459 **54**
Auce, *Latvia* L43+564 **47**
Auch, *France* M86+437 **55**
Auchterarder, *Scotland* N22+563 **41**
Auckland, *New Zealand* A31-369 **112**
Auckland Is., *Pacific Ocean* A85-550 **106**
Aude, dep., *France* M75+431 **55**
Audegle, *Somalia* K02+018 **83**
Audenarde, *Belgium* M68+508 **44**
Audierne, B. d', *France* N27+479 **54**
Audubon, *Iowa* U30+416 **95**
Aughnacloy, *N. Ireland* N42+544 **42**
Aughrim, *Ireland, Rep.* N38+528 **43**
Augsburg, *W. Germany* M25+484 **48**
Augusta, *Arkansas* U08+353 **97**

Augusta, *Georgia* T42+334 **97**
Augusta, *Kansas* U42+377 **95**
Augusta, *Kentucky* T54+387 **97**
Augusta, *Maine* S59+444 **90**
Augusta, *Sicily* L89+372 **57**
Augusta, *Wisconsin* U07+447 **91**
Augustów, *Poland* L43+538 **49**
Augustus, Mt., *W. Australia* E12-246 **110**
Auletta, *Italy* L87+406 **57**
Aumale, *Algeria* M68+360 **80**
Aunis, prov., *France* N08+461 **54**
Aura, *Finland* L44+606 **47**
Auraiya, *India* G63+264 **73**
Aurangabad, *India* G33+247 **73**
Aurangabad, *India* G88+199 **70**
Auray, *France* N18+477 **54**
Aurillac, *France* M76+449 **55**
Aurora, *Illinois* T80+418 **91**
Aurora, *Ontario* T27+440 **91**
Aus, *S.-W. Africa* L82-266 **84**
Au Sable, *Michigan* T50+445 **91**
Au Sable Forks, *New York* S82+445 **91**
Austin, *Minnesota* U18+437 **93**
Austin, *Nevada* V73+395 **92**
Austin, *Texas* U46+303 **95**
Austin, L., *W. Australia* E12-276 **110**
Austral Is., *Pacific Oc.* Y00-250 **107**
Australia, *Australasia* **110-111**
Australian Alps, *Vic.-N.S.W.* C10-368 **109**
Australian Capital Terr.
  Australia C06-355 **109**
Austria, *Central Europe* M06+474 **50**
Autlan, *Mexico* U87+197 **100**
Autun, *France* M64+470 **54**
Auvergne, prov., *France* M72+454 **55**
Auxerre, *France* M69+478 **54**
Aux Sources, Mt.,
  Lesotho L06-288 **84**
Ava, *Burma* F54+218 **71**
Avallon, *France* M66+475 **54**
Avalon Pen., *Newfoundland* R52+473 **90**
Avanoas, *S.-W. Africa* M12-184 **84**
Avare, *Brazil* R24-231 **105**
Avaviken, *Sweden* L68+656 **46**
Aveiro, *Brazil* R60-034 **105**
Aveiro, *Portugal* N52+406 **52**
Avelgem, *Belgium* M69+508 **44**
Avellanada, *Argentina* R80-347 **103**
Avellino, *Italy* M01+409 **57**
Avenir, *French Guiana* R53+048 **105**
Averoy, *Norway* M45+630 **46**
Aversa, *Italy* M05+410 **57**
Avesnes, *France* M66+501 **54**
Avesta, *Sweden* L83+601 **47**
Aveyron, dep., *France* M73+441 **55**
Avezzano, *Italy* M09+419 **57**
Aviá Teria, *Argentina* S04-266 **103**
Aviemore, *Scotland* N23+572 **40**
Avigliano, *Italy* L86+408 **57**
Avignon, *France* M61+440 **55**
Avila, *Spain* N28+406 **52**
Aviz, *Portugal* N47+391 **52**
Avoca, *Iowa* U32+414 **95**
Avoca, *Tasmania* C14-418 **109**
Avoca, *Victoria* C39-371 **109**
Avola, *Sicily* L89+369 **57**
Avon, co., *England* N15+515 **38**
Avon R., *England* N10+523 **37**
Avon R., *Scotland* N20+574 **40**
Avranches, *France* N08+487 **54**
Awaji Shima, *Japan* D00+344 **68**
Awakino, *New Zealand* A32-387 **112**
Awe L., *Scotland* N32+563 **41**
Awjilah, *Libya* L52+292 **81**
Awusa L., *Ethiopia* K40+070 **83**
Axat, *France* M77+428 **55**
Axel, *Netherlands* M67+513 **44**
Axel Heiberg, *North-West*
  Territories U15+790 **89**
Axminster, *England* N18+508 **38**
Ayabaca, *Peru* T28-046 **104**
Ayacucho, *Argentina* R82-371 **103**
Ayacucho, *Peru* S85-132 **104**
Ayaguz, *Kazakh* G59+480 **62**
Ayakhta, *U.S.S.R.* F66+593 **63**
Ayamonte, *Spain* N44+372 **52**
Ayan, *U.S.S.R.* C70+563 **63**
Ayancik, *Turkey* K61+419 **74**
Ayaviri, *Peru* S64-147 **104**
Aydin, *Turkey* L13+379 **74**
Ayerbe, *Spain* N04+423 **53**
Ayia, *Greece* L43+397 **59**
Ayion Oros, *Greece* L35+403 **59**
Ayios Evstratios, *Greece* L30+395 **59**
Aylesbury, *England* N05+518 **39**
Aylmer, *Ontario* T36+428 **91**
Aylmer, L., *N.-W. Territories* V20+643 **88**
Aylsham, *England* M82+528 **39**
Aylwin, *Quebec* T06+460 **91**
Aymores, *Brazil* Q67-196 **105**
Ayon Ostrov, *U.S.S.R.* A65+700 **63**
Ayora, *Spain* N06+390 **53**
Ayr, *Queensland* C15-195 **111**
Ayr & R., *Scotland* N28+555 **41**
Ayun, *Saudi Arabia* K08+265 **74**
Ayutla, *Guatemala* U13+147 **100**
Ayutla, *Mexico* U55+169 **100**
Ayutthaya, *Thailand* F27+144 **69**
Ayvalik, *Turkey* L20+394 **74**
Aywaille, *Belgium* M56+505 **44**
Azaila, *Spain* N03+413 **53**
Azamgarh, *India* G41+261 **73**
Azare, *Nigeria* M28+116 **81**
Azaz, *Syria* K48+366 **76**
Azerbaydzhanskaya, rep.,
  U.S.S.R. J80+410 **62**
Azi, *Latvia* L27+563 **47**
Azogues, *Ecuador* T17+026 **104**
Azores Is. *See* Açores Is.
Azov, Sea of, *U.S.S.R.* K48+460 **60**
Azpeitia, *Spain* N14+432 **53**
Aztec, *New Mexico* V15+367 **98**
Azua, *Dominican Rep.* S64+184 **101**
Azuaga, *Spain* N34+382 **52**
Azul, *Argentina* R89-367 **103**
Azzan, *Yemen, D.R.* J74+144 **74**
Az Zubayr, *Iraq* J74+304 **74**
Baabda, *Lebanon* K57+338 **76**
Baalbek, *Lebanon* K53+340 **76**
Baarle Nassau, *Netherlands* M60+514 **44**
Baarn, *Netherlands* M58+522 **44**

Babahoya, *Ecuador* T26-018 **104**
Babar, I., *Indonesia* D32-080 **65**
Babati, *Tanzania* K56-042 **83**
Babel I., *Tasmania* C11-399 **109**
Bab el Mandeb, *Red Sea* K10+120 **30**
Babine L., *Brit. Columbia* W38+550 **88**
Babispe, *Mexico* V23+305 **100**
Babol, *Iran* J44+366 **75**
Babura, *Nigeria* M40+126 **82**
Babuyan Is., *Philippines* D80+192 **64**
Babylon, *Iraq* K03+326 **74**
Bacabal, *Brazil* R69-053 **105**
Bacadehuachi, *Mexico* V24+298 **100**
Bacalar, *Mexico* T81+187 **100**
Bacan, I., *Indonesia* D45+006 **65**
Bacău, *Romania* L18+465 **58**
Bacchus Marsh, *Victoria* C33-377 **109**
Bacerac, *Mexico* V23+303 **100**
Bach long Vi, I., *N. Vietnam* E74+202 **69**
Back R., *N.-W. Territories* U40+660 **88**
Backbone Mts., *W. Va.-Md.* T27+393 **96**
Bäckefors, *Sweden* M17+588 **47**
Backergunge, *Bangladesh* F88+224 **71**
Backstairs Pass., *S. Aust.* C72-357 **109**
Bac-Ninh, *N. Vietnam* E83+212 **69**
Bacoachi, *Mexico* V40+296 **100**
Bacoachic, *Mexico* V28+309 **100**
Bacolod, *Philippines* D72+106 **65**
Bacup, *England* N13+537 **37**
Bada, *Saudi Arabia* K48+269 **74**
Badajoz, *Brazil* R17-026 **105**
Badajoz, *Spain* N41+389 **52**
Badalona, *Spain* M77+415 **53**
Badarma, *U.S.S.R.* F15+578 **63**
Badas, *Brunei* E33+046 **65**
Bad Axe, *Michigan* T48+438 **91**
Bad Ems, *W. Germany* M44+503 **48**
Baden, *Germany* M43+480 **48**
Baden, *Switzerland* M40+475 **45**
Baden-Baden, *Germany* M40+487 **48**
Badin, *Pakistan* H36+246 **70**
Badiya, *Oman* J09+225 **75**
Bad Kissingen, *W. Germany* M29+502 **48**
Bad Lands, *Nebraska, etc.* U80+426 **98**
Badnur, *India* G72+218 **70**
Badon, *Senegal* N74+128 **80**
Badrinath, *India* G63+308 **70**
Baduen, *Somalia* J74+070 **83**
Badulla, *Sri Lanka* G53+070 **70**
Baena, *Spain* N26+376 **52**
Baerle-Duc, *Belgium* M60+514 **44**
Baetas, *Brazil* S14-061 **104**
Baffin B., *N.-W. Territories* S30+714 **89**
Baffin I., *N.-W. Territories* S60+680 **89**
Bafia, *Cameroun* M24+046 **81**
Bafoulabé, *Mali* N64+136 **80**
Baf'q, *Iran* J28+316 **75**
Bafra, *Turkey* K54+415 **74**
Baft, *Iran* J21+291 **75**
Bagata, *Zaire* L72-038 **82**
Bage, *Brazil* R54-312 **103**
Bagenalstown. *See* Muine Bheag
Baghdad, *Iraq* K04+334 **74**
Bagherhat, *Bangladesh* G01+227 **73**
Baghin, *Iran* J19+302 **75**
Baghpat, *India* G76+290 **72**
Baginbum Hd., *Ireland, Rep.* N41+522 **43**
Bagley, *Minnesota* U32+475 **93**
Bagnell, *Missouri* U16+382 **97**
Bagnols-sur-Ceze, *France* M62+442 **55**
Bagotville, *Quebec* S65+484 **90**
Baguio, *Philippines* D86+165 **65**
Bahaar-i-Gaz, *Iran* J37+368 **75**
Bahadurgarh, *India* G79+287 **72**
Bahama I., Grand, *Bahamas, The* T20 + 266 **101**
Bahamas, The, *West Indies* T10 + 250 **101**
Bahawalpur, *Pakistan* H19+294 **72**
Baheri, *India* G63+287 **73**
Bahia. *See* Salvador
Bahia Blanca, *Argentina* S13-386 **103**
Bahia de Caráquez, *Ecuador* T33-007 **104**
Bahia Laura, *Argentina* S39-483 **103**
Bahia Negra, *Paraguay* R79-202 **103**
Bahia Solano, *Colombia* T14+063 **104**
Bahra, *Saudi Arabia* K33+214 **74**
Bahraich, *India* G50+276 **73**
Bahrain, *The Gulf* J57 + 261 **75**
Bahret el Ateibe, *Syria* K50+335 **76**
Bahret el Hijane, *Syria* K50+333 **76**
Bahret Homs, *Syria* K51+346 **76**
Bahu Kalat, *Iran* H81+257 **75**
Bahus, *Brazil* R48-184 **105**
Baiao, *Brazil* R26-028 **105**
Baibokoum, *Chad* L86+078 **81**
Baiburt, *Turkey* K30+403 **74**
Baidaratskaya B., *U.S.S.R.* H60+700 **62**
Baie St Paul, *Quebec* S63+474 **91**
Baie Verte, *New Brunswick* S25+460 **90**
Baiji, *Iraq* K09+350 **74**
Baikit, *U.S.S.R.* F51+617 **63**
Baikonur, *Kazakh* H53+479 **62**
Baile-Atha-Cliath. *See* Dublin
Bailen, *Spain* N21+381 **52**
Baillie, *N.-W. Territories* W50+706 **88**
Baimak Tanalykovo, *U.S.S.R.* J14+526 **61**
Bainbridge, *Georgia* T57+309 **97**
Bairnsdale, *Victoria* C14-378 **109**
Baital Faqih, *Yemen* K10+146 **74**
Baitik Bogdo, *China* F80+450 **64**
Baixo Longa, *Angola* L66-164 **84**
Baja, *Hungary* L66+462 **58**
Baja California, state, *Mexico* V60+300 **100**
Baján, *Mexico* U68+265 **100**
Bajmok, *Yugoslavia* L64+460 **58**
Bakaly, *U.S.S.R.* J37+552 **61**
Bakel, *Senegal* N74+148 **80**
Baker, *Montana* U86+463 **93**
Baker, *Oregon* V77+448 **92**
Baker I., *Pacific Ocean* Z70+004 **106**
Baker L., *N.-W. Territories* U40+644 **88**
Baker, Mt., *Washington* W10+483 **98**
Baker Butte, *Arizona* V38+344 **94**
Bakersfield, *California* V84+354 **92**
Bakhasar, *India* H23+247 **70**
Baklansk, *U.S.S.R.* H64+558 **61**
Bakloh, *India* G85+325 **72**
Bako, *Ethiopia* K50+058 **83**
Bakonyerdo, *Hungary* L72+473 **49**
Bala, *Wales* N22+529 **38**

Balabac Str., *Philippines* E20+076 **65**
Balagnat, *India* G58+220 **70**
Balakhta, *U.S.S.R.* F79+552 **63**
Balaklava, *U.S.S.R.* K68+445 **60**
Balaklava, *S. Australia* C70-342 **109**
Balancan, *Mexico* U10+178 **100**
Balaquer, *Spain* M83+418 **53**
Balashov, *U.S.S.R.* K11+515 **61**
Balasore, *India* G18+215 **71**
Balat, *Egypt* L04+256 **81**
Balaton, L., *Hungary* L74+469 **49**
Balazote, *Spain* N13+389 **53**
Balboa, *Panama* T27+090 **101**
Balbriggan, *Ireland, Rep.* N37+536 **42**
Balcarce, *Argentina* R80-379 **103**
Balchik, *Bulgaria* L11+434 **58**
Balclutha, *New Zealand* A62-463 **112**
Bald Knob, *Arkansas* U10+353 **95**
Bald Knob, *W. Virginia* T30+384 **97**
Baldwin, *Illinois* U02+382 **97**
Baldwin, *Michigan* T65+439 **91**
Baldwinsville, *New York* T08+431 **96**
Baldy Pk., *Arizona* V28+340 **98**
Baldy Pk., *New Mexico* V04+358 **94**
Baleares, Is. *See* Balares
Balearic Is. *See* Baleares
Balen, *Belgium* M59+512 **44**
Baler, *Philippines* D81+158 **65**
Balestrand, *Norway* M51+612 **47**
Baley, *U.S.S.R.* E20+517 **63**
Balfour, *N. Dakota* U63+479 **93**
Balfour, *Tasmania* C30-413 **109**
Bali, I., *Indonesia* E30-084 **65**
Balikesir, *Turkey* L13+397 **74**
Balikpapan, *Borneo* E19-012 **65**
Balk, *Netherlands* M57+529 **44**
Balkh, *Afghanistan* H49+368 **75**
Balkhash & Oz., *Kazakh* H00+469 **62**
Ballabgarh, *India* G76+283 **72**
Ballachulish, *Scotland* N31+567 **41**
Ballaghaderreen, *Ireland, Rep.* N51+539 **42**
Ballantrae, *Scotland* N33+550 **41**
Ballara, *Queensland* C60-210 **111**
Ballarat, *Victoria* C37-376 **109**
Ballater, *Scotland* N18+570 **40**
Ballé, *Mali* N52+154 **80**
Ballenas, B. de, *Mexico* V50+268 **100**
Ballenas Channel, *Mexico* V52+292 **100**
Balleny Is., *Antarctica* B10-670 **27**
Balia, *India* G35+257 **73**
Ballina, *Ireland, Rep.* N55+541 **42**
Ballina, *New S. Wales* B69-289 **109**
Ballinasloe, *Ireland, Rep.* N49+533 **43**
Ballindine, *Ireland, Rep.* N54+537 **42**
Ballingarry, *Ireland, Rep.* N53+525 **43**
Ballinluig, *Scotland* N22+566 **41**
Ballinrobe, *Ireland, Rep.* N55+536 **42**
Ballinskelligs B., *Ireland, Rep.* N62+518 **43**
Ballston Spa, *New York* S83+430 **96**
Ballybay, *Ireland, Rep.* N41+541 **42**
Ballybofey, *Ireland, Rep.* N47+548 **42**
Ballybunion, *Ireland, Rep.* N56+525 **43**
Ballycastle, *Ireland, Rep.* N56+543 **42**
Ballycastle, *N. Ireland* N37+552 **42**
Ballyclare, *N. Ireland* N36+547 **42**
Ballyconnell, *Ireland, Rep.* N45+541 **42**
Ballycotton B., *Ireland, Rep.* N47+518 **43**
Ballyduff, *Ireland, Rep.* N48+521 **43**
Ballygar, *Ireland, Rep.* N50+535 **43**
Ballygawley, *N. Ireland* N42+545 **42**
Ballyhaise, *Ireland, Rep.* N44+540 **42**
Ballyhaunis, *Ireland, Rep.* N53+538 **42**
Ballyhoura Hills, *Ireland, Rep.* N51+523 **43**
Ballyjamesduff, *Ireland, Rep.* N43+539 **42**
Ballymahon, *Ireland, Rep.* N47+534 **43**
Ballymena, *N. Ireland* N37+549 **42**
Ballymoney, *N. Ireland* N39+551 **42**
Ballymote, *Ireland, Rep.* N51+541 **42**
Ballynahinch, *N. Ireland* N35+544 **42**
Ballyquintin Pt., *N. Ireland* N33+543 **42**
Ballyragget, *Ireland, Rep.* N44+528 **43**
Ballyshannon, *Ireland, Rep.* N49+545 **42**
Ballyvaghan, *Ireland, Rep.* N55+531 **43**
Balmoral, *Victoria* C49-372 **109**
Balombo, *Angola* M00-124 **82**
Balotra, *India* H16+258 **70**
Balrampur, *India* G47+274 **73**
Balranald, *New S. Wales* C39-346 **109**
Balsam, L., *Ontario* T23+446 **91**
Balta, *Ukraine* L02+479 **60**
Baltanas, *Spain* N26+419 **52**
Baltic Sea, *N.-W. Europe* **47**
Baltim, *Egypt* K84+316 **81**
Baltimore, *Ireland, Rep.* N56+515 **43**
Baltimore, *Maryland* T10+393 **91**
Baltinglass, *Ireland, Rep.* N40+529 **43**
Baltistan, *Kashmir* G84+354 **72**
Baltiysk, *U.S.S.R.* L60+547 **47**
Baluchistan, *Pakistan* H60+275 **70**
Balurghat, *India* G07+252 **73**
Bam, *Iran* J1C+290 **75**
Bama, *Nigeria* M08+116 **81**
Bamako, *Mali* N48+126 **80**
Bambari, *Cent. Afr. Rep.* L56+056 **81**
Bamberg, *W. Germany* M25+499 **48**
Bamenda, *Cameroun* M30+058 **81**
Bamfield, *Michigan* T53+446 **91**
Bamian, *Afghanistan* H43+348 **75**
Bampton, *England* N21+510 **38**
Bampur, *Iran* H87+272 **75**
Bam Tso, *Tibet* G04+281 **71**
Banaras, *India* G42+254 **73**
Banat, *Romania* L65+460 **58**
Banayyan, *Saudi Arabia* J53+232 **75**
Banbridge, *N. Ireland* N38+544 **42**
Ban Chamai, *Thailand* F32+082 **69**
Banchory, *Scotland* N15+570 **40**
Bancroft, *Ontario* T17+450 **91**
Banda, *India* G58+255 **73**
Banda Atjeh, *Sumatra* F59+056 **65**
Banda Sea, *Indonesia* D50-055 **65**
Bandar. *See* Machilipatnam
Bandar Abbas, *Iran* J22+272 **75**
Bandarawela, *Sri Lanka* G54+068 **70**
Bandar e Deylam, *Iran* J59+302 **75**
Bandar e Lengeh, *Iran* J31+266 **75**
Bandar e Rig, *Iran* J56+295 **75**
Bandar e Shapur, *Iran* J64+304 **74**

Bandar Jissah, *Oman* J08+235 **75**
Bandar Shah, *Iran* J36+370 **75**
Bandera, *Argentina* S13-289 **103**
Banderas, B., *Mexico* V03+206 **100**
Bandiagara, *Mali* N22+140 **80**
Bandikui, *India* G81+269 **70**
Bandin Tologoi, *China* F07+412 **64**
Band-i-Qir, *Iran* J66+316 **74**
Bandirma, *Turkey* L12+404 **74**
Bandol, *France* M56+431 **55**
Bandon & R., *Ireland, Rep.* N52+517 **43**
Bandundu, *Zaire* L76-034 **82**
Bandung, *Java* E75-068 **65**
Baned, *India* G78+315 **72**
Banes, *Cuba* T05+210 **101**
Bañeza, la, *Spain* N35+422 **52**
Banff, *Scotland* N15+577 **40**
Banff & Park, *Alberta* V63+510 **88**
Bangada, *Congo* L12+040 **83**
Bangalore, *India* G74+131 **70**
Bangassou, *Cent. Afr. Rep.* L42+048 **81**
Bangka, I., *Indonesia* E84-022 **65**
Bangkok, (Krung Thep),
  Thailand G27+138 **69**
Bangkok, Bight of, *Thailand* F28+131 **69**
Bangladesh, *S. Asia* G05+246 **71**
Bang Mun Nak, *Thailand* F28+160 **65**
Bangor, *Maine* S53+448 **90**
Bangor, *N. Ireland* N34+546 **42**
Bangor, *Pennsylvania* T02+408 **96**
Bangor, *Wales* N25+532 **38**
Bang Saphan Yai, *Thailand* F33+113 **69**
Bangui, *Cent. Afr. Rep.* L68+044 **81**
Bangweulu L., *Zambia* L02-112 **83**
Ban Houei Sai, *Laos* F27+203 **69**
Bania, *Cent. Afr. Rep.* M40+042 **82**
Bani Bu 'Ali, *Oman* J05+221 **75**
Banica, *Dominican Rep.* S69+190 **101**
Baniyas, *Syria* K54+352 **76**
Baniyas, *Syria* K56+332 **76**
Banja Luka, *Yugoslavia* L77+448 **56**
Banjarmasin, *Indonesia* E32-034 **65**
Ban Jaruga, *Yugoslavia* L79+454 **56**
Banjul, *Gambia* P10+134 **80**
Banka, *India* G18+249 **73**
Banki, *India* G26+203 **71**
Bankipore, *India* G29+256 **73**
Banks I., *N.-W. Territories* W00+730 **88**
Banks I., *Queensland* C46-102 **111**
Banks Is., *Pacific Ocean* A72-145 **106**
Banks Pen., *New Zealand* A40-437 **112**
Banks Str., *Tasmania* C12-406 **109**
Bankura, *India* G17+232 **73**
Bann R., *Ireland, Rep.* N39+525 **43**
Bann R., *N. Ireland* N37+544 **42**
Banningville. *See* Bandundu
Bannu, *Pakistan* H26+330 **72**
Bañolas, *Spain* M73+421 **53**
Baños de Montemayor, *Spain* N35+403 **52**
Ban-pot, *Thailand* F31+160 **69**
Bansda, *India* H09+208 **70**
Bansi, *India* G43+272 **73**
Banswara, *India* H03+236 **70**
Bantalor, *New Brunswick* S38+463 **90**
Ban Thakham, *Thailand* F34+089 **69**
Bantry & B., *Ireland, Rep.* N57+517 **43**
Banu, *Afghanistan* H34+356 **75**
Banur, *India* G80+305 **72**
Banyak Kep., *Indonesia* F46+022 **65**
Banyo, *Cameroun* M20+068 **81**
Banyuwang, *Java* E34-082 **65**
Banzare Coast, *Antarctica* D65-660 **27**
Banzyville, *See* Yasanyama
Bapaume, *France* M73+501 **54**
Baquedano, *Chile* S58-230 **103**
Ba'quba, *Iraq* K02+337 **74**
Bar, *Yugoslavia* L65+421 **58**
Bara, *Sudan* K88+138 **81**
Barabanki, *India* G53+270 **73**
Barabinsk, *U.S.S.R.* G70+553 **62**
Baraboo, *Wisconsin* T89+435 **91**
Baracoa, *Cuba* S87+203 **101**
Barada, *Syria* K47+359 **76**
Baradine & R., *N.S.W.* C06-309 **109**
Baraimi, *U.A.E.* J26+243 **75**
Barak R., *India* F70+250 **71**
Baramula, *Kashmir* H04+342 **72**
Baranagar, *India* G09+227 **73**
Baranof I., *Alaska* X00+570 **99**
Baranovichi, *U.S.S.R.* L23+532 **60**
Baranów, *Poland* L51+505 **49**
Baraque Michel, *Belgium* M53+505 **44**
Barataria B., *Louisiana* U00+292 **95**
Baratta, *S. Australia* C65-320 **109**
Baraunda, *India* G57+250 **73**
Baraut, *India* G76+291 **72**
Barbacena, *Brazil* Q83-212 **105**
Barbacoas, *Colombia* T19+016 **104**
Barbadillo del Mercada, *Spain* N20+421 **52**
Barbados, I., *Windward Is.* R88+132 **101**
Barbastro, *Spain* M89+420 **53**
Barbezieux, *France* N01+455 **54**
Barbuda, I., *Leeward Is.* S10+177 **101**
Barca d'Alva, *Portugal* N41+410 **52**
Barcaldine, *Queensland* C28-234 **111**
Barcarrota, *Spain* N41+385 **52**
Barce. *See* Marj, el
Barcellona Pozza di Gotto,
  Sicily L89+382 **57**
Barcelos, *Brazil* S18-010 **104**
Barcelona, *Spain* M76+414 **53**
Barcelona, *Venezuela* S57+101 **104**
Barcelonnette, *France* M50+444 **55**
Barcelos, *Portugal* N52+415 **52**
Barco de Avila, el, *Spain* N33+404 **52**
Barcoo, R., *Queensland* C34-242 **111**
Bardera, *Somalia* K15+022 **83**
Bardi, *India* G45+245 **73**
Bardia, *Libya* L30+318 **81**
Bardsey, I., *Wales* N29+528 **38**
Bardstown, *Kentucky* T63+378 **97**
Bareilly, *India* G63+284 **73**
Barents Sea, *Arctic Ocean* K30+750 **62**
Barentsøya, I., *Arctic Ocean* L50+785 **62**
Barfurush. *See* Babol
Bargal, *Somalia* J54+112 **83**
Barh, *India* G26+255 **73**

Index

Barhaj, India G37+263 73
Bar Harbor, Maine S49+444 90
Bari, India G74+267 73
Bari, Italy L79+411 57
Bari Doab, Pakistan H12+304 72
Barinas, Venezuela S61+086 104
Baring, C., N.-W. Territories V72+700 88
Baringa, Zaire L56+008 82
Barisal, Bangladesh F88+227 71
Barisan, Pegunungar., Sum. F25–014 65
Barito, R., Indonesia E32–028 65
Barkah, Oman J12+238 75
Barkald, Norway M24+620 47
Barkhan, Pakistan H33+299 72
Barkly Tableland, Australia C70–192 111
Bârlad, Romania L14+462 58
Bar le Duc, France M60+488 54
Barlee, L., W. Australia E03–290 110
Barlee Ra., W. Australia E20–236 110
Barletta, Italy L83+413 57
Barmedman, New S. Wales C15–341 109
Barmer, India H21+257 70
Barmera, S. Australia C57–342 109
Barmouth, Wales N24+527 38
Barnaby River, N.B. S33+469 90
Barnard Castle, England N11+545 37
Barnato, New S. Wales C30–316 109
Barnaul, U.S.S.R. G33+535 62
Barn Bluff, Tasmania C25–417 109
Barne Inlet, Antarctica B30–800 27
Barnegat B., New Jersey S85+398 91
Barnesville, Minnesota U39+466 93
Barneveld, Netherlands M56+521 44
Barnsley, England N09+536 37
Barnstable, Massachusetts S62+417 96
Barnstaple, England N24+511 38
Baroda, India H10+222 70
Barotseland, Zambia L41–160 84
Baroyeca, Mexico V24+279 100
Barpeta, India F84+263 71
Barquinha, Portugal N51+394 52
Barquisimeto, Venezuela S56+100 104
Barra, Saudi Arabia J85+249 74
Barra Hd., Scotland N45+568 41
Barra, I., Scotland N45+570 40
Barra, Sd. of, Scotland N44+571 40
Barraba, New S. Wales B87–304 109
Barrackpore, India G10+228 73
Barracon, Argentina R52–263 103
Barra de Tonala, Mexico U23+160 100
Barra do Corda, Brazil R01–055 105
Barra do Pirai, Brazil Q83–224 105
Barra do Rio Doce, Brazil Q59–196 105
Barra do Rio Grande, Brazil Q80–111 105
Barra dos Bugres, Brazil R73–150 104
Barra Mansa, Brazil Q85–224 105
Barran, Somalia J68+102 83
Barranca, Peru T10–048 104
Barranca Bermeja, Colombia S83+071 104
Barrancas, Venezuela S13+088 104
Barrancos, Portugal N42+382 52
Barranqueras, Argentina R84–276 103
Barranquilla, Colombia S89+109 104
Barre, Vermont S75+442 91
Barreiras, Brazil R00–122 105
Barreirinha, Brazil R72–029 105
Barreirinhas, Brazil Q77–026 105
Barreiro, Portugal N54+387 52
Barreiros, Brazil Q31–087 105
Barreme, France M52+440 55
Barrie, Ontario T28+444 91
Barrier I., Great, N.Z. A27–360 112
Barrier I., Little, N.Z. A29–362 112
Barrington, Mt., N.S.W. B82–321 109
Barringun, New S. Wales C26–290 109
Barron, Wisconsin U11+454 93
Barrow, Argentina S02–382 103
Barrow-in-Furness, England N19+541 37
Barrow R., Ireland, Rep. N42+524 43
Barrow Str., N.-W. Terr. U45+736 88
Barrow Creek, N. T., Aust. D08–214 111
Barry, Wales N20+514 38
Barry Mts., Victoria C20–372 109
Barsi, India G85+182 70
Bar-sur-Aube, France M62+482 54
Bar-sur-Seine, France M64+481 54
Bartibog, New Brunswick S34+473 90
Bartica, Guyana R82+063 104
Bartle Frere Mt., Queensland C35–176 111
Bartlesville, Oklahoma U36+367 95
Baruva, India G32+190 71
Barvaux, Belgium M57+503 44
Barwa. India G34+232 73
Barwani, India H01+220 70
Barwon, R., New S. Wales C26–302 109
Basel (Basle), Switzerland M44+476 45
Baselland, canton, Switz. M43+474 45
Bashi, Iran J53+286 75
Bashi Chan., Phil.-Taiwan D80+215 67
Bashkirskaya, aut. rep., U.S.S.R. J30+550 62
Basia, India G30+229 73
Basilan, I., Philippines D77+066 65
Basilicata, reg., Italy L83+405 57
Basingstoke, England N07+513 39
Baskatong L., Quebec T05+468 91
Bàsmo, Norway M06+663 46
Basongo, Zaire L58–044 82
Basra, Iraq J73+305 74
Bas-Rhin, dep., France M42+486 54
Bass Str., Vict.-Tasm. C30–395 111
Bassac, Laos E85+149 69
Bassein, Burma F61+168 71
Bassein, India H13+196 70
Basses, Gt. & Lit., Sri Lanka G50+061 70
Basses-Alpes. See Alpes-de-Haute Provence
Basses-Pyrénées. See Pyrénées Atlantiques.
Basse Terre, Leeward Is. S09+160 101
Bassevelde, Belgium M68+512 44
Båstad, Sweden M13+564 47
Bastak, Iran J33+272 75
Basti, India G43+268 73
Bastia, Corsica M33+427 56
Bastogne, Belgium M56+500 44
Bastrop, Louisiana U11+328 95
Basura, Mexico V43+311 100
Basutoland. See Lesotho
Bata, Equatorial Guinea M32+018 82
Bataan, Philippines D88+147 65
Batabano, Cuba T43+227 101
Batacosa, Mexico V24+278 100

Batala, India G89+318 72
Batalha, Portugal N53+397 52
Batan Is., Philippines D78+210 64
Batangas, Philippines D84+137 65
Batavia, See Jakarta
Batavia, Argentina S35–348 103
Batavia, New York T19+430 96
Bataysk, U.S.S.R. K31+471 61
Batchawana, Ontario T55+472 91
Batchelor, N. Terr.. Aust. D24–131 110
Batdambang, Khmer F11+130 69
Bateman's B., New S. Wales B89–358 109
Batenburg, Netherlands M56+518 44
Batesburg, S. Carolina T39+339 97
Batesville, Arkansas U10+358 95
Batesville, Mississippi U00+344 97
Bath, England N14+514 38
Bath, Maine S59+439 90
Bath, New York T14+423 96
Bathgate, Scotland N22+559 41
Bathurst. See Banjul
Bathurst, New Brunswick S34+476 90
Bathurst, New S. Wales C03–334 109
Bathurst Inl., N.-W. Terr. V15+670 88
Bathurst I., N. Terr., Aust. D28–116 110
Bathurst I., N.-W. Terr. U60+756 88
Batie, Upper Volta N18+098 80
Batiscan, Quebec S74+465 91
Batlow, New South Wales C12–355 109
Batna, Algeria M52+356 80
Baton Rouge, Louisiana U07+304 95
Batopilas, Mexico V14+270 100
Batraki, U.S.S.R. J68+532 61
Batroun, Lebanon K56+342 76
Batticaloa, Sri Lanka G50+077 70
Battice, Belgium M55+506 44
Battih, Saudi Arabia J67+150 74
Battle Creek, Michigan T61+424 91
Battleford, Saskatchewan V20+529 88
Battleford, N., Saskatchewan V20+530 88
Battle Harbour, Labrador R65+526 89
Battle Mountain, Nevada V72+406 92
Batu, Indonesia F40–005 65
Batumi, U.S.S.R. K20+418 62
Baturaja, Sumatra F05–040 65
Baturi, Mexico V23+258 100
Baturite, Brazil Q34–004 105
Baud, India G34+208 71
Baudette, Minnesota U28+488 93
Baudo, Colombia T13+052 104
Baudouinville. See Moba
Bauge, France M88+475 54
Baunt, U.S.S.R. E40+553 63
Baures, Bolivia S22–137 104
Bauru, Brazil R24–221 105
Bauska, Latvia L35+564 47
Bautzen, E. Germany M03+512 48
Bawal, India G80+281 72
Bawean, I., Indonesia E44–058 65
Bawiti, Egypt L08+282 81
Bawku, Ghana N00+110 80
Bawtry, England N06+534 37
Bay Is., Honduras T68+164 101
Bayamo, Cuba T11+204 101
Bayana, India G77+269 73
Bayan Aul, Kazakh G86+507 62
Bayan Dzurikhe, Mongolia E76+477 64
Bayanga, Cent. Afr. Rep. L84+054 81
Bayan Kara Shan, China F30+335 64
Bayan Tumen, Mongolia E34+480 64
Bayazit, Turkey K08+396 74
Bay City, Michigan T36+436 91
Bay City, Texas U36+290 95
Bayern, W. Germany M18+490 48
Bayeux, France N05+493 54
Bayir, Jordan K50+308 76
Baykal, Oz, Russia E80+533 63
Bay Minette, Alabama T77+308 97
Bayona, Spain N53+421 52
Bayonne, France N09+435 55
Bayou Bodcau Res., La.-Ark. U20+329 95
Bayovar, Peru T36–058 104
Bayram Ali, Turkmen H77+375 62
Bayreuth, W. Germany M21+499 48
Bayrischer Wald, W. Germany M12+490 48
Bays, L. of, Ontario T24+453 91
Baza, Sa. de, Spain N08+375 53
Bazar Musa Khel, Pakistan H31+309 72
Bazaruto, I., Mozambique K58–218 84
Bazas, France N01+444 55
Bazias, Romania L52+448 58
Bazman, Iran J00+278 75
Beach, N. Dakota U84+470 93
Beachport, S. Australia C60–374 109
Beachy Hd., England M89+508 39
Beacon, New York S84+415 96
Beaconsfield, Tasmania C20–412 109
Beal Ra., Queensland C52–250 111
Bear Is. See Medvezhi Osa.
Bear L. & R., Ida.-Ut. V38+420 94
Beardmore Gl., Antarctica A70–850 27
Bearn, prov., France N03+432 55
Bear Paw Mts., Montana V26+483 94
Beata, I., Dominican Rep. S69+ 75 101
Beatenberg, Switzerland M43+467 45
Beatrice, Nebraska U40+403 95
Beattock, Scotland N21+553 41
Beattyville, Kentucky T52+376 97
Beaucaire, France M61+437 55
Beaufort, S. Carolina T34+325 97
Beaufort, Victoria C40–374 109
Beaufort Basin, Arctic Oc. X30–750 26
Beaufort Sea, Arctic Ocean W63+720 26
Beaufort West, Cape Prov. L44–324 84
Beaugency, France M80+478 54
Beauly & Firth, Scotland N27+575 40
Beaumaris, Wales N25+533 38
Beaumont, Belgium M65+502 44
Beaumont, France M76+491 54
Beaumont, New Zealand A62–458 112
Beaumont, Texas U25+302 95
Beaune, France M61+470 54
Beauport, Quebec S67+469 91
Beauraing, Belgium M60+501 44
Beauvais, France M78+494 54
Beauvoir-sur-Mer, France N12+469 54
Beaver, Oklahoma U64+368 94
Beaver, Utah V46+383 94

Beaver I., Michigan T63+457 91
Beaver R., Saskatchewan V25+542 88
Beaver Dam, Wisconsin T83+435 91
Beaver Falls, Pennsylvania T32+408 91
Beaverhead Mts., Idaho V53+454 92
Beawar, India H04+261 70
Beazley, Argentina S40–337 103
Bebedouro, Brazil R21–209 105
Becerrea, Spain N43+429 52
Bechuanaland. See Botswana
Becleau, Romania L35+472 49
Beda, Yemen J84+142 74
Bedak, Afghanistan H44+345 75
Bedar, Spain N12+372 53
Beddgelert, Wales N25+530 38
Bedford, Pennsylvania T21+400 96
Bedford, Quebec S78+451 91
Bedford, Virginia T27+373 97
Bedford & co., England N03+521 39
Bedretto, Switzerland M39+465 45
Bedr Honein, Saudi Arabia K38+237 74
Beduval, Saskatchewan W16+552 88
Bedzin, Poland L66+504 49
Beebe, Arkansas U11+351 97
Beechey, L., N.-W. Terr. V10+653 88
Beechworth, Victoria C20–364 109
Beecroft Hd., N.S.W. B85–350 109
Beek, Zaire L54+004 82
Beek, Netherlands M54+518 44
Beek, Netherlands M55+509 44
Beekbergen, Netherlands M54+522 44
Beenoskee, Ireland, Rep. N60+522 43
Beerlegem, Belgium M68+509 44
Beernem, Belgium M70+511 44
Beers, Netherlands M55+517 44
Beersheba, Israel K61+312 76
Beeville, Texas U46+284 94
Befale, Zaire L54+040 82
Befandriana, Madagascar J68–154 83
Bega, New South Wales C01–367 109
Behbehan, Iran J57+306 75
Beho, Belgium M54+502 44
Beidha, Saudi Arabia K30+208 74
Beilen, Netherlands M51+529 44
Beilul, Ethiopia K16+130 83
Beinwil, Switzerland M41+473 45
Beira, Mozambique K60–198 84
Beirut (Beyrouth), Lebanon K57+339 76
Beisan, Israel K57+325 76
Beitbridge, Rhodesia L00–222 84
Beit-et-Din, Lebanon K56+337 76
Beit Guvrin, Israel K60+316 76
Beius, Romania L46+467 58
Beja, Portugal N47+380 52
Béjar, Spain N35+404 52
Bejestan, Iran J11+346 75
Bejucal, Cuba T44+230 101
Békéscsaba, Hungary L54+467 49
Bela, Pakistan H52+261 70
Bela, India G47+259 73
Belair, Louisiana T89+298 97
Belang, Celebes D61+010 65
Belangpidie, Sumatra F50–038 65
Belaya Tserkov, Ukraine K89+498 60
Belcher Is., N.-W. Terr. T25+560 89
Belchirag, Afghanistan H58+358 75
Belchite, Spain N04+413 53
Belcoo, Ireland, Rep. N47+543 42
Beldanga, India G10+240 73
Belebey, U.S.S.R. J35+541 61
Belem, Argentina V32+278 96
Belém (Pará), Brazil R21–014 105
Belen, Argentina S42–278 103
Belen, New Mexico V11+346 94
Belen, Panama T35+090 101
Belfast, Maine S54+444 90
Belfast & L., N. Ireland N35+546 42
Belfield, Netherlands M53+513 44
Belfield, N. Dakota U79+469 93
Belford, England N11+556 37
Belfort, France M49+476 54
Belgaum, India H02+159 70
Belgium, Europe M63+507 50
Belgorod, U.S.S.R. K51+507 60
Belgorod Onestrovskiy, Ukr. K88+462 60
Belgrade. See Beograd
Belgrano, Argentina R82–358 103
Belin, France N05+445 55
Belitung, I., Indonesia E72–029 65
Belize, Belize T80+176 101
Belize, Central America T84+170 101

Bell I., Newfoundland R63+507 90
Bellac, France M84+461 54
Bella Coola, Brit. Columbia W40+521 88
Bellaire, Michigan T61+450 91
Bellaire, Ohio T35+400 91
Bellary, India G78+152 70
Bellavista, Peru T22–056 104
Bellbrook, New S. Wales B75–308 109
Belledune, New Brunswick S35+478 90
Bellefontaine, Ohio T53+404 91
Bellefonte, Pennsylvania T17+409 96
Belle Fourche, S. Dakota U83+447 93
Belle Ile, France N19+473 54
Belle Isle, New Brunswick S34+457 90
Belle Isle, Newfoundland R62+518 90
Belle Isle, Str. of, Nfd., etc. R72+513 90
Belleme, France M87+484 54
Belle Plain, Iowa U14+418 95
Bellerive, Tasmania C16–429 109
Belleville, France M82+461 54
Belleville, Kansas U46+398 95
Belleville, Illinois U00+385 95
Belleville, Ontario T14+422 91
Bellevue, Iowa U03+423 95
Bellevue, Ontario T55+467 91
Belley, France M56+458 54
Belle Yella, Liberia N60+076 80
Bellinger, New S. Wales B74–304 109
Bellingham, England N13+551 37
Bellingham, Washington W14+485 98
Bellingshausen Sea, Antarc. T60–670 27
Bellinzona, Switzerland M36+462 45
Bellows Falls, Vermont S75+431 96
Belluno, Italy M16+462 56
Bell Ville, Argentina S16–325 103
Belmez, Spain N32+383 52
Belmond, Iowa U22+429 95
Belmont, Missouri T85+367 95
Belmont, New York T18+422 96

Belmont L., Pennsylvania T03+418 96
Belmonte, Brazil S47–058 104
Belmonte, Brazil Q54–158 105
Belmonte, Portugal N44+404 52
Belmullet, Ireland, Rep. N60+542 42
Belo Horizonte, Brazil Q84–200 105
Beloit, Kansas U48+394 95
Beloit, Wisconsin T84+425 95
Belomorsk, Karelskaya K61+645 62
Belorado, Spain N19+424 52
Beloretsk, U.S.S.R. J10+540 61
Belorusskaya S.S.R. See Byelo-Russia
Belostok. See Bialystok
Beloye Oz., U.S.S.R. K44+602 60
Beloyo More, U.S.S.R. K30+658 62
Belp, Switzerland M45+469 45
Belt, Lille, Denmark M31+553 47
Belt, Store, Denmark M24+555 47
Beltana, S. Australia C70–308 109
Belterra, Brazil R60–026 105
Belton, S. Carolina C68–322 109
Belturbet, Ireland, Rep. N45+541 42
Belvedere Marittimo, Italy L85+396 57
Belver, Portugal N48+395 52
Belvidere, Illinois T83+422 95
Belvidere, New Jersey T01+408 96
Belyy, Os., U.S.S.R. H30+730 62
Bemidji, Minnesota U30+474 93
Benagerie, S. Australia C58–315 109
Ben Alder, Scotland N27+568 41
Benapol, India G07+230 73
Benares, See Varanasi
Benavente, Spain N34+420 52
Benbecula, I., Scotland N44+574 40
Benbury, Ireland, Rep. N59+536 42
Ben Cruachan, Scotland N31+564 41
Bencubbin, W. Australia E11–308 110
Bend, Oregon W08+441 92
Ben Dearg, Scotland N30+578 40
Bendery, Moldavia L03+469 60
Bendigo, Victoria C34–368 109
Bendoc, Victoria C07–371 109
Benevento, Italy M01+412 57
Bengal, B. of, India, etc. G00+180 71
Bengal, East, Bangladesh G03+240 73
Bengal, West, India G14+235 73
Ben Gardane, Tunisia M24+330 81
Benghazi, Libya L60+320 81
Benguela, Angola M10–126 82
Benha, Egypt K82+304 81
Ben Hope, Scotland N28+584 40
Beni, Bolivia S43–130 104
Beni-Abbès, Algeria N14+302 80
Benicarlo, Spain M88+404 53
Benin, rep., W. Africa M80+098 80
Benin, Bight of, W. Africa M80+050 80
Benin City, Nigeria M56+064 80
Beni Saf, Algeria N08+354 80
Beni Suef, Egypt K84+290 81
Benito, Rio Muni M32+014 82
Benjamin Constant, Brazil S61–044 104
Benkelman, Nebraska U70–400 95
Benkovac, Yugoslavia L87+441 56
Ben Lawers, Scotland N25+565 41
Ben Ledi, Scotland N26+563 41
Ben Lomond, N.S.W. B80–301 109
Ben Lomond, Scotland N28+562 41
Ben Lomond, Tasmania C15–416 109
Ben Macdhui, Scotland N22+571 40
Ben More, Scotland N27+564 41
Ben More Assynt, Scotland N29+581 40
Bennett, Brit. Columbia X00+599 88
Bennettsville, S. Carolina T28+346 97
Ben Nevis, Scotland N30+568 41
Bennington, Vermont S79+429 96
Benson, Arizona V32+320 94
Benson, Minnesota U34+453 93
Benson Mines, New York T00+442 91
Bentinck's I., Burma F21+171 71
Benton, Arkansas U16+345 97
Benton Harbor, Michigan T69+421 91
Benue R., Nigeria M40+080 81
Ben Vorlich, Scotland N25+563 41
Benwee Hd., Ireland, Rep. N59+545 42
Ben Wyvis, Scotland N27+577 40
Beograd, Yugoslavia L57+448 58
Beppu, Japan D21+332 68
Berar, India G74+205 70
Berat, Albania L60+407 59
Berawinnia, New S. Wales C33–290 109
Berber, Sudan K66+180 81
Berbera, Somalia K00+104 83
Berberati, Cent. Afr. Rep. L86+044 81
Berdichev, Ukraine L09+498 60
Berdigyastyakh, U.S.S.R. D46+623 63
Berdyansk, Ukraine K50+468 60
Bere Regis, England N13+507 39
Beresford, S. Dakota U42+430 93
Beresti, Romania L13+461 58
Berezniki, U.S.S.R. J20+594 62
Berezovo, U.S.S.R. H60+641 62
Berg, Norway L77+695 46
Berga, Spain M79+421 53
Bergamo, Italy M32+457 56
Bergen, E. Germany M10+544 48
Bergen, Norway T01+408 46
Bergen, W. Germany M31+528 48
Bergen-op-Zoom, Neth. M64+515 44
Bergerac, France M87+449 55
Bergisch Gladbach, W. Germany M46+510 48
Bergün, Switzerland M32+466 45
Berhampur, India G10+241 73
Berhampur, India G31+192 71
Beri, India G80+287 72
Bering, U.S.S.R. Z62+648 63
Beringen, Belgium M59+510 44
Bering Sea, Asia-America A00+590 99
Bering Str., Asia-America Z30+652 99
Berislavl, Ukraine K69+468 60
Berjeik, Netherlands M58+513 44
Berkåk, Norway M30+629 46
Berkeley, California W14+379 92
Berkhamsted, England N07+518 39
Berkovitsa, Bulgaria L42+433 58
Berkshire (Berks), co., Eng. N08+515 39
Berkshire Hills, Massachusetts S79+423 96
Berlin, Germany M10+525 48
Berlin, New Hampshire S75+445 91
Berlin, Wisconsin T83+440 91
Bermagui, N.S.W. C00–364 109

Bermillo de Savago, *Spain* N37+414 **52**
Bermudas, Is., *Atlantic Oc.* S30+320 **99**
Bern & canton, *Switzerland* M45+469 **45**
Bernalillo, *New Mexico* V10+353 **94**
Bernasconi, *Argentina* S23−379 **103**
Bernay, *France* M86+492 **54**
Bernburg, *E. Germany* M20+518 **48**
Berne. *See* Bern
Berneau, *Belgium* M56+507 **44**
Berneck, *Switzerland* M32+474 **45**
Berner Alpen, *Switzerland* M46+463 **45**
Bernina, Passo del, *Switz.* M30+464 **45**
Beromunster. *See* Munster
Berri, *S. Australia* C57−343 **109**
Berri, prov., *France* M76+471 **54**
Berriedale, *Scotland* N21+582 **40**
Berrigan, *New S. Wales* C25−357 **109**
Berry, *New South Wales* B86−348 **109**
Berry Is., *Bahamas, The* T18+256 **101**
Berryville, *Virginia* T18+391 **96**
Bersillies, *Belgium* M65+503 **44**
Berthierville, *Quebec* S79+461 **91**
Berthold, *N. Dakota* U71+483 **93**
Bertoua, *Cameroun* M08+046 **81**
Bertraghboy B., *Ireland, Rep.* N59+534 **43**
Bertrix, *Belgium* M59+499 **44**
Berwick, *Pennsylvania* T08+411 **96**
Berwick-upon-Tweed, *Eng.* N12+558 **37**
Berwyn Mts., *Wales* N20+529 **38**
Berzee, *Belgium* M64+503 **44**
Bescançon, *France* M54+473 **54**
Beskidy Zachodnie, mts.,
    Central Europe L54+495 **49**
Besni, *Turkey* K43+378 **74**
Bessala, *Congo* L86−026 **82**
Bessemer, *Alabama* T72+334 **97**
Best, *Netherlands* M58+515 **44**
Betanzos, *Spain* N49+434 **52**
Betbetti, *Sudan* L34+152 **81**
Bethanie, *S.-W. Africa* L76−264 **84**
Bethany, *Missouri* U24+403 **95**
Bethel, *Maine* S65+444 **90**
Bethlehem, *O.F.S.* L10−284 **84**
Bethlehem, *Israel* K59+317 **76**
Bethlehem, *Pennsylvania* T02+406 **96**
Betling Sib., *India* F75+238 **71**
Betsiamites, *Quebec* S52+490 **90**
Betsiamites R., *Quebec* S58+493 **90**
Bettiah, *India* G32+268 **73**
Beugen, *Netherlands* M54+517 **44**
Beulah, *Victoria* C46−360 **109**
Beveland, Noord, I.,
    Netherlands M67+516 **44**
Beveland, Zuid, I.,
    Netherlands M66+515 **44**
Beveren, *Belgium* M65+512 **44**
Beverley, *England* N02+538 **37**
Beverlo, *Belgium* M59+511 **44**
Beverly, *Massachusetts* S65+426 **96**
Beverst, *Belgium* M57+509 **44**
Bewdley, *England* N14+524 **38**
Bex, *Switzerland* M48+463 **45**
Beyla, *Guinea* N52+088 **80**
Beypazari, *Turkey* K79+402 **74**
Beypore, *India* G85+113 **70**
Beysehir, *Turkey* K80+376 **74**
Bezdán, *Yugoslavia* L67+458 **58**
Bezhitsa, *U.S.S.R.* K64+533 **60**
Beziers, *France* M71+434 **55**
Bezwada, *India* G56+165 **70**
Bhabua, *India* G38+250 **73**
Bhadarwah, *Kashmir* G85+329 **72**
Bhadaur, *India* G88+305 **72**
Bhadaura, *India* G76+248 **73**
Bhadohi, *India* G44+254 **73**
Bhadra, *India* G89+291 **72**
Bhadreswar, *India* G10+228 **73**
Bhagalpur, *India* G18+252 **73**
Bhakkar, *Pakistan* H23+317 **72**
Bhamo, *Burma* F46+242 **71**
Bhandara, *India* G62+211 **70**
Bhannis, *Lebanon* K56+339 **76**
Bhanrer Ra., *India* G63+234 **73**
Bharatpur, *India* G75+272 **73**
Bhatgaon, *Nepal* G27+276 **73**
Bhatinda, *India* H00+302 **72**
Bhatnair, *India* H04+295 **72**
Bhatpara, *India* G09+229 **73**
Bhavnagar, *India* H17+216 **70**
Bhawani Patna, *India* G40+200 **71**
Bhera, *Pakistan* H12+325 **72**
Bhilwara, *India* H02+254 **70**
Bhima R., *India* G82+172 **70**
Bhind, *India* G67+265 **73**
Bhir (Bir), *India* G85+190 **70**
Bhiwani, *India* G83+288 **72**
Bhojpur, *India* G35+255 **73**
Bhong Chu, R., *Tibet* G17+286 **71**
Bhopal, *India* G75+233 **73**
Bhuj, *India* H32+232 **70**
Bhusawal, *India* G85+210 **70**
Bhutan, *S. Asia* G00+270 **71**
Biafra, Bight of, *W. Africa* M38+026 **80**
Biak, I., *New Guinea* C84−010 **65**
Białogard, *Poland* L84+540 **49**
Białowieza, *Poland* L37+527 **49**
Białystok, *Poland* L41+531 **49**
Biarritz, *France* N09+435 **55**
Biasca, *Switzerland* M36+464 **45**
Biberach, *Germany* M32+481 **48**
Bibon, *Wisconsin* U07+464 **91**
Bic, *Quebec* S52+484 **90**
Bicknell, *Indiana* T74+388 **91**
Bida, *Nigeria* M54+092 **80**
Bidar, *India* G74+179 **70**
Biddeford, *Maine* S63+435 **96**
Bideford & B., *England* N25+510 **38**
Bidon, *Algeria* M84+222 **80**
Biel, *Switzerland* M47+471 **45**
Bielefeld, *Germany* M39+520 **48**
Bieler See, *Switzerland* M47+471 **45**
Bielopole, *Ukraine* K64+512 **60**
Bielsk, *Poland* L41+528 **49**
Bienne. *See* Biel
Bière, *Switzerland* M52+466 **45**
Bietschhorn, mt., *Switz.* M43+464 **45**
Big I., *N.-W. Territories* S63+620 **89**
Big L., *Arkansas* U01+357 **95**
Biga, *Turkey* L16+404 **74**

Big Bell, *W. Australia* E13−272 **110**
Big Belt Mts., *Montana* V40+468 **93**
Big Bend Nat. Pk., *Texas* U80+292 **94**
Big Blue R., *Kan.-Neb.* U40+400 **95**
Bigelow, *Maine* S63+451 **90**
Biggar, *Saskatchewan* V18+518 **88**
Biggar, *Scotland* N21+556 **41**
Biggleswade, *England* N02+521 **39**
Big Hatchet Mts., *New Mex.* V20+316 **94**
Bighorn Mts., *Wyoming* V15+444 **98**
Bighorn R., *Montana, etc.* V19+450 **93**
Bignona, *Senegal* P08+128 **80**
Big Rapids, *Michigan* T63+437 **91**
Big Salmon R., *Yukon* W80+612 **88**
Big Sandy R., *Kentucky, etc.* T45+380 **93**
Big Spring, *Texas* U68+322 **94**
Bigtimber, *Montana* V30+458 **93**
Big Trout L., *Ontario* T88+540 **89**
Bihac, *Yugoslavia* L85+448 **56**
Bihar, *India* G26+252 **73**
Bihar, *India* G30+248 **71**
Biharamulo, *Tanzania* K82−026 **83**
Bihorului, Mti, *Romania* L45+464 **58**
Bijagos, Arqui. Dos.,
    Guinea-Bissau P04+114 **80**
Bijapur, *India* G85+168 **70**
Bijar, *Iran* J74+359 **74**
Bijawar, *India* G63+246 **73**
Bijeljina, *Yugoslavia* L65+448 **58**
Bijnabad, *Iran* J12+280 **75**
Bijnor, *India* G71+294 **72**
Bikaner, *India* H10+280 **72**
Bikin, *U.S.S.R.* D04+467 **63**
Bikini, I., *Marshall Is.* A85+120 **106**
Bilaspur, *India* G79+312 **72**
Bilaspur, *India* G47+220 **73**
Bilauktaung Ra.,
    Burma-Thailand F38+145 **65**
Bilbao, *Spain* N18+433 **52**
Bileća, *Yugoslavia* L70+429 **58**
Bilecik, *Turkey* L00+402 **74**
Bilé Karpaty, *Czechoslovakia* L74+490 **49**
Bilimbaevski, *U.S.S.R.* J02+568 **61**
Bilin, *Burma* F47+173 **71**
Bilisht, *Albania* L54+406 **59**
Bilkis, *Iran* J15+371 **75**
Billabong, R. *See* Moulamein
Billeroo, *S. Australia* C60−312 **109**
Billings, *Montana* V21+458 **93**
Billiton, I. *See* Belitung
Bilma, *Niger* m12+184 **81**
Bilo Goro, *Yugoslavia* L78+458 **56**
Biloxi, *Mississippi* T84+304 **95**
Bilsi, *India* G67+282 **73**
Bilta, *Norway* L50+693 **46**
Bilthoven, *Netherlands* M59+t21 **44**
Bilugyun, I., *Burma* F45+164 **71**
Bilyarsk, *U.S.S.R.* J58+550 **61**
Bilzen, *Belgium* M55+509 **44**
Bimbe, *Angola* L84−120 **82**
Bimberi, Mt., *New S. Wales* C08−356 **109**
Bimlipatam, *India* G39+178 **71**
Binaiya, mt., *Ceram I., Indon.* D34-032 **65**
Binche, *Belgium* M65+504 **44**
Bindki, *India* G56+261 **73**
Bindura, *Rhodesia* K82−172 **84**
Binefar, *Spain* M88+418 **53**
Bingara, *New South Wales* B86−299 **109**
Bingen, *W. Germany* M43+500 **48**
Bingerville, *Ivory Coast* N24+054 **80**
Bingham, *England* N06+529 **37**
Bingham, *Maine* S59+451 **90**
Bingham Canyon, *Utah* V43+406 **94**
Binghamton, *New York* T06+422 **96**
Bingiri, *Zaire* L28−054 **82**
Bingol, *Turkey* K28+390 **74**
Binh Dinh (An Nhon),
    S. Viet. E65+139 **69**
Binn, *Switzerland* M41+464 **45**
Binnaway, *New S. Wales* C06−315 **109**
Bint, *Iran* J03+263 **75**
Bintan, I.,
    Riau Arch., Indonesia F02+011 **65**
Bintuni, Tk., *New Guinea* D12−024 **65**
Bir Ali, *Yemen, South* J70 + 140 **74**
Birao, *Japan* C40+423 **68**
Birchip, *Victoria* C43−360 **109**
Birchwood, *New Zealand* A73−459 **112**
Birdsboro, *Pennsylvania* T05+403 **96**
Birdsville, *Queensland* C64−278 **111**
Birdum,
    N. Terr., Australia D11−156 **110**
Birecik, *Turkey* K42+371 **74**
Birein, *Syria* K50+350 **76**
Bir Fadhil, *Saudi Arabia* J61+222 **74**
Bir Gara, *Chad* L84+132 **81**
Birhan, mt., *Ethiopia* K42+108 **83**
Birjand, *Iran* J04+328 **75**
Birkao, *Somalia* K20−012 **83**
Birkenhead, *England* N18+534 **37**
Bir Malusi, *Iraq* K30+335 **74**
Bir Maqran, *Saudi Arabia* J61+217 **74**
Birmingham, *Alabama* T71+335 **93**
Birmingham, *England* N11+525 **37**
Birmingham, *Michigan* T49+426 **91**
Birney, *Montana* V10+452 **93**
Birni-n-Kebbi, *Nigeria* M64+122 **80**
Birni-n' Konni, *Niger* M58+136 **80**
Birobidzhan, *U.S.S.R.* D12+488 **63**
Birq, *Saudi Arabia* K21+181 **74**
Birr, *Ireland, Rep.* N47+531 **43**
Birrie, R., *New South Wales* C18−294 **109**
Birsilpur, *India* H16+282 **72**
Birsk, *U.S.S.R.* J28+554 **61**
Birzhay, *Lithuania* L31+562 **47**
Bisalpur, *India* G61+283 **73**
Bisauli, *India* G66+283 **73**
Bisbee, *Arizona* V29+334 **94**
Bisbee, *N. Dakota* U56+486 **93**
Biscay, B. of, *France-Spain* N24+460 **50**
Bischofszell, *Switzerland* M34+475 **45**
Biscoe, B., *Antarctica* Y00−770 **27**
Biscoe, I., *Antartica* S40−660 **27**
Biscotasing, *Ontario* T43+472 **91**
Bisha, *Saudi Arabia* K09+201 **74**
Bishnath, *India* F71+266 **71**
Bishnupur, *India* G16+230 **73**
Bishop Mt., *Wyoming* V24+410 **93**
Bishop Auckland, *England* N10+547 **37**
Bishop's Falls, *Nfd.* R63+490 **90**
Bishops Stortford, *England* M89+519 **39**

Bishri, Jebel el, *Syria* K36+354 **74**
Bisisthal, *Switzerland* M37+469 **45**
Biskia, *Ethiopia* K46+154 **83**
Bismarck, *N. Dakota* U65+468 **93**
Bismarck Arch., *Pacific Oc.* C00−050 **106**
Bismarck C., *Greenland* P25+770 **26**
Bison, *S. Dakota* U75+455 **93**
Bissau, *India* G89+282 **72**
Bissau, *Guinea-Bissau* P04+118 **80**
Bissett, *Ontario* T18+462 **91**
Bistcho, L., *Alberta* V85+598 **88**
Bithur, *India* G58+266 **73**
Bitlis, *Turkey* K18+385 **74**
Bitola, *Yugoslavia* L52+411 **58**
Bitterfeld, *E. Germany* M16+516 **48**
Bitter Root Mts., *Idaho* V64+469 **92**
Bivio, *Switzerland* M32+465 **45**
Biwa Ko, *Japan* C84+352 **68**
Biysk, *U.S.S.R.* G27+526 **62**
Bizerte, *Tunisia* M32+372 **81**
Bjelóvar, *Yugoslavia* L79+459 **56**
Björkö, *Sweden* L66+599 **47**
Björna, *Sweden* L68+636 **46**
Bjørnør, *Norway* M29+642 **46**
Bjørnøya, I., *Barents Sea* L63+743 **62**
Black Hd., *Ireland, Rep.* N55+532 **43**
Black Hills, *S. Dakota* U85+442 **98**
Black Isle, *Scotland* N25+576 **40**
Black Mt., *Pakistan* H13+345 **72**
Black Mts., *Arizona* V57+358 **92**
Black Mts., *Wales* N19+519 **38**
Black Ra., *New Mexico* V17+330 **94**
Black R., *Arkansas, etc.* U08+360 **95**
Black Sea, *Europe-Asia* K60+440 **30**
Blackall, *Queensland* C27−242 **111**
Blackburn, *England* N15+537 **37**
Blackdown Hills, *England* N19+509 **38**
Blackfoot, *Idaho* V44+432 **92**
Blackpool, *England* N18+538 **37**
Blackriver, *Michigan* T50+448 **91**
Black River Falls, *Wisconsin* U05+443 **91**
Black Rock, *Arkansas* U07+361 **97**
Black Rock Des., *Nevada* V84+412 **92**
Blacksod B., *Ireland, Rep.* N61+541 **42**
Black Sugar Loaf, mt.,
    New South Wales B81−314 **109**
Blackville, *New Brunswick* S35+467 **90**
Blackville, *S. Carolina* T38+333 **97**
Black Volta R., *Ghana* N14+094 **80**
Blackwater, *Ireland, Rep.* N38+524 **43**
Blackwater L., *N.-W. Terr.* W28+644 **88**
Blackwater Res., *Scotland* N29+567 **41**
Blackwater R.,
    Cork, etc. Ireland, Rep. N47+520 **43**
Blackwater R.,
    Meath, Ireland, Rep. N40+537 **42**
Blackwater R., *N. Ireland* N40+545 **42**
Blackwell, *Oklahoma* U44+368 **95**
Blaenavon, *Wales* N19+518 **38**
Blagoveshchensk, *U.S.S.R.* D44+504 **63**
Blagoveshchensk, *U.S.S.R.* J24+550 **61**
Blagoevgrad, *Bulgaria* L42+420 **58**
Blair, *Nebraska* U37+416 **95**
Blair Atholl, *Scotland* N23+568 **41**
Blairgowrie, *Scotland* N20+566 **41**
Blairmore, *Alberta* V56+496 **88**
Blaj, *Romania* L36+462 **58**
Blanc, C., *Mauritania* P12+208 **80**
Blanc, le, *France* M83+466 **54**
Blanc, Mt., *France-Italy* M48+458 **54**
Blanca, B., *Argentina* S10−394 **103**
Blanca Pk., *Colorado* V03+378 **98**
Blanca, Sierra, *New Mexico* V05+332 **94**
Blanche, L., *S. Australia* C62−292 **109**
Blanche Town, *S. Australia* C62−343 **109**
Blanchewater, *S. Australia* C63−295 **109**
Blanco, C., *Oregon* W28+428 **92**
Blanco Pico, *Costa Rica* T50+095 **101**
Bland, *Virginia* T37+371 **97**
Blandford, *England* N13+509 **39**
Blanes, *Spain* M73+417 **53**
Blaney Park, *Michigan* T65+462 **91**
Blangy, *France* M80+499 **54**
Blankenberge, *Belgium* M71+513 **44**
Blantyre-Limbe, *Malawi* K60−158 **83**
Blaregnies, *Belgium* M67+504 **44**
Blasket Sd., *Ireland, Rep.* N63+521 **43**
Blaton, *Belgium* M68+505 **44**
Blaye, *France* N04+451 **55**
Blayney, *New South Wales* C04−336 **109**
Blenheim, *New Zealand* A36−415 **112**
Blenheim, *Ontario* T42+424 **91**
Blessington, *Ireland, Rep.* N39=532 **43**
Blida, *Algeria* M72+364 **80**
Blind River, *Ontario* T48+462 **91**
Blinman, *S. Australia* C68−311 **109**
Blitta, *Togo* M84+084 **80**
Blitzen, Mt., *Nevada* V68+414 **92**
Block I., *Rhode Island* S70+412 **96**
Bloemfontein, *O.F.S.* L22−290 **84**
Blois, *France* M82+476 **54**
Blokzijl, *Netherlands* M54+527 **44**
Bloody Foreland,
    Ireland, Rep. N50+552 **42**
Bloomfield, *Iowa* U14+408 **95**
Bloomington, *Illinois* T84+407 **95**
Bloomsburg, *Pennsylvania* T09+410 **96**
Blossburg, *Pennsylvania* T12+417 **96**
Blount Springs, *Alabama* T70+340 **97**
Blue Mt., *India* F72+227 **71**
Blue Mts., *Jamaica* T10+180 **101**
Blue Mts., *New S. Wales* B88−334 **109**
Blue Mts., *Oregon* V81+450 **92**
Blue Mts., *Pennsylvania* T04+407 **96**
Blue Earth, *Minnesota* U25+437 **93**
Bluefield, *W. Virginia* T37+373 **97**
Bluefields, *Nicaragua* T53+120 **101**
Blue Lake, *Michigan* T60+448 **91**
Blue Ridge, mts., *U.S.A.* T48+350 **99**
Blue Stack Mts.,
    Ireland, Rep. N49+547 **42**
Bluff, *New Zealand* A70−466 **112**
Bluff, *Utah* V28+371 **98**
Bluff Knoll, *W. Australia* E15−344 **110**
Blumenau, *Brazil* R25−270 **103**
Blyth, *England* N09+551 **37**
Blytheville, *Arkansas* U00+359 **95**
Blytheville, *Arkansas* U00+359 **95**
Blytherkerovsk, *U.S.S.R.* D70+552 **63**
Bo, *Sierra Leone* N70+082 **80**

Boac, *Philippines* D79+134 **65**
Boaco, *Nicaragua* T65+124 **101**
Boafé, *Brazil* S71−072 **104**
Boardman, *N. Carolina* T24+345 **97**
Boat of Garten, *Scotland* N22+572 **40**
Boa Vista, *Brazil* Q59−088 **105**
Boa Vista, *Brazil* S03+027 **104**
Boa Vista Tocantins, *Brazil* R15−064 **105**
Bobadah, *New S. Wales* C20−323 **109**
Bobi, *Paraguay* R67−269 **103**
Bobo Dioulasso, *Upper Volta* N26+112 **80**
Bobolice, *Poland* L81+539 **49**
Bobrov, *U.S.S.R.* K30+510 **61**
Bobruysk, *Belorussia* L05+532 **60**
Bocas del Toro, *Panama* T43+094 **101**
Bocca do Curua, *Brazil* R56−054 **105**
Bocca do Tauary, *Brazil* S69−082 **104**
Bochnia, *Poland* L57+500 **49**
Bocholt, *Belgium* M57+512 **44**
Bocholt, *W. Germany* M50+519 **48**
Bochum, *W. Germany* M47+515 **48**
Bocota, *Mozambique* K70−228 **84**
Bodalla, *New South Wales* C00−361 **109**
Bodaybo, *U.S.S.R.* E34+578 **63**
Boden, *Sweden* L50+658 **46**
Boden See, *Switzerland-*
    Germany M33+476 **45**
Boderg L., *Ireland, Rep.* N48+539 **42**
Bodmin & Moors, *England* N28+505 **38**
Bodø, *Norway* M04+672 **46**
Boela, *Ceram I., Indonesia* D27−032 **65**
Boende, *Congo* L56−004 **82**
Boentok, *Borneo* E31−016 **65**
Boeol, *Célébes* D82+011 **65**
Boertange, *Netherlands* M47+530 **44**
Bofin L., *Ireland, Rep.* N48+538 **42**
Bogalusa, *Louisiana* T89+308 **95**
Bogan, R., *New S. Wales* C18−312 **109**
Bogandé, *Upper Volta* N00+128 **80**
Bogan Gate, *New S. Wales* C14−331 **109**
Bogbonga, *Zaire* L64+014 **82**
Bogdarin, *U.S.S.R.* E39+544 **63**
Bogdo Ula, *China* G02+434 **64**
Boggabri, *New South Wales* C00−307 **109**
Boggeragh Mts.,
    Ireland, Rep. N54+520 **43**
Boghari. *See* Ksar El Boukhari
Bognor Regis, *England* N04+508 **39**
Bogong, Mt., *Victoria* C16−367 **109**
Bogor, *Java, Indonesia* E80−065 **65**
Bogorodskoye, *U.S.S.R.* J67+524 **61**
Bogorodskoye, *U.S.S.R.* C57+525 **63**
Bogota, *Colombia* S83+046 **104**
Bogotol, *U.S.S.R.* G03+561 **62**
Bogra, *Bangladesh* G09+248 **73**
Bohemia, *Czechoslovakia* M06+496 **48**
Böhmer Wald, *Germany-*
    Czechoslovakia M12+492 **48**
Bohol, I., *Philippines* D64+100 **65**
Boiestown, *New Brunswick* S38+465 **90**
Boigu, I., *Papua*
    New Guinea C47−093 **111**
Boim, *Brazil* R61−027 **105**
Bois, L. des, *N.-W. Terr.* W17+668 **88**
Bois Blanc I., *Michigan* T57+458 **91**
Boisé, *Idaho* V68+436 **92**
Boise City, *Oklahoma* U75+368 **94**
Bois-le-Duc. *See* 'sHertogenbosch
Boissevain, *Manitoba* U60+493 **88**
Boké, *Guinea* N86+110 **80**
Bokhara, R., *New S. Wales* C16−294 **109**
Bokki, *Cameroun* M10+088 **81**
Bokoro, *Chad* L76+122 **81**
Bolan, *Pakistan* H42+295 **70**
Bolangir, *India* G38+206 **71**
Bolbec, *France* M87+496 **54**
Bole, *Ghana* N14+090 **80**
Bölebyn, *Sweden* L52+654 **46**
Bolgrad, *Ukraine* L08+457 **60**
Bolintin, *Romania* L25+444 **58**
Bolivar, *Argentina* S07−362 **105**
Bolivar, *Colombia* T11+018 **104**
Bolivar, *Missouri* U20+376 **95**
Bolivia, rep., *S. America* — **104**
Bollstabruk, *Sweden* L74+630 **46**
Bolmen, L., *Sweden* M08+569 **47**
Bolobo, *Zaire* L82−022 **82**
Bologna, *Italy* M22+445 **56**
Bologoye, *U.S.S.R.* K66+578 **60**
Bolotnoye, *U.S.S.R.* G34+554 **62**
Bolsena, L. di, *Italy* M19+426 **56**
Bolshevik, Ostrov, *U.S.S.R.* F10+787 **63**
Bolshoy Lyakhovskiy, Ostrov,
    U.S.S.R. C45+735 **63**
Boltaña, *Spain* N00+425 **53**
Bolton, *England* N15+536 **37**
Bolu, *Turkey* K82+408 **74**
Bolus Hd., *Ireland, Rep.* N62+518 **43**
Bolzano, *Italy* M22+465 **56**
Bomal, *Belgium* M57+504 **44**
Bomba, Gulf of, *Libya* L40+322 **81**
Bombala, *New S. Wales* C04−369 **109**
Bombarral, *Portugal* N55+393 **52**
Bombay, *India* H13+190 **70**
Bomfim, *Brazil* Q61−104 **105**
Bomfim, *Brazil* R22−166 **105**
Bomhus, *Sweden* L77+606 **47**
Bom Jardim, *Brazil* S63−067 **104**
Bom Jesus do Gurgueia,
    Brazil Q86−092 **105**
Bømlo, I., *Norway* M59+597 **47**
Bomnak, *U.S.S.R.* D36+547 **63**
Bomoseen, L., *Vermont* S79+437 **96**
Bonaduz, *Switzerland* M33+468 **45**
Bonaire, I., *Neth. Antilles* S49+122 **94**
Bonar Bridge, *Scotland* N26+579 **40**
Bonaventure I., *Quebec* S25+485 **90**
Bonavista, *Newfoundland* R49+482 **90**
Bonavista B., *Newfoundland* R48+489 **90**
Bondo, *Zaire* L36+038 **82**
Bône ('Annaba), *Algeria* M44+368 **81**
Bone, G. of, *Célébes* D86−035 **65**
Bo'ness, *Scotland* N50+560 **41**
Bongor, *Chad* L88+104 **81**
Bonham, *Texas* U37+336 **95**
Bonifacio & B. de, *Corsica* M35+414 **57**
Bonn, *Germany* M48+507 **48**
Bonne Bay, *Newfoundland* R78+496 **90**

Bonne Terre, *Missouri* U04+379 **97**
Bonneval, *France* M82+482 **54**
Bonneville Salt Flats, *Utah* V54+410 **94**
Bonney, L., *S. Aust.* C58-376 **109**
Bonnie Rock, *W. Australia* E09-304 **110**
Bonny, *France* M73+475 **54**
Bonny, *Nigeria* M46+044 **80**
Book Plat., *Colorado* V20+397 **94**
Boolaboolka L., *N.S.W.* C40-326 **109**
Booleroo Centre, *S. Australia* C70-329 **109**
Booligal, *New S. Wales* C31-339 **109**
Boom, *Belgium* M64+511 **44**
Boone, *Iowa* U23+422 **95**
Boone, *N. Carolina* T40+362 **97**
Booneville, *Mississippi* T82+346 **97**
Boonville, *Missouri* U16+390 **95**
Boonville, *New York* T02+435 **96**
Boorindal, *New S. Wales* C23-304 **109**
Booroorban, *New S. Wales* C32-348 **109**
Boorowa, *New S. Wales* C08-344 **109**
Boort, *Victoria* C38-360 **109**
Boothia, G. of, *N.-W. Terr.* T70+700 **89**
Boothia Pen., *N.-W. Terr.* U20+706 **89**
Bootle, *England* N20+543 **37**
Bootle, *England* N18+534 **37**
Boqueron, *Cuba* T01+200 **101**
Boquete, *Panama* T45+088 **101**
Boramo, *Somalia* K10+100 **83**
Borås, *Sweden* M12+577 **47**
Borazjan, *Iran* J53+292 **75**
Borba, *Brazil* R88-044 **104**
Bordeaux, *France* N04+448 **55**
Borders, reg., *Scotland* N16+555 **41**
Bordertown, *S. Australia* C55-363 **109**
Borga, *Sweden* M00+648 **46**
Borge Fjell, *Norway* M08+653 **46**
Borger, *Netherlands* M49+529 **44**
Borger, *Texas* U68+357 **94**
Borgholm, *Sweden* L80+569 **47**
Borgne, *Haiti* S75+198 **101**
Borisoglebsk, *U. S. S. R.* K17+514 **61**
Borisov, *Byelo-Russia* L09+551 **60**
Bo River Post, *Sudan* L12+068 **81**
Borja, *Spain* N09+418 **53**
Borjas Blancas, *Spain* M83+415 **53**
Borkum I., *Germany* M49+536 **48**
Borlänge, *Sweden* L88+605 **47**
Borneo, *Indonesia* — **65**
Bornholm, I., *Denmark* M00+551 **47**
Bor Nor, *China* E14+476 **64**
Borodino, *U.S.S.R.* K56+554 **60**
Borogontsy, *U.S.S.R.* D20+630 **63**
Borovë, *Albania* L57+397 **59**
Borovichi, *U.S.S.R.* K67+586 **60**
Borris, *Ireland, Rep.* N41+526 **43**
Borrisoleigh, *Ireland, Rep.* N48+527 **43**
Borroloola, *N. Terr., Aust.* C81-161 **111**
Borskoe, *U.S.S.R.* J50+530 **61**
Borūjerd, *Iran* J67+339 **74**
Borzya, *U.S.S.R.* E21+506 **63**
Bosco, *Switzerland* M39+463 **45**
Boscobel, *Wisconsin* U04+431 **91**
Bosiljgrad, *Yugoslavia* L45+425 **58**
Boskoop, *Netherlands* M62+521 **44**
Bosna-Hercegovina, *Yugosl.* L72+443 **58**
Boso Pen., *Japan* C57+353 **68**
Bosobolo, *Zaire* L60+040 **82**
Bosoli, *Botswana* L14-210 **84**
Bosporus, *Turkey* L06+413 **74**
Bossier City, *Louisiana* U22+325 **95**
Bosso, *Niger* M10+136 **81**
Bostan, *Pakistan* H48+304 **70**
Boston, *England* N00+530 **37**
Boston, *Massachusetts* S66+424 **91**
Boston Mts., *Arkansas* U24+358 **95**
Botany B., *New S. Wales* B84-340 **109**
Botera, *Angola* M04-118 **82**
Bothaville, *O.F.S.* L20-274 **84**
Bothnia, G. of, *N.-W. Europe* — **46-47**
Botswana (Bechuanaland) L30-216 **84**
Bouake, *Ivory Coast* N30+078 **80**
Bour, *Cent. Afr. Rep.* L86+060 **81**
Bou Arfa, *Morocco* N12+326 **80**
Bouches-du-Rhône, dep., *Fr.* M59+436 **55**
Bou Djébéha, *Mali* N16+184 **80**
Boudoukou, *Ivory Coast* N18+082 **80**
Boudry, *Switzerland* M49+470 **45**
Bougainville, I., *Solomon Is.* B60-060 **106**
Bougaroun C., *Algeria* M48+368 **80**
Bougie (Begaia), *Algeria* M60+366 **80**
Bougouni, *Mali* N46+114 **80**
Bouillon, *Belgium* M60+498 **44**
Boularderie I., *Nova Scotia* S03+463 **90**
Boulder, *Colorado* V02+400 **94**
Boulder, *W. Australia* D81-309 **110**
Boulder Mt., *Idaho* V56+440 **98**
Boulia, *Queensland* C61-227 **111**
Boulogne, *France* M80+508 **54**
Bouna, *Ivory Coast* N18+092 **80**
Boundary, *Brit. Columbia* W71+564 **88**
Bountiful, *Utah* V42+408 **94**
Bounty Is., *Pacific Ocean* A05-475 **106**
Bourbonnais, prov., *France* M71+465 **54**
Bourem, *Mali* N02+168 **80**
Bourg, *France* M59+462 **54**
Bourg Argental, *France* M63+453 **55**
Bourges, *France* M76+471 **54**
Bourget, L. du, *France* M55+457 **54**
Bourgogne, prov., *France* M61+471 **54**
Bourg St Pierre, *Switz.* M47+460 **45**
Bourke, *New S. Wales* C24-302 **109**
Bourkes, *Ontario* T31+483 **91**
Bournemouth, *England* N11+507 **39**
Bouvet I., *Atlantic Ocean* M70-540 **27**
Bovigny, *Belgium* M55+502 **44**
Bovino, *Italy* L41+413 **57**
Bow R., *Alberta* V44+502 **88**
Bowbells, *N. Dakota* U74+488 **93**
Bowen, *Queensland* C10-200 **111**
Bowen, C., *N.-W. Terr.* S88+720 **89**
Bowie, *Texas* U47+336 **95**
Bowling Green, *Kentucky* T68+370 **97**
Bowling Green, *Missouri* U08+394 **95**
Bowling Green, *Ohio* T52+414 **91**
Bowling Green, *Virginia* T14+380 **97**
Bowman, *N. Dakota* U81+462 **93**
Bowman B., *N.-W. Terr.* T00+656 **89**
Bowman I., *Antarctica* F20-650 **27**
Bowmanville, *Ontario* T22+439 **91**
Bowral, *New South Wales* B88-345 **109**

Bowser, *Victoria* C22-363 **109**
Box Elder, *Montana* V30+483 **93**
Boxholm, *Sweden* M00+582 **47**
Boxmeer, *Netherlands* M54+516 **44**
Box Tank, *New S. Wales* C47-322 **109**
Boxtel, *Netherlands* M58+516 **44**
Boydton, *Virginia* T20+367 **97**
Boyle, *Ireland, Rep.* N50+540 **42**
Boyne, R., *Ireland, Rep.* N38+537 **42**
Boyne City, *Michigan* T60+453 **91**
Boyoma Falls, *Zaire* L26+002 **82**
Bozeman, *Montana* V36+457 **93**
Bozoum, *Cent. Afr. Rep.* L82+062 **81**
Bra, *Italy* M43+447 **56**
Brabant, prov. *Belgium* M62+508 **44**
Brabant, Noord, prov., *Neth.* M60+516 **44**
Brac, I., *Yugoslavia* L80+433 **56**
Bracadale L., *Scotland* N39+573 **40**
Bracebridge, *Ontario* T26+450 **91**
Bräcke, *Sweden* L88+628 **46**
Bracknell, *England* N05+514 **39**
Brad, *Romania* L43+461 **58**
Braddock, *N. Dakota* U60+465 **93**
Braddock, *Pennsylvania* T29+404 **96**
Bradford, *England* N10+538 **37**
Bradford, *Pennsylvania* T22+419 **96**
Braemar, *Scotland* N20+570 **40**
Braeriach, *Scotland* N22+571 **40**
Braga, *Portugal* N51+416 **52**
Bragado, *Argentina* S03-352 **103**
Bragança, *Brazil* R11-011 **105**
Bragança, *Portugal* N41+418 **52**
Bragança Paulista, *Brazil* R10-228 **105**
Brahmanbaria, *Bangladesh* F83+240 **71**
Brahmaputra R., *India* F70+265 **71**
Braidwood, *Illinois* T79+413 **91**
Braidwood, *New S. Wales* C01-354 **109**
Brail, *Switzerland* M30+466 **45**
Brăila, *Romania* L12+452 **58**
Braine l'Alleud, *Belgium* M64+507 **44**
Braine le Comte, *Belgium* M65+506 **44**
Brainerd, *Minnesota* U25+463 **93**
Braintree, *England* M87+519 **39**
Brak, *Libya* M04+276 **81**
Brampton, *Ontario* T29+437 **91**
Branchville, *S. Carolina* T35+333 **97**
Brandenburg, *E. Germany* M15+524 **48**
Brandon, *England* M86+524 **39**
Brandon, *Manitoba* U59+498 **88**
Brandon B. and Head,
  Ireland, Rep. N61+523 **43**
Brandon Mt., *Ireland, Rep.* N42+525 **43**
Brandsen, *Argentina* R80-352 **193**
Brandvlei, *Cape Province* L56-304 **84**
Branford, *Florida* T48+300 **97**
Braniewa, *Poland* L61+544 **49**
Bransfield Str., *Antarctica* R60-620 **27**
Bransk, *Poland* L43+527 **49**
Brantford, *Ontario* T32+431 **91**
Brantôme, *France* M86+453 **55**
Branxholme, *Victoria* C49-379 **109**
Bras d'or L., *Nova Scotia* S05+459 **90**
Brasilia, *Brazil* R23-160 **105**
Brasov, *Romania* L27+456 **58**
Brassus, le, *Switzerland* M53+466 **45**
Bratislava, *Czechoslovakia* L78+482 **49**
Bratsk, *U.S.S.R.* F19+561 **63**
Brattleboro, *Vermont* S76+425 **96**
Braunau, *Austria* M12+482 **48**
Braunlage, *W. Germany* M27+523 **48**
Braunschweig, *W. Germany* M36+469 **45**
Braunwald, *Switzerland* M36+469 **45**
Brava, *Somalia* K06+012 **83**
Brawley, *California* V63+330 **92**
Bray & Hd., *Ireland, Rep.* N36-532 **43**
Bray Hd., *Ireland, Rep.* N63+519 **43**
Brazil, *Indiana* T73+395 **95**
Brazil, rep., *S. America* — **104-105**
Brazos R., *Texas* U34+294 **95**
Brazos Santiago, *Texas* U43+260 **96**
Brazzaville, *Congo* L88-042 **82**
Brčko, *Yugoslavia* L67+449 **58**
Bream B., *New Zealand* A32-358 **112**
Brechin, *Scotland* N16+567 **41**
Breckenridge, *Minnesota* U40+463 **93**
Brecknock, Pen., *Chile* S70-546 **103**
Brecknock, See Powys
Břeclav, *Czechoslovakia* L73+488 **49**
Brecon, *Wales* N20+520 **38**
Brecon Beacons, *Wales* N20+519 **38**
Breda, *Netherlands* M61+5 6 **44**
Bredasdorp, *Cape Province* L60+346 **84**
Bredene, *Belgium* M72+512 **44**
Bredoo, *New South Wales* C06-360 **109**
Bredy, *U.S.S.R.* J59+526 **61**
Bree, *Belgium* M56+511 **44**
Breidha fjördhur, *Iceland* P54+652 **46**
Breil, *France* M45+439 **55**
Breithorn, mt., *Switzerland* M43+465 **45**
Brejo, *Brazil* Q77-036 **105**
Bremangerland, *Norway* M60+618 **46**
Bremen, *W. Germany* M37+531 **48**
Bremerhaven, *W. German* M39+536 **48**
Bremerton, *Washington* W16+475 **92**
Bremgarten, *Switzerland* M40+474 **45**
Brenham, *Texas* U38+302 **95**
Brenner Pass, *Austria-Italy* M21+470 **56**
Breno, *Italy* M28+459 **56**
Brent, *Ontario* T21+461 **91**
Brentford, *England* N02+515 **39**
Brentwood, *England* M88+516 **39**
Brescia, *Italy* M29+455 **56**
Breskens, *Netherlands* M69+514 **44**
Breslau. See Wroclaw
Bressay I., *Scotland* N66+601 **40**
Bressuire, *France* N03+468 **54**
Brest, *France* N27+484 **54**
Brest, *Byelo-Russia* L38+521 **60**
Brest-Litovsk. See Brest
Bretagne, prov., *France* N17+480 **54**
Bretcu, *Romania* L22-460 **58**
Breton Sd., *Louisiana* T74+295 **95**
Breugel, *Netherlands* M57+515 **44**
Brevard, *N. Carolina* T46+352 **97**
Breves, *Brazil* R33-16 **105**
Brevik, *Norway* M32+590 **47**
Brewarrina, *New S. Wales* C19-300 **109**
Brewer, *Maine* S52+448 **90**
Brewster Mt., *Antarctica* A75-730 **27**
Brewton, *Alabama* T72+311 **97**
Brežice, *Yugoslavia* L86+459 **56**

Březová, *Czechoslovakia* L75+486 **49**
Brezova, *Czechoslovakia* L81+496 **49**
Bria, *Cent. Afr. Rep.* L48+066 **81**
Briançon, *France* M50+449 **55**
Briare, *France* M73+476 **54**
Bribbaree, *New S. Wales* C12-341 **109**
Bridgehampton, *New York* S74+409 **96**
Bridgend, *Wales* N21+515 **38**
Bridgeport, *Connecticut* S79+412 **91**
Bridgeport, *Nebraska* U79+418 **94**
Bridgeport L., *Texas* U48+332 **95**
Bridgeton, *New Jersey* T01+395 **96**
Bridgetown, *Nova Scotia* S31+449 **90**
Bridgman C., *Arctic Ocean* Q00+840 **26**
Bridgnorth, *England* N15+525 **38**
Bridgton, *Maine* S64+440 **90**
Bridgwater & B., *England* N18+511 **38**
Bridlington & B., *England* N01+541 **37**
Bridport, *Tasmania* C16-410 **109**
Brielle, *Netherlands* M65+519 **44**
Brienz, *Switzerland* M42+468 **45**
Brienzer See, *Switzerland* M42+467 **45**
Brier I., *Nova Scotia* S38+443 **90**
Brig, *Switzerland* M42+463 **45**
Brigels, *Switzerland* M36+468 **45**
Brigham, *Utah* V42+415 **94**
Bright, *Victoria* C18-367 **109**
Brightlingsea, *England* M84+518 **39**
Brighton, *Colorado* U89+400 **94**
Brighton, *England* N01+508 **39**
Brighton, *S. Australia* C33-351 **109**
Brighton, *Tasmania* C16-427 **109**
Brignoles, *France* M54+434 **55**
Brindaban, *India* G74+275 **72**
Brindisi, *Italy* L72+406 **57**
Brinkley, *Arkansas* U08+349 **97**
Brinkworth, *S. Australia* C70-337 **109**
Brione, *Switzerland* M37+463 **45**
Brioude, *France* M70+453 **55**
Brissago, *Switzerland* M38+461 **45**
Bristol, *England* N15+515 **38**
Bristol, *New Brunswick* S45+465 **90**
Bristol, *Pennsylvania* T00+401 **96**
Bristol, *Rhode Island* S68+417 **96**
Bristol, *Tennessee* T43+366 **97**
Bristol B., *Alaska* Y60+580 **99**
Bristol Channel, *England* N23+513 **38**
Bristol I., *South Sandwich Is.* P80-580 **27**
British Columbia, prov. *Canada* — **88**
British Guiana, *See Guyana*
British Honduras, *See Belize*
British Isles, *N.-W. Europe* — **34**
Brito, *Nicaragua* T65+114 **101**
Britonto, *Italy* L79+411 **57**
Britstown, *Cape Province* L38-306 **84**
Brive-la-Gaillarde, *France* M81+452 **55**
Briviesca, *Spain* N20+425 **52**
Brno, *Czechoslovakia* L80+492 **49**
Broach, *India* H12+216 **70**
Broad B., *Scotland* N37+582 **40**
Broadalbin, *New York* S85+431 **91**
Broadford, *Pennsylvania* T27+401 **96**
Broadford, *Scotland* N36+572 **40**
Broadhaven, *Ireland, Rep.* N60+543 **42**
Broadus, *Montana* V02+455 **93**
Brock I., *N.-W. Territories* V50+776 **88**
Brockton, *Massachusetts* S66+421 **96**
Brockville, *Ontario* T04+446 **91**
Brod, *Yugoslavia* L53+415 **58**
Brodeur Pen., *N.-W. Terr.* T75+723 **89**
Brodhead, *Wisconsin* T86+427 **91**
Brodick, *Scotland* N31+556 **41**
Brodribb, *Victoria* C08-377 **109**
Broek-in-Waterland,
  Netherlands M60+524 **44**
Broglio, *Switzerland* M38+464 **45**
Broken B., *New S. Wales* B83-336 **109**
Broken Bow, *Nebraska* U58+414 **95**
Broken Hill, *Zambia* L10-144 **83**
Broken Hill, *New S. Wales* C51-319 **109**
Bromberg. *See Bydgoszcz*
Bromley, *England* N00+514 **39**
Bromptonville, *Quebec* S72+455 **91**
Brønnøysund, *Norway* M16+655 **46**
Bronte, *Sicily* M01+378 **57**
Brookfield, *Missouri* U18+498 **95**
Brookhaven, *Mississippi* U02+316 **95**
Brookings, *Oregon* W26+421 **92**
Brookings, *S. Dakota* U40+444 **93**
Brooklyn, *Iowa* U14+417 **95**
Brooklyn, *New York* S84+406 **96**
Brooklyn, *Nova Scotia* S28+441 **90**
Brooks Ra., *Alaska* Y50+674 **99**
Brook's Point, *Philippines* E13+089 **65**
Brookville, *Pennsylvania* T25+411 **96**
Broom L., *Scotland* N31+579 **40**
Broome, *W. Australia* D76-178 **110**
Brora, *Scotland* N23+580 **40**
Brosna R., *Ireland, Rep.* N48+532 **43**
Brough Hd., *Orkney, Scot.* N20+592 **40**
Broughton, *England* N19+543 **37**
Broughty Ferry, *Scotland* N17+565 **41**
Broumov, *Czechoslovakia* L82+506 **49**
Brouwershaven, *Netherlands* M67+517 **44**
Brown, Mt., *S. Australia* C72-325 **109**
Brown's Valley, *Minnesota* U41+456 **93**
Brownsville, *Kentucky* T68+372 **97**
Brownsville, *Tennessee* T86+356 **97**
Brownsville, *Texas* U45+259 **94**
Brownville, *Maine* S58+453 **90**
Brownwood, *Texas* U54+316 **95**
Brownwood, L., *Texas* U55+318 **95**
Broxburn, *Scotland* N21+559 **41**
Brozas, *Spain* N41+396 **52**
Bruce Coast, *Antarctica* P25-730 **27**
Bruce Mt., *W. Australia* E08-226 **110**
Bruce Mines, *Ontario* T53+463 **91**
Bruck an der Mur, *Austria* M13+473 **48**
Bruff, *Ireland, Rep.* N51+525 **43**
Bruges, *Belgium* M71+512 **44**
Brugg, *Switzerland* M41+475 **45**
Brugge, *See Bruges*
Bruin Pk., *Utah* V32+394 **94**
Bruly, *Belgium* M63+500 **44**
Brummen, *Netherlands* M53+521 **44**
Brunei & state, *Borneo* E31+050 **65**
Brunette Downs, *N.T., Aust.* C85-184 **111**
Brunflo, *Sweden* M01+631 **46**
Brunn. *See Brno*
Brunner, *New Zealand* A52-425 **112**

Brunssum, *Netherlands* M54+509 **44**
Brunswick. *See Braunschweig*
Brunswick, *Georgia* T39+312 **97**
Brunswick, *Maine* S60+439 **90**
Brunswick, *Maryland* T15+393 **96**
Brunswick B., *W. Australia* D61-152 **110**
Brunswick, Pen. de, *Chile* S70-535 **103**
Bruny I., *Tasmania* C16-434 **109**
Brusa. *See Bursa*
Brusartsi, *Bulgaria* L42+437 **58**
Brush, *Colorado* U82+402 **94**
Brusio, *Switzerland* M29+463 **45**
Brussel (Brussels). *See Bruxelles*
Bruthen, *Victoria* C13-377 **109**
Bruxelles (Brussels),
  Belgium M64+508 **44**
Bruzual, *Venezuela* S56+079 **104**
Bryan Coast, *Antarctica* T30-750 **27**
Bryansk, *U.S.S.R.* K64+533 **60**
Bryce Canyon Nat. Park, *Ut.* V47+377 **92**
Brynmawr, *Wales* N19+518 **38**
Bryson, *Quebec* T10+457 **91**
Bryson City, *N. Carolina* T51+354 **97**
Brzeg, *Poland* L75+509 **49**
Brzesko, *Poland* L56+500 **49**
Bsharri, *Lebanon* K54+343 **76**
Bua, *Angola* M10-072 **82**
Buayan, *Philippines* D59+061 **65**
Bubasa, *Ethiopia* K16+088 **83**
Bubiyan I., *The Gulf* J71+298 **74**
Bubulu, *Uganda* K64+008 **83**
Bucaramanga, *Colombia* S79+072 **104**
Buchach, *Ukraine* L27+491 **60**
Buchan, *Victoria* C11-374 **109**
Buchan Ness, *Scotland* N11+575 **40**
Buchanan, L., *Queensland* C25-216 **111**
Buchanan L., *Texas* U51+308 **95**
Buchardo, *Argentina* S21-347 **103**
Bucharest. *See Bucuresti*
Buchs, *Switzerland* M33+472 **45**
Buckhannon, *West Virginia* T31+389 **97**
Buckie, *Scotland* N18+577 **40**
Buckingham, *Quebec* T03+456 **91**
Buckingham & co., *England* N06+520 **39**
Buckley, *New Zealand* A10-384 **112**
Bucksport, *Maine* S53+446 **90**
Buctouche, *New Brunswick* S28+465 **90**
Bucuresti, *Romania* L23+444 **58**
Bud, *Norway* M48+630 **46**
Budaia, *Saudi Arabia* K10+230 **74**
Budapest, *Hungary* L66+475 **49**
Budaun, *India* G65+282 **73**
Bud Bud, *India* G14+233 **73**
Buddh Gaya, *India* G30+247 **73**
Budesti, *Romania* L21+442 **58**
Budhana, *India* G76+293 **72**
Budleigh Salterton, *England* N20+506 **38**
Budva, *Yugoslavia* L67+423 **58**
Buea, *Cameroun* M36+042 **81**
Buenaventura, *Colombia* T12+040 **104**
Buena Vista, *Georgia* T57+323 **97**
Buena Vista, *Virginia* T26+377 **97**
Buenos Aires, *Argentina* R81-346 **103**
Buenos Aires, *Colombia* S60-032 **104**
Buenos Aires, L.,
  Chile-Argentina S76-465 **103**
Bufa, mt., *Mexico* U89+207 **100**
Buffalo, *Minnesota* U23+452 **93**
Buffalo, *Missouri* U19+397 **97**
Buffalo, *New York* T23+429 **91**
Buffalo L., *N.-W. Terr.* V63+602 **88**
Buffalo, *S. Dakota* U82+456 **93**
Buffalo, *Wyoming* V10+444 **93**
Buff City, *Tennessee* T44+365 **97**
Bufumine, *Chad* L84+150 **81**
Bug. R., *Poland, etc.* L51+525 **49**
Buga, *Colombia* T08+038 **104**
Buglma, *U.S.S.R.* J43+545 **61**
Buguruslan, *U.S.S.R.* J46+536 **61**
Builth Wells, *Wales* N20+521 **38**
Buinsk, *U.S.S.R.* J70+550 **61**
Buique, *Brazil* Q43-086 **105**
Buitenpost, *Netherlands* M53+532 **44**
Bujumbura, *Barundi* L04-034 **83**
Buka, I., *Solomon Is.* B60-050 **106**
Bukama, *Zaire* L24-092 **82**
Bukavu, *Zaire* L06-026 **83**
Bukene, *Tanzania* K74-042 **83**
Bukhara, *Uzbek* H64+398 **62**
Bukoba, *Tanzania* K78-014 **83**
Bukwimba, *Tanzania* K70-028 **83**
Bülach, *Switzerland* M39+475 **45**
Bulagan, *Mongolia* F09+488 **64**
Bulan, *Philippines* D67+125 **65**
Bulandshahr, *India* G73+284 **72**
Bulawayo, *Rhodesia* L08-204 **84**
Bulgaria, *Europe* L30+425 **51**
Bulinski, *U.S.S.R.* D70+680 **63**
Bullange, *Belgium* M52+504 **44**
Buller, Mt., *Victoria* C21-371 **109**
Bulli, *New S. Wales* B84-343 **109**
Bulloo Cr., *Queensland* C40-280 **111**
Bull Shoals Res., *Arkansas* U17+365 **95**
Bulnes, *Chile* S74-366 **103**
Bulo Burti, *Somalia* J86+038 **83**
Bulsar, *India* H12+206 **70**
Bulu, mt., *Borneo* E15+028 **65**
Bulun, *U.S.S.R.* D84+709 **63**
Bulun Tokhor, *China* G15+470 **64**
Bumba, *Zaire* L44+020 **82**
Buna, *Kenya* K30-012 **83**
Buna, *Papua New Guinea* C10-087 **111**
Bunbury, *W. Australia* E26-332 **110**
Bunclody, *Ireland, Rep.* N46+526 **43**
Buncrana, *Ireland, Rep.* N45+551 **42**
Bundaberg, *Queensland* B76-248 **111**
Bundarra, *New S. Wales* B84-302 **109**
Bundi, *India* G86+254 **70**
Bundoran, *Ireland, Rep.* N50+545 **42**
Bungay, *England* M81+525 **39**
Bungo, *Angola* L86-074 **82**
Bungo Str., *Japan* D16+330 **68**
Buninyong, *Victoria* C37-377 **109**
Bunker, *Missouri* U08+374 **97**
Bunkie, *Louisiana* U13+309 **95**
Bunschoten, *Netherlands* M58+522 **44**
Buochs, *Switzerland* M39+470 **45**
Buolkalakh, *U.S.S.R.* E02+731 **63**

Buorkhaya, Guba, *U.S.S.R.* D20+720 63
Buq, *Iran* H81+286 75
Buraida, *Saudi Arabia* K05+265 74
Bur Akaba, *Somalia* K06+026 83
Buram, *Sudan* L30+108 81
Burao, *Somalia* J86+094 83
Buraq, *Syria* K51+332 76
Burazjun, *Iran* J35+299 75
Burchun, *China* G19+477 64
Burd, Jebel, *Saudi Arabia* K35+272 74
Burdekin, R., *Queensland* C20-200 111
Burdur, *Turkey* K88+377 74
Burdwan, *India* G12+232 73
Bureå, *Sweden* L53+646 46
Bureinskiy Khrebet, *U.S.S.R.* D10+500 63
Bureir, *Israel* K62+316 76
Büren, *Switzerland* M46+471 45
Bureya, *U.S.S.R.* D31+496 63
Burg, Den, *Netherlands* M68+517 44
Burgas, *Bulgaria* L15+425 58
Burgaw, *N. Carolina* T18+346 97
Burgdorf, *Switzerland* M44+471 45
Burgenland, prov., *Austria* L82+473 49
Burgess Hill, *England* N01+509 39
Burgos, *Spain* N22+423 52
Burhanpur, *India* G82+213 70
Buria, *India* G76+302 72
Burity, *Brazil* Q78-039 105
Burkesville, *Kentucky* T62+368 97
Burketown, *Queensland* C63-176 111
Burkeville, *Virginia* T19+372 97
Burks Falls, *Ontario* T26+457 91
Burley, *Idaho* V54+426 94
Burlington, *Colorado* U74+392 94
Burlington, *Iowa* U07+408 95
Burlington, *New Jersey* S89+402 96
Burlington, *Ontario* T29+434 91
Burlington, *Vermont* S79+445 91
Burlington, *Wisconsin* T80+427 95
Burlyuk, *U.S.S.R.* K68+448 80
Burma, *S. Asia* F50+210 31
Burnak, *U.S.S.R.* K21+518 61
Burnham, *England* N18+512 38
Burnham-on-Crouch, *Eng.* M85+516 39
Burnie, *Tasmania* C25-411 109
Burnley, *England* N14+538 37
Burns, *New South Wales* C54-321 109
Burns, *Oregon* V85+436 92
Burnside R., *N.-W. Terr.* V25+661 88
Burntisland, *Scotland* N19+561 41
Burra, *S. Australia* C66-336 109
Burren Junction, *N.S.W.* C06-301 109
Burriana, *Spain* N01+399 53
Burrinjuck & Res., *N.S.W.* C09-350 109
Burrow Hd., *Scotland* N26+547 41
Burry Port & Inlet, *Wales* N26+517 38
Bursa, *Turkey* L06+402 74
Burt L., *Michigan* T58+455 91
Burton-in-Kendal, *England* N16+542 37
Burtonport, *Ireland, Rep.* N50+549 42
Burton-upon-Trent, *England* N10+528 37
Burträsk, *Sweden* L56+645 46
Burtundy, *New S. Wales* C47-337 109
Buru I., *Indonesia* D50-034 65
Burullus L., *Egypt* K86+314 81
Burum, *Yemen, South* J66+143 74
Burundi, *Cent. Africa* L00-035 83
Burunurt, *Mongolia* E39+467 64
Bury, *England* N14+536 37
Buryatskaya A.S.S.R.,
  U.S.S.R. E60+527 63
Bury St Edmunds,
  England M86+522 39
Busembatia, *Uganda* K68+006 83
Bushehr (Bushire), *Iran* J54+289 75
Bushmills, *N. Ireland* N39+552 42
Bushnell, *Florida* T43+286 97
Busra, *Syria* K51+325 76
Bussa, *Nigeria* M62+102 80
Bussaco, *Portugal* N50+404 52
Busselton, *W. Australia* E28-338 110
Bussum, *Netherlands* M59+523 44
Bustam, *Iran* J30+365 75
Buta, *Zaire* L30+028 82
Butana, *India* G80+292 72
Buta Ranquil, *Argentina* S59-370 103
Butaritari, I., *Gilbert Is.* A40+040 106
Bute, *S. Australia* C72-339 109
Bute I., *Scotland* N31+558 41
Bütgenbach, *Belgium* M53+504 44
Buthidaung, *Burma* F74+210 71
Butler, *Missouri* U26+382 95
Butler, *Pennsylvania* T29+409 91
Butschwil, *Switzerland* M35+474 45
Butte, *Montana* V45+460 92
Buttes, *Switzerland* M51+469 45
Buttevant, *Ireland, Rep.* N52+522 43
Button Is., *Quebec* S27+606 89
Butuan, *Philippines* D57+090 65
Butung I., *Indonesia* D73-050 65
Buturlinovka, *U.S.S.R.* K26+508 61
Buxar, *India* G36+255 73
Buxton, *England* N11+533 37
Buy, *U.S.S.R.* K21+586 60
Buyaga, *U.S.S.R.* D47+597 63
Buyr Nuur, lake, *Mongolia* E15+475 63
Buzancais, *France* M82+469 54
Buzău, *Romania* L19+451 58
Buzuluk, *U.S.S.R.* J46+528 61
Buzzards B., *Massachusetts* S65+416 96
Bwahit, mt., *Ethiopia* K40+132 83
Byam Martin Channel
  North-West Territories V00+762 88
Bydgoszcz, *Poland* L72+531 49
Byelaya, R., *U.S.S.R.* J36+558 61
Byelokatay, *U.S.S.R.* J06+557 61
Byelo-Russia (White Russia)
  U.S.S.R. L12+540 60
Byelyy, Os., *U.S.S.R.* H30+730 62
Bygland, *Norway* M43+588 47
Byglandsfjord, *Norway* M43+586 47
Bylot I., *N.-W. Territories* T20+728 89
Byng Inlet, *Ontario* T34+457 91
Byrock, *New S. Wales* C22-306 109
Byron, C., *New S. Wales* B68-286 111
Byske, *Sweden* L53+649 46
Bytom, *Poland* L66+504 49
Bytow, *Poland* L75+542 49
Caaguazu, *Paraguay* R66-254 103

Caballo Res., *New Mexico* V14+330 94
Caballo Cocha, *Peru* S63-038 104
Caballos, Sierra de los,
  New Mexico V13+329 94
Cabañas, *Cuba* T47+229 101
Cabanatuan, *Philippines* D84+155 65
Cabar, *Yugoslavia* M02+456 56
Cabedello, *Brazil* Q28-070 105
Cabellos, *Uruguay* R74-307 103
Cabezas, *Bolivia* S20-188 104
Cabezo del Buey, *Spain* N31+387 52
Cabinda, *Angola* M16-050 82
Cabonga Res., *Quebec* T10+473 91
Cabot Hd., *Ontario* T38+453 91
Cabot Str., *Nfd., etc.* S00+475 90
Cabo Blanco, *Argentina* S35-472 103
Cabo Frio, *Brazil* Q75-226 105
Cabosa I., *Burma* F43+128 71
Cabo Verde, Arquipelago de,
  See Cape Verde Is.
Cabra, *Spain* N27+375 52
Cabrera I., *Balearic Is., Spain* M72+391 53
Cabrobo, *Brazil* Q56-086 105
Cabuérniga, *Spain* N26+432 52
Cabure, *Venezuela* S58+112 104
Čačak, *Yugoslavia* L58+439 58
Cacapon R., *W. Virginia* T21+394 96
Cacequy, *Brazil* R58-299 103
Cáceres, *Spain* N38+394 52
Cachinal, *Chile* S57-250 103
Cachipoque, *Angola* L64-120 82
Cachoeira, *Brazil* Q54-127 105
Cachoeira de Iguacu, *Arg.* R58-257 103
Cachoeira do Sul, *Brazil* R47-300 103
Caconda, *Angola* M00-138 82
Cacouna, *Quebec* S57+479 90
Cadaqués, *Spain* M71+423 53
Caddo L., *Louisiana* U24+328 95
Cadereyta, *Mexico* U60+256 100
Cader Idris, *Wales* N24+527 38
Cadillac, *Michigan* T63+443 91
Cadiz, *Spain* N38+365 52
Cadiz, Gulf of, *Spain* N43+368 52
Caen, *France* N02+492 54
Caerleon, *Wales* N18+516 38
Caernarvon B., *Wales* N27+525 38
Caernarvon, *Wales* N26+531 38
Caerphilly, *Wales* N19+516 38
Cagayan de Oro, *Philippines* D62+084 65
Cagayan Sulu, I., *Phil.* E09+071 65
Cagliari & G. di, *Sardinia* M35+392 56
Caguas, *Puerto Rico* S36+183 101
Caha Mts., *Ireland, Rep.* N59+517 43
Cahirsiveen, *Ireland, Rep.* N61+519 43
Cahore Pt., *Ireland, Rep.* N37+526 43
Cahors, *France* M81+444 55
Caibarien, *Cuba* T27+226 101
Caicara, *Bolivar, Venezuela* S37+074 104
Caicara, *Brazil* S31-032 104
Caicara, *Monagas, Venezuela* S22+098 104
Caicos Is., *Bahama Is.* T30+216 101
Caihaique, *Chile* S70-454 103
Cailloma, *Peru* S70-152 104
Caillou B., *Louisiana* U06+291 95
Caimanera, *Cuba* T02+200 101
Caird Coast, *Antarctica* P40-750 27
Cairn Gorm, *Scotland* N22+571 40
Cairns, *Queensland* C25-168 111
Cairn Toul, *Scotland* N22+570 40
Cairo, *Egypt* K82+300 81
Cairo, *Georgia* T55+308 97
Cairo, *Illinois* T85+370 95
Caister, *England* M80+527 39
Caistor, *England* N02+535 37
Caiza, *Bolivia* S21-217 104
Caiamarca, *Peru* T21-072 104
Čakovec, *Yugoslavia* L82+464 56
Cala, *Spain* N38+380 52
Calabar, *Nigeria* M40+050 80
Calabozo, *Venezuela* S44+089 104
Calabria, dep., *Italy* L80+391 57
Calacoto, *Bolivia* S53-172 104
Calafat, *Romania* L42+440 58
Calafate, *Argentina* S70-503 103
Calais, *France* M79+510 54
Calais, *Maine* S44+452 90
Calama, *Brazil* S17-079 104
Calama, *Chile* S53-224 103
Calamar, *Colombia* S89+102 104
Calamar, *Colombia* S71+019 104
Calamian Group, *Phil.* E00+120 65
Calamocha, *Spain* N08+409 53
Calang, *Sumatra* F57+047 65
Calaoria. *See* Reggio
Calatayud, *Spain* N10+414 53
Calava C., *Sicily* M00+382 57
Calbuco, *Chile* S79-417 103
Calcasieu L., *Louisiana* U20+296 95
Calceta, *Ecuador* T31-008 104
Calchaqui, *Argentina* S02-299 103
Calcutta, *India* G09+226 73
Caldas da Rainha, *Portugal* N55+394 52
Calder R., *England* N10+537 37
Caldera, *Chile* S65-271 103
Caldwell, *Idaho* V70+437 92
Caldwell, *Texas* U40+305 95
Caledonia, *Minnesota* U09+436 93
Calella, *Spain* M73+416 53
Calenzana, *Corsica* M38+369 55
Caleta Buena, *Chile* S61-199 103
Caleta Olivia, *Argentina* S45-464 103
Calgary, *Alberta* V54+510 88
Cali, *Colombia* T09+036 104
Calicut, *India* G86+114 70
California, G. of, *Mexico* V40+280 100
California, state, *U.S.A.* V17+404 98
Calimali, *Mexico* V50+282 100
Calingasta, *Argentina* S57-313 103
Calla, *Spain* N08+405 53
Callabonna & L., *S. Aust.* C59-298 109
Callan, *Ireland, Rep.* N44+525 43
Callander, *Ontario* T26+462 91
Callander, *Scotland* N25+562 41
Callanna, *S. Australia* C73-296 109
Callao, *Peru* T13-120 104
Calmon, *Brazil* R36-267 103
Calmpthout, *Belgium* M63+514 44
Calpulalpam, *Mexico* U74+221 100
Caltagirone, *Sicily* M03+372 57

Caltanissetta, *Sicily* M06+375 57
Calulo, *Angola* M00-100 82
Calumet I., *Quebec* T10+458 91
Calunda, *Angola* L40-122 82
Calvados, dep., *France* N03+490 54
Calverton, *Virginia* T16+386 97
Calvillo, *Mexico* U77+218 100
Calvinia, *Cape Province* L60-316 84
Camabatela, *Angola* L88-084 82
Camaguey, *Cuba* T18+212 101
Camaguey, Is. de, *Cuba* T18+223 101
Camana, *Peru* S77-166 104
Camara, *Brazil* S10-188 104
Camarat C., *France* M50+432 55
Camargo, *Bolivia* S32-210 104
Camargo, *Mexico* U52+262 100
Camargo, *Mexico* V01+277 100
Camarones & B., *Argentina* S35-448 103
Camataqui, *Bolivia* S32-210 104
Ca-Mau, *S. Vietnam* E89+092 69
Ca-Mau, *S. Vietnam* F01+086 69
Camaxilo, *Angola* L66-084 82
Cambados, *Spain* N53+425 52
Cambay, *India* H14+223 70
Cambay, G. of, *See* Khambat
Cambodia, *S. E. Asia* F00+120 69
Cambodia, C. *See* Ca-mau, Pt.
Cambrai, *France* M71+502 54
Cambrian Mts., *Wales* N22+525 38
Cambridge, *Massachusetts* S67+424 96
Cambridge, *New Zealand* A27-379 112
Cambridge and Isle of Ely, co.
  England N00+524 37
Camden, *Arkansas* U17+336 95
Camden, *Maine* S54+443 90
Camden, *New Jersey* T01+399 96
Camden, *New South Wales* B86-340 109
Camden, *New York* T04+433 91
Camden, *S. Carolina* T34+343 97
Camden Haven, *N.S.W.* B74-317 109
Camedo, *Switzerland* M38+462 45
Cameron, *Missouri* U26+398 95
Cameron, *Texas* U42+308 95
Cameron Mts., *New Zealand* A78-460 112
Camerota, *Italy* L88+400 57
Cameroun, *W. Africa* M16+050 82
Cameta, *Brazil* R27-022 105
Camilla, *Georgia* T55+312 97
Camina, *Chile* S57-194 103
Caminha, *Portugal* N53+418 52
Caminreal, *Spain* N08+408 53
Camoa, *Mexico* V25+276 100
Camocim, *Brazil* Q65-030 105
Camooweal, *Queensland* C71-200 111
Camorta I., *Nicobar Is.* F69+081 71
Campana, *Argentina* R84-341 103
Campana, I., *Chile* T02-482 103
Campania, dep., *Italy* M01+411 57
Campas, *Mexico* V28+300 100
Campbell, *Missouri* U00+365 97
Campbell B., *N.-W. Terr.* U85+676 88
Campbell I., *Pacific Ocean* A62-528 106
Campbell I., *Yukon* X21+646 88
Campbellford, *Ontario* T17+443 91
Campbellpore, *Pakistan* H16+338 72
Campbellton, *N.B.* S40+480 90
Campbelltown, *N.S.W.* B85-341 109
Campbell Town, *Tasmania* C15-419 109
Campbeltown, *Scotland* N33+554 41
Campeche & state, *Mexico* U03+198 100
Campeche, G. of, *Mexico* U24+190 100
Camperdown, *Victoria* C41-383 109
Campiglia Marittima, *Italy* M27+431 56
Campillos, *Spain* N28+370 52
Campina Grande, *Brazil* Q35-074 105
Campinas, *Brazil* R12-228 105
Campobasso, *Italy* M02+416 57
Campo Belo, *Brazil* T02-210 105
Campobello I., *N.B* S42+449 90
Campo Formoso, *Brazil* Q62-104 105
Campo Formoso, *Brazil* R20-170 105
Campo Gallo, *Argentina* S18-266 103
Campo Grande, *Brazil* R59-206 105
Campo Largo, *Brazil* Q87-116 105
Campo Maior, *Brazil* Q73-048 105
Campo Maior, *Portugal* N42+390 52
Campos, *Brazil* Q67-217 105
Campo Sales, *Brazil* Q63-070 105
Campos Novos, *Brazil* R38-274 103
Camosie Fells, *Scotland* N25-560 41
Camrose, *Alberta* V46+532 88
Camsell Mt., *N.-W. Terr.* W21+617 88
Canaan, *New Brunswick* S30+463 90
Canaan, *New Hampshire* S72+436 91
Canaca, *North America* 88-89
Canadian, *Texas* U62+359 94
Canadian Channel, *Quebec* S18+499 90
Canadian R., *Oklahoma, etc* U67+359 98
Cañadon de las Vacas, *Arg.* S56-506 103
Canakkale, *Turkey* L22+401 74
Canama, *Brazil* S72-056 104
Canancaigua, *New York* T14+429 96
Canancaigua L., *New York* T14+428 96
Cananea, *Mexico* V33+310 100
Cananeia, *Brazil* R18-250 103
Canarias, Islas, *Atlantic Oc.* P00+280 80
Canarreos, Arch. de los,
  Cuba T44+220 101
Canary Is. *See* Canarias, Islas
Canas, *Portugal* N47+405 52
Canaseraga, *New York* T17+425 96
Canatlar, *Mexico* U89+244 100
Cañaveral, *Spain* N38+398 52
Canaveral, C., *Florida* T34+284 99
Cañaveras, *Spain* N15+404 53
Canaveiras, *Brazil* Q54-156 105
Canbelego, *N. South Wales* C22-316 109
Canberra, *Cap. Terr., Aust.* C06-353 109
Canby, *Minnesota* U38+447 93
Candasnos, *Spain* N00+415 53
Candelo, *New South Wales* C02-368 109
Candia. *See* Iráklion
Canea. *See* Khania
Canella, *Brazil* R35-294 103
Canelones, *Uruguay* R67-345 103
Canete, *Chile* S80-378 103
Canete, *Peru* T09-131 104
Cañete, *Spain* N10+400 53

Cangamba, *Angola* L60-136 82
Cangandala, *Angola* L81-098 82
Cangas, *Spain* N39+431 52
Canguaretama, *Brazil* Q31-064 105
Canha, *Portugal* N52+388 52
Canicatti, *Sicily* M07+373 57
Cankiri, *Turkey* K68+406 74
Canna, I., *Scotland* N40+571 40
Cannanore, *India* G88+120 70
Cannelton, *Indiana* T71+379 97
Cannes, *France* M48+435 55
Cannock, *England* N12+527 38
Cannon Ball, *N. Dakota* U64+464 93
Canobla, *New South Wales* C16-313 109
Canon City, *Colorado* V02+384 94
Canora, *Saskatchewan* U74+514 88
Canosa, *Italy* L84+412 57
Canowindra, *New S. Wales* C08-336 109
Canso & C., *Nova Scotia* S06+454 90
Canso, Str. of, *Nova Scotia* S07+455 90
Cantabrica, Cord., *Spain* N24+429 52
Cantal, dep., *France* M73+452 55
Cantanhede, *Portugal* N52+403 52
Canterbury, *England* M84+513 39
Canterbury, *New Brunswick* S45+459 90
Canterbury Bight, *N.Z.* A46-440 112
Canterbury Plains, *N.Z.* A50-440 112
Can Tho, *S. Vietnam* E85+100 69
Canton (Kwangchow), *China* E40+232 67
Canton, *Mississippi* U00+326 95
Canton, *New York* T11+446 91
Canton, *Ohio* T38+408 91
Canton, *S. Dakota* U34+432 93
Canton I., *Phoenix Is.* Z42-030 106
Canton Res., *Oklahoma* U52+362 95
Canuelas, *Argentina* R83-351 103
Canutama, *Brazil* S27-066 104
Canyon de Chelly Nat. Mon.,
  Arizona V26+362 94
Capabarida, *Venezuela* S63+112 104
Capakcur. *See* Bingol.
Capana, *Brazil* S10-058 104
Capao Bonito, *Brazil* R21-240 103
Cap Chat, *Quebec* S40+491 90
Cap de la Madeleine, *Quebec* S75+464 91
Cape Barren I., *Tasmania* C12-404 109
Cape Breton I., *Nova Scotia* S06+460 90
Cape Breton Highlands Nat.
  Park, *Nova Scotia* S04+470 90
Cape Charles, *Virginia* T06+372 97
Cape Clear, *Ireland, Rep.* N57+514 43
Cape Coast, *Ghana* N08+052 80
Cape Cod B., *Massachusetts* S61+419 96
Cape Fear R., *N. Carolina* T22+346 97
Cape Girardeau, *Missouri* T88+373 95
Cape Haitien, *Haiti* S73+198 101
Cape May, *New Jersey* T00+389 96
Cape May Court House,
  New Jersey S89+391 96
Cape Province, *South Africa* L40-300 84
Cape Tormentine, *N.B.* S23+461 90
Cape Town, *Cape Province* L70-340 84
Cape Verde Is., *Atlantic Ocean* P60+160 80
Cape York Pen., *Queensland* C45-132 111
Capelle, la, *France* M67+500 54
Capilla, *Argentina* R85-343 103
Capilla del Monte, *Argentina* S28-309 103
Capitan Mts., *New Mexico* V02+336 94
Caplan, *Quebec* S34+481 90
Capoompeta, mt., *N.S.W.* B78-294 109
Capote Mt., *Texas* U86+300 94
Cappoquin, *Ireland, Rep.* N47+521 43
Capraia, I., *Italy* M31+430 56
Capreol, *Ontario* T35+467 91
Caprera, I., *Sardinia* M33+413 57
Capri, I., *Italy* M04+404 57
Capricorn Chan., *Queensland* B75-226 111
Caprivi Strip, *S.-W. Africa* L40-180 84
Carabaya, Cord. de, *Peru* S62-140 104
Caracarai, *Brazil* S05+023 104
Caracas, *Venezuela* S42+105 104
Caracol, *Brazil* Q79-093 105
Caragh L., *Ireland, Rep.* N59+521 43
Caraguatay, *Paraguay* R71-250 103
Caransebes, *Romania* L47+454 58
Caraomer, *Romania* L11+438 58
Carapegua, *Paraguay* R73-257 103
Caraquet, *New Brunswick* S30+478 90
Caras, *Peru* T17-092 104
Caratasca Lag., *Honduras* T54+154 101
Caratiá, *Brazil* S26-060 104
Carauari, *Brazil* S42-048 104
Caravaca, *Spain* N13+381 53
Caravelas, *Brazil* Q56-178 105
Caraveli, *Peru* S81-158 104
Carballino, *Spain* N48+424 52
Carballo, *Spain* N52+432 52
Carbonara C., *Sardinia* M33+391 57
Carbondale, *Illinois* T86+377 95
Carbondale, *Pennsylvania* T03+415 96
Carbon Hill, *Alabama* T75+339 97
Carcajou, *Alberta* V72+580 88
Carcassone, *France* M76+432 55
Carcoar, *New South Wales* C05-337 109
Carcross, *Yukon* W89+601 88
Carcura, *Libya* L60+312 81
Cardamom Hills, *India* G77+100 70
Cardenas, *Cuba* T37+230 101
Cardiel, L., *Argentina* S68-490 103
Cardiff, *Wales* N19+515 38
Cardigan, *Wales* N28+525 38
Cardigan B., *Wales* N27+525 38
Cardona, *Spain* M76+419 53
Cardston, *Alberta* V50+492 88
Cardwell, *Queensland* C24-180 111
Carey, L., *W. Australia* D76-288 110
Carhaix, *France* N21+483 54
Carhue. *See* Adolfo Alsina
Caribbean Sea, *S. & Cent. America* 101
Caribou, *Maine* S48+469 90
Caribou, *Newfoundland* S06+478 90
Caribou Mts., *Alberta* V65+591 88
Čaribrod. *See* Dimitrovgrad
Carichic, *Mexico* V11+278 100
Carinda, *New South Wales* C14-305 109
Cariñena, *Spain* N07+413 53
Caripito, *Venezuela* S19+100 104
Carius, *Brazil* Q57-062 105
Carl, L., *Oklahoma* U44+362 95

Carlet, *Spain* N03+392 **53**
Carleton, *Quebec* S36+481 **90**
Carleton, Mt., *N.B.* S42+473 **90**
Carleton Place, *Ontario* T07+451 **91**
Carlingford & L.
  Ireland, Rep. N37+540 **42**
Carlinville, *Illinois* U00+392 **95**
Carlisle, *England* N18+549 **37**
Carlisle, *Kentucky* T54+383 **97**
Carlisle, *Pennsylvania* T14+402 **96**
Carlisle, *S. Carolina* 139+346 **97**
Carlos Casares, *Argentina* S08-356 **103**
Carlow & co., *Ireland, Rep.* N42+528 **43**
Carlsbad, *New Mexico* U86+324 **94**
Carlsbad Caverns Nat. Park,
  New Mexico U87+320 **98**
Carlton, *Minnesota* U15+467 **93**
Carmacks, *Yukon* X10+617 **88**
Carman, *Manitoba* U46+496 **88**
Carmarthen, *Wales* N26+518 **38**
Carmarthen B., *Wales* N27+516 **38**
Carmaux, *France* M77+440 **55**
Carmel, *New York* S82+414 **96**
Carmel, Mt., *Israel* K60+327 **76**
Carmelo, *Uruguay* R80-340 **99**
Carmen, *Bolivia* S47-115 **104**
Carmen, *Colombia* T01+097 **104**
Carmen, *Mexico* U11+186 **100**
Carmen I., *Mexico* V36+259 **100**
Carmen de Patagones,
  Argentina S17-407 **103**
Carmensa, *Argentina* S46-352 **103**
Carmi, *Illinois* T79+382 **97**
Carmona, *Spain* N34+375 **52**
Carnarvon, *Cape Province* L48-312 **84**
Carnarvon, *W. Australia* E37-249 **110**
Carndonagh, *Ireland, Rep.* N44+552 **42**
Carnegie, L., *W. Australia* D74-260 **110**
Carnot, *Cent. Afr. Rep.* L84+050 **81**
Carnoustie, *Scotland* N16+565 **41**
Carnsore Pt., *Ireland, Rep.* N38+522 **43**
Caro, *Michigan* T50+435 **91**
Carolina, *Brazil* R15-072 **105**
Carolina, *Transvaal* K88-262 **84**
Caroline I., *Pacific Ocean* Y00-100 **107**
Caroline Is., *Pacific Ocean* C00+050 **106**
Carora, *Venezuela* S60+102 **104**
Carpathian Mts., *Cent. Europe* L42+490 **49**
Carpatii Meridionali, *Rom.* L42+450 **58**
Carpentaria, G. of, *Aust.* C66-140 **111**
Carrantuohill, *Ireland, Rep.* N59+520 **43**
Carrara, *Italy* M29+441 **56**
Carrathool, *New S. Wales* C28-344 **109**
Carrbridge, *Scotland* N23+573 **40**
Carreño, *Spain* N35+434 **52**
Carrickfergus, *N. Ireland* N35+547 **42**
Carrickmacross, *Ireland, Rep.* N40+540 **42**
Carrick-on-Shannon,
  Ireland, Rep. N49+539 **42**
Carrick-on-Suir, *Ireland, Rep.* N45+523 **43**
Carrieton, *S. Australia* C69-324 **109**
Carrington, *N. Dakota* U55+474 **93**
Carrión-de-los-Condes, *Sp.* N28+424 **52**
Carrizo Mts., *Arizona* V26+368 **94**
Carrizo Springs, *Texas* U59+286 **94**
Carrizozo, *New Mexico* V05+336 **94**
Carroll, *Iowa* U30+422 **95**
Carrollton, *Alabama* T79+332 **97**
Carrollton, *Kentucky* T61+387 **91**
Carrollton, *Missouri* U22+394 **95**
Carrowmore L., *Ireland, Rep.* N59+542 **42**
Carroz, le, *Switzerland* M53+466 **45**
Carsamba, *Turkey* K50+411 **74**
Carse of Gowrie, *Scotland* N19+564 **41**
Carson City, *Nevada* V89+392 **92**
Carson Sink, *Nevada* V82+397 **92**
Carstairs, *Scotland* N22+557 **41**
Carstensz G., mt... (Pk. Sukarno)
  Irian Jaya, Indon. C76-040 **65**
Cartagena, *Colombia* T03+105 **104**
Cartagena, *Spain* N06+377 **53**
Cartago, *Colombia* T05+047 **104**
Cartago, *Costa Rica* T53+099 **101**
Cartaxo, *Portugal* N53+391 **52**
Cartaya, *Spain* N43+373 **52**
Carter, *Wyoming* V32+414 **93**
Carter Bar, *Scot.-Eng.* N15+553 **41**
Carteret, *France* N11+494 **54**
Cartersville, *Georgia* T59+342 **97**
Carterton, *New Zealand* A27-410 **112**
Carthage, *Illinois* U07+404 **95**
Carthage, *Missouri* U26+372 **95**
Carthage, *New York* T03+440 **91**
Carthage, *N. Carolin* T27+354 **97**
Carthage, *Tennessee* T66+363 **97**
Cartier, *Ontario* T39+467 **91**
Cartwright, *Labrador* R72+530 **89**
Carumbay, *Bolivia* S13-190 **104**
Carupano, *Venezuela* S19+106 **104**
Carutaperá, *Brazil* R06-012 **105**
Caruthersville, *Missouri* T88+362 **95**
Carvoeiro, *Brazil* S12-014 **104**
Casablanca, *Chile* S69-333 **103**
Casablanca, *Morocco* N46+336 **80**
Casaccia, *Switzerland* M32+464 **45**
Casa Grande, *Arizona* V40+328 **99**
Casas Ibañez, *Spain* N09+393 **53**
Cascade, *Montana* V40+473 **93**
Cascade Ra., *Oregon, etc.* W14+426 **98**
Cascais, *Portugal* N56+387 **52**
Casco B., *Maine* S60+437 **90**
Caserta, *Italy* M04+411 **57**
Caseville, *Michigan* T49+439 **91**
Cashel, *Ireland, Rep.* N47+525 **43**
Casilda, *Argentina* S07-331 **103**
Casilda, *Cuba* T30+217 **101**
Casino, *New South Wales* B72-288 **109**
Casma, *Peru* T20-096 **104**
Casmalia, *California* W04+347 **92**
Caspe, *Spain* N00+413 **53**
Casper, *Wyoming* V08+428 **93**
Caspian Sea, *Europe-Asia* J60+400 **30**
Cassai, *Angola* L48-108 **82**
Cassamba, *Angola* L58-132 **82**
Cassel, *France* M75+508 **54**
Casselton, *N. Dakota* U42+470 **93**
Cassiar Mts., *Brit. Columbia* W55+592 **88**
Cassilis, *New South Wales* C00-320 **109**
Cassinga, *Angola* L84-152 **84**
Cassino, *Brazil* R44-323 **99**
Cassino, *Italy* M07+415 **57**

Cassipore, *Brazil* R37+034 **104**
Cassis, *France* M57+432 **55**
Cassopolis, *Michigan* T66+419 **91**
Cassou, *Upper Volta* N12+116 **80**
Cassville, *Missouri* U23+368 **95**
Castanhal, *Brazil* S14-064 **104**
Castanheiro, *Brazil* S34-002 **104**
Castaño, *Argentina* S58-310 **103**
Castasegna, *Switzerland* M33+463 **45**
Casteljaloux, *France* N00+443 **55**
Castellammare & G. di, *Sic.* M13+380 **57**
Castellammare di Stabia,
  Italy M03+407 **57**
Castellane, *France* M51+439 **55**
Castellar de Santiago, *Spain* N19+386 **52**
Castelli, *Argentina* R77-360 **103**
Castello, *Brazil* Q69-053 **105**
Castellón de la Plana, *Spain* N00+400 **53**
Castellote, *Spain* N01+408 **53**
Castelnaudary, *France* M78+433 **55**
Castelo Branco, *Portugal* N45+398 **52**
Castelo de Vide, *Portugal* N44+394 **52**
Castelsarrasin, *France* M83+440 **55**
Castelvetrano, *Sicily* M13+377 **57**
Casterton, *Victoria* C52-376 **109**
Castets, *France* N07+439 **55**
Castillo, mt., *Chile* S74-460 **103**
Castine, *Maine* S53+444 **90**
Castlebar, *Ireland, Rep.* N56+539 **42**
Castlebellingham, *Ireland, Rep.* N38+539 **42**
Castleblayney, *Ireland, Rep.* N40+541 **42**
Castlecomer, *Ireland, Rep.* N43+528 **43**
Castlederg, *N. Ireland* N46+547 **42**
Castledermot, *Ireland, Rep.* N41+529 **43**
Castle Douglas, *Scotland* N24+549 **41**
Castleisland, *Ireland, Rep.* N57+522 **43**
Castlemaine, *Ireland, Rep.* N58+522 **43**
Castlemaine, *Victoria* C35-371 **109**
Castlemartyr, *Ireland, Rep.* N48+519 **43**
Castlepollard, *Ireland, Rep.* N44+537 **42**
Castlerea, *Ireland, Rep.* N51+538 **42**
Castlereagh, R., *N.S.W.* C10-308 **109**
Castle Rock, *Utah* V37+412 **94**
Castle Rock, mt., *Oregon* V79+440 **92**
Castle Rock Buttes, *S. Dak.* U81+453 **93**
Castletown, *Scotland* N20+586 **40**
Castletown Bere, *Ireland, Rep.* N60+517 **43**
Castlewellan, *N. Ireland* N35+542 **42**
Castres, *France* M77+436 **55**
Castro, *Brazil* R30-248 **103**
Castro, *Chile* S83-424 **103**
Castro Marin, *Portugal* N44+372 **52**
Castropol, *Spain* N42+435 **52**
Castrovillari, *Italy* L83+398 **57**
Castuera, *Spain* N33+388 **52**
Cat I., *Bahamas, The* T04 + 243 **101**
Catabola, *Angola* L76-122 **82**
Catak, *Turkey* K14+382 **74**
Catamarca, *Argentina* S35-285 **103**
Catanduanes, I., *Philippines* D64+ 37 **65**
Catania & G. di, *Sicily* M00+375 **57**
Catanzaro, *Italy* L80+389 **57**
Catarina la Grande, *Mexico* U19+163 **100**
Catarman, *Philippines* D62+124 **65**
Catastrophe, C., *S. Australia* C84-350 **111**
Catabalogan, *Philippines* D60+11**0 65**
Catahoula L., *Louisiana* U13+345 **95**
Cateau, le, *France* M69+501 **54**
Cathcart, *New S. Wales* C04-368 **109**
Cathedral Mt., *Texas* U82+302 **94**
Catingueiro, *Brazil* R20-113 **105**
Catlettsburg, *Kentucky* T46+384 **97**
Catonsville, *Maryland* T10+393 **96**
Catorce, *Mexico* U66+237 **100**
Catrilo, *Argentina* S21-363 **103**
Catskill, *New York* S83+422 **96**
Catskill Mts., *New York* S86+422 **96**
Cattaraugus, *New York* T23+424 **96**
Cauquenes, *Chile* S74-359 **103**
Causapscal, *Quebec* S43+484 **90**
Cauto, R., *Cuba* T13+206 **101**
Cauvery R., *India* G72+113 **70**
Caux, *French Guiana* R42+043 **105**
Cavalcante, *Brazil* R15-139 **105**
Cavallo Pass, *Texas* U38+283 **94**
Cavan & co., *Ireland, Rep.* N44+540 **42**
Cave, *New Zealand* A54-443 **112**
Cavendish, *Victoria* C48-375 **109**
Cavergno, *Switzerland* M38+463 **45**
Caviana, I., *Brazil* R31+002 **105**
Cawnpore. See Kanpur
Caxias, *Brazil* R31-046 **105**
Caxias, *Brazil* Q80-048 **105**
Caxias do Sul, *Brazil* R37-295 **103**
Cayambe, *Ecuador* T19+011 **104**
Cayenne, *French Guiana* R44+048 **105**
Cayes, Les, *Haiti* S83+182 **101**
Cayo, *Belize* T80+172 **101**
Cayuga, *Ontario* T29+430 **91**
Cayuga, L., *New York* T10+427 **96**
Cazage, *Angola* L56-112 **82**
Cazalla de la Sierra, *Spain* N35+379 **52**
Cazenovia, *New York* T05+429 **96**
Cazin, *Yugoslavia* L85+450 **56**
Cazorla, *Spain* N18+379 **52**
Ceara. See Fortaleza
Ceannannus Mór, see Kells
Ceara Mirim, *Brazil* Q32-056 **105**
Cebaco, I., *Panama* T37+075 **101**
Cebollar, *Argentina* S39-291 **103**
Cebollera, *Spain* N16+420 **53**
Cebu, *Philippines* D66+104 **65**
Cecil, *Georgia* T50+310 **97**
Cecina, *Italy* N41+398 **52**
Cedar, *Utah* V34+394 **94**
Cedar L., *Texas* U74+328 **94**
Cedar Mts., *Oregon* V77+432 **92**
Cedar Ra., *Utah* V44+388 **94**
Cedarburg, *Wisconsin* T78+433 **91**
Cedar City, *Utah* V48+376 **94**
Cedar Falls, *Iowa* U14+425 **95**
Cedar Key, *Florida* T49+293 **99**
Cedar Rapids, *Iowa* U10+420 **95**
Cedar Springs, *Michigan* T63+433 **91**
Cedral, *Mexico* U64+238 **100**
Cedros, I., *Mexico* V62+281 **100**
Ceduna, *S. Australia* D08-320 **111**
Cefalu, *Sicily* M06+380 **57**
Cegled, *Hungary* L61+472 **49**
Cehegin, *Spain* N11+381 **53**
Ceiba, *Honduras* T72-157 **101**

Cejita Blanca, *New Mexico* V12+363 **94**
Celanova, *Spain* N48+422 **52**
Celaya, *Mexico* U65+206 **100**
Celébes (Sulawesi). *Indonesia* E00-023 **65**
Celebes Sea, *Indonesia* E00+038 **65**
Celje, *Yugoslavia* L88+462 **56**
Celle, *Germany* M30+526 **48**
Celles, *Belgium* M69+507 **44**
Cemisgezek, *Turkey* K36+391 **74**
Center, *Texas* U25+318 **95**
Centerville, *Alabama* T73+329 **97**
Centerville, *Iowa* U17+407 **95**
Centerville, *Missouri* U06+373 **97**
Centerville, *Tennessee* T75+357 **97**
Central. reg., *Scotland* N26+562 **41**
Central African Rep., *Afr.* L60+070 **81**
Central America* T66+140 **101**
Central City, *Nebraska* U48+410 **95**
Centralia, *Illinois* T85+386 **95**
Centralia, *Washington* W18+467 **92**
Central Lake, *Michigan* T62+452 **91**
Centreville, *New Brunswick* S46+465 **90**
Cephalonia. See Kefallinia
Ceram Sea, *Indonesia* D40-030 **65**
Cerignola, *Italy* L85+413 **57**
Cerigo. See Kithira I.
Cerigotto. See Andikithira I.
Cerknica, *Yugoslavia* M04+458 **56**
Cermik, *Turkey* K33+382 **74**
Cernauti. See Chernovtsy
Cerralvo, *Mexico* U59+261 **100**
Cerralvo, I., *Mexico* V29+243 **100**
Cerreto Sannita, *Italy* M03+413 **57**
Cerro de Pasco, *Peru* T08-107 **104**
Cervera de Pisuerga, *Spain* N27+429 **52**
Cesena, *Italy* M17+441 **56**
Cesis, *Latvia* L29+573 **47**
Ceská Lipa, *Czechoslovakia* M03+507 **48**
Ceské Budéjovice, *Czech.* M03+489 **48**
Cessnock, *New S. Wales* B82-329 **109**
Cetinje, *Yugoslavia* L66+424 **58**
Cetraro, *Italy* L84+395 **57**
Cette. See Sete
Ceuta, *N. Africa* N32+358 **80**
Ceuta, B. de, *Mexico* V13+241 **100**
Cevennes, *France* M68+445 **55**
Ceyhan, *Turkey* K58+370 **74**
Ceylon I., & rep. See Sri Lanka
Chabatok, *Quebec* S83+504 **90**
Chablis, *France* M67+478 **54**
Chacabuco, *Argentina* S03-346 **103**
Chacance, *Chile* S58-223 **103**
Chachapoyas, *Peru* T17-064 **104**
Chachoengsao, *Thailand* F24+136 **69**
Chaco, R., *New Mexico* V18+360 **94**
Chad, rep., *Cent. Agrica* L70+150 **81**
Chad (Tchad), L., *Chad* M04+134 **81**
Chadron, *Nebraska* U78+428 **94**
Chadwick, *Missouri* U18+369 **97**
Chagai, *Pakistan* H62+293 **70**
Chagda, *U.S.S.R.* D26+586 **63**
Chagny, *France* M61+469 **54**
Chagos Arch., *Indian Ocean* H13-057 **77**
Chah Bahar, *Iran* H86+253 **75**
Chaibassa, *India* G25+225 **73**
Chaise Dieu, *France* M68+453 **55**
Chakansur, *Afghanistan* H77+311 **75**
Chakia, *India* G40+251 **73**
Chaksam, *Tibet* F85+293 **71**
Chakwal, *Pakistan* H13+329 **72**
Chala, *Peru* S86-158 **104**
Chalcis. See Khalkis
Chaleur B., *Quebec-N.B.* S34+479 **90**
Chalham, I., *Chile* S86-507 **103**
Chalhuanca, *Peru* S81-143 **104**
Chaling, *China* E38+269 **67**
Chalisgaon, *India* H00+205 **70**
Chalk River, *Ontario* T14+460 **91**
Challapata, *Bolivia* S41-189 **104**
Chalons-sur-Marne, *France* M64+489 **54**
Chalon-sur-Saône, *France* M61+468 **54**
Chalus, *France* M84+456 **54**
Cham, *Germany* M14+492 **48**
Chama, *New Mexico* V08+368 **94**
Chaman, *Pakistan* H51+309 **70**
Chamba, *India* G83+326 **72**
Chambal R., *India* G84+257 **70**
Chamberlain L., *Maine* S56+462 **90**
Chamberlain, *S. Dakota* U56+438 **93**
Chambersburg, *Pennsylvania* T17+399 **96**
Chambéry, *France* M54+456 **54**
Chambivas, *Brazil* R22-066 **105**
Chambord, *Quebec* S28+484 **90**
Chamdo, *China* F46+312 **64**
Chamical, *Argentina* S37-304 **103**
Chamo, L., *Ethiopia* K44+058 **83**
Chamonix, *France* M49+459 **54**
Champa, *India* G44+220 **73**
Champagne, prov., *France* M65+489 **54**
Champaign, *Illinois* T80+402 **95**
Champerico, *Guatemala* U11+142 **100**
Champlain L., *N.Y.-Vermont* S80+442 **91**
Champlitte, *France* M57+476 **54**
Champlon, *Belgium* M57+501 **44**
Chamusca, *Portugal* N51+393 **52**
Chanco, *Chile* S75-356 **103**
Chancy, *Switzerland* M54+462 **45**
Chanda, *India* G60+200 **70**
Chandausi, *India* G68+284 **73**
Chandeleur Is & Sd., *La.* T84+298 **95**
Chanderi, *India* G71+247 **73**
Chandernagore, *India* G10+228 **73**
Chandigarh, *India* G79+307 **72**
Chandod, *India* H08+220 **70**
Chandpur, *Bangladesh* F86+233 **71**
Chandpur, *India* G70+292 **73**
Chanduria, *Bangladesh* G06+229 **73**
Changchih, *China* E42+361 **66**
Changchow, *China* E14+244 **67**
Changchow, *China* E01+318 **66**
Changchun, *China* D57+438 **64**
Ch'angkang, *China* E68+192 **64**
Changkiakow, *China* E31+408 **66**
Changlo, *China* E69+367 **66**
Changpeh, *China* E31+411 **66**
Changping, *China* E22+403 **66**
Changpu, *China* E13+242 **67**
Changsha, *China* E42+282 **67**
Changshan, *China* E09+289 **67**

Changte. See Anyang
Changteh, *China* E51+290 **67**
Changting, *China* E22+257 **67**
Changyeh, *China* F26+389 **64**
Channel Is., *English Chan.* N15+494 **54**
Chantada, *Spain* N47+426 **52**
Chanthaburi, *Thailand* F17+126 **69**
Chantilly, *France* M75+492 **54**
Chanute, *Kansas* U33+376 **95**
Chany, Oz., *U.S.S.R.* G75+550 **62**
Chao, R., *Thailand* F27+150 **65**
Chaoan, *China* E20+237 **67**
Chaochow, *China* E20+237 **67**
Chao Hu, *China* F08+273 **66**
Chapala, L., *Mexico* U78+202 **100**
Chapayevsk, *U.S.S.R.* J62+530 **61**
Chapleau, *Ontario* T50+478 **91**
Chapell Is., *Tasmania* C14-403 **109**
Chapra, *India* G31+258 **73**
Char, *Mauritania* N78+216 **80**
Chara, *U.S.S.R.* E10+570 **63**
Charagua, *Bolivia* S19-197 **104**
Charana, *Bolivia* S57-175 **104**
Charcot, I., *Antarctica* S85-700 **27**
Chard, *England* N18+509 **38**
Chardzhou, *Turkmen* H70+390 **62**
Charente, dep., *France* M89+458 **54**
Charente, R., *France* N04+457 **54**
Charente-Maritime, dep.,
  France N06+458 **54**
Chari R., *Chad* L80+108 **81**
Charikar, *Afghanistan* H35+350 **75**
Charité, la, *France* M72+472 **54**
Chariton, *Iowa* U20+410 **95**
Charkhari, *India* G62+254 **73**
Charleroi, *Belgium* M63+504 **44**
Charles R., *Massachusetts* S68+424 **96**
Charles City, *Iowa* U16+430 **95**
Charleston, *Illinois* T80+394 **95**
Charleston, *Mississippi* U00+340 **97**
Charleston, *Missouri* T86+370 **95**
Charleston, *Queensland* C38-186 **111**
Charleston, S., *Carolina* T30+328 **97**
Charleston, *W. Virginia* T40+384 **97**
Charleston Pk., *Nevada* V64+362 **92**
Charlestown, *Indiana, Rep.* N52+539 **42**
Charles Town, *W. Virginia* T17+393 **96**
Charleville (Rath Luire),
  Ireland, Rep. N52+523 **43**
Charleville, *France* M62+498 **54**
Charleville, *Queensland* C23-264 **111**
Charlevoix, *Michigan* T62+453 **91**
Charlotte, *Michigan* T59+426 **91**
Charlotte, *N. Carolina* T35+352 **97**
Charlotte, *New York* T16+433 **91**
Charlotte Amalie, *Virgin Is.* S29+184 **101**
Charlotte Harbor, *Florida* T43+270 **97**
Charlottenburg, *Germany* M10+525 **48**
Charlottesville, *Virginia* T21+381 **97**
Charlottetown, *P.E.I.* S19+463 **90**
Charlton, *Victoria* C40-363 **109**
Charlton I., *N.-W. Terr.* T26+517 **89**
Charmey, *Switzerland* M47+466 **45**
Charnwood Forest, *England* N08+527 **37**
Charolles, *France* M64+464 **54**
Charrote, Sierra, *Texas* U72+308 **94**
Charsadda, *Pakistan* H19+342 **72**
Charters Towers, *Queensland* C23-200 **111**
Chartres, *France* M81+485 **54**
Charvonnex, *France* M53+460 **45**
Chascomus, *Argentina* R78-356 **103**
Chaska, *Minnesota* U22+448 **93**
Chasseneuil, *France* M87+458 **54**
Châteaubriant, *France* N08+477 **54**
Château Chinon, *France* M67+471 **54**
Château-du-Loir, *France* M87+477 **54**
Châteaudun, *France* M82+481 **54**
Chateau Gontier, *France* N04+478 **54**
Château-la-Valliere, *France* M88+475 **54**
Chateaulin, *France* N25+482 **54**
Châteauneuf-en-Thymerais,
  France M82+486 **54**
Châteaurenault, *France* M85+479 **54**
Châteauroux, *France* M81+468 **54**
Château Salins, *France* M51+488 **54**
Château Thierry, *France* M70+491 **54**
Châteauvillain, *France* M60+480 **54**
Châtelet, *Belgium* M63+504 **44**
Châtellerault, *France* M87+468 **54**
Châtel-St Denis, *Switzerland* M49+465 **45**
Chatfield, *Minnesota* U13+438 **93**
Chatham, *England* M87+514 **39**
Chatham, *New Brunswick* S33+471 **90**
Chatham, *New York* S82+424 **91**
Chatham, *Ontario* T43+424 **91**
Chatham, *Virginia* T27+368 **97**
Chatham Is., *Pacific Ocean* Z70-442 **106**
Chatillon-sur-Seine, *France* M63+478 **54**
Chatra, *India* G31+242 **73**
Chatrapur, *India* G30+194 **71**
Châtre, la, *France* M78+466 **54**
Chattahoochee R., *Georgia* T59+309 **99**
Chattanooga, *Tennessee* T62+350 **97**
Chaudiere R., *Quebec* S67+467 **91**
Chau-doc, *S. Vietnam* E89+108 **69**
Chauka R., *India* G52+274 **73**
Chaumont-en-Bassigny, *Fr.* M59+481 **54**
Chaunskaya Guba, *U.S.S.R.* A60+695 **63**
Chausa, *India* G36+255 **73**
Chautauqua L., *New York* T26+422 **96**
Chaux de Fonds, la, *Switz.* M49+471 **45**
Chaves, *Brazil* R29-003 **105**
Chaves, *Portugal* N45+418 **52**
Chayu, *Tibet* F47+284 **64**
Chazon, *Argentina* S20-332 **103**
Cheadle, *England* N12+530 **37**
Cheb, *Czechoslovakia* M16+501 **48**
Cheboksary, *U.S.S.R.* J76+562 **61**
Cheboygan, *Michigan* T57+456 **91**
Checmu, *Mexico* T70+213 **100**
Cheduba & I., *Burma* F68+189 **71**
Che foo. See Yentai
Chehalis, *Washington* W18+466 **92**
Chekiang, prov., *China* E00+292 **67**
Chekunda, *U.S.S.R.* D16+508 **63**
Chelforó, *Argentina* S39-391 **103**
Chelkar, *Kazakh* J04+479 **62**
Chelm, *Poland* L39+511 **49**
Chelmsford, *England* M87+517 **39**
Chelsea, *Vermont* S75+440 **91**

Chelsea, *Wisconsin* U02+453 **91**
Cheltenham, *England* N12+519 **39**
Chelva, *Spain* N06+397 **53**
Chelyabinsk, *U.S.S.R.* H81+551 **61**
Chemba, *Mozambique* K62-172 **84**
Chembar, *U.S.S.R.* K10+529 **61**
Chemnitz. *See* Karl Marx Stadt
Chenab R., *Pakistan* H22+303 **72**
Chenchow. *See* Hwaiyang
Chengchow, *China* E37+346 **66**
Chengho, *China* E07+274 **67**
Chênghsien, *China* E37+348 **66**
Chengshan Tow, *China* D74+373 **64**
Chêng-têhshih, *China* E12+410 **66**
Chengtu, *China* F06+306 **66**
Chenhsien, *China* E42+258 **67**
Chennan. *See* Tehpao
Chenoa, *Illinois* T83+408 **91**
Chenting, *China* E32+381 **66**
Chenyüan, *China* E69+271 **67**
Chepen, *Peru* T27-072 **104**
Chepes, *Argentina* S40-313 **103**
Cher, R. & dep., *France* M85+473 **54**
Cherbourg, *France* N10+497 **54**
Cherchell, *Algeria* M76+364 **80**
Cheremkhovo, *U.S.S.R.* F11+532 **63**
Cherepovets, *U.S.S.R.* K39+592 **60**
Cherkassy, *Ukraine* K78+494 **60**
Chermoz, *U.S.S.R.* J24+587 **62**
Chernigov, *Ukraine* K82+515 **60**
Chernikovsk, *U.S.S.R.* J25+548 **61**
Chernovsk, *U.S.S.R.* J71+580 **61**
Chernovtsy, *Ukraine* L24+483 **60**
Chernyakhovsk, *U.S.S.R.* L49+546 **47**
Cherokee, *Iowa* U34+427 **95**
Cherokees, L. o' the, *Okla.* U29+367 **95**
Cherra Pungi, *India* F79+252 **71**
Cherryfield, *Maine* S47+446 **90**
Cherskogo, Khrebet, *U.S.S.R.* C20+640 **63**
Chertkovo, *Ukraine* K29+494 **60**
Chervenbyreg, *Bulgaria* L35+433 **58**
Cherwell R., *England* N08+517 **39**
Chesapeake B., *Maryland* T08+388 **99**
Cheshire, co., *England* N15+532 **37**
Cheshskaya Guba, *U.S.S.R.* J80+675 **62**
Chesley, *Ontario* T36+443 **91**
Chester, *England* N17+532 **37**
Chester, *Illinois* T89+379 **97**
Chester, *Pennsylvania* T03+398 **96**
Chester, S. *Carolina* T38+347 **97**
Chesterfield, *England* N09+532 **37**
Chesterfield, S. *Carolina* T31+348 **97**
Chesterfield Inlet, *North-West Territories* U10+639 **89**
Chesterfield Is., *Pacific Oc.* B40+190 **106**
Chester-le-Street, *England* N09+549 **37**
Chestertown, *Maryland* T07+392 **96**
Chesuncook L., *Maine* S56+460 **90**
Chethang, *Tibet* F79+293 **71**
Chetumal & B., *Mexico* T77+184 **100**
Cheviot, *New Zealand* A40-429 **112**
Cheviot, The, *England* N13+555 **37**
Cheviot Hills, *Eng.-Scot.* N14+553 **37**
Cheyenne, *Wyoming* U88+412 **93**
Cheyenne R., S. *Dakota* U70+445 **93**
Chhachrauli, *India* G75+303 **72**
Chhata, *India* G75+277 **72**
Chhatarpur, *India* G62+249 **73**
Chhibramau, *India* G63+271 **73**
Chhindwara, *India* G66+221 **73**
Chiai, *Taiwan* D87+235 **67**
Chiang Mai, *Thailand* F36+188 **69**
Chiang Rai, *Thailand* F31+199 **69**
Chiapa, *Mexico* U18+167 **100**
Chiapas R. & state, *Mexico* U16+170 **100**
Chiasso, *Switzerland* M36+458 **45**
Chiavari, *Italy* M34+443 **56**
Chiba, *Japan* C59+356 **68**
Chibia, *Angola* M08-154 **84**
Chibougamau L., *Quebec* S86+498 **90**
Chicago, *Illinois* T76+418 **95**
Chichagof I., *Alaska* X05+578 **99**
Chichester, *England* N03+508 **39**
Chickasha, *Oklahoma* U48+350 **95**
Chiclayo, *Peru* T29-068 **104**
Chico, *California* W11+397 **92**
Chicoana, *Argentina* S33-252 **103**
Chicopee & R., *Massachusetts* S76+422 **96**
Chicoutimi, *Quebec* S66+484 **90**
Chicundo, *Transvaal* K86-228 **84**
Chidambaram, *India* G62+115 **70**
Chidley, C., *Quebec* S27+603 **89**
Chiang-kan, *Thailand* F20+179 **69**
Chiengue, *Angola* L82-116 **82**
Chienou, *China* E19+268 **67**
Chieti, *Italy* M05+424 **56**
Chièvres, *Belgium* M67+506 **44**
Chigha Khur, *Iran* J54+320 **75**
Chignecto B., *New Brunswick-Nova Scotia* S31+454 **90**
Chignik, *Alaska* Y42+555 **26**
Chichow. *See* Kweichih
Chih-fêng, *China* E06+423 **66**
Chihi, *Tanzania* K50-094 **83**
Chikiang, *China* E62+274 **67**
Chihsien, *China* E34+354 **66**
Chihuahua & state, *Mexico* V06+286 **100**
Chik-Ballapur, *India* G74+135 **70**
Chikien, *China* D85+522 **63**
Chikmagalur, *India* G84+133 **70**
Chikwawa, *Malawi* K60-160 **83**
Chilas, *Kashmir* H05+354 **72**
Childress, *Texas* U62+346 **94**
Chile, rep., S. *America* **103**
Chilecito, *Argentina* S45-292 **103**
Chilete, *Peru* T23-073 **104**
Chilia Veche, *Romania* L04+454 **58**
Chilka L., *India* G27+196 **71**
Chilko L., *Brit. Columbia* W25+512 **88**
Chilko R., *Brit. Columbia* W20+518 **88**
Chillan, *Chile* S73-364 **103**
Chillicothe, *Missouri* U22+398 **95**
Chillicothe, *Ohio* T48+394 **91**
Chillingollah, *Victoria* C42-353 **109**
Chiliwack, *Brit. Columbia* W10+493 **88**
Chiloe, I. de, *Chile* S84-426 **103**
Chilonga, *Zambia* K82-122 **83**
Chilpancingo, *Mexico* U56+174 **100**
Chiltern, *Victoria* C20-362 **109**
Chiltern Hills, *England* N04+518 **39**

Chilton, *Wisconsin* T79+441 **91**
Chiluane, *Moçambique.* K60-206 **84**
Chilubula, *Zambia* K86-102 **83**
Chilung, *Taiwan* D80+251 **67**
Chilwa L., *Malawi* K56-154 **83**
Chimay, *Belgium* M64+501 **44**
Chimbai, *Uzbek* J01+430 **62**
Chimbote, *Peru* T21-091 **104**
Chimkent, *Kazakh* H33+423 **62**
Chimpek, *Kazakh* H06+450 **62**
China, rep., *Asia* E60+330 **31**
Chinandega, *Nicaragua* T73+126 **101**
Chincha, *Peru* T07-135 **104**
Chinchaga R., *Alberta* V85+580 **88**
Chinchon, *Spain* N21+402 **52**
Chinchow, *China* D82+412 **64**
Chindwin R., *Burma* F60+225 **71**
Ching Hai, *China* F28+64
Chingleput, *India* G59+128 **70**
Ching Shan, *China* E54+314 **66**
Chingtao, *China* D88+361 **66**
Chinguetta, *Mauritania* N74+204 **80**
Chinhai, *China* D79+300 **67**
Chin Hill, *Burma* F68+227 **71**
Chini, *India* G70+315 **72**
Chiniot, *Pakistan* H12+316 **72**
Chinishk, *Iran* J06+322 **75**
Chinju, *Korea* D42+353 **64**
Chinkiang. *China* E03+322 **66**
Chin Ling Shan, *China* E80+345 **64**
Chinook, *Montana* V25+486 **93**
Chinsura, *India* G10+229 **73**
Chinwangtao, *China* E02+399 **66**
Chioggia, *Italy* M16+452 **56**
Chios. *See* Khios, I..
Chipchiahue, *Argentina* S51-421 **103**
Chipili, *Zambia* L06-110 **83**
Chipman, *New Brunswick* S35+462 **90**
Chippewa Falls, *Wisconsin* U09+449 **95**
Chippewa, R., *Wisconsin* U06+456 **99**
Chipping Norton, *England* N09+519 **39**
Chipping Sodbury, *England* N14+515 **38**
Chiputneticook Ls., *Maine-New Brunswick* S47+457 **90**
Chiquian, *Peru* T12-102 **104**
Chiquimula, *Guatemala* T87+147 **100**
Chiquinquira, *Colombia* S83+056 **104**
Chiras, *Afghanistan* H55+353 **75**
Chirawa, *India* G86+282 **72**
Chi-ri-cahua Mts., *Arizona* V27+320 **93**
Chiriqui, Lag. de, *Panama* T42+093 **101**
Chiriqui Grande, *Panama* T43+090 **101**
Chirpan, *Bulgaria* L28+422 **58**
Chirripo Grande, mt., *Costa Rica* T52+097 **101**
Chisamba Falls, *Zambia* K86-101 **83**
Chishmy, *U.S.S.R.* J28+545 **61**
Chisimaio, *Somalia* K14-002 **83**
Chisinau. *See* Kishinev
Chistopol, *U.S.S.R.* J56+554 **61**
Chita, *U.S.S.R.* E39+520 **63**
Chitipa, *Malawi* K70+098 **83**
Chitorgarh, *India* H01+248 **70**
Chitradurga, *India* G81+142 **70**
Chitral & R., *Pakistan* H19+358 **72**
Chitre, *Panama* T33+080 **101**
Chittagong, *Bangladesh* F79+223 **71**
Chittoor, *India* G65+133 **70**
Chiusi, *Italy* M18+430 **56**
Chiuta, L., *Malawi* K56-146 **83**
Chiva, *Spain* N04+395 **53**
Chivasso, *Italy* M43+452 **56**
Chivay, *Peru* S69-156 **104**
Chivilcoy, *Argentina* S00-349 **103**
Chivota, Sierra, *New Mexico* V14+354 **93**
Chivyu, *U.S.S.R.* J36+635 **62**
Chiwanda, *Tanzania* K60-114 **83**
Chmielnik, *Poland* L55+506 **49**
Choapam, *Mexico* U35+174 **100**
Choban Bey, *Syria* K45+366 **76**
Chocaya, *Bolivia* S38-209 **104**
Chocen, *Czechoslovakia* L83+500 **49**
Cho-chow, *China* E24+395 **66**
Choco, Cord. de, *Colombia* T13+070 **104**
Choconta, *Colombia* S82+052 **104**
Choele Choel, *Argentina* S34-393 **103**
Choiseul, *Solomon Is.* B48-070 **106**
Choix, *Mexico* V17+272 **100**
Chojna, *Poland* M03+529 **48**
Choke Mts., *Ethiopia* K44+106 **83**
Cholet, *France* N05+471 **54**
Cholon, S. *Vietnam* E80+108 **69**
Choluteca, *Honduras* T74+133 **101**
Choma, *Zambia* L18-168 **84**
Chomutov, *Czechoslavakia* M10+505 **48**
Chone, *Ecuador* T31-006 **104**
Chongjin, *Korea* D32+418 **64**
Chong Kal, *Khmer* F09+139 **69**
Chonos, Arch. de los, *Chile* T00-450 **103**
Chorillos, *Peru* T12-124 **104**
Chorley, *England* N16+537 **37**
Chorrera, *Panama* T28+089 **101**
Chorzele, *Poland* L54+533 **49**
Chorzow, *Poland* L66+503 **49**
Chosi, *Japan* C55+357 **68**
Chos Malal, *Argentina* S62-373 **103**
Chota, *Peru* T22-066 **104**
Choushan I., *China* D77+300 **67**
Christchurch, *England* N11+508 **39**
Christchurch, *New Zealand* A44-435 **112**
Christiansburg, *Virginia* T32+371 **97**
Christianshaab, *Greenland* R40+690 **89**
Christie, Mt., *Yukon* W58+634 **88**
Christmas I., *Indian Ocean* E86-104 **65**
Christmas, I., *Pacific Ocean* Y45+020 **107**
Chrudim, *Czechoslovakia* L85+499 **49**
Chrzanów, *Poland* L64+502 **49**
Chuale L., *Mozambique* K72-250 **84**
Chuambara, *Mozambique* K68-154 **84**
Chuanchow, *China* E09+249 **67**
Chuanhsien, *China* E54+260 **67**
Chubut & R., *Argentina* S40-435 **103**
Chuchow, *China* E40+278 **67**
Chuchow. *See* Lishui
Chucul, *Argentina* S25-330 **103**
Chudovo, *U.S.S.R.* K81+591 **60**
Chudskoye, Oz., *Eston.-U.S.S.R.* L16+58 **47**
Chuho, *China* D42+451 **64**
Chühsien, *China* E07+355 **66**
Chuhsien, *China* E07+289 **67**
Chukai, *Malaya* F09+042 **65**

Chukhloma, *U.S.S.R.* K14+588 **61**
Chukotskiy Khrebet, *U.S.S.R.* A30+682 **63**
Chulman, *U.S.S.R.* D61+567 **63**
Chulym, *U.S.S.R.* G55+551 **62**
Chumbi, *Tibet* G06+274 **71**
Chumikan, *U.S.S.R.* C88+547 **63**
Chuna, R., *U.S.S.R.* F40+572 **63**
Chunar, *India* G43+250 **73**
Chunchön, *Korea* D43+380 **64**
Chungan, *China* E12+277 **67**
Chunghsien, *China* E72+303 **67**
Chungking, *China* E81+295 **67**
Chungshan, *China* E53+246 **67**
Chungsiang, *China* E44+312 **66**
Chungtien, *China* F32+277 **64**
Chunian, *Pakistan* H06+309 **72**
Chunya, *Tanzania* K70-086 **83**
Chuquibambilla, *Peru* S77-140 **104**
Chuquicamata, *Chile* S53-222 **103**
Chur, *Switzerland* M33+469 **45**
Churapcha, *U.S.S.R.* D16+621 **63**
Churchill C., *Manitoba* U21+590 **89**
Churchill L., *Saskatchewan* V20+560 **88**
Churchill, R. & Falls, .*Lab.* S10+530 **89**
Churchill R., *Manitoba* U35+570 **88**
Church's Ferry, *N. Dakota* U55+483 **93**
Churia Ghati Hills, *Nepal* G24+269 **73**
Churu, *India* H00+283 **72**
Chusca, Sierra, *New Mexico* V20+362 **94**
Chusovoi, *U.S.S.R.* J12+582 **62**
Chuvashskaya, aut. rep., *U.S.S.R.* J80+560 **62**
Chwan Ho. *See* Yangtze Kiang
Cibao, Cord. de, *Dom. Rep.* S62+190 **101**
Cicero, *Illinois* T77+418 **95**
Cidones, *Spain* N16+418 **53**
Ciechanow, *Poland* L56+529 **49**
Ciego de Avila, *Cuba* T22+218 **101**
Cienaga, *Colombia* S85+110 **104**
Cienfuegos, *Cuba* T33+222 **101**
Cierfs, *Switzerland* M28+466 **45**
Cieszyn, *Poland* L67+498 **49**
Cieza, *Spain* N08+383 **53**
Cifuentes, *Spain* N16+408 **53**
Cilacap, *Java* E67+077 **65**
Cimalterec, *U.S.S.R.* U39+163 **100**
Cimarron R., *Oklahoma, etc.* U60+370 **98**
Cincinnati, *Ohio* T57+391 **91**
Cioara, *Romania* L15+448 **58**
Ciotat, *France* M57+432 **55**
Circeo C., *Italy* M12+412 **57**
Circle, *Alaska* X56+668 **99**
Circle, *Montana* V04+474 **93**
Circleville, *Ohio* T48+396 **91**
Cirebon, *Java* E69+066 **65**
Cirencester, *England* N12+517 **39**
Ciro, *Italy* L78+394 **57**
Cirque Mt., *Labrador* S22+591 **89**
Citlaltepetl, mt., *Mexico* U44+190 **100**
Citrusdal, *Cape Province* L66-326 **84**
Cittanova, *Italy* L83+384 **57**
Ciudad Bolivar, *Venezuela* S21+082 **104**
Ciudad Chetumal, *Mexico* T79+183 **100**
Ciudad Juarez, *Mexico* V09+316 **100**
Ciudad Madero, *Mexico* U48+223 **100**
Ciudad Real, *Spain* N23+390 **52**
Ciudad Rodrigo, *Spain* N39+406 **52**
Ciudad Victoria, *Mexico* U54+238 **100**
Civray, *France* M88+461 **54**
Civril, *Turkey* L02+383 **74**
Cizre, *Turkey* K17+374 **74**
Clackmannan, *Scotland* N22+561 **41**
Clacton-on-Sea, *England* M83+518 **39**
Claire, L., *Alberta* V42+587 **88**
Clamecy, *France* M69+474 **54**
Clara, *Ireland, Rep.* N46+533 **43**
Clara I., *Burma* F43+108 **71**
Clare, *Michigan* T59+438 **91**
Clare, S. *Australia* C69-338 **109**
Clare, co., *Ireland, Rep.* N53+528 **43**
Clare I., *Ireland, Rep.* N60+538 **42**
Clarecastle, *Ireland, Rep.* N54+528 **43**
Claremont, *New Hampshire* S74+434 **96**
Claremore, *Oklahoma* U34+364 **95**
Claremorris, *Ireland, Rep.* N54+537 **42**
Clarence, *Ireland, Rep.* N46+538 **42**
Clarence, I., *Antarctica* R54-610 **27**
Clarence, I., *Chile* S72-541 **103**
Clarence, R., *New S. Wales* B74-294 **109**
Clarence, R., *New Zealand* A40-423 **112**
Clarence Str., *N. Terr., Aust.* D24-120 **110**
Clarendon, *Arkansas* U08+347 **97**
Clarinda, *Iowa* U30+406 **95**
Clarion, *Iowa* U22+428 **95**
Clarion, *Pennsylvania* T26+412 **96**
Clarion R., *Pennsylvania* T24+413 **96**
Clark, S. *Dakota* U44+449 **93**
Clarke I., *Tasmania* C12-405 **109**
Clarkesville, *Texas* U30+336 **95**
Clarksburg, *West Virginia* T32+393 **91**
Clarksdale, *Mississippi* U04+342 **97**
Clarksville, *Tennessee* T74+365 **95**
Claro, *Switzerland* M36+463 **45**
Clay Center, *Kansas* U43+394 **95**
Claydon, *England* M83+521 **39**
Clayton, *Alabama* T63+319 **97**
Clayton, *New Jersey* T01+397 **91**
Clayton, *New Mexico* U80+365 **94**
Clear I., *Ireland, Rep.* N57+514 **43**
Clear L., *California* W17+390 **92**
Clearfield, *Pennsylvania* T21+410 **96**
Clear Lake, *Iowa* U18+432 **95**
Clearmont, *Wyoming* V08+446 **93**
Clearwater L., *Quebec* T00+558 **89**
Clearwater R., *Idaho* V63+461 **92**
Cleburne, *Texas* U44+324 **95**
Clent Hills, *England* N12+524 **37**
Clermont, *Queensland* C15-226 **111**
Clermont, *Transvaal* L12-236 **84**
Clermont-Ferrand, *France* M71+458 **54**
Cleveland, *Ohio* T40+415 **91**
Cleveland, *Tennessee* T59+351 **97**
Cleveland, *Texas* U30+302 **95**
Cleveland Hills, *England* N07+544 **37**
Clew Bay, *Ireland, Rep.* N59+538 **42**
Clifden, *Ireland, Rep.* N60+535 **43**
Clifton, *Arizona* V26+330 **94**
Clifton, *Tennessee* T78+354 **97**
Clifton Forge, *Virginia* T29+378 **97**

Clifton Ville, *Wisconsin* T83+447 **91**
Clinch Mts., *Tenn.-Va.* T48+364 **97**
Clinton, *Arkansas* U16+356 **97**
Clinton, *Illinois* T84+402 **95**
Clinton, *Iowa* U02+418 **95**
Clinton, *Massachusetts* S70+424 **96**
Clinton, *Missouri* U22+384 **95**
Clinton, *Oklahoma* U54+354 **95**
Clinton, *Ontario* T39+436 **91**
Clinton Colden L., *N.W.T.* V18+632 **88**
Clinton Dam, *Tennessee* T55+362 **97**
Clipperton I., *Pacific Ocean* V25+100 **107**
Clisson, *France* N08+471 **54**
Clitheroe, *England* N13+539 **37**
Clogham, *Ireland, Rep.* N47+532 **43**
Clogher, *N. Ireland* N43+544 **42**
Clonakilty & B., *Ireland, Rep.* N53+516 **43**
Cloncurry, *Queensland* C57-207 **111**
Clones, *Ireland, Rep.* N43+542 **42**
Clonmel, *Ireland, Rep.* N46+524 **43**
Clonegal, *Ireland, Rep.* N40+527 **43**
Cloquet, *Minnesota* U15+467 **93**
Clorinda, *Argentina* R77-252 **103**
Cloud Pk., *Wyoming* V12+446 **93**
Clover, *Virginia* T22+369 **97**
Clovis, *New Mexico* U80+344 **94**
Cloyne, *Ireland, Rep.* N49+519 **43**
Cluj, *Romania* L38+468 **58**
Clun Forest, *Wales* N20+524 **38**
Clunes, *Victoria* C37-373 **109**
Clusone, *Italy* M30+458 **56**
Clyde, *New Zealand* A64-451 **112**
Clyde, Firth of, *Scotland* N30+555 **41**
Clyde, Inlet, *N.-W. Terr.* S50+704 **89**
Clyde R., *Scotland* N26+559 **41**
Clydebank, *Scotland* N26+559 **41**
Coahuila, state, *Mexico* U74+270 **100**
Coalcoman, *Mexico* U78+188 **100**
Coamo, *Puerto Rico* S38+180 **101**
Coari, *Brazil* S19-040 **104**
Coast Mts., *Brit. Columbia* W30+510 **88**
Coast Ra., *Oregon, etc.* W33+418 **92**
Coatbridge, *Scotland* N24+558 **41**
Coatepeque, *Guatemala* U11+147 **100**
Coatesville, *Pennsylvania* T05+399 **96**
Coaticook, *Quebec* S71+451 **91**
Coats I., *N.-W. Terr.* T45+620 **89**
Coats Ld., *Antarctica* N75-750 **27**
Cobalt, *Ontario* T28+474 **91**
Coban, *Guatemala* U02+155 **100**
Cobar, *New S. Wales* C25-316 **109**
Cobargo. *New S. Wales* C01-364 **109**
Cobb, Mt., *New Zealand* A45-410 **112**
Cobden, *Victoria* C42-384 **109**
Cobequid Mts., *Nova Scotia* S26+455 **90**
Cobh, *Ireland, Rep.* N50+518 **43**
Cobija, *Bolivia* S53-110 **104**
Cobleskill, *New York* S87+427 **91**
Coboconk, *Ontario* T23+447 **91**
Cobourg, *Ontario* T19+440 **91**
Cobourg Pen., *N. Terr., Aust.* D15-114 **110**
Cobram, *Victoria* C26-359 **109**
Cobre, El, *Cuba* T06+201 **101**
Coburg, *W. Germany* M24+502 **48**
Coburg I., *N.-W. Terr.* T20+760 **89**
Cocahacra, *Peru* S71-170 **104**
Cocamá, *Peru* S68-105 **104**
Cochabamba, *Bolivia* S36-174 **104**
Cochin, *India* G82+100 **70**
Cochin China, S. *Vietnam* F00+102 **69**
Cochinoca, *Argentina* S35-227 **103**
Cochran, *Georgia* T50+324 **97**
Cochrane, *Ontario* T36+492 **89**
Cochrane, L., *Chile-Argent.* S72-472 **103**
Cockburn, S. *Australia* C54-321 **109**
Cockburn I., *Ontario* T50+459 **91**
Cockburn, Mt., *W. Australia* D45-157 **110**
Cockburnspath, *Scotland* N14+559 **41**
Cockermouth, *England* N20+547 **37**
Cockscomb Mts., *Belize* T84+166 **101**
Coco, I. del, *Pacific Ocean* T70+045 **107**
Cocos Is. (Keeling), *Indian Oc.* F45-120 **77**
Cocula, *Mexico* U83+203 **100**
Cocuy, *Columbia* S75+064 **104**
Cod C., *Massachusetts* S60+421 **96**
Codajas, *Brazil* S12-036 **104**
Codfish I., *New Zealand* A74+557 **41**
Codó *Brazil* Q83-044 **105**
Cod's Hd., *Ireland, Rep.* N61+517 **43**
Cody, *Wyoming* V24+445 **93**
Coe Hill, *Ontario* T17+448 **91**
Coeur d'Alene, *Idaho* V71+477 **92**
Coevorden, *Netherlands* M49+527 **44**
Coeymans, *New York* S83+425 **96**
Coffeyville, *Kansas* U34+370 **95**
Coff's Harbour, *N.S.W.* B71-303 **109**
Cognac, *France* N02+457 **54**
Cogolludo, *Spain* N19+410 **52**
Cohoes, *New York* S82+428 **96**
Cohuna, *Victoria* C35-358 **109**
Coiba, I., *Panama* T40+075 **101**
Coimbatore, *India* G78+110 **70**
Coimbra, *Portugal* N50+402 **52**
Coin, *Spain* N28+366 **52**
Coire. *See* Chur
Cojimies, *Ecuador* T30+003 **104**
Coko Ra., *New S. Wales* C51-305 **109**
Colac, *Victoria* C39-384 **109**
Colair L., *India* G52+166 **70**
Colbeck Arch., *Antarctica* H85-680 **27**
Colby, *Kansas* U66+394 **94**
Colcha, *Bolivia* S47-208 **104**
Colchester, *England* M85+519 **39**
Coldingham, *Scotland* N13+559 **41**
Coldstream, *Scotland* N13+557 **41**
Coldwater, *Mississippi* U00+347 **97**
Colebrook, *New Hampshire* S69+449 **91**
Coleman, *Alberta* V57+496 **88**
Coleman, *Texas* U56+318 **95**
Coleraine, *N. Ireland* N40+551 **42**
Coleraine, *Victoria* C50-375 **109**
Coleridge, L., *New Zealand* A51-433 **112**
Colgong, *India* G16+252 **73**
Colhué Huapi, L., *Argentina* S53-455 **103**
Colima & state, *Mexico* U82+192 **100**
Colinas, *Honduras* T80+150 **101**
Coll, I., *Scotland* N39+557 **41**
Collahuasi, *Chile* S52-210 **103**
Collarenebri, *New S. Wales* C09-296 **109**
Collie, *New South Wales* C10-317 **109**

Collie, W. Australia E21-333 110
Collier B., W. Australia D65-160 110
Collines-de-Normandie,
  France N06+490 54
Collingwood, Ontario T31+445 91
Collingwood, Queensland C45-222 111
Collo, Algeria M50+368 80
Collooney, Ireland, Rep. N51+542 42
Colmar, France M46+481 54
Colmars, France M50+442 55
Colmena, Argentina S01-286 103
Colmenar de Oreja, Spain N21+401 52
Colmenar Viejo, Spain N23+406 52
Colmi, Honduras T64+150 101
Colmonell, Scotland N29+551 41
Colne, England N13+539 37
Colne R., England M85+519 39
Cologne. See Köln
Colomb-Bechar (Bechar),
  Algeria N12+314 80
Colombia, Brazil R23-202 105
Colombia, rep., S. America 104
Colombier, Switzerland M49+470 45
Colombo, Sri Lanka G62+070 70
Colon, Argentina R79-321 103
Colon, Argentina S07-338 103
Colon, Cuba T34+227 111
Colon, Panama T28+093 111
Colon, Venezuela S74+080 104
Colonel Fer. Gomez, Brazil R36+008 105
Colonelganj, India G49+271 73
Colonia, Uruguay R77-344 103
Colonia Alvear, Argentina S46-350 103
Colonia Sarmiento, Argent. S55-457 103
Colonsay, I., Scotland N37+561 41
Colorado, Texas U65+323 94
Colorado, state, U.S.A. V17+391 98
Colorado Des., California V66+349 92
Colorado Des., Wyoming V28+424 93
Colorado Plat., Arizona V30+360 94
Colorado, R., Argentina S22-393 103
Colorado R., Texas U36+292 95
Colorado R., U.S.A. V57+333 98
Colorado R., Utah, etc. V30+380 94
Colorado R., Little, Arizona V38+358 94
Colorados, Arch. de los, Cuba T56+224 101
Colorado Springs, Colorado U89+388 94
Colotlan, Mexico U80+223 100
Colpoy B., Ontario T36+449 91
Colquechaca, Bolivia S37-190 104
Colton, California V74+341 92
Columbia, Alabama T61+313 97
Columbia, Indiana T63+412 91
Columbia, Kentucky T62+371 97
Columbia, Louisiana U13+321 97
Columbia, Mississippi T89+312 99
Columbia, Missouri U14+390 95
Columbia, Pennsylvania T09+400 96
Columbia, S. Carolina T36+340 97
Columbia, Tennessee T72+356 97
Columbia C., Canada S60+830 26
Columbia, Dist. of, U.S.A. T12+386 91
Columbia, Mt., Alberta V75+524 88
Colombia Plat., Wash., etc. V80+469 98
Colombia R., Canada-
  U.S.A. W06+457 92
Columbiana, Alabama T70+332 97
Columbus, Georgia T60+325 97
Columbus, Indiana T65+392 91
Columbus, Kansas U30+372 95
Columbus, Mississippi T80+336 95
Columbus, Montana V26+456 93
Columbus, Nebraska U42+414 95
Columbus, Ohio T48+400 91
Columbus, Texas U39+297 95
Colville L., N.-W. Terr. W25+678 88
Colville Ra., New Zealand A26-370 112
Colwyn Bay, Wales N22+533 38
Comacchio, Valli di, Italy M18+447 56
Comana, Romania L23+442 58
Comayagua, Honduras 176+144 101
Combarbala, Chile S66-311 103
Comber, N. Ireland N34+545 42
Comblain, Belgium M57+505 44
Comeragh Mts., Ireland, Rep. N45+522 43
Comino C., Sardinia M31+405 57
Comiso, Sicily M02+369 57
Comitan, Mexico U12+162 100
Commissioners L., Quebec S73+482 90
Commonwealth Ra., Antarc. Z80-850 27
Como, Italy M36+458 56
Como, L. di, Italy M35+460 56
Comores, Arch. des, See Comoro Is.
Comorin C., India G74+081 70
Comoro Is., Ind. Oc. K06-122 83
Compiègne, France M73+494 54
Comporta, Portugal N53+384 52
Compostela, Mexico U89+213 100
Comrie, Scotland N24+564 41
Conakry, Guinea N82+096 80
Conceicao do Araguaya,
  Brazil R27-086 105
Conceicao do Arroio, Brazil R33-299 103
Concepcion, Argentina S17-312 103
Concepcion, Argentina R78-284 103
Concepcion, Bolivia S40-114 104
Concepcion, Chile S78-368 103
Concepcion, Paraguay R75-234 103
Concepcion del Oro, Mexico U68+245 100
Concepcion del Uruguay,
  Argentina R80-325 103
Conception B. Nfd. R48+478 90
Conception I.,Bahamas,The T01+239 101
Conception, Pt., California W03+346 98
Conchas Res., New Mexico U86+354 94
Conchi, Chile S52-219 103
Concord, Massachusetts S68+425 96
Concord, New Hampshire S69+432 91
Concord, N. Carolina T34+354 97
Concordia, Argentina R79-313 103
Concordia, Kansas U46+395 95
Concordia, Mexico V06+232 100
Concordia, Peru S63-185 104
Condobolin, New S. Wales C18-331 109
Condom, France M88+440 55
Condor, Cord. del, Peru T20-040 104
Conemaugh, Pennsylvania T24+404 96
Conesa, Argentina S28-401 103
Confolens, France M86+460 54
Congo, rep., Cent. Africa. See Zaire.
Congo, rep., Cent Africa M00+002 82

Congo R. (Zaire) Cent. Afr. L76-016 82
Coniston Water, England N19+543 37
Coney I., New York S83+405 96
Conlin, Montana V00+469 93
Conn L., Ireland, Rep. N56+540 42
Connacht, prov.,
  Ireland, Rep. N51+538 42
Connecticut R., Conn., etc. S74+413 96
Connecticut R., Vermont S75+428 91
Connecticut, state, U.S.A. S80+415 99
Connellsville, Pennsylvania T28+400 96
Connemara, Ireland, Rep. N58+535 43
Connors, New Brunswick S53+472 90
Conrad, Montana V42+482 93
Conroe, Texas U33+302 95
Conshohocken, New Jersey T02+401 96
Conselheiro Lafaiete, Brazil Q80-204 105
Constance. See Konstanz
Constance, L. See Boden See
Constanta, Romania L08+442 58
Constantine, Algeria M50+362 80
Constitucion, Chile S75-354 103
Consuegra, Spain N22+394 52
Contamana, Peru T00-073 104
Conthey, Switzerland M46+462 45
Contreras, I., Chile T00-519 103
Contwoyto L., N.-W. Terr. V42+657 88
Conway, Arkansas U14+351 95
Conway, Missouri U18+376 95
Conway, New Hampshire S67+440 91
Conway, S. Carolina T 24+339 97
Conwy, Wales N23+533 38
Coober Pedy, S. Australia D03-287 111
Cooch Behar, India G03+263 73
Cook, B. de, Chile S60-552 103
Cook Inl., Alaska Y15+590 99
Cook Is., Pacific Ocean Y60-200 106
Cook, Mt., New Zealand A59-436 112
Cook Str., New Zealand A32-414 112
Cook's Passage, Queensland C29-147 111
Cookshire, Quebec S70+454 91
Cookstown, N. Ireland N40+546 42
Cooktown, Queensland C28-154 111
Coolabah, New S. Wales C20-311 109
Coolah, New S. Wales C02-318 109
Coolamon, New S. Wales C17-348 109
Coolgardie, W. Australia D83-309 110
Cooma, New South Wales C06-362 109
Coomacarrea,
  Ireland, Rep. N60+520 43
Coonabarabran, N.S.W. C04-313 109
Coonalpym, S. Australia C61-357 109
Coonamble, New S. Wales C09-309 109
Coondiwindi, Queensland B88-283 111
Cooper Cr., S. Australia C66-278 111
Cooperstown, New York T00+427 96
Coorg, India G83+122 70
Coorong, The, S. Australia C62-360 109
Cootamundra, New S. Wales C12-347 109
Cootehill, Ireland, Rep. N42+541 42
Copenhagen. See Köbenhavn.
Copetonas, Argentina S03-386 103
Copiapo, Chile S62-273 103
Copley, S. Australia C69-306 109
Coporaque, Peru S70-148 104
Copper Cliff, Ontario T37+465 91
Coppermine, North-West
  Territories V65+672 88
Coppermine R., N.-W. Terr. V60+664 88
Coppet, Switzerland M53+463 45
Coquar, Quebec T02+481 91
Coquilhatville (Mbandaka),
  Zaire L70+001 82
Coquimbo & B. de, Chile S68-299 103
Corabia, Romania L33+438 58
Coracoes, Brazil R02-217 105
Coraki, New S. Wales B71-288 109
Corangamite, L., Victoria C40-382 109
Corato, Italy L82+411 57
Corazon, Sierra, Texas U82+295 94
Corcaigh. See Cork
Corcovado, G. del, Chile S80-434 103
Corcovado, mt. Chile S76-432 103
Corcubion, Spain N55+429 52
Cordell, Oklahoma U54+352 95
Cordoba, Mexico U42+190 100
Cordoba, Peru T00-139 104
Córdoba, Spain N29+379 52
Cordoba and Sa. de,
  Argentina S26-314 103
Cordova, Alaska X70+605 99
Corfu. See Kérkira, I.
Corfu, Str. of Greece L60+395 59
Coria, Spain N39+400 52
Corigliano Calabro, Italy L81+396 57
Corindi, New S. Wales B71-300 109
Coringa, India G47+168 71
Corinth. See Korinthos
Corinth, Mississippi T81+349 95
Corinto, Brazil Q87-184 105
Corinto, Nicaragua T57+136 101
Coristine, Ontario T24+461 91
Cork & co., Ireland, Rep. N51+519 43
Cork Harb., Ireland, Rep. N49+518 43
Corleone, Sicily M10+378 57
Corner Inl., Victoria C22-387 109
Corner Brook, Nfd. R78+490 90
Corning, Iowa U28+410 95
Corning, New York T13+421 96
Cornwall, New York S84+414 96
Cornwall, Ontario S88+450 91
Cornwall, co., England N26+438 38
Coro, Venezuela S58+114 104
Coroata, Brazil Q85-040 105
Corocoro, Bolivia S52-171 104
Coroico, Bolivia S47-161 104
Corofin, Ireland, Rep. N54+529 43
Corona, New S. Wales C52-312 109
Coronada, B., Costa Rica T52+090 101
Coronation G., N. W. Terr. V40+678 88
Coronation I., Antarctica 605-610 27
Coronel, Chile S79-370 103
Coronel Pringles, Argentina S09-380 103
Coronel Suarez, Argentina S11-376 103
Coronie, Surinam R69+058 105
Coropuna, mt., Peru S76-156 104
Corowa, New South Wales C22-360 109
Corozal, Belize T81+184 101
Corpen Aike, Argentina S56-496 103
Corpus Christi & B., Texas U44+278 94
Corpus Christi L., Texas V29+282 94

Corpus Christi Pass, Texas U43+276 94
Corque, Bolivia S46-183 104
Corrales, Uruguay R64-314 103
Corralitos, Mexico V17+306 100
Corregidor, I., Philippines D87+144 65
Correze, dep., France M78+453 54
Corrib L. Ireland, Rep. N55+534 43
Corrientes, Argentina R83-276 103
Corrientes, C., Argentina R76-381 103
Corrientes, C., Mexico V04+204 100
Corrigin, W. Australia E12-322 110
Corrimal, New S. Wales B85-344 109
Corry, Pennsylvania T28+419 96
Corryvreckan, G. of, Scot. N35+561 41
Corse, I., France M36+420 56
Corsewall Pt., Scotland N31+550 41
Corsica. See Corse, I.
Corsicana, Texas U39+322 95
Cortes, G. de, Cuba T54+220 101
Cortland, New York T07+426 96
Cortona, Italy M18+433 56
Coruche, Portugal N51+390 52
Coruh, R., Turkey K24+407 74
Corum, Turkey K61+405 74
Corumba, Brazil R75-190 105
Corunna. See La Coruña,
Corvallis, Oregon W20+446 92
Corwen, Wales N20+530 38
Corwin, Alaska Y85+685 99
Corydon, Iowa U20+408 95
Cosalo, Mexico V09+244 100
Coseguina, Vol., Nicaragua T75+130 101
Cosenza, Italy L82+393 57
Cosquin, Argentina S27-312 103
Cossonay, Switzerland M51+466 45
Costa Rica, rep.,
  Central America T54+100 101
Costermansville. See Bukavu
Costillo Pk., New Mexico U92+368 94
Cotabato, Philippines D65+072 65
Cotagaita, Bolivia S34-208 104
Cotahuasi, Peru S78-152 104
Cote Blanche B., Louisiana U10+296 95
Cote D'Ivoire. See Ivory Coast
Côte-d'Or, dep., France M60+474 54
Côtes-du-Nord, dep., France N18+484 54
Cöthen, Germany M18+517 48
Cotonou, Benin M76+064 80
Cotswold, Hills, England N12+519 39
Cottbus, E. Germany M04+518 48
Cottica, Surinam R56+038 105
Cotulla, Texas U55+284 94
Coudersport, Pennsylvania T18+417 96
Coudres, I. aux, Quebec S62+474 91
Coulagh B., Ireland, Rep. N60+517 43
Coulman, I., Antarctica A62-730 27
Council Bluffs, Iowa U35+412 95
Council Grove, Kansas U39+386 95
Coupar-Angus, Scotland N20+565 41
Courantyne, R., Guyana, etc. R77+042 104
Couronne C., France M60+433 55
Courtenay, B. Dakota U51+472 93
Courtmacsherry,
  Ireland, Rep. N52+516 43
Courtrai, Belgium M70+508 44
Court St Etienne, Belgium M62+506 44
Couterne, France N02+485 54
Couthuin, Belgium M59+505 44
Couvin, Belgium M63+501 44
Covenas, Colombia T04+094 104
Coventry, England N09+524 37
Covilhã, Portugal N45+403 52
Covington, Kentucky T57+391 91
Covington, Tennessee T88+356 97
Covington, Virginia T30+378 97
Cowal, L., New S. Wales C15-336 109
Cowan, L., W. Australia D79-318 110
Cowangie, Victoria C51-352 109
Cowbridge, Wales N20+514 38
Cowdenbeath, Scotland N20+561 41
Cowell, S. Australia C79-334 111
Cowes, I. of W., England N08+508 39
Cowra, New South Wales C07-339 109
Coxsackie, New York S83+424 96
Cox's Bazar, Bangladesh F78+214 71
Coyame, Mexico V01+294 100
Coyuca, Mexico U64+183 100
Cozumel, I., Mexico T70+204 100
Crabbs, Newfoundland R83+482 90
Craboon, N.S.W. C03-321 109
Cracow. See Krakow
Cradle Mt., Tasmania C24-417 109
Craig, Colorado V16+404 94
Craigavon, N. Ireland N38+544 42
Craig Harbour, N.-W. Terr. T35+760 89
Craigue, Ireland, Rep. N42+528 43
Craigville, Minnesota U22+479 93
Crail, Scotland N16+563 41
Craiova, Romania L37+443 58
Cranberry, England N11+509 38
Cranbrook, Brit. Columbia V65+496 88
Crandon, Wisconsin T83+455 91
Crane I., Quebec S63+471 91
Cranleigh, England N03+511 39
Crans, Switzerland M45+463 45
Crater Lake National Park,
  Oregon W14+430 92
Crateus, Brazil Q64-052 105
Crato, Brazil S39+304 104
Crato, Brazil Q56-072 105
Cravo, Colombia S62+056 104
Crawford, Nebraska U80+427 94
Crawford, Scotland N22+555 41
Crazy Mts., Montana V32+461 93
Creag Meagaidh, Scotland N28+569 41
Crediton, England N22+508 38
Cree L., Saskatchewan V10+578 88
Cree I., Saskatchewan V07+584 88
Cree R., Scotland N27+550 41
Cremona, Italy M30+452 56
Cres, I., Yugoslavia M04+448 56
Cresco, Iowa U14+434 95
Cressy, Victoria C38-381 109
Crest, Quebec T24+465 91
Cresta, Switzerland M33+465 45
Creston, Iowa U26+410 95
Creswell B., N.-W. Terr. U20+722 89
Creswick, Victoria C37-374 109
Crete (Kriti), Greece L30+350 59
Crete, Nebraska U42+406 95

Crete, Sea of, Greece L30+359 59
Creuse, dep., France M78+460 54
Creusot, le, France M64+468 54
Crewe, England N15+531 37
Crewkerne, England N17+509 38
Criccieth, Wales N25+529 38
Crickhowell, Wales N19+519 38
Cricklade, England N11+516 39
Crieff, Scotland N23+564 41
Crimea (Krym), U.S.S.R. K66+450 60
Crimmitschau, E. Germany M16+508 48
Cripple Creek, Colorado V02+387 94
Crisana, Romania L48+468 58
Cristobal, Panama T29+093 101
Crnagora, Yugoslavia L64+430 58
Croagh Patrick, Ireland, Rep. N58+538 42
Crockett, Texas U33+313 95
Croisic le, France N15+472 54
Croker I., N. Terr., Aust. D14-111 110
Cromarty, & Firth, Scotland N24+577 40
Cromer, England M82+529 39
Cromwell, New Zealand A64-449 112
Crooked I., Bahamas, The S86+228 101
Crookston, Minnesota U40+478 93
Crookwell, New S. Wales C03-345 109
Croom, Ireland, Rep. N52+525 43
Croppa Creek, New S. Wales B88-291 109
Cross Fell, England N15+547 37
Crosshaven, Ireland, Rep. N50+518 43
Crossmolina, Ireland, Rep. N56+541 42
Cross Point, Quebec S40+481 90
Crotone, Italy L77+391 57
Crow Agency, Montana V15+455 93
Crowes, Victoria C40-387 109
Crowley, Louisiana U13+302 95
Crown Prince Olav Ld.,
  Antarctica K25-690 27
Crown Princess Martha Ld.,
  Antarctica N30-720 27
Crows Nest Pass, Alberta V58+498 88
Croydon, England N01+514 39
Croydon, Queensland C47-181 111
Crozet Is., Indian Ocean J60-463 77
Crozier, C., Antarctica A65-770 27
Cruden B., Scotland N11+574 40
Crumlin, N. Ireland N37+546 42
Cruz, Utah V47+388 92
Cruz Alta, Argentina S11-330 103
Cruz Alta, Brazil R52-286 103
Cruz del Eje, Argentina S29-308 103
Cruzeiro do Sul, Brazil S76-078 104
Cruz Grande, Chile S68-294 103
Cruz Grande, Mexico U55+167 100
Crystal Brook, S. Australia C71-333 109
Crystal Falls, Michigan T80+461 91
Crystal Springs, Mississippi U01+320 97
Cuamba, Mozambique K50-148 83
Cuango, Angola L72-092 82
Cuanza R., Angola M10-092 82
Cuareim, Brazil R76-302 103
Cuatro Cienegas, Mexico U73+269 100
Cuba, New Mexico V12+360 94
Cuba, New York T20+423 91
Cuba, Portugal N47+382 52
Cuba, I., West Indies T30+220 101
Cuchi, Angola L78-146 82
Cuchillo-Co, Argentina S28-384 103
Cuchillo Parado, Mexico U89+294 100
Cucumbi, Angola L66-104 82
Cucuta, Colombia S75+079 104
Cudahy, Wisconsin T77+430 91
Cuddalore, India G62+117 70
Cuddapah, India G66+144 70
Cudgewa, Victoria C13-362 109
Cue, W. Australia E12-274 100
Cuellar, Spain N26+414 52
Cuenca, Ecuador T24-028 104
Cuenca, Spain N13+401 53
Cuencame, Mexico U83+248 100
Cuernavaca, Mexico U55+188 100
Cuero, Texas U44+290 95
Cuevo, Bolivia S21-204 104
Cuglieri, Sardinia M39+402 57
Cuiabá, Brazil R80-072 104
Cuiaba, Brazil R66-156 105
Cuicuina, Nicaragua T57+136 101
Cuilcagh, Ireland, Rep. N47+542 42
Cuillin Hills, Scotland N38+572 40
Cuillin Sd., Scotland N38+571 40
Cuiña, P. de, Spain N41+429 52
Cuito Cuanavale, Angola L64-152 84
Culcairn, New South Wales C18-357 109
Culebra, I., West Indies S32+184 101
Culebra, G. de la, Costa Rica T64+108 101
Culgoa, R., New S. Wales C20-296 109
Culgoa, R., Queensland C15-286 111
Culiacan, Mexico V15+249 100
Cullarin Ra., New S. Wales C03-346 109
Cullera, Spain N01+392 53
Cullompton, England N21+509 38
Cully, Switzerland M50+465 45
Culpeper, Virginia T18+384 97
Culverden, New Zealand A43-427 112
Cumana, Venezuela S24+104 104
Cumaria, Peru S84-099 104
Cumberland, Brit. Columbia W31+496 88
Cumberland, Maryland T22+397 96
Cumberland, Virginia T20+375 97
Cumberland, Wisconsin U12+456 93
Cumberland I., Georgia T39+308 97
Cumberland Mts., Tenn., etc. T52+365 97
Cumberland Pen.,N.-W. Terr. T66+664 89
Cumberland Plat., Tenn. T66+351 97
Cumberland Sd., Kentucky, etc. T78+368 97
Cumberland Sd., N.-W. Terr. S30+650 89
Cumbres, Great, I., Scotland N30+558 41
Cumbrae, co., England N18+547 37
Cumbrian Mts., England N18+545 37
Cumbum, India G65+156 70
Cumnock, New S. Wales C07-330 109
Cumnock, Scotland N26+554 41
Cunene R., Angola M16-172 84
Cuneo, Italy M45+444 56
Cunnamulla, Queensland C26-280 111
Cupar, Scotland N18+563 41
Cuprija, Yugoslavia L56+440 58
Cura, Venezuela S45+100 104
Curaca, Brazil Q59-090 105
Curaçoa, I., Caribbean Sea S53+122 104
Curaglia, Switzerland M37+467 45
Curiapo, Venezuela S07+086 104

Curico, *Chile* S67–350 **103**
Curiplaya, *Colombia* S89+003 **104**
Curitiba, *Brazil* R25–256 **103**
Curitibanos, *Brazil* R34–273 **103**
Curlewis, *New South Wales* B88–311 **109**
Curnamona, *S. Australia* C63–316 **109**
Curora, *Mozambique* K42–116 **83**
Currabubula, *New S. Wales* B86–312 **109**
Curraes Novos, *Brazil* Q39–062 **105**
Curralinho, *Brazil* R28–017 **105**
Currane L., *Ireland, Rep.* N61+518 **43**
Curraun Pen., (Corraun),
  Ireland, Rep. N59+539 **42**
Currituck Sd., *N. Carolina* T04+364 **97**
Curtis, I., *Pacific Ocean* Z80–305 **106**
Curua, *Brazil* R52+010 **105**
Curuay, Gde. do, L., *Brazil* R62–022 **105**
Curuca, *Brazil* R17–006 **105**
Curupachi, *Brazil* R76–076 **105**
Curuzú Cuatia, *Argentina* R78–298 **103**
Curwensville, *Pennsylvania* T21+410 **96**
Cury, *Brazil* R63–039 **105**
Cushendall, *N. Ireland* N36+551 **42**
Cushendun, *N. Ireland* N36+551 **42**
Cushing, *Oklahoma* U40+359 **95**
Custer, *S. Dakota* U82+437 **93**
Cut Bank, *Montana* V44+486 **93**
Cuthbert, *Georgia* T59+318 **97**
Cutra L., *Ireland, Rep.* N53+530 **43**
Cuttack, *India* G24+204 **71**
Cuxhaven, *W. Germany* M38+539 **48**
Cuzco, *Peru* S72–135 **104**
Cycládes, See Kikladhes, Is.
Cygnet, *Tasmania* C18–432 **109**
Cynthiana, *Kentucky* T56+385 **97**
Cyprus, I. and rep., *Medi-*
  terranean Sea K72+350 **76**
Cyrenaica, *Libya* L50+292 **81**
Cyrene. See Shahhat
  Czechoslovakia, rep.,
    Central Europe **50-51**
Czersk, *Poland* L72+538 **49**
Czestochowa, *Poland* L65+508 **49**
Dabakala, *Ivory Coast* N26+084 **80**
Dabaro, *Somalia* J68+064 **83**
Dabeiba, *Colombia* T07+070 **104**
Dabhoi, *India* H09+220 **70**
Dabie, *Poland* M02+534 **48**
Dabola, *Guinea* N66+108 **80**
Dabrowa Górnicza, *Poland* L65+504 **49**
Dacca, *Bangladesh* F87+237 **71**
Dadanawa, *Guyana* R88+028 **104**
Dade City, *Florida* T43+284 **97**
Dadri, *India* G82+286 **72**
Dagana, *Senegal* P04+164 **80**
Dagarita, *Somalia* K06+106 **83**
Dagash, *Sudan* K70+190 **81**
Dagda, *Latvia* L15+561 **47**
Dagenham, *England* M89+515 **39**
Dagupan, *Philippines* D88+160 **65**
Dahlak Arch., *Ethiopia* K28+156 **83**
Dahomey, rep., See Benin
Daimiel, *Spain* N22+391 **52**
Daireaux, *Argentina* S11–365 **103**
Dairen, See Luta
Dairut, *Egypt* K86+276 **81**
Daisetsuzan Nat. Park, *Japan* C44+435 **68**
Daishoji, *Japan* C82+363 **68**
Dajarra, *Queensland* C63–218 **111**
Dakar, *Senegal* P14+146 **80**
Dakhla, *Mauritania* P06 + 236 **80**
Dal, *Norway* M22+603 **47**
Dal Alv, *Sweden* L80+602 **47**
Dala, *Angola* L58–112 **82**
Dalan Dszadagad, *Mongolia* F02+437 **64**
Dalat, *S. Vietnam* E70+120 **69**
Dalbandin, *Pakistan* H63+290 **70**
Dalbeattie, *Scotland* N23+549 **41**
Dalbo Sjön, *Sweden* M12+589 **47**
Dalby, *Queensland* B83–270 **111**
Dalby, *Sweden* M12+606 **47**
Dalen, *Netherlands* M49+527 **44**
Dalen, *Norway* M42+595 **47**
Dalgety, *New S. Wales* C07–364 **109**
Dalhart, *Texas* U75+360 **98**
Dalhousie, *India* G84+325 **72**
Dalhousie, *New Brunswick* S38+481 **90**
Dalkeith, *Scotland* N18+559 **41**
Dalkey, *Ireland, Rep.* N36+533 **43**
Dallas, *Oregon* W20+449 **92**
Dallas, *Texas* U41+328 **95**
Dallas, L., *Texas* U42+332 **95**
Dalles, The, *Oregon* W07+456 **92**
Dalmacio Velez, *Argentina* S22–327 **103**
Dalmally, *Scotland* N30+564 **41**
Dalmatia, *Yugoslavia* L82+437 **56**
Dalmatovo, *U.S.S.R.* H73+562 **61**
Dalmau, *India* G54+261 **73**
Dalmellington, *Scotland* N26+553 **41**
Daloa, *Ivory Coast* N38+070 **80**
Dalry, *Scotland* N28+557 **41**
Dalrymple, Mt., *Queensland* C15–206 **111**
Dalton, *England* N19+542 **37**
Dalton, *Ontario* T54+481 **91**
Daltonganj, *India* G35+240 **73**
Dalwhinnie, *Scotland* N25+569 **40**
Daly, *N. Terr., Australia* D22–126 **110**
Daly R., *N. Terr., Australia* D23–142 **110**
Daly Waters, *N. Terr., Aust.* D10–162 **111**
Dam, *Surinam* R60+046 **105**
Daman, *India* H12+204 **70**
Damanhur, *Egypt* K88+310 **81**
Damar, I., *Indonesia* D38–072 **65**
Damascus (Damas), *Syria* K52+335 **75**
Damávand, mt., *Iran* J48+360 **75**
Dambe, *Angola* L88–068 **82**
Damghan, *Iran* J34+362 **75**
Damietta, *Egypt* K80+314 **81**
Damiya, *Jordan* K57+321 **76**
Dammam Al, *Saudi Arabia* J57+265 **75**
Damoh, *India* G63+238 **73**
Dampier Arch., *W. Aust.* E22–204 **110**
Dampier Land, *W. Australia* D73–174 **110**
Dampier Str., *Indonesia* D26–007 **65**
Damqawt, *Yemen, South* J43 + 166 **75**
Dana, Mt., *California* V85+379 **92**
Danbury, *Connecticut* S81+414 **96**
Danby, *California* V62+347 **92**
Dandenong, *Victoria* C29–380 **109**
Danforth, *Maine* S47+457 **90**
Danger Pt., *Cape Province* L64–348 **84**

Dangra Yum L:, *Tibet* G20+310 **71**
Danilov, *U.S.S.R.* K29+582 **60**
Dankaz, *Ethiopia* K44+124 **83**
Danmark Fd., *Greenland* P85+810 **26**
Dannemora, *Sweden* L74+603 **34**
Dannevirke, *New Zealand* A23–400 **112**
Danube (Dunarea, Donau), R.,
  Cent. Europe L70+450 **51**
Danville, *Illinois* T76+401 **95**
Danville, *Kentucky* T59+376 **97**
Danville, *Pennsylvania* T10+410 **96**
Danville, *Virginia* T26+366 **97**
Danzig. See Gdansk
Danzig, G. of, *Poland* L66+546 **49**
Daolatabad, *Afghanistan* H60+364 **75**
Daqq-e-Patargan,
  Iran-Afghanistan H88+341 **75**
Daraban Kalan, *Pakistan* H28+317 **72**
Daraw, *Egypt* K72+240 **81**
Darb, *Saudi Arabia* K16+175 **74**
Darbhanga, *India* G24+262 **73**
Dardanelles, *Turkey* L23+400 **74**
Darende, *Turkey* K45+386 **74**
Dar-es-Salaam, *Tanzania* K34–070 **83**
Dargai, *Pakistan* H19+345 **72**
Dargaon, *India* G33+217 **71**
Dargaville, *New Zealand* A37–359 **112**
Dargo, *Victoria* C16–375 **109**
Darien, *Georgia* T39+314 **97**
Darien, G. of, *Colombia* T10+082 **104**
Dariyah, *Saudi Arabia* J81+247 **74**
Darjeeling, *India* G10+270 **73**
Darling Ra., *W. Australia* E22–314 **110**
Darling, R., *New S. Wales* C44–336 **109**
Darling Downs, *Queensland* C00–276 **111**
Darlington, *England* N09+545 **37**
Darlington, *S. Carolina* T29+343 **97**
Darlington, *Wisconsin* U01+426 **95**
Darlington Point, *N.S.W.* C24–346 **109**
Darłowo, *Poland* L82+544 **49**
Darmstadt, *W. Germany* M38+499 **48**
Daroca, *Spain* N08+411 **53**
Dart, C., *Antarctica* W10–720 **27**
Dart R., *England* N22+505 **38**
Dartmoor, *England* N23+506 **38**
Dartmoor, *Victoria* C53–380 **109**
Dartmouth, *England* N21+503 **38**
Dartmouth, *Nova Scotia* S21+447 **90**
Daru, I., *Papua New Guinea* C41–091 **111**
Darun, *Iran* J58+330 **75**
Daruvar, *Yugoslavia* L77+456 **56**
Darwen, *England* N15+537 **37**
Darwin, *N. Terr., Australia* D24–124 **110**
Darwin, mt., *Chile* S56–548 **103**
Darwin Mt., *Rhodesia* K80–168 **84**
Daryabad, *India* G51+269 **73**
Daryácheh e Baktegán L.,
  Iran J36+295 **75**
Daryácheh-ye-Namak, *Iran* J50+348 **75**
Daryácheh-ye-Rezá'îyeh, *Iran* J88+378 **74**
Dasara, *Bangladesh* G00+239 **73**
Dashibalbar, *Mongolia* E34+495 **64**
Dasht R., *Pakistan* H78+256 **70**
Dasht Ab, *Iran* J21+289 **75**
Dashtiari, *Iran* H82+255 **75**
Daska, *Pakistan* H04+323 **72**
Daspalla, *India* G31+203 **71**
Daspur, *India* G23+220 **73**
Dasuya, *India* G86+318 **72**
Dataganj, *India* G63+280 **73**
Datia, *India* G69+256 **73**
Daudnagar, *India* G33+250 **73**
Daugavgriva, *Latvia* L36+570 **47**
Daugavpils, *Latvia* L21+559 **47**
Daulatabad, *India* G88+200 **70**
Daulat Yar, *Afghanistan* H55+345 **75**
Daule, *Ecuador* T30–018 **104**
Dauletabad, *Iran* J35+361 **75**
Dauphin, *Manitoba* U60+509 **88**
Dauphine, prov., *France* M56+449 **55**
Davao & G., *Philippines* D57+070 **65**
Davenport, *Iowa* U04+415 **95**
Davenport Ra., *N.T., Aust.* D00–209 **111**
Daventry, *England* N07+523 **37**
David, *Panama* T44+085 **101**
David City, *Nebraska* U43+412 **95**
Davignab, *S.-W. Africa* L62–276 **84**
Davis Mts., *Texas* U84+308 **94**
Davis Sea, *Antarctica* F60–650 **27**
Davis Str., *Greenland* R80+660 **26**
Davos Dorf, *Switzerland* M31+468 **45**
Davos Platz, *Switzerland* M31+468 **45**
Davy Sd., *Greenland* P40+720 **26**
Dawna Ra., *Burma* F41+170 **71**
Dawson, *Georgia* T57+318 **97**
Dawson, *Minnesota* U36+449 **93**
Dawson, *New Mexico* V00+366 **94**
Dawson, *N. Dakota* U59+469 **93**
Dawson, *Yukon* X25+643 **88**
Dawson Ra., *Yukon* X22+629 **88**
Dawson B., *Queensland* C02–255 **111**
Dawson Creek, *B.C.* W02+558 **88**
Dawsonville, *Georgia* T55+344 **97**
Dax, *France* N06+437 **55**
Daylesford, *Victoria* C35–374 **109**
Dayton, *Tennessee* T60+355 **97**
Dayton, *Ohio* T55+398 **91**
Daytona Beach, *Florida* T36+292 **97**
De Aar, *Cape Province* L36–308 **84**
Dead Sea, *Jordan-Israel* K56+314 **76**
Deadwood, *S. Dakota* U82+446 **98**
Deal, *England* M82+512 **39**
Dean, Forest of, *England* N15+518 **38**
Dean Funes, *Argentina* S27–304 **103**
Dease Arm, *N.-W. Terr.* W00+664 **88**
Dease Lake, *Brit. Columbia* W78+445 **90**
Dease R., *Brit. Columbia* W55+592 **88**
Dease Str., *N.-W. Terr.* V20+682 **88**
Death Valley, *California* V72+366 **92**
Deauville, *France* N00+494 **54**
Debar, *Yugoslavia* L57+416 **58**
Debec, *New Brunswick* S46+461 **90**
Debess, *U.S.S.R.* J36+576 **61**
Deblin, *Poland* L49+506 **49**
Debno, *Poland* L92+527 **48**
Debra Markos, *Ethiopia* K42+104 **83**
Debrecen, *Hungary* L51+475 **49**
Decatur, *Alabama* T72+346 **97**
Decatur, *Georgia* T56+338 **97**
Decatur, *Illinois* T84+398 **95**

Decaturville, *Tennessee* T79+355 **97**
Deccan, *India* G80+130 **70**
Deception, I., *South Shetlands* S04–630 **27**
Děčin, *Czechoslovakia* M05+508 **48**
Decize, *France* M69+468 **54**
Decorah, *Iowa* U11+412 **95**
Dedeagach. See Alexandroupolis
Dedham, *Massachusetts* S67+423 **96**
Dédougou, *Upper Volta* N20+122 **80**
Dedza, *Malawi* K64–142 **83**
Dee R., *Scotland* N12+571 **40**
Dee R., *Wales* N18+530 **38**
Deel R., *Ireland, Rep.* N54+526 **43**
Deep Creek L., *Maryland* T26+395 **96**
Deepwater, *New S. Wales* B79–294 **109**
Deer I., *Maine* S52+442 **90**
Deer Lake, *Newfoundland* R74+492 **90**
Deerlijk, *Belgium* M70+508 **44**
Deer Lodge, *Montana* V46+464 **92**
Deer River, *Minnesota* U23+473 **93**
Defferrari, *Argentina* R87–384 **103**
De Funiak Springs, *Florida* T67+307 **97**
Degana, *India* H02+270 **70**
Degerfors, *Sweden* L62+642 **46**
Degrad, *Brazil* R39+021 **105**
De Grey, R., *W. Australia* E02–204 **110**
Deh Bid, *Iran* J41+306 **75**
Dehdez, *Iran* J58+318 **75**
Dehra, (Dehra Dun) *India* G71+303 **72**
Dehrud, *Iran* J50+290 **75**
Deim Zubeir, *Sudan* L22+078 **81**
Deinze, *Belgium* M69+510 **44**
Deir Abu Said, *Jordan* K56+325 **76**
Deir 'Ali, *Syria* K52+332 **76**
Deir Atiye, *Syria* K49+341 **76**
Deir ez Zor, *Syria* K29+354 **74**
Deir Hafir, *Syria* K44+361 **76**
Deir Shemil, *Syria* K52+352 **76**
Dej, *Romania* L37+471 **49**
Dekalb, *Illinois* T82+419 **95**
De Kalb, *Mississippi* T82+328 **97**
De Kastri, *U.S.S.R.* C55+515 **63**
Dekoven, *Kentucky* T79+376 **97**
Delano Mt., *Utah* V45+385 **98**
Delano Pk., *Utah* V44+384 **94**
Delavan, *Wisconsin* T82+427 **91**
Delaware N.J., etc. T02+418 **91**
Delaware, *Ohio* T49+403 **91**
Delaware, state, *U.S.A.* T03+391 **99**
Delaware B., Del.-New Jersey T01+391 **96**
Delaware City, *Delaware* T03+396 **96**
Delaware R., *New York, etc.* T01+405 **96**
Delden, *Netherlands* M50+523 **44**
Delegate, *New S. Wales* C06–370 **109**
Deleitosa, *Spain* N33+396 **52**
De Lemmer, *Netherlands* M56+528 **44**
Delémont, *Switzerland* M46+474 **45**
Delfshaven, *Netherlands* M63+519 **44**
Delft, *Netherlands* M64+520 **44**
Delfzijl, *Netherlands* M48+533 **44**
Delgado C., *Mozambique* K26–108 **83**
Delger, *Mongolia* E56+457 **64**
Delgo, *Sudan* K86+200 **81**
Delhi, *India* G77+286 **72**
Delhi, *New York* T00+423 **96**
Dellenbaugh, Mt., *Arizona* V51+363 **92**
Dellys, *Algeria* M66+366 **80**
Delmenhorst, *W. Germany* M39+530 **48**
Del Norte, *Colorado* V08+376 **94**
Deloraine, *Tasmania* C20–415 **109**
Del Rio, *Texas* U66+294 **94**
Delta, *Colorado* V18+387 **94**
Delta, *Louisiana* U06+324 **97**
Delta, *Missouri* T89+372 **97**
Delta, *Pennsylvania* T08+397 **96**
Delta, *Utah* V46+396 **94**
Delungra, *New S. Wales* B85–296 **109**
Demanda, Sa. de la, *Spain* N18+422 **52**
Demchok, *Tibet* G63+326 **70**
Deming, *New Mexico* V18+323 **94**
Demirji Dagh, *Turkey* L10+391 **74**
Demmin, *E. Germany* M12+539 **48**
Demopolis, *Alabama* T77+325 **97**
Denbigh, *Wales* N20+532 **38**
Denderleeuw, *Belgium* M66+509 **44**
Dendermonde, *Belgium* M65+511 **44**
Dendi, mt., *Ethiopia* K42+086 **83**
Denekamp, *Netherlands* M48+524 **44**
Den Haag. See s' Gravenhage
Denham Ra., *Queensland* C08–260 **111**
Denia, *Spain* M89+388 **53**
Deniliquin, *New S. Wales* C30–356 **109**
Denison, *Iowa* U32+420 **95**
Denison, *Texas* U39+338 **95**
Denizli, *Turkey* L05+377 **74**
Denman, *New S. Wales* B86–324 **109**
Denmark, *S. Carolina* T37+333 **97**
Denmark, kingdom, *W. Eur.* **35**
Denmark Str., *Greenland, etc.* Q00+670 **25**
Der Oever, *Netherlands* M60+529 **44**
Dert Blanche, mt., *Switz.* M44+460 **45**
Denton, *Maryland* T05+389 **91**
Denton, *Texas* U42+332 **95**
D'Entrecasteaux, Is.,
  Papua New Guinea B80–100 **111**
D'Entrecasteaux Pt.,
  W. Australia E24–348 **110**
Denver, *Colorado* V00+397 **94**
Deoband, *India* G74+297 **72**
Deobhog, *India* G44+200 **71**
Deogarh, *India* G32+214 **71**
Deogiar, *India* G12+245 **73**
Deoli *India* G88+257 **70**
Deoria, *India* G37+265 **73**
De Panne, *Belgium* M74+511 **44**
De Pere, *Wisconsin* T78+445 **91**
Deposit, *New York* T03+421 **91**
Depot Harbor, *Ontario* T31+453 **91**
Dera, *Syria* K53+326 **76**
Dera Bugti, *Pakistan* H35+291 **70**
Dera Ghazi Khan, *Pakistan* H26+301 **72**
Dera Ismail Khan, *Pakistan* H25+318 **72**
Dera Nanak, *India* G89+320 **72**
Derbent, *U.S.S.R.* J71+422 **62**
Derby, *W. Australia* D68–172 **110**
Derby & co., *England* N09+529 **37**
Derecske, *Hungary* L51+474 **49**
Derg L., *Ireland, Rep.* N47+546 **42**
Derg L., *Ireland, Rep.* N50+530 **43**
Derg R., *N. Ireland* N46+547 **42**

De Ridder, *Louisiana* U20+308 **95**
De Rijp, *Netherlands* M61+525 **44**
Dermott, *Arkansas* U07+336 **95**
Derna, (Dernah), *Libya* L44+326 **81**
Dernberg C., *S.-W. Africa* L86–278 **84**
Derravaragh L., *Ireland, Rep.* N44+537 **42**
Derryveagh Mts.,
  Ireland, Rep. N49+550 **42**
Derudeb, *Sudan* K54+174 **81**
De Ruyter, *New York* T05+428 **96**
Derventa, *Yugoslavia* L73+450 **56**
Derwent, R., *England* N12+548 **37**
Derwent R., *England* N05+538 **37**
Derwent R., *Tasmania* C22–424 **109**
Derwent Water, *England* N19+546 **37**
Des Arc, *Arkansas* U09+350 **97**
Descalvados, *Brazil* R76–167 **104**
Deschaillons, *Quebec* S72+466 **91**
Deseado, R., *Argentina* S50–468 **103**
Deshambault L., *Sask.* V00+546 **88**
Des Moines R., *Iowa* U22+416 **95**
Desna, R., *Ukraine* K84+512 **60**
Desolacion, I., *Chile* S84–532 **103**
Desolation C., *Greenland* R25+610 **26**
De Soto, *Missouri* U04+382 **95**
Dessau, *E. Germany* M16+518 **48**
Deta, *Romania* L53+454 **58**
Detroit, *Michigan* T48+424 **91**
Detroit Lakes, *Minnesota* U35+468 **93**
Dett, *Rhodesia* L18–186 **84**
Deurne, *Netherlands* M55+515 **44**
Deux Rivières, *Ontario* T20+463 **91**
Deux-Sèvres, dep., *France* N03+466 **54**
Déva, *Romania* L43+459 **58**
Dévavanya, *Hungary* L54+471 **49**
Deventer, *Netherlands* M53+523 **44**
Deveron R., *Scotland* N15+577 **40**
Devil's Elbow, *Scotland* N21+569 **41**
Devils Lake, *N. Dakota* U53+481 **93**
Devin, *Bulgaria* L34+417 **58**
Devizes, *England* N12+513 **39**
Devon, co., *England* N22+508 **38**
Devonport, *England* N25+504 **38**
Devonport, *New Zealand* A31–368 **112**
Devonport, *Tasmania* C22–412 **109**
De Witt, *Arkansas* U08+343 **97**
Dewsbury, *England* N10+537 **37**
Dexter, *Maine* S56+450 **90**
Dexter, *Missouri* U00+368 **95**
Dezful, *Iran* J70+324 **74**
Dhaba, *Saudi Arabia* K56+274 **74**
Dhahran, *Saudi Arabia* J58+263 **75**
Dhak, *Pakistan* H15+325 **72**
Dhamar, *Yemen* K04+147 **74**
Dhampur, *India* G69+293 **73**
Dhamra, *India* G18+208 **71**
Dhamtari, *India* G50+208 **70**
Dhang Ra., *Nepal* G48+282 **73**
Dhangain, *India* G34+252 **73**
Dhank, *Oman* J23+236 **75**
Dhankuta, *Nepal* G16+270 **73**
Dhariya, *Saudi Arabia* K13+247 **74**
Dharmjaygarh, *India* G41+224 **73**
Dharmkot, *India* G88+309 **72**
Dharmsala, *India* G82+322 **72**
Dharwar, *India* H00+156 **70**
Dhaulagiri, mt., *Nepal* G40+287 **73**
Dhiban, *Jordan* K55+315 **76**
Dhidhimótikhon, *Greece* L21+413 **58**
Dhionisiadhes. See Yianisahes Is.
Dholera, *India* H27+222 **70**
Dholpur, *India* G73+267 **73**
Dhond, *India* G00+260 **73**
Dhubri, *India* G00+260 **73**
Dhula, *Yemen, South* J71+150 **74**
Dhulia, *India* H01+209 **70**
Dhurma, *Saudi Arabia* J84+246 **74**
Dhurwai, *India* G66+255 **73**
Dia I., *Crete* L29+354 **59**
Diamante, *Argentina* S04–320 **103**
Diamantina, *Brazil* Q81–182 **105**
Diamantina, R., *Queensland* C53–242 **111**
Diamond, I., *Burma* F64+159 **71**
Diamond Harbour, *India* G10+222 **73**
Dibah, *U.A.E.* J22+257 **75**
Dibai, *U.A.E.* J28+253 **75**
Dibbah, Jebel, *Saudi Arabia* K56+278 **74**
Dibbéla, *Niger* M14+176 **81**
Dibit, *Somalia* J72+060 **83**
Dibrugarh, *India* F60+274 **71**
Dickinson, *N. Dakota* U77+469 **93**
Dickson, *Tennessee* T75+362 **95**
Die, *France* M60+448 **55**
Diefenbaker L., *Saskatchewan* V10+510 **88**
Diego Garcia, I., *Indian Oc.* H35–100 **23**
Diego Suarez, *Madagascar* J64–124 **83**
Dien Bien Phu, *N. Vietnam* F12+212 **69**
Dieppe, *France* M84+499 **54**
Diest, *Belgium* M60+510 **44**
Dieverbrug, *Netherlands* M52+529 **44**
Dig, *India* G76+274 **72**
Digby, *Nova Scotia* S35+446 **90**
Digby Neck, *Nova Scotia* S37+444 **90**
Dighal, *Yemen, South* J70+146 **74**
Digne, *France* M53+441 **55**
Digoin, *France* M66+465 **54**
Diguel, R., *Irian Jaya,*
  Indon. C60–072 **65**
Dijon, *France* M60+473 **54**
Diksmuide, *Belgium* M73+510 **44**
Dikwa, *Nigeria* M06+120 **81**
Dilam, *Saudi Arabia* J76+240 **74**
Dili, *Timor I., Indonesia* D56–086 **65**
Dillon, *Montana* V46+452 **92**
Dilolo, *Angola* L48–118 **82**
Dilolo, *Zaire* L46–106 **82**
Dimbokro, *Ivory Coast* N28+068 **80**
Dimitrovo (Pernik), *Bulgaria* L42+426 **58**
Dimitrovgrad, *Yugoslavia* L43+431 **58**
Dimla, *Bangladesh* G06+261 **73**
Dimotika. See Dhidhimótikhon.
Dinagat, I., *Philippines* D56+100 **65**
Dinajpur, *Bangladesh* G08+256 **73**
Dinan, *France* N12+485 **54**
Dinant, *Belgium* M60+503 **44**
Dinanagar, *India* G87+322 **72**
Dinapur, *India* G29+256 **73**
Dinar, *Turkey* K89+381 **74**
Dinard, *France* N13+486 **54**

Dinarske Planina, *Yugoslavia* L82+440 **56**
Dinas Mawddwy, *Wales* N22+527 **38**
Dindigul, *India* G72+104 **70**
Dingle & B., *Ireland, Rep.* N62+521 **43**
Dingwall, *Scotland* N27+576 **40**
Dinosaur Nat. Mon., *Colo.* V23+406 **94**
Dinteloord, *Netherlands* M64+516 **44**
Diourbel, *Senegal* P08+146 **80**
Dipalpur, *Pakistan* H08+306 **72**
Dipton, *New Zealand* A69–459 **112**
Dir, *Pakistan* H18+352 **72**
Direction, C., *Queensland* C39–129 **111**
Diredawe, *Ethiopia* K20+094 **83**
Diriamba, *Nicaragua* T66+117 **101**
Dirk Hartogs I., *W. Aust.* E42–258 **110**
Dirksland, *Netherlands* M65+518 **44**
Dirranbandi, *Queensland* C11–284 **111**
Disappointment, C., *Wash.* W24+463 **92**
Disappointment Is.,
  Tuamotu Arch. X38–145 **107**
Disappointment, L., *W. Aust.* D73–234 **110**
Disaster B., *New S. Wales* C00–373 **109**
Discovery B., *Victoria* C54–382 **109**
Disentis, *Switzerland* M37+467 **45**
Disko B., *Greenland* R35+690 **26**
Disko, I., *Greenland* R35+700 **26**
Disna, *Byelo-Russia* L11+552 **60**
Dison, *Belgium* M55+506 **44**
District of Columbia, *U.S.A.* T12+386 **91**
Diu, *India* H23+208 **70**
Diver, *Ontario* T28+468 **91**
Dividing Range, mts., *Aust.* C10–260 **111**
Diviso, *Colombia* T20+014 **104**
Divrigi, *Turkey* K41+394 **74**
Diwan Chah, *Iran* H85+299 **75**
Diwangiri, *India* F81+268 **71**
Diwaniyah, *Iraq* K01+320 **74**
Dix, *Quebec* T07+482 **91**
Dixmude, *Belgium* M73+510 **44**
Dixon, *Illinois* T87+418 **95**
Dixon, *Kentucky* T76+375 **97**
Dixon Entrance, *B.C.* W75+545 **88**
Diyarbakir, *Turkey* K28+380 **74**
Dizah, *Iran* H76+272 **75**
Djaid, *U.A.E.* J24+254 **75**
Djajapura, *See* Jayapura
Djakarta, *See* Jakarta
Djambi, *See* Jambi
Djawa, *See* Java
Djelfa, *Algeria* M70+346 **80**
Djeneien, *Tunisia* M30+318 **81**
Djerba, I., *Tunisia* M26+338 **81**
Djibouti, *F.T.A.I.* K12+114 **83**
Djidjelh, *Algeria* M54+366 **80**
Djolu, *Zaire* L46+08 **82**
Djougou, *Benin* M80+098 **80**
Djursholm, *Sweden* L72+594 **47**
Dmitriya Lapteva Proliv,
  U.S.S.R. C40+730 **63**
Dnepr R., *Ukraine* K68+470 **60**
Dneprodzerzhinsk, *Ukraine* K62+486 **60**
Dnepropetrovsk, *Ukraine* K60+485 **60**
Dnester (Dniester), R., *Ukr.* L28+489 **60**
Doaktown, *New Brunswick* S37+466 **90**
Dobbyn, *Queensland* C60–198 **111**
Dobele, *Latvia* L40+566 **47**
Doberan, *E. Germany* M19+541 **48**
Dobra, *Czechoslovakia* L50+491 **49**
Dobřany, *Czechoslovakia* M11+497 **48**
Dobrich, *See* Tolbukhin.
Dobruja, *Romania* L10+455 **58**
Dobryanka, *U.S.S.R.* J22+584 **61**
Dobrzyn, *Poland* L66+531 **49**
Doce Leguas, Cayos de las,
  Cuba T25+210 **101**
Doctor Arroyo, *Mexico* U61+238 **100**
Dodecanese, *Greece* L18+360 **59**
Dodge City, *Kansas* U60+378 **95**
Dodgeville, *Wisconsin* U01+430 **95**
Dodman Pt., *England* N29+502 **38**
Dodoma, *Tanzania* K56–062 **83**
Dodson, *Montana* V20+484 **93**
Doel, *Belgium* M64+513 **44**
Doesburg, *Netherlands* M53+520 **44**
Doetinchem, *Netherlands* M52+520 **44**
Dogger Bank, *North Sea* M78+545 **34**
Doha, *Qatar, Arabia* J51+253 **75**
Dohad, *India* H04+228 **70**
Doka, *Saudi Arabia* K23+199 **74**
Dokka, *Yemen* K05+131 **74**
Dokkum, *Netherlands* M54+533 **44**
Dol, *France* N10+485 **54**
Dolbeau, *Quebec* S73+488 **90**
Dolcigno. *See* Ulcinj.
Dôle, *France* M57+471 **54**
Dolent, Mt., *Switzerland* M48+459 **45**
Dolgellau, *Wales* N23+527 **38**
Dollar, *Scotland* N22+562 **41**
Dolo, *Ethiopia* K18+040 **83**
Dolomitiche, Alpi, *Italy* M18+464 **56**
Dolores, *Argentina* R76–364 **103**
Dolores, *Mexico* V35+251 **100**
Dolores, *Spain* N05+381 **53**
Dolphin, C., *Falkland Is.* R84–512 **103**
Dolunnor. *See* Tolun.
Dom, mt., *Irian Jaya,*
  Indon. C78–027 **65**
Domariaganj, *India* G44+272 **73**
Dombås, *Norway* M35+621 **46**
Domburg, *Netherlands* M69+516 **44**
Domel, I., *Burma* F41+115 **71**
Dome Rock Mts., *Arizona* V54+336 **92**
Domfront, *France* N04+486 **54**
Dominica, I., *West Indies* S07+154 **101**
Dominican Rep., *West Indies* S60+190 **101**
Dömitz, *E. Germany* M23+531 **48**
Dom Pedrito, *Brazil* R58–310 **103**
Domuyo, mt., *Argentina* S63–366 **103**
Domvraina, *Greece* L42+383 **59**
Don R., *England* N07+535 **37**
Don, R., *U.S.S.R.* K20+481 **62**
Don, R., *Scotland* N13+572 **40**
Donaghadee, *N. Ireland* N33+546 **42**
Donald, *Victoria* C42–364 **109**
Donaldson, *Louisiana* U06+301 **95**
Donau, R., *Central Europe* M14+489 **48**
Donaueschingen, *W. Germany* M39+479 **48**
Don Benito, *Spain* N35+388 **52**
Doncaster, *England* N07+535 **37**
Dondo, *Angola* M04–096 **82**
Donegal & co., *Ireland, Rep.* N49+546 **42**

Donegal B., *Ireland, Rep.* N52+545 **42**
Donegal Pt., *Ireland, Rep.* N58+527 **43**
Donets, R., *U.S.S.R.* K25+480 **61**
Donetsk, *Ukraine* K43+479 **60**
Donga, *Nigeria* M30+076 **81**
Dongara, *W. Australia* E30–290 **110**
Donggala, *Celèbes, Indon.* E02–008 **65**
Dong-hoi, *N. Vietnam* E80+174 **69**
Dongo, *Angola* L86–146 **82**
Dongola, *Sudan* K88+190 **81**
Doniphan, *Missouri* U05+366 **97**
Donji Miholjac, *Yugoslavia* L72+457 **56**
Dønna, *Norway* M15+661 **46**
Don Pia-fai, mt., *Thailand* F22+144 **69**
Doon R. & L., *Scotland* N26+553 **41**
Doon Otok, I., *Yugoslavia* M00+440 **56**
Doorn, *Netherlands* M58+520 **44**
Dora, L., *W. Australia* D72–221 **110**
Doranda, *India* G28+233 **73**
Dorat, le, *France* M83+462 **54**
Dorchester, *England* N15+507 **38**
Dorchester, *New Brunswick* S27+459 **90**
Dorchester, C., *N.-W. Terr.* T20+654 **89**
Dordogne, dep., *France* M85+451 **54**
Dordogne R., *France* N03+450 **55**
Dordrecht, *Netherlands* M62+518 **44**
Dore L., *Saskatchewan* V14+548 **88**
Dore, Mt., *France* M72+454 **54**
Dores, *Brazil* R39–306 **103**
Dori, *Upper Volta* N00+140 **80**
Dorking, *England* N02+512 **39**
Dornie, *Scotland* N33+573 **40**
Dornoch & Firth, *Scotland* N24+579 **40**
Dorotea, *Sweden* L81+643 **46**
Dorrego, *Argentina* S08–387 **103**
Dorrigo, *New S. Wales* B75–304 **109**
Dorset, co., *England* N14+508 **38**
Dorsey, *Montana* V34+464 **93**
Dortmund, *W. Germany* M45+515 **48**
Dos Bahias, C., *Argentina* S33–450 **103**
Doshi, *Afghanistan* H37+356 **75**
Dospat, *Bulgaria* L36+416 **58**
Dosso, *Cameroun* M70+130 **80**
Dossor, *Kazakh* J43+475 **62**
Dothan, *Alabama* T62+312 **97**
Douai, *France* M71+504 **54**
Douala, *Cameroun* M32+040 **81**
Douarnenez, *France* N25+481 **54**
Doubs, dep., *France* M51+471 **54**
Doubtless B., *New Zealand* A39–349 **112**
Doucet, *Quebec* T10+482 **91**
Douglas, *Arizona* V27+313 **94**
Douglas, *Cape Province* L32–290 **84**
Douglas, *Georgia* T47+315 **97**
Douglas, I. of Man *N27+542* **37**
Douglas, Mt., *Montana* V32+454 **93**
Douglas, *Wyoming* V02+428 **93**
Douglastown, *Quebec* S26+488 **90**
Douglasville, *Georgia* T58+337 **97**
Doullens, *France* M76+502 **54**
Doulus Hd., *Ireland, Rep.* N62+520 **43**
Doume, *Cameroun* M08+044 **81**
Doune, *Scotland* N24+562 **41**
Dounreay, *Scotland* N22+586 **40**
Douro, & R., *Spain-Portugal* N49–411 **52**
Dover, *Delaware* T03+392 **96**
Dover, *England* M82+511 **39**
Dover, *New Hampshire* S65+434 **96**
Dover, *New Jersey* S87+409 **96**
Dover, *Ohio* T39+406 **91**
Dover, *Tasmania* C18–433 **109**
Dover, *Tennessee* T77+365 **97**
Dover, Str. of,
  England-France M81+505 **54**
Dover Foxcroft, *Maine* S55+452 **90**
Dovrefjell, *Norway* M36+622 **46**
Dow L., *Botswana* L32–214 **84**
Dowa, *Malawi* K66–136 **83**
Down, co., *N. Ireland* N36+543 **42**
Downham Market, *England* M88+526 **39**
Downpatrick, *N. Ireland* N34+543 **42**
Downpatrick Hd.,
  Ireland, Rep. N56+543 **42**
Doyles, *Newfoundland* R85+479 **90**
Doylestown, *Pennsylvania* T01+403 **96**
Drăgășani, *Romania* L34+446 **58**
Draguignan, *France* M51+436 **55**
Drake, *New S. Wales* B76–289 **109**
Drake Str., *Antarctica* S00–580 **27**
Drakensberg, mts., *S. Africa* L04–270 **84**
Dráma, *Greece* L35+411 **58**
Drammen, *Norway* M28+598 **47**
Dranov I., *Romania* L04+449 **58**
Dras, *Kashmir* G85+344 **72**
Drawsko, *Poland* L85+535 **49**
Drayton, *N. Dakota* U43+486 **93**
Drazinda, *Pakistan* H37+372 **94**
Drem, *Scotland* N16+560 **41**
Drenthe, prov., *Netherlands* M50+528 **44**
Dresden, *E. Germany* M07+511 **48**
Dresden, *Ontario* T44+426 **91**
Dreux, *France* M82+487 **54**
Drimoleague, *Ireland, Rep.* N56+516 **43**
Drin G., *Albania* L63+417 **58**
Drina, R., *Yugoslavia* L66+436 **58**
Drøbak, *Norway* M26+597 **47**
Drogheda & B., *Ireland, Rep.* N38+537 **42**
Droitwich, *England* N13+523 **39**
Drome, dep. & R., *France* M65+447 **55**
Dromod, *Ireland, Rep.* N47+539 **42**
Dromore West, *Ireland, Rep.* N53+542 **42**
Dromore, *N. Ireland* N37+544 **42**
Dromore, *N. Ireland* N45+545 **42**
Drongen, *Belgium* M68+511 **44**
Drum Hills, *Ireland, Rep.* N46+520 **43**
Drumheller, *Alberta* V45+513 **88**
Drummond I., *Michigan* T52+460 **91**
Drummondville, *Quebec* S75+459 **91**
Drumnadrochit, *Scotland* N27+573 **40**
Drumshanbo, *Ireland, Rep.* N48+540 **42**
Drunen, *Netherlands* M59+517 **44**
Druten, *Netherlands* M56+519 **44**
Druz, Jeb. ed, *Syria* K49+326 **76**
Dryden, *Ontario* U15+498 **89**
Drymen, *Scotland* N27+561 **41**
Drysdale River, *W. Australia* D49–141 **110**
Dschang, *Cameroun* M30+056 **82**
Dubawnt L., *N.-W. Terr.* J70+636 **88**
Dubbo, *New S. Wales* C08–323 **109**
Dublin, *Georgia* T47+324 **99**
Dublin & co., *Ireland, Rep.* N38+533 **43**

Dublin, *Texas* U50+322 **95**
Dubno, *Ukraine* L26+504 **60**
Du Bois, *Pennsylvania* T23+411 **96**
Dubrovnik, *Yugoslavia* L71+427 **58**
Dubuque, *Iowa* U04+425 **95**
Duchcov, *Czechoslovakia* M08+506 **48**
Duchesne, *Utah* V32+402 **94**
Ducie I., *Pacific Ocean* W26–254 **107**
Duck Is., *Ontario* T48+457 **91**
Dudinka, *U.S.S.R.* G26+693 **62**
Dudley, *England* N13+525 **37**
Duero R., *Spain* N27+416 **52**
Duffel, *Belgium* M61+511 **44**
Dufftown, *Scotland* N19+574 **40**
Dugi Otok, I., *Yugoslavia* M00+440 **56**
Duifken Pt., *Queensland* C50–124 **111**
Duisburg, *W. Germany* M50+515 **48**
Dujana, *India* G80+287 **72**
Duke of Gloucester Grp.,
  Tuamotu Archipelago W80–208 **107**
Duke of York Arch.,
  N.-W. Territories V50+678 **88**
Duk Faiwil, *Sudan* K82+076 **81**
Dulce, G., *Costa Rica* T49+086 **101**
Duluth, *Minnesota* U13+468 **93**
Dulverton, *England* N21+510 **38**
Duma, *Syria* K52+335 **76**
Dumas, *Arkansas* U09+338 **97**
Dumas, *Texas* U71+358 **94**
Dumbarton, *Scotland* N27+559 **41**
Dum-Dum, *India* G09+226 **73**
Dumeir, *Syria* K50+336 **76**
Dumfries, *Scotland* N22+551 **41**
Dumfries & Galloway, reg., *Scot.*
  N26+550 **41**
Dumka, *India* G16+243 **73**
Dumraon, *India* G35+255 **73**
Dunarea (Danube), R., *Cent.*
  Europe L24+441 **51**
Dunbar, *Scotland* N15+560 **41**
Dunblane, *Scotland* N24+562 **41**
Dunboyne, *Ireland, Rep.* N39+534 **43**
Duncan, *Arkansas* U08+346 **97**
Duncan, *Oklahoma* U48+345 **95**
Duncan Pass., *Andaman Is.* F75+112 **71**
Duncannon, *Ireland, Rep.* N41+522 **43**
Duncansby Hd., *Scotland* N18+586 **40**
Dundalk & B., *Ireland, Rep.* N38+540 **42**
Dundas, *Ontario* T30+433 **91**
Dundas Str., *N. Terr., Aust.* D20–110 **110**
Dun Dealgan. *See* Dundalk
Dundee, *Natal* K88–282 **84**
Dundee, *Scotland* N18+565 **41**
Dundee I., *Antarctica* R62–630 **27**
Dundrum & B., *N. Ireland* N35+543 **42**
Dunedin, *New Zealand* A 57–459 **112**
Dunedoo, *New S. Wales* C04–320 **109**
Dunfanaghy, *Ireland, Rep.* N48+552 **42**
Dunfermline, *Scotland* N21+561 **41**
Dungannon, *N. Ireland* N41+545 **42**
Dungarpur, *India* H08+238 **70**
Dungarven & Harb.,
  Ireland, Rep. N46+521 **43**
Dungbure Ra., *Tibet* G30+350 **71**
Dungeness, *England* M84+509 **39**
Dungiven, *N. Ireland* N41+549 **42**
Dungloe, *Ireland, Rep.* N50+549 **42**
Dungu, *Zaire* L08+034 **83**
Dungunab, *Sudan* K54+218 **81**
Dunkeld, *Scotland* N22–566 **41**
Dunkerque (Dunkirk), *France* M76+511 **54**
Dunkirk, *New York* T26+425 **96**
Dunkur, *Ethiopia* K54+118 **83**
Dunkwa, *Ghana* N12+060 **80**
Dunlap, *Iowa* U36+420 **95**
Dunlavin, *Ireland, Rep.* N40+530 **43**
Dunleer, *Ireland, Rep.* N38+538 **42**
Dunlop, *Scotland* N27+557 **41**
Dunmanus B., *Ireland, Rep.* N59+516 **43**
Dunmanway, *Ireland, Rep.* N55+517 **43**
Dunmore, *Ireland, Rep.* N52+536 **42**
Dunn, *N. Carolina* T22+353 **97**
Dunnet Hd & B., *Scotland* N20+586 **40**
Dunolly, *Victoria* C38–369 **109**
Dunoon, *Scotland* N30+559 **41**
Duns, *Scotland* N14+558 **41**
Dunstable, *England* N03+519 **39**
Dunvegan & L., *Scotland* N39+574 **40**
Dupulan, *India* J56+320 **75**
Du Quain, *Illinois* T86+380 **97**
Duque de York, I., *Chile* T01–506 **103**
Dura, *Jordan* K60+315 **76**
Durango, *Colorado* V17+372 **94**
Durango & state, *Mexico* U88+240 **100**
Durant, *Mississippi* T89+330 **97**
Durant, *Oklahoma* U38+340 **95**
Durazno, *Uruguay* R69–334 **103**
Durazzo. *See* Durrës
Durban, *Natal* K84–298 **84**
Durbe, *Latvia* L52+566 **47**
Durbuy, *Belgium* M57+503 **44**
Durdevac, *Yugoslavia* L78+460 **56**
Durdurch, *Somalia* J68+112 **83**
Dureikish, *Syria* K53+349 **76**
Duren, *W. Germany* M51+508 **48**
Durga Str., *New Guinea* C70–073 **111**
Durham, *N. Carolina* T23+360 **97**
Durham, *Ontario* T35+442 **91**
Durham & co., *England* N09+548 **37**
Durness & Kyle of, *Scotland* N28+586 **40**
Durrës, *Albania* L63+413 **58**
Durrow, *Ireland, Rep.* N44+528 **43**
Dursey I. & Hd., *Ireland, Rep.* N61+516 **43**
Dursley, *England* N14+517 **38**
Duruh, *Iran* H86+322 **75**
Durukhsh, *Iran* J01+331 **75**
D'Urville I., *New Zealand* A37–408 **112**
Dushanbe, *Tadzhik* H37+386 **62**
Dushore, *Pennsylvania* T09+415 **96**
Dusky Sound, *New Zealand* A81–457 **112**
Düsseldorf, *W. Germany* M49+513 **48**
Duszniki Zdrój, *Poland* L82+504 **49**
Dutch Harb., *Aleutian Is.* Z10+540 **99**
Dutch Guiana. *See* Surinam
Dutton, Mt., *Utah* V44+380 **94**
Duvan, *U.S.S.R.* J12+557 **61**
Duwadami, *Saudi Arabia* K04+248 **74**

Duwwah, *Oman* J07+205 **75**
Dvina, R., *Latvia* L32+568 **47**
Dyatkovo, *U.S.S.R.* K64+535 **60**
Dyce, *Scotland* N13+572 **40**
Dyer, C., *N.-W. Territories* S07+665 **89**
Dyersburg, *Tennessee* T87+360 **97**
Dyfed, co., *Wales* N26+520 **38**
Dyfi R., *Wales* N23+526 **38**
Dyle R., *Belgium* M63+510 **44**
Dyurtyuli, *U.S.S.R.* J31+554 **61**
Dzamyn Ude, *Mongolia* E55+446 **64**
Dzep, *Yugoslavia* L47+427 **58**
Dzerzhinsk, *U.S.S.R.* K09+563 **61**
Dzerzhinsh, *Byelo-Russia* L17+536 **60**
Dzhagdy Khrebet, *U.S.S.R.* D30+538 **63**
Dzhalinda, *U.S.S.R.* D67+536 **63**
Dzhalal Abad, *Kirgiz.* H12+407 **62**
Dzhambul, *Kazakh.* H21+428 **62**
Dzhetygara, *Kazakh.* H82+524 **62**
Dzhezkazgan, *Kazakh.* H44+480 **62**
Dzhugdzhur Khrebet,
  U.S.S.R. C70+580 **63**
Dzhungarskiy Ala-Tau,
  Kazakh. G60+450 **62**
Dzierzoniow, *Poland* L80+508 **49**
Dzogchen, *China* F36+322 **64**
Eagle, *Alaska* X37+645 **99**
Eagle I., *Ireland, Rep.* N60+543 **42**
Eagle L., *Maine* S56+463 **90**
Eagle L., *Maine* S50+471 **90**
Eagle Grove, *Iowa* U24+427 **95**
Eagle Mountain L., *Texas* U45+328 **95**
Eagle Pass, *Texas* U62+287 **94**
Eagle River, *Wisconsin* T86+459 **91**
Eagles Nest, *Ireland, Rep.* N58+518 **43**
Ealing, *England* N02+515 **39**
Eardisley, *England* N18+521 **38**
Earith, *England* M89+523 **39**
Earlston, *Scotland* N16+556 **41**
Earlville, *New York* T04+427 **96**
Earn L., *Scotland* N25+564 **41**
Earn, R., *Scotland* N20+564 **41**
Easington, *England* N08+548 **37**
East Anglia, *S.E. England* **39**
East Arlington, *Vermont* S79+431 **91**
East Aurora, *New York* T22+428 **96**
Eastbourne, *England* M88+508 **39**
Eastbourne, *New Zealand* A30–413 **112**
East Dereham, *England* M84+527 **39**
Easter I., *Pacific Ocean* V25–265 **107**
Eastern B., *Maryland* T08+388 **96**
Eastern States, *India* G50+230 **70**
East Grand Forks, *Minnesota* U42+479 **93**
East Kilbride, *Scotland* N25+558 **41**
Eastland, *Texas* U53+324 **95**
East Liverpool, *Ohio* T34+406 **91**
East London, *Cape Province* L12–330 **84**
East Lothian, co., *See* Lothian
Eastmain R., *Quebec* T05+526 **89**
Eastman, *Georgia* T49+322 **97**
Easton, *Maryland* T06+388 **96**
Easton, *Pennsylvania* T02+407 **96**
Eastport, *Maine* S42+449 **90**
East Retford, *England* N06+533 **37**
East Riding, *Yorks.,* *See* Humberside
East St Louis, *Illinois* U01+386 **95**
East Sioux Falls, *S. Dakota* U40+435 **93**
Eastville, *Virginia* T06+373 **97**
Eaton Rapids, *Michigan* T58+425 **91**
Eau Claire, *Wisconsin* U19+448 **93**
Ebbw Vale, *Wales* N19+518 **38**
Eberswalde, *E. Germany* M07+528 **48**
Eboli, *Italy* M00+406 **57**
Ebolowa, *Cameroun* M24+028 **82**
Ebro, R., *Spain* N09+421 **53**
Ecaussines, *Belgium* M65+506 **44**
Ecclefechan, *Scotland* N19+550 **41**
Echallens, *Switzerland* M50+466 **45**
Echo L., *Tasmania* C20–422 **109**
Echo Cliffs, *Arizona* V40+364 **94**
Echt, *Netherlands* M55+511 **44**
Echten, *Netherlands* M52+527 **44**
Echternach, *Luxembourg* M51+498 **48**
Echuca, *Victoria* C31–362 **109**
Eck L., *Scotland* N30+561 **41**
Ecuador, rep., *S. America* **104**
Edam, *Netherlands* M60+525 **44**
Eday, I., *Orkney Is., Scot.* N16+592 **40**
Ed Damer, *Sudan* K66+176 **81**
Ed Damur, *Lebanon* K57+337 **76**
Ed Debba, *Sudan* K86+180 **81**
Eddrachillis B., *Scotland* N31+583 **40**
Ed Dueim, *Sudan* K76+140 **81**
Ede, *Netherlands* M56+521 **44**
Edebäck, *Sweden* M08+601 **47**
Eden, *Maine* S50+444 **90**
Eden, *New South Wales* C01–371 **109**
Eden, *New York* T23+426 **96**
Eden R., *England* N17+548 **37**
Edenburg, *Orange Free State* L24–296 **84**
Edendale, *New Zealand* A67–463 **112**
Edenderry, *Ireland, Rep.* N42+533 **43**
Edenhope, *Victoria* C52–370 **109**
Edensburg, *Pennsylvania* T23+405 **96**
Edenton, *N. Carolina* T10+361 **97**
Edeowie, *S. Australia* C69–314 **109**
Ederengin Nuru, *Mongolia* F40+434 **64**
Edge Hill, *England* N09+521 **39**
Edgeley, *N. Dakota* U52+464 **93**
Edgemont, *S. Dakota* V24+434 **93**
Edgerton, *Wisconsin* T84+429 **91**
Edgeøya, I., *Arctic Ocean* L45+780 **62**
Edgeworthstown, *Ireland, Rep.* N45+537 **42**
Edhessa, *Greece* L48+408 **59**
Edievale, *New Zealand* A64–458 **112**
Edina, *Missouri* U13+402 **95**
Edinburg, *Texas* U49+264 **94**
Edinburgh, *Scotland* N19+559 **41**
Edirne, *Turkey* L23+417 **59**
Edithburgh, *S. Australia* C74–351 **109**
Edith Cavell, Mt., *Alberta* V78+530 **88**
Edmonton, *Alberta* V52+538 **88**
Edmundston, *New Brunswick* S50+474 **90**
Edremit, *Turkey* L18+397 **74**
Edsele, *Sweden* L81+634 **46**
Edson, *Alberta* V68+538 **88**
Eduni, Mt., *North-West*
  Territories W48+644 **88**
Edward (Amin) L.,
  Zaire-Uganda L02–004 **83**

Index

Edward, R., *New S. Wales* C34-352 **109**
Edwardesabad. *See* Bannu.
Edwards, *New York* T01+443 **91**
Edwards Plat., *Texas* U66+308 **94**
Edwardsville, *Illinois* U00+388 **95**
Eekloo, *Belgium* M69+512 **44**
Efate, I., *New Hebrides* A68-185 **106**
Eferding, *Austria* M06+483 **48**
Effingham, *Illinois* T82+391 **95**
Egadi Is., *Sicily* M17+379 **57**
Egan, *S. Dakota* U40+440 **93**
Egana, *Argentina* R85-369 **103**
Eganville, *Ontario* T13+455 **91**
Eger, *Czechoslovakia*. *See* Cheb.
Eger, *Hungary* L58+479 **49**
Egersund, *Norway* M54+584 **47**
Egg L., *Quebec* S78+544 **89**
Eggenfelden, *W. Germany* M13+484 **48**
Eghezee, *Belgium* M60+506 **44**
Egin, *Turkey* K39+392 **74**
Eglinton, C., *N.-W. Terr.* S55+707 **89**
Egmont B., *Prince Edward I.* S25+466 **90**
Egmont, Mt., *New Zealand* A35-393 **112**
Egremont, *England* N21+545 **37**
Egridir, *Turkey* K85+378 **74**
Egypt, *N. Africa* L00+250 **81**
Eibergen, *Netherlands* M50+521 **44**
Eichstätt, *Germany* M23+489 **48**
Eidsvoll, *Norway* M22+603 **47**
Eifel, mts., *W. Germany* M50+501 **48**
Eigg I., *Scotland* N37+569 **41**
Eights Coast, *Antarctica* T80-750 **27**
Eighty Mile Beach, *W. Aust.* D95-196 **110**
Eil, *Somalia* J60+078 **83**
Eil L., *Scotland* N31+568 **41**
Eilat, *Israel* K60+296 **76**
Eindhoven, *Netherlands* M57+514 **44**
Eire, *See* Ireland, Rep. of.
Eisden, *Netherlands* M56+508 **44**
Eisenach, *E. Germany* M28+509 **48**
Eisenerz, *Austria* M01+475 **48**
Eisleben, *E. Germany* M21+515 **48**
Ejutla, *Mexico* U40+166 **100**
Ekaterinoslav. *See* Dnepropetrovsk.
Eke, *Belgium* M68+510 **44**
Ekeren, *Belgium* M64+513 **44**
Eketahana, *New Zealand* A26-406 **112**
Ekhinádbes Is., *Greece* L54+384 **59**
Ekimchan, *U.S.S.R.* D12+530 **63**
Eksjö, *Sweden* M00+577 **47**
Ekträsk, *Sweden* L61+644 **46**
Ekwan R., *Ontario* T52+537 **89**
El Aaiun, *Western Sahara* N80+268 **80**
El Abde, *Lebanon* K54+346 **76**
Elafónisi Chan, *Greece* L42+364 **59**
Élafos I., *Greece* L42+365 **59**
El Agheila (Al'Uqaylah)
   Libya L64+302 **81**
El Aguila, *Argentina* S43-363 **103**
El Aina, *Jordan* K55+310 **76**
El Alamein, *Egypt* L07+308 **81**
Elasson, *Greece* L47+399 **59**
Elâzig, *Turkey* K34+386 **74**
Elba, I., *Italy* M28+428 **56**
El Bab, *Syria* K45+364 **76**
El Bahluliye, *Syria* K54+356 **76**
El Banco, *Colombia* S84+090 **104**
El Barco de Valdeorras, *Sp.* N42+424 **52**
Elbasan, *Albania* L60+412 **58**
El Baul, *Venezuela* S50+090 **104**
Elbe R., *Germany* M25+532 **48**
Elbert, Mt., *Colorado* V08+391 **98**
Elbeuf, *France* M83+493 **54**
Elbing. *See* Elblag.
El-Birka, *Saudi Arabia* K27+223 **74**
Elbistan, *Turkey* K47+383 **74**
Elblag, *Poland* L64+542 **49**
El Br'aij, *Syria* K49+343 **76**
Elbrus. mt., *U.S.S.R.* K17+432 **62**
Elburg, *Netherlands* M55+524 **44**
Elburz Mts., *Iran* J56+363 **75**
El Carmen, *Bolivia* S22-145 **104**
El Carmen, *See* Carmen
El Centro, *California* V63+329 **92**
Elche, *Spain* N04+383 **53**
El Chorro, *Argentina* S14-232 **103**
El Cuy, *Argentina* S50-399 **103**
El Dab, *Somalia* J82+088 **83**
El Diwân, *Egypt* K78+224 **81**
El Donfar, *Somalia* J66+104 **83**
Eldora, *Iowa* U18+424 **95**
El Dorado, *Arkansas* U16+332 **95**
El Dorado, *Kansas* U42+378 **95**
El Dorado, *Mexico* V14+242 **100**
El Dorado, *Venezuela* S10+066 **104**
Eldoret, *Kenya* K58+006 **83**
El Djezair (Algiers), *Algeria* M72+366 **55**
El Encanto, *Colombia* S82-012 **104**
Elephant Butte Res., *New*
   Mexico V13+334 **94**
Elephant I., *Antarctica* R60-610 **27**
El Ergh, *Libya* L50+290 **81**
Eleşkirt, *Turkey* K13+399 **74**
Eleuthera I., *Bahamas, The* T10+250 **101**
Elewijt, *Belgium* M63+510 **44**
El Faiyum, *Egypt* K84+294 **81**
El Fasher, *Sudan* L28+136 **81**
El Fuwara, *Saudi Arabia* K15+262 **74**
Elgena, *Ethiopia* K38+170 **83**
El Geneina, *Sudan* L46+134 **81**
El Geteina, *Sudan* K76+146 **81**
Elgg, *Switzerland* M37+475 **45**
El Ghobbe, *Saudi Arabia* K31+239 **74**
Elgin, *Illinois* T80+420 **95**
Elgin, *New Brunswick* S31+458 **90**
Elgin, *Scotland* N20+576 **40**
El Giof. *See* El Jauf.
El Giza, *Egypt* K82+300 **81**
El Golea, *Algeria* M74+306 **80**
Elgon, Mt., *Uganda* K62+012 **83**
El Hamidiya, *Syria* K49+354 **76**
El Hamra, *Syria* K48+353 **76**
El Hamra, *Saudi Arabia* K48+345 **76**
El Hasa, *Saudi Arabia* J67+272 **74**
El-Hayath, *Saudi Arabia* K25+261 **74**
El Hijane, *Syria* K51+333 **76**
El Hilla, *Sudan* L16+134 **81**
El Husn, *Jordan* K55+325 **76**
Elie, *Scotland* N17+562 **41**
Elisabethville. *See* Lubumbashi.
Elisavetgrad. *See* Kirovograd.

Elizabeth, *New Jersey* T86+406 **96**
Elizabeth I., *Massachusetts* S65+414 **96**
Elizabeth, *West Virginia* T38+390 **91**
Elizabeth City, *N. Carolina* T08+363 **97**
Elizabethtown, *Kentucky* T65+377 **97**
Elizondo, *Spain* N09+433 **53**
El Jafr, *Jordan* K53+303 **76**
El Jauf, *Libya* L40+238 **81**
El Judeide, *Syria* K53+336 **76**
Elk Mts., *New Mexico* V18+337 **94**
Elk, *Poland* L46+538 **49**
Elk City, *Oklahoma* U57+354 **95**
El Kerak, *Jordan* K56+312 **76**
El Kharga, *Egypt* K86+254 **81**
Elkhart, *Indiana* T66+417 **91**
Elkhead Mts., *Colorado* V14+408 **94**
Elkhorn, Mt., *Idaho* V45+424 **92**
El Khushniye, *Syria* K55+330 **76**
Elkins, *West Virginia* T29+389 **91**
Elko, *Nevada* V65+408 **92**
Elk Point, *S. Dakota* U40+427 **93**
Elk River, *Minnesota* U22+453 **93**
Elkton, *Maryland* T05+396 **96**
El Lâdhiqîya. *See* Latakia.
El Laghodeh, *Somalia* J66+094 **83**
Ellas, *Greece* L42+385 **59**
Ellef Ringnes I., *N.-W. Terr.* U65+784 **88**
Ellen, Mt., *Utah* V35+382 **94**
Ellenabad, *India* H02+294 **72**
Ellendale, *N. Dakota* U51+460 **93**
Ellensburg, *Washington* W04+470 **92**
Ellerslie, *Prince Edward I.* S23+466 **90**
Ellesmere I., *N.-W. Terr.* T30+780 **89**
Ellesmere, I., *New Zealand* A44-439 **112**
Ellesmere Port, *England* N17+533 **37**
Ellezelles, *Belgium* M68+507 **44**
Ellice Is., *See* Tuvalu
Ellice R., *N.-W. Territories* V05+666 **88**
Ellichpur, *India* G75+212 **70**
Ellicott City, *Maryland* T11+393 **96**
Elliot, *Cape Province* L12-314 **84**
Elliot B., *N.-W. Territories* U35+676 **88**
Elliot Group, *China* D74+393 **66**
Ellon, *Scotland* N12+574 **40**
Ellora, *India* G88+201 **70**
Ellsworth, *Maine* S50+445 **96**
Ellsworth Mts., *Antarctica* U00-770 **27**
Elm, *Switzerland* M35+469 **45**
El Ma'arra, *Syria* K49+360 **76**
Elma Dagh, *Turkey* K72+398 **74**
El Madhiq, *Saudi Arabia* K32+233 **74**
El Mansura, *Egypt* K82+310 **81**
El Mazar, *Jordan* K56+311 **76**
El Mazra'a, *Jordan* K57+313 **76**
El Meget, *Somalia* J80+032 **83**
El Menzil, *Jordan* K54+311 **76**
Elmira, *New York* T11+421 **96**
El Minya, *Egypt* K86+280 **81**
El Molar, *Spain* N22+408 **52**
Elmore, *Victoria* C32-365 **109**
El Muwaqqar, *Jordan* K53+318 **76**
El Obeid, *Sudan* K88+132 **81**
El Odaiya, *Sudan* L10+120 **81**
Elora, *Tennesse* T68+350 **97**
El Oro, *Mexico* V02+259 **100**
El Pardo, *Spain* N24+405 **52**
El Paso, *Illinois* T84+408 **95**
El Paso, *Texas* V09+316 **98**
Elphin, *Ireland, Rep.* N49+538 **42**
Elphinstone I., *Burma* F42+123 **71**
El Pico, *Bolivia* S28-158 **104**
El Pilar, *Venezuela* S18+104 **104**
El Pintado, *Argentina* S08-246 **103**
El Puente del Arzobispo, *Sp.* N31+398 **52**
El Qadmus, *Syria* K53+351 **76**
El Qanawat, *Syria* K50+327 **76**
El Qaryatein, *Syria* K46+342 **76**
El Qathma, *Saudi Arabia* K17+238 **74**
El Qatrana, *Jordan* K54+312 **76**
El Qatrun, *Libya* M02+250 **81**
El Quds esh Sherif. *See* Jerusalem
El Quneitra, *Syria* K55+331 **76**
El Quseir, *Syria* K50+345 **76**
El Quweira, *Jordan* K58+298 **76**
El Reno, *Oklahoma* U48+353 **95**
Elroy, *Wisconsin* U01+437 **91**
El Sadi. *See* Wajir
El Salvador, *Cent. America* T80+135 **101**
Elsenborn, *Belgium* M53+505 **44**
Elsloo, *Netherlands* M55+509 **44**
Elspeet, *Netherlands* M55+523 **44**
Elst, *Netherlands* M55+519 **44**
Elsterwerda, *E. Germany* M09+515 **48**
Eltham, *New Zealand* A34-394 **112**
El Tigre, *Venezuela* S25+089 **104**
El Toro, *Spain* N04+400 **53**
El Transito, *Chile* S61-288 **103**
Eluru, *India* G53+168 **70**
El Valle, *Colombia* T14+062 **104**
Elvas, *Portugal* N43+389 **52**
El Vigia, *Venezuela* S69+086 **104**
Elvira, C., *N.-W. Territories* V12+728 **88**
Ely, *England* M89+524 **37**
Ely, *Minnesota* U12+478 **93**
Ely, *Nevada* V60+393 **92**
Ely, Isle of, *England* M89+525 **37**
Emanguiova, *U.S.S.R.* J28+522 **61**
Emba R., *Kazakh* J28+470 **62**
Embarcacion, *Argentina* S25-232 **103**
Embóna, *Greece* L13+362 **59**
Embrun, *France* M51+445 **55**
Emden, *W. Germany* M47+534 **48**
Emerald, *Queensland* C11-232 **111**
Emerald I., *N.-W. Terr.* V58+756 **88**
Emerson, *Manitoba* U42+492 **88**
Emilia-Romagna, reg., *Italy* M26+445 **56**
Eminabad, *Pakistan* H04+321 **72**
Eminence, *Missouri* U08+372 **97**
Emmaste, *Estonia* L44+587 **47**
Emmaville, *New S. Wales* B81-294 **109**
Emmen, *Netherlands* M49+528 **44**
Emmetsburg, *Iowa* U28+431 **95**
Emmons, Mt., *Utah* V32+406 **94**
Emory Pk., *Texas* U80+292 **94**
Empalme, *Mexico* V34+281 **100**
Empedrado, *Argentina* R83-279 **103**
Empire, *Michigan* T66+448 **91**
Emporia, *Kansas* U37+384 **95**
Emporia, *Virginia* T15+367 **95**
Emporium, *Pennsylvania* T20+415 **96**

Emptinne, *Belgium* M59+503 **44**
Ems, *W. Germany* M44+503 **48**
Enard B., *Scotland* N32+581 **40**
Encarnacion, *Paraguay* R65-273 **103**
Encontrados, *Venezuela* S73+091 **104**
Encounter B., *S. Australia* C68-357 **109**
Encruzilhada, *Brazil* R45-305 **103**
Ende, *Flores I., Indonesia* D80-088 **65**
Enderbury I., *Phoenix Is.* Z36-032 **106**
Enderby Ld., *Antarctica* J60-680 **27**
Enderlin, *N. Dakota* U46+466 **93**
Endicott, *New York* T07+421 **96**
Endicott Mts., *Alaska* Y10+674 **99**
Enez, *Turkey* L23+407 **74**
Enez, G. of, *Greece* L25+407 **59**
Enfe, *Lebanon* K55+343 **76**
Enfield, *England* N00+516 **39**
Engano, C., *Philippines* D76+186 **65**
Engelberg, *Switzerland* M40+468 **45**
Engels, *U.S.S.R.* J83+514 **61**
Enggano, I., *Indonesia* F16-054 **65**
Enghien, *Belgium* M66+507 **44**
England, *Great Britain* N12+520 **34**
Englehart, *Ontario* T29+478 **91**
Englewood, *New Jersey* S84+408 **96**
English Chan., *France-Eng.* N12+500 **54**
English R., *Ontario* U25+502 **88**
English Bazar, *India* G11+250 **73**
English Coast, *Antarctica* T00-740 **27**
Enid, *Oklahoma* U48+364 **95**
Enkhuizen, *Netherlands* M58+527 **44**
Enköping, *Sweden* L78+597 **47**
Enna, *Sicily* M04+375 **57**
En Nahud, *Sudan* L10+126 **81**
En Naqura, *Lebanon* K59+331 **76**
En Nebk, *Syria* K50+340 **76**
Ennell L., *Ireland, Rep.* N44+535 **43**
En Nemara, *Syria* K46+329 **76**
Enngonia, *New S. Wales* C25-294 **109**
Ennis, *Ireland, Rep.* N54+528 **43**
Enniscorthy, *Ireland, Rep.* N39+525 **43**
Enniskillen, *N. Ireland* N46+543 **42**
Ennistimon, *Ireland, Rep.* N56+529 **43**
Enns, *Austria* M03+482 **48**
Enns. R., *Austria* M04+475 **48**
Enontekiö, *Finland* L39+684 **46**
Enriquillo, L.,
   Dominican Rep. S70+186 **101**
Ensanche Colonia Sarmiento,
   Argentina S60-453 **103**
Ensay, *Victoria* C13-374 **109**
Enschede, *Netherlands* M48+522 **44**
Ensenada, *Argentina* R78-348 **103**
Ensenada, *Mexico* V70+317 **100**
Enshih, *China* E63+302 **67**
Entebbe, *Uganda* K76+001 **83**
Enterprise, *Mississippi* T83+322 **95**
Entraygues, *France* M75+446 **55**
Entre Rios, *Brazil* Q48-120 **105**
Entre Rios, *Brazil* Q79-220 **105**
Eolie, Isole, *Italy* M02+387 **57**
Epe, *Netherlands* M54+523 **44**
Epernay, *France* M66+490 **54**
Ephraim, *Utah* V40+394 **94**
Episkopi & B., *Cyprus* K73+346 **76**
Epping & Forest, *England* M89+517 **39**
Epsom, *England* N02+513 **39**
Equatorial Guinea, *W. Afr.* M30+016 **82**
Ercis, *Turkey* K11+390 **74**
Erd, *Hungary* L66+474 **49**
Erebus Gulf, *Antarctica* R75-640 **27**
Erebus Mt., *Antarctica* B30-780 **27**
Eregli, *Turkey* K81+414 **74**
Ereğli, *Turkey* K67+375 **74**
Erepecú, L., *Brazil* R69-013 **105**
Eressós, *Greece* L25+391 **59**
Erexim, *Brazil* R43-279 **103**
Erfurt, *E. Germany* M24+510 **48**
Erh Hai, *China* F29+256 **64**
Erhlien, *China* E42+422 **63**
Ericht L., *Scotland* N27+568 **41**
Erie, *Pennsylvania* T31+421 **91**
Erie, L., *U.S.A.-Canada* T40+420 **99**
Ericau, *Ontario* T42+423 **91**
Eriha, *Syria* K50+358 **76**
Erisort L., *Scotland* N38+581 **40**
Erlach, *Switzerland* M47+470 **45**
Erlangen, *W. Germany* M24+496 **48**
Erlenbach, *Switzerland* M45+467 **45**
Ermelo, *Netherlands* M56+523 **44**
Ermenek, *Turkey* K73+366 **74**
Ernakulam, *India* G82+100 **70**
Erne L., *N. Ireland* N47+545 **42**
Erne L., Up., *N. Ireland* N45+542 **42**
Ernee, *France* N06+483 **54**
Eromanga, I., *New Hebrides* A65-192 **106**
Erquelinnes, *Belgium* M65+503 **44**
Er Rabba, *Jordan* K56+312 **76**
Er Rahad, *Sudan* K86+128 **81**
Er Ramle, *Syria* K46+357 **76**
Er Rastan, *Syria* K50+349 **76**
Errigal, *Ireland, Rep.* N49+550 **42**
Erris Hd., *Ireland, Rep.* N60+543 **42**
Er Rumman, *Jordan* K55+322 **76**
Erudina, *S. Australia* C64-315 **109**
Erval, *Brazil* R49-319 **103**
Erz Geb., *E. Germany* M12+506 **48**
Erzincan, *Turkey* K34+398 **74**
Erzurum, *Turkey* K22+399 **74**
Erzvilkas, *Lithuania* L44+553 **47**
Esashi, *Japan* C45+450 **68**
Esbjerg, *Denmark* M39+555 **47**
Escada, *Brazil* Q31-082 **105**
Escala, la, *Spain* M71+421 **53**
Escalante, *Utah* V40+378 **94**
Escalon, *Mexico* U85+266 **100**
Escanaba & R., *Michigan* T73+458 **91**
Escaut, R., *Belgium* M65+511 **44**
Esch, *Luxembourg* M54+495 **48**
Escholzmatt, *Switzerland* M42+469 **45**
Escudo de Veragua, *Panama* T39+091 **101**
Escuinapa, *Mexico* V04+228 **100**
Escuintla, *Guatemala* U04+142 **100**
Esc. minac Pt., *N.B.* S29+471 **90**
Esfahan, *Iran* J50+327 **75**
Eshcwe, *Natal* K80-288 **84**
Esk R., *England* N21+547 **37**
Eskdale, *New Zealand* A19-393 **112**
Eske L., *Ireland. Rep.* N48+547 **42**
Eskilstuna, *Sweden* L81+594 **47**

Eskimo, C., *N.-W. Terr.* U25+610 **89**
Eskisehir, *Turkey* K87+398 **74**
Esla R., *Spain* N35+418 **52**
Eslöv, *Sweden* M10+559 **47**
Esmeralda, I., *Chile* T02-489 **103**
Esmeraldas, *Ecuador* 128+010 **104**
Espalion, *France* M73+445 **55**
Espanola, *Ontario* T40+463 **91**
Esperance, *W. Australia* D79-337 **110**
Esperanza, *Argentina* S06-314 **103**
Espiel, *Spain* N30+382 **52**
Espinho, *Portugal* N52+410 **52**
Espinosa de los Monteros, *Sp.* N21+431 **52**
Espirito Santo, *Brazil* S02-061 **104**
Espirito Santo, *Brazil* Q61-204 **105**
Espiritu Santo, B. del, *Mex.* T74+193 **100**
Espiritu Santo, I., *Argentina* S51-526 **103**
Espiritu Santo, I., *Mexico* V32+244 **100**
Espiritu Santo, I.,
   New Hebrides A76-158 **106**
Esquel, *Argentina* S68-428 **103**
Esquimalt, *Brit. Columbia* W21+484 **88**
Esquina, *Argentina* R87-300 **103**
Es Sa'an, *Syria* K46+353 **76**
Es Safi, *Jordan* K57+310 **76**
Es Salt, *Jordan* K56+320 **76**
Es Samra, *Jordan* K53+322 **76**
Es Sanamein, *Syria* K53+331 **76**
Esse & Alv, *Finland* L41+636 **46**
Essen, *Belgium* M63+515 **44**
Essen, *Germany* M48+516 **48**
Essequibo, R., *Guyana* R81+068 **104**
Essex, *Ontario* T47+422 **91**
Essex, co., *England* M87+518 **39**
Essex Mt., *Wyoming* V25+419 **98**
Esslingen, *W. Germany* M34+487 **48**
Es Sukhne, *Syria* K37+348 **74**
Es Suweidîya, *Syria* K51+327 **76**
Estabutchie, *Mississippi* T86+314 **97**
Estados, I., de los, *Argentina* S26-548 **103**
Estavayer, *Switzerland* M49+469 **45**
Estcourt, *Natal* L00-290 **84**
Esteli, *Nicaragua* T69+130 **101**
Esternay, *France* M69+487 **54**
Estevan, *Saskatchewan* U79+493 **88**
Estherville, *Iowa* U29+434 **95**
Estin Gol, *China* F26+410 **64**
Estonia, rep., *U.S.S.R.* **47**
Estoril, *Portugal* N56+387 **52**
Estreito, *Brazil* R40-318 **103**
Estremoz, *Portugal* N45+388 **52**
Estrondo, Sa. des, *Brazil* R20-076 **105**
E'Sufeina, *Saudi Arabia* K27+233 **74**
Etah, *India* G68+275 **73**
Etalle, *Belgium* M56+497 **44**
Étampes, *France* M77+484 **54**
Étaples, *France* M80+505 **54**
Etawah, *India* G66+268 **73**
Etawney L., *Manitoba* U47+584 **88**
Eternity Ra., *Antarctica* S20-720 **27**
Ethe, *Belgium* M56+496 **44**
Ethiopia, *E. Africa* **83**
Etivaz, I', *Switzerland* M47+464 **45**
Etive L., *Scotland* N31+565 **41**
Etna, Mt., *Sicily* M00+378 **57**
Eton, *England* N04+515 **39**
Ettelbrück, *Luxembourg* M53+499 **48**
Etten, *Netherlands* M62+516 **44**
Ettrick, *New Zealand* A63-457 **112**
Ettrick R., *Scotland* N18+555 **41**
Euabalong, *New S. Wales* C21-331 **109**
Euboea. *See* Evvoia, I.
Eucla, *W. Australia* D37-316 **110**
Eudunda, *S. Australia* C66-341 **109**
Eufaula, *Alabama* T61+318 **99**
Eufaula & Res., *Oklahoma* U34+353 **95**
Eugene, *Oregon* W19+441 **96**
Eugmö, *Finland* L43+638 **46**
Eugowra, *New S. Wales* C09-334 **109**
Eumungerie, *New S. Wales* C08-320 **109**
Eunice, *Louisiana* U14+304 **95**
Eupen, *Belgium* M54+506 **44**
Euphrates, R., *Iraq, etc.* J89+315 **74**
Eure, dep., *France* M85+491 **54**
Eureka, *California* W25+408 **92**
Eureka, *Kansas* U38+378 **95**
Eureka, *Nevada* V66+396 **92**
Eureka, *Utah* V41+400 **94**
Eure-et-Loir, dep., *France* M28+484 **54**
Euriowie, *New S. Wales* C50-314 **109**
Euroa, *Victoria* C27-367 **109**
Eursinge, *Netherlands* M51+528 **44**
Euston, *New S. Wales* C44-346 **109**
Eutaw, *Alabama* T77+329 **97**
Eutsuk L., *Brit. Columbia* W40+536 **88**
Evale, *Angola* L86-166 **84**
Evandale, *Tasmania* C17-416 **109**
Evans, L., *Quebec* T12+508 **89**
Evanston, *Illinois* T76+421 **95**
Evanston, *Wyoming* V36+412 **93**
Evansville, *Indiana* T76+380 **97**
Evansville, *Minnesota* U34+461 **93**
Eva Peron, La Plata, *Argent.* R78-349 **103**
Evaux, *France* M75+462 **54**
Eveleth, *Minnesota* U16+472 **93**
Everard, L., *S. Australia* D00-312 **111**
Everest, Mt., *Nepal-Tibet* G18+280 **71**
Everett, *Washington* W12+478 **98**
Evergem, *Belgium* M68+511 **44**
Everglades, The, *Florida* T35+256 **99**
Everglades Nat. Park, *Florida* T36+255 **97**
Evergreen, *Alabama* T72+315 **97**
Evesham & Vale of, *England* N12+521 **39**
Evijärvi, *Finland* L39+634 **46**
Evje, *Norway* M43+586 **47**
Evolène, *Switzerland* M45+461 **45**
Evora, *Portugal* N47+386 **52**
Evreux, *France* M83+490 **54**
Evros, *Greece* L23+413 **58**
Evrykhou, *Cyprus* K73+350 **76**
Évvoia. G. of, *Greece* L40+387 **59**
Evvoia, I., *Greece* L36+386 **59**
Ewarton, *Jamaica* T13+182 **101**
Ewe, L., *Scotland* N34+578 **40**
Exaltacion, *Bolivia* S33-134 **104**
Exe R., *England* N21+507 **38**
Exeter, *England* N21+507 **38**
Exeter, *New Hampshire* S66+430 **96**
Exloo, *Netherlands* M49+529 **44**
Exminster, *England* N21+507 **38**

Exmoor, England N21+512 38
Exmouth, England N20+506 38
Exmouth G., W. Australia E33-218 110
Expedition Ra., Queensland C06-242 111
Exuma Is., Bahamas, The T10+244 101
Exuma Sd., Bahamas, The T08+244 101
Eyasi L., Tanzania K60-036 83
Eye L., Quebec T10+532 89
Eyemouth, Scotland N12+559 41
Eymoutiers, France M79+457 54
Eyre, W. Australia D52-321 110
Eyre Cr., S. Australia C67-266 111
Eyre, L., S. Australia C76-282 111
Eyre Pen., S. Australia C85-334 111
Eyrecourt, Ireland, Rep. N49+532 43
Eyzies, les, France M84+449 55
Ezcaray, Spain N18+423 52
Fab, Somalia J72+048 83
Fåborg, Denmark M28+551 47
Facatativa, Columbia S86+047 104
Fada, Chad L50+172 81
Fadan' Gourma, Upper Volta M88+120 80
Faddeyevskiy, Ostrov, Russia C35+750 63
Faenza, Italy M19+443 56
Faeröerne, N. Atlantic Ocean N40+620 34
Faeroes. See Faeroerne.
Fafa, Mali M86+152 80
Făgăras, Romania L30+458 58
Fagarg, Sudan L20+118 81
Fagerli, Norway L83+671 46
Fagernes, Norway M34+610 47
Fagnano, L., Argentina S46-546 103
Faid, Saudi Arabia K14+271 74
Faido, Switzerland M37+465 45
Fai-fo, (Hoi An), S. Vietnam E70+158 69
Fair I., Scotland N10+595 40
Fairbanks, Alaska X75+643 99
Fairbury, Illinios T81+408 91
Fairbury, Nebraska U43+402 95
Fairfield, Illinois T80+384 95
Fairfield, Iowa U12+410 95
Fairfield, Maine S58+446 90
Fairhaven, Massachusetts S65+416 96
Fair Head, N. Ireland N37+552 42
Fairlie, New Zealand A55-441 112
Fairmont, Minnesota U27+437 95
Fairmont, West Virginia T31+395 91
Fairview, Alberta V82+559 88
Fairville, New Brunswick S37+453 90
Fairweather, Mt., Alaska X15+590 99
Faith, S. Dakota U73+450 93
Faizabad, Afghanistan H26+371 75
Faizabad, India G47+267 73
Fajr, Saudi Arabia K44+289 74
Fakfak, Irian Jaya, Indon. D17-029 65
Fakiya, Bulgaria L18+422 58
Falam, Burma F68+230 71
Falama, Guinea N52+106 80
Fâlciu, Romania L11+463 58
Falcon, Res., Texas U56+269 94
Falcone, C. of, Sardinia M41+410 57
Falkenberg, Sweden M15+569 47
Falkirk, Scotland N23+560 41
Falkland, Scotland N19+562 41
Falkland Is., S. Atlantic Oc. S00-517 103
Falkland Is. Dependencies,
 Antarctica R00-550 27
Falknov, Czechoslovakia M14+502 48
Fallöping, Sweden M09+581 47
Fall River, Massachusetts S67+417 96
Falls City, Nebraska U34+402 95
Falmagne, Belgium M61+502 44
Falmouth, Jamaica T16+185 101
Falmouth, Kentucky T56+387 91
Falmouth & B., England N30+501 38
False B., Cape Province L68-344 84
False Point, India G19+204 71
Falset, Spain M85+411 53
Falso, C., Mexico V30+229 100
Falster, I., Denmark M18+548 47
Faluja, Israel K61+316 76
Falun, Sweden L86+606 47
Famagusta & B., Cyprus K66+351 76
Famatina, Argentina S45-290 103
Fanad Hd., Ireland, Rep. N46+553 42
Fannich L., Scotland N30+576 40
Fanning, I., Pacific Ocean Y58+040 107
Fanö, I., Denmark M39+554 47
Fanö Bugt, Denmark M41+553 47
Fanshawe, C., N.-W. Terr. T10+730 89
Fanuch, Iran J02+266 75
Fao, Iraq J69+300 74
Faradje, Congo L02+036 83
Farafangana, Madagascar J74-230 83
Farah, Afghanistan H77+324 75
Farajja, Saudi Arabia J56+218 75
Faranah, Guinea N64+100 80
Faranlep, I., Caroline Is. C40+082 106
Farasan Is., Red Sea K18+168 74
Farewell C., Greenland Q70+590 26
Fargo, N. Dakota U41+469 93
Faribault, Minnesota U20+443 93
Faridabad, India G76+284 72
Faridkot, India H02+307 72
Faridpur, India G63+282 73
Faridpur, Bangladesh G01+236 73
Fariman, Iran J02+360 75
Farina, S. Australia C70-301 109
Farmington, Maine S61+447 90
Farmington, Missouri U03+378 97
Farmington, New Mexico V20+367 94
Farmington, Utah V42+409 94
Farmville, Virginia T20+373 97
Farnborough, England N00+514 39
Farne Is., England N10+556 37
Farnes, Norway M43+613 47
Farnham, Quebec S78+453 91
Farnworth, England N14+535 37
Faro, Brazil R71-020 105
Färön, I., Sweden L65+579 47
Farrukhabad, India G63+274 73
Farrukhnagar, India G79+284 72
Farsala, Greece L46+393 59
Farsi, Afghanistan H71+338 75
Farsund, Norway M49+581 47
Farwell, Michigan T59+438 91
Farwell, Texas U78+340 98
Fasa, Iran J38+289 75
Fatahabad, India G87+295 72

Fatait ibn Kanat,
 Saudi Arabia K10+293 74
Fatehabad, India G70+271 73
Fatehgarh, India G62+273 73
Fatehpur, India H00+280 72
Fatehpur, India G55+259 73
Father L., Quebec T02+495 89
Fatmomakke, Sweden L89+650 46
Fatshan, China E41+231 67
Fatu Hiva, I., Marquesas Is. X20-108 107
Fawley, England N08+508 39
Faxaflói, Iceland P50+645 46
Faxina, Brazil R24-238 105
Faya. See Largeau.
Fayette, Alabama T77+337 95
Fayette, Missouri U16+391 95
Fayetteville, Arkansas U25+361 93
Fayetteville, N. Carolina T23+350 97
Fayetteville, Pennsylvania T14+399 96
Fayetteville, W. Virginia T37+380 97
Fazilka, India H06+304 72
Fderik, Mauritania N76+226 80
Feale R., Ireland Rep. N58+525 43
Fear,·C., N. Carolina T16+336 99
Featherton, Mt., Victoria C17-369 109
Fécamp, France M87+498 54
Fedaracion, Argentina R78-309 103
Feeagh L., Ireland, Rep. N57+539 42
Fehmarn, I., Germany M23+544 48
Feifu. See Faifo.
Feilding, New Zealand A26-400 112
Feira de Santana, Brazil Q53-124 105
Feldbach, Austria L85+470 49
Feldkirch, Austria M33+472 48
Felipe Carrillo Puerto, Mex. T73+196 100
Femund, L., Norway M19+623 46
Feng chèn, China E41+405 66
Fengshien, China E20+346 66
Fenghwang, China E63+279 67
Fengkieh, China E63+311 66
Fengsiang, China E77+343 66
Fengyang, China E12+328 66
Fenit, Ireland, Rep. N59+523 43
Fenny Stratford, England N04+520 39
Fens, The, England N00+526 37
Fenton, Michigan T52+428 91
Fenyang, China E50+373 66
Feodosiya & B., U.S.S.R. K58+450 60
Fergus, Ontario T32+437 91
Fergus Falls, Minnesota U36+463 93
Ferguson, Missouri U02+387 97
Ferguson, Quebec S81+478 91
Fergusson I., Papua New Guinea
 B86-095 111
Fermanagh, co., N. Ireland N46+543 42
Fermoy, Ireland, Rep. N50+521 43
Fernando Poo, I., See Macias Nguema
Fernie, Brit. Columbia V59+496 88
Ferns, Ireland, Rep. N39+526 43
Ferozepore, India H02+309 72
Ferrar Gl., Antarctica B70-790 27
Ferrara, Italy M20+448 56
Ferrato C., Sardinia M32+393 57
Ferreira do Zezere, Portugal N50+357 52
Ferrol del Caudillo, Spain N49+434 52
Fertile, Minnesota U38+476 93
Fertö tó, See Neusiedler See
Fes, Morocco N30+340 80
Festus, Missouri U02+382 97
Fethard, Ireland, Rep. N46+524 43
Fetlar I., Scotland N05+606 40
Fez. See Fes
Ffestiniog, Wales N24+529 38
Fiambala, Argentina S46-277 103
Ficalho, Portugal N44+380 52
Fichtel Geb., W. Germany M18+501 48
Fideris, Switzerland M31+469 45
Fier, Albania L63+407 59
Fiesch, Switzerland M41+464 45
Fife, reg., Scotland N18+563 41
Fife Ness, Scotland N15+563 41
Figeac, France M78+466 55
Figline Vald, Italy M21+436 56
Figueira de Castelo Rodrigo,
 Portugal N42+409 52
Figueras, Spain M72+423 53
Figuig, Morocco N08+320 80
Fiji Is., Pacific Ocean A00-175 106
Filakovo, Czechoslovakia L61+483 49
Filchner Ice Shelf,
 Antarctica R30-790 27
Filey, England N02+542 37
Filiátes, Greece L58+396 59
Filicudi, I., Italy M03+386 57
Filipow, Poland L44+542 49
Filisur, Switzerland M32+467 45
Fincastle, Virginia T29+374 97
Findhorn & R., Scotland N22+577 40
Findlay, Ohio T52+410 91
Findlay Grp., N.-W. Terr. V00+772 88
Fingal, Ontario T45+483 91
Fingal, Tasmania C13-417 109
Finhaut, Switzerland M48+461 45
Finistère, dep., France N24+483 54
Finisterre, C., Spain N55+428 52
Finke, R., N. Terr., Aust. D01-255 111
Finland, rep., N. Europe 46
Finland, G. of, N.-W. Europe 47
Finlay R., Brit. Columbia W25+564 88
Finlay Forks, Brit. Columbia W23+559 88
Finley, New S. Wales C28-357 109
Finschhafen,
 Papua New Guinea C13-065 111
Finspäng, Sweden L85+587 47
Finsteraarhorn, Switzerland M41+465 45
Fintona, N. Ireland N44+545 42
Fionn L., Scotland N33+577 40
Fionnay, Switzerland M46+460 45
Fiq, Syria K56+328 76
Firat, R., Turkey K36+397 74
Firdaus, Iran J11+340 75
Firenze, Italy M23+438 56
Firmat, Argentina S09-334 103
Firnis, Turkey K49+379 74
Firozabad, India G70+272 73
Firozpur Jhirka, India G78+277 72
Firuzabad, Iran J45+288 75
Firuze, Iran J12+378 75
Fish Camp, Kenya K56+036 83
Fisher Str., N.-W. Terr. T50-635 89

Fishers I., New York S72+412 96
Fishbuard & B., Wales N30+520 38
Fitchburg, Massachusetts S71+426 96
Fitful Hd., Scotland N08+599 40
Fitzcarrald, Peru S70-117 104
Fitzgerald, Alberta V40+599 88
Fitzgerald, Tasmania C21-428 109
Fitzpatrick, Alabama T65+322 97
Fitzroy, W. Australia D56-181 110
Fitz Roy, C., N.-W. Terr. T30+755 89
Fitzroy, R., Queensland C02-230 111
Fitzroy, R., W. Australia D63-179 110
Fitzwilliam I., Ontario T41+455 91
Fiume. See Rijeka
Fivemiletown, N. Ireland N44+544 42
Fjällåsen, Sweden L59+675 46
Flagstaff, Arizona V40+35 94
Flamborough Hd., England N00+542 37
Flamingo Tk.,
 Irian Jaya, Indon. C76-057 65
Flat, Alaska Y48+624 99
Flathead, L., Montana V55+478 92
Flattery, C., Queensland C28-150 111
Flattery, C., Washington W28+479 98
Flèche, la, France N00+477 54
Fleetwood, England N18+539 37
Flekkefjord, Norway M50+583 47
Flemington, New Jersey S89+405 96
Flensburg, W. Germany M34+547 48
Flers, France N03+488 54
Fleurance, France M86+439 55
Fleurier, Switzerland M50+469 45
Fleuru, Belgium M63+505 44
Flims, Switzerland M34+468 45
Flinders I., S. Australia D03-335 111
Flinders I., Tasmania C12-400 109
Flinders Ra., S. Australia C70-322 111
Flinders, R., Queensland C52-194 111
Flin Flon, Manitoba U71+548 88
Flint, Michigan T52+431 91
Flint, Wales N19+532 38
Flint I., Pacific Ocean Y15-105 107
Flint R., Georgia T57+310 99
Flisa, Norway M18+606 47
Flora, Illinois T81+386 95
Florac, France N00+443 55
Floreffe, Belgium M61+504 44
Florence. See Firenze.
Florence, Alabama T76+348 97
Florence, Arizona V40+330 94
Florence, Colorado V02+384 94
Florence, S. Carolina T29+342 97
Florence, Wisconsin T80+460 91
Florencia, Argentina R86-280 103
Florencia, Colombia T04+017 104
Florennes, Belgium M62+502 44
Florenville, Belgium M58+497 44
Flores, Guatemala T89+170 100
Flores, I., Atlantic Ocean Q08+394 80
Flores, I. & Sea, Indonesia D80-085 65
Floriano, Brazil Q78-068 105
Floriano Peixoto, Brazil S44-092 104
Florianopolis, Brazil R21-276 103
Florida, state, U.S.A. T64+306 99
Florida B., Florida T41+250 99
Florida, C., Florida T31+257 99
Florida Mts., New Mexico V16+322 94
Florida Str., Bahamas, The T30+250 101
Florida Str., Florida T39+244 99
Florida City, Florida T33+254 99
Florida Keys, Florida T34+250 97
Floridia, Uruguay R67-340 103
Florina, Greece L51+408 59
Flöro, Norway M61+617 46
Flotta, I., Orkney Is. Scot. N19+588 40
Floydada, Texas U68+340 94
Flüelen, Switzerland M38+469 45
Flushing. See Vlissingen
Flushing, New York S83+407 96
Fly, R., Papua New Guinea C50-078 111
Flying Fish C., Antarctica U65-730 27
Foča, Yugoslavia L67+435 58
Focsani, Romania L17+456 58
Fofa Cahuel, Argentina S65-423 103
Foggia, Italy L87+415 57
Fogo I., Newfoundland R55+497 90
Föhr, I., Germany M39+547 48
Foix, France M80+430 55
Fokis, Greece L46+386 59
Folda, I., Norway M04+676 46
Folégandros, I., Greece L30+366 59
Foleyet, Ontario T45+483 91
Foligno, Italy M14+430 56
Folkestone, England M83+511 39
Folkston, Georgia T42+309 97
Folkstone, N. Carolina T15+345 97
Follega, Netherlands M56+529 44
Fonda, New York S86+429 96
Fond du Lac, Minnesota-
 Wisconsin U09+469 91
Fond du Lac, Saskatchewan V13+595 88
Fond du Lac, Wisconsin T81+438 91
Fonsagráda, Spain N42+431 52
Fonseca, G. of, Honduras T76+132 101
Fontaine, Belgium M64+504 44
Fontainebleau, France M74+484 54
Fontana, L., Argentina S69-449 103
Fontenay le Comte, France M71+465 54
Fontenay le Comte, France N05+465 54
Foochow, China E04+261 67
Forbes, New S. Wales C52-333 109
Forbes, Mt., Alberta V70+516 88
Forcados, Nigeria M58+052 80
Forcalquier, France M56+440 55
Förde, Norway M55+615 47
Ford Ranges, Antarctica X40-770 27
Ford's Bridge, New S. Wales C57-298 109
Fordyce, Arkansas U14+338 95
Forel, Mt., Greenland Q10+670 26
Forest, Ontario T42+431 91
Forestier Pen., Tasmania C13-429 109
Forfar, Scotland N17+566 41
Fork, R., N., Idaho V42+440 98
Forli, Italy M18+442 56
Forlorn Pt., Ireland, Rep. N39+522 43
Formentera I., Balearic Is. M81+387 53
Formia, Italy M08+413 57
Formosa, Argentina R79-261 103
Formosa, Brazil R13-156 105
Formosa. See Taiwan, I.

Formosa Str. See Taiwan Hai Hsia
Fornos d'Algódres, Portugal N45+407 52
Forres, Scotland N22+576 40
Forrest, W. Australia D41-308 110
Forrest, Victoria C48-386 109
Forrest City, Arkansas U04+350 95
Forsa, Sweden L79+617 47
Forsayth, Queensland C39-185 111
Forsnäs, Sweden L68+662 46
Forssa, Finland L38+608 47
Forsyth, Montana V10+462 93
Fort Albany, Ontario T40+525 89
Fort Alexander, Manitoba U37+504 88
Fortaleza, Amazonas, Brazil S52-064 104
Fortaleza, Ceara, Brazil Q52-037 105
Fortaleza, state of, Acre,
 Brazil S58-100 104
Fort Ann, New York S80+435 96
Fort Archambault, See Sarh
Fort Atkinson, Wisconsin T83+429 95
Fort Augustus, Scotland N28+571 40
Fort Beaufort, Cape Province L20-328 84
Fort Bennett, S. Dakota U64+447 93
Fort Benton, Montana V34+478 93
Fort Brabant, N.-W. Terr. V42+707 88
Fort Bragg, California W23+395 92
Fort Chipewyan, Alberta V36+590 88
Fort Collins, Colorado V00+406 94
Fort Coulonge, Quebec T11+459 91
Fort Crampel, Central
 African Republic L64+070 81
Ford Dauphin, Madagascar J78-250 83
Fort Dodge, Iowa U25+426 95
Fort Edward, New York S82+433 91
Fortescue, R., W. Australia E18-214 110
Fort Fairfield, Maine S47+467 90
Fort Flatters, Algeria M50+280 80
Fort Fraser, Brit. Columbia W28+541 88
Fort George, Scotland N24+576 40
Fort George, R., Quebec T20+540 89
Fort Gouraud, See Fdérik
Fort Grahame, B.C. W27+563 88
Fort Grey, New S. Wales C52-289 109
Forth, Firth of, Scotland N18+561 41
Forth R., Scotland N24+561 41
Fort Haka, Burma F68+226 71
Fort Hall, Kenya K48-008 83
Fort Henrique, S.-W. Africa M00-174 84
Fort Hertz, Burma F45+273 71
Fort Hill, See Chitipa
Fort Howard, Wisconsin T78+445 91
Fort Hunter, New York S85+429 96
Fortin Teniente Montania,
 Paraguay S00-220 103
Fortin Camacho, Paraguay S02-221 103
Fortin Lopez, Paraguay R89-214 103
Fortin Munoz, Paraguay S04-235 103
Fortin Saavedra, Paraguay S00-234 103
Fort Jameson, Zambia K74-138 83
Fort Kent, Maine S52+472 90
Fort Keogh, Montana V05+464 93
Fort Lallemand, Algeria M52+312 80
Fort Lamy, See N'Djamena
Fort Laperrine. See Tamanrasset
Fort Laramie, Wyoming U87+422 93
Fort Madison, Iowa U08+406 95
Fort Maginnis, Montana V25+472 93
Fort Morgan, Alabama T78+303 97
Fort Morgan, Colorado U83+402 94
Fort Munro, Pakistan H30+229 72
Fort Nelson & R., B.C. W17+590 88
Fort Ogden, Florida T41+271 97
Fort Peck, Montana V08+480 93
Fort Peck Res., Montana V16+476 93
Fort Pierre, S. Dakota U62+443 93
Fort Plain, New York S88+429 96
Fort Polignac, Alveria M40+262 80
Fort Portal, Uganda K88+006 83
Fort Randall, Alaska Y75+547 26
Fort Rice, N. Dakota U64+465 93
Fort Roseberry, Zambia L06-112 83
Fort St George. See Madras
Fort St John, B.C. W07+560 88
Fort Sandeman, Pakistan H31+314 72
Fort Saskatchewan, Alberta V48+539 88
Fort Scott, Kansas U28+378 95
Fort Sibut, Cent. Afr. Rep. L66+058 81
Fort Sill, Oklahoma U50+346 95
Fort Smith, Arkansas U26+353 95
Fort Smith, N.-W. Terr. V41+600 88
Fort Stedman, Burma F48+205 71
Fort Stockton, Texas U76+308 94
Fort Sumner, New Mexico U85+344 94
Fortuna, California T45+483 91
Fortuna, Spain N07+382 53
Fortune B., Newfoundland R66+471 90
Fort Valley, Georgia T53+326 97
Fort Vermilion, Alberta V65+586 88
Fort Victoria, Rhodesia K84-202 84
Fort Warren, Wyoming U89+412 93
Fort Wayne, Indiana T61+411 91
Fort White, Burma F67+234 71
Fort William, Scotland N31+568 41
Fort Worth, Texas U44+328 95
Fort Yates, N. Dakota U64+461 93
Fort Yukon, Alaska X60+663 99
Forville, Belgium M60+506 44
Fosse, Belgium M62+504 44
Foster, Victoria C23-386 109
Foster Ls., Saskatchewan V03+564 88
Fougeres, France N07+484 54
Foul I., Egypt K56+234 81
Foul, I., Burma F65+182 71
Foula, I., Scotland N12+602 34
Foulness I., England M85+516 39
Fouly, la, Switzerland M47+459 45
Foúrnoi, Is., Greece L21+376 59
Foveaux Strait, New Zealand A72-466 112
Fowchow. See Fowling.
Fowlers B., S. Australia D14-320 110
Fowling, China E76+297 67
Fowning, China E00+338 66
Fowyang, China E24+330 66
Fox Is., Aleutian Is. Z20+530 99
Fox R., Manitoba U27+556 88
Foxe Basin, N.-W.
 Territories T20+670 89
Foxe Chan., N.-W.
 Territories T30+650 89
Foxe Pen., N.-W. Terr. T10+647 89

Foxford, *Ireland, Rep.* N55+540 **42**
Fox River, *Quebec* S26+490 **90**
Foxton, *New Zealand* A28–404 **112**
Foyle L., *N. Ireland* N43+551 **42**
Foyle R., *N. Ireland* N44+550 **42**
Foynes, *Ireland, Rep.* N55+526 **43**
Foz do Acre, *Brazil* S44–088 **104**
Foz do Cunene, *Angola* M18–172 **84**
Foz Embira, *Brazil* S61–074 **104**
Fraire, *Belgium* M63+503 **44**
Framboise, *Nova Scotia* S02+457 **90**
Frameries, *Belgium* M67+504 **44**
Framingham, *Massachusetts* S69+423 **96**
Franca, *Brazil* R15–206 **105**
Francavilla Fontana, *Italy* L75+405 **57**
France, *W. Europe* M78+470 **50**
Frances, *S. Australia* C54–367 **109**
Frances L., *Yukon* W55+610 **88**
Franceville, *Gabon* M04–018 **82**
Franche-Comte, prov., *France* M50+472 **54**
Francistown, *Botswana* L14–214 **84**
Francois L., *British Columbia* W35+541 **88**
Frankfort, *Kansas* U39+397 **95**
Frankfort, *Kentucky* T59+383 **97**
Frankfort, *Michigan* T67+446 **91**
Frankfurt-am-Main, *W. Germany* M38+501 **48**
Frankfurt-an-der-Oder, *E. Germany* M03+523 **48**
Fränkischer Jura, *W. Germany* M21+492 **48**
Franklin, *Louisiana* U08+298 **95**
Franklin, *New Hampshire* S70+434 **96**
Franklin, *New Jersey* S87+411 **96**
Franklin, *N. Carolina* T50+352 **97**
Franklin, *Pennsylvania* T29+414 **96**
Franklin, *Tasmania* C19–432 **111**
Franklin, *Tennessee* T71+358 **97**
Franklin, *Virginia* T12+367 **97**
Franklin, *W. Virginia* T26+386 **97**
Franklin Dist., *N.-W. Terr.* **88–89**
Franklin, I., *Antarctica* A68–760 **27**
Franklin Mts., *N.-W. Territories* W25+656 **88**
Franklin City, *Virginia* T02+380 **97**
Franklin Falls, *N.H.* S70+434 **91**
Frantsa Iosifa Zemlya, *Arctic Ocean* J30+810 **62**
Franz Josef Fd., *Greenland* P85+740 **26**
Franz Josef Land, *See* Frantsa Iosifa Zemlya.
Fraser R., *British Columbia* W13+514 **88**
Fraserburg, *Cape Province* L50–320 **84**
Fraserburgh, *Scotland* N12+577 **40**
Frasertown, *New Zealand* A15–390 **112**
Frasnes, *Belgium* M68+507 **44**
Frater, *Ontario* T57+473 **91**
Frauenfeld, *Switzerland* M37+476 **45**
Fray Bentos, *Uruguay* R80–332 **103**
Fredericia, *Denmark* M31+556 **47**
Frederick, *Maryland* T14+394 **96**
Frederick, *Oklahoma* U54+344 **95**
Frederick, *S. Dakota* U51+458 **93**
Fredericksburg, *Virginia* T15+383 **97**
Fredericktown, *Missouri* U02+375 **95**
Fredericton, *New Brunswick* S40+460 **90**
Frederikshåb, *Greenland* R30+620 **26**
Frederikshavn, *Denmark* M27+575 **47**
Fredonia, *Colombia* T04+060 **104**
Fredonia, *Kansas* U35+376 **95**
Fredonia, *New York* T26+425 **96**
Fredrika, *Sweden* L70+641 **46**
Fredrikstad, *Norway* M24+592 **47**
Freehold, *New Jersey* S85+402 **96**
Freeling, *S. Australia* C67–345 **109**
Freeport, *Illinois* T88+423 **95**
Freeport, *Pennsylvania* T29+407 **96**
Freetown, *Sierra Leone* N80+086 **80**
Fregenal de la Sierra, *Spain* N40+382 **52**
Fréhel, C., *France* N14+487 **54**
Freiberg, *E. Germany* M10+510 **48**
Freiburg, *W. Germany* M43+480 **48**
Freirina, *Chile* S67–284 **103**
Freistadt, *Austria* M03+485 **48**
Freital, *E. Germany* M08+511 **48**
Freixiel, *Portugal* N44+413 **52**
Freixo, *Portugal* N41+411 **52**
Fremantle, *W. Australia* E25–320 **110**
Fremont, *Nebraska* U38+414 **95**
Fremont, *Ohio* T49+414 **91**
Fremont Pk., *Wyoming* V28+432 **93**
Fremont R., *Utah* V35+386 **94**
French I., *Victoria* C28–383 **109**
French R., *Ontario* T32+460 **91**
French Guiana, rep., *S. America* R50+036 **105**
Frenchman R., *Saskatchewan* V20+493 **93**
Frenchman Cap, *Tasmania* C24–423 **109**
Frenchpark, *Ireland, Rep.* N50+539 **42**
French River, *Ontario* T36+459 **91**
French Territory of the Afars and the Issas (F.T.A.I.), *E. Africa* K10+115 **83**
Fresko, *Ivory Coast* N36+050 **80**
Fresnillo, *Mexico* U77+232 **100**
Fria, C., *S.-W. Africa* M18–184 **84**
Fresno, *California* V89+368 **92**
Frias, *Spain* N20+428 **52**
Fribourg & canton, *Switz.* M47+468 **45**
Fridtjof Nansen Mt., *Antarctica* A10–850 **27**
Friedland, *E. Germany* M09+536 **48**
Friend, *Nebraska* U44+406 **95**
Friesische Is., Nord., *W. Ger.* M39+546 **47**
Friesische Is., Ost., *W. Germany* M52+538 **48**
Friesland, prov., *Netherlands* M54+531 **44**
Friuli-Venezia Giulia, reg., *Italy* M12+462 **56**
Frobisher B., *N.-W. Terr.* S30+618 **89**
Frobisher L., *Saskatchewan* V20+564 **88**
Fro Havet, *Norway* M35+638 **46**
Frome, *England* N14+512 **38**
Frome, L., *S. Australia* C61–308 **109**
Front Ra., *Colorado* V04+400 **94**
Fronteira, *Portugal* N46+390 **52**
Frontera, *Mexico* U16+186 **100**
Fronteras, *Mexico* V27+310 **100**
Front Royal, *Virginia* T18+389 **96**
Frosinone, *Italy* M10+416 **57**
Frostburg, *Maryland* T24+397 **96**

Frøya, *Norway* M38+637 **46**
Frozen Str., *N.-W. Terr.* T55+658 **89**
Frunze, *Kirgiz.* H02+429 **62**
Frutigen, *Switzerland* M44+466 **45**
Frvdek, *Czechoslovakia* L70+497 **49**
F.T.A.I. (French Territory of the Afars and the Issas), *E. Africa* K10+114 **83**
Fthiótis, *Greece* L45+388 **59**
Fuchin, *China* D20+474 **64**
Fuchow, *China* E22+280 **67**
Fu-chow, *China* D81+397 **66**
Fuente-Alamo de Murcia, *Sp.* N07+378 **53**
Fuente del Arco, *Spain* N35+382 **52**
Fuentes de Onoro, *Spain* N41+406 **52**
Fuerteventura, I., *Canary Islands* N82+284 **80**
Fuerte, El, *Mexico* V20+268 **100**
Fuerte, R., *Mexico* V22+262 **100**
Fuhsin, *China* D80+421 **66**
Fuji yama (Fuji san), *Japan* C66+354 **68**
Fukien, prov., *China* E12+260 **67**
Fukuei Chiao, *Taiwan* D80 + 255 **64**
Fukui, *Japan* C82+360 **68**
Fukuoka, *Japan* D28+335 **68**
Fukushima, *Japan* C57+377 **68**
Fukuyama, *Japan* C59+415 **68**
Fukuyama, *Japan* D16+345 **68**
Fulda, R., *W. Germany* M33+511 **48**
Fullerton, *Nebraska* U48+414 **95**
Fulton, *Kentucky* T83+365 **97**
Fulton, *Mississippi* T81+343 **97**
Fulton, *Missouri* U12+388 **95**
Fulton, *New York* T07+433 **96**
Fulton Chain Ls., *New York* S89+437 **96**
Funchal, *Madeira I.* P10+326 **80**
Fundão, *Portugal* N45+402 **52**
Fundy, B. of, *N.S., N.B.* S37+448 **90**
Fünen, *See* Fyn.
Fünfkirchen, *See* Pécs.
Funing, *See* Siapu.
Fure, *Japan* C49+446 **68**
Furg, *Iran* J29+283 **75**
Furneaux Grp., *Tasmania* C13–400 **109**
Furnes, *See* Veurne.
Furqlus, *Syria* K47+346 **76**
Fürth, *W. Germany* M24+494 **48**
Furue, *Japan* D25+314 **68**
Fusagasuga, *Colombia* S86+042 **104**
Fushih, *China* E63+365 **66**
Fushimi, *Japan* C85+350 **68**
Fu-shun, *China* D66+419 **66**
Fusio, *Switzerland* M38+464 **45**
Fuyu, *China* D61+452 **64**
Fyn, *Denmark* M28+553 **47**
Fyne, L., *Scotland* N31+561 **41**
Gabaidu, *Iran* K28–018 **83**
Gabandi, *Iran* J41+272 **75**
Gaberones, *Botswana* L24–246 **84**
Gabès & G. of, *Tunisia* M30+338 **81**
Gabin, *Poland* L62+524 **49**
Gabon, rep., *Cent. Africa* M26–006 **82**
Gabrovo, *Bulgaria* L28+429 **58**
Gach Saran, *Iran* J50+302 **75**
Gadag, *India* G86+155 **70**
Gadsden, *Alabama* T66+340 **97**
Gael Hamkes B., *Greenland* P34+740 **26**
Gaeşti, *Romania* L28+447 **58**
Gaeta & G. di, *Italy* M09+412 **57**
Gafsa, *Tunisia* M38+344 **81**
Gagetown, *New Brunswick* S37+457 **90**
Gagnon, *Quebec* S43+516 **89**
Gaibanda, *Bangladesh* G02+253 **73**
Gáidharos, I., *Greece* L18+375 **59**
Gáillac, *France* M78+439 **55**
Gaiman, *Argentina* S34–433 **103**
Gainesboro, *Tennessee* T64+363 **97**
Gainesville, *Alabama* T79+328 **97**
Gainesville, *Florida* T44+296 **97**
Gainesville, *Georgia* T53+342 **97**
Gainesville, *Missouri* U15+366 **97**
Gainsborough, *England* N05+534 **37**
Gainsville, *Texas* U42+336 **95**
Gairdner, L., *S. Australia* C85–316 **111**
Gairloch, *Scotland* N34+577 **40**
Gairlochy, *Scotland* N30+569 **40**
Gala Water, *Scotland* N17+556 **41**
Galag, *Iran* J03+255 **75**
Galangue, *Angola* L82–138 **82**
Galapagos Is., *Pacific Ocean* U00–007 **107**
Galashiels, *Scotland* N17+556 **41**
Galatea, *New Zealand* A20–384 **112**
Galathea B., *Nicobar Is.* F67+066 **71**
Galati, *Romania* L12+454 **58**
Galatz. *See* Galaţi.
Galax, *Virginia* T36+366 **97**
Galcaio, *Somalia* J76+066 **83**
Galdhøpiggen, mt., *Norway* M40+616 **47**
Galeana, *Mexico* U60+248 **100**
Galeana, *Mexico* V15+301 **100**
Galena, *Illinois* U03+424 **95**
Galesburg, *Illinois* U02+410 **95**
Galeton, *Pennsylvania* T16+417 **96**
Galich, *U.S.S.R.* K16+584 **61**
Galilee, L., *Queensland* C25–222 **111**
Galilee, Sea of. *See* Tiberias L.
Galiuro Mts., *Arizona* V32+326 **94**
Gallatin, *Tennessee* T69+364 **97**
Galle, *Sri Lanka* G59+060 **70**
Gallego, *Mexico* V08+298 **94**
Gallegos R., *Argentina* S56–516 **103**
Galley Hd., *Ireland, Rep.* N54+515 **43**
Gallipoli (Gelibolu), *Turkey* L20+408 **59**
Gallipoli, *Italy* L72+401 **57**
Gällivare, *Sweden* L56+670 **46**
Gallo Mts., *New Mexico* V20+341 **94**
Galloway, Mull of, *Scotland* N29+546 **41**
Gallup, *New Mexico* V23+356 **94**
Galong, *New South Wales* C09–346 **109**
Galt, *Ontario* T32+434 **91**
Galty Mts., *Ireland, Rep.* N49+523 **43**
Galtymore, *Ireland, Rep.* N49+524 **43**
Galva, *Illinois* U01+412 **91**
Galveston and B., *Texas* U29+293 **95**
Galvez, *Argentina* S07–320 **103**
Galway (Gaillimh), *Ireland, Rep.* N54+533 **43**
Galway B., *Ireland Rep.* N55+532 **43**
Gambaga, *Ghana* N02+106 **80**
Gambia, rep., *W. Africa* P05+130 **80**
Gambia, R., *W. Africa* P00+136 **80**

Gambo, *Newfoundland* R55+488 **90**
Gams, *Switzerland* M33+472 **45**
Gananoque, *Ontario* T07+443 **91**
Gand. *See* Gent
Gandak R., *India* G32+267 **73**
Gandava, *Pakistan* H45+286 **70**
Gander (Airport) & L., *Nfd.* R58+489 **90**
Gandesa, *Spain* M88+411 **53**
Gandia, *Spain* N01+390 **53**
Ganganagar, *India* H07+290 **72**
Gangaw, *Burma* F65+221 **71**
Ganges (Ganga), R., *India* G33+256 **73**
Gangoh, *India* G76+298 **72**
Gangtok, *Sikkim* G08+273 **73**
Ganjam, *India* G29+194 **71**
Ganmam, *New South Wales* C18–348 **109**
Gannat, *France* M71+461 **54**
Gannett Pk., *Wyoming* V28+432 **93**
Gantheame B., *W. Australia* E37–274 **110**
Ganza, *Cent. Afr. Rep.* L44+078 **81**
Gao, *Mali* N00+162 **80**
Gaoual, *Guinea* N80+118 **80**
Gara L., *Ireland, Rep.* N51+539 **42**
Garachine, *Panama* T19+080 **101**
Garah, *New South Wales* C02–290 **109**
Garanhuns, *Brazil* Q38–089 **105**
Garba Tula, *Kenya* K38+004 **83**
Gard, dep., *France* M64+440 **55**
Garda, L. di, *Italy* M26+457 **56**
Gardafui, C., *Somalia* J52+118 **83**
Garden, *Michigan* T69+458 **91**
Garden City, *Kansas* U66+380 **94**
Gardiner, *Maine* S59+442 **90**
Gardiner, *Montana* V35+450 **93**
Gardiner, *Oregon* W24+438 **92**
Gardiners, B. & I., *New York* S73+411 **96**
Gardner I., *Hawaiian Is.* Z15+250 **106**
Gardula, *Ethiopia* K44+058 **83**
Garelochhead, *Scotland* N29+561 **41**
Garfield, *Utah* V43+408 **94**
Gar Gunsa, *Tibet* G60+321 **70**
Garha, *India* G72+250 **73**
Garhmuktesar, *India* G73+288 **72**
Garhshankar, *India* G82+312 **72**
Garibaldi, *Brazil* R40–293 **103**
Garibaldi Park, *B.C.* W20+500 **88**
Garies, *Cape Province* L72–306 **84**
Gariganus, *S.-W. Africa* L72–262 **84**
Garissa, *Kenya* K30–006 **83**
Garland, *Montana* V06+459 **93**
Garm, *Tadzhik* H27+390 **62**
Garmsar, *Iran* J47+353 **75**
Garo Hills, *India* F87+254 **71**
Garonne, R., *France* M83+438 **55**
Garoua, *Cameroun* M10+092 **81**
Garraway, *Liberia* N48+046 **80**
Garrison & Res., *N. Dakota* U69+477 **93**
Garron Pt., *N. Ireland* N36+550 **42**
Garrovillas, *Spain* N39+397 **52**
Garry, L., *N.-W. Territories* U60+659 **88**
Garsen, *Kenya* K30–024 **83**
Garstang, *England* N17+539 **37**
Gartok, *Tibet* G58+318 **70**
Garvagh, *N. Ireland* N40+550 **42**
Gary, *Indiana* T74+416 **91**
Garza, *Argentina* S22–281 **103**
Garzon, *Colombia* T04+021 **104**
Gascogne, G. de, *Fr.-Sp.* N12+437 **55**
Gascogne, prov., *France* M88+435 **55**
Gasconade R., *Missouri* U11+380 **97**
Gascoyne, R., *W. Australia* E16–252 **110**
Gasharbrum, mt., *Kashmir* G80+358 **72**
Gaspé, *Quebec* S37+488 **90**
Gaspé, B. & C., *Quebec* S25+488 **90**
Gaspé Pen., *Quebec* S33+488 **90**
Gaspésia Park, *Quebec* S38+488 **90**
Gasselte, *Netherlands* M49+530 **44**
Gastonia, *N. Carolina* T37+352 **97**
Gastre, *Argentina* S56–421 **103**
Gat (Ghat), *Libya* M30+246 **81**
Gata, *Spain* N39+402 **52**
Gata, C., *Cyprus* K72+345 **76**
Gate City, *Virginia* T45+366 **97**
Gateshead, *England* N09+550 **37**
Gatineau R., *Quebec* T06+460 **91**
Gatooma, *Rhodesia* L00–184 **84**
Gatun L., *Panama* T29+092 **101**
Gaud-i-Zirreh, *Afghanistan* H80+297 **75**
Gauhati, *India* F79+262 **71**
Gaurihar, *India* G38+256 **73**
Gavdhos, I., *Crete* L36+348 **59**
Gaviao, *Portugal* N48+394 **52**
Gävle, *Sweden* L78+607 **47**
Gävle Bukten, *Sweden* L75+608 **47**
Gawler, *S. Australia* C68–346 **109**
Gawler Ra., *S. Australia* C85–325 **111**
Gaya, *India* G30+248 **73**
Gaya, *Niger* M70+118 **80**
Gayaza, *Uganda* K86–008 **83**
Gaylord, *Michigan* T58+450 **91**
Gaza, *Cent. Afr. Rep.* L88+046 **81**
Gaza, *Egypt* K63+315 **76**
Gazeh Manzil, *Iran* H85+258 **75**
Gazi Antep, *Turkey* K46+371 **74**
Cazik, *Iran* H89+330 **75**
Gdansk, *Poland* L68+544 **49**
Gdynia, *Poland* L69+545 **49**
Gebit, *Sudan* K50+190 **81**
Gedaref, *Sudan* K56+140 **81**
Gedinne, *Belgium* M60+500 **44**
Geel, *Belgium* M60+512 **44**
Geelong, *Victoria* C34–382 **109**
Geeraardsbergen, *Belgium* M67+508 **44**
Geeveston, *Tasmania* C19–432 **109**
Geh, *Iran* H89+262 **75**
Geikie R., *Saskatchewan* U88+571 **88**
Gela, *Sicily* M04+371 **57**
Gelderland, *Netherlands* M54+521 **44**
Geldrop, *Netherlands* M57+514 **44**
Ge ibolu, *Turkey* L20+405 **74**
Ge inden, *Belgium* M58+508 **44**
Geisenkirchen, *Germany* M47+516 **48**
Gemas, *Malaya* F14+026 **69**
Gemblowx, *Belgium* M62+506 **44**
Gemena, *Zaire* L60+032 **82**
Gemert, *Netherlands* M56+516 **44**
Gemmenich, *Belgium* M54+507 **44**
Gemmi Pass, *Switzerland* M44+464 **45**
Gemville, *New South Wales* C43–309 **109**
Genappe, *Belgium* M63+506 **44**
Gendringen, *Netherlands* M52+519 **44**

Genemuiden, *Netherlands* M54+526 **44**
General Acha, *Argentina* S28–374 **103**
General Alvear, *Argentina* S00–360 **103**
General Capdevila, *Argentina* S09–274 **103**
General Grant Nat. Pk., *Cal.* V84+367 **92**
General Guido, *Argentina* R77–366 **103**
General La Madrid, *Argent.* S08–373 **103**
General Lavalle, *Argentina* R72–364 **103**
General MacArthur, *Phil.* D57+115 **65**
General Pico, *Argentina* S23–356 **103**
General Pinto, *Argentina* S12–348 **103**
General Roca, *Argentina* S46–390 **103**
General Viamonte, *Argentina* S06–350 **103**
General Villegas, *Argentina* S18–350 **103**
Geneseo, *New York* T17+428 **96**
Geneva, *Nebraska* U46+405 **95**
Geneva, *New York* T12+428 **96**
Geneva. L. of. *See* Leman, Lac
Genève (Geneva), *Switz.* M53+462 **45**
Genipapo, *Brazil* R04–044 **105**
Genkai Nada, *Japan* D30+337 **68**
Gennargentu, Mte. del, *Sardinia* M34+400 **57**
Gennep, *Netherlands* M54+517 **44**
Genoa. *See* Genova
Genoa, *Victoria* C03–374 **109**
Genova, *Italy* M37+444 **56**
Genova, G. di, *Italy* M36+440 **56**
Gent, *Belgium* M47+349 **45**
Geographe B., *W. Australia* E28–334 **110**
Geographe Chan., *W. Aust.* E38–250 **110**
Georga Zemlya, *Arctic Oc.* J70+805 **62**
George L., *New S. Wales* C04–352 **109**
George L., *New York* S81+436 **96**
George R., *Quebec* S33+580 **89**
George Town, *Gr. Cayman, W.I.* T38+194 **101**
Georgetown, *Guyana* R79+066 **104**
Georgetown, *Delaware* T02+387 **91**
Georgetown, *Quebec* T61+319 **91**
George Town, *Pinang I., Malaya* F28+054 **69**
Georgetown, *Pr. Edward I.* S15+462 **90**
Georgetown, *S. Carolina* T26+333 **97**
George Town, *Tasmania* C19–411 **109**
Georgetown, *Virginia* T13+389 **96**
Georgia, state, *U.S.A.* T50+330 **99**
Georgian B., *Ontario* T36+455 **91**
Georgian B. Is. Nat. Pk., *Ont.* T30+450 **91**
Georgiyevka, *Kazakh.* G51+493 **62**
Georgiyevsk, *U.S.S.R.* K09+442 **62**
Georgina, R., *Queensland* C71–216 **111**
Gera, *E. Germany* M17+509 **48**
Geraldine, *New Zealand* A53–440 **112**
Geraldton, *W. Australia* E32–286 **110**
Geremoabo, *Brazil* Q50–101 **105**
Gérgal, *Spain* N08+371 **53**
Gerlach, *Nevada* V85+408 **92**
Germania, *Argentina* S12–346 **103**
Germania Land, *Greenland* P30+770 **26**
Germany, E. & W., *Central Europe* **48**
Gerona, *Spain* M73+420 **53**
Gers, dep., *France* M87+437 **55**
Gerze, *Turkey* K58+418 **74**
Getafe, *Spain* N22+403 **52**
Gethsemani, *Quebec* S03+503 **90**
Gettysburg, *Pennsylvania* T14+398 **96**
Gettysburg, *S. Dakota* U60+450 **93**
Getz Ice Shelf, *Antarctica* W10–750 **27**
Gevar, *Turkey* K04+376 **74**
Gevgelija, *Yugoslavia* L45+412 **58**
Ghabaghib, *Syria* K53+332 **76**
Ghaghra, R., *India* G42+266 **73**
Ghaida, *Yemen, South* J67+142 **74**
Ghail, *Saudi Arabia* J82+226 **74**
Ghana, W. Afr. N10+081 **80**
Gharandal, *Jordan* K59+301 **76**
Ghardaia, *Algeria* M68+322 **80**
Gharian, *Libya* M12+322 **50**
Ghat, *Saudi Arabia* K00+260 **74**
Ghatal, *India* G13+227 **73**
Ghatampur, *India* G59+261 **73**
Ghatghat, *Saudi Arabia* J82+245 **74**
Ghats, Eastern, *India* G56+172 **70**
Ghats, Western, *India* H06+177 **70**
Ghauta, *Saudi Arabia* J79+222 **74**
Ghaziabad, *India* G75+286 **72**
Ghazipur, *India* G38+256 **73**
Ghazir, *Lebanon* K56+340 **76**
Ghazni, *Afghanistan* H39+336 **75**
Ghazir, *Afghanistan* H81+344 **75**
Ghotki, *Pakistan* H34+280 **70**
Giant's Causeway, *N. Ireland* N39+552 **42**
Giaour Dagh, *Turkey* K52+366 **74**
Giarabub, *Libya* L34+296 **81**
Giarre, *Sicily* L89+377 **57**
Gibara, *Cuba* T07+211 **101**
Gibeon, *S.-W. Africa* L74–252 **84**
Gibraltar, *Spain* N32+361 **52**
Gibraltar, Str. of, *Spain-Morocco* N33+359 **52**
Gibson Desert, *W. Aust.* D60–237 **110**
Giddings, *Texas* U42+302 **95**
Gien, *France* M74+477 **54**
Giessen, *Germany* M38+505 **48**
Gifford, *Scotland* N16+559 **41**
Gifhorn, *W. Germany* M27+525 **48**
Gifu, *Japan* C79+353 **68**
Giganta, La, *Mexico* V39+261 **100**
Gijon, *Spain* N34+435 **52**
Gila Desert, *Arizona* V50+323 **98**
Gila R., *Arizona, etc.* V30+330 **94**
Gilau, *Romania* L40+467 **58**
Gilbert Is., *Pacific Ocean* A35+007 **106**
Gilbert, R., *Queensland* C47–172 **111**
Gilbués, *Brazil* Q89–096 **105**
Gilehdar, *Iran* J43+276 **75**
Gilgandra, *New S. Wales* C08–317 **109**
Gilgil, *Kenya* K30+003 **83**
Gilgit & R., *Kashmir* H04+359 **72**
Gilgunnia, *New S. Wales* C24–324 **109**
Gill L., *Ireland, Rep.* N50+542 **42**
Gillett, *Arkansas* U09+341 **97**
Gillette, *Wyoming* V03+443 **93**

Gillingham, *England* M87+514 **39**
Gimel, *Switzerland* M52+465 **45**
Ginir, *Ethiopia* K26+070 **83**
Ginzo, *Spain* N46+420 **52**
Gioia, G. di, *Italy* L86+385 **57**
Giornico, *Switzerland* M37+464 **45**
Girardot, *Colombia* S89+042 **104**
Girdle Ness, *Scotland* N12+571 **40**
Giresun, *Turkey* K40+409 **74**
Girga, *Egypt* K78+264 **81**
Giridih, *India* G22+242 **73**
Girilambone, *New S. Wales* C19–312 **109**
Girishk, *Afghanistan* H62+318 **75**
Gironde, dep., *France* N02+448 **55**
Gironde, R., *France* N06+453 **54**
Girvan & R., *Scotland* N29+553 **41**
Gisborne, *New Zealand* A12–387 **112**
Gisors, *France* M79+493 **54**
Giswil, *Switzerland* M41+468 **45**
Gitch, mt., *Ethiopia* K40+132 **83**
Giurgiu, *Romania* L24+439 **58**
Givry, *Belgium* M66+504 **44**
Gizhiga, *U.S.S.R.* B26+621 **63**
Giżycko, *Poland* L49+541 **49**
Gjinokaster, *Albania* L59+401 **59**
Gjoa Haven, *N.-W. Terr.* U43+681 **88**
Gjøvik, *Norway* M26+608 **47**
Glabbeek-Zuurbemde, *Belg.* M60+509 **44**
Glace Bay, *Nova Scotia* S00+462 **90**
Glacier, *British Columbia* V75+511 **88**
Glacier Nat. Park, *Montana* V50+485 **98**
Gladstone, *Michigan* T72+459 **91**
Gladstone, *New S. Wales* B73–310 **109**
Gladstone, *Queensland* B82–237 **111**
Gladstone, *S. Australia* C70–332 **109**
Gladstone, *Tasmania* C13–410 **109**
Gladwin, *Michigan* T57+440 **91**
Glamis, *Scotland* N18+566 **41**
Glamoc, *Yugoslavia* L79+441 **56**
Glamorgan, W. Mid. & S., co., *Wales* N22+517 **38**
Glanaruddery Mts., *Ireland, Rep.* N57+523 **43**
Glärnisch, mt., *Switzerland* M36+470 **45**
Glarus & canton, *Switz.* M36+471 **45**
Glasgow, *Kentucky* T65+370 **97**
Glasgow, *Montana* V10+482 **93**
Glasgow, *Scotland* N26+558 **41**
Glass L., *Scotland* N27+577 **40**
Glassboro, *New Jersey* T00+397 **96**
Glauchau, *E. Germany* M15+508 **48**
Glazov, *U.S.S.R.* J44+582 **61**
Glen, *New Hampshire* S67+441 **91**
Glen Affric, *Scotland* N30+572 **40**
Glenarm, *N. Ireland* N36+550 **42**
Glenburnie, *S. Australia* C54–378 **109**
Glencoe, *Minnesota* U25+448 **93**
Glendale, *Arizona* V44+334 **94**
Glendale, *California* V80+342 **92**
Glencoe, *S. Australia* C57–377 **109**
Glendive, *Montana* U88+471 **93**
Glendowan Mts., *Ireland, Rep.* N48+550 **42**
Gleneagles, *Scotland* N22+563 **41**
Glenelg, *Scotland* N34+572 **40**
Glenelg, *S. Australia* C69–350 **109**
Glenfinnan, *Scotland* N33+568 **41**
Glengad Hd., *N. Ireland* N43+553 **42**
Glengariff, *Ireland, Rep.* N57+517 **43**
Glen Garry, *Scotland* N30+571 **40**
Glenhope, *New Zealand* A44–416 **112**
Glen Innes, *New S. Wales* B80–298 **109**
Glenluce, *Scotland* N29+549 **41**
Glen Lyon, *Scotland* N26+566 **41**
Glennamaddy, *Ireland, Rep.* N51+536 **42**
Glenreagh, *New S. Wales* B73–300 **109**
Glenrock, *Wyoming* V05+428 **93**
Glenrothes, *Scotland* N19+562 **41**
Glens Falls, *New York* S82+433 **91**
Glen Shee, *Scotland* N20+567 **41**
Glenties, *Ireland, Rep.* N50+548 **42**
Glenville, *West Virginia* T35+389 **91**
Glenwood, *Iowa* U34+410 **95**
Glenwood, *Minnesota* U33+457 **93**
Glenwood Springs, *Colorado* V14+395 **94**
Gletsch, *Switzerland* M40+466 **45**
Glittertind, mt., *Norway* M38+613 **47**
Gliwice, *Poland* L68+503 **49**
Globe, *Arizona* V35+333 **94**
Głogau. See Głogów.
Głogów, *Poland* L84+517 **49**
Gloppen, *Norway* M53+618 **46**
Glossop, *England* N12+535 **37**
Gloucester, *Massachusetts* S64+426 **96**
Gloucester, *New Jersey* T01+399 **96**
Gloucester, *New S. Wales* B79–320 **109**
Gloucester, *Virginia* T09+374 **97**
Gloucester & co., *England* N13+519 **39**
Gloversville, *New York* S86+430 **96**
Glukhov, *Ukraine* K66+516 **60**
Glyndebourne, *England* N00+509 **39**
Gmünd, *Austria* M09+469 **48**
Gmünd, *W. Germany* M31+488 **48**
Gmunden, *Austria* M07+479 **48**
Gniew, *Poland* L92+526 **48**
Gniezno, *Poland* L75+525 **49**
Goa, Daman & Diu, *India* H06+155 **70**
Goalpara, *India* F86+261 **71**
Goalundo, *Bangladesh* G01+238 **73**
Gobabis, *S.-W. Africa* L66–224 **84**
Gobi, des., *Mongolia, etc.* F00+430 **63**
Gobindpur, *India* G20+238 **73**
Godavari R., *India* G63+186 **70**
Godda, *India* G16+248 **73**
Godech, *Bulgaria* L42+430 **58**
Goderich, *Ontario* T40+437 **91**
Godhra, *India* H07+228 **70**
Gods L., *Manitoba* U35+548 **88**
Gods R., *Manitoba* U20+552 **89**
Godthåb, *Greenland* R32+640 **26**
Goes, *Netherlands* M67+515 **44**
Gogama, *Ontario* T41+476 **91**
Gogebic Ra., *Michigan* T88+467 **91**
Gog Magog Hills, *England* M87+522 **39**
Gogrial, *Sudan* L10+086 **81**
Gohana, *India* G80+291 **72**
Goiánia, *Brazil* R26–166 **105**
Goias, *Brazil* R31–158 **105**
Goil L., *Scotland* N29+561 **41**
Goirle, *Netherlands* M60+515 **44**
Goksun, *Turkey* K51+381 **74**

Golaghat, *India* F66+265 **71**
Golchikha, *U.S.S.R.* G37+718 **62**
Golconda, *Illinois* T81+374 **97**
Golconda, *India* G69+174 **70**
Gołdap, *Poland* L46+543 **49**
Gold Coast. See Ghana.
Golden, *Colorado* V02+398 **94**
Golden B., *New Zealand* A42–407 **112**
Golden Lake, *Ontario* T14+455 **91**
Golden Vale, *Ireland, Rep.* N45+525 **43**
Goldfield, *Nevada* V74+379 **92**
Goldsboro, *N. Carolina* T18+354 **97**
Goleniow, *Poland* M01+535 **48**
Gol Gol, *New South Wales* C46–342 **109**
Golmo, *China* F60+362 **64**
Golspie, *Scotland* N24+580 **40**
Goltva, *Ukraine* K67+494 **60**
Gomal Pass, *Pakistan* H29+321 **72**
Gomalcalco, *Mexico* U20+182 **100**
Gombe, *Nigeria* M24+102 **81**
Gomel, *Byelo Russia* K84+525 **60**
Gomera, I., *Canary Is.* P14+280 **80**
Gómez Farias, *Mexico* U66+248 **100**
Gomez Palacio, *Mexico* U81+256 **100**
Gonaïves, *Haiti* S75+194 **101**
Gonave, I. de la, *Haiti* S78+189 **101**
Gonda, *India* G48+271 **73**
Gondal, *India* H25+220 **70**
Gondo, *Switzerland* M41+462 **45**
Gongka Ling, *China* F26+286 **64**
Gongolgon, *New S. Wales* C19–304 **139**
Gondiadz, *Poland* L43+535 **49**
Gonzales, *Texas* U44+294 **95**
Goodenough I., *Papua New Guinea* B89–094 **111**
Gooderham, *Ontario* T20+449 **91**
Good Hope, *N.-W. Terr.* W52+661 **88**
Good Hope, C. of,
Cape Province L70–344 **84**
Goodland, *Kansas* U70+392 **94**
Goodooga, *New S. Wales* C16–292 **109**
Goodrich, *Wisconsin* U01+452 **91**
Goodwin Sands, *England* M79+512 **39**
Goole, *England* N05+537 **37**
Goomalling, *W. Australia* E19–312 **110**
Goombalie, *New S. Wales* C28–300 **109**
Goor, *Netherlands* M50+522 **44**
Goose L., *Oregon-California* W03+42) **92**
Goose Bay, *Labrador* S02+534 **89**
Gopalpur, *India* G31+192 **71**
Göppingen, *W. Germany* M32+487 **48**
Gor, *Spain* N18+374 **52**
Gora, *China* F36+292 **64**
Gorakhpur, *India* G40+268 **73**
Gordola, *Switzerland* M37+462 **45**
Gordon, *S. Australia* C71–321 **109**
Gordon, *Nebraska* U74+428 **94**
Gordon R., *Tasmania* C26–426 **109**
Gordonsville, *Virginia* T19+381 **97**
Gore, *Ethiopia* K56+080 **83**
Goré, *Chad* L80+078 **81**
Gore, *New Zealand* A66–461 **112**
Gore Bay, *Ontario* T45+459 **91**
Gorebridge, *Scotland* N18+558 **41**
Gorey, *Ireland, Rep.* N38+527 **43**
Gorgan, *Iran* J33+368 **75**
Gorgona, I., *Italy* M31+434 **56**
Gorinchem, *Netherlands* M60+518 **44**
Gorizia, *Italy* M08+460 **56**
Gor'kiy, *U.S.S.R.* K06+564 **61**
Gorlice, *Poland* L54+496 **49**
Görlitz, *E. Germany* L90+512 **48**
Gorlovka, *Ukraine* K42+484 **60**
Gormanstown, *Tasmania* C26–421 **109**
Gorodets, *U.S.S.R.* K10+567 **61**
Gorodishche, *U.S.S.R.* J86+533 **61**
Gorodnitsa, *Ukraine* L16+508 **60**
Goroke, *Victoria* C51–367 **109**
Gorontalo, *Celebes* D72+006 **65**
Gorrahei, *Ethiopia* K04+066 **83**
Gorsel, *Netherlands* M53+522 **44**
Gort, *Ireland, Rep.* N53+531 **43**
Gorumna I., *Ireland, Rep.* N58+532 **43**
Gorzów Wielkopolski,
Poland L89+527 **48**
Gosai Than, mt., *Nepal-Tibet* G25+283 **71**
Göschenen, *Switzerland* M38+467 **45**
Gosford, *New South Wales* B83–334 **109**
Goshanak, *Pakistan* H60+264 **70**
Goshen, *New York* S86+413 **96**
Gospić, *Yugoslavia* L88+446 **56**
Gosport, *England* N07+508 **39**
Gossa, *Norway* M49 + 629 **46**
Gossau, *Switzerland* M34+474 **45**
Gosselies, *Belgium* M63+505 **44**
Gostivar, *Yugoslavia* L54+418 **58**
Göta Älv, *Sweden* M17+581 **47**
Göteborg, *Sweden* M18+577 **47**
Gotha, *E. Germany* M26+510 **48**
Gothenburg. See Göteborg.
Gothenburg, *Nebraska* U61+409 **94**
Gotland, I., *Sweden* L68+575 **47**
Goto Retto, *Japan* D36+330 **68**
Gotska Sandon, *Sweden* L65+583 **47**
Göttingen, *W. Germany* M30+5 5 **48**
Gottwaldov, *Czechoslovakia* L74+492 **49**
Gouda, *Netherlands* M62+520 **44**
Goudswaard, *Netherlands* M65+518 **44**
Gough I., *Atlantic Ocean* M14–85 **8**
Gouin Res., *Quebec* S88+486 **90**
Goulburn, *New South Wales* C02–348 **109**
Goulburn R., *Victoria* C29–362 **109**
Gounarou, *Benin* M74 + 108 **80**
Goundam, *Mali* N22+164 **80**
Gouré, *Niger* M28+140 **81**
Gournay, *France* M80+495 **54**
Gourock, Ra., *New S. Wales* C04–358 **109**
Gouverneur, *New York* T03+4÷3 **91**
Gowanda, *New York* T34+424 **91**
Gower, pen., *Wales* N25+516 **38**
Gowna L., *Ireland, Rep.* N45+539 **42**
Goya, *Argentina* R86–291 **103**
Gozo, I. (Malta),
Mediterranean Sea M04+36 **57**
Graaff Reinet, *Cape Province* L32–324 **84**
Grabow, *Poland* L71+515 **49**
Gračac, *Yugoslavia* L85+443 **56**
Gracefield, *Quebec* T07+461 **91**
Gracias, *Honduras* T82+146 **101**
Gracias a Dios, *Nicaragua* T50+149 **101**

Gradets, *Bulgaria* L21+428 **58**
Grado, *Spain* N37+433 **52**
Grafton, *New South Wales* B73–297 **109**
Grafton, *N. Dakota* U44+484 **93**
Grafton, *W. Virginia* T30+393 **91**
Grafton, Is., *Chile* S80–542 **101**
Grahaju, *Brazil* Q79–068 **105**
Graham, *Texas* U51+331 **95**
Graham Ld. See Antarctic Pen. S25–660 **27**
Graham Bell, Os., *Arctic Oc.* H65+811 **62**
Grahamstown, *Cape Province* L20–332 **84**
Grain, *England* M86+514 **39**
Grajewo, *Poland* L45+537 **49**
Grammont. See Geeraardsbergen.
Grampian Mts., *Scotland* N26+567 **41**
Grampian, reg., *Scotland* N17+573 **40**
Grampians, mts., *Victoria* C45–372 **109**
Gramsbergen, *Netherlands* M50+526 **44**
Granada, *Nicaragua* T66+120 **101**
Granada, *Spain* N22+372 **52**
Granard, *Ireland, Rep.* N45+538 **43**
Granby, *Quebec* S77+454 **91**
Gran Canaria, I., *Canary Is.* P04+278 **80**
Gran Chaco, *Argentina* S14–270 **103**
Grand Can., *China* E24+375 **64**
Grand I., *Michigan* T70+465 **91**
Grand I., *New York* T24+430 **96**
Grand L., *Louisiana* U08+298 **95**
Grand L., *Louisiana* U16+298 **95**
Grand L., *Maine-N.B.* S45+456 **90**
Grand L., *New Brunswick* S36+460 **90**
Grand L., *Newfoundland* R74+490 **90**
Grand R., *Colorado* V06+400 **94**
Grand R., *Michigan* T61+429 **91**
Grand R., *S. Dakota* U80+456 **98**
Grand Bassa, *Liberia* N60+060 **80**
Grand Bassam, *Ivory Coast* N22+052 **80**
Grand Canyon, *Arizona* V50+356 **98**
Grand Canyon Nat. Park,
Arizona V45+362 **98**
Grand Cayman, I., *W. I.* T38+193 **101**
Grand Coulee Dam, *Wash.* V84+479 **98**
Grande, B., *Argentina* S50–505 **103**
Grande, Rio, *Brazil* R30–198 **105**
Grande, Sa, *Brazil* Q66–046 **105**
Grande Anse, *N.B.* S31+478 **90**
Grande Comore, I.,
Comoro Is., Africa K10–116 **83**
Grande de Santiago, R.,
Mexico U84+212 **100**
Grand Falls, *N.B.* S47+471 **90**
Grand Falls, *Newfoundland* R64+490 **90**
Grand Forks, *B.C.* V81+491 **88**
Grand Forks, *N. Dakota* U42+479 **93**
Grand Haven, *Michigan* T67+431 **91**
Grandin, L., *N.-W. Terr.* V88+640 **88**
Grand Island, *Nebraska* U50+408 **95**
Grand Junction, *Colorado* V22+390 **94**
Grand Junction, *Tennessee* T85+350 **97**
Grand Lahou, *Ivory Coast* N30+052 **80**
Grande Ledge, *Michigan* T58+428 **91**
Grand Manan I., *N.B.* S41+448 **90**
Grand Marais, *Minnesota* U02+477 **91**
Grand Mère, *Quebec* S76+466 **91**
Grand Mesa, *Colorado* V18+391 **94**
Grandola, *Portugal* N51+381 **52**
Grand Piles, *Quebec* S76+467 **91**
Grand Prarie, *Alberta* V84+554 **88**
Grand Rapids, *Michigan* T64+430 **91**
Grand Rapids, *Minnesota* U21+472 **93**
Grandrieu, *Belgium* M65+502 **44**
Grand River, *Quebec* S27+484 **90**
Grandson, *Switzerland* M50+468 **45**
Grand Teton Mt. & Nat. Park,
Wyoming V35+434 **98**
Grand Tower, *Illinois* T87+376 **97**
Grand Victoria L., *Quebec* T14+476 **91**
Grane, *Norway* M10+656 **46**
Graney L., *Ireland, Rep.* N52+530 **43**
Grangemouth, *Scotland* N22+560 **41**
Granger, *Wyoming* V30+416 **93**
Granite City, *Illinois* U02+387 **95**
Granite Falls, *Minnesota* U33+448 **93**
Granity, *New Zealand* A48–416 **112**
Granja, *Brazil* Q65–031 **105**
Grankulla, *Finland* L32+602 **47**
Granollers, *Spain* M76+416 **53**
Granön, *Sweden* L64+642 **46**
Grant, *Ontario* T69+501 **89**
Grant Ra., *Nevada* V63+388 **92**
Grant City, *Missouri* U26+404 **95**
Grantham, *England* N04+529 **37**
Granton, *Scotland* N19+560 **41**
Grantown-on-Spey, *Scotland* N21+573 **40**
Grants, *New Mexico* V17+351 **94**
Grants Pass, *Oregon* W20+425 **92**
Grantsville, *Utah* V45+406 **94**
Granville, *New York* S79+434 **96**
Granville, *N. Dakota* U65+483 **93**
Granville L., *Manitoba* U65+562 **88**
Granvin, *Norway* M50+605 **47**
Gras, L., de, *N.-W. Terr.* V35+646 **88**
Grasett, *Ontario* T57+485 **91**
Graskop, *Transvaal* K86–250 **84**
Grasmere, *England* N18+545 **37**
Gräsö, *Sweden* L70+604 **47**
Grassano, *Italy* L82+406 **57**
Grasse, *France* M49+437 **55**
Grassier. *Switzerland* M53+464 **45**
Graubünden, canton, *Switz.* M35+467 **45**
Graus, *Spain* M88+422 **53**
Gravarne, *Sweden* M22+583 **47**
Grave, *Netherlands* M56+518 **44**
Gravelbourg, *Saskatchewan* V09+499 **88**
's Gravenhage, *Netherlands* M64+521 **44**
Gravenhurst, *Ontario* T26+449 **91**
's Gravenzande, *Netherlands* M65+520 **44**
Gravesend, *England* M88+514 **39**
Gravesend, *New S. Wales* B88–296 **109**
Gray, *France* M57+474 **54**
Grayling, *Michigan* T59+447 **91**
Grayville, *Illinois* T78+383 **97**
Graz, *Austria* L87+471 **49**
Great L., *Tasmania* C20–419 **109**
Great Pt., *Massachusetts* S60+414 **96**
Great Australian Bight, *Aust.* D30–336 **110**
Great Barrier Reef, *Aust.* C05–190 **111**
Great Barrington, *Mass.* S80+422 **96**
Great Basin, *Nevada* V75+402 **98**
Great Bear L., *N.-W. Terr.* W00+658 **88**

Great Bend, *Kansas* U53+384 **95**
Great Basket I.,
Ireland, Rep. N63+521 **43**
Great Dividing Ra., *Aust.* C10–260 **111**
Great Driffield, *England* N03+540 **37**
Great Falls, *Montana* V38+475 **93**
Great Geysir, *Iceland* P31+643 **46**
Great Lake. See Tonle Sap.
Great Long L., *Quebec* S65+562 **89**
Great Malvern, *England* N14+521 **38**
Great North Mts., *W.Va., etc.* T23+389 **96**
Great Rapids, *Manitoba* U57+534 **88**
Great Salt L., *Utah* V46+419 **92**
Great Salt Lake Des., *Utah* V51+409 **92**
Great Sand Dunes Nat. Mon.,
Colorado V04+378 **94**
Great Sandy !. (Fraser I.),
Queensland B71–252 **111**
Great Slave L., *N.-W. Terr.* V60+610 **88**
Great Smoky Mts., *Tennessee* T52+356 **97**
Great Smoky Mts. Nat. Park,
Tennessee T52+357 **97**
Great South B., *New York* S79+406 **96**
Great Torrington, *England* N25+509 **38**
Great Victoria Des.,
W. Aust. D40–280 **110**
Great Wass I., *Maine* S46+445 **90**
Great Western Tiers,
Tasmania C22–418 **109**
Great Yarmouth, *England* M80+526 **39**
Grebbestad, *Sweden* M22+587 **47**
Greco C., *Cyprus* K65+349 **76**
Greece, S. *Europe* L48+380 **51**
Greeley, *Colorado* U88+404 **94**
Green B., *Wisconsin* T77+448 **91**
Green Mts., *Vermont* S77+438 **91**
Green Mts., *Wyoming* V14+424 **93**
Green R., *Kentucky* T3+375 **97**
Green R., *Utah, etc.* V30+386 **94**
Green Bay, *Wisconsin* T78+445 **91**
Greencastle, *Indiana* T70+396 **95**
Greenfield, *Indiana* T65+398 **91**
Greenfield, *Iowa* U26+412 **95**
Greenfield, *Massachusetts* S75+426 **96**
Greenland, *N. America* Q60+700 **26**
Greenland Sea, *Greenland* N50+760 **26**
Greenock, *Scotland* N29+559 **41**
Greenore Pt., *Ireland, Rep.* N38+522 **43**
Greenport, *New York* S74+411 **91**
Green River, *Utah* V31+390 **94**
Green River, *Wyoming* V27+415 **93**
Greensboro, *Georgia* T49+335 **97**
Greensboro, *N. Carolina* T29+361 **97**
Greensburg, *Kansas* U56+376 **95**
Greensburg, *Kentucky* T63+373 **97**
Greensburg, *Pennsylvania* T28+404 **96**
Greenville, *Alabama* T70+318 **97**
Greenville, *Illinois* T86+389 **95**
Greenville, *Kentucky* T73+372 **97**
Greenville, *Liberia* N54+050 **80**
Greenville, *Maine* S58+455 **90**
Greenville, *Michigan* T62+432 **91**
Greenville, *Mississippi* U00+334 **95**
Greenville, *Missouri* U03+372 **95**
Greenville, *N. Carolina* T14+356 **97**
Greenville, *S. Carolina* T45+348 **97**
Greenville, *Tennessee* T47+362 **97**
Greenville, *Texas* U36+332 **95**
Greenwich, *Connecticut* S82+410 **95**
Greenwich, *England* N00+515 **39**
Greenwich, *Rhode Island* S69+417 **96**
Greenwood, *S. Carolina* T43+342 **97**
Greenwood, *Wisconsin* U04+449 **91**
Greenwood L., *N.Y.-N.J.* S86+412 **96**
Gregory, *S. Dakota* U56+432 **93**
Gregory, L., *S. Australia* C66–290 **109**
Gregory Ra., *Queensland* C40–186 **111**
Greifen See, *Switzerland* M38+474 **45**
Greifswald, *Germany* M10+541 **48**
Grein, *Austria* M01+483 **48**
Greiz, *Germany* M17+506 **48**
Grenå, *Denmark* M25+564 **47**
Grenada, *Mississippi* T89+338 **97**
Grenada, I., *Windward Is.* S10+121 **101**
Grenadines, Is.,
Windward Is. S08+127 **101**
Grenchen, *Switzerland* M46+472 **45**
Grenfell, *New South Wales* C11–339 **109**
Grenoble, *France* M56+452 **55**
Grenora, *N. Dakota* U83+487 **93**
Grenville, C., *Queensland* C41–119 **111**
Gretna, *Louisiana* U00+298 **95**
Gretna, *Virginia* T27+369 **97**
Gretna Green, *Scotland* N18+550 **41**
Grevená, *Greece* L51+401 **59**
Grey Ra., *Qnsld.-N.S.W.* C50–288 **111**
Greybull, *Wyoming* V18+444 **93**
Greycliff, *Montana* V28+457 **93**
Greylock Mt., *Massachusetts* S79+427 **96**
Greymouth, *New Zealand* A52–425 **112**
Greys Butte, mt., *Oregon* V89+429 **92**
Greystones, *Ireland, Rep.* N36+531 **43**
Greytown, *New Zealand* A27–411 **112**
Greytown. See San Juan del Norte.
Griesalp, *Switzerland* M43+466 **45**
Griffin, *Georgia* T56+332 **97**
Griffith, *New South Wales* C24–343 **109**
Grim C., *Tasmania* C31–407 **109**
Grimsby, *England* N01+535 **37**
Grimstad, *Norway* M38+583 **47**
Grindelwald, *Switzerland* M42+466 **45**
Grindstone, *Michigan* T47+440 **91**
Grinnell, *Iowa* U16+417 **95**
Grinnell Pen., *N.-W. Terr.* U25+766 **88**
Griquatown, *Cape Province* L40–238 **84**
Griva *Latvia* L21+559 **47**
Grobina, *Latvia* L53+565 **47**
Gröbming, *Austria* M07+474 **48**
Grodno, *Byelo Russia* L37+537 **60**
Grodzisk, *Poland* L82+522 **49**
Groenlo, *Netherlands* M50+520 **44**
Groningen & prov.,
Netherlands M50+532 **44**
Grono, *Switzerland* M35+463 **45**
Groote Eylandt,
N. Terr., Aust C80–140 **111**
Grootfontein, *S.-W. Africa* L80–252 **84**
Grootfontein, *S.-W. Africa* L70–196 **84**

17

Groot Natuna, I., *Indonesia* E70+039 **65**
Grossevichi, *U.S.S.R.* C63+479 **63**
Gross Glockner, *Austria* M15+471 **48**
Grosswardein. *See* Oradea
Groton, *New York* T09+426 **96**
Groton, *S. Dakota* U49+455 **93**
Groznyy, *U.S.S.R.* J87+435 **62**
Grudziadz, *Poland* L67+535 **49**
Grues, l. aux, *Quebec* S63+471 **91**
Gruinard B., *Scotland* N33+579 **40**
Grüsch, *Switzerland* M32+470 **45**
Gruyère, Lac de, *Switz.* M47+467 **45**
Gruz, *Yugoslavia* L71+427 **58**
Gruzinskaya (Georgia), rep.,
  U.S.S.R. K10+422 **62**
Grybów, *Poland* L55+496 **49**
Gsteig, *Switzerland* M46+464 **45**
Guabito, Panama T46+096 **101**
Guacanayabo, G. de, *Cuba* T14+206 **101**
Guachipas, *Argentina* S33-256 **103**
Guadalaja, *Spain* N19+406 **52**
Guadalajara, *Mexico* U80+206 **100**
Guadalcanal, *Spain* N35+381 **52**
Guadalcanal, I., *Solomon Is.* B30-095 **106**
Guadalcazar, *Mexico* U62+226 **100**
Guadalquivir, R., *Spain* N30+376 **52**
Guadalupe, *Mexico* U75+227 **100**
Guadalupe I., *Mexico* V82+290 **100**
Guadalupe Mts.,
  New Mexico, Texas V00+320 **94**
Guadalupe R., *Texas* U47+296 **98**
Guadalupe-y-Calvo, *Mexico* V11+262 **100**
Guadarrama, *Spain* N25+407 **52**
Guadarrama, Sa. de, *Spain* N24+410 **52**
Guadeloupe, I., *Leeward Is.* S10+162 **101**
Guadiana, R., *Spain* N45+383 **52**
Guadix, *Spain* N19+373 **52**
Guafo & G. de, *Chile* S88-436 **103**
Guaitecas, Is., *Chile* S82-439 **103**
Guajar-a-Mirim, *Brazil* S32-108 **104**
Guajaratuba, *Brazil* S17-050 **104**
Gualeguaychu, *Argentina* R81-330 **103**
Guam, I., *Pacific Ocean* C30+140 **106**
Guamini, *Argentina* S15-370 **103**
Guamo, *Colombia* T00+040 **104**
Guanabacoa, *Cuba* T43+232 **101**
Guanabara, *Brazil* Q82-228 **105**
Guanacevi, *Mexico* V06+259 **100**
Guanahani. *See* San Salvador
Guanajuato, *Mexico* U67+212 **100**
Guanare, *Venezuela* S58+090 **104**
Guanarito, *Venezuela* S54+087 **104**
Guandacol, *Argentina* S52-295 **103**
Guane, *Cuba* T54+223 **101**
Guanica, *Puerto Rico* S41+180 **101**
Guanta, *Venezuela* S27+102 **104**
Guantanamo, *Cuba* T02+202 **101**
Guapi, *Colombia* T17+026 **104**
Guapiles, *Costa Rica* T53+102 **101**
Guapore, *Brazil* R41-289 **103**
Guapore (Rondonia), *Brazil* S31-118 **104**
Guapore, R., *Brazil-Bolivia* S16-128 **104**
Guaqui, *Bolivia* S54-166 **104**
Guarapuava, *Brazil* R40-255 **103**
Guarda, *Portugal* N43+406 **52**
Guasabas, *Mexico* V25+298 **100**
Guasdualito, *Venezuela* S64+072 **104**
Guasipati, *Venezuela* S11+074 **104**
Guatemala, *Guatemala* U03+146 **100**
Guatemala, rep.
  Cent. America U00+154 **100**
Guatrache, *Argentina* S22-378 **103**
Guaviare, R., *Colombia* S56+036 **104**
Guaxupe, *Brazil* R10-212 **105**
Guayabal, *Venezuela* S43+080 **104**
Guayama, *Puerto Rico* S36+181 **101**
Guayaquil, *Ecuador* T29-022 **104**
Guaymas, *Mexico* V35+279 **100**
Guazapares, *Mexico* V15+273 **100**
Guben, *E. Germany* M02+520 **48**
Gubin. *See* Guben
Gudiyatam, *India* G67+130 **70**
Guelma, *Algeria* M46+361 **80**
Guelph, *Ontario* T32+436 **91**
Guemes, *Argentina* S30-246 **103**
Guéret, *France* M79+462 **54**
Guernsey, I., *Channel Is.* N15+495 **54**
Guernsey Res., *Wyoming* U89+424 **93**
Guerrero, *Mexico* V13+284 **100**
Guerrero, *Tamaulipas, Mex.* U56+267 **100**
Guerrero, state, *Mexico* U60+176 **100**
Gugera, *Pakistan* H10+309 **72**
Guiana Highlands, *S. Amer.* R80+028 **104**
Guija, *Mozambique* K74-244 **84**
Guildford, *England* N03+512 **39**
Guildford, *Maine* S56+452 **90**
Guillaumes, *France* M49+441 **55**
Guilo, *Angola* L64-076 **82**
Guimaraes, *Brazil* Q88-020 **105**
Guimarães, *Portugal* N50+414 **52**
Guinea-Bissau, *N.-W. Afr.* P00+120 **80**
Guinea, *West Africa* N60+110 **80**
Guinea, G. of, *N.-W. Africa* M70+030 **82**
Guines, *Cuba* T42+231 **101**
Guingamp, *France* N19+485 **54**
Guiria, *Venezuela* S13+106 **104**
Guise, *France* M68+499 **54**
Guisisil, Vol., *Nicaragua* T67+127 **101**
Gujarat, state, *India* H07+218 **70**
Gujar Khan, *Pakistan* H11+333 **72**
Gujranwala, *Pakistan* H05+321 **72**
Gujrat, *Pakistan* H05+326 **72**
Gulargambone, *N.S.W.* C09-314 **109**
Gulbarga, *India* G78+173 **70**
Gulbene, *Latvia* L20+571 **47**
Gulfport, *Mississippi* T84+304 **95**
Gulgong, *New South Wales* C03-326 **109**
Gulistan, *Pakistan* H50+306 **70**
Gul Koh, *Afghanistan* H42+334 **75**
Gull L., *Quebec* T11+498 **89**
Gullane, *Scotland* N17+560 **41**
Gulpaigan, *Iran* J59+334 **75**
Gulpen, *Netherlands* M55+508 **44**
Gulran, *Afghanistan* H80+351 **75**
Gulu, *Uganda* K76+026 **83**
Gum, *India* K20+116 **83**
Gummersbach, *W. Germany* M45+510 **48**
Gümüljina, *See* Komotini
Gümüsane, *Turkey* K33+404 **74**
Guna, *India* G76+246 **73**
Gunbad-i-Qabuz, *Iran* J28+373 **75**

Gunbar, *New South Wales* C28-341 **109**
Gunchu, *Japan* D14+338 **68**
Gundagai, *New S. Wales* C12-351 **109**
Gunisao R., *Manitoba* U40+540 **88**
Gunnedah, *New S. Wales* B88-310 **109**
Gunning, *New South Wales* C05-348 **109**
Gunnislake, *England* N25+505 **38**
Gunnison, *Colorado* V12+386 **94**
Gunnison, *Utah* V42+392 **94**
Gunnison R., *Colorado* V14+385 **94**
Guntakal, *India* G75+152 **70**
Guntersville & L., *Alabama* T68+344 **97**
Guntur, *India* G57+164 **70**
Gurais, *Kashmir* H01+346 **72**
Gurdaspur, *India* G87+320 **72**
Gurdon, *Arkansas* U19+338 **95**
Gurgaon, *India* G78+285 **72**
Gurgl, *Austria* M24+469 **48**
Gurha, *India* H20+252 **70**
Gurkha, *Nepal* G32+280 **73**
Gurla Mandhata, mt., *Tibet* G51+304 **70**
Gurnigel, *Switzerland* M45+468 **45**
Gursköy, *Norway* M56+623 **46**
Gurupa, *Brazil* R39-015 **105**
Gurupa, I., *Brazil* R39-010 **105**
Guru Sikhar, *India* H13+247 **70**
Gur'yev, *Kazakh* J50+470 **62**
Gusev, *U.S.S.R.* L47+546 **47**
Gusht, *Iran* H78+277 **75**
Guspini, *Sardinia* M38+396 **57**
Gustav Holm, Kap, *Greenland* Q05+670 **26**
Güstrow, *E. Germany* M17+538 **48**
Guthrie, *Iowa* U27+416 **95**
Guthrie, *Kentucky* T73+367 **97**
Guthrie, *Oklahoma* U44+358 **95**
Guyana, *S. America* R84+050 **104**
Guyenne, prov., *France* M82+446 **55**
Guymon, *Oklahoma* U68+368 **94**
Guyra, *New South Wales* B80-302 **109**
Guzman, *Mexico* U82+196 **100**
Gwa, *Burma* F62+176 **71**
Gwabegar, *New S. Wales* C06-306 **109**
Gwadar, *Pakistan* H76+251 **70**
Gwalior, *India* G71+262 **73**
Gwanda, *Rhodesia* L06-210 **84**
Gwatar, *Iran* H81+251 **75**
Gweebarra B., *Ireland, Rep.* N51+549 **42**
Gwelo, *Rhodesia* L02-194 **84**
Gwent, co., *Wales* N18+517 **38**
Gwydir, R., *New S. Wales* B83-304 **109**
Gwyned, co., *Wales* N24+530 **38**
Gyangtse, *Tibet* G03+289 **71**
Gydanski Pol., *U.S.S.R.* G80+700 **62**
Gympie, *Queensland* B74-261 **111**
Györ, *Hungary* L74+477 **49**
Gypsumville, *Manitoba* U51+516 **88**
Gyula, *Hungary* L52+465 **49**
Gzhatsk, *U.S.S.R.* K60+555 **60**
Haacht, *Belgium* M62+510 **44**
Haag, *Switzerland* M33+472 **45**
Haaksbergen, *Netherlands* M49+522 **44**
Haarlem, *Netherlands* M62+524 **44**
Habana, *Cuba* T44+232 **101**
Habban, *Yemen, South* J77 + 146 **74**
Habbaniyah, *Iraq* K07+334 **74**
Habigang, *Bangladesh* F81+244 **71**
Hachinohe, *Japan* C51+405 **68**
Hadda, *Saudi Arabia* K32+214 **74**
Haddington, *Scotland* N16+560 **41**
Hadera, *Israel* K60+324 **76**
Haderslev, *Denmark* M33+552 **47**
Hadhramaut, *Yemen, South* J76 + 155 **74**
Hadjin, *Turkey* K52+375 **74**
Haeju, *Korea* D58+380 **64**
Haerhpin, *China* D45+455 **64**
Hafar, *Saudi Arabia* J84+284 **74**
Hafar al Ats, *Saudi Arabia* J80+260 **74**
Haffe. *See* Babenna
Hafnarfjördhur, *Iceland* P41+641 **46**
Hagen, *W. Germany* M45+514 **48**
Hageri, *Estonia* L32+591 **47**
Hagerstown, *Maryland* T16+397 **96**
Hagi, *Japan* D21+344 **68**
Hague, C. de la, *France* N12+497 **54**
Hahnville, *Louisiana* U03+299 **97**
Haibak, *Afghanistan* H42+362 **75**
Hai cheng, *China* D74+409 **66**
Haichow. *See* Tunghai
Haidar Pasha, *Turkey* L05+410 **74**
Haifa, *Israel* K60+328 **76**
Haig, *W. Australia* D54-309 **110**
Haik'ou, *China* E58+200 **67**
Hail, *Saudi Arabia* K19+275 **74**
Hailar, *China* E02+490 **64**
Haileybury, *Ontario* T28+475 **91**
Hailun, *China* D48+472 **64**
Hailuoto, *Finland* L32+650 **46**
Hainan I., *China* E60+190 **67**
Hainan Str., *China* E60+200 **67**
Hainaut, prov., *Belgium* M66+505 **44**
Haines, *Alaska* X02+594 **88**
Haiphong, *N. Vietnam* E80+208 **69**
Hair, *Saudi Arabia* J79+244 **74**
Haiten I., *China* E01+256 **67**
Haiti, rep., *West Indies* S74+190 **101**
Hajduböszörmény, *Hungary* L52+477 **49**
Hajima, Jebel, *Saudi Arabia* K44+245 **74**
Hajipur, *India* G28+257 **73**
Hajjar, *China* F72+369 **64**
Hakkâri, *Turkey* K07+376 **74**
Hakodate, *Japan* C55+418 **68**
Hala, *Pakistan* H40+258 **70**
Halacho, *Mexico* U01+204 **100**
Halba, *Lebanon* K54+346 **76**
Halbe, *Saudi Arabia* K11+198 **74**
Halberstadt, *E. Germany* M24+519 **48**
Halden, *Norway* M21+591 **47**
Haleb. *See* Aleppo
Halebiye, *Syria* K31+357 **74**
Halen, *Belgium* M59+509 **44**
Halesworth, *England* M81+524 **39**
Hali, *Saudi Arabia* K20+189 **74**
Halia, *India* G46+248 **73**
Halib, *Saudi Arabia* J31+227 **75**
Haliburton, *Ontario* T21+450 **91**
Halifax, *England* N11+537 **37**
Halifax, *N. Carolina* T16+363 **97**
Halifax & Harb., *N.S.* S22+446 **90**
Halifax B., *Queensland* C18-190 **111**
Halkett C., *Alaska* Y10+708 **99**
Hall, *W. Germany* M32+491 **48**

Hall Is., *Caroline Is.* B76+080 **106**
Hall Ld., *Greenland* R30+810 **26**
Halle, *E. Germany* M18+515 **48**
Halle, *Belgium* M65+507 **44**
Hallein, *Austria* M11+476 **48**
Halley B., *Antarctica* Q15-738 **27**
Halliste, *Estonia* L27+581 **47**
Hällnäss, *Sweden* L62+643 **46**
Hallock, *Minnesota* U42+488 **93**
Hallowell, *Maine* S59+443 **90**
Halls Creek, *W. Australia* D43-181 **110**
Hallstavik, *Sweden* L69+601 **47**
Hallviken, *Sweden* L87+637 **46**
Halmahera, I., *Indonesia* D42+006 **65**
Halmstad, *Sweden* M14+561 **47**
Halsa, *Norway* M41+631 **46**
Hälsingborg, *Sweden* M14+561 **47**
Halstead, *Kansas* U46+360 **95**
Halys, C., *Turkey* K54+417 **74**
Hama, *Syria* K50+351 **76**
Hamada, *Japan* D17+349 **68**
Hamadan, *Iran* J70+348 **74**
Hamaidan, *Saudi Arabia* J37+208 **75**
Hamam, *Saudi Arabia* J86+208 **74**
Hamamatsu, *Japan* C74+347 **68**
Haman, *Iraq* K05+312 **74**
Hamar, *Saudi Arabia* J83+224 **74**
Hamar, *Norway* M23+608 **47**
Hambantota, *Sri Lanka* G53+061 **70**
Hamburg, *W. Germany* M30+536 **48**
Hamburg, *Iowa* U34+406 **95**
Hamburg, *New York* T23+427 **96**
Hamburg, *Pennsylvania* T06+405 **96**
Hamburg, *S. Carolina* T41+335 **97**
Hämeenlinna, *Finland* L33+610 **47**
Hameln, *W. Germany* M34+521 **48**
Hami, *Yemen, South* J61 + 148 **74**
Hamidiya, *Syria* K54+347 **76**
Hamilton, *Alabama* T78+342 **97**
Hamilton, *New York* T04+428 **96**
Hamilton, *New Zealand* A28-378 **112**
Hamilton, *N. Carolina* T14+359 **97**
Hamilton, *Ohio* T57+394 **91**
Hamilton, *Ontario* T29+433 **91**
Hamilton, *Scotland* N24+558 **41**
Hamilton, *Tasmania* C19-426 **109**
Hamilton, *Victoria* C48-378 **109**
Hamilton, *Washington* W08+480 **88**
Hamilton Inl., *Labrador* R75+543 **89**
Hamilton, L., *Arkansas* U18+344 **95**
Hamilton, L., *Texas* U51+308 **98**
Hamilton R. (Churchill), *Lab.* S10+530 **89**
Hamina, *Finland* L16+605 **47**
Hamirpur, *India* G59+259 **73**
Hamlet, *N. Carolina* T28+349 **97**
Hamley Bridge, *S. Australia* C68-344 **109**
Hamm, *W. Germany* M43+517 **48**
Hamme, *Belgium* M65+511 **44**
Hammerdal, *Sweden* L88+636 **46**
Hammerfest, *Norway* L38+706 **46**
Hammersley Ra., *W. Aust.* E15-220 **110**
Hammond, *Indiana* T75+416 **91**
Hammond, *Louisiana* U02+305 **95**
Hammond, *New Brunswick* S45+474 **90**
Hammond, *S. Australia* C70-325 **109**
Hammonton, *New Jersey* S85+396 **96**
Hamont, *Belgium* M57+512 **44**
Hampden, *New Zealand* A55-453 **112**
Hampden, *N. Dakota* U52+486 **93**
Hampshire, co., *England* N08+510 **39**
Hampton, *Arkansas* U15+335 **97**
Hampton, *New Brunswick* S34+455 **90**
Hampton, *New Hampshire* S65+430 **90**
Hampton, *S. Carolina* T37+329 **97**
Hamun-i-Helmand,
  Iran-Afghanistan H82+314 **75**
Hamun-i-Puzak, *Afghanistan* H80+314 **75**
Han, *Belgium* M59+501 **44**
Hanakiya, *Saudi Arabia* K24+253 **74**
Hanau, *W. Germany* M36+501 **48**
Hanchung, *China* E78+331 **66**
Hancock, *Michigan* T81+473 **99**
Hancock, *New York* T02+419 **96**
Handegg, *Switzerland* M40+466 **45**
Handeni, *Tanzania* K42-054 **83**
Hanford, *California* V88+363 **92**
Hanford, *Washington* W37+466 **92**
Hangchow, *China* D89+303 **67**
Hangchow B., *China* D80+306 **66**
Hangu, *Pakistan* H24+335 **72**
Han Kiang, *China* E60+328 **64**
Hankinson, *N. Dakota* U41+461 **93**
Hankong, *China* E04+254 **64**
Hankow (Wuhan), *China* E34+306 **66**
Hanle, *Kashmir* G66+328 **70**
Hanley, *England* N13+530 **37**
Hanmer, *New Zealand* A43-425 **112**
Hanna, *Alberta* V41+514 **88**
Hanna, *Wyoming* V06+414 **93**
Hannibal, *Missouri* U08+396 **95**
Hannover, *Germany* M32+524 **48**
Hanover, *Belgium* M60+507 **44**
Hanö-bukten, *Sweden* M02+558 **47**
Hanoi, *N. Vietnam* E85+210 **69**
Hanover, *Ontario* T36+442 **91**
Hanover, *Pennsylvania* T12+398 **96**
Hanover, *Virginia* T14+377 **97**
Hanover, I., *Chile* S88-510 **103**
Hansi, *India* G84+291 **72**
Hansweert, *Netherlands* M66+515 **44**
Hanumangarh. *See* Bhatnair
Hanyang, *China* E34+305 **67**
Hanyin, *China* E68+329 **66**
Hanza, *Kashmir* H02+364 **72**
Hao, I., *Tuamotu Arch.* X20-190 **107**
Haparanda, *Sweden* L35+658 **46**
Hapora, *Japan* C59+440 **68**
Hapur, *India* G73+287 **72**
Haqal, *Saudi Arabia* K60+292 **74**
Heraiya, *India* G45+268 **73**
Herak, *Saudi Arabia* K48+256 **74**
Harar, *Ethiopia* K18+092 **83**
Hara Usu Nur, *Mongolia* F76+480 **64**
Harbin. *See* Haerhpin
Harbor Beach, *Michigan* T46+438 **91**
Harbor Spring, *Michigan* T60+455 **91**
Harburg Wilhelmsburg, *Ger.* M30+534 **48**
Harda, *India* G77+223 **70**

Hardanger Fjell, *Norway* M42+609 **47**
Hardanger Fd., *Norway* M54+601 **47**
Hardenberg, *Netherlands* M50+526 **44**
Harderwijk, *Netherlands* M56+523 **44**
Hardin, *Montana* V16+457 **93**
Harding, *Natal* L00-306 **84**
Hardoi, *India* G59+274 **73**
Hardwar, *India* G71+299 **72**
Hardwicke B., *S. Australia* C76-348 **109**
Hardy, Pen., *Chile* S52-555 **103**
Hare B., *Newfoundland* R64+512 **90**
Hare I., *Quebec* S58+479 **91**
Hareidland, *Norway* M54+624 **46**
Harelbeke, *Belgium* M70+509 **44**
Hargeisa, *Somalia* K06+094 **83**
Hari, R., *Sumatra, Indon* F10-016 **65**
Harib, *Saudi Arabia* J85+152 **74**
Harihar, *India* G85+146 **70**
Harim, *Syria* K51+362 **76**
Haripur, *Pakistan* H12+340 **72**
Hariq, *Saudi Arabia* J81+237 **74**
Harishpur, *India* G21+201 **71**
Harlan, *Iowa* U32+416 **95**
Harlan, *Kentucky* T47+368 **99**
Harlech, *Wales* N25+529 **38**
Harlem, *Montana* V22+485 **93**
Harlequin Hills, *Nevada* V84+415 **92**
Harlingen, *Netherlands* M57+532 **44**
Harlingen, *Texas* U46+262 **94**
Harlowton, *Montana* V29+464 **93**
Harmanli. *See* Kharmanli
Harnai, *Pakistan* H42+302 **70**
Harney L., *Oregon* V85+432 **92**
Harney Pk., *S. Dakota* U81+438 **93**
Harney Basin, *Oregon* W00+436 **98**
Harnösand, *Sweden* L73+626 **46**
Har Nuur, lake, *Mongolia* F73+480 **63**
Harper, *Liberia* N46+044 **80**
Harran, *Turkey* K35+370 **74**
Harray, L. of, *Orkney, Scot.* N19+590 **40**
Harrington Harbour, *Quebec* R87+505 **90**
Harris, I. & Sd., of *Scotland* N41+578 **40**
Harrisburg, *Arkansas* U04+355 **95**
Harrisburg, *Illinois* T82+378 **95**
Harrisburg, *Pennsylvania* T12+403 **96**
Harrison, *Arkansas* U18+362 **95**
Harrison, *Michigan* T59+440 **91**
Harrison, C., *Labrador* R67+548 **89**
Harrison L., *Brit. Columbia* W10+498 **88**
Harrisonburg, *Louisiana* U10+318 **97**
Harrisonburg, *Virginia* T23+384 **97**
Harrisonville, *Missouri* U26+386 **95**
Harrisville, *Michigan* T50+447 **91**
Harrodsburg, *Kentucky* T59+378 **97**
Harrogate, *England* N09+540 **37**
Harrow, *England* N02+516 **39**
Hârsova, *Romania* L12+447 **58**
Harspranget, *Sweden* L61+668 **46**
Harstad, *Norway* L81+689 **46**
Hart, *Michigan* T68+437 **91**
Hartford, *Connecticut* S76+418 **96**
Hartland, *New Brunswick* S45+464 **90**
Hartlepool, *England* N07+547 **37**
Hartsville, *Tennessee* T67+364 **97**
Hartville, *Missouri* U18+373 **97**
Harvard, *Illinois* T82+425 **91**
Harvard, Mt., *Colorado* V08+385 **98**
Harvey, *New Brunswick* S42+457 **90**
Harvey, *N. Dakota* U60+478 **93**
Harwell, *England* N08+516 **39**
Harwich, *England* M82+519 **39**
Haryana, state, *India* G84+291 **72**
Harz, mts., *Germany* M27+516 **48**
Hasan Dagh, *Turkey* K66+382 **74**
Hasan Kuli, *Turkmen* J37+378 **62**
Hasanpur, *India* G70+293 **73**
Hasbeya, *Lebanon* K56+334 **76**
Hassan, *India* G83+130 **70**
Hassayampa, *Arizona* V46+334 **98**
Hasselt, *Belgium* M58+509 **44**
Hasselt, *Netherlands* M53+526 **44**
Hastiere, *Belgium* M61+502 **44**
Hastings, *England* M86+509 **39**
Hastings, *Michigan* T62+427 **91**
Hastings, *Minnesota* U16+448 **93**
Hastings, *Nebraska* U50+406 **95**
Hastings, *New Zealand* A19-396 **112**
Hasting's Ra., *New S. Wales* B80-312 **109**
Hateg, *Romania* L42+456 **58**
Hatfield, *England* N06+536 **37**
Hatfield, *New South Wales* C37-339 **109**
Hatha, *Saudi Arabia* K27+228 **74**
Hathras, *India* G71+276 **73**
Ha-tinh, *N. Vietnam* E85+184 **69**
Hatteras, C., *N. Carolina* T03+352 **97**
Hattiesburg, *Mississippi* T86+312 **95**
Hatton Headline, *N.-W. Terr.* S30+611 **89**
Hatvan, *Hungary* L62+477 **49**
Hat Yai, *Thailand* F27+071 **65**
Haudères, les, *Switzerland* M45+461 **45**
Haugesund, *Norway* M58+594 **47**
Haukipudas, *Finland* L28+652 **46**
Haukivesi, *Finland* L10+622 **46**
Haura, *Yemen, South* J74 + 139 **74**
Hauraki Gulf, *New Zealand* A30-367 **112**
Haurangi Mts.,
  New Zealand A28-414 **112**
Hauroko, L., *New Zealand* A76-460 **112**
Hausa, *Jordan* K43+299 **76**
Hausstock, mt., *Switzerland* M36+468 **45**
Haut, Isle, *Maine* S52+441 **90**
Hauta, *Yemen, South* J80 + 135 **74**
Hauta, *Saudi Arabia* J79+236 **74**
Haut Atlas, mts., *Morocco* N50+320 **80**
Haute-Garonne, dep., *France* M81+434 **55**
Haute-Loire, dep., *France* M67+451 **55**
Haute-Marne, dep., *France* M58+482 **54**
Hautes-Alpes, dep., *France* M53+446 **55**
Haute-Saône, dep., *France* M51+477 **54**
Haute Savoie, dep., *France* M49+458 **55**
Haute Vienne, dep., *France* M85+459 **54**
Haute Volta. *See* Upper Volta
Havana. *See* Habana
Havasu L., *Cal.-Ariz.* V56+346 **92**
Havelange, *Belgium* M59+504 **44**
Havelland, *E. Germany* M14+527 **48**
Havelock, *New Brunswick* S32+460 **90**
Havelock I., *Andaman Is.* F72+119 **71**

Havelock North, *N.Z.* A18–397 **112**
Haverfordwest, *Wales* N30+518 **38**
Haverhill, *Massachusetts* S67+428 **96**
Haverstraw, *New York* S84+412 **96**
Havre, *Belgium* M66+505 **44**
Havre, *Montana* V28+485 **93**
Havre de Grace, *Maryland* T07+396 **96**
Hawaii I., *Hawaiian Is.* Y30+200 **107**
Hawaiian Is., *Pacific Ocean* Y60+250 **106**
Hawarden, *Iowa* U38+430 **95**
Hawea Flat, *New Zealand* A64–445 **112**
Hawera, *New Zealand* A34–396 **112**
Hawesville, *Kentucky* T71+379 **97**
Hawick, *Scotland* N16+554 **41**
Hawizeh, *Iran* J71+315 **74**
Hawke, C., *New S. Wales* B76–322 **109**
Hawker, *S. Australia* C70–319 **109**
Hawke's B., *New Zealand* A16–393 **112**
Hawkesbury, *Ontario* S88+456 **91**
Hawr al Hammar, *Iraq* J76+308 **74**
Hawr Saniyah, *Iraq* J80+320 **74**
Hay, *New South Wales* C31–346 **109**
Hay R., *Alberta* V72+595 **88**
Hayes Halvø, *Greenland* S50+770 **26**
Hayling I., *England* N06+508 **39**
Hayneville, *Alabama* I70+322 **97**
Hay-on-Wye, *Wales* N19+521 **38**
Hay River, *North-West
　　Territories* V65+606 **88**
Hays, *Kansas* U56+388 **95**
Hayward, *Wisconsin* U08+460 **93**
Hazara Highlands, *Afghan.* H60+339 **75**
Hazard, *Kentucky* T49+373 **97**
Hazaribagh, *India* G28+240 **73**
Hazaribagh Ra., *India* G36+232 **73**
Hazarjuft, *Afghanistan* H65+310 **75**
Hazelton, *British Columbia* W45+553 **88**
Hazil, *Saudi Arabia* K15+299 **74**
Hazlehurst, *Georgia* T45+318 **97**
Hazleton, *Pennsylvania* T06+410 **96**
Hazro, *Pakistan* H15+339 **72**
Headford, *Ireland, Rep.* N55+535 **43**
Healesville, *Victoria* C27–376 **109**
Heard I., *Indian Ocean* H12–520 **77**
Hearst, *Ontario* T52+498 **89**
Heathcote, *Victoria* C32–369 **109**
Hebbronville, *Texas* U52+274 **94**
Heber, *Utah* V38+406 **94**
Heber Springs, *Arkansas* U12+355 **97**
Hebrides, Outer, *Scotland* N42+580 **40**
Hebron, *Jordan* K59+315 **76**
Hebron, *Labrador* S16+585 **89**
Hebron, *Nebraska* U46+401 **95**
Hebron, *N. Dakota* U72+469 **93**
Hecate Str., *Brit. Columbia* W65+534 **88**
Hecelchakan, *Mexico* U01+202 **100**
Hechingen, *Germany* M36+483 **48**
Hechtel, *Belgium* M58+512 **44**
Hectanooga, *Nova Scotia* S36+442 **90**
Hector, Mt., *New Zealand* A28–409 **112**
Hede, *Sweden* M09+624 **46**
Hedemora, *Sweden* L84+603 **47**
Heemstede, *Netherlands* M62+523 **44**
Heer, *Netherlands* M56+508 **44**
Heerenveen, *Netherlands* M54+530 **44**
Heerlen, *Netherlands* M54+509 **44**
Heiberg I., *N.-W. Terr.* U00+782 **89**
Heide, *W. Germany* M36+542 **48**
Heidelberg, *W. Germany* M38+494 **48**
Heidelburg, *Transvaal* L10–266 **84**
Heiden, *Switzerland* M33+474 **45**
Heijen, *Netherlands* M54+517 **44**
Heilbronn, *W. Germany* M35+491 **48**
Heinola, *Finland* L23+612 **47**
Heist, *Belgium* M71+513 **44**
Hejaz (Hijaz), *Saudi Arabia* K40+253 **74**
Hekla, Mt., *Iceland* P28+640 **46**
Helchteren, *Belgium* M58+511 **44**
Helder, Den, *Netherlands* M61+530 **44**
Helena, *Arkansas* U04+346 **95**
Helena, *Montana* V42+466 **93**
Helensburgh, *Scotland* N28+560 **41**
Helensville, *New Zealand* A33–367 **112**
Helgoland, I., *W. Germany* M43+542 **48**
Helgoländer, Bucht,
　　W. Germany M42+543 **48**
Hell Gate, *British Columbia* W34+593 **88**
Hellin, *Spain* N10+385 **53**
Helmand Des., *Afghanistan* H60+304 **75**
Helmand R., *Afghanistan* H70+305 **75**
Helme, *Estonia* L25+580 **47**
Helmond, *Netherlands* M56+515 **44**
Helmsdale, *Scotland* N22+581 **40**
Helsingfors. *See Helsinki*
Helsingør, *Denmark* M15+560 **47**
Helsinki, *Finland* L30+602 **47**
Helston, *England* N32+501 **38**
Helvellyn, *England* N18+545 **37**
Helvick Hd., *Ireland, Rep.* N45+520 **43**
Hemelum, *Netherlands* M57+529 **44**
Hemnes, *Norway* M08+662 **46**
Hemse, *Sweden* L70+572 **47**
Hendaye, *France* N10+434 **55**
Henderson, *Kentucky* T76+378 **95**
Henderson, *Minnesota* U24+445 **93**
Henderson, *New York* T07+438 **91**
Henderson, *N. Carolina* T20+363 **97**
Henderson, *Tennessee* T82+354 **97**
Henderson I., *Pacific Ocean* W50–246 **107**
Hendersonville, *N. Carolina* T45+353 **97**
Hengchow. *See Hengyang*
Hengelo, *Netherlands* M49+523 **44**
Henghsien, *China* E64+226 **67**
Hengshan, *China* E43+272 **67**
Hengyang, *China* E44+270 **67**
Henjam, I., *Iran* J25+266 **75**
Henjareh, *Iran* J00+282 **75**
Henley-on-Thames, *England* N05+515 **39**
Henlopen, C., *New Jersey* T00+388 **96**
Hennebont, *France* N20+478 **54**
Henrietta, *Texas* U49+338 **95**
Henrietta Maria C., *Ontario* T44+549 **89**
Henrique de Carvalho,
　　Angola L58–096 **82**
Henry Mts., *Utah* V36+380 **94**
Henryetta, *Oklahoma* U36+354 **95**
Henty, *New South Wales* C18–355 **109**
Henzada, *Burma* F58+176 **71**
Heran, *Yemen* K13+161 **74**
Herat, *Afghanistan* H77+344 **75**
Herault, dep., *France* M71+435 **55**

Herberton, *Queensland* C28–172 **111**
Herbertville, *New Zealand* A21–405 **112**
Herbertville, *Quebec* S69+484 **90**
Herbesthal, *Belgium* M54+506 **44**
Herceg Novi, *Yugoslavia* L69+420 **58**
Heredia, *Costa Rica* T54+100 **101**
Hereford, *Texas* U74+348 **94**
Heref. & Worcs., co., *England* N15+522 **38**
Hereheretue, I., *Pacific Oc.* X60–200 **107**
Herford, *W. Germany* M38+521 **48**
Heriot, *New Zealand* A64–458 **112**
Herisau, *Switzerland* M34+474 **45**
Herkimer, *New York* T00+430 **96**
Herma Ness, *Shetland, Scot.* N06+608 **40**
Hermann, *Missouri* U09+387 **95**
Hermidale, *New S. Wales* C20–316 **109**
Hermil, *Lebanon* K52+344 **76**
Hermitage B., *Newfoundland* R72+475 **90**
Hermite, Is., *Chile* S46–560 **103**
Hermon, Mt. *See Sheikh, Jebel esh*
Hermosillo, *Mexico* V36+291 **100**
Herne, *Belgium* M66+507 **44**
Herne Bay, *England* M83+514 **39**
Herning, *Denmark* M36+561 **47**
Herowabad, *Iran* J68+377 **74**
Herräng, *Sweden* L68+601 **47**
Herrera, *Argentina* S19–285 **103**
Herrera di Pisuerga, *Spain* N26+426 **52**
Herrick, *Tasmania* C13–411 **109**
Herrington, *Kansas* U42+386 **95**
Hersey, *Michigan* T63+439 **91**
Herselt, *Belgium* M61+511 **44**
Herstmonceux, *England* M88+509 **39**
Hertford, *N. Carolina* T09+362 **97**
Hertford & co., *England* N00+518 **39**
's Hertogenbosch, *Netherl'ds* M58+517 **44**
Herval, *Brazil* R39–274 **103**
Hervas, *Spain* N35+402 **52**
Hervé, *Belgium* M59+506 **44**
Hervey B., *Queensland* B73–246 **111**
Hervey Is., *Cook Is.* Y50–200 **106**
Herzberg, *E. Germany* M11+517 **48**
Herzliya, *Israel* K61+322 **76**
Herzogenbuchsee, *Switz.* M44+472 **45**
Hesdin, *France* M78+504 **54**
Hessen, *W. Germany* M38+506 **48**
Heught, Mt., *N. Terr., Aust.* D23–228 **110**
Heusden, *Netherlands* M58+517 **44**
Hève, C. de la, *France* M89+495 **54**
Hexham, *England* N13+550 **37**
Heytesbury, *England* N13+512 **39**
Heywood, *Victoria* C50–381 **109**
Hiakiang, *China* E67+258 **67**
Hiawatha, *Kansas* U34+398 **95**
Hibbing, *Minnesota* U18+474 **93**
Hidalgo, *Mexico* U59+277 **100**
Hidalgo, state, *Mexico* U54+204 **100**
Hieflau, *Austria* M02+476 **48**
Hierro, I., *Canary Is.* P30+276 **80**
Highland, reg., *Scotland* N30+576 **40**
Highland Park, *Illinois* T78+422 **95**
Highmore, *S. Dakota* U57+445 **93**
High Point, *N. Carolina* T30+360 **97**
Highwood Mts., *Montana* V32+475 **93**
Hiimeji, *Japan* D02+348 **68**
Hiiumaa, I., *Estonia* L44+589 **47**
Hijar, *Spain* N03+411 **53**
Hikone, *Japan* C82+353 **68**
Hildesheim, *W. Germany* M30+521 **48**
Hili, *Saudi Arabia* J26+244 **75**
Hillah, al, *Iraq* K03+325 **74**
Hill City, *Kansas* U60+394 **95**
Hill City, *S. Dakota* U22+470 **93**
Hillman, *Michigan* T54+451 **91**
Hillsboro, *Illinois* T87+392 **95**
Hillsboro, *N. Carolina* T24+362 **97**
Hillsboro, *Texas* U42+320 **95**
Hillsborough, *N.B.* S28+459 **90**
Hillsdale, *Michigan* T58+419 **91**
Hillston, *New South Wales* C27–335 **109**
Hillsville, *Virginia* T35+368 **97**
Hilversum, *Netherlands* M59+522 **44**
Hilwa, *Saudi Arabia* J80+233 **74**
Hilvan, *Saudi Arabia* K23+222 **74**
Himachal Pradesh, *India* G75+320 **72**
Himalaya Mts., *India, etc.* G60+300 **30**
Himanka, *Finland* L38+641 **46**
Himare, *Albania* L62+401 **59**
Hinckley, *Minnesota* U18+461 **93**
Hindeloopen, *Netherlands* M58+529 **44**
Hindman, *Kentucky* T48+373 **97**
Hindmarsh, L., *Victoria* C49–360 **109**
Hindubagh, *Pakistan* H42+309 **70**
Hindu Kush, mts.,
　　Afghanistan-Pakistan H20+364 **70**
Hindupur, *India* G75+139 **70**
Hingan. *See Ankang*
Hinganghat, *India* G66+205 **70**
Hingham, *Montana* V33+485 **93**
Hingho, *China* E38+410 **66**
Hinghwa, *China* E50+330 **66**
Hinghwa (Putien), *China* E05+255 **67**
Hingi, *China* F00+251 **67**
Hinglaj, *Pakistan* H57+255 **70**
Hingol R., *Pakistan* H56+250 **70**
Hingoli, *India* G76+196 **70**
Hinnøya, *Norway* L84+687 **46**
Hinsdale, *Montana* V12+484 **93**
Hinsdale, *New Hampshire* S75+428 **96**
Hinton, *W. Virginia* T35+377 **97**
Hiro, *Japan* C40+423 **68**
Hirosaki, *Japan* C57+406 **68**
Hiroshima, *Japan* D15+344 **68**
Hisaronu, *Turkey* K77+416 **74**
Hisban, *Jordan* K55+318 **76**
Hispaniola, I., *West Indies* S70+190 **101**
Hissar, *India* G86+291a **72**
Hissmofors, *Sweden* M03+634 **46**
Hisua, *India* G27+248 **73**
Hisya, *Syria* K49+344 **76**
Hit, *Iraq* K14+336 **74**
Hitra, *Norway* M38+636 **46**
Hivaoa, I., *Marquesa Is.* X24–100 **107**
Hiwasa, *Japan* D03+338 **68**
Hjälmaren, L., *Sweden* L86+595 **47**
Hjørring, *Denmark* M35+575 **47**
Hkamti, *Burma* F56+260 **71**
Hkok, *Ireland, Rep.* N42+521 **43**
Hobart, *Oklahoma* U54+350 **95**
Hobart, *Tasmania* C16–430 **109**
Hobbs, *New Mexico* U78+326 **94**

Hoboken, *Belgium* M64+512 **44**
Hobro, *Denmark* M31+566 **47**
Hochwan, *China* E82+300 **67**
Hodal, *India* G76+279 **72**
Hodeida, *Yemen* K12+148 **74**
Hodgson, *Manitoba* U46+512 **88**
Hodmezövasárhely, *Hungary* L58+464 **49**
Hoek van Holland,
　　Netherlands M65+520 **44**
Hoyes Bridge, *Kenya* K58+010 **83**
Hof, *W. Germany* M19+503 **48**
Hofei, *China* E16+319 **66**
Hofmeyr, *S.-W. Africa* L70–244 **84**
Höfs Jökull, *Iceland* P24+648 **46**
Hofuf, *Saudi Arabia* J62+254 **74**
Höganäs, *Sweden* M15+562 **47**
Hohe Tauern, *Austria* M15+472 **48**
Hohsien, *China* E51+244 **67**
Hoihong, *China* E59+209 **67**
Hokianga Harb., *N.Z.* A39–354 **112**
Hokitika, *New Zealand* A54–427 **112**
Hokkaidô I., *Japan* C42+430 **68**
Holbaek, *Denmark* M20+557 **47**
Holberg, *British Columbia* W48+506 **88**
Holbrook, *Arizona* V31+348 **94**
Holbrook, *New South Wales* C17–358 **109**
Holdenville, *Oklahoma* U38+351 **95**
Holdredge, *Nebraska* U54+444 **95**
Holguin, *Cuba* T08+208 **101**
Holinkoerh, *China* E50+404 **66**
Holland, *Michigan* T67+428 **91**
Holland, New, *New S. Wales* C18–316 **109**
Holland, Noord, prov., *Neth.* M61+526 **44**
Holland, Zuid, prov., *Neth.* M63+520 **44**
Holland, *Michigan* T75+428 **91**
Hollange, *Belgium* M56+499 **44**
Hollidaysburg, *Pennsylvania* T21+404 **96**
Hollis, *Oklahoma* U59+347 **95**
Holly, *Colorado* U72+381 **94**
Holly, *Michigan* T52+428 **91**
Holly Springs, *Mississippi* T87+348 **95**
Hollywood, *California* V80+341 **92**
Holmestrand, *Norway* M28+595 **47**
Holmsund, *Sweden* L58+637 **46**
Holstebro., *Denmark* M38+563 **47**
Holstein, *Germany* M32+539 **48**
Holsteinsborg, *Greenland* R40+670 **26**
Holsworthy, *England* N26+508 **38**
Holten, *Netherlands* M51+523 **44**
Holton, *Kansas* U36+394 **95**
Holwerd, *Netherlands* M55+534 **44**
Holy I., *England* N11+557 **37**
Holy I., *Wales* N28+533 **38**
Holy Cross, *Alaska* Y60+624 **99**
Holy Cross, Mt. of the,
　　Colorado V09+396 **98**
Holyhead, *Wales* N28+533 **38**
Holyoke, *Colorado* U74+406 **94**
Holyoke, *Massachusetts* S76+422 **91**
Holywood, *N. Ireland* N35+546 **42**
Home B., *N.-W. Territories* S30+678 **89**
Homer, *Alaska* Y10+559 **99**
Homer, *Louisiana* U18+328 **95**
Homer, *New York* T08+427 **91**
Homestead, *Pennsylvania* T29+404 **91**
Homfray Str., *Andaman Is.* F72+124 **71**
Hommelvik, *Norway* M26+634 **46**
Homs, *Libya* M04+326 **81**
Homs, *Syria* K50+347 **76**
Honan. *See Loyang*
Honan, prov., *China* E42+340 **66**
Honda, *Columbia* S89+052 **104**
Honda, B., *Cuba* T49+229 **101**
Hondo, *Mexico* U65+277 **100**
Honduras, rep., *C. America* T76+150 **101**
Honduras, C., *Honduras* T66+160 **101**
Honduras, G. of, *Cent. Amer* T70+165 **101**
Hønefoss, *Norway* M28+602 **47**
Honesdale, *Pennsylvania* T02+415 **96**
Honfleur, *France* N00+494 **54**
Honghai B., *China* E28+227 **67**
Hong Kong I., *S.-E. Asia* E34+223 **67**
Honiara, I., *Solomon Is.* B30–095 **106**
Honiton, *England* N19+508 **38**
Honolulu, *Hawaiian Is.* Y30+208 **107**
Honor, *Michigan* T66+447 **91**
Honshū, I., *Japan* **68**
Hood, Mt., *Oregon* W10+453 **92**
Hoofdplaat, *Netherlands* M68+514 **44**
Hooger Smilde, *Netherlands* M52+529 **44**
Hoogeveen, *Netherlands* M51+527 **44**
Hoogezand, *Netherlands* M49+532 **44**
Hooghalen, *Netherlands* M51+529 **44**
Hooghly, *India* G10+230 **73**
Hooghly R., *India* G12+216 **73**
Hook Hd., *Ireland, Rep.* N42+521 **43**
Hookina, *S. Australia* C71–318 **109**
Hoopeston, *Illinois* T76+405 **91**
Hoorn Den, *Netherlands* M60+526 **44**
Hoosick Falls, *New York* S80+429 **91**
Hoover Dam, *Arizona* V57+359 **92**
Hope, *Aransas* U21+336 **95**
Hope, *British Columbia* W08+494 **88**
Hopedale, *Labrador* S03+554 **89**
Hopeh, prov., *China* E24+386 **66**
Hopen, I., *Barents Sea* L30+766 **62**
Hopes Advance, C., *Quebec* S36+607 **89**
Hopetoun, *Victoria* C46–357 **109**
Hope Town, *Andaman Is.* F74+117 **71**
Hopetown, *Cape Province* L36–296 **84**
Hopewell, *Virginia* T14+372 **97**
Hopkinsville, *Kentucky* T75+368 **95**
Hoppo, *China* E64+216 **67**
Horaždovice, *Czechoslovakia* M08+493 **48**
Horcasitas, *Mexico* V34+294 **100**
Horgen, *Switzerland* M38+473 **45**
Horka, *E. Germany* L90+513 **48**
Hormuz, *Iran* J31+276 **75**
Hormuz I., *Iran* J21+271 **75**
Hormuz. Str. of,
　　Saudi Arabia-Iran J24+266 **75**
Horn, *Austria* L86+487 **48**
Horn, *Iceland* P44+665 **46**
Horn, *Netherlands* M54+512 **44**
Horn, C., *Chile* S46–560 **103**
Horn Mts., *N.-W. Terr.* V85+617 **88**
Hornavan, *Sweden* L74+662 **46**
Horncastle, *England* N01+532 **37**

Hornefors, *Sweden* L61+637 **46**
Hornell, *New York* T16+423 **96**
Hornopiren, mt., *Chile* S75–418 **103**
Hornos, C. de *Chile* S44–560 **103**
Hornsby, *New South Wales* B84–337 **109**
Hornsea, *England* N01+539 **37**
Horonobe, *Japan* C49+451 **68**
Horqueta, *Paraguay* R72–232 **103**
Horseheads, *New York* T11+422 **96**
Horsens, *Denmark* M31+559 **47**
Horse Shoe, *W. Australia* E09–255 **110**
Horseshoe Res., *Arizona* V40+340 **94**
Horsham, *England* N02+511 **39**
Horsham, *Victoria* C47–367 **109**
Horšovský Tyn., *Czech.* M13+495 **48**
Horst, *Netherlands* M54+515 **44**
Horten, *Norway* M27+594 **47**
Horton, *Kansas* U34+396 **95**
Horton, *Montana* V06+463 **93**
Horton R., *N.-W. Terr.* W12+682 **88**
Hose Ra., *Sarawak* E38+019 **65**
Hoshangabad, *India* G73+227 **73**
Hoshiarpur, *India* G83+315 **72**
Hospel, *India* G81+153 **70**
Hospenthal, *Switzerland* M39+466 **45**
Hossegor, *France* N08+437 **55**
Hoste, I., *Chile* S56–552 **103**
Hosur, *India* G73+128 **70**
Hotagen, *Sweden* M05+640 **46**
Hotsch, *China* E28+353 **66**
Hot Springs, *N. Carolina* T47+359 **97**
Hot Springs, *S. Dakota* U81+434 **93**
Hot Springs Nat. Pk., *Ark.* U18+346 **95**
Hotton, *Belgium* M57+503 **44**
Houdelaincourt, *France* M57+485 **54**
Houffalize, *Belgium* M55+501 **44**
Houghton L., *Michigan* T59+444 **91**
Houlton, *Maine* S47+461 **90**
Houma, *Louisiana* U04+296 **95**
Hourn, L., *Scotland* N34+571 **40**
Housatonic, R., *Conecticut* S79+414 **96**
House Ra., *Utah* V50+395 **94**
Houstan, *Mississippi* T84+339 **97**
Houston, *Missouri* U12+374 **95**
Houston, *Texas* U32+298 **95**
Houten, *Netherlands* M59+520 **44**
Houtman Abrolhos,
　　W. Aust. E42–284 **110**
Hovd, *Mongolia* E80+402 **64**
Hove, *England* N01+508 **39**
Hovsgöl Nuur, lake
　　Mongolia F25+520 **63**
Howard, *Michigan* T63+434 **91**
Howard, *Pennsylvania* T16+410 **96**
Howard, *S. Dakota* U45+440 **93**
Howell, *Michigan* T54+426 **91**
Howick, *Natal* L00+294 **84**
Howland I., *Pacific Ocean* Z70+005 **106**
Howley, *Newfoundland* R72+492 **90**
Howrah, *India* G10+226 **73**
Howth, *Ireland, Rep.* N36+534 **43**
Hoy, I. *Orkney, Scotland* N20+588 **40**
Hoyes, *Spain* N41+401 **52**
Hoyt, *New Brunswick* S39+456 **90**
Hoyun, *China* E42+237 **64**
Hozat, *Turkey* K34+393 **74**
Hrubieszów, *Poland* L37+508 **49**
Hsenwi, *Burma* F42+234 **71**
Hsiachwan Shan, *China* E44+216 **67**
Hsiamen, *China* E11+244 **67**
Hsinchu, *Taiwan* D84+248 **67**
Hsinking. *See Changchun*
Hsipaw, *Burma* F46+226 **71**
Hsuchang, *China* E36+340 **66**
Hsuchow. *See Hsuchang*
Huachi, *Bolivia* S44–156 **104**
Huacho, *Peru* T12–088 **104**
Huacrachuco, *Peru* T12–088 **104**
Hualgayoo, *Peru* T22–068 **104**
Hualienkang, *Taiwan* D80+240 **67**
Huambo, *Angola* L86–128 **82**
Huanay, *Bolivia* S48–155 **104**
Huancabamba, *Peru* T27–052 **104**
Huancane, *Peru* S58–152 **104**
Huancavelica, *Peru* T01–126 **104**
Huancayo, *Peru* T01–120 **104**
Huanchaca, *Bolivia* S40–203 **104**
Huanchaco, *Peru* T25–081 **104**
Huanta, *Peru* S85–126 **104**
Huanuco, *Peru* T08–098 **104**
Huaras, *Peru* T16–095 **104**
Huari, *Chile* S59–200 **103**
Huariaca, *Peru* T07–105 **104**
Huarmey, *Peru* T19–101 **104**
Huasco, *Chile* S67–284 **103**
Huatusco, *Mexico* U42+192 **100**
Huaylas, *Peru* T17–090 **104**
Hubli, *India* G88+154 **70**
Huchow, *China* D88+308 **66**
Hucknall Torkard, *England* N07+531 **37**
Huddersfield, *England* N11+536 **37**
Hudiksvall, *Sweden* L77+617 **47**
Hudson, *Maine* S53+451 **90**
Hudson, *Wisconsin* U16+450 **93**
Hudson & R., *New York* S83+423 **96**
Hudson B., *Canada* T60+580 **89**
Hudson R., *New York* S83+420 **91**
Hudson Str., *Canada* S80+620 **89**
Hudson Falls, *New York* S81+433 **91**
Hue, *S. Vietnam* E75+165 **69**
Hueco Mts., *New Mex.-Texas* V06+320 **94**
Huedin, *Romania* L42+469 **58**
Huehuetenango, *Guatemala* U08+154 **100**
Huejutla, *Mexico* U51+212 **100**
Huelva, *Spain* N41+372 **52**
Huereal Overa, *Spain* N12+374 **53**
Huete, *Spain* N16+402 **53**
Hughenden, *Queensland* C35–209 **111**
Hugo, *Oklahoma* U33+340 **95**
Huhehot, *China* E50+408 **66**
Huiarau Ra., *New Zealand* A18–387 **112**
Hüichôn, *Korea* D52+402 **64**
Huj, *Israel* K62+315 **76**
Hukawng Valley, *Burma* F50+266 **71**
Hukow, *China* E23+297 **64**
Hukuntsi, *Botswana* L50–240 **84**
Hula L., *Israel* J77+331 **76**
Hulaiba, *Iraq* J47+321 **74**
Hulin, *China* D10+460 **64**
Hull, *England* N02+537 **37**

Hull, *Quebec* T04+455 **91**
Hulst, *Netherlands* M66+513 **44**
Hulun. *See* Hailar
Hulun Chih, *China* E16+448 **64**
Hulutao, *China* D84+407 **64**
Huma, *China* D50+515 **63**
Humacao, *Puerto Rico* S34+183 **101**
Humaita, *Paraguay* R81–271 **103**
Humansdorp, *Cape Province* L32–340 **84**
Humayta, *Brazil* S18–074 **104**
Humber, R., *England* N02+537 **37**
Humbermouth, *Nfd.* R77+490 **90**
Humberside, co., *England* N03+538 **37**
Humboldt, *Iowa* U26+428 **95**
Humboldt, *Saskatchewan* V01+519 **88**
Humboldt, *Tennessee* T84+358 **97**
Humboldt B., *California* W30+408 **98**
Humboldt Glacier, *Greenland* R30+790 **26**
Humboldt R., *Nevada* V80+404 **92**
Hume Res., *New S. Wales* C18–360 **109**
Humenne, *Czechoslovakia* L49+490 **49**
Humphreys, Mt., *Arizona* Y39+354 **94**
Humphreys, Mt., *California* V82+373 **92**
Humphreys, Mt., *Wyoming* V31+443 **93**
Hun, *Libya* L84+292 **81**
Húnaflói, *Iceland* P36+659 **46**
Hunan, prov., *China* E54+266 **67**
Hungary, *Central Europe* L60+470 **51**
Hungchiang, *China* E11+273 **67**
Hungerford, *England* N09+514 **39**
Hungnam, *Korea* D43+400 **64**
Hungtse, *China* E08+332 **66**
Hunsrück, mts., *W. Germany* M46+499 **48**
Hunstanton, *England* M87+529 **39**
Hunter Is., *Tasmania* C31–405 **109**
Hunter Ra., *New S. Wales* C00–330 **109**
Hunter R., *New S. Wales* B82–326 **109**
Huntersville, *W. Virginia* T30+382 **97**
Huntingburg, *Indiana* T72+384 **97**
Huntingdon, *Pennsylvania* T18+405 **96**
Huntingdon and Peterborough, co.
See Cambridgeshire
Huntington, *New York* S81+408 **96**
Huntington, *Utah* V36+394 **94**
Huntington, *W. Virginia* T45+384 **97**
Huntley, *Montana* V20+458 **93**
Huntly, *New Zealand* A29–376 **112**
Huntly, *Scotland* N17+574 **40**
Huntsville, *Alabama* T69+347 **97**
Huntsville, *Ontario* T25+453 **91**
Huntsville, *Tennessee* T57+364 **97**
Huntsville, *Texas* U32+307 **95**
Hunucma, *Mexico* T89+210 **100**
Hun-yüan-chow, *China* E38+397 **66**
Hunza, *Kashmir* H02+364 **72**
Huon Is., *Pacific Ocean* B10–180 **106**
Huon Pen.,
Papua New Guinea C20–064 **111**
Huon, R., *Tasmania* C20–431 **109**
Hupeh, prov., *China* E42+315 **66**
Hurd, C., *Ontario* T40+452 **91**
Hurghada, *Egypt* K68+270 **81**
Huron, S. *Dakota* U50+444 **93**
Huron, L., *U.S.A.-Canada* T40+450 **99**
Hurtsboro, *Alabama* T63+323 **97**
Huskvarna, *Sweden* M04+578 **47**
Husum, *W. Germany* M36+545 **48**
Hutchinson, *Kansas* U48+381 **95**
Hutchinson, *Minnesota* U26+450 **93**
Hüttenberg, *Austria* M03+469 **48**
Huttwil, *Switzerland* M43+471 **45**
Huy, *Belgium* M59+505 **44**
Hvar, I., *Yugoslavia* L79+431 **56**
Hwahsien, *China* E40+235 **67**
Hwaian, *China* E04+335 **66**
Hwaijen, *China* E42+399 **66**
Hwaining, *China* E17+305 **67**
Hwaiyang, *China* E30+337 **66**
Hwaiyn. *See* Tsingkiang
Hwangchow. See Hwangkang
Hwang-Hai. *See* Yellow Sea
Hwang Ho, R., *China* E24+360 **64**
Hwanghsien, *China* D87+377 **66**
Hwangkang, *China* E30+307 **66**
Hweichow. *See* Sihsien
Hweimin, *China* E15+375 **66**
Hweinan, *China* D53+428 **64**
Hweitseh, *China* F11+264 **67**
Hwohsien, *China* E50+365 **66**
Hyde, *England* N13+535 **37**
Hyden, *Kentucky* T51+372 **97**
Hyden, *W. Australia* E06–322 **110**
Hyde Park, *Vermont* S75+446 **91**
Hyderabad, *India* G69+173 **70**
Hyderabad, *Pakistan* H40+254 **70**
Hyères, *France* M53+431 **55**
Hyères, Is. d', *France* M51+430 **55**
Hyland R., *Yukon* W50+602 **88**
Hyndman Pk., *Idaho* V54+438 **98**
Hyogo, *Japan* D00+347 **68**
Hyrum, *Utah* V42+416 **94**
Hyrynsalmi, *Finland* L08+647 **46**
Hythe, *England* M84+511 **39**
Hythe, *England* N08+509 **39**
Iasi, *Romania* L14+471 **60**
Ibadan, *Nigeria* M66+074 **80**
Ibague, *Colombia* T02+044 **104**
Ibarra, *Ecuador* T18+005 **104**
Ibb, *Yemen* K05+140 **74**
Ibembo, *Zaire* L38+026 **82**
Ibicui, *Brazil* R70–294 **103**
Ibiza, I., *Balearic Is.* M80+390 **53**
Ibresi, *U.S.S.R.* J77+553 **61**
Ibri, *Oman* J22+231 **75**
Ibwe Munyama, *Zambia* L08–162 **84**
Ica, *Peru* T04–140 **104**
Ica, R., *Brazil* S50–028 **104**
Icel, *Turkey* K62+369 **51**
Iceland, I. & rep., *N. Atl. Oc.* **—34**
Ichak, *India* G28+242 **73**
Ichang, *China* E52+307 **66**
Icheng, *China* E46+317 **66**
Ichow. *See* Lini.
Ichun, *China* E33+277 **67**
Idabel, *Oklahoma* U28+338 **95**
Ida Grove, *Iowa* U33+424 **95**
Idah, *Nigeria* M50+072 **80**
Idaho, state, *U.S.A.* V67+444 **98**
Idaho Falls, *Idaho* V42+435 **92**
Ideles, *Algeria* M54+236 **80**
Idfu, *Egypt* K74+250 **81**
Idhra, I., *Greece* L39+374 **59**

Idirtu, *China* F50+374 **64**
Idlib, *Syria* K50+359 **76**
Idutywa, *Cape Province* L10–322 **84**
Ierissós, G. of, *Greece* L36+405 **59**
Ifakara, *Tanzania* K50–082 **83**
Iférouane, *Niger* M48+188 **80**
Ifni, terr., *N.-W. Africa* N64+288 **80**
Igan, *Sarawak* E49+028 **65**
Igarapé, Mirim, *Brazil* R23–020 **105**
Igarka, *U.S.S.R.* G20+675 **62**
Iglesias, *Sardinia* M39+393 **56**
Igli, *Algeria* N12+304 **80**
Igoma, *Tanzania* ' K70–078 **83**
Igra, *U.S.S.R.* J41+574 **61**
Iguaçú, & R., *Brazil* R58–256 **103**
Iguala, *Mexico* U56+183 **100**
Iguapé, *Brazil* R16–247 **103**
Iguatu, *Brazil* Q56–064 **105**
Igumira, *Tanzania* K70–068 **83**
Ihosy, *Madagascar* J84–224 **83**
Ihtiman, *Bulgaria* L37+424 **58**
Iida, *Japan* C73+355 **68**
Iisalmi, *Finland* L17+635 **46**
Ijebu-Ode, *Nigeria* M66+068 **80**
IJsselmonde, *Netherlands* M63+519 **44**
IJsselmuiden, *Netherlands* M54+526 **44**
IJsselstein, *Netherlands* M60+520 **44**
IJssel Meer, *Netherlands* M58+527 **44**
IJssel R., *Netherlands* M53+523 **44**
Ijui, *Brazil* R54–284 **103**
Ijzendijke, *Netherlands* M68+513 **44**
Ikaria, I., *Greece* L23+376 **59**
Ikisu, *Tanzania* K66–020 **83**
Ikla, *Estonia* L33+579 **47**
Ikonde, *Tanzania* K88–064 **83**
Ilagan, *Philippines* D79+171 **65**
Ilam, *Nepal* G12+269 **73**
Ilam, *Iran* J82+337 **74**
Ilanz, *Switzerland* M35+468 **45**
Iława. *Poland* L63+536 **49**
Iławka, *Poland* L56+544 **490**
Ile-à-la Crosse, L., *Sask.* V18+554 **88**
Ile-de-France, prov., *France* M75+490 **54**
Ilford, *England* M89+516 **39**
Ilfracombe, *England* N25+512 **38**
Ilhavo, *Portugal* N52+406 **52**
Ilhéus, *Brazil* Q54–148 **105**
Ili, *Kazakh.* G76+438 **62**
Ilia, *Greece* L51+378 **59**
Ilic, *Turkey* K39+394 **74**
Ilich, *Kazakh.* H40+410 **62**
Iligan, *Philippines* D64+080 **65**
Ilimsk, *U.S.S.R.* F08+569 **63**
Iliodhrómia, I., *Greece* L37+392 **59**
Ilion, *New York* T00+430 **96**
Ilkeston, *England* N08+530 **37**
Ilkley, *England* N11+539 **37**
Illapel, *Chile* S67–315 **103**
Ille-et-Vilaine, dep., *France* N11+482 **54**
Illescas, *Spain* N23+401 **52**
Illimani, mt., *Bolivia* S47–166 **104**
Illinois, state, *U.S.A.* U03+398 **99**
Illinois R., *Illinois* U04+398 **95**
Illora, *Spain* N23+373 **52**
Ilmen Oz., *U.S.S.R.* K83+583 **60**
Ilminster, *England* N17+509 **38**
Ilo, *Peru* S68–175 **104**
Iloilo, *Philippines* D75+108 **65**
Ilorin, *Nigeria* M62+084 **80**
Ilpi, *U.S.S.R.* A41+615 **63**
Imabaru, *Japan* D12+340 **68**
Iman, *U.S.S.R.* D07+459 **63**
Imandra, Oz., *U.S.S.R.* K73+675 **62**
Imerimandroso, *Madagascar* J68–176 **83**
Imi, *Ethiopia* K16+064 **83**
Immendingen, *Germany* M38+479 **48**
Immingham, *England* N01+536 **37**
Imperatriz, *Brazil* S44–054 **104**
Imperatriz, *Brazil* R14–056 **105**
Imperia, *Italy* M42+439 **56**
Imperial Dam, *Arizona* V57+331 **98**
Imphal, *India* F66+247 **71**
Imroz, I., *Turkey* L26+402 **74**
Imtan, *Syria* K49+324 **76**
Inagua, I. Gt., *Bahamas, The* S80 + 211 **101**
Inagua, I. Lit., *Bahamas, The* S78 + 215 **101**
Inarijärvi, *Finland* L18 + 688 **46**
Inari L., *Finland* L12+690 **46**
Inch, *Ireland, Rep.* N37+527 **43**
Inchkeith, *Scotland* N19+560 **41**
Inchön, *Korea* D50+375 **64**
Incourt, *Belgium* M61+507 **44**
Indaal, L., *Scotland* N38+557 **41**
Indals Älv. *Sweden* L80+629 **46**
Indaw, *Burma* F53+242 **71**
Indawgyi L., *Burma* F52+253 **71**
Independence, *Iowa* U12+425 **95**
Independence, *Kansas* U34+372 **95**
Independence, *Missouri* U26+390 **95**
Independencia, *Argentina* S50–317 **103**
India, rep., *S. Asia* **— 70–71**
Indian Des. *See* Thar Des.
Indian L., *New York* S86+437 **96**
Indiana, *Pennsylvania* T55+407 **96**
Indiana. state, *U.S.A.* T72+402 **99**
Indianapolis, *Indiana* T67+398 **91**
Indian Head, *Saskatchewan* U82+505 **88**
Indian House L., *Quebec* S29+562 **89**
Indianola, *Iowa* U22+413 **95**
Indiga, *U.S.S.R.* J67+676 **62**
Indigirka, R., *U.S.S.R.* C30+678 **63**
Indonesia, rep., *S.-E. Asia* E30–050 **65**
Indore, *India* G84+226 **70**
Indre, dep., *France* M80+467 **54**
Indre-et-Loire, dep., *France* M86+472 **54**
Indur. *See* Nizamabad
Indus, R., *Pakistan, etc.* H10+354 **70**
Inebolu, *Turkey* K66+419 **74**
Inez, *Kentucky* T45+378 **97**
Infantes, *Spain* N18+387 **52**
Ingelmunster, *Belgium* M70+509 **44**
Ingersoll, *Ontario* T35+431 **91**
Ingham, *Queensland* C23–188 **111**
Inglefield Inlet, *Greenland* S58+770 **26**
Inglefield Ld., *Greenland* S00+790 **26**
Inglewood, *New Zealand* A34–391 **112**
Inglewood, *Victoria* C37–366 **109**
Ing Luiggi, *Argentina* S27–353 **103**
Ingolstadt, *W. Germany* M22+488 **48**
Ingrid Christensen Coast,
Antarctica G70–700 **27**

Inhambane, *Mozambique* K58–240 **84**
Ining, *China* G51+440 **62**
Inishark I., *Ireland, Rep* N62+536 **42**
Inishcrone, *Ireland, Rep.* N54+542 **42**
Inishbofin, I., *Ireland, Rep.* N61+536 **42**
Inisheer, I., *Ireland, Rep.* N57+531 **43**
Inishkea I., *Ireland, Rep.* N61+541 **42**
Inishmaan, I., *Ireland, Rep.* N58+531 **43**
Inishmore, I., *Ireland, Rep.* N58+531 **43**
Inishmurray, I., *Ireland, Rep.*, N52+544 **42**
Inishowen & Hd.,
Ireland, Rep. N42+552 **42**
Inishtrahull, *Ireland, Rep.* N43+554 **42**
Inishtrahull Sd., *Ireland, Rep.* N44+554 **42**
Inishturk, I., *Ireland, Rep.* N61+537 **42**
Inklin R., *British Columbia* W75+590 **88**
Inner Sd., *Scotland* N36+574 **40**
Innerleithen, *Scotland* N18+556 **41**
Inner Mongolia, *China* F00+410 **64**
Innertkirchen, *Switzerland* M40+467 **45**
Innisfail, *Queensland* C24–172 **111**
Innsbruck, *Austria* M22+473 **48**
Inny R., *Ireland, Rep.* N47+535 **43**
Inowrocław, *Poland* L71+528 **49**
Inquisivi, *Bolivia* S43–167 **104**
Ins, *Switzerland* M47+470 **45**
In Salah, (Ain Salah) *Alg.* M76+270 **80**
Insar, *U.S.S.R.* K04+538 **61**
Insein, *Burma* F53+168 **71**
In Shan, *China* E72+417 **66**
Insterburg. *See* Chernyakhovsk.
Interlaken, *Switzerland* M43+467 **45**
International Falls, *Minnesota* U20+486 **93**
Interview I., *Andaman Is.* F75+130 **71**
Intragna, *Switzerland* M38+462 **45**
Inutil, B., *Chile* S60–536 **103**
Inveraray, *Scotland* N31+562 **41**
Inverbervie, *Scotland* N14+568 **41**
Invercargill, *New Zealand* A69–464 **112**
Inverell, *New South Wales* B84–288 **109**
Invergordon, *Scotland* N25+577 **40**
Inverkeithing, *Scotland* N20+560 **41**
Inverness, *Nova Scotia* S08+463 **90**
Inverness, *Scotland* N25+575 **40**
Invershin, *Scotland* N26+579 **40**
Inverurie, *Scotland* N14+573 **40**
Investigator Str., *S. Aust.* C75–356 **111**
Inyati, *Rhodesia* L08–196 **84**
Inza, *U.S.S.R.* J82+538 **61**
Inzer, *U.S.S.R.* J14+542 **61**
Ioannina, *Greece* L55+397 **59**
Iola, *Kansas* U34+379 **95**
Iona, *Nova Scotia* S05+460 **90**
Iona I., *Scotland* N39+563 **41**
Ionia, *Michigan* T60+430 **91**
Ionia, *Montana* V14+453 **93**
Ionian Is., *Greece* L56+387 **59**
Ionian Sea, *Italy, etc* L72+380 **51**
Ios, I., *Greece* L28+367 **59**
Iowa state, *U.S.A.* U27+418 **99**
Iowa City, *Iowa* U09+416 **95**
Iowa Falls, *Iowa* U20+426 **95**
Ipala, *Mexico* V03+202 **100**
Ipiales, *Colombia* T15+008 **104**
Ipin, *China* F03+287 **67**
Ipiros, *Greece* L55+395 **59**
Ipoh, *Malaya* F24+046 **69**
Ippy, *Cent. Afr. Rep.* L54+060 **81**
Ipswich, *England* M83+520 **39**
Ipswich, *Queensland* B73–274 **111**
Ipswich, *S. Dakota* U54+454 **93**
Ipu, *Brazil* Q63–043 **105**
Iquique, *Chile* S61–202 **103**
Iquitos, *Peru* S79–038 **104**
Iracoubo, *French Guiana* R49+054 **105**
Iráklia, I., *Greece* L27+368 **59**
Iráklion, *Kriti* L29+353 **59**
Iran (Persia), *S. W. Asia* J40+330 **75**
Irapa, *Venezuela* S15+105 **104**
Irapuato, *Mexico* U68+206 **100**
Iraq, rep., *S.-W. Asia* L10+330 **74**
Irazu, Vol., *Costa Rica* T53+102 **101**
Irbid, *Jordan* K55+326 **76**
Irbit, *U.S.S.R.* H72+576 **61**
Ireland, I., *British Isles* **— 42–43**
Ireland, Rep. of
British Isles N48+520 **34**
Irendyk Mts., *U.S.S.R.* J12+520 **61**
Irgiz, *Kazakh* H83+485 **62**
Irian Jaya, *New Guinea* C60–054 **65**
Iringa, *Tanzania* K56–078 **83**
Irish Sea, *British Isles* N30+536 **34**
Irkutsk, *U.S.S.R.* F04+524 **63**
Iron Mt., *Missouri* U03+375 **97**
Iron City, *Tennessee* T76+350 **97**
Irondale, *Ontario* T21+448 **91**
Iron Knob, *S. Australia* C76–327 **111**
Iron Mountain, *Michigan* T78+458 **91**
Iron River, *Michigan* T82+461 **91**
Iron River, *Wisconsin* U09+465 **93**
Ironton, *Missouri* U04+376 **95**
Ironton, *Ohio* T46+386 **97**
Ironwood, *Michigan* U01+465 **91**
Iroquois, *Ontario* T42+499 **91**
Iroquois Chute, *Quebec* S78+477 **91**
Irrawaddy, *Burma* F60+172 **71**
Irrawaddy, R., *Burma* F54+228 **71**
Irthing R., *England* N17+549 **37**
Irtysh R., *U.S.S.R.* H35+595 **62**
Irumu, *Zaire* L00–014 **83**
Irvine & R., *Scotland* N31+556 **41**
Irvinestown, *N. Ireland* N46+545 **42**
Isa, Mt., *Queensland* C64–208 **111**
Isabela I., *Galapagos Is.* U10–007 **107**
Isaccea, *Romania* L09+452 **58**
Isafjördhur, *Iceland* P48+661 **46**
Isai Kalat, *Pakistan* H66+269 **70**
Isa Khel, *Pakistan* H22+327 **72**
Isangi, *Zaire* L34+006 **82**
Isari, *Greece* L48+374 **59**
Ischia, I., *Italy* M07+407 **57**
Ise B., *Japan* C81+347 **68**
Iseghem. See Izegem
Iselin, *Pennsylvania* T26+406 **96**
Iseltwald, *Switzerland* M42+467 **45**
Isère & R., *France* M57+452 **55**
Isernia, *Italy* M05+416 **57**
Isha Baidoa, *Somalia* K08+030 **83**
Ishan, *China* E68+245 **67**
Ishikari, R., *Japan* C40+435 **68**
Ishim, *U.S.S.R.* H34+562 **62**

Ishimbai, *U.S.S.R.* J23+534 **61**
Ishinomaki B., *Japan* C52+383 **68**
Ishkamish, *Afghanistan* H35+364 **75**
Ishkasham, *Afghanistan* H20+366 **75**
Ishpeming, *Michigan* T76+465 **91**
Ishqanan, *Iran* J38+272 **75**
Isil Kul, *U.S.S.R.* H23+549 **62**
Isiolo, *Kenya* K44+004 **83**
Isisford, *Queensland* C35–241 **111**
Iskenderun, *Turkey* K53+366 **74**
Iskilip, *Turkey* K64+407 **74**
Iskitim, *U.S.S.R.* G40+547 **62**
Iskut R., *British Columbia* W65+568 **88**
Islamabad, *Pakistan* H11+338 **72**
Islampur, *India* G29+249 **73**
Island L., *Manitoba* U25+538 **88**
Island Pond, *Vermont* S71+449 **91**
Islands, B. of, *Newfoundland* R84+493 **90**
Islands, B. of, *New Zealand* A35–353 **112**
Islay I., *Scotland* N37+558 **41**
Isle of Man., *British Is.* N28+542 **37**
Isle of Wight, *England* N08+507 **39**
Isleta, *New Mexico* V11+348 **94**
Isle Verte, *Quebec* S56+480 **90**
Ismailia, *Egypt* K76+306 **81**
Isna, *Egypt* K74+252 **81**
Isoka, *Zambia* K74–104 **83**
Isparta, *Turkey* K87+378 **74**
Israel, rep., *S.-W. Asia* K62+320 **76**
Issoudun, *France* M78+469 **54**
Issyk Kul, Oz., *Kirgiz* G80+424 **62**
Istanbul, *Turkey* L07+411 **74**
Istmina, *Colombia* T15+053 **104**
Istra, *Yugoslavia* M06+452 **56**
Itabaiana, *Brazil* Q31–073 **105**
Itacare, *Brazil* Q54–144 **105**
Itacoatiara, *Brazil* R8J–030 **104**
Itaete, *Brazil* Q67–130 **105**
Itaituba, *Brazil* R64–043 **105**
Itajai, *Brazil* R22–270 **103**
Italy, *Central Europe* M18+440 **50**
Itapecuru-mirim, *Brazil* Q86–033 **105**
Itapemirim, Cachoeiro de,
Brazil Q67–208 **105**
Itapetininga, *Brazil* R19–235 **105**
Itapura, *Brazil* R39–207 **105** '
Itaqui, *Brazil* R70–292 **103**
Itarsi, *India* G72+225 **70**
Itasca, L., *Minnesota* U33+472 **98**
Itauna, *Brazil* Q88–201 **105**
Itéa, *Greece* L46+385 **59**
Ithaca, *Michigan* T58+433 **91**
Ithaca, *New York* T09+424 **96**
Itháci. *See* Ithaka
Ithaka, *Greece* L56+384 **59**
Itiés, *Greece* L50+401 **59**
Itula, *Congo* L12–036 **83**
Iturbe, *Argentina* S32–231 **103**
Ivailovgrad, *Bulgaria* L23+415 **58**
Ivanhoe, *New South Wales* C34–329 **109**
Ivanic Grad, *Yugoslavia* L82+457 **56**
Ivano-Frankovsk, *Ukraine* L34+490 **60**
Ivanovka, *U.S.S.R.* J55+525 **61**
Ivanovo, *U.S.S.R.* K24+570 **60**
Ivdel, *U.S.S.R.* H87+608 **62**
Iviza, I. See Ibiza, I.
Ivory Coast, *W. Africa* N40+080 **80**
Iwakuni, *Japan* D17+341 **68**
Iwaniska, *Poland* L52+507 **49**
Ixiamas, *Bolivia* S49–137 **104**
Ixtla, *Mexico* U55+186 **100**
Ixtlan de Juarez, *Mexico* U39+174 **100**
Iyang, *China* E16+284 **67**
Iyo Nada, *Japan* D18+336 **68**
Izabal & L., *Guatemala* T85+154 **100**
Izamal, *Mexico* T83+208 **100**
Izegem, *Belgium* M71+509 **44**
Izhevsk, *U.S.S.R.* J40+568 **61**
Izhma R., *U.S.S.R.* J37+650 **62**
Izki, *Oman* J14+229 **75**
Izmail, *Ukraine* L07+454 **60**
İzmir, *Turkey* L17+384 **74**
İzmit, *Turkey* L01+408 **74**
Izra, *Syria* K52+329 **76**
Iztapa, *Guatemala* U04+139 **100**
Izu Pen., *Japan* C66+348 **68**
Izu Shichito, *Japan* C62+343 **68**
Izyum, *Ukraine* K47+492 **60**
Jääski, *Kazakh.* L06+610 **47**
Jabalpur, *India* G60+232 **73**
Jabbeke, *Belgium* M72+512 **44**
Jabbul, *Syria* K45+361 **76**
Jablonec, *Czechoslovakia* L89+507 **48**
Jabrin Oasis, *Saudi Arabia* J66+232 **75**
Jaburú, *Brazil* S39–040 **104**
Jaca, *Spain* N03+426 **53**
Jacarezinho, *Brazil* R30–232 **105**
Jachal, *Argentina* S33–303 **103**
Jacitara, *Brazil* S32–019 **104**
Jacksboro, *Tennessee* T55+363 **97**
Jackson, *Kentucky* T50+375 **97**
Jackson, *Louisiana* U07+308 **95**
Jackson, *Michigan* T56+423 **91**
Jackson, *Minnesota* U30+436 **93**
Jackson, *Mississippi* U01+323 **95**
Jackson, *Missouri* T88+374 **97**
Jackson, *N. Carolina* T15+364 **97**
Jackson, *Ohio* T46+391 **91**
Jackson, *Tennessee* T83+356 **97**
Jackson, *Wyoming* V36+434 **93**
Jackson Mts., *Nevada* V81+414 **92**
Jacksonville, *Florida* T40+303 **97**
Jacksonville, *Illinois* U02+398 **95**
Jacksonville, *N. Carolina* T15+348 **97**
Jacksonville, *Texas* U32+320 **95**
Jacmel, *Haiti* S75+183 **101**
Jacobabad, *Pakistan* H49+282 **80**
Jacobina, *Brazil* Q63–112 **105**
Jacques Cartier, Mt., *Que.* S36+490 **90**
Jacquet River, *N.B.* S36+479 **90**
Jade Mines, *Burma* F53+256 **71**
Jadib, *Yemen, South* J42+166 **75**
Jaén, *Spain* N22+377 **52**
Jafarabad, *India* H22+209 **70**
Jaffa (Yafo), *Israel* K62+320 **76**
Jaffna, *Sri Lanka* G68+097 **70**
Jagadhri, *India* G76+301 **72**
Jagdispur, *India* G33+254 **73**
Jagodina, *Yugoslavia* L53+440 **58**
Jagraon, *India* G87+308 **72**
Jaguarão, *Brazil* R51–324 **103**

Jaguari, *Brazil* R58–295 **103**
Jaguariaira, *Brazil* R28–242 **105**
Jaguaruna, *Brazil* R24–286 **103**
Jahanabad, *India* G30+252 **73**
Jahangirabad, *India* G71+284 **72**
Jahra, *Kuwait* J74+294 **74**
Jahrum, *Iran* J38+284 **75**
Jaicos, *Brazil* Q66–074 **105**
Jaipur, *India* G84+268 **70**
Jaipur, *India* G21+208 **71**
Jais, *India* G51+263 **73**
Jaisalmer, *India* H24+268 **70**
Jajarm, *Iran* J22+370 **75**
Jakarta, *Java, Indonesia* E79+062 **65**
Jäkkvik, *Sweden* L78+663 **46**
Jakobi, *Estonia* L21+592 **47**
Jakobstad. *See Pietarsaari*
Jalalabad, *Afghanistan* H28+345 **72**
Jalalpur, *India* G44+263 **73**
Jalalpur, *Pakistan* H22+295 **72**
Jalalpur, *Pakistan* H04+327 **72**
Jalapa, *Nicaragua* T65+139 **101**
Jalapa Enriquez, *Mexico* U42+195 **100**
Jalasjärvi, *Finland* L43+625 **46**
Jalaun, *India* G64+260 **73**
Jalgaon, *India* G68+210 **70**
Jalisco, state, *Mexico* U80+200 **100**
Jalk, *Iran* H74+276 **75**
Jalor, *India* H14+252 **70**
Jalpaiguri, *India* G07+265 **73**
Jaluit, I., *Marshall Is.* A64+060 **106**
Jamaica, I., *West Indies* T14+181 **101**
Jamaja, *Estonia* L48+580 **47**
Jamalabad, *Iran* J73+373 **74**
Jamalpur, *Bangladesh* G00+249 **73**
Jamalpur, *India* G21+253 **73**
Jamberoo, *New S. Wales* B86–346 **109**
Jambi, *Sumatra, Indonesia* F08-016 **65**
Jamdena, I., *See Yamdena*
James B., *Canada* T30+530 **89**
James Ras., *N. Terr., Aust.* D15–241 **110**
James R., *S. Dakota* U50+442 **98**
James R., *Virginia* I20+377 **97**
Jamesburg, *California* W10+364 **92**
James Ross, I., *Antarctica* R75–640 **27**
Jamestown, *New York* T25+421 **91**
Jamestown & Res., *N. Dakota* U52+469 **93**
Jamestown, *S. Australia* C68–332 **109**
James W. Ellsworth Ld.,
  Antarctica U40–770 **27**
Jamiltepec, *Mexico* U47+162 **100**
Jammer Bugt, *Denmark* M36+573 **47**
Jammu & Kashmir, *India* H01+327 **72**
Jammu & Kashmir, *India–*
  Pakistan H00+350 **70**
Jamnagar, *India* H30+224 **70**
Jampur, *Pakistan* H26+296 **72**
Jamrad, *Afghanistan* H42+331 **75**
Jamrao, *Pakistan* H35+255 **70**
Jämsä *Finland* L29+619 **47**
Jamshedpur, *India* G22+228 **73**
Jamui, *India* G22+249 **73**
Jamuna R., *Bangladesh* G02+250 **73**
Jandaq, *Iran* J34+341 **75**
Jandiala, *India* G89+315 **72**
Janesville, *Wisconsin* T84+427 **95**
Jangipur, *India* G11+245 **73**
Jani Khel, *Pakistan* H27+328 **72**
Janjira, *India* H12+184 **70**
Jan Mayen, I., *Arctic Ocean* N55+710 **62**
Janos, *Mexico* V18+310 **100**
Jansath, *India* G73+293 **72**
Jansenville, *Cape Province* L30–330 **84**
Januaria, *Brazil* Q86–154 **105**
Janze, *France* N09+480 **54**
Jaoho, *China* D06+472 **64**
Jaora, *India* G89+236 **70**
Japan & Sea of, *E. Asia* C60+400 **64**
Japen, I., *See Yapen I.*
Japur R., *Brazil* S45+019 **104**
Japvo Mt., *India* F65+256 **71**
Jaragua, *Brazil* R25–265 **103**
Jaragua, *Brazil* R26–157 **105**
Jarales, *New Mexico* V12+346 **94**
Jaramillo, *Argentina* S43–472 **103**
Jarandilla, *Spain* N34+402 **52**
Jardim, *Brazil* Q40–065 **105**
Jardines de la Reina, *Cuba* T24+211 **101**
Jarji, *Nigeria* M46+108 **80**
Jarocin, *Poland* L75+520 **49**
Jaremer, *Czechoslovakia* L85+504 **49**
Jarosław, *Poland* L44+500 **49**
Järpen, *Sweden* M09+634 **46**
Jarrow, *England* N09+550 **37**
Jarvis I., *Pacific Ocean* Y60–002 **106**
Järvsö, *Sweden* L83+617 **47**
Jashpurnagar, *India* G35+229 **73**
Jask, *Iran* J13+257 **75**
Jason I., *Falkland Is.* S07–510 **103**
Jasper, *Florida* T48+305 **97**
Jasper, *Georgia* T57+345 **97**
Jasper, *Texas* U24+310 **95**
Jasper & Park, *Alberta* V80+533 **88**
Jassy. *See Iasi.*
Jastrowie, *Poland* L79+534 **49**
Jaswantnagar, *India* G66+269 **73**
Jaszberény, *Hungary* L60+475 **49**
Jath, *India* G88+170 **70**
Jativa, *Spain* N03+390 **53**
Jatoba, *Brazil* Q50–092 **105**
Jaú, *Brazil* R21–222 **105**
Jauche, *Belgium* M60+507 **44**
Jauf, *Saudi Arabia* K31+299 **74**
Jaulfari, *Saudi Arabia* J46+165 **75**
Jauja, *Peru* T02–117 **104**
Jaumave, *Mexico* U57+234 **100**
Jaunjelgava, *Latvia* L29+566 **47**
Jaunpur, *India* G44+258 **73**
Java, I., *Indonesia* E60–073 **65**
Javari, R., *Peru-Brazil* S78–065 **104**
Javier, I., *Chile* S86–471 **103**
Jawa, *Nigeria* M24+128 **81**
Jawalamukhi, *India* G82+318 **72**
Jayapura, *Indonesia* F76+026 **65**
Jazir, *Oman* J20+186 **75**
Jebba, *Nigeria* M62+090 **80**
Jeble, *Syria* K54+354 **76**
Jech Doab, *Pakistan* H14+321 **72**
Jedabya, *Libya* L58+306 **81**
Jedburgh, *Scotland* N15+555 **41**

Jedede, *Saudi Arabia* K29+218 **74**
Jefferson, *Georgia* T51+341 **97**
Jefferson, *Wisconsin* T82+430 **95**
Jefferson, Mt., *Oregon* W11+446 **92**
Jefferson City, *Missouri* U13+386 **95**
Jeffersonville, *Indiana* T64+383 **97**
Jehol. *See Chêng-têhshih.*
Jekabpils, *Latvia* L25+565 **47**
Jelgava, *Latvia* L37+566 **47**
Jelsava, *Czechoslovakia* L59+486 **49**
Jemeppe, *Belgium* M62+505 **44**
Jena, *E. Germany* M21+509 **48**
Jenin, *Jordan* K58+325 **76**
Jenipapo, *Brazil* R84–064 **104**
Jennings, *Louisiana* U16+302 **95**
Jenolan Caves, *New S. Wales* C00–339 **109**
Jeparit, *Victoria* C48–362 **109**
Jeppo, *Finland* L44+634 **46**
Jerablus, *Syria* K42+368 **76**
Jerash, *Jordan* K55+323 **76**
Jeremie, *Haiti* S84+187 **101**
Jerez, *Mexico* U78+228 **100**
Jerez de la Frontera, *Spain* N37+367 **52**
Jeriban, *Somalia* J66+072 **83**
Jericho, *Jordan* K57+319 **76**
Jericho, *Queensland* C24–234 **111**
Jerilderie, *New S. Wales* C26–354 **109**
Jerome, *Arizona* V43+348 **94**
Jerruck, *Pakistan* H40+250 **70**
Jersey, I., *Channel Is.* N13+492 **54**
Jersey City, *New Jersey* S84+407 **96**
Jerseyshore, *Pennsylvania* T14+412 **96**
Jerusalem, *Israel-Jordan* K59+318 **76**
Jervis B., *New South Wales* B86–351 **109**
Jervois Ra., *N. Terr., Aust.* C83–225 **111**
Jesenik, *Czechoslovakia* L77+503 **49**
Jesselton, *N. Borneo* E24+060 **65**
Jessore, *Bangladesh* G04+231 **73**
Jesup, *Georgia* T41+316 **97**
Jesus I., *Quebec* S81+457 **91**
Jesus Maria, *Argentina* S25–310 **103**
Jesus Maria, *Mexico* V16+282 **100**
Jetalsar, *India* H26+217 **70**
Jeypore, *India* G44+189 **71**
Jezzin, *Lebanon* K57+335 **76**
Jhal, *Pakistan* H45+282 **70**
Jhalrapatan, *India* G82+246 **70**
Jhang Maghiana, *Pakistan* H16+313 **72**
Jhansi, *India* G68+254 **73**
Jhau, *Pakistan* H56+262 **70**
Jhelum, *Pakistan* H08+330 **72**
Jhelum R., *Pakistan* H14+325 **72**
Jhunjhunu, *India* G87+281 **72**
Jiachan, *Tibet* G53+316 **70**
Jianpur, *India* G40+262 **73**
Jibhalanta, *Mongolia* F49+480 **63**
Jicaro, *Nicaragua* T65+138 **101**
Jičin, *Czechoslovakia* L88+505 **49**
Jidd, *Iraq* K32+328 **74**
Jidda, *Saudi Arabia* K35+215 **74**
Jiggitai L., *Tibet* G19+350 **71**
Jihlava, *Czechoslovakia* L87+494 **49**
Jildiah, *Jebel, Saudi Arabia* K15+277 **74**
Jimena de la Frontera, *Spain* N32+365 **52**
Jimenez, *Mexico* U64+290 **100**
Jimenez, *Mexico* V00+270 **100**
Jimma, *Ethiopia* K48+076 **83**
Jim Thorpe, *Pennsylvania* T05+408 **96**
Jind, *India* G82+293 **72**
Jinotega, *Nicaragua* T66+131 **101**
Jipijapa, *Ecuador* T33–012 **104**
Jirgalanta, *Mongolia* F80+480 **63**
Jirm, *Afghanistan* H25+368 **75**
Jisha, *Saudi Arabia* J61+253 **74**
Jisresh Shughur, *Syria* K52+358 **76**
Jiul R., *Romania* L37+441 **58**
Jiza, *Jordan* K54+317 **76**
João Pessoa, *Brazil* Q28–071 **105**
Jodhpur, *India* H12+263 **70**
Joensuu, *Finland* L01+626 **46**
Jofane, *Mozambique* K64–214 **84**
Jogjakarta, *See Yogyakarta*
Johannesburg, *Transvaal* L12–262 **84**
John o' Groats, *Scotland* N18+586 **40**
Johnsonburg, *Pennsylvania* T22+415 **96**
Johnson City, *Tennessee* T44+363 **97**
Johnston I., *Pacific Ocean* Z28+170 **106**
Johnstown, *Ireland, Rep.* N41+534 **43**
Johnstown, *New York* S85+430 **96**
Johnstown, *Pennsylvania* T24+403 **96**
Johore Baharu, *Malaya* F08+015 **69**
Joinville, *Brazil* R23–263 **103**
Joinville, *France* M59+484 **54**
Joinville I., *Antarctica* R60–630 **27**
Jokkmökk, *Sweden* L61+666 **46**
Jol Plat., *Saudi Arabia* J65+154 **74**
Joliet, *Illinois* T78+415 **95**
Joliette, *Quebec* S81+460 **91**
Jolo, I., *Philippines* D82+059 **65**
Jonava, *Lithuania* L34+551 **47**
Jonesboro, *Arkansas* U04+358 **95**
Jonesboro, *Georgia* T56+335 **97**
Jonesboro, *Illinois* T86+374 **97**
Jonesboro, *Louisiana* U16+322 **95**
Jonesport, *Maine* S46+445 **90**
Joniškis, *Lithuania* L39+562 **47**
Jönköping, *Sweden* M05+578 **47**
Jonquière, *Quebec* S67+484 **90**
Jonuta, *Mexico* U13+180 **100**
Joplin, *Missouri* U27+372 **95**
Jordan, *Minnesota* U22+447 **93**
Jordan, *Montana* V12+473 **93**
Jordan, S.-W. *Asia* K53+313 **74**
Jordan, R., *Israel* K57+323 **76**
Jordan, R., *Utah* V42+407 **94**
Jorhat, *India* F65+267 **71**
Jorje Montt, I., *Chile* S88–513 **103**
Jorna da Del Muerto,
  New Mexico V11+330 **94**
Joseph Bonaparte Gulf,
  W. Australia D40–130 **110**
Jostedalsbre Glacier, *Norway* M47+616 **47**
Jotunheimen, *Norway* M42+615 **34**
Joux, L. de, *Switzerland* M52+466 **45**
Jowai, *India* F76+254 **71**
Juan de Fuca Str.,
  U.S.A.-Canada W20+479 **98**
Juan Fernandez I.,
  Pacific Ocean T25–345 **107**
Juan Stuven, I., *Chile* T00–479 **103**
Juárez, *Argentina* R89–376 **103**

Juarez, *Mexico* U01+188 **100**
Juba, *Sudan* K80+050 **81**
Jubba, *Saudi Arabia* K23+280 **74**
Jubbulpore. *See Jabalpur*
Jubeil, *Lebanon* K56+341 **76**
Jubi, C., *Morocco* N78+280 **80**
Jucaro, *Cuba* T23+216 **101**
Juchitan, *Mexico* U31+164 **100**
Judenburg, *Austria* M02+471 **48**
Judique, *Nova Scotia* S09+459 **90**
Judith, *Montana* V28+477 **93**
Judith Pt., *Rhode Island* S67+414 **91**
Juian, *China* D85+278 **67**
Juichow. *See Kaoan*
Juist, I., *Germany* M48+537 **48**
Juiz de Fora, *Brazil* Q80–217 **105**
Jujuy, *Argentina* S32–242 **103**
Jukao, *China* D66+427 **66**
Jukkasjarvi, *Sweden* L52+679 **34**
Julaco, *Bolivia* S46–209 **104**
Julesburg, *Colorado* U74+410 **94**
Juli, *Peru* S57–162 **104**
Juliaca, *Peru* S61–156 **104**
Julianstown, *Ireland, Rep.* N38+537 **42**
Julio de Castilhos, *Brazil* R52–293 **103**
Jullundur, *India* G86+313 **72**
Jumaima, *Iraq* K08+298 **74**
Jumet, *Belgium* M63+504 **44**
Jumilla, *Spain* N08+385 **53**
Jumin, *Iran* J08+345 **75**
Jumla, *Nepal* G47+293 **73**
Jumna (Yamuna), R., *India* G58+260 **73**
Junagarh, *India* H17+216 **70**
Junan, *China* E33+330 **66**
Junction City, *Kansas* U41+390 **95**
Jundiai, *Brazil* R11–232 **105**
Juneau, *Alaska* W86+585 **99**
Junee, *New South Wales* C14–349 **109**
Jungfrau, mt., *Switzerland* M42+465 **45**
Jungfraujoch, *Switzerland* M42+465 **45**
Jungkiang, *China* E68+259 **67**
Junin, *Argentina* S67–400 **103**
Junin, *Argentina* S06–345 **103**
Junin, *Chile* S61–198 **103**
Junin, *Peru* S66–114 **104**
Juning. *See Junan*
Juniper, *New Brunswick* S43+466 **90**
Juniye, (Jounie) *Lebanon* K56+340 **76**
Junsele, *Sweden* L78+637 **46**
Juojarvi, *Finland* L08+628 **46**
Jupia, *Brazil* R39–208 **105**
Juquila, *Mexico* U45+163 **100**
Jura, dep., *France* M54+467 **54**
Jura, mts., *France-Switz.* M54+463 **54**
Jura I. & Sd. of, *Scotland* N35+560 **41**
Jurado, *Colombia* T17+072 **104**
Jurbarkas, *Lithuania* L43+551 **47**
Jurf ed Darawish, *Jordan* K55+307 **76**
Jüri, *Estonia* L30+594 **47**
Juruá, R., *Brazil* S40–045 **104**
Juruena & R., *Brazil* R83–128 **104**
Juruty, *Brazil* R67–020 **105**
Jusiye, *Syria* K50+344 **76**
Jussy, *Switzerland* M52+462 **45**
Justlahuaca, *Mexico* U48+174 **100**
Justo Daract, *Argentina* S31–338 **103**
Jutahy, *Brazil* S42–027 **104**
Juticalpa, *Honduras* T64+146 **101**
Jutland. *See Jylland.*
Juuka, *Finland* L05+632 **46**
Juwain, *Afghanistan* H80+316 **75**
Juwara, *Oman* J16+190 **75**
Jylland, *Denmark* M36+562 **47**
Jylland, South, *Denmark* M36+552 **47**
Jyväskylä, *Finland* L26+623 **46**

K2, Mt, *Kashmir* G81+359 **72**
Kabaena, I., *Indonesia* D79–054 **65**
Kabala, *Sierra Leone* N70+096 **80**
Kabale, *Uganda* L00–014 **83**
Kabalega Falls, *Uganda* K80+020 **83**
Kabba, *Nigeria* M54+078 **80**
Kabia, I., *Indonesia* D87–061 **65**
Kabinda, *Zaire* L26–074 **82**
Kabongo, *Zaire* L26–074 **82**
Kabul & R., *Afghanistan* H34+346 **75**
Kabunda, *Zaire* L04–126 **83**
Kabwe, *Zambia* L10–144 **83**
Kačanik, *Yugoslavia* L53+424 **58**
Kachiry, *Kazakh* G84+530 **62**
Kachkar, *U.S.S.R.* H84+544 **61**
Kachuga, *U.S.S.R.* E84+540 **63**
Kadaura, *India* G61+260 **73**
Kadina, *S. Australia* C74–340 **109**
Kadiri, *India* G70+141 **70**
Kadiyevka, *Ukraine* K39+486 **60**
Kadoka, *S. Dakota* U69+438 **93**
Kadom, *U.S.S.R.* K15+546 **61**
Kadugli, *Sudan* L02+110 **81**
Kadur, *India* G84+136 **70**
Kadyy, *U.S.S.R.* K11+577 **61**
Kadzand, *Netherlands* M70+514 **44**
Kaesong, *Korea* D52+380 **64**
Kaf, *Saudi Arabia* K46+315 **74**
Kafakumba, *Congo* L38–096 **82**
Kafanchan, *Nigeria* M40+096 **80**
Kafia Kingi, *Sudan* L34+092 **81**
Kafr, *Chad* L44+162 **81**
Kafr Behum, *Syria* K50+351 **76**
Katrun, *Syria* K52+348 **76**
Kagan, *Uzbek* H63+396 **61**
Kagi. *See Chiai*
Kagmar, *Sudan* K88+144 **81**
Kagoshima, *Japan* D27+316 **68**
Kagoshima B., *Japan* D28+311 **68**
Kagul, *Moldavia* L11+459 **60**
Kahama, *Tanzania* K74–038 **83**
Kahoka, *Missouri* U10+404 **95**
Kahra, *Yemen* J89+141 **74**
Kahror, *Pakistan* H18+296 **72**
Kahta, *Turkey* K38+381 **74**
Kahuta, *Pakistan* H09+336 **72**
Kai-Kep, *Indonesia* D14–058 **65**
Kaiama, *Nigeria* M66+096 **80**
Kaiapoi, *New Zealand* A44–434 **112**
Kai-chow, *China* E30+357 **66**
Kaieteur Fall, *Guyana* R87+052 **104**
Kai feng, *China* E33+348 **66**
Kaigo, *Sudan* K80+060 **81**
Kaihwa. *See Wenshan*

Kaikoura, *New Zealand* A38–424 **112**
Kaikoura Ra., *New Zealand* A40–421 **112**
Kailas Ra., *India-Tibet* G78+352 **70**
Kaimanawa Mts., *N.Z.* A24–390 **112**
Kaimganj, *India* G64+275 **73**
Kaimur Ra., *India* G48+245 **73**
Kaipara Harb., *New Zealand* A35–364 **112**
Kaira, *India* H13+226 **70**
Kairana, *India* G77+294 **72**
Kairouan, *Tunisia* M30+358 **81**
Kairovo, *U.S.S.R.* J16+558 **61**
Kaisarie. *See Kayseri*
Kaišedorys, *Lithuania* L33+549 **47**
Kaiserslautern, *W. Germany* M43+494 **48**
Kaiser Wilhelm II Ld.,
  Antarctica G00–670 **27**
Kaitangata, *New Zealand* A61–463 **112**
Kaithal, *India* G81+297 **72**
Kai-yuan, *China* D66+427 **66**
Kajaani, *Finland* L13+642 **46**
Kajiado, *Kenya* K50–018 **83**
Kajiki, *Japan* D26+317 **68**
Kajuri Kach, *Pakistan* H31+321 **72**
Kakamari, *Uganda* K64+034 **83**
Kakamega, *Kenya* K60+002 **83**
Kakh, *Iran* J08+342 **75**
Kakhovskoye Vdkhr., *Ukr.* K62+471 **60**
Kakia, *Botswana* L40–248 **84**
Kakisa, L., *N.-W. Terr.* V76+607 **88**
Kakori, *India* G55+269 **73**
Kakoyarra, *New S. Wales* C51–317 **109**
Kaksha, *U.S.S.R.* J80+582 **61**
Kalabagh, *Pakistan* H21+330 **72**
Kalabaka, *Greece* L50+397 **59**
Kalabo, *Zambia* L44–150 **84**
Kalabsha, *Egypt* K74+234 **81**
Kalach, *U.S.S.R.* K24+504 **61**
Kaladan, *Burma* F72+211 **71**
Kalahari Des., *Botswana* L40–238 **84**
Kalajoki, *Finland* L36+643 **46**
Kalakan, *U.S.S.R.* E19+552 **63**
Kalakepen, *Sumatra* F43+028 **65**
Kálámai, *Greece* L47+370 **59**
Kalamáta. *See Kálámai.*
Kalamazoo, *Michigan* T63+424 **91**
Kalamboa, *Sudan* L30+126 **81**
Kalamos I., *Greece* L55+386 **59**
Kala Nao, *Afghanistan* H71+350 **75**
Kalanaur, *India* G82+289 **72**
Kalangali, *Tanzania* K66–062 **83**
Kalannie, *W. Australia* E18–302 **110**
Kala Sarkari, *Afghanistan* H46+358 **75**
Kalat, *Pakistan* H50+270 **70**
Kalat-i-Ghilzai, *Afghanistan* H49+320 **75**
Kalat-i-Nadiri, *Iran* J01+371 **75**
Kalaw, *Burma* F50+207 **71**
Kale, *Burma* F65+232 **71**
Kalediran, *Turkey* K74+362 **74**
Kalemié, *Zaire* L04-060 **83**
Kalewa, *Burma* F64+232 **71**
Kalgan. *See Changkiakow*
Kalgoorlie, *W. Australia* D82–307 **110**
Kalikino, *U.S.S.R.* J35+528 **61**
Kalimnos, I., *Greece* L19+370 **59**
Kalingapatnam, *India* G35+184 **70**
Kalinin, *U.S.S.R.* K56+568 **60**
Kaliningrad, *U.S.S.R.* L57+547 **47**
Kalinino, *U.S.S.R.* E70+599 **63**
Kalispell, *Montana* V56+479 **98**
Kalisz, *Poland* L71+518 **49**
Kaliua, *Tanzania* K80–050 **83**
Kalix Älv, *Sweden* L56+676 **46**
Kalixfors, *Sweden* L59+677 **46**
Kalka, *India* G78+308 **72**
Kalkaska, *Michigan* T61+448 **91**
Kalkfeld, *S.-W. Africa* L84–208 **84**
Kalkfontein, *Botswana* L54–222 **84**
Kalkwerk, *S.-W. Africa* L76–268 **84**
Kallavesi, *Finland* L14+628 **46**
Kallim, *Chad* L54+128 **81**
Kalloni, *Greece* L23+392 **59**
Kall Sjön, *Sweden* M12+637 **46**
Kalmar, *Sweden* L82+567 **47**
Kalmar Sund, *Sweden* L82+565 **47**
Kalmykovo, *Kazakh* J50+490 **62**
Kalna, *India* G10+232 **73**
Kalocsa, *Hungary* L66+465 **49**
Kalokhorio, *Cyprus* K72+351 **76**
Kalol, *India* H14+234 **70**
Kalpi, *India* G62+261 **73**
Kaltag, *Alaska* Y50+640 **99**
Kaluga, *U.S.S.R.* K52+545 **60**
Kalule, *Zaire* L24–096 **82**
Kalundborg, *Denmark* M83+557 **47**
Kalundu, *Zambia* L02–104 **83**
Kalutara, *Sri Lanka* G61+065 **70**
Kalyan, *India* H11+192 **70**
Kalyazin, *U.S.S.R.* K44+572 **60**
Kama, R., *U.S.S.R.* J22+608 **62**
Kamah, *Labrador* S22+590 **89**
Kamaishi, *Japan* C48+393 **68**
Kamalampaka, *Tanzania* K86–056 **83**
Kamalia, *Pakistan* H08+307 **72**
Kaman, *India* G77+276 **72**
Kamaran, I., *Red Sea* K14+154 **74**
Kamasin, *India* G46+254 **73**
Kamassa, *Cameroun* M10+078 **81**
Kamchatka, *U.S.S.R.* B40+560 **63**
Kamen, *U.S.S.R.* G52+538 **62**
Kamenets Podolskiy, *Ukraine* L21+488 **60**
Kamenskoye, *U.S.S.R.* B00+625 **63**
Kamensk Shakhtinski,
  U.S.S.R. K28+483 **61**
Kamensk Ural'skiy, *U.S.S.R.* H79+564 **61**
Kamet, Mt., *India* G64+309 **70**
Kami Iwani, *Japan* D10+351 **68**
Kamina, *Zaire* L30–088 **82**
Kamloops, *Brit. Columbia* W02+507 **88**
Kamnik, *Yugoslavia* M02+462 **56**
Kamouraska, *Quebec* S59+476 **90**
Kampa Dzong, *Tibet* G09+283 **71**
Kampala, *Uganda* K74+002 **83**
Kampen, *Netherlands* M54+526 **44**
Kampot, *Khmer* F05+106 **69**
Kamptee, *India* G64+212 **70**
Kamsack, *Saskatchewan* U71+513 **88**
Kamyshin, *U.S.S.R.* J88+501 **61**
Kamyshlov, *U.S.S.R.* H74+568 **61**
Kanab, *Utah* V45+370 **94**
Kannauj, *India* G61+270 **73**

Kanawha, R., W. Virginia T38+382 97
Kanayama, Japan C77+356 68
Kanazawa, Japan C80+366 68
Kanchanaburi, Thailand F33+140 69
Kanchipuram, India G61+126 70
Kanchenjunga, mt., Nepal G11+277 73
Kandahar, Afghanistan H56+316 75
Kandalaksha, U.S.S.R. K73+674 62
Kandavu, I., Fiji A10-190 106
Kandhla, India G76+293 72
Kandi, India G11+239 73
Kandole, Zaire L38-034 82
Kandos, New South Wales C00-329 109
Kandy, Sri Lanka G57+073 70
Kane, Pennsylvania T23+416 96
Kane Basin, Greenland S60+790 26
Kanev, Ukraine K81+497 60
Kangan, Iran J47+278 75
Kangar, Malaya F28+064 69
Kangaroo I., S. Australia C76-358 111
Kangāvar, Iran J72+346 74
Kangmar, Kashmir G70+334 70
Kango, Gabon M30+002 82
Kangpao, China E31+418 66
Kangra, India G82+321 72
Kangsa R., Bangladesh F88+250 71
Kanhsien, China E30+259 67
Kani, Burma F61+224 71
Kaniva, Victoria C53-364 109
Kankakee, Illinois T77+411 95
Kankan, Guinea N56+104 80
Kanker, India G50+202 70
Kankesanturai, Sri Lanka G60+098 70
Kan Kiang, China E28+274 64
Kannus, Finland L37+639 46
Kano, Nigeria M38+118 80
Kanpetlet, Burma F67+214 71
Kanpur, India G58+265 73
Kansas, state, U.S.A. U60+387 98
Kansas R., Kansas U36+390 95
Kansas City, Kansas U28+391 95
Kansas City, Missouri U28+390 95
Kansk, U.S.S.R. F55+563 63
Kansu, prov., China E84+350 66
Kantai, India G28+262 73
Kantchari, Upper Volta M82+124 80
Kanturk, Ireland, Rep. N53+522 43
Kanuma, Japan C61+365 68
Kanus, S.-W. Africa L68-278 84
Kanyinchaung, Burma F76+210 71
Kaoan, China E27+284 67
Kao-bang, Indo-China E82+227 69
Kaocheng, China E30+349 66
Kaohsiung, Taiwan D88+226 67
Kaolack, Senegal P06+142 80
Kaolan. See Lanchow
Kao Lu-ang, mt., Thailand F32+086 69
Kaomi, China E01+363 66
Kaoyi, China E31+376 66
Kaoyu, China E03+328 66
Kaoyu Hu, China E04+328 66
Kapal, Kazakh G65+452 62
Kapalu, Kashmir G82+352 72
Kapfenberg, Austria L88+473 48
Kapiri Mposhi, Tanzania L06–140 83
Kapiskau R., Ontario T52+526 89
Kapiti I., New Zealand A31-408 112
Kapoeas, R., Borneo E52+001 65
Kapoeta, Sudan K68+048 81
Kaposvár, Hungary L73+464 58
Kapsabet, Kenya K60+002 83
Kapsukas, Lithuania L40+545 47
Kapunda, S. Australia C66-343 109
Kapurthala, India G88+313 72
Kapuskasing, Ontario T46+496 89
Kara, U.S.S.R. H66+692 62
Kara Sea, U.S.S.R. H00+750 62
Kara Bogaz Gol, Turkmen. J40+413 62
Karabuk, Turkey K74+411 74
Karabuta, Iran J73+370 74
Karacabey, Turkey L10+402 74
Karaca Dagh, Turkey K74+394 74
Karachev, U.S.S.R. K60+531 60
Karachi, Pakistan H47+248 70
Karaga, U.S.S.R. B11+592 63
Karaganda, Kazakh H10+500 62
Karaginskiy Os., U.S.S.R. B05+590 63
Karak, Tibet G67+322 70
Kara Kalpakskaya, Uzbek. J12+430 62
Karakelong, I., Indonesia D49+042 65
Karakoram Ra., Kashmir G84+364 72
Karakose, Turkey K12+398 74
Karamea, New Zealand A47–412 112
Karamea Bight, N.Z. A50-413 112
Karamsur Pass, Pakistan H08+368 72
Karand, Iran J82+343 74
Karasa, U.S.S.R. J56+547 61
Karasburg, S.-W. Africa L66–282 84
Kara Shahr, Sinkiang, China G22+421 62
Karasjok, Norway L27+694 46
Karatina, Kenya K46–004 83
Karatsu, Japan D30+336 68
Karaul, U.S.S.R. G37+701 62
Karauli, India G78+265 73
Karaurgan, Turkey K17+404 74
Kardam, Tibet G54+304 70
Kardhitsa, Greece L48+394 59
Karelskaya A.S.S.R. (Karelia),
    rep., U.S.S.R. K80+642 62
Karenni, Burma F45+194 71
Karesuando, Sweden L45+684 46
Karganrud, Iran J66+379 74
Karghalik, Sinkiang, China G75+379 72
Kargil, Kashmir G83+345 72
Kargopol, U.S.S.R. K36+615 60
Karhal, India G66+270 73
Kariba, Dam & L.,
    Zam.-Rhod. L06–164 84
Karibib, S.-W. Africa L84–218 84
Karikal, India G61+110 70
Karimata, I., Indonesia E67-015 65
Karin, Somalia J86+108 83
Karis, (Karjaa), Finland L38+601 47
Kariz, Iran H85+349 75
Karkaralinsk, U.S.S.R. G87+495 62
Karkkila, Finland L34+605 47
Karla Marksa, Pik, mt., Tad. H16+372 75

Karl-Marx Stadt,
    E. Germany M09+508 48
Karlovac, Yugoslavia L87+455 56
Karlovy Vary, Czechoslovakia M13+502 48
Karlsbad. See Karlovy Vary
Karlsborg, Sweden M03+585 47
Karlshamn, Sweden M01+562 47
Karlskrona, Sweden L86+561 47
Karlsruhe, W. Germany M38+490 48
Karlstad, Sweden M09+595 47
Karlukovo, U.S.S.R. B43+688 63
Karmöy, I., Norway M58+593 47
Karnal, India G78+297 72
Karnataka, India G79+123 70
Karnes, Texas U47+289 94
Karnten, prov., Austria M06+467 48
Karona Fall, Guyana R88+040 104
Karoonda, S. Australia C61–352 109
Karora, Sudan K40+176 83
Karpáthos, I. & Str., Greece L17+356 59
Karperón, Greece L50+400 59
Karroo Great, Cape Province L46–326 84
Kars, Turkey K12+406 74
Karsakpai, Kazakh H50+480 62
Kärsämäki, Finland L25+640 46
Kārsava, Latvia L14+568 47
Karshi, Uzbek H56+388 62
Karstula, Finland L31+629 46
Karsun, U.S.S.R. J78+542 61
Kartaly, U.S.S.R. H86+530 61
Kartarpur, India G87+314 72
Kartse, Kashmir G83+343 72
Karungi, Sweden L37+661 46
Karungu, Kenya K66–010 83
Karunki, Finland L36+661 46
Karur, India G71+112 70
Karvina, Czechoslovakia L69+498 49
Karwar, India H05+149 70
Karymskoye, U.S.S.R. E34+517 63
Kasai R., Zaire L60–034 82
Kasama, Zambia K82–104 83
Kasanga, Tanzania K84–084 83
Kasauli, India G78+309 72
Kasba L., N.-W. Territories U74+604 88
Kasempa, Zambia L26–134 82
Kasenga, Zaire L08–106 83
Kasenga, Zambia L20–158 84
Kasganj, India G68+278 73
Kashan, Iran J53+340 75
Kashgar, China G83+395 62
Kashing, China D85+308 66
Kashira, U.S.S.R. K40+548 60
Kashiwazaki, Japan C68+374 68
Kashmir, see Jammu and Kashmir
Kashmor, Pakistan H32+283 70
Kasimov, U.S.S.R. K22+549 61
Kasinka, Botswana L34–184 84
Kaskinen, (Kasko) Finland L53+624 46
Kasongo, Zaire L20–044 82
Kásos, I., Greece L19+354 59
Kásós Str., Crete L20+352 59
Kaspichan, Bulgaria L17+433 58
Kassala, Sudan K52+154 83
Kassandra, Greece L39+400 59
Kassel, W. Germany M33+515 48
Kastamonu, Turkey K66+414 74
Kastélli, Crete L38+355 59
Kasterlee, Belgium M60+512 44
Kastoria, Greece L53+405 59
Kastrosikiá, Greece L56+391 59
Kasulu, Tanzania L00–046 83
Kasungu, Malawi K70–132 83
Kasur, Pakistan H03+311 72
Katahdin, Mt., Maine S53+459 90
Katahdin Iron Works, Maine S55+455 90
Katákolon, Greece L52+377 59
Katanga, See Shaba
Katanning, W. Australia E14–336 110
Katav Ivanovsk, U.S.S.R. J11+548 61
Katerini, Greece L45+403 59
Katha, Burma F52+242 71
Kathawachaga, L., N.-W.T. V40+661 88
Katherine, N. Terr., Aust. D16–144 110
Kathmandu, Nepal G28+277 73
Kathua, Kashmir G87+324 72
Katihar, India G14+256 73
Katmai Vol., Alaska T32+580 99
Káto Akhaia, Greece L51+381 59
Káto Nevrokópion, Greece L37+413 58
Katoomba, New S. Wales B88–338 109
Katowice, Poland L66+503 49
Katrine, L., Scotland N27+563 41
Katrineholm, Sweden M33+590 47
Katsina, Nigeria M44+128 80
Kattegat, Sweden-Denmark M24+570 47
Kattowitz. See Katowice
Katwa, India G11+236 236 73
Katwewe, Zaire L10–084 83
Katwijk-aan-Zee, Netherlands M64+522 44
Kauai, I., Hawaiian Is. Y58+220 107
Kaufbeuren, W. Germany M26+478 48
Kauhava, Finland L42+631 46
Kaukauna, Wisconsin T80+443 91
Kaunas, Lithuania L36+549 47
Kauriya, India G44+212 71
Kautokeino, Norway L42+689 46
Kavak, Turkey K54+411 74
Kavali, India G60+150 70
Kaválla, Greece L33+411 58
Kaválla, Greece L34+409 59
Kavkas, Bolshoi & Maly, mts.,
    U.S.S.R. K80+415 62
Kawakawa, New Zealand A35–354 112
Kawambwa, Zambia L06–098 83
Kawanoe, Japan D08+340 68
Kawardha, India G53+220 73
Kawasaki, Japan C62+355 68
Kawhia, New Zealand A31–381 112
Kawich Ra., Nevada V71+379 92
Kawkareik, Burma F40+165 71
Kaw Peunan, Thailand F30+097 69
Kaw Samui, Thailand F30+094 69
Kayes, Mali N68+142 80
Kayseri, Turkey K58+387 74
Kaysville, Utah V42+410 94
Kazachye, U.S.S.R. C82+707 63
Kazakhskaya, rep., U.S.S.R. H60+470 62
Kazalinsk, Kazakh H78+457 62
Kazan, U.S.S.R. J66+558 61
Kazanlŭk, Bulgaria L28+426 58
Kazérun, Iran J50+296 75

Kazvin, Iran J60+363 74
Kdyne, Czechoslovakia M12+494 48
Kéa (Tziá), I., Greece L34+374 59
Kearney, Nebraska U54+406 95
Keban Maden, Turkey K38+388 74
Ke-bao I., N. Vietnam E75+212 69
Kecherma, Niger M12+172 81
Kechika R., Brit. Columbia W40+588 88
Kecskemét, Hungary L62+469 49
Kedainiai, Lithuania L36+553 47
Kedgwick, New Brunswick S44+476 90
Kediri, Java, Indonesia E48–079 65
Keele R., N.-W. Territories W38+642 88
Keelung (Chilung), Taiwan D80+251 67
Keene, New Hampshire S74+429 96
Keeper Hill, Ireland, Rep. N50+527 43
Keeseville, New York S81+445 91
Keetmanshoop, S.-W. Africa L72–266 84
Keewatin, Dist., N.-W. Terr. — 88-89
Keewong, New S. Wales C30–323 109
Kefallinia, Greece L57+382 59
Kegaska, Quebec S07+502 90
Keighley, England N11+539 37
Keila, Estonia L33+593 47
Keita, Chad L42+174 81
Keitele, Finland L22+631 46
Keith, Scotland N18+575 40
Keith, S. Australia C58–361 109
Keith B., N.-W. Territories W10+654 88
Kelamet, Ethiopia K38+160 83
Kelang, Malaya F22+031 69
Kelcyre, Albania L59+403 59
Kellet, C., N.-W. Terr. W32+718 88
Kelloselkä, Finland L01+670 34
Kells, Ireland, Rep. N41+537 42
Kelme, Lithuania L42+557 47
Kelowna, British Columbia V86+500 88
Kelso, Scotland N15+556 41
Kem, Karelia, U.S.S.R. K62+651 62
Kemal Paşa, Turkey L16+383 74
Kemerovo, U.S.S.R. G24+553 62
Kemi, Finland L33+657 46
Kemijärvi, Finland L15+667 46
Kemijoki, Finland L28+662 46
Kemmerer, Wyoming V34+418 93
Kemp, L., Texas U55+336 95
Kemp Ld., Antarctica J05-670 27
Kempele, Finland L27+649 46
Kempsey, New South Wales B74–311 109
Kempt L., Quebec S86+475 91
Kempten, Germany M28+477 48
Kenai Pen., Alaska Y00+605 99
Kendal, England N16+543 37
Kendall, New York T18+333 96
Kendall, C., N.-W. Terr. T72+640 89
Kendari, Célèbes, D75–038 65
Kendawangan, Borneo E59–024 65
Kenema, Sierra Leone N68+080 80
Ken-tung, Burma F32+212 71
Kenhardt, Cape Province L52–292 84
Kenilworth, England N09+524 37
Kenitra, Morocco N40+344 80
Kenmare, N. Dakota U72+487 93
Kenmare & R., Ireland, Rep. N58+519 43
Kenmore, Scotland N24+566 41
Kennebec, S. Dakota U59+439 93
Kennebec R., Maine S59+443 90
Kennebunk, Maine S63+434 96
Kennet R., England N06+514 39
Kennett, Missouri U01+363 97
Kenogami & L., Quebec S68+483 90
Keno Hill, Yukon X01+643 88
Kenora, Ontario U27+499 88
Kenosha, Wisconsin T77+426 95
Kensington, Prince Edward I. S21+464 90
Kent, New Brunswick S32+466 90
Kent, co., England M86+512 39
Kent I., Maryland T08+389 96
Kent Peninsula, N.-W.
    Territories V15+680 88
Kentford, England M87+523 39
Kentucky, state, U.S.A. T70+374 95
Kentucky L., N. Dakota T78+362 95
Kentville, Nova Scotia S27+450 90
Kenya, E. Africa K40+010 83
Kenya, Mt., Kenya K46–004 83
Keokuk, Iowa U08+404 95
Keonjhar, India G26+215 71
Keos (Tzia). See Kea, I.
Kepler Mts., New Zealand A76–454 112
Keppel, I., Falkland Is. S00–512 103
Ke-ala, state, India G80+100 70
Kerang, Victoria C37–357 109
Kerava, Finland L29+604 47
Kerch, U.S.S.R. K51+454 60
Kerchoual, Mali M88+170 80
Keren, Ethiopia K40+158 83
Kerema, Papua New Guinea C26–081 111
Kerguelen Is., Indian Ocean H30–495 77
Ker cho, Kenya K58–004 83
Ker nci, mt., Sumatra F22-016 65
Kertenbosch. See Zuidwolde
Kerkenna Is., Tunisia M24+346 81
Kerki, Turkmen. H58+377 62
Kérkira & I., Greece L61+396 59
Kerkrade, Netherlands M54+509 44
Kermadec Is., Pacific Ocean Z80–295 106
Kermān, Iran J17+303 75
Kerman Desert, Iran J04+290 75
Kermanshah, Iran J77+343 74
Kerry, co., Ireland, Rep. N58+520 43
Kerry Hd., Ireland, Rep. N60+524 43
Kerzers, Switzerland M47+470 45
Kesagami L., Ontario T30+502 89
Kesariya, India G30+264 73
Kesteren, Netherlands M57+519 44
Kestilä, Finland L22+644 46
Keswick, England N19+546 37
Keszthely, Hungary L76+468 49
Ketapang, Borneo E60–017 65
Ketchikan, Alaska W65+555 99
Ketrzyn, Poland L52+541 49
Kettering, England N04+524 37
Keuka L., New York T13–425 96
Kewanee, Illinois U00+412 95
Kewatin, Wisconsin T75+445 91
Keweenaw B., Michigan T80+469 91
Keweenaw Pen., Wisconsin T84+466 99

Key L., Ireland, Rep. N50+540 42
Key Harbour, Ontario T34+459 91
Key Largo, Florida T32+251 97
Keyser, W. Virginia T24+395 96
Keysville, Virginia T21+371 97
Key West, Florida T41+246 97
Kezhma, U.S.S.R. F24+590 63
Khabab, Syria K52+330 76
Khabarovsk, U.S.S.R. D00+483 63
Khaburah, Oman J18+240 75
Khadasan, Mongolia F06+478 64
Khadhra, Saudi Arabia K09+285 74
Khadro, Pakistan H37+261 70
Khafs Maqran, Saudi Arabia J83+214 74
Khagaul, India G29+255 73
Khaibar, Saudi Arabia K33+258 74
Khairabad, India G55+274 73
Khairpur, Pakistan H37+275 70
Khairpur, Pakistan H16+296 72
Khaiwan, Yemen K07+165 74
Khalis-ed-Daff, Saudi Arabia K35+220 74
Khalki, I., Greece L14+362 59
Khalkidhki, Greece L40+404 59
Khalkis, Greece L38+385 59
Khal-Mer-Sede, U.S.S.R. G69+675 62
Khalturin, U.S.S.R. J66+586 61
Khaluf, Saudi Arabia J12+204 75
Kham, Iran J25+290 75
Khambat, G. of, H14 + 223 70
Khamiab, Afghanistan H55+374 75
Khamis, Mushait,
    Saudi Arabia K10+183 74
Kham-kheut, Laos F03+182 69
Khamr, Yemen K06+161 74
Khanabad, Afghanistan H35+367 75
Khanaqin, Iraq J88+344 74
Khān Baghdādi, Iraq K14+339 74
Khandela, India G87+275 72
Khandwa, India G81+218 70
Khan-ez-Zebib, Jordan K53+315 76
Khanfar, Yemen, South J89 + 133 74
Khangai Shan, Mongolia F50+480 31
Khangarh, Pakistan H23+299 72
Khanh-hoa, S. Vietnam E66+122 69
Khania, Crete L36+355 59
Khaniadhana, India G71+250 73
Khanka Oz., U.S.S.R. D15+449 63
Khanntor, Syria K47+344 76
Khanpur, Pakistan H26+286 72
Khan Sheikhun, Syria K50+354 76
Khan Tengri, Kirgiz. G58+420 62
Khanty Mansiysk, U.S.S.R. H35+610 62
Khanu, Iran J13+280 75
Khan Yunis, Egypt K64+314 76
Kharaghoda, India H19+232 70
Kharan, Pakistan H57+285 70
Kharar, India G13+227 73
Kharkov, Ukraine K53+500 60
Kharmanli, Bulgaria L25+419 58
Kharovsk, U.S.S.R. K29+599 60
Kharsawan, India G25+228 73
Khartaksho, Kashmir G83+349 72
Khartoum, Sudan K74+156 81
Khasab, U.A.E. J23+262 75
Khasfa, Saudi Arabia J35+197 75
Khasi Hills, India F80+254 71
Khasmel Girba, Sudan K56+150 81
Khatanga, U.S.S.R. F16+721 63
Khatangsky Guba, U.S.S.R. E50+745 63
Kheralu, India H14+236 70
Kheri, India G55+279 73
Kherlen R., Mongolia E44+480 64
Kherson, Ukraine K74+466 60
Khetri, India G85+280 72
Khilok, U.S.S.R. E56+515 63
Khinis, Turkey K19+394 74
Khinjan, Afghanistan H37+355 75
Khios & I., Greece L24+384 59
Khisfin, Syria K55+329 76
Khiva, Uzbek H86+413 62
Khmel'nitskiy, Ukraine L18+494 60
Khmer, See Cambodia
Kholm, U.S.S.R. K83+572 60
Kholmsk, U.S.S.R. C47+469 63
Không, Laos E84+139 69
Khor, U.S.S.R. D00+479 63
Khóra Sfakion, Crete L35+352 59
Khor Dhahiya, Saudi Arabia J50+189 75
Khor Kalba, Saudi Arabia J22+252 75
Khorramabad, Iran J70+336 74
Khormali, China G04+452 64
Khorramshahr, Iran J70+305 74
Khotan, Sinkiang, China G61+369 62
Khrisoúpolis, Greece L32+410 58
Khrojna, Bulgaria L32+418 58
Khudhfiya, Saudi Arabia J53+190 75
Khujur, Iran J69+358 74
Khulna, Bangladesh G02+228 73
Khumain, Iran J59+338 75
Khungcha, Burma F71+218 71
Khunsar, Iran J58+332 75
Khur, Iran J09+329 75
Khur, Iran J30+338 75
Khurai, India G70+241 73
Khurja, India G73+282 72
Khurma, Saudi Arabia K17+218 74
Khusf, Iran J06+328 75
Khushab, Pakistan H16+323 72
Khvalynsk, U.S.S.R. J72+525 61
Khvoy, Iran K00+386 74
Khyber Pass, Pakistan H23+340 72
Kiama, New South Wales B86–347 109
Kiambi, Zaire L20–056 82
Kiambi, Zaire L12–074 83
Kiamichi Mts., Oklahoma U28+346 95
Kiamusze, China D28+468 64
Kian, China E30+271 67
Kiangchow. See Kiangling
Kiangling, China E46+303 67
Kiangpeh, China E80+296 67
Kiangsi, prov., China E24+274 67
Kiangsu, prov., China E00+332 66
Kiangsu. See Yangchow
Kiangyin, China D88+317 66
Kiantajarvi, Finland L05+650 46
Kiao-chow B., China D88+360 66
Kiaohsien, China D89+362 66
Kiating. See Loshan
Kibangula, Zaire L16–048 82
Kibombo, Zaire L24–040 82

Kibondo, *Tanzania* K86–036 **83**
Kicevo, *Yugoslavia* L54+415 **58**
Kichiga, *U.S.S.R.* B09+598 **63**
Kichiginsk, *U.S.S.R.* H82+545 **61**
Kicking Horse Pass, *Alberta* V68+512 **88**
Kidal, *Mali* M82+182 **80**
Kidderminster, *England* N14+524 **37**
Kidnappers, C., *New Zealand* A17–396 **112**
Kidodi, *Tanzania* K48–076 **83**
Kiel, *W. Germany* M29+543 **48**
Kiel (Nord-Ostsee) Kanal.
  W. Germany M35+540 **84**
Kielce, *Poland* L56+510 **49**
Kieldrecht, *Belgium* M65+513 **44**
Kieler Bucht, *W. Germany* M27+545 **48**
Kienchang. *See* Nanchang
Kiencheng, *China* E62+282 **67**
Kienko, *China* E87+321 **66**
Kienning. *See* Kienow
Kienow, *China* E09+271 **67**
Kienping, *China* E02+419 **66**
Kienshui, *China* F13+237 **64**
Kienteh, *China* E03+296 **67**
Kiev. *See* Kiyev
Kiffa, *Mauritania* N68+166 **80**
Kigali, *Rwanda* L00–020 **83**
Kiganga, *Tanzania* K60–078 **83**
Kigoma, *Tanzania* L02–048 **83**
Kihsien, *China* E16+401 **66**
Kii Chan., *Japan* D00+336 **68**
Kijabe, *Kenya* K50–010 **83**
Kikhchik, *U.S.S.R.* B53+535 **63**
Kikinda, *Yugoslavia* L57+458 **58**
Kikkertaksoak I., *Quebec* S27+603 **89**
Kikládhes, Is., *Greece* L30+370 **59**
Kikori & R., *Papua New Guinea* C35–074 **111**
Kikwit, *Zaire* L66–054 **82**
Kila Drosh, (Drosh), *Pak.* H19+355 **72**
Kilbeggan, *Ireland, Rep.* N45+534 **43**
Kilbourn, *Wisconsin* T89+437 **91**
Kilbrennan Sd., *Scotland* N33+556 **41**
Kilchu, *Korea* D34+410 **64**
Kilcormac, *Ireland, Rep.* N46+532 **43**
Kilcullen, *Ireland, Rep.* N40+531 **43**
Kildare & co., *Ireland, Rep.* N41+532 **43**
Kilfinnane, *Ireland, Rep.* N51+524 **43**
Kilgarvan, *Ireland, Rep.* N57+519 **43**
Kilian, *China* G73+372 **72**
Kilifi, *Kenya* K30–036 **83**
Kilimanjaro Mt., *Tanzania* K46–030 **83**
Kilindini, *Kenya* K32–040 **83**
Kilkee, *Ireland, Rep.* N58+527 **43**
Kilkeel, *N. Ireland* N36+540 **42**
Kilkenny & co., *Ireland, Rep.* N43+526 **43**
Kilkieran B., *Ireland, Rep.* N58+533 **43**
Kilkis, *Greece* L44+411 **58**
Kilkis, *Greece* L43+409 **59**
Kilkivan, *Queensland* B77–260 **111**
Kill, *Ireland, Rep.* N39+533 **43**
Killala B., *Ireland, Rep.* N55+542 **42**
Killaloe, *Ireland, Rep.* N51+528 **43**
Killarney, *Ireland, Rep.* N57+520 **43**
Killarney, *Ontario* T39+460 **91**
Killary Harb., *Ireland, Rep.* N60+536 **42**
Killashandra, *Ireland, Rep.* N45+540 **42**
Killiecrankie, Pass of,
  Scotland N22+568 **41**
Killimor, *Ireland, Rep.* N50+532 **43**
Killin, *Scotland* N26+565 **41**
Killini, *Greece* L53+379 **59**
Killorglin, *Ireland, Rep.* N59+521 **43**
Killybegs, *Ireland, Rep.* N51+546 **42**
Killyleagh, *N. Ireland* N34+544 **42**
Kilmacthomas, *Ireland, Rep.* N45+522 **43**
Kilmallock, *Ireland, Rep.* N51+524 **43**
Kilmarnock, *Scotland* N27+556 **41**
Kilmore, *Victoria* C30–373 **109**
Kilosa, *Tanzania* K48–068 **83**
Kilrea, *N. Ireland* N39+549 **42**
Kilrush, *Ireland, Rep.* N57+526 **43**
Kilsyth, *Scotland* N24+560 **41**
Kiltamagh, *Ireland, Rep.* N54+538 **42**
Kilwa Kivinje, *Tanzania* K34–088 **83**
Kilwinning, *Scotland* N28+557 **41**
Kima, *Zaire* L18–016 **82**
Kimball, *S. Dakota* U54+437 **93**
Kimberley, *Cape Province* L32–288 **84**
Kimi, *Greece* L35+386 **59**
Kimito, (Kemiö), *Finland* L44+601 **47**
Kimolos, I., *Greece* L33+368 **59**
Kimvula, *Zaire* L84–058 **82**
Kinabulu, mt., *Sabah* E20+062 **65**
Kinbrace, *Scotland* N24+583 **40**
Kincardine, *Ontario* T40+442 **91**
Kincardine, *Scotland* N14+569 **40**
Kincardine-on-Forth, *Scot.* N22+561 **41**
Kinchow Wan, *China* D80+391 **66**
Kincraig, *Scotland* N24+571 **40**
Kindat, *Burma* F63+237 **71**
Kindersley, *Saskatchewan* V22+512 **88**
Kindia, *Guinea* N76+100 **80**
Kindu-Port Empain, *Zaire* L24–030 **82**
Kinel, *U.S.S.R.* J56+532 **61**
Kinel Cherkkassy, *U.S.S.R.* J49+535 **61**
Kineo, *Maine* S84+457 **90**
Kineshma, *U.S.S.R.* K17+575 **61**
King I., *Burma* F40+125 **71**
King I., *Tasmania* C36–400 **111**
King and Queen, *Virginia* T11+376 **97**
King Christian IX Ld.,
  Greenland Q10+680 **26**
King Edward VIII Fall,
  Guyana R88+056 **104**
King Edward VII Land,
  Antarctica Y40–770 **27**
Kingfisher, *Oklahoma* U48+358 **95**
King Frederick VIII Ld.,
  Greenland P40+790 **26**
King Frederick VI Ld.,
  Greenland Q70+630 **26**
Kingfu, *China* F04+284 **64**
King George I,
  South Shetlands R75–620 **27**
King George Is., *Pacific Oc.* X60–150 **107**
King George, Mt, *B.C.* V61+504 **88**
King George Sd., *W. Aust.* E10–351 **110**
King George V Ld., *Antarc.* C00–790 **27**
King George VI Sd., *Antarc.* S50–700 **27**
King George VI Falls,
  Guyana S08+058 **104**

Kingku, *China* F25+236 **64**
King Leopold Ra., *W. Aust.* D60–170 **110**
King Leopold & Queen Astrid
  Coast, *Antarctica* G40–670 **27**
Kingman, *Kansas* U49+376 **95**
Kingmen, *China* E47+310 **66**
Kings Pk., *Utah* V32+407 **94**
King's Canyon Nat. Park,
  California V84+371 **92**
Kingsclere, *England* N08+513 **39**
Kingscote, *S. Australia* C74–356 **109**
Kingscourt, *Ireland, Rep.* N41+539 **42**
King's Lynn, *England* M88+528 **39**
King Sound, *W. Australia* D70–166 **110**
Kingsport, *Tennessee* T46+366 **97**
Kingston, *Jamaica* T11+179 **101**
Kingston, *New York* S84+419 **96**
Kingston, *New Zealand* A68–453 **112**
Kingston, *Ontario* T09+443 **91**
Kingston, *S. Australia* C61–368 **109**
Kingston Ra., *California* V71+366 **92**
Kingstree, *S. Carolina* T29+336 **97**
Kingswear, *England* N21+503 **38**
Kingtung, *China* F24+243 **64**
Kingushi, *Zaire* L80–052 **82**
Kingussie, *Scotland* N24+571 **40**
Kingyüan, *See* Ishan
Kinhsien, *China* D80+391 **66**
Kinhwa, *China* E02+291 **67**
Kinki, *China* E83+378 **66**
Kinlochewe, *Scotland* N32+576 **40**
Kinlochleven, *Scotland* N30+567 **41**
Kinloch Rannoch, *Scotland* N25+567 **41**
Kinross, *Scotland* N21+562 **41**
Kinsale, *Ireland, Rep.* N51+517 **43**
Kinsale, Old Hd. of, *Ireland,
  Rep.* N51+516 **43**
Kinshasa, *Zaire* L88–044 **82**
Kintap, *Borneo* E29–038 **65**
Kintyre, *Scotland* N34+556 **41**
Kintyre, Mull of, *Scotland* N35+553 **41**
Kinvarra, *Ireland, Rep.* N54+531 **43**
Kinyangiri, *Tanzania* K62–044 **83**
Kiowa, *Kansas* U51+370 **95**
Kiparissia, *Greece* L50+372 **59**
Kiparissia, G. of, *Greece* L52+374 **59**
Kipawa & L., *Quebec* T24+468 **91**
Kipini, *Kenya* K26–026 **83**
Kirá Panayiá, *See* Pélagos, I.
Kirchberg, *Switzerland* M45+471 **45**
Kirensk, *U.S.S.R.* E72+580 **63**
Kirgizskaya, rep., *U.S.S.R.* H10+420 **62**
Kiri, *Zaire* L16–014 **82**
Kirin, *China* D50+438 **64**
Kirit, *Somalia* J84+088 **83**
Kiriwina, I.,
  Papua New Guinea B84–086 **111**
Kirkagac, *Turkey* L14+390 **74**
Kirkby Lonsdale, *England* N16–542 **37**
Kirkcaldy, *Scotland* N19+561 **41**
Kirkcudbright., *Scot.,* N24+548 **41**
Kirkee, *India* H06+186 **70**
Kirkenes, *Norway* L00+697 **46**
Kirkintilloch, *Scotland* N25+559 **41**
Kirkland Lake, *Ontario* T30+482 **91**
Kirksville, *Missouri* U16+402 **95**
Kirkuk, *Iraq* K04+357 **74**
Kirkwall, *Orkney, Scot.* N18+390 **40**
Kirong Dzong, *Nepal* G28+284 **73**
Kirov, *U.S.S.R.* K64+541 **60**
Kirov, *U.S.S.R.* J62+586 **61**
Kirovgrad, *U.S.S.R.* J01+574 **61**
Kirovograd, *Ukraine* K77+485 **60**
Kirovsk, *U.S.S.R.* K67+675 **62**
Kirriemuir, *Scotland* N18+567 **41**
Kirsanov, *U.S.S.R.* K14+526 **61**
Kirsehir, *Turkey* K65+391 **74**
Kirthar Ra., *Pakistan* H46+270 **70**
Kirun. *See* Chilung
Kiruna, *Sweden* L58+678 **46**
Kisamba, *Zaire* L36–074 **82**
Kisbér, *Hungary* L72+475 **49**
Kisangani, *Zaire* L28+006 **82**
Kishanganj, *India* G12+261 **73**
Kishangarh, *India* H01+264 **70**
Kishangarh, *India* H27+270 **72**
Kishi, *Nigeria* M66+090 **80**
Kishinev, *Moldavia* L77+470 **60**
Kishtwar, *Kashmir* G85+333 **72**
Kisii, *Kenya* K62–008 **83**
Kisiju, *Tanzania* K34–074 **83**
Kiska, I., *Aleutian Is.* A15+511 **99**
Kiskisink, *Quebec* S73+479 **90**
Kiskunfélégyháza, *Hungary* L61+467 **49**
Kispest, *Hungary* L65+475 **49**
Kissaraing I., *Burma* F35+118 **71**
Kissidougou, *Guinea* N69+092 **80**
Kisujszállás, *Hungary* L55+472 **49**
Kisumu, *Kenya* K60–002 **83**
Kisvárda, *Hungary* L48–482 **49**
Kiswe, *Syria* K52+333 **76**
Kita, *Mali* N56+130 **80**
Kitab, *Uzbek.* H48+390 **62**
Kitakyushu, *Japan* D25+338 **68**
Kitchener, *Ontario* T33+434 **91**
Kitchioh, *China* E25+228 **67**
Kitgum, *Uganda* K72+030 **83**
Kithira I., *Greece* L42–363 **59**
Kithirai Chan, *Greece* L42+360 **59**
Kithnos, I., *Greece* L33+374 **59**
Kitima, *Cyprus* K76+348 **76**
Kittanning, *Pennsylvania* T28+408 **96**
Kittatinny Mts., *New Jersey* S89+411 **96**
Kittila, *Finland* L30+676 **46**
Kitui, *Kenya* K42–012 **83**
Kityang, *China* E22+235 **67**
Kitzingen, *Germany* M29+497 **48**
Kiuchuan, *China* F38+397 **64**
Kiungchow. *See* Kiungshan
Kiungchow Str. *See* Hai Nan
Kiungchow Hai Hsia,
  China E60+202 **67**
Kiungshan, *Hainan I., China* E57+200 **67**
Kiuruvesi, *Finland* L20+637 **46**

Kivijarvi, *Finland* L29+632 **46**
Kivu L., *Zaire-Rwanda* L06–020 **83**
Kiwai I., *Papua New Guinea* C39–087 **111**
Kiyev, *Ukraine* K87+505 **60**
Kiyma, *Kazakh* H44+518 **62**
Kizel, *U.S.S.R.* J23+592 **62**
Kizil Irmak, *Turkey* K68+400 **74**
Kizil Jilga, *Kashmir* K65+353 **70**
Kizyl Arvat, *Turkmen* J24+390 **62**
Kjerringøy, *Norway* M02+675 **46**
Kladanj, *Yugoslavia* L68+442 **58**
Kladno, *Czechoslovakia* M06+501 **48**
Klagenfurt, *Austria* M04+466 **48**
Klaipeda, *Lithuania* L53+558 **47**
Klamath R., *California* W22+414 **92**
Klamath Falls, *Oregon* W11+422 **92**
Klamath Mts., *California* W18+414 **92**
Klang, *See* Kelang
Klar Älv, *Sweden* M12+607 **47**
Klerksdorp, *Transvaal* L20–268 **84**
Kleszczele, *Poland* L40+525 **49**
Klimpfjall, *Sweden* M01+650 **46**
Klisura, *Bulgaria* L33+427 **58**
Kliuchi, *U.S.S.R.* J89+526 **61**
Ključ, *Yugoslavia* L79+445 **56**
Klodawa, *Poland* L66+523 **49**
Klofta, *Norway* M23+601 **47**
Klomnice, *Poland* L64+510 **49**
Klondike R., *Yukon* X15+642 **88**
Kloosterzande, *Netherlands* M66+513 **44**
Klosters, *Switzerland* M31+469 **45**
Kluane, L., *Yukon* X22+610 **88**
Klundert, *Netherlands* M63+517 **44**
Knighton, *Wales* N18+523 **38**
Knin, *Yugoslavia* L83+440 **56**
Knob, C., *W. Australia* E05–345 **110**
Knobel, *Arkansas* U04+364 **97**
Knockboy, *Ireland, Rep.* N57+518 **43**
Knockbrack, *Ireland, Rep.* N57+519 **43**
Knockmealdown Mts.,
  Ireland, Rep. N48+522 **43**
Knockower, *Ireland, Rep.* N58+517 **43**
Knokke, *Belgium* M70+513 **44**
Knox, *Pennsylvania* T28+412 **96**
Knox Coast, *Antarctica* F10–660 **27**
Knoxville, *Iowa* U18+412 **95**
Knoxville, *Tennessee* T54+360 **97**
Knysna, *Cape Province* L40–340 **84**
Knyszyn, *Poland* L43+534 **49**
Kobarid, *Yugoslavia* M09+463 **56**
Kōbe, *Japan* C88+348 **68**
København, *Denmark* M14+557 **47**
Koblenz, *W. Germany* M45+504 **48**
Kobrin, *Belorussia* L34+522 **60**
Kobroör, I., *Indonesia* D02–063 **65**
Kocaeli. *See* Izmit
Kočane, *Yugoslavia* L46+419 **58**
Kočevje, *Yugoslavia* M01+456 **56**
Kochi, *Japan* D09+335 **68**
Kochiki Retto, *Japan* D32+317 **68**
Kochow. *See* Mowming
Kodavere, *Estonia* L17+587 **47**
Kodiak I., *Alaska* Y20+578 **99**
Koeala (Kuala), *Sumatra* F40+034 **65**
Koemai, *Borneo* E50–026 **65**
Koepang (Kupang), *Timor I.,
  Indonesia* D69–102 **65**
Koetai, R., *Borneo* E26+004 **65**
Koffiefontein, *Orange Free
  State* L30–294 **84**
Koforidua, *Ghana* N02+062 **80**
Kofu, *Japan* C68+356 **68**
Kogaluk R., *Quebec* T05+594 **89**
Køge B., *Greenland* Q58+650 **26**
Kohat, *Pakistan* H21+336 **72**
Koh Chang, *Thailand* F16+120 **69**
Kohima, *India* F65+257 **71**
Koh Kong, *Cambodia* F12+113 **69**
Koh Kut, *Thailand* F15+116 **69**
Koh Rong, *Cambodia* F10+107 **69**
Kohima, *India*
Kojnic, *Yugoslavia* L72+439 **58**
Kojonup, *W. Australia* E17–338 **110**
Kokand, *Uzbek* H24+408 **75**
Kokchetav, *Kazakh* H33+533 **62**
Kokhtla Yarva, *Estonia* L15+594 **47**
Kokkola, *Finland* L41+639 **46**
Koko, *Chad* L70+096 **81**
Kokoda,
  Papua New Guinea C13–090 **111**
Kokomo, *Indiana* T67+405 **91**
Koko Nor. *See* Ching Hai
Kokoshili Ra., *Tibet* G30+357 **71**
Kokpekty, *Kazakh.* G46+488 **62**
Kokstad, *Cape Province* L04–306 **84**
Kokura, *Japan* D25+338 **68**
Kokyar, *Sinkiang, China* G77+374 **72**
Ko-lan-chow, *China* E50+389 **66**
Kolar, *India* G71+132 **70**
Kolari, *Finland* L38+673 **46**
Kolarovgrad, *Bulgaria* L19+433 **58**
Kolberg, *See* Kolobrzeg
Kolda, *Senegal* P00+130 **80**
Kolding, *Denmark* M33+555 **47**
Kole, *Zaire* L28+020 **82**
Kolguyev Ostrov, *U.S.S.R.* J65+690 **62**
Kolhapur, *India* H05+168 **70**
Kolin, *Czechoslovakia* L89+500 **48**
Kolkas Rags, *Latvia* L44+577 **47**
Kollick Kenyon Plateau,
  Antarctica V00–770 **27**
Köln, *W. Germany* M48+509 **48**
Kolno, *Poland* L48+534 **49**
Kolo. *Poland* L68+522 **49**
Kolobrzeg, *Poland* L86+542 **49**
Kologriv, *U.S.S.R.* K04+588 **61**
Kolokani, *Mali* N48+134 **80**
Kolomna, *U.S.S.R.* K38+550 **60**
Kolomyya, *Ukraine* L30+486 **60**
Kolossia, *Kenya* K56+016 **83**
Kolozsvár, *See* Cluj
Kolpashevo, *U.S.S.R.* G42+583 **62**
Kolwezi, *Zaire* L26–108 **82**
Kolyma, R., *U.S.S.R.* B60+675 **63**
Kolymskiy, Khrebet, *U.S.S.R.* B30+634 **63**
Komandorskiye Ostr., *U.S.S.R.* A80+550 **63**
Komariya, *Sri Lanka* G49+070 **70**
Komarno, *Czechoslovakia* L71+478 **49**
Komatsu, *Japan* C81+364 **68**
Komi, aut. rep., *U.S.S.R.* J40+650 **62**
Komintern, *U.S.S.R.* K31+477 **61**

Kommunarsk, *Ukraine* U38+485 **60**
Kommunizma, Pk., *Tadzhik.* H17+388 **62**
Komotini, *Greece* L28+410 **58**
Kompong Chan, *Khmer* E87+120 **69**
Kompong Chnang, *Khmer* F02+123 **69**
Kompong Som, *Khmer* F07+111 **69**
Kompong-thom, *Khmer* F01+127 **69**
Komsomolets Ostrov, *U.S.S.R.* F60+808 **63**
Komsomolsk, *U.S.S.R.* C77+505 **63**
Kondoa, *Tanzania* K56–048 **83**
Kong, *Ivory Coast* N28+092 **80**
Kong Karl's Land, *Arctic Oc.* L05+790 **62**
Kongmoon, *China* E41+226 **67**
Kongor, *Sudan* K82+072 **81**
Kongsberg, *Norway* M32+597 **47**
Kongsmoen, *Norway* M16+648 **46**
Kongsvinger, *Norway* M18+602 **47**
Kongwa, *Tanzania* K52–064 **83**
Königsberg, *See* Kaliningrad
Konispol, *Albania* L59+397 **59**
Konotop, *Ukraine* K71+513 **60**
Konstantinovka, *Ukraine* K43+485 **60**
Konstantinovsk, *U.S.S.R.* K23+476 **61**
Konstanz, *Switz.* M35+476 **48**
Kontiomaki, *Finland* L11+643 **46**
Konya, *Turkey* K76+380 **74**
Konza, *Kenya* K48–018 **83**
Koondrook, *Victoria* C35–357 **109**
Koonenberry, *New S. Wales* C46–305 **109**
Koorawatha, *New S. Wales* C50–341 **109**
Kootenay Park, *B.C.* V70+506 **88**
Kootwijk, *Netherlands* M55+522 **44**
Koo-wee-rup, *Victoria* C27–382 **109**
Kopeisk, *U.S.S.R.* H80+550 **61**
Kopervik, *Norway* M58+593 **47**
Köping, *Sweden* L84+595 **47**
Kopparberg, *Sweden* M00+599 **47**
Koppigen, *Switzerland* M44+471 **45**
Koprivnica, *Yugoslavia* L79+462 **56**
Kora, *India* G58+261 **73**
Korce, *Albania* L56+407 **59**
Korcheva, *U.S.S.R.* K50+568 **60**
Korcula, I., *Yugoslavia* L78+429 **56**
Korea, N., *Asia* D30+412 **64**
Korea, S., *Asia* D30+368 **64**
Korea Strait, *Asia* D36+393 **64**
Korinthia, & Argolis, *Greece* L43+378 **59**
Kórinthos, *Greece* L42+379 **59**
Kórinthos, G. of, *Greece* L44+382 **59**
Koritza. *See* Korce
Kormakiti, *Cyprus* K72+354 **76**
Kornat, I., *Yugoslavia* L88+438 **56**
Korneuburg, *Austria* L82+484 **49**
Korogwe, *Tanzania* K40–052 **83**
Koroit, *Victoria* C46–383 **109**
Korong Vale, *Victoria* C38–364 **109**
Körös R., *Hungary* L58+468 **58**
Korosten, *Ukraine* L08+510 **60**
Koro Toro, *Chad* L70+160 **81**
Korppoo, *Finland* L50+602 **47**
Korsakov, *U.S.S.R.* C46–464 **63**
Korsnas, *Finland* L53+628 **46**
Korsnes, *Norway* L84+683 **46**
Kortessem, *Belgium* M58+509 **44**
Kortgem, *Netherlands* M67+516 **44**
Korti, *Sudan* K80+180 **81**
Kortrijk (Courtrai), *Belgium* M70+508 **44**
Korumburra, *Victoria* C25–384 **109**
Korwai, *India* G72+241 **73**
Koryakskiy Khrebet, *U.S.S.R.* A60+623 **63**
Korzum, *Turkey* L03+371 **74**
Kos, I., *Greece* L17+368 **59**
Koscierzyna, *Poland* L72+541 **49**
Kosciusko, *Mississippi* T88+330 **95**
Kosciusko, Mt., *N.S.W.* C10–364 **109**
Kosha, *Sudan* K86+206 **81**
Koshchagyl, *Kazakh.* J37+470 **62**
Koshki, *U.S.S.R.* J57+542 **61**
Kosi, *India* G75+277 **72**
Košice, *Czechoslovakia* L52+497 **49**
Kosima, *Kuwait* J73+295 **74**
Koslan, *U.S.S.R.* J66+634 **62**
Köslin, *See* Koszalin
Koso Gol, *Mongolia* F28+510 **63**
Kosovo Metohija, *Yugoslavia* L54+425 **58**
Kostainica, *Yugoslavia* L81+452 **56**
Kosti, *Sudan* K74+132 **81**
Kostroma, *U.S.S.R.* K24+578 **60**
Koszalin, *Poland* L83+542 **49**
Kota Baharu, *Malaya* F17+061 **69**
Kotah, *India* G85+252 **70**
Kota Kinabalu, *Sabah* E24+060 **65**
Kotalpur, *India* G14+230 **73**
Kota Tinggi, *Malaya* F07+018 **69**
Kotcha L., *British Columbia* W08+592 **88**
Kotehandpur,
  Bangladesh G06+234 **73**
Kotel, *Bulgaria* L21+429 **58**
Kotelnich, *U.S.S.R.* J70+584 **61**
Kotelnyy, Ostrov, *U.S.S.R.* C65+754 **63**
Kotido, *Uganda* K68+030 **83**
Kotka, *Finland* L18+605 **47**
Kot Kapura, *India* H01+306 **72**
Kotma, *India* G79+280 **72**
Kot Kasim, *India* G74+311 **72**
Kotlas, *U.S.S.R.* J80+612 **62**
Kotli, *Kashmir* H07+335 **72**
Kotonkoro, *Nigeria* M54+110 **80**
Kotri, *Pakistan* H41+253 **70**
Kotturu, *India* G82+148 **70**
Kotzebue Sd., *Alaska* Z00+665 **99**
Kouango, *Cent. Afr. Rep.* L60+050 **81**
Koudougou, *Upper Volta* N13+120 **80**
Koulikoro, *Mali* N46+128 **80**
Kounde, *Cent. Afr. Rep.* M02+060 **81**
Kourou, *French Guiana* R46+052 **105**
Koutiala, *Mali* N32+122 **80**
Kouvola, *Finland* L19+608 **47**
Kovel, *Ukraine* L34+512 **60**
Kovno. *See* Kaunas
Kovrov, *U.S.S.R.* K22+563 **61**
Kowloon, *China* E35+224 **67**
Koyiu, *China* E45+231 **67**
Koyukuk, R., *Alaska* Y30+655 **99**
Kozan, *Turkey* K55+375 **74**
Kozani, *Greece* L49+403 **59**
Kozhikode. *See* Calicut
Kra & Isthmus of, *Thailand* F37+104 **69**
Kracheh, *Khmer* E84+125 **69**
Kragerø, *Norway* M34+588 **47**
Kragujevac, *Yugoslavia* L53+440 **58**

Krakow, *Poland* L60+501 **49**
Kramatorsk, *Ukraine* K45+487 **60**
Krammer, *Netherlands* M65+517 **44**
Kranj, *Yugoslavia* M04+463 **56**
Kranystaw, *Poland* L41+510 **49**
Kranz, *U.S.S.R* L57+549 **47**
Krapina, *Yugoslavia* L85+462 **56**
Krasino, *Novaya Zemlya* J35+708 **62**
Krasnobród, *Poland* L44+505 **49**
Krasnodar, *U.S.S.R.* K37+451 **62**
Krasnograd, *Ukraine* K58+494 **60**
Krasnoufimsk, *U.S.S.R.* J14+566 **61**
Krasnovisher, *U.S.S.R.* J17+602 **62**
Krasnovodsk, *Turkmen* J44+401 **62**
Krasnoyarsk, *U.S.S.R.* F71+562 **63**
Krasnyi Kholm, *U.S.S.R.* K48+581 **60**
Krasny Kut, *U.S.S.R.* J78+509 **61**
Krasnyy Yar, *U.S.S.R.* K02+507 **61**

Krefeld, *W. Germany* M51+513 **48**
Kremenchug, *Ukraine* K69+491 **60**
Kremensk, *U.S.S.R.* K10+497 **61**
Krems, *Austria* L87+484 **49**
Kretinga, *Lith.* L53+559 **47**
Kreuzlingen, *Switzerland* M35+476 **45**
Kribi, *Cameroun* M30+030 **81**
Krimml, *Austria* M17+472 **48**
Krishna, R., *India* G63+166 **70**
Krishnanagar, *India* G09+234 **73**
Krishnaraja Res., *India* G81+126 **70**
Kristiansand, *Norway* M42+581 **47**
Kristianstad, *Sweden* M05+561 **47**
Kristiansund, *Norway* M43+631 **46**
Kristiinankaupunki, *Finland* L52+623 **46**
Kriti, I., *Greece* L30+350 **59**
Kriva Palanka, *Yugoslavia* L45+422 **58**
Krivoy Rog, *Ukraine* K70+478 **60**
Krizevci, *Yugoslavia* L81+460 **56**
Krk, I., *Yugoslavia* M02+451 **56**
Krnov, *Czechoslovakia* L74+501 **49**
Kroken, *Norway* M04+653 **46**
Kroměřiz, *Czechoslovakia* L76+493 **49**
Kronoby, *Finland* L42+637 **46**
Kronshtadt, *U.S.S.R.* L02+600 **60**
Kroonstad, *Orange Free State* L16+276 **84**
Kropotkin, *U.S.S.R.* K28+454 **62**
Krotoszyn, *Poland* L76+517 **49**
Krško, *Yugoslavia* L87+459 **56**
Krugersdorp, *Transvaal* L14+262 **84**
Kruishoutem, *Belgium* M69+509 **44**
Krujë, *Albania* L62+415 **58**
Krumbach, *W. Germany* M28+482 **48**
Krumlov, *Czechoslovakia* M04+488 **48**
Krunga, *Kenya* K22-018 **83**
Krung Thep, *Thailand* F27+138 **69**
Krupnik, *Bulgaria* L40+418 **58**
Krusevac, *Yugoslavia* L52+436 **58**
Krustpils, *Latvia* L24+565 **47**
Krzyz, *Poland* L84+529 **49**
Ksar el Boukhari, *Algeria* M74+358 **80**
Kuala, *Sumatra* E40+034 **65**
Kuala Kangsar, *Malaya* F25+049 **69**
Kuala Kerai, *Malaya* F16+054 **65**
Kuala Klawang, *Malaya* F18+030 **69**
Kuala Lipis, *Malaya* F17+042 **69**
Kuala Lumpur, *Malaya* F20+032 **69**
Kuandang, *Celébes* D72+008 **65**
Kuantan, *Malaya* F10+037 **65**
Kub, *S.-W. Africa* L74-242 **84**
Kucha, *Sinkiang, China* G43+418 **62**
Kuching, *Sarawak* E58+016 **65**
Kuchow. See Jungkiang
Kudat, *Sabah* E20+069 **65**
Kudymkar, *U.S.S.R.* J33+593 **62**
Kuhak, *Iran* H71+271 **75**
Kuhak, *Iran* H79+309 **75**
Kuh Banan, *Iran* J22+315 **75**
Kuh-e-Bul, *Iran* J55+305 **75**
Kuh Furgan, *Iran* J22+279 **75**
Kuh-i-Bul, *Iran* J43+308 **75**
Kuh-i-Dinar, *Iran* J51+310 **75**
Kuh-i-Kashigah, *Iran* J28+284 **75**
Kuhmo, *Finland* L03+641 **46**
Kuhpayeh, *Iran* J45+327 **75**
Kuhrud, *Iran* J53+337 **75**
Kuhsan, *Afghanistan* H82+347 **75**
Kuibis, *S.-W. Africa* L80-268 **84**
Kuibyshevka, *U.S.S.R.* D39+509 **63**
Kuikiang, *China* E23+297 **67**
Kuinre, *Netherlands* M55+528 **44**
Kukan, *Thailand* F05+146 **69**
Kukatush, *Ontario* T43+481 **91**
Kukawa, *Nigeria* M08+128 **81**
Kukes, *Albania* L58+421 **58**
Kukong, *China* E41+249 **64**
Kukong (Shiukwan), *China* E38+248 **67**
Kulachi, *Pakistan* H27+320 **72**
Kulaikh, *Saudi Arabia* K25+212 **74**
Kuldiga, *Latvia* L48+570 **47**
Kuldja, *Sinkiang, China* G51+440 **62**
Kulhakangri Mt., *Tibet* F87+280 **71**
Kulin, *China* E85+281 **67**
Kulmbach, *W. Germany* M21+501 **48**
Kulu, *India* G78+319 **72**
Kulunda, *U.S.S.R.* G67+526 **62**
Kulwin, *Victoria* C44-350 **109**
Kumai, *Borneo, Indon.* E50-026 **65**
Kumamoto, *Japan* D26+328 **68**
Kumara, *New Zealand* A52-426 **112**
Kumara, *U.S.S.R.* D48+517 **63**
Kumasi, *Ghana* N10+068 **80**
Kumbakonam, *India* G63+110 **70**
Kumher, *India* G76+273 **73**
Kumora, *U.S.S.R.* E52+559 **63**
Kumta, *India* H04+144 **70**
Kunda, *Estonia* L21+595 **47**
Kunduz, *Afghanistan* H36+367 **75**
Kungchang. See Lungsi
Kungnung, *India* F70+240 **71**
Kungrad, *Uzbek* J06+431 **62**
Kungur, *U.S.S.R.* J19+574 **61**
Kunhsien, *China* E53+327 **66**
Kunlun Shan, *China-Tibet* **30-31**
Kunming, *China* F14+250 **64**
Kunsan, *Korea* D50+360 **64**
Kuopio, *Finland* L14+629 **46**
Kupa R., *Yugoslavia* M00+455 **56**
Kupang, *Timor I., Indon.* D69-102 **65**
Kupishkis, *Lithuania* L30+558 **47**
Kupyansk, *Ukraine* K45+497 **60**

Kure, *Japan* D15+342 **68**
Kure, I., *Hawaiian Is.* Z80+288 **106**
Kureika, *U.S.S.R.* G05+670 **62**
Kuressare, *Estonia* L45+582 **47**
Kurgan, *U.S.S.R.* H57+556 **62**
Kuria Muria Is., *Arabian Sea* J22+175 **75**
Kurigram, *Bangladesh* G02+258 **73**
Kurilskiye Ostrova, *U.S.S.R.* C00+458 **63**
Kurnool, *India* G72+159 **70**
Kurow, *New Zealand* A57-446 **112**
Kurram, *Pakistan* H29+339 **72**
Kursk, *U.S.S.R.* K53+517 **60**
Kurski Zaliv, *U.S.S.R.* L55+550 **47**
Kurtalan, *Turkey* K18+384 **74**
Kuru, *Finland* L37+619 **47**
Kuruman, *Cape Province* L40-276 **84**
Kurume, *Japan* D27+332 **68**
Kurunegala, *Sri Lanka* G58+076 **70**
Kusa, *U.S.S.R.* J04+553 **61**
Kusaie, I., *Caroline Is.* B10+053 **106**
Kushersk, *U.S.S.R.* J30+584 **61**
Kushiro, *Japan* C33+430 **68**
Kushk, *Afghanistan* H75+348 **75**
Kushka, *Turkmen.* H77+352 **62**
Kushtia, *Bangladesh* G05+239 **73**
Kushva, *U.S.S.R.* J02+584 **61**
Kuskokwim B., *Alaska* Y80+590 **99**
Kusma, *Nepal* G38+282 **73**
Kustanay, *Kazakh* H70+531 **62**
Kütahya, *Turkey* L01+393 **74**
Kutai, R., *Borneo, Indon.* E26+004 **65**
Kut-al-Hai, *Iraq* J84+322 **74**
Kutatjane, *Sumatra, Indon.* F44+034 **65**
Kutch, & Gulf of, *India* H23+232 **70**
Kutch, Rann of, *India* H30+240 **70**
Kutchan, *Japan* C56+429 **68**
Kutin, *Yugoslavia* L80+455 **56**
Kutno, *Poland* L64+522 **49**
Kütsing, *China* F07+255 **67**
Kutu, *Ethiopia* K64+090 **83**
Kutum, *Sudan* L32+140 **81**
Kuuaamo, *Finland* L05+659 **46**
Kuusjärvi, *Finland* L07+627 **46**
Kuwait & state, *The Gulf* J72+294 **74**
Kuyang, *China* E60+414 **66**
Kuybyshev, *U.S.S.R.* J58+531 **61**
Kuybyshev, *U.S.S.R.* G68+559 **62**
Kuybyshevskoye Vdkhr.,
  U.S.S.R. J60+548 **61**
Kuytan, *U.S.S.R.* F22+544 **63**
Kuzhbal, *U.S.S.R.* K05+585 **61**
Kuzino, *U.S.S.R.* J04+571 **61**
Kuzmin, *Yugoslavia* L64+450 **58**
Kuznetsk, *U.S.S.R.* J81+530 **61**
Kuzovatovo, *U.S.S.R.* J75+536 **61**
Kvaløy, N., *Norway* L65+702 **46**
Kvaløy, S., *Norway* L68+697 **46**
Kvarken, Östra, *Sweden* L56+634 **46**
Kvarner, G. of, *Yugoslavia* M05+448 **56**
Kvarneric, G. of, *Yugoslavia* M01+445 **56**
Kvesmenes, *Norway* L60+693 **46**
Kwajalein, Is., *Marshall Is.* A80+088 **106**
Kwakhanai, *Botswana* L52-218 **84**
Kwakoegron, *Surinam* R62+051 **105**
Kwangchang, *China* E23+267 **67**
Kwangchow, *China* E40+232 **67**
Kwangchow Wan, *China* E56+210 **67**
Kwang-nam, *S. Vietnam* E79+159 **69**
Kwangnan, *China* F00+241 **67**
Kwangping. See Yungnien
Kwangsichuang prov., *China* E72+238 **67**
Kwangsin. See Shangjao
Kwangtung, prov., *China* E36+235 **67**
Kwania L., *Uganda* K74+016 **83**
Kwan-tung (Luta) Pen., *Ch.* D86+388 **66**
Kweichih, *China* E15+307 **66**
Kweichow. See Fengkieh
Kweichow, prov., *China* E84+268 **67**
Kweihwa. See Tzeyun
Kweihwa. See Huhehot
Kweilin, *China* E59+254 **67**
Kweiping, *China* E59+233 **67**
Kweisui. See Huhehot
Kweiteh, *China* F22+360 **64**
Kweiteh. See Shangkiu
Kweiyang, *China* E80+266 **67**
Kweiyang, *China* E45+258 **67**
Kwi-chu, *N. Vietnam* E88+194 **69**
Kwidzyn, *Poland* L66+538 **49**
Kwitao, *Burma* F44+257 **71**
Kwoka, mt., *New Guinea* D15-006 **65**
Kyabram, *Victoria* C30-363 **109**
Kyakhta, *U.S.S.R.* E81+504 **63**
Kyalite Crossing, *N.S.W.* C40-349 **109**
Kyangin, *Burma* F58+182 **71**
Kyaring Nor, *China* F46+348 **64**
Kyaukiaw, *Burma* F72+208 **71**
Kyaukpyu, *Burma* F69+195 **71**
Kyaukse, *Burma* F53+215 **71**
Kybybolite, *S. Australia* C54-369 **109**
Kyelang, *India* G78+326 **72**
Kyi R., *Tibet* F80+298 **71**
Kymi, *Finland* L19+605 **47**
Kyneton, *Victoria* C33-373 **109**
Kyoga L., *Uganda* K74+014 **83**
Kyoto, *Japan* C85+350 **68**
Kyrenia, *Cyprus* K70+353 **76**
Kyshtym, *U.S.S.R.* H86+557 **61**
Kythrea, *Cyprus* K69+352 **76**
Kyūshū, I., *Japan* D24+330 **68**
Kyustendil, *Bulgaria* L48+422 **58**
Kyusyur, *U.S.S.R.* D45+708 **63**
Kywong, *New South Wales* C20-350 **109**
Kyzl, *U.S.S.R.* F63+517 **63**
Kyzyl Kum, *Uzbek, etc.* H70+423 **62**
Kyzylsk, *U.S.S.R.* J06+526 **61**
Kzyl Orda, *Kazakh* H57+450 **62**

Laanila, *Finland* L16+684 **46**
La Argentina, *Argentina* S70+503 **103**
La Ascención, *Mexico* V18+310 **100**
La Asuncion, *Venezuela* S23+110 **104**
Laban, *Jordan* K56+309 **76**
La Banda, *Argentina* S25-277 **103**
Labang, *Sarawak* E40+033 **65**
Labe, *Guinea* N74+114 **80**
Labelle, *Quebec* S89+463 **91**
Laberge, L., *Yukon* X00+610 **88**
Labouheyre, *France* N06+442 **55**
Laboulaye, *Argentina* S20-341 **103**

Labrador, *Canada* **89**
Labrea, *Brazil* S28-072 **104**
La Brea, *Honduras* T76+134 **101**
La Brea, *Trinidad* S08+102 **104**
Labuan, I., *Sabah* E29+054 **65**
Labuk B., *Sabah* E14+061 **65**
La Canoa, *Venezuela* S23+086 **104**
La Carlota, *Argentina* S20-334 **103**
La Carolina, *Spain* N22+383 **52**
La Ceiba, *Venezuela* S66+094 **104**
Lacepede B., *S. Australia* C62-367 **109**
Lac Frontiere, *Quebec* S60+467 **90**
Lachen, *Switzerland* M37+472 **45**
Lachine, *Quebec* S82+455 **91**
Lachlan R., *New S. Wales* C30-338 **109**
Lachmangarh, *India* G89+278 **72**
Lachute, *Quebec* S87+457 **91**
Lackawanna, *New York* T23+428 **96**
Lackawaxen, *Pennsylvania* T00+415 **96**
Lacken Res., *Ireland, Rep.* N39+532 **43**
La Cocha, *Argentina* S33-278 **103**
Lacombe, *Alberta* V53+522 **88**
La Concordia, *Salvador* T85+134 **101**
Laconia, *New Hampshire* S69+435 **96**
La Copelina, *Argentina* S46-372 **103**
La Coruña, *Spain* N51+433 **52**
La Crosse, *Wisconsin* U07+438 **93**
La Cruz, *Columbia* T11+015 **104**
La Cruz, *Mexico* V01+279 **100**
Ladakh Ra., *Tibet* G60+322 **70**
Ladis, *Iran* H82+289 **75**
Ladoga, L. See Ladozhskoye Ozero
La Dorada, *Columbia* S88+055 **104**
Ladozhskoye Oz., *Russia* K84+606 **60**
Ladwa, *India* G77+300 **72**
Lady Neunes B., *Antarctica* A70-730 **27**
Ladysmith, *British Columbia* W23+490 **88**
Ladysmith, *Natal* L02-288 **84**
Ladysmith, *Wisconsin* U07+455 **93**
Lae, *Papua New Guinea* C18-068 **111**
Laeken, *Belgium* M69+509 **44**
Laesö, I., *Denmark* M24+573 **47**
La Esperanza, *Honduras* T81+143 **101**
La Estrada, *Spain* N51+427 **52**
Lafayette, *Georgia* T62+347 **97**
La Fayette, *Indiana* T71+404 **91**
Lafayette, *Louisiana* U12+302 **95**
La Florencia, *Argentina* S13-241 **103**
Lafontaine, *Quebec* S59+471 **90**
Lagakalaka, *Somalia* J66+060 **83**
Lagan R., *N. Ireland* N35+546 **42**
Lages, *Brazil* Q37-056 **105**
Laggan, *Scotland* N26+570 **40**
Laggan L., *Scotland* N27+570 **40**
Laghouat, *Algeria* M72+332 **80**
Lagonegro, *Italy* L85+401 **57**
Lagos, *Mexico* U72+214 **100**
Lagos, *Nigeria* M70+064 **80**
Lagos, *Portugal* N52+371 **52**
La Grande, *Oregon* V79+453 **92**
Lagrange, *Georgia* T60+330 **97**
Lagrange, *Indiana* T62+416 **91**
Lagrange, *Kentucky* T62+384 **97**
La Grange, *W. Australia* D79-186 **110**
La Granja, *Spain* N24+409 **52**
La Guaira, *Venezuela* S41+106 **104**
La Guardia, *Argentina* S33-295 **103**
La Guardia, *Spain* N53+419 **52**
Laguna, *Brazil* R23-284 **103**
Lagunas, *Peru* T04-053 **104**
Lagunillas, *Bolivia* S22-196 **104**
Laharpur, *India* G54+276 **73**
Lanej, *Yemen, South* K00+130 **74**
Lahijan, *Iran* J60+372 **75**
Laholm, *Sweden* M12+565 **47**
Lahore, *Pakistan* H04+316 **72**
Lahti, *Finland* L26+610 **47**
Lai, C., *N. Vietnam* E77+171 **69**
Laibach. See Ljubljana
Lai-chau, *N. Vietnam* F11+222 **69**
Laichow. See Yehsien
Laigle, *France* M86+488 **54**
Laila, *Saudi Arabia* J79+223 **74**
Laingsburg, *Cape Province* L56-330 **84**
Lairg, *Scotland* N26+580 **40**
Laishev, *U.S.S.R.* J63+554 **61**
Laives, *Italy* M22+465 **45**
Laja, L., *Chile* S68-374 **103**
Lajao, *Brazil* Q69-192 **105**
La Jaonesa, *Argentina* S39-386 **103**
Lajes, *Brazil* R32-278 **103**
La Junquera, *Spain* M73+424 **53**
La Junta, *Colorado* U81+380 **94**
Lakatrask, *Sweden* L53+663 **46**
Lake Andes, *S. Dakota* U52+432 **93**
Lake Butler, *Florida* T45+300 **97**
Lake Charles, *Louisiana* U19+302 **95**
Lake City, *Florida* T46+302 **97**
Lake City, *Michigan* T61+444 **91**
Lake District, *England* N19+546 **37**
Lake Edward, *Quebec* S73+477 **91**
Lakefield, *Ontario* T20+444 **91**
Lake Geneva, *Wisconsin* T80+426 **91**
Lake George, *New York* S82+434 **96**
Lake Harbour, *N.-W. Terr.* S59+632 **89**
Lakeland, *Florida* T42+280 **97**
Lake Mejella, *California* W12+365 **92**
Lake Pleasant, *New York* S86+434 **96**
Lake Providence, *Louisiana* U07+328 **95**
Lakes Entrance, *Victoria* C12-378 **109**
Lakeview, *Minnesota* U12+469 **93**
Lakeview, *Oregon* W02+422 **92**
Lakewood, *New Jersey* S85+400 **96**
Lakewood, *Ohio* T40+415 **91**
Lakhimpur, *India* F65+272 **71**
Lakhimpur, *India* G55+280 **73**
Lakki, *Pakistan* H24+325 **72**
Lakkor Tso, *Tibet* G36+320 **71**
Lakonia, *Greece* L45+369 **59**
Lakonia, G. of, *Greece* L44+366 **59**
Lakota, *Ivory Coast* N34+060 **80**
Lakota, *N. Dakota* U50+464 **93**
Lakse Fd., *Norway* L20+705 **46**
Lakshadweep, *Indian Ocean* H13+115 **70**
Laktsang, *Tibet* G42+303 **71**
Lala Musa, *Pakistan* H06+327 **72**
Lalbagh, *India* G10+242 **73**
Lalganj, *India* G29+259 **73**
La Libertad, *Ecuador* T35-022 **104**

La Libertad, *Guatemala* U01+167 **100**
La Libertad, *Nicaragua* T61+123 **101**
La Ligua, *Chile* S67-324 **103**
Lalin, *Spain* N49+426 **52**
Lalitpur, *India* G69+247 **73**
La Maddalena, I., *Sardinia* M34+413 **57**
La Malbaie, *Quebec* S61+476 **91**
Lamar, *Colorado* U76+381 **94**
Lamar, *Missouri* U26+374 **95**
Lamastre, *France* M63+450 **55**
Lambach, *Austria* M07+481 **48**
Lamballe, *France* N15+485 **54**
Lambay I., *Ireland, Rep.* N36+535 **43**
Lambert's Ld., *Greenland* P30+790 **26**
Lambertville, *New Jersey* T00+403 **96**
Lámbia, *Greece* L49+379 **59**
Lamb's Hd., *Ireland, Rep.* N61+517 **43**
Lamé, *Chad* M02+092 **81**
Lamego, *Portugal* N47+411 **52**
Lameroo, *S. Australia* C57-354 **109**
Lamesa, *Texas* U70+326 **94**
Lamia, *Greece* L45+389 **59**
Lamlash, *Scotland* N31+555 **41**
Lammermuir Hills, *Scotland* N16+559 **41**
Lamotrek Is., *Caroline Is.* C30+075 **106**
Lampa, *Peru* S80-153 **104**
Lampazos, *Mexico* U62+270 **100**
Lampedusa, I., *Medit. Sea* M12+355 **81**
Lampeter, *Wales* N25+521 **38**
Lamphun, *Thailand* F35+186 **69**
Lampi, I., *Burma* F41+108 **71**
Lampton, C., *N.-W. Terr.* W20+710 **88**
Lamu, *Kenya* K24-024 **83**
Lamud, *Peru* T17-063 **104**
Lanark, *Scotland* N23+557 **41**
Lancashire, co., *England* N16+537 **37**
Lancaster, *England* N17+540 **37**
Lancaster, *Missouri* U16+404 **95**
Lancaster, *New Hampshire* S69+445 **91**
Lancaster, *New York* T22+429 **96**
Lancaster, *Pennsylvania* T08+401 **96**
Lancaster, *S. Carolina* T34+347 **97**
Lancaster, *Wisconsin* U04+429 **91**
Lancaster Sd., *N.-W. Terr.* T60+734 **89**
Lanchow, *China* F07+360 **66**
Landeck, *Austria* M27+471 **48**
Landen, *Belgium* M60+508 **44**
Lander, *Wyoming* V22+429 **93**
Landerneau, *France* N26+484 **54**
Landes, dep., *France* N04+440 **55**
Landfall, I., *Chile* S85-534 **103**
Landi Khana, *Pakistan* H23+342 **72**
Landi Kotal, *Pakistan* H23+342 **72**
Landon, *Sweden* M04+636 **46**
Landovery, *Wales* N23+520 **38**
Landsberg, *W. Germany* M25+481 **48**
Landsberg. See Gorzow Wielkopolski
Land's End, *England* N34+500 **38**
Landshut, *W. Germany* M17+490 **48**
Landskrona, *Sweden* M13+559 **47**
Langá, *Denmark* M31+563 **47**
Langadhas, *Greece* L41+408 **59**
Langana L., *Ethiopia* K38+076 **83**
Langchung, *China* E84+315 **66**
Langeac, *France* M70+451 **55**
Langeland, I., *Denmark* M26+549 **47**
Längelmavesi, *Finland* L34+615 **47**
Langenthal, *Switzerland* M43+472 **45**
Langholm, *Scotland* N18+552 **41**
Langkawi, I., *Malaya* F31+063 **69**
Langlade, I., *Atlantic Oc.* R68+468 **90**
Langogne, *France* M67+447 **55**
Langon, *France* N02+445 **55**
Langøya, *Norway* M00+687 **46**
Langport, *England* N17+511 **38**
Langres, *France* M58+478 **54**
Langsa, *Sumatra* F42+045 **65**
Långsele, *Sweden* L78+632 **46**
Lang-Son, *N. Vietnam* E79+218 **69**
Långträsk, *Sweden* L58+654 **46**
Languedoc, prov., *France* M66+430 **55**
Lanklaar, *Belgium* M56+510 **44**
Lankor Tso, *Tibet* G42+325 **71**
Lannion, *France* N21+488 **54**
Lansdale, *Pennsylvania* T02+402 **96**
Lansing, *Michigan* T57+428 **91**
Lansingburg, *New York* S82+428 **91**
Lan Tao, *China* E36+223 **67**
Lanzarote, I., *Canary Is.* N82+290 **80**
Laoag, *Philippines* D87+182 **65**
Lao Bao, *S. Vietnam* E80+165 **69**
Lao-chang-Ho R., *China* E23+378 **66**
Lao-Cai, *N. Vietnam* F07+225 **69**
Laon, *France* M69+496 **54**
La Oroya, *Peru* T06-115 **104**
Laos, *S.-E. Asia* F10+192 **69**
Lao shan, *China* D86+363 **66**
Lapalisse, *France* M68+462 **54**
La Palma, I., *Canary Is.* D30+286 **80**
La Paragua, *Venezuela* S21+070 **104**
La Paz, *Argentina* R88-307 **103**
La Paz, *Argentina* S45-334 **103**
La Paz, *Bolivia* S49-165 **104**
La Paz, *Honduras* T76+143 **101**
La Paz, *Mexico* V32+241 **100**
Lapchung L., *Tibet* G27+300 **71**
Lapeer, *Michigan* T50+431 **91**
La Pelada, *Argentina* S06-309 **103**
Lapinlahti, *Finland* L16+634 **46**
Lapithos, *Cyprus* K71+353 **76**
La Plata, *Argentina* R78+349 **103**
La Porte, *Indiana* T70+416 **95**
Laporte, *Pynnsylvania* T09+414 **96**
La Porte City, *Iowa* U13+424 **95**
Lapovo, *Yugoslavia* L54+442 **58**
Lappa Järvi, *Finland* L38+631 **46**
Lappeenranta, *Finland* L11+610 **47**
Lappland, *N. Europe* L57+680 **46**
Lapptrask, *Sweden* L39+660 **46**
Laprida, *Argentina* S06-378 **103**
Laptevykh Sea, *U.S.S.R.* D70+750 **63**
Lăpusul Românesc *Romania* L36+475 **49**
Lapy, *Poland* L43+530 **49**
Laqit, *Kuwait* J71+290 **74**
La Quiaca, *Argentina* S34-222 **103**
Lar, *Iran* J33+276 **75**
Larache, *Morocco* N38+350 **80**
Laragne, *France* M55+443 **55**

24

Laramate, *Peru* S89-142 **104**
Laramie, *Wyoming* V04+413 **93**
Laramie Mts., *Wyoming* V06+424 **93**
Laramie Pk., *Wyoming* V02+422 **93**
Larangeiras, *Brazil* S11-132 **104**
La Rasse, *Switzerland* M49+471 **45**
Larbert, *Scotland* N23+560 **41**
Larchwood, *Ontario* T38+466 **91**
Laredo, *Texas* V39+275 **94**
Largeau (Faya), *Chad* L66+180 **81**
Largo, *New Mexico* V17+366 **94**
Largs, *Scotland* N29+558 **41**
Larino, *Italy* M01+418 **57**
La Rioja, *Argentina* S41-294 **103**
Larisa, *Greece* L44+396 **59**
Larkana, *Pakistan* H41+275 **70**
Larnaca & B., *Cyprus* K68+349 **76**
Larne & L., *N. Ireland* N35+549 **42**
Larned, *Kansas* U56+382 **95**
La Robla, *Spain* N34+428 **52**
Laroche, *Belgium* M56+502 **44**
La Rochelle, *France* N07+462 **54**
La Roda, *Spain* N13+392 **53**
Lars Christensen Coast,
    Antarctic H50-680 **27**
Laruns, *France* N03+430 **55**
Larvik, *Norway* M30+590 **47**
Laryak, *U.S.S.R.* G60+612 **62**
La Salle, *Illinois* T84+413 **95**
Las Animas, *Colorado* U80+380 **94**
Las Anod, *Somalia* J76+082 **83**
Las Cejas, *Argentina* S29-269 **103**
Las Coloradas, *Argentina* S64-396 **103**
Las Cruces, *New Mexico* V11+323 **94**
Las Cruces, *New Mexico* V11+325 **98**
La Serena, *Chile* S67-299 **103**
Last Flores, *Argentina* R86-361 **103**
Lasgird, *Iran* J43+353 **75**
Lash, *Afghanistan* H81+316 **75**
Las Heras, *Argentina* S53-465 **103**
Lashio, *Burma* F43+228 **71**
Lashkar, *India* G71+262 **73**
Lasithi, *Crete* L24+350 **59**
Las Khoreh, *Somalia* J70+110 **83**
Las Lajas, *Argentina* S62-385 **103**
Las Lomitas,*Argentina* S03-247 **103**
Las Palmas, *Canary Is.* P04+280 **80**
Las Plumas, *Argentina* S44-436 **103**
Lassen Pk., *California* W09+405 **92**
Lassen Peak Nat. Park, *Cal.* W08+405 **98**
Las Tablas, *Panama* T31+078 **101**
Last Mountain L., *Sask.* V00+510 **88**
Lastovo, I., *Yugoslavia* L79+427 **56**
Las Vacas, *Mexico* U67+295 **100**
Las Vegas, *Nevada* V60+362 **92**
Las Vegas, *New Mexico* V02+356 **94**
Latacunga, *Ecuador* T22-009 **104**
Latakia, *Syria* K55+355 **76**
La Tamba, *Guinea* N60+108 **80**
Laterrière, *Quebec* S67+483 **90**
Latheron, *Scotland* N20+583 **40**
Latrobe, *Pennsylvania* T27+404 **96**
Latrobe, *Tasmania* C22-412 **109**
Latrun, *Jordan* K60+318 **76**
La Tuque, *Quebec* S77+475 **91**
Latvia, rep., *U.S.S.R.* **47**
Lauder, *Scotland* N16+557 **41**
Laufen, *Switzerland* M45+474 **45**
Launceston, *England* N26+506 **38**
Launceston, *Tasmania* C18-414 **109**
Laune R., *Ireland, Rep.* N59+519 **43**
Launggyang, *Burma* F40+260 **71**
La Union, *Chile* S78-403 **103**
La Union, *Mexico* U70+180 **100**
La Union, *Salvador* T77+134 **101**
La Union, *Spain* N05+377 **53**
Laura, *Queensland* C33-156 **111**
Laura, *S. Australia* C70-331 **109**
La Urbana, *Venezuela* S41+070 **104**
Laurel, *Maryland* T11+391 **96**
Laurel, *Mississippi* T83+316 **95**
Laurel, *Montana* V22+456 **93**
Laurel Hill, *Pennsylvania* T25+402 **96**
Laurens, *S. Carolina* T42+345 **97**
Laurent, *Quebec* S73+471 **91**
Laurentide Mts., *Quebec* S82+465 **90**
Laurentides Park, *Quebec* S68+477 **91**
Lauria, *Italy* L85+400 **57**
Laurie, I., *South Orkneys* Q87-610 **27**
Laurinburg, *N. Carolina* T27+348 **97**
Lausanne, *Switzerland* M50+465 **45**
Lautaro, *Chile* S75-384 **103**
Lautem, *Timor I., Indonesia* D48-084 **65**
Lauzon, *Quebec* S67+468 **91**
Lavacherie, *Belgium* M57+501 **44**
Laval, *France* N05+481 **54**
Laval B., *Quebec* S54+487 **90**
Lavalle, *Argentina* S52-327 **103**
Lavalleja, *Uruguay* R60-340 **103**
Lavamund, *Austria* L90+466 **48**
Lavardac, *France* M88+442 **55**
La Vega, *Dominican Rep.* S63+193 **101**
La Vela, *Venezuela* S57+114 **104**
Laverton, *W. Australia* D75-284 **110**
Laviana, *Spain* N33+432 **52**
Lavina, *Montana* V24+463 **93**
Lavongai, *Bismarck Arch.* B96-030 **106**
Lavos, *Portugal* N53+401 **52**
Lavras, *Brazil* R00-213 **105**
Lavras, *Brazil* R53-308 **103**
Lavras, *Brazil* Q54-068 **105**
Lavrentiya, *U.S.S.R.* Z36+654 **63**
Lávrion, *Greece* L36+377 **59**
Lawk Sawk, *Burma* F48+212 **71**
Lawra, *Ghana* N16+106 **80**
Lawrence, *Kansas* U32+390 **95**
Lawrence, *Massachusetts* S67+427 **96**
Lawrence, *New Zealand* A61-459 **112**
Lawrenceburg, *Tennessee* T75+352 **97**
Lawrenceville, *Illinois* T76+387 **95**
Lawton, *Oklahoma* U50+345 **95**
Laxford L., *Scotland* N31+584 **40**
Laysan I., *Hawaiian Is.* Z42+260 **106**
Lazarevac, *Yugoslavia* L59+444 **58**
Lazio, dep., *Italy* M16+420 **57**
Lead, *S. Dakota* U83+444 **93**
Leadhills, *Scotland* N22+554 **41**
Leadville, *Colorado* V08+392 **94**
Leaf R., *Quebec* S65+587 **89**
Leakesville, *Mississippi* T81+311 **97**
Leaksville, *N. Carolina* T28+365 **97**

Leamington, *England* N09+523 **37**
Leamington, *Ontario* T46+421 **91**
Leane L., *Ireland, Rep.* N57+520 **43**
Leatherhead, *England* N03+513 **39**
Leavenworth, *Indiana* T68+382 **97**
Leavenworth, *Kansas* U30+393 **95**
Łeba, *Poland* L74+547 **49**
Lebanon, *Kentucky* T61+375 **97**
Lebanon, *Missouri* U16+377 **95**
Lebanon, *New Hampshire* S74+437 **96**
Lebanon, *Pennsylvania* T09+403 **96**
Lebanon, rep., *W. Asia* K56+340 **74**
Lebesby, *Norway* L18+705 **46**
Lebombo Mts., *S. Africa* K78-250 **84**
Lebork, *Poland* L74+545 **49**
Lebu, *Chile* S82-375 **103**
Lebye, *Lebanon* K52+342 **76**
Lecce, *Italy* L71+404 **57**
Lecco, *Italy* M34+458 **56**
Lectourre, *France* M86+439 **55**
Ledbury, *England* N15+520 **38**
Ledesma, *Argentina* S29-238 **103**
Ledesma, *Spain* N36+411 **52**
Ledo, *India* F55+272 **71**
Lee R., *Ireland, Rep.* N51+519 **43**
Leech Lake, *Minnesota* U28+472 **93**
Leeds, *England* N09+538 **37**
Leende, *Netherlands* M57+513 **44**
Leerbeek, *Belgium* M65+508 **44**
Leerdam, *Netherlands* M59+519 **44**
Leesburg, *Virginia* T15+391 **96**
Leesville, *Louisiana* U20+311 **95**
Leeton, *New South Wales* C21-346 **109**
Leeuwarden, *Netherlands* M55+532 **44**
Leeuwin, C., *W. Australia* E29-340 **110**
Leeward Is., *West Indies* S10+172 **101**
Lefka, *Cyprus* K73+351 **76**
Lefkara, *Cyprus* K70+348 **76**
Lefkoniko, *Cyprus* K67+353 **76**
Lefroy, L., *W. Australia* D80-312 **110**
Legaspi, *Philippines* D68+130 **65**
Legge Pk., *Tasmania* C14-416 **109**
Leghorn, *See* Livorno
Legnica, *Poland* L83+512 **49**
Leh, *Kashmir* G74+342 **72**
Le Havre, *France* M89+495 **54**
Lehi, *Utah* V41+404 **94**
Lehututu, *Botswana* L48-240 **84**
Leiah, *Pakistan* H24+310 **72**
Leicester & co., *England* N07+526 **37**
Leichhardt, R., *Queensland* C62-136 **111**
Leiden, *Netherlands* M63+522 **44**
Leigh Creek, *S. Australia* C70-305 **109**
Leighlinbridge, *Ireland, Rep.* N42-527 **43**
Leighton Buzzard, *England* N04+519 **39**
Leignon, *Belgium* M59+503 **44**
Leimuiden, *Netherlands* M62+522 **44**
Leinster, prov., *Ireland, Rep.* N42+520 **43**
Leinster, Mt., *Ireland, Rep.* N41+526 **43**
Leipzig, *E. Germany* M16+514 **48**
Leisele, *Belgium* M74+510 **44**
Leitchfield, *Kentucky* T68+375 **97**
Leith, *Scotland* N19+560 **41**
Leitrim, co., *Ireland, Rep.* N49+543 **42**
Leix (Laois), co., *Ireland,*
    Rep. N44+534 **43**
Leixlip, *Ireland, Rep.* N39+534 **43**
Leiyang, *China* E43+264 **67**
Leka, *Norway* M20+650 **46**
Le Kef, *Tunisia* M38+360 **81**
Leksands Noret, *Sweden* M00+607 **47**
Leksvik, *Norway* M26+637 **46**
Leland, *Michigan* T64+451 **91**
Leland, *Mississippi* U05+334 **95**
Leleque, *Argentina* S66-424 **103**
Le Maire, Estrecho de, *Arg.* S30-550 **103**
Léman, Lac, *Switzerland* M51+464 **45**
Le Mans, *France* M89+480 **54**
Le Mars, *Iowa* U37+428 **95**
Lemberg. *See* Lvov
Lemnos. *See* Limnos, I.
Lemvethna, *Burma* F59+174 **71**
Lena, R., *U.S.S.R.* D65+692 **63**
Lenina Pk., *Kirgiz.* H13+393 **62**
Leninabad, *Uzbek* H33+403 **62**
Leninakan, *Armyanskaya* K04+408 **62**
Leningrad, *U.S.S.R.* K88+599 **60**
Leninka, *U.S.S.R.* A14+647 **63**
Leninogorsk, *Kazakh.* G40+5(5 **62**
Leninsk, *Turkmen.* H70+390 **62**
Leninsk Kuznetskiy, *U.S.S.R.* G23+545 **62**
Lenk, *Switzerland* M45+465 **45**
Lennox, I., *Chile & Argent.* S42-553 **103**
Lenoir, *N. Carolina* T39+359 **97**
Lens, *France* M73+504 **54**
Lent, *Netherlands* M55+519 **44**
Lentiira, *Finland* L01+644 **46**
Lenvik, *Norway* L71+694 **46**
Lenz, *Switzerland* M32+467 **45**
Lenzerheide, *Switzerland* M32+467 **45**
Leoben, *Austria* L89+473 **48**
Leola, *S. Dakota* U54+458 **93**
León, *France* N08+439 **55**
Leon, *Mexico* U70+212 **100**
Leon, *Nicaragua* T72+125 **101**
León, *Spain* N33+426 **52**
León, Monts de, *Spain* N3'+426 **52**
Leongatha, *Victoria* C25-384 **109**
Leonidhion, *Greece* L43+372 **59**
Leonora, *W. Australia* D83-286 **110**
Leonteva, *U.S.S.R.* K50+590 **60**
Leopoldsburg, *Belgium* M58+511 **44**
Leopold II L., *See* Mai-Ndomba L.
Leopoldville. *See* Kinshasa
Lepepe, *Botswana* L24-234 **84**
Lepontine, Alpi, *Switz.-Italy* M41+463 **45**
Lepreau, *New Brunswick* S39+452 **90**
Lercara Friddi, *Sicily* M03+378 **57**
Lerdo, *Mexico* U82+255 **100**
Lerida, *Spain* M86+416 **53**
Lerma, *Argentina* S34-250 **103**
Lerma, *Spain* N22+420 **51**
Lermoos, *Austria* M25+474 **48**
Léros, I., *Greece* L19+372 **59**
Le Roy, *New York* T18+429 **91**
Lerwick, *Shetland, Scot.* N07+601 **40**
Lesbos. *See* Lesvos I.
Les Escoumains, *Quebec* S56+483 **90**

Leskovac, L48+430 **58**
Lesotho (Basutoland), *Afr.* L10-294 **84**
Lesozavodsk, *U.S.S.R.* D09+454 **63**
Lesparre, *France* N06+453 **55**
Lesser Slave L., *Alberta* V65+554 **88**
Lessines, *Belgium* M67+507 **44**
Lestijärvi, *Finland* L32+635 **46**
Lesvos, I., *Greece* L22+392 **59**
Leszno, *Poland* L81+518 **49**
Letcher, *S. Dakota* U49+439 **93**
Letchworth, *England* N01+520 **39**
Letea I., *Romania* L04+453 **58**
Lethbridge, *Alberta* V46+497 **88**
Leti Kep., *Indonesia* D42-084 **65**
Letpadan, *Burma* F56+177 **71**
Lette, *New South Wales* C42-344 **109**
Letterfrack, *Ireland, Rep.* N60+535 **43**
Letterkenny, *Ireland, Rep.* N46+550 **42**
Letty Harbour, *N.-W. Terr.* W28+690 **88**
Letur, *Spain* N13+384 **53**
Leucate, *France* M72+429 **55**
Leucite Hills, *Wyoming* V24+418 **93**
Leuk, *Switzerland* M44+463 **45**
Leuser, mt., *Sumatra* F47+038 **65**
Leuven (Louvain), *Belgium* M62+509 **44**
Leuze, *Belgium* M68+506 **44**
Levádhia, *Greece* L43+385 **59**
Levanger, *Norway* M22+638 **46**
Leven, *Scotland* N18+562 **41**
Leven L., *Scotland* N20+562 **41**
Levêque, C., *W. Australia* D72-163 **110**
Levice, *Czechoslovakia* L69+483 **49**
Levick, Mt., *Antarctica* B20-740 **27**
Levin, *New Zealand* A28-406 **112**
Levis, *Quebec* S67+468 **91**
Levitha, I., *Greece* L21+370 **59**
Levkás, I., *Greece* L56+387 **59**
Levoča, *Czechoslovakia* L57+490 **49**
Lewes, *England* N00+509 **39**
Lewes R., *Yukon* X05+616 **88**
Lewis, Butt of, *Scotland* N37+585 **40**
Lewis I., *Scotland* N40+581 **40**
Lewis Ra., *Montana* V52+482 **98**
Lewisburg, *Pennsylvania* T11+410 **91**
Lewisburg, *Tennessee* T73+354 **97**
Lewisburg, *W. Virginia* T33+378 **97**
Lewiston, *Idaho* V72+464 **92**
Lewiston, *Maine* S61+441 **90**
Lewiston, *Michigan* T56+449 **91**
Lewiston, *N. Carolina* T13+362 **97**
Lewiston, *Illinois* U01+404 **91**
Lewistown, *Montana* V27+470 **93**
Lewistown, *Pennsylvania* T16+406 **96**
Lexington, *Georgia* T49+338 **97**
Lexington, *Kentucky* T57+380 **97**
Lexington, *Missouri* U23+392 **95**
Lexington, *Nebraska* U58+408 **95**
Lexington, *N. Carolina* T32+358 **97**
Lexington, *Tennessee* T80+356 **97**
Lexington, *Virginia* T27+377 **97**
Leydsdorp, *Transvaal* K86-240 **84**
Leyte, I., *Philippines* D60+108 **65**
Lezajsk, *Poland* L46+503 **49**
Lha-kang Dzong, *Tibet* F83+281 **71**
Lhasa, *Tibet* F83+296 **71**
Lha-tse Dzong, *Tibet* G14+291 **71**
Lhontse Dzong, *Tibet* F76+284 **71**
Lianchow, *See* Wuwei
Liangsiang, *China* E22+396 **66**
Liant, C., *Thailand* F26+127 **69**
Liao R., *China* D70+422 **64**
Liaocheng, *China* E24+365 **66**
Liaohsien, *China* E39+370 **66**
Liao-tung, G. of, *China* D86+398 **66**
Liao yang-chow, *China* D71+412 **66**
Liard, *N.-W. Territories* W23+602 **88**
Liard R., *N.-W. Territories* W23+608 **88**
Liari, *Pakistan* H51+256 **70**
Liberal, *Kansas* U66+370 **94**
Liberdade, *Brazil* S70-072 **104**
Liberec, *Czechoslovakia* L90+508 **48**
Liberia, *Costa Rica* T61+106 **101**
Liberia, rep., *W. Africa* N60+070 **80**
Libertad, *Mexico* V46+298 **100**
Liboi, *Kenya* K24+004 **83**
Libourne, *France* N02+449 **55**
Libreville, *Gabon* M32+004 **82**
Libya, *N. Africa* L60+250 **81**
Licata, *Sicily* M00+371 **57**
Licheng. *See* Tsinan
Lichfield, *England* N11+527 **37**
Licking R., *Kentucky* T56+387 **97**
Lida, *Belorussia* L29+539 **60**
Lida-di-Roma, *Italy* M16+417 **57**
Liddel R., *Scot.-Eng.* N17+551 **41**
Liddes, *Switzerland* M47+460 **45**
Liddon G., *N.-W. Terr.* V45+750 **88**
Lidjombo, *Cameroun* L84+026 **82**
Lidköping, *Sweden* M11+585 **47**
Lidzbark, *Poland* L57+541 **49**
Liechtenstein, *Europe* M32+472 **45**
Liège & prov., *Belgium* M57+506 **44**
Liegnitz. *See* Legnica
Lieksa, *Finland* L00+633 **46**
Lienkong, *China* E23+263 **67**
Lienyunkang, *China* E03+347 **66**
Lienz, *Austria* M14+468 **48**
Liepāja, *Latvia* L54+565 **47**
Lierneux, *Belgium* M55+503 **44**
Lierre, *Belgium* M63+511 **44**
Liers, *Belgium* M57+507 **44**
Liestal, *Switzerland* M44+475 **45**
Lievre, R. du, *Quebec* T03+467 **91**
Lifford, *Ireland, Rep.* N45+548 **42**
Lifu, I., *Loyalty Is.* A12-226 **106**
Ligure, Appennino, *Italy* M36+446 **56**
Liguria, dep. *Italy* M38+445 **56**
Ligurian Sea, *Italy* M39+433 **56**
Lihsien, *China* E50+296 **67**
Likiang, *China* F28+268 **64**
Likimi, *Zaire* L56+028 **82**
Liling, *China* E38+277 **67**
Lilla Edet, *Sweden* M17+581 **47**
Lille, *Belgium* M61+507 **44**
Lille, *France* M71+507 **54**
Lillehammer, *Norway* M27+611 **47**
Lillesand, *Norway* M39+582 **47**
Lillo, *Belgium* M64+513 **44**
Lillo, *Spain* N20+397 **52**

Lillooet, *British Columbia* W11+506 **88**
Lilongwe, *Malawi* K66-140 **83**
Lim Fd., *Denmark* M40+566 **47**
Lima, *Ohio* T55+408 **91**
Lima, *Peru* T12-120 **104**
Limache, *Chile* S68-330 **103**
Limassol, *Cyprus* K72+347 **76**
Limavady, *N. Ireland* N42+550 **42**
Limay, R., *Argentina* S52-392 **103**
Limay Mahuida, *Argentina* S40-372 **103**
Limbazhi, *Latvia* L32+575 **47**
Limbourg, *Belgium* M54+506 **44**
Limburg, *Germany* M42+504 **48**
Limburg, prov. *Belgium* M58+510 **44**
Limchow. *See* Hoppo.
Limeira, *Brazil* R14-225 **105**
Limerick (Luimneach)
    Ireland, Rep. N52+527 **43**
Limes, *Belgium* M58+496 **44**
Limestone, *Maine* S47+470 **90**
Limmen, *Netherlands* M62+526 **44**
Limmen Bight,
    N. Terr., Australia C86-148 **111**
Limni, *Greece* L40+388 **59**
Limnos, I., *Greece* L29+400 **59**
Limoges, *France* M82+458 **54**
Limon, *Colorado* U83+392 **94**
Limon, *Costa Rica* T48+100 **101**
Limousin, prov., *France* M78+454 **54**
Limoux, *France* M77+431 **55**
Limpopo R.,
    Moçambique. etc. K68-250 **84**
Lina, mt., *New Guinea* D07-014 **65**
Linares, *Chile* S70-358 **103**
Linares, *Mexico* U57+248 **100**
Linares, *Spain* N22+381 **52**
Lincheng, *China* E16+349 **66**
Linchwan. *See* Fuchow
Lincoln, *Argentina* S09-349 **103**
Lincoln, *England* N03+532 **37**
Lincoln, *Illinois* T86+402 **95**
Lincoln, *Maine* S51+454 **90**
Lincoln, *Michigan* T51+447 **91**
Lincoln, *Nebraska* U40+408 **95**
Lincoln, *New Zealand* A45-436 **112**
Lincoln, co., *England* N01+532 **37**
Lincoln Sea, *Arctic Ocean* R35+840 **26**
Lincoln Wolds, *England* N01+534 **37**
Lincolnton, *N. Carolina* T37+355 **97**
Lindau, *W. Germany* M32+475 **48**
Lindesay, Mt., *Queensland* B68-281 **111**
Lindesnes, *Norway* M47+580 **47**
Lindi, *Tanzania* K32-100 **83**
Lindley, *Orange Free State* L12-278 **84**
Lindos, *Greece* L11+361 **59**
Lindsay, *Ontario* T23+444 **91**

Line Is., *Pacific Ocean* Y30+020 **107**
Linfen, *China* E51+360 **66**
Lingchwan, *China* E58+255 **67**
Lingen, *W. Germany* N46+525 **48**
Lingga, I., *Riau Kep.,*
    Indonesia F02-003 **65**
Lingling, *China* E51+263 **67**
Lingueré, *Senegal* P00+154 **80**
Lingyun, *China* E81+244 **67**
Linhai, *China* D83+290 **67**
Linhares, *Brazil* Q61-194 **105**
Linho, *China* E75+408 **66**
Linhsien, *China* E45+248 **67**
Lini, *China* E10+351 **66**
Linkiang, *China* D49+416 **64**
Linkiang (Tsingkiang), *China* E27+280 **67**
Linköping, *Sweden* L86+584 **47**
Linkuva, *Lithuania* L36+561 **47**
Linlithgow, *Scotland* N21+560 **41**
Linn, *Missouri* U11+385 **97**
Linnhe, L., *Scotland* N33+566 **41**
Linosa, I., *Medit. Sea* M13+359 **57**
Linping, *China* E33+244 **67**
Lins, *Brazil* R29-218 **103**
Linsi, *China* E11+434 **64**
Lintan, *China* F10+348 **66**
Linth, R., *Switzerland* M36+472 **45**
Linthal, *Switzerland* M36+469 **45**
Linton, *Quebec* S73+473 **91**
Linyu, *China* E01+400 **66**
Linz, *Austria* M04+483 **48**
Lion, G. du, *France* M66+430 **55**
Lion Pt., *N.-W. Territories* W25+727 **88**
Lio Porgyul, *Tibet* G67+320 **70**
Liouesso, *Congo* L86+010 **82**
Lipa, *Yugoslavia* L84+447 **56**
Lipari. & I., *Italy* M01+385 **57**
Lipetsk, *U.S.S.R.* K33+526 **60**
Liping, *China* E66+263 **67**
Lipovets, *Ukraine* L06+492 **60**
Lippstadt, *W. Germany* M40+517 **48**
Lipsoi, I., *Greece* L19+373 **59**
Lira, *Uganda* K74+022 **83**
Lircay, *Peru* S89-130 **104**
Liria, *Spain* N04+396 **53**
Lisala, *Zaire* L50+022 **82**
Lisboa, *Portugal* N55+387 **52**
Lisbon. *See* Lisboa
Lisburn, *N. Ireland* N36+545 **42**
Lisburne, C. *Alaska* Z00+685 **99**
Liscannor B., *Ireland, Rep.* N57+529 **43**
Lisdoonvarna, *Ireland, Rep.* N56+530 **43**
Lishih, *China* E53+375 **66**
Lishui, *China* E00+285 **67**
Lisianski, I., *Hawaiian Is.* Z55+260 **106**
Lisieux, *France* M89+492 **54**
Liskeard, *England* N27+504 **38**
L'Isle, *Switzerland* M52+466 **45**
L'Islet, *Quebec* S62+471 **91**
Lismore, *Ireland, Rep.* N48+521 **43**
Lismore, *New South Wales* B70-286 **111**
Lismore I., *Scotland* N33+565 **41**
Lisnaskea, *N. Ireland* N45+542 **42**
Lissar, *Iran* J66+380 **74**
Listowel, *Ireland, Rep.* N57+524 **43**
Listowel, *Ontario* T36+437 **91**
Lisu, *Ethiopia* K50+100 **83**
Litchfield, *Illinois* T88+392 **95**
Litchfield, *Minnesota* U27+451 **93**
Lith Ai, *Saudi Arabia* K28+202 **74**
Lithgow, *New South Wales* B89-335 **109**
Lithinon, C., *Crete* L32+349 **59**
Lithuania, rep., *U.S.S.R.* **47**

Litoměřice, Czechoslovakia M05+505 **48**
Little R., Missouri T88+363 **97**
Little Belt Mts., Montana V34+468 **93**
Little Current, Ontario T42+460 **91**
Little Falls, Minnesota U26+460 **93**
Little Falls, New York S89+430 **96**
Little Horn Mts., Arizona V52+334 **92**
Little River, Newfoundland R85+478 **90**
Little River, New Zealand A43-437 **112**
Little Rock, Arkansas U14+348 **95**
Little Rocky Mts., Montana V22+479 **93**
Little Smoky R., Alberta V74+546 **88**
Littleton, Colorado V00+396 **94**
Littleton, New Hampshire S70+443 **91**
Little Valley, New York T23+423 **96**
Littoria, Italy M13+415 **57**
Liuan, China E22+318 **64**
Liuchow, China E64+243 **67**
Liupan Shan, China E84+356 **66**
Liusvaara, Karelia K77+626 **46**
Live Oak, Florida T48+303 **97**
Liverpool, New South Wales B85-339 **109**
Liverpool, Nova Scotia S28+440 **90**
Liverpool & B., England N18+534 **37**
Liverpool Coast, Greenland P35+710 **26**
Liverpool Plains, N.S.W. C00-312 **109**
Liverpool Ra., New S. Wales B88-318 **109**
Livingston, Alabama T79+326 **97**
Livingston, Guatemala T82+158 **100**
Livingston, Montana V33+457 **93**
Livingston, Tennessee T62+364 **97**
Livingston, Texas U30+307 **95**
Livingston, I., S. Shetlands S04-630 **27**
Livingstone, See Maramba
Livingstonia, Malawi K66-108 **83**
Livno, Yugoslavia L78+438 **56**
Livny, U.S.S.R. K45+524 **60**
Livo Joki, Finland L18+655 **46**
Livorno, Italy M28+435 **56**
Livramento, Brazil R63-308 **103**
Liwa, Oman J21+246 **75**
Liwale, Tanzania K42-098 **83**
Lizard & Pt., England N31+500 **38**
Ljubljana, Yugoslavia M03+461 **56**
Ljubuški, Yugoslavia L75+432 **56**
Ljungdalen, Sweden M13+628 **46**
Ljusdal, Sweden L83+618 **47**
Llandaff, Wales N19+515 **38**
Llandeilo, Wales N24+519 **38**
Llandrindod Wells, Wales N20+522 **38**
Llandudno, Wales N23+533 **38**
Llanelli, Wales N25+517 **38**
Llanerchymedd, Wales N26+533 **38**
Llanes, Spain N29+434 **52**
Llangollen, Wales N19+530 **38**
Llanguihuie, L., Chile S76-411 **103**
Llanllyfni, Wales N26+530 **38**
Llano Estacado, New Mex. U78+340 **94**
Llanrhaiadr, Wales N20+528 **38**
Llanrwst, Wales N23+531 **38**
Llerena, Spain N36+383 **52**
Lleyn Pen., Wales N27+529 **38**
Lliamna, L., Alaska Y30+595 **99**
Llico, Chile S72-347 **103**
Lloydminster, Saskatchewan V30+534 **88**
Lluchmayor, Balearic Is. M72+395 **53**
Loango, Congo M20-046 **82**
Lobbes, Belgium M64+504 **44**
Loberia, Argentina R83-382 **103**
Lobito, Angola M08-124 **82**
Lobos, Argentina R86-352 **103**
Lobstick L., Labrador S30+540 **89**
Locarno, Switzerland M37+462 **45**
Lochalsh, Ontario T56+484 **91**
Lochalsh, Kyle of, Scotland N34+573 **40**
Lochbuie, Scotland N35+564 **41**
Lochcarron, Scotland N33+574 **40**
Lochearnhead, Scotland N26+564 **41**
Lochem, Netherlands M51+522 **44**
Lochgelly, Scotland N20+561 **41**
Lochgilphead, Scotland N33+560 **41**
Lochgoilhead, Scotland N29+562 **41**
Lochinver, Scotland N31+582 **40**
Lochmaben, Scotland N21+551 **41**
Lochmaddy, Scotland N43+576 **40**
Lochnagar, Scotland N20+570 **40**
Lochy, L., Scotland N29+570 **40**
Lockerbie, Scotland N20+551 **41**
Lockhart, New South Wales C21-353 **109**
Lock Haven, Pennsylvania T15+411 **96**
Lockport, New York T22+431 **96**
Locle, le, Switzerland M49+471 **45**
Loc Ninh, S. Vietnam E81+118 **65**
Lochristi, Belgium M67+511 **44**
Lodeynoye Pole, U.S.S.R. K69+608 **60**
Lodhran, Pakistan H20+295 **72**
Lodi, Wisconsin T87+434 **91**
Lødingen, Norway L84+684 **46**
Lodwar, Kenya K56+030 **83**
Lodz, Poland L63+518 **49**
Loenen, Netherlands M54+521 **44**
Loewoek, Celébes D73-010 **65**
Lofer, Austria M14+476 **48**
Lofoten, Is., Norway M16+680 **46**
Logan, Montana V39+459 **93**
Logan, Utah V42+418 **94**
Logan, Mt., Quebec S40+489 **90**
Logan, Mt., Yukon X30+606 **88**
Logansport, Indiana T68+408 **95**
Logone R., Cameroun-Chad. M00+104 **81**
Logrona, Spain N15+424 **53**
Lohardaga, India G32+234 **73**
Loharu, India G85+285 **72**
Loikaw, Burma F46+197 **71**
Loir, R., France N02+476 **54**
Loire, dep., France M67+457 **54**
Loire R., France N09+472 **54**
Loire Atlantique, dep., Fr. N11+474 **54**
Loiret, dep., France M77+479 **54**
Loir-et-Cher, dep., France M82+475 **54**
Loja, Ecuador T25-040 **104**
Loja, Spain N25+372 **52**
Lokerer, Belgium M66+511 **44**
Lokka, Finland L14+678 **46**
Løkken, Denmark M32+574 **47**
Lökken, Norway M32+631 **46**
Loko, Sudan K84+044 **81**
Lokoja, Nigeria M50+078 **80**
Loks I., N.-W. Territories S26+620 **89**
Lola, Angola M08-144 **82**
Lolland, Denmark M20+546 **47**

Lom, Bulgaria L41+438 **58**
Loman, Minnesota U23+485 **93**
Lomas, Argentina R80-348 **103**
Loma Tina, mt., Dom. Rep. S64+186 **101**
Lombard, Montana V39+461 **93**
Lombardia, dep., Italy M30+457 **56**
Lomblen, I., Indonesia D70-085 **65**
Lombok, I. & Str., Indonesia E24-088 **65**
Lome, Togo M84+062 **80**
Lomela, Zaire L40-022 **82**
Lomie, Cameroun M08+032 **81**
Lommel, Belgium M58+512 **44**
Lomond Hills, Scotland N20+562 **41**
Lomond L., Scotland N28+562 **41**
Łomża, Poland L48+532 **49**
Loncoche, Chile S77-394 **103**
Loncopue, Argentina S64-381 **103**
Londiani, Kenya K54-002 **83**
London, England N01+515 **39**
London, Ontario T37+430 **91**
Londonderry, & co., Northern Ireland N44+550 **42**
Londonderry, C., W. Aust. D49-138 **110**
Londonderry, I., Chile S64-550 **103**
Long Beach. S. Carolina T23+334 **99**
Long I., Bahamas, The T01 + 234 **101**
Long I., New York S78+408 **96**
Long I., Nova Scoia S38+443 **90**
Long L., Maine S56+466 **90**
Long L., Ontario T70+496 **89**
Long L., Scotland N29+562 **41**
Long Ra., Newfoundland R74+500 **90**
Longa, Brazil Q73-054 **105**
Long Beach, California V79+338 **92**
Long Beach, New Jersey S85+396 **96**
Long Branch, New Jersey S84+403 **96**
Longchamps, Belgium M56+500 **44**
Longford, Tasmania C18-416 **109**
Longford & co., Ireland, Rep. N47+537 **42**
Long Island Sd., N.Y., etc. S77+411 **96**
Long Island City, New York S84+407 **96**
Long Melford, England M86+521 **39**
Longmont, Colorado V01+402 **94**
Long Point I., Ontario T32+426 **91**
Long Prairie, Minnesota U29+460 **93**
Longreach, Queensland C35-232 **111**
Longs Pk., Colorado V04+402 **94**
Longtown, England N18+550 **37**
Longué, France N01+474 **54**
Longueuil, Quebec S81+456 **91**
Longuyon, France M57+494 **54**
Longview, Texas U28+324 **95**
Longview, Washington W18+461 **92**
Longwy, France M55+495 **54**
Long-Xuyen, S. Vietnam E87+104 **69**
Lonneker, Netherlands M48+522 **44**
Lons Saunier, France M57+467 **54**
Looc, Philippines D78+123 **65**
Looe, E. & W., England N27+504 **38**
Lookout, C., N. Carolina T37+374 **99**
Loolmalasin, mt., Tanzania K56-030 **83**
Loop Hd., Ireland, Rep. N60+526 **43**
Lopei, China D24+476 **64**
Lopez C., Gabon M38-006 **82**
Lopik, Netherlands M60+520 **44**
Lop Nor, Sinkiang, China F88+404 **64**
Lopphavet, Norway L54+704 **46**
Lora Hamun, Pakistan H61+292 **70**
Lorain, Ohio T43+414 **91**
Loralai, Pakistan H38+304 **70**
Lorca, Spain N10+377 **53**
Lord Howe I., Pacific Ocean B35-314 **106**
Lordsburg, New Mexico V22+324 **94**
Loreno, Brazil R00-226 **105**
Loreto, Brazil R02-073 **105**
Loreto, Mexico V38+260 **100**
Lorica, Colombia T04+092 **104**
Lorient, France N12+478 **54**
Lorne, Victoria C36-386 **109**
Lorn, Firth of, Scotland N34+563 **41**
Lorrach, W. Germany M44+476 **48**
Lorraine, prov., France M53+487 **54**
Los Andes, Chile S64-328 **103**
Los Angeles, California V79+341 **92**
Los Angeles, Chile S74-375 **103**
Los Blancos, Argentina S16-235 **103**
Loshan, China F08+296 **67**
Lošinj I., Yugoslavia M04+445 **56**
Los Lamentos, Mexico V04+305 **100**
Los Menucos, Argentina S49-408 **103**
Los Pozos, Chile S62-265 **103**
Los Santos, Panama T32+080 **101**
Los Santos de Maimona, Spain N38+385 **52**
Lossie R., Scotland N20+577 **40**
Lossiemouth, Scotland N20+577 **40**
Los Teques, Venezuela S42+103 **104**
Los Tigres, Argentina S16-258 **103**
Lostwithiel, England N28+504 **38**
Los Vilos, Chile S69-319 **103**
Lot, dep., France M80+446 **55**
Lot, R., France M85+445 **55**
Lota, Chile S79-371 **103**
Lotbinière, Quebec S72+466 **91**
Lot-et-Garonne, dep., France M87+443 **55**
Lothian, reg., Scotland N18+559 **41**
Lottigna, Switzerland M36+465 **45**
Loubet Coast, Antarctica S25-680 **27**
Loudeac, France N16+482 **54**
Loudima, Congo M12-042 **82**
Loudon, Malawi K69-122 **83**
Loudon, Tennessee T56+357 **97**
Loudun, France N00+470 **54**
Louga, Senegal P08+154 **80**
Loughborough, England N07+528 **37**
Loughborough's I., Burma F43+104 **71**
Loughor, Wales N24+517 **38**
Loughrea, Ireland, Rep. N51+532 **43**
Louhans, France M59+466 **54**
Louisa, Kentucky T46+381 **97**
Louisburg, N. Carolina T20+362 **97**
Louiseville, Quebec S78+463 **91**
Louisiade Arch. Papua New Guinea B70-110 **111**
Louisiana, state, U.S.A. U20+306 **99**
Louis Trichardt, Transvaal L00-232 **84**
Louisville, Colorado V02+400 **94**
Louisville, Kentucky T65+383 **97**
Louisville, Mississippi T84+331 **97**
Loule, Portugal N48+371 **52**
Loup City, Nebraska U54+412 **95**
Lourdes, France N01+431 **55**

Lourenço Marques, See Maputo
Lourical, Portugal N53+401 **52**
Lourinha, Portugal N56+392 **52**
Louth, England N00+534 **37**
Louth, New South Wales C29-306 **109**
Louth & co., Ireland, Rep. N39+539 **42**
Louvain, Belgium M62+509 **44**
Louveigne, Belgium M56+505 **44**
Louviers, France M83+492 **54**
Lövanger, Sweden L52+643 **46**
Loveland, Colorado V00+404 **94**
Lovell, Wyoming V21+448 **93**
Lovisa (Lovisa), Finland L23+605 **47**
Lovington, New Mexico U80+329 **94**
Lövlid, Sweden L80+647 **46**
Low, C., N.-W. Territories T64+634 **89**
Lowa, Zaire L24-014 **82**
Lowell, Massachusetts S68+427 **91**
Lowell, Michigan T62+429 **91**
Lower Brule, S. Dakota U39+441 **93**
Lowestoft, England M80+525 **39**
Lowicz, Poland L60+521 **49**
Lowland, N. Carolina T09+353 **97**
Lowriet, Belize T81+182 **101**
Lowville, New York T03+438 **91**
Loxton, S. Australia C57-345 **109**
Loyalty Is., Pacific Ocean A80-210 **106**
Loyang, China E45+348 **66**
Loyung, China E63+244 **67**
Lozère, dep., France M68+444 **55**
Loznica, Yugoslavia L65+445 **58**
Luampa, Zambia L34-152 **84**
Luan. See Changchih
Luanda, Angola M10-090 **82**
Luang Prabang, Laos F17+198 **69**
Luarca, Spain N40+435 **52**
Luashi, Zaire L38-110 **82**
Lubana, Latvia L20+569 **47**
Lubartow, Poland L45+515 **49**
Lubben, E. Germany M07+520 **48**
Lubbock, Texas U70+336 **94**
Lübeck, W. Germany M26+539 **48**
Lübeck, Victoria C45-368 **109**
Lübecker B., E. & W. Germany M24+541 **48**
Lubefu, Zaire L34-046 **82**
Lubin, Poland L82+514 **49**
Lublin, Poland L45+512 **49**
Lubliniec, Poland L68+507 **49**
Lubnaig, L., Scotland N26+563 **41**
Lubumbashi, Zaire L14-118 **83**
Luc, le, France M52+434 **55**
Lucala, Angola L88-094 **82**
Lucan. Ireland, Rep. N39+534 **43**
Lucania. See Basilicata.
Lucca, Italy M27+439 **56**
Lucca, Jamaica T19+185 **101**
Luce B., Scotland N29+548 **41**
Lucena, Spain N27+374 **52**
Lučenec, Czechoslovakia L62+483 **49**
Lucera, Italy L88+415 **57**
Lucerne. See Luzern.
Luch, U.S.S.R. K17+570 **61**
Luchow, China E88+288 **67**
Luchow (Hofei), China E17+319 **66**
Lucinda, Pennsylvania T27+413 **96**
Lucindale, S. Australia C58-370 **109**
Luckau, E. Germany M08+519 **48**
Luckenwalde, E. Germany M11+521 **48**
Lucknow, India G54+268 **73**
Lucknow, Ontario T39+440 **91**
Luçon, France N07+465 **54**
Luderitz, S.-W. Africa L88-266 **84**
Ludhiana, India G85+309 **72**
Ludington, Michigan T69+440 **91**
Ludlow, England N16+524 **38**
Ludvika, Sweden L89+601 **47**
Ludwigshafen, W. Germany M40+495 **48**
Ludwigslust, E. Germany M21+533 **48**
Ludza, Latvia L14+565 **47**
Luebo, Zaire L52-054 **82**
Luga, U.S.S.R. L01+587 **60**
Lugano & L. di, Switz. M36+460 **45**
Lugansk, Ukraine K34+486 **60**
Lugh Ferrandi, Somalia K14+036 **83**
Lugo, Spain N45+430 **52**
Lugoj, Romania L49+457 **58**
Lugovaia, Kazakh. H13+430 **62**
Luhaiya, Yemen K14+157 **74**
Luhit R., India F54+276 **71**
Luhsien. See Luchow.
Luhwang Shan I., China D77+297 **67**
Luichow. See Hoihong
Luichow Pen., China E66+208 **64**
Luime, Angola L84-108 **82**
Luitpold Cst., Antarctica Q20-770 **27**
Lujan, Argentina R85-345 **103**
Lujan, Argentina S53-330 **103**
Lujan, Paraguay R75-252 **103**
Lukala, Zaire M04-056 **82**
Lukovit, Bulgaria L35+432 **58**
Lukoyanov, U.S.S.R. K03+550 **61**
Lukula, Zaire M12-054 **82**
Lule Älv, Sweden L54+663 **46**
Lulea, Sweden L47+656 **46**
Luluabourg, Zaire L46-058 **82**
Luling, China E07+398 **66**
Lumberton, N. Carolina T24+346 **97**
Lumbres, France M78+507 **54**
Lummen, Belgium M59+510 **44**
Lumsden, New Zealand A69-457 **112**
Luna, Arkansas U06+334 **97**
Lunan B., Scotland N15+566 **41**
Lund, Sweden M11+557 **47**
Lundy I., England N28+512 **38**
Lune, R., England N16+542 **37**
Lüneburg, W. Germany M28+533 **48**
Lunel, France M66+437 **55**
Luneville, France M51+486 **54**
Lungan. See Pingwu.
Lungki, China E13+246 **67**
Lungnan, China E32+248 **67**
Lungai, China F03+349 **66**
Lungyen, China E18+252 **67**
Luni, India H11+260 **70**
Lunino, U.S.S.R. J89+536 **61**
Lunz, Austria L90+478 **48**
Lupeh, China D83+446 **64**
Lupiro, Tanzania K50-084 **83**
Lupkow, Poland L48+493 **49**

Luputa, Zaire L38-072 **82**
Luray, Virginia T21+387 **91**
Lurgan, N. Ireland N38+544 **42**
Luribay, Bolivia S46-170 **104**
Lurøy, Norway M13+664 **46**
Lusaka, Zambia L10-154 **84**
Lusambo, Zaire L40-050 **82**
Lusambo, Zaire L44-084 **82**
Lushai Hills, India F72+233 **71**
Lushnjë, Albania L62+409 **59**
Lushun, China D82+388 **66**
Lusk, Wyoming U86+427 **93**
Luss, Scotland N28+561 **41**
Lut Des., Iran J10+310 **30**
Lüta, China ·D80+389 **66**
Luther, Michigan T65+441 **91**
Luton, England N02+519 **39**
Lutsen, Minnesota U04+476 **91**
Lutsk, Ukraine L28+508 **60**
Luttre, Belgium M64+505 **44**
Luvia, Finland L50+613 **47**
Luxembourg, and Grand-duchy of, N.-W. Europe M54+497 **48**
Luxembourg, prov., Belg. M57+500 **44**
Luxeuil, France M52+478 **54**
Luxor, Egypt K74+256 **81**
Luzern & canton, Switz. M40+471 **45**
Luzon, I., Philippines D85+150 **65**
Luzon Str. Philippines D75+200 **64**
Luzy, France M66+468 **54**
Lvov, Ukraine L36+498 **60**
Lwanhsien, China E07+397 **66**
Lwan-ping, China D82+409 **66**
Lyallpur, Pakistan H15+314 **72**
Lybster, Scotland N20+583 **40**
Lycksele, Sweden L68+646 **46**
Lydavénai, Lithuania L41+556 **47**
Lydda, Israel K61+320 **76**
Lydenburg, Transvaal K88-252 **84**
Lydney, England N16+517 **38**
Lyell, Mt., Brit. Columbia V72+ 17 **88**
Lyell, Mt., California V85+378 **92**
Lyell Ra., New Zealand A46-416 **112**
Lykens, Pennsylvania T11+405 **96**
Lyme B., England N18+506 **38**
Lyme Regis, England N18+507 **38**
Lymington, England N09+508 **39**
Lynchburg, Virginia T25+374 **97**
Lyndhurst, S. Australia C70-303 **109**
Lynn, Massachusetts S65+425 **96**
Lynton, England N23+512 **38**
Lyon, France M61+458 **54**
Lyon, Montana V39+448 **93**
Lyonnais, prov., France M65+458 **54**
Lyons, Georgia T44+322 **97**
Lyons, Kansas U49+384 **95**
Lyons, New York T12+430 **96**
Lyons, R., W. Australia E27-243 **110**
Lysamis, Kenya K42+016 **83**
Łyse, Poland L51+534 **49**
Lysekil, Sweden M21+583 **47**
Lyss, Switz. M46+471 **45**
Lyster, Quebec S69+464 **91**
Lysva, U.S.S.R. J14+581 **61**
Lytham St Annes, England N18+537 **37**
Lyttelton, New Zealand A43-436 **112**
Lytton, British Columbia W09+502 **88**
Ma'an, Jordan K56+302 **76**
Maarheeze, Netherlands M57+513 **44**
Maarianhamina. See Mariehamn.
Ma'arret en Numan, Syria K50+357 **76**
Maas, R., Netherlands M55+518 **44**
Maasbree, Netherlands M54+514 **44**
Maaseik, Belgium M55+511 **44**
Ma'asir, Saudi Arabia K41+307 **74**
Maassluis, Netherlands M65+519 **44**
Maastricht, Belgium M56+508 **44**
Maatsuyker Is., Tasmania C22-436 **109**
Mabote, Mozambique K66-222 **84**
Mabrouk, Mali N08+194 **80**
Mabuki, Tanzania K70-030 **83**
McAdam, New Brunswick S44+456 **90**
Macahe, Brazil Q71-225 **105**
Macahyba, Brazil Q32-059 **105**
McAlester, Oklahoma U34+350 **95**
McAlister, mt., New S. Wales C02-345 **109**
Macaloje, Mozambique K52-120 **83**
Macao (Port.), China E38+223 **67**
Macapa, Brazil R36+001 **105**
Macás, Ecuador T19-024 **104**
Macau, Brazil Q40-051 **105**
McCammon, Idaho V43+426 **94**
Macclesfield, England N13+533 **37**
McClintock Chan., N.-W. Ter. U70+714 **88**
McClure, C., N.-W. Terr. W08+746 **88**
McClure Str., N.-W. Terr. V70+738 **88**
McComb, Mississippi U03+312 **97**
McConnellsburg, Pa. T18+399 **96**
McCook, Nebraska U66+402 **94**
Macdonald, L., W. Australia D37-234 **110**
Macdonnell Ranges, N. Terr., Aust. D15-232 **110**
McDouall Ra., N. Terr. Aust. D00-196 **111**
Macdougall, L., N.-W. Terr. U50+660 **88**
Maceio, Brazil Q34-095 **105**
Macerata, Italy M09+433 **56**
McGill, Nevada V59+395 **92**
Macgillycuddy's Reeks, Ireland, Rep. N59+520 **43**
McGregor, Texas U44+314 **95**
McGregor Ra., Queensland C43-268 **111**
Mach, Pakistan H48+298 **70**
Machala, Ecuador T29-032 **104**
Machareti, Bolivia S19-208 **104**
Machias, Maine S45+448 **90**
Machias B., Maine S44+446 **90**
Machiasport, Maine S44+448 **90**
Machicha, Mozambique K58-240 **84**
Machilipatnam (Bandar), India G52+162 **70**
Machiques, Venezuela S75+100 **104**
Machiwara, India G83+309 **72**
Machu Picchu, Peru S77-128 **104**
Machynlleth, Wales N23+526 **38**
Macias Nguema, Equat - Guinea M38+036 **80**
Măcin, Romania L11+452 **58**
McIntosh, S. Dakota U59+459 **93**
Mackay, Alberta V40+570 **88**
Mackay, Queensland C00-211 **111**
Mackay L., N.-W. Terr. V32+640 **88**
Mackay, L., W. Australia D37-226 **110**
McKeesport, Pennsylvania T29+404 **96**

Mackenna, *Argentina* S27-338 **103**
McKenzie, *Tennessee* T81+361 **97**
Mackenzie B., *Antartica* H05-680 **27**
Mackenzie Dist., *N.-W. Terr.* W00+640 **88**
Mackenzie B., *N.-W. Terr.* X15+688 **88**
Mackenzie Mts., *N.-W. Terr.* W60+642 **88**
Mackenzie R., *N.-W. Terr.* W45+654 **88**
Mackenzie King I., *N.-W. T.* V30+776 **88**
Mackillop, L., *Queensland* C52-262 **111**
Mackinac I. & Str. of, *Mich.* T58+458 **91**
Mackinaw, *Michigan* T59+458 **91**
McKinley, Mt., *Alaska* Y05+628 **99**
Macksville, *New S. Wales* B74-308 **109**
Maclean, *New S. Wales* B71-294 **109**
McLeansboro, *Illinois* T81+381 **97**
Macleay, R., *New S. Wales* B76-308 **109**
Macleod, *Alberta* V50-498 **88**
McLeod R., *N.-W. Terr.* V35+632 **88**
Macloutsi, *Botswana* L10-222 **84**
MacMahon Fort, *Algeria* M80+292 **80**
McMillan, L., *New Mexico* U86+326 **94**
Macmillan Ra., *Yukon* X10+636 **94**
Macmillan R., *Yukon* W85+635 **88**
McMinnville, *Tennessee* T65+357 **97**
McMullen Pk., *Arizona* V24+330 **94**
McMurdo Sd., *Antarctica* A90-770 **27**
McNary, *Arizona* V29+340 **94**
Macomb, *Illinois* U06+404 **95**
Macomer, *Sardinia* M37+402 **57**
Macon, *Belgium* M65+501 **44**
Mâcon, *France* M61+463 **54**
Macon, *Georgia* T52+328 **97**
Macon, *Mississippi* T82+331 **95**
Macon, *Missouri* U15+398 **95**
McPherson, *Kansas* U46+384 **95**
McPherson, *N.-W. Terr.* W89+672 **88**
Macpherson Ra., *Queensland* B75-280 **111**
Macquarie Harb., *Tasmania* C28-423 **109**
Macquarie I., *Pacific Ocean* B35-510 **106**
Macquarie, L., *New S. Wales* B81-331 **109**
Macquarie Mt., *N.S.W.* C05-337 **109**
Macquarie, R., *N.S.W.* C15-306 **109**
Macquarie, R., *Tasmania* C17-417 **109**
McRae, *Georgia* T48+320 **97**
Mac-Robertson Ld., *Antarc.* H75-690 **27**
Macroom, *Ireland, Rep.* N54+519 **43**
Macuje, *Colombia* S80+004 **104**
Macusani, *Peru* S62-140 **104**
McVicar Arm, *N.-W. Terr.* V85+652 **88**
Madaba, *Jordan* K55+317 **76**
Madadi, *Chad* L56+182 **81**
Madagascar I., *Indian Oc.* J76-200 **83**
Madahy, *Brazil* Ro6-050 **105**
Madain Salih, *Saudi Arabia* K41+269 **74**
Madan, *Iran* J10+366 **74**
Madaripur, *Bangladesh* F89+232 **71**
Madawaska, *Ontario* T18+455 **91**
Madeira Is., *Atlantic Ocean* P10+326 **80**
Madeira, R., *Brazil* S08-056 **104**
Madeleine, C. de la, *Quebec* S32+493 **90**
Madhepur, *India* G22+262 **73**
Madhipura, *India* G19+259 **73**
Madhopur, *India* G81+260 **70**
Madhopur, *India* G86+323 **72**
Madhubani, *India* G23+264 **73**
Madhupur, *India* G20+243 **73**
Madhya Pradesh, *India* G75+236 **70**
Madinat ash Sh'ab,
  Yemen, South K01+127 **74**
Madison, *Georgia* T51+338 **97**
Madison, *Kansas* U37+382 **95**
Madison, *Nebraska* U45+418 **95**
Madison, *New Jersey* S87+407 **96**
Madison, *N. Carolina* T30+364 **97**
Madison, *S. Dakota* U42+440 **93**
Madison, *Wisconsin* T86+430 **95**
Madisonville, *Kentucky* T75+372 **97**
Madoc, *Ontario* T15+445 **91**
Madona, *Latvia* L23+569 **47**
Madras, *India* G58+132 **70**
Madre, Laguna, *Texas* U44+266 **94**
Madre, Sa., *Mexico* V04+250 **100**
Madre, Sierra, *Wyoming* V12+412 **93**
Madre Austral, Lag. de la,
  Mexico U47+246 **100**
Madre de Dios, I., *Chile* T00-502 **103**
Madre de Dios, R., *Peru-Bol.* S54-123 **104**
Madre del Sur, Sa., *Mexico* U65+174 **100**
Madrid, *New Mexico* V08+354 **94**
Madrid, *Spain* N22+404 **52**
Madridejos, *Spain* N21+395 **52**
Madura, I., *Indonesia* G72+100 **70**
Madurai, I., *Indonesia* E40+069 **65**
Maebashi, *Japan* C65+364 **68**
Maeseyck, *Belgium* M55+511 **44**
Maestra, Sa., *Cuba* T10+202 **101**
Mafeking, *Cape Province* L26-260 **84**
Mafia I., *Tanzania* K32-078 **83**
Mafra, *Portugal* N56+390 **52**
Mafraq, *Jordan* K53+324 **76**
Magad Plat. *See Jol Plat*
Magadan, *Russia* B86+595 **63**
Magadi & L., *Kenya* K52-020 **83**
Magadino, *Switzerland* M37+462 **45**
Magallanes. *See Punta Arenas*
Magallanes, Estrecho de,
  Chile S82-532 **103**
Magangue, *Colombia* S89+092 **104**
Magas, *Iran* H80+271 **75**
Magaz, *Spain* N27+420 **52**
Magburaka, *Sierra Leone* N72+088 **80**
Magdala, *Ethiopia* K34+112 **83**
Magdalen Is., *Quebec* S13+474 **90**
Magdalena, *Bolivia* S25-133 **104**
Magdalena, *Mexico* V35+306 **100**
Magdalena, *New Mexico* V14+342 **94**
Magdalena, B., *Mexico* V42+245 **100**
Magdalena, I., *Chile* S78-447 **103**
Magdalena, R., *Colombia* S88+095 **104**
Magdalena, R., *Mexico* V45+308 **100**
Magdeburg, *E. Germany* M20+521 **48**
Magee I., *N. Ireland* N34+548 **42**
Magellan, Str. of, *Chile* S60-528 **103**
Mageroya, *Norway* L26+709 **46**
Maggia, *Switzerland* M38+462 **45**
Maggiore, L., *Italy* M37+460 **56**
Maghang Tsangpo, R., *Tibet* G25+292 **71**
Maghara, Geb., *Egypt* K70+306 **76**
Magharee Is., *Ireland, Rep.* N60+523 **43**
Maghera, *N. Ireland* N50+548 **42**

Magherafelt, *N. Ireland* N40+548 **42**
Maglaj, *Yugoslavia* L71+446 **58**
Maglie, *Italy* L70+401 **57**
Magnetic Pole, N., *N.-W. T.* U70+760 **88**
Magnitogorsk, *Russia* J06+533 **61**
Magnolia, *Alabama* T76+322 **97**
Magnolia, *Arkansas* U19+332 **95**
Magnolia, *Mississippi* U02+311 **95**
Magnolia, *N. Carolina* T20+350 **97**
Magog, *Quebec* S73+453 **91**
Magpie, *Quebec* S27+503 **90**
Magpie L., *Quebec* S28+510 **90**
Maguse L., *N.-W. Terr.* U44+614 **88**
Magwe, *Burma* F60+202 **71**
Mahabad, *Iran* J86+368 **74**
Mahabaleshwar, *India* H07+180 **70**
Mahaban, *India* G73+274 **72**
Mahabharat Ra., *Nepal* G30+274 **73**
Mahadeo Hills, *India* G72+223 **73**
Mahail, *Saudi Arabia* K17+190 **74**
Mahajamba B. de, *Madag.* J78-154 **83**
Mahajan, *India* H07+287 **72**
Mahalapye, *Botswana* L20-232 **84**
Mahallat, *Iran* J58+339 **75**
Maham, *India* G82+290 **72**
Mahanadi R., *India* G31+206 **71**
Mahanoro, *Madagascar* J68-200 **83**
Mahanoy City,
  Pennsylvania T07+408 **96**
Maharashtra, state, *India* H00+190 **70**
Mahbubnagar, *India* G71+168 **70**
Mahdia, *Tunisia* M24+354 **81**
Mahé, *India*, G87+117 **70**
Mahendragiri, mt., *India* G33+192 **71**
Mahia Pen., *New Zealand* A12-392 **112**
Mahmed-Hussein-magala,
  Iran J55+368 **75**
Mahmudabad, *India* G53+273 **73**
Mahmudabad. *Iran* J47+366 **75**
Mahot I., *Saudi Arabia* J12+205 **75**
Mahunda, *Mozambique* K32-118 **83**
Mahuva, *India* H18+211 **70**
Maibud, *Iran* J35+322 **75**
Maida, *Yemen* K13+163 **74**
Maidan, *Afghanistan* H49+324 **75**
Maidenhead, *England* N04+515 **39**
Maidstone, *England* M87+513 **39**
Maiduguri, *Nigeria* M10+118 **81**
Maienfeld, *Switzerland* M33+470 **45**
Maihar, *India* G55+243 **73**
Maikal Ra., *India* G52+224 **73**
Maikop, *U.S.S.R.* K29+445 **62**
Maimana, *Afghanistan* H60+358 **75**
Mai-Ndombe, L., *Zaire* L70-020 **82**
Main, R., *Germany* M33+498 **48**
Main R., *N. Ireland* N38+547 **42**
Main Barrier Ra., *N.S.W.* C52-316 **109**
Maine, prov., *France* N01+483 **54**
Maine, state, *U.S.A.* S60+450 **99**
Maine, G. of, *Maine, etc.* S54+433 **90**
Maine-et-Loire, dep.,
  France N04+472 **54**
Maing Kaing, *Burma* F58+248 **71**
Maingkwan, *Burma* F50+263 **71**
Mainpuri, *India* G66+272 **73**
Mainstream, *Maine* S57+449 **90**
Mainz, *W. Germany* M40+500 **48**
Maipo, mt., *Argentina* S59-342 **103**
Maipu, *Argentina* R77-368 **103**
Maique R., *Ireland, Rep.* N53+526 **43**
Maison Carrée (El Harrach),
  Algeria M72+366 **80**
Maissin, *Belgium* M59+500 **44**
Mait & I., *Somalia* J78+108 **83**
Maitland, *New South Wales* B81-327 **109**
Maitland, *S. Australia* C74-343 **109**
Maitland, L., *W. Australia* D83-269 **110**
Maiz, *Mexico* U58+224 **100**
Maizura, *Japan* C88+354 **68**
Maja, I., *Indonesia* E63-011 **65**
Majagua, *Colombia* S88+085 **104**
Majitha, *India* H00+317 **72**
Majmaa, *Saudi Arabia* J88+259 **74**
Majorca. *See Mallorca*
Majunga, *Madagascar* J82-158 **83**
Majuro, Is., *Marshall Is.* A50+0e5 **106**
Makale, *Ethiopia* K32+134 **83**
Makania, *Tanzania* K44-044 **83**
Makariev, *U.S.S.R.* K07+578 **61**
Makarvey, *U.S.S.R.* J89+561 **61**
Makasar, *Celébes, see Ujung Pardang*
Makassar Str., *Indonesia* E15-C32 **65**
Makatea, I., *Tuamotu Arch.* X80-158 **107**
Makedhonia, *Greece* L48+407 **59**
Makemo, I., *Tuamotu Arch.* X54-162 **107**
Makhachkala, *U.S.S.R.* J76+430 **62**
Makhai, *China* F66+381 **64**
Makikihi, *New Zealand* A53-446 **112**
Makindu, *Kenya* K42-024 **83**
Makkinga, *Netherlands* M53+530 **44**
Makla, Jebel el, *Saudi Arabia* K58+286 **74**
Mako, *Hungary* L57+462 **58**
Makongolosi, *Tanzania* K70-084 **83**
Makorako, mt., *N.Z.* A23-391 **112**
Makram, *Saudi Arabia* K32+205 **74**
Makri, *India* G48+198 **70**
Makri, *Turkey* L05+367 **74**
Maksamaa, *Finland* L47+632 **46**
Maku, *Iran* K03+393 **74**
Makum, *India* F57+274 **71**
Makurdi, *Nigeria* M38+078 **80**
Makwiro, *Rhodesia* K88-178 **84**
Makeyevka, *Ukraine* K42+448 **60**
Mal B., *Ireland, Rep.* N57+528 **43**
Mal B., *Quebec* S25+486 **90**
Mala, *Peru* T10-127 **100**
Malå, *Sweden* L68+652 **46**
Malabang, *Philippines* D65+076 **65**
Malabar Coast, *India* H00+120 **70**
Malabo, *Macias Nguema* M37+038 **80**
Malacca, Str. of,
  Sumatra-Malaya F26+025 **65**
Malad City, *Idaho* V44+422 **94**
Maladeta, mt., *Spain* M86+226 **53**
Malaga, *Spain* N26+367 **52**
Malaita, *Solomon Is.* B25-C90 **106**
Malakal, *Sudan* K80+094 **81**
Malakand & Pass, *Pakistan* H19+345 **72**
Malang, *Java* E43-080 **65**

Malange, *Angola* L82-096 **82**
Malaren, L., *Sweden* L78+595 **47**
Malargue, *Argentina* S57-355 **103**
Malas, *Ethiopia* K42+164 **83**
Malawi (Nyasaland), *E. Afr.* K66-120 **83**
Malaya, *E. Asia* **65**
Malayir, *Iran* J68+343 **74**
Malaysia, *S. E. Asia* **65**
Malazgirt, *Turkey* K13+391 **74**
Malbork, *Poland* L66+540 **49**
Malchow, *E. Germany* M15+535 **48**
Malda, *India* G11+250 **73**
Maldegem, *Belgium* M69+512 **44**
Malden, *Massachusetts* S66+424 **96**
Malden, *Missouri* U00+366 **95**
Malden, I., *Pacific Ocean* Y30-045 **107**
Maldive Is., *Indian Ocean* H10+050 **30**
Maldon, *England* M86+517 **39**
Maldonado, *Uruguay* R60-349 **103**
Maléa, C., *Greece* L41+365 **59**
Malé Karpaty, *Czech.* L77+484 **49**
Malekula, I., *New Hebrides* A73-173 **106**
Máleme, *Crete* L37+355 **59**
Maler Kotla, *India* G85+305 **72**
Malesherbes, *France* M75+483 **54**
Malheur L., *Oregon* V83+433 **92**
Mali, rep., *W. Africa* N00+160 **80**
Malia, *India* H25+230 **70**
Malihabad, *India* G56+269 **73**
Malin Hd., *Ireland, Rep.* N44+554 **42**
Malinau, *Borneo* E20+036 **65**
Malindi, *Kenya* K30-032 **83**
Malines, *Belgium* M61+510 **44**
Malkangiri, *India* G48+185 **71**
Malko Trnovo, *Bulgaria* L15+420 **58**
Mallacoota & Inl., *Victoria* C02-376 **109**
Mallaig, *Scotland* N35+570 **40**
Mállia, G., *Crete* L27+354 **59**
Malloggia, *Switzerland* M32+464 **45**
Mallorca I., *Balearic Is.* M72+395 **53**
Mallow, *Ireland, Rep.* N52+521 **43**
Malmberget, *Sweden* L56+671 **46**
Malmesbury, *England* N13+516 **39**
Malmö, *Sweden* M12+556 **47**
Malmyzh, *U.S.S.R.* J56+565 **61**
Malombe L., *Malawi* K58-146 **83**
Malone, *New York* S86+449 **91**
Malonga, *Zaire* L40-106 **82**
Malpeque B., *P.E.I.* S23+466 **90**
Malta, *Montana* V17+484 **93**
Malta Chan., *Medit. Sea* M02+364 **57**
Malta, I., *Mediterranean Sea* M03+359 **57**
Malters, *Switzerland* M41+470 **45**
Malton, *England* N05+541 **37**
Malung, *Sweden* M08+607 **47**
Malvaglia, *Switzerland* M36+464 **45**
Malvan, *India* H09+161 **70**
Malvern, *Arkansas* U16+344 **95**
Malvern Hills, *England* N14+521 **38**
Malvina, *Quebec* S69+452 **91**
Malvinas, Islas. *See Falkland Is.*
Mama, *U.S.S.R.* E42+583 **63**
Maman, *U.S.S.R.* K50+160 **83**
Mamantel, *Mexico* U07+184 **100**
Mambasa, *Zaire* L06+012 **83**
Mammoth Cave, *Kentucky* T66+372 **97**
Mammoth Cave Nat. Park,
  Kentucky T68+372 **97**
Mamonal, *Colombia* T03+104 **104**
Mamou, *Guinea* N72+104 **80**
Mampoko, *Zaire* L68+008 **82**
Maputo, *Mozambique* K74-260 **84**
Mamu, *Afghanistan* H67+296 **75**
Mamudju, *Celébes,* E07-026 **65**
Man, *Ivory Coast* N46+076 **80**
Man, I. of, *Irish Sea* N27+542 **37**
Manacapuru, *Brazil* S03-033 **104**
Manacor, *Balearic Is.* M71+395 **53**
Manado, *Celébes,* D61+015 **65**
Managua, *Nicaragua* T68+122 **101**
Managua L., *Nicaragua* T68+124 **101**
Manakha, *Yemen* K08+151 **74**
Manama, *Bahrain I.* J57+263 **75**
Mananjary, *Madagascar* J70-214 **83**
Manankoro, *Mali* N44+104 **80**
Manantenina, *Madagascar* J76-244 **83**
Manapouri L., *New Zealand* A75-455 **112**
Manasarowar L., *Tibet* G52+307 **70**
Manasquan, *New Jersey* S85+401 **91**
Manassas, *Virginia* T15+387 **91**
Manaus, *Brazil* S00-030 **104**
Mancelona, *Michigan* T61+449 **91**
Manche, dep., *France* N09+492 **54**
Manchester, *England* N13+535 **37**
Manchester, Greater, co., *Eng.* N14+535 **37**
Manchester, *Iowa* U09+424 **95**
Manchester, *New Hampshire* S69+429 **91**
Manchester, *Tennessee* T67+354 **97**
Manchester, *Virginia* T15+375 **97**
Manchouli, *China* E14+492 **64**
Manchuria, *China* D60+460 **64**
Mancinik, *Turkey* K48+392 **74**
Manda, *Tanzania* K62-106 **83**
Mandal, *Norway* M45+580 **47**
Mandalay, *Burma* F53+220 **71**
Mandal Gobi, *Mongolia* E83+452 **64**
Mandan, *N. Dakota* U65+468 **93**
Mandarin B., *China* E58+209 **67**
Mander, *Netherlands* M49+524 **44**
Mandera, *Kenya* K20+038 **83**
Mandeville, *Louisiana* U01+304 **97**
Mandi, *India* G78+317 **72**
Mandie, *Mozambique* K68+164 **84**
Mandla, *India* G58+226 **73**
Mandritsara, *Madagascar* J68-158 **83**
Mandvi, *India* H34+228 **70**
Manfred, *New South Wales* C37-334 **109**
Manfredonia, G., di, *Italy* L84+416 **57**
Manfuha, *Saudi Arabia* J79+246 **74**
Mangaia, I., *Cook Is* Y50-220 **107**
Mangaldai, *India* F77+264 **71**
Mangalme, *Chad* L62+127 **81**
Mangalore, *India* H01+129 **70**
Mangareva, I., *Tuamotu*
  Archipelago W88-235 **107**
Mangawhena, *New Zealand* A26-398 **112**
Mangfall Geb., *W. Germany* M18+476 **48**
Manglaralto, *Ecuador* T34-018 **104**
Mangoche, *Malawi* K58-144 **84**
Mangoni, *New Zealand* A39-350 **112**

Mangrol, *India* H30+210 **70**
Mangualde, *Portugal* N47+406 **52**
Mangueria, L. da, *Brazil* R48-332 **103**
Manhatten, *Kansas* U40+392 **95**
Manhay, *Belgium* M56+503 **44**
Manhuassu, *Brazil* Q72-204 **105**
Manicoré, *Brazil* S07-058 **104**
Manifold, C., *Queensland* B85-225 **111**
Manihiki, I., *Pacific Ocean* Y66-105 **106**
Manikarchar, *India* G01+256 **73**
Manikganj. *See Dasara*
Manikpur, *Bangladesh* F77+218 **71**
Manikuagan R., *Quebec* S52+508 **90**
Manila, *Philippines* D84+146 **65**
Manilla, *New South Wales* B86-307 **109**
Manipur, *India* F65+250 **71**
Manisa, *Turkey* L15+386 **74**
Manistee, *Michigan* T68+443 **91**
Manistee R., *Michigan* T64+445 **91**
Manistique, *Michigan* T68+460 **91**
Manitoba, prov., *Canada* **88**
Manitoba, L., *Manitoba* U52+510 **88**
Manitou Gorge, *Quebec* S57+578 **89**
Manitou Is., *Michigan* T66+451 **91**
Manitoulin I., *Ontario* T42+457 **91**
Manitowaning, *Ontario* T41+457 **91**
Manitowoc, *Wisconsin* T76+442 **9**
Maniwaki, *Quebec* T06+464 **91**
Maniya, *Iraq* K12+308 **74**
Manizales, *Colombia* T03+051 **104**
Manja, *Madagascar* K04-214 **83**
Manjhi, *India* G32+258 **73**
Manjimup, *W. Australia* E23-340 **110**
Manka, *Taiwan* D81+250 **67**
Mankato, *Minnesota* U24+442 **93**
Mankheri, *India* G33+237 **73**
Manlleu, *Spain* M76+420 **53**
Manly, *New South Wales* B83-338 **109**
Manmad, *India* H03+203 **70**
Mannahill, *S. Australia* C60-324 **109**
Mannar, *Sri Lanka* G61+090 **70**
Mannar, G. of, *India* G67+086 **70**
Mannargudi, *India* G64+107 **70**
Mannheim, *W. Germany* M39+495 **48**
Manning, *S. Carolina* T31+337 **97**
Mannum, *S. Australia* C64-349 **109**
Manoa, *Bolivia* S33-097 **104**
Manoel Vieira, *Brazil* S02-104 **104**
Manokwari, *New Guinea* D06-008 **65**
Manono, *Zaire* L16-074 **82**
Manorhamilton, *Ireland, Rep.* N49+543 **42**
Manosque, *France* M55+439 **55**
Manresa, *Spain* M79+417 **53**
Mansehra, *Pakistan* H10+344 **72**
Mansel I., *North-West*
  Territories T30+616 **89**
Mansfield, *England* N07+531 **37**
Mansfield, *Louisiana* U22+320 **95**
Mansfield, *Massachusetts* S67+421 **91**
Mansfield, *Ohio* T45+408 **91**
Mansfield, *Pennsylvania* T13+418 **96**
Mansfield, *Victoria* C24-370 **109**
Mansfield, Mt., *Vermont* S77+446 **91**
Mansi, *Burma* F54+248 **71**
Mansilla de Las Mulas, *Spain* N33+425 **52**
Manta, *Ecuador* T34+009 **104**
Manti, *Utah* V40+392 **94**
Mantilla, *Argentina* R82-288 **103**
Mantova, *Italy* M25+451 **56**
Mantua. *See Mantova*
Manu, *Peru* S65-123 **104**
Manu'a, I., *Samoa Is.* Z28-150 **106**
Manuel Rodrigue, I., *Chile* S84-528 **103**
Manujan, *Iran* J15+274 **75**
Manus I., *Admiralty Is.* C20-023 **106**
Many, *Louisiana* U21+315 **95**
Manyoni, *Tanzania* K42-058 **83**
Manzala L., *Egypt* K78+312 **81**
Manzanares, *Spain* N20+390 **52**
Manzanillo, *Cuba* T13+204 **101**
Manzanillo, *Mexico* U86+190 **100**
Manzanillo, Pta., *Panama* T27+096 **101**
Mao, *Chad* L88+140 **81**
Mapia Is., *Pacific Ocean* D00+005 **106**
Mapimi, *Mexico* U83+259 **100**
Maping. *See Liuchow*
Mapire, *Venezuela* S28+076 **104**
Maple Creek, *Saskatchewan* V26+499 **88**
Maqainama, *Saudi Arabia* J67+223 **74**
Maqatin, *Yemen, South* J81+135 **74**
Maqna, *Suadi Arabia* K62+284 **74**
Maquela do Zombo, *Angola* L88-062 **82**
Maquinchao, *Argentina* S43-412 **103**
Maquoketa, *Iowa* U04+420 **95**
Mara, *Transvaal* L04+232 **84**
Maraã, *Brazil* S33-019 **104**
Maraba, *Brazil* R24-053 **105**
Maracá, I. de, *Brazil* R32+020 **105**
Maracaibo, *Venezuela* S70+106 **104**
Maracaibo, L. de, *Venezuela* S70+100 **104**
Maracana, *Brazil* R15-008 **105**
Maracassume, *Brazil* R06-020 **105**
Maracay, *Venezuela* S45+103 **104**
Marada, *Libya* L64+290 **81**
Maradi, *Niger* M46+132 **80**
Maragheh, *Iran* J82+374 **74**
Maragogi, *Brazil* Q32-090 **105**
Marakei, I., *Gilbert Is.* A40+025 **106**
Marakwet, *Kenya* K56+010 **83**
Maralinga, *S. Aust.* D20-302 **110**
Maramba, *Zambia* L24-178 **84**
Marand, *Iran* J86+384 **74**
Maranguape, *Brazil* Q52-038 **105**
Marañon, R., *Peru* T34-034 **104**
Maras, *Turkey* K48+376 **74**
Marau, *Brazil* Q54-141 **105**
Maravilha, *Brazil* S48-061 **104**
Marazion, *England* N33+501 **38**
Mabella, *Spain* N29+365 **52**
Marble Bar, *W. Australia* E02-211 **110**
Marblehead, *Massachusetts* S65+425 **96**
Marcellino, *Brazil* S44+008 **104**
Marche, *Belgium* M58+502 **44**
Marche, dep., *Italy* M11+433 **56**
Marche, prov. *France* M80+462 **54**
Marchena, *Spain* N32+373 **52**
Marchin, *Belgium* M58+505 **44**
Mar Chiquita, *Argentina* S16-306 **103**
Marcus I., *Pacific Ocean* B70+250 **106**
Marcy, Mt., *New York* S84+441 **91**

Mardan, *Pakistan* H17+342 **72**
Mar del Plata, *Argentina* R76-379 **103**
Mardin, *Turkey* K26+373 **74**
Mare, I., *Loyalty Is.* A70-220 **106**
Marechal Deodoro, *Brazil* Q34-098 **105**
Maree L., *Scotland* N33+577 **40**
Marengo, *Wisconsin* U05+465 **91**
Margarita, I., *Venezuela* S24+110 **104**
Margarites, *Crete* L32+354 **59**
Margate, *England* M82+514 **39**
Maria I., *Tasmania* C12-427 **109**
Marianao, *Cuba* T45+230 **101**
Marianas, Is., *Pacific Ocean* C25+150 **106**
Marianna, *Arkansas* U05+347 **97**
Marianna, *Florida* T62+308 **97**
Marianske Lázně, *Czech.* M14+499 **48**
Marias, *Montana* V33+479 **93**
Marias R., *Montana* V48+483 **98**
Marib, *Yemen* K00+157 **74**
Maribor, *Yugoslavia* L86+466 **56**
Maridi, *Sudan* L04+050 **81**
Marie Byrd Ld., *Antarctica* W60-780 **27**
Mariefred, *Sweden* L77+592 **47**
Marie Galante, I., *Leeward Is.* S07+159 **101**
Mariehamn, *Finland* L60+601 **47**
Marienbad. *See* Marianske Lázně.
Marienberg, *Netherlands* M51+525 **44**
Marienbourg, *Belgium* M63+501 **44**
Marienburg. *See* Malbork
Mariental, *S.-W. Africa* L72-244 **84**
Marienville, *Pennsylvania* T25+415 **96**
Mariestad, *Sweden* M07+587 **47**
Marietta, *Georgia* T57+339 **97**
Marietta, *Ohio* T39+394 **91**
Mari Indus, *Pakistan* H20+329 **72**
Mariiskaya, aut. rep., *U.S.S.R.* J70+564 **62**
Marina Fall, *Guyana* R88+055 **104**
Marine City, *Michigan* T45+427 **91**
Marinette, *Wisconsin* T76+451 **91**
Marinha Grande, *Portugal* N54+398 **52**
Marion, *Arkansas* U02+352 **97**
Marion, *Illinois* T84+377 **95**
Marion, *Iowa* U10+420 **95**
Marion, *Indiana* T64+406 **91**
Marion, *Kentucky* T80+372 **97**
Marion, *N. Carolina* T42+357 **97**
Marion, *N. Dakota* U50+466 **93**
Marion, *Ohio* T49+406 **91**
Marion, *Virginia* T39+368 **97**
Marion B., *Tasmania* C12-428 **109**
Maritsa R., *Bulgaria, etc* L24+419 **58**
Mariyampole. *See* Kapsukas
Marj, Al., *Libya* L54+324 **81**
Marjamaa, *Estonia* L33+589 **47**
Markala, *Mali* N34+140 **80**
Markapur, *India* G60+157 **70**
Markelo, *Netherlands* M51+522 **44**
Marken, I., *Netherlands* M59+524 **44**
Market Deeping, *England* N02+527 **37**
Market Drayton, *England* N15+529 **37**
Market Harborough, *Eng.* N05+525 **37**
Markethill, *N. Ireland* N39+543 **42**
Markham, L., *Tibet* G42+350 **71**
Markham, Mt., *Antartica* B50-830 **27**
Markovo, *U.S.S.R.* A57+644 **63**
Marks, *U.S.S.R.* J79+517 **61**
Markstay, *Ontario* T33+465 **91**
Marlboro, *Massachusetts* S69+424 **96**
Marlborough, *Guyana* R82+075 **104**
Marlborough, *England* N10+514 **39**
Marlette, *Michigan* T48+433 **91**
Marlo, *Victoria* C09-378 **109**
Marmande, *France* M89+445 **55**
Marmara, Sea of, *Turkey* L10+407 **74**
Marmaris, *Turkey* L10+369 **74**
Marne, dep., *France* M64+488 **54**
Marnoo, *Victoria* C43-367 **109**
Maroni, R., *Fr. Guiana* R53+029 **105**
Maroua, *Cameroun* M04+106 **81**
Marquesas, Is., *Pacific Oc.* X30-100 **107**
Marquette, *Michigan* T74+465 **91**
Marquina, *Spain* N15+433 **53**
Marra, R., *New S. Wales* C17-306 **109**
Marrakech, *Morocco* N48+316 **80**
Marrawah, *Tasmania* C32-410 **109**
Marree, *S. Australia* C72-296 **109**
Marsabit, *Kenya* K42+022 **83**
Marsa Hali, *Saudi Arabia* K22+187 **74**
Marsala, *Sicily* M15+378 **57**
Marsden, *New South Wales* C14-338 **109**
Marseille, *France* M58+433 **55**
Marsh, I., *Louisiana* U12+295 **95**
Marshall, *Illinois* T76+394 **95**
Marshall, *Michigan* T60+423 **91**
Marshall, *Minnesota* U35+445 **93**
Marshall, *Missouri* U20+391 **95**
Marshall, *Texas* U26+326 **95**
Marshall Is., *Pacific Ocean* A60+075 **106**
Marshall Pass, *Colorado* V08+382 **98**
Marshalltown, *Iowa* U17+421 **95**
Marshfield, *Missouri* U18+374 **95**
Marshfield, *Oregon* W26+434 **92**
Marshfield, *Wisconsin* U01+447 **91**
Mars Hill, *Maine* S48+465 **90**
Marstrand, *Sweden* M20+579 **47**
Marsum, *Netherlands* M56+532 **44**
Martaban, *Burma* F45+166 **71**
Martaban, G. of, *Burma* F50+155 **71**
Martelange, *Belgium* M56+498 **44**
Marthas Vineyard, I., *Mass.* S64+412 **96**
Martigny-Ville, *Switzerland* M48+461 **45**
Martin, *S. Dakota* U71+432 **93**
Martin L., *Alabama* T65+328 **97**
Martina, *Switzerland* M27+469 **45**
Martinho, *Brazil* R71-059 **105**
Martinique, I., *Windward Is.* S06+146 **101**
Martinsburg, *W. Virginia* T18+395 **96**
Martinsville, *Virginia* T29+367 **97**
Marton, *New Zealand* A27-401 **112**
Martos, *Spain* N24+377 **52**
Martre, Lac la, *N.-W. Terr.* V85+634 **88**
Maruf, *Afghanistan* H48+315 **75**
Marugame, *Japan* D07+342 **68**
Marum, *Netherlands* M52+531 **44**
Marutea, I., *Tuamotu Arch.* X45-180 **107**
Marvejols, *France* M71+445 **55**
Mary, *Turkmen.* H79+375 **62**
Maryborough, *Queensland* B74-255 **111**
Maryborough. *See* Portlaoise
Maryborough, *Victoria* C38-371 **109**
Marydale, *Cape Province* L48-294 **84**

Maryland, state, *U.S.A.* T10+392 **99**
Maryport, *England* N21+547 **37**
Marysville, *California* W10+391 **92**
Marysville, *New Brunswick* S39+460 **90**
Maryville, *Kansas* U40+398 **95**
Maryville, *Missouri* U30+404 **95**
Mas-afuera, *Pacific Ocean* T35-345 **107**
Masaka, *Uganda* K80-004 **83**
Masangena, *Mozambique* K72-216 **84**
Masara, *Mozambique* K66-182 **84**
Masasi, *Tanzania* K38-108 **83**
Masaya, *Nicaragua* T67+120 **101**
Masbate, I., *Philippines* D70+121 **65**
Mascara, *Algeria* N00+354 **80**
Maseru, *Lesotho* L14-292 **84**
Mashaki, *Afghanistan* H40+333 **75**
Masharbrum, mt., *Kashmir* G82+356 **72**
Mashhad, *Iran* J02+363 **75**
Mashkol, Hamun-i-, *Pak.* H72+281 **70**
Masi-Manimba, *Zaire* L72-048 **82**
Masindi, *Uganda* K80+016 **83**
Masira Chan., *Saudi Arabia* J08+207 **75**
Masira, G. of, *Saudi Arabia* J10+197 **75**
Masira I., *Oman* J08+204 **75**
Masjed Soleymān, *Iran* J63+314 **74**
Mask L., *Ireland, Rep.* N56+536 **42**
Masoala C., *Madagascar* J58-160 **83**
Mason, *Michigan* T57+426 **91**
Mason City, *Iowa* U19+432 **95**
Masoy, *Norway* L30+709 **46**
Massa, *Italy* M29+440 **56**
Massachusetts, state, *U.S.A.* S80+421 **99**
Massachusetts B., *Mass.* S63+424 **96**
Massafra, *Italy* L77+406 **57**
Massakori, *Chad* L86+130 **81**
Massapé, *Brazil* Q62-034 **105**
Massawa, *Ethiopia* K34+156 **83**
Massena, *New York* S89+449 **91**
Massènya, *Chad* L82+114 **81**
Masseube, *France* M87+434 **55**
Massey, *Ontario* T42+462 **91**
Massillon, *Ohio* T39+409 **91**
Masterton, *New Zealand* A26-409 **112**
Mastuj, *Pakistan* H15+363 **72**
Mastung, *Pakistan* H49+298 **70**
Mastura, *Saudi Arabia* K37+231 **74**
Masulipatnam (Bandar),
   India G52+162 **70**
Masyaf, *Syria* K52+351 **76**
Mat, *India* G73+276 **72**
Mata Amarilla, *Argentina* S68-496 **103**
Matagalpa, *Nicaragua* T65+130 **101**
Matagorda, B. & Pen., *Texas* U36+286 **94**
Matagorda, I., *Texas* U40+282 **94**
Matakana I., *New Zealand* A23-376 **112**
Matale, *Sri Lanka* G57+076 **70**
Matam, *Senegal* N80+156 **80**
Matamoros, *Mexico* U79+256 **100**
Matamoros, *Mexico* U45+258 **100**
Matane, *Quebec* S45+488 **90**
Matang, *Malaya* F26+048 **69**
Matanuska, *Alaska* Y00+614 **99**
Matanzas, *Cuba* T39+230 **101**
Matapedia, *Quebec* S42+480 **90**
Matapedia, L., *Quebec* S45+486 **90**
Matapozuelos, *Spain* N28+414 **52**
Matara, *Sri Lanka* G57+060 **70**
Mataram, *Lombok I., Indon.* E24-085 **65**
Mataro, *Spain* M75+415 **53**
Matatiele, *Cape Province* L08-304 **84**
Mataule, *Brazil* R47+015 **105**
Mataura, *New Zealand* A66-462 **112**
Matehuala, *Mexico* U63+236 **100**
Matera, *Italy* L80+407 **57**
Mátészalka, *Hungary* L46+479 **49**
Mateur, *Tunisia* M32+370 **81**
Matfors, *Sweden* L78+624 **46**
Mathew Town, *Bahamas, The* S82+210 **101**
Mathura, *India* G74+274 **73**
Matiara, *India* G16+263 **71**
Matlock, *England* N09+531 **37**
Matna, *Sudan* K60+138 **81**
Matrah, *Oman* J09+236 **75**
Matruh, *Egypt* L16+312 **81**
Matsue, *Japan* D12+354 **68**
Matsumoto, *Japan* C69+362 **68**
Matsushima, *Japan* C53+384 **68**
Matsuyama, *Japan* D13+338 **68**
Mattawa, *Ontario* T22+463 **91**
Matterhorn, mt., *Switz.-It.* M44+460 **45**
Matto Grosso, *Brazil* S00-150 **104**
Mattoon, *Illinois* T80+394 **95**
Matucana, *Peru* T09-118 **104**
Matun, *Afghanistan* H30+334 **75**
Matura, *Brazil* S49-035 **104**
Maturin, *Venezuela* S19+097 **104**
Matvaieva, *U.S.S.R.* J13+578 **61**
Mau, *India* G59+222 **73**
Mau Aimma, *India* G48+257 **73**
Maubeuge, *France* M66+503 **54**
Maubin, *Burma* F56+166 **71**
Maubourguet, *France* N00+435 **55**
Maudaha, *India* G59+257 **73**
Maude, *New South Wales* C34-345 **109**
Mauele, *Mozambique* K66-244 **84**
Maues, *Brazil* R73-034 **105**
Mauganj, *India* G48+246 **73**
Maugerville, *New Brunswick* S39+459 **90**
Maui, I., *Hawaiian Is.* Y30+208 **107**
Mauleon Licharre, *France* N04+432 **55**
Maurawan, *India* G55+264 **73**
Maurice, L., *S. Australia* D24-292 **110**
Mauritania, rep., *W. Africa* N60+200 **80**
Mauritius, I., *Indian Ocean* J17-200 **77**
Maurs, *France* M77+448 **55**
Mauston, *Wisconsin* U01+438 **91**
Maumturk Mts., *Ireland, Rep.* N58+535 **43**
Mawk Mai, *Burma* F43+202 **71**
Mawson, *Antarctica* H78-680 **27**
Maxcanu, *Mexico* U00+205 **100**
Maxton, *N. Carolina* T26+348 **97**
Maxwelltown, *Scotland* N22+551 **41**
May, C., *New Jersey* T00+389 **96**
May, I. of, *Scotland* N16+562 **41**
Maya, I., *Indonesia* E63-O11 **65**
Mayaguez, *Puerto Rico* S42+182 **101**
Mayari, *Cuba* T04+207 **101**
Mayavaram, *India* G62+112 **70**
Mayen, *W. Germany* M46+503 **48**
Mayenne, dep., *France* N05+482 **54**
Mayersville, *Mississippi* U06+329 **97**

Mayfield, *Kentucky* T82+367 **97**
Maymyo, *Burma* F51+220 **71**
Maynooth, *Ireland, Rep.* N39+534 **43**
Maynooth, *Ontario* T18+452 **91**
Mayo, co., *Ireland, Rep.* N56+537 **42**
Mayoumba, *Gabon* M26-036 **82**
Mayran, L., *Mexico* U77+258 **100**
Mays Landing, *New Jersey* S88+394 **96**
Maysville, *Kentucky* T52+386 **97**
Mayville, *New York* T22+423 **96**
Maza, *Argentina* S20-367 **103**
Mazabuka, *Zambia* L14-158 **84**
Mazagan (El Jadida), *Morocco* N52+330 **80**
Mazagão, *Brazil* R39-002 **105**
Mazamet, *France* M76+435 **55**
Mazan, *Argentina* S39-288 **103**
Mazan, *Peru* S78-036 **104**
Mazapil, *Mexico* U70+247 **100**
Mazara del Vallo, *Sicily* M14+376 **57**
Mazaredo, *Argentina* S40-470 **103**
Mazar-i-Sharif, *Afghanistan* H47+366 **75**
Mazarron, *Spain* N08+377 **53**
Mazatenango, *Guatemala* U09+144 **100**
Mazatlán, *Mexico* V09+232 **100**
Mazheikyai, *Lithuania* L45+563 **47**
Mbabane, *Swaziland* K82-264 **84**
Mbalama, *Mozambique* K38-134 **83**
Mbale, *Uganda* K66+008 **83**
Mbandaka, *Zaire* L70+001 **82**
Mbarangandu, *Tanzania* K50-104 **83**
Mbarara, *Uganda* K86-006 **83**
Mbeya, *Tanzania* K70-090 **83**
Mbozi, *Tanzania* K72-090 **83**
Mbuji-Mayi, *Zaire* L38-062 **82**
Mcuburi, *Mozambique* K36-146 **83**
Mead L., *Nevada, etc.* V57+361 **92**
Meadville, *Pennsylvania* T31+416 **91**
Meaford, *Ontario* T33+446 **91**
Meath, co., *Ireland, Rep.* N39+537 **42**
Mecatina I. Gt. *Quebec* R83+508 **90**
Mecatina I. Lit., *Quebec* R86+506 **90**
Mecca, *Saudi Arabia* K31+214 **74**
Mechanicville, *New York* S82+429 **96**
Mechelen, *Belgium* M56+509 **44**
Mechelen (Malines), *Belg.* M63+510 **44**
Mecheria, *Algeria* N02+332 **80**
Mecklenburg, *W. Germany* M18+535 **48**
Medak, *India* G70+181 **70**
Medak, *Yugoslavia* L87+444 **56**
Medan, *Sumatra* F38+036 **65**
Medanos, *Argentina* S17-389 **103**
Medellin, *Colombia* T04+061 **104**
Medemblik, *Netherlands* M59+528 **44**
Medenine, *Tunisia* M28+334 **81**
Meder, *Ethiopia* K26+146 **83**
Medford, *Oregon* W17+423 **92**
Medford, *Wisconsin* U02+451 **91**
Medgidia, *Romania* L10+443 **58**
Media, *Pennsylvania* T02+399 **96**
Medias, *Romania* L34+461 **58**
Medicine Bow Ra., *Wyo.-Colo.* V06+408 **93**
Medicine Hat, *Alberta* V34+500 **88**
Medina, *Saudi Arabia* K30+246 **74**
Medina, *New York* T20+432 **96**
Medina, *N. Dakota* U56+469 **93**
Medina, *Ohio* T41+411 **91**
Medinaceli, *Spain* N15+412 **53**
Medina del Campo, *Spain* N29+413 **52**
Medina de Rioseco, *Spain* N30+419 **52**
Medina Sidonia, *Spain* N36+365 **52**
Médine, *Mali* N68+142 **80**
Mediterranean Sea, *S. Europe* **50-51**
Mednogorsk, *U.S.S.R.* J14+518 **61**
Medora, *N. Dakota* U81+469 **93**
Medvezhegorsk, *Karelia* K64+628 **62**
Medvezhi Osa., *U.S.S.R.* B20+710 **63**
Medvezhi Yar, *U.S.S.R.* F80+706 **63**
Medway R., *England* M87+513 **39**
Meekatharra, *W. Australia* E10-266 **110**
Meenin. *See* Menin
Meerle, *Belgium* M61+515 **44**
Meerlo, *Netherlands* M54+515 **44**
Meersburg, *W. Germany* M35+477 **48**
Meersen, *Netherlands* M55+509 **44**
Meerut, *India* G74+290 **72**
Meeuwen, *Belgium* M57+511 **44**
Mega, *Ethiopia* K40+040 **83**
Megalópolis, *Greece* L47+374 **59**
Mégantic, & L., *Quebec* S65+456 **91**
Mégara, *Greece* L40+380 **59**
Meghalaya, state, *India* F82+254 **71**
Megiskan, *Quebec* T13+483 **91**
Mehar, *Pakistan* H43+272 **70**
Meherpur, *Bangladesh* G08+238 **73**
Mehndawal, *India* G41+270 **73**
Meihsien, *China* E23+244 **67**
Meiktila, *Burma* F55+208 **71**
Meiningen, *E. Germany* M28+505 **48**
Meiringen, *Switzerland* M41+467 **45**
Meissen, *E. Germany* M09+512 **48**
Meitene, *Latvia* L38+564 **47**
Mejillones, *Chile* S62-230 **103**
Mekatina, *Ontario* T55+471 **91**
Meknes, *Morocco* N34+340 **80**
Me-kong R., *S.-E. Asia* E84+125 **69**
Melaka, *Malaya* F17+022 **69**
Melanesia, *Pacific Oc.* B30-050 **106**
Melbourne, *Victoria* C30-378 **109**
Meleuz, *U.S.S.R.* J24+528 **61**
Melfi, *Italy* L86+410 **57**
Melfort, *Saskatchewan* U87+531 **88**
Meligalá, *Greece* L48+372 **59**
Melilla, *Morocco* N18+352 **80**
Melipilla, *Chile* S67-336 **103**
Melitopol, *Ukraine* K58+469 **60**
Melk, *Austria* L88+483 **48**
Melle, *France* N01+462 **54**
Mellier, *Belgium* M57+498 **44**
Me lingen, *Switzerland* M40+474 **45**
Melo, *Uruguay* R56-322 **103**
Melona, *Israel* K59+330 **76**
Melreux, *Belgium* M57+503 **44**
Melrose, *Minnesota* U29+457 **93**
Melrose, *Scotland* N16+556 **41**
Melun, *France* M74+485 **54**
Melvich, *Scotland* N24+586 **40**
Melville, *Saskatchewan* U77+508 **88**
Melville B., *Greenland* S00+760 **26**
Melville, C., *Queensland* C32-142 **111**

Melville I., *N. Terr., Aust.* D23-116 **110**
Melville I., *N.-W. Terr.* V30+756 **88**
Melville L., *Labrador* R85+538 **89**
Melville Pen., *N.-W. Terr.* T55+679 **89**
Melvin L., *N. Ireland-*
   Ireland, Rep. N49+544 **42**
Memba & B., *Mozambique* K26-142 **83**
Membij, *Syria* K42+365 **76**
Memel. *See* Klaipeda
Memphis, *Tennessee* U00+352 **97**
Memphremagog, L., *Quebec* S74+451 **91**
Mena, *Arkansas* U26+346 **95**
Menai Bridge, *Wales* N25+532 **38**
Menai Str., *Wales* N26+531 **38**
Menairi, *Chad* L44+152 **81**
Ménaka, *Mali* M76+158 **80**
Menasha, *Wisconsin* T80+442 **91**
Mendak, *Saudi Arabia* K22+203 **74**
Mendawai, R., *Borneo* E40-017 **65**
Mende, *France* M69+445 **55**
Mendebo Mts., *Ethiopia* K32+068 **83**
Menderez, R., *Turkey* L08+379 **74**
Mendip Hills, *England* N16+513 **38**
Mendocino, C., *California* W27+404 **92**
Mendota, *Illinois* T85+416 **91**
Mendota, L., *Wisconsin* T86+431 **95**
Mendoza, *Argentina* S53-328 **103**
Mendrisio, *Switzerland* M36+459 **45**
Menfi, *Sicily* M12+376 **57**
Menga, *Cameroun* M16+062 **81**
Meng Chai Nat, *Thailand* F29+152 **69**
Meng Chumporn, *Thailand* F35+106 **69**
Meng Fang, *Thailand* F35+198 **69**
Meng Kalamasai, *Thailand* F09+165 **69**
Meng Kemmarat, *Thailand* E98+160 **69**
Meng Krabin, *Thailand* F19+139 **69**
Meng Kuwi, *Thailand* F31+121 **69**
Meng Pran Kao, *Thailand* F31+124 **69**
Meng Pre, *Thailand* F29+182 **69**
Meng Teun, *Thailand* F35+176 **69**
Mengtsz, *China* F10+232 **64**
Meng Uthen, *Thailand* F03+175 **69**
Menin, *Belgium* M71+508 **44**
Menindee, *New S. Wales* C45-324 **109**
Menindee L., *New S. Wales* C46-324 **109**
Meningie, *S. Australia* C64-357 **109**
Menjapa, mt., *Borneo* E24+011 **65**
Menominee & R., *Michigan* T76+451 **91**
Menomonie, *Wisconsin* U12+448 **93**
Menorca I., *Balearic Is.* M65+400 **53**
Mentawai Is., *Indonesia* F40+020 **31**
Mentok, *Bangka I., Indonesia* E89+020 **65**
Menton, *France* M45+438 **55**
Menzelinsk, *U.S.S.R.* J41+557 **61**
Menzies, *W. Australia* D84-296 **110**
Meoqui, *Mexico* V03+282 **100**
Me-ping, R., *Thailand* F30+540 **69**
Meppel, *Netherlands* M53+527 **44**
Merabello G., *Crete* L25+352 **59**
Merano, *Italy* M23+467 **56**
Merasheen I., *Nfld.* R55+475 **90**
Merauke, *New Guinea* C57-085 **65**
Mercara, *India* G85+126 **70**
Merced, *California* W03+373 **92**
Mercedaria, mt., *Argentina* S61-320 **103**
Mercedes, *Argentina* R86-346 **103**
Mercedes, *Argentina* R79-293 **103**
Mercedes, *Bolivia* S41-126 **104**
Mercedes, *Uruguay* R78-333 **103**
Mercer, *New Zealand* A29-373 **112**
Mercer, *Pennsylvania* T32+413 **91**
Merchtem, *Belgium* M65+510 **44**
Mercy, C., *N.-W. Terr.* S20+650 **89**
Meredith, *Michigan* T57+442 **91**
Meredith, C., *Falkland Is.* S04-522 **103**
Mereg, *Somalia* J76+038 **83**
Mergentheim, *W. Germany* M32+494 **48**
Mergui, *Burma* F38+124 **71**
Mergui Arch., *Burma* F48+116 **71**
Meribah, *S. Australia* C55-347 **109**
Merida, *Mexico* T88+209 **100**
Merida, *Spain* N38+390 **52**
Merida & Cord. de, *Venez.* S67+084 **104**
Meriden, *Connecticut* S77+415 **96**
Meridian, *Mississippi* T82+324 **97**
Meringur, *Victoria* C52-344 **109**
Merioneth, co., *see* Gwyned
Merj Uyun, *Lebanon* K53+334 **76**
Merka, *Somalia* K01+018 **83**
Merksplas, *Belgium* M61+514 **44**
Merowe, *Sudan* K80+182 **81**
Merredin, *W. Australia* E09-314 **110**
Merrill, *Wisconsin* T88+452 **91**
Merrimack R., *New Hamp.-*
   Mass. S68+427 **96**
Merriwa, *New S. Wales* B88-322 **109**
Merrygoen, *New S. Wales* C05-319 **109**
Mersey R., *England* N16+534 **37**
Merseyside, co., *England* N18+534 **37**
Mersin, *Turkey* K62+369 **74**
Mersing, *Malaya* F07+024 **65**
Mersis, *Somalia* J84+046 **83**
Mersrags, *Latvia* L41+573 **47**
Merta, *India* H06+266 **70**
Merthyr Tydfil, *Wales* N20+518 **38**
Mertola, *Portugal* N46+376 **52**
Meru, *Kenya* K44+002 **83**
Merwe, *Zambia* K82-142 **83**
Merzig, *W. Germany* M50+494 **48**
Mesa, *Arizona* V40+334 **94**
Mesabi Ra., *Minnesota* U20+477 **93**
Mesagne, *Italy* L73+405 **57**
Mesará B., *Crete* L32+350 **59**
Mesa Verde Nat. Park, *Colo.* V22+376 **98**
Mesen, *Belgium* M73+508 **44**
Meshghara, *Lebanon* K56+336 **76**
Meskene, *Syria* K41+360 **76**
Mesmiye, *Syria* K52+331 **76**
Mesocco, *Switzerland* M35+464 **45**
Mesolóngion, *Greece* L51+384 **59**
Messancy, *Belgium* M55+496 **44**
Messina, *Sicily* L89+382 **57**
Messina, Str. di, *Italy* L87+380 **57**
Messinia, *Greece* L49+372 **59**
Messinia, G. of, *Greece* L48+367 **59**
Mesudiye, *Turkey* K43+405 **74**
Metan, *Argentina* S30-255 **103**
Metangula, *Mozambique* K60-128 **83**
Metaripuá, *Brazil* S40-077 **104**
Méthana Pen., *Greece* L40+376 **59**

Methil (Buckhaven & Methil),
   Scotland N18+562 41
Methven, New Zealand A50-436 112
Metis Ls., Quebec S46+483 90
Metis Beach, Quebec S48+487 90
Metkovic, Yugoslavia L74+430 58
Metlakatla, Alaska W65+551 99
Metlika, Yugoslavia L88+456 56
Metropolis, Illinois T83+372 95
Metropolitan, Michigan T77+460 91
Métsovon, Greece L53+398 59
Mettet, Belgium M62+503 44
Mettlen, Switzerland M42+470 45
Mettur Dam, India G74+119 70
Metulla, Israel K57+333 76
Metz, France M53+491 54
Meulebeke, Belgium M70+510 44
Meurthe-et-Moselle, dep.,
   France M51+485 54
Meuse, dep., France M57+490 54
Meuse, R., Belgium, etc. M56+490 54
Mexcala & R., Mexico U58+177 100
Mexiana, I., Brazil R27+000 105
Mexicali, Mexico V62+326 100
Mexico, Mexico U55+194 100
Mexico, New York T07+434 96
Mexico, rep. Cent. America 100
Mexico B., New York T08+435 96
Mexico, G. of U00+250 100
Meyadin, Syria K27+350 74
Meyersdale, Pennsylvania T24+398 96
Meymac, France M77+455 54
Mèze, France M68+435 55
Mezen, U.S.S.R. J94+658 62
Mezieres, France M62+497 54
Mezöbereny Bèkés, Hungary L54+468 49
Mezökövesd, Hungary L57+478 49
Mesötúr, Hungary L56+470 49
Mezquitic, Mexico U82+226 100
Mgori, Tanzania K60-050 83
Mhow, India G85+224 70
Miahuatlan, Mexico U39+165 100
Miajadas, Spain N35+391 52
Miami, Arizona V36+333 94
Miami, Florida T31+257 97
Miami, Oklahoma U30+369 95
Miandowab, Iraq K05+326 74
Miandrivazo, Madagascar J88-196 83
Mianeh, Iran J73+374 74
Miani, India G86+317 72
Miani, Pakistan H11+325 72
Mian Kalai, Pakistan H20+348 72
Mianwali, Pakistan H21+325 72
Miao-tao I., China D86+383 66
Miass, U.S.S.R. J00+558 61
Miastko, Poland L78+540 49
Micay, Colombia T15+029 104
Michailovsk, U.S.S.R. H80+536 61
Micheh, China E59+378 66
Michigan, state, U.S.A. T73+462 99
Michigan, L., U.S.A.-Canada T70+434 99
Michigan City, Indiana T71+417 91
Michipicoten, Ontario T60+482 89
Michipicoten I. & B., Ont. T64+477 91
Michoacan, state, Mexico U72+188 100
Michurinsk, U.S.S.R. K27+529 61
Mickelson, Michigan T59+444 91
Micronesia, Pacific Oc. B30+100 106
Mid Canyon, Montana V41+471 93
Middleboro, Massachusetts S65+419 96
Middelburg, Netherlands M68+515 44
Middelburg, Transvaal L04-258 84
Middelharnis, Netherlands M65+518 44
Middelkerke, Belgium M73+512 44
Middleburg, New York S86+426 91
Middleburg, Pennsylvania T13+408 96
Middlebury, Vermont S79+441 91
Middleham, England N11+543 37
Middlemarch, New Zealand A59-455 112
Middleport, New York T21+431 96
Middlesboro, Kentucky T52+366 97
Middlesbrough, England N07+546 37
Middlesex, Belize T80+172 101
Middleton, Nova Scotia S30+449 90
Middleton-in-Teesdale, Eng. N13+546 37
Middletown, Connecticut S76+416 96
Middletown, Delaware T04+394 91
Middletown, New York S87+414 96
Middletown, Ohio T56+395 91
Middletown, Pennsylvania T11+402 96
Midland, Michigan T55+436 91
Midland, Ontario T29+447 91
Midland, Texas U72+320 94
Midlands, West, co., Eng. N11+525 37
Midleton, Ireland, Rep. N49+519 43
Midlothian, co., see Lothian
Midnapur, India G16+224 73
Midway Is., Hawaiian Is. Z60+290 106
Midwest, Wyoming V08+435 93
Midye, Turkey L12+416 74
Miécourt, Switzerland M47+474 45
Miedzyrzec, Poland L44+520 49
Mienning, China F30+239 64
Mienyang, China E40+302 67
Mienyang, China F01+313 66
Mier, Mexico U55+264 100
Mieres, Spain N35+432 52
Mifflintown, Pennsylvania T15+405 96
Migdal Gad, Israel K62+317 76
Mikhailovgrad, Bulgaria L41+434 58
Mikhaylovka, U.S.S.R. K10+500 61
Mikkeli, Finland L16+617 47
Mikonos, I., Greece L28+375 59
Milaca, Minnesota U22+458 93
Milan, Italy. See Milano
Milan, Missouri U19+402 95
Milan, New Hampshire S67+446 91
Milan, Tennessee T82+364 95
Milang, S. Australia C67-354 109
Milano, Italy M35+455 56
Milas, Turkey L14+373 74
Milazzo, Sicily L89+382 57
Milbank, S. Dakota U40+452 93
Mildenhall, England M87+523 39
Mildura, Victoria C47-342 109
Miléai, Greece L41+393 59
Miles, Queensland C00-267 111
Milesburg, Pennsylvania T17+409 96
Miles City, Montana V05+464 93
Milford, Delaware T02+389 96
Milford, Massachusetts S69+422 96
Milford, Nova Scotia S21+451 90

Milford, Pennsylvania S89+413 96
Milford, Utah V48+384 94
Milford Haven, Wales N30+517 38
Milford Sound, N.Z. A72-447 112
Mili Is., Marshall Islands A44+060 106
Miliana, Algeria M76+362 80
Milk R., Montana V16+486 93
Milkovo, U.S.S.R. B37+549 63
Mill, Netherlands M55+517 44
Mill I., Antarctica F26-650 27
Mill Is., N.-W. Territories T15+642 89
Millau, France M72+441 55
Millbridge, Ontario T16+447 91
Mille Lacs, Minnesota U22+462 93
Miller, S. Dakota U54+446 93
Millerovo, U.S.S.R. K28+489 61
Millersburg, Ohio T41+406 91
Miller's Flat, New Zealand A63-457 112
Mille Vaches, Quebec S55+486 90
Millford, Ireland, Rep. N46+551 42
Millicent, S. Australia C58-376 109
Millinocket, Maine S52+457 90
Millport, Scotland N29+558 41
Millridge, Maine S47+445 90
Millstreet, Ireland, Rep. N54+520 43
Milltown Malbay,
   Ireland, Rep. N56+528 43
Millville, New Jersey T00+394 96
Milne B., Papua New Guinea B86+05 111
Milnor, N. Dakota U45+463 93
Milo, Maine S54+452 90
Milos, I., Greece L33+367 59
Milparinka, New S. Wales C49-294 109
Milton, New Zealand A70-461 112
Milton, Ontario T29+435 91
Milton, Pennsylvania T12+410 96
Milwaukee, Wisconsin T78+430 95
Mimika, New Guinea C82-047 65
Mina al Ahmadi, Kuwait J71+293 74
Minab, Iran J18+271 75
Minaki, Ontario U27+500 88
Minas, Uruguay R62-343 103
Minas de Riotinto, Spain N39+377 52
Minas Novas, Brazil Q76-174 105
Minatitlan, Mexico U27+180 100
Minbu, Burma F60+202 71
Minch Little, Scotland N39+577 40
Minch North, Scotland N36+580 40
Mindanao, I., Philippines D60+074 65
Mindarie, S. Australia C59-349 109
Minden, Germany M37+523 48
Minden, Louisiana U20+326 95
Mindoro, I. & Str., Phil. D86+125 65
Mine Hd., Ireland, Rep. N46+520 43
Minehead, England N21+512 38
Mineola, New York S82+407 96
Mineral Ra., Michigan T88+467 91
Mineral Point, Wisconsin U01+429 91
Mineral Wells, Texas U49+328 95
Minga, Zambia K84-144 83
Mingan Is., Quebec S23+502 90
Mingary, S. Australia C55-321 109
Mingin, Burma F63+229 71
Minglanilla, Spain N10+395 53
Mingoyo, Tanzania K32-102 83
Mingshui, China F53+422 64
Minhla, Burma F59+199 71
Minho, Spain-Portugal N49+422 52
Minhow, China E04+261 67
Minicoy, I., Laccadives H11+082 70
Minna, Nigeria M50+096 80
Minneapolis, Minnesota U20+450 93
Minnedosa, Manitoba U60+502 88
Minnesota, state, U.S.A. U36+464 98
Minnesota R., Minn. etc. U36+450 98
Minnik, Syria K48+391 74
Minorca. See Menorca
Minot, N. Dakota U68+483 93
Min Shan, China F12+343 66
Minsk, Belorussia L15+538 60
Minsk Mazowiecki, Poland L51+522 49
Minto, N. Dakota U44+483 93
Minto Inl., N.-W. Terr. V70+712 88
Minto L., Quebec T02+568 89
Minusinsk, U.S.S.R. E79+537 63
Minya Konka, China F19+295 64
Minyip, Victoria C33-365 109
Mio, Michigan T54+446 91
Miquelon Is.,
   Atlantic Ocean R68+470 90
Mirador, Brazil Q88-063 105
Miraflores, Colombia S78+051 104
Miramar, Argentina R78-382 103
Mirambeau, France N04+453 55
Miramichie B., N.B. S29+472 90
Miramont, France M87+446 55
Miram Shah, Pakistan H29+330 72
Miranda, Argentina R86-364 103
Miranda, Brazil R69-202 105
Miranda, Nicaragua T57+140 101
Miranda de Ebro, Spain N18+427 52
Miranda do Corgo, Portugal N50+401 52
Miranda do Douro, Portugal N37+415 52
Mirande, France M88+435 55
Mirandela, Portugal N43+415 52
Mirandilla, Spain N37+391 52
Mirbat, Oman J34+170 75
Mirebeau, France M89+468 54
Mirim, L., Brazil R48-327 103
Mirjavèh, Iran H81+290 75
Mirnoe, U.S.S.R. G04+623 62
Mirosi, Romania L30+444 58
Mirpur, Kashmir H07+332 72
Mirpur Khas, Pakistan H36+255 70
Mirtoan Sea, Greece L38+368 59
Mirtos, Crete L27+350 59
Mirt Padam, India F58+284 71
Mirzapur, India G44+251 73
Miscou I., New Brunswick S27+480 90
Mishikamau, L., Labrador S25+542 89
Mishrif, Saudi Arabia K01+205 74
Miska, Saudi Arabia K13+249 74
Misoöl, I., New Guinea D30-018 65
Misquah Hills, Minnesota U62+478 91
Misque, Bolivia S37-178 104
Missis, Turkey K56+370 74
Mississippi, state, U.S.A. U00+328 99
Mississippi Delta, Louisiana T70+290 95
Mississippi R., U.S.A. U03+380 99

Mississippi Sd., Mississippi T84+303 95
Missolónghi. See Mesolóngion.
Missoula, Montana V54+469 92
Missouri, state, U.S.A. U20+381 99
Missouri R., U.S.A. U33+408 98
Missouri Valley, Iowa U36+416 95
Mistassini L., Quebec S83+508 89
Mistretta, Sicily M04+379 57
Misurata, (Misrátah), Libya M00+322 81
Mitala Maria, Uganda K76+001 83
Mitchell, Ontario T37+435 91
Mitchell, Queensland C13-264 111
Mitchell, S. Dakota U48+437 93
Mitchell, Mt., N. Carolina T44+358 97
Mitchell, R., Queensland C47-160 111
Mitchelstown, Ireland, Rep. N50+523 43
Mithankot, Pakistan H28+289 72
Mithi, Pakistan H31+246 70
Mithimna, Greece L23+393 59
Mitho, S. Vietnam E82+104
Mitilini, Lesvos, I., Greece L21+391 59
Mito, Japan C57+364 68
Mitsiz, Gabon M22+008 82
Mittagong, New S. Wales B88-344 109
Mitta Mitta, Victoria C15-365 109
Mittelmark, Germany M10+522 48
Mittelmark, W. Germany M10+522 48
Mitu, Colombia S60+009 104
Mitumba Mts., Zaire L10-016 104
Miyako, Japan C48+397 68
Miyanduab, Iran J83+370 74
Miyazaki, Japan D21+319 68
Mizda, Libya M12+314 81
Mizen Hd., Ireland, Rep. N36+528 43
Mizen Hd., Ireland, Rep. N59+514 43
Mizil, Romania L21+450 58
Mizpah, Montana V01+462 93
Mjölby, Sweden L89+583 47
Mjosa, L., Norway M24+607 47
Mladá Boleslav, Czech. M01+504 48
Mlanje, Mt., See Mulanje Mt.
Mlawa, Poland L58+531 49
Mljet, I., Yugoslavia L75+427 56
Mo, Norway M05+663 46
Moab, Utah V28+386 94
Moama, New South Wales C32-361 109
Mo Ångsåg, Sweden L41+636 46
Moapa, Nevada V59+367 92
Moate, Ireland, Rep. N54+534 43
Moba, Zaire L00+070 82
Mobile & B., Alabama T78+307 97
Mobridge, S. Dakota U63+456 93
Mocajuba, Brazil R26-025 105
Moçambique, Mozambique K26-150 83
Moçâmedes, Angola M16-152 82
Mocha, Yemen K10+133 74
Mocimboa-da-Praia, Mozamb. K28-114 83
Mocksville, N. Carolina T33+358 97
Mocoa, Colombia T10+011 104
Mocorito, Mexico V18+256 100
Moctezuma, Mexico U66+228 100
Moctezuma, Mexico U29+298 100
Modane, France M50+452 55
Modave, Belgium M58+504 44
Modena, Italy M24+446 56
Modesto, California W06+376 92
Modica, Sicily M02+369 57
Modjamboli, Zaire L48+022 82
Mo-duc, S. Vietnam E66+149 69
Modung, China F50+291 64
Moe, Victoria C22-382 109
Moena, I., Indonesia D75-050 65
Moengo, Surinam R57+056 105
Mofa, Ethiopia K28+106 83
Moffat, Scotland N21+553 41
Mogadiscio (Mogadishu),
   Somalia J88+020 83
Mogador (Essaouira), Mor. N60+314 80
Mogadouro, Portugal N39+414 52
Mogar, Ethiopia K42+080 83
Mogaung, Burma F48+253 71
Mogilev, Belorussia K88+539 60
Mogilev Podolskiy, Ukraine L13+485 60
Mogocha, U.S.S.R. E02+537 63
Mogochin, U.S.S.R. G39+577 62
Mogok, Burma F51+229 71
Mogollan Mt., New Mexico V22+336 94
Mogollon Mesa, Arizona V34+344 94
Moguer, Spain N41+372 52
Mogur, Ethiopia K28+050 83
Mohacs, Hungary L68+460 58
Mohako, New Zealand A20-391 112
Mohawk, New York T00+430 96
Mohawk R., New York S84+430 96
Moheli, I., Comoro Is. K08-124 83
Moher, Cliffs of, Ireland, Rep. N57+530 43
Mohill, Ireland, Rep. N47+539 42
Moho, China D75+534 63
Mohoro, Tanzania K34-082 83
Moia, Sudan L12+050 81
Moine, L. du, Quebec T18+469 91
Moirang, India F67+245 71
Moisaküla, Estonia L29+581 47
Moisie, Quebec S35+503 90
Moissac, France M84+441 55
Mojave, California V79+351 92
Moji, Japan C57+364 68
Moju & R., Brazil R22-019 105
Mokai, New Zealand A24-385 112
Mokameh, India G24+254 73
Mokolo, Cameroun M08+108 81
Mokpo, Korea D52+348 64
Mokshany, U.S.S.R. K08+534 61
Moldava, Czechoslovakia L54+486 49
Moldavia, Romania L18+467 58
Moldavia, rep., U.S.S.R. L12+474 60
Molde & Fd., Norway M47+628 46
Molepolole, Botswana L26-244 84
Môle St Nicolas, Haiti S80+198 101
Molfetta, Italy L80+412 57
Molina, Chile S67-350 103
Molina, Spain N07+381 53
Molina, Spain N11+409 53
Moline, Illinois U03+414 95
Molino, Florida T74+307 97
Moliro, Zaire K86-084 83
Moll, Belgium M59+512 44
Mollendo, Peru S72-170 104
Mollis, Switzerland M35+471 45
Mollosund, Sweden M21+581 47
Molndal, Sweden M18+577 47

Molong, New South Wales C07-331 109
Molotov. See Perm.
Molotovsk (Severodvinsk)
   U.S.S.R. K30+645 62
Molucca Pass., Indonesia D58-007 65
Moluccas, Is., Indonesia D45-012 65
Moma, Mozambique K34-166 83
Mombasa, Kenya K32-040 83
Momchilgrad, Bulgaria L28+415 58
Momeik. See Mong-mit.
Momignies, Belgium M65+500 44
Momotombo, Nicaragua T69+125 101
Mompós. Columbia S87+092 104
Møn. I., Denmark M16+550 47
Monà Fd., Finland L48+635 46
Mona, I., Puerto Rico S48+182 101
Mona Pass., West Indies S50+180 101
Monach, Sd. of, Scotland N45+576 40
Monaco, princip., S. Europe M46+437 55
Monadhliath Mts., Scotland N26+571 40
Monaghan & co.,
   Ireland, Rep. N42+542 42
Monango, N.Dakota U52+462 93
Monar L., Scotland N30+574 40
Monaro Ra., New S. Wales C07-364 109
Monasterace Marina, Italy L81+385 57
Monasterevin, Ireland, Rep. N42+531 43
Monastir. See Bitola.
Monastir, Sardinia M36+394 57
Monastir, Tunisia M24+358 81
Monbetsu, Japan C40+443 68
Monbuey, Spain N38+420 52
Mönchengladbach, W. Ger. M52+512 45
Monchique, Portugal N51+373 52
Monclova, Mexico U69+269 100
Moncton, New Brunswick S29+461 90
Mondo, Chad L86+138 81
Mondonedo, Spain N44+434 52
Mondovi, Wisconsin U10+446 93
Mondul, Tanzania K52-032 83
Monemvasia, Greece L42+367 59
Monessen, Pennsylvania T30+402 96
Monetny, U.S.S.R. H85+570 61
Monett, Missouri U24+370 95
Moneva, Spain N05+411 53
Monforte, Portugal N45+390 52
Monforte, Spain N45+425 52
Monga, Zaire L42+040 82
Mongalla, Sudan K80+052 81
Monger, L., W. Australia E17-290 110
Möng-Hsu, Burma F40+218 71
Monghyr, India G21+254 73
Mongka, Burma F33+226 71
Möng Kiang, Burma F40+219 71
Mongkol-borey, Cambodia F12+135 69
Möng Kung, Burma F44+216 71
Möng-Kyet, Burma F39+231 71
Mong-mit, Burma F49+231 71
Mongo, Chad L66+122 81
Mongolia, rep., E. Asia F00+450 31
Mongolia, Inner, China F20+404 64
Mongonu, Nigeria M08+126 81
Mongoumba, Cent. Afr. Rep. L70+036 81
Möng-pai, Burma F48+198 71
Möng Pan, Burma F40+203 71
Möng Pawn, Burma F45+208 71
Möng-Sit, Burma F43+205 71
Mongu, Zambia L42-154 84
Moniaive, Scotland N23+552 41
Moniquira, Colombia S82+059 104
Monivea, Ireland Rep. N52+534 43
Monmouth, Illinois U04+409 95
Monmouth, Wales N16+518 38
Monnikendam, Netherlands M60+525 44
Mono L., California V84+380 92
Monomay I. & Pt., Mass. S60+415 96
Monopoli, Italy L76+409 57
Monovar, Spain N05+385 53
Monreal del Campo, Spain N08+408 53
Monroe, Louisiana U13+325 97
Monroe, Michigan T50+419 91
Monroe, N. Carolina T33+350 97
Monroe, Wisconsin T88+426 95
Monroeville, Alabama 174+315 97
Monrovia, Liberia N64+064 80
Mons, Belgium M66+504 44
Monsanto, Portugal N43+401 52
Monsâo, Portugal N50+421 52
Monserrato, Sardinia M35+393 57
Monson, Massachusetts S74+422 96
Monster, Netherlands M65+520 44
Mönsterås, Sweden L81+570 47
Mont, Belgium M55+502 44
Montague Tremblante Park,
   Quebec T00+469 91
Montague, Michigan T68+435 91
Montagu I., S. Sandwich Is. P80-580 27
Montaigu, Belgium M60+510 44
Montana, state, U.S.A. V38+468 94
Montanchez, Spain N37+393 52
Montargis, France M73+480 54
Montauban, France M82+440 55
Montbard, France M64+476 54
Montblanch, Spain M83+414 53
Montbrison, France M66+456 54
Montclair, New Jersey M66+497 54
Mont de Marsan, France N03+439 55
Montdidier, France M75+496 54
Mont Dore, le, France M66+456 54
Monte Alegre, Brazil R54-019 105
Monte Azul, Brazil R24-189 105
Montebello, Quebec T00+457 91
Monte Carlo, Monaco M46+437 55
Montecollina, S. Australia C60-294 109
Monte Coman, Argentina S47-346 103
Monte Cristi, Dominican
   Republic S69+199 101
Monte Cristi, Sa. de,
   Dominican Rep. S64+196 101
Montecristo, I., Italy M28+423 56
Montefrio, Spain N24+373 52
Montego Bay, Jamaica T17+186 101
Montélimar, France M62+446 55
Montello, Wisconsin T86+438 91
Montemorelos, Mexico U59+252 100
Montenegro, Yugoslavia L64+426 58
Montereau, France M72+484 54
Monterey, California W11+366 92

Monterey, *Virginia* T27+384 97
Monterey, B. of, *California* W14+367 92
Monteriá, *Colombia* T05+087 104
Monteros, *Argentina* S34–272 103
Monterrey, *Mexico* U61+257 100
Monte San Angelo, *Italy* L84+417 57
Montes Claros, *Brazil* Q82–167 105
Montevideo, *Minnesota* U35+449 93
Montevideo, *Uruguay* R67–349 103
Monte Vista, *Colorado* V08+376 94
Montezuma, *Georgia* T54+324 97
Montfort-sur-Meu, *France* N12+481 54
Montgomery, *Alabama* T68+324 97
Montgomery, *Missouri* U09+390 95
Montgomery, *Wales* N19+526 38
Monthey, *Switzerland* M48+463 45
Monticello, *Arkansas* U10+336 95
Monticello, *Georgia* T52+333 97
Monticello, *Maine* S47+463 90
Monticello, *New York* S88+416 91
Monticello, *Utah* V26+380 94
Montijo, B. de, *Panama* T36+076 101
Montilla, *Spain* N28+375 52
Mont Joli, *Quebec* S49+486 90
Mont Laurier, *Quebec* T03+465 91
Montlucon, *France* M74+464 54
Montmagny, *Quebec* S63+470 90
Montmédy, *France* M58+495 54
Montmirail, *France* M69+489 54
Montmorency, *Quebec* S67+469 91
Montoursville, *Pennsylvania* T12+412 96
Montpelier, *Idaho* V38+423 94
Montpelier, *Vermont* S76+443 91
Montpellier, *France* M67+436 55
Montreal, *Quebec* S82+455 91
Montreal L., *Saskatchewan* V05+542 88
Montrejeau, *France* M87+431 55
Montreuil, *France* M79+505 54
Montreuil Bellay, *France* N01+471 54
Montreux, *Switzerland* M48+464 45
Montrose, *Colorado* V17+384 94
Montrose, *Pennsylvania* T06+418 96
Montrose, *Scotland* N15+567 41
Monts, Pt. des, *Quebec* S44+493 90
Mont-St Jean, *Belgium* M64+507 44
Mont-St-Michel & B., *Fr.* N09+487 54
Montserrat, I., *Leeward Is.* S13+168 101
Monywa, *Burma* F58+220 71
Monza, *Italy* M35+456 56
Monze, *Zambia* L16–162 84
Monzon, *Spain* M89+419 53
Moolawatana, *S. Australia* C62–299 109
Moonbi Ra., *New S. Wales* B84–308 109
Moonta, *S. Australia* C75–341 109
Moora, *W. Australia* E24–306 110
Moorcroft, *Wyoming* V00+443 93
Moore, L., *W. Australia* E15–294 110
Moorefield, *W. Virginia* T24+391 96
Moorfoot Hills, *Scotland* N19+557 41
Moorhead, *Minnesota* U41+469 93
Moorsel, *Belgium* M65+509 44
Moorslede, *Belgium* M72+509 44
Moose L., *Manitoba* U62+540 88
Moose R., *Ontario* T42+505 89
Moosehead L., *Maine* S58+456 90
Moose Jaw, *Saskatchewan* V04+504 88
Moosic, Mts., *Pennsylvania* T03+417 96
Moosomin, *Saskatchewan* U70+501 88
Moosonee, *Ontario* T34+511 89
Mopti, *Mali* N24+142 80
Moquegua, *Peru* S66–172 104
Mora, *Ethiopia* K54+104 83
Mora, *Cameroun* M06+110 81
Mora, *Minnesota* U20+459 93
Mora, *Portugal* N49+389 52
Mora, *Spain* N23+397 52
Mora, *Sweden* M03+610 47
Moradabad, *India* G67+288 73
Mora de Rubielos, *Spain* N05+403 53
Moramanga, *Malagasy Rep.* J70–190 83
Morano Calabro, *Italy* L83+399 57
Morar, *India* G70+262 73
Morar L., *Scotland* N34+569 40
Morat. *See* Murten
Moratalla, *Spain* N11+382 53
Morava R., *Yugoslavia* L53+444 58
Moravia, *Czechoslovakia* L75+493 49
Moravska Trebova, *Czech.* L79+498 49
Morawhanna, *Guyana* R88+083 104

Moray Firth, *Scotland* N22+577 40
Morbihan, dep., *France* N18+479 54
Morden, *Manitoba* U50+493 88
Mordialloc, *Victoria* C29–380 109
Mordova, *U.S.S.R.* K22+536 61
Mordovskava, aut. rep.,
  U.S.S.R. K10+544 62
Morea, *Greece* L46+376 59
Moreau R., *S. Dakota* U72+452 98
Morecambe & B., *England* N17+451 37
Moreda, *Spain* N20+374 52
Moree, *New South Wales* C01–295 109
Moreira, *Brazil* S21–006 104
Mörel, *Switzerland* M42+464 45
Morelia, *Mexico* U67+196 100
Morella, *Spain* N01+406 53
Morelos, *Mexico* U65+284 100
Morelos, *Mexico* V13+267 100
Morelos, state, *Mexico* U54+186 100
Morena, *India* G76+261 73
Morena, Sa., *Spain* N24+383 52
Morenci, *Arizona* V26+332 94
Morere, *New Zealand* A13–390 112
Morez, *France* M54+465 54
Morgan, *S. Australia* C62–340 10
Morgan City, *Louisiana* U07+297 95
Morganton, *N. Carolina* T40+357 97
Morgat, *France* N27+482 54
Morges, *Switzerland* M51+465 45
Morgins, *Switzerland* M49+462 45
Moriana, *India* F64+267 71
Morice L., *Brit. Columbia* W47+540 88
Morinville, *Alberta* V52+540 88
Morioka, *Japan* C53+397 68
Morisset, *New South Wales* B82–332 109
Morlaix, *France* N23+485 54
Mormugao, *India* H07+155 70
Mornington, *Victoria* C29–382 109
Mornington, I., *Chile* T02–498 103
Moro G., *Philippines* D70+069 65

Morobe, *Papua New Guinea* C15–078 111
Morocco, *N.-W. Africa* N30+326 80
Morogoro, *Tanzania* K44–068 83
Morokwen, *Cape Province* L36–262 84
Moron, *Cuba* T22+221 101
Morón, *Venezuela* S49+110 104
Morona, *Ecuador* T15–028 104
Morondava, *Malagasy Rep.* K04–204 83
Morón de la Frontera, *Spain* N33+371 52
Morotai, I., *Indonesia* D40+022 65
Moroto, *Uganda* K62+026 83
Morpeth, *England* N10+552 37
Morpeth, *New South Wales* B81–328 109
Morphou & B., *Cyprus* K72+352 76
Morrillton, *Arkansas* U16+352 95
Morrinhos, *Brazil* R25–178 105
Morrinsville, *New Zealand* A27–377 112
Morris, *Illinois* T80+414 95
Morris, *Manitoba* U45+495 88
Morris, *Minnesota* U36+456 93
Morrisburg, *Ontario* T01+449 91
Morris Jesup C., *Arctic Oc.* Q55+840 25
Morrison, *Illinois* U00+418 91
Morristown, *New Jersey* S87+408 96
Morrisville, *New York* T04+430 91
Morro, *Ecuador* T32–026 104
Morrosquillo, G. de, *Colom.* T04+095 104
Mors, *Denmark* M38+568 47
Morshansk, *U.S.S.R.* K19+534 61
Mortagne, *France* M87+485 54
Mortagua, *Portugal* N49+404 52
Mortain, *France* N06+486 54
Mortlake, *Victoria* C43–381 109
Morundah, *New S. Wales* C22–349 109
Moruya, *New S. Wales* B80–360 109
Morven, *New Zealand* A53–448 112
Morven, *Queensland* C18–264 111
Morvi, *India* H24+228 70
Morwell, *Victoria* C22–382 109
Moscow, *Idaho* V03+467 92
Moscow. *See* Moskva
Moselle, dep., *France* M48+489 54
Moselle R., *France* M53+489 54
Mosera, I. *See* Masira I.
Mosgiel, *New Zealand* A58–458 112
Moshupa, *Botswana* L28–248 84
Mosjøen, *Norway* M11+658 46
Moskenesøya, *Norway* M12+680 46
Moskva, *U.S.S.R.* K45+558 60
Mosqueiro, *Brazil* R21–012 105
Mosquera, *Colombia* T21+024 104
Mosquito Bank, *Nicaragua* T46+132 101
Moss, *Norway* M26+595 47
Mossamedes, *Angola* M16–152 84
Mossburn, *New Zealand* A70–457 112
Mossel B., *Cape Province* L46–342 84
Mossendio, *Congo* M14+030 82
Mossgiel, *New South Wales* C33–333 109
Mossoro, *Brazil* Q44–052 105
Mossurize, *Mozambique* K72+206 84
Moss Vale, *New S. Wales* B88–346 109
Most, *Czechoslovakia* M08+505 48
Mostaganem, *Algeria* N00+358 80
Mostar, *Yugoslavia* L73+433 58
Mostardas, *Brazil* R35–310 103
Mosul, *Iraq* K12+365 74
Mota del Marques, *Spain* N31+416 52
Motala, *Sweden* M00+585 47
Motatan, *Venezuela* S63+094 104
Motherwell, *Scotland* N24+558 41
Mötier, *Switzerland* M48+469 45
Môtiers, *Switzerland* M50+469 45
Motihari, *India* G30+266 73
Motöt, *Switzerland* M45+461 45
Motril, *Spain* N22+367 52
Mott, *N. Dakota* U75+464 93
Motueka, *New Zealand* A42–411 112
Motul, *Mexico* T84+211 100
Moturoa, *New Zealand* A36–390 112
Moudala, *Chad* L68+088 81
Moudhros, *Greece* L29+399 59
Moudon, *Switzerland* M49+467 45
Mouila, *Gabon* M24–020 82
Moukden. *See* Shenyang
Moulamein & R., *N.S.W.* C36–351 109
Moulins, *France* M70+466 54
Moulmein, *Burma* F44+164 71
Moulouya R., *Morocco* N22+330 80
Moulton, *Alabama* T74+344 97
Mound City, *Illinois* T85+370 97
Mountain Grove, *Missouri* U14+371 97
Mountain Home, *Arkansas* U15+363 97
Mountain Sheep Bluffs, *Montana*
  V03+473 93
Mountain View, *Arkansas* U13+358 97
Mount Ayr, *Iowa* U26+407 95
Mount Barker, *S. Australia* C67–351 109
Mount Bellew, *Ireland, Rep.*
  N51+535 43
Mount Carmel, *Illinois* T76+384 95
Mount Carmel, *Pennsylvania* T09+408 96
Mount Carroll, *Illinois* U00+421 91
Mount Clemens, *Michigan* T47+426 91
Mount Desert I. (Acadia Nat.
  Park), *Maine* S50+443 90
Mount Drysdale, *N.S.W.* C25–312 109
Mount Forest, *Ontario* T35+440 91
Mount Gambier, *S. Aust.* C55–379 109
Mount Holly, *New Jersey* S89+400 96
Mount Hope, *N.S.W.* C25–329 109
Mount Jewett, *Pennsylvania* T22+417 96
Mount Lofty Ra., *S. Aust.* C66–350 109
Mount Magnet, *W. Aust.* E12–280 110
Mount Manara, *N.S.W.* C36–324 109
Mountmellick, *Ireland, Rep.* N44+531 43
Mount Morgan, *Queensland* C00–237 111
Mount Morris, *New York* T17+427 96
Mount Murray, *Alberta* V39+564 88
Mount Olive, *Mississippi* T88+317 95
Mount Olive, *N. Carolina* T18+352 97
Mount Pleasant, *Iowa* U10+409 95
Mount Pleasant, *Michigan* T59+436 91
Mount Pleasant, *Pa.* T27+402 96
Mount Pleasant, *S. Aust.* C66–348 109
Mount Pleasant, *Tennessee* T75+355 95
Mount Pleasant, *Texas* U30+332 95
Mount Pleasant, *Utah* V40+394 94
Mountrath, *Ireland, Rep.,* N45+530 43
Mount Robson Park, *B.C.* W00+530 88
Mounts B., *England* N33+500 38
Mount Sterling, *Kentucky* T54+381 97

Mount Stewart, *P.E.I.* S17+464 90
Mount Union, *Pennsylvania* T18+404 96
Mount Vernon, *Illinois* T84+384 95
Mount Vernon, *Indiana* T77+380 95
Mount Vernon, *Kentucky* T57+374 97
Mount Vernon, *Virginia* T13+387 91
Moura, *Brazil* S10–016 104
Moura, *Portugal* N45+381 52
Mourão, *Portugal* N44+384 52
Mourne Mts., *N. Ireland* N36+542 42
Mourne R., *N. Ireland* N45+548 42
Moussoro, *Chad* L80+136 81
Moutier, *Switzerland* M46+473 45
Moutohora, *New Zealand* A14–383 112
Mowlaik, *Burma* F64+236 71
Mowming, *China* E54+217 67
Mowping, *China* D80+374 66
Moy R., *Ireland, Rep.* N55+541 42
Moyale, *Kenya* K36+034 83
Moyobamba, *Peru* T12–062 104
Mozambique. rep., *E. Africa* K70–200 84
Moehga, *U.S.S.R.* J45+565 61
Mozyr, *Belorussia* L05+520 60
Mpanda, *Tanzania* K84–064 83
Mporokoso, *Zambia* K88–094 83
Mstislavl, *Belorussia* K80+541 60
Mtakuja, *Tanzania* K86–072 83
Mtarica, *Mozambique* K48–128 83
Mtito Andei, *Kenya* K40–028 83
Mtoko, *Rhodesia* K76–174 84
Mtsensk, *U.S.S.R.* K51+533 60
Mu, R., *Burma* F57+228 71
Muadhdham, el, *Saudi Arabia* K43+278 74
Muang Chaiya, *Thailand* F35+093 69
Muang Chana, *Thailand* F26+070 69
Muang Langsuan, *Thailand* F35+100 69
Muang Nan, *Thailand* F26+188 69
Muang Palien, *Thailand* F32+073 69
Mubarraz, *Saudi Arabia* J62+256 74
Mubende, *Uganda* K82+004 83
Muchinga Mts., *Zambia* K80–116 83
Muckish, *Ireland, Rep.* N48+551 42
Muckros Hd., *Ireland, Rep.* N52+546 42
Mudanya, *Turkey* L07+404 74
Mudawwara, *Jordan* K54+294 76
Muddusjarvi, *Finland* L19+691 46
Mudgee, *New S. Wales* C02–327 109
Mudhnib, *Saudi Arabia* K04+259 74
Mugford C., *Labrador* S13+582 89
Muggendorf, *W. Germany* M23+498 48
Mugia, *Spain* N55+431 52
Mugla, *Turkey* L10+372 74
Muglad, *Sudan* L14+110 81
Muhamdi, *India* G58+279 73
Muhammadabad, *Iran* J05+375 75
Muhammadgarh, *India* G71+237 73
Muharraq, *The Gulf* J56 + 264 75
Mühldorf. *W. Germany* M15+482 48
Mühlehorn, *Switzerland* M35+471 45
Mühlhausen, *E. Germany* M27+512 48
Muhu, *Estonia* L41+586 47
Muhu Väin, *Estonia* L40+588 47
Muinak, *Uzbek.* J06+438 62
Muine Bheag, *Ireland, Rep.* N42+527 43
Mukalla, *Yemen, South* J65+146 74
Mukdahan, *Thailand* F01+164 69
Mukden. *See* Shenyang
Mukhtuya, *U.S.S.R.* E30+607 63
Muktinath, *Nepal* G37+288 73
Muktsar, *India* H03+305 72
Muktui, *Mongolia* E80+492 64
Mula, *Spain* N08+380 53
Mulanje, Mt., *Malawi* K56–156 83
Mulchen, *Chile* S73–377 103
Mulege, *Mexico* V42+268 100
Mulgrave, *Nova Scotia* S08+456 90
Mulheim, *W. Germany* M48+510 48
Mulheim, *W. Germany* M49+515 48
Mulhouse, *France* M46+477 54
Mulki, *India* H01+131 70
Mull Hd., *Orkney, Scot.* N18+594 40
Mull, I., *Scotland* N36+564 41
Mull, Sd. of, *Scotland* N35+565 41
Mullaghareirk Mts., *Ireland, Rep.* N55+523 43
Mullaittivu, *Sri Lanka* G55+093 70
Mullaley, *New South Wales* C01–311 109
Muller Peg., *Borneo* E40+003 65
Mullet L., *Michigan* T57+455 91
Mullewa, *W. Australia* E27–284 110
Müllheim, *Switzerland* M36+476 45
Mullingar, *Ireland, Rep.* N44+535 43
Mullion Creek, *N.S.W.* C05–332 109
Muloorina, *S. Australia* C73–292 109
Muloowurtina, *S Australia* C60–301 109
Mulroy B., *Ireland, Rep.* N46+552 42
Multan, *Pakistan* H21+302 72
Multia, *Finland* L31+624 46
Multia, *Zambia* L18–150 82
Muna, *Indonesia* D75+050 65
Mundo Novo, *Brazil* Q63–118 105
Munfordville, *Kentucky* T65+373 97
Mungari, *Mozambique* K68–174 84
Mungindi, *N.S.W.-Qnsld.* C06–289 109
Munich. *See* Munchen
Muniesa, *Spain* N05+410 53
Munising, *Michigan* T70+464 91
Munkfors, *Sweden* M09+599 47
Munnerstadt, *W. Germany* M29+502 48
Munoz Gamero, Pen., *Chile* S80–526 103
Munroe, *Louisiana* U12+324 95
Münster, *W. Germany* M44+520 48
Münster, *Switzerland* M27+466 45
Münster, *Switzerland* M41+465 45
Munster, *Switzerland* M41+472 45
Munster, prov., *Ireland, Rep.* N52+523 43
Muong Attopeu, *Laos* E78+149 69
Muong Borikan, *Laos* F08+186 69
Muong Het, *Laos* F05+208 69
Muong Sing, *Laos* F23+212 69
Muong Son, *Laos,* Swed.-Fin. L39+677 46
Muonionalusta, *Sweden* L40+679 46
Muotathal, *Switzerland* M37+470 45
Mur, *Yemen* K12+156 74
Murakami, *Japan* C63+382 68
Murat, R., *Turkey* K28+388 74
Murat Dagh, *Turkey* L02+389 74

Murbat, *Oman* J31+171 75
Murça, *Portugal* N45+414 52
Murcheh Khur, *Iran* J52+331 75
Murchison, C., *N.-W. Terr.* S24+636 89
Murchison Falls, *see* Kabalega Falls
Murchison Mts., *N.Z.* A76–452 112
Murchison, R., *W. Aust.* E22–266 110
Murcia, *Spain* N07+380 53
Murdo, *S. Dakota* U65+438 93
Muresul (Maros), R.,
  Romania L54+462 58
Murfreesboro, *Tennessee* T68+358 93
Muri, *Switzerland* M40+473 45
Murias de Paredes, *Spain* N37+429 52
Müritz. *See, E. Germany* M14+534 48
Murjo, mt., *Java* E55–066 65
Murmansk, *U.S.S.R.* K70+690 62
Murom, *U.S.S.R.* K18+555 61
Muroran, *Japan* C54+423 68
Muros, *Spain* N54+428 52
Murphy, *N. Carolina* T54+351 97
Murphysboro, *Illinois* T86+378 95
Murray, *Kentucky* T80+366 95
Murray, *Utah* V42+406 98
Murray, R., *N.S.W.*, etc. C39–352 109
Murray Bridge, *S. Australia* C65–352 109
Murray Harbour, *P.E.I.* S15+460 90
Murray River, *P.E.I.* S16+460 90
Murrayville, *Victoria* C53–353 109
Murree, *Pakistan* H10+339 72
Mürren, *Switzerland* M43+466 45
Murrumbidgee, R., *N.S.W.* C35–346 109
Murrumburrah & Harden,
  New South Wales C10–346 109
Murrurundi, *New S. Wales* B85–318 109
Mursan, *India* G72+275 72
Murshidabad, *India* G10+243 73
Mursir, *Oman* J22+249 75
Murten & See, *Switzerland* M47+469 45
Murtoa, *Victoria* C45–367 109
Mururoa I., *Tuamotu Arch.* X10–215 107
Murwara, *India* G57+238 73
Murzuq, *Libya* M06+258 81
Mus, *Turkey* K21+388 74
Musa Kala, *Afghanistan* H61+323 75
Musalamiya, *Saudi Arabia* J65+275 74
Muscat (Masqat), *Oman* J09+236 75
Muscat & Oman. *See* Oman
Muscatine, *Iowa* U06+414 95
Musemir, *Yemen, South* K02+134 74
Musgrave Harb., *Nfd.* R52+495 90
Musgrave Ra., *New Guinea* C40–063 111
Musgrave Ra., *S. Australia* D20–260 110
Musheramore, *Ireland, Rep.* N54+520 43
Mushie, *Zaire* L78–030 82
Muskeget Chan., *Mass.* S62+413 96
Muskegon, *Michigan* T68+432 91
Muskegon R., *Michigan* T62+440 91
Muskogee, *Oklahoma* U33+359 95
Muskwaro, L., *Quebec* S06+506 90
Musmar, *Sudan* K56+180 81
Musoma, *Tanzania* K66–016 83
Mussau I., *Pacific Ocean* C00–020 106
Musselburgh, *Scotland* N18+559 41
Mussidan, *France* M88+450 55
Mussuma, *Angola* L48–142 82
Mustahil, *Ethiopia* K02+052 83
Mustajidda, *Saudi Arabia* K19+266 74
Mustang, *Nepal* G37+291 73
Mustang I., *Texas* U43+276 94
Musters, L., *Argentina* S56–455 103
Muswellbrook, *N.S.W.* B85–323 109
Mut, *Egypt* L06+254 81
Mut, *Turkey* K70+366 74
Mutanda, *Zambia* L22–124 82
Mutano, *Angola* M01–166 84
Mutorai, *U.S.S.R.* F27+615 63
Mutshatsha, *Zaire* L34–056 82
Mutsu B., *Japan* C53+411 68
Mutton I., *Ireland, Rep.* N57+528 43
Mutumbo, *Angola* L76–134 82
Mutupet, *India* G66+104 70
Muwale, *Tanzania* K68–064 83
Muy, le, *France* M50+435 55
Muya, *Japan* D02+342 68
Muya, *U.S.S.R.* E24+563 63
Muzaffarabad, *Kashmir* H09+344 72
Muzaffargarh, *Pakistan* H23+301 72
Muzaffarnagar, *India* G74+294 72
Muzaffarpur, *India* G27+261 73
Muzhi, *U.S.S.R.* H63+655 62
Muzquiz, *Mexico* U69+278 100
Muztagh Ata, *Sinkiang, China* G89+383 72
Mwanza, *Tanzania* K72–026 83
Mweelrea, *Ireland, Rep.* N59+536 42
Mweru L., *Zaire* L08–090 83
Mwinilunga, *Zambia* L34–120 82
Myanaung, *Burma* F58+182 71
Myall, L., *New S. Wales* B77–325 109
Myadaung, *Burma* F52+238 71
Myaungmya, *Burma* F60+166 71
Myebon, *Burma* F69+201 71
Myenmoletkhat, Mt., *Burma* F37+134 71
Myingyan, *Burma* F57+214 71
Myitkyina, *Burma* F45+254 71
Myjava, *Czechoslovakia* L74+488 49
Mymensingh, *Bangladesh* F87+248 71
Myohaung, *Burma* F53+219 71
Myohaung, *Burma* F71+206 71
Myrdal, *Norway* M47+607 47
Myrtle Creek, *S. Australia* C71–304 109
Myrtleford, *Victoria* C19–366 109
Myslowice, *Poland* L67+502 49
Mysore. *See* Karnataka
Mystic, *S. Dakota* U82+441 93
Mziha, *Tanzania* K44–058 83
Mzimba, *Malawi* K68–120 83
Naaf, *Bangladesh* F75+210 71
Naarden, *Netherlands* M59+523 44
Naas, *Ireland, Rep.* N40+532 43
Nabadwip, *India* G10+234 73
Naband, *Iran* J43+274 75
Nabatiye, *Lebanon* K57+334 76
Nabberu, L., *W. Australia* D87–257 110
Nabha, *India* G83+304 72
Nablus, *Jordan* K59+322 76
Nacaome, *Honduras* T75+136 101
Nachvak B., *Labrador* S21+592 89
Nacimiento. *Mexico* U71+279 100
Nackara, *S. Australia* C65–328 109

Naco, *Arizona* V30+313 **94**
Nacogdoches, *Texas* U28+316 **95**
Nacozari de Garcia, *Mexico* V29+305 **100**
Nadia. *See* Nabadwip
Nadiad, *India* H12+226 **70**
Naerøy, *Norway* M22+648 **46**
Naestved, *Denmark* M20+552 **47**
Nafels, *Switzerland* M36+471 **45**
Naga, *Yemen, D.R.* J64+149 **74**
Naga, *Philippines* D70+136 **65**
Naga Hills, *India* F60+262 **71**
Nagaland, *India* F64+262 **71**
Nagambie, *Victoria* C29–368 **109**
Nagano, *Japan* C71+366 **68**
Nagaoka, *Japan* C67+374 **68**
Nagappattinam, *India* G61+108 **70**
Nagar, *India* G77+321 **72**
Nagar, *Kashmir* H01+362 **72**
Nagar Karnul, *India* G70+164 **70**
Nagar Parkar, *India* H25+243 **70**
Nagasaki, *Japan* D31+327 **68**
Nagaur, *India* H07+270 **70**
Nagda, *India* G87+232 **70**
Nagercoil, *India* G74+083 **70**
Nagha Kalat, *Pakistan* H59+274 **70**
Nagina, *India* G69+295 **73**
Nagoya, *Japan* C78+351 **68**
Nagpur, *India* G65+210 **70**
Nagu, (Nauvo), *Finland* L49+602 **47**
Nagykanizsa, *Hungary* L78+465 **49**
Naha, *Japan* D44+262 **68**
Nahael Niyeu, *Argentina* S39–405 **103**
Nahan, *India* G76+305 **72**
Nahariya, *Israel* K59+330 **76**
Naibandan, *Iran* J15+323 **75**
Naifa, *Saudi Arabia* J53+199 **75**
Naifar, *Iraq* J89+322 **74**
Naihati, *India* G09+229 **73**
Nain, *Labrador* S11+563 **89**
Nain, *Iran* J41+329 **75**
Naini Tal, *India* G63+294 **73**
Nain Sing Ra., *Tibet* G50+326 **70**
Nairn, *Scotland* N23+576 **40**
Nairobi, *Kenya* K52–001 **83**
Naisecho, *Kenya* K48+018 **83**
Naismith, *Montana* V41+484 **93**
Naivasha, & L., *Kenya* K52–008 **83**
Najera, *Spain* N16+424 **53**
Najibabad, *India* G70+296 **73**
Najira, *Saudi Arabia* J70+280 **74**
Nakajo, *Japan* C64+381 **68**
Nakatsu, *Japan* D23+336 **68**
Nakawn Pathom, *Thailand* F30+138 **69**
Nakfa, *Ethiopia* K40+166 **83**
Nakhala, *Saudi Arabia* J53+243 **75**
Nakhaun Phantom, *Thailand* F02+174 **69**
Nakhichevan, *U.S.S.R.* J85+390 **62**
Nakhon Ratchasima, *Thai.* F17+149 **69**
Nakhon Sawan, *Thailand* F30+158 **69**
Nakhon Si Thammarat, *Thai.* F30+084 **69**
Nakina, *Ontario* T70+501 **89**
Nakl Mubarak, *Saudi Arabia* K40+243 **74**
Nakodar, *India* G87+311 **72**
Nakuru, *Kenya* K54–004 **83**
Nalagarh, *India* G79+310 **72**
Nalgonda, *India* G64+170 **70**
Nallamalai Hills, *India* G67+159 **70**
Nalut, *Libya* M24+318 **81**
Namangan, *Uzbek.* H20+412 **62**
Namasagali, *Uganda* K72+010 **83**
Namatail, *Mozambique* K32–158 **83**
Nambala, *Zambia* L18–152 **84**
Nambucca, *New S. Wales* B73–306 **109**
Namcha Barwa, *China* F58+295 **64**
Nam-dinh, *N. Vietnam* E83+204 **69**
Namhoi. *See* Fatshan
Namib Desert, *S.-W. Africa* M04–250 **84**
Namibia. *See* South-West Africa
Namlea, *Buru I., Indonesia* D48–034 **65**
Namling Dzong, *Tibet* G06+296 **71**
Nam Mao R., *Burma* F47+236 **71**
Namoi, *New South Wales* B88–310 **109**
Namonuito, Is., *Caroline Is.* C00+085 **106**
Namorona, *Madagascar* J72–218 **83**
Nampa, *Idaho* V70+436 **92**
Nampula, *Mozambique* K34–152 **83**
Nams Vatn, *Norway* M08+651 **46**
Namsen, R., *Norway* M14+647 **46**
Namsos, *Norway* M21+645 **46**
Namtsy, *U.S.S.R.* D31+627 **63**
Namtu, *Burma* F45+229 **71**
Namur & prov., *Belgium* M61+503 **44**
Namutoni, *S.-W. Africa* L78–188 **84**
Namwala, *Zambia* L22–158 **84**
Namyang, *China* E33+252 **67**
Nanaimo, *Brit. Columbia* W34+492 **88**
Nana Kru, *Liberia* N52+048 **80**
Nanan. *See* Tayu
Nanao, *Japan* C78+370 **68**
Nanchang, *China* E24+286 **67**
Nancheng (Hanchung), *China* E78+331 **66**
Nancheng (Kienchang), *China* E20+275 **67**
Nanchung, *China* E83+308 **66**
Nancy, *France* M55+487 **54**
Nanda Devi, mt., *India* G60+304 **70**
Nanded, *India* G75+192 **70**
Nandewar Ra., *N.S.W.* B86–302 **109**
Nanga Parbat, *Kashmir* H03+352 **72**
Nanguar, *Mozambique* K42–124 **83**
Nanjangud, *India* G79+121 **70**
Nankang. *See* Tsingtze
Nanking, *China* E07+320 **66**
Nannine, *W. Australia* E10–268 **110**
Nanning, *China* E70+228 **67**
Nanortalik, *Greenland* Q72+600 **26**
Nanpara, *India* G51+278 **73**
Nanping, *China* E11+267 **67**
Nanripo, *Mozambique* K36–140 **83**
Nan Shan, *China* F30+384 **62**
Nantan, *China* E74+251 **67**
Nantes, *France* N09+472 **54**
Nanticoke, *Pennsylvania* T06+412 **96**
Nantucket I., *Massachusetts* S60+412 **96**
Nantucket Sd., *Massachusetts* S62+414 **96**
Nantung, *China* D85+320 **66**
Nantwich, *England* N15+531 **37**
Nanyang, *China* E45+330 **66**
Nanyuki, *Kenya* K48+001 **83**
Naoetsu, *Japan* C70+371 **68**
Napa, *California* W14+383 **92**

Napanee, *Ontario* T12+442 **91**
Napas, *U.S.S.R.* G48+599 **62**
Napier, *New Zealand* A18–395 **112**
Naples. *See* Napoli
Napoleon, *N. Dakota* U58+465 **93**
Napoli, *Italy* M05+409 **57**
Napoli, G. di, *Italy* M07+406 **57**
Naqb Ashtar, *Jordan* K57+300 **76**
Nara, *Mali* N44+152 **80**
Nara, *Japan* C85+347 **68**
Naracoorte, *S. Australia* C56–370 **109**
Naradhan, *New S. Wales* C22–336 **109**
Narativat, *Thailand* F19+064 **69**
Narayanganj, *Bangladesh* F82+236 **71**
Narbada R., *India* G68+230 **73**
Narberth, *Wales* N28+518 **38**
Narbonne, *France* M72+432 **55**
Nares Ld., *Greenland* R25+820 **26**
Nari R., *Pakistan* H43+284 **70**
Narino. *See* Japura
Narken, *Sweden* L44+670 **46**
Narnaul, *India* G85+281 **72**
Narok, *Kenya* K56–012 **83**
Narooma, *New South Wales* B89–363 **109**
Narovchat, *U.S.S.R.* K08+538 **61**
Narowal, *Pakistan* H01+321 **72**
Narrabri, *New South Wales* C01–303 **109**
Narrabri West, *N.S.W.* C02–304 **109**
Narragansett B., *Rhode I.* S69+414 **96**
Narran L. & R., *N.S.W.* C16–296 **109**
Narranderra, *New S. Wales* C21–348 **109**
Narrogin, *W. Australia* E17–328 **110**
Narromine, *New S. Wales* C10–323 **109**
Narsinghgarh, *India* G77+238 **70**
Narsinghpur, *India* G65+229 **73**
Naruta, *Japan* D02+342 **68**
Narva, *Estonia* L11+593 **47**
Narva Laht, *Estonia* L16+596 **47**
Narvik, *Norway* L75+685 **46**
Narwar, *India* G73+257 **73**
Naryan Mar, *U.S.S.R.* J40+677 **62**
Narykary, *U.S.S.R.* H60+634 **62**
Narym, *U.S.S.R.* G50+589 **62**
Naryn, *Kirgiz.* G84+414 **62**
Naseby, *New Zealand* A59–450 **112**
Nashua and R., *N.H.* S69+428 **96**
Nashville, *Arkansas* U22+339 **95**
Nashville, *Illinois* T86+384 **95**
Nashville, *N. Carolina* T18+360 **97**
Nashville, *Tennessee* T71+361 **97**
Nasijarvi, *Finland* L38+616 **47**
Nasia, *Ghana* N04+100 **80**
Nasik, *India* H07+200 **70**
Nasirabad, *India* H01+262 **70**
Naskaupi R., *Labrador* S10+542 **89**
Nassau, *Bahama Is.* T15+250 **101**
Nassau, G. de, *Chile* S46–555 **103**
Nassau, I., *Pacific Ocean* Z03–114 **106**
Nasser, L., *Egypt* K82+216 **81**
Nassjo, *Sweden* M02+577 **47**
Nata, *Panama* T33+084 **101**
Natal, *Brazil* Q31–058 **105**
Natal, *Brazil* S01–068 **104**
Natal, *South Africa* L00–286 **84**
Natal, *Sumatra* F35+006 **65**
Natanes Plat., *Arizona* V26+334 **94**
Natanya, *Israel* K61+323 **76**
Natashquan, *Quebec* S11+502 **90**
Natashquan R., *Quebec* S10+514 **89**
Natchez, *Mississippi* U08+316 **93**
Natimuk, *Victoria* C48–367 **109**
National City, *California* V73+325 **92**
Natividade, *Brazil* R16–115 **105**
Natron L., *Tanzania* K54–024 **83**
Nattavaara, *Sweden* L54+667 **46**
Naturaliste, C., *W. Aust.* E82–384 **110**
Naturawit L., *N.-W. Terr.* U51+635 **88**
Naukhas, *S.-W. Africa* L82–236 **84**
Naumburg, *E. Germany* M19+512 **48**
Naumestis, *Lithuania* L43+548 **47**
Naumiestis, *Lithuania* L50+554 **47**
Nauplia. *See* Navplion
Naur, *Jordan* K55+319 **76**
Nauru, I., *Pacific Ocean* A78–003 **106**
Naushahra. *See* Nowshera
Naushahro, *Pakistan* H41+268 **70**
Naushk, *U.S.S.R.* E84+505 **62**
Nauta, *Peru* S81–045 **104**
Nautla, *Mexico* U41+202 **96**
Nauvoo, *Illinois* T86+406 **95**
Nava del Rey, *Spain* N30+414 **52**
Navajo, Mt., *Utah* V36+370 **94**
Navalcarnero, *Spain* N24+403 **52**
Navalmoral, *Spain* N33+399 **52**
Navan, *Ireland, Rep.* N40+537 **42**
Navarino, I., *Chile* S46–550 **99**
Navarre, *Victoria* C42–369 **109**
Navarre, prov., *France* N07+433 **55**
Navojoa, *Mexico* V26+272 **96**
Navplion, *Greece* L43+376 **59**
Navrongo, *Ghana* N06+108 **80**
Navsari, *India* H12+209 **70**
Nawa, *Syria* K54+329 **76**
Nawabganj, *India* G47+269 **73**
Nawabganj, *India* G53+269 **73**
Nawada, *India* G26+249 **73**
Nawah Basoda, *India* G70+236 **73**
Nawahganj, *India* G62+285 **73**
Nawai, *India* G84+264 **70**
Nawalgarh, *India* G88+278 **72**
Naxos, I., *Greece* L27+370 **59**
Nayakhan, *U.S.S.R.* B38+620 **63**
Nayarit, state, *Mexico* V00+220 **96**
Nayarit, Sa. de, *Mexico* U84+226 **96**
Nayoro, *Japan* C44+443 **63**
Nazaré de Mata, *Brazil* Q3 –077 **105**
Nazareth, *Belgium* M69+509 **44**
Nazareth, *Israel* K58+327 **76**
Nazas, *Mexico* U85+252 **96**
Nazca, *Peru* S88–148 **104**
Naze, The, *England* M82+519 **39**
Naze, The (Lindesnes), *Nor.* M47+580 **47**
Nazilli, *Turkey* L10+379 **74**
Nazimovo, *U.S.S.R.* F83+595 **63**
Ncheu, *Malawi* K62–148 **83**
Ndala, *Tanzania* K70–046 **83**
Ndeni, I., *Santa Cruz Is.* A82–105 **106**
N'Djamena, *Chad* M00+122 **81**
Ndola, *Zambia* L08–130 **83**
Neagh L., *N. Ireland* N38+546 **42**
Neapolis, *Crete* L26+353 **59**

Near Is., *Aleutian Islands* A40+517 **95**
Neath, *Wales* N23+517 **38**
Nebikon, *Switzerland* M42+472 **45**
Nebit-Dag, *Turkmen.* J36+392 **62**
Nebo Mt., *Utah* V41+398 **94**
Nebraska, state, *U.S.A.* U73+416 **98**
Nebraska City, *Nebraska* U35+406 **95**
Necedah, *Wisconsin* U00+440 **91**
Neckar, R., *W. Germany* M36+492 **48**
Necochea, *Argentina* R83–386 **103**
Nederweert, *Netherlands* M56+513 **44**
Neede, *Netherlands* M50+521 **44**
Needham Market, *England* M84+522 **39**
Needles, *California* V58+348 **92**
Needles, The, *N.S.W.* C55+345 **92**
Needles, The, *England* N10+507 **39**
Neemuch, *India* H00+245 **70**
Neenah, *Wisconsin* T81+442 **91**
Neerpelt, *Belgium* M57+512 **44**
Nefud Des., *Saudi Arabia* K30+288 **74**
Negaunee, *Michigan* T75+465 **91**
Negocio, *Argentina* S35–418 **103**
Negombo, *Sri Lanka* G61+073 **70**
Negra Pta., *Peru* T36–060 **104**
Negrais, C., *Burma* F65+160 **71**
Negro, R., *Argentina* S30–398 **103**
Negro, R., *Brazil* S20–004 **104**
Negro, R., *Uruguay* R60–324 **103**
Negros, I., *Philippines* D72+100 **65**
Nehavend, *Iran* J71+343 **74**
Nehbandan, *Iran* J00+315 **75**
Neilsville, *Wisconsin* U04+446 **91**
Neisse. *See* Nysa
Neiva, *Colombia* T02+027 **104**
Nejd, *Saudi Arabia* K18+256 **74**
Neksø, *Bornholm I., Den.* L89+551 **47**
Nelia Gaari, *New S. Wales* C43–321 **109**
Nelkan, *U.S.S.R.* C84+577 **63**
Nelligen, *New South Wales* B89–356 **109**
Nellore, *India* G60+145 **70**
Nelma, *U.S.S.R.* C65+475 **63**
Nelson, *Brit. Columbia* V73+495 **88**
Nelson, *New Zealand* A40–413 **112**
Nelson, *Victoria* C54–381 **109**
Nelson, C., *Victoria* C51–384 **109**
Nelson Hd., *N.-W. Terr.* W10+710 **88**
Nelson L., *Manitoba* U63+557 **88**
Nelson, Mt., *Brit. Columbia* V68+504 **88**
Nelson R., *Manitoba* U25+562 **88**
Nema, *Mauritania* N44+166 **80**
Nemecke Pravno, *Czech.* L68+489 **49**
Nemikachi L., *Quebec* S87+475 **91**
Nemours, (Ghazaouet), *Alg.* N10+350 **80**
Nemours, *France* M74+482 **54**
Nemunas, R., *Lithuania* L40+551 **47**
Nemuro, *Japan* C26+433 **68**
Nemuro B., *Japan* C28+434 **68**
Nen R., *England* N03+526 **37**
Nenagh, *Ireland, Rep.* N49+528 **43**
Nendeln, *Liechtenstein* M33+472 **45**
Neodesha, *Kansas* U35+374 **95**
Neosho, *Missouri* U26+368 **95**
Nepa, *U.S.S.R.* E71+592 **63**
Nepal, *Asia* G50+270 **30**
Nepalganj, *Nepal* G50+280 **73**
Nephi, *Utah* V42+396 **94**
Nephin, *Ireland, Rep.* N56+540 **42**
Nephin Beg, *Ireland, Rep.* N58+540 **43**
Nérac, *France* M88+441 **55**
Nerchinsk, *U.S.S.R.* E19+520 **63**
Nerpio, *Spain* N14+382 **53**
Nerriga, *New South Wales* C00–352 **109**
Nes, *U.S.S.R.* K03+667 **62**
Nesna, *Norway* M12+662 **46**
Nespawa, *Manitoba* U57+503 **88**
Ness L., *Scotland* N27+573 **40**
Ness City, *Kansas* U60–384 **95**
Nesset, *Norway* M42+628 **46**
Nesslau, *Switzerland* M35+472 **45**
Nesthorn, mt., *Switzerland* M42+464 **45**
Nesttun, *Norway* M58+603 **47**
Nettilling L., *N.-W. Terr.* S65+662 **89**
Nettuno, *Italy* M14+415 **57**
Neubrandenburg, *E. Germany* M10+535 **48**
Neuburg, *W. Germany* M23+487 **48**
Neuchâtel & canton, *Switz.* M48+470 **45**
Neuchâtel, L. de, *Switz.* M49+445 **45**
Neufchâteau, *Belgium* M57+498 **44**
Neufchâtel, *France* M56+483 **54**
Neufchâtel, *France* M82+498 **54**
Neufelden, *Austria* M06+485 **48**
Neuhausen, *Switzerland* M38+477 **45**
Neumünster, *W. Germany* M30+541 **48**
Neunkirch, *Switzerland* M39+477 **45**
Neuquen, *Argentina* S49–389 **103**
Neuse R., *N. Carolina* T14+353 **97**
Neusiedler See, *Austria* L79+477 **49**
Neuss, *W. Germany* M50+512 **48**
Neustadt, *W. Germany* M25+541 **48**
Neustettin. *See* Szczecinek
Neustrelitz, *E. Germany* M12+533 **48**
Neu Ulm, *W. Germany* M30+484 **48**
Neuva, I., *Chile & Argent.* S40–552 **103**
Neuva Esperanza, *Bolivia* S28–158 **104**
Neuva Lubeca, *Argentina* S63–446 **103**
Neuve Eglise, *Belgium* M73+508 **44**
Neuveville, *Switzerland* M47+471 **45**
Neuvitas, *Cuba* T14+215 **101**
Nevada, *Iowa* U20+422 **95**
Nevada, *Missouri* U26+378 **95**
Nevada, state, *U.S.A.* V81+395 **98**
Nevada, Sa., *U.S.A.* V12+411 **98**
Nevada, Sa., *Spain* N20+370 **52**
Nevel, *U.S.S.R.* L00+560 **60**
Nevel'sk, *U.S.S.R.* C48+465 **63**
Nevers, *France* M71+470 **54**
Nevertire, *New South Wales* C14–319 **109**
Nevesinje, *Yugoslavia* L71+432 **58**
Neveyezhkino, *U.S.S.R.* K01+512 **61**
Nevis, I., *Leeward Islands* S15+172 **101**
Nevshir, *Turkey* K62+386 **74**
Nevyansk, *U.S.S.R.* H89+574 **61**
New Albany, *Indiana* T65+383 **99**
New Albany, *Mississippi* T84+345 **95**
New Amsterdam, *Guyana* R76+061 **105**
Newark, *Delaware* T04+397 **96**
Newark, *England* N05+531 **37**
Newark, *New Jersey* S85+407 **96**

Newark, *Ohio* T45+401 **91**
Newaygo, *Michigan* T65+434 **91**
New Bedford, *Massachusetts* S65+416 **96**
New Bern, *N. Carolina* T12+351 **97**
Newbern, *Tennessee* T86+362 **97**
Newberry, *Michigan* T63+463 **91**
Newberry, *S. Carolina* T40+343 **97**
New Bloomfield, *Pa* T14+404 **96**
New Britain, *Bismarck Archipelago* B85–060 **106**
New Britain, *Connecticut* S76+417 **96**
New Brunswick, *New Jersey* S87+405 **96**
New Brunswick, prov., *Canada* S36+470 **89**
Newburg, *New Brunswick* S45+463 **90**
Newburgh, *New York* S84+414 **96**
Newburgh, *Scotland* N19+563 **41**
Newbury, *England* N08+514 **39**
Newburyport, *Massachusetts* S65+428 **96**
Newby Bridge, *England* N18+543 **37**
New Caledonia, *Pacific Oc.* A85–212 **106**
New Carlisle, *Quebec* S32+480 **90**
Newcastle, *Delaware* T03+397 **91**
Newcastle, *Natal* L00–278 **84**
Newcastle, *New Brunswick* S34+470 **90**
New Castle, *New Jersey* T04+397 **96**
Newcastle, *New South Wales* B80–330 **109**
Newcastle, *N. Ireland* N35+542 **42**
New Castle, *Pennsylvania* T32+411 **91**
Newcastle, *Wyoming* U86+439 **93**
Newcastle Emlyn, *Wales* N27+520 **38**
Newcastle-under-Lyme, *Eng.* N13+530 **37**
Newcastle-upon-Tyne, *Eng.* N10+550 **37**
Newcastle Waters, *N.T., Australia* D09–173 **111**
Newchwang. *See* Yingkow
New City, *New York* S84+411 **96**
New Cumberland, *W. Va.* T34+405 **91**
New England Ra., *N.S.W.* B80–306 **109**
Newfane, *Vermont* S76+430 **96**
New Forest, *England* N10+508 **39**
Newfoundland, prov., *Canada* R70+490 **89**
New Galloway, *Scotland* N25+551 **41**
New Georgia, I., *Soloman Is.* B48–080 **105**
New Glasgow, *Nova Scotia* S16+456 **90**
New Guinea, *Pacific Ocean* C60–060 **31**
New Hampshire, state, *U.S.A.* S70+435 **99**
New Hampton, *Iowa* U14+430 **95**
New Haven, *Connecticut* S78+413 **91**
Newhaven, *England* N00+508 **39**
New Haven, *Missouri* U08+386 **97**
New Hebrides, Is., *Pac. Oc.* A70–170 **106**
New Iberia, *Lousiana* U11+300 **95**
New Ireland, *Bismarck Arch.* B75–040 **106**
New Jersey, state, *U.S.A.* S89+404 **99**
New Liskeard, *Ontario* T28+475 **91**
Newe London, *Connecticut* S73+413 **96**
New London, *Wisconsin* T83+445 **91**
New Madrid, *Missouri* T88+366 **95**
Newmarket, *England* M88+522 **39**
Newmarket, *Ireland, Rep.* N54+522 **43**
Newmarket, *Ontario* T27+441 **91**
New Mexico, state, *U.S.A.* V20+344 **98**
Newnes, *New South Wales* B89–332 **109**
Newnham, *England* N16+518 **38**
New Norfolk, *Tasmania* C18–428 **109**
New Orleans, *Louisiana* U00+300 **95**
New Plymouth, *N.Z.* A36–390 **112**
Newport, *Arkansas* U08+356 **97**
Newport, *Ireland, Rep.* N57+539 **42**
Newport, *I. of W., England* N08+507 **39**
Newport, *Kentucky* T57+391 **91**
Newport, *New Hampshire* S73+434 **96**
Newport, *Quebec* S29+483 **90**
Newport, *Rhode Island* S68+415 **91**
Newport, *Vermont* S73+449 **91**
Newport, *Wales* N18+516 **38**
Newport News, *Virginia* T08+370 **97**
Newport-on-Tay, *Scotland* N18+564 **41**
New Providence, I., *Bahamas, The* T15+250 **101**
Newquay, *England* N30+504 **38**
New Quay, *Wales* N26+522 **38**
New Radnor, *Wales* N19+522 **38**
New Richmond, *Quebec* S35+482 **90**
New Richmond, *Wisconsin* U15+452 **93**
New Rochelle, *New York* S82+409 **96**
New Rockford, *N. Dakota* U55+477 **93**
New Ross, *Ireland, Rep.* N42+524 **43**
New Salem, *N. Dakota* U68+469 **93**
New Siberian Islands, *See* Novosibirskiye Ostrova
New South Wales, state, *Aust — * **111**
Newton, *Iowa* U18+416 **95**
Newton, *Kansas* U44+381 **95**
Newton, *Massachusetts* S67+424 **96**
Newton, *New Jersey* S89+410 **96**
Newton-Abbot, *England* N22+505 **38**
Newtonmore, *Scotland* N25+571 **40**
Newton-Stewart, *Scotland* N27+550 **41**
Newtown, *Wales* N20+525 **38**
Newtownards, *N. Ireland* N34+546 **42**
Newtown Butler, *N. Ireland* N44+542 **42**
Newtown Hamilton, *N. Ire.* N39+542 **42**
Newtonstewart, *N. Ire.* N44+547 **42**
New Ulm, *Minnesota* U27+443 **93**
New Waterford, *Nova Scotia* S00+463 **90**
New Westminster, *B.C.* W18+492 **88**
New World I., *Nfd.* R59+496 **90**
New York, *New York* S84+408 **91**
New York, state, *U.S.A.* T20+425 **99**
New Zealand, *Australasia — * **112**
Nexö. *See* Neksö.
Neya, *U.S.S.R.* K06+583 **61**
Nezhin, *Ukraine* K79+511 **60**
Ngami, L., *Botswana* L40–210 **84**
Nganglaring Tso, *Tibet* G42+315 **71**
N'Gaoundéré, *Cameroun* M08+074 **81**
Ngapara, *New Zealand* A55–450 **112**
Ngaruawehia, *New Zealand* A29–377 **112**
Ngatik, I., *Caroline Islands* B47+050 **106**
Ngauruhoe, Mt., *N.Z.* A26–391 **112**
Ngeuni, *Sudan* L14+060 **81**
Ngong, *Kenya* K50–014 **83**
Ngoring Nor, *China* F42+348 **64**
Nguigmi, *Niger* M12+142 **81**

Ngulu, I., *Pacific Ocean* C78+075 **106**
Ngwasi, *Tanzania* K46-086 **83**
Nha-Trang, *S. Vietnam* E65+123 **69**
Nhill, *Victoria* C50-363 **109**
Niafounke, *Mali* N24+160 **80**
Niagara, *Ontario* T25+433 **91**
Niagara Falls, *New York* T24+431 **91**
Niagara Falls, *Ontario* T24+431 **91**
Niah, *Sarawak* E38+037 **65**
Niamey, *Niger* M78+134 **80**
Nia Nia, *Zaire* L14+014 **83**
Niapa, mt., *Borneo* E15+017 **65**
Nias, I., *Indonesia* F44+011 **65**
Nicaragua, rep., *Cent. Amer.* T62+130 **101**
Nicaragua L., *Nicaragua* T63+116 **101**
Nicastro, *Italy* L82+390 **57**
Nic Doit Soe Pk., *Arizona* V36+364 **94**
Nice, *France* M47+437 **55**
Nicobar Is., *Indian Ocean* F70+085 **71**
Nicolet, *Quebec* S76+462 **91**
Nicoque, *Mozambique* K36-128 **83**
Nicosia, *Cyprus* K70+352 **76**
Nicoya & Pen., *Costa Rica* T62+100 **101**
Nidau, *Switzerland* M47+471 **45**
Nidd R., *England* N10+540 **37**
Nidzica, *Poland* L57+533 **49**
Niedere Tauern, *Austria* M06+473 **48**
Niedersachsen, *W. Germany* M42+528 **48**
Nielle, *Ivory Coast* N34+102 **80**
Niére, *Chad* L50+142 **81**
Nieuw Amsterdam, *Surinam* R60+058 **105**
Nieuwendijk, *Netherlands* M61+518 **44**
Nieuwersluis, *Netherlands* M60+522 **44**
Nieuwkoop *Netherlands* M61+522 **44**
Nieuw Nickerie, *Surinam* R73+058 **105**
Nieuwpoort, *Belgium* M73+511 **44**
Nieuwpoort, *Netherlands* M61+519 **44**
Nieves, *Mexico* U78+240 **100**
Nièvre, dep., *France* M68+471 **54**
Nigde, *Turkey* K62+380 **74**
Niger, rep., *W. Africa* M30+156 **81**
Niger R., *W. Africa* N10+150 **80**
Nigeria, *W. Africa* M40+100 **80**
Nighasan, *India* G55+282 **73**
Nigula, *Estonia* L20+595 **47**
Niigata, *Japan* C66+379 **68**
Niihau, I., *Hawaiian Is.* Y60+220 **106**
Niitaka Chain, *Taiwan* D84+240 **67**
Nijil, *Jordan* K57+305 **76**
Nijkerk, *Netherlands* M58+522 **44**
Nijmegen, *Netherlands* M55+518 **44**
Nikaria. *See* Ikaria, I.
Nikiforos, *Greece* L34+412 **58**
Nikki, *Benin* M72+098 **80**
Nikko Nat. Park, *Japan* C64+368 **68**
Nikolayevskiy, *U.S.S.R.* J87+501 **61**
Nikolayev, *Ukraine* K78+470 **60**
Nikolayevsk-na-Amure, *U.S.S.R.* C56+533 **63**
Nikolo Kozelsk, *Ukraine* K71+476 **60**
Nikolskaya Pestrovka, *U.S.S.R.* J84+538 **61**
Nikolsk Berezovka, *U.S.S.R.* J35+561 **61**
Nikopol, *Ukraine* K63+476 **60**
Niksar, *Turkey* K48+407 **74**
Nikšić, *Yugoslavia* L66+428 **58**
Nila, I., *Indonesia* D33-068 **65**
Nile, R., *N. Africa* K72+250 **81**
Niles, *Michigan* T68+418 **91**
Nilgiri, *India* G19+214 **71**
Nilgiri Hills, *India* G81+116 **70**
Nilphamari, *Bangladesh* G07+259 **73**
Nimach, (Neemuch), *India* H00+245 **70**
Nimes, *France* M64+439 **55**
Nimgiri, Mt., *India* G39+196 **71**
Nimmitabel, *New S. Wales* C05-365 **109**
Nine de Julio, *Argentina* S05-354 **99**
Ninety Mile Beach, *Victoria* C16-382 **109**
Nineveh, *Iraq* K11+366 **74**
Ningan, *China* D33+444 **64**
Ninganpao, *China* E86+373 **66**
Ningerh, *China* F25+231 **64**
Ninghai, *China* D81+293 **67**
Ninghsien, *China* E37+267 **67**
Ninghsien. *See* Ningpo
Ningiang, *China* E44+283 **67**
Ningkwo. *See* Suancheng
Ninglingting. *See* Kinki
Ningpo, *China* D80+298 **67**
Ning-sia. *See* Yingchwan
Ningteh, *China* E03+267 **67**
Ning-wu-fu, *China* E46+390 **66**
Ning-yüan chow, *China* D86+405 **66**
Ning-yüan-ting, *China* E44+403 **66**
Ninh-binh, *N. Vietnam* E84+203 **69**
Ninh Hoa, *S. Vietnam* E66+140 **65**
Ninove, *Belgium* M66+508 **44**
Niobrara R., *Nebraska* U71+424 **98**
Nioet, mt., *Borneo* E60+010 **65**
Nioro, *Mali* N58+152 **80**
Niort, *France* N03+463 **54**
Nios. *See* Ios, I.
Nipe, B. de, *Cuba* T04+208 **101**
Nipigon, *Ontario* T80+492 **89**
Nipigon, L., *Ontario* T80+500 **89**
Nipissing, L., *Ontario* T29+462 **91**
Nirmal, *India* G69+191 **70**
Nis, *Yugoslavia* L49+433 **58**
Nisab, *Saudi Arabia* J81+149 **74**
Nisehu, *Kashmir* G65+346 **70**
Nish. *See* Nis
Nishapur. *See* Neyshābūr,
Nishio, *Japan* C77+348 **68**
Nisiros, I., *Greece* L17+384 **59**
Nissan, *Solomon Islands* B60-053 **106**
Nissi, *Estonia* L34+591 **47**
Niteroi, *Brazil* Q79-228 **105**
Nith, R., *Scotland* N22+550 **41**
Nitra, *Czechoslovakia* L71+483 **49**
Niue, I. *Cook Islands* Z30-190 **106**
Nivala, *Finland* L30+639 **46**
Nivelles, *Belgium* M64+506 **44**
Nivernais, prov., *France* M68+471 **54**
Nizamabad, *India* G71+187 **70**
Nizampatnam, *India* G55+159 **70**
Nizana, *Israel* K63+309 **76**
Nizhne Chirskaya, *U.S.S.R.* K12+484 **61**
Nizhne Udinsk, *U.S.S.R.* F35+549 **63**
Nizhi Pesha, *U.S.S.R.* J73+668 **62**
Nizhniye Serogozy, *Ukraine* K64+469 **60**
Nizhniy Kresty, *U.S.S.R.* B25+687 **63**
Nizhiy Lomov, *U.S.S.R.* K02+536 **61**

Nizhniy Tagil, *U.S.S.R.* J01+579 **61**
Nizke Tatry, *Czechoslovakia* L63+490 **49**
Njombe, *Tanzania* K60-094 **83**
Nkhota-Kota, *Malawi* K64-130 **84**
N'Kongsamba, *Cameroun* M30+050 **81**
Nmai R., *Burma* F41+264 **71**
Noagarh, *India* G47+204 **71**
Noakhali. *See* Sudharam
Noanama, *Colombia* T13+047 **104**
Noatak R., *Alaska* Y60+675 **99**
Nobber, *Ireland, Rep.* N40+538 **42**
Nochistlan, *Mexico* U44+174 **100**
Noerbø, *Norway* M56+587 **47**
Nogales, *Arizona* V36+313 **94**
Nogaro, *France* N00+438 **55**
Nogent-le-Rotrou, *France* M85+483 **54**
Nogent-sur-Seine, *France* M69+485 **54**
Noginsk, *U.S.S.R.* K40+558 **60**
Nohar, *India* H02+292 **72**
Noirmoutier, I. de, *France* N14+470 **54**
Nokhtuysk, *U.S.S.R.* E11+600 **63**
Nola, *Cent. Afr. Rep.* L84+034 **82**
Nola, *Italy* M03+409 **57**
Nome, *Alaska* Z00+642 **99**
Nomining Ls., *Quebec* T00+465 **91**
Nomoi, Is., *Caroline Islands* B65+060 **106**
Nonacho L., *N.-W. Terr.* V30+614 **88**
Nonancourt, *France* M83+488 **54**
Nong-han, *Thailand* F11+174 **69**
Nong Khai, *Thailand* F13+179 **69**
Nongoma, *Natal* K80-280 **84**
Nonni, R. (Nun), *China* D64+488 **64**
Nonoava, *Mexico* V10+274 **100**
Nonouti, I., *Gilbert Islands* A35-005 **106**
Nöo, *Estonia* L21+583 **47**
Noojee, *Victoria* C24-379 **109**
Noonthorungee, *N.S.W.* C46-310 **109**
Noordeloos, *Netherlands* M60+519 **44**
Noordwolde, *Netherlands* M53+529 **44**
Nootka I., *Brit. Columbia* W41+498 **88**
Nootongoro, *Tanzania* K62-032 **83**
Nora, *Sweden* M00+595 **47**
Noranda, *Quebec* T25+482 **91**
Nord, dep., *France* M71+505 **54**
Nord Cap (Horn), *Iceland* P44+665 **46**
Norddal, *Norway* M47+623 **46**
Nordenshelda, Arkh., *U.S.S.R.* F55+762 **63**
Nordhausen, *E. Germany* M25+515 **48**
Nordkapp, *Norway* L72+709 **46**
Nordkyn Halvøy, *Norway* L12+709 **46**
Nördlingen, *W. Germany* M27+489 **48**
Nordost Rundingen, *Greenland* N60+810 **26**
Nordreisa, *Norway* L54+688 **46**
Nordrhein-Westfalen, *W. Ger.* M48+518 **48**
Nord Slesvig. *See* Jylland, South
Nordstrand I., *W. Germany* M37+545 **48**
Nordvik, *U.S.S.R.* E53+739 **63**
Nore, *Norway* M36+601 **47**
Nore R., *Ireland, Rep.* N42+523 **43**
Norfolk, *Nebraska* U44+422 **95**
Norfolk, *Virginia* T08+369 **97**
Norfolk, co., *England* M84+527 **39**
Norfolk Broads, *England* M81+527 **39**
Norfolk I., *Pacific Ocean* A72-290 **106**
Norfolk Res., *Arkansas* U14+364 **95**
Norgama, *Pakistan* H50+286 **70**
Norheimsund, *Norway* M53+603 **47**
Norily, *U.S.S.R.* G06+694 **62**
Norman, *N.-W. Territories* W32+649 **88**
Norman, *Oklahoma* U44+352 **95**
Normandie, prov., *France* N00+488 **54**
Normanby I., *Papua New Guinea* B84-100 **111**
Normanton, *Queensland* C53-176 **111**
Norman Wells, *N.-W. Terr.* W40+652 **88**
Norquin, *Argentina* S64-377 **103**
Norquinco, *Argentina* S66-418 **103**
Norris, L., *Tennessee* T54+364 **97**
Norris Arm, *Newfoundland* R61+491 **90**
Norristown, *Pennsylvania* T02+402 **96**
Norrköping, *Sweden* L83+586 **47**
Norrsundet, *Sweden* L78+610 **47**
Norrtalje, *Sweden* L68+598 **47**
Norseman, *W. Australia* D80-321 **110**
Norsholm, *Sweden* L84+585 **47**
North C., *Antarctica* A80-700 **27**
North C., *New Zealand* A42-344 **112**
North Chan., *Scot.-N. Ire.* N33+550 **42**
North Chan., *Scot.-N. Ire.* T50+461 **91**
North Downs, *England* M87+513 **39**
North I., *New Zealand* **112**
North Pt., *Prince Edward I.* S24+471 **90**
North Sea, *W. Europe* **34**
North Adams, *Massachusetts* S78+427 **96**
Northallerton, *England* N08+543 **37**
Northam, *W. Australia* E20-316 **110**
Northampton, *Massachusetts* S76+424 **96**
Northampton, *W. Australia* E32-282 **110**
Northampton & co., *Eng.* N05+523 **37**
North Bay, *Ontario* T27+463 **91**
North Bend, *Oregon* W25+434 **96**
North Berwick, *Scotland* N16+560 **41**
North Borneo (Sabah), *Borneo* E21+054 **65**
North Bourke, *N.S.W.* C24-300 **109**
Northbridge, *Massachusetts* S70+422 **96**
North Carolina, state, *U.S.A.* T40+358 **99**
North Creek, *New York* S84+437 **91**
North Dakota, state, *U.S.A.* U78+472 **98**
Northern Circars, *India* G50+165 **70**
Northern Ireland, *Brit. Isles* N40+544 **34**
Northern Territory, *Aust.* **110-111**
Northfield, *Minnesota* U19+445 **93**
North Land. *See* Severnaya Zemlya
North Lisbon, *Wisconsin* U01+439 **91**
North Little Rock, *Arkansas* U13+348 **99**
North Platte, *Nebraska* U64+411 **94**
North Pole, *Arctic Ocean* **26**
North Riding, *see* North Yorkshire
North Ronaldsay, I. & Firth, *Orkney, Scotland* N14+594 **40**
North Shields, *England* N09+550 **37**
North Sydney, *Nova Scotia* S02+462 **90**
North Tonawanday. *N.Y.* T23+430 **96**
North Truchas Pk., *N. Mex.* V04+360 **94**
Northumberland, co., *Eng.* N13+553 **37**
Northumberland, *Pa.* T11+409 **96**

Northumberland Str., *New Brunswick, etc.* S27+465 **90**
North Vancouver, *B.C.* W19+494 **88**
Northville, *New York* S86+433 **91**
North West C., *W. Aust.* E35-218 **110**
North-West River, *Labrador* S01+537 **89**
North-West Territories, *Can.* **88-89**
Northwich, *England* N15+532 **37**
Northwood, *Iowa* U19+434 **95**
Norton, *Kansas* U60+398 **95**
Norton, *New Brunswick* S34+456 **90**
Norton Sd., *Alaska* Z00+636 **99**
Norwalk, *Connecticut* S81+411 **96**
Norwalk, *Ohio* T46+413 **91**
Norway, king., *N.-W. Europe* **46-47**
Norwich, *Connecticut* S72+415 **96**
Norwich, *England* M82+526 **39**
Norwich, *New York* T03+425 **96**
Norwood, *Massachusetts* S67+422 **96**
Norwood, *New York* T00+447 **91**
Noshiro, *Japan* C60+402 **68**
Nossegem, *Belgium* M63+509 **44**
Nosy Be. I., *Madagascar* J70-134 **83**
Noto, *Sicily* L89+368 **57**
Noto Pen., *Japan* C80+372 **68**
Notodden, *Norway* M38+595 **47**
Notre Dame B., *Nfd.* R60+497 **90**
Notre Dame Mts., *Quebec* S60+470 **90**
Notre Dame-du-Lac, *Quebec* S53+476 **90**
Nottawasaga B., *Ontario* T32+446 **91**
Nottingham & co., *England* N07+530 **37**
Nottingham I., *N.-W. Terr.* T17+636 **89**
Nouakchott, *Mauritania* P06+180 **80**
Nova Chaves, *Angola* L32-108 **82**
Nova Cruz, *Brazil* Q32-064 **105**
Nova Gaia, *Angola* L74-102 **82**
Nova Goa (Panjim), *Goa, Daman & Diu* H07+156 **70**
Nova Lisboa. *See* Huambo
Novara, *Italy* M38+454 **56**
Nova Scotia, prov., *Canada* S20+450 **89**
Nova Venecia, *Brazil* Q63-188 **105**
Novaya Sibir, Ostrov, *U.S.S.R.* C10+750 **63**
Novaya Zemlya, *U.S.S.R.* J20+730 **62**
Nova York, *Brazil* Q84-068 **105**
Nové Zámky, *Czech.* L71+480 **49**
Novgorod, *U.S.S.R.* K82+586 **60**
Novi, *Yugoslavia* M01+451 **56**
Novi Pazar, *Bulgaria* L17+434 **58**
Novi Pazar, *Yugoslavia* L57+431 **58**
Novi Sad, *Yugoslavia* L61+453 **58**
Novo Alekseyevka, *Kasakh.* H66+453 **62**
Novocherkassk, *U.S.S.R.* K29+474 **61**
Novokuznetsk, *U.S.S.R.* G17+538 **62**
Novo Mesto, *Yugoslavia* M01+458 **56**
Novomoskovsk, *U.S.S.R.* K43+479 **60**
Novo Moskovsk, *Ukraine* K58+487 **60**
Novo Nikolayevskiy, *U.S.S.R.* K13+510 **61**
Novo Redondo, *Angola* -M06-114 **82**
Novorossiysk, *U.S.S.R.* K44+448 **62**
Novoshakhtinsk, *U.S.S.R.* K31+477 **61**
Novosibirsk, *U.S.S.R.* G42+550 **62**
Novosibirskiye Ostrova, *U.S.S.R.* C60+755 **63**
Novo Troitsk, *U.S.S.R.* J21+545 **61**
Novourgench, *Uzbek* H86+415 **62**
Novska, *Yugoslavia* L78+453 **56**
Novy Jičin, *Czechoslovakia* L72+496 **49**
Novyy Port, *U.S.S.R.* H12+676 **62**
Nowa Wilejka, *Lithuania* L27+547 **47**
Nowendoc, *New S. Wales* B80-316 **109**
Nowgong, *India* F74+263 **71**
Nowinga, *Victoria* C40-352 **109**
Nowra, *New South Wales* B87-349 **109**
Nowshera, *Pakistan* H18+340 **72**
Nowy Sacz, *Poland* L56+496 **49**
Nowy Targ, *Poland* L60+495 **49**
Nowy Tomysl, *Poland* L83+523 **49**
Noya, *Spain* N53+427 **52**
Nozay, *France* N10+476 **54**
Ntungamo, *Uganda* K86-008 **83**
Nuanetsi, *Rhodesia* K8-214 **84**
Nueces R., *Texas* U48+280 **94**
Nueltin L., *N.-W. Terr.* U56+602 **88**
Nueva Imperial, *Chile* S78-386 **103**
Nuevo, G., *Argentina* S28-426 **103**
Nuevo Laredo, *Mexico* U57+274 **100**
Nuevo Leon, state, *Mexico* U60+262 **100**
Nûgssuaq, Pen., *Greenland* R35+700 **26**
Nuits St Georges, *France* M60+471 **54**
Nukualofa, I., *Marquesas Is.* X30-100 **107**
Nukuhiva, I., *Marquesas Is.* X30-100 **107**
Nukuoro, I., *Caroline Is.* B60+040 **106**
Nukus, *Uzbek* J02+424 **62**
Nules, *Spain* N01+398 **53**
Nullagine, *W. Australia* E00-218 **110**
Nullarbor Plain, *W. Aust.* D40-306 **110**
Numata, *Japan* C66+366 **68**
Numazu, *Japan* C67+351 **68**
Numfoor, I., *New Guinea* D01-010 **65**
Nunchia, *Colombia* S74+056 **104**
Nuneaton, *England* N09+525 **37**
Nunivak I., *Alaska* Z15+600 **99**
Nunkiang, *China* D59+490 **64**
Nuqui, *Colombia* T14+057 **104**
Nurmes, *Finland* L05+636 **46**
Nurpur, *India* G84+323 **72**
Nurri, *Sardinia* M35+397 **57**
Nürnberg, *Germany* M24+494 **48**
Nusaybin, *Turkey* K23+371 **74**
Nushki, *Pakistan* H54+296 **70**
Nutrias, *Venezuela* S56+079 **104**
Nuwara Eliya, *Sri Lanka* G56+070 **70**
Nyada, *Sweden* M19+611 **47**
Nyah, *Victoria* C40-352 **109**
Nyåker, *Sweden* L54+638 **46**
Nyala, *Sudan* L30+120 **81**
Nyal kungu, *Tanzania* K70-026 **83**
Nyarilell, *Sudan* L18+092 **81**
Nyandoma, *U.S.S.R.* K29+617 **62**
Nyantakana, *Tanzania* K82-030 **83**
Nyanza, *Rwanda* L00-024 **83**
Nyasa, L., *Malawi* K64-118 **83**
Nyasaland, (Malawi), *E. Afr.* K66-120 **83**
Nyazepetrovsk, *U.S.S.R.* J03+561 **61**
Nyda, *U.S.S.R.* H11+667 **62**
Nyeri, *Kenya* K48-004 **83**
Nyhammar, *Sweden* M00+603 **47**

Nyiregyháza, *Hungary* L50+479 **49**
Nykobing, *Denmark* M19+547 **47**
Nykøbing, *Denmark* M37+568 **47**
Nyköping, *Sweden* L78+587 **47**
Nylstroom, *Transvaal* L10-246 **84**
Nyamagee, *New South Wales* C22-321 **109**
Nymboida & R., *N.S.W.* B75-299 **109**
Nyngan, *New South Wales* C17-316 **109**
Nyon, *Switzerland* M53+464 **45**
Nyonga, *Tanzania* K78-068 **83**
Nyons, *France* M59+444 **55**
Nysa, *Poland* L76+505 **49**
Nysted, *Denmark* M19+546 **47**
Nyurba, *U.S.S.R.* E10+634 **63**
Nyuya, *U.S.S.R.* E22+606 **63**
Nzega, *Tanzania* K70-042 **83**
Oababatiya, *Israel* K58+324 **76**
Oacoma, *S. Dakota* U56+438 **93**
Oahe Res., *S. Dakota* U62+450 **93**
Oahu, I., *Hawaiian Islands* Y45+212 **107**
Oakan, *Japan* C34+434 **68**
Oakbank, *S. Australia* C57-331 **109**
Oakes, *N. Dakota* U48+462 **93**
Oakham, *England* N04+527 **37**
Oakland, *California* W14+378 **92**
Oakland, *Maryland* T26+394 **91**
Oakley, *Kansas* U66+390 **94**
Oakville, *Ontario* T28+435 **91**
Oamaru, *New Zealand* A54-451 **112**
Oates Ld., *Antarctica* B50-700 **27**
Oatlands, *Tasmania* C16-423 **109**
Oaxaca & state, *Mexico* U40+170 **100**
Ob, R., *U.S.S.R.* H55+655 **62**
Obama, *Japan* C85+355 **68**
Oban, *New Zealand* A71-469 **112**
Oban, *Scotland* N33+564 **41**
Obatogamau L., *Quebec* S88+496 **90**
Obbia, *Somalia* J68+054 **83**
Obeh, *Afghanistan* H71+345 **75**
Oberammergau, *W. Germany* M24+476 **48**
Oberhausen, *W. Germany* M49+515 **48**
Oberlin, *Kansas* U63+398 **94**
Oberon, *New South Wales* C01-337 **109**
Oberriet, *Switzerland* M33+473 **45**
Oberwald, *Switzerland* M40+465 **45**
Obi, I., *Indonesia* D44-016 **65**
Obidos, *Brazil* R63-018 **105**
Obidos, *Portugal* N55+394 **52**
Obihiro, *Japan* C40+428 **68**
Obo, *Cent. Afr. Rep.* L20+052 **81**
Oahe Res., *S. Dakota* U62+448 **88**
Obock, *F.T.A.I.* K10+118 **83**
Oborona, *U.S.S.R.* K25+521 **61**
Obrayera, *Nicaragua* T53+143 **101**
Obskaya Guba, *U.S.S.R.* H10+700 **62**
Ocala, *Florida* T43+292 **97**
Ocampo, *Mexico* U57+229 **100**
Ocana, *Colombia* S80+081 **104**
Ocana, *Spain* N21+399 **52**
Occidental, Cord., *Colombia* T10+050 **104**
Ocean I., *Pacific Ocean* A63-012 **106**
Oceana, *W. Virginia* T40+377 **97**
Ocean City, *New Jersey* S87+393 **96**
Ochil Hills, *Scotland* N22+562 **41**
Ocland, *Romania* L28+461 **58**
Ocoa, B. de, *Dominican Rep.* S64+183 **101**
Ocona, *Peru* S78-165 **104**
Oconto, *Wisconsin* T77+449 **91**
Ocos, *Guatemala* U13+145 **100**
Ocotal, *Nicaragua* T58+134 **101**
Ocumare, *Venezuela* S41+101 **104**
Oda, *Ghana* N06+060 **80**
Oda, *Japan* D15+352 **68**
Odaka, *Japan* C54+375 **68**
Odate, *Japan* C57+403 **68**
Odawara, *Japan* C65+352 **68**
Odemira, *Portugal* N52+376 **52**
Odemis, *Turkey* L12+382 **74**
Odense, *Denmark* M28+554 **47**
Oder R., *Germany* M04+527 **48**
Odessa, *Texas* U74+318 **94**
Odessa, *Ukraine* K86+465 **60**
Odienné, *Ivory Coast* N46+096 **80**
Odoorn, *Netherlands* M49+529 **44**
Odorhei, *Romania* L28+463 **58**
Odra R., *Poland* M04+527 **48**
Odzala, *Congo* M02+006 **82**
Oedelem, *Belgium* M70+512 **44**
Oeiras, *Brazil* Q73-070 **105**
Oelwein, *Iowa* U11+426 **95**
Oetling, *Argentina* S00-273 **103**
Of, *Turkey* K27+410 **74**
Offaly (Ui Failghe), co., *Ireland, Rep.* N45+533 **43**
Offenbach, *Germany* M38+501 **48**
Ogaki, *Japan* C79+354 **68**
Ogallala, *Nebraska* U70+411 **94**
Ogden, *Utah* V42+412 **94**
Ogdensburg, *New York* T03+447 **91**
Ogilvie, *Yukon* X28+638 **88**
Ogilvie Ra., *Yukon* X00+448 **88**
Ogoja, *Nigeria* M38+068 **81**
Ogoki R., *Ontario* T70+506 **89**
Ogr, *Sudan* L16+120 **81**
Ogulin, *Yugoslavia* L89+452 **56**
Ohakune, *New Zealand* A27-393 **112**
Ohau, L., *New Zealand* A61-442 **112**
Ohey, *Belgium* M59+504 **44**
O'Higgins, mt., *Chile* S80-488 **103**
Ohio, state, *U.S.A.* T53+405 **99**
Ohio R., *U.S.A.* T68+378 **99**
Ohrid, *Yugoslavia* L55+411 **58**
Ohridsko Jezero, *Yugoslavia* L56+410 **58**
Ohura, *New Zealand* A30-389 **112**
Oich L., *Scotland* N29+571 **40**
Oignies, *Belgium* M62+500 **44**
Oil City, *Pennsylvania* T43+414 **96**
Oil Springs, *Ontario* T43+428 **91**
Oirot Tura, *U.S.S.R.* G24+518 **62**
Oirschot, *Netherlands* M58+515 **44**
Oise, dep., *France* M76+494 **54**
Oise, R., *France* M76+490 **54**
Oita, *Japan* D20+332 **68**
Ojinaga, *Mexico* U87+295 **100**
Ojiya, *Japan* C67+373 **68**
Ojocaliente, *Mexico* U73+225 **100**
Ojo de Agua, *Argentina* S23-294 **103**
Ojo del Toro, Pico, *Cuba* T14+200 **101**
Oka R., *U.S.S.R.* K16+558 **61**

Okahandja, S.-W. Africa L78–220 **84**
Okanagan Lake, B.C. W00+499 **88**
Okanogan R., Washington W00+478 **98**
Okaukweyo, S.-W. Africa L86–190 **84**
Okavango, R. & Swamp,
  Botswana L40–198 **84**
Okayama, Japan D06+346 **68**
Okeechobee, L., Florida T34+269 **97**
Okehampton, England N24+507 **38**
Okha, U.S.S.R. C42+537 **63**
Okhansk, U.S.S.R. J28+576 **61**
Okhotsk, U.S.S.R. C40+593 **63**
Okhotsk, Sea of, U.S.S.R. C10+550 **63**
Okigunto, Japan D12+362 **68**
Okinawa Gunto, Japan D42+265 **68**
Oklahoma, state, U.S.A. U54+357 **98**
Oklahoma City, Oklahoma U45+354 **95**
Okmulgee, Oklahoma U36+356 **95**
Okolona, Mississippi T82+342 **97**
Oktyabrskoy Revolyutsiy, Os.,
  U.S.S.R. F50+790 **63**
Okučani, Yugoslavia L77+453 **56**
Okuru, New Zealand A66–439 **112**
Okushiri I., Japan C63+422 **68**
Okusi Ambeno, Port. Timor D65–094 **110**
Olaine, Latvia L36+568 **47**
Olanchito, Honduras T68+156 **101**
Öland, I., Sweden L80+567 **47**
Olary, S. Australia C58–323 **109**
Olasan, Ethiopia K00+052 **83**
Olavarria, Argentina S02–368 **103**
Olawa, Poland L76+510 **49**
Olbia, Sardinia M33+409 **57**
Olcott, New York T22+433 **96**
Oldcastle, Ireland, Rep. N43+538 **42**
Oldenburg, W. Germany M25+543 **48**
Oldenburg, W. Germany M41+532 **48**
Oldenzaal, Netherlands M48+523 **44**
Old Forge, Pennsylvania T04+413 **96**
Oldham, England N13+535 **37**
Old Orchard, Maine S62+435 **90**
Old Orchard Beach, Maine S62+435 **96**
Oldtown, Maine S52+450 **90**
Olean, New York T21+421 **96**
Olecko, Poland L45+540 **49**
Olekminsk, U.S.S.R. D89+603 **63**
Olenek, U.S.S.R. E45+685 **63**
Olenek, U.S.S.R. D80+727 **63**
Olenekskiy Zaliv, U.S.S.R. D85+734 **63**
Oléron, I. d', France N08+460 **54**
Olga, U.S.S.R. C88+436 **63**
Olifants Kloof, Botswana L60–222 **84**
Olimbos. See Olympus.
Oiva de Jerez, Spain N41+383 **52**
Olivares, Spain N15+397 **53**
Olivares, Co. de, Argentina S59–303 **103**
Oliveira, Brazil Q78–122 **105**
Olivenza, Spain N42+387 **52**
Olivone, Switzerland M36+465 **45**
Ollague, Chile S50–212 **103**
Ollague, mt., Bolivia S49–212 **104**
Olmedo, Spain N28+413 **52**
Olney, Illinois T78+387 **95**
Olomouc, Czechoslovakia L77+496 **49**
Olot, Spain M75+422 **53**
Olovyannaya, U.S.S.R. E26+510 **63**
Olpe, Germany M43+510 **48**
Olst, Netherlands M53+523 **44**
Olsztyn, Poland L57+538 **49**
Olten, Switzerland M43+473 **45**
Oltu, Turkey K18+406 **74**
Oltul R., Romania L33+458 **58**
Olvera, Spain N31+369 **52**
Olympia, Greece L50+376 **59**
Olympia, Washington W17+470 **92**
Olympic Nat. Park, Wash. W26+476 **98**
Olympus (Olimbos), mts.,
  Greece L46+400 **59**
Olympus, Mt., Washington W23+475 **98**
Olyutorskiy Zaliv, U.S.S.R. A70+600 **63**
Omagh, N. Ireland N44+546 **42**
Omaguas, Peru S80–042 **104**
Omaha, Nebraska U36+412 **95**
Oman, Arabia J26+238 **75**
Oman, G. of, Arabia-Iran J10+248 **75**
Omaruru, S.-W. Africa L84–212 **84**
Ombombo, S.-W. Africa M06–186 **84**
Omdurman, Sudan K76+156 **81**
Omeo, Victoria C15–371 **109**
Omer, Michigan T53+440 **91**
Ometepec, Mexico U50+166 **100**
Ommen, Netherlands M51+525 **44**
Omoa, Honduras T79+156 **101**
Omsk, U.S.S.R. H10+550 **62**
Omuta, Japan D27+330 **68**
Omutninsk, U.S.S.R. J46+586 **61**
Ona, R., U.S.S.R. F50+570 **63**
Onawa, Iowa U36+420 **95**
Onaway, Michigan T55+453 **91**
Onega & R., Russia K39+640 **62**
Onehunga, New Zealand A31–370 **112**
Oneida, New York T04+431 **96**
Oneida L., New York T06+432 **96**
O'Neill, Nebraska U52+424 **95**
Oneonta, New York T00+425 **96**
Onezhskoye Oz., U.S.S.R. K60+618 **62**
Ongole, India G59+156 **70**
Ongudai, U.S.S.R. G23+508 **62**
Onich, Scotland N31+567 **41**
Onipa, S.-W. Africa L82–178 **84**
Onitsha, Nigeria M50+062 **80**
Onoto, Venezuela S31+098 **104**
Onotoa, I., Gilbert Islands A30–020 **106**
Onslow, W. Australia E30–217 **110**
Onslow B., N. Carolina T12+343 **97**
Ontario, prov., Canada **89**
Ontario, L., U.S.A.-Canada T20+439 **99**
Onteniente, Spain N04+388 **53**
Ontiñena, Spain N00+417 **53**
Oodnadatta, S. Australia C88–273 **111**
Ooldea, S. Australia D19–305 **110**
Oostburg, Netherlands M69+513 **44**
Oostende (Ostende), Belgium M73+512 **44**
Ooster Schelde, Netherlands M66+516 **44**
Oosterwolde, Netherlands M52+530 **44**
Oosthuizen, Netherlands M60+526 **44**
Oostkamp, Belgium M71+512 **44**
Oostmalle, Belgium M62+513 **44**
Oostvoorne, Netherlands M66+519 **44**
Ootacamund, India G79+114 **70**
Opala, U.S.S.R. B50+520 **63**

Opari, Sudan K78+040 **81**
Opatija, Yugoslavia M04+453 **56**
Opava, Czechoslovakia L73+499 **49**
Opelousas, Louisiana U12+304 **95**
Ophir, Mt., Malaya F15+024 **69**
Ophoven, Belgium M55+511 **44**
Opis, Iraq K04+339 **74**
Opochka, U.S.S.R. L08+568 **60**
Opodepe, Mexico V34+300 **100**
Opole, Poland L73+507 **49**
Oporto. See Porto
Opotiki, New Zealand A16–380 **112**
Oppa B., Japan C51+386 **68**
Oppeln. See Opole
Opunake, New Zealand A37–394 **112**
Oputo, Mexico V25+300 **100**
Oqair, Saudi Arabia J59+257 **75**
Oradea, Romania L48+470 **58**
Orai, India G63+260 **73**
Oran, Algeria N04+356 **80**
Orange, France M61+442 **55**
Orange, Massachusetts S74+427 **96**
Orange, New South Wales C05–334 **109**
Orange Texas U22+301 **95**
Orange, Virginia T19+382 **97**
Orange R., S. Africa L70–284 **84**
Orange City, Iowa U36+430 **95**
Orangeburg, S. Carolina T35+335 **97**
Orange Free State, S. Africa L20–284 **84**
Orangeville, Ontario T31+439 **91**
Orange Geb., Surinam R60+030 **105**
Oranmore, Ireland, Rep. N53+533 **43**
Oras, Philippines D58+121 **65**
Orăstie, Romania L41+458 **58**
Oravita, Romania L50+451 **58**
Oravská Magura, Czech. L65+493 **49**
Orbe, Switzerland M51+467 **45**
Orbost, Victoria C09–377 **109**
Orcera, Spain N16+383 **53**
Orchha, India G68+253 **73**
Ord, Mt., W. Australia D60–175 **110**
Ordenes, Spain N50+431 **52**
Ord River, W. Australia D37–174 **110**
Ordu, Turkey K42+409 **74**
Ordzhonikidze, Russia K02+430 **62**
Ordzhonikidzegrad. See Bezhitsa
Örebro, Sweden L89+593 **47**
Oregon, Illinois T86+419 **95**
Oregon, state, U.S.A. W15+440 **98**
Oregon City, Oregon W16+455 **92**
Öregrund, Sweden L69+603 **47**
Orekhovo Zuyevo, Russia K35+558 **60**
Orel, U.S.S.R. K53+530 **60**
Orellana, Peru T01–070 **104**
Orellana, Spain N33+390 **52**
Orenburg, Russia J29+517 **61**
Orense, Spain N47+423 **52**
Orepuki, New Zealand Q73–463 **112**
Öresund, Denmark-Sweden M14+560 **47**
Orgaña, Spain M82+422 **53**
Orgaz, Spain N23+396 **52**
Oriental, Cord., Colombia S84+050 **104**
Oriental, Cord., Peru T04–375 **104**
Orihuela, Spain N06+381 **53**
Orillia, Ontario T27+446 **91**
Orinoco, R., Venezuela S20+083 **104**
Orissa, state, India G35+2.0 **71**
Oristano & G. di, Sardinia M39+399 **57**
Orivesi, Finland L04+623 **46**
Oriximiná, Brazil R65–016 **105**
Orizaba, Mexico U43+183 **100**
Orizare, Bulgaria L14+427 **58**
Orkanger, Norway M31+633 **46**
Orkhon R., Mongolia F08+484 **64**
Orkney Is., Scotland N18+590 **40**
Ørland, Norway M32+637 **46**
Orlando, Florida T38+285 **97**
Orleanais, prov., France M79+478 **54**
Orleans, France M79+479 **54**
Orleans, I. of, Quebec S66+469 **91**
Orleansville, (El Asnam), Alg. M82+360 **80**
Orman, Syria K49+325 **76**
Ormara, Pakistan H62+251 **70**
Ormondville, New Zealand A22–401 **112**
Ormskirk, England N18+536 **37**
Ornach, Pakistan H53+268 **70**
Orne, dep., France N00+487 **54**
Örnsköldsvik, Sweden L67+633 **46**
Orochen, Russia D55+584 **63**
Orocue, Colombia S58+046 **104**
Oroluk, I., Caroline Islands B50+073 **106**
Oron, U.S.S.R. F70+644 **63**
Orono, Maine S52+449 **90**
Oronsay I., Scotland N38+560 **41**
Orontes, R., Syria K52+356 **74**
Orosei, & G. di, Sardinia M32+402 **57**
Orosi, Vol., Costa Rica T62+110 **101**
Orrin R., Scotland N27+576 **40**
Orroroo, S. Austral'a C68–328 **109**
Orsa, Sweden M02+611 **47**
Orsha, Belorussia K88+545 **60**
Orsières, Switzerland M47+460 **45**
Orsk, U.S.S.R. J08+512 **61**
Orsova, Romania L45+447 **58**
Ortegal, C., Spain N47+435 **52**
Orthez, France N05+453 **55**
Ortiz, Mexico V03+282 **100**
Ortiz, Venezuela S43+096 **104**
Orugueira, Spain N47+434 **52**
Orulgan, Khrebet, U.S.S.R. D50+677 **63**
Oruro, Bolivia S43–180 **104**
Orust, Sweden M20+582 **47**
Oryekhovo, U.S.S.R. K04+505 **61**
Osa, U.S.S.R. J27+572 **61**
Osage, Iowa U16+412 **95**
Osage City, Karsas U36+386 **95**
Osaka, Japan C87+347 **68**
Osakis, Minnesota U31+459 **93**
Osawatomie, Kansas U30+385 **95**
Osborne, Kansas U52+394 **95**
Oscar II Coast, Antarctica S05–640 **27**
Osceola, Arkansas U00+358 **97**
Osceola, Iowa U22+410 **95**
Oschiri, Sardinia M35+407 **57**
Oscoda, Michigan T50+444 **91**
Osen, Norway M27+643 **46**
Osh, Kirgiz H13+405 **62**
Oshawa, Ontario T23+439 **91**
O Shima, Japan C64+347 **68**
Oshkosh, Wisconsin T81+440 **91**
Oshnoviveh, Iran K00+370 **74**

Osijek, Yugoslavia L68+455 **58**
Osilo, Sardinia M36+408 **57**
Osipenko, U.S.S.R. C81+525 **63**
Osipovichi, Belorussia L08+533 **60**
Osire Sud, S.-W. Africa L76–212 **84**
Oskaloosa, Iowa U16+412 **95**
Oskarshamn, Sweden L81+573 **47**
Oslo, Norway M25+599 **47**
Oslo Fd., Norway M26+592 **47**
Osmanabad, India G83+180 **70**
Osmancik, Turkey K60+409 **74**
Osnabrück, W. Germany M42+523 **48**
Osorno, Chile S79–405 **103**
Osorno, Spain N26+424 **52**
Osowiec, Poland L44+535 **49**
Oss, Netherlands M57+518 **44**
Ossining, New York S83+412 **96**
Ostavall, Sweden L87+625 **46**
Ostende, Belgium M73+512 **44**
Österreich, Nieder, prov.,
  Austria L85+486 **49**
Österreich, Ober, prov.,
  Austria M04+484 **48**
Östersund, Sweden M02+632 **46**
Osthammar, Sweden L70+603 **47**
Ostrava, Czechoslovakia L70+498 **49**
Ostroda, Poland L60+537 **49**
Ostrołeka, Poland L50+537 **49**
Ostrov, Romania L11+449 **58**
Ostrov, U.S.S.R. L09+574 **60**
Ostrovnoe, U.S.S.R. B00+680 **63**
Ostrowiec, Poland L52+509 **49**
Ostrów Mazowiecka, Poland L49+528 **49**
Ostuni, Italy L75+407 **57**
Østvagøy, Norway M02+683 **46**
Ōsumikaikyō. Japan D24+308 **68**
Osuna, Spain N30+372 **52**
Oswego & R., New York T09+434 **96**
Oswestry, England N18+529 **38**
Otago Peninsula, N.Z. A52–458 **112**
Otaki, New Zealand A29–407 **112**
Otaru & B., Japan C54+432 **68**
Otasuts, Japan C56+433 **68**
Otavalo, Ecuador T19+002 **104**
Otepaa, Estonia L21+580 **47**
Othris, mts., Greece L45+390 **59**
Otira, New Zealand A50–428 **112**
Otis, New Brunswick S43+460 **90**
Otjiwarongo, S.-W. Africa L80–204 **84**
Otocac, Yugoslavia L89+449 **56**
Otoineppu, Japan C47+448 **68**
Otorohanga, New Zealand A28–382 **112**
Otpor, (Zabaykal'sk), U.S.S.R. E15+497 **63**
Otranto, Str. of, It.-Albania L66+402 **59**
Otsego, L., New York S89+428 **96**
Otsu, Japan C85+350 **68**
Ottawa, Illinois T83+414 **95**
Ottawa, Kansas U32+386 **95**
Ottawa, Ontario T04+454 **91**
Ottawa Is., N.-W. Terr. T30+596 **89**
Ottawa R., Quebec, etc. T16+462 **91**
Otterlo, Netherlands M55+521 **44**
Otterøy, Norway M49+628 **46**
Ottignies, Belgium M63+507 **44**
Otting, W. Germany M14+484 **48**
Ottumwa, Iowa U14+410 **95**
Otus, U.S.S.R. K59+450 **60**
Otway, B., Chile S84–535 **103**
Otway, C., Victoria C39–389 **109**
Otwock, Poland L52+521 **49**
Ötz, Austria M25+472 **48**
Ötztaler Alpen, Italy M23+470 **56**
Ouachita L., Arkansas, etc. U30+345 **99**
Ouachita R., Arkansas U23+340 **99**
Ouagadougou, Volta N08+122 **80**
Ouahigouya, Volta N14+134 **80**
Ouangolodougou, Ivory
  Coast N30+100 **80**
Ouargla, Algeria M58+316 **80**
Oubangui R., Congo and Zaire L74+004 **82**
Ouddorp, Netherlands M66+518 **44**
Oudekapelle, Belgium M73+510 **44**
Oudenaarde, Belgium M68+508 **44**
Oudenbosch, Netherlands M63+516 **44**
Oudtshoorn, Cape Province L46–336 **84**
Ouessant, I. d', France N30+484 **54**
Oughterard, Ireland, Rep. N56+534 **43**
Ouidah, Benin M78+064 **80**
Oukês, Albania L58+411 **58**
Oulu, Finland L18+644 **46**
Oulujärvi, Finland L18+644 **46**
Oulujoki, Finland L23+648 **46**
Oum Chalauoba, Chad L58+158 **81**
Ounasjoki, Finland L32+672 **46**
Ouricury, Brazil O61–078 **105**
Ourinhos, Brazil Q80–205 **105**
Ouro Preto, Brazil Q80–204 **105**
Ouse R., Norfolk, etc., England
  M88+525 **39**
Ouse R., Yorks, England N07+539 **37**
Outarde B., Quebec S51+490 **90**
Outardes, R. aux, Quebec S54+500 **90**
Outjo, S.-W. Africa L84–200 **84**
Outtrim, Victoria C26–385 **109**
Ouyen, Victoria C46–351 **109**
Ovalle, Chile S68–306 **103**
Ovar, Portugal N52+408 **52**
Over Flakkee I., Netherlands M65+517 **44**
Overijssel, prov., Netherlands M51+524 **44**
Overkalix, Sweden L43+663 **46**
Overmark, Finland L51+626 **46**
Overpelt, Belgium M58+512 **44**
Overtornea, Sweden L38+664 **46**
Oviedo, Spain N35+433 **52**
Ovruch, Ukraine L07+512 **60**
Owaka, New Zealand A62–464 **112**
Owasco L., New York T09+428 **96**
Owatonna, Minnesota U18+440 **93**
Owego, New York T08+421 **96**
Owen, Wisconsin U04+450 **91**
Owen's I., Burma F39+110 **71**
Owens L., California V78+364 **92**
Owensboro, Kentucky T73+378 **97**
Owen Sound, Ontario T36+446 **91**
Owen Stanley Ra.,
  Papua New Guinea C14–092 **111**
Owensville, Indiana T77+383 **97**
Owenton, Kentucky T59+386 **97**
Owerri, Nigeria M48+054 **80**
Owl Creek Mts., Wyoming V25+436 **93**

Owo, Nigeria M56+072 **80**
Owosso, Michigan T55+430 **91**
Owyhee R., Oregon V75+432 **92**
Ox Mts., Ireland, Rep. N54+541 **42**
Oxford, Maryland T07+387 **91**
Oxford, Mississippi T87+344 **97**
Oxford, New York T04+424 **91**
Oxford, N. Carolina T21+363 **97**
Oxford & co., England N08+518 **39**
Oxley, New South Wales C35–342 **109**
Oxley's Pk., New S. Wales B88–318 **109**
Oyapock, R., Brazil, etc. R42+034 **105**
Oyem, Gabon M20+016 **82**
Oymyakon, U.S.S.R. C40+630 **63**
Oyo, Nigeria M66+080 **80**
Oyster B., Tasmania C11–423 **109**
Ozark Mts., Ark.-Mo. U20+360 **95**
Ozark Plat., Missouri, etc. U24+364 **99**
Ozarks, L. of the, Missouri U18+382 **95**
Ozd, Hungary L58+482 **49**
Ozerki, U.S.S.R. J87+520 **61**
Ozhogino, U.S.S.R. C16+692 **63**
Ozieri, Sardinia M36+406 **57**
Ozun, Romania L25+458 **58**
Paan, Burma F44+170 **71**
Paan, China F36+299 **64**
Paarl, Cape Province L66–338 **84**
Pabianice, Poland .L64+517 **49**
Pabna, Bangladesh G04+240 **73**
Pacaraima, Sa., Brazil, etc. S18+040 **104**
Pacasmayo, Peru T27–074 **104**
Pachbhadra, India H17+260 **70**
Pachow. See Pachung
Pachuca, Mexico U52+200 **100**
Pachung, China E80+318 **66**
Pacific, Missouri U05+385 **97**
Pacific Ocean **102-103**
Paços, Portugal N51+413 **52**
Padam, Kashmir G79+334 **72**
Padang, Sumatra F28–009 **65**
Paderborn, W. Germany M37+517 **48**
Padilla, Bolivia S26–192 **104**
Padova, Italy M19+454 **56**
Padrauna, India G36+269 **73**
Padre I., Texas U44+268 **94**
Padstow, England N30+505 **38**
Padua. See Padova
Paducah, Kentucky T82+370 **97**
Paducah, Texas U61+340 **94**
Padul, Spain N22+370 **52**
Paeroa, New Zealand A26–374 **112**
Pafuri, Mozambique K82–226 **84**
Pagai Is., Indonesia F26–030 **65**
Pagalu I., Gulf of Guinea M57+014 **82**
Pagan, Burma F60+211 **71**
Pagan, I., Mariana Is. C25+170 **106**
Pagasai, G. of, Greece L42+392 **59**
Pago, I., Yugoslavia M00+444 **56**
Pagong L., Kashmir-Tibet G66+336 **70**
Pagosa Springs, Colorado V12+372 **94**
Paharpur, Pakistan H24+321 **72**
Pahiatua, New Zealand A25–404 **112**
Pahlavi Dezh, Iran J33+370 **75**
Pahlevi Bandar-e, Iran J63+375 **74**
Pahsien, China E21+391 **66**
Pahsien. See Chungking
Paide, Estonia L26+589 **47**
Paignton, England N21+504 **38**
Paiho, China E59+328 **66**
Päijänne, L., Finland L27+615 **47**
Pai-Khoi Khrebet, U.S.S.R. H60+675 **62**
Pailam, India G57+257 **73**
Pailingmiao, China E56+416 **64**
Paimpol, France N18+487 **54**
Painted Des., Arizona V35+360 **98**
Paintsville, Kentucky T47+378 **97**
Paisley, Ontario T38+443 **91**
Paisley, Scotland N26+558 **41**
Paita, Peru T36–051 **104**
Pai Tu Hu, China E17+308 **66**
Paiz do Vinho, Portugal N47+412 **52**
Pajakumbuh, Sumatra F27–001 **65**
Pajala, Sweden L40+672 **46**
Pajares, Spain N34+430 **52**
Pakakku, Burma F59+213 **71**
Pakanbaru, Sumatra F22+006 **65**
Pakaur, India G13+246 **73**
Pakchan, Burma F37+105 **71**
Pak-Loi, China E65+214 **67**
Pakistan, S. Asia H60+280 **70**
Pak-lay, Laos F21+182 **69**
Pakpattan, Pakistan H10+303 **72**
Pakrac, Yugoslavia L77+454 **56**
Paks, Hungary L67+467 **49**
Pakse, Laos E85+151 **69**
Palafrugell, Spain M71+419 **53**
Palaiokhóra, Crete L38+352 **59**
Palamau, India G34+239 **73**
Palamcottah, India G73+087 **70**
Palamós, Spain M71+418 **53**
Palamuse, Estonia L20+587 **47**
Palana, U.S.S.R. B30+590 **63**
Palanpur, India H15+241 **70**
Palatka, Florida T40+296 **97**
Palau Is., Pacific Ocean D02+074 **65**
Palaw, Burma F38+130 **69**
Palawan, I., Phillippines E10+100 **65**
Paldiski, Estonia L35+594 **47**
Palembang, Sumatra F01–030 **65**
Palena, Chile S78–438 **103**
Palenque, Mexico U12+174 **100**
Paleokhorio, Cyprus K71+349 **76**
Palermo, Argentina S24–236 **103**
Palermo, N. Dakota U73+483 **93**
Palermo, Sicily M10+381 **57**
Palestina, Chile S56–240 **103**
Palestine, Texas U34+317 **95**
Palestine, W. Asia K60+320 **74**
Paletwa, Burma F72+213 **71**
Palghat, India G79+108 **70**
Palgrave Pt., S.-W. Africa M10–204 **84**
Palgu Tso, Tibet G26+289 **71**
Palhiers, France M80+431 **55**
Palhoca, Brazil Q82–278 **103**
Pali, India H10+257 **70**
Palime, Togo M86+068 **80**
Palisade, Nevada V67+406 **92**
Paliseul, Belgium M59+499 **44**
Palizada, Mexico U12+182 **100**
Palk Str., India G60+100 **70**
Palkot, India G32+229 **73**

Palliser B., *New Zealand* A30–415 **112**
Palma, *Balearic Islands* M74+396 **53**
Palma, *Brazil* Q74–212 **105**
Palma, *Brazil* R16–124 **105**
Palma, *Mozambique* K28–110 **83**
Palma, I., *Canary Is* P30+286 **80**
Palmaras, *Brazil* R33–303 **103**
Palmas, *Brazil* R42–265 **103**
Palmas, B., *Mexico* V28+237 **100**
Palmas C., *Liberia* N46+044 **80**
Palmas, G. of, *Sardinia* M39+390 **57**
Palm Beach, *Florida* T30+267 **97**
Palmeira, *Brazil* R50–279 **103**
Palmer Land, *Antarctica* S24–725 **27**
Palmerston, *Ontario* T35+439 **91**
Palmerston I., *Cook Islands* Y80–158 **106**
Palmerston North, *N.Z.* A26–403 **112**
Palmerston South, *N.Z.* A56–454 **112**
Palmira, *Colombia* T08+037 **104**
Palms, *Michigan* T47+436 **91**
Palmyra, *Missouri* U07+398 **95**
Palmyra, *Syria* K41+346 **74**
Palmyra I., *Pacific Ocean* Y72+060 **106**
Palni Hills, *India* G76+104 **70**
Paloh, *Borneo* E64+016 **65**
Paloich, *Sudan* K74+104 **81**
Palo Santo, *Argentina* R86–255 **103**
Palpa, *Nepal* G38+279 **73**
Palu, *Turkey* K30+388 **74**
Palwal, *India* G76+281 **72**
Pambon Chan., *India* G66+092 **70**
Pamekasan, *Indonesia* E39–070 **65**
Pamir, mts., *U.S.S.R.* H15+374 **62**
Pamlico Sd., *N. Carolina* T06+352 **97**
Pampa, *Texas* U66+356 **94**
Pampas, *Peru* S89–122 **104**
Pamplona, *Colombia* S76+076 **104**
Pamplona, *Spain* N10+428 **53**
Panache L., *Ontario* T38+462 **91**
Panagyurishte, *Bulgaria* L35+425 **58**
Panaji, *Goa, Daman & Diu* H07 + 156 **70**
Panama & rep.,
 Central America T27+090 **101**
Panama Can., *Panama* T28+080 **89**
Panama, G. of, *Panama* T26+080 **101**
Panama City, *Florida* T64+302 **97**
Panarea, I., *Italy* M00+386 **57**
Panat, *Thailand* F23+134 **69**
Panay, I., *Philippines* D75+112 **65**
Pancevo, *Yugoslavia* L56+449 **58**
Panciu, *Romania* L17+459 **58**
Pandan, *Philippines* D77+116 **65**
Pan de Azucar, *Chile* S64–261 **103**
Pandharpur, *India* G88+177 **70**
Pando, *Uruguay* R66–347 **103**
Paneviys, *Lithuania* L34+558 **47**
Panfilov, *Kazakh.* G59+441 **62**
Panfilov, *U.S.S.R.* K12+503 **61**
Pangala, *Congo* M02–034 **82**
Pangbourne, *England* N07+515 **39**
Pangkiang, *China* E41+426 **64**
Panguitch, *Utah* V45+378 **94**
Pania Mutombo, *Zaire* L36–054 **82**
Panipat, *India* G78+294 **72**
Panja, *China* F82+400 **64**
Panjim. *See* Panaji
Panjnad R., *Pakistan* H25+290 **72**
Pannerden, *Netherlands* M54+519 **44**
Panruti, *India* G62+118 **70**
Pantanaw, *Burma* F58+169 **71**
Pantar, I., *Indonesia* D66–084 **65**
Pantelleria, I., *Medit. Sea* M18+368 **57**
Pánuco, *Mexico* U67+266 **100**
Pao-an-chow, *China* E29+403 **66**
Paochang, *China* E26+420 **66**
Pão de Assucar. *Brazil* Q45–097 **105**
Pão dos Ferros. *Brazil* Q49–061 **105**
Paoking. *See* Shaoyang
Paola, *Italy* L84+394 **57**
Paola, *Kansas* U30+386 **95**
Paoli, *Indiana* T69+385 **97**
Paoning. *See* Langchung
Paosham, *China* F36+252 **64**
Paoting, *China* E27+389 **66**
Pao-tow, *China* E60+406 **66**
Papakura, *New Zealand* A30–371 **112**
Papantla, *Mexico* U44+205 **100**
Papa Stour I., *Scotland* N10+603 **40**
Papa Westray, I., *Scotland* N17+594 **40**
Papenburg, *W. Germany* M46+531 **48**
Papendrecht, *Netherlands* M62+518 **44**
Paphos, *Cyprus* K76+347 **76**
Paposo, *Chile* S63–250 **103**
Papua, G. of, *Papua New Guinea*
 C30–086 **111**
Papua New Guinea
 Pacific Ocean C60–060 **31**
Papun, *Burma* F45+181 **71**
Pará, *Brazil* R21–014 **105**
Para, R., *Brazil* R20–010 **105**
Paracatu, *Brazil* R11–172 **105**
Paracel Is & Reefs,
 S. China Sea E50+165 **69**
Parachilna, *S. Australia* C70–311 **109**
Parachinar, *Pakistan* H29+339 **72**
Paracin, *Yugoslavia* L52+439 **58**
Paracuro, *Brazil* Q54–034 **105**
Parag, *Iran* H86+255 **75**
Paragould, *Arkansas* U03+361 **99**
Paraguari, *Paraguay* R73–256 **103**
Paraguay, rep., *S. America* --- **103**
Paraguay R., *Argent., etc.* R80–267 **103**
Parah, *Afghanistan* H79+342 **75**
Parakes, *Botswana* L48–186 **84**
Parakou, *Benin* M74 + 094 **80**
Paramaribo, *Surinam* R62+057 **105**
Paramonga, *Peru* T17–007 **104**
Paramoshiri, *U.S.S.R.* B55+505 **63**
Parana, *Argentina* S03–318 **103**
Paraná, R., *Argentina* R86–292 **103**
Paranaiba & R., *Brazil* R37–197 **105**
Parang, *Philippines* D84+059 **65**
Paranga, *Uganda* K72+024 **83**
Parapola, I., *Greece* L39+369 **59**
Parattah, *Tasmania* C16–424 **109**
Parbati R., *India* G78+235 **70**
Parbhani, *India* G79+193 **70**
Parchim, *E. Germany* M19+534 **48**
Pardubice, *Czechoslovakia* L84+500 **49**
Parecis, *Brazil* R72–140 **105**

Parecis, Sa. dos, *Brazil* S10–119 **104**
Paren, *U.S.S.R.* B10+624 **63**
Parent, *Quebec* S88+480 **90**
Pareora, *New Zealand* A52–445 **112**
Parika, *Guyana* R81+068 **104**
Parinari, *Peru* S87–044 **104**
Paringa, *S. Australia* C55–342 **109**
Parintins, *Brazil* R69–025 **105**
Paris, *France* M76+488 **54**
Paris, *Illinois* T76+396 **95**
Paris, *Kentucky* T55+382 **97**
Paris, *Ontario* T33+432 **91**
Paris, *Tennessee* T80+362 **95**
Paris, *Texas* U34+336 **95**
Parita, B. de, *Panama* T32+081 **101**
Pariz, *Iran* J26+299 **75**
Park Ra., *Colorado* V08+400 **94**
Park Ra., *Wyoming* V14+413 **98**
Parker, *S. Dakota* U10+624 **93**
Parker, C., *N.-W. Terr.* T25+750 **89**
Parker Dam, *Arizona* V55+342 **98**
Parkersburg, *W. Virginia* T39+393 **91**
Parkes, *New South Wales* C11–332 **109**
Park Falls, *Wisconsin* U03+459 **91**
Park Rapids, *Minnesota* U30+469 **93**
Parkston, *S. Dakota* U48+434 **93**
Parma, *Italy* M28+448 **56**
Parmele, *N. Carolina* T13+358 **93**
Parnagua, *Brazil* Q86–103 **105**
Parnahyba, *Brazil* Q71–029 **105**
Parnaiba, R., *Brazil* Q76–037 **105**
Parnu & G., *Estonia* L33+583 **47**
Paro, *Bhutan* G04+274 **73**
Paron, *India* G78+249 **70**
Paroo, R., *New South Wales* C34–300 **109**
Páros, I., *Greece* L29+371 **59**
Parowan, *Utah* V48+388 **94**
Parral, *Chile* S71–361 **103**
Parral, *Mexico* V04+269 **100**
Parramatta, *New S. Wales* B85–338 **109**
Parras, *Mexico* U73+255 **100**
Parrett R., *England* N18+511 **38**
Parry I., *Ontario* T31+453 **91**
Parry Is., *N.-W. Terr.* V30+762 **88**
Parry Sound, *Ontario* T30+454 **91**
Parsa, *India* G30+259 **73**
Parsnip R., *Brit. Columbia* W20+556 **88**
Parsons, *Kansas* U32+374 **95**
Parsons, *W. Virginia* T28+391 **96**
Partabgarh, *India* H01+239 **70**
Partabgarh, *India* G48+259 **73**
Partabpur, *India* G40+234 **73**
Parthenay, *France* N01+466 **54**
Partinico, *Sicily* M11+381 **57**
Partridge I., *Tibet* G20+330 **71**
Partry Mts., *Ireland, Rep.* N57+537 **42**
Pas, The, *Manitoba* U68+540 **88**
Pasadena, *California* V79+341 **92**
Pasargadae, *Iran* J42+302 **75**
Pascagoula, *Mississippi* T81+304 **97**
Pas-de-Calais, dep., *France* M76+505 **54**
Paseagoula & R., *Mississippi* T81+304 **95**
Paskuh, *Iran* H80+276 **75**
Pasley, C., *W. Australia* D69–340 **110**
Pasni, *Pakistan* H70+252 **70**
Paso de Indios, *Argentina* S54–438 **103**
Paso de los Libres, *Argent.* R72–297 **103**
Paso de los Toros, *Uruguay* S39–326 **103**
Paso Limay, *Argentina* S63–405 **103**
Paso Robles, *California* W05+356 **92**
Paspebiac, *Quebec* S31+481 **90**
Pasrur, *Pakistan* H02+322 **72**
Passamaquoddy B., *N.B.* S42+451 **90**
Passau, *W. Germany* M09+486 **48**
Passendale, *Belgium* M72+509 **44**
Passero C., *Sicily* L89+367 **57**
Passiac, *New Jersey* S85+408 **96**
Passo Fundo, *Brazil* R44–281 **103**
Passos, *Brazil* R10–206 **105**
Pasto, *Colombia* T14+012 **104**
Pastrana, *Spain* N18+404 **52**
Pasvik Elv, *Norway* L04+693 **46**
Pásztó, *Hungary* L62+479 **49**
Patan, *India* H16+238 **70**
Patan, *India* H07+174 **70**
Patan, *Nepal* G28+276 **73**
Pataudi, *India* G79+283 **72**
Pataz, *Peru* T16–076 **104**
Patchewollock, *Victoria* C47–354 **109**
Patchogue, *New York* S78+407 **96**
Patea, *New Zealand* A33–397 **112**
Patencia, *Spain* N28+420 **52**
Paterno, *Sicily* M01+375 **57**
Paterson, *New Jersey* S85+409 **96**
Pathankot, *India* G86+323 **72**
Pathari, *India* G71+239 **73**
Pathfinder Res., *Wyoming* V11+424 **93**
Patiala, *India* G81+303 **72**
Pa-tiao, mt., *Laos* F15+193 **69**
Patkai Hills, *Burma* F55+268 **71**
Pátmos, I., *Greece* L20+373 **59**
Patna, *India* G41+207 **71**
Patna, *India* G28+236 **73**
Patos, *Brazil* Q43–070 **105**
Patos, L. dos, *Brazil* R40–314 **103**
Patquia, *Argentina* S41–301 **103**
Pátrai, *Greece* L49+383 **59**
Pátrai, G. of, *Greece* L50+383 **59**
Patras. *See* Pátrai.
Patrasayar, *India* G15+232 **73**
Patricio Lynch, I., *Chile* T02–485 **103**
Patrocinio, *Brazil* R12–190 **105**
Pattani, *Thailand* F22+068 **69**
Patten, *Maine* S51+460 **90**
Patterson, *Louisiana* U08+297 **97**
Patti, *Sicily* M00+381 **57**
Patutahi, *New Zealand* A12–386 **112**
Patzcuaro, *Mexico* U69+194 **100**
Pau, *France* N02+433 **55**
Pau d'Arco, *Brazil* R26–079 **105**
Paul, L., *N.-W. Territories* V30+651 **88**
Paulista, *Brazil* Q67–082 **105**
Paul's Valley, *Oklahoma* U42+347 **95**
Paungde, *Burma* F57+183 **71**
Pauni, *India* G62+208 **70**
Pautrask. *Sweden* L75+648 **46**
Pavia, *Italy* M35+452 **56**
Pāvilosta, *Latvia* L53+569 **47**
Pavlodar, *Kazakh.* G79+522 **62**
Pavlograd, *Ukraine* K55+486 **60**

Pavlovka, *U.S.S.R.* K10+519 **61**
Pavlovo, *U.S.S.R.* K11+560 **61**
Pavlovsk, *U.S.S.R.* K29+504 **61**
Pavlovski, *U.S.S.R.* K38+558 **60**
Pawnee City, *Nebraska* U37+402 **95**
Paw Paw, *Michigan* T65+422 **91**
Pawtucket, *Rhode Island* S69+419 **96**
Paxoi, I., *Greece* L59+392 **59**
Paxton, *Illinois* T78+405 **95**
Payerne, *Switzerland* M48+468 **45**
Payne L., *Quebec* S75+598 **89**
Payne R., *Quebec* S70+601 **89**
Paynesville, *Minnesota* U29+454 **93**
Payo Obispo. *See* Ciudad Chetumal
Paysandu, *Uruguay* R79–322 **103**
Payson, *Utah* V41+401 **94**
Paz, R., *Salvador* U00+138 **101**
Pazardzhik, *Bulgaria* L34+422 **58**
Pazaung, *Burma* F46+190 **71**
Peace R., *Brit. Columbia* W20+560 **88**
Peace River, *Alberta* V75+560 **88**
Peak, The, *England* N11+534 **37**
Peak Hill, *New S. Wales* C10–328 **109**
Peak Hill, *W. Australia* E08–257 **110**
Peale, Mt., *Utah* V26+384 **94**
Pearce Point, *N.-W. Terr.* W17+690 **88**
Pearl R., *Mississippi* T88+306 **95**
Pearl Harbor, *Hawaiian Is.* Y45+212 **107**
Pearsall, *Texas* U54+290 **94**
Peary Ld., *Greenland* Q35+830 **26**
Pebane, *Mozambique* K40-168 **83**
Pebble I., *Falkland Islands* R88–512 **103**
Pébo, *Cent. Afr. Rep.* L68+080 **81**
Pec, *Yugoslavia* L58+427 **58**
Pechenga, *U.S.S.R.* K84+696 **62**
Pechora, *U.S.S.R.* J14+648 **62**
Pechora, R., *U.S.S.R.* J47+660 **62**
Pecos, *New Mexico* V04+356 **94**
Pecos, *Texas* U82+314 **94**
Pecos R., *Texas, etc.* U72+310 **94**
Pecs, *Hungary* L71+461 **58**
Pedernales, *Venezuela* S13+098 **104**
Pedhoulas, *Cyprus* K73+350 **76**
Pedregal, *Panama* T44+084 **101**
Pedro Pt., *Sri Lanka* G58+198 **70**
Pedroll, *Brazil* Q69–045 **105**
Pedro Luro, *Argentina* S16–396 **103**
Pedrotallagalla, mt., *Sri Lanka* G56+071 **70**
Peebinga, *S. Australia* C54–349 **109**
Peebles, *Scotland* N19+556 **41**
Peekskill, *New York* S83+413 **96**
Peel R., *Yukon* X05+658 **88**
Peenemünde, *E. Germany* M07+541 **48**
Peery L., *New S. Wales* C38–308 **109**
Peetri, *Estonia* L25+589 **47**
Pegasus, & B., *New Zealand* A41–432 **112**
Pega Yoma, *Burma* F55+190 **71**
Pegu, *Burma* F51+173 **71**
Pegunungan Maoke,
 New Guinea C80–038 **65**
Pehan, *China* D52+482 **64**
Pehowa, *India* G80+299 **72**
Pehuajó, *Argentina* S11–357 **103**
Peinsta, mt., *Chile* S81–503 **103**
Peip ng. *See* Peking
Peipus, L., *See* Chudskoye Oz.
Peixe, *Brazil* R21–120 **105**
Pekan, *Malaya* F10+036 **69**
Pekin, *Illinois* T88+406 **91**
Peking, *China* E21+400 **66**
Pelagie Is., *Medit. Sea* M13+355 **81**
Pélagos, I., *Greece* L36+393 **59**
Peledui, *U.S.S.R.* E42+597 **63**
Pelée L., *Ontario* T46+418 **91**
Peleng, I., *Indonesia* D70–014 **65**
Peljesac Pen., *Yugoslavia* L76+430 **57**
Pelkosenniemi, *Finland* L15+670 **46**
Pella, *Greece* L48+409 **59**
Pella, *Iowa* U18+414 **95**
Pellegrini, *Argentina* S19–362 **103**
Pellworr I., *W. Germany* M38+545 **48**
Pelly Pt., *N.-W. Terr.* U66+701 **88**
Pelly Ra., *Yukon* W70+612 **88**
Pelly R., *Yukon* W83+618 **88**
Peloncillo Ra., *Arizona* V25+326 **94**
Peloponnisos, *Greece* L48+370 **59**
Pelotas, *Brazil* R45–318 **103**
Pemba I., *E. Africa* K52–052 **83**
Pembroke, *Ontario* T13+458 **91**
Pembroke, *Wales* N30+517 **38**
Pembroke, C., *Falkland Is.* R76–516 **103**
Pembroke, C., *N.-W. Terr.* T35+635 **89**
Penafiel, *Portugal* N50+412 **52**
Peñafiel, *Spain* N25+413 **52**
Penalva, *Brazil* R00–031 **105**
Penambo Ra., *Sarawak* E30+030 **65**
Peña Negra, Sa. de, *Spain* N37+421 **52**
Penápolis, *Brazil* R30–215 **105**
Peñaranda de Bracamonte,
 Spain N31+409 **52**
Peñarroya, *Spain* N28+383 **52**
Penarth, *Wales* N19+514 **38**
Penas, G. de, *Chile* T00–472 **103**
Pendembu, *Sierra Leone* N64+082 **80**
Pendleton, *Arkansas* U09+340 **97**
Pendleton, *Oregon* V83+457 **92**
Pend Oreille, L., *Idaho* V70+480 **98**
Penedo, *Brazil* Q39–103 **105**
Penedono, *Portugal* N45+410 **52**
Penggaram, *Malaya* F13+019 **69**
Penghu, Is., *China* E03+234 **67**
Penglai, *China* D85+378 **66**
Pengpu, *China* E15+328 **64**
Penguin, *Tasmania* C24–411 **109**
Penhalonga, *Rhodesia* K74–188 **84**
Peniche, *Portugal* N56+394 **52**
Penicuik, *Scotland* N19+558 **41**
Peñiscola, *Spain* M88+404 **53**
Penn, *N. Dakota* U54+483 **93**
Pennfield, *New Brunswick* S40+451 **90**
Pennine, Alpi, *Switzerland* M46+460 **45**
Pennine Chain, *England* N14+540 **37**
Penns Grove, *New Jersey* T03+397 **96**
Pennsylvania, state, *U.S.A.* T25+408 **99**
Penn Yan, *New York* T12+427 **96**
Penobscot B., *Maine* S54+441 **90**
Penola, *S. Australia* C55–374 **109**
Penong, *S. Australia* D12–318 **110**
Penonome, *Panama* T32+082 **101**
Penrith, *England* N17+547 **37**

Penrith, *New South Wales* B86–338 **109**
Pensacola, *Florida* T73+304 **93**
Penshurst. *Victoria* C46–379 **109**
Pentland Firth, *Scotland* N20+587 **40**
Pentland Hills, *Scotland* N21+558 **41**
Pentwater, *Michigan* T68+438 **91**
Penza, *U.S.S.R.* K00+532 **61**
Penzance, *England* N33+501 **38**
Penzhino, *U.S.S.R.* A71+633 **63**
Penzhinskaya Guba, *U.S.S.R.* B20+610 **63**
Peoria, *Illinois* T88+407 **95**
Peperga, *Netherlands* M54+528 **44**
Pepinster, *Belgium* M55+506 **44**
Peqin, *Albania* L62+411 **58**
Perak, *Malaya* F54+054 **69**
Peralta, *Spain* N11+424 **53**
Perce, *Quebec* S26+485 **90**
Perdido, Mte., *Spain* M87+427 **53**
Pereira, *Colombia* T04+048 **104**
Perello, *Spain* M86+409 **53**
Perez, *Chile* S60–260 **103**
Pergamno, *Argentina* S04–338 **103**
Perho, *Finland* L33+632 **46**
Peribonca R., *Quebec* S68+510 **90**
Perico, *Argentina* S31–244 **103**
Perigueux, *France* M85+452 **55**
Perija, Sa. de, *Venezuela* S76+100 **104**
Perim I., *Red Sea* K09+127 **74**
Peripery, *Brazil* Q71–042 **105**
Peristéra, I., *Greece* L36+392 **59**
Perlas & Lag. de las, *Nic.* T52+124 **101**
Perlas, Arch. de las, *Pan.* T26+084 **101**
Perm, *U.S.S.R.* J23+580 **61**
Pernambuco (Recife), *Braz.* Q30–080 **105**
Peronne, *France* M72+499 **54**
Péronnes, *Belgium* M65+504 **44**
Perpignan, *France* M73+427 **55**
Perranporth, *England* N31+503 **38**
Perrot I., *Quebec* S84+454 **91**
Perry, *Iowa* U24+418 **95**
Perry, *New York* T18+428 **96**
Perry, *Oklahoma* U44+362 **95**
Perry R., *N.-W. Terr.* U80+666 **88**
Perryville, *Missouri* T89+377 **97**
Persepolis, *Iran* J42+300 **75**
Persia. *See* Iran
Persian Gulf, *See* The Gulf
Perth, *New Brunswick* S46+467 **90**
Perth, *Ontario* T08+449 **91**
Perth, *W. Australia* E25–319 **110**
Perth, *Scotland* N21+564 **41**
Perth Amboy, *New Jersey* S86+405 **96**
Peru, *Indiana* T67+407 **91**
Peru, rep., *S. America* **104**
Perufune, *Japan* C40+424 **68**
Perugia, *Italy* M20+431 **56**
Peruibe, *Brazil* R12–242 **105**
Peruwelz, *Belgium* M68+505 **44**
Pervijze, *Belgium* M73+511 **44**
Pervomaisk, *Ukraine* K85+481 **60**
Perwez, *Belgium* M61+506 **44**
Pesaro, *Italy* M12+439 **56**
Pescadores Is. *See* Penghu Is.
Pescara, *Italy* M05+425 **56**
Peschici, *Italy* L84+419 **57**
Peshawar, *Pakistan* H20+340 **72**
Peshtigo R., *Wisconsin* T80+455 **91**
Pesqueira, *Brazil* Q40–084 **105**
Pestravka, *U.S.S.R.* J60+524 **61**
Petah Tiqva, *Israel* K61+321 **76**
Petalioi. G. of. *Greece* L35+379 **59**
Petalioi. I., *Greece* L34+380 **59**
Petaluma, *California* W16+383 **92**
Peterborough, *England* N03+526 **37**
Peterborough, *Ontario* T20+443 **91**
Peterborough, *S. Australia* C67–329 **109**
Peter I. Øy, *Antarctica* U05–690 **27**
Peterhead, *Scotland* N11+575 **40**
Peterlee, *England* N08+548 **37**
Petermann Fd., *Greenland* S05+810 **26**
Petermann Pk., *Greenland* Q00+730 **26**
Petermann Ra., *W. Aust.* D35–250 **110**
Peter Pond L., *Sask.* V22+558 **88**
Petersburg, *Alaska* W75+568 **99**
Petersburg, *Virginia* T15+372 **97**
Peterupe. *Latvia* L33+573 **47**
Petit Bois I., *Alabama* T80+302 **95**
Petit Francois. *Fr. Guiana* R44+031 **105**
Petit Nord Pen., *Nfd.* R70+509 **90**
Petitot R., *Brit. Columbia* W08+598 **88**
Petitsikapau L., *Labrador* S40+544 **89**
Peto, *Mexico* T82+201 **100**
Petone, *New Zealand* A31–412 **112**
Petoroa, *Chile* S66–321 **103**
Petoskey, *Michigan* T60+454 **91**
Petra, *Jordan* K57+303 **76**
Petra Velikogo Zaliv, *U.S.S.R.* D18+428 **63**
Petrich, *Bulgaria* L41+414 **58**
Petrified Forest Nat. Mon.,
 Arizona V28+348 **94**
Petrinja, *Yugoslavia* L82+454 **56**
Petrodvorets, *U.S.S.R.* L02+598 **60**
Petrolia, *Ontario* T43+429 **91**
Petrolina, *Brazil* Q63–094 **105**
Petropavlovsk, *Kazakh.* H35+549 **62**
Petropavlovsk, *U.S.S.R.* B36+530 **63**
Petropolis, *Brazil* Q80–225 **105**
Petrovac, *Yugoslavia* L51+444 **58**
Petrovsk, *U.S.S.R.* J22+536 **61**
Petrovsk, *U.S.S.R.* E66+513 **63**
Petrovsk, *U.S.S.R.* J88+523 **61**
Petrozavodsk, *U.S.S.R.* K65+618 **62**
Petsamo. *See* Pechenga
Pettigoe, *Ireland, Rep.* N47+545 **42**
Pevas, *Peru* S71–032 **104**
Pewsey, *England* N11+513 **39**
Pézenas, *France* M70+435 **55**
Pforzheim, *W. Germany* M38+489 **48**
Phagwara, *India* G85+312 **72**
Phalodi, *India* H16+270 **70**
Phanom Dang Rae,
 Thailand F16 + 143 **69**
Phan Rang, *S. Vietnam* E65+116 **69**
Phan-Thiet & B. of,
 S. Vietnam E71+110 **69**
Phaphund, *India* G63+266 **73**
Phatthalung, *Thailand* F29+076 **69**
Phenix City, *Alabama* T60+325 **97**
Phet Buri, *Thailand* F31+132 **69**
Philadelphia, *Pennsylvania* T01+400 **91**
Philip, *S. Dakota* U70+441 **93**
Philippeville, *Belgium* M63+502 **44**

Philippeville & G. of,
(Skikda), *Algeria* M48+366 **80**
Philippi, *W. Virginia* T30+391 **91**
Philippi, L., *Queensland* C66-244 **111**
Philippines. Is., *Pacific Oc.* **65**
Philippopolis. See Plovdiv
Philiaur, *India* G85+310 **72**
Phillip I., *Victoria* C28-384 **109**
Phillip Edward I., *Ontario* T38+459 **91**
Phillips, *Maine* S62+448 **90**
Phillips, *Wisconsin* U03+457 **91**
Phillipsburg, *Kansas* U56+398 **95**
Phillipsburg, *New Jersey* T01+406 **96**
Philomena, *Alberta* V39+551 **88**
Phitsanulok Muang, *Thailand* F29+170 **69**
Phnom-Penh, *Khmer* F00+115 **69**
Phoenix, *Arizona* V43+334 **94**
Phoenix I., *Phoenix Is.* Z36-040 **106**
Phoenix Is., *Pacific Ocean* Z40-040 **106**
Phoenixville, *Pennsylvania* T03+401 **96**
Pho-mo-chang-thang Tso,
Tibet F87+286 **71**
Phu-dien, *N. Vietnam* E86+190 **69**
Phulji, *Pakistan* H43+270 **70**
Phulpur, *India* G47+255 **73**
Phu-Quoc, I., *Khmer* F06+102 **69**
Phu-yen, *S. Vietnam* E65+134 **69**
Piacenza, *Italy* M32+450 **56**
Pian. R., *New S. Wales* C06-302 **109**
Piangil, *Victoria* C41-351 **109**
Pianosa, I., *Italy* M29+426 **56**
Pias, *Portugal* N45+380 **52**
Piatra Neamt, *Romania* L22+469 **58**
Piazza Armerina, *Sicily* M04+373 **57**
Piazzi, I.. *Chile* S84-518 **103**
Pibor Post, *Sudan* K72+068 **81**
Picardie, prov., *France* M78+500 **54**
Piceno. See Ascoli.
Pichanal, *Argentina* S26-233 **103**
Picher, *Oklahoma* U30+370 **95**
Pichilemu, *Chile* S71-344 **103**
Pickens, *Mississippi* U00+329 **97**
Pickering, *England* N05+542 **37**
Pickwick L., *Tennessee, etc.* T78+349 **95**
Picola, *Victoria* C29-360 **109**
Picos, *Brazil* Q85-059 **105**
Picton, *New South Wales* B87-342 **109**
Picton, *New Zealand* A36-413 **112**
Picton, *Ontario* T13+440 **91**
Picton, Mt., *Tasmania* C21-432 **109**
Pictou, *Nova Scotia* S15+458 **90**
Pictou I., *Nova Scotia* S17+457 **90**
Picun Leufu, *Argentina* S55-395 **103**
Pidark, *Pakistan* H71+257 **70**
Piedad, La, *Mexico* U73+203 **100**
Piedmont, *Missouri* U05+371 **97**
Piedmont, *Quebec* S84+459 **91**
Piedmont, *S. Carolina* T45+347 **97**
Piedmont, *S. Dakota* U81+442 **93**
Piedrahita, *Spain* N32+405 **52**
Piedras Negras, *Mexico* U63+288 **100**
Piedra Sola, *Uruguay* R67-320 **103**
Pieksämäki, *Finland* L17+623 **46**
Pielinen, *Finland* L04+633 **46**
Pieman R., *Tasmania* C30-417 **109**
Piemonte, dep., *Italy* M44+450 **56**
Pierre, *S. Dakota* U62+444 **93**
Pierreville, *Quebec* S77+461 **91**
Pietarsaari (Jakobstad), *Fin.* L44+637 **46**
Pietermaritzburg, *Natal* K88-296 **84**
Pietersburg, *Transvaal* L04-238 **84**
Piggot, *Arkansas* U02+364 **95**
Pigue, *Argentina* S15-376 **103**
Pihtipudas, *Finland* L26+634 **46**
Pikes Pk., *Colorado* V00+388 **94**
Pikeville, *Kentucky* T45+374 **97**
Pila, *Argentina* R80-360 **103**
Piła, *Poland* L80+532 **49**
Pilao Arcado, *Brazil* Q75-102 **105**
Pilar, *Argentina* S07-314 **103**
Pilar, *Brazil* R28-147 **105**
Pilar, *Paraguay* R80-269 **103**
Pilar, C., *Chile* S88-528 **103**
Pilcaniyeu, *Argentina* S64-410 **103**
Pilibhit, *India* G61+286 **73**
Pilliga, *New South Wales* C07-304 **109**
Pillinger, *Tasmania* C27-424 **109**
Pilos, *Greece* L50+369 **59**
Pilot, The, *New S. Wales* C11-368 **109**
Pilot Knob, *Missouri* U04+374 **97**
Pilsen. See Plzen.
Piltene, *Latvia* L50+547 **47**
Pi Mai, *Thailand* F15+152 **69**
Pimentel, *Peru* T29-067 **104**
Pina, *Spain* N03+415 **53**
Pinaki I., *Tuamotu Arch.* X20-195 **107**
Pinaleno Ra., *Arizona* V30+326 **94**
Pinang I., *Malaya* F28+051 **69**
Pinarbasi, *Turkey* K52+387 **74**
Pinar del Rio, *Cuba* T52+224 **101**
Pincknevville, *Illinois* T87+381 **97**
Pind Dadan Khan, *Pakistan* H12+326 **72**
Pindhos, mts., *Greece* L50+393 **59**
Pindi Gheb, *Pakistan* H16+332 **72**
Pine I., *Florida* T43+266 **97**
Pine Mts., *Kentucky* T52+369 **97**
Pine Bluff, *Arkansas* U12+342 **97**
Pine City, *Minnesota* U18+458 **93**
Pine Creek, *N. Territory,*
Australia D18-138 **110**
Pinedale, *Wyoming* V28+429 **93**
Pinehurst, *N. Carolina* T27+352 **97**
Pineola, *N. Carolina* T42+362 **97**
Pine River, *Minnesota* U26+467 **93**
Pinetown, *Natal* K86-298 **84**
Pineville, *Kentucky* T52+367 **97**
Pineville, *Missouri* U26+366 **95**
Pineville, *W. Virginia* T38+376 **97**
Piney Buttes, *Montana* V12+475 **93**
Ping-chuan-chow, *China* E07+410 **66**
Pingelap, I., *Caroline Is.*
B25+045 **106**
Pingelly, *W. Australia* E18-324 **110**
Pingkiang, *China* E38+285 **67**
Pingliang, *China* E80+354 **66**
Pinglo, *China* E55+246 **67**
Pingrup, *W. Australia* E07-333 **110**
Ping-ting-chow, *China* E39+378 **66**
Pingwu, *China* F02+323 **66**
Pingyang. See Linfen.

Pingyüan, *China* E21+371 **66**
Pinhel, *Portugal* N42+408 **52**
Pini, I., *Indonesia* F38+002 **65**
Pinjarra, *W. Australia* E25-326 **110**
Pinnacles, *New South Wales* C52-321 **109**
Pinnaroo, *S. Australia* C55-353 **109**
Pinos, *Mexico* U69+228 **100**
Pinos, I. de, *Cuba* T47+216 **101**
Pinos, Mt., *California* V85+348 **92**
Pinrang, *Celébes,* E02-038 **65**
Pinsk, *Belorussia* L24+521 **60**
Pintados, *Chile* S58-207 **103**
Pinto, *Argentina* S16-292 **103**
Pioneer, Os., *U.S.S.R.* F80+800 **63**
Piotrkow, *Poland* L62+509 **49**
Pipar, *India* H08+264 **70**
Pipestone, *Minnesota* U36+440 **98**
Pipinas, *Argentina* R74-355 **103**
Pipmuacan L., *Quebec* S62+496 **90**
Pippli, *India* G15+216 **71**
Piqua, *Ohio* T56+401 **91**
Piracuruca, *Brazil* Q70-039 **105**
Piraeus. See Piraievs.
Piraievs, *Greece* L38+379 **59**
Piramide, mt., *Chile* S81-490 **103**
Piranhas, *Brazil* Q47-095 **105**
Pirapora, *Brazil* R00-173 **105**
Piratini, *Brazil* R49-314 **103**
Piray, *Argentina* R59-266 **103**
Pirgos, *Greece* L45+366 **59**
Pirgos, *Greece* L51+377 **59**
Pirgos, *Crete* L29+350 **59**
Pirin Planina, *Bulgaria-*
Greece L40+415 **58**
Piritu, *Venezuela* S30+101 **104**
Pirmasens, *W. Germany* M45+492 **48**
Pirna, *E. Germany* M06+510 **48**
Pirot, *Yugoslavia* L45+431 **58**
Pir Panjal Ra., *Kashmir* H04+340 **72**
Pisa, *Italy* M44+437 **56**
Pisagua, *Chile* S62-196 **103**
Pisco, *Peru* T08-136 **104**
Pisek, *Czechoslovakia* M05+493 **48**
Pishin, *Pakistan* H48+305 **70**
Pishin, *Iran* H79+261 **75**
Pisticci, *Italy* L80+404 **57**
Pitanguy, *Brazil* Q89-198 **105**
Pitarpunga L., *N.S.W.* C40-344 **109**
Pitcairn I., *Pacific Ocean* W60-25⊂ **107**
Pite Älv, *Sweden* L64+660 **46**
Piteå, *Sweden* L51+653 **46**
Piterka, *U.S.S.R.* J75+506 **61**
Pitesti, *Romania* L31+449 **58**
Pithiviers, *France* M77+482 **54**
Pithoria, *India* G69+241 **73**
Pitlochry, *Scotland* N22+567 **41**
Pitt, Mt., *Oregon* W14+424 **92**
Pitt R., *California* W11+409 **92**
Pittsboro, *N. Carolina* T25+357 **93**
Pittsburg, *Kansas* U28+371 **99**
Pittsburgh, *Pennsylvania* T30+405 **91**
Pittsfield, *Illinois* U05+396 **95**
Pittsfield, *Maine* S56+448 **90**
Pittsfield, *Massachusetts* S79+424 **91**
Pittston, *Pennsylvania* T05+41⊃ **96**
Piua-Petri, *Romania* L13+446 **58**
Piaura, *Peru* T34-052 **104**
Piza, *Latvia* L48+576 **47**
Placentia B., *Newfoundland* R58+468 **90**
Placer Guadalupe, *Mexico* VC2+292 **100**
Plainfield, *New Jersey* S87+4⊆6 **91**
Plainview, *Nebraska* U49+42⊂ **95**
Plainview, *Texas* U70+342 **94**
Plainwell, *Michigan* T64+425 **91**
Pláka B., *Crete* L34+352 **59**
Plakoti C., *Cyprus* K65+355 **76**
Plana, *Czechoslovakia* M13-498 **48**
Planaltina, *Brazil* R16-156 **105**
Planina, *Yugoslavia* M05+458 **56**
Plant City, *Florida* T43+280 **97**
Plascencia, *Spain* N36+401 **52**
Plaski, *Yugoslavia* L88+45C **56**
Plassen, *Norway* M15+611 **47**
Plaster Rock, *N.B.* S44+470 **90**
Plastun, *U.S.S.R.* C82+446 **63**
Plata. R. de la,
Argent., etc. R70-350 **103**
Platamon. *Greece* L44+400 **59**
Plati, *Greece* L45+405 **59**
Platres, *Cyprus* K73+349 **76**
Platt Nat. Park, *Oklahoma* U42+345 **98**
Platte R., *Nebraska* U60+408 **95**
Platteville, *Wisconsin* U03+428 **95**
Plattsburg, *Missouri* U27+396 **95**
Plattsburg, *New York* S81+447 **91**
Plattsmouth, *Nebraska* U36+410 **95**
Plauen, *E. Germany* M17+505 **48**
Plav, *Yugoslavia* L60+426 **58**
Plavnica, *Yugoslavia* L55+423 **58**
Playas L., *New Mexico* V23+317 **98**
Plaza Huincul, *Argentina* S55-389 **103**
Pleasant B., *Maine* S47+445 **90**
Pleasant Grove, *Utah* V41+404 **94**
Pleasantville, *New Jersey* S84+392 **96**
Pleiku, *S. Vietnam* E⁻2+140 **65**
Plenty, B. of, *New Zealand* A18-378 **112**
Plentywood, *Montana* U88+488 **93**
Plessisville, *Quebec* S70+462 **91**
Plettenberg B., *Cape Prov.* L38-324 **84**
Pleven, *Bulgaria* L3⁻+434 **58**
Pljevlja, *Yugoslavia* L64+434 **58**
Płock, *Poland* L61+525 **49**
Ploiesti, *Romania* L24+449 **58**
Plomarion, *Greece* ⊥22+389 **59**
Plomosa Mts., *Arizona* V53+338 **92**
Plon, *W. Germany* M28+541 **48**
Plonge, Lac la, *Saskatchewan* V13+552 **88**
Plovdiv, *Bulgaria* ⊥32+421 **58**
Plumtree, *Rhodesia* L12-206 **84**
Plymouth, *Indiana* T68+414 **91**
Plymouth, *Massachusetts* S64+420 **91**
Plymouth, *New Jersey* S44+420 **91**
Plymouth, *N. Carolina* T10+359 **97**
Plymouth, *Pennsy vania* T06+413 **96**
Plymouth, *Wisconsin* T78+438 **91**
Plymouth & Sd., *England* N25+504 **38**
Plynlimmon, *Wales* N22+525 **38**
Plzeň, *Czechoslovakia* M10+492 **48**
Poaí, *China* E4 +352 **66**
Pobedy, Pik, mt., *China, etc.* G60+420 **62**

Pobla de Segur, *Spain* M84+422 **53**
Pocahontas, *Arkansas* U06+362 **95**
Pocahontas, *Virginia* T38+373 **97**
Pocatello, *Idaho* V45+428 **94**
Pochinki, *U.S.S.R.* K01+547 **61**
Pochutla, *Mexico* U39+158 **100**
Pocklington, *England* N05+539 **37**
Podkagernaya, *U.S.S.R.* B19+604 **63**
Podkamennaya Tunguska,
U.S.S.R. G00+616 **63**
Podlubovo, *U.S.S.R.* J25+543 **61**
Podolsk, *U.S.S.R.* K45+554 **60**
Pogamasing, *Ontario* T41+469 **91**
Pohai, G. of, *China* E06+385 **66**
Pohai, Str. of, *China* D84+385 **66**
Point L., *N.-W. Territories* V50+652 **88**
Pointe à Pitre. *Leeward Is.* S08+164 **101**
Pointe du Chene, *N.B.* S27+462 **90**
Poitiers, *France* M88+466 **54**
Poitou, prov., *France* N02+465 **54**
Poix, *Belgium* M58+500 **44**
Poix, *France* M78+498 **54**
Pokaakku, I., *Pacific Ocean* A65+140 **106**
Pokaran, *India* H20+268 **70**
Pokataroo, *New S. Wales* C08-296 **109**
Pokemouche, *N.B.* S29+477 **90**
Pokhara, *Nepal* G36+282 **73**
Pokka, *Finland* L26+681 **46**
Pokrovsk, *U.S.S.R.* K14+531 **61**
Pokrovsk, *U.S.S.R.* K36+474 **61**
Pokrovsk. See Engels.
Pokrovskoe, *U.S.S.R.* D34+613 **63**
Pola. See Pula.
Pola de Siero, *Spain* N34+434 **52**
Poland, rep., *Cent. Europe* L72+520 **51**
Polesk, *U.S.S.R.* L53+548 **47**
Polevskoi, *U.S.S.R.* H89+564 **61**
Polgahawela, *Sri Lanka* G58+074 **70**
Polgar, *Hungary* L53+478 **49**
Poli, *Cameroun* M10+084 **81**
Poliaigos, I., *Greece* L32+368 **59**
Policastro, G. di, *Italy* L86+400 **57**
Poligny, *France* M56+468 **54**
Polillo Is., *Philippines* D78+148 **65**
Pólinos, See Poliaigos, I.
Polis, *Cyprus* K75+350 **76**
Pollensa, *Balearic Islands* M71+399 **53**
Polotsk, *Belorussia* L08+555 **60**
Polson, *Montana* V55+477 **92**
Poltava, *Ukraine* K62+496 **60**
Poluostrov Buzachi, *Kazakh.* J50+448 **62**
Põlva, *Estonia* L18+580 **47**
Polynesia, *Pacific Oc.* Z30-100 **106**
Poman, *Argentina* S37-283 **103**
Pomaro, *Mexico* V75+184 **100**
Pombal, *Brazil* Q47-067 **105**
Pombal, *Portugal* N52+399 **52**
Pombets, *Japan* C38+431 **68**
Pomene, *Mozambique* K56-230 **84**
Pomeroy, *N. Ireland* N41+546 **42**
Pommersche B., *E. Germany* M04+542 **48**
Pomorie, *Bulgaria* L15+426 **58**
Pomorze, *Poland* L72+536 **49**
Pomos Pt., *Cyprus* K75+352 **76**
Pompey's Pillar, *Montana* V17+460 **93**
Ponape, I., *Caroline Islands* B45+070 **106**
Ponca City, *Oklahoma* U42+366 **95**
Ponce, *Puerto Rico* S39+180 **101**
Pondicherry, *India* G61+120 **70**
Ponente, Riviera di, *Italy* M40+437 **56**
Ponferrada, *Spain* N39+425 **52**
Ponoi, *U.S.S.R.* K24+670 **61**
Pons, *France* N03+456 **54**
Pons, *Spain* M83+419 **53**
Ponta Grossa, *Brazil* R31-252 **103**
Pontardawe, *Wales* N23+517 **38**
Pont-Audemer, *France* M87+494 **54**
Pontchartrain, L., *Louisiana* U00+302 **95**
Pont Chateau, *France* N12+474 **54**
Pont d'Ain, *France* M58+461 **54**
Ponte Boa, *Brazil* S36-026 **104**
Ponte da Barca, *Portugal* N51+418 **52**
Ponte de Sôr, *Portugal* N48+392 **52**
Pontefract, *England* N08+537 **37**
Ponte Nova, *Brazil* Q78-204 **105**
Pontevedra, *Spain* N52+424 **52**
Pontiac, *Illinois* T82+409 **91**
Pontiac, *Michigan* T50+427 **91**
Pontianak, *Borneo* E64-002 **65**
Pontivy, *France* N18+481 **54**
Pontoise, *France* M77+491 **54**
Pontotoc, *Mississippi* T84+342 **97**
Pontresina, *Switzerland* M31+465 **45**
Ponts, les, *Switzerland* M50+470 **45**
Pontypool, *Wales* N18+517 **38**
Pontypool, *Ontario* T22+441 **91**
Pontypridd, *Wales* N20+516 **38**
Ponza, I., *Italy* M12+410 **57**
Poole, *England* N12+507 **39**
Poole, Mt., *New. S. Wales* C50-297 **109**
Poolewe. *Scotland* N34+578 **40**
Poona, *India* H06+186 **70**
Pooncarie, *New South Wales* C46-334 **109**
Poopelloe, L., *New S. Wales* C36-316 **109**
Poopo, *Bolivia* S42-184 **104**
Poopo, L., *Bolivia* S43-188 **104**
Popa Mt., *Burma* F58+209 **71**
Popakai, *Surinam* R62+032 **105**
Popayan, *Colombia* T09+025 **104**
Poperinge, *Belgium* M74+508 **44**
Poplar, *Montana* V01+481 **93**
Poplar R., *Manitoba* U37+528 **88**
Poplar Bluff, *Missouri* U02+368 **97**
Poplarville, *Mississippi* T87+308 **97**
Popocatepetl, mt., *Mexico* U52+192 **100**
Popovača, *Yugoslavia* L80+456 **56**
Poppel, *Belgium* M60+514 **44**
Porahat, *India* G27+226 **73**
Porbandar, *India* H33+216 **70**
Porcupine R., *Alaska* X40+698 **99**
Poreč, *Yugoslavia* M08+452 **56**
Pori, *Finland* L50+615 **47**
Porjus, *Sweden* L61+670 **46**
Porkhov, *U.S.S.R.* L03+578 **60**
Porkkala, *Finland* L34+600 **47**
Porlamar, *Margarita I.,*
Venezuela S23+109 **104**
Pornic. *France* N13+471 **54**
Poronaysk, *U.S.S.R.* C42+492 **63**
Poros I., *Greece* L39+375 **59**

Poro Tso, *Tibet* G38+310 **71**
Porsanger Fd., *Norway* L28+704 **46**
Porsanger-halvøya, *Norway* L36+700 **46**
Porsgrund, *Norway* M32+591 **47**
Portachuela, *Bolivia* S20-171 **104**
Port Adelaide, *S. Australia* C69-349 **109**
Portadown, *N. Ireland* N39+544 **42**
Portaferry, *N. Ireland* N33+544 **42**
Portage, *Wisconsin* T87+436 **91**
Portage I., *New Brunswick* S30+472 **90**
Portage la Prairie, *Manitoba* U50+500 **88**
Portage River, *N. B.* S30+474 **90**
Portageville, *New York* T18+426 **96**
Portal, *N. Dakota* U75+490 **93**
Portal, *N. Saskatchewan* U76+491 **88**
Port Albert, *Victoria* C20-386 **109**
Portalegre, *Portugal* N45+393 **52**
Portales, *New Mexico* U80+341 **94**
Port Alfred, *Quebec* S65+484 **90**
Port Allen, *Louisiana* U07+304 **91**
Port Antonio, *Jamaica* T08+182 **101**
Portarlington, *Ireland, Rep.* N44+532 **43**
Port Arthur. See Lushun
Port Arthur, *Tasmania* C13-432 **109**
Port Arthur, *Texas* U23+299 **95**
Port Augusta, *S. Australia* C74-325 **109**
Port au Port B., *Nfd.* R84+490 **90**
Port au Prince, *Haiti* S73+186 **101**
Port aux Baxques, *Nfd.* R85+476 **90**
Port Blandford, *Nfd.* R55+484 **90**
Port Borden, *Pr. Edward I.* S22+462 **90**
Port Broughton, *South*
Australia C73-336 **109**
Port Campbell, *Victoria* C42-386 **109**
Port Chalmers, *N.Z.* A56-457 **112**
Port Chester, *New York* S81+410 **96**
Port Clinton, *Ohio* T48+415 **91**
Port Cornwallis,
Andaman Islands F72+134 **71**
Port Dalhousie, *Ontario* T26+432 **91**
Port Daniel *Quebec* S29+482 **90**
Port Darwin, *Falkland Is.* R84-518 **103**
Port Davey, *Tasmania* C24-434 **109**
Port de Paix, *Haiti* S76+199 **101**
Port Dickson, *Malaya* F19+02 **69**
Port Douglas, *Queensland* C28-164 **111**
Port Dover, *Ontario* T31+428 **91**
Portel, *Brazil* R34-019 **105**
Port Elgin, *Ontario* T38+445 **91**
Port Elizabeth, *Cape Prov.* L26-340 **84**
Port Ellen, *Scotland* N37+556 **41**
Port Etienne, *Mauritania* P12+210 **80**
Port Eynon, *Wales* N25+516 **38**
Port Fairy, *Victoria* C47-384 **109**
Port Germein, *S. Australia* C72-330 **109**
Port Gibson, *Mississippi* U06+320 **95**
Port Glasgow, *Scotland* N27+559 **41**
Porglenone, *N. Ireland* N39+549 **42**
Portgordon, *Scotland* N18+577 **40**
Port Harcourt, *Nigeria* M48+048 **80**
Port Hedland, *W. Australia* E08-205 **110**
Porthmadog, *Wales* N25+529 **38**
Port Hope, *Michigan* T46+440 **91**
Port Hope, *Ontario* T20+439 **91**
Port Huron, *Michigan* T45+430 **91**
Portimão, *Portugal* N51+371 **52**
Port Jackson, *New. S. Wales* B83-339 **109**
Port Jervis, *New York* S88+414 **96**
Port Joli, *Nova Scotia* S38+438 **90**
Port Kelang, *Malaya* F22+030 **69**
Port Kembla, *New S. Wales* B85-345 **109**
Portland, *Arkansas* U09+332 **97**
Portland, *Maine* S62+437 **90**
Portland, *New South Wales* C00-334 **109**
Portland, *Oregon* W16+455 **92**
Portland, *Victoria* C51-383 **109**
Portland C., *Tasmania* C13-407 **109**
Portland Harb. & I., *Eng.* N14+506 **38**
Portland Point, *Jamaica* T13+178 **101**
Portland Prom., *Quebec* T20+590 **89**
Port Laoise, *Ireland, Rep.* N44+530 **43**
Port Lavaca, *Texas* U40+286 **94**
Portlaw, *Ireland, Rep.* N44+522 **43**
Port Lincoln, *S. Australia* C85-347 **111**
Port Loko, *Sierra Leone* N76+088 **80**
Port Lyautey. See Kenitra N40+344 **80**
Port M'Donnell, *S. Aust.* C56-380 **109**
Port M'Nicoll, *Ontario* T29+448 **91**
Port Macquarie, *N.S.W.* B73-314 **109**
Port Medway, *Nova Scotia* S27+441 **90**
Port Menier, *Anticosti I., Que.* S26+498 **90**
Port Moresby, *Papua New Guinea*
C17-094 **111**
Portnacroish, *Scotland* N32+566 **41**
Port Nelson (abandoned),
Manitoba U18+567 **89**
Portneuf, *Quebec* S71+467 **91**
Port Nolloth, *Cape Province* L78-292 **84**
Port Norris, *New Jersey* T00+392 **91**
Porto, *Portugal* N52+411 **52**
Porto Acre, *Brazil* S46-097 **104**
Porto Alegre, *Brazil* Q57-180 **105**
Porto Alegre, *Brazil* R37-300 **103**
Porto Alegre, *Brazil* Q74-034 **105**
Porto Alexandre, *Angola* M18-158 **84**
Porto Amelia, *Mozambique* K26-130 **83**
Porto Barreirão, *Brazil* R20-126 **105**
Portobelo, *Panama* T28+096 **101**
Porto Botte, *Sardinia* M39+391 **57**
Porto Camargo, *Brazil* R53-234 **105**
Porto Civitanova, *Italy* M08+433 **56**
Porto d'Ascoli, *Italy* M07+429 **56**
Porto de Moz, *Brazil* R42-018 **105**
Porto de Moz, *Portugal* N53+394 **52**
Porto do Jeronymo, *Brazil* R31-186 **105**
Porto Empedocle, *Sicily* M09+373 **57**
Porto Esperanca, *Brazil* R74-197 **105**
Porto Espiridião, *Brazil* R79-158 **104**
Porto Franco, *Brazil* R26-086 **105**
Porto Franco, *Brazil* R13-099 **105**
Porto Franco, *Brazil* R14-064 **105**
Port of Spain, *Trinidad* S08+107 **104**
Porto Guaira, *Brazil* R55-240 **105**
Port Okha, *India* H36+223 **70**
Portola, *California* W03+398 **92**
Porto Lucena, *Brazil* R60-277 **103**
Porto Mendes, *Brazil* R56-244 **105**
Porto Nacional, *Brazil* R20-108 **105**
Porto Novo, *Benin* M74+064 **80**
Porto Novo, *India* G62+116 **70**

Port Ontario, *New York* T07+435 **96**
Porto Seguro, *Brazil* Q54-163 **105**
Porto Torres, *Sardinia* M40+408 **57**
Porto Vecchio, *Corsica* M35+416 **57**
Porto Velho, *Brazil* S23-088 **104**
Portoviejo, *Ecuador* T32-010 **104**
Port Patrick, *Scotland* N31+548 **41**
Port Pegasus, *New Zealand* A73-472 **112**
Port Phillip B., *Victoria* C31-382 **109**
Port Pirie, *S. Australia* C72-332 **109**
Port Pleasant, *New Jersey* S85+401 **91**
Port Radium, *N.-W. Terr.* V75+659 **88**
Portree, *Scotland* N37+574 **40**
Port Rowan, *Ontario* T33+427 **91**
Port Royal, *Jamaica* T11+179 **101**
Port Royal, *S. Carolina* T34+324 **97**
Portrush, *N. Ireland* N40+552 **42**
Port Safaga, *Egypt* K66+261 **81**
Port Said, *Egypt* K76+312 **81**
Port St John's, *Cape Prov.* L02-318 **84**
Portsalon, *Ireland, Rep.* N46+552 **42**
Port Shepstone, *Natal* K88-308 **84**
Port Simpson, *B.C.* W63+546 **88**
Portsmouth, *England* N07+508 **39**
Portsmouth, *New Hampshire* S65+431 **90**
Portsmouth, *Ohio* T48+387 **91**
Portsmouth, *Virginia* T08+368 **97**
Portsonachan, *Scotland* N31+563 **41**
Portsoy, *Scotland* N16+577 **40**
Port Stanley, *Ontario* T37+427 **91**
Port Stephens, *N.S.W.* B78-328 **109**
Port Sudan, *Sudan* K46+196 **81**
Port Talbot, *Wales* N23+516 **38**
Port Tampa City, *Florida* T45+278 **97**
Port Taufiq, *Egypt* K74+300 **81**
Portugal, *W. Europe* N48+400 **50**
Portugalia, *Angola* L56-074 **82**
Portuguese Guinea, *See* Guinea-Bissau
Portumna, *Ireland, Rep.* N49+531 **43**
Port Vendres, *France* M71+425 **55**
Port Victoria, *Kenya* K66+002 **83**
Port Wakefield, *S. Aust.* C71-342 **109**
Port Washington, *Wisconsin* T77+434 **91**
Port Weller, *Ontario* T25+432 **91**
Porvenir, *Chile* S62-533 **103**
Porvoo, (Borga) *Finland* L26+604 **47**
Posadas, *Argentina* R66-273 **103**
Posadowsky B., *Antarctica* G05-670 **27**
Poschiavo, *Switzerland* M30+463 **45**
Poseh, *China* E81+239 **67**
Posen. *See* Poznan
Poshan, *China* E13+365 **66**
Posht-i-kuh, *Iran* J84+336 **74**
Poso, *Celébes* D86-014 **65**
Poso Danau, *Celébes* D87-018 **65**
Possession I., *Antarctica* A50-720 **27**
Post, *Texas* U68+332 **94**
Posušje, *Yugoslavia* L76+435 **56**
Potapovo, *U.S.S.R.* G21+687 **62**
Potchefstroom, *Transvaal* L16-266 **84**
Poteau, *Oklahoma* U28+350 **95**
Potemkino, *U.S.S.R.* J84+504 **61**
Potenza, *Italy* L85+407 **57**
Poti, *Gruzinskaya, U.S.S.R.* K20+422 **62**
Potiskum, *Nigeria* M24+116 **81**
Potomac R., *Maryland, etc.* T20+396 **96**
Potosi, *Bolivia* S34-197 **104**
Potosi, *Missouri* U05+379 **97**
Potrerillos, *Chile* S57-265 **103**
Potsdam, *E. Germany* M12+524 **48**
Pottstown, *Pennsylvania* T04+403 **91**
Pottsville, *Pennsylvania* T07+407 **91**
Pouce Coupe, *B.C.* W00+554 **88**
Poughkeepsie, *New York* S83+417 **91**
Pouso Alegre, *Brazil* R72-118 **104**
Pouso Alegre, *Brazil* R06-212 **105**
Povenets, *Karelskaya* K62+628 **62**
Poverty B., *New Zealand* A12-388 **112**
Povoa de Varzim, *Portugal* N53+414 **52**
Povorina, *U.S.S.R.* K16+512 **61**
Povungnituk, *Quebec* T25+602 **89**
Povungnituk R., *Quebec* T05+602 **89**
Powder R., *Montana* V04+453 **98**
Powder River Ra., *Montana* V00+454 **93**
Powderville, *Montana* V01+458 **93**
Powell, L., *Utah* V36+370 **98**
Powell Mts., *Pa.-Va.* T49+366 **97**
Powell Creek, *N.-T. Aust.* D09-179 **111**
Powys, co., *Wales* N23+523 **38**
Poyang, *China* E20+290 **67**
Poyang Hu, *China* E22+290 **67**
Poza de la sal, *Spain* N21+427 **52**
Požarevac, *Yugoslavia* L53+446 **58**
Požega, *Yugoslavia* L74+453 **58**
Poznan, *Poland* L78+524 **49**
Pozo Almonte, *Chile* S58-203 **103**
Pozoblanco, *Spain* N29+384 **52**
Prachin Buri, *Thailand* F22+140 **69**
Prado, *Brazil* Q56-173 **105**
Praga, *Poland* L54+523 **49**
Prague. *See* Praha
Praha, *Czechoslovakia* M04+501 **48**
Praid, *Romania* L29+466 **58**
Prainha, *Brazil* S02-072 **104**
Prairie, *Queensland* C32-209 **111**
Prairie du Chien, *Wisconsin* U06+430 **95**
Prairie du Sac, *Wisconsin* T89+433 **91**
Pratapgarth, *India* G48+259 **73**
Prato, *Italy* M24+439 **56**
Pratt, *Kansas* U53+376 **95**
Pratt City, *Alabama* T71+335 **97**
Pravia, *Spain* N37+434 **52**
Pregolya, R., *U.S.S.R.* L51+546 **47**
Prenay, *Lithuania* L36+546 **47**
Prentice, *Wisconsin* U02+455 **91**
Prerov, *Czechoslovakia* L75+495 **49**
Prescott, *Arizona* V45+345 **92**
Prescott, *Ontario* T03+447 **91**
President R. Sáenz-Pena,
  Argentina S02-266 **103**
Presidente Hermes, *Brazil* S11-113 **104**
Presidente Roma, *Brazil* S11-108 **104**
Prešov, *Czechoslovakia* L53+490 **49**
Prespansko Jezero,
  Albania, etc. L54+409 **59**
Presque Isle, *Maine* S48+466 **90**
Pressburg. *See* Bratislava
Přeštice, *Czechoslovakia* M10+495 **48**
Preston, *England* N16+538 **37**
Preston, *Idaho* V41+421 **94**

Preston, *Minnesota* U13+437 **93**
Prestonpans, *Scotland* N18+560 **41**
Prestonsburg, *Kentucky* T47+377 **97**
Prestwick, *Scotland* N28+555 **41**
Pretoria, *Transvaal* L10-258 **84**
Pretty Boy L., *Maryland* T10+396 **96**
Préveza, *Greece* L56+390 **59**
Pribilof Is. Bering Sea Z30+568 **99**
Pribram, *Czechoslovakia* M06+497 **48**
Price and R., *Utah* V34+396 **94**
Priego, *Spain* N25+374 **52**
Prieska, *Cape Province* L44-296 **84**
Prignitz, *E. Germany* M18+531 **48**
Prijedor, *Yugoslavia* L80+450 **56**
Prijepolje, *Yugoslavia* L62+434 **58**
Prilep, *Yugoslavia* L51+414 **58**
Priluki, *Ukraine* K76+506 **60**
Prim Pt., *Prince Edward I.* S19+461 **90**
Primrose L., *Saskatchewan* V28+549 **88**
Prince Albert, *Cape Province* L48-332 **84**
Prince Albert, *Saskatchewan* V05+534 **88**
Prince Albert Mts., *Antarc.* B25-770 **27**
Prince Albert Park, *Sask.* V00+540 **88**
Prince Albert Pen., *N.-W. T.* V60+718 **88**
Prince Albert Sd., *N.-W. T.* V55+704 **88**
Prince Alfred, C., *N.-W. T.* W29+734 **88**
Prince Charles I., *N.W.T.* T10+672 **89**
Prince Edward I., *Canada* S20+464 **89**
Prince Edward Is., *Indian Oc.* K40-460 **77**
Prince Edwad Pen., *Ont.* T14+440 **91**
Prince George, *B.C.* W17+541 **88**
Prince Harald Ld., *Antarc.* K80-710 **27**
Prince of Wales, C., *Alaska* Z15+653 **99**
Prince of Wales I., *Alaska* W75+556 **99**
Prince of Wales I., *N.-W. T.* U60+720 **88**
Prince of Wales I., *Qnsld.* C47-107 **111**
Prince of Wales Str., *N.-W. T.* V80+724 **88**
Prince Patrick I., *N.-W. T.* W00+756 **88**
Prince Regent Inl., *N.-W. T.* U00+728 **89**
Prince Rupert, *B.C.* W61+543 **88**
Princes Lake, *Ontario* T18+454 **91**
Princess Astrid Ld., *Antarc.* M30-710 **27**
Princess Charlotte B.,
  Queensland C36-142 **111**
Princess Elizabeth Ld.,
  Antartica G70-720 **27**
Princess Ragnhild Ld.,
  Antartica L00-710 **27**
Princess Royal I., *B.C.* W52+530 **88**
Princeton, *Illinois* T87+414 **95**
Princeton, *Indiana* T76+384 **95**
Princeton, *Kentucky* T77+372 **95**
Princeton, *Maine* S46+452 **90**
Princeton, *Wisconsin* T85+438 **91**
Princetown, *England* N24+505 **38**
Princetown, *Pr. Edward I.* S22+465 **90**
Prince William Sd., *Alaska* X70+600 **99**
Principe I., *G. of Guinea* M46+016 **82**
Principe da Beira, *Brazil* S27-124 **104**
Pringles, *Argentina* S23-404 **103**
Prins Karl's Forland,
  Arctic Ocean M25+785 **62**
Prinzapolca, *Nicaragua* T51+134 **101**
Pripyat (Pripet) Marshes,
  Byelo-Russia L18+520 **60**
Pripyat (Pripet), R.,
  Byelo-Russia L03+518 **60**
Pristina, *Yugoslavia* L53+427 **58**
Pritzwalk, *E. Germany* M17+532 **48**
Privalnoye, *U.S.S.R.* J83+509 **61**
Prizren, *Yugoslavia* L56+422 **58**
Prizzi, *Sicily* M09+377 **57**
Progreso, *Mexico* 188-212 **100**
Prokop'yevsk, *U.S.S.R.* G20+541 **62**
Prokuplje, *Yugoslavia* L51+433 **58**
Prome, *Burma* F58+188 **71**
Prong, *Ghana* N06+080 **80**
Propria, *Brazil* Q41-103 **105**
Proskurov. *Ukraine* L18+494 **60**
Provence, prov., *France* M54+438 **55**
Providence, *Kentucky* T78+373 **97**
Providence, *N.-W. Terr.* V75+611 **88**
Providence, *Rhode Island* S68+418 **91**
Providence, C., *N.-W. Terr.* V45+736 **88**
Providence I., *Indian Ocean* J50-090 **77**
Provins, *France* M70+485 **54**
Provo, *Utah* V40+402 **94**
Prozor, *Yugoslavia* L74+438 **56**
Prudentopolis, *Brazil* R36-253 **103**
Prudhoe L., *Greenland* S45+780 **26**
Prüm, *W. Germany* M51+502 **48**
Prut, R. *U.S.S.R., etc.* L11+468 **58**
Przasnysz, *Poland* L55+530 **49**
Przemysl, *Poland* L43+498 **49**
Przhevalsk, *Kirgiz.* G70+425 **62**
Psará, I., *Greece* L26+386 **59**
Pskov, *U.S.S.R.* L10+578 **60**
Pskovskoye Oz., *U.S.S.R.*
  Estonia L12+580 **60**
Ptuj, *Yugoslavia* L85+464 **56**
Puan, *Argentina* S17-376 **103**
Pucacuro, *Peru* T04-028 **104**
Pucallpa, *Peru* S87-086 **104**
Puchezh, *U.S.S.R.* K11+570 **61**
Puchow. *See* Yungtsi
Puck, *Poland* L69+547 **49**
Pudasjärvi, *Finland* L19+654 **46**
Pudukkottai, *India* G68+104 **70**
Puebla & state, *Mexico* U49+188 **100**
Puebla Bonito, *New Mexico* V17+360 **99**
Puebla de Alcocer, *Spain* N31+390 **52**
Puebla de Sanabria, *Spain* N40+420 **52**
Puebla de Trives, *Spain* N42+425 **52**
Pueblo, *Colorado* U88+383 **94**
Pueblo Hundido, *Chile* S60-203 **103**
Puelches, *Argentina* S35-382 **103**
Puente Caldelas, *Spain* N51+423 **52**
Puentedeume, *Spain* N49+432 **52**
Puerco, R., *Arizona* V28+350 **94**
Puerhken, *Mongolia* F87+460 **63**
Puerto Armuelles, *Panama* T47+084 **101**
Puerto Asis, *Colombia* T09+005 **104**
Puerto Ayacucho, *Venezuela* S46+057 **104**
Puertck Aysen, *Chile* S78-453 **103**
Puerto Barrios, *Guatemala* T80+158 **100**
Puerto Bermudez, *Peru* S89-102 **104**
Puerto Berrio, *Colombia* S87+065 **104**
Puerto Bello, *Venezuela* S48+049 **104**
Puerto Cabezas, *Nicaragua* T50+140 **101**
Puerto Carreno, *Colombia* S44+060 **104**
Puerto Casado, *Paraguay* R77-223 **103**

Puerto Chicama, *Peru* T27-078 **104**
Puerto Colombia, *Colombia* T00+109 **104**
Puerto Cordoba, *Colombia* S59-014 **104**
Puerto Cortes, *Honduras* T78+157 **101**
Puerto Coyle, *Argentina* S56-508 **103**
Puerto Cumarebo, *Venez.* S56+114 **104**
Puerto de Carrizal, *Chile* S67-281 **103**
Puerto de Chanaral, *Chile* S64-263 **103**
Puerto de Santa Maria, *Spain* N37+366 **52**
Puerto Deseado, *Argentina* S36-476 **103**
Puerto Eten, *Peru* T29-068 **104**
Puerto Harberton, *Argent.* S44-548 **103**
Puerto Heath, *Bolivia* S52-124 **104**
Puerto Ichilo, *Bolivia* S26-170 **104**
Puerto Isabel, *Mexico* V59+317 **100**
Puerto Leguisamo, *Colombia* S88-003 **104**
Puerto Libertad, *Salvador* T86+134 **101**
Puertollano, *Spain* N25+387 **52**
Puerto Lobos, *Argentina* S30-420 **103**
Puerto Lomas, *Peru* S89-155 **104**
Puerto Madryn, *Argentina* S30-427 **103**
Puerto Maldonado, *Peru* S56-126 **104**
Puerto Mexico, *Mexico* U27+180 **100**
Puerto Montt, *Chile* S78-413 **103**
Puerto Morelos, *Mexico* T70+209 **100**
Puerto Natales, *Chile* S76-516 **103**
Puerto Patillos, *Chile* S61-208 **103**
Puerto Pirámide, *Argentina* S26-426 **103**
Puerto Plata, *Dom. Rep.* S64+198 **101**
Puerto Princesa, *Phil.* E08+097 **65**
Puerto Principe, *Colombia* S85+004 **104**
Puerto Quellen, *Chile* S81-428 **103**
Puerto Quijarro, *Bolivia* R77-178 **104**
Puerto Raso, *Argentina* S32-444 **103**
Puerto Rico, I., *West Indies* S38+183 **101**
Puerto Suarez, *Bolivia* R77-190 **104**
Puerto Sucre, *Bolivia* S32-108 **104**
Puerto Toledo, *Bolivia* S16-175 **104**
Puerto Varas, *Chile* S78-413 **103**
Puerto Victoria, *Peru* T00-098 **104**
Puerto Villamizar, *Colombia* S75+082 **104**
Puerto Visser, *Argentina* S43-454 **103**
Puerto Wilches, *Colombia* S83+073 **104**
Pueyrredón, L., *Argentina* S71-476 **103**
Pugachev, *U.S.S.R.* J67+520 **61**
Pugal, *India* H14+286 **72**
Puget, *France* M49+440 **55**
Puget Sd., *Washington* W18+474 **98**
Puglia, dep. *Italy* L80+409 **57**
Pühalepa, *Estonia* L42+589 **47**
Puimro, *Brazil* R58+010 **105**
Pukaki, L., *New Zealand* A59-441 **112**
Pukapaka I., *Tuamotu Arch.* X22-150 **107**
Pukapuka I., *Pacific Ocean* Z06-108 **106**
Pukchong, *Korea* D39+404 **64**
Pukekohe, *New Zealand* A31-372 **112**
Puket, *Thailand* F40+079 **69**
Pukow, *China* E08+321 **66**
Pula, *Yugoslavia* M07+449 **56**
Pulacayo, *Bolivia* S40-204 **104**
Pulap, I., *Caroline Islands* C25+073 **106**
Pulaski, *New York* T07+436 **91**
Pulaski, *Tennessee* T72+352 **97**
Pulaski, *Virginia* T35+371 **97**
Palicat I., *India* G59+140 **70**
Palkkila, *Finland* L25+643 **46**
Pullen I. (Richards I.).
  N.-W. Territories X00+686 **88**
Pullen, *Ontario* T40+494 **89**
Pultneyville, *New York* T13+432 **96**
Puma, *Tanzania* K62-050 **83**
Puma, I., *Ecuador* T31-030 **104**
Purakha, *Bhutan* G01+276 **73**
Punch, *Kashmir* H05+338 **72**
Pundri, *India* G80+298 **72**
Punab, *India* G84+305 **72**
Puno, *Peru* S60-159 **104**
Punta Alta, *Argentina* S12-388 **103**
Punta Arenas, *Chile* S66-532 **103**
Punta Colorado, *Chile* S66-292 **103**
Punta del Faro, *Sicily* L87+383 **57**
Punta de Pedras, *Brazil* R23-014 **105**
Punta Gorda, *Belize* T83+162 **101**
Puntarenas, *Costa Rica* T58+100 **101**
Punta Salinas, *Venezuela* S61+117 **104**
Punxsutawney, *Pennsylvania* T24+409 **96**
Puolanka, *Finland* L14+649 **46**
Purang Chaka, *Tibet* G47+329 **71**
Purbeck Downs, *England* N15+507 **38**
Purgatcire R., *Colorado* U82+376 **94**
Puri, *India* G22+198 **71**
Purificaeion, *Colombia* T00+038 **104**
Purna, *India* G76+192 **70**
Purnea, *India* G15+258 **73**
Pursat, *Khmer* F06+125 **69**
Purulia, *India* G21+233 **73**
Purus, R., *Brazil, etc.* S32-074 **104**
Purwa, *India* G85+265 **73**
Pusan, *Korea* D36+351 **64**
Pu-san, m:., *Laos* F11+198 **69**
Pushchino, *U.S.S.R.* E62+580 **63**
Pust-i-Badam, *Iran* J27+328 **75**
Putao, *Burma* F43+274 **71**
Putbus, *W. Germany* M09+543 **48**
Putien, *China* E05+255 **67**
Putignano, *Italy* L77+408 **57**
Putnam, *Connecticut* S71+419 **96**
Putnok, *Hungary* L58+483 **49**
Putorana, Gory, *U.S.S.R.* R60+690 **63**
Puttalam, *Sri Lanka* G61+081 **70**
Putte, *Belgium* M64+514 **44**
Putte, *Belgium* M62+511 **44**
Putten, *Netherlands* M56+522 **44**
Putumayo, R., *Colombia, etc.* S88-006 **104**
Putussibau, *Borneo* E42+008 **65**
Puula Vesi, *Finland* L20+617 **47**
Puurs, *Belgium* M64+511 **44**
Puy, le, *France* M67+450 **55**
Puyallup, *Washington* W14+472 **98**
Puy-de-Dôme, dep., *France* M70+456 **54**
Pwllheli, *Wales* N27+529 **38**
Pyapon, *Burma* F56+162 **71**
Pyatistennoe, *U.S.S.R.* B20+680 **63**
Pyevyek, *U.S.S.R.* A53+698 **63**
Pyhäjärvi, *Finland* L24+636 **46**
Pyhäjärvi, *Finland* L46+610 **47**
Pyhäntä, *Finland* L22+641 **46**
Pyinmana, *Burma* F52+197 **71**
Pyöngyang, *Korea* D54+393 **64**
Pyramid L., *Nevada* V87+400 **92**

Pyramid Pk., *California* W01+389 **92**
Pyramid Hill, *Victoria* C35-361 **109**
Pyrénées, Mt., *France-Spain* **53**
Pyrénées-Orientales dep.,
  France M76+425 **55**
Pyrzyce, *Poland* M01+531 **48**
Pyu, *Burma* F51+185 **71**
Pyzdry, *Poland* L74+522 **49**
Qafar, *Saudi Arabia* K19+274 **74**
Qaiya, *Saudi Arabia* J88+241 **74**
Qala, *Afghanistan* H14+369 **75**
Qala Mashiz, *Iran* J20+299 **75**
Qal'at al Akhdhar,
  Saudi Arabia K45+281 **74**
Qal'at ed Dab'a, *Jordan* K54+316 **76**
Qal'at el Marqan, *Syria* K54+352 **76**
Qal'at el Mudiq, *Syria* K51+355 **74**
Qal'at Uneiza, *Jordan* K55+305 **76**
Qalqiliya, *Jordan* K60+322 **76**
Qamr B., *Yemen, South* J44+160 **75**
Qara, *Egypt* L20+298 **81**
Qardaha, *Syria* K54+355 **76**
Qartaba, *Lebanon* K55+341 **76**
Qasim, *Saudi Arabia* K21+272 **74**
Qasr Amij, *Iraq* K19+334 **74**
Qasr el Azraq, *Jordan* K49+319 **76**
Qasr e Qand, *Iran* H85+262 **75**
Qasr Haiyaniya,
  Saudi Arabia K14+286 **74**
Qasr ibn Aliya, *Saudi Arabia* K10+291 **74**
Qasr-i-Shirin, *Iran* J86+346 **74**
Qa'taba, *Yemen* K01+139 **74**
Qatana, *Syria* K53+334 **76**
Qatar, *The Gulf* J52+250 **75**
Qatif, *Saudi Arabia* J60+267 **74**
Qayen, *Iran* J05+338 **75**
Qena, *Egypt* K74+262 **81**
Qeshm I., *Iran* J26+267 **75**
Qeys, I., *Iran* J36+265 **75**
Qishn, *Yemen, D.R.* J50+155 **75**
Qishran, I., *Saudi Arabia* K30+202 **74**
Qizan, *Saudi Arabia* K14+169 **74**
Qom, *Iran* J55+347 **75**
Qotur, *Iran* K04+385 **74**
Qoz Bal 'Air, *Saudi Arabia* K21+192 **74**
Quabbin Res., *Massachusetts* S74+424 **96**
Quadda, *Cent. Afr. Rep.* L46+082 **81**
Quakenbruck, *W. Germany* M42+527 **48**
Quambatook, *Victoria* C39-359 **109**
Quambone, *New S. Wales* C13-309 **109**
Quang Tri, *S. Vietnam* E77+168 **65**
Quantock Hills, *England* N19+511 **38**
Quarai, *Brazil* R69-304 **103**
Quatre Bras, *Belgium* M63+506 **44**
Qubeiyat, *Lebanon* K52+346 **76**
Quchan, *Iran* J10+371 **75**
Queanbeyan, *New S. Wales* C04-354 **109**
Quebec, *Quebec* S67+468 **91**
Quebec, prov., *Canada* **89**
Queen Alexandra Ra.,
  Antarctica . B20-840 **27**
Queen Anne, *Maryland* T06+388 **96**
Queen Charlotte B.
  Falkland Islands S04-517 **103**
Queen Charlotte Is., *B.C.* W75+530 **88**
Queen Charlotte Sd., *B.C.* W50+514 **88**
Queen Charlotte Str., *B.C.* W45+508 **88**
Queen Elizabeth Is., *N.-W.T.* V40+770 **88**
Queen Mary Ld., *Antarctica* F65-670 **27**
Queen Maud G.,
  N.-W. Territories U60+676 **88**
Queen Maud Ld., *Antarc.* L60-720 **27**
Queen Maud Ra., *Antarc.* Y50-870 **27**
Queen's Chan., *N. Terr.,
  Australia* D33-147 **110**
Queenscliff, *Victoria* C32-383 **109**
Queenscliffe, *S. Australia* C74-356 **109**
Queensland, state, *Australia* **111**
Queenstown, *Cape Province* L18-320 **84**
Queenstown, *New Zealand* A68-450 **112**
Queenstown. *See* Cobh
Queenstown, *Tasmania* C27-421 **109**
Queimadas, *Brazil* Q58-110 **105**
Quelimane, *Mozambique* K48-178 **84**
Quemu Quemú, *Argentina* S21-360 **103**
Quequen, *Argentina* R82-385 **103**
Queretaro, *Mexico* U62+206 **100**
Quesnel, *Brit. Columbia* W15+532 **88**
Quesnel L., *Brit. Columbia* W08+528 **88**
Quetta, *Pakistan* H48+302 **70**
Quetzalapa, *Mexico* U49+170 **100**
Quezaltenango, *Guatemala* U09+148 **100**
Quezon City, *Philippines* D83+149 **65**
Quibdo, *Colombia* T10+057 **104**
Quiberon B. de., *France* N18+475 **54**
Quievrain, *Belgium* M68+504 **44**
Quila, *Mexico* V13+245 **100**
Quilca, *Peru* S75-166 **104**
Quilino, *Argentina* S28-301 **103**
Quillabamba, *Peru* S77-128 **104**
Quillan, *France* M77+429 **55**
Quillota, *Chile* S68-328 **103**
Quilon (Kollam), *India* G90+111 **70**
Quilpie, *Queensland* C35-266 **111**
Quimper, *France* N25+480 **54**
Quimperle, *France* N21+479 **54**
Quincy, *Illinois* U08+399 **95**
Quincy, *Massachusetts* S66+423 **91**
Quincy, *Michigan* T59+420 **91**
Quines, *Argentina* S34-321 **103**
Quinnimont, *W. Virginia* T36+378 **97**
Quintana de la Serena, *Sp.* N34+388 **52**
Quintanar de la Orden, *Sp.* N19+396 **52**
Quintana Roo, state, *Mexico* T78+194 **100**
Quipapa, *Brazil* Q36-087 **105**
Quirindi, *New South Wales* B86-316 **109**
Quiriquire, *Venezuela* S18+100 **104**
Quiroga, *Spain* N43+424 **52**
Quissanga, *Mozambique* K28-124 **83**
Quissico, *Mozambique* K62-248 **84**
Quitapa, *Angola* L70-106 **82**
Quito, *Ecuador* T21-002 **104**
Quixada, *Brazil* Q55-050 **105**
Quixeramobim, *Brazil* Q56-052 **105**
Qunsuliye, *Saudi Arabia* K13+221 **74**
Quoich L., *Scotland* N31+571 **40**
Quorn, *S. Australia* C72-323 **109**
Quryat, *Oman* J07+233 **75**
Qus, *Egypt* K74+260 **81**
Qusayar, *Yemen, South* J58+150 **75**

Quseir, *Egypt* K64+260 **81**
Qusuriya, *Saudi Arabia* K03+238 **74**
Quteife, *Syria* K50+337 **76**
Quyon, *Quebec* T08+455 **91**
Raahe, *Finland* L33+646 **46**
Rab., *I., Yugoslavia* M02+448 **56**
Raba, *Sumbawa, I., Indon.* E07-085 **65**
Rabat, *Morocco* N42+340 **80**
Rabat Kerim, *Iran* J53+355 **75**
Rabigh, *Saudi Arabia* K36+228 **74**
Rabkob. See Dharmjaygarh
Race, C., *Newfoundland* R49+466 **90**
Race, The, *Conn.-New York* S73+412 **96**
Rach-zhia, *S. Vietnam* E89+100 **69**
Raciborz, *Poland* L71+501 **49**
Racine, *Wisconsin* T77+427 **91**
Rada, *Yemen* K01+146 **74**
Radak Chain, *Marshall Is.* A40+100 **106**
Rădăuti, *Romania* L24+479 **60**
Radford, *Virginia* T33+371 **97**
Radhanpur, *India* H21+238 **70**
Radhwa, Jebel, *Saudi Arabia* K41+245 **74**
Radnevo, *Bulgaria* L24+423 **58**
Radnor, See Powys
Radnor Forest, *Wales* N20+522 **38**
Radom, *Poland* L53+504 **49**
Radomir, *Bulgaria* L42+425 **58**
Radomsko, *Poland* L64+511 **49**
Radstadt, *Austria* M09+474 **48**
Radviliškis, *Lithuania* L39+558 **47**
Radzyn, *Poland* L44+518 **49**
Rae, *N.-W. Territories* V65+633 **88**
Rae Isthmus, *N.-W. Terr.* T70+666 **89**
Rae R., *N.-W. Territories* V70+676 **88**
Rae Bareli, *India* G53+263 **73**
Raeside, L., *W. Australia* D82-290 **110**
Raetihi, *New Zealand* A28-394 **112**
Rafaela, *Argentina* S09-312 **103**
Rafah, *Egypt* K65+313 **76**
Rafsinjan, *Iran* J25+305 **75**
Raga, *Sudan* L26+084 **81**
Ragaine, *Lithuania* L48+550 **47**
Ragaz Bad, *Switzerland* M33+470 **45**
Raghugarh, *India* G77+244 **73**
Raghunathpur, *India* G20+235 **73**
Raglan, *New Zealand* A31-378 **112**
Raglan Ra., *New Zealand* A41-420 **112**
Ragunda, *Sweden* L81+631 **46**
Ragusa. See Dubrovnik
Ragusa, *Sicily* M02+369 **57**
Rahaeng. See Tak
Raheita, *Ethiopia* K12+126 **83**
Rahhyut, *Oman* J40+168 **75**
Raiatea, I., *Society Islands* Y10-168 **107**
Raichur, *India* G76+162 **70**
Raida, *Yemen, South* J74+148 **74**
Raida, *Yemen, South* J57+151 **75**
Raiganj, *India* G11+256 **73**
Raikot, *India* G86+306 **72**
Rainbow, *Victoria* C48-359 **109**
Raingarh, *India* G73+311 **72**
Rainier, Mt., *Washington* W10+468 **92**
Rainy L., *Ontario* U18+488 **89**
Raipur, *India* G50+213 **70**
Raivavae, I., *Austral Is.* X75-245 **107**
Raiwind, *Pakistan* H05+312 **72**
Raja, mt., *Borneo* E44-008 **65**
Rajahmundry, *India* G48+170 **70**
Rajakhera, *India* G71+269 **73**
Rajang, R., *Sarawak* E46+020 **65**
Rajanpur, *Pakistan* H28+291 **72**
Rajapalaiyam, *India* G74+095 **70**
Rajasthan, *India* H10+270 **70**
Rajburi, *Thailand* F32+136 **69**
Rajgarh, *India* G88+286 **72**
Rajkot, *India* H25+222 **70**
Rajmahal, *India* G13+250 **73**
Rajmahal Hills, *India* G24+245 **73**
Rajpura, *India* G80+305 **72**
Rajshahi, *Bangladesh* G08+243 **73**
Rajura, *India* G64+197 **70**
Rakahanga, I., *Pacific Oc.* Y66-100 **106**
Rakaposhi, mt., *Kashmir* H03+361 **72**
Raka Tsangpo, R., *Tibet* G20+296 **71**
Rakvere, *Estonia* L22+593 **47**
Raleigh, *New South Wales* B73-305 **109**
Raleigh, *N. Carolina* T22+356 **99**
Raleigh B., *N. Carolina* T06+348 **97**
Ralik Chain, *Marshall Is.* A70+080 **106**
Ram, *Jordan* K57+296 **76**
Rama, *Ethiopia* K30+124 **83**
Rama, *Israel* K58+329 **76**
Ramadi, *Iraq* K10+334 **74**
Ramallah, *Jordan* K59+319 **76**
Ramallo, *Argentina* S00-335 **103**
Ramanthapuran, *India* G67+094 **70**
Rambouillet, *France* M79+487 **54**
Ramee, *Burma* F66+192 **71**
Rathmelton, *Ireland, Rep.* N46+550 **42**
Rameswaram, *India* G64+092 **70**
Ramgarh, *India* H00+281 **72**
Ramgarh, *India* G54+228 **73**
Ramgarh, *India* G26+236 **73**
Ram Hormuz, *Iran* J63+312 **74**
Ramishk, *Iran* J06+269 **75**
Ramkola, *India* G42+236 **73**
Ramle, *Israel* K61+319 **76**
Ramnagar, *India* G57+226 **73**
Ramnagar, *Kashmir* G88+328 **72**
Ramnagar, *Pakistan* H07+323 **72**
Râmnicul Sărat, *Romania* L18+454 **58**
Râmnicu Valcea, *Romania* L34+451 **58**
Ramore, *Ontario* T32+484 **91**
Ramoutsa, *Botswana* L26-248 **84**
Rampart House, *Yukon* X35+671 **88**
Rampur, *India* G33+210 **71**
Rampur, *India* G74+315 **72**
Rampur, *India* G66+288 **73**
Ramsay, *Ontario* T44+474 **91**
Ramsbottom, *England* N14+537 **37**
Ramsele, *Sweden* L81+635 **46**
Ramsey, *Isle of Man* N26+543 **37**
Ramsey I., *Wales* N32+519 **38**
Ramsgate, *England* M82+513 **39**
Ramsgate, *Tasmania* C19-435 **109**
Ramsjö, *Sweden* L86+621 **47**
Ramskapelle, *Belgium* M73+511 **44**
Ramtha, *Jordan* K54+326 **76**
Ramtok, *India* G63+215 **70**
Rana, Fd., *Norway* M12+662 **46**
Ranaghat, *India* G09+231 **73**

Rancagua, *Chile* S65-341 **103**
Rance, *Belgium* M64+501 **44**
Ranchi, *India* G28+234 **73**
Ranchito, *Mexico* U71+233 **100**
Rand, *New South Wales* C21-356 **109**
Randalstown, *N. Ireland* N38+547 **42**
Randazzo, *Sicily* M00+379 **57**
Randers, *Denmark* M30+564 **47**
Randolph, *Vermont* S76+439 **91**
Random I., *Newfoundland* R52+481 **90**
Randsfjord, *Norway* M27+603 **47**
Ranenburg, *U.S.S.R.* K30+532 **61**
Ranfurly, *New Zealand* A59-451 **112**
Rangamati, *Bangladesh* F77+227 **71**
Rangeley, *Maine* S64+450 **90**
Rangeley Ls., *Maine* S65+449 **90**
Rangemore, *New S. Wales* C34-354 **109**
Ranger, *Texas* U52+322 **98**
Rangiora, *New Zealand* A44-433 **112**
Rangitaiki, R., *New Zealand* A20-385 **112**
Rangitikei, R., *New Zealand* A27-401 **112**
Rangitoto Ra., *New Zealand* A26-385 **112**
Rangoon & R., *Burma* F53+168 **71**
Rangpur, *Bangladesh* G04+257 **73**
Rania, *India* H01+295 **72**
Ranibennur, *India* G86+147 **70**
Raniganj, *India* G12+259 **73**
Raniganj, *India* G17+236 **73**
Ranikhet, *India* G63+296 **73**
Rankin Inl., *N.-W. Terr.* U15+632 **89**
Rankins Springs, *N.S.W.* C22-339 **109**
Rannoch, L., *Scotland* N26+567 **41**
Rannoch Moor, *Scotland* N28+566 **41**
Ranong, *Thailand* F39+100 **65**
Rantauparapat, *Sumatra* F31+021 **65**
Rantekombola, mt., *Celebes* E00-034 **65**
Rantsila, *Finland* L26+645 **46**
Ranua, *Finland* L21+659 **46**
Rapa, I., *Austral Islands* X65-275 **107**
Rapadama, *Upper Volta* N06+122 **80**
Raphoe, *Ireland, Rep.* N45+549 **42**
Rapid City, *S. Dakota* U80+441 **93**
Rapla, *Estonia* L31+590 **47**
Rappahannock R., *Virginia* T10+381 **97**
Rapperswil, *Switzerland* M37+472 **45**
Raqqa, *Syria* K36+359 **74**
Rarotonga, I., *Cook Islands* Y60-210 **106**
Ras al Had, *Oman* J01+225 **75**
Ras al Khaymah, *U.A.E.* J24+259 **75**
Rashad, *Sudan* K84+118 **81**
Rashadiya, *Jordan* K56+307 **76**
Rasheiye, *Lebanon* K55+335 **76**
Rashin, *Korea* D28+420 **64**
Rashm, *Iran* J34+352 **75**
Rasht, *Iran* J62+373 **74**
Raška, *Yugoslavia* L56+433 **58**
Ras Lanuf, *Libya* L67+304 **81**
Rason, L., *W. Australia* D64-286 **110**
Rasova, *Romania* L12+442 **58**
Rasskazovo, *U.S.S.R.* K19+526 **61**
Ratangarh, *India* H02+280 **72**
Rat Buri, *Thailand* F32+136 **69**
Rathdrum, *Ireland, Rep.* N37+529 **43**
Rathfriland, *N. Ireland* N37+542 **42**
Ratheale, *Ireland, Rep.* N54+525 **43**
Rathlin I., *N. Ireland* N37+553 **42**
Rathnew, *Ireland, Rep.* N36+530 **43**
Ratibor. See Raciborz.
Ratnagiri, *India* H10+170 **70**
Raton, *New Mexico* U67+369 **94**
Rattlesnake Ra., *Wyoming* V14+428 **93**
Rattray Hd., *Scotland* N11+576 **40**
Rättvik, *Sweden* L89+609 **47**
Rauch, *Argentina* R85-367 **103**
Raudha, *Yemen* K05+155 **74**
Raukumara Ra., *N.Z.* A12-380 **112**
Rauma, *Finland* L51+611 **47**
Rautavaara, *Finland* L10+635 **46**
Rautio, *Finland* L35-641 **46**
Rauwaq, Jebel er, *Syria* K48+341 **74**
Ravar, *Iran* J20+314 **75**
Ravenna, *Italy* M17+444 **56**
Ravi R., *Pakistan* H03+317 **72**
Ravar, *Iran* J20+314 **75**
Rawaidha, *Saudi Arabia* K02+239 **74**
Rawalpindi, *Pakistan* H11+336 **72**
Rawandiz, *Iraq* K30+367 **74**
Rawatsar, *India* H04+292 **72**
Rawene, *New Zealand* A39-354 **112**
Rawlinna, *W. Australia* D58-309 **110**
Rawlins, *Wyoming* V14+418 **93**
Rawson, *Argentine* S31-433 **103**
Ray, C., *Newfoundland* R86+476 **90**
Rayadrug, *India* G79+148 **70**
Raymond, *Alberta* V47+495 **88**
Raymondville, *Texas* U46+266 **94**
Rayon, *Mexico* U58+218 **100**
Rayon, *Mexico* V34+296 **100**
Rays Hill, *Pennsylvania* T20+398 **96**
Razelm L., *Romania* L06+448 **58**
Razgrad, *Bulgaria* L21+435 **58**
Razmak, *Pakistan* H31+327 **72**
Ré, I. de, *France* N08+462 **54**
Reading, *England* N06+514 **39**
Reading, *Pennsylvania* T05+404 **91**
Real, Cord., *Bolivia* S50-162 **104**
Real, Cord., *Ecuador, etc.* T24-020 **104**
Real Castillo, *Mexico* V67+320 **100**
Realico, *Argentina* S25-351 **103**
Realp, *Switzerland* M39+466 **45**
Reata, *Mexico* U67+262 **100**
Rebun, I., *Japan* C54+454 **68**
Recalde, *Argentina* S07-365 **103**
Recherche Arch., *W. Aust.* D73-346 **110**
Rechna Doab, *Pakistan* H15+310 **72**
Recht, *Belgium* M54+503 **44**
Recife, *Brazil* Q30-080 **105**
Reconquista, *Argentina* R88-291 **103**
Recreio, *Brazil* R77-080 **105**
Red Des., *Wyoming* V18+420 **93**
Red L., *Minnesota* U30+480 **93**
Red R., *Louisiana, etc.* U12+313 **95**
Red R., *Minn. Man.* U42+479 **88**
Red R. See Song-koi.
Red Sea, *Africa-Arabia* K50+200 **30**
Redbank, *New Jersey* S85+403 **96**
Red Bluff Res., *New Mex.-Texas* U84+320 **94**
Redby, *Minnesota* U29+479 **93**
Red Cliffs, *Victoria* C47-344 **109**

Red Deer, *Alberta* V53+520 **88**
Red Deer R., *Alberta* V38+510 **88**
Redding, *California* W14+406 **92**
Redditch, *England* N12+523 **37**
Redempção, *Brazil* R65-106 **105**
Redfield, *Arkansas* U13+344 **97**
Redfield, *S. Dakota* U55+449 **93**
Red Hill, *S. Australia* C71-336 **109**
Red Hill, *Victoria* C30-384 **109**
Red Indian L., *Nfd.* R70+488 **90**
Redlands, *California* V73+341 **92**
Red Lodge, *Montana* V26+452 **93**
Red Oak, *Iowa* U31+410 **95**
Redon, *France* N13+477 **54**
Redondeta, *Spain* N51+422 **52**
Red Pine, *New Brunswick* S34+474 **90**
Redruth, *England* N31+502 **38**
Red Salt L., *Tibet* G18+338 **71**
Red Wing, *Minnesota* U15+448 **93**
Redwood Falls, *Minnesota* U31+445 **93**
Ree L., *Ireland, Rep.* N48+535 **43**
Reed City, *Michigan* T63+439 **91**
Reedsburg, *Wisconsin* U00+435 **91**
Reefton, *New Zealand* A49-421 **112**
Reelfoot, L., *Tennessee* T86+364 **95**
Refresco, *Chile* S59-254 **103**
Regensburg, *Germany* M17+490 **48**
Reggan, *Algeria* M88+264 **80**
Reggio, *Italy* L86+381 **57**
Reggio nell'Emilia, *Italy* M26+447 **56**
Reghin, *Romania* L32+468 **58**
Regina, *Saskatchewan* U87+504 **88**
Registro do Araguaia, *Brazil* R41-157 **105**
Regua, *Portugal* N47+412 **52**
Rehoboth, S.-W. Africa* L78-232 **84**
Rehovo, *Israel* K61+319 **76**
Reichenbach, E. *Germany* M16+506 **48**
Reidsville, *N. Carolina* T28+364 **97**
Reigate, *England* N01+512 **39**
Reigi, *Estonia* L45+589 **47**
Reims, *France* M66+493 **54**
Reina Adelaide, Arch. de la, *Chile* T00-522 **103**
Reindeer L., *Saskatchewan* U75+570 **88**
Reinosa, *Spain* N25+430 **52**
Reitan, *Norway* M22+629 **46**
Reitz, *Orange Free State* L10-278 **84**
Rekinniki, *U.S.S.R.* B07+608 **63**
Relizane, (Ighil-Izane), *Alg.* M86+356 **80**
Remanso, *Brazil* Q73-096 **105**
Remarkable, Mt., *S. Aust.* C71-328 **109**
Rembang, *Java* E52-067 **65**
Remedios, *Cuba* T27+225 **101**
Remedios, *Panama* T40+083 **101**
Remiremont, *France* M51+480 **54**
Remoulins, *France* M63+440 **55**
Remscheid, *W. Germany* M47+512 **48**
Remüs, *Switzerland* M28+468 **45**
Rena, *Norway* M22+611 **47**
Renaix, *Belgium* M68+507 **44**
Renca, *Argentina* S32-327 **103**
Rendsburg, *Germany* M32+543 **48**
Renfrew, *Ontario* T10+455 **91**
Renfrew, *Scotland* N26+559 **41**
Rengat, *Sumatra* F14-006 **65**
Reni, *India* H00+287 **72**
Renigunta, *India* G63+138 **70**
Renk, *Sudan* K72+118 **81**
Renkum, *Netherlands* M56+520 **44**
Renmark, *S. Australia* C56-342 **109**
Rennell, I., *Solomon Islands* B29-120 **106**
Rennes, *France* N10+481 **54**
Reno, *Nevada* V89+395 **92**
Renovo, *Pennsylvania* T16+413 **91**
Rensselaer, *New York* S82+426 **91**
Renswoude, *Netherlands* M57+521 **44**
Renville, *Minnesota* U32+448 **93**
Reo, *Flores I., Indonesia* D87-083 **65**
Réole la, *France* N00+445 **55**
Repartição, *Brazil* R67-048 **105**
Republic Dominican, *W.I.* S64+190 **101**
Republican R., *Nebraska* U54+400 **95**
Repulse B., *N.-W. Terr.* T66+662 **89**
Repulse B., *Queensland* C05-206 **111**
Requena, *Peru* S81-049 **104**
Requena, *Spain* N07+395 **53**
Resistencia, *Argentina* R84-274 **103**
Resita, *Romania* L49+453 **58**
Resolution, *New Zealand* A80-457 **112**
Resolution I., *N.-W. Terr.* V52+609 **88**
Resolution I., *N.-W. Terr.* S30+614 **89**
Rethel, *France* M64+495 **54**
Réthimnon, *Crete* L33+354 **59**
Retie, *Belgium* M61+513 **44**
Réunion, I., *Indian Ocean* J30-210 **77**
Reusel, *Netherlands* M59+514 **44**
Reutlingen, *W. Germany* M35+485 **48**
Reutte, *Austria* M26+475 **48**
Revda, *U.S.S.R.* J00+568 **61**
Revel. See Tallinn.
Revelstoke, *B.C.* V79+509 **88**
Revilla Gigedo Is., *Mexico* V42+190 **100**
Revivum, *Israel* K61+310 **76**
Rewa, *India* G52+245 **73**
Rewari, *India* G80+282 **72**
Rey, I. del, *Panama* T25+084 **101**
Reydarharfjord, *Iceland* N81+650 **46**
Reyes, *Mexico* U74+196 **100**
Reykjavik, *Iceland* P41+641 **46**
Reynosa, *Mexico* U50+260 **100**
Rezé-Izeau, *France* N00+376 **54**
Rezekne, *Latvia* L16+565 **47**
Rhatikon, mts., *Switzerland-Austria* M32+470 **45**
Rhayader, *Wales* N21+523 **38**
Rheden, *Netherlands* M54+520 **44**
Rhein R., *Germany, etc.* M46+506 **48**
Rheine, W. *Germany* M46+523 **48**
Rheinland-Pfalz, *W. Germany* M48+502 **48**
Rhenen, *Netherlands* M57+520 **44**
Rheydt, W. *Germany* M51+512 **48**
Rhine, R. N.-W. Europe* M50+510 **50**
Rhinelander, *Wisconsin* T87+457 **91**
Rhode I., *Rhode Island* S68+415 **96**
Rhode Island, state, *U.S.A.* S70+416 **99**
Rhodes. See Rodhos, I.
Rhodesia, N. See Zambia
Rhodesia, S.E.Africa* L00-200 **84**
Rhon Geb., W. *Germany* M30+504 **48**
Rhondda, *Wales* N21+516 **38**

Rhône, dep., *France* M62+459 **54**
Rhône, R..*France, etc.* M62+445 **55**
Rhyl, *Wales* N21+533 **38**
Riaño, *Spain* N30+430 **52**
Riau, Kep., arch., *Indon.* F04+004 **65**
Riaza, *Spain* N21+413 **52**
Ribadeo, *Spain* N42+433 **52**
Ribadesella, *Spain* N30+434 **52**
Ribble R., *England* N14+539 **37**
Ribe, *Denmark* M38+553 **47**
Ribeirão Preto, *Brazil* R17-212 **105**
Ribera, *Sicily* M11+375 **57**
Riberalta, *Bolivia* S36-110 **104**
Riccall, *England* N06+538 **37**
Riccarton, *New Zealand* A44-435 **112**
Rice Lake, *Wisconsin* U10+455 **93**
Richards C., *Arctic Ocean* T30+830 **26**
Richardson Mts., *N.Z.* A68-448 **112**
Richey, *Montana* U74+469 **93**
Richfield, *Utah* V43+388 **92**
Richibucto, *New Brunswick* S29+467 **90**
Richland, *Washington* V86+463 **92**
Richland Center, *Wisconsin* U02+433 **91**
Richmond, *California* W15+379 **92**
Richmond, *Cape Province* L38-314 **84**
Richmond, *England* N10+544 **37**
Richmond, *England* N02+514 **39**
Richmond, *Indiana* T59+399 **91**
Richmond, *Kentucky* T56+378 **97**
Richmond, *Maine* S59+441 **90**
Richmond, *New South Wales* B86-336 **109**
Richmond, *New York* S85+406 **91**
Richmond, *New Zealand* A41-413 **112**
Richmond, *Quebec* S73+457 **91**
Richmond, *Queensland* C41-208 **111**
Richmond, *Utah* V41+419 **94**
Richmond, *Virginia* T15+375 **97**
Richmond R., *New S. Wales* B70-289 **109**
Richwood, *Minnesota* U35+469 **93**
Richwood, W. *Virginia* T33+382 **97**
Rickmansworth, *England* N03+516 **39**
Ricla, *Spain* N09+415 **53**
Riddes, *Switzerland* M47+462 **45**
Ridgetown, *Ontario* T41+425 **91**
Ridgway, *Pennsylvania* T22+414 **91**
Ridi, *Nepal* G39+280 **73**
Riding Mount Park, *Man.* U60+506 **88**
Ridout, *Ontario* T48+476 **91**
Riesa, E. *Germany* M10+513 **48**
Rietavas, *Lithuania* L48+557 **47**
Rieti, *Italy* M13+424 **56**
Rifle, *Colorado* V17+395 **94**
Riga, *Latvia* L35+569 **47**
Riga, G. of *Latvia* L36+577 **47**
Rigan, *Iran* J06+286 **75**
Rigmati, *Iran* J11+276 **75**
Rignasco, *Switzerland* M38+463 **45**
Rigolet, *Labrador* R80+542 **89**
Rihand Dam, *India* G43+241 **73**
Rijeka, *Yugoslavia* M04+453 **56**
Rijswijk, *Netherlands* M64+521 **44**
Rimatara, I., *Austral Is.* Y20-230 **107**
Rimini, *Italy* M15+440 **56**
Rimouski, *Quebec* S51+484 **90**
Rincon, *Cuba* T44+230 **101**
Rincon, *New Mexico* V12+326 **98**
Rindal, *Norway* M35+631 **46**
Rineanna, *Ireland, Rep.* N53+527 **43**
Ringarooma B., *Tasmania* C14-408 **109**
Ringelspitz, mt., *Switz.* M34+469 **45**
Ringkøbing, *Denmark* M40+561 **47**
Ringvassøy, I., *Norway* L66+700 **46**
Ringwood, *Victoria* C29-378 **109**
Rinihue, *Chile* S75-397 **103**
Riobamba, *Ecuador* T22-018 **104**
Rio Branco, *Brazil* R27-251 **103**
Rio Branco, *Brazil* S48-100 **104**
Rio Branco, R., *Brazil* S09+015 **104**
Rio Branco, *Uruguay* R51-325 **103**
Rio Bueno, *Chile* S78-404 **103**
Rio Chico, *Argentina* S52-498 **103**
Rio Chico, *Venezuela* S35+103 **104**
Rio Colorado, *Argentina* S25-389 **103**
Rio Conchos, *Mexico* V00+292 **100**
Rio Cuarto, *Argentina* S26-332 **103**
Rio de Janeiro, *Brazil* Q80-229 **105**
Rio de Oro, *Colombia* S80+084 **104**
Rio-de-Oro, *W. Sahara* N80+250 **80**
Rio Fenix, *Argentina* S66-464 **103**
Rio Florido, *Mexico* V01+265 **100**
Rio Gallegos & R., *Argent.* S56+516 **103**
Rio Grande, *Argentina* S47-538 **103**
Rio Grande, *Brazil* R43-320 **103**
Rio Grande City, *Texas* U43+264 **94**
Rio Grande del Norte, *Mexico-U.S.A.* V02+308 **100**
Rio Hacha, *Colombia* S77+115 **104**
Rio Hondo, *Argentina* S29-275 **103**
Rio Muerto, *Argentina* S10-262 **103**
Rio Mulato, *Bolivia* S41-196 **104**
Rio Muni, *W. Africa* M30+016 **82**
Rio Negro, *Brazil* R29-261 **103**
Rio Pardo, *Brazil* R53-203 **105**
Rio Verde, *Brazil* R35-178 **105**
Rio Verde, *Ecuador* T26+010 **104**
Rio Verde, *Mexico* U60+220 **100**
Rioz, *France* M54+475 **54**
Riozinho, *Brazil* S40-100 **104**
Ripats, *Sweden* L56+669 **46**
Ripley, *California* V59+335 **92**
Ripley, *England* N09+531 **37**
Ripley, *Mississippi* T84+347 **97**
Ripley, *New York* T28+422 **96**
Ripley, *Tennessee* T88+358 **97**
Ripley, W. *Virginia* T40+388 **97**
Ripon, *England* N09+541 **37**
Ripon, *Quebec* T01+459 **91**
Ripon, *Wisconsin* T83+439 **91**
Risafe, *Syria* K37+357 **74**
Risalpur, *Pakistan* H18+341 **72**
Risbäck, *Sweden* L59+673 **46**
Rishiri, I., *Japan* C53+452 **68**
Rishon-le-Zion, *Israel* K61+320 **76**
Risør, *Norway* M34+587 **47**
Ristijärvi, *Finland* L10+645 **46**
Risut, *Oman* J36+170 **75**
Ritchie's Arch., *Andaman Is.* F70+122 **71**

Rivadavia, Argentina S18–241 **103**
Rivas, Nicaragua T65+115 **101**
Rivera, Argentina S20–371 **103**
Rivera, Uruguay R64–310 **103**
Riverhead, New York S76+409 **91**
Rivero, I., Chile S86–456 **103**
Riversdale, New Zealand A67–459 **112**
Riverside, California V74+340 **92**
Riverside Mt., California V57+340 **92**
Riverton, New Zealand A71–463 **112**
Riverton, S. Australia C67–342 **109**
Riverton, Wyoming V20+430 **93**
Riviera di Levante. Italy M34+440 **54**
Riviera di Ponente, Italy M42+438 **54**
Rivière a Pièrre, Quebec S73+470 **91**
Rivière du Loup, Quebec S57+479 **90**
Riyadh (Ar Riyâd).
  Saudi Arabia J80+246 **74**
Riyaq, Lebanon K54+339 **76**
Rizaiyeh. See Rezā'īveh
Rize, Turkey K25+413 **74**
Rizokarpaso, Cyprus K64+356 **76**
Rizzuto C., Italy L77+389 **57**
Roa, Spain N24+417 **52**
Roanne, France M66+461 **54**
Roanoke, Alabama T62+332 **97**
Roanoke, Virginia T30+373 **97**
Roanoke R., N. Carolina T18+366 **97**
Roaringwater B.,
  Ireland, Rep. N57+515 **43**
Roatan I., Honduras T69+164 **101**
Robat Thana, Pakistan H84+298 **70**
Robbins I., Tasmania C30–407 **109**
Robe, S. Australia C62–372 **109**
Robe, Mt., New S. Wales C53–316 **109**
Robe R., Ireland, Rep. N55+536 **42**
Roberts, Montana V25+454 **93**
Robertsfors, Sweden L55+642 **46**
Robertsganj, India G41+247 **73**
Robertsport, Liberia N68+068 **80**
Robertstown, Ireland, Rep. N41+532 **43**
Robertstown, S. Australia C66–340 **109**
Roberval, Quebec S73+485 **90**
Robeson Ch., Arctic Ocean S00+820 **26**
Robinson, Illinois T76+390 **95**
Robinson Crusoe, I., Chile T25–335 **107**
Robinson's, Newfoundland R83+483 **90**
Robinvale, Victoria C43–345 **109**
Robore, Bolivia R87–183 **104**
Robson, Mt., B.C. V84+533 **88**
Robstown, Texas U46+278 **94**
Roca, la, Spain N40+391 **52**
Rocha, Uruguay R55–344 **103**
Rochdale, England N13+536 **37**
Rochefort, Belgium M59+502 **44**
Rochefort, France N06+459 **54**
Rochester, England M87+514 **39**
Rochester, Michigan T49+427 **91**
Rochester, Minnesota U15+441 **93**
Rochester, New Hampshire S66+433 **91**
Rochester, New York T16+432 **91**
Rochester, Victoria C32–364 **109**
Roche-sur-Yon, la, France N09+467 **54**
Rock Pt., New Zealand A47–409 **112**
Rock, The, New S. Wales C18–353 **109**
Rockall, I., Atlantic Ocean N82+575 **34**
Rockefeller Plateau, Antarc. X40–800 **27**
Rockford, Alabama T68+329 **97**
Rockford, Illinois T85+423 **91**
Rockhampton, Queensland B86–232 **111**
Rock Hill, S. Carolina T36+349 **97**
Rockingham, N. Carolina T29+349 **97**
Rock Island, Illinois U04+415 **91**
Rockland, Maine S55+441 **90**
Rockland, Massachusetts S65+421 **96**
Rockland, Ontario T02+455 **91**
Rockport, Indiana T72+379 **97**
Rockport, Missouri U34+404 **95**
Rock Springs, Wyoming V26+416 **93**
Rockstone, Guyana R81+058 **104**
Rockville, Maryland T13+391 **96**
Rockwell City, Iowa U28+424 **95**
Rockwood, Tennessee T58+358 **97**
Rocky Mts., N. America V30+550 **88**
Rockyford, Colorado U82+381 **94**
Rocky Mount, N. Carolina T16+360 **97**
Rockymount, Virginia T29+370 **97**
Rocky Mt. Nat. Park, Colo. V09+406 **98**
Rocroi, France M63+499 **54**
Rødby, Denmark M22+547 **47**
Rodez, France M75+443 **55**
Rodhopi, Greece L28+412 **58**
Rodhos, Greece L14+364 **59**
Rodhos, I., Greece L12+362 **59**
Rodkhan, Pakistan H64+261 **70**
Rodney, Mississippi U07+319 **97**
Rodopi Planina, Bulg.-Greece L36+415 **59**
Rodosto. See Tekirdag
Rodriguez, I., Indian Ocean H70–195 **77**
Roe R., N. Ireland N42+551 **42**
Roebourne, W. Australia E17–208 **110**
Roermond, Netherlands M54+512 **44**
Roesbrugge, Belgium M74+509 **44**
Roeselare, Belgium M71+509 **44**
Roes Welcome Sound,
  N.-W. Territories T70+650 **89**
Roeulx, Belgium M65+505 **44**
Rogachev, Byelo-Russia L00+531 **60**
Rogers City, Michigan T53+455 **91**
Rogersville, New Brunswick S33+468 **90**
Rogersville, Tennessee T48+364 **97**
Rogliano, Corsica M33+374 **55**
Rohri, Pakistan H36+276 **70**
Rohtak, India G80+289 **72**
Roi Et, Thailand F08+161 **69**
Roisin, Belgium M68+503 **44**
Rojas, Argentina S04–342 **103**
Rokishkis, Lithuania L25+560 **47**
Rolde, Netherlands M50+530 **44**
Rolla, Missouri U11+380 **97**
Rolle, Switzerland M52+465 **45**
Rolvsøya, Norway L36+709 **46**
Roma, Queensland C07–265 **111**
Roma, Sweden L69+575 **47**
Roma, Italy M15+419 **57**
Romaing I., Indonesia D46–077 **65**
Romaine R., Quebec S21+514 **90**
Roman, Romania L19+469 **58**
Romania, S.-E. Eur. L24+460 **51**
Romans, France M60+451 **55**

Romanshorn, Switzerland M34+476 **45**
Romanzof, C., Alaska Z10+618 **99**
Rome, Georgia T61+342 **97**
Rome, New York T03+432 **91**
Rome. See Roma.
Romerée, Belgium M62+501 **44**
Romford, England M89+516 **39**
Romney, W. Virginia T23+393 **91**
Romney Marsh, England M85+511 **39**
Romny, Ukraine K69+508 **60**
Rømø. I., Denmark M39+551 **47**
Romodanovo, U.S.S.R. J88+544 **61**
Romont, Switzerland M48+467 **45**
Romsdalshorn, Norway M43+625 **46**
Romsey, England N09+510 **39**
Ron, N. Vietnam E81+178 **69**
Ronda, Kashmir N31+367 **72**
Rondà, Spain N31+367 **52**
Rondeau, Ontario T42+423 **91**
Rondonia, state, Brazil S31–118 **104**
Ronge Lac la, Sask. V00+552 **88**
Rønne, Bornholm, I., Den. M01+551 **47**
Ronneby, Sweden L88+562 **47**
Ronne Entrance, Antarctica T00–720 **27**
Ronne Ice Shelf, Antarctica S00–770 **27**
Ronse, Belgium M68+507 **44**
Roosendaal, Netherlands M63+515 **44**
Roosevelt, I., Antarctica Y65–800 **27**
Roosevelt Res., Arizona V33+340 **98**
Roosevelttown, New York S88+450 **91**
Roosky, Ireland, Rep. N47+538 **42**
Roper, R., N. Terr., Aust. D00–154 **111**
Roquefort, France N02+440 **55**
Rora Hd., Orkney N21+589 **40**
Rori, India G89+297 **72**
Røros, Norway M21+626 **46**
Rorschach, Switzerland M33+475 **45**
Røs Vatn, Norway M06+658 **46**
Rosa, la, Switzerland M30+464 **45**
Rosa, Monte, Switz.-Italy M43+459 **45**
Rosablanche, mt., Switz. M46+461 **45**
Rosarinho, Brazil R85–036 **104**
Rosario, Argentina S04–329 **103**
Rosario, Brazil Q86–029 **105**
Rosario, Chile S60–243 **103**
Rosario, Mexico V03+263 **100**
Rosario, Mexico V64+301 **100**
Rosario, Mexico V05+229 **100**
Rosario de la Frontera,
  Argentina S30–258 **103**
Rosario Oeste, Brazil R68–148 **105**
Rosario Tala, Argentina R85–323 **103**
Rosas, Spain M71+423 **53**
Rosas, G. of, Spain M70+422 **53**
Roscommon, Michigan T58+445 **91**
Roscommon & co.,
  Ireland, Rep. N49+536 **42**
Roscrea, Ireland, Rep. N47+529 **43**
Rose, i., Samoa Z18–150 **106**
Roseau, Minnesota U34+488 **93**
Rosebery, Tasmania C27–418 **109**
Rosebud, S. Dakota U65+432 **93**
Roseburg, Oregon W20+432 **92**
Rosedale, Mississippi U06+338 **97**
Roseires, Sudan K64+118 **81**
Rosenheim, W.Germany M17+478 **48**
Rosetown, Saskatchewan V16+514 **88**
Rosetta (Rashid), Egypt K88+314 **81**
Rosier, C., Quebec S25+489 **91**
Rosignano Marittamo, Italy M27+433 **56**
Rosignol, Guyana R76+063 **104**
Roslavl, U.S.S.R. K73+540 **60**
Rosport, Luxembourg M51+498 **44**
Ross, England N16+519 **38**
Ross, New Zealand A55–429 **112**
Ross, Tasmania C15–420 **109**
Ross Ice Shelf, Antarctica Z80–810 **27**
Ross, I., Burma F42+122 **71**
Ross R., Yukon W70+618 **88**
Ross Sea, Antarctica Z30–750 **27**
Rossa, Switzerland M35+464 **45**
Ross & Cromarty, co., See Highland
Rossano, Italy L80+396 **57**
Rosscarberry, Ireland, Rep. N54+516 **43**
Rosseau L., Ontario T28+452 **91**
Rossel I., Papua New Guinea B66–114 **111**
Rossignol, Belgium M57+497 **44**
Rossignol L., Nova Scotia S31+442 **90**
Rossland, British Columbia V78+492 **88**
Rosslare Harb., Ireland, Rep. N38+523 **43**
Rosslyn, Virginia T13+389 **96**
Rosta, Norway L61+690 **46**
Rosthern, Saskatchewan V09+529 **88**
Rostock, E. Germany M18+541 **48**
Rostov, U.S.S.R. K32+472 **61**
Rostov, U.S.S.R. K34+572 **60**
Roswell, New Mexico U87+334 **94**
Rosyth, Scotland N21+560 **41**
Rota, I., Mariana Islands C27+148 **106**
Rothenburg, Germany M29+494 **48**
Rotherham, England N08+534 **37**
Rothesay, Scotland N30+558 **41**
Roti, I., Indonesia D72–108 **65**
Roto, New South Wales C27–331 **109**
Rotorua, New Zealand A22–381 **112**
Rotterdam, Netherlands M63+519 **44**
Rotuma, I., Fiji A17–130 **106**
Roubaix, France M71+507 **54**
Rouen, France M84+495 **54**
Rôuge, Estonia L18+577 **47**
Roulers, Belgium M71+509 **44**
Round Mt., New S. Wales B77–304 **109**
Roundup, Montana V22+464 **93**
Roura, Fr. Guiana R44+046 **105**
Rous, Pen., Chile S55–555 **103**
Rousay I., Orkney, Scotland N18+592 **40**
Rouse's Point, New York S80+450 **91**
Rousseau, S. Dakota U61+443 **93**
Roussillon, prov., France M47+428 **55**
Rouveen, Netherlands M53+526 **44**
Rouyn, Quebec T25+482 **91**
Rovaniemi, Finland L26+665 **46**
Roveredo, Switzerland M35+462 **45**
Rovigo, Italy M19+451 **56**
Rovinari, Romania L41+449 **58**
Rovno, Ukraine L22+506 **60**
Rowena, New South Wales C07–298 **109**
Roxburgh, New Zealand A64–457 **112**
Roxburgh, Scotland N15+556 **41**
Roxbury, New York S87+423 **96**
Royal Canal, Ireland, Rep. N38–534 **43**

Royale, I., Michigan T84+480 **91**
Royan.France N06+456 **54**
Rozet, Wyoming V02+443 **93**
Rožňava. Czechoslovakia L57+485 **49**
Rtishchevo, U.S.S.R. K07+523 **61**
Ruabon, Wales N18+530 **38**
Ruahine Ra., New Zealand A24–400 **112**
Ruapehu, Mt., New Zealand A26–393 **112**
Rubtsovsk, U.S.S.R. G53+513 **62**
Ruby, Alaska Y30+645 **99**
Rucava, Latvia L53+561 **47**
Rudali, India G49+267 **73**
Rudbar, Afghanistan H74+301 **75**
Ruddervoorde, Belgium M71+511 **44**
Rudkøbing. Denmark M26+549 **47**
Rudnaya Pristan, U.S.S.R. C84+442 **63**
Rudok, Tibet G62+334 **70**
Rudolf L., Kenya K54+034 **83**
Rueiba, Sudan L08+156 **81**
Ruel, Ontario T39+472 **91**
Ruffec, France M89+460 **54**
Rugby, England N08+524 **37**
Rugby, N. Dakota U60+484 **93**
Rugeley, England N12+528 **37**
Rügen, I., E. Germany M10+544 **48**
Rui Khaf, Iran H89+346 **75**
Rūjiena, Latvia L28+579 **47**
Ruk, Pakistan H38+278 **70**
Rukumkot, Nepal G44+286 **73**
Rukwa L., Tanzania K76–080 **83**
Rumania. See Romania.
Rum, I., Scotland N38+570 **40**
Rumbek, Sudan L02+068 **81**
Rumburk, Czechoslovakia M03+509 **48**
Rumegies, France M70+505 **44**
Rumford Falls, Maine S63+445 **90**
Rumigny, France M66+498 **44**
Rumillies, Belgium M69+506 **44**
Rum Jungle, N. Terr., Aust. D24–123 **110**
Rumoi, Japan C50+439 **68**
Rumuruti, Kenya K50+002 **83**
Runanga, New Zealand A52–424 **112**
Runcorn, England N16+533 **37**
Rungwa, Tanzania K68–070 **83**
Rungwe Mt., Tanzania K66–092 **83**
Rupar, India G81+309 **72**
Rupsa, India G75+270 **73**
Rupert, Idaho V54+426 **94**
Rurrenabaque, Bolivia S45–145 **104**
Rurutu I., Tubuai Islands X60–250 **107**
Rusape, Rhodesia K78–186 **84**
Ruse (Ruschuk), Bulgaria L24+438 **58**
Ruseifa, Jordan K54+320 **76**
Rusele, Sweden L72+648 **46**
Rusaworth, Victoria C30–366 **109**
Rusne, R., Lithuania L51+552 **47**
Russas, Brazil Q48–049 **105**
Russel, C., N.-W. Terr. V75+753 **88**
Russelkonda, India G32+200 **71**
Russell, Kansas U54+388 **95**
Russell, New Zealand A35–353 **112**
Russel Pt., N.-W. Terr. V62+729 **88**
Russellville, Alabama T76+345 **95**
Russelville, Kentucky T72+368 **97**
Russian Soc. Federated Soviet
  Reps (Russia). U.S.S.R. 62-63
Russkoye Ustye, U.S.S.R. C07+713 **63**
Russo, Switzerland M38+462 **45**
Rustak, Afghanistan H31+371 **75**
Rustburg, Virginia T25+372 **97**
Ruston, Louisiana U16+326 **95**
Rutba, Iraq K29+329 **74**
Rutherfordton, N. Carolina T42+353 **97**
Ruthi, Switzerland M33+473 **45**
Ruthin, Wales N20+531 **38**
Rutland, Vermont S78+436 **91**
Rutland, co., See Leicester & co.
Rutland I., Andaman Is. F74+114 **71**
Ruurlo, Netherlands M51+521 **44**
Ruvuma R., Mozambique K30–108 **83**
Ruwenzori Mts., Uganda L00+004 **83**
Ružomberok, Czechoslovakia L64+491 **49**
Rwanda, Central Africa L00–025 **83**
Ryan, L., Scotland N30+550 **41**
Ryazan, U.S.S.R. K32+546 **60**
Ryazhsk, U.S.S.R. K30+537 **60**
Rybachiy, Pcl., U.S.S.R. K75+694 **62**
Rybinsk, U.S.S.R. K37+580 **60**
Rybinskoye Res., U.S.S.R. K40+586 **60**
Rybnoe, U.S.S.R. E85+729 **63**
Ryde, I. of W., England N07+507 **39**
Rye, England M86+510 **39**
Rye Patch Res., Nevada V80+406 **92**
Rylstone, New South Wales C00–328 **109**
Rymarov, Czechoslovakia L77+499 **49**
Rypin, Poland L64+531 **49**
Ryukyu Retto, Japan D50+250 **64**
Rzeszów, Poland L48+501 **49**
Rzhev, U.S.S.R. K64+563 **60**

Saalfeld, E. Germany M22+506 **48**
Saanen, Switzerland M46+465 **45**
Saarbrücken, W. Germany M48+492 **48**
Saaremaa, I., Estonia L44+584 **47**
Saariselkä, Finland L12+682 **46**
Saarland, W. Germany M46+493 **48**
Saarlouis, W. Germany M50+493 **48**
Saas Grund, Switzerland M42+461 **45**
Saavedra, Argentina S15–378 **103**
Saavedra, Chile S80–387 **19**
Saba, Iran J69+308 **74**
Sabac, Yugoslavia L62+448 **58**
Sabah (N. Borneo), Borneo **65**
Sabalgarh, India G78+262 **70**
Sabana, Arch. de, Cuba T30+232 **101**
Sabanalarga, Colombia T00+106 **104**
Sabancuy, Mexico U06+190 **100**
Sab Biyar, Syria K54+338 **76**
Sabile, Latvia L44+570 **47**
Sabiñanigo, Spain N03+425 **53**
Sabine and L.. Texas U23+296 **95**
Sabine R., Texas U22+300 **95**
Sabine Mt.. Antarctica A65–720 **27**
Sable, France N02+473 **54**
Sable, C., Florida T37+252 **99**
Sable, C., Nova Scotia S33+435 **90**
Sable I., Nova Scotia S00+439 **90**
Sables d'Olonne, les, France N10+465 **54**
Sabrina Coast, Antarctica E45–660 **27**
Sabzawar (Shindand), Afghan. H77+334 **75**
Sabzawar (Iran) J14+362 **75**

Sacandaga Res. & R.,
  New York S85+431 **96**
Sac City, Iowa U30+424 **95**
Sacedon, Spain N17+405 **53**
Sachigo R., Ontario U05+546 **89**
Sachsen-Anhalt, W. Germany M22+520 **48**
Sackets Harbor, New York T07+439 **91**
Sackville, New Brunswick S26+459 **90**
Saco, Maine S63+435 **90**
Saco, Montana V14+485 **93**
Sacramento, Brazil R14–199 **105**
Sacramento, California W09+385 **92**
Sacramento Mts., New Mex. V03+332 **94**
Sacramento R., California W12+392 **92**
Sada, Yemen K07+169 **74**
Sádaba, Spain N07+423 **53**
Sadabad, India G72+274 **73**
Sada Bandeira, Angola M08–148 **82**
Sadad, Syria K48+343 **76**
Saddleback Mt., Maine S63+449 **90**
Sadhaura, India G77+304 **72**
Sadij, Iran J07+257 **75**
Sadiya, India F56+278 **71**
Sa'diya. Jebel, Saudi Arabia K29+207 **74**
Sadmarda, Afghanistan H47+356 **75**
Sado, I., Japan C70+380 **68**
Sadra, India H13+233 **70**
Saduan, Saudi Arabia K11+192 **74**
Saeki, Japan D19+330 **68**
Safad, (Zefat), Israel K57+330 **76**
Safed Koh Ra., Afghan.-Pak. H26+340 **72**
Saffuriya, Israel K58+327 **76**
Safi, Morocco N56+320 **80**
Safidabeh, Iran H87+308 **75**
Safif, Saudi Arabia J53+214 **75**
Safita, Syria K53+348 **76**
Safranbolu, Turkey K73+412 **74**
Saga, Japan D28+332 **68**
Sagaing, Burma F54+218 **71**
Sagami B., Japan C64+352 **68**
Sagar, India G67+238 **73**
Sagar I., India G10+217 **73**
Sagata, Ethiopia K60+058 **83**
Sagauli, India G31+267 **73**
Sage Plains, Oregon W06+437 **92**
Saginaw, Michigan T54+435 **91**
Saginaw B., Michigan T52+440 **91**
Sagone, G. de, Corsica M39+421 **56**
Sagres, Portugal N53+370 **52**
Sagua la Grande, Cuba T30+228 **101**
Saguenay R., Quebec S64+483 **90**
Sagunto, Spain N01+397 **53**
Saham, Oman J19+242 **75**
Sahambavany. Malagasy Rep. J60–142 **83**
Sahand, mt., Iran J82+376 **74**
Sahara Desert. Africa 80-81
Saharanpur, India G74+297 **72**
Saharien Atlas Mts., Algeria M80+334 **80**
Sahaswan, India G67+281 **73**
Sahiadriparvat Ra., India G85+206 **70**
Sahibganj, India G14+252 **73**
Sahiwal, Pakistan H11+307 **72**
Sahuajo, Mexico U76+200 **100**
Sahuaripa, Mexico V24+288 **100**
Sahugun. Spain N30+423 **52**
Sahun. Yemen. South J72+141 **74**
Sahy, Czechoslovakia L66+481 **49**
Sahyadri Mts., India H03+150 **70**
Saibai, I., Papua New Guinea C44–095 **111**
Saida. See Sidon
Saidabad, Iran J26+295 **75**
Saidapet, India G58+130 **70**
Said Bundas, Sudan L32+084 **81**
Saidpur, India G41+256 **73**
Saidu, Pakistan H16+348 **70**
Saignelégier. Switzerland M48+473 **45**
Saigon, S. Vietnam E80+108 **69**
Saihut, Yemen, South J53+153 **75**
Sailana, India H00+235 **70**
Saimaa Kanal, Fin.-U.S.S.R. L10+610 **47**
Saimaa, L., Finland L12+613 **47**
St Abb's Hd.. Scotland N13+559 **41**
St Affrique, France M73+440 **55**
St Agatha, Maine S50+472 **90**
St Agreve, France M64+450 **55**
St Albans, England N02+517 **39**
St Albans, Vermont S79+448 **91**
St Amour, France M58+464 **54**
St Andre, Quebec S58+477 **91**
St André C., Madagascar K04–164 **83**
St Andrews, New Brunswick S42+451 **90**
St Andrews, New Zealand A53–445 **112**
St Andrews, Scotland N17+563 **41**
Ste Anne, Quebec S60+474 **91**
Ste Anne de Beaupré, Quebec S66+470 **91**
Ste Anne de la Pérage, Que. S73+466 **91**
Ste Anne des Monts, Quebec S39+491 **90**
St Anns Bay, Jamaica T13+185 **101**
St Anthonis, Netherlands M55+516 **44**
St Anthony, Idaho V41+440 **98**
St Antônien, Switzerland M31+470 **45**
St Arnaud, Victoria C41–367 **109**
St Asaph, Wales N21+532 **38**
St Augustin, C. de,
  Madagascar K10–238 **83**
St Augustine, Florida T38+299 **97**
St Austell & B., England N29+503 **38**
Ste Barbara, Venezuela S22+096 **104**
St Barthélemy. I.. Leeward Is. S17+179 **101**
St Béat, France M86+429 **55**
St Bečej, Yugoslavia L60+456 **58**
St Bernard Pass, Gd.,
  Switzerland-Italy M46+457 **56**
St Boniface, Manitoba U40+500 **88**
St Bride's B., Wales N32+518 **38**
St Brieuc, France N17+485 **54**
St Calais, France M86+480 **54**
St Catherines, Ontario T25+432 **91**
Ste Cécile. Quebec S66+457 **91**
St Chamond. France M63+455 **54**
St Charles, Michigan T55+433 **91**
St Charles, C., Labrador R64+524 **89**
St Chély d'Apcher, France M70+448 **55**
St Christopher, I. (St Kitts).
  Leeward Islands S16+173 **101**
St Clair, Michigan T45+429 **91**
St Clair, L., Mich.-Ont. T46+425 **91**
St Clair L., Tasmania C22–421 **109**
St Cloud, Minnesota U25+456 **93**
Ste Croix, Switzerland M51+468 **45**
St Croix, R., Wisconsin U16+457 **99**

St Davids & Hd., *Wales* N32+519 **38**
St Denis, *France* M76+489 **54**
St di Nova Siri, *Italy* L80+402 **57**
St Dizier, *France* M60+486 **54**
St Elias Mt., *Alaska* X40+604 **99**
St Elias Ra., *Yukon* X30+602 **88**
Saintes, *France* N04+457 **54**
St Etienne. *France* M64+454 **54**
St Eustatius, I., *Leeward Is.* S17+175 **101**
St Fabien, *Quebec* S53+483 **90**
St Fargeau, *France* M72+477 **54**
St Felicien, *Quebec* S74+486 **90**
Saintfield, *N. Ireland* N35+545 **42**
St Filipsland, *Netherlands* M65+516 **44**
St Fillans, *Scotland* N25+564 **41**
St Finans B., *Ireland, Rep.* N58+518 **43**
St Florent & G. de, *Corsica* M35+428 **56**
St Florentin, *France* M68+480 **54**
St Flour, *France* M72+450 **55**
St Francis, *Maine* S54+472 **90**
St Francis B., *S.-W. Africa* M02-252 **84**
St Francis, L., *Quebec* S67+459 **91**
St Francis, L., *Quebec* S86+452 **91**
St Francis R., *Arkansas* U03+358 **97**
St Francis R., *Quebec* S76+459 **91**
St Fulgent, *France* N07+469 **54**
St Gabriel de Brandon, *Que.* S80+463 **91**
St Gallen & canton, *Switz.* M34+474 **45**
St Gaudens, *France* M86+431 **55**
Ste Genevieve, *Missouri* U00+380 **97**
St George, *New Brunswick* S41+452 **90**
St George Hd., *N.S.W.* B86-352 **109**
St George I., *Bering Sea* Z29+564 **99**
St Georges, *Fr. Guiana* R41+037 **105**
St George's B., *Nfd.* R86+483 **90**
St George's Chan., *Ire.-Wales* N34+520 **38**
St Georges de Beauce, *Que.* S44+461 **90**
St Gérard, *Belgium* M62+502 **44**
St Germain, *France* M77+488 **54**
St German, *Puerto Rico* S42+181 **101**
St Gheorghe I., *Romania* L03+450 **58**
St Ghislain, *Belgium* M67+504 **44**
St Gilgen, *Austria* M10+477 **48**
St Gilles, *France* M64+437 **55**
St Gillis, *Belgium* M65+510 **44**
St Gillis-Waas, *Belgium* M65+512 **44**
St Gingolph, *Switzerland* M49+464 **45**
St Girons, *France* M83+430 **55**
St Gotthard, pass. *Switz.* M38+466 **45**
St Guenolé, *France* N26+478 **54**
St Helena, *Atlantic Ocean* N36-158 **85**
St Helena B.,*Cape Province* L72-328 **84**
St Helens, *England* N17+535 **37**
St Helens, Mt., *Washington* W12+461 **92**
St Hilaire, *New Brunswick* S51+473 **90**
St Hubert, *Belgium* M58+500 **44**
St Hyacinthe, *Quebec* S78+457 **91**
St Ignace, *Michigan* T59+459 **91**
St Imier, *Switzerland* M48+472 **45**
St Irénée. *Quebec* S61+476 **91**
St Ives, *England* N01+524 **37**
St Ives & B., *England* N33+502 **38**
St Jacques, *New Brunswick* S51+475 **90**
St James, *Minnesota* U28+440 **93**
St James, C., *B.C.* W67+518 **88**
St Jan, *Belgium* M73+509 **44**
St Jean, *France* M52+453 **54**
St Jean. *Quebec* S79+453 **91**
St Jean d'Angély. *France* N03+459 **54**
St Jean de Luz, *France* N10+434 **55**
St Jérôme. *Quebec* S84+458 **91**
St Joachim, *Quebec* S65+471 **91**
St John, *New Brunswick* S36+453 **90**
St John, West, *N.B.* S37+452 **90**
St John B., *Newfoundland* R76+509 **90**
St John, L., *Quebec* S72+486 **90**
St John, Mt., *Quebec* S22+504 **90**
St Johns, *Arizona* V27+345 **94**
St John's, Michigan* T57+430 **91**
St Johns, *Newfoundland* R46+475 **90**
St John's Pt., *Ireland, Rep.* N51+546 **42**
St John's Pt., *N. Ireland* N34+542 **42**
St Johns R., *Florida* T39+300 **97**
St Johnsbury, *Vermont* S72+445 **91**
St Joseph, *Louisiana* U07+319 **97**
St Joseph, *Michigan* T68+422 **91**
St Joseph, *Missouri* U30+398 **95**
St Joseph, *Quebec* S65+463 **90**
St Joseph I., *Ontario* T54+462 **91**
St Joseph I., *Texas* V42+280 **94**
St Joseph L., *Ontario* U02+510 **89**
Ste Justine, *Quebec* S62+464 **91**
St Kilda, Is., *Scotland* N51+578 **40**
St Kitts, I., *West Indies* S16+173 **101**
St Laurent, *Fr. Guiana* R55+054 **105**
St Lawrence, *Queensland* C03-222 **111**
St Lawrence, G. of, *Canada* S12+486 **90**
St Lawrence I., *Alaska* Z30+632 **99**
St Lawrence, R., *Quebec* S62+474 **89**
St Lawrence Seaway,
  N. America T01+448 **91**
St Leger, *Belgium* M56+496 **44**
St Léonard. *France* M81+458 **54**
St Leonard, *New Brunswick* S47+472 **90**
St Leonards, *England* M87+509 **39**
St Lewis, C., *Labrador* R44+528 **89**
St Lin, *Quebec* S83+458 **91**
St Lô, *France* N06+491 **54**
St Louis, *Mauritania* P10+160 **80**
St Louis, *Michigan* T58+434 **91**
St Louis, *Missouri* U02+386 **97**
St Louis, L., *Quebec* S83+454 **91**
St Louis de Kent, *N.B.* S30+467 **90**
St Lucia C., *Natal* K74+284 **84**
St Lucia, I., *Windward Is.* S05+140 **101**
St Lucia L., *Natal* K76+280 **84**
St Luke's I., *Burma* F41+102 **71**
St Maartensdijk, *Netherlands* M66+515 **44**
St Magnus B., *Scotland* N09+604 **40**
St Maixent, *France* N01+464 **54**
St Malo & Gulf, *France* N12+487 **54**
St Marc, *Haiti* S76+192 **101**
St Mard, *Belgium* M57+496 **44**
Ste Marie C., *Madagascar* J88-256 **83**
Ste Marie I.. *Madagascar* J60-170 **83**
St Marks, *Florida* T55+302 **97**
St Martin, I., *Leeward Is.* S18+181 **101**
St Martins, *New Brunswick* S33+454 **90**
St Mary B., *Nova Scotia* S37+442 **90**
St Mary Is., *India* H03+135 **70**

St Mary's, *Ontario* T37+433 **91**
St Marys, *Pennsylvania* T22+414 **96**
St Marys, *Tasmania* C11-416 **109**
St Mary's B., *Newfoundland* R53+467 **90**
St Mary's L., *Scotland* N19+555 **41**
St Mary's Pk., *S. Australia* C65-315 **111**
St Matthew I.. *Alaska* Z45+603 **99**
St Matthew's I., *Burma* F41+100 **71**
St Maurice, *Switzerland* M48+462 **45**
St Maurice R., *Quebec* S77+475 **91**
St Mazimin, *France* M55+435 **55**
St Meen, *France* N13+482 **54**
St Michael, *Alaska* Y70+631 **99**
St Michaels, *Maryland* T05+389 **91**
St Moritz, *Switzerland* M31+465 **45**
St Nazaire, *France* N15+473 **54**
St Neots, *England* N02+522 **37**
St Nicolaasga, *Netherlands* M56+529 **44**
St Nicolas. See St Niklaas
St Niklaas, *Belgium* M65+512 **44**
St Niklau, *Switzerland* M43+462 **45**
St Odilienberg, *Netherlands* M54+512 **44**
St Omer, *France* M77+508 **54**
Saintonge, prov.. *France* N02+454 **54**
St Paul I., *Bering Sea* Z32+570 **99**
St Paul, I., *Indian Ocean* G76-386 **77**
St Paul de Fenouillet, *France* M75+428 **55**
St Peter, *Minnesota* U24+443 **93**
St Peter, *Prince Edward I.* S15+464 **90**
St Peter, L., *Quebec* S78+461 **91**
St Petersburg, *Florida* T46+278 **97**
St Petersburg, *Pennsylvania* T22+412 **96**
St Pierre, *Martinique, W.I.* S06+147 **101**
St Pierre. I., *Quebec* S64+469 **91**
St Pierre. I., *Atlantic Ocean* R67+468 **90**
St Pol, *France* M76+504 **54**
St Polten, *Austria* L87+482 **49**
St Pons, *France* M73+435 **55**
St Pourçain, *France* M70+463 **54**
St Quentin, *France* M70+499 **54**
St Raymond, *Quebec* S71+469 **91**
St Rémi d'Amherst. *Quebec* S89+461 **91**
St Roch, *Quebec* S61+473 **90**
St Sébastien I., *Madagascar* J68-124 **83**
St Sernin-sur-Rance, *France* M75+439 **55**
St Servan, *France* N12+486 **54**
St Sever, *France* N03+438 **55**
St Simeon, *Quebec* S59+478 **91**
St Simon. *Quebec* S54+482 **91**
St Stephen, *New Brunswick* S44+452 **90**
St Thecle, *Quebec* S75+469 **91**
Ste Thérèse. L., *N.-W. Terr.* W07+646 **88**
St Thomas, *Ontario* T37+428 **91**
St Thomas, I., *Virgin Is.* S30+184 **101**
St Tronde. See St Truiden
St Tropez, *France* M50+433 **55**
St Truiden, *Belgium* M59+508 **44**
St Valery, *France* M80+502 **54**
St Valery-en-Caux, *France* M86+499 **54**
St Veit, *Austria* M04+468 **48**
St Vincent, *Windward Is.* S07+132 **101**
St Vincent C., *Madagascar* J20-220 **83**
St Vincent, G., *S. Australia* C72-346 **109**
St Vith, *Belgium* M53+503 **44**
St Xavier, *Montana* V16+454 **93**
Saipan, I., *Mariana Is.* C25+152 **106**
Saiping, *China* E36+326 **64**
Saiun, *Yemen, South* J66+160 **74**
Saivomuotka, *Sweden* L41+681 **46**
Saiyidwala, *Pakistan* H09+311 **72**
Saka Dzong, *Tibet* G28+295 **71**
Sakai, *Japan* C87+346 **68**
Sakaka, *Saudi Arabia* K29+299 **74**
Sakakawea, L., *N. Dakota* U74+476 **93**
Sakania, *Zaire* L08-128 **83**
Sakaria, R., *Turkey* K86+400 **74**
Sakata, *Japan* C61+389 **68**
Sakesar, *Pakistan* H17+324 **72**
Sakha, *Saudi Arabia* K08+232 **74**
Sakhalin, *U.S.S.R.* C40+510 **63**
Sakhalinskiy Zaliv, *U.S.S.R.* C55+539 **63**
Saki, *U.S.S.R.* K68+451 **60**
Šakiai. *Lithuania* L42+549 **47**
Sakishima Gunto, *Japan* D66+244 **68**
Sakr, *Yemen, D.R.* J48+156 **75**
Sakti, *India* G42+220 **73**
Säkylä, *Finland* L46+610 **47**
Sala, *Czechoslovakia* L73+482 **49**
Sala, *Sweden* L80+599 **47**
Salada, L., *Mexico* V63+322 **100**
Salado. R.. *Argentina* S14-292 **103**
Salado, R., *Texas* U58+270 **94**
Salaga, *Ghana* N04+086 **80**
Salahiye, *Syria* K26+348 **74**
Salala, *Oman* J35+171 **75**
Salama, *Guatemala* U02+151 **100**
Salamanca, *Mexico* U67+206 **100**
Salamanca, *New York* T22+422 **91**
Salamanca, *Spain* N34+409 **52**
Salamaua, *Papua New Guinea* C18-072 **111**
Salamina, *Colombia* T03+054 **104**
Salamis I.. *Greece* L39+379 **59**
Salangen, *Norway* L74+690 **46**
Salas, *Spain* N38+434 **52**
Salas de los Infantes, *Spain* N19+420 **52**
Salaverry, *Peru* T24-083 **104**
Sala-y-Gomez I., *Pacific Oc.* V00-258 **107**
Salbris, *France* M78+474 **54**
Saldana, *Spain* N29+425 **52**
Saldus, *Latvia* L45+567 **47**
Sale, *Victoria* C18-381 **109**
Salekhard, *U.S.S.R.* H51+664 **62**
Salem, *Illinois* T84+386 **95**
Salem, *India* G71+118 **70**
Salem, *Massachusetts* S65+425 **91**
Salem, *Missouri* U10+376 **97**
Salem, *New Jersey* T03+396 **91**
Salem, *Oregon* W18+449 **92**
Salem, *Virginia* T31+373 **97**
Salemi, *Sicily* M13+378 **57**
Sälen, *Sweden* M11+612 **47**
Salerno, *Italy* M02+407 **57**
Salerno, G. di, *Italy* M02+405 **57**
Salford, *England* N14+535 **37**
Salida, *Colorado* V06+386 **94**
Salina, *Kansas* U46+388 **95**
Salina, *Malawi* K64-136 **83**
Salina, *Utah* V41+390 **94**
Salina, I., *Italy* M01+386 **57**

Salina Cruz, *Mexico* U32+162 **100**
Salinas, *California* W10+366 **92**
Salinas, *Ecuador* T35-022 **104**
Salinas, *Mexico* U70+226 **100**
Salinas, *Mexico* U61+259 **100**
Salinas Pk., *New Mexico* V09+334 **94**
Salinas R., *California* W09+364 **92**
Salinitas, *Chile* S60-250 **103**
Salinópolis. *Brazil* R15-007 **105**
Salisbury, *England* N11+511 **39**
Salisbury, *Maryland* T03+385 **99**
Salisbury, *New Brunswick* S30+460 **90**
Salisbury, *N. Carolina* T33+356 **97**
Salisbury, *Rhodesia* K84-178 **84**
Salisbury, *S. Australia* C68-348 **109**
Salisbury I., *N.-W. Terr.* T12+639 **89**
Salisbury Plain, *England* N11+512 **39**
Salisbury I., *Uganda* K66+016 **83**
Salkhad, *Syria* K50+325 **76**
Salyan, *Nepal* G47+284 **73**
Salmon, *Idaho* V62+452 **92**
Salmon River Mts., *Idaho* V58+444 **92**
Salo, *Finland* L41+604 **47**
Salon, *France* M60+436 **55**
Salon, *India* G51+260 **73**
Salonica. See Thessaloniki
Salonta, *Romania* L50+469 **58**
Salop, co., *England* N16+544 **37**
Salqin, *Syria* K51+361 **76**
Salsette I., *India* H13+192 **70**
Salt Fd., *Norway* M06+672 **46**
Salt L., *Utah* V46+392 **94**
Salt L., *W. Australia* E37-240 **110**
Salt Ls., *W. Australia* D40-290 **110**
Salt Ra., *Pakistan* H18+326 **70**
Salt R., *Arizona* V34+338 **94**
Salta, *Argentina* S33+248 **103**
Saltash, *England* N25+504 **38**
Saltcoats, *Scotland* N29+556 **41**
Saltdal, *Norway* L87+671 **46**
Saltee, Is., *Ireland, Rep.* N40+521 **43**
Saltillo, *Mexico* U65+255 **100**
Salt Lake City, *Utah* V42+408 **94**
Salto, *Argentina* S02-343 **103**
Salto, *Uruguay* R78-314 **103**
Salto Grande, *Brazil* Q60-160 **105**
Salton Sea, *California* V66+334 **92**
Salt Plains Res., *Oklahoma* U50+368 **95**
Salt Sulphur Springs, *W.Va.* T34+376 **97**
Saltville, *Virginia* T41+369 **97**
Saluda, *Virginia* T09+377 **97**
Salûm & G. of, *Egypt* L30+316 **81**
Salur, *India* G40+186 **71**
Salut, Is. du, *Fr. Guiana* R46+054 **105**
Saluzzo, *Italy* M45+446 **56**
Salvador (Bahia), *Brazil* Q51-130 **105**
Salvador, L., *Louisiana* U01+296 **95**
Salvador, El, rep., *Cent. Amer.* T84+136 **101**
Salvaterra, *Portugal* N53+390 **52**
Salvatierra, *Mexico* U65+202 **100**
Salzburg, *Austria* M12+478 **48**
Salzwedel, *E. Germany* M23+528 **48**
Samahala, *Botswana* L38-196 **84**
Samalut, *Egypt* K86+282 **81**
Samana & B. de, *Dom. Rep.* S56+192 **101**
Samar, I., *Philippines* D60+117 **65**
Samarai, *Papua New Guinea* B87-107 **111**
Samarinda, *Borneo* E17-006 **65**
Samarkand, *Uzbek.* H48+395 **62**
Samarra Balad, *Iraq* K06+342 **74**
Samastipur, *India* G25+259 **73**
Samawa, *Iraq* J89+312 **74**
Sambalpur, *India* G35+214 **71**
Sambeek, *Netherlands* M54+516 **44**
Sambhal, *India* G69+285 **73**
Sambhar, *India* G88+268 **70**
Sambor, *Ukraine* L40+496 **60**
Samborombón, B.. *Argent.* R70-359 **103**
Sambre, R., *Belgium* M64+504 **44**
Same, *Japan* C51+405 **68**
Samedan, *Switzerland* M31+465 **45**
Sami, *Pakistan* H70+260 **70**
Samira, *Saudi Arabia* K17+264 **74**
Sam Ka, *Burma* F48+202 **71**
Sam-nua, *Laos* F05+204 **69**
Samoa Is., *Pacific Ocean* Z40-150 **106**
Samokov, *Bulgaria* L39+423 **58**
Samorogan, *Upper Volta* N30+114 **80**
Samos, I., *Greece* L19+337 **59**
Samothrace. See Samothraki I.
Samothráki I., *Greece* L27+405 **59**
Sampacho, *Argentina* S28-334 **103**
Sampit, *Borneo* E41-028 **65**
Samrée, *Belgium* M56+502 **44**
Samsat, *Turkey* K39+376 **74**
Samshui, *China* E42+232 **67**
Samsø, I., *Denmark* M26+558 **47**
Samsu, *Korea* D42+413 **64**
Samsun, *Turkey* K52+414 **74**
Samthar, *India* G67+258 **73**
Samuie Str., *Thailand* F30+092 **69**
San, *Mali* N28+130 **80**
San'a, *Yemen* K05+154 **74**
Sanam, *Jebel, Iraq* J75+301 **74**
San Ambrosio I., *Pacific Oc.* T30-250 **107**
Sanandaj, *Iran* J77+354 **74**
San Andres Mts., *New Mex.* V08+330 **94**
San Angelo, *Texas* U61+313 **98**
San Antioco, I., *Sardinia* M40+390 **57**
San Antonio *Chile* S70-336 **103**
San Antonio, *Texas* U51+294 **95**
San Antonio, C., *Argentina* R70-366 **103**
San Antonio, C., *Cuba* T59+218 **101**
San Antonio Pk., *New Mex.* V06+368 **94**
San Antonio R. & B., *Texas* U44+286 **94**
San Antonio Oeste, *Argent.* S30-408 **103**
San Bartolomeu de Nessines,
  Portugal N50+372 **52**
San Benedetto del Tronto, *It.* M07+430 **56**
San Benito, *Mexico* U14+147 **100**
San Benito, *Texas* U46+261 **94**
San Benito Is., *Mexico* V64+282 **100**
San Bernardino, *California* V74+341 **92**
San Bernardino R., *Cal.* V66+340 **92**
San Bernardo, *Chile* S64-335 **103**
San Blas, *Argentina* S14-405 **103**
San Blas, *Mexico* V02+215 **100**

San Blas, *Mexico* V22+262 **100**
San Blas, C., *Florida* T62+297 **99**
San Blas, G. de, *Panama* T23+096 **101**
San Borja, *Mexico* V52+288 **100**
Sanborn, *N. Dakota* U49+469 **93**
San Carlos, *Argentina* S35-260 **103**
San Carlos, *Argentina* S55-337 **103**
San Carlos, *Argentina* S31-312 **103**
San Carlos, *Chile* S71-363 **103**
San Carlos, *Mexico* U53+244 **100**
San Carlos, *Nicaragua* T58+111 **101**
San Carlos,
  Amazonas, Venez. S42+019 **104**
San Carlos, *Cojedes, Venez.* S52+097 **104**
San Carlos, L. *Arizona* V32+332 **94**
San Carlos de Bariloche,
  Argentina S68-411 **103**
San Carlos del Zulia, *Venz.* S70+090 **104**
Sanchez, *Dominican Rep.* S58+192 **101**
San Clemente, *Spain* N15+394 **53**
San Cosme, *Paraguay* R68-272 **103**
San Cristobal, *Mexico* S07-303 **103**
San Cristobal, *Mexico* U15+168 **100**
San Cristobal, *Venezuela* S73+078 **104**
San Cristobal I., *Galapagos Is.* U00-007 **107**
San Cristobal, I., *Solomon Is.* B20-110 **106**
Sancti Spiritus, *Cuba* T27+218 **101**
Sand, *Norway* M52+595 **47**
Sandakan. *N. Borneo* E11+059 **65**
Sanday I. & Sd., *Orkney, Scot.* N15+592 **40**
Sandbach, *England* N14+532 **37**
Sandefjord, *Norway* M29+591 **47**
Sandefjord B., *Antarctica* G80-700 **27**
Sanders, *Arizona* V26+352 **94**
Sandgate, *England* M83+511 **39**
Sandgate, *Queensland* B72-272 **111**
Sandhornøy, *Norway* M06+671 **46**
Sandia, *Peru* S57-143 **104**
San Diego, *California* V73+327 **92**
San Diego, *Texas* U50+277 **94**
San Diego, C., *Argentina* S31-547 **99**
San Diego de Cabrutica,
  Venezuela S28+084 **104**
Sandikli, *Turkey* K88+384 **74**
Sandila, *India* G56+270 **73**
San Dimas, *Mexico* V04+241 **100**
Sandnes, *Norway* M56+589 **47**
Sandoa, *Zaire* L44-098 **82**
San Domingos, *Portugal* N45+377 **52**
Sandown, *I. of Wight, Eng.* N07+507 **39**
Sandpoint, *Idaho* V70+480 **98**
Sandringham, *England* M87+528 **39**
Sandstone, *Minnesota* U17+461 **93**
Sandstone, *W. Australia* E05-279 **110**
Sandträsk, *Sweden* L52+661 **46**
Sandusky, *Michigan* T47+434 **91**
Sandusky, *Ohio* T46+414 **91**
Sandvig, *Bornholm, I., Den.* M01+553 **47**
Sandwich, *England* M82+513 **39**
Sandwich, *Ontario* T48+423 **91**
Sandy, C., *Queensland* B70-246 **111**
Sandy L., *Manitoba* U68+598 **88**
Sandy L., *Ontario* U18+531 **89**
San Esteban de Formaz,
  Spain N19+415 **52**
San Felipe, *Chile* S65-327 **103**
San Felipe, *Guatemala* U10+146 **100**
San Felipe, *Mexico* U01+179 **100**
San Felipe, *Mexico* U67+215 **100**
San Felipe, *Venezuela* S52+104 **104**
San Feliu de Guixals, *Spain* M72+418 **53**
San Feliu de Llobregat, *Sp.* M78+414 **53**
San Félix, *Venezuela* S16+083 **104**
San Felix I., *Pacific Ocean* U05-250 **107**
San Fernando, *Chile* S66-344 **103**
San Fernando, *Mexico* U49+248 **100**
San Fernando, *Mexico* V63+300 **100**
San Fernando, *Philippines* D88+166 **65**
San Fernando, *Trinidad* S08+103 **104**
San Fernando de Apure,
  Venezuela S45+077 **104**
San Fernando de Atabapo,
  Venezuela S47+040 **104**
Sanford, *Florida* T38+288 **97**
Sanford, *Maine* S65+435 **90**
Sanford, *N. Carolina* T25+355 **97**
Sanford, Mt., *Alaska* X60+620 **99**
San Francisco, *Argentina* S13-314 **103**
San Francisco, *California* W15+378 **92**
San Francisco Mts., *Arizona* V40+355 **94**
San Francisco Pk., *Arizona* V40+355 **98**
Sanga, *Angola* L88-114 **82**
Sangareddipet, *India* G71+176 **70**
Sanger, *N. Dakota* U66+472 **93**
Sanggau, *Borneo* E56+002 **65**
Sangihe Kep., *Indonesia* D58+027 **65**
San Giovanni in Fiore, *Italy* L80+393 **57**
Sangkulirang, *Borneo* E12+010 **65**
Sangla Hill, *Pakistan* H09+316 **72**
Sangre de Cristo Mts., *Colo.-*
  New Mexico V01+370 **94**
Sangre Grande Town,
  Trinidad S06+106 **104**
Sangrur, *India* G85+302 **72**
Sangwin, *Liberia* N56+054 **80**
San Ignacio, *Bolivia* S33-150 **104**
San Ignacio, *Bolivia* S05-162 **104**
San Ignacio, *Mexico* V07+241 **100**
San Ignacio, *Mexico* V48+271 **100**
San Ignacio, *Paguay* R72-269 **103**
Sanish, *N. Dakota* U75+480 **93**
San Javier, *Argentina* S00-305 **103**
San Javier, *Chile* S70-356 **103**
São João, *Portugal* N44+412 **52**
San Joaquin, *Bolivia* S29-132 **104**
San Jorge, C., *Argentina* S40-460 **103**
San José, *Bolivia* S04-176 **104**
San José. *California* W12+373 **92**
San José, *Colombia* S71+025 **104**
San José, *Costa Rica* T54+099 **101**
San José, *Guatemala* U05+139 **100**
San José, *Uruguay* R70-342 **103**
San José, G., *Argentina* S26-422 **103**
San José, I., *Mexico* V34+250 **100**
San José Carpizo, *Mexico* U58+193 **100**
San José de Amacuro, *Venez.* S03+085 **104**
San José de Feliciano, *Argent.* R83-303 **103**
San José del Cabo, *Mexico* V28-230 **100**
San José de Ocune, *Colombia* S61+041 **104**
San Juan, *Bolivia* R88-177 **104**
San Juan, *Puerto Rico* S36+185 **101**

San Juan, *Venezuela* S50+111 **104**
San Juan & R., *Argentina* S51-316 **103**
San Juan, C., *Argentina* S22-548 **103**
San Juan Mts., *Colorado* V12+374 **94**
San Juan, R., *Mexico* U32+181 **100**
San Juan, R., *Nicaragua* T54+108 **101**
San Juan R., *Utah, etc.* V30+372 **94**
San Juan de Camarones,
  Mexico V06+250 **100**
San Juan de Guadalupe,
  Mexico U77+245 **100**
San Juan del Norte, *Nic.* T52+110 **101**
San Juan de los Lagos, *Mex.* U73+213 **100**
San Juan del Rio, *Mexico* U59+204 **100**
San Juan del Sur, *Nicaragua* T65+114 **101**
San Juan Sabinas, *Mexico* U68+278 **100**
San Julian, *Argentina* S47-493 **103**
San Justo, *Argentina* S03-307 **103**
Sankuri Post, *Kenya* K32-004 **83**
San Lazaro, C., *Mexico* V43+247 **100**
San Leandro, *California* W13+377 **92**
San Lorenzo, *Argentina* S04-327 **103**
San Lorenzo, *Ecuador* T23+013 **104**
San Lorenzo, *Honduras* T74+134 **101**
San Lorenzo, *Mexico* V35+306 **100**
San Lorenzo, *Peru* S56-115 **104**
San Lorenzo Is., *Mexico* V46+286 **100**
San Lorenzo del Escorial, *Sp.* N25+406 **52**
Sanlucar la Mayor, *Spain* N37+374 **52**
San Lucas, *Bolivia* S31-200 **104**
San Lucas, C., *Mexico* V29+229 **100**
San Luis, *Argentina* R81-276 **103**
San Luis, *Argentina* S39-332 **103**
San Luis, *Cuba* T02+203 **101**
San Luis de la Paz, *Mexico* U61+212 **100**
San Luis Obispo, *California* W04+353 **92**
San Luis Potosi & state,
  Mexico U65+222 **100**
Sanluri, *Sardinia* M37+396 **57**
San Marcos, *Colombia* T01+086 **104**
San Marino, rep., *Italy* M15+441 **56**
San Martin, *Argentina* S64-440 **103**
San Martin, *Colombia* S82+038 **104**
San Martin, L., *Chile-Argent.* S76-489 **103**
San Martin de los Andes,
  Argentina S68-402 **103**
San Martin de Valdeiglesais,
  Spain N26+403 **52**
San Martinho, *Portugal* N55+395 **52**
San Mateo, *Florida* T39+296 **97**
San Mateo, *Spain* M89+404 **53**
San Mateo Pk., *New Mexico* V15+339 **94**
San Matias, *Bolivia* R79-164 **104**
San Matias, G., *Argentina* S26-414 **103**
San Maura. *See* Levkás I.
San Miguel, *Bolivia* S05-166 **104**
San Miguel, *Mexico* U65+209 **100**
San Miguel, *Peru* S83-130 **104**
San Miguel, *Salvador* T79+135 **101**
San Miguel. *See* Rey, I. del
San Miguel, B. de, *Panama* T19+084 **101**
San Miguel I., *California* W02+341 **92**
San Miguel, R., *Bolivia* S20-160 **104**
San Miguel de Tucuman,
  Argentina S32-268 **103**
San Nicolás, *Argentina* S01-334 **103**
Sano Nocera, *Italy* M02+407 **57**
San Pablo, *Bolivia* S40-216 **104**
San Pablo, C., *Argentina* S40-543 **103**
San Pedro, *Argentina* R87-338 **103**
San Pedro, *Bolivia* S37-181 **104**
San Pedro, *Belize* T78+180 **101**
San Pedro, *California* V80+337 **92**
San Pedro, *Ivory Coast* N40+048 **80**
San Pedro, *Mexico* U78+259 **100**
San Pedro, *Paraguay* R72-240 **103**
San Pedro Chan, *California* V87+336 **92**
San Pedro R., *Arizona* V32+326 **94**
San Pedro de Arimeña,
  Colombia S70+044 **104**
San Pedro del Gallo, *Mexico* U87+256 **100**
San Pedro de Lloc, *Peru* T26-076 **104**
San Pedro de Macoris,
  Dominican Rep. S56+186 **101**
San Pedro do Sul, *Portugal* N48+407 **52**
San Pedro Soloma, *Guat.* U08+157 **100**
San Pedro Sula, *Honduras* T78+155 **101**
San Pietro I., *Sardinia* M40+392 **56**
San Quintin & B., *Mexico* V66+304 **100**
San Rafael, *Argentina* S50-346 **103**
San Rafael, *California* W15+379 **92**
San Rafael, *New Mexico* V18+352 **98**
San Ramon, *Mexico* V66+308 **100**
San Ramon, *Peru* T01-111 **104**
San Remo, *Italy* M43+438 **56**
San Roque, *Argentina* R82-286 **103**
San Salvador, *Angola* M04-062 **82**
San Salvador, *Bahamas, The* S88 + 240 **101**
San Salvador, *Salvador* T86+137 **101**
Sansanne Mango, *Togo* M86+104 **80**
San Sebastian, *Spain* N12+433 **53**
San Sebastian & B. de,
  Argentina S51-533 **103**
San Severo, *Italy* L88+417 **57**
Sans Souci, *Ontario* T29+451 **91**
Santa, *Peru* T22-090 **104**
Santa Ana, *Bolivia* S34-138 **104**
Santa Ana, *Bolivia* R82-186 **104**
Santa Ana, *California* V77+337 **92**
Santa Ana, *Ecuador* T32-012 **104**
Santa Ana, *Mexico* V35+305 **100**
Santa Ana, *Peru* S77-129 **104**
Santa Ana, *Salvador* T87+140 **101**
Santa Anna (Bananal), I. de,
  Brazil R32-114 **105**
Santa Antonio da Gloria,
  Brazil Q50-093 **105**
Santa Barbara, *California* V88+344 **92**
Santa Barbara, *Honduras* T80+149 **101**
Santa Barbara Chan., *Cal.* W06+343 **92**
Santa Barbara Is., *California* W00+340 **98**
Santa Barbara de Samana,
  Dominican Rep. S56+192 **101**
Santa Carolina, *Brazil* S44-077 **104**
Santa Catalina, *Chile* S58-252 **103**
Santa Catalina I., *California* V80+334 **92**
Santa Catalina I., *Mexico* V34+257 **100**
Santa Catalina, mt., *Mexico* V63+309 **100**
Santa Catalina Ra., *Arizona* V34+324 **94**
Santa Catarina, *Mexico* V28+231 **100**
Santa Catarina, I., *Brazil* R21-276 **103**
Santa Clara, *Brazil* S58-028 **104**

Santa Clara, *Cuba* T30+224 **101**
Santa Clara, Sa., *Mexico* V54+273 **100**
Santa Coloma de Farnes, *Sp.* M74+418 **53**
Santa Cruz, *Argentina* S52-500 **103**
Santa Cruz, *Bolivia* S20-177 **104**
Santa Cruz, *Brazil* Q61-200 **105**
Santa Cruz, *Brazil* S75-059 **104**
Santa Cruz, *California* W12+370 **92**
Santa Cruz, *Chile* S68-346 **103**
Santa Cruz, *Mexico* V02+258 **100**
Santa Cruz, *Mexico* V34+312 **100**
Santa Cruz, *Nicaragua* T66+134 **101**
Santa Cruz, *Peru* T05-056 **104**
Santa Cruz, *Philippines* D81+140 **65**
Santa Cruz Chan. & I., *Cal.* V89+340 **92**
Santa Cruz Is., *Pacific Ocean* A80-112 **106**
Santa Cruz de Bravo, *Mex.* T76+196 **100**
Santa Cruz de la Zarza, *Sp.* N20+400 **52**
Santa Cruz del Sur, *Cuba* T19+208 **101**
Santa Cruz de Tenerife,
  Canary Is. P08+284 **80**
Santa Elena, *Ecuador* T35-023 **104**
Santa Eufemia, G. di, *Italy* L84+389 **57**
Santa Fé, *Argentina* S05-316 **103**
Santa Fé, *Cuba* T46+217 **101**
Santa Fé, *New Mexico* V14+356 **94**
Santa Helena, *Brazil* R56-249 **103**
Santa Helena, *Brazil* R02-024 **105**
Santai, *China* F00+311 **66**
Santa Innes, B., *Mexico* V41+269 **100**
Santa Isabel, *Argentina* S41-362 **103**
Santa Isabel, *See* Macias Nguema
Santalnes, I., *Chile* S76-539 **103**
Santa Lucia, *Cuba* T06+210 **101**
Santa Luzia, *Brazil* R18-162 **105**
Santa Margarita, I., *Mexico* V41+244 **100**
Santa Maria, *Argentina* S36-266 **103**
Santa Maria, *Brazil* R52-297 **103**
Santa Maria, *California* W03+349 **92**
Santa Maria, I., *Atlantic Oc.* P61+372 **80**
Santa Maria, I., *Chile* S81-370 **103**
Santa Maria, mt., *Argentina* S56-362 **103**
Santa Maria del Rio, *Mex.* U64+218 **100**
Santa Maria di Leuca C., *It.* L70+398 **57**
Santa Maria la Real de Nieva,
  Spain N26+411 **52**
Santa Maria Nova, *Brazil* R28-092 **105**
Santa Marta, *Colombia* S85+112 **104**
Santa Monica, *California* V81+341 **92**
Santa Monica B., *California* V88+338 **92**
Santander, *Colombia* T08+030 **104**
Santander, *Spain* N23+434 **52**
Santa Paula, *California* V84+342 **92**
Santa Philomena, *Brazil* R04-091 **105**
Santa Quiteria, *Brazil* Q76-034 **105**
Santarem, *Brazil* Q55-137 **105**
Santarem, *Portugal* N52+392 **52**
Santa Rita, *Venezuela* S68+104
Santa Rosa, *Argentina* S31-323 **103**
Santa Rosa, *Argentina* S49-331 **103**
Santa Rosa, *Bolivia* S07-170 **104**
Santa Rosa, *Brazil* R57-278 **103**
Santa Rosa, *California* W16+384 **92**
Santa Rosa, *Honduras* T84+147 **101**
Santa Rosa, *New Mexico* U88+348 **94**
Santa Rosa, *Uruguay* R76-303 **103**
Santa Rosa I., *California* W01+340 **92**
Santa Rosa de Toay, *Argent.* S25-365 **103**
Santa Rosalia, *Mexico* V44+272 **100**
Santa Vitoria do Palmar,
  Brazil R50-336 **103**
Santerem, *Brazil* R58-024 **105**
Santiago, *Brazil* R59-291 **103**
Santiago, *Chile* S64-334 **103**
Santiago, *Mexico* V28+336 **100**
Santiago, *Mexico* V01+217 **100**
Santiago, *Panama* T35+081 **101**
Santiago, *Dominican Rep.* S64+194 **101**
Santiago Mts., *Texas* U81+300 **94**
Santiago de Compostela, *Sp.* N51+429 **52**
Santiago, Cerro, *Panama* T40+087 **101**
Santiago, Sa. de, *Bolivia* S00-183 **104**
Santiago de Cuba, *Cuba* T05+201 **101**
Santiago del Estero, *Argent.* S26-278 **103**
Santiago Papasquiaro, *Mex.* V02+248 **100**
Santilland, *Spain* N24+433 **52**
Santipur, *India* G08+232 **73**
Santis, mt., *Switzerland* M34+472 **45**
Santo Angelo, *Brazil* R56-283 **103**
Santo Antonio, *Brazil* S2-089 **104**
Santo Antonio, *Brazil* S21-124 **104**
Santo Antonio, *Brazil* R43-009 **105**
Santo Antonio do Zaire,
  Angola M16-064 **82**
Santo Corazon, *Bolivia* R82-179 **104**
Santo Domingo, *Cuba* T31+226 **101**
Santo Domingo,
  Domin. Rep. S59+186 **101**
Santo Domingo, *Mexico* V65+307 **100**
San Tomé, *Venezuela* S24+091 **104**
Santorini, *See* Thira, I.
Santos, *Brazil* R08-238 **105**
Santo Thome, *Argentina* R67-285 **103**
Santo Tomas, *Mexico* V68+315 **100**
Santo Tomas, *Peru* S74-144 **104**
Santvliet, *Belgium* M64+513 **44**
San Urbano, *Argentina* S09-336 **103**
San Vicente, *Salvador* T82+136 **101**
San Vito C., *Italy* L77+404 **57**
São Anna do Livramento,
  Brazil R63-309 **103**
São Antonio de Balsas,
  Brazil R06-076 **105**
São Antonio do Ica, *Brazil* S48-031 **104**
São Benedicto, *Brazil* S10-002 **104**
São Bento do Norte, *Brazil* Q36-051 **105**
São Borja, *Brazil* R66-287 **103**
São Carlos, *Brazil* R17-221 **105**
São Christovão, *Brazil* Q44-110 **105**
São Domingos, *Brazil* R07-135 **105**
São Domingos, *Brazil* R17-016 **105**
São Felippe, *Brazil* S59-065 **104**
São Felippe, *Brazil* S44-004 **104**
São Felix, *Brazil* R44-065 **105**
São Francisco, *Brazil* Q58-038 **105**
São Francisco, *Brazil* Q77-063 **105**
São Francisco, *Brazil* Q89-160 **105**
São Francisco, *Brazil* R56-046 **105**
São Francisco do Sul & I. de,
  Brazil R22-263 **103**

São Francisco, R., *Brazil* Q56-089 **105**
São Hill, *Tanzania* K60-084 **83**
São Jeronimo, *Brazil* R36-237 **105**
São Jeronymo, *Brazil* R40-299 **103**
São Joao da Barra, *Brazil* Q66-216 **105**
São Joao da Boa Vista, *Brazil* R11-218 **105**
São Joao del Rei, *Brazil* Q85-210 **105**
São João do Araguaya, *Brazil* R22-053 **105**
São João do Piauhy, *Brazil* Q74-084 **105**
São Joaquim, *Brazil* S44 000 **104**
São Joaquin, *Brazil* R66-048 **105**
São José, *Brazil* R42-320 **103**
São José, *Brazil* R22-276 **103**
São José, *Brazil* S38-003 **104**
São José do Duro, *Brazil* R08-113 **105**
São José do Mipibu, *Brazil* Q31-061 **105**
São José dos Martyrios,
  Brazil R20-063 **105**
São Jose do Rio Prêto, *Brazil* R26-207 **105**
São Jose dos Mattoes, *Brazil* Q79-054 **105**
São José do Tocantins, *Brazil* R21-144 **105**
São Lourenco & R., *Brazil* R61-165 **105**
São Luis, *Brazil* Q86-026 **105**
São Luis, I. de, *Brazil* Q86-025 **105**
São Luiz do Caceres, *Brazil* R76-162 **105**
São Luiz Gonzaga, *Brazil* R60-283 **103**
São Marcello, *Brazil* R01-110 **105**
São Mateus do Sul, *Brazil* R32-260 **103**
São Matheus, *Brazil* Q59-188 **105**
São Miguel, *Brazil* R14-016 **105**
São Miguel, I., *Atlantic Oc.* P64+380 **80**
Saona, I. *Dominican Rep.* S52+182 **101**
Saône, R., *France* M60+463 **54**
Saône-et-Loire, dep., *France* M61+466 **54**
Sao Paulo, *Brazil* R10-234 **105**
Sao Paulo de Olivenca, *Brazil* S53-035 **104**
São Raymundo Nonato,
  Brazil Q76-090 **105**
São Sebastião & I. da, *Brazil* R02-238 **105**
São Simão, *Brazil* R15-214 **105**
São Thomé I., *G. of Guinea* M50+002 **82**
Saoura, *Algeria* N24+278 **80**
São Vicente, *Brazil* R09-238 **105**
São Vicente, *Brazil* R19-058 **105**
Sapaya, *Ecuador* T24+008 **104**
Sapiéntza I., *Greece* L50+367 **59**
Saposoa, *Peru* T10-070 **104**
Sapporo, *Japan* C52+430 **68**
Sapri, *Italy* L86+400 **57**
Sapulpa, *Oklahoma* U37+360 **95**
Saqqez, *Iran* J82+363 **74**
Saragossa (Zaragoza), *Spain* N05+416 **53**
Saraikela, *India* G24+227 **73**
Sarajevo, *Yugoslavia* L70+438 **58**
Sarala, *U.S.S.R.* G04+550 **62**
Saranac Lake, *New York* S85+444 **91**
Saranda, *India* G28+222 **73**
Sarandi del Yi, *Uruguay* R64-333 **103**
Sarangarh, *India* G41+215 **71**
Saranovo, *Bulgaria* L35+422 **58**
Saransk, *U.S.S.R.* J89+542 **61**
Sarapul, *U.S.S.R.* J38+565 **61**
Sarasota, *Florida* T45+273 **97**
Saratoga, *Wyoming* V11+415 **93**
Saratoga, L., *New York* S82+430 **96**
Saratoga Springs, *New York* S82+431 **91**
Saratov, *U.S.S.R.* J84+515 **61**
Saratsi-ting, *China* E53+407 **66**
Sarawak, *Borneo* E54+013 **65**
Sarbaz, *Iran* H82+266 **75**
Sárbogárd, *Hungary* L68+469 **49**
Sarco, *Chile* S69-288 **103**
Sardarshahr, *India* H03+285 **103**
Sardasht, *Iran* J87+361 **74**
Sardegna, I., *Italy* M36+400 **57**
Sardhana, *India* G74+291 **72**
Sardinia. *See* Sardegna.
Sardis, *Mississippi* T89+344 **97**
Sardis Res., *Mississippi* T88+345 **95**
Sardoal, *Portugal* N49+396 **52**
Sareks Nat. Park, *Sweden* L76+673 **46**
Sargans, *Switzerland* M33+471 **45**
Sarh, *Chad* L70+092 **81**
Sari, *Iran* J42+366 **75**
Sarikamis, *Turkey* K15+404 **74**
Sarina, *Queensland* C04-215 **111**
Sariñena, *Spain* N01+418 **53**
Sar-i-Pul, *Afghanistan* H54+361 **75**
Sar-i-Pul, *Iran* J85+345 **74**
Sarir, *Libya* L46+276 **81**
Sark, I., *Channel Islands* N14+494 **54**
Sarkad, *Hungary* L52+468 **49**
Sarlat, *France* M83+449 **55**
Sarles, *N. Dakota* U54+490 **93**
Sarmi, *New Guinea* C68-019 **65**
Sarmiento, mt., *Chile* S65-545 **103**
Sarna, *Sweden* M11+617 **47**
Sarnen, *Switzerland* M40+469 **45**
Sarnia, *Ontario* T44+430 **91**
Saronic G., *Greece* L38+376 **59**
Saronno, *Italy* M35+456 **56**
Sarpsborg, *Norway* M23+593 **47**
Sarpul, *Iran* J58+371 **75**
Sarrebourg, *France* M48+487 **54**
Sarreguemines, *France* M48+491 **54**
Sarre Union, *France* M47+489 **54**
Sarria, *Spain* N44+428 **52**
Sart, *Belgium* M54+505 **44**
Sartene, *Corsica* M36+416 **57**
Sarthe R. & dep., *France* M89+480 **54**
Sarufutso, *Japan* C48+452 **68**
Sarur, *Saudi Arabia* J12+233 **75**
Sarvar, *Hungary* L79+472 **49**
Sasa Baneh, *Ethiopia* K08+078 **83**
Sasaram, *India* G35+249 **73**
Sasawara, *Tanzania* K48-116 **83**
Sasebo, *Japan* D32+331 **68**
Sasovo, *U.S.S.R.* K18+543 **61**
Sassandra & R., *Ivory Coast* N36+050 **80**
Sassari, *Sardinia* M39+407 **57**
Sassnitz, *E. Germany* S11-318 **103**
Sastre, *Argentina* S11-318 **103**
Sas-van-Gent, *Netherlands* M67+512 **44**
Satacougou, *Mali* N68+126 **80**
Satara, *India* H05+178 **70**

Säter, *Sweden* L86+603 **47**
Satevo, *Mexico* V06+279 **100**
Satins, *France* M55+470 **54**
Satka, *U.S.S.R.* J06+550 **61**
Satkhira, *Bangladesh* G05+227 **73**
Satoraljaujhely, *Hungary* L50+484 **49**
Satpura Ra., *India* H05+217 **70**
Satul, *Thailand* F30+066 **69**
Satu Mare, *Romania* L43+478 **49**
Sauda, *Norway* M52+597 **47**
Saudhárkrókur, *Iceland* P28+657 **46**
Saudi Arabia, *S.-W. Asia* **74**
Saugeen Pen., *Ontario* T38+451 **91**
Saugerties, *New York* S84+421 **91**
Sauk Center, *Minnesota* U30+457 **93**
Sauk Rapids, *Minnesota* U25+456 **93**
Saulieu, *France* M65+473 **54**
Sault Ste Marie, *Michigan* T56+465 **91**
Sault Ste Marie, *Ontario* T56+465 **91**
Saumur, *France* N01+473 **54**
Saunders, I., *S. Sandwich Is.* P80-570 **27**
Sauqira B., *Oman* J16+185 **75**
Saurashtra, *India* H25+220 **70**
Sava, R., *Yugoslavia* L61+447 **58**
Savai'i, I., *Samoa Islands* Z45-140 **106**
Savalan, mt., *Iran* J73+383 **74**
Savanna, *Illinois* U01+421 **91**
Savannah, *Georgia* T37+321 **97**
Savannah, *Missouri* U30+399 **95**
Savannah R., *Georgia-S. Car.* T46+340 **97**
Savannakhet, *Laos* F02+166 **69**
Savanna la Mar, *Jamaica* T19+183 **101**
Savantvadi, *India* H07+160 **70**
Savanur, *India* G87+150 **70**
Save, *Benin* M76 + 080 **80**
Save R., *Mozambique* K60-210 **84**
Saveh, *Iran* J58+352 **75**
Savenay, *France* N12+473 **54**
Savoie, dep., *France* M49+455 **54**
Savoie, prov., *France* M53+457 **54**
Savona, *Italy* M39+443 **56**
Savonlinna, *Finland* L07+619 **46**
Savu Sea, *Indonesia* D80-096 **65**
Savukoski, *Finland* L11+673 **46**
Sawa, *Yemen, South* J74 + 159 **74**
Sawatch Mts., *Colorado* V10+388 **94**
Sawel, *N. Ireland* N42+548 **42**
Saxmundham, *England* M81+522 **39**
Saxnäs, *Sweden* L88+649 **46**
Saxton, *Pennsylvania* T20+402 **96**
Saya, *Syria* K54+351 **76**
Sayan, *Peru* T13-110 **104**
Sayan, Vostochnya, *U.S.S.R.* F30+525 **63**
Sayan, Zapadnyy, *U.S.S.R.* F60+535 **63**
Sayre, *Oklahoma* U56+354 **95**
Sayre, *Pennsylvania* T09+420 **96**
Sayula, *Mexico* U82+198 **100**
Scafell Pike, *England* N19+544 **37**
Scalea, *Italy* L85+398 **57**
Scanteia, *Romania* L15+470 **58**
Scapa Flow, *Orkney, Scot.* N18+589 **40**
Scarba, I., *Scotland* N34+562 **41**
Scarboro, *Maine* S62+436 **90**
Scarborough, *England* N02+543 **37**
Scariff I., *Ireland, Rep.* N62+517 **43**
Scărisoara, *Romania* L43+465 **58**
Scatari I., *Nova Scotia* R88+460 **90**
Schafer, *N. Dakota* U79+478 **93**
Schaffhausen & canton,
  Switzerland M38+477 **45**
Schelde, Ooster & Wester,
  Netherlands M66+515 **44**
Schenectady, *New York* S83+428 **91**
Scheveningen, *Netherlands* M64+521 **44**
Schiedam, *Netherlands* M64+519 **44**
Schiermonnikoog I,
  Netherlands M53+535 **44**
Schiphol, *Netherlands* M61+523 **44**
Schleins, *Switzerland* M27+469 **45**
Schleswig, *W. Germany* M33+545 **48**
Schleswig-Holstein,
  Germany M33+540 **48**
Schneidemühl. *See* Pila.
Schoharie, *New York* S86+427 **96**
Schönbuhl, *Switzerland* M45+470 **45**
Schonebeck, *E. Germany* M25+520 **48**
Schongau, *W. Germany* M25+478 **48**
Schoonhoven, *Netherlands* M61+519 **44**
Schötz, *Switzerland* M42+472 **45**
Schouten, I., *Tasmania* C11-424 **109**
Schouwen I., *Netherlands* M67+517 **44**
Schuchinsk, *Kazakh* H28+530 **62**
Schull, *Ireland, Rep.* N57+515 **43**
Schuls, *Switzerland* M28+468 **45**
Schuyler, *Nebraska* U42+414 **95**
Schwabach, *W. Germany* M24+493 **48**
Schwägalp, *Switzerland* M34+473 **45**
Schwandorf, *W. Germany* M17+493 **48**
Schwaner, Peg., *Borneo* E46-011 **65**
Schwarzhorn, mt., *Switz.* M43+462 **45**
Schwarzwald, *W. Germany* M38+486 **48**
Schwedt, *E. Germany* M04+531 **48**
Schweidnitz. *See* Swidnica.
Schweinfurt, *W. Germany* M29+501 **48**
Schwerin, *E. Germany* M22+536 **48**
Schwyz & canton, *Switz.* M38+470 **45**
Sciacca, *Sicily* M12+375 **57**
Scilly, Is. of, *England* N38+500 **38**
Scituate, *Massachusetts* S64+422 **96**
Scobey, *Montana* V02+488 **93**
Scone, *New South Wales* B85-320 **109**
Scone, *Scotland* N20+564 **41**
Scoresby, C., *N.-W. Terr.* U20+714 **89**
Scoresby Ld., *Greenland* P85+730 **26**
Scoresby Sd., *Greenland* P38+700 **26**
Scotia, *Ontario* T26+455 **91**
Scotia Sea, *Antarctica* R90-580 **27**
Scotland, *Great Britain* N24+560 **34**
Scotland, *S. Dakota* U46+431 **93**
Scott, C., *Brit. Columbia* W51+507 **88**
Scott Inl., *N.-W. Territories* S65+710 **89**
Scott I., *Antarctica* A02-670 **27**
Scott, Mt., *Oregon* W12+432 **98**
Scott City, *Kansas* U66+384 **94**
Scottsbluff, *Nebraska* U82+416 **93**
Scottsdale, *Tasmania* C16-412 **109**
Scourie, *Scotland* N31+584 **40**
Scranton, *Pennsylvania* T04+414 **91**
Scridain, L., *Scotland* N37+563 **41**
Scugog L., *Ontario* T23+442 **91**
Scunthorpe, *England* N04+536 **37**

Index

Scutari (Shkodër), *Albania* L63+421 **58**
Scutari (Uskudar), *Turkey* L06+411 **74**
Seaford, *Delaware* T04+386 **91**
Seahorse Pt., *N.-W. Terr.* T30+641 **89**
Sea Isle City, *New Jersey* S88+392 **91**
Scal R., *Manitoba* U40+590 **88**
Sea Lake, *Victoria* C43-356 **109**
Sea Lion Is., *Falkland Is.* R84-524 **103**
Searcy, *Arkansas* U10+352 **95**
Seattle, *Washington* W14+476 **92**
Sebago L., *Maine* S63+439 **90**
Sebastián Vizcaino B. de, *Mexico* V58+282 **100**
Sebenico. *See* Sibenik
Sebewaing, *Michigan* T50+437 **91**
Sebha, (Sabhah), *Libya* M04+270 **81**
Sebin Karahisar, *Turkey* K40+403 **74**
Sebree, *Kentucky* T75+376 **97**
Sečovce, *Czechoslovakia* L50+487 **49**
Secretary I., *New Zealand* A78-452 **112**
Secunderabad, *India* G68+175 **70**
Seda, *Lithuania* L47+561 **47**
Sedalia, *Missouri* U20+389 **99**
Sedan, *France* M60+497 **54**
Sedan, *S. Australia* C64-346 **109**
Sedano, *Spain* N23+427 **52**
Sedbergh, *England* N15+543 **37**
Seddon, *New Zealand* A35-417 **112**
Seddonville, *New Zealand* A48-415 **112**
Sedhiou, *Senegal* P04+128 **80**
Sedom, *Israel* K57+311 **76**
Sedrun, *Switzerland* M37+467 **45**
Seeheim, *S.-W. Africa* L72-270 **84**
Seelisberg, *Switzerland* M38+470 **45**
Sées, *France* M89+486 **54**
Seewis, *Switzerland* M32+470 **45**
Sefrou, *Morocco* N30+340 **80**
Sefton, *New Zealand* A41-432 **112**
Sefton, Mt., *New Zealand* A59-437 **112**
Segorbe, *Spain* N03+398 **53**
Ségou, *Mali* N38+132 **80**
Segovia, *Spain* N25+409 **52**
Segovia, R., *Nicaragua* 154+147 **101**
Seguela, *Fr. W. Africa* N42+080 **80**
Sehkukeh, *Iran* H81+307 **75**
Sehwan, *Pakistan* H43+264 **70**
Seibo, *Dominican Rep.* S54+190 **101**
Seiland, *Norway* L40+704 **46**
Seine, R., *France* M87+495 **54**
Seine-et-Marne, dep., *France* M73+487 **54**
Seine-et-Oise, dep., *France* M79+488 **54**
Seine-Maritime, dep., *Fr.* M86+497 **54**
Seitler, *U.S.S.R.* K61+454 **60**
Seiyala, *Egypt* K74+226 **81**
Sejal, *Colombia* S48+026 **104**
Sekenke, *Tanzania* K66-044 **83**
Seki, *Japan* C78+354 **68**
Sekieshan I., *China* D76+303 **67**
Sekondi, *Ghana* N10+050 **80**
Sektyakh, *U.S.S.R.* D60+700 **63**
Selby, *England* N06+538 **37**
Selby, *S. Dakota* U60+454 **93**
Selemiya, *Syria* K48+350 **76**
Selenga, R., *Mong.-U.S.S.R.* E80+515 **63**
Selima Oasis, *Sudan* L04+212 **81**
Selinsgrove, *Pennsylvania* T11+408 **96**
Selkirk, *Manitoba* U42+502 **88**
Selkirk, *Yukon* X14+631 **88**
Selkirk, *Scotland* N17+555 **41**
Selkirk Mts., *Brit. Columbia* V70+500 **88**
Selle, Sa. de la, *Haiti* S72+184 **101**
Selles, *France* M81+473 **54**
Selma, *Alabama* T72+324 **97**
Selma, *N. Carolina* T20+355 **97**
Selous Mt., *Yukon* W68+634 **88**
Selva, *Argentina* S13-297 **103**
Selwyn, *Queensland* C56-215 **111**
Selwyn Ra., *Queensland* C60-214 **111**
Selwyn R., *Yukon* W60+634 **88**
Selzaete, *Belgium* M67+512 **44**
Sem, *Norway* M28+593 **47**
Semarang, *Java* E58-070 **65**
Semawe, pref., *Israel* K62+304 **76**
Seminoe Res., *Wyoming* V11+420 **93**
Semipalatinsk, *Kazakh* G59+505 **62**
Semnan, *Iran* J40+356 **75**
Senador Pompeu, *Brazil* Q56-055 **105**
Senatobia, *Mississippi* U00+346 **97**
Sendai, *Japan* C53+383 **68**
Seneca L., *New York* T11+427 **91**
Seneca Falls, *New York* T11+429 **96**
Sénégal, rep., *W. Africa* P00+146 **80**
Senev, *Michigan* T66+463 **91**
Senga Hill, *Zambia* K82-094 **83**
Sengilei, *U.S.S.R.* J67+540 **61**
Senise, *Italy* L82+402 **57**
Senj, *Yugoslavia* M01+450 **56**
Senja, *Norway* L76+693 **46**
Senna Madureira, *Brazil* S53-092 **104**
Senneterre, *Quebec* T14+484 **91**
Sens, *France* M70+482 **54**
Senta, *Yugoslavia* L59+459 **58**
Sentinel Ra., *Antarctica* T80-770 **27**
Seondha, *India* G67+262 **73**
Seoni, *India* G63+221 **73**
Seoni-Malwa, *India* G75+225 **73**
Seoul (Sóul), *Korea* D48+377 **64**
Separation Pt., *New Zealand* A42-407 **112**
Seperior, *Nebraska* U48+400 **95**
Sepólno, *Poland* L74+535 **49**
Sepulveda, *Spain* N22+413 **52**
Sequeros, *Spain* N36+405 **52**
Sequoia Nat. Park., *Cal.* V83+365 **92**
Serai, *Syria* K54+358 **76**
Serakhs, *Turkmen* H83+365 **62**
Seram I., *Indonesia* D40-030 **65**
Serampore, *India* G10+228 **73**
Serbia, *Yugoslavia* L52+430 **58**
Serdeles, *Libya* M26+258 **81**
Serdobol, *Karelia* K86+617 **46**
Serdobsk, *U.S.S.R.* K04+525 **61**
Serengeti Nat. Pk., *Tanzania* K60-020 **83**
Sergach, *U.S.S.R.* J88+556 **61**
Sergiyevsk, *U.S.S.R.* J53+540 **61**
Serifos, I., *Greece* L33+372 **59**
Sermata, I., *Indonesia* D36-085 **65**
Serov, *U.S.S.R.* H88+599 **62**
Serowe, *Botswana* L20-224 **84**
Serpa, *Portugal* N45+379 **52**
Serpins, *Portugal* N49+402 **52**
Serpukhov, *U.S.S.R.* K46+549 **60**

Sérrai, *Greece* L39+411 **58**
Serra San Bruno, *Italy* L82+386 **57**
Serrezuela, *Argentina* S32-306 **103**
Sertã, *Portugal* N49+398 **52**
Sertig, *Switzerland* M31+467 **45**
Sérvia, *Greece* L48+401 **59**
Serviceton, *Victoria* C54-364 **109**
Sesheke, *Zambia* L30-174 **84**
Sete, *France* M68+434 **55**
Sete Lagoas, *Brazil* Q85-194 **105**
Setif, *Algeria* M58+360 **80**
Setubal, *Portugal* N53+385 **52**
Seul, Lac, *Ontario* U15+502 **89**
Sevan, Oz., *Armyan, U.S.S.R.* K00+403 **62**
Sevastopol, *U.S.S.R.* K68+446 **60**
Sevelen, *Switzerland* M33+471 **45**
Seven Islands (Sept'Iles), *Quebec* S38+503 **90**
Sevenoaks, *England* M89+513 **39**
Severac-le-Château, *France* M72+443 **55**
Severn, *Cape Province* L42-268 **84**
Severn, *Ontario* T77+558 **89**
Severn R., *England* N15+526 **37**
Severn, R., *Ontario* T88+543 **89**
Severnaya Dvina, *U.S.S.R.* K10+628 **62**
Severnaya Zemlya, *U.S.S.R.* F50+800 **63**
Sevier L., *Utah* V49+390 **92**
Sevier R., *Utah* V44+394 **92**
Sevilla, *Spain* N36+374 **52**
Seville. *See* Sevilla
Seward, *Alaska* X86+602 **99**
Seward Pen., *Alaska* Y80+651 **99**
Seybaplaya, *Mexico* U04+196 **100**
Seychelles, Is., *Indian Ocean* J30-050 **77**
Seydhisfjördhur. *Iceland* N84+653 **46**
Seymchan, *U.S.S.R.* B76+630 **63**
Seymour, *Indiana* T66+390 **91**
Seymour, *Victoria* C29-370 **109**
Seyne, *France* M51+444 **55**
Sezanne, *France* M68+487 **54**
Sfakiá. *See* Khóra Sfakion.
Sfäntu Gheorghe, *Romania* L25+459 **58**
Sfax, *Tunisia* M26+348 **81**
Sfira, *Syria* K46+361 **76**
Sgurr Mor., *Scotland* N30+577 **40**
Shaam, *U.A.E.* J23+260 **75**
Shaba, *Zaire* L50 + 100 **82**
Shadegan, *Iran* J68+306 **74**
Shadrinsk, *U.S.S.R.* H69+560 **61**
Shaduela, *Ethiopia* K18+134 **83**
Shadwan, I., *Egypt* K64+274 **81**
Shafa Amr, *Israel* K59+328 **76**
Shaftesbury, *England* N13+510 **39**
Shag Rocks, *Atlantic Ocean* Q85-540 **27**
Shahabad, *India* G79+302 **72**
Shahabad, *India* G60+276 **73**
Shah Abdul Azim, *Iran* J52+356 **75**
Shahba, *Syria* K50+328 **76**
Shahbandar, *Pakistan* H43+241 **70**
Shah Dad, *Iran* J14+306 **75**
Shahdadkot, *Pakistan* H42+278 **70**
Shahdadpur, *Pakistan* H38+258 **70**
Shahdara, *India* G76+287 **72**
Shahdol, *India* G51+230 **73**
Shahganj. *India* G44+260 **73**
Shahi, *Iran* J43+365 **75**
Shahin, *Iran* J81+367 **74**
Shahjahanpur, *India* G61+278 **73**
Shahjui, *Afghanistan* H44+325 **75**
Shahpur, *Pakistan* H15+323 **72**
Shähpür, *Iran* K02+382 **74**
Shahpura, *India* H01+257 **70**
Shah Rakht, *Iran* J00+338 **75**
Shahr-i-Babak, *Iran* J30+320 **75**
Shahriza, *Iran* J49+320 **75**
Shahr-i-Zabul, *Iran* H81+310 **75**
Shahrud, *Iran* J30+364 **75**
Shahsien, *China* E14+264 **67**
Shaiba, *Saudi Arabia* K12+280 **74**
Shajara, *Saudi Arabia* J84+223 **74**
Shakhty, *U.S.S.R.* K28+476 **61**
Shakopee, *Minnesota* U21+448 **93**
Shakubetsueki, *Japan* C37+428 **68**
Shala L., *Ethiopia* K38+074 **83**
Shalasha, *Sudan* L20+106 **81**
Shamil, *Iran* J20+274 **75**
Shammar, Jebel, *Saudi Arabia* K24+277 **74**
Shamokin, *Pennsylvania* T10+408 **91**
Shanghai, *China* D81+312 **66**
Shangjao, *China* E12+285 **67**
Shangkiu, *China* E26+345 **66**
Shangtung Pen., *China* D86+370 **64**
Shangyiu, *China* E32+260 **67**
Shan-hai-kwan. *See* Linyu.
Shansien, *China* E53+347 **66**
Shanklin, I. of W., *England* N07+506 **39**
Shanna, *Saudi Arabia* J54+190 **75**
Shannon, *New Zealand* A27-405 **112**
Shannon, I., *Greenland* P25+750 **26**
Shannon, R. & Airport, *Ireland, Rep.* N52+527 **43**
Shansi, *China* E48+380 **66**
Shantarskiye Os., *U.S.S.R.* C73+550 **63**
Shantung, prov., *China* E12+360 **66**
Shaohing, *China* D86+300 **67**
Shaowu, *China* E15+273 **67**
Shaoyang, *China* E51+272 **67**
Shap, *England* N16+545 **37**
Shapinsay, I., *Orkney Is., Scot.* N17+590 **40**
Shaqa, *Qatar, Saudi Arabia* K25+198 **74**
Shaqiq, *Saudi Arabia* J51+257 **75**
Shaqra, *Saudi Arabia* J89+252 **74**
Sharakpur, *Pakistan* H05+315 **72**
Sharjah, *U.A.E.* J72+254 **75**
Shark B., *W. Australia* E40-254 **110**
Sharon, *Pennsylvania* T33+413 **91**
Sharqi, Jeb. esh, *Leb.-Syria* K52+340 **76**
Sharr, Jebel el, *Saudi Arabia* K55+276 **74**
Sharya, *U.S.S.R.* J87+584 **61**
Shasi, *China* E46+302 **67**
Shasta, *California* W15+407 **92**
Shasta, Mt., *California* W13+415 **92**
Shasta Res., *California* W12+408 **92**
Shatra, *Iraq* J84+314 **74**
Shatt-al-Arab, *Iraq* J73+307 **74**
Shaubek, *Jordan* K57+305 **76**
Shawano, *Wisconsin* T82+448 **91**
Shawinigan Falls, *Quebec* S77+465 **91**
Shawnee, *Oklahoma* U42+353 **95**
Shawneetown, *Illinois* T79+377 **97**
Shchors, *Ukraine* K78+518 **60**

Sheboygan, *Wisconsin* T76+438 **91**
Shediac, *New Brunswick* S27+462 **90**
Sheelin L., *Ireland, Rep.* N44+538 **42**
Sheenjik R., *Alaska* X55+673 **80**
Sheep Haven, *Ireland, Rep.* N48+552 **42**
Sheep's Hd., *Ireland, Rep.* N59+515 **43**
Sheerness, *England* M85+514 **39**
Sheffield, *Alabama* T76+348 **95**
Sheffield, *England* N09+534 **37**
Sheffield, *New Zealand* A48-434 **112**
Sheffield, *Tasmania* C22-414 **109**
Sheikh, Jeb. esh, *Syria* K55+334 **76**
Sheikh 'Abd er Rahman. *See* Arka.
Sheikh Miskin, *Syria* K53+328 **76**
Sheik 'Othman, *Yemen, South* K00 + 129 **74**
Sheik Seraq, *Syria* K46+330 **76**
Shekha, *Yemen, South* J64 + 151 **74**
Shekhupura, *Pakistan* H05+317 **72**
Sheklung, *China* E36+231 **67**
Shelburne, *Nova Scotia* S32+438 **90**
Shelburne, *Ontario* T31+441 **91**
Shelby, *Michigan* T68+436 **91**
Shelby, *Montana* V41+485 **93**
Shelby, *N. Carolina* T38+352 **97**
Shelbyville, *Illinois* T84+394 **95**
Shelbyville, *Kentucky* T61+382 **97**
Shelbyville, *Tennessee* T69+356 **97**
Sheldon, *Iowa* U35+412 **95**
Shelikhova Zaliv, *U.S.S.R.* B45+600 **63**
Shellharbour, *New South Wales* B85-346 **109**
Shelter I., *New York* S74+411 **96**
Shenandoah, *Iowa* U32+408 **95**
Shenandoah, *Pennsylvania* T07+409 **91**
Shenandoah R., *Virginia* T18+392 **96**
Shenandoah Junct., *W. Va.* T17+394 **96**
Shenandoah Nat. Park, *Va.* T20+384 **97**
Shenchow. *See* Yuanling.
Shendam, *Nigeria* M34+088 **81**
Shendi, *Sudan* K70+166 **81**
Shëngjin, *Albania* L63+418 **58**
Shenkursk, *U.S.S.R.* K12+623 **62**
Shensi, prov., *China* E66+350 **66**
Shenyang, *China* D70+418 **66**
Sheopur, *India* G80+256 **70**
Shepetovka, *Ukraine* L17+502 **60**
Shepparton, *Victoria* C27+364 **109**
Sheppey, I. of, *England* M85+514 **39**
Sherada, *Ethiopia* K52+072 **83**
Sherard Osborn Fd., *Greenland* R30+820 **26**
Sherbro I., *Sierra Leone* N76+078 **80**
Sherbrooke, *Quebec* S72+454 **91**
Sheridan, *Wyoming* V12+448 **93**
Sheridan, Mt., *Wyoming* V34+443 **93**
Sherman, *Texas* U40+336 **95**
Sherpur, *Bangladesh* G82+246 **73**
Sherridon, *Manitoba* U66+551 **88**
Shetland (Zetland), *Scotland* N06+604 **40**
Shevaroy Hills, *India* G68+119 **70**
Sheyenne, *N. Dakota* U55+479 **93**
Shiant Is. & Sd. of, *Scotland* N38+579 **40**
Shibam, *Yemen, South* J68 + 159 **74**
Shibarghan, *Afghanistan* H55+366 **75**
Shibata, *Japan* C64+379 **68**
Shibin el Kom, *Egypt* K84+306 **81**
Shickshock Mts., *Quebec* S44+488 **90**
Shiel, L., *Scotland* N34+568 **41**
Shieldaig, *Scotland* N34+575 **40**
Shigatse, *Tibet* G07+293 **71**
Shihnan. *See* Enshih.
Shih Pao Shan, *China* E64+294 **64**
Shihshow, *China* E45+296 **67**
Shihtao, *China* D76+369 **66**
Shihtsien, *China* E70+275 **67**
Shikarpur, *Pakistan* H38+278 **70**
Shikohabad, *India* G68+271 **73**
Shikoku, I., *Japan* D06+340 **68**
Shilka & R., *U.S.S.R.* E23+519 **63**
Shülelagh, *Ireland, Rep.* N39+527 **43**
Shillong, *India* F79+255 **71**
Shiloh, *Tennessee* T80+350 **97**
Shilongol, *China* E24+434 **64**
Shimoga, *India* G86+140 **70**
Shimoni, *Kenya* K34-046 **83**
Shimonoseki, *Japan* D24+340 **68**
Shimoshima, *Japan* D29+324 **68**
Shimshal & Pass, *Kashmir* G88+364 **72**
Shin, L., *Scotland* N27+581 **40**
Shinas, *Oman* J22+247 **75**
Shinghar, *Pakistan* H31+317 **72**
Shingu, *Japan* C84+337 **68**
Shinjo, *Japan* C58+388 **68**
Shinshar, *Syria* K49+346 **76**
Shinyanga, *Tanzania* K70-036 **83**
Shipets, *Japan* C29+436 **68**
Shippigan, *New Brunswick* S28+477 **90**
Shippigan I., *New Brunswick* S28+478 **90**
Shiraishi, *Japan* C56+380 **68**
Shiraz, *Iran* J45+296 **75**
Shireza, *Pakistan* H56+277 **70**
Shirley, *Montana* V04+466 **93**
Shirley Mts., *Wyoming* V09+422 **93**
Shirokaya, *U.S.S.R.* B47+619 **63**
Shisur, *Saudi Arabia* J39+182 **75**
Shiuhing. *See* Koyiu.
Shiukwan, *China* E38+248 **67**
Shivpuri, *India* G74+254 **73**
Shizugawa, *Japan* C51+387 **68**
Shizuoka, *Japan* C69+350 **68**
Shklov, *U.S.S.R.* K88+542 **60**
Shkoder, *Albania* L63+421 **58**
Shoal Harbour, *Newfoundland* R54+482 **90**
Shoalhaven R., *N.S.W.* B86-348 **109**
Shoeburyness, *England* M85+515 **39**
Shoka, *Taiwan* D86+241 **67**
Sholapur, *India* G84+176 **70**
Shonai. *See* Tsuruoka.
Shorkot, *Pakistan* H17+308 **72**
Short, *Missouri* U06+368 **97**
Short Mts., *W. Virginia* T22+392 **96**
Short Pine Hills, *S. Dakota* U80+453 **93**
Shoshone Falls, *Idaho* V57+424 **97**
Shoshone Mts.. *Wyoming* V28+442 **93**
Shoshone Res., *Wyoming* V25+442 **98**
Shovo Tso, *Tibet* G40+313 **71**
Shreveport, *Louisiana* U22+325 **95**
Shrewsbury, *England* N17+527 **37**
Shropshire (Salop), *Eng.* See Salop.
Shtora, *Lebanon* K55+338 **76**
Shubuta, *Mississippi* T82+318 **97**
Shuikow, *China* E07+263 **67**

Shujabad, *Pakistan* H22+299 **72**
Shumagin Is., *Alaska* Y60+549 **99**
Shumaisa, *Saudi Arabia* J87+249 **74**
Shumen, *Bulgaria* L19+433 **58**
Shumerlya, *U.S.S.R.* J81+555 **61**
Shunking. *See* Nanchung.
Shunteh. *See* Singtai.
Shuqra, *Yemen, South* J86 + 134 **74**
Shurab. *Iran* J21+338 **75**
Shurma, *Saudi Arabia* K18+232 **74**
Shuru Tso, *Tibet* G22+302 **71**
Shushal, *Kashmir* G68+335 **70**
Shushtar, *Iran* J67+321 **74**
Shusp, *Iran* J00+317 **75**
Shuttleton, *New S. Wales* C24-322 **109**
Shuya, *U.S.S.R.* K21+568 **61**
Shuyang, *China* E07+342 **66**
Shwebo, *Burma* F56+225 **71**
Shwedaung, *Burma* F59+186 **71**
Shwegyin, *Burma* F48+180 **71**
Sialkot, *Pakistan* H03+325 **72**
Siam. *See* Thailand.
Siam, G. of, *Thailand, etc.* F20+110 **69**
Sian, *China* E66+342 **66**
Siangtan, *China* E43+279 **67**
Siangyang, *China* E47+320 **66**
Siangyin, *China* E42+286 **67**
Siao Hingan Ling, *China* D42+488 **64**
Siapu, *China* E00+269 **67**
Siargao, I., *Philippines* D54+100 **65**
Siaton, *Philippines* D72+091 **65**
Siauliai, *Lithuania* L40+559 **47**
Sib, *Oman* J11+237 **75**
Sibenik, *Yugoslavia* L85+437 **56**
Siberut, I., *Indonesia* F36-014 **65**
Sibi, *Pakistan* H42+296 **70**
Sibiu, *Romania* L35+458 **58**
Sibolga, *Sumatra* F37+018 **65**
Sibsagar, *India* F61+270 **71**
Sibu, *Sarawak* E49+022 **65**
Sicasica, *Bolivia* S46-174 **104**
Sichang, *China* F16+278 **64**
Sicie C., *France* M55+430 **55**
Sicilia, I., *Italy* M06+380 **57**
Sicilian Channel, *Mediterranean Sea* M18+373 **57**
Sicily. *See* Sicilia, I.
Sicuani, *Peru* S67-143 **104**
Sid, *Yugoslavia* L65+452 **58**
Sidaka, *Iraq* K02+369 **74**
Sideby (Siipyy), *Finland* L52+621 **47**
Siderno Marina, *Italy* L82+383 **57**
Sidhout, *India* G66+145 **70**
Sidi Barrani, *Egypt* L24+316 **81**
Sidi Beben, *Libya* L70+306 **81**
Sidi-bel-Abbes, *Algeria* N04+352 **80**
Sidi Ifni, *Ifni, N.-W. Africa* N69+288 **80**
Sidlaw Hills, *Scotland* N19+565 **41**
Sidnaw, *Michigan* T82+465 **91**
Sidney, *Montana* U86+477 **93**
Sidney, *Nebraska* U78+412 **94**
Sidney, *New York* T02+423 **91**
Sidon (Saida), *Lebanon* K58+336 **76**
Sidra, Gulf of, *Libya* L70+316 **81**
Siedlce, *Poland* L47+522 **49**
Siegen, *W. Germany* M42+509 **48**
Siem-Reap, *Khmer* F06+133 **69**
Siena, *Italy* M26+433 **56**
Sieradz, *Poland* L68+516 **49**
Sierra Colorada, *Argentina* S46-406 **103**
Sierra Grande, *Argentina* S32-414 **103**
Sierra Leone, *W. Africa* N70+088 **80**
Sierra Mojada, *Mexico* U82+273 **100**
Sierra Rosaria, *Argentina* S48-427 **103**
Sifnos, I., *Greece* L32+370 **59**
Sigean, *France* M72+430 **55**
Sighet, *Romania* L37+479 **49**
Sighisoara, *Romania* L31+462 **58**
Siglufjördhur, *Iceland* P23+662 **46**
Sigmaringen, *W. Germany* M35+481 **48**
Sigourney, *Iowa* U14+412 **95**
Sigsig, *Ecuador* T23-030 **104**
Sigüenza, *Spain* N16+411 **53**
Siguiri, *Guinea* N56+114 **80**
Sigulda, *Latvia, U.S.S.R.* L31+572 **47**
Sihl See, *Switzerland* M37+471 **45**
Sihsien, *China* E09+288 **67**
Siilinjärvi, *Finland* L14+630 **46**
Sikandarabad, *India* G74+285 **72**
Sikandra Rao, *India* G70+277 **73**
Sikar, *India* G89+275 **72**
Sikasso, *Mali* N34+112 **80**
Si Kiang, R., *China* E54+232 **64**
Siking. *See* Sian.
Sikinos, I., *Greece* L29+367 **59**
Sikkim, *India* G09+275 **73**
Sila, La., *Italy* L81+392 **57**
Silao, *Mexico* U69+290 **100**
Silchar, *India* F73+248 **71**
Silenen, *Switzerland* M38+468 **45**
Silenrieux, *Belgium* M64+502 **44**
Silesia, *Montana* V23+455 **93**
Silgarhi, *Nepal* G67+364 **74**
Silifke, *Turkey* K67+364 **74**
Silistra, *Bulgaria* L16+441 **58**
Siljan, L., *Sweden* M02+609 **47**
Silkeborg, *Denmark* M33+561 **47**
Silloth, *England* N26+548 **37**
Sils, *Switzerland* M31+464 **45**
Silvaplana, *Switzerland* M31+465 **45**
Silva Porto, *Angola* L78-124 **82**
Silver L., *Oregon* W06+431 **92**
Silver City, *New Mexico* V20+328 **94**
Silverton, *Colorado* V17+378 **94**
Silverton, *New S. Wales* C53-320 **109**
Silves, *Brazil* R80-027 **105**
Silves, *Portugal* N50+372 **52**
Silvretta, mts., *Austria-Switzerland* M30+469 **45**
Simand, L., *Quebec* T22+477 **91**
Simcoe, *Ontario* T32+429 **91**
Simcoe, L., *Ontario* T26+444 **91**
Simeulue, I., *Indonesia* F54+025 **65**
Simferopol, *U.S.S.R.* K66+450 **60**
Simi, I., *Greece* L13+366 **59**
Simla, *India* G77+310 **72**
Simleul Silvaniei, *Romania* L43+472 **49**
Simo, *Finland* L11+657 **46**
Simola, *Finland* L11+609 **47**
Simon, L., *Quebec* T01+460 **91**
Simpelveld, *Netherlands* M54+508 **44**

Simplon and Pass, *Switzerland* M42+462 **45**
Simpson, Fort, *N.-W. Terr.* W11+614 **88**
Simpson, C., *Alaska* Y25+709 **88**
Simpson Des., *Australia* C80–254 **111**
Simpson, I., *Chile* S83–459 **103**
Simuna, *Estonia* L22+590 **47**
Sinai, pen., *Egypt* K70+290 **81**
Sinaloa, state, *Mexico* V12+250 **100**
Sinaloa & R., *Mexico* V20+260 **100**
Sinamaica, *Venezuela* S71+110 **104**
Sinbo, *Burma* F48+247 **71**
Sinchang, *China* D84+295 **67**
Sin-chow, *China* E43+385 **66**
Sind, *Pakistan* H40+255 **70**
Sindel, *Bulgaria* L15+431 **58**
Sindhuli Garhi, *Nepal* G25+272 **73**
Sind Sagar Doab, *Pakistan* H21+311 **72**
Sines, *Portugal* N53+379 **52**
Singa, *Sudan* K66+132 **81**
Singapore & Str., *S. Asia* F07+012 **69**
Singaraja, *Bali I., Indon.* E29–081 **65**
Singen, *W. Germany* M38+477 **48**
Singhbhum, *India* G27+224 **73**
Singida, *Tanzania* K62–046 **83**
Singitic G., *Greece* L36+402 **59**
Singkawang, *Borneo* E66+010 **65**
Singkep, I.,
  Riouw Arch., Indon. F04–006 **65**
Singleton, *New South Wales* B83–326 **109**
Singora. *See* Songkhla
Singsingsia, *China* F58+418 **64**
Singtai, *China* E33+371 **66**
Sinho, *China* E28+375 **66**
Sinhsien, *China* E44+384 **64**
Sinhwa, *China* E52+277 **67**
Sining, *China* F18+363 **64**
Siniscola, *Sardinia* M32+406 **57**
Sinj, *Yugoslavia* L80+437 **56**
Sinjar, & Jebel, *Iraq* K18+364 **74**
Sinjil, *Palestine* K58+320 **76**
Sinkiang, *China* G30+400 **30**
Sin-min-fu, *China* D74+420 **66**
Sinnamary, *Fr. Guiana* R47+053 **105**
Sinning, *China* E55+266 **67**
Sinoe L., *Romania* L06+446 **58**
Sinoia, *Rhodesia* K88–172 **84**
Sinop, *Turkey* K58+420 **74**
Sinton, *Texas* U44+280 **94**
Sintra, *Portugal* N56+388 **52**
Sinuiju, *N. Korea* D64+401 **64**
Sinyang, *China* E35+322 **66**
Sion, *Switzerland* M46+462 **45**
Sioux City, *Iowa* U38+426 **95**
Sioux Falls, *S. Dakota* U40+435 **93**
Sioux Lookout, *Ontario* U11+502 **89**
Siparia, *Trinidad* S09+102 **104**
Sipoiilo, *Rhodesia* K86–166 **84**
Sipora, I., *Indonesia* F32–022 **65**
Siquisique, *Venezuela* S58+106 **104**
Sira, *India* G78+138 **70**
Sira. *See* Siros, I.
Siracusa, *Sicily* M88+371 **57**
Sirajganj, *Bangladesh* G01+245 **73**
Sir Douglas, Mt., *Alberta* V60+505 **88**
Sir Edward Pellew Group,
  N. Territory, Australia C77–157 **111**
Siretul, R., *Romania* L18+462 **58**
Sirhind, *India* G81+306 **72**
Siri, *Ethiopia* K36+080 **83**
Sirjan, *Iran* J28+296 **75**
Sirna, I., *Greece* L20+363 **59**
Sironcha, *India* G60+188 **70**
Sironj, *India* G74+241 **73**
Siros, I., *Greece* L30+374 **59**
Sirsa, *India* H00+295 **72**
Sirsi, *India* G68+286 **73**
Sirsi, *India* H00+146 **70**
Sirte (Surt), *Libya* L80+312 **81**
Sisak, *Yugoslavia* L82+454 **56**
Sisaket, *Thailand* F04+150 **69**
Sisal, *Mexico* U00+211 **100**
Sisi, *Botswana* L16–218 **84**
Sisopon, *Khmer* F12+136 **69**
Sister I., E., *Tasmania* C13–397 **109**
Sister I., W., *Tasmania* C14–397 **109**
Sisteron, *France* M54+442 **55**
Sitamarhi, *India* G27+266 **73**
Sitamau, *India* G87+240 **70**
Sitapur, *India* C56+275 **73**
Sitara, *Saudi Arabia* J83+227 **74**
Sithonia, *Greece* L37+401 **59**
Sitia, *Crete* L23+352 **59**
Sitka, *Alaska* X04+569 **99**
Sitpur, *Pakistan* H25+292 **72**
Sittang, *Burma* F49+174 **71**
Sittang, R., *Burma* F51+192 **71**
Sittard, *Netherlands* M55+510 **44**
Sitten. *See* Sion
Sivand, *Iran* J42+301 **75**
Sivas, *Turkey* K48+398 **74**
Siverek, *Turkey* K34+378 **74**
Sivrihisar, *Turkey* K81+395 **74**
Sivry, *Belgium* M65+502 **44**
Siwa, *Egypt* L28+292 **81**
Siwalik Hills, *India* G73+304 **70**
Siwan, *India* G34+262 **73**
Sixmilebridge, *Ireland, Rep.* N53+527 **43**
Sixteen, *Montana* V36+462 **93**
Sjælland, *Denmark* M18+556 **47**
Sjötorp, *Sweden* M06+588 **47**
Skadarsko Jezero, *Yugosl.-Alb.* L64+422 **58**
Skagafjord, *Iceland* P28+660 **46**
Skagen, *Denmark* M26+577 **47**
Skagerrak, *Norway-Denmark* M42+573 **47**
Skagway, *Alaska* X00+592 **99**
Skaneateles, L., *New York* T08+428 **96**
Skara, *Sweden* M09+584 **47**
Skardu, *Kashmir* G86+353 **72**
Skarnes, *Norway* M20+602 **47**
Skeena R., *Brit. Columbia* W52+546 **88**
Skegness, *England* M88+531 **37**
Skellefte Alv, *Sweden* L68+654 **46**
Skelleftea, *Sweden* L54+647 **46**
Skiathos, I., *Greece* L39+392 **59**
Skibbereen, *Ireland, Rep.* N56+515 **43**
Skiddaw, mt., *England* N19+546 **37**
Skien, *Norway* M32+592 **47**
Skierniewice, *Poland* L59+520 **49**
Skiftet Kihti, *Finland* L54+600 **47**
Skipton, *England* N12+540 **37**
Skiros, I., *Greece* L32+389 **59**
Skive, *Denmark* M36+566 **47**

Skofia Loka, *Yugoslavic* M04+462 **56**
Skópelos, I., *Greece* L36+391 **59**
Skopin, *U.S.S.R.* K33+538 **60**
Skopje, *Yugoslavia* L51+420 **58**
Skövde, *Sweden* M07+584 **47**
Skovorodino, *U.S.S.R.* D67+540 **63**
Skowhegan, *Maine* S58+448 **90**
Skradin, *Yugoslavia* L85+438 **56**
Skrunda, *Latvia* L48+567 **47**
Skudenshamn, *Norway* M58+592 **47**
Skuodas, *Lithuania* L51+562 **47**
Skye, I., *Scotland* N38+574 **40**
Slagelse, *Denmark* M22+554 **47**
Slamet, mt., *Java* E66–072 **65**
Slammannon, *New S. Wales* C38–320 **109**
Slane, *Ireland, Rep.* N39+537 **42**
Slaney R., *Ireland, Rep.* N39+524 **43**
Slapin, L., *Scotland* N36+571 **40**
Slatina, *Yugoslavia* L74+457 **58**
Slatina, *Romania* L34+444 **58**
Slatington, *Pennsylvania* T03+407 **96**
Slave R., *N.-W. Territories* V48+604 **88**
Slăveni, *Romania* L33+441 **58**
Slavgorod, *U.S.S.R.* G70+532 **62**
Slavonia, *Yugoslavia* L72+454 **58**
Slavonski Brod, *Yugoslavia* L72–452 **56**
Slavyansk, *Ukraine* K44+488 **60**
Slea Hd., *Ireland, Rep.* N63+521 **43**
Sleaford, *England* N02+530 **37**
Sleat, Sd. of, *Scotland* N35+571 **40**
Sleepers, The, *N.-W. Terr.* T36+572 **89**
Sleydinge, *Belgium* M68+511 **44**
Slide Mt., *New York* S86+420 **91**
Sliedrecht, *Netherlands* M61+518 **44**
Slievanea, *Ireland, Rep.* N61+522 **43**
Slieve Anierin, *Ireland, Rep.* N48+541 **42**
Slieve Aughty, Mts.,
  Ireland, Rep. N51+531 **43**
Slieve Bernagh, *Ireland, Rep.* N51+528 **43**
Slieve Bloom Mts.,
  Ireland, Rep. N45+530 **43**
Slieve Car, *Ireland, Rep.* N58+541 **42**
Slieve Donard, *N. Ireland* N35+542 **42**
Slievefelim Mts., *Ireland, Rep.* N50+527 **43**
Slieve Gamph Mts.,
  Ireland, Rep. N54+541 **42**
Slieve League, *Ireland, Rep.* N52+546 **42**
Slieve Mish, mts., *Ireland, Rep.* N59+522 **43**
Slieve Miskish, *Ireland, Rep.* N60+516 **43**
Slievemore, *Ireland, Rep.* N60+540 **42**
Slievenakilla, *Ireland, Rep.* N48+542 **42**
Slievenamon, *Ireland, Rep.* N45+524 **43**
Slieve Snaght, *Ireland, Rep.* N44+552 **42**
Slieve Tooey, *Ireland, Rep.* N52+548 **42**
Sligo & co., *Ireland, Rep.* N51+542 **42**
Sligo B., *Ireland, Rep.* N53+543 **42**
Slite, *Sweden* L67+577 **47**
Sliven, *Bulgaria* L22+427 **58**
Slobodskoy, *U.S.S.R.* J58+587 **61**
Sloka, *Latvia* L38+569 **47**
Slonim, *Byelo-Russia* L28+530 **60**
Sloten, *Netherlands* M56+529 **44**
Slough, *England* N04+515 **39**
Slovakia, *Czechoslovakia* L60+485 **49**
Slovenija, *Yugoslavia* M00+459 **56**
Slovensko, *Czechoslovakia* L60+488 **49**
Sluis, *Netherlands* M70+513 **44**
Sluiskil, *Netherlands* M67+513 **44**
Slunj, *Yugoslavia* L86+451 **56**
Słupsk, *Poland* L78+545 **49**
Slussfors, *Sweden* L82+655 **46**
Slutsk, *Byelo-Russia* L15+530 **60**
Slyne Hd., *Ireland, Rep.* N61+534 **43**
Slyudyanka, *U.S.S.R.* F08+516 **63**
Smerwick Harb., *Ireland, Rep.* N62+522 **43**
Smethport, *Pennsylvania* T21+448 **96**
Smilde, *Netherlands* M51+530 **44**
Smiltene, *Latvia* L25+574 **47**
Smith, *Alberta* V54+551 **88**
Smith B., *N.-W. Territories* T20+770 **89**
Smith B., Gt. Bear L.,
  N.-W.Territories W15+661 **88**
Smith I., *Quebec* T24+606 **89**
Smith I., *South Shetlands* S12–630 **27**
Smithers, *British Columbia* W42+548 **88**
Smithfield, *N. Carolina* T20+355 **97**
Smithfield, *Virginia* T11+370 **97**
Smithfield, *Utah* V41+418 **94**
Smithland, *Kentucky* T80+371 **97**
Smiths Falls, *Ontario* T06+449 **91**
Smithton, *Tasmania* C29–409 **109**
Smoky R., *Alberta* V78+552 **88**
Smoky Hill R., *Kansas* U65+388 **98**
Smøla, *Norway* M42+634 **46**
Smolensk, *U.S.S.R.* K78+548 **60**
Smoothstone L., *Sask.* V13+542 **88**
Smyrna. *See* Izmir
Snaefell, *Isle of Man* N27+543 **37**
Snake, R. & Canyon,
  Washington, etc. V83+464 **92**
Snake R., *Yukon* W77+657 **88**
Snares Is., *New Zealand* A81–481 **112**
Snåsa, *Norway* M16+642 **46**
Snåsa Vatn, *Norway* M18+642 **46**
Sneek, *Netherlands* M56+530 **44**
Sneen, *Ireland, Rep.* N59+518 **43**
Snizort, L., *Scotland* N39+576 **40**
Snøhetta, mt., *Norway* M34+623 **46**
Snow Flake, *Arizona* V31+345 **94**
Snow Lake, *Manitoba* U60+548 **88**
Snow Pk., *Wyoming* V09+414 **98**
Snowdon, mt., *Wales* N24+530 **38**
Snowtown, *S. Australia* C71–338 **109**
Snow Water L., *Nevada* V60+406 **94**
Snowy Mts., *Vict.-N.S.W.* C12–366 **109**
Snowy R., *Victoria* C11–386 **109**
Snyder, *Texas* U66+326 **94**
Soanzano, *Italy* L80+403 **57**
Soazza, *Switzerland* M35+463 **45**
Sobakin, *U.S.S.R.* J71+538 **61**
Soboko, *Cent. Afr. Rep.* L30+068 **81**
Sobrado, *Brazil* R49–055 **105**
Sobral, *Brazil* Q62–037 **105**
Sobrance, *Czechoslovakia* L47+487 **49**
Sobraon, *India* H00+311 **72**
Sochi, *U.S.S.R.* K34+438 **62**
Social Circle, *Georgia* T52+336 **97**
Society Is., *Pacific Ocean* Y20–150 **107**
Socorro, *Colombia* S80+064 **104**
Socorro, *New Mexico* V12+341 **94**
Socorro I., *Mexico* V36+188 **100**
Socotra, I., *Indian Ocean* J36+124 **83**

Soc-trang, *S. Vietnam* E84+096 **69**
Sodankylä, *Finland* L20+674 **46**
Soda Springs, *Idaho* V40+426 **94**
Söderfors, *Sweden* L77+604 **47**
Söderhamn, *Sweden* L78+613 **47**
Söderköping, *Sweden* L82+585 **47**
Södertälje, *Sweden* L74+592 **47**
Sodiri, *Sudan* L06+142 **81**
Sodus, *New York* T12+432 **96**
Sodus Pt., *New York* T12+432 **96**
Soela (Sulu) Eiln, *Indonesia* D58–018 **65**
Soemba (Sumba), I., *Indon.* E00–100 **65**
Soembawa (Sumbawa), I.,
  Indonesia E10–088 **65**
Soerabaja, *See* Surabaya
Soest, *W. Germany* M41+516 **48**
Soest, *Netherlands* M58+522 **44**
Sofala, *Mozambique* K62–202 **84**
Sofala, *New South Wales* C02–331 **109**
Sofiya (Sofia), *Bulgaria* L40+427 **58**
Sogamosa, *Colombia* S77+057 **104**
Sogndal, *Norway* M52+583 **47**
Sogne Fd., *Norway* M54+611 **47**
Söğüt, *Turkey* K89+401 **74**
Sohag, *Egypt* K80+266 **81**
Sohagpur, *India* G51+233 **73**
Sohan R., *Pakistan* H16+330 **72**
Sohar, *Oman* J20+244 **75**
Sohawal, *India* G55+246 **73**
Soheb, *Yemen, South* J79 + 139 **74**
Sohna, *India* G77+283 **72**
Soignies, *Belgium* M66+506 **44**
Soissons, *France* M70+494 **54**
Soke, *England* N02+526 **37**
Soke, *Turkey* L16+378 **74**
Sok Gomba, *Tibet* F68+320 **64**
Sok Karmalinsk, *U.S.S.R.* J45+541 **61**
Sokki, *Chad* L68+112 **81**
Sokode, *Togo* M84+090 **80**
Sokol, *U.S.S.R.* K29+594 **60**
Sokolo, *Mali* N36+146 **80**
Sokota, *Ethiopia* K36+126 **83**
Sokoto, *Nigeria* M58+128 **80**
Sola Consilina, *Italy* L87+404 **57**
Solai, *Kenya* K52+001 **83**
Solbad Hall, *Austria* M21+473 **48**
Soledad, *Venezuela* S21+082 **104**
Soledade, *Brazil* S55–066 **104**
Solent, The, *England* N08+508 **39**
Solenzara, *Corsica* M34+418 **57**
Sol Iletsk, *U.S.S.R.* J29+511 **61**
Solimoes (Amazonas), R.,
  Brazil S40–020 **104**
Solingen, *W. Germany* M48+512 **48**
Solleftea, *Sweden* L76+632 **46**
Sollum, *see* Salûm,
Solok, *Sumatra* F25–007 **65**
Solomon Is., *Pacific Ocean* B30–060 **106**
Solomon R., *Kansas* U59+396 **98**
Solon, *India* G77+309 **72**
Solothurn & canton, *Switz.* M45+472 **45**
Solsona, *Spain* M81+420 **53**
Solstad, *Norway* M17+651 **46**
Soltau, *W. Germany* M31+530 **48**
Solund, I., *Norway* M60+611 **47**
Solway, *Minnesota* U31+475 **93**
Solway Firth, *Eng.-Scot.* N22+548 **37**
Solwezi, *Zambia* L22–122 **82**
Soma, *Turkey* L14+392 **74**
Somalia, *E. Africa* K00+050 **83**
Sombor, *Yugoslavia* L66+458 **58**
Sombreiro Chan., *Nicobar Is.* F70+076 **71**
Sombrerete, *Mexico* U81+238 **100**
Sombrero, I., *Leeward Is.* S21+187 **101**
Somcuta Mare, *Romania* L39+475 **49**
Somcren, *Netherlands* M56+514 **44**
Somerset, *Kentucky* T58+371 **97**
Somerset, *Pennsylvania* T24+400 **91**
Somerset, *Queensland* C45–108 **111**
Somerset, co., *England* N18+510 **38**
Somerset I., *N.-W. Terr.* U20+730 **89**
Somerset Res., *Vermont* S77+430 **96**
Somerville, *New Jersey* S88+405 **96**
Somerville, *Tennessee* T86+353 **97**
Somme, *Belgium* M58+503 **44**
Somme, dep., *France* M76+500 **54**
Somme, R., *France* M79+502 **54**
Sommierea, *France* M66+438 **55**
Somoto, *Nicaragua* T70+136 **101**
Somovit, *Bulgaria* L31+437 **58**
Somzee, *Belgium* M63+503 **44**
Son R., *India* G32+253 **73**
Sonamukhi, *India* G16+232 **73**
Sonbarsa, *India* G18+253 **73**
Sönderborg, *Denmark* M31+549 **47**
Sonepat, *India* G78+290 **72**
Song-Cau, *S. Vietnam* E65+135 **69**
Songea, *Tanzania* K56–108 **83**
Songkhla, *Thailand* F27+071 **69**
Song-koi, R., *N. Vietnam* F10+229 **69**
Sonhat, *India* G45+235 **73**
Sonkajärvi, *Finland* L15+637 **46**
Sonkovo, *U.S.S.R.* K47+578 **60**
Sonmiani, *Pakistan* H50+258 **70**
Sonneberg, *E. Germany* M23+503 **48**
Sonogno, *Switzerland* M37+463 **45**
Sonora, state & R., *Mexico* V38+288 **100**
Sonoyta, *Mexico* V47+319 **100**
Sonpur, *India* G36+208 **73**
Sonpur, *India* G29+257 **73**
Sonson, *Colombia* T01+057 **104**
Soochow, *China* D86+313 **66**
Soping. *See* Yuyu
Sopley, *England* N.1+508 **39**
Soppero, *Sweden* L50+681 **46**
Sopron, *Hungary* L80+476 **56**
Sopur, *Kashmir* H03+343 **72**
Sora, *Italy* M08+417 **57**
Sorata, *Bolivia* S52–158 **104**
Sorbas, *Spain* N11+351 **53**
Sorell, *Tasmania* C15–428 **109**
Sörenberg, *Switzerland* M42+468 **45**
Sorfold, *Norway* L87+575 **46**
Sorgono, *Sardinia* M35+400 **57**
Soria, *Spain* N15+418 **53**
Soriano, *Uruguay* R80–336 **103**
Sornico, *Switzerland* M38+464 **45**
Sorocaba, *Brazil* R15–234 **105**
Soroki, *Moldavia* L10+482 **60**
Sorol, I., *Caroline Is.* C55+075 **106**
Soromesis, *Botswana* L46–194 **84**
Soron, *India* G67+279 **73**

Sorong, *New Guinea* D22–008 **65**
Sororoca, *Brazil* S09+008 **104**
Soroti, *Uganda* K68+016 **83**
Sorøya I., *Norway* L44+705 **46**
Sorrento, *Italy* M04+406 **57**
Sorsele, *Sweden* L75+655 **46**
Sortavala, *Karelia* K86+617 **46**
Sosnovka, *U.S.S.R.* K21+532 **61**
Sosnovo Ozerskoye, *U.S.S.R.* E50+526 **63**
Sosnowiec, *Poland* L66+504 **49**
Sosva, *U.S.S.R.* H80+592 **62**
Soto la Marina, *Mexico* U49+237 **100**
Sotra, I., *Norway* M60+603 **47**
Sotuta, *Mexico* T83+205 **100**
Souanke, *Congo* M06+020 **82**
Soudan, *N. Terr. Aust.* C77–200 **111**
Souflion, *Greece* L23+411 **58**
Souillac, *France* M81+449 **55**
Soûl. *See* Seoul
Soure, *Brazil* R21–007 **105**
Soure, *Portugal* N52+401 **52**
Souris, *Manitoba* U62+497 **88**
Souris, *Prince Edward I.* S13+464 **90**
Sousse, *Tunisia* M26+358 **81**
Souterraine. la. *France* M81+462 **54**
South Africa, rep., *Africa* L30–280 **84**
South Downs, *England* N04+507 **39**
South I., *New Zealand* **112**
Southampton, *England* N08+509 **39**
Southampton, *New York* S74+409 **91**
Southampton, *Ontario* T38+445 **91**
Southampton, C., *N.-W. Terr.* T52+618 **89**
Southampton I., *N.-W. Terr.* T60+646 **89**
South Australia, state, *Aust.* **110-111**
South Bend, *Indiana* T68+417 **91**
South Bend, *Washington* W23+467 **92**
Southbridge, *Massachusetts* S72+422 **96**
Southbridge, *New Zealand* A46–438 **112**
South Boston, *Virginia* T24+367 **97**
South Carolina, state, *U.S.A.* T40+341 **99**
South China Sea, *Asia* E60+100 **31**
South Dakota, state, *U.S.A.* U78+448 **98**
South-East C., *Tasmania* C19–436 **109**
South-East C., *Victoria* C22–390 **109**
Southend-on-Sea, *England* M86+515 **39**
Southern Alps, *New Zealand* A60–436 **112**
Southern Cross, *W. Australia* E04–311 **110**
South Foreland, *England* M83+511 **39**
South Georgia, I., *Atlant. Oc.* Q40–540 **27**
South Hadley Falls, *Mass.* S76+422 **96**
South Haven, *Michigan* T68+424 **91**
South Indian L., *Manitoba* U52+568 **88**
South Jacksonville, *Florida* T40+303 **97**
South Milwaukee, *Wisconsin* T77+430 **91**
South Nahanni R.,
  N.-W. Territories W40+616 **88**
South Orkneys, Is., *Atlantic*
  Ocean R00–610 **27**
South Paris, *Maine* S63+443 **90**
South Pittsburg, *Tennessee* T64+350 **97**
South Polar Plateau, *Antarc.* B30–870 **27**
South Pole, *Antarctica* **27**
Southport, *England* N18+536 **37**
Southport, *Prince Edward I.* S18+463 **90**
Southport, *Queensland* B70–279 **111**
South River, *New Jersey* S87+404 **96**
South Ronaldsay I., *Scot.* N18+588 **40**
South Sandwich Is., *Atl. Oc.* P80–570 **27**
South Shetland Is., *Antarc.* S00–630 **27**
South Shields, *England* N08+550 **37**
South-West C., *Tasmania* C23–435 **109**
South-West Africa, S. *Africa* L76–250 **84**
South Yorkshire, co., *Eng.* N08+535 **37**
South Yemen, *Asia* J80 + 150 **74**
Souza, *Brazil* Q49–067 **105**
Souzel, *Brazil* R44–024 **105**
Souzel, *Portugal* N46+389 **52**
Sovetsk, *U.S.S.R.* L48+551 **47**
Sovetsk, *U.S.S.R.* J66+576 **61**
Sovetskaya Gavan, *U.S.S.R.* C57+488 **63**
Soy, *Kenya* K58+008 **83**
Soya & B., *Japan* C50+454 **68**
Soya Misaki, *Japan* C49+455 **68**
Soyopa, *Mexico* V26+290 **100**
Spa, *Belgium* M55+505 **44**
Spain, *W. Europe* N24+400 **50**
Spalato. *See* Split
Spalding, *England* N01+528 **37**
Spalding, *S. Australia* C68–334 **109**
Spandau, *W. Berlin* M11+525 **48**
Spanish, *Ontario* T44+462 **91**
Spanish Fork. *Utah* V40+401 **94**
Spanish Town, *Jamaica* T12+180 **101**
Sparks, *Nevada* V89+395 **92**
Sparta, *Illinois* T88+382 **95**
Sparta, *N. Carolina* T37+365 **97**
Sparta, *Wisconsin* U05+439 **91**
Sparta (Sparti), *Greece* L46+371 **59**
Spartanburg, *S. Carolina* T42+350 **97**
Spartivento C., *Italy* L83+379 **57**
Spask, *U.S.S.R.* J64+550 **61**
Spask, *U.S.S.R.* K11+538 **61**
Spassk, *U.S.S.R.* D13+447 **63**
Spencer, *Iowa* U30+432 **95**
Spencer, *S. Dakota* U46+437 **93**
Spencer G., *S. Australia* C78–340 **111**
Spenser Mts., *New Zealand* A44–420 **112**
Sperrin Mts., *N. Ireland* N42+548 **42**
Spetsai I.. *Greece* L41+372 **59**
Spey, R., *Scotland* N19+576 **40**
Speyer, *W. Germany* M39+493 **48**
Spezand, *Pakistan* H48+299 **70**
Spezia, La, *Italy* M31+441 **56**
Sphinx, *Montana* V36+452 **93**
Spilsby, *England* M89+532 **37**
Spinazzola, *Italy* L83+410 **57**
Spiringen, *Switzerland* M38+469 **45**
Spirit Lake, *Iowa* U30+434 **95**
Spitsbergen, *Arctic Ocean* L40+800 **62**
Spitsbergen, Vest, *Arctic*
  Ocean L80+790 **62**
Spittal, *Austria* M09+468 **48**
Split, *Yugoslavia* L81+435 **56**
Split L., *Manitoba* U38+560 **88**
Splügen, *Switzerland* M34+466 **45**
Splügen Pass, *Switzerland-Italy*
  M30+465 **45**
Spofford, *Texas* U62+292 **94**
Spokane, *Washington* V75+476 **92**
Spoleto, *Italy* M14+428 **56**
Spontin, *Belgium* M60+503 **44**
Sporadhes, *Aegean Sea* L18+370 **59**

Sporadhes, Voriai, *Aegean Sea* L32+392 59
Spotsylvania, *Virginia* T16+382 97
Spree R., *E. Germany* M06+523 48
Spremberg, *E. Germany* M04+516 48
Sprimont, *Belgium* M56+505 44
Springbok, *Cape Province* L72-296 84
Spring City, *Tennessee* T59+356 97
Springdale, *Arkansas* U24+362 93
Springdale, *Montana* V32+457 93
Springer, *New Mexico* U88+364 94
Springerville, *Arizona* V26+342 94
Springfield, *Colorado* U76+374 94
Springfield, *Georgia* T38+323 97
Springfield, *Illinois* T88+398 91
Springfield, *Massachusetts* S75+421 91
Springfield, *Missouri* U20+372 95
Springfield, *Ohio* T53+399 91
Springfield, *Vermont* S75+433 96
Springfontein, *Orange Free State* L26-304 84
Springhill, *Nova Scotia* S24+456 90
Spring Hope, *N. Carolina* T19+360 97
Springlands, *Guyana* R73+058 105
Spring Place, *Georgia* T59+348 97
Springsure, *Queensland* C12-239 111
Springville, *New York* T22+425 91
Springville, *Utah* V40+402 94
Spruce Brook, *Newfoundland* R79+488 90
Spruce Knob, *W. Virginia* T28+387 96
Spruga, *Switzerland* M39+462 45
Squillace, G. di, *Italy* L78+387 57
Srbija (Serbia), *Yugoslavia* L58+435 58
Srebrenica, *Yugoslavia* L65+441 58
Sredinnyy Khrebet, *U.S.S.R.* B30+570 63
Sredne Kamchatsk, *U.S.S.R.* B31+555 63
Sredne Kolyma, *U.S.S.R.* B80+670 63
Sredne Vilyuysk, *U.S.S.R.* D70+639 63
Srem, *Poland* L78+521 49
Srepok, R., *Khmer* E78+136 65
Sretensk, *U.S.S.R.* E12+524 63
Srikakulam, *India* G36+183 71
Sri Lanka, *S. Asia* G55+076 70
Sri Madhopur, *India* G86+274 72
Srinagar, *Kashmir* H01+341 72
Srirangapatnam, *India* G79+124 70
Srivilliputtur, *India* G74+095 70
Srnetica, *Yugoslavia* L81+445 56
Sroda, *Poland* L76+522 49
Stackpool, *Ontario* T41+479 91
Stack's Mts., *Ireland, Rep.* N57+523 43
Stadacona, *Quebec* S73+474 91
Staden, *Belgium* M72+510 44
Staffa, I., *Scotland* N38+564 41
Stafford, *Arizona* V28+328 94
Stafford, *England* N13+528 37
Stafford, *Kansas* U52+379 95
Stafford, *Virginia* T15+384 97
Stafford, co., *England* N12+529 37
Staines, *England* N03+514 39
Stambaugh, *Michigan* T81+461 91
Stamford, *Connecticut* S81+411 91
Stamford, *England* N03+526 37
Stamprooi, *Netherlands* M56+512 44
Stanberry, *Missouri* U28+403 95
Stanchik, *U.S.S.R.* B89+710 63
Standerton, *Transvaal* L04-270 84
Standish, *Michigan* T54+439 91
Stange, *Norway* M23+607 47
Stanislav, *Ukraine* L34+490 49
Stanley, *Falkland Is.* R78-516 99
Stanley, *Tasmania* C28-408 109
Stanley Falls, *See* Boyoma Falls
Stanleyville. *See* Kisangani L28+006 82
Stann Creek, *Belize* T80+170 101
Stanovoy Khrebet, *U.S.S.R.* D60+557 63
Stans, *Switzerland* M40+470 45
Stansmore Ra., *W. Australia* D45-214 110
Stanthorpe, *Queensland* B78-285 111
Stanton, *Michigan* T61+433 91
Stanton, *N. Dakota* U69+473 93
Staphorst, *Netherlands* M53+526 44
Staples, *Minnesota* U29+463 93
Stara Planina, *Bulgaria* L30+427 59
Staraya Russa, *U.S.S.R.* K80+580 60
Stara Zagora, *Bulgaria* L26+424 58
Starbuck, I., *Pacific Ocean* Y32-055 107
Star City, *Arkansas* U11+340 97
Stargard, *Poland* L90+533 48
Starkville, *Mississippi* T84+334 95
Starkweather, *N. Dakota* U53+485 93
Starobel'sk, *Ukraine* K36+492 60
Starodub, *U.S.S.R.* K73+526 60
Starogard, *Poland* L69+540 49
Staro Konstantinov, *Ukraine* L16+498 60
Staryy Oskol, *U.S.S.R.* K43+512 60
Staten I., *Argentina. See* Estados, I. de los
Staten I., *New York* S85+406 96
Statesville, *N. Carolina* T35+357 97
Stattlandet, *Norway* M58+622 46
Staunton, *Virginia* T25+382 97
Stavanger, *Norway* M56+590 47
Stavelot, *Belgium* M54+504 44
Stavenisse, *Netherlands* M66+516 44
Stavern, *Norway* M30+590 47
Staveren, *Netherlands* M58+529 44
Stavropol, *U.S.S.R.* K20+450 62
Stawell, *Victoria* C43-371 109
Steckborn, *Switzerland* M36+477 45
Steele, *N. Dakota* U60+469 93
Steelton, *Pennsylvania* T11+402 96
Steelville, *Missouri* U08+380 95
Steenbergen, *Netherlands* M64+516 44
Steensel, *Netherlands* M58+514 44
Steenwijk, *Netherlands* M53+528 44
Stefanie L., *Ethiopia* K48+046 83
Steiermark, prov., *Austria* M00+472 48
Stein, *Switzerland* M37+477 45
Steinkjer, *Norway* M21+640 46
Stekene, *Belgium* M66+512 44
Stellarton, *Nova Scotia* S16+456 90
Stenay, *France* M59+495 54
Stendal, *E. Germany* M19+526 48
Stenness, L. of, *Orkney. Scot.* N19+590 40
Stenträsk, *Sweden* L61+663 46
Stephenson, *Michigan* T76+454 91
Stephenville, *Newfoundland* R81+485 90
Stepnoy, *U.S.S.R.* K05+465 62
Stepnyak, *Kazakh.* H25+531 62
Sterea, *Greece* L48+387 59
Sterling, *Colorado* U79+406 94
Sterling, *Illinois* T88+418 95

Sterlitamak, *U.S.S.R.* J24+536 61
Šternberk, *Czechoslovakia* L77+497 49
Sterrebeek, *Belgium* M63+509 44
Stettin. *See* Szczecin
Stettler, *Alberta* V45+520 88
Steubenville, *Ohio* T34+404 91
Stevens Point, *Wisconsin* T88+445 91
Stewart, *Brit. Columbia* W60+557 88
Stewart River, *Yukon* X26+636 88
Stewart, I., *Chile* S68-548 103
Stewart Is., *New Zealand* A73-470 112
Stewart R., *Yukon* X05+640 88
Stewart Sd., *Andaman Is.* F72+130 71
Steyr, *Austria* M04+480 48
Stia, *Italy* M20+438 56
Stikine R., *Brit. Columbia* W70+568 88
Stillwater, *Minnesota* U17+451 93
Stillwater, *Oklahoma* U42+362 95
Štimlje, *Yugoslavia* L54+424 58
Štip, *Yugoslavia* L47+417 58
Stirling, *Scotland* N24+561 41
Stirling Ra., *W. Australia* E10-342 110
Stjernøya, *Norway* L44+703 46
Stockholm, *Sweden* L72+594 47
Stockinbingal, *New South Wales* C13-346 109
Stockport, *England* N13+534 37
Stockton, *California* W08+379 92
Stockton, *Kansas* U56+394 95
Stockton, *New South Wales* B80-329 109
Stockton-on-Tees, *England* N08+546 37
Stoer, Pt. of, *Scotland* N32+583 40
Stoke-on-Trent, *England* N13+530 37
Stolbovaya, *U.S.S.R.* B69+645 63
Stolp. *See* Słupsk
Ston, *Yugoslavia* L74+428 56
Stonehaven, *Scotland* N13+569 40
Stony L., *Ontario* T19+445 91
Stony Crossing, *New South Wales* C39-351 109
Stony Stratford, *England* N06+520 39
Stor Sjön, *Sweden* M04+633 46
Stora Lulevatten, *Sweden* L64+672 46
Stora Sjöfallets Nat. Park, *Sweden* L74+676 46
Storavan, *Sweden* L70+657 46
Stord, I., *Norway* M58+598 47
Støren, *Norway* M28+631 46
Storforshei, *Norway* M03+664 46
Storlien, *Sweden* M17+634 46
Storm B., *Tasmania* C15-432 109
Storm Lake, *Iowa* U31+426 95
Stornoway, *Scotland* N38+582 40
Storsund, *Sweden* L56+656 46
Storuman, *Sweden* L77+650 46
Storvik, *Sweden* L82+606 47
Stour, R., *England* M84+520 39
Stourbridge, *England* N13+525 37
Stourport, *England* N14+524 37
Stowmarket, *England* M84+522 39
Strabane, *N. Ireland* N45+548 42
Strachan, *Quebec* T00+480 91
Strachan I., *Papua N. Guin.,* C47-090 111
Stradbally, *Ireland, Rep.* N43+530 43
Strahan, *Tasmania* C28-422 109
Stralsund, *E. Germany* M12+543 48
Strand, *Norway* M54+590 47
Stranda, *Norway* M48+623 46
Strangford, *N. Ireland* N33+544 42
Strangford L., *N. Ireland* N33+545 42
Strangways Springs, *South Australia* C80-289 111
Stranorlar, *Ireland, Rep.* N46+548 42
Stranraer, *Scotland* N30+549 41
Strasbourg, *France* M43+485 54
Strasburg, *Virginia* T20+390 96
Strässa, *Sweden* L89+598 47
Stratford, *Connecticut* S78+412 96
Stratford, *Michigan* T60+445 91
Stratford, *New Zealand* A34-393 112
Stratford, *Ontario* T36+434 91
Stratford, *Victoria* C18-379 109
Stratford-upon-Avon, *England* N10+522 37
Strathalbyn, *S. Australia* C67-352 109
Strathclyde, reg., *Scotland* N32+558 41
Strathcona Park, *B.C.* W35+498 88
Strathpeffer, *Scotland* N27+576 40
Strathroy, *Ontario* T40+430 91
Strathy Pt., *Scotland* N24+586 40
Strathyre, *Scotland* N26+563 41
Straubing, *W. Germany* M15+489 48
Štrba, *Czech.* L60+491 49
Streaky B., *S. Australia* D05-324 111
Streator, *Illinois* T83+411 95
Strelka, *U.S.S.R.* B79+618 63
Strelka, *U.S.S.R.* F14+617 63
Strelka, *U.S.S.R.* F70+581 63
Strencis, *Latvia* L26+576 47
Stribro, *Czechoslovakia* M12+497 48
Strijbeek, *Netherlands* M61+515 44
Strijen, *Netherlands* M63+517 44
Strimón, G. of, *Greece* L36+406 59
Strokestown, *Ireland, Rep.* N48+538 42
Stroma, I., *Scotland* N19+586 40
Stromboli, I., *Italy* L89+388 57
Stromeferry, *Scotland* N33+573 40
Stromness, *Orkney, Scot.* N20+590 40
Strömsberg, *Sweden* L75+604 47
Strömsbruk, *Sweden* L76+619 47
Strömstad, *Sweden* M23+590 47
Strömsund, *Sweden* L86+639 46
Ströms Vattudäl, *Sweden* M04+644 46
Strömtorp, *Sweden* M03+593 47
Strongoli, *Italy* L78+393 57
Stronsay I., & Firth, *Scot.* N15+591 40
Stroud, *England* N13+517 39
Stroudsburg, *Pennsylvania* T01+410 96
Struga, *Yugoslavia* L56+412 58
Strule, R., *N. Ireland* N44+547 42
Struma, R., *Bulgaria-Greece* L42+418 58
Strumica, *Yugoslavia* L44+414 58
Stryy, *Ukraine* L37+493 60
Strzelecki Pk., *Tasmania* C13-402 109
Strzelin, *Poland* L78+508 49
Stuart, *Florida* T32+272 97
Stuart, *Virginia* T32+366 97
Stuart Ra., *S. Australia* D05-290 111
Stuart Highway, *N.T., Aust.* D06-186 111
Stugun, *Sweden* L86+632 46
Stung-Treng, *Khmer* E84+135 69

Sturgis, *S. Dakota* U82+444 93
Sturt Des., *S. Australia, etc.* C54-282 111
Sturt, Mt., *New S. Wales* C50-296 109
Stuttgart, *Arkansas* U10+345 97
Stuttgart, *W. Germany* M35+488 48
Suakin, *Sudan* K46+196 81
Suancheng, *China* E07+309 66
Süan-hwa, *China* E29+406 66
Suaqui, *Mexico* V27+286 100
Subeimanieh, *Iran* J54+358 75
Subh, Jebel, *Saudi Arabia* K36+237 74
Subotica, *Yugoslavia* L62+461 58
Sucha, *Poland* L62+498 49
Suchan, *U.S.S.R.* D11+430 63
Süchow (Tungshan), *China* E15+343 66
Suck R., *Ireland, Rep.* N49+533 43
Sucre, *Bolivia* S32-192 104
Sudan. rep. *Africa* — 81
Sudbury, *England* M86+520 39
Sudbury, *Ontario* T36+465 91
Suddie, *Guyana* R81+070 104
Sudety, mts., *Czech., etc.* L84+507 49
Sudharam, *Bangladesh* F83+228 71
Suez, *Egypt* K74+300 81
Suez Canal, *Egypt* K75+310 81
Suez, Gulf of, *Egypt* K72+286 81
Suffolk, *England* T09+367 97
Suffolk, co., *England* M84+523 39
Suggsville, *Alabama* T76+316 97
Suhl, *E. Germany* M26+506 48
Suifu. *See* Ipin
Suihwa, *China* D47+466 64
Suining, *China* E12+339 66
Suipacha, *Bolivia* S33-215 104
Suir R., *Ireland, Rep.* N43+523 43
Suiteh, *China* E59+374 66
Sujangarh, *India* H02+277 72
Sujanpur, *India* G86+323 72
Sujanpur, *India* G81+318 72
Sujica, *Yugoslavia* L71+438 56
Sukarnapura. *See* Djajapura
Sukarno, Pk. *See* Puntjak Djaja
Sukhumi, *Gruzinskaya* K25+430 62
Sukkur, *Pakistan* H37+276 70
Suklek B., *Labrador* S20+588 89
Sukow, *China* E45+375 66
Sukumo, *Japan* D13+330 68
Sulaiman Ra., *Pakistan* H30+310 70
Sulaimiya, *Saudi Arabia* J75+242 74
Sulaiyil, *Saudi Arabia* J87+204 74
Sulaymānīya. *Iraq* J87+356 74
Sulecin, *Poland* L87+521 49
Sulgen, *Switzerland* M35+475 45
Sulina, *Romania* L02+451 58
Sulitelma, mt., *Norway* L82+671 46
Sullana, *Peru* T34-049 104
Sullivan, *Illinois* T82+396 95
Sullivan, *Indiana* T74+390 95
Sullivan, *Missouri* U07+382 97
Sulmona, *Italy* M07+419 57
Sulphur Springs, *Texas* U34+332 95
Sultan Bulak, *Iran* J65+358 74
Sultan Dagh, *Turkey* K84+383 74
Sultan Hamud, *Kenya* K46-020 83
Sultaniyeh, *Iran* J67+365 74
Sultanpur, *India* G47+262 73
Sultanpur, *India* H00+312 72
Sulu Arch., *Philippines* D82+055 65
Sulu Sea, *Indonesia* D58-018 65
Sulu Sea, *Philippines* E00-081 65
Sumagana, *Japan* C48+434 68
Sumatra. I. *Indonesia* F39+005 65
Sumba, I.. *Indonesia* E00-100 65
Sumbawa, I., *Indonesia* E10-088 65
Sumbur, *Mongolia* E68+465 64
Sumburgh Hd., *Scotland* N08+599 40
Sümeg, *Hungary* L77+470 49
Sumiswald, *Switzerland* M44+470 45
Summerside, *Pr. Edward I.* S22+464 90
Summit, *S. Dakota* U42+453 93
Sumperk, *Czechoslovakia* L79+500 49
Sumter, *S. Carolina* T32+339 97
Sumy, *Ukraine* K61+509 60
Suna, *Tanzania* K62-056 83
Sunapee, *New Hampshire* S72+434 96
Sunart L., *Scotland* N34+567 41
Sunbury, *Pennsylvania* T11+409 91
Suncho Corral, *Argentina* S21-279 103
Sunchow. *See* Kweiping
Suncook, *New Hampshire* S69+431 91
Sunda Str., *Indonesia* F00-064 65
Sundance, *Wyoming* U86+444 93
Sundargarh, *India* G35+221 73
Sunderland, *England* N08+549 37
Sundridge, *Ontario* T27+458 91
Sundsvall, *Sweden* L76+624 46
Sungari Res., *China* D50+430 64
Sungari R., *China* D60+456 64
Sungkiang. *China* D81+311 66
Sunndal, *Norway* M38+627 46
Sunnyside, *Utah* V32-395 94
Suntar, *U.S.S.R.* E14-622 63
Sunyaqi, *Ghana* N14-074 80
Suonnejoki, *Finland* L17+625 46
Supaul, *India* G20+261 73
Superior, *Wisconsin* U12+467 93
Superior L., *U.S.A.-Canada* T80+475 99
Supiori, I., *New Guinea, Indonesia* C87-006 65
Suq ash Shuyukh, *Iraq* J81+309 74
Sur, *Oman* J03+226 75
Sur (Tyre), *Lebanon* K59+333 76
Sura R., *U.S.S.R.* J81+551 61
Surab, *Pakistan* H52+283 70
Surabaya, *Java* E43-072 65
Surajgarh, *India* G85+283 72
Surakarta, *Java* E25-075 65
Suran, *Syria* K49+353 76
Surapur, *India* G76+166 70
Surat, *India* H12+211 70
Suratgarh, *India* H06+293 72
Surat, Thani, *Thailand* F34+091 69
Surendranagar, *India* H20+227 70
Surgères, *France* N05+461 54
Surgut, *U.S.S.R.* G70+613 62
Suri, *India* G15+239 73
Surigao Str., *Philippines* D60+092 65
Surin, *Thailand* F09+148 69
Surinam (Dutch Guiana) *S. America* R70+040 105

Suriname, R., *Surinam* R63+042 105
Suriya, *Yemen, South* J84+135 74
Surling, Mt., *S. Vietnam* E73+115 69
Surrey, co., *England* N03+513 39
Sursee, *Switzerland* M41+472 45
Sursk, *Ukraine* K61+484 60
Süs (Susch), *Switzerland* M30+468 45
Susa, *Iran* J70+323 74
Susak, *Yugoslavia* M03+447 56
Susquehanna R., *Pa., etc.* T08+398 91
Sussex, *New Brunswick* S33+457 90
Sussex, E. & W., co., *England* N01+510 39
Susteren, *Netherlands* M55+511 44
Sutherland, *Cape Province* L56-324 84
Sutherland, co., *See* Highland
Suting. *See* Tahsien.
Sutlej R., *Pakistan* H12+302 72
Sutsien, *China* E10+339 66
Sutton, *Ontario* T26+443 91
Suure Jaani, *Estonia* L27+585 47
Suvavesi, *Finland* L11+626 46
Suvorov, I., *Pacific Ocean* Y80-138 106
Suwair, *Saudi Arabia* K28+301 74
Suwałki, *Poland* L43+541 49
Suwayh, *Oman* J02+222 75
Suwayq, *Oman* J15+239 75
Suweilih, *Jordan* K55+320 76
Suwo Nada, *Japan* D21+338 68
Svalbard, *Arctic Ocean* L60+790 62
Svanstein, *Sweden* L37+666 46
Svappavaara, *Sweden* L54+677 46
Svørholt-halvøya, *Norway* L24+704 46
Svartenhuk Pen., *Greenland* R38+720 26
Svartisen, *Norway* M06+666 46
Svartvik, *Sweden* L76+623 46
Švekšna, *Lithuania* L50+556 47
Svendborg, *Denmark* M26+551 47
Sventoji, *Lithuania* L53+560 47
Sverdlovsk, *U.S.S.R.* H86+568 61
Sverdrup Is., *N.-W. Terr.* U30+778 88
Sverdrup, Os., *U.S.S.R.* G64+745 62
Svishtov, *Bulgaria* L28+436 58
Svitavy, *Czechoslovakia* L80+497 49
Svobodny, *U.S.S.R.* D41+514 63
Svolvaer, *Norway* M02+682 46
Swabi, *Pakistan* H15+341 72
Swakopmund, *S.-W. Africa* M02-226 84
Swale R., *England* N09+543 37
Swan, R., *W. Australia* E22-314 110
Swan Hill, *Victoria* C39-354 109
Swan Reach, *S. Australia* C62-346 109
Swan River, *Manitoba* U66+524 88
Swansea, *Tasmania* C12-422 109
Swansea & B., *Wales* N24+516 38
Swanton, *Vermont* S79+449 91
Swarzewo, *Poland* L70+547 49
Swastika, *Ontario* T31+481 91
Swat & R., *Pakistan* H15+350 72
Swatow, *China* E20+234 67
Swaziland, *S. Africa* K80-264 84
Sweden, *N.-W. Europe* 46-47
Sweet Grass Hills, *Montana* V37+489 93
Sweetwater, *Texas* U62+324 94
Swellendam, *Cape Province* L58-340 84
Swidnica, *Poland* L81+509 49
Swietochlowice, *Poland* L67+503 49
Swift Current, *Saskatchewan* V17+502 88
Swilly, L., *Ireland, Rep.* N45+552 42
Swinburne, C., *N.-W. Terr.* U54+710 88
Swindon, *England* N11+515 39
Swinemünde. *See* Swinioujscie
Swinford, *Ireland, Rep.* N54+539 42
Swinoujscie, *Poland* M04+539 48
Switzerland, *Central Europe* M42+470 50
Swords, *Ireland, Rep.* N37+534 43
Syasstroy, *U.S.S.R.* K75+602 60
Sycamore, *Illinois* T82+420 91
Sydney, *New South Wales* B83-339 109
Sydney, *Nova Scotia* S01+461 90
Sydney Mines, *Nova Scotia* S01+463 90
Syeti Vrach, *Bulgaria* L40+416 58
Sylhet, *Bangladesh* F78+250 71
Sylt, I., *W. Germany* M40+549 48
Sylte, *Norway* M46+623 46
Syracuse, *Kansas* U70+380 94
Syracuse, *New York* T06+430 96
Syracuse, *Sicily* M88+371 57
Syr Darya, *Kazakh.* H50+440 62
Syria, *W. Asia* K40+350 74
Syrian Des., *Iraq, etc.* K30+323 74
Sysert, *U.S.S.R.* H86+566 61
Syzran, *U.S.S.R.* J68+532 68
Szarvas, *Hungary* L56+469 49
Székesféhervar, *Hungary* L69+472 49
Szekszard, *Hungary* L68+463 58
Szemao, *China* F23+227 64
Szenan, *China* E69+279 67
Szengen, *China* E72+235 67
Szentes, *Hungary* L58+467 49
Szolnok, *Hungary* L59+472 49
Szombathely, *Hungary* L80+472 56
Szreńsk, *Poland* L59+530 49
Szrotawa, *Poland* L87+516 49
Taba, *Saudi Arabia* K16+269 74
Tabab, *Saudi Arabia* K15+187 74
Tabala, *Saudi Arabia* K15+197 74
Tabas, *Iran* J19+337 75
Tabasara, Sierra de, *Panama* T36+086 101
Tabasco, state, *Mexico* U20+180 100
Tabas Sunnikhana, *Iran* H89+327 75
Tabatinga, *Brazil* R22-216 105
Tabatinga, *Brazil* S60-045 104
Tabelbala, *Algeria* N20+292 80
Table B. & Mt., *Cape Prov.* L69-339 84
Taboieiro, *Brazil* R81-052 104
Tábor, *Czechoslovakia* M00+494 48
Tabora, *Tanzania* K74-050 83
Tabriz, *Iran* J82+381 74
Tabu, *Ivory Coast* N44+046 80
Tabuk, *Saudi Arabia* K49+285 74
Tabut, *Yemen South* J47+159 75
Tacambaro. *Mexico* U67+190 100

Tache, L., N.-W. Territories W03+642 88
Tacloban, Philippines D60+111 65
Tacna, Peru S62-180 104
Taco, Argentina S20-256 103
Tacoma, Washington W15+473 92
Taconic Mts., N.Y.-Mass. S80+425 96
Tacuarembo, Uruguay R66-317 103
Tadcaster, England N08+539 37
Tadjoura & G. of, F.T.A.I. K12+116 83
Tadoussac, Quebec S58+481 90
Tadzhikskaya, rep., U.S.S.R. H30+390 62
Taegu, Korea D38+358 64
Taejón, Korea D44+363 64
Taf R., Wales N27+518 38
Tafalla, Spain N10+425 53
Taff R., Wales N20+515 38
Tafila, Jordan K56+309 76
Taft, Iran J34+318 75
Taftville, Connecticut S72+415 96
Taganrog & G., U.S.S.R. K36+473 61
Taga Zong, Bhutan G00+270 71
Tagish, Yukon W86+602 88
Tagula, I., Papua New Guinea B70-115 111
Tagus, N. Dakota U72+484 93
Tagus, R. See Tajo R.
Tahakopa, New Zealand A63+465 112
Tahat Mt., Algeria M56+230 80
Tahcheng, China G42+467 62
Ta Hingan Ling, China D84+480 64
Tahiti, I., Society Islands X82-180 107
Tahoe, L., California W00+391 92
Tahora, New Zealand A31-390 112
Tahoua, Niger M58+148 80
Tahsien, China E75+313 66
Tahta, Egypt K82+268 81
Tahuna, Indonesia D58+037 65
Tai-an, China E17+362 66
Taichow. See Linhai.
Taichung, Taiwan D86+242 67
Taieri, R., New Zealand A58-456 112
Taif, Saudi Arabia K28+211 74
Tai-hang-shan, China E36+370 66
Taihape, New Zealand A25-396 112
Taihsien, China E00+325 66
Taihsien, China E43+391 66
Tai Hu, China D88+312 66
Taiku, China E46+374 66
Tailem Bend, S. Australia C63-353 109
Taima, Saudi Arabia K36+277 74
Tainan, Taiwan D88+230 67
Taipale, Finland L04+627 46
Taipei, Taiwan D82+250 67
Taiping. See Tsungtso.
Taiping, Malaya F26+049 69
Taiping. See Tangtu.
Taipingchwan, China D72+444 64
Taipinghs. See Wanyuan.
Taira, Japan C54+371 68
Tairadate Str., Japan C56+411 68
Taishan I., China D77+303 67
Taishet, U.S.S.R. F41+560 63
Taishun, China E01+275 67
Taitao, Pen. de. Chile S88-462 103
Taiwan, I., China D84+240 67
Taiwan Hai Hsai, China E06+240 67
Taiwara, Afghanistan H63+335 75
Taiyetos, mts., Greece L46+370 59
Taiyiba, Jordan K57+303 76
Taiyuan, China E45+378 66
Ta'izz, Yemen K06+136 74
Tajan, Borneo E59-001 65
Tajo, R., Spain-Portugal N44+397 52
Tajrish, Iran J52+358 75
Tajumulco, mt., Guatemala U11+151 100
Tak, Thailand F35+169 69
Takada, Japan C70+371 68
Takahashi, Japan D08+348 68
Takaka, New Zealand A43-409 112
Takamatsu, Japan D06+343 68
Takao. See Kaohsiung.
Takaoka, Japan C78+368 68
Takapuna, New Zealand A31-368 112
Takasaki, Japan C66+363 68
Takaungu, Kenya K30-038 83
Takayama, Japan C76+362 68
Takefu, Japan C83+358 68
Takhta Bazar, Turkmen H74+360 62
Takht-i-Sulaiman, Pakistan H30+316 72
Takingeur, Sumatra F49+047 65
Takla L., British Columbia W35+554 88
Takla Makan, des., Sinkiang,
China G40+380 30
Takoradi, Ghana N12+050 80
Ta-ku, China E14+389 66
Takuapa, Thailand F40+088 69
Talagang, Pakistan H15+329 72
Talaimanar, Sri Lanka G62+091 70
Talasski Ala Tau, Kirgiz. H20+423 62
Talar Ra., Pakistan H64+254 70
Talara, Peru T38-045 104
Talavera de la Reina, Spain N29+399 52
Talca, Chile S70-354 103
Talcahuano, Chile S79-367 103
Tali, China E61+348 66
Tali, China F30+257 64
Taliabu, I., Indonesia D60-018 65
Taliwang, Sumbawa I.,
Indonesia E19-088 65
Talladega, Alabama T67+334 97
Tallahassee, Florida T56+304 97
Tallangatta, Victoria C16-362 109
Tallata-Mafara, Nigeria M54+124 80
Tallinn, Estonia L31+595 47
Tallow, Ireland, Rep. N48+521 43
Tallulah, Louisiana U07+324 95
Tallulah Falls, Georgia T50+347 97
Talmenka, U.S.S.R. G39+538 62
Talou Shan, China E82+284 64
Talsi, Latvia L45+572 47
Taltal, Chile S63-254 103
Tamale, Ghana N04+094 80
Tamanrasset, Algeria M58+226 80
Tamaqua, Pennsylvania T06+408 96
Tamar R., England N25+505 38
Tamar R., Tasmania C19-412 109
Tamarite de Litera, Spain M87+419 53
Tamási, Hungary L71+467 49
Tamatave, Madagascar J64-182 83
Tamaulipas, state, Mexico U53+235 100
Tamaya, Chile S69-305 103
Tamba, Rhodesia L02-214 84
Tambach, Kenya K56+006 83

Tambacounda, Senegal N82+138 80
Tambo de Mora, Peru T07-135 104
Tambohorano, Madagascar K06-176 83
Tamboril, Brazil Q63-048 105
Tambov, U.S.S.R. K22+527 61
Tambura, Sudan L14+056 81
Tame, Colombia S71+066 104
Tamel Aiken, Argentina S66-482 103
Tamiahua & L., Mexico U46+212 100
Tamil Nadu, state, India G70+114 70
Tamins, Switzerland M33+468 45
Tamluk, India G12+223 73
Tammisaari (Ekenäs), Finland L39+600 47
Tammu, Burma F54+242 71
Tampa, Florida T45+280 97
Tampa B., Florida T46+278 99
Tampere, Finland L37+615 47
Tampico, Mexico U48+222 100
Tamra, Saudi Arabia J88+204 74
Tamsalu, Estonia L23+591 47
Tamtsak Bulak, Mongolia E13+470 64
Tamworth, England N10+526 37
Tamworth, New S. Wales B85-311 109
Tana Fd., Norway L1C+707 46
Tana, I., New Hebrides A65-195 106
Tana L., Ethiopia K46-118 83
Tana, R., Norway L23-698 46
Tanabe, Japan C88+338 68
Tanabu, Japan C52+413 68
Tanaga I., Aleutian Is. Z80+512 99
Tanah Merah, Malaya F17+057 69
Tanahmerah, New Guinea C60-062 65
Tanami, N. Terr., Australia D32-200 110
Tanana, Alaska Y10+652 99
Tanana, R., Alaska X60+635 99
Tananarive (Antananarivo),
Madagascar J76-190 83
Tancanhuitz, Mexico U54+216 100
Tancheng, China E09+345 66
Tanda, India G44+266 73
Tanda Urmar, India G86+316 72
Tandil, Argentina R85-372 103
Tandou L., New S. Wales C47-326 109
Taneatua, New Zealand A18-380 112
Tanega Shima, Japan D24+306 68
Tanen-taung-gyi Mts.,
Thailand-Burma F42+151 69
Tanga, Tanzania K36-050 83
Tanganyika. See Tanzania
Tanganyika, L., E. Cent. Afr. L00-050 83
Tangen, Norway M22+606 47
Tangermünde, E. Germany M18+526 48
Tangier, (Tanger), Morocco N34+356 80
Tang-shan, China E11+396 66
Tangshan, China E21+344 66
Tangtu, China E09+316 66
Tangui, U.S.S.R. F24+555 63
Tanimbar Kep., Indon. D22-074 65
Tanjungpandan,
Billiton I., Indonesia E74-027 65
Tanjungperiuk, Java, Indon. E78+060 65
Tanjungredeb, Borneo E16+023 65
Tanjungselor, Borneo E16+028 65
Tank, Pakistan H27+322 72
Tankapirtti, Finland L16+682 46
Tankse, Kashmir G70+340 70
Tännäs, Sweden M14+625 46
Tanta, Egypt K84+308 81
Tantung, China D63+401 66
Tanuf, Oman J17+230 75
Tanzania, E. Africa K60-050 83
Tao, Burma F71+228 71
Taoan, China F23+310 64
Taochow. See Lintan.
Taofu, China F23+310 64
Taormina, Sicily L88+378 57
Taos, New Mexico V04+364 94
Tapa, Estonia L24+592 47
Tapachula, Mexico U13+149 100
Tapah, Malaya F22+042 69
Tapajos, R., Brazil R63-040 105
Tapalque, Argentina S00-362 103
Tapan, Sumatra F24-021 65
Tapanui, New Zealand A64-455 112
Tapa Shan, China E67+320 66
Tapauá, Brazil S26-057 104
Tapera do Retiro, Brazil S11-099 104
Taplang Dzong, Nepal G14+274 73
Tappahannock, Virginia T11+381 97
Tapti R., India G78+216 70
Tapuaenuku, mt., N.Z. A38-420 112
Taqa, Oman J33+171 75
Taquanalsinho, Brazil R80-092 104
Taquara, Brazil R35-297 103
Taquaretinga, Brazil Q36-079 105
Tara, U.S.S.R. H05+567 62
Tàrabulus esh Shàm, (Tripoli),
Lebanon K55+344 76
Taradale, New Zealand A18-395 112
Tarago, New South Wales C02-351 109
Tarahumare, Sa., Mexico V16+280 100
Tarakan, Borneo E14+034 65
Tarakli, Turkey K87+404 74
Taralga, New South Wales C01-344 109
Tarana, New South Wales C01-336 109
Taranaki Bight, N., N.Z. A36-388 112
Taranaki Bight, S., N.Z. A38-397 112
Tarancón, Spain N18+400 52
Taranto, Italy L76+404 57
Taranto, G. di, Italy L77+400 57
Tarapoto, Peru T08-065 104
Taraqua, Brazil S49-002 104
Tararua Ra., New Zealand A28-409 112
Tarascon, France M80+428 55
Tarasp, Switzerland M28+468 45
Tarata, Peru S61-177 104
Tarauaca, Brazil S65-084 104
Tarawa, I., Gilbert Is. A40+020 106
Tarawera, New Zealand A65-434 112
Tarazona, Spain N10+419 53
Tarazona de la Mancha, Sp. N12+392 53
Tarbagatai Khrebet, Kazakh. G40+470 62
Tarbat Ness, Scotland N23+579 40
Tarbert, Ireland, Rep. N56+526 43
Tarbert, Scotland N32+558 41
Tarbert, Scotland N41+579 40
Tarbes, France N00+432 55
Tarboro, N. Carolina T15+359 97
Tarchan, Tibet G52+310 70
Tarcoola, S. Australia D02-307 111
Tarcoon, New South Wales C20-303 109
Tarcutta, New South Wales C14-353 109

Taree, New South Wales B76-320 109
Tärendö, Sweden L44+672 46
Târgovişte, Romania L27+449 58
Târgu Mures, Romania L33+466 58
Târgul Ocna, Romania L20+463 58
Tarija, Bolivia S29-214 104
Tarim, Basin & R., Sinkiang G30+400 30
Tarlac, Philippines D87+156 65
Tarma, Peru T05-114 104
Tarn, dep. & R., France M77+438 55
Tärna, Sweden L88+657 46
Tarn-et-Garonne, dep., Fr. M81+442 55
Tarnobrzeg, Poland L50+506 49
Tarnów, Poland L54+500 49
Tarnowskie Gory, Poland L67+505 49
Tarn Taran, India H00+314 72
Tarnu Mâgurele, Romania L31+437 58
Taroudant, Morocco N54+304 80
Tarragona, Spain M82+411 53
Tarran Hills, New S. Wales C23-326 109
Tarrega, Spain M83+416 53
Tarsale, China G70+648 62
Tarso Muri, mt., Libya L68+212 81
Tarsus, Turkey K61+370 74
Tartagal, Argentina S22-227 103
Tartas, France N05+438 55
Tartna Point, New S. Wales C45-330 109
Tartu, Estonia L19+583 47
Tartus, Syria K55+349 76
Tarum, Iran J26+281 75
Taseevo, U.S.S.R. F61+573 63
Taseko Ls., Brit. Columbia W22+514 88
Tashi Bhup Tso, Tibet G30+322 71
Tashihto, China F82+438 64
Tashkent, Uzbek. H34+415 62
Tashkurghan, Afghanistan H43+367 75
Tash Kurghan, China G88+377 72
Tashmalik, China G86+392 72
Tasil, Syria K54+328 76
Taskan, U.S.S.R. B89+630 63
Tasköprü, Turkey K62+416 74
Tasman B., New Zealand A40-410 112
Tasman, Mt., New Zealand A58-435 112
Tasman Mts., New Zealand A45-410 112
Tasman Pen., Tasmania C13-431 109
Tasmania I. & state, Aust. C20-420 111
Tassgong, Bhutan F80+272 71
Tata, Hungary L70+478 49
Tatakoto, Tuamotu Arch. X20-175 107
Tatarsk, U.S.S.R. G84+552 62
Tatarskaya, aut. rep., U.S.S.R. J60+553 62
Tatarskiy Proliv, U.S.S.R. C50+500 63
Tathlina, L., N.-W. Terr. V75+604 88
Tating, China E86+271 67
Tatinnai L., N.-W. Terr. U47+606 88
Tatnam C., Manitoba U05+578 89
Tatong, Victoria C24-367 109
Tatranská Lomnica, Czech. L59+491 49
Tatry, mts., Poland-Czech. L60+493 49
Tatta, Pakistan H43+247 70
Tatu R., China F22+320 64
Tatuhy, Brazil R16-232 105
Ta-tung, China E41+401 66
Tatung Ho, China F14+370 64
Tauapeçaçú, Brazil S06-025 104
Taubate, Brazil R03-230 105
Tauha, Brazil Q62-060 105
Taumarunui, New Zealand A28-388 112
Taungdwingyi, Burma F56+200 71
Taunggyi, Burma F48+209 71
Taungup, Burma F64+189 71
Taunton, England N18+510 38
Taunton, Massachusetts S67+419 91
Taunus, mts., W. Germany M40+503 48
Taupo & L., New Zealand A24-387 112
Tauranga & Harb., N.Z. A23-377 112
Tauste, Spain N07+419 53
Tauysk, U.S.S.R. C03+598 63
Tavda, U.S.S.R. H57+581 62
Taverne, Switzerland M36+461 45
Tavistock, England N25+505 38
Tavolara, I., Sardinia M32+409 57
Tavoy & R., Burma F41+140 71
Tavoy I., Burma F40+130 71
Tavsanli, Turkey L03+396 74
Tawang, India F78+276 71
Tawas City, Michigan T51+443 91
Tawau, Sabah E12+043 65
Tawitawi, I., Philippines E00+052 65
Taxco, Mexico U57+184 100
Tay, Firth of & R., Scotland N19+564 41
Tay, L., Scotland N25+565 41
Tayga, U.S.S.R. G27+558 62
Taylor, Mt., New Mexico V18+352 94
Taylorsville, Alabama T69+345 97
Taylorsville, N. Carolina T37+359 97
Tayport, Scotland N17+564 41
Tayside, reg., Scotland N23+567 41
Taytay, Philippines E04+108 65
Tayü, China E34+255 67
Tayung, China E57+292 67
Taza, Morocco N24+342 80
Tazewell, Virginia T39+371 97
Tazovskaya G., U.S.S.R. G85+692 62
Tbilisi, Gruzinskaya, U.S.S.R. K01+418 62
Tchad. See Chad
Tchaourôu, Benin M76+088 80
Tczew, Poland L67+541 49
Te Anau, L., New Zealand A73-452 112
Teano Ra., W. Australia E10-245 110
Teapa, Mexico U18+174 100
Te Aroha, New Zealand A26-376 112
Te Awamutu, New Zealand A28-380 112
Teboursouk, Tunisia M34+364 81
Tebyulyakh, U.S.S.R. C31+648 63
Tecamachalco, Mexico U46+188 100
Tecka & R., Argentina S65-434 103
Tecolutla, Mexico U43+205 100
Tecoripe, Mexico V28+290 100
Tecpan, Mexico U62+172 100
Tecuniseh, Michigan T54+420 91
Tedzhen, Turkmen. H87+373 62
Tegerhi, Libya M04+240 81
Tegucigalpa, Honduras T72+141 101
Teheruak L., N.-W. Terr. U72+663 88
Tehpao, China B80+233 67
Tehri, India G69+304 70
Tehsien, China E22+375 66
Tehuacan, Mexico U44+185 100

Tehucan, Mexico U44+185 100
Tehuantepec, Mexico U32+164 100
Tehuantepec, G. of, Mexico U30+158 100
Tehuantepec, Isth. of, Mex., U28+172 100
Teian. See Anlu
Teifi, R., Wales N26+520 38
Teign, R., England N22+506 38
Teignmouth, England N21+505 38
Teith, R., Scotland N24+561 41
Tekapo, L., New Zealand A57-439 112
Te Karaka, New Zealand A13-384 112
Tekari, India G31+250 73
Tekirdag, Turkey L15+410 74
Te Kuiti, New Zealand A29-383 112
Tela, Honduras T75+158 101
Tel-Aviv-Yafo, Israel K62+321 76
Telegraph Creek, B.C. W67+581 88
Telford, England N15+527 37
Telichie, S. Australia C61-317 109
Telkalakh, Syria K52+347 76
Tel Kochek, Syria K17+370 74
Tell Bise, Syria K49+348 76
Tell Ejine, Syria K48+358 76
Tell el Milh, Israel K60+312 76
Tellicherry, India G87+118 70
Teloloapan, Mexico U60+182 100
Tel Or, Israel K56+326 76
Telpos-iz, U.S.S.R. J05+637 62
Telsen, Argentina S41-424 103
Tel'shvay, Lithuania L46+560 47
Telukbetung, Sumatra, Indon. E89-054 65
Teluk Cenarawasih, New Guinea D00-024 65
Tembeling, Malaya F16+040 69
Temblador, Venezuela S17+090 104
Teme, R., England N15+523 37
Temesvar. See Timisoara
Temir, Kazakh. J18+491 62
Temir Tau, U.S.S.R. G16+532 62
Temnikov, U.S.S.R. K10+546 61
Temora, New South Wales C15-345 109
Temosachic, Mexico V15+288 100
Tempe, Arizona V41+334 94
Tempio, Sardinia M35+409 57
Temple, Texas U44+310 95
Templemore, Ireland, Rep. N47+528 43
Temse, Belgium M65+511 44
Temta, U.S.S.R. J84+575 61
Temuco, Chile S76-386 103
Temuka, New Zealand A52-440 112
Tenanzingo, Mexico U57+189 100
Tenasique, Mexico U09+174 100
Tenasserim, Burma F36+120 71
Tenasserim R., Burma F37+136 71
Tenby, Wales N28+517 38
Ten Degree Chan.,
Andaman Islands F75+098 71
Tenerife, I., Canary Is. P10+282 80
Ténès, Algeria M84+362 80
Tengchow. See Penglai
Tengiz, Oz., Kazakh. H35+504 62
Tennant's Creek,
N. Territory, Australia D05-195 111
Tennessee, state, U.S.A. T80+357 99
Tennessee Pass, Colorado V07+394 98
Tennessee R., Kentucky, etc. T79+368 97
Tenterfield, New S. Wales B78-290 109
Ten Thousand Is., Florida T37+256 99
Ten Thousand Smokes, Val. of,
Alaska Y35+578 99
Teocaltiche, Mexico U77+215 100
Teocuitatlan, Mexico U80+200 100
Téophilo Otoni, Brazil Q69-178 105
Tepatitlan, Mexico U77+208 100
Tepehuanes, Mexico V05+254 100
Tepelene, Albania L60+403 59
Tepic, Mexico U89+215 100
Teramo, Italy M08+426 56
Terang, Victoria C43-383 109
Ter Apel, Netherlands M48+529 44
Terban, Jebel, Saudi Arabia K18+197 74
Terborg, Netherlands M52+519 44
Terenceville, Newfoundland R58+477 90
Teresina, Brazil Q77-050 105
Teressa I., Nicobar Is F71+083 71
Terewah L., New South Wales C16-296 109
Terezin, Czechoslovakia M05+505 48
Teri, Pakistan H23+332 72
Teri Nam Tso, Tibet G26+310 71
Termez, Uzbek. H47+370 62
Termini Imerese, Sicily M08+380 57
Termoli, Italy M00+420 57
Termonde, Belgium M65+510 44
Ternate, Halmahera I. D46+008 65
Terneuzen, Netherlands M67+513 44
Terni, Italy M14+426 56
Ternopol, Ukraine L27+496 60
Terowie, S. Australia C67-331 109
Terpeniya, Zal, U.S.S.R. C40+485 63
Terracina, Italy M10+413 57
Terralba, Sardinia M38+397 57
Terra Nova, Newfoundland R55+485 90
Terra Santa, Brazil R69-019 105
Terrazas, Mexico V17+303 100
Terrebonne B., Louisiana U04+292 95
Terre Haute, Indiana T74+395 91
Terrel, Texas U38+327 95
Terror Mt., Antarctica B30-790 27
Terry, Montana V02+468 93
Terschelling I., Netherlands M58+534 44
Teruel, Spain N07+404 53
Tervola, Finland L31+661 46
Tervuren, Belgium M63+508 44
Teshekpuk, L., Alaska Y20+705 88
Tesin, Mongolia F44+492 64
Tesio, Japan C50+459 68
Teslin L., Yukon W75+600 88
Teslin R., Yukon W84+609 88
Tessaoua, Niger M40+134 80
Tessenderlo, Belgium M59+511 44
Tete, Mozambique K68-162 84
Teton Ra., Wyoming V36+436 93
Tetouan (Tetuan), Morocco N32+356 80
Tetyukhe, U.S.S.R. See Rudnaya Pristan
Tetyushi, U.S.S.R. J67+549 61
Teulada, Sardinia M37+390 57
Teulada C., Sardinia M38+389 57
Teutoburger Wald,
W. Germany M41+521 48

Tevere. See Tiber
Teviot, R., Scotland N15+555 41
Tevriz, U.S.S.R. H16+573 62
Te Waewae B., N.Z. A76–463 112
Texarkana, Arkansas U24+334 95
Texas, state, U.S.A. U67+318 98
Texcoco, Mexico U53+195 100
Texel I., Netherlands M61+531 44
Texoma, L., Oklahoma U40+340 95
Tezpur, India F73+266 71
Thachap Kangri, Tibet G46+334 70
Thadiq, Saudi Arabia J86+252 74
Thailand, S.-E. Asia F30+160 69
Thakhek, Laos F01+174 69
Thal, Pakistan H26+334 72
Thale Sap, L., Thailand F28+075 69
Thalkirch, Switzerland M34+466 45
Thames, New Zealand A27–372 112
Thames, Firth of, N.Z. A28–370 112
Thames R., Connecticut S73+414 96
Thames, R., England N00+515 39
Thana, India H12+194 70
Thanesar, India G79+299 72
Thanh-hoa, N. Vietnam E86+198 69
Thanjavur, India G65+108 70
Thann, France M47+478 54
Thar Des., India H27+257 70
Tharrawaddy, Burma F55+176 71
Tharsis, Spain N42+376 52
Thásos I., Greece L32+407 59
Thásos Str., Greece L32+408 59
Thatcher, Arizona V28+328 94
Thaton, Burma F46+169 71
Thaungdut, Burma F62+244 71
Thayer, Missouri U10+365 97
Thayetmyo, Burma F59+193 71
Thazi, Burma F53+208 71
The Gulf, Arabia, etc. 74-75
Thelon R., N.-W. Territories U84+645 88
Theodore, Queensland B89–250 111
Theodore Roosevelt L., Ariz. V37+337 94
Thérmai, G. of, Greece L43+402 59
Thérmiá, See Kithnos, I.
Thermopolis, Wyoming V19+437 93
Thesprotia, Greece L58+395 59
Thessalia, Greece L46+395 59
Thessaloniki, Greece L42+406 59
Thetford, England M85+524 39
Thetford Mines, Quebec S67+461 91
Theux, Belgium M55+505 44
Thibodaux, Louisiana U04+298 95
Thief River Falls, Minnesota U38+482 93
Thielsen, Mt., Oregon W12+432 92
Thielt, Belgium M70+510 44
Thies, Senegal P12+148 80
Thimbu, Bhutan G06+275 73
Thingvalla vatn, Iceland P37+642 46
Thio, Ethiopia K24+146 83
Thionville, France M53+494 54
Thira, I., Greece L27+364 59
Thirsk, England N08+542 37
Thirtyone Mile L., Quebec T05+461 91
Thisted, Denmark M38+570 47
Thistilfjord, Iceland P02+663 46
Thityabin, Burma F56+233 71
Thiviers, France M84+455 54
Thjórsá, R., Iceland P23+645 46
Thok Jalung, Tibet G51+323 70
Tholen & I., Netherlands M65+515 44
Thomaston, Georgia T56+329 97
Thomastown, Ireland, Rep. N43+525 43
Thomasville, Georgia T54+308 97
Thompsonville, Connecticut S76+420 96
Thomson Ville, Michigan T65+445 91
Thongwa, Burma F51+167 71
Thorn. See Torun
Thornhill, Scotland N23+552 41
Thórshavn, Faeröe Is. N41+618 34
Thórshöfn, Iceland P01+662 46
Thouars, France N01+469 54
Thourout. See Torhout
Thousand Isles, New York T06+443 91
Thousand Lake Mt., Utah V39+384 94
Thraki, Greece L24+412 58
Three Hummock I., Tasmania C30+404 109
Three Kings Is., N.Z. A47–341 112
Three Points C., Ghana N14+048 80
Three Rivers, Michigan T64+420 91
Three Rivers (Trois Rivières),
Quebec S76+464 89
Throssel Ra., W. Australia D80–220 110
Thueyts, France M65+447 55
Thuin, Belgium M64+503 44
Thule, Greenland S58+760 26
Thule I. South Sandwich Is. P80–590 27
Thumail, Iraq K13+331 74
Thun, Switzerland M44+468 45
Thunder B., Michigan T50+450 91
Thunder Bay, Ontario T86+486 89
Thuner See, Switzerland M44+467 45
Thur, R., Switzerland M37+476 45
Thurgau, canton, Switz. M36+476 45
Thüringen, W. Germany M24+507 48
Thüringer Wald, E. Germany M24+505 48
Thurles, Ireland, Rep. N47+527 43
Thurloo Downs, N.S.W. C40–293 109
Thursday I., Queensland C47–105 111
Thurso & R., Scotland N21+586 40
Thusis, Switzerland M33+467 45
Tia, New South Wales B80–312 109
Tiaret, Algeria M82+354 80
Tiassale, Ivory Coast N30+060 80
Tibati, Cameroun M16+064 81
Tiber (Tevere), R., Italy M15+420 57
Tiberias & L., Israel K56+328 76
Tibet, China G30+325 30
Tibnin, Lebanon K58+332 76
Tibooburra, New S. Wales C48–293 109
Tiburón, Haiti S86+184 101
Tiburon I., Mexico V45+289 100
Ticino, canton, Switzerland M38+463 45
Ticonderoga, New York S80+439 91
Ticul, Mexico T87+204 100
Tidjikja, Mauritania N70+184 80
Tidworth, England N10+512 39
Tiebissou, Ivory Coast N30+072 80
Tiefencastel, Switzerland M32+467 45
Tieh-ling, China D67+423 66
Tiel, Netherlands M57+519 44
Tielt, Belgium M70+510 44
Tien Chih, China F14+246 64
Tien-chwang-tai, China D78+409 66

Tienen (Tirlemont), Belgium M61+508 44
Tienpaoshan, China E15+419 66
Tiensha Pass, China E79+341 66
Tien Shan, Central Asia G70+430 30
Tienshui, China E84+344 66
Tientsin (Tienching), China E17+391 66
Tiermas, Spain N06+426 53
Tierra del Fuego,
Chile-Argentina S50–540 103
Tiffin, Ohio T49+411 91
Tifton, Georgia T51+314 97
Tigănești, Romania L23+447 58
Tighina. See Bendery.
Tighnabruaich, Scotland N31+559 41
Tigil, U.S.S.R. B37+577 63
Tignish, Prince Edward I. S24+470 90
Tigris, R., Iraq J86+325 74
Tihwa, China G14+437 62
Tijuana, Mexico V74+324 100
Tikhvin, U.S.S.R. K70+596 60
Tikrit, Iraq K08+346 74
Tiksi, U.S.S.R. D36+716 63
Tilburg, Netherlands M60+516 44
Tilbury, England M88+514 39
Tilcara, Argentina S32–236 103
Tilichiki, U.S.S.R. A83+605 63
Tilamook, Oregon W23+454 92
Tillangchong I., Nicobar Is. F68+085 71
Tillsonburg, Ontario T34+429 91
Tílos, I., Greece L16+364 59
Tilpa, New South Wales C33–310 109
Tilsit. See Sovetsk.
Timanski Kryazh, U.S.S.R. J60+650 62
Timaru, New Zealand A52–444 112
Timbalier B., Louisiana U02+292 95
Timber Lake, S. Dakota U46+453 93
Timboon, Victoria C42–385 109
Timbuktu. See Tombouctou.
Timiskaming, Quebec T25+467 91
Timisoara, Romania L53+458 58
Timmins, Ontario T38+485 91
Timor, I. & Sea, Indonesia D60–100 65
Timote, Argentina S14–354 103
Tinaca Pt., Philippines D58+056 65
Tinahely, Ireland, Rep. N39+528 43
Tindouf, Algeria N46+274 80
Tineo, Spain N39+433 52
Tingchow. See Changting.
Tingha, New South Wales B83–300 109
Tinghsien, China E29+385 66
Tingnan, China E31+246 67
Tingo Maria, Peru T05–091 104
Tingri Dzong, Tibet G20+285 71
Tinian, I., Mariana Is. C26+140 106
Tinkhannock, Pennsylvania T06+415 96
Tinnevelly. See Tirunelveli.
Tinogasta, Argentina S46–281 103
Tinos, I., Greece L29+376 59
Tinsukia, India F57+274 71
Tintigny, Belgium M57+497 44
Tintina, Argentina S16–270 103
Tintinara, S. Australia C59–358 109
Tinwald, New Zealand A49–439 112
Tioman, Pulau, I., Malaya F05+028 69
Tionesta, Pennsylvania T27+415 96
Tipperary & co., Ireland, Rep. N49+525 43
Tipton, Iowa U06+418 95
Tiracumba, Sa. de, Brazil R10–036 105
Tiran, I., Saudi Arabia K63+280 74
Tirana. See Tiranë.
Tiranë, Albania L62+413 58
Tiraspol, Moldavia L02+468 60
Tire, Turkey L14+380 74
Tireboli, Turkey K37+409 74
Tiree, I., Scotland N41+565 41
Tirgu Jiu, Romania L40+450 58
Tirich Mir, Pakistan H19+363 72
Tirlemont, Belgium M60+508 44
Tirlyanski, U.S.S.R. J08+542 61
Tírnavos, Greece L46+397 59
Tirol, Austria M22+471 48
Tiruchirapalli, India G68+107 70
Tiruchendur, India G71+084 70
Tiru Kona Malai. See Trincomalee.
Tirunelveli, India G73+088 70
Tirupati, India G64+136 70
Tiruvannamalai, India G65+123 70
Tisiye, Syria K51+324 76
Tissa, Nigeria M28+074 81
Tisza (Tisa), R., Hungary-
Yugoslavia L56+475 51
Titalyah, Bangladesh G09+265 73
Titicaca, L., Bolivia-Peru S56–158 104
Titisee, W. Germany M41+479 48
Titograd, Yugoslavia L65+424 58
Titovo Uzice, Yugoslavia L61+439 58
Titu, Romania L27+447 58
Titusville, Pennsylvania T28+417 91
Tiwi, Oman A04+228 75
Tixkokob, Mexico T85+210 100
Tixtla, Mexico U55+176 100
Tizimin, Mexico T77+211 100
Tizi Ouzou, Algeria M66+366 80
Tjalang, See Calang
Tjilatjap, See Cilacap
Tjirebon, See Cirebon
Tjörn, I., Sweden M20+580 47
Tlacotalpan, Mexico U34+186 100
Tlaltenango, Mexico U80+218 100
Tlapa, Mexico U51+176 100
Tlaxcala & state, Mexico U50+193 100
Tlaxiaco, Mexico U40+173 100
Tlemcen, Algeria N08+350 80
Tméssa, Libya L86+264 81
Toay, Argentina S26+368 103
Toba, Japan C79+345 68
Tobago, I., Trinidad S04+112 101
Toba Meer, Sumatra F37+026 65
Tobarro, Spain N10+386 53
Tobel, Switzerland M36+475 45
Tobelo, Halmahera I., Indon. D42+016 65
Tobermory, Ontario T40+452 91
Tobermory, Scotland N36+566 41
Toboali, Bangka I., Indonesia E81–030 65
Toboli, Celebes, D89–008 65
Tobolsk, U.S.S.R. H39+581 62
Tobruq (Tobruk), Libya L36+320 81
Toccoa, Georgia T50+346 97
Toco, Chile S58–220 103
Tocopilla, Chile S62–220 103
Tocumwal, New S. Wales C28–359 109

Tocuyo, Venezuela S59+098 104
Todenyang, Kenya K54+044 83
Todmorden, England N13+537 37
Todos Santos, Mexico V31+235 100
Todos Santos, B., Mexico V71+317 100
Toe Hd., Ireland, Rep. N55+515 43
Togarakaikyo, Japan D28+301 68
Toghraqbulaq, China F68+404 64
Togo, rep., W. Africa M88+080 80
Tojo, rep., W. Africa D11+348 68
To Huping Tso, Tibet G41+342 71
Tojo, Japan D11+348 68
Tokanga, U.S.S.R. K33+680 62
Tokanui, New Zealand A66–465 112
Tokar, Sudan K44+182 83
Tokara Retto, Japan D32+296 68
Tokat, Turkey K50+403 74
Tokatidake, Japan C42+434 68
Tokelau Is., Pacific Ocean Z45–090 106
Tokmak, Kirgiz. G88+429 62
Tokomaru, New Zealand A10–382 112
Tokoto, China E53+403 66
Tokushima, Japan D03+341 68
Tokuyama, Japan D19+340 68
Tōkyō & B., Japan C62+357 68
Tolaga Bay, New Zealand A10–384 112
Tolbukhin, Bulgaria L13+435 58
Toledo, Chile S63–273 103
Toledo, Ohio T51+417 91
Toledo, Spain N26+399 52
Toledo, Mtes. de, Spain N26+397 52
Tolmin, Yugoslavia M08+462 56
Tolo, G. of, Celébes, D76–022 65
Tolsta Hd., Scotland N37+583 40
Toluca, Mexico U58+193 100
Toluca, Montana V17+457 93
Tolun, China E22+423 66
Tölz, Bad, Germany M21+478 48
Tomah, Wisconsin U03+440 91
Tomahawk, Wisconsin T88+455 91
Tomar, Portugal N51+396 52
Tomari, U.S.S.R. C46+477 63
Tomaszów Mazowiecki, Pol. L60+515 49
Tomatin, Scotland N24+573 40
Tomatumari, Guyana R84+053 104
Tombigbee R., Alabama T77+315 99
Tombouctou, Mali N18+168 80
Tome, Chile S78–366 103
Tomiko, Ontario T27+466 91
Tomini, G. of, Celébes, D86–004 65
Tomintoul, Scotland N20+572 40
Tomkinson Ra., Australia D38–260 110
Tomsk, U.S.S.R. G30+563 62
Tom's River, New Jersey S85+399 91
Tonala, Mexico U22+158 100
Tonate, French Guiana R44+049 105
Tonawanda, New York T23+430 96
Tonbridge, England M88+512 39
Tønder, Denmark M37+549 47
Tondi, India G66+098 70
Tonga, Sudan K84+094 81
Tonga, Is., Pacific Ocean Z60–220 106
Tongala, Victoria C31–363 109
Tongareva, I., Pacific Ocean Y50–092 107
Tongeren, Belgium M57+508 44
Tongobory, Madagascar K04–236 83
Tongoy, Chile S69–304 103
Tongres. See Tongeren.
Tongue & Kyle of, Scotland N26+585 40
Tongue R., Montana V08+454 98
Tonichi, Mexico V25+288 100
Tonk, India G85+262 70
Tonkin, N. Vietnam F00+214 69
Tongking, G. of, S.E. Asia E70+204 69
Tonkhil, Mongolia F68+464 64
Tonkova, U.S.S.R. G00+607 62
Tonle Sap, Khmer F06+129 69
Tonneins, France M88+444 55
Tonnerre, France M66+478 54
Tonopah, Nevada V73+382 92
Tønsberg, Norway M27+593 47
Tooele, Utah V44+405 92
Toowoomba, Queensland B78–274 111
Top Oz., Karelskaya K80+657 62
Topeka, Kansas U34+390 95
Topolčany, Czechoslovakia L71+486 49
Torez, Ukraine K40+480 61
Torhout (Thourout), Belg. M71+511 44
Tori, India G31+237 73
Toriñana, C., Spain N56+430 52
Torino, Italy M87+454 56
Torit, Sudan K74+044 81
Torma, Estonia L19+588 47
Torne Trask, Sweden L66+684 46
Tornetrask, Sweden L62+682 46
Tornio, Finland L35+659 46
Tornionjoki, Sweden L48+676 46
Tornquist, Argentina S13–382 103
Törökszentmiklós, Hungary L58+472 49
Toroni, G. of, Greece L38+401 59
Toronto, New South Wales B81–330 109
Toronto, Ontario T26+437 91
Toronto, S. Dakota U40+446 93
Tororo, Uganda K64+006 83
Toros Dağlari, Turkey K80+370 74
Torquay, England N21+505 38
Torre Annunziata, Italy M03+408 57
Torreblanca, Spain N21+408 52
Torre del Greco, Italy M04+408 57
Torrelaguna, Spain N21+408 52
Torrelapaja, Spain N12+415 53
Torrelavega, Spain N24+433 52
Torrens, L., S. Australia C74–310 109
Torrente, Spain N03+394 53
Torreon, Mexico V34+287 100
Torres, Mexico V34+287 100
Torres Is., Pacific Ocean Z60–220 106
Torres Str., Queensland C50–104 111
Torres Novas, Portugal N51+395 52
Torres Vedras, Portugal N55+391 52
Torrevieja, Spain N04+380 53
Torridon, L., Scotland N34+576 40
Torrijos, Spain N28+400 52
Torrington, Connecticut S79+418 96
Torrington, Wyoming U86+421 93
Torrowangee, New S. Wales C51–314 109
Torrox, Spain N24+367 52
Torsby, Sweden M12+602 47
Tortola, I., Virgin Is. S28+185 101
Tortorici, Sicily M01+380 57
Tortosa, Spain M87+407 53
Tortue, I., Haiti S76+201 101

Tortuga I., Mexico V42+274 100
Torun, Poland L68+531 49
Tory, I. Ireland. Rep. N49+552 42
Torzhok, U.S.S.R. K61+571 60
Tosa B., Japan D08+334 68
Toscana, dep., Italy M23+434 56
Tosco-Emiliano, Appinnino,
mts., Italy M26+444 56
Tossa, Spain M73+417 53
Tostado, Argentina S11–292 103
Totana, Spain N15+378 53
Totling, Tibet G61+314 70
Totma, U.S.S.R. K14+600 62
Totnes, England N22+504 38
Totonicapam, Guatemala U08+150 100
Totskoye, U.S.S.R. J43+525 61
Tottenham, New S. Wales C16–322 109
Tottori, Japan D05+355 68
Touba, Ivory Coast N46+084 80
Toubkal, mt., Morocco N48+310 80
Touggourt, Algeria M54+328 80
Toul, France M55+487 54
Toulon, France M55+431 55
Toulouse, France M82+436 55
Toungoo, Burma F51+190 71
Touquet, le, France M80+505 54
Touraine, prov., France M86+471 54
Tourane (Da Nang), S. Viet. E71+161 69
Tourbis, L., Quebec S85+473 91
Tourcoing, France M71+507 54
Tour-du-Pin, la, France M58+456 54
Tournai, Belgium M70+506 44
Tournon, France M61+451 55
Tournus, France M61+465 54
Tours, France M86+474 54
Touws River, Cape Province L58–334 84
Towamba, New South Wales C02–371 109
Towanda, Pennsylvania T09+417 96
Towari, Celebes D81–046 65
Towcester, England N06+521 39
Tower City, N. Dakota U46+469 93
Townsend, Montana V39+463 93
Townsend, Mt., N.S.W. C10–364 109
Townsville, Queensland C19–193 111
Towoeti Danau, Celébes, D82–028 65
Towson, Maryland T09+394 96
Towy, R., Wales N25+519 38
Toyah L., Texas U81+313 94
Toyama & B., Japan C76+367 68
Tozeur, Tunisia M42+338 81
Trabzon, Turkey K33+410 74
Tracadie, New Brunswick S30+475 90
Tracy, Minnesota U34+442 93
Tradom, Tibet G36+303 71
Traer, Iowa U14+422 95
Trahiry, Brazil Q56–033 105
Trahynas, Brazil R22–144 105
Traiguen, Chile S76–382 103
Traiguen, I., Chile S83–455 103
Trail, British Columbia V76+493 88
Tralee & B., Ireland, Rep. N58+523 43
Tramore, Ireland, Rep. N43+522 43
Tranas. Sweden M00+581 47
Trancas, Argentina S32–263 103
Trancoso, Portugal N44+408 52
Trang, Thailand F33+076 69
Trangan, I., Indonesia D04–067 65
Trangie, New South Wales C12–321 109
Tranquebar, India G61+111 70
Tranqueira, Brazil Q82–082 105
Transcona, Manitoba U42+500 88
Transilvania, Romania L32+465 58
Transvaal, S. Africa L00–250 84
Transylvanian Alps,
Romania L42+450 58
Trapani, Sicily M15+380 57
Traralgon, Victoria C21–382 109
Trasimeno, L., Italy M17+431 56
Trasparga, Spain N47+431 52
Traunstein, Germany M14+478 48
Travancore, India G80+090 70
Travellers L., New S. Wales C47–333 109
Traverse B., Michigan T63+451 91
Traversay Is., Atlantic Ocean P85–560 27
Traverse City, Michigan T64+448 91
Travis, L., Texas U48+304 95
Trawbreaga B., Ireland, Rep. N44+553 42
Trèvic. Czechoslovakia L85+492 49
Trebinje, Yugoslavia L70+427 58
Trebizond. See Trabzon
Tree River Post, N.-W. Terr. V47+672 88
Tregaron, Wales N24+522 38
Treig, L., Scotland N28+568 41
Treinta-y-Tres, Uruguay R57–332 103
Trelew, Argentina S32–432 103
Trelleborg, Sweden M11+554 47
Tremadoc B., Wales N26+528 38
Tremblant, Mt., Quebec S87+463 91
Tremiti Is., Italy L87+420 56
Tremont, Maine S50+443 90
Tremp, Spain M85+422 53
Trencin, Czechoslovakia L72+489 49
Trenel, Argentina S26–355 103
Trenque Lauquen, Argentina S17–359 103
Trent. See Trento
Trent Canal, Ontario T24+445 91
Trent, R., England N04+530 37
Trentino-Alto Adige, reg.,
Italy M22+465 56
Trento, Italy M23+461 56
Trenton, Georgia T63+348 97
Trenton, Michigan T49+422 91
Trenton, Missouri U22+401 95
Trenton, New Jersey S89+402 96
Trenton, Ontario T16+442 91
Trenton, Tennessee T84+360 97
Tréport, le, France M82+501 54
Tres Arroyos, Argentina S02–384 103
Tres Lomas, Argentina S17–364 103
Tres Marias, Is., Mexico V10+215 100
Tres Montes, Pen., Chile T02–469 103
Tres Virgenes, Las, Mexico V46+274 100
Treves. See Trier
Trevino, Mexico U68+260 100
Treviso, Italy M17+457 56
Trevna, Bulgaria L27+424 58
Triabunna, Tasmania C13–425 109
Triana, Spain N36+374 52
Tricase, Italy L70+399 57
Trichinopoly. See Tiruchirapalli
Trichur, India G82+106 70
Trida, New South Wales C30–330 109

Trier, *Germany* M50+497 48
Trieste, *Italy* M07+457 56
Trikeri Str., *Greece* L41+390 59
Trikkala, *Greece* L50+396 59
Trikomo, *Cyprus* K67+353 76
Trim, *Ireland, Rep.* N41+536 43
Trincomalee, *Sri Lanka* G53+086 70
Trinidad, *Bolivia* S28-148 104
Trinidad, *Colorado* U87+372 94
Trinidad, *Cuba* T29+218 97
Trinidad, *Uruguay* R72-336 103
Trinidad, I., *Argentina* S12-392 103
Trinidad, I., *Atlantic Ocean* P87-203 85
Trinidad I., *West Indies* S07+105 104
Trinity & B., *Newfoundland* R50+482 90
Trinity, *Texas* U32+310 95
Trinity Pen, *Antarctica* R75-640 27
Trinity R., *Tezas* U30+312 95
Trionto C., *Italy* L78+396 57
Tripoli, *Lebanon* K55+345 76
Tripoli (Tarābulus), *Libya* M10+328 81
Tripolis, *Greece* L46+375 59
Tripolitania, *Libya* M00+300 81
Tripura, *India* F80+240 71
Tristan da Cunha, *Atlantic Oc.* N76-372 85
Triunfo, *Mexico* V31+239 100
Trivandrum, *India* G79+085 70
Trmbesh, *Bulgaria* L27+434 58
Trn, *Bulgaria* L44+428 58
Trnava, *Czechoslovakia* L75+484 49
Trobriand Is.,
   Papua New Guinea B84-086 111
Trogir, *Yugoslavia* L82+435 56
Trios Pistoles, *Quebec* S55+481 90
Trois Ponts, *Belgium* M55+504 44
Trois Rivières, *Quebec* S76+464 91
Troitsk, *U.S.S.R.* H81+540 61
Troitsk, *U.S.S.R.* K07+541 61
Troitsko Pechorsk, *U.S.S.R.* J23+629 62
Trollhättan, *Sweden* M16+583 47
Trollheimen, *Norway* M36+629 46
Tromen, mt., *Argentina* S60-371 103
Tromsø, *Norway* L66+697 46
Trondheim & Fd., *Norway* M28+635 46
Troödos, *Cyprus* K73+349 76
Troon, *Scotland* N28+555 41
Tropea, *Italy* L85+387 57
Troppau. *See Opava*
Trosa, *Sweden* L75+589 47
Trossachs, *Scotland* N26+562 41
Trout Lake, *Michigan* T60+462 91
Trowbridge, *England* N13+513 39
Troy, *New York* S82+427 91
Troy, *Turkey* L22+400 74
Troyes, *France* M66+483 54
Truba, *Saudi Arabia* K11+283 74
Truer Ra., *Northern*
   Territory, Australia D21-222 110
Trujillo, *Honduras* T66+158 101
Trujillo, *Peru* T24-082 104
Trujillo, *Spain* N35+395 52
Trujillo, *Venezuela* S62+093 104
Truk, I., *Caroline Is.* B82+070 106
Truksum, *Tibet* G40+300 71
Trumbull, *Mt., Arizona* V50+364 92
Trundle, *New South Wales* C15-329 109
Truns, *Switzerland* M36+467 45
Truro, *England* N30+502 38
Truro, *Nova Scotia* S19+454 90
Truro, *S. Australia* C65-344 109
Truskmore, *Ireland, Rep.* N50+544 42
Trutnov, *Czechoslovakia* L85+506 49
Trzebnica, *Poland* L78+514 49
Tržič, *Yugoslavia* M04+464 56
Tsabong, *Botswana* L46-262 84
Tsagan Olom, *Mongolia* F50+467 64
Tsahura, *Yemen, South* J70+148 74
Tsangbe, *Bhutan* G05+271 73
Tsanghsien. *See Wuchow*
Tsangwu, *China* E51+235 67
Tsaochow. *See Hotseh*
Tsaokiang. *China* E28+376 66
Tsaritsyn. *See Volgograd*
Tsavo Nat. Park, *Kenya* K40-028 83
Tschenstochau. *See Czestochowa*
Tschiertschen, *Switzerland* M32+468 45
Tseelim, *Israel* K63+313 76
Tsehchow. *See Tsincheng*
Tselinograd, *Kazakh* H21+512 52
Tsemah, *Israel* K56+327 76
Tsengshing, *China* E37+233 67
Tses, *S.-W. Africa* L70-260 84
Tshikapa, *Zaire* L56-064 82
Tsho Mirari L., *Kashmir* G70+329 72
Tsimlyanskoye Vdkhr.,
   U.S.S.R. K12+470 61
Tsinan, *China* E17+367 66
Tsincheng, *China* E43+353 66
Tsinchow. *See Tienshui*
Tsing-chow, *China* E29+381 66
Tsingchow. *See Yitu*
Tsing Hai. *See Ching Hai*
Tsingkiang, *China* 27+280 67
Tsingkiang, *China* E06+336 66
Tsingkow, *China* E05+348 66
Tsingtao, *China* D88+361 66
Tsingtze (Singtze), *China* E23+294 67
Tsingyüan, *See Paoting*
Tsingyün, *China* E42+237 67
Tsining, *China* E20+354 64
Tsinkiang, *China* E09+249 67
Tsinsien, *China* E22+284 67
Tsinyang, *China* E42+351 66
Tsitsihar, *China* D66+474 64
Tsivilsk, *U.S.S.R.* J71+558 61
Tsivory, *Madagascar* J84-242 83
Tskhinvali, *Gruzinskaya* K07+425 62
Tso-motre-tung, L., *Tibet* G10+284 71
Tsu, *Japan* C81+347 68
Tsugaru Str., *Japan* C54+416 68
Tsugitaka, mt., *Taiwan* D82+248 64
Tsungfa, *China* E38+236 67
Tsungming, *China* D81+316 66
Tsungtso, *China* E76+224 64
Tsunhwa, *China* E12+403 66
Tsunyi, *China* E79+277 67
Tsuruga, *Japan* C83+356 68
Tsuruoka, *Japan* C61+387 68
Tsuyama, *Japan* D06+350 68
Tsuyung, *China* F20+250 64
Tua, *Portugal* N45+412 52
Tua, *Zaire* L80-036 82

Tuakau, *New Zealand* A30-373 112
Tuam, *Ireland, Rep.* N53+535 43
Tuamarina, *New Zealand* A36-414 112
Tuamotu Arch., *Pacific Oc.* X30-200 107
Tuao, *Philippines* D82+178 65
Tuapse, *U.S.S.R.* K36+441 62
Tuatapere, *New Zealand* A74-461 112
Tubai, I., *Society Islands* Y10-160 107
Tubarão, *Brazil* R24-285 103
Tubas, *Jordan* K58+323 76
Tubbercurry, *Ireland, Rep.* N52+540 42
Tubingen, *Germany* M36+485 48
Tubize, *Belgium* M65+507 44
Tubuai, I., *Austral Islands* X88-210 107
Tubutama, *Mexico* V39+308 100
Tucacas, *Venezuela* S49+108 104
Tuckernuck I., *Massachusetts* S61+413 96
Tuckerton, *New Jersey* S86+396 91
Tucson, *Arizona* V36+322 94
Tucson Ra., *Arizona* V37+324 94
Tucumcari, *New Mexico* U82+352 94
Tucunare, *Brazil* R63-051 105
Tucupita, *Venezuela* K08-204 104
Tucurui, *Brazil* R26-038 105
Tudela, *Spain* N10+421 53
Tufi, *Papua New Guinea* C04-092 111
Tug, *Turkey* K16+385 74
Tuguegarao, *Philippines* D80+176 65
Tugur, *U.S.S.R.* C79+537 63
Tukums, *Latvia* L41+569 47
Tula, *Mexico* U55+200 100
Tula, *Mexico* U58+230 100
Tula, *U.S.S.R.* K44+542 60
Tulan, *China* F38+369 64
Tulancingo, *Mexico* U50+201 100
Tularosa, *New Mexico* V06+339 94
Tularosa Basin, *New Mexico* V09+329 94
Tulcan, *Ecuador* T16+008 104
Tulcea, *Romania* L07+452 58
Tulchin, *Ukraine* L07+487 60
Tulear, *Madagascar* K08-234 83
Tuli, *Rhodesia* L04-220 84
Tulkarm, *Jordan* K60+323 76
Tullahoma, *Tennessee* T68+353 97
Tullamore, *Ireland, Rep.* N45+533 43
Tullamore, *New S. Wales* C15-327 109
Tulle, *France* M79+453 55
Tullow, *Ireland, Rep.* N40+528 43
Tulsa, *Oklahoma* U36+362 95
Tulsk, *Ireland, Rep.* N49+538 43
Tulu, *Ethiopia* K22+072 83
Tulua, *Colombia* T08+041 104
Tulun, *U.S.S.R.* F27+545 63
Tumaco & Rado de,
   Colombia T22+017 104
Tumany, *U.S.S.R.* B55+611 63
Tumbarumba, *N.S.W.* C12-358 109
Tumbes, *Peru* T33-035 104
Tumit-Guna, *China* E55+414 66
Tumkur, *India* G77+132 70
Tumlong, *India* G08+274 73
Tummel, R., *Scotland* N24+567 41
Tummo, *Libya* M06+224 81
Tump, *Pakistan* H76+260 70
Tumu, *Ghana* N12+108 80
Tumucumaque, Sa., *Brazil* R52+018 105
Tumupasa, *Bolivia* S48-142 104
Tumut & R., *New S. Wales* C11-354 109
Tunas de Zaza, *Cuba* T28+216 101
Tunbridge Wells, *England* M88+511 39
Tuncurry, *New South Wales* B76-321 109
Tundla, *India* G72+272 70
Tundubai, *Sudan* L44+146 81
Tunduru, *Tanzania* K46-112 83
Tungan, *China* E53+264 67
Tungchang. *See Liaocheng*
Tungchow. *See Tali*
Tungchwan. *See Hweitseh*
Tungchwan. *See Santai*
Tunghai, *China* E04+346 66
Tungho, *China* D38+460 64
Tunghsien, *China* E20+398 66
Tunghwa, *China* D56+416 64
Tungjen, *China* E65+277 67
Tungkun, *China* E37+230 67
Tungkwan, *China* E59+346 66
Tungkwan, *China* E65+350 66
Tungliao, *China* D76+436 64
Tungshan. *See Suchow*
Tungtai, *China* D87+329 66
Tung Ting Hu, *China* E45+290 67
Tunguska, R., *U.S.S.R.* F30+640 63
Tunhwang, *China* F61+402 64
Tuni, *India* G44+173 71
Tunica, *Mississippi* U02+347 97
Tunis, *Tunisia* M30+368 81
Tunisia, *N. Africa* M30+350 81
Tunja, *Colombia* S81+056 104
Tunnsjø, *Norway* M10+647 46
Tunuyan & R., *Argentina* S55-335 103
Tuoy Khaya, *U.S.S.R.* E51+622 63
Tuparoa, *New Zealand* A10-379 112
Tupelo, *Mississippi* T82+343 97
Tupilco, *Mexico* U20+184 100
Tupinambaranas, I., *Brazil* R80-034 104
Tupiza, *Bolivia* S34-213 104
Tupper Lake, *New York* S87+442 91
Tuquarussu, *Brazil* R20-102 105
Tuquerres, *Colombia* T15+010 104
Tura, *India* F89+255 71
Tura, *U.S.S.R.* F30+641 63
Turaba, *Saudi Arabia* K20+208 74
Turakom, *Laos* T15+184 69
Turbat-i-Heideri, *Iran* J06+353 75
Turbat-i-Jam, *Iran* H86+353 75
Turbo, *Colombia* T10+081 104
Turda, *Romania* L37+466 58
Tureia I., *Tuamotu Arch.* X20-208 107
Turfan, *Sinkiang, China* G02+429 64
Turgay, *Kazakh* H69+499 62
Turgutlu, *Turkey* L14+385 74
Türi, *Estonia* L27+588 47
Turiaçu, *Brazil* R02-018 105
Turiamo, *Venezuela* S46+105 104
Turin. *See Torino*
Turkestan, *Kazakh, etc.* H40+432 62
Turkey, rep., *Europe-Asia* K78+390 51
Turkmenskaya, rep., *U.S.S.R.* J10+405 62
Turks Is., *Bahamas, The* S67+214 101
Turku, *Finland* L47+604 47
Turneffe Is., *Belize* T77+174 101
Turnhout, *Belgium* M60+513 44

Tūrnoovo. *Bulgaria* L27+430 58
Turnu Severin, *Romania* L44+446 58
Turquino, Pico de, *Cuba* T10+200 101
Turr, *Ethiopia* K08+064 83
Turrialba, *Costa Rica* T52+100 101
Turshiz, *Iran* J10+352 75
Turtkul, *Uzbek.* H84+415 62
Turtle Mts., *N. Dakota* U61+490 93
Turukta, *U.S.S.R.* E30+610 63
Turukhansk, *U.S.S.R.* G11+657 62
Turun, *Iran* J20+355 75
Turut, *Iran* J29+355 75
Turzovka, *Czechoslovakia* L68+494 49
Tus, *Iran* J03+366 75
Tuscaloosa, *Alabama* T76+332 97
Tuscarora Mts., *Pa.* T17+402 96
Tuscola, *Illinois* T80+398 91
Tuscumbia, *Alabama* T76+347 97
Tuscumbia, *Missouri* U15+383 97
Tuticorin, *India* G71+090 70
Tuttlingen, *W. Germany* M37+479 48
Tutuila, I., *Samoa* Z33-150 106
Tutuvalu, *Pacific Ocean* A15-090 106
Tuwairifa, *Saudi Arabia* J62+216 74
Tuweiq, Jeb. el, *Jordan* K46+295 76
Tuxpan, *Mexico* U44+210 100
Tuxpan, *Mexico* V01+218 100
Tuxtepec, *Mexico* U37+181 100
Tuxtla & Vol. de, *Mexico* U31+185 100
Tuxtla Gutierrez, *Mexico* U18+168 100
Tuy, *Spain* N52+421 52
Tuyen-Quang, *N. Vietnam* E89+217 69
Tuy-hoa, *S. Vietnam* E64+131 69
Tuyun, *China* E75+263 67
Tuz Gölu, *Turkey* K70+386 74
Tuzla, *Yugoslavia* L68+446 58
Tväran, *Sweden* L54+656 46
Tvurditsa, *Bulgaria* L26+427 58
Twante, *Burma* F54+166 71
Tweed, *Ontario* T14+445 91
Tweed, R., *Scotland* N13+557 41
Tweedsmuir Hills, *Scotland* N20+554 41
Tweedsmuir Park, *B.C.* W35+534 88
Twelve Pins, *Ireland, Rep.* N59+535 43
Twenty-five de Mayo, *Argent.* S46-380 103
Twenty-five de Mayo, *Argent.* S01-354 103
Twin Buttes, *Montana* V02+486 93
Twin Falls, *Idaho* V57+425 92
Twofold B., *New S. Wales* C00-370 109
Two Harbors, *Minnesota* U10+470 93
Two Mountains, L. of, *Que* S86+455 91
Two Rivers, *Wisconsin* T76+442 91
Tyler, *Texas* U31+322 98
Tygda, *U.S.S.R.* D52+532 63
Tyler, *Texas* U32+324 95
Tyndinski, *U.S.S.R.* D61+553 63
Tyndall, Mt., *New Zealand* A55-433 112
Tyne & Wear, co., *England* N09+550 37
Tynemouth, *England* N08+550 37
Tynset, *Norway* M25+623 46
Tyr (Sour), *Lebanon* K59+330 76
Tyrone, *Pennsylvania* T19+407 96
Tyrone, co., *N. Ireland* N43+546 42
Tyrrell, L., *Victoria* C43+354 109
Tyrrhenian Sea, *Italy* M18+400 57
Tyumen, *U.S.S.R.* H57+572 62
Tywyn, *Wales* N24+526 38
Tzechung, *China* E33+364 66
Tzeya Ho, *China* E26+380 64
Tzeyang, *China* E18+356 66
Tzeyun, *China* E82+256 67

Ulster, prov.,
   Ireland, Rep.-N. Ire. N48+548 42
Ulster Canal,
   Ireland, Rep.-N. Ire. N42+542 42
Ultima, *Victoria* C41-355 109
Ulua, *Honduras* T76+158 101
Ulukişla, *Turkey* K63+376 74
Ulva, I., *Scotland* N37+565 41
Ulverston, *England* N19+542 37
Ulverstone, *Tasmania* C23-412 109
Ulyanovsk, *U.S.S.R.* J70+544 61
Ülzen, *W. Germany* M27+530 48
Uman, *Ukraine* K88+488 60
Umanak Fd., *Greenland* R35+710 26
Umarkot, *Pakistan* H31+253 70
Umbria, reg., *Italy* M15+429 56
Umea, *Sweden* L58+638 46
Umm Ar Rusays, *Oman* J07+205 75
Umm el Qulban, *Saudi Arabia* K20+279 74
Umm Kuteira, *Sudan* L30+146 81
Umm Lej, *Saudi Arabia* K46+250 74
Umm Qasr, *Iraq* J73+300 74
Umm Ruwaba, *Sudan* K84+128 81
Umnak I., *Aleutian Is.* Z20+529 99
Umtali, *Rhodesia* K74-188 84
Umtata, *Cape Province* L08-318 84
Umvuma, *Rhodesia* K86-194 84
Una, *India* G82+315 72
Una R., *Yugoslavia* L80+452 56
Unadilla, *New York* T02+423 96
Unalakleet, *Alaska* Y65+637 99
Unalaska, *Aleutian Is.* Z10+535 99
Uncastillo, *Spain* N06+424 53
Uncia, *Bolivia* S39-185 104
Uncompahgre Plat., *Colorado* V20+385 94
Underbool, *Victoria* C49-352 109
Undur Khan, *Mongolia* E57+474 64
Ungarie, *New South Wales* C18-336 109
Ungava B., *Quebec* S45+594 89
União, *Brazil* Q77-045 105
União, *Brazil* S69-096 104
União da Victoria, *Brazil* R36-262 103
União Marara, *Brazil* S11-008 104
Uniejów, *Poland* L67+520 49
Unimak I., *Aleutian Is.* Y85+544 99
Unini, *Peru* S84-106 104
Union, *Argentina* S35-352 103
Union, *Argentina* S50-292 103
Union, *Missouri* U06+384 97
Union, *S. Carolina* T40+347 97
Union City, *Tennessee* T85+364 97
Union of Soviet Socialist Republics,
   (U.S.S.R.), *Europe-Asia* 30-31
Uniontown, *Kentucky* T77+378 97
Uniontown, *Pennsylvania* T29+396 96
Unionville, *Missouri* U18+405 95
Unionville, *Nevada* V80+404 92
United Arab Emirates,
   S.-W. Asia J35+240 75
United Kingdom of Gt. Britain
   & N. Ire., *N.-W. Europe* 34
United States of America
   (U.S.A.) 98-99
United States Ra. *N.-W. Terr.* T30+810 26
Unnao, *India* G57+265 73
Unst, I., *Scotland* N05+607 40
Unterwalden, canton, *Switz.* M41+469 45
Unzha, *U.S.S.R.* K06+580 61
Uozu, *Japan* C75+368 68
Upata, *Venezuela* S15+081 104
Upemba L., *Zaire* L22-086 82
Upernivik, *Greenland* R40+730 26
Upington, *Cape Province* L52-284 84
Upolu, I., *Samoa* Z40-140 106
Upper Marlboro, *Maryland* T10+388 96
Upper Sandusky, *Ohio* T50+408 91
Upper Seal L., *Quebec* S84+558 89
Upper Volta, rep., *W. Afr.* N15+130 80
Uppsala, *Sweden* L74+599 47
Ur, *Iraq* J85+310 74
Uracoa, *Venezuela* S14+091 104
Urakawa, *Japan* C43+422 68
Ural, R., *U.S.S.R.* J54+508 62
Uralla, *New South Wales* B82-306 109
Uralsk, *U.S.S.R.* J52+513 62
Uralskiye Khrebet, *U.S.S.R.* J10+535 62
Urana, *New South Wales* C23-354 109
Uranium City, *Saskatchewan* V20+598 88
Urapunga, *N. Terr., Aust.* D03-147 110
Ura Tyube, *U.S.S.R.* H36+400 62
Urawa, *Japan* C62+358 68
Urbakh, *U.S.S.R.* J78+512 61
Urcos, *Peru* S70-137 104
Urda, *U.S.S.R.* J75+488 62
Urdzhar, *U.S.S.R.* G50+470 62
Ure R., *England* N11+543 37
Ures, *Mexico* V32+292 100
Urfa, *Turkey* K37+372 74
Urgun, *Afghanistan* H35+329 75
Uri, canton, *Switzerland* M38+468 45
Uribe, *Colombia* S85+031 104
Uribia, *Colombia* S73+116 104
Urisino, *New South Wales* C38-297 109
Urnasch, *Switzerland* M34+473 45
Urtazymsk, *U.S.S.R.* H07+520 61
Urtuin, *Mongolia* E26+462 64
Uruapan, *Mexico* U72+194 100
Urubamba & R., *Peru* S74-134 104
Urucará, *Brazil* R76-024 105
Urucu, *Brazil* Q64-177 105
Urucui, *Brazil* Q87-072 105
Uruguaiana, *Brazil* R72-297 103
Uruguay, rep., *S. America* 103
Uruguay, R., *Uruguay, etc.* R81-334 103
Urumchi, *Sinkiang, China* G14+437 62
Urumes Surhra, *Syria* K48+361 76
Urussanga, *Brazil* R26-286 103
Urville, Tg. d', *New Guinea* C73-015 65
Uryupinsk, *U.S.S.R.* K18+508 61
Urzhum, *U.S.S.R.* J60+571 61
Urziceni, *Romania* L20+446 58
Usak, *Turkey* L04+387 74
Usakos, *S.-W. Africa* L86-220 84
Usborne, mt., *Falkland Is.* R84-516 103
Usedom, *E. Germany* M06+540 48
Ushant I. *See Quessant, I. d'*
Ushirombo, *Tanzania* K78-034 83
Ush Tobe, *U.S.S.R.* G69+455 62
Ushuaia, *Argentina* S50-548 103
Usk, *Wales* N17+517 38
Usk, R., *Wales* N19+518 38
Uska, *India* G41+272 73

Index

Uskedal, *Norway* M55+599 **47**
Uskudar, *Turkey* L06+411 **74**
Usole, Siberskoye, *U.S.S.R.* F09+528 **63**
Uspenskiy, *U.S.S.R.* H13+488 **62**
Usquil, *Peru* T21-079 **104**
Ussel, *France* M76+456 **54**
Ussuri, R., *U.S.S.R.* D08+465 **63**
Ussuriysk, *U.S.S.R.* D18+437 **63**
Ust Aldan, *U.S.S.R.* D35+635 **63**
Ust Amginskoye, *U.S.S.R.* D01+628 **63**
Ust Apuka, *U.S.S.R.* A61+605 **63**
Ust Belaya, *U.S.S.R.* A40+652 **63**
Ust' Bolsheretsk, *U.S.S.R.* B52+527 **63**
Ust' Chaun, *U.S.S.R.* A57+688 **63**
Uster, *Switzerland* M38+473 **45**
Usti nad Labem, *Czech.* M05+507 **48**
Ust Ishim, *U.S.S.R.* H25+575 **62**
Ust Kamenogorsk, *Kazakh.* G45+500 **62**
Ust Khayryuzovo, *U.S.S.R.* B49+570 **63**
Ust Kut, *U.S.S.R.* E85+570 **63**
Ust Maya, *U.S.S.R.* D02+604 **63**
Ust' Nera, *U.S.S.R.* C31+644 **63**
Ust Sopochnoye, *U.S.S.R.* B55+560 **63**
Ust Tsilma, *U.S.S.R.* J48+654 **62**
Ust Uda, *U.S.S.R.* F10+543 **63**
Ust Urt. plat., *U.S.S.R.* J30+440 **62**
Ust Usa, *U.S.S.R.* J18+660 **62**
Ust Uskoye, *U.S.S.R.* H66+543 **61**
Ust Yenisei Port, *U.S.S.R.* G34+698 **62**
Ustyuzhna, *U.S.S.R.* K52+588 **60**
Usumacinta, R., *Mexico* U08+168 **100**
Usumbura (Bujumbura), *Burma* L04-034 **83**
Utah, state, *U.S.A.* V45+391 **98**
Utah L., *Utah* V41+402 **92**
Utajarvi, *Finland* L22+647 **46**
Utena, *U.S.S.R.* L27+555 **47**
Utete, *Tanzania* K38-080 **83**
Uthal, *Pakistan* H50+257 **70**
Utiarity, *Brazil* R80-131 **104**
Utica, *New York* T01+431 **91**
Utiel, *Spain* N07+396 **53**
Utikuma L., *Alberta* V63+557 **88**
Utraula, *India* G46+273 **73**
Utrecht, *Natal* K88-276 **84**
Utrecht & prov., *Netherlands* M59+521 **44**
Utrera, *Spain* N35+372 **52**
Utsjoki, *Finland* L18+699 **46**
Utsunomiya, *Japan* C60+366 **68**
Uttar Pradesh, *India* G65+280 **70**
Uttaradit, *Thailand* F30+176 **69**
Uusikaarlepyy, *Finland* L45+635 **46**
Uusikaupunki, *Finland* L51+608 **47**
Uvac, *Yugoslavia* L63+436 **58**
Uvat, *U.S.S.R.* H38+591 **62**
Uvéa. I., *Loyalty Islands* A78-205 **106**
Uvira, *Zaire* L06-034 **83**
Uvs Nuur, lake, *Mongolia* F73+503 **63**
Uxbridge, *Massachusetts* S70+421 **96**
Uxbridge, *Ontario* T25+441 **91**
Uxmal, *Mexico* T89+204 **100**
Uyu Chaung R., *Burma* F55+252 **71**
Uyuni, *Bolivia* S41-205 **104**
Uzbekskaya, rep., *U.S.S.R.* H60+400 **62**
Uzdin, *Yugoslavia* L56+452 **58**
Uzgen, *U.S.S.R.* H10+406 **62**
Uzhgorod, *U.S.S.R.* L46+486 **60**
Uzyansk, *U.S.S.R.* J12+536 **61**
Vaal R., *S. Africa* L30-282 **84**
Vaalwater, *Transvaal* L10-242 **84**
Vaasä, *Finland* L50+631 **46**
Vac, *Hungary* L65+478 **49**
Vache, I. La, *Haiti* S82+181 **101**
Vadsø, *Norway* L02+701 **46**
Vaduz, *Liechtenstein* M33+471 **45**
Værøy, *Norway* M14+677 **46**
Vags Fd., *Norway* L78+690 **46**
Vah, R., *Czechoslovakia* L73+485 **49**
Vaila, I., *Scotland* N09+602 **40**
Vairowal, *India* G89+314 **72**
Valais, canton, *Switzerland* M47+462 **45**
Val Brillant, *Quebec* S45+485 **90**
Valcheta, *Argentina* S37-407 **103**
Valday, *U.S.S.R.* K69+579 **60**
Valday Hills, *U.S.S.R.* K72+576 **60**
Valdepeñas. *Spain* N21+388 **52**
Valderredible, *Spain* N24+428 **52**
Valderrobres, *Spain* M89+409 **53**
Valdez, *Alaska* X70+610 **99**
Valdez, Pen., *Argentina* S24-422 **103**
Valdivia, *Chile* S80-398 **103**
Valdosta. *Georgia* T50+308 **97**
Valea-lui-Mihai, *Romania* L47+475 **49**
Valença, *Brazil* Q71-066 **105**
Valençay. *France* M81+471 **54**
Valence, *France* M61+450 **55**
Valencia, *Spain* N02+395 **53**
Valencia, *Venezuela* S48+102 **104**
Valencia, Gulf of, *Spain* N87+394 **53**
Valencia de Alcantara, *Spain* N43+394 **52**
Valencia de Don Juan, *Spain* N33+423 **52**
Valenciennes, *France* M69+503 **54**
Väleni de Munte. *Romania* L24+452 **58**
Valencia I., *Ireland, Rep.* N62+519 **43**
Valentin, mt., *Chile* S80-465 **103**
Valentine, *Nebraska* U64+428 **94**
Valera, *Venezuela* S63+093 **104**
Valga, *U.S.S.R.* L24+578 **47**
Valjala, *U.S.S.R.* L43+584 **47**
Valjevo, *Yugoslavia* L61+443 **58**
Valkeakoshi, *Finland* L35+612 **47**
Valkenburg, *Netherlands* M55+509 **44**
Valladolid, *Mexico* T77+205 **100**
Valladolid, *Spain* N28+416 **52**
Valldemosa, *Balearic Is.* M74+397 **53**
Valle-D'Aosta, reg., *Italy* M47+457 **58**
Valle de La Pascua, *Venez.* S36+092 **104**
Valle de Santiago, *Mexico* U68+203 **100**
Valledupar, *Colombia* S79+104 **104**
Vallejo, *California* W13+381 **92**
Vallenar, *Chile* S65-284 **103**
Valletta, *Malta* M03+359 **57**
Valley City, *N. Dakota* U48+469 **93**
Valleyfield, *Quebec* S85+453 **91**
Vallgrund, *Finland* L52+632 **46**
Vallorbe, *Switzerland* M52+467 **45**
Valmaseda, *Spain* N19+432 **52**
Valmiera, *U.S.S.R.* L27+575 **47**
Valognes, *France* N09+495 **54**
Valona. See Vlone
Valona B., *Albania* L63+404 **59**
Valoria la Buena, *Spain* L63+418 **52**
Valparaiso, *Chile* S70-330 **103**

Valparaiso, *Indiana* T72+414 **95**
Valparaiso, *Mexico* U81+228 **100**
Vals Platz, *Switzerland* M35+466 **45**
Valtimo, *Finland* L07+637 **46**
Valverde de Jucar. *Spain* N14+397 **53**
Valverde del Caming, *Spain* N40+376 **52**
Van & Gölu, *Turkey* K10+385 **74**
Vana Vändra. *Estonia* L30+587 **47**
Van Buren, *Arkansas* U26+354 **99**
Van Buren, *Maine* S48+471 **90**
Van Buren, *Missouri* U06+370 **97**
Vanceboro, *Maine* S45+455 **90**
Vancouver, *Brit. Columbia* W19+493 **88**
Vancouver, *Washington* W16+456 **92**
Vancouver I., *Brit. Columbia* W34+500 **88**
Vancouver, Mt., *Yukon* X26+605 **88**
Vandalia, *Illinois* T85+389 **95**
Van Diemen. C.. *N.T., Aust.* D27-111 **110**
Van Diemen G.;
  N. Territory, Australia D18-119 **110**
Vanegas, *Mexico* U66+239 **100**
Vänern. L., *Sweden* M12+589 **47**
Vänersborg. *Sweden* M16+584 **47**
Vangaindrano, *Madagascar* J74-234 **83**
Van Horn Mts., *Texas* V00+308 **94**
Vankarem, *U.S.S.R.* Z66+678 **63**
Vanndale, *Arkansas* U05+353 **97**
Vannes, *France* N17+477 **54**
Vannøy, *Norway* L60+701 **46**
Vanovara, *U.S.S.R.* F15+604 **63**
Vanrhynsdorp, *South Africa* L68-316 **84**
Vansittart I., *N.-W. Terr.* T55+659 **89**
Vanua Levu, I., *Fiji* A04-170 **106**
Var, dep., *France* M52+435 **55**
Varanasi, *India* G42+254 **73**
Varanger-halvøya, *Norway* L00+700 **46**
Varanger Halvøy, *Norway* L06+704 **46**
Varaždin, *Yugoslavia* L82+463 **56**
Varberg, *Sweden* M16+571 **47**
Vardar R., *Greece, etc.* L46+414 **58**
Vardø, *Norway* K84+703 **46**
Vares, C. de, *Spain* N46+435 **52**
Varese, *Italy* M38+458 **56**
Varkaus, *Finland* L13+623 **46**
Varna, *Bulgaria* L12+432 **58**
Varnavin, *U.S.S.R.* K00+574 **61**
Värtsilä, *Finland* K86+622 **46**
Vasht, *Iran* H83+282 **75**
Vasknarva, *U.S.S.R.* L14+590 **47**
Vassar, *Michigan* T51+434 **91**
Vastanfors, *Sweden* L85+600 **47**
Västerås, *Sweden* L81+597 **47**
Väster Dal Älv. *Sweden* M10+611 **47**
Västervik, *Sweden* L80+578 **47**
Vasvar, *Hungary* L78+471 **49**
Vatican City (Citta del
  Vaticano), *Italy* M15+417 **57**
Vaticano C., *Italy* L85+387 **57**
Vatna Jökull, *Iceland* P12+645 **46**
Vatomandry, *Madagascar* J66-194 **83**
Vättern. L., *Sweden* M04+580 **47**
Vättis, *Switzerland* M33+469 **45**
Vaucluse, dep., *France* M59+440 **55**
Vaud, canton, *Switzerland* M51+466 **45**
Vaughn, *New Mexico* V00+348 **94**
Vaxjö, *Sweden* M01+569 **47**
Vaygach, Ostrov, *U.S.S.R.* J00+700 **62**
Vechel, *Netherlands* M55+516 **44**
Vedia, *Argentina* S10-344 **103**
Vedrin, *Belgium* M61+505 **44**
Veere, *Netherlands* M68+516 **44**
Vega & Fd., *Norway* M18+656 **46**
Vegornitis, L., *Greece* L49+407 **59**
Vegreville, *Alberta* V43+536 **88**
Vejle, *Denmark* M33+557 **47**
Vela, *Argentina* R88-374 **103**
Velaines, *Belgium* M69+507 **44**
Velebit Planina, *Yugoslavia* L88+445 **56**
Veles, *Yugoslavia* L49+417 **58**
Velestinon, *Greece* L43+394 **59**
Velez Rubio, *Spain* N12+377 **53**
Veliki Ustyug, *U.S.S.R.* J83+609 **62**
Velikiye Luki, *U.S.S.R.* K87+564 **60**
Velizh, *U.S.S.R.* K83+556 **60**
Velletri, *Italy* M13+417 **57**
Vellore, *India* G66+129 **70**
Velp, *Netherlands* M54+520 **44**
Velsen, *Netherlands* M62+525 **44**
Velsk, *U.S.S.R.* K17+611 **60**
Venado, *Mexico* U66+230 **100**
Venado Tuerto, *Argentina* S12-337 **103**
Vendee, dep., *France* N10+467 **54**
Vendôme, *France* M84+478 **54**
Venendaal, *Netherlands* M57+520 **44**
Veneto, reg., *Italy* M16+454 **56**
Venezia, & G. di, *Italy* M16+454 **56**
Venezuela, rep., *S. America* **104**
Venezuela, G. de, *Venezuela* S66+115 **104**
Vengurla, *India* H08+159 **70**
Venice. *See* Venezia
Venlo, *Netherlands* M53+514 **44**
Vennacher, L., *Scotland* N26+562 **41**
Venraij, *Netherlands* M54+515 **44**
Ventotene, I., *Italy* M10+408 **57**
Ventspils, *U.S.S.R.* L50+574 **47**
Ventura, *California* V86+343 **92**
Venus B., *Australia* C26-388 **109**
Vera, *Argentina* S02-294 **103**
Vera, *Spain* N11+372 **53**
Veracuz and state, *Mexico* U37+191 **100**
Veramin, *Iran* J49+354 **75**
Veraval, *India* H28+209 **70**
Verbania, *Switzerland* M39+460 **45**
Vercelli, *Italy* M39+453 **56**
Verde, C., *See* Vert, C.
Verde R., *Arizona* V40+338 **94**
Verdun, *France* M58+491 **54**
Verdun, *Quebec* S82+455 **91**
Vereshchagino, *U.S.S.R.* G15+641 **62**
Vereshchagino, *U.S.S.R.* J31+581 **61**
Vereya, *U.S.S.R.* K54+553 **61**
Verga C., *Guinea* N88+104 **80**
Vergara, *Uruguay* R53-329 **103**
Vergennes, *Vermont* S79+441 **91**
Verin, *Spain* N44+419 **52**
Verkhne Imbatskoe, *U.S.S.R.* G12+632 **62**
Verkhne Uralsk, *U.S.S.R.* J06+538 **61**
Verkhne Vilyuysk, *U.S.S.R.* D88+633 **63**
Verkhoturye, *U.S.S.R.* H67+589 **62**
Verkhoyansk, *U.S.S.R.* D09+672 **63**
Verkhoyanskiy Khr., *U.S.S.R.* D30+650 **63**
Vermilion, *S. Dakota* U42+428 **93**

Vermilion B., *Louisiana* U12+296 **95**
Vermont, state, *U.S.A.* S80+437 **99**
Vernal, *Utah* V28+404 **94**
Verneuil, *France* M86+487 **54**
Vernon, *British Columbia* V85+503 **88**
Veroia, *Greece* L47+405 **59**
Verona, *Italy* M24+454 **56**
Vernon, *Texas* U55+342 **95**
Verrieres, les, *Switzerland* M51+469 **45**
Versailles, *France* M77+488 **54**
Versailles, *Kentucky* T59+381 **97**
Versam, *Switzerland* M34+468 **45**
Vert, C., *Senegal* P16+148 **80**
Verte, I., *Quebec* S57+480 **90**
Vertrijk, *Belgium* M61+508 **44**
Verviers, *Belgium* M55+506 **44**
Vervins, *France* M66+498 **54**
Vesanto, *Finland* L21+629 **46**
Vesoul, *France* M53+476 **54**
Vessem, *Netherlands* M58+514 **44**
Vest Fd., *Norway* M06+678 **46**
Vesta, *Costa Rica* T48+097 **101**
Vesterälen. Is., *Norway* M00+693 **46**
Vest Vägøy, *Norway* M06+682 **46**
Vesyegonsk, *U.S.S.R.* K47+587 **60**
Veszprem, *Hungary* L73+471 **49**
Vetluga, *U.S.S.R.* J85+579 **61**
Vetluga, R., *U.S.S.R.* J89+573 **62**
Veurne, *Belgium* M74+511 **44**
Vevey, *Switzerland* M49+465 **45**
Vex, *Switzerland* M46+462 **45**
Viacha, *Bolivia* S50-166 **104**
Viana, *Brazil* Q88-031 **105**
Viana do Castelo, *Portugal* **52**
Viangchan, *Laos* F15+180 **69**
Viborg, *Denmark* M34+564 **47**
Vibo Valentia, *Italy* L83+387 **57**
Vicente de la Barquera, S.,
  Spain N26+434 **52**
Vicenza, *Italy* M21+455 **56**
Vich, *Spain* M76+419 **53**
Vichuquen, *Chile* S72-348 **103**
Vichy, *France* M69+461 **54**
Vicksburg, *Mississippi* U06+324 **97**
Vicosa, *Brazil* Q66-036 **105**
Victor Harbour, *S. Australia* C69-356 **109**
Victoria, *Argentina* S01-325 **103**
Victoria, *British Columbia* W20+485 **88**
Victoria, *Hong Kong* E34+220 **64**
Victoria, *Texas* U42+288 **94**
Victoria, state, *Australia* — **111**
Victoria Falls, *Rhodesia* L24-178 **84**
Victoria I., *N.-W. Territories* V30+710 **88**
Victoria L., *New S. Wales* C52-340 **109**
Victoria I., *Uganda, etc.* K70-010 **83**
Victoria Ld., *Antarctica* B30-740 **27**
Victoria, Mt., *Burma* F67+214 **71**
Victoria, Mt.,
  Papua New Guinea C17-088 **111**
Victoria, R., *N.Terr., Aust.* D26-154 **110**
Victoria do Mearim, *Brazil* Q87-034 **105**
Victoria Point, *Burma* F39+100 **71**
Victoria River Downs
  N. Territory, Australia D14-162 **110**
Victoriaville, *Quebec* S72+461 **91**
Victoria West, *South Africa* L42-314 **84**
Victorica, *Argentina* S32-361 **103**
Vicuna, *Chile* S64-300 **103**
Vidago, *Portugal* N45+417 **52**
Vidin, *Bulgaria* L43+440 **58**
Viedma, *Argentina* S18-407 **103**
Viedma, L., *Argentina* S74-496 **103**
Vienna (Wien), *Austria* L82+482 **49**
Vienne, *France* M61+455 **54**
Vienne, dep., *France* M88+465 **54**
Vienne R., *France* M87+471 **54**
Vientiane, *Laos* F15+180 **69**
Vieques, I. de, *West Indies* S32+182 **101**
Vierlingsbeek, *Netherlands* M54+516 **44**
Vierwaldstatter See, *Switz.* M39+470 **45**
Vierzon Ville, *France* M78+472 **54**
Vietnam N., *S.E.Asia* E70+195 **69**
Vietnam S., *S.E.Asia* E65+130 **69**
Vigan, *Philippines* D87+176 **65**
Vigan, le, *France* M68+440 **55**
Vigia, *Brazil* R19-008 **105**
Vigia Chico, *Mexico* T74+197 **100**
Vigo & R., *Spain* N52+422 **52**
Vigrestad, *Norway* M56+585 **47**
Vihanti, *Finland* L30+645 **46**
Vijayanagar, *India* G80+154 **70**
Vijayavada, *India* G56+165 **70**
Vijosë R., *Albania* L62+406 **59**
Vikaviskis, *U.S.S.R.* L42+546 **47**
Vikna, *Norway* M24+649 **46**
Vila Arriage, *Angola* M10-146 **82**
Vila de Cangombe, *Angola* L60-144 **82**
Vila de João Belo, *Mozamb.* K68-252 **84**
Vila Lugela, *Mozambique* K48-170 **84**
Vila Luso, *Angola* L60-120 **82**
Vila Machado, *Mozambique* K64-194 **84**
Vila Manica, *Mozambique* K72-190 **84**
Vilanculos, *Mozambique* K58-220 **84**
Vilani, *U.S.S.R.* L18+566 **47**
Vila Nova de Famalicão.
  Portugal N51+414 **52**
Vila Nova de Gerveira, *Port.* N52+419 **52**
Vila Pereira de Eca, *Angola* L78-162 **84**
Vila Pery, *Mozambique* K70-194 **84**
Vila Real. *Portugal* N47+413 **52**
Vilar Formoso, *Portugal* N41+406 **52**
Vila Serpa Pinto, *Angola* L80-146 **82**
Vila Velha de Rodao, *Port.* N46+397 **52**
Vila Verissimo, *Angola* L56-082 **82**
Vila Viçosa, *Portugal* N44+388 **52**
Vilcheka, Os., *Arctic Ocean* H85+807 **62**
Vilhelmina, *Sweden* L80+649 **46**
Vilhena, *Brazil* S01-126 **104**
Viljandi, *U.S.S.R.* L26+584 **47**
Villa Angela, *Argentina* S04-275 **103**
Villa Bella, *Bolivia* S32-105 **104**
Villa Bens, *W. Sahara* N81+274 **80**
Villa Bittencourt, *Brazil* S56-015 **104**
Villablino, *Spain* N38+430 **52**
Villacañas. *Spain* N20+396 **52**
Villach, *Austria* M07+465 **48**
Villa Cisneros, *See* Dakhla
Villa Constitucion, *Argentina* S02-332 **103**
Villa del Rosario, *Paraguay* R73-245 **103**
Villa de Rosario, *Argentina* S22-316 **103**
Villa Dolores, *Argentina* S31-319 **103**
Villafranca, *Spain* N41+426 **52**
Villafranca del Cid. *Spain* N02+404 **53**

Villafranca del Panadés. *Sp.* M80+413 **53**
Villaguay, *Argentina* R84-319 **103**
Villa Guillermina, *Argentina* R87-282 **103**
Villa Hermosa, *Mexico* U18+179 **100**
Villa Hidalgo, *Mexico* U87+261 **100**
Villa Iris, *Argentina* S20-382 **103**
Villa Jordão, *Brazil* S73-095 **104**
Villajoyosa, *Spain* N01+385 **53**
Villalba, *Spain* N46+432 **52**
Villaldama, *Mexico* U62+264 **100**
Villalón de Campos, *Spain* N30+421 **52**
Villalonga, *Argentina* S16-400 **103**
Villalpando, *Spain* N33+419 **52**
Villa Maria, *Argentina* S20-324 **103**
Villa Mercedes, *Argentina* S33-336 **103**
Villa Montes, *Bolivia* S21-212 **104**
Villa Murtinho, *Brazil* S32-104 **104**
Villanueva de Cordoba, *Sp.* N28+383 **52**
Villa Nova, *Brazil* R77-068 **105**
Villa Nova, *Brazil* Q39-104 **105**
Villanova, *Greece* L11+364 **59**
Villa Novo, *Brazil* R41-012 **105**
Villanueva-de-la-Serena, *Sp.* N35+390 **52**
Villanueva-y Geltrú, *Spain* M81+413 **53**
Villaodrid, *Spain* N43+433 **52**
Villaputzu, *Sardinia* M33+395 **57**
Villarcayo, *Spain* N21+429 **52**
Villareal, *Spain* N01+399 **53**
Villarrica, *Chile* S74-392 **103**
Villarrica, *Paraguay* R68-257 **103**
Villarrobledo, *Spain* N16+393 **53**
Villa Sanjurjo, *Morocco* N24+352 **80**
Villavicencio, *Colombia* S76+040 **104**
Villaviciosa, *Spain* N32+435 **52**
Villa Viejo, *Colombia* T02+030 **104**
Villazon, *Bolivia* S34-220 **104**
Villefort, *France* M67+444 **55**
Villefranche-de-Rouergue,
  France M78+443 **55**
Ville Marie, *Quebec* T27+473 **91**
Villena, *Spain* N05+386 **53**
Villeneuve-sur-Lot, *France* M86+444 **55**
Villeurbanne, *France* M61+458 **54**
Villingen, *W. Germany* M39+481 **48**
Villisca, *Iowa* U30+409 **95**
Villo-Duca-Abruzzi, *Somalia* J86+026 **83**
Villupuram, *India* G62+121 **70**
Vilnyus (Vilna), *Lithuania* L28+546 **47**
Vilvoorde, *Belgium* M63+509 **44**
Vilyui, R., *U.S.S.R.* E30+670 **63**
Vilyuysk, *U.S.S.R.* D80+637 **63**
Vimioso, *Portugal* N39+417 **52**
Vimperk, *Czechoslovakia* M08+490 **48**
Viña del Mar, *Chile* S70-330 **103**
Vinai Haven I., *Maine* S53+441 **90**
Vinaroz, *Spain* M87+405 **53**
Vincennes, *Indiana* T75+386 **95**
Vinchiaturo, *Italy* M02+415 **57**
Vindel Alv, *Sweden* L70+651 **46**
Vindhya Ra., *India* G80+222 **70**
Vineland, *New Jersey* T00+395 **96**
Vineyard Sd., *Massachusetts* S64+414 **96**
Vinh, *N. Vietnam* E86+187 **69**
Vinh Loi, *S. Vietnam* E85+093 **69**
Vinita, *Oklahoma* U32+366 **95**
Vinkovci, *Yugoslavia* L67+453 **58**
Vinnitsa, *Ukraine* L10+492 **60**
Vintes, *Ecuador* T28-015 **104**
Vinton, *Iowa* U12+422 **95**
Viransehir. *Turkey* K31+374 **74**
Virden, *Manitoba* U65+498 **88**
Virgin Is., *West Indies* S28+185 **101**
Virginia, *Ireland, Rep.* N42+539 **42**
Virginia, *Minnesota* U15+475 **93**
Virginia, state, *U.S.A.* T27+374 **99**
Virginia City, *Montana* V42+452 **93**
Virginia Falls, *N.-W. Terr.* W32+616 **88**
Viroqua, *Wisconsin* U05+436 **91**
Virovitica, *Yugoslavia* L76+458 **58**
Virpazar, *Yugoslavia* L65+423 **58**
Virtasalmi, *Finland* L15+621 **46**
Virton, *Belgium* M57+496 **44**
Virtsu, *Estonia* L39+586 **47**
Viru, *Peru* T22-084 **104**
Vis, I., *Yugoslavia* L83+430 **56**
Visalia, *California* V86+363 **92**
Visby, *Gotland, Sweden* L70+577 **47**
Viscount Melville Sd.,
  N.-W. Territories V30+732 **88**
Visé. *Belgium* M56+507 **44**
Viseu, *Portugal* N47+407 **52**
Vishakhapatnam, *India* G40+177 **71**
Viski, *Latvia* L19+561 **47**
Viso, Mte., *Italy* M48+447 **56**
Visoko, *Yugoslavia* L71+440 **58**
Visp, *Switzerland* M43+463 **45**
Vista Alegre, *Brazil* S06+017 **104**
Vistula (Wisła), R., *Poland* L50+515 **49**
Vitebsk, *Byelo-Russia* K89+551 **60**
Viterbo, *Italy* M17+424 **56**
Vitigudino, *Spain* N38+410 **52**
Viti Levu, I., *Fiji* A10-177 **106**
Vitim, R., *U.S.S.R.* E40+590 **63**
Vitoria, *Brazil* Q62-203 **105**
Vitoria, *Spain* N16+429 **53**
Vitry-le-François, *France* M62+487 **54**
Vitteaux, *France* M63+474 **54**
Vittoria, *Sicily* M03+369 **57**
Viver, *Spain* N04+399 **53**
Vivero, *Spain* N45+434 **52**
Vivi, *U.S.S.R.* F41+640 **63**
Vivonne & B., *S. Australia* C77-359 **109**
Vivorata, *Argentina* R76-378 **103**
Vizeu, *Brazil* R07-012 **105**
Vizianagram, *India* G39+181 **71**
Vizirul *Romania* L14+449 **58**
Vizovice, *Czechoslovakia* L73+492 **49**
Vizzini, *Sicily* M02+372 **57**
Vlaanderen, Oost, *Belgium* M68+509 **44**
Vlaanderen, West, *Belgium* M72+510 **44**
Vlaardingen, *Netherlands* M64+519 **44**
Vladimir, *U.S.S.R.* K28+561 **60**
Vladimirovka, *U.S.S.R.* J83+484 **61**
Vladivostok, *U.S.S.R.* D18+430 **63**
Vlieland I., *Netherlands* M60+533 **44**
Vlissingen, *Netherlands* M69+514 **44**
Vlone, *Albania* L63+405 **59**
Vltava R., *Czechoslovakia* M03+504 **48**
Voghera, *Italy* M36+450 **56**
Vohemar, *Madagascar* J60-134 **83**
Vohma, *Estonia* L27+586 **47**
Voi, *Kenya* K38-034 **83**

Voiotía, *Greece* L39+382 **59**
Voiron, *France* M57+452 **54**
Voitsberg, *Austria* L89+470 **48**
Voiviis, L., *Greece* L43+395 **59**
Vojvodina, *Yugoslavia* L60+454 **58**
Volcano B., *Japan* C56+424 **68**
Volga R., *U.S.S.R.* J85+477 **62**
Volgograd, *U.S.S.R.* K04+487 **61**
Volissos, *Greece* L24+385 **59**
Volkhov, R., *U.S.S.R.* K78+596 **60**
Vollenhove, *Netherlands* M54+527 **44**
Volochanka, *U.S.S.R.* F64+710 **63**
Volochisk, *Ukraine* L23+495 **60**
Vologda, *U.S.S.R.* K32+592 **60**
Volokolamsk, *U.S.S.R.* K54+561 **60**
Vólos. *Greece* L42+394 **59**
Volosinov, *Yugoslavia* L59+456 **58**
Volovets, *Ukraine* L40+488 **60**
Volozhin, *Belorussia* L22+541 **60**
Volsk, *U.S.S.R.* K60+595 **60**
Volsk, *U.S.S.R.* J75+521 **61**
Volta R., *Ghana* M88+060 **80**
Voltveti, *Estonia* L30+582 **47**
Vonèche. *Belgium* M60+501 **44**
Voorburg, *Netherlands* M64+521 **44**
Voorschoten, *Netherlands* M63+521 **44**
Voorst, *Netherlands* M53+522 **44**
Voorthuizen, *Netherlands* M56+522 **44**
Vopnafjordhur, *Iceland* N88+658 **46**
Vorab, mt., *Switzerland* M35+469 **45**
Vorarlberg, *Austria* M31+472 **48**
Vorauen, *Switzerland* M36+470 **45**
Vorkuta, *U.S.S.R.* H67+674 **62**
Vormsi, I., *Estonia* L40+590 **47**
Voronezh, *U.S.S.R.* K35+517 **60**
Voroshilovgrad, *Ukraine* K34+486 **60**
Vosges, dep. & mts., *France* M50+482 **54**
Voss, *Norway* M51+606 **47**
Vostock I., *Pacific Ocean* Y15–100 **107**
Votkinsk, *U.S.S.R.* J36+570 **61**
Voulijoki, *Finland* L18+642 **46**
Vouvry, *Switzerland* M49+463 **45**
Vouziers, *France* M62+493 **54**
Voxna, *Sweden* L86+613 **47**
Voyampolka, *U.S.S.R.* B33+584 **63**
Voznesensk *U.S.S.R.* K82+475 **60**
Vrancv, *Czechoslovakia* L50+489 **49**
Vrangelya, Ostrov, I., *U.S.S.R.* A00+718 **63**
Vranje, *Yugoslavia* L49+425 **58**
Vratsa, *Bulgaria* L39+432 **58**
Vrbitsa, *Bulgaria* L20+430 **58**
Vrchovina Českomoravska.
  Czechoslovakia L84+495 **49**
Vredefort, *O.F.S.* L16–270 **84**
Vrin, *Switzerland* M36+467 **45**
Vrindaban, *India* G73+276 **73**
Vroomshoop, *Netherlands* M51+524 **44**
Vršac. *Yugoslavia* L52+451 **58**
Vrutky. *Czechoslovakia* L67+491 **49**
Vryburg, *Cape Province* L32–270 **84**
Vučitrn, *Yugoslavia* L54+428 **58**
Vukovar, *Yugoslavia* L66+454 **58**
Vulcan, *Missouri* U04+374 **97**
Vulcano, I., *Italy* M00+384 **57**
Vulpera, *Switzerland* M28+468 **45**
Vyatka (Kirov), *U.S.S.R.* J62+586 **61**
Vyatka, R., *U.S.S.R.* J65+577 **62**
Vyazemski, *U.S.S.R.* D01+475 **63**
Vyazma, *U.S.S.R.* K63+551 **60**
Vyazniki, *U.S.S.R.* K17+563 **61**
Vyborg, *U.S.S.R.* L07+606 **60**
Vyrnwy, L., *Wales* N21+528 **38**
Vyrtsyarv Oz., *Estonia* L24+583 **47**
Vyru, *Estonia* L18+578 **47**
Vyshniy Volochek, *U.S.S.R.* K63+576 **60**
Vyskov, *Czechoslovakia* L78+493 **49**
Vytegra, *U.S.S.R.* K52+610 **60**
Wa, *Ghana* N14+102 **80**
Waalwijk, *Netherlands* M60+517 **44**
Wabash R., *Indiana* T76+392 **95**
Wabiskaw R., *Alberta* V55+568 **88**
Waboose Dam, *Ontario* T78+506 **89**
Wabos, *Ontario* T55+468 **91**
Wabra, *Saudi Arabia* J56+274 **74**
Wabuda, I.,
  Papua New Guinea C38–084 **111**
Waco, *Texas* U43+315 **95**
Wad, *Pakistan* H51+272 **70**
Waddamana, *Tasmania* C20–421 **109**
Wadden Zee, *Netherlands* M57+533 **44**
Waddington Mt., *B.C.* W33+513 **88**
Wadebridge, *England* N29+505 **38**
Wadena, *Minnesota* U31+464 **93**
Wadesboro, *N. Carolina* T31+350 **97**
Wad Hamid, *Sudan* K74+166 **81**
Wadi-es-Sir, *Jordan* K55+320 **76**
Wadi Gemal I., *Egypt* K60+246 **81**
Wadi Halfa, *Sudan* K82+216 **81**
Wadi Musa, *Jordan* K57+303 **76**
Wadi Medani, *Sudan* K70+144 **81**
Wafi, *Saudi Arabia* K07+249 **74**
Wageningen, *Netherlands* M56+520 **44**
Wager B., *N.-W. Territories* U00+654 **89**
Wagga Wagga, *N.S.W.* C16–351 **109**
Wagin, *W. Austrlia* E15–332 **110**
Wagoner, *Oklahoma* U34+360 **95**
Wahabis, *Saudi Arabia* K20+243 **74**
Wahla, *Saudi Arabia* K20+180 **74**
Wahoo, *Nebraska* U40+412 **95**
Waiau, *New Zealand* A41–426 **112**
Waichow. See Waiyeung
Waigeo, I., *New Guinea* D26–002 **65**
Waiheke I., *New Zealand* A20–368 **112**
Waihi, *New Zealand* A25+374 **112**
Waikaia, *New Zealand* A67–457 **112**
Waikare Moana, *N.Z.* A17–387 **112**
Waikari, *New Zealand* A44–429 **112**
Waikato, R., *New Zealand* A25–382 **112**
Waikerie, *S. Australia* C60–342 **109**
Waikouaiti, *New Zealand* A55–456 **112**
Waimakariri, R., *N.Z.* A46–434 **112**
Waimate, *New Zealand* A54–447 **112**
Waimes, *Belgium* M53+504 **44**
Wainfleet, *England* M89+531 **37**
Wainganga R., *India* G61+212 **70**
Waingapu, *Sumba I., Indon.* D89–096 **65**
Wainwright, *Alaska* Y60+705 **99**
Waipara, *New Zealand* A41–430 **112**
Waipawa, *New Zealand* A20–399 **112**
Waipukurau, *New Zealand* A20–400 **112**
Wairarapa, L., *New Zealand* A28–412 **112**
Wairau, R., *New Zealand* A40–416 **112**

Wairio, *New Zealand* A72–458 **112**
Wairoa, *New Zealand* A16–391 **112**
Wais, *Iran* J66+335 **74**
Waitara, *New Zealand* A34–390 **112**
Waitomo, *New Zealand* A29–383 **112**
Waiuku, *New Zealand* A32–372 **112**
Waiyeung, *China* E33+231 **67**
Wajir, *Kenya* K30+016 **83**
Wakamatsu, *Japan* C6C+375 **68**
Wakasa B., *Japan* C86+357 **68**
Wakatipu, L., *N.Z.* A68–451 **112**
Wakayama, *Japan* C89+342 **68**
Wakba, *Jordan* K54+305 **74**
Wake I., *Pacific Ocean* A80+192 **106**
Wakefield, *England* N09–537 **37**
Wakonichi L., *Quebec* S84+501 **90**
Wakrah, *Qatar, Arabia* J51+252 **75**
Waksa, *Iraq* K07+308 **74**
Wakuan Hu, *China* E18+524 **64**
Walachia, *Romania* L24+448 **58**
Walbrzych, *Poland* L82+508 **49**
Walcha, *New South Wales* B81–310 **109**
Walcheren I., *Netherlands* M69+515 **44**
Wald, *Switzerland* M37+473 **45**
Waldia, *Ethiopia* K32+118 **83**
Waldoboro, *Maine* S56+441 **90**
Waldport, *Oregon* W24+444 **92**
Walen See, *Switzerland* M35+471 **45**
Walenstadt, *Switzerland* M34+471 **45**
Wales, *Great Britain* N20+524 **34**
Walgett, *New South Wales* C11–300 **109**
Walgreen Coast, *Antarctica* U50–720 **27**
Walhalla, *S. Carolina* T48+347 **97**
Walhalla, *Victoria* C21–379 **109**
Walker, *Minnesota* U28+471 **93**
Walker, L., *Nevada* V82+388 **92**
Walker's Ra., *Oregon* W10+434 **92**
Walkerton, *Ontario* T37+441 **91**
Walkerville, *Ontario* T48+424 **91**
Wallace, *Idaho* V65+475 **92**
Wallaceburg, *Ontario* T43+426 **91**
Wallal, *Western Australia* D85–198 **110**
Wallaroo, *S. Australia* C75–340 **109**
Wallasey, *England* N18+534 **37**
Wallaston, Mt.,
  N. Territory, Australia D15–166 **110**
Walla Walla, *New S. Wales* C19–358 **109**
Walla-Walla, *Washington* V80+461 **92**
Wallenpaupack, L., *Pa.* T01+414 **96**
Wallingford, *England* N07+516 **39**
Wallis L., *New South Wales* B76–322 **109**
Wallowa Mts., *Oregon* V74+452 **92**
Wallsend, *New S. Wales* B81–329 **109**
Walney I., *England* N20+541 **37**
Walnut Cove, *N. Carolina* T31+362 **97**
Walsall, *England* N12+526 **37**
Walsenburg, *Colorado* U88+376 **94**
Walsoorden, *Netherlands* M66+514 **44**
Walterboro, *S. Carolina* T34+329 **97**
Waltham, *England* M87+518 **39**
Waltham, *Massachusetts* S67+424 **96**
Waltham, *Quebec* T12+459 **91**
Walton, *New York* T01+422 **96**
Walvis Bay, *S.-W. Africa* M02–230 **84**
Walwale, *Ghana* N04+104 **80**
Wamba, *Zaire* L12+020 **83**
Wamel, *Netherlands* M57+519 **44**
Wampsville, *New York* T04+430 **91**
Wana, *Pakistan* H33+323 **72**
Wanaaring, *New S. Wales* C35–297 **109**
Wanaka & L., *New Zealand* A65–445 **112**
Wanbi, *S. Australia* C58–348 **109**
Wandiwash, *India* G62+126 **70**
Wandre, *Belgium* M56+507 **44**
Wandsbek, *W. Germany* M30+536 **48**
Wan Fou Shan, *China* E32+292 **67**
Wanganella, *New S. Wales* C31–352 **109**
Wanganui & R., *N.Z.* A30–399 **112**
Wangaratta, *Victoria* C22–364 **109**
Wangyehmiao, *China* D77+460 **64**
Wanhsien, *China* E70+308 **66**
Wankie, *Rhodesia* L20–184 **84**
Wanping, *China* E21+398 **66**
Wantage, *England* N08+516 **39**
Wanyuan, *China* E70+321 **66**
Wapeelo, *Iowa* U08+412 **95**
Wappapello Res., *Missouri* U02+370 **95**
Wapheton, *N. Dakota* U40+462 **98**
Wapiti R., *Alberta* V87+548 **88**
Warandab, *Ethiopia* K06+070 **83**
Warangal, *India* G62+180 **70**
Waratah, *Tasmania* C27–415 **109**
Waratah B., *Victoria* C24–388 **109**
Warburton, *Victoria* C26–378 **109**
Wardair, *Ethiopia* J89+068 **83**
Wardha & R., *India* G68+208 **70**
Ware, *England* N00+518 **39**
Waremme, *Belgium* M58+507 **44**
Warialda, *New South Wales* B86–296 **109**
Warka, *Poland* L53+518 **49**
Warmbad, *S.-W. Africa* L66–284 **84**
Warmbaths, *Transvaal* L10–250 **84**
Warm Springs, *Virginia* T28+380 **97**
Warnemünde. *E. Germany* M17+542 **48**
Warner L., *Oregon* V89+423 **92**
Warneton, *Belgium* M72+507 **44**
Warora, *India* G62+203 **70**
Warracknabeal, *Victoira* C45–363 **109**
Warragul, *Victoria* C25–382 **109**
Warrego, R., *New S. Wales* C28–296 **109**
Warren, *Arkansas* U13+336 **97**
Warren, *Illinois* U00+425 **91**
Warren. *Minnesota* U40+482 **93**
Warren, *New South Wales* C13–318 **109**
Warren, *Ohio* T35+413 **91**
Warren, *Pennsylvania* T25+418 **96**
Warrenpoint, *N. Ireland* N37+541 **42**
Warrensburg, *Missouri* U22+388 **95**
Wellington, I, *Chile* T00–495 **103**
Warrenton, *Virginia* T17+387 **96**
Warri, *Nigeria* M56+056 **81**
Warrington, *England* N16+534 **37**
Warrnambool, *Victoria* C45–384 **109**
Warroad, *Minnesota* U32+489 **93**
Warroh, *Ethiopia* K12+086 **83**
Warrumbungle Ra., *N.S.W.* C03–313 **109**
Warsaw, *Indiana* T65+412 **91**
Warsaw, *New York* T19+427 **96**
Warsaw, *N. Carolina* T19+350 **97**
Warsaw. See Warszawa
Warszawa, *Poland* L54+523 **49**
Warta, *Poland* L68+517 **49**

Warta R., *Poland* L71+524 **49**
Wartburg, *Tennessee* T57+361 **97**
Warwick, *Queensland* B78–280 **111**
Warwick, *Rhode Island* S68+417 **96**
Warwick & co., *England* N09+524 **37**
Wasatch Mts., *Utah* V36+400 **94**
Waseca, *Minnesota* U20+440 **93**
Wasen, *Switzerland* M43+471 **45**
Wash, The, *England* M88+530 **37**
Washakie Needle, *Wyoming* V27+438 **93**
Washburn, *Wisconsin* U06+467 **93**
Washington,
  District of Columbia T12+389 **91**
Washington, *Indiana* T72+386 **95**
Washington, *Iowa* U10+413 **95**
Washington, *Missouri* U07+386 **97**
Washington, *New Jersey* T00+407 **96**
Washington, *N. Carolina* T12+355 **97**
Washington, *Ohio* T51+396 **91**
Washington, *Pennsylvania* T32+402 **91**
Washington, *Virginia* T19+387 **96**
Washington, state, *U.S.A.* W12+475 **98**
Washington I., *Pacific Ocean* Y60+048 **106**
Washington Ld., *Greenland* S00+800 **26**
Washington, Mt., *N.H.* S67+443 **91**
Washir, *Afghanistan* H66+321 **75**
Washuk, *Pakistan* H61+277 **70**
Wasmes, *Belgium* M67+504 **44**
Wassen, *Switzerland* M38+467 **45**
Wataroa, *New Zealand* A58–433 **112**
Watchet, *England* N20+512 **38**
Waterbury, *Connecticut* S78+415 **96**
Waterford, *New Brunswick* S32+457 **90**
Waterford (Port Láirge).
  Ireland, Rep. N43+522 **43**
Waterford Harb., *Ireland, Rep.* N42+522 **43**
Waterloo, *Belgium* M64+507 **44**
Waterloo, *Illinois* U01+384 **97**
Waterloo, *Iowa* U14+425 **95**
Waterloo, *Ontario* T33+435 **91**
Waterloo, *Quebec* S75+454 **91**
Watertown, *New York* T06+440 **91**
Watertown, *S. Dakota* U43+449 **93**
Watertown, *Wisconsin* T82+432 **91**
Waterville, *Maine* S58+446 **90**
Watervliet. *New York* S82+428 **96**
Waterways, *Alberta* V38+564 **88**
Watford, *England* N03+517 **39**
Watford City, *N. Dakota* U80+479 **93**
Watkins Glen, *New York* T12+424 **96**
Watlings I., *Bahamas, The* S88 + 240 **101**
Watonga, *Oklahoma* U51+358 **95**
Watou, *Belgium* M74+508 **44**
Watrous, *Saskatchewan* V02+513 **88**
Watsa, *Zaire* L02+028 **83**
Watseka, *Illinois* T76+408 **95**
Watson, *Utah* V24+398 **94**
Watsonville, *California* W11+369 **92**
Watt, *New Brunswick* S43+454 **90**
Watts Bar L., *Tennessee* T58+355 **97**
Wattsville, *Alabama* T67+336 **97**
Wau, *Papua New Guinea* C20–074 **111**
Wau, *Sudan* L12+078 **81**
Wauchope, *New South Wales* B74–315 **109**
Wauchula, *Florida* T41+276 **97**
Waukaringa, *S. Australia* C64–323 **109**
Waukegan, *Illinois* T77+424 **95**
Waukesha, *Wisconsin* T78+430 **95**
Waupaca, *Wisconsin* T85+444 **91**
Waupun, *Wisconsin* T82+436 **91**
Waurika, *Oklahoma* U48+342 **95**
Wausau, *Wisconsin* T88+450 **91**
Wautoma, *Wisconsin* T86+442 **91**
Wauwatosa, *Wisconsin* T79+431 **91**
Wave Hill, *N. Terr., Aust.* D24–175 **110**
Waveney R., *England* M81+525 **39**
Waverley, *Iowa* U14+428 **95**
Waverly, *New York* T09+420 **96**
Waverly, *Ohio* T48+392 **91**
Wavre, *Belgium* M62+507 **44**
Waxahachie, *Texas* U41+324 **95**
Waycross, *Georgia* T44+312 **97**
Wayland, *New York* T53+480 **91**
Wayne, *W. Virginia* 145+382 **97**
Waynesboro, *Georgia* T42+330 **97**
Waynesboro, *Pennsylvania* T16+398 **96**
Waynesville, *N. Carolina* T48+355 **97**
Waynoka, *Oklahoma* U54+366 **95**
Wazirabad, *Pakistan* H05+324 **72**
Weald, The, *England* M89+511 **39**
Wear, R., *England* N10+548 **37**
Weatherford, *Texas* U46+328 **95**
Weatherly, *Pennsylvania* T06+410 **96**
Weaver, R., *England* N16+532 **37**
Webb City, *Missouri* U26+372 **95**
Webbwood, *Ontario* T41+463 **91**
Webster, *S. Dakota* U45+453 **93**
Webster City, *Iowa* U22+425 **95**
Webster Springs, *W. Virginia* T33+385 **97**
Wecheelderzande, *Belgium* M61+513 **44**
Weda B., *Halmahera, Indon.* D40+002 **65**
Weddell I., *Falkland Islands* S06–518 **103**
Weddell Sea, *Antarctica* Q00–700 **27**
Wedderburn, *Victoria* C39–364 **109**
Wedgeport, *Nova Scotia* S36+437 **90**
Wednesbury, *England* V12+526 **37**
Weed, *California* W14+414 **92**
Weedon, *Quebec* S68+458 **91**
Weedsport, *New York* T09+430 **96**
Weeping Water, *Nebraska* U37+408 **95**
Weert, *Netherlands* M56+512 **44**
Weesen, *Switzerland* M35+471 **45**
Weisshorn, mt., *Switzerland* M44+461 **45**
Weesp, *Netherlands* M60+523 **44**
Wee Waa, *New S. Wales* C04–302 **109**
Weichang, *China* E11+418 **66**
Weiden, *W. Germany* M17+496 **48**
Weifang, *China* E06+367 **66**
Wei-hai, *China* D78+374 **66**
Wei Ho, R., *China* E76+342 **64**
Weihwei. See Chihsien
Welmoringle, *New S. Wales* C19–292 **109**
Weimar, *E. Germany* M22+509 **48**
Weipa, *Queensland* C48–130 **111**
Weinfelden, *Switzerland* M35+476 **45**
Weiser, *Idaho* V72+442 **92**
Wei Shan Hu, *China* E18+350 **66**
Weissenfels, *E. Germany* M18+512 **48**
Weisshorn, mt., *Switzerland* M44+461 **45**
Weissmies, mt., *Switzerland* M34+470 **45**
Weisstannen, *Switzerland* M34+470 **45**
Wejh, *Saudi Arabia* K51+263 **74**
Welch, *W. Virginia* T38+375 **97**

Weldon, *N. Carolina* T16+364 **97**
Welford, *Queensland* C38–251 **111**
Welland, *Ontario* T25+430 **91**
Welland, R., *England* N03+527 **37**
Wellesley Is., *Queensland* C63–164 **111**
Wellin, *Belgium* M59+501 **44**
Wellingborough, *England* N04+523 **37**
Wellington, *Kansas* U42+372 **95**
Wellington, *New S. Wales* C06–326 **109**
Wellington, *New Zealand* A31–413 **112**
Wellington, *S. Australia* C64–354 **109**
Wellington, I., *Chile* T00–495 **103**
Wellington L., *Victoria* C16–380 **109**
Wells, *Norfolk, England* M85+530 **39**
Wells, *Somerset, England* N16+512 **38**
Wells, *Nevada* V60+411 **92**
Wellsboro, *Pennsylvania* T14+418 **96**
Wellsville, *Missouri* U10+390 **95**
Wellsville, *New York* T18+421 **96**
Wels, *Austria* M06+482 **48**
Welsford, *New Brunswick* S38+455 **90**
Welshpool, *Wales* N17+526 **37**
Welwyn Garden City, *Eng.* N01+518 **39**
Wema, *Zaire* L50–006 **82**
Wembo Niama, *Zaire* L32–042 **82**
Wemyss Bay, *Scotland* N29+559 **41**
Wenatchee, *Washington* W02+474 **92**
Wenchow, *China* D86+280 **67**
Wenshan, *China* F04+236 **67**
Wensi, *China* E53+353 **66**
Wentworth, *New S. Wales* C48–341 **109**
Weobley, *England* N17+522 **38**
Werribee, *Victoria* C32–379 **109**
Werris Creek, *New S. Wales* B86–313 **109**
Wervershoof, *Netherlands* M59+527 **44**
Wervik, *Belgium* M72+508 **44**
Wesel, *W. Germany* M50+517 **48**
Wesenberg, *E. Germany* M12+532 **48**
Weser, R., *W. Germany* M36+526 **48**
Wessel Is., *N. Terr., Aust.* C81–112 **111**
Wesson, *Mississippi* U02+317 **97**
West B., *Louisiana* T75+291 **95**
West Allis, *Wisconsin* T79+431 **91**
West Barra, *Scotland* N08+601 **40**
West Bay City, *Michigan* T54+436 **91**
West Bend, *Wisconsin* T79+435 **91**
West Bengal, *India* G15+224 **71**
West Branch, *Michigan* T55+443 **91**
West Bromwich, *England* N12+525 **37**
Westbrook, *Maine* S62+437 **90**
Westbury, *Tasmania* C19–415 **109**
Westby, *New South Wales* C16–355 **109**
West Calder, *Scotland* N21+559 **41**
West Chester, *Pennsylvania* T04+399 **96**
Westerly, *Rhode Island* S71+413 **96**
Westende, *Belgium* M73+512 **44**
Western Australia, state, *Aust.* **110**
Western Sahara, *W. Africa* N80 + 260 **80**
Wester Schelde, *Netherlands* M67+514 **44**
Westfalen, *W. Germany* M42+518 **48**
Westfield, *Massachusetts* S76+421 **91**
Westfield, *New Brunswick* S38+454 **90**
Westfield, *New York* T28+423 **96**
Westfield, *Pennsylvania* T16+419 **96**
West Frankfort, *Illinois* T84+379 **95**
West Hartlepool, *England* N07+547 **37**
West Indies, *Caribbean Sea* S70+200 **85**
West Irian (Irian Barat), *See Irian Jaya*
West Linton, *Scotland* N20+557 **41**
West Lothian, co., *See Lothian*
Westmeath, co., *Ireland, Rep.* N45+535 **43**
Westminster, *Maryland* T12+396 **96**
Westmorland, co., *See Cumbria*
West Nicholson, *Rhodesia* L04–212 **84**
Weston, *Sabah* E26+053 **65**
Weston, *West Virginia* T33+390 **91**
Weston-super-Mare, *England* N18+513 **38**
Westplains, *Missouri* U12+368 **95**
West Point, *Arkansas* U10+352 **97**
West Point, *Georgia* T61+329 **97**
West Point, *Mississippi* T82+336 **95**
Westpoint, *Nebraska* U40+418 **95**
West Point, *New York* S84+413 **96**
West Point, *Virginia* T11+375 **97**
Westport, *Ireland, Rep.* N57+538 **42**
Westport, *New Zealand* A50–417 **112**
Westport, *Ontario* T09+447 **91**
Westray I. & Firth, *Scot.* N18+593 **40**
West Riding, *See West Yorkshire*
West Union, *Iowa* U12+430 **95**
West Virginia, state, *U.S.A.* T40+384 **99**
Westwoud, *Netherlands* M59+527 **44**
West Yorkshire, *Eng.* N10+537 **37**
Wetar, I. & Str., *Indonesia* D52–080 **65**
Wetaskiwin, *Alberta* V50+532 **88**
Wetterhorn, mt., *Switzerland* M41+466 **45**
Wetumpka, *Alabama* T67+326 **97**
Wewoka, *Oklahoma* U40+352 **95**
Wexford & co., *Ireland, Rep.* N39+523 **43**
Wexford B. & Harb., *Ireland, Rep.*
  N37+523 **43**
Wey, R., *England* N03+514 **39**
Weybridge, *England* N03+514 **39**
Weyburn, *Saskatchewan* U83+497 **88**
Weymont, *Quebec* S83+479 **91**
Weymouth, *England* N15+506 **38**
Weymouth, *Nova Scotia* S36+444 **90**
Whakataki, *New Zealand* A22–408 **112**
Whakatane, *New Zealand* A18–380 **112**
Whale R., *Quebec* S44+574 **89**
Whale, R., Gt., *Quebec* T15+551 **89**
Whale, R., Lit., *Quebec* T08+555 **89**
Whales, B. of, *Antarctica* Z00–790 **27**
Whalsay, I., *Scotland* N06+604 **40**
Whangarei, *New Zealand* A34–358 **112**
Wharanui, *New Zealand* A31–416 **112**
Wharfe, R., *England* N09+539 **37**
Wharton, *Texas* U36+293 **95**
Wheatland, *Wyoming* V00+420 **93**
Wheatland Res., *Wyoming* V04+418 **93**
Wheaton, *Minnesota* U39+458 **93**
Wheeler Dam & L., *Alabama* T73+348 **97**
Wheeler Pk., *Nevada* V56+391 **92**
Wheeling, *W. Virginia* T34+401 **91**
Whetstone Buttes, *N. Dakota* U77+462 **93**
Whitbourne, *Newfoundland* R51+474 **90**
Whitby, *England* N04+545 **37**
Whitby, *Ontario* T24+439 **91**
Whitchurch, *Salop, Eng.* N16+530 **37**
Whitchurch, *Hants, Eng.* N08+512 **39**

White B., *Newfoundland* R68+500 **90**
White L., *Louisiana* U14+298 **95**
White Mts., *New Hampshire* S68+443 **91**
White R., *Arkansas* U12+360 **95**
White R., *Indiana* T74+385 **97**
White R., *S. Dakota* U73+439 **98**
White R., *Utah, etc.* V24+400 **94**
White R., *Yukon* X32+632 **88**
White Cliffs, *New S. Wales* C42-309 **109**
White Earth, *N. Dakota* U77+484 **93**
Whitefish, *Montana* V58+483 **98**
Whitefish B., *Michigan* T59+469 **91**
Whitehall, *Michigan* T68+434 **91**
Whitehall, *New York* S80+435 **91**
Whitehaven, *England* N21+545 **37**
Whitehorse, *Yukon* X00+606 **88**
White Horse Hills, *England* N10+515 **39**
White Mark, *Tasmania* C13-401 **109**
White Pass, *Brit. Columbia* W88+596 **88**
White Plains, *New York* S83+410 **96**
White River, *Ontario* T61+488 **89**
White River, *S. Dakota* U65+435 **93**
White River Junction,
  Vermont S74+434 **99**
White Russia (Byelo-Russia),
  rep., *U.S.S.R.* L12+536 **60**
White Sulphur Springs,
  Montana V36+465 **93**
White Volta, R., *Ghana* N06+088 **80**
Whitfield, *Victoria* C22-368 **109**
Whiting, *New Jersey* S86+399 **91**
Whitley Bay, *England* N09+551 **37**
Whitney, *Ontario* T19+455 **91**
Whitney, Mt., *California* V80+366 **92**
Whittier, *California* V78+339 **92**
Whittlesea, *Victoria* C29-375 **109**
Whitton, *New South Wales* C23-345 **109**
Wholdaia L., *N.-W. Terr.* U86+604 **88**
Whyalla, *S. Australia* C75-330 **109**
Wiarton, *Ontario* T37+447 **91**
Wichita, *Kansas* U44+377 **95**
Wichita Falls & R., *Texas* U50+338 **95**
Wichita Mts., *Oklahoma* U54+347 **95**
Wick, *Scotland* N19+584 **40**
Wickliffe, *Missouri* T86+370 **95**
Wicklow & co., *Ireland, Rep.* N36+530 **43**
Wicklow Hd., *Ireland, Rep.* N36+530 **43**
Wicklow Mts., *Ireland, Rep.* N39+530 **43**
Widnes, *England* N16+534 **37**
Wielbark, *Poland* L54+534 **49**
Wielen, *Poland* L83+528 **49**
Wieliczka, *Poland* L60+500 **49**
Wielun, *Poland* L69+512 **49**
Wien, *Austria* L82+482 **49**
Wiener Neustadt, *Austria* L83+478 **49**
Wierzbnik, *Poland* L53+511 **49**
Wiesbaden, *W. Germany* M41+501 **48**
Wiesen, *Switzerland* M32+467 **45**
Wigan, *England* N16+536 **37**
Wight, I. of, *England* N08+507 **39**
Wigton, *England* N19+548 **37**
Wigtown, *Scotland* N27+549 **41**
Wigtown B., *Scotland* N25+548 **41**
Wijhe, *Netherlands* M53+524 **44**
Wijk, *Netherlands* M56+508 **44**
Wijk, *Netherlands* M58+520 **44**
Wil, *Switzerland* M36+475 **45**
Wilcannia, *New S. Wales* C41-316 **109**
Wildhorn, mt., *Switzerland* M46+464 **45**
Wildstrubel, mt., *Switzerland* M45+464 **45**
Wildwood, *Florida* T42+288 **97**
Wildwood, *New Jersey* S89+390 **91**
Wilhelmshaven, *W. Germany* M41+535 **48**
Wilkes Ld., *Antarctica* E20-690 **27**
Wilkes Barre, *Pennsylvania* T05+412 **96**
Wilkesboro, *N. Carolina* T37+362 **97**
Wilkin's Str., *Antarctica* S80-710 **27**
Wilkolaz, *Poland* L46+510 **49**
Willamette R., *Oregon* W19+449 **92**
Willcox, *Arizona* V29+323 **94**
Willemsdorp, *Netherlands* M62+517 **44**
Willemstad, *Curaçao I.* S53+121 **104**
Willemstad, *Netherlands* M63+517 **44**
William, Mt., *Victoria* C44-374 **109**
Williams, *Arizona* V43+352 **94**
Williams Pt., *North-West*
  Territories V68+688 **88**
Williamsburg, *Kentucky* T55+368 **97**
Williamsburg, *Virginia* T10+372 **97**
Williamsport, *Indiana* T74+403 **95**
Williamsport, *Pennsylvania* T13+413 **96**
Williamston, *N. Carolina* T13+358 **97**
Williamsville, *Missouri* U03+397 **97**
Willimantie, *Connecticut* S73+417 **96**
Williston, *Cape Province* L54-314 **84**
Williston, *N. Dakota* U82+481 **93**
Willmar, *Minnesota* U30+451 **93**
Willochra, *S. Australia* C71-322 **109**
Willow L., *N.-W. Territories* W07+620 **88**
Willow Creek, *Montana* V40+458 **93**
Willow Lake R., *N.-W. Terr.* W15+620 **88**
Willowmore, *Cape Province* L38-332 **84**
Willow Springs, *Missouri* U12+370 **95**
Wills Mt., *Pennsylvania* T22+399 **96**
Wilmette, *Illinois* T77+422 **91**
Wilmington, *California* V80+338 **92**
Wilmington, *Delaware* T03+397 **96**
Wilmington, *N. Carolina* T18+342 **97**
Wilmington, *S. Australia* C72-326 **109**
Wilnis, *Netherlands* M61+522 **44**
Wilno, *Ontario* T15+455 **91**
Wilson, *N. Carolina* T18+357 **97**
Wilson's Prom., *Victoria* C22-388 **109**
Wilsonville, *Alabama* T69+332 **97**
Willunga, *S. Australia* C69-353 **109**
Wiltshire (Wilts), co., *Eng.* N11+514 **39**
Wiluna, *W. Australia* D88-266 **110**
Wimbledon, *S. Australia* C51+472 **93**
Wimmera, R., *Victoria* C47-368 **109**
Winburg, *Orange Free State* L18-286 **84**
Winchendon, *Massachusetts* S72+427 **91**
Winchester, *England* N08+511 **39**
Winchester, *Kentucky* T55+380 **97**
Winchester, *Ontario* T02+451 **91**
Winchester, *Tennessee* T69+352 **97**
Winchester, *Virginia* T19+392 **96**
Wind R., *Yukon* X00+654 **88**
Wind Cave Nat. Pk., *S. Dak.* U82+434 **93**
Windermere & L., *England* N18+544 **37**
Windhoek, *S.-W. Africa* L78-226 **84**
Windom, *Minnesota* U31+439 **93**

Wind River Pk. & Mts.,
  Wyoming V25+424 **98**
Windsor, *Colorado* V00+405 **94**
Windsor, *Connecticut* S76+419 **96**
Windsor, *England* N04+515 **39**
Windsor, *Missouri* U21+386 **95**
Windsor, *N. Carolina* T12+361 **97**
Windsor, *New South Wales* B86-337 **109**
Windsor, *Nova Scotia* S25+450 **90**
Windsor, *Ontario* T48+423 **91**
Windsor, *Quebec* S72+456 **91**
Windsor, *Vermont* S75+435 **91**
Windward Is., *West Indies* S06+138 **101**
Windward Pass., *West Indies* S84+200 **101**
Winfield, *Kansas* U42+372 **95**
Winfield, *W. Virginia* T41+385 **97**
Wingen, *New South Wales* B85-319 **109**
Wingene, *Belgium* M70+510 **44**
Wingham, *New South Wales* B77-319 **109**
Wingham, *Ontario* T38+439 **91**
Winisk R., *Ontario* T70+548 **89**
Winnebago, *Minnesota* U25+438 **93**
Winnebago L., *Wisconsin* T81+440 **91**
Winnemucca, *Nevada* V76+410 **92**
Winnemucca L., *Nevada* V86+400 **92**
Winner, *S. Dakota* U42+434 **93**
Winnett, *Montana* V20+470 **93**
Winnfield, *Louisiana* U16+319 **97**
Winnipeg, *Manitoba* U43+499 **88**
Winnipeg, L., *Manitoba* U45+526 **88**
Winnipegosis, *Manitoba* U60+514 **88**
Winnipegosis, L., *Manitoba* U60+530 **88**
Winnipesaukee, L., *N.H.* S68+436 **91**
Winnsboro, *S. Carolina* T37+344 **97**
Winona, *Minnesota* U10+441 **93**
Winschoten, *Netherlands* M48+533 **44**
Winslow, *Arizona* V34+350 **94**
Winsted, *Connecticut* S78+419 **96**
Winston Salem, *N. Carolina* T32+361 **97**
Winter Ra., *Oregon* W09+430 **92**
Winterhaven, *California* V58+327 **92**
Winter Haven, *Florida* T39+281 **97**
Winterport, *Maine* S53+446 **90**
Winterset, *Iowa* U24+413 **95**
Winterswijk, *Netherlands* M49+520 **44**
Winterthur, *Switzerland* M38+475 **45**
Winton, *New Zealand* A26-462 **112**
Winton, *Queensland* C41-222 **111**
Wirksworth, *England* N09+531 **37**
Wirrabara, *S. Australia* C71-330 **109**
Wirral Pen., *England* N18+533 **37**
Wirrega, *S. Australia* C56-362 **109**
Wirt, *Minnesota* U23+478 **93**
Wisbech, *England* M89+527 **37**
Wisconsin, state, *U.S.A.* U07+447 **99**
Wisconsin R., *Wisconsin* T89+452 **91**
Wisconsin Rapids, *Wisconsin* T89+444 **91**
Wise, *Virginia* T46+370 **97**
Wishaw, *Scotland* N23+558 **41**
Wishek, *N. Dakota* U58+462 **93**
Wisla (Vistula), R., *Poland* L51+517 **49**
Wismar, *E. Germany* M22+539 **48**
Witham, R., *England* N02+532 **37**
Withlacoochee B., *Florida* T57+290 **99**
Witputs, *S.-W. Africa* L80-276 **84**
Witry, *Belgium* M56+498 **44**
Witten, *W. Germany* M46+515 **48**
Wittenberg, *E. Germany* M14+519 **48**
Wittenberge, *E. Germany* M19+530 **48**
Wittenoon, *Western Aust.* E09-213 **110**
Wittingen, *W. Germany* M26+527 **48**
Wittstock, *E. Germany* M15+532 **48**
Wivenhoe, *England* M84+518 **39**
Wloclawek, *Poland* L66+526 **49**
Wodonga, *Victoria* C19-361 **109**
Woerden, *Netherlands* M61+521 **44**
Wognum, *Netherlands* M60+527 **44**
Wohlen, *Switzerland* M40+473 **45**
Wokam, I., *Indonesia* D03-058 **65**
Wolbrom, *Poland* L61+504 **49**
Woleai, I., *Caroline Islands* C40+065 **106**
Wolfe I., *Ontario* T08+442 **91**
Wolfe City, *Texas* U36+332 **95**
Wolf Point, *Montana* V04+481 **93**
Wolfeboro, *New Hampshire* S67+436 **91**
Wolfsberg, *Austria* M01+468 **48**
Wolfville, *Nova Scotia* S25+450 **90**
Wolgast, *E. Germany* M08+540 **48**
Wolhusen, *Switzerland* M42+471 **45**
Wollaston, *England* N04+522 **39**
Wollaston Foreland,
  Greenland P28+740 **26**
Wollaston, Is., *Chile* S44-557 **103**
Wollaston L., *Saskatchewan* U80+584 **88**
Wollongong, *New S. Wales* B85-344 **109**
Wolseley, *S. Australia* C54-364 **109**
Wolstenholme, C., *Quebec* T15+621 **89**
Wolvega, *Netherlands* M54+529 **44**
Wolverhampton, *England* N13+526 **37**
Wolverton, *Belgium* M64+509 **44**
Wolverton, *England* N05+521 **39**
Woman River, *Ontario* T46+475 **91**
Wonoka, *S. Australia* C70-317 **109**
Wonsan, *Korea* D45+391 **64**
Wonthaggi, *Victoria* C27-386 **109**
Wood R., *Saskatchewan* V12+500 **88**
Woodbridge, *England* M82+527 **39**
Wood Buffalo Park, *Alberta* V50+594 **88**
Woodburn, *New South Wales* B70-290 **109**
Woodbury, *New Jersey* T01+398 **96**
Woodford, *Newfoundland* R49+474 **90**
Woodlark I., *Papua New Guinea*
  B74+093 **111**
Woodroffe, Mt., *S. Australia* D23-264 **110**
Woods, L., *N. Terr., Aust.* D10-179 **110**
Woods, L. of the, *Ontario* U30+494 **88**
Woods Hole, *Massachusetts* S64+415 **96**
Woodside, *Utah* V32+392 **94**
Woodside, *Victoria* C19-385 **109**
Woodstock, *Illinois* T80+424 **95**
Woodstock, *New Brunswick* S45+461 **90**
Woodstock, *Ontario* T35+432 **91**
Woodstock, *Vermont* S75+436 **96**
Woodstock, *Virginia* T21+388 **96**
Woodsville, *New Hampshire* S72+441 **91**
Woodville, *New Zealand* A24-403 **112**
Woodward, *Oklahoma* U57+364 **95**
Wooler, *England* N12+555 **37**
Wooltana, *S. Australia* C64-305 **109**
Woolwich, *England* N00+515 **39**
Woomera, *S. Australia* C82-312 **111**

Woonsocket, *Rhode Island* S69+420 **96**
Woonsocket, *S. Dakota* U50+441 **93**
Worcester, *Cape Province* L64-338 **84**
Worcester, *England* N13+522 **37**
Worcester, *Massachusetts* S71+423 **91**
Worcester, co., *See* Hereford & Worcs.
Workington, *England* N21+546 **37**
Worksop, *England* N07+533 **37**
Workum, *Netherlands* M57+530 **44**
Worland, *Wyoming* V18+440 **93**
Worms, *W. Germany* M40+496 **48**
Worthing, *England* N02+508 **39**
Worthington, *Minnesota* U32+436 **93**
Worthington, *Ontario* T39+464 **91**
Wotho, I., *Marshall Islands* A85+100 **106**
Woudenberg, *Netherlands* M57+521 **44**
Woudrichem, *Netherlands* M60+518 **44**
Wounta, *Nicaragua* T51+135 **101**
Wour, *Chad* L86+212 **81**
Wouw, *Netherlands* M64+515 **44**
Wowoni, I., *Indonesia* D72-041 **65**
Wrangel I. *See* Vrangelya, Ostrov
Wrangell, *Alaska* W70+564 **99**
Wrangell, Mt., *Alaska* X62+616 **99**
Wrath C., *Scotland* N30+586 **40**
Wray, *Colorado* U74+400 **94**
Wrexham, *Wales* N18+530 **38**
Wright, Mt., *New S. Wales* C46-312 **109**
Wrightsville, *Georgia* T46+327 **97**
Wrightsville Beach, *North*
  Carolina T17+342 **97**
Wrigley, *N.-W. Territories* W25+637 **88**
Wroclaw, *Poland* L78+511 **49**
Wroxham, *England* M82+527 **39**
Wuchang, *China* D46+449 **64**
Wuchang, *China* E34+305 **67**
Wuchow (Tsangwu), *China* E51+235 **67**
Wuchwan, *China* E51+411 **66**
Wudam, *Saudi Arabia* J15+238 **75**
Wuhan, *China* E32+304 **66**
Wuhing. *See* Huchow
Wuhsien. *See* Soochow
Wuhu, *China* E09+314 **66**
Wukang, *China* E56+268 **67**
Wukari, *Nigeria* M32+078 **81**
Wukiang, *China* E25+380 **66**
Wu Kiang, R., *China* E72+280 **64**
Wular L., *Kashmir* H02+344 **72**
Wuntho, *Burma* F55+239 **71**
Wuppertal, *W. Germany* M47+513 **48**
Wurttemberg, *W. Germany* M36+485 **48**
Wurzburg, *W. Germany* M30+498 **48**
Wurzen, *E. Germany* M14+514 **48**
Wushih, *Hainan Island* E62+192 **64**
Wusiang, *China* E42+368 **66**
Wusih, *China* D88+316 **66**
Wuti, *China* E14+377 **66**
Wutsin, *China* E00+318 **66**
Wuustwezel, *Belgium* M63+514 **44**
Wuwei, *China* F14+379 **66**
Wu Yi Shan, *China* E21+270 **67**
Wuyüan, *China* E70+411 **66**
Wuyuon, *China* D32+490 **64**
Wyalong, West, *New S. Wales* C17-339 **109**
Wyandotte, *Michigan* L49+422 **91**
Wyangala Res., *New South*
  Wales C06-339 **109**
Wye, R., *England-Wales* N16+520 **38**
Wyk, *W. Germany* M39+547 **48**
Wymondham, *England* M83+526 **39**
Wyndham, *New Zealand* A66-463 **112**
Wyndham, *W. Australia* D41-154 **110**
Wynne, *Arkansas* U05+352 **95**
Wynyard, *Tasmania* C26-410 **109**
Wyoming, state, *U.S.A.* V26+436 **98**
Wyoming Pk., *Wyoming* V34+426 **93**
Wyong, *New South Wales* B82-333 **109**
Wysokie Mazowieckie, *Poland* L45+529 **49**
Wyszkow, *Poland* L51+526 **49**
Wytheville, *Virginia* T37+369 **97**

Xanthi, *Greece* L31+412 **58**
Xanxere, *Brazil* R45-268 **103**
Xapuri, *Brazil* S52-107 **104**
Xenia, *Montana* V31+486 **93**
Xeró, *See* Peristera I.
Xibury, *Brazil* S43-053 **104**
Xilokastron, *Greece* L44+381 **59**
Xingu, *Brazil* S55-082 **104**
Yaan, *China* F11+300 **64**
Yaapeet, *Victoria* C48-358 **109**
Yaate, *Lebanon* K53+340 **76**
Yablonovy Khrebet Mts.,
  U.S.S.R. E50+510 **63**
Yabrud, *Syria* K50+339 **76**
Yackandandah, *Victoria* C17-362 **109**
Yacuiba, *Bolivia* S22-218 **104**
Yagvildino, *U.S.S.R.* J21+558 **61**
Yakhtul, *Yemen* K10+135 **74**
Yakima, *Washington* W03+466 **92**
Yako, *Volta* N14+128 **80**
Yakoma, *Zaire* L46+038 **82**
Yaku Kaikyo, *Japan* D25+303 **68**
Yaku Shima, *Japan* D27+303 **68**
Yakutsk, *U.S.S.R.* D31+621 **63**
Yale, *British Columbia* W08+496 **88**
Yale, *Michigan* T47+432 **91**
Yalgoo, *W. Australia* E20-282 **110**
Yalinga, *Cent. Afr. Rep.* L40+065 **81**
Yallourn, *Victoria* C22-381 **109**
Yalouke, *Cent. Afr. Rep.* L78+054 **81**
Yalpunga, *New S. Wales* C48-289 **109**
Yalta, *U.S.S.R.* K64+446 **60**
Yalu, *China* D77+483 **64**
Yalu, R., *China, etc.* D60+407 **64**
Yalung R., *China* F28+314 **64**
Yalutorovsk, *U.S.S.R.* H53+568 **62**
Yamada, *Japan* C79+345 **68**
Yamagata, *Japan* C58+382 **68**
Yamaguchi, *Japan* D21+342 **68**
Yamal, Pol., *U.S.S.R.* H30+715 **62**
Yamba, *New South Wales* B70-294 **109**
Yambol, *Bulgaria* L21+425 **58**
Yamdena I., *Indonesia* D22+077 **65**
Yamdok Tso, *Tibet* F85+290 **71**
Yamethin, *Burma* F43+153 **71**
Yampol, *U.S.S.R.* L10+483 **60**
Yampol, *U.S.S.R.* L23+499 **60**
Yamsk, *U.S.S.R.* B66+593 **63**
Yamuna R., *India* G58+260 **73**
Yanac, *U.S.S.R.* C51-361 **109**
Yanam, *India* G47+168 **71**
Yanaoca, *Peru* S69-143 **104**

Yancannia, *New S. Wales* C44-303 **109**
Yanco, *New South Wales* C22-346 **109**
Yanda, *N., New South Wales* C25-310 **109**
Yandoon, *Burma* F56+170 **71**
Yangchow, *China* E04+323 **66**
Yanghissar, *Sinkiang, China* G83+389 **72**
Yang-kao, *China* E38+404 **66**
Yangku. *See* Taiyuan
Yangtze Kiang, R., *China* E70+308 **66**
Yangyuan, *China* E34+401 **66**
Yankton, *S. Dakota* U44+429 **93**
Yannina. *See* Ioannina
Yantabulla, *New South Wales* C30-294 **109**
Yaoundé, *Cameroun* M20+038 **81**
Yap, I., *Pacific Ocean* C70+093 **106**
Yapen I., *Irian Jaya, Indon.* C82+018 **65**
Yaraka, *Queensland* C36-248 **111**
Yarda, *Chad* L66+184 **81**
Yare R., *England* M81+526 **39**
Yarensk, *U.S.S.R.* J65+623 **62**
Yarim, *Yemen* K04+145 **74**
Yarkand, *Sinkiang, China* G77+384 **72**
Yarmouth, *I. of Wight, Eng.* N09+507 **39**
Yarmouth, *Maine* S61+438 **90**
Yarmouth, *Nova Scotia* S37+438 **90**
Yarmouth, Great, *England* M80+526 **39**
Yaroslavl, *U.S.S.R.* K30+576 **60**
Yarram, *Victoria* C20-385 **109**
Yarrawonga, *Victoria* C24-360 **109**
Yarrow, R., *Scotland* N18+555 **41**
Yartsevo, *U.S.S.R.* G00+602 **63**
Yarumal, *Colombia* T03+070 **104**
Yarylgach, *U.S.S.R.* K73+456 **60**
Yasanyama, *Zaire* L53+042 **81**
Yasin, *Kashmir* H10+364 **72**
Yasothon, *Thailand* F04+158 **65**
Yass & R., *New S. Wales* C07-348 **109**
Yatakala, *Niger* M88+146 **80**
Yathkyed L., *N.-W. Terr.* U35+630 **88**
Yatsushiro, *Japan* D26+325 **68**
Yatta, *Jordan* K59+314 **76**
Yatung, *Tibet* G06+274 **71**
Yauca, *Peru* S87-157 **104**
Yautepec, *Mexico* U54+188 **100**
Yavarete, *Colombia* S54-002 **104**
Yawata, *Japan* D25+338 **68**
Yazd, *Iran* J33+319 **75**
Yazdan, *Iran* H85+337 **75**
Yazoo City, *Mississippi* U02+328 **95**
Ybbs, *Austria* M00+482 **48**
Ye, *Burma* F43+153 **71**
Yea, *Victoria* C27-372 **109**
Yecla, *Spain* N07+386 **53**
Yecora, *Mexico* V22+288 **100**
Yéfira, *Greece* L44+407 **59**
Yefremov, *U.S.S.R.* K42+532 **60**
Yegros, *Paraguay* R68-265 **103**
Yehcheng. *See* Karghalik
Yehkiatsi, *China* E24+318 **64**
Yehpaishow, *China* E01+413 **66**
Yehsien, *China* E00+372 **66**
Yelabuga, *U.S.S.R.* J47+558 **61**
Yelan, *U.S.S.R.* K08+509 **61**
Yelatma, *U.S.S.R.* K20+550 **61**
Yeldyak, *U.S.S.R.* J20+556 **61**
Yelets, *U.S.S.R.* K39+526 **60**
Yelizarovo, *U.S.S.R.* H45+615 **62**
Yell, I. & Sd., *Scotland* N07+606 **40**
Yellandu, *India* G59+177 **70**
Yellow Mt., *New S. Wales* C19-327 **109**
Yellow R. *See* Hwang Ho
Yellow Sea, *China* D78+350 **66**
Yellowhead Pass, *Alberta* V80+532 **88**
Yellowstone L., *Wyoming* V32+440 **98**
Yellowstone Nat. Pk., *Wyo.* V34+447 **98**
Yellowstone R., *Montana, etc.* U86+473 **93**
Yellowtail Res., *Montana* V20+450 **93**
Yemanzhelinka, *U.S.S.R.* H82+548 **61**
Yemen, *Asia* K10+173 **74**
Yemen, *South Asia* J80+150 **74**
Yenakiyevo, *Ukraine* K41+482 **60**
Yenan (Fushih), *China* E63+366 **66**
Yenangyaung, *Burma* F60+204 **71**
Yen-Bay, *N. Vietnam* F02+216 **69**
Yenbo, *Saudi Arabia* K42+242 **74**
Yencheng, *China* D89+333 **66**
Yenchih, *China* F50+420 **64**
Yenchow. *See* Tzeyang
Yenchow. *See* Kienteh
Yenda, *New South Wales* C23-343 **109**
Yenise, R., *U.S.S.R.* G20+680 **62**
Yeniseisk, *U.S.S.R.* F78+583 **63**
Yeniseyskiy Zaliv, *U.S.S.R.* G60+724 **62**
Yenki, *China* D32+428 **64**
Yenki (Kara Shahr), *China* G22+421 **62**
Yenping. *See* Nanping
Yentai, *China* D82+375 **66**
Yeoval, *New South Wales* C08-328 **109**
Yeovil, *England* N16+510 **38**
Yeper, *Belgium* M73+508 **44**
Yeráki, *Greece* L44+370 **59**
Yerbogachen, *U.S.S.R.* E73+614 **63**
Yerevan, *Armyanskaya, U.S.S.R.* K03+402 **62**
Yerofei Pavlovich, *U.S.S.R.* D78+540 **63**
Yeropol, *U.S.S.R.* A66+651 **63**
Yeshbum, *Yemen, South* J79+145 **74**
Yessei, *Russia* F17+683 **63**
Yeste, *Spain* N14+384 **53**
Yesud ha Ma'ala, *Israel* K56+331 **76**
Yetman, *New South Wales* B86+289 **109**
Ye-u, *Burma* F57+228 **71**
Yeu, I. d', *France* N14+467 **54**
Yeungkong, *China* E48+217 **64**
Yevseyevo, *U.S.S.R.* B69+673 **63**
Yeysk, *U.S.S.R.* K40+465 **62**
Yhu, *Paraguay* R66-250 **103**
Yi, R., *Uruguay* R71-333 **103**
Yianisadhes Is., *Crete* L22+354 **59**
Yiannitsá, *Greece* L46+407 **59**
Yidha, *Greece* L45+406 **59**
Yihsien, *China* E26+394 **66**
Yingchia. *See* Yanghissar
Yingchow. *See* Fowyang
Yingchwan, *China* E82+385 **66**
Yinghsien, *China* E41+395 **66**
Yingtak, *China* E40+242 **67**
Yinkanie, *S. Australia* C58-343 **109**
Yioúra, I., *Greece* L32+376 **59**

Yithion, *Greece* L45+368　59
Yitu, *China* E09+367　66
Yiyang, *China* E46+287　67
Yocalla, *Bolivia* S36–192　104
Yochow. *See* Yoyang
Yogovsk, *U.S.S.R.* J22+576　61
Yogyakarta, *Java* E58+079　65
Yoho Park, *Brit. Columbia* V70+512　88
Yokkaichi, *Japan* C80+350　68
Yoko, *Cameroun* M16+056　81
Yokohama, *Japan* C62+354　68
Yokosuku, *Japan* C62+352　68
Yokote, *Japan* C57+393　68
Yola, *Nigeria* M16+092　81
Yonago, *Japan* D10+354　68
Yone Zawa, *Japan* C59+379　68
Yonkers, *New York* S83+409　96
Yonne, dep., *France* M69+478　54
York, *Alabama* T80+325　97
York, *England* N07+539　37
York, *Nebraska* U46+408　95
York, *Pennsylvania* T11+400　96
York, *W. Australia* E19–319　110
York C., *Greenland* S50+760　26
York, C., *Queensland* C45–108　111
York R., *Virginia* T10+374　97
York Sd., *W. Australia* D58–150　110
Yorke Pen., *S. Australia* C74–346　109
Yorketown, *S. Australia* C75–350　109
York Factory, *Manitoba* U16+567　89
Yorkshire, North, co., *Eng.* N08+542　37
Yorkshire Moors, *England* N05+544　37
Yorkshire Wolds, *England* N03+540　37
Yorkton, *Saskatchewan* U75+511　88
Yorktown, *Virginia* T09+372　97
York Village, *Maine* S64+432　90
Yoro, *Honduras* T71+150　101
Yosemite Nat. Park. *Cal.* V88+379　92
Yoshkar Ola, *U.S.S.R.* J72+568　61
Youghal & Harb., *Ireland, Rep.* N47+519　43
Youghiogheny River Res.,
　Penn. etc. T27+397　96
Youkadouma, *Cameroun* M00+036　81
Young, *New South Wales* C10+343　109
Younghusband Pen., *S. Aust.* C64–360　109
Youngstown, *Ohio* T34+411　91
Yount Pk., *Wyoming* V30+440　93
Yoyang, *China* E40+294　67
Yozgat, *Turkey* K62+398　74
Ypres (Yeper), *Belgium* M73+508　44
Ypsilanti, *Michigan* T52+423　91
Yreka, *California* W16+417　92
Ysabel, I., *Solomon Islands* B35–080　106
Yssingeaux, *France* M65+451　55
Ystad, *Sweden* M07+555　47
Ytterhogdal, *Sweden* M01+622　46
Yüanchow. *See* Chihkiang
Yüanchow. *See* Ichun
Yüanling, *China* E58+285　67
Yubalia, *S. Australia* C58–336　109
Yubi C., *Morocco* N78+280　80
Yucamani, mt., *Peru* S60–170　104
Yucatan, state, *Mexico* T84+208　100
Yucatan Chan., *Mex.-Cuba* T66+216　101
Yugoslavia (Jugoslavia),
　Cent. Europe L70+440　51
Yuhsien, *China* E32+398　66
Yuhwan, *China* D82+282　67
Yukhnov, *U.S.S.R.* K59+548　60

Yukon Terr., *Canaaa* W80+610　88
Yukon, R., *Alaska* Y60+626　99
Yulin, *China* E62+383　66
Yuma, *Arizona* V58+329　98
Yuma, *Colorado* U76+401　94
Yumen, *China* F50+410　63
Yungchow. *See* Lingling
Yungera, *Victoria* C41–348　109
Yungfu, *China* E60+250　67
Yungki. *See* Kirin
Yungkia. *See* Wenchow
Yungnien, *China* E31+368　66
Yungning (Nanning), *China* E70+228　67
Yungning, *China* F25–277　64
Yungping. *See* Lulung
Yungshun, *China* E61+290　67
Yungsin, *China* E33+270　67
Yungsui, *China* E63+286　67
Yungtsi, *China* E59+349　66
Yunhsien, *China* E54+329　66
Yunsi, *China* E57+331　66
Yunta, *S. Australia* C63–326　109
Yurievets, *U.S.S.R.* K11+574　61
Yurimaguas, *Peru* T07–059　104
Yurlovka, *U.S.S.R.* J79+536　61
Yurmysh, *U.S.S.R.* H70+572　61
Yushu, *China* F50+332　64
Yütze, *China* E44+377　66
Yuyang, *China* E67+288　67
Yuyu, *China* E46+402　66
Yverdon, *Switzerland* M50–468　45
Ywathit, *Burma* F45+192　71
Zaachila, *Mexico* U41+168　100
Zaandam, *Netherlands* M61–524　44
Zabid, *Yemen* K11+141　74
Zabrze, *Poland* L67+504　49
Zacapa, *Guatemala* T88+149　100
Zacapoaxtla, *Mexico* U46+198　100
Zacatecas & state, *Mexico* U76+228　100
Zadar, *Yugoslavia* L89+441　56
Zadonsk, *U.S.S.R.* K36+524　60
Zafarabad, *Iran* J75+390　74
Zafarwal, *Pakistan* H01+323　72
Zafra, *Spain* N38+384　52
Zagazig, *Egypt* K80+306　81
Zagreb, *Yugoslavia* L84+458　56
Zahedan, *Iran* H84+295　75
Zahle, *Lebanon* K55+338　76
Zahran, *Saudi Arabia* K06+174　74
Zaidiya, *Yemen* K12+152　74
Zainsk, *U.S.S.R.* J47+553　61
Zaire, rep., *Cent. Africa* L50–050　82
Zaisan, *Kazakh.* G30+474　62
Zaječar, *Yugoslavia* L46+439　58
Zakho, *Iraq* K13+373　74
Zakin, *Afghanistan* H81+326　75
Zakinthos, I., *Greece* L56+378　59
Zakroczyn, *Poland* L55+498　49
Zákros, *Crete* L22+351　59
Zalău, *Romania* L42+472　49
Zalew Wiślany. *Poland* L62+544　49
Zalma, *Missouri* U01+370　97
Zambia, *Africa* L30–150　84
Zambezi R., *S.-E. Africa* L52–186　84
Zamboanga, *Philippines* D77+070　65
Zamora, *Ecuador* T22–042　104
Zamora de Hadalgo, *Mex.* U74+199　100
Zamora, *Spain* N34+415　52
Zandberg, *Netherlands* M48+529　44

Zandvoort, *Netherlands* M63+524　44
Zanesville, *Ohio* T42+399　91
Zangla, *Kashmir* G78+336　72
Zanjan, *Iran* J69+367　74
Zante. *See* Zakinthos I.
Zanzibar & I., *E. Africa* K34–062　83
Zapala, *Argentina* S61–388　103
Zapallar, *Argentina* R87–265　103
Zapata Pen., *Cuba* T40+223　101
Zaporozhye, *Ukraine* K59+479　60
Zara. *See* Zadar
Zaragoza, *Colombia* S89+074　104
Zaragoza, *Mexico* U57+241　100
Zaragoza, *Spain* N05+416　53
Zaragozo, *Mexico* U81+260　100
Zaraguro, *Ecuador* T25–036　104
Zarand, *Iran* J20+308　75
Zarasai, *Lithuania* L22+558　47
Zarauz, *Spain* N13+433　53
Zaraza, *Venezuela* S32+094　104
Zaria, *Nigeria* M44+110　80
Zarki, *Poland* L64+507　49
Zarqa, *Jordan* K53+321　76
Zarnūqa, *Saudi Arabia* J61+250　74
Zarzis, *Tunisia* M35+335　81
Zatec, *Czechoslovakia* M09+503　48
Zavitinsk, *U.S.S.R.* D33+500　63
Zawiercie, *Poland* L63+505　49
Zaysan, Oz., *Kazakh* G35+480　62
Zbaszyn, *Poland* L84+522　49
Zdunska Wola, *Poland* L66+516　49
Zealand, *New Brunswick* S41+461　90
Zealand. *See* Sjaelland
Zebak, *Afghanistan* H21+364　75
Zebdani, *Syria* K53+337　76
Zebid Qadhima, *Saudi Arabia* K35+224　74
Zeebrugge, *Belgium* M71+513　44
Zeehan. *Tasmania* C28–419　109
Zeeland, prov., *Netherlands* M67+515　44
Zeerust, *Transvaal* L24–256　84
Zegharta, *Lebanon* K55+344　76
Zeila, *Somalia* K10+112　83
Zeist, *Netherlands* M58+521　44
Zeitz, *E. Germany* M17+510　48
Zelaf, *Syria* K46+329　76
Zele, *Belgium* M66+511　44
Železná Ruda. *Czech.* M11+491　48
Zella, *Libya* L76+284　81
Zelman, *U.S.S.R.* J84+507　61
Zemio, *Cent. Afr. Rep.* L30+050　81
Zemun, *Yugoslavia* L57+448　58
Zenica, *Yugoslavia* L73+442　58
Zepce, *Yugoslavia* L72+445　58
Zermatt, *Switzerland* M43+460　45
Zernez, *Switzerland* M29+467　45
Zetland (Shetland), *Scot.* N07+604　40
Zevenbergen, *Netherlands* M62+516　44
Zeya, *U.S.S.R.* D47+537　63
Zeyma, *Saudi Arabia* K29+217　74
Zgierz, *Poland* L63+519　49
Zgorzelec. *See* Görlitz.
Zhdanov, *Ukraine* K44+471　60
Zhigansk, *U.S.S.R.* D70+667　63
Zhitomir, *Ukraine* L08+504　60
Zhmerinka, *Ukraine* L10+490　60
Ziarat, *Pakistan* H43+304　70
Ziba. *See* Dhaba.
Zidani Most, *Yugoslavia* L89+461　56

Ziemupe, *Latvia* L53+568　47
Zierikzee, *Netherlands* M66+516　44
Zijpe, *Netherlands* M66+517　44
Zikhron Ya'aqoy, *Israel* K60+325　76
Zile, *Turkey* K54+402　74
Zilfi, *Saudi Arabia* K02+262　74
Zilina, *Czechoslovakia* L67+492　49
Zima, *U.S.S.R.* F18+540　63
Zimapan, *Mexico* U56+207　100
Zindajan, *Afghanistan* H79+344　75
Zinder, *Niger* M36+138　81
Zingst, pen., *E. Germany* M14+544　48
Zion Nat. Park, *Utah* V48+374　92
Zira, *India* H00+310　72
Ziraquira, *Colombia* S84+050　104
Zirc, *Hungary* L73+473　49
Zitacuaro, *Mexico* U63+193　100
Zittau, *E. Germany* M01+509　48
Zizers, *Switzerland* M32+469　45
Zlatoust, *U.S.S.R.* J02+551　61
Zmeinogorsk, *U.S.S.R.* G47+511　62
Znin, *Poland* L74+528　49
Znojmo, *Czechoslovakia* L84+489　49
Zoar, *Labrador* S19+558　89
Zofingen, *Switzerland* M42+473　45
Zoisa, *Tanzania* K50–058　83
Zolder, *Belgium* M58+510　44
Zollino, *Italy* L71+402　57
Zolotoye, *U.S.S.R.* J85+508　61
Zomba, *Malawi* K58–154　83
Zonguldak, *Turkey* K78+416　74
Zorita, *Spain* N34+393　52
Zoute, Het, *Belgium* M70+514　44
Zoutkamp, *Netherlands* M52+533　44
Zrenjanin, *Yugoslavia* L58+454　58
Zuara, *Libya* M18+328　81
Zuevka, *U.S.S.R.* J55+585　61
Zug & canton, *Switzerland* M39+472　45
Zuger See, *Switzerland* M39+471　45
Zuhab, *Iran* J85+347　74
Zuid Beijerland, *Netherlands* M64+518　44
Zuider Zee. *See* IJsselmeer
Zuidland, *Netherlands* M65+518　44
Zuid Natoena Eiln., *Indon.* E66+028　65
Zuidwolde, *Netherlands* M51+527　44
Zuila, *Libya* L88+262　81
Zukur, Jab., *Yemen* K13+140　74
Zula, *Ethiopia* K32+152　83
Zulfikar, *Afghanistan* H82+356　75
Zumbo, *Mozambique* K88–156　84
Zumpango, *Mexico* U54+198　100
Zundert, *Netherlands* M62+515　44
Zungeru, *Nigeria* M54+098　80
Zuni, Mt.. *New Mexico* V18+352　94
Zürich & canton. *Switz.* M39+474　45
Zürich See, *Switzerland* M38+472　45
Zurzach, *Switzerland* M40+476　45
Zutphen, *Netherlands* M53+522　44
Zwai L., *Ethiopia* K38+078　83
Zwartsluis, *Netherlands* M54+526　44
Zweelo, *Netherlands* M50+528　44
Zweibrucken, *W. Germany* M47+493　48
Zweisimmen, *Switzerland* M46+466　45
Zwickau, *E. Germany* M15+507　48
Zwoleń. *Poland* L51+513　49
Zwolle, *Netherlands* M53+525　44
Zyrardów. *Poland* L57+521　49
Zyryanka, *U.S.S.R.* B85+645　63
Zyryanovsk, *Kazakh.* G35+498　62
Zyyi, *Cyprus* K70+347　76